MEDICAL APPLICATIONS OF THE BEHAVIORAL SCIENCES

Medical Applications of the Behavioral Sciences

EDITORS

JONATHAN J. BRAUNSTEIN, M.D.
*Associate Dean for Medical Education
Associate Professor of Medicine
University of Miami School of Medicine
Miami, Florida*

RICHARD P. TOISTER, Ph.D.
*Adjunct Associate Professor of Pediatrics and Psychology
University of Miami School of Medicine;
Director, Department of Psychology and Behavioral Medicine
Grant Center Hospital
Miami, Florida*

YEAR BOOK MEDICAL PUBLISHERS, INC.
CHICAGO • LONDON

Copyright © September 1981 by Year Book Medical Publishers, Inc. All rights reserved. No part of this publication may be reproduced, stored in a retrieval system, or transmitted, in any form or by any means, electronic, mechanical, photocopying, recording, or otherwise, without prior written permission from the publisher. Printed in the United States of America.

Library of Congress Cataloging in Publication Data
Main entry under title:

Medical applications of the behavioral sciences.
    Includes index.
    1. Medicine and psychology. 2. Social medicine. I. Braunstein, Jonathan J. II. Toister, Richard P. [DNLM: 1. Behavior therapy. 2. Behavior WM 425 M489]
R726.5 M4   616   81-3435
ISBN 0-8151-1194-0   AACR2

*To my MOTHER, and the memory of my FATHER—
for encouraging me to strive for the best in life; and
to the memory of SAM and JESSIE FELMAN—
for helping to remove a seemingly insurmountable
obstacle from my path*

J.J.B.

*To ELLEN for her understanding and encouragement;
to PHILIP, STEVEN, and LAURA for their patience;
and, in memory, to MURRAY TOISTER and
LAWRENCE EPSTEIN,
who taught by example*

R.P.T.

Contributors

PAUL J. BENKE, M.D., Ph.D.
  Associate Professor of Pediatrics, University of Miami School of Medicine, Miami, Florida

JONATHAN J. BRAUNSTEIN, M.D.
  Associate Dean for Medical Education, Associate Professor of Medicine, University of Miami School of Medicine, Miami, Florida

DONALD R. CRAMPTON, M.D.
  Acting Chairman, Department of Pediatrics, Mount Sinai Hospital, Miami, Florida

LUCY ESTRIN, A.C.S.W.
  Adjunct Assistant Professor of Psychiatry, University of Miami School of Medicine, Miami, Florida

MICHAEL C. HUGHES, M.D.
  Clinical Associate Professor of Psychiatry, University of Miami School of Medicine, Miami, Florida

SANFORD JACOBSON, M.D.
  Clinical Professor of Psychiatry, University of Miami School of Medicine, Miami, Florida

MALCOLM KUSHNER, Ph.D.
  Adjunct Associate Professor of Psychiatry and Family Medicine, University of Miami School of Medicine; President, Florida School of Professional Psychology, Miami, Florida

HARRIET P. LEFLEY, Ph.D.
  Associate Professor of Psychiatry, Director of Research and Evaluation, University of Miami; Jackson Memorial Community Mental Health Center, Miami, Florida

ANTHONY NOWELS, M.D.
  Medical Director, Grant Center Hospital; Clinical Associate Professor of Psychiatry, University of Miami School of Medicine, Miami, Florida

IRENE MOLNER SCHATZ, A.C.S.W.
  Adjunct Assistant Professor of Family Medicine, University of Miami School of Medicine, Miami, Florida

NEIL SCHNEIDERMAN, Ph.D.
  Professor of Psychology, Director of Behavioral Medicine Research Program, University of Miami, Miami, Florida

CLARISSA S. SCOTT, Ph.D.
  Assistant Professor of Social Anthropology, Department of Psychiatry, University of Miami School of Medicine, Miami, Florida

JEFFREY M. SEIBERT, Ph.D.
  Assistant Professor of Pediatrics, Mailman Center for Child Development, University of Miami School of Medicine, Miami, Florida

MARC SILBRET, M.D.
  Assistant Professor of Psychiatry and Neurological Surgery, University of Miami, Florida

GAIL SILVERMAN, Ph.D.
Adjunct Assistant Professor in Family Medicine, University of Miami School of Medicine, Miami, Florida

RICHARD P. TOISTER, Ph.D.
Adjunct Associate Professor of Pediatrics and Psychology, University of Miami School of Medicine; Director, Department of Psychology and Behavioral Medicine, Grant Center Hospital, Miami, Florida

WALLACE WILKINS, Ph.D.
Professor of Psychology, Director of Clinical Training, Old Dominion University, Norfolk, Virginia

Contents

Preface xiii
PART I The Biology of Behavior

1. Genetics, Development, and Behavior. *Donald R. Crampton, M.D., Paul J. Benke, M.D., Ph.D.,* and *Jonathan J. Braunstein, M.D.* 3
   Basic Genetic Concepts in Medicine, 3. Genetics of Mental Retardation, 9. Specific Behaviors, 17. Genetics of Psychiatric Disorders, 18. Genetic Counseling, 21. Summary, 23.

2. Neurologic Basis of Behavior. *Neil Schneiderman, Ph.D.* 26
   Neuronal Transmission, 26. The Effects of Psychoactive Drugs on Brain Function and Behavior, 33. Relationships Between the Organization of the Nervous System and Behavior, 37. Summary, 53.

3. The Biochemistry of the Functional Psychoses. *Jonathan J. Braunstein, M.D.,* and *Sanford Jacobson, M.D.* 55
   Biochemical Aspects of the Affective Disorders, 55. Biochemical Aspects of Schizophrenia, 64. Summary, 74.

4. Normal Sleep and Sleep Disorders. *Jonathan J. Braunstein, M.D.,* and *Sanford Jacobson, M.D.* 77
   Normal Sleep Patterns, 77. Drugs and Sleep, 79. Sleep Disorders, 81. Summary, 92.

PART II Psychological Factors in Behavior

5. Theories of Psychological Function: Psychoanalytic Theory—*Sanford Jacobson, M.D.,* and *Jonathan J. Braunstein, M.D.*; Learning Theory and Behavior Therapy—*Malcolm Kushner, Ph.D.,* and *Richard P. Toister, Ph.D.* 97
   Psychoanalytic Theory, 97. Learning Theory and Behavior Therapy, 105. Summary, 116.

6. The Classification and Evaluation of Psychological Dysfunction. *Sanford Jacobson, M.D., Richard P. Toister, Ph.D.,* and *Jonathan J. Braunstein, M.D.* 119
   What Constitutes Psychological Dysfunction?, 119. Categories of Psychological Disorders, 124. Evaluation of Psychological Function by Means of the Mental Status Examination, 128. Psychological Testing, 131. Summary, 141.

7. Reactions to Stress. *Jonathan J. Braunstein, M.D.* 143
   Definition of Stress, 143. Physiological Responses, 146. Psychological Responses, 151. Relationship Between Physiological and Psychological Responses, 154. Life Stress and Illness, 155. Summary, 161.

8. Behavioral Medicine (Psychosomatic or Psychophysiological Disorders). *Neil Schneiderman, Ph.D., Wallace Wilkins, Ph.D., Jonathan J. Braunstein, M.D.,* and *Marc Silbret, M.D.*   163
  General Considerations, 163. Circulatory Disorders, 169. Bronchial Asthma, 174. Peptic Ulcer Disease, 178. Therapeutic Considerations in Psychosomatic Disorders, 181. Summary, 187.

PART III Behavior in Social and Cultural Perspective

9. Social Aspects of Medicine. *Harriet P. Lefley, Ph.D.*   195
  Some Sociological Correlates of Health and Illness, 196. Socialization and Health, 205. The Family in Medicine, 208. Summary, 215.

10. Culture, Ethnicity, and Medicine. *Clarissa S. Scott, Ph.D.*   218
  Health Culture, 219. Culturally Determined Concepts About the Body and Its Functions, 221. The Influence of Ethnicity on Patients' Symptoms, 225. Culturally Related Differences in the Incidence of Disease, 227. Culture-Bound Syndromes, 230. Cultural Differences in Etiologic Explanations, 233. Differences in Choice of Therapies and Therapists, 235. Summary, 237.

11. Life-Styles and Health. *Marc Silbret, M.D., Neil Schneiderman, Ph.D.,* and *Jonathan J. Braunstein, M.D.*   241
  Life-Style in Our Modern Urban Society, 241. Cancer, 246. Atherosclerotic Cardiovascular Disease, 250. Summary, 261.

12. Substance Abuse. *Jonathan J. Braunstein, M.D., Neil Schneiderman, Ph.D.,* and *Marc Silbret, M.D.*   264
  General Concepts, 264. Obesity, 269. The Use and Abuse of Alcohol, 274. Licit and Illicit Drugs (Other Than Alcohol), 283. Summary, 291.

PART IV The Life Cycle

13. Introduction to Human Development. *Michael C. Hughes, M.D.,* and *Jonathan J. Braunstein, M.D.*   295
  Essential Human Needs, 296. General Concepts of Development, 297. Culture and Development, 302. Methods of Study, 303. Summary, 305.

14. The Early Years. *Jeffrey M. Seibert, Ph.D.,* and *Richard P. Toister, Ph.D.*   307
  The Infant, 307. The Toddler, 318. Summary, 324.

15. Preschool and School Age. *Richard P. Toister, Ph.D.,* and *Jeffrey M. Seibert, Ph.D.*   327
  Preschool Age (3–6 Years), 327. School-Age Period (6–12 Years), 336. Summary, 348.

16. Child Abuse—A Problem of Family Dysfunction. *Irene Molner Schatz, A.C.S.W.,* and *Lucy Estrin, A.C.S.W.*   351
  General Concepts of Family Function, 351. Child Abuse, 353. Summary, 361.

CONTENTS

17. An Introduction to Adolescent Development. *Anthony Nowels, M.D., Richard P. Toister, Ph.D.*, and *Jonathan J. Braunstein, M.D.* ... 363
    General Concepts, 363. Early Adolescence (Ages 11–13 in Girls and 13–15 in Boys), 366. Mid-Adolescence (Ages 14–16 in Girls and 15–17 in Boys), 369. Late Adolescence, 374. Problems of Adjustment in Adolescence, 378. Summary, 381.

18. Young and Middle Adulthood. *Clarissa S. Scott, Ph.D.* ... 383
    Theoretical Basis for the Stages of Adulthood, 383. Women During Adulthood—Myths and Realities, 391. Activities and Issues in the Adult Years, 395. Summary, 399.

19. The Geriatric Period. *Jonathan J. Braunstein, M.D.* ... 401
    Demographic Aspects of Aging in the United States, 401. Biologic Changes With Aging, 403. Psychosocial Aspects of Aging, 408. Medical Care of the Elderly, 414. Summary, 415.

20. Death and Dying. *Jonathan J. Braunstein, M.D.* ... 417
    Modern Changes in Death, 417. The Terminally Ill Patient, 420. The Responses of Medical Personnel to the Dying, 423. Caring for the Dying Patient, 426. The Family, 428. Summary, 430.

PART V The Patient and the Doctor

21. Concepts of Health, Illness, and Disease. *Jonathan J. Braunstein, M.D.* ... 435
    What Are Concepts?, 436. Concepts of Ill Health—Illness Versus Disease, 437. Concepts of Health, 443. The Practical Application of the Concepts of Health and Ill Health, 445. Summary, 452.

22. Illness Behavior. *Jonathan J. Braunstein, M.D.* ... 454
    The Period Prior to Contact With the Health-Care System, 455. The Period of Medical Care, 460. Summary, 468.

23. Patient Compliance. *Clarissa S. Scott, Ph.D.* ... 470
    Definition and Scope of the Problem, 470. Methodological Problems of the Study of Compliance, 471. Current State of Knowledge, 473. Health Belief Model, 477. Strategies for Improving Compliance, 479. Summary, 482.

24. The Physician-Patient Relationship: Communication Between the Physician and the Patient—*Jonathan J. Braunstein, M.D.;* The Traditional and Humanistic Models, *Gail Silverman, Ph.D.* ... 484
    Communication Between the Physician and the Patient, 484. The Traditional and Humanistic Models of the Physician-Patient Relationship, 494. Summary, 500.

Name Index ... 503
Subject Index ... 513

Preface

WHAT IS COMMONLY referred to as the "art of medicine" is in reality nothing more than the provision of appropriate medical care in such a way as to meet the individual needs of a particular patient. It is a concept that is based on the fact that no two people are alike, that they are affected by and react differently to illness, and, consequently, the care that they receive should take into account these differences. In the past it has been assumed that some clinicians were just intuitively better than others in this phase of medicine, that the "art of medicine" could not be learned. In a sense, the emergence of the behavioral sciences as bona fide medical disciplines has put this notion to rest and provided a scientific basis for this so-called art. By carefully considering a person's psychological make up and reactions, his social and cultural background, his family structure and relationships, and the environment in which he lives and works, *plus* being aware of the available behavioral science information relative to his particular problem(s) and situation, much can be done to make the practice of medicine an artful application of medical science. Although the foregoing might seem obvious, it is only within the past decade or so that the behavioral sciences have found a place, albeit a limited one, alongside the biologic sciences in medical education.

A large body of medically relevant information about the psychological, sociological, and cultural aspects of human behavior exists. It is the purpose of this book to introduce clinically oriented medical personnel to these behavioral science facts and theories and to demonstrate the usefulness of this material in the practice of medicine. Although it was written with the physician in mind, other health professionals involved in patient care should find it helpful in understanding and in responding appropriately to their patients' needs.

There are a number of cogent reasons for medical personnel to be knowledgeable in the behavioral sciences. First, behavioral factors such as faulty nutrition, inadequate physical activity, cigarette smoking, excessive alcohol use, drug abuse, improper driving habits, and the presence of certain harmful personality traits play a critical role in the pathogenesis of some of the most common and serious diseases affecting our population. Since diseases related to behavioral and environmental factors account for approximately 70% of American deaths, one means of substantially improving the health of our nation is to modify or eliminate these factors.

A second reason for health professionals to be well informed about the behavioral aspects of medicine is that psychosocial and cultural factors are important in the diagnosis, treatment, and outcome of many illnesses. Because of their influence on (1) people's attitudes and beliefs about health and illness, (2) the behavior of the sick, and (3) the interaction that takes place between a physician and a patient, these factors can determine, for example, if and when someone with symptoms seeks medical help, how well he adapts to the stress associated with illness and medical care, and whether or not he complies with medical advice.

A significant percentage of patients, particularly those seen in primary care practices, have complaints related to emotional or social problems. They may express these complaints directly or as physical symptoms which they feel are acceptable to the physician. Although these problems are usually due to the stress of daily living, developmental crises, or physical ailments, they also result from specific mental disorders that, if carefully looked for, can be found in at least 15% of the patients in primary care practices. Since nonpsychiatric physicians are responsible for the initial interpretation and management of a wide range of psychosocial problems, a knowledge of the fundamental concepts of human behavior and development should be a goal for these physicians.

Differing in several respects from the other available behavioral science texts, this work is an outgrowth of ten years of teaching the behavioral sciences to freshman and sophomore students at the University of Miami Medical School. It has been designed to meet the needs of both medical students and practitioners, to give the reader a fairly broad exposure to the material encompassed in the behavioral sciences, and to go into sufficient depth to be intellectually challenging to the reader. For those who are interested in delving even further into a particular topic, an extensive and up-to-date bibliography can be found at the end of most chapters.

To achieve a proper balance between the presentation of behavioral science theory and its clinical application, both behavioral scientists and clinicians are included in the authorship.

Human behavior results from the complex interplay of biologic, psychological, sociological, and cultural factors, and the organization of the text is based on this theme. The first three parts deal with general concepts in each of the major behavioral disciplines. In part I, the biologic substrate for normal and abnormal behavior is discussed. Recent information about the genetics and biochemistry of the major psychoses, sleep disorders, and the action of psychoactive drugs is presented, both from a theoretical standpoint and in terms of the practical use of this information in patient care.

Part II focuses on the psychological aspects of human behavior, dealing with topics such as psychoanalytic and learning theory, the mental status examination, psychological testing, the nature of stress and its relationship to illness, and the concept of psychosomatic disease. Although this is not a text in psychiatry, the material in this section will expose the reader to current thinking with respect to important clinical aspects of psychological function and dysfunction.

Part III, on the social and cultural aspects of health and illness, begins with two introductory chapters (9 and 10) on medical sociology and anthropology. These chapters discuss the influence of social and cultural factors on (1) the distribution of disease, (2) symptom expression, (3) the definition and treatment of illness, (4) the utilization of traditional and nontraditional health-care systems, and (5) the outcome of illness. The manner in which social roles and family dynamics affect the behavior of the sick is also described. Chapters 11 and 12 deal with the clinical application of many of the sociological and anthropological concepts introduced in the two preceding chapters. Chapter 11, on life-styles and health, reviews the effects of some behavioral and environmental factors on the health of our population, with specific emphasis on the role of these factors in the etiology of the three major causes of death in this country, i.e., coronary artery disease, stroke, and cancer. Chapter 12, on substance abuse, describes the interplay of psychological, sociological, and cultural factors in the pathogenesis of this widespread medical and community problem.

Part IV consists of a series of clinically oriented chapters on human development which survey the principal tasks facing individuals in each phase of life and some of the ways in which people cope with these challenges. The physical, psychological, and social changes that occur during human development are discussed, along with the implications of these changes for the evaluation and care of patients. Also, examples of specific medical disorders are presented that illustrate important physical and psychosocial issues. Particularly noteworthy is chapter 18, on the adult period of life, and chapter 19, on the geriatric period. Many of the concepts of development in these chapters come from relatively recent studies.

The material in the final part (V) has a

strong clinical orientation, illustrating how psychological, social, and cultural factors affect such vital matters as illness behavior, the physician-patient relationship, and patient compliance. The gist of the message in this section is that the behavior of physicians and patients, rather than being governed solely by rational problem-solving motives, is frequently molded by complex psychosocial and cultural forces of which they are often unaware. Understanding the nature of these forces and how they operate is helpful to medical personnel by enabling them to interact in a more effective and humane way with their patients.

It has been the editors' hope in preparing this work that it may be instrumental in getting physicians and other health professionals to consider the patient, his psyche, his social and cultural background, and his behavior patterns in carrying out treatment. If this is done, the patient will benefit greatly, medical practice will become an artful application of medical science, and the goal of the editors will be realized.

Particular thanks for their assistance in preparing the book must go to our contributors and to Liliana Martin, who as typist and secretary had a major role in the successful completion of the work. Without their help, the realization of the editors' dreams could not have been achieved.

JONATHAN J. BRAUNSTEIN

RICHARD P. TOISTER

PART I

The Biology of Behavior

1 / Genetics, Development, and Behavior

DONALD R. CRAMPTON, M.D., PAUL J. BENKE, M.D., Ph.D., and JONATHAN J. BRAUNSTEIN, M.D.

IT IS GENERALLY ACCEPTED that human behavior is influenced by both genetic and environmental factors. These factors are not simply additive in their effects; rather, they interact in a much more complex fashion—an idea that has been expressed by Dobzhansky:

> There seems little point in belaboring the truism that behavior as such is not inherited. Only genes can be inherited, in the sense of being handed down from parents to offspring. Even so, I have mostly division products, true copies of the genes I have inherited from my parents, rather than these genes themselves. The skin color is not inherited either, because the skin pigment is not carried in the sex cells. However, I am yet to meet anybody who would contend that one's genes have nothing to do with one's skin color. Human, as well as animal, behavior is the outcome of a process of development in which the genes and the environment are components of a system of feedback relationships. The same statement can be made equally validly with respect to one's skin color, the shape of one's head, blood chemistry, and somatic, metabolic, and mental diseases.[1]

In this chapter, we will review some basic genetic concepts and then describe some genetic defects that are responsible for specific developmental and behavioral disorders. While the focus of this discussion is on the importance of hereditary factors in human development and behavior, the reader should not forget the critical role played by the environment.

BASIC GENETIC CONCEPTS IN MEDICINE

Chromosomes and Genes in Man

Modern explanations of the growth of an entire human organism from a single cell, the fertilized egg, were developed within the last century. An idea of the primitive theories can be gained from Figure 1–1, which depicts a

A HOMUNCULUS SUPPOSEDLY CARRIED IN THE SPERM OF MAN

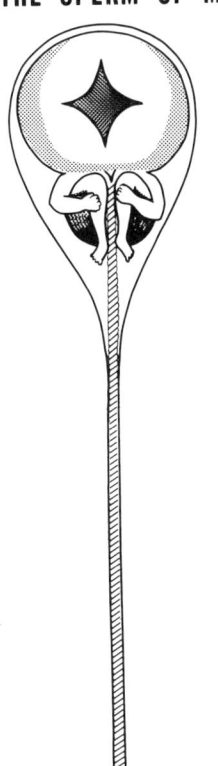

Fig 1–1.—Early view of the human sperm cell, which was thought to contain a miniature human being.

preformationist view of the composition of the human sperm cell. The cell was thought to contain a miniature but fully formed human being.

Chromosomes

Genes, the basic units of inheritance, are components of intranuclear structures called chromosomes. In humans, each diploid cell has 46 chromosomes—22 pairs of somatic chromosomes (autosomes) and 1 pair of sex chromosomes, XY in males and XX in females. The different chromosomes are distinguished from one another by size, position of the centromere (i.e., the point of attachment), and the presence of specific banding patterns (when stained).

Large abnormalities in chromosome morphology can be directly observed under the light microscope with special staining techniques. In order to do this, cultured blood lymphocytes are stimulated to divide and then treated with a mitotic inhibiting agent. The chromosomes are stained and a photograph of the total complement of visible chromosomes is taken. The individual chromosomes are then arranged systematically for analysis. The resulting diagrammatic arrangement of chromosomes is called a karyotype (Fig 1–2).

By means of karyotype analysis, abnormalities in the number and structure of chromosomes can be identified that are characteristic of certain hereditary disorders in which impaired mental function is a prominent part of the clinical picture. These abnormalities are usually due to an aberration in the normal process of cell division. An example of this is *nondisjunction,* in which a pair of chromosomes fails to separate during cell division, so that one daughter cell contains an extra chromosome that is missing from the other daughter cell. If nondisjunction of chromosome 21 occurs during the maturation of a gamete (ovum or spermatozoon) and the daughter cell with the extra 21 chromosome is fertilized by a normal gamete, the fetus that develops from this union has three 21 chromosomes (trisomy 21), a total of 47 chromosomes, and the clinical features of Down syndrome.

Chromosomal anomalies also result from an aberration in cell division called *translocation,* in which there is an interchange of material between chromosomes of different

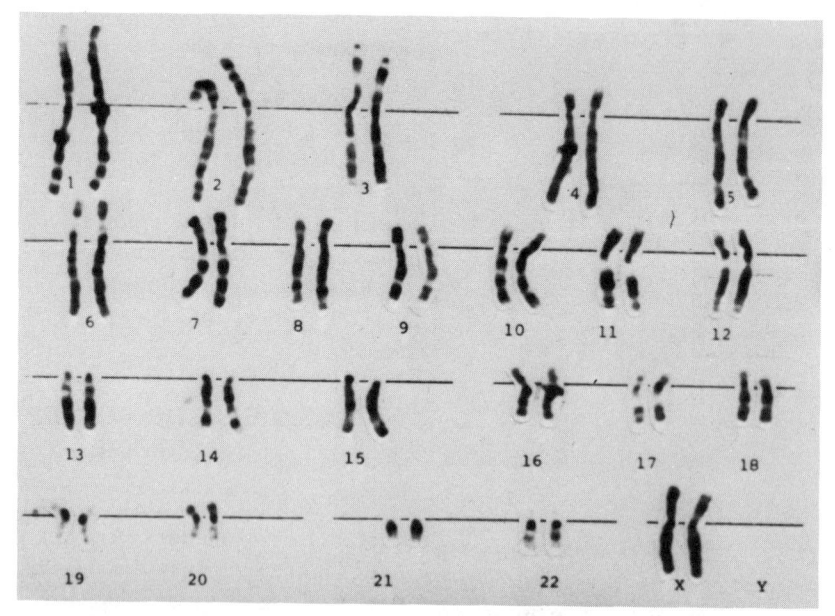

Fig 1–2.—Karyotype of a normal female. (Compliments of Dr. Paul Ing, Department of Pediatrics, University of Miami School of Medicine.)

pairs. During cell division part or all of a chromosome becomes attached to another, so that one of the daughter cells contains extra chromosomal material. Karyotype analysis of some persons with Down syndrome has demonstrated that there is a fusion of chromosome 21 material with another autosome (usually 14 or 15) due to translocation. These persons have the normal number of 46 chromosomes; however, one of them (14 or 15) is oversized because it has extra 21 chromosomal material attached to it. Either parent of a child with translocation Down syndrome may be the carrier of the abnormal chromosome, passing it on to the child at the time of fertilization.

Genes

Each "unit" of genetic information governing the production of a specific protein is called a gene. This genetic information is contained in a series of deoxyribonucleotides arranged in a particular sequence. The sequence of the nucleotides represents the code for the formation of an amino acid chain. Initially, the code is transcribed to a molecule of messenger ribonucleic acid (mRNA), which then acts as a template for the synthesis of a polypeptide chain in cytoplasmic structures called ribosomes. A sequence of three consecutive nucleotide bases on a molecule of mRNA (called a codon) is responsible for the laying down of a single amino acid. The proteins that are ultimately formed as a result of this process may be either structural or enzymatic in nature.

The localization of gene loci on specific chromosomes has been accomplished through the use of special study techniques such as the following[2]:
1. *The analysis of chromosome translocations.*
2. *The study of hybrid cells,* as for example cells formed by the fusion of human and mouse cells. These cells retain some (but not all) of the chromosomes of both species. As they replicate in tissue culture, the human chromosomes are preferentially lost with successive cell divisions. The demonstration that a human gene product is associated with the retention or loss of a specific human chromosome in the hybrid preparation is evidence that the gene's locus is on that chromosome.
3. *Linkage studies,* or studies of gene segregation in kindred groups. Genes are said to be "linked" when they lie very close to each other on the same chromosome. Such genes segregate together during meiosis so that the characteristics or traits that they control are inherited together. When the location of a "marker" gene that determines a particular trait is known to be on a specific chromosome, this information can be used to find the locus of a gene that determines a second trait. If the two traits are found to be inherited together in repeated studies of family pedigrees, it can be assumed that the two genes lie close together on the same chromosome.

Based on information obtained from these and other types of studies, human gene maps have been constructed showing the location of gene loci on specific chromosomes.[3] Approximately 230 autosomal genes and 110 X-linked genes have been assigned,[2] some of which appear on the gene map in Figure 1–3.

Mutations are caused by changes in the deoxyribonucleotide sequence of a gene. This affects the production of an amino acid and, hence, alters the structure and function of a protein molecule. If the altered protein is an enzyme, then there may be abnormalities in body metabolism. Such is the case in persons with phenylketonuria, a disorder associated with mental retardation, which is caused by a genetically induced deficiency of the liver enzyme, phenylalanine hydroxylase. If the defective protein is a structural one, the disturbance that results can also be detrimental, as, for example, the disorder of sickle cell anemia, which is due to a genetically induced amino acid substitution in the hemoglobin molecule. However, not all mutations are harmful to an organism; some are neutral in their effects and lead only to genetic variability, while others may even be beneficial.

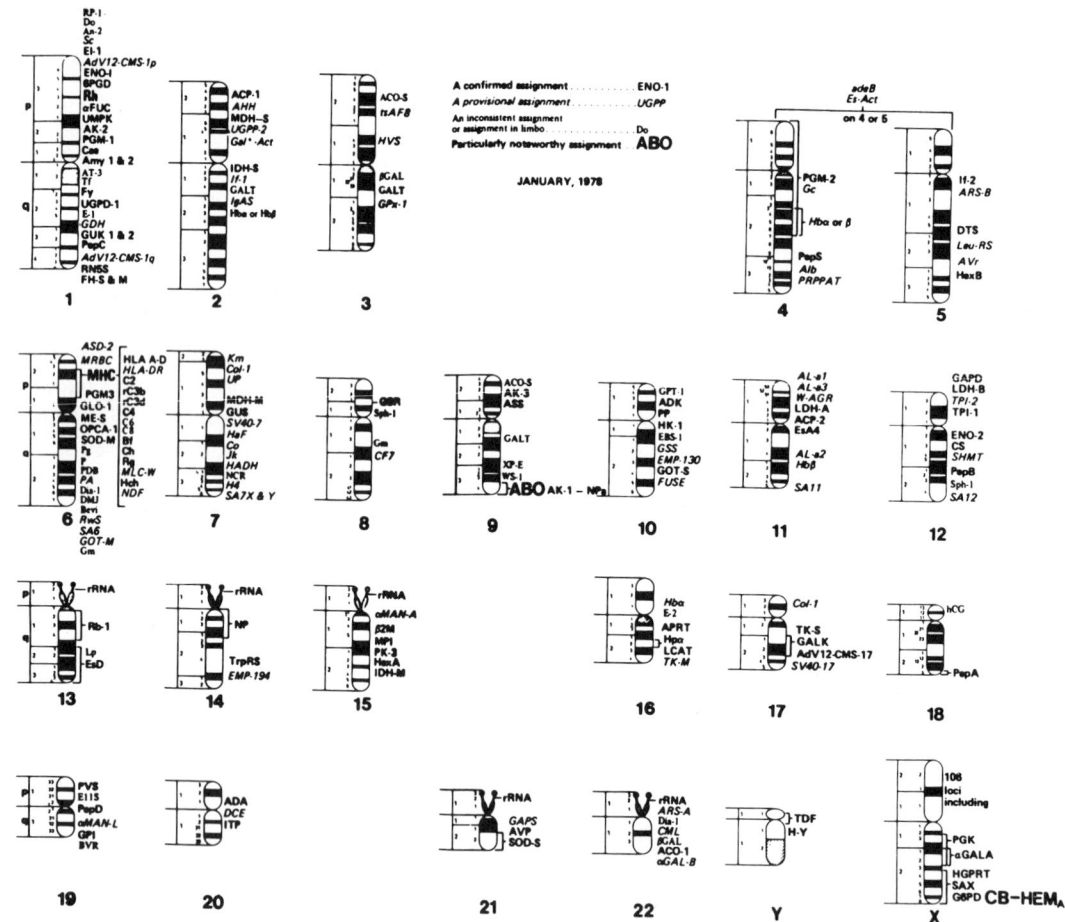

Fig 1-3.—A genetic map showing the chromosomes of man with the location of specific genetic loci. (From McKusick V.A.: *Mendelian Inheritance in Man.* Baltimore, The Johns Hopkins University Press, 1978.)

Genetic Function during Early Growth and Development

In mammals and higher organisms, fertilization of the egg results in rapid production of protein at the site of the maternally derived ribosomes. Messages from the new zygote nucleus are not needed for the first several cell divisions. However, subsequent embryonic development follows a fixed schedule that is genetically determined and characteristic of the species. The genetic program of an organism determines when and where different types of cells will form, what proteins they will make, and how they will function. Anatomical and physiological differences among vertebrate species are primarily the result of characteristic differences in the timing of genetic events during morphogenesis rather than the amounts of gene products,[4] and variations in the chemistry of structural proteins from species to species are actually relatively small.[5]

The influence of genes on the structure and function of the body may be latent or overt. Research shows that in bacteria many genes are expressed only when there is a physiological need for their products. Similar mechanisms turn genes on and off during differentiation in higher organisms. Entire chromosomes can be activated or silenced by changes in the activity of a single modification enzyme,[6] and it is likely that similar mechanisms exist for small segments of the genome.

What causes a cell to differentiate into specific cell types, such as red blood cells, muscle cells, or neurons, is not yet known. However, much information is available about general factors in embryogenesis and differentiation. The direction of a cell's differentiation at each stage of development is determined by its embryologic position in relation to other cells. Differential expression of a cell's genes is also controlled by chemical signals. For example, lithium, sodium, and calcium ions induce the differentiation of neurons from ectoderm in the frog.[7]

As each cell differentiates, information from the cell surface is transmitted to the nucleus and new proteins are made. As cell lines move down specific developmental pathways, they rapidly lose their multipotential capacity for development and have more limited options for differentiation. With time, the structure of cells becomes more specialized and their function more limited. Specific cell differentiation is a function of the age of a cell, as the stages of differentiation take place sequentially. The generation of a series of sequential cell inductions* necessary for differentiation requires that developing cells (1) become sensitive to new inducers or transduce previous signals into a new internal messenger or (2) develop a new set of responses to changes in the same internal signal with time.[8] It is likely that both cyclic adenosine monophosphate and cyclic guanosine monophosphate play a role in these changes during differentiation.[9] Developmental anomalies take place when drugs, mutations, or other agents interfere with these processes.

Clinical Problems in Early Growth and Development

Pare, in the 16th century, postulated that the birth of malformed children was due to the following factors: the will of God, overabundance or deficiency in the amount of "seed," ingestion of maternal toxins, narrow or malpositioned uterus, injury to the mother, inheritance of deformity or disease, or craft or subtlety of the devil and his agents.

While Pare's notion of the influence of God and the devil is no more amenable to scientific inquiry today than it was in the 16th century, the other factors are recognized by modern physicians to be important causes of congenital anomalies. Some examples of these factors (using Pare's terminology) are: (1) *amount of "seed"*—abnormalities in the total number of chromosomes or aneuploidy; (2) *maternal toxins*—maternal medications, alcohol, and cigarette smoking; (3) *uterine factors*—anatomical abnormalities of the placenta and uterus; (4) *injury to the mother*—maternal infections with syphilis, toxoplasmosis, or viruses such as rubella, cytomegalovirus, and herpes simplex type II; and (5) *inheritance*—genetic causes of defective fetal growth and development.

A number of these factors (e.g., maternal alcohol consumption, chromosome abnormalities) are associated with major physical and mental defects in the fetus, while others are associated with relatively minor problems (e.g., maternal cigarette smoking). The nature of the injuries caused by most of these factors depends on when in the gestational period the fetus is exposed to them. Rubella infection may cause congenital heart defects and other organ anomalies if contracted by the mother during the first several weeks of pregnancy, but infection after the third gestational month leads primarily to neurosensory hearing loss.[10] Thalidomide causes phocomelia and other anomalies only if ingested by the mother 28–42 days after conception.[11]

Towbin has shown that mechanical and anoxic damage to the central nervous system is a frequent finding in infants who die in the perinatal period.[12-14] Gestational age is a major factor in determining the nature and location of the lesions caused by these insults when they are due to a difficult vaginal delivery.[13] There is reason to believe that the incidence of perinatal damage to the central nervous system is higher than clinical reports indicate.

---

*Induction during development is the alteration of a cell's genetically mediated production of proteins.

By extrapolating the data from studies of the neuropathologic findings in infants who die in the perinatal period from complications of the puerperium, one would predict that more abnormalities would be found during the neurologic examination of surviving infants and children than are actually recorded.

Contrary to the widely held belief that many cases of mental retardation and learning disorders are caused by transient neonatal insults, prospective studies of infants exposed to these insults show that those who survive and are raised in a supportive environment usually recover from them.[15] Moreover, infants and toddlers with mild neurologic abnormalities related to perinatal injury are usually indistinguishable from children born of uncomplicated pregnancies when the two groups are tested in the early school years.[15, 16] Clearly, there are strong self-righting forces in neurologic development.

Much of the growth and differentiation of the central nervous system of humans and higher apes takes place after birth. This increases the vulnerability of this organ system to perinatal environmental factors that have a detrimental effect on the genetic control of its development. The impact of these factors illustrates the critical interaction that takes place between heredity and environment in human development. Recent studies have shown that even relatively brief periods of severe malnutrition in infant rats result in decreased cell number and total DNA content of the brain.[17] It has also been demonstrated that the learning capacities of children who were malnourished as infants are adversely affected.[18, 19]

Social variables contribute in a major way to the environmental influences on genetically programmed development. It has been clearly shown that children born to mothers from lower socioeconomic classes have a much higher incidence of developmental disabilities than do the offspring of mothers in the upper social strata. One reason for this disparity may be that mothers in the lower classes have less access to modern prenatal and perinatal care. Not only are children of disadvantaged mothers at greater risk during gestation, but also they fail to show the same degree of recovery from perinatal insults as children exposed to similar insults who are raised in an advantaged environment.[20]

Many gestational and puerperal factors that increase the risk of fetal injury can be identified by taking a good medical history of the mother. Attention must be paid to both biologic and social aspects. On the basis of a historical evaluation, 10–20% of pregnancies can be identified as high risk for the fetus. More than half of the cases of prenatal and perinatal mortality and morbidity are associated with these pregnancies.

Patterns of Inheritance in Man

Mendelian Inheritance

In classical or mendelian genetics, single genetic traits are attributed to the action of paired genes, one of which comes from the mother and the other from the father. Genes for a specific trait are located at the same site on homologous chromosomes and are called alleles.

Genotype refers to the genetic constitution of an individual, while *phenotype* refers to the individual's appearance or physiological state as determined by the genotype. If two alleles are chemically identical, the individual is said to be *homozygous* for that trait; if they are not, the individual is said to be *heterozygous*.

Any disease inherited in one of the mendelian patterns is caused by a defect in a single protein, either structural or enzymatic. When a trait is passed from parent to offspring with a 50% probability, the trait is said to be *dominantly* inherited. Only one dose of a gene—i.e., the heterozygous state—is necessary for the expression of a dominant trait. The capacity to synthesize structural proteins is transmitted by this type of inheritance. Genetic diseases with a dominant pattern of transmission are commonly associated with bone, connective tissue, and membrane defects. On the other hand, *recessively* inherited traits require two doses of a gene—i.e., the homozygous state—for full clinical expression. Recessive disorders are passed from both parents to their offspring with a

25% probability. They are due in most instances to enzyme deficiencies. The heterozygote, while often demonstrating a small decrease in activity of the enzyme on biochemical analysis, is usually well clinically because the reduction in activity does not interfere with cell function. The homozygote has a more severe deficiency of the enzyme and, consequently, frequently develops clinical illness.

According to the Lyon hypothesis, early in embryogenesis one of the two X chromosomes in the female is randomly inactivated.[21] The inactive or so-called late-replicating X chromosome forms the sex chromatin or Barr body seen in interphase nuclei—a cellular finding often used to screen for the genetic sex of an individual. The pattern of inheritance associated with genes on their X chromosome is called X-linked. Males with a defective gene on their X chromosome have that gene expressed in their phenotype because there is no allelic gene present on the nonhomologous Y chromosome. Classical hemophilia, Duchenne muscular dystrophy, and color blindness are examples of *recessive X-linked diseases*. In these disorders, sons of mothers who carry the defective gene have a 50% chance of receiving the X chromosome with the defective gene and thus of exhibiting the disorder. In addition, half the daughters of these mothers carry the unexpressed abnormal gene and have the same chance of producing abnormal sons as their mothers. In an *X-linked dominant inheritance pattern*, female carriers show the phenotypic effects of the abnormal gene, just as do males who carry it on their X chromosome.

V. A. McKusick, in *Mendelian Inheritance in Man*, catalogs more than 2,000 conditions that are known or believed to be single-gene defects, and the number of newly recognized disorders of this type has been increasing exponentially.[22] About 90% of these defects are autosomal and 10% are X-linked. Of the autosomal disorders, about half are dominantly inherited and half are recessively inherited. A significant proportion of dominantly inherited disorders are the result of spontaneous new mutations—a fact that has great significance in estimating the recurrence rate for disease in families with an affected individual. Collectively, mendelian disorders have a frequency of occurrence in the general population of about 2 in 100.[23]

Polygenic Inheritance

In contrast to mendelian traits, which are determined by single genes, polygenic traits are due to the interaction of multiple genes. Isolated cleft palate, cleft lip with or without cleft palate, neural tube defects such as meningomyelocele and anencephaly, pyloric stenosis, clubfoot deformity, congenital hip dislocation, and some forms of congenital heart disease are examples of disorders with this type of inheritance. Polygenic-determined disorders characteristically involve a single organ system, although defects in nearby organs can occur as a result of their proximity to the affected tissue during embryogenesis, the so-called field effect.[23] For example, individuals who have meningomyelocele as a primary development defect may exhibit abnormalities of the urinary system and other pelvic organs, probably as a result of the proximity of these tissues to the neural tube or because neural innervation is required for their normal development.

Riccardi has outlined the risks of recurrence for polygenic disorders as follows[23]:

1. Increased risk, compared to the general population, for occurrence of the disorder among first-, second-, and third-degree relatives.
2. Two to five percent risk for first-degree relatives to the proband; about half that risk for second-degree relatives.
3. Increasing risk with increasing numbers of affected genetic relatives, especially first- and second-degree relatives.
4. Increasing risk if a relative is of the sex usually affected.
5. Increasing risk with increasing severity of the defect in the proband.

GENETICS OF MENTAL RETARDATION

Mental retardation is a syndrome that arises during the developmental period and comprises two main clinical features: subnormal intelligence and inadequate social adaptation. Both of these characteristics should be present before a diagnosis of retardation is made. The finding of a low IQ alone is insufficient, since many individuals with mild reductions in IQ are able to function perfectly well from a social standpoint. By definition, the diagnosis is restricted to those who develop the clinical picture before age 18.

The definition of intelligence and the measurement of this attribute are covered in some detail in chapter 6; however, the following aspects of intelligence are particularly relevant to the topic of mental retardation and, therefore, will be dealt with here: (1) the genetic influence on IQ, and (2) the distribution of IQ scores according to social class and race.

Current information indicates that intelligence, like most other kinds of human behavior, is the result of the complex interaction of genetic and environmental factors. Mussen, Conger, and Kagen have summarized the evidence for the role of genetic factors in determining intelligence-test performance:[24]

1. A child's or adolescent's IQ is more highly correlated with that of his parents or other immediate relatives than with that of randomly selected nonrelatives. (This finding could, of course, also be explained by differences in the environmental conditions to which the test subjects are exposed.)
2. The IQs of children adopted at a very early age have a higher correlation with the IQs of their biologic parents than with those of their adoptive parents.
3. There is a positive correlation between intelligence levels and genetic closeness. For example, the IQs of monozygotic (identical) twins reared together are more highly correlated than those of either dizygotic (nonidentical) twins or nontwin siblings who are also reared together. Since monozygotic twins have an identical genetic makeup, this would be expected if genetic factors are operative.

However, these authors point out that there are data from twin studies indicating that environmental factors are also important determinants of intelligence. For example, the degree of correlation between the IQs of identical twins *reared apart* is significantly lower than it is for those *raised together*.

While there has been a great deal of controversy about the degree to which intelligence is influenced by heredity, it can be reliably concluded from the present state of knowledge that genetic (or biologic) factors account for the *potential* for intellectual functioning possessed by an individual, and that they may set a ceiling on this level of function.[24] It is probable that the environmental conditions to which a person is exposed ultimately determine the realization of his intellectual potential.

The importance of the environment is indicated by the correlation of intelligence-test performance with social class standing. Typically, lower-class children and adolescents score lower on these tests than those in the middle and upper social classes.[24] Presumably, this finding is explained by differences in psychosocial variables such as parent-child interaction, the quality of schooling, the values of the peer group, and the general opportunities for intellectual growth—all of which place the lower-class child at a disadvantage.

It is reported that black children in this country score on the average 10–15 points lower than white children on intelligence tests. Jensen, who attributes intelligence primarily to the effects of heredity, has suggested that this difference is due to genetic factors.[25] However, it is a mistake to assume that if a trait, such as intelligence, has a significant genetic component, differences between groups with respect to this trait must be genetically determined. An alternative explanation is that a higher proportion of the black children tested come from socially disadvantaged families and that their lower IQ scores are related to environmental deficiencies associated with lower social class membership. This interpretation is supported by studies showing that if black children with low IQs are exposed to an intellectually enriching environment (i.e., through adoption or special educational programs), many will improve their performance.

About 1% of our population is mentally retarded, with males outnumbering females. Systems of classification of this disorder are based on intelligence testing, a score of at least two standard deviations below the mean (i.e., below 70) being required for this diagnosis. Persons with mental retardation can be divided into two broad categories depending on the level of their IQ: "mild" cases with an IQ between 50 and 70, and "moderate" to "severe" cases with an IQ of less than 50. The vast majority (about 75%) of the 2 million retardates in this country fall into the "mild" category.

This division has implications in terms of the etiology of mental retardation. A large proportion of the mildly affected group is made up of individuals who are members of the lower socioeconomic classes. They do not have organic brain disease and appear to represent the lower end of a normal distribution in intellectual performance. Their condition is often familial and seems to be related to both genetic and environmental (psychosocial deprivation) factors. On the other hand, the population of moderate and severe mental retardates is composed principally of persons with brain damage or malformation due either to genetic or to acquired physical and biochemical defects.

A categorization of the causative factors in moderate and severe mental retardation (i.e., IQ less than 50) is found in Figure 1–4. Genetic disorders are etiologically responsible for nearly 50% of the half million of these cases in the United States. Clinically, this group of individuals is quite distinct from those with the mild form of retardation and is characterized by the following features: (1) they have a high incidence of physical or laboratory abnormalities; (2) they come from all socioeconomic classes; and (3) they are significantly less mentally competent than most of their close family relatives.

Mental retardation is usually first suspected by a parent or teacher who recognizes that a child is not making adequate progress in accomplishing the tasks of cognitive learning and that he has difficulty in acquiring the skills of everyday social life. This impression is confirmed when the child fails to perform normally on a standardized test of intelli-

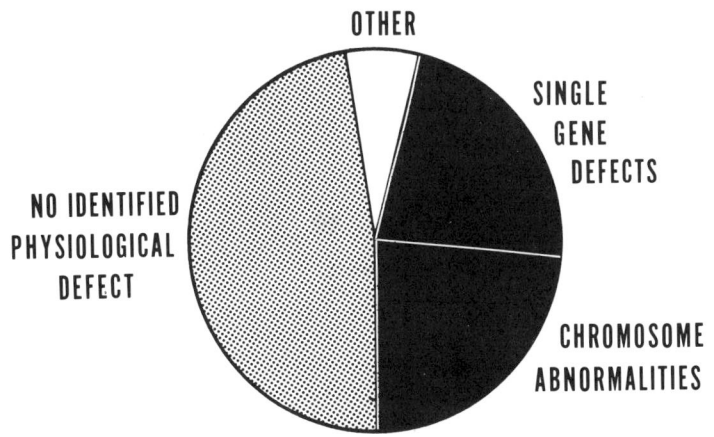

Fig 1–4.—Factors in the cause of moderate and severe mental retardation.

gence. Every retarded person exhibits his own unique constellation of attention, memory, learning, and other response deficits, as well as his own repertoire of socially inappropriate behaviors. The degree of insight which the mentally retarded have with respect to their intellectual ability and their capacity for good judgment or "common sense" varies greatly. Those with mild or moderate retardation often have great difficulty with emotional adjustment, which compounds their intellectual handicap. Many of those with moderate or severe retardation have associated neurologic abnormalities, such as seizures, gait disturbances, poor coordination, and sensory defects (deafness or poor vision).

Now let us examine some of the specific genetic disorders associated with mental retardation.

Chromosome Anomalies and Mental Retardation

The number of moderate and severe mental retardates with chromosome aberrations is relatively high. *Aneuploidy* refers to the situation in which there is a deviation from the normal number of 46 chromosomes. Most instances of aneuploidy are the result of sporadic events. Autosomal aneuploidy is regularly associated with mental retardation and abnormal physical findings. In Table 1–1, several examples of these conditions are listed, along with a description of the chromosomal abnormality and clinical findings.

The most common autosomal aneuploidy is *Down syndrome*, or mongolism, which results from extra chromosome 21 material in one of three forms: trisomy 21, trisomy 21 mosaic (in which some cells have trisomy 21 and others are normal), and translocation trisomy 21. Regardless of the type of chromosome abnormality present, persons with Down syndrome have similar physical findings and, with rare exceptions, are moderately to severely retarded. Trisomy 21 is directly related to maternal age, being more common in children born to older mothers (especially those over 35 years). The overall incidence of this defect is 1 in 600 births, whereas in mothers over 45 it is as high as 1 in 50 births. Persons who have a mosaic karyotype may be more mildly affected than those with the other two types of Down syndrome.

About one third of persons with Down syndrome and a translocation karyotype have inherited this defect; in the other two thirds, the anomaly arises de novo. Persons with a balanced translocation defect involving chromosome 21 (a situation in which there are 45 chromosomes with one of the 21 chromosomes translocated to chromosome 14 or 15) are normal but are carriers of the defect. They may pass it on to their offspring and produce a child with Down syndrome. For a mother with a balanced translocation, the risk of having an affected child is about 10–15% regardless of her age; for the father, it is about 2–4%. It is important to identify these carriers, so that they can receive proper genetic counseling.

Children with Down syndrome have a typical facial appearance characterized by slanting eyes, epicanthal folds, protruding tongue with micrognathus, folded ears, and increased incidence of congenital heart disease. They are frequently described as being good-natured, passive, and easily managed from a behavioral standpoint—characterizations that are interesting observations but not well defined scientifically.

Sex chromosome aneuploidy is common, occurring in about 1 in 200 live births. Mental retardation is only occasionally present in persons with these disorders, and if it is, it is less severe than in those with autosomal aneuploidy. Also, the physical findings are more variable and less severe than in the autosomal aneuploidy conditions. The most common abnormality of sex chromosome number in liveborn children is found in *Klinefelter syndrome*. In this disorder, chromosome analysis usually reveals the presence of 47 chromosomes due to an extra X chromosome (47 XXY, see Table 1–1), which is derived from the mother in more than half the cases. Persons who have this disorder are phenotypically male but have a Barr body (sex chromatin) in their somatic cells due to the extra X

TABLE 1–1.—CHROMOSOMAL IMBALANCE SYNDROMES*

SYNDROME	DIAGNOSTIC MANIFESTATIONS Craniofacial	Limbs	Other	MENTAL DEFICIENCY	SHORT STATURE	GENETIC TRANSMISSION
Down syndrome (mongolism)	Upward slant to palpebral fissures; flat facies	Short hands; clinodactyly of 5th finger	Hypotonia	+	+/−	21 Trisomy
18 Trisomy	Microstomia; short palpebral fissure	Clenched hand, 2d finger over 3d; low arches on fingertips	Short sternum	+	+	18 Trisomy
13 (D₁) Trisomy	Defects of eye, nose, lip, and forebrain of holoprosencephaly type	Polydactyly; narrow, hyperconvex fingernails	Skin defects, posterior scalp	+	+	13 Trisomy
XXY (Klinefelter) syndrome		Long legs	Hypogenitalism; hypogonadism; behavioral aberrations	+/−		XXY
XO (Turner) syndrome	Heart-shaped facies; prominent ears	Congenital lymphedema or its residua	Broad chest with widely spaced nipples; low posterior hairline	+/−	+	XO
XYY syndrome	Long head; prominent glabella	Tend to be tall	Poor coordination; aberrant behavior	+/−		XYY

*The chromosomal abnormalities give rise to particular patterns of multiple defects that allow for clinical recognition. They are grouped together to aid the clinician in deciding which patients clearly merit chromosomal study for confirmatory diagnosis and genetic counsel.
Adapted from Vaughan V.C., McKay R.J., Behrman R.E.: *Nelson Textbook of Pediatrics*, ed. 11. Philadelphia, W.B. Saunders Co., 1979.

chromosome. The incidence of this syndrome is 1 in 500 male births and, like those with Down syndrome, children with Klinefelter syndrome are born more frequently to older mothers.[26] Clinically, these persons have a eunuchoid habitus, gynecomastia (30%), and evidence of hypogonadism with small testes, azospermia, and infertility. There is an increased incidence of behavioral disorders including mental retardation, which occurs in 25% of cases. The diagnosis of Klinefelter syndrome is often missed until after puberty when signs of hypogonadism develop.

Turner syndrome, a condition in which there are 44 autosomes and only one X chromosome (see Table 1–1), is the only genetic disorder in which there is a complete deletion of a chromosome. Only about 1 in 40 fetuses with Turner syndrome survives the gestational period. The incidence of this disorder, excluding XO/XX mosaics, is 1 in 5,000 newborns. Those who have this syndrome are phenotypically female but no Barr body is found in their somatic cells as they have only one X chromosome. No association exists between maternal age at conception and the risk of producing a child with Turner syndrome. Clinically, these persons may have short stature, sexual underdevelopment, and a webbed neck. Mental retardation occurs in 10% of them. In addition, one third of these persons have congenital cardiac defects; anomalies of the urinary tract and neurosensory hearing loss are also common.

Another aneuploid disorder involving the sex chromosomes is the *XYY karyotype* (see Table 1–1). Individuals with this disorder are phenotypically males who are fertile and able to procreate chromosomally normal offspring. A highly variable pattern of minor malformations has been described in persons with this syndrome, including a long narrow face, large teeth, and the presence of nodulocystic acne in adolescence. In such persons, there is possibly a minimal increase in the risk of mental retardation. Females with an *XXX karyotype* have a normal appearance, are fertile, and as a rule produce children with normal chromosomes. They have two Barr bodies in their somatic cells. A small number of these individuals have mild mental retardation.

Metabolic Disorders

Phenylketonuria (PKU) is the most common single-gene defect associated with mental retardation. In this country, the incidence of PKU is about 1 in 11,500 live births.[27] This disorder has an autosomal recessive pattern of inheritance and is due to a deficiency in the liver enzyme, phenylalanine hydroxylase. It can be detected by testing for increased levels of phenylalanine in blood and urine after the feeding of a protein food source. If dietary management using a low-phenylalanine formula is instituted in the first weeks of life, affected children can be spared the neurologic sequelae of this disorder, which include mental retardation, irritability, seizures, and autistic behavior. Strict dietary management is advised from birth to age 6—the period of rapid brain growth; however, the toxic effects of phenylalanine on mental function may occur at any age. The consequences of this genetic deficit if untreated are variable. Occasionally, untreated individuals with PKU have normal intelligence despite their metabolic defect, and their disorder is not detected until they develop psychiatric problems in adulthood or give birth to retarded children.[28]

More is known about the mechanism of mental retardation in PKU than in any other genetic or metabolic disorder. The developing brain of humans and animals is markedly affected by a chronic excess of phenylalanine in the blood.[29, 30] Increased levels of phenylalanine are associated with a deficiency in the total myelin content[31, 32] and a decrease in the level of unsaturated fatty acids in the brain.[33] In experimental animals, excessive amounts of phenylalanine interfere with protein-synthesizing organelles in the brain by impairing the transport of tryptophan into the central nervous system.[34, 35] These effects are noted only in the neonatal period of these animals.[33-35] Aminoacylation of transfer RNA, gluconeogenesis, and pyruvate metabolism may also be affected by excess phenylalanine.[36, 37] Only phenylalanine, not its metabolites, is associated with these abnormalities. Dietary precautions in persons with PKU prevent the toxic effects of phenylalanine by reducing elevated levels of it in the blood.

Because phenylalanine is concentrated by the placenta, elevated levels in the mother are even higher in the fetus. In spite of dietary management, almost all infants (including those who do not have PKU themselves) born to mothers with PKU are retarded.[38]

A wide range of other genetically induced metabolic conditions cause mental retardation in humans. Most of them are rare, and many are treatable by dietary and metabolic manipulation. Like PKU, maple syrup urine disease is managed by lowering the amount of amino acids in the diet, in this case, leucine, isoleucine, and valine. Some disorders of amino acid metabolism can be treated by the administration of a vitamin cofactor. They are associated with an enzyme abnormality that leads to a high Michaelis constant (K_m) for the enzyme. As a result, increased amounts of the vitamin cofactor are needed to effect enzyme catalysis. Pyridoxine-dependent seizures, pyridoxine-dependent homocystinuria, and vitamin B_{12}–responsive methylmalonic acidemia are examples of these disorders. In persons with these conditions, if the metabolic abnormality is not identified and treated, mental retardation occurs. A disorder of carbohydrate metabolism, galactosemia, produces mental retardation, cataracts, and cirrhosis of the liver unless the affected infant is treated with a galactose-free diet early in life.

Some genetic defects cause mental retardation because of an abnormality in the *transport* of neurologically important substances. Wilson disease, which is due to a defect in the metabolism and transport of copper, may be associated with behavioral abnormalities, mental retardation, and liver damage. Hartnup disease, which is due to defective transport of neutral amino acids in the intestine and kidneys, is characterized by cerebellar ataxia, a pellagra-like skin rash, mental retardation, and aminoaciduria.

The *storage* of abnormal compounds may destroy nervous tissues. For example, Tay-Sachs disease, which is due to an absence of hexosaminidase A, causes accumulation of a specific glycolipid in the neurons of the cerebral gray matter. Neurologic deterioration begins in the first year of life. Other diseases associated with the storage of abnormal compounds in the brain are the mucopolysaccharidoses and the mucolipidoses.

The Phakomatoses

The phakomatoses are examples of single-gene defects associated with mental retardation. Tuberous sclerosis is an autosomal dominant disorder characterized by a butterfly-shaped facial rash, areas of hypopigmentation of the skin, and seizures. Mental retardation occurs frequently but not in all cases. Retinal phakomas, cystic changes in the phalanges, and intracranial calcifications are also found frequently. There is a relatively high incidence of this disorder among mentally retarded individuals in institutions. It is a disorder with a wide range of expression, and its incidence may be higher than the 1 in 100,000 previously estimated.[39]

Neurofibromatosis is a neurocutaneous disorder with an autosomal dominant pattern of inheritance. The estimated incidence is 1 in 2,500–3,300 live births.[23] Multiple subcutaneous neurofibromas and café-au-lait spots on the skin are the clinical hallmarks of the disease. The fibrous tumors may also involve any part of the central or peripheral nervous system. Bone and joint abnormalities, as well as endocrine and growth disturbances, are also found. Mental retardation is mild when present, except where intracranial growth of neurofibromas results in seizures and atrophy of contiguous brain tissue. Mental retardation appears to precede clinical manifestations of the disorder for reasons that are not clear. The nature of the genetic defect in this disorder is unknown.

Multiple Congenital Anomaly (MCA)/ Mental Retardation (MR) Syndromes

It is likely that this large group of rare disorders is recessively inherited because of the increased incidence of the disorder in siblings and in consanguineous marriages. The diag-

TABLE 1-2.—EXAMPLES OF GENETIC MULTIPLE CONGENITAL ANOMALY (MCA)/MENTAL RETARDATION (MR) SYNDROMES

SYNDROME	COMMON PHYSICAL FINDINGS	INHERITANCE*
Smith-Lemli-Opitz	Failure to thrive, ptosis, syndactyly of toes 2 and 3, abnormalities of external genitalia	A/R
De Sanctis-Cacchione	Xeroderma pigmentosa, microcephaly, hypogonadism	A/R
Seckel	Prenatal growth deficiency, microcephaly, prominent nose	A/R
Cockayne	Growth failure with senility, retinal degeneration, deafness, photosensitivity	A/R
Sjögren-Larssen	Ichthyosis, spasticity, shortness	A/R
Congenital myotonic dystrophy	Mother affected, severe hypotonia, clubfeet, myopathic facies	A/D
Craniosynostosis syndromes	Synostosis of cranium, maxillary hypoplasia, syndactyly, thumb anomalies or polydactyly	A/D or A/R
Multiple lentigines	Cutaneous lentigines, deafness, pulmonic stenosis, hypertelorism, growth failure	A/D

*Abbreviations: A/R—autosomal recessive: A/D—autosomal dominant.
Source: Crandall B.F.: Genetic disorders and mental retardation, *J. Am. Acad. Child Psychiatry* 16(1):88–108, 1977. (Used by permission.)

TABLE 1-3.—MCA/MR SYNDROMES ATTRIBUTED TO SPECIFIC DRUG EXPOSURE DURING PREGNANCY

DRUG	MR	PHYSICAL FINDINGS
Alcohol (fetal alcohol syndrome)[43]	+	Prenatal growth deficiency, microcephaly, short palpebral fissures, joint anomalies
Tridione[44]	+	Growth deficiency, maxillary hypoplasia, ptosis or strabismus, heart defect
Hydantoin[45]	+/−	Growth deficiency, cleft lip and palate, dysplasia of terminal phalanges, occasional cardiac abnormalities
Progesterone[46]	+/−	Limb defects, congenital heart defects
Warfarin[47]	+	Hypoplastic nasal cartilage, stippled epiphyses, hypotonia, seizures

Source: Crandall B.F.: Genetic disorders and mental retardation, *J. Am. Acad. Child Psychiatry* 16(1):88–108, 1977. (Used by permission.)

nosis of these defects is usually made at a genetic center. A list of some of the more common genetic MCA/MR syndromes appears in Table 1–2. Some MCA/MR syndromes are caused by the teratogenic effects of maternal medication taken during early pregnancy, rather than by genetic defects (Table 1–3).

X-Linked Mental Retardation

In studies of the mentally retarded in institutions, it has repeatedly been found that there are from 30% to 50% more males than females.[40] This can be attributed in part to X-linked forms of the disorder.

One of these forms is associated with a constriction near the end of the long arm of the X chromosome, referred to as the "fragile site" marker.[41] It is estimated that about one third of families with X-linked mental retardation have the fragile-X syndrome.[42] Affected males have few abnormal physical findings except for enlarged testes that become evident at puberty. A recent study of female carriers has shown that some have a mild degree of mental retardation.[42] The importance of the fragile-X syndrome lies in the fact that, next to trisomy 21, it is the most common cause of mental retardation that can be specifically diagnosed by chromosomal analysis.[40]

Malformations of the Central Nervous System

The etiology of malformations of the central nervous system, like malformations of other organs, includes genetic as well as acquired disorders. Secondary abnormalities of the skull and face frequently occur along with the neurologic defects. In these conditions, mental retardation is usually profound and many newborns with such defects do not survive infancy.

Hydrocephalus can be present at birth or develop in early infancy. It has many causes, including several genetically induced forms. One of these is X-linked, an obstructive type resulting from a stenosis of the aqueduct of Sylvius. Autosomal recessive and polygenically inherited forms are also known. Cases associated with multiple congenital anomaly syndromes have been identified. The prognosis for mental development is improved by early correction of the abnormal dynamics of cerebral spinal fluid.

The related neural tube defects, *anencephaly, encephalocele,* and *myelomeningocele,* constitute a relatively common group of malformations that have an incidence of 1 in 600 live births. The risk of recurrence is in the range of 5%. Mental retardation may result from anomalies of the nervous system or from complications such as hydrocephalus and meningitis. Approximately half of all persons with meningomyelocele show mental retardation. In this condition, determination of the level of α-fetoprotein in the amniotic fluid establishes a presumptive prenatal diagnosis with 90% accuracy. This allows parents of an affected child to consider future pregnancies with the knowledge that a prenatal diagnosis can be made and the pregnancy terminated if there is an abnormality.

"Pure" Mental Retardation

The label "pure" is used to refer to cases of mild to severe mental retardation without specific identifying features, such as physical anomalies or metabolic abnormalities. Current evidence suggests that there are genetic components in the etiology of these cases. The mild form may be multifactorial (i.e., determined by the additive effects of many genetic and nongenetic factors) or polygenic. In some instances, severe mental retardation may be recessively inherited, particularly in those individuals with a small head size. In a recent study, about 20% of the siblings of this group had mild or severe mental retardation, whereas their parents were usually of normal intelligence.[48]

SPECIFIC BEHAVIORS

Dyslexia

Dyslexia is a specific reading disability that occurs in children who have normal intelligence, adequate educational opportunities, and intact neurologic function (see also chap. 15). It is seen in at least 5% of the population, and up to 50% of cases may be inherited, with an autosomal dominant inheritance being most common.[49] Males tend to be more severely affected than females. Genetic linkage studies have suggested that there is a high correlation with chromosome 15 heteromorphisms.[50]

Stuttering

Stuttering is a defect in timing in the transition from one sound to another. The onset of this disorder occurs before age 12. More males than females are affected, and usually to a more severe degree. Most individuals recover, and the defect is not associated with neurologic disorders or mental retardation.

Stuttering is frequently familial. When probands of adults are studied, the average frequency of affected siblings is 28.6% for males and 10.1% for females. By contrast, the frequency of this disorder in the general population is 4.5% and 1.5% in males and females, respectively.[51] The mechanism by which this trait might be inherited and the degree of its expressivity are still under investigation.

GENETICS OF PSYCHIATRIC DISORDERS

The following methods of genetic investigation have been used in an attempt to define the role played by heredity in the distribution of psychiatric conditions such as schizophrenia and the primary affective disorders:

1. *Family risk studies.* A comparison is made between the expectancy rate (the cases that may arise during a designated period of time) for a disorder in the biologic relatives of an affected individual (index case) and that in the general population. There is also an attempt to see whether this risk figure correlates with the closeness of familial relationship.
2. *Twin studies.* The concordance rate (the frequency with which a co-twin is affected by a disorder which the other has) is determined for monozygotic (MZ) and dizygotic (DZ) twins. If there is a significant genetic component to the illness, the rate will be much higher in the MZ twins. The rate for DZ twins should approximate that of nontwin full siblings.
3. *Adoption studies.* In these studies, the incidence of a disorder is determined in adoptees and their biologic and adoptive parents. If a genetic factor(s) is influencing its distribution, the rate of the disorder in the adopted offspring of affected individuals will be higher than that in a control group of adoptees whose biologic parents do not have the condition. Alternatively, the rate in the biologic relatives of adoptees with the disorder will exceed that in (1) the biologic relatives of a control group of unaffected adoptees, and (2) the adoptive relatives of both the affected and the unaffected children.

In the next two sections, we will briefly review some of the evidence from these kinds of studies indicating that schizophrenia and the primary affective disorders have a hereditary basis. In schizophrenia, the importance of genetic factors in the etiology of the chronic forms has been fairly well established, although the exact mode of inheritance has not been established. The same is true for unipolar depression. With respect to manic-depressive (bipolar) illness, there is evidence, albeit controversial, that in some families this disorder is inherited as an X-linked trait.

Schizophrenia

The prevalence of schizophrenia in our population is about 1%, a rate similar to that in other Western countries. In the late 1930s, Kallmann reported that a study of the families of over 1,000 schizophrenics showed that their biologic relatives had a greatly increased risk of developing this condition.[52] Subsequent investigations have confirmed Kallmann's general observations, although the expectancy rates found in these studies varied somewhat from his figures. A summary of the results of the studies in the literature dealing with the morbidity risks to the different categories of family members of schizophrenic patients appears in Table 1–4. These data show

TABLE 1–4.—MORBIDITY RISK OF SCHIZOPHRENIA*

RELATIVES OF SCHIZOPHRENICS	RISK (%)
First-degree	
Parents	4.4
Siblings	8.5
Neither parent schizophrenic	8.2
One parent schizophrenic	13.8
Children	12.3
Both parents schizophrenic	36.6
Second-degree	
Uncles and aunts	2.0
Nephews and nieces	2.2
Grandchildren	2.8
Half-siblings	3.2
Third-degree	
First cousins	2.9
General population†	0.86

*Based on Slater and Cowie (1971)[53]; data mainly derived from pooled data on Zerbin-Rudin (1967)[54], correction for age usually by shorter Weinberg method, risk 15–39; only cases of definite schizophrenia counted.

†Compiled from 19 investigations in 6 countries.

Source: Tsuang M.T.: Genetic factors in schizophrenia, in Grenell R.G., Gabay S. (eds.): *Biological Foundations of Psychiatry.* New York, Raven Press, 1976, vol. 2. (Used by permission.)

that not only is there an increased risk of the disorder in the biologic relatives of an affected person over that experienced by the general population but also that the closer the familial relationship, the greater the risk. The findings from some family risk studies indicate that it is the chronic, not the acute, form of the illness that tends to occur with greater frequency among the biologic relatives of schizophrenics.[55]

Twin studies have provided additional evidence for the role of heredity in this illness. Once again, Kallmann made some of the initial observations, reporting in the 1940s that a study of over 900 twins showed that the concordance rate for schizophrenia was much higher in MZ than in DZ pairs. A summary of the available data on twin studies done prior to 1967 showed the concordance rate for DZ twins to be 6–12%, or no greater than the morbidity risk for a full nontwin sibling, whereas the rate for MZ twins averaged 58%.[56] Table 1–5 lists the results of more recent and better controlled twin studies performed in four countries including the United States. These support the general conclusion of the earlier research, that there is a significantly higher concordance rate for MZ twins.

Some of the most compelling evidence for a genetic basis for schizophrenia has come from studies of adopted children.[55, 56] Heston reported one of the first of these studies, in which 47 children born to schizophrenic mothers confined to a psychiatric hospital were the experimental subjects.[57] The children were permanently separated from their mothers early in the postnatal period and given up for adoption. A control group of 50 children born to nonschizophrenic mothers and also given up for adoption were chosen from the registers of the adoption agencies that handled the experimental subjects. Both groups of children were followed over many years and an attempt was made to ascertain the incidence of psychiatric illness among them. A much higher concentration of psychiatric disability and schizophrenia was found in the adopted offspring of the schizophrenic mothers than in the control children.

In more recent studies, conducted in Denmark, the distribution of schizophrenia in the biologic and adoptive relatives of adoptees with this disorder was determined.[56, 59] From a large number of adopted children, those who later developed schizophrenia were identified as experimental subjects. The incidence of the illness in the biologic relatives of these subjects was compared with that in the biologic relatives of a control group of adoptees without schizophrenia. The occurrence of schizophrenia in the adoptive families of the two groups of adoptees was also evaluated. The incidence of the disorder in the biologic relatives (parents, siblings, and half-siblings) of the schizophrenics was found to be 8%, as contrasted to a rate of only 2% in the biologic relatives of the nonschizophrenics. This difference was statistically significant. The rate of illness in the adoptive relatives of the experimental and control adoptees was 1.5% to 3%, respectively, considerably lower than that in the biologic relatives of the schizophrenics.

Additional data favoring a role for genetic

TABLE 1–5.—CONCORDANCE RATES OF SCHIZOPHRENIA IN TWINS*

		MZ PAIRS			DZ PAIRS		
REFERENCE	COUNTRY	No. of Pairs	Concordance† a	b	No. of Pairs	Concordance† a	b
Tienari (1968)	Finland	16	6%	36%	20	5%	14%
Kringlen (1968)	Norway	55	25	38	90	4	10
Fischer et al. (1969)	Denmark	21	24	48	41	10	19
Pollin et al. (1969)	United States	80	14	35	146	4	10

*Based on Gottesman and Shields (1972).[58]
†a, Diagnostically certain cases only; b, also including probable schizophrenics.
Source: Tsuang M.T.: Genetic factors in schizophrenia, in Grenell R.G., Gabay S. (eds.): *Biological Foundations of Psychiatry*. New York, Raven Press, 1976, vol. 2. (Used by permission.)

factors in this condition have come from studies of MZ twins raised apart. These have shown a concordance rate for schizophrenia of 64%.[56]

While the evidence that has accumulated so far on the hereditary nature of schizophrenia indicates that this illness, at least in its chronic form, has a genetic component, the precise mode of transmission of the trait is uncertain. No chromosome anomalies have been discovered and neither a monogenic nor a polygenic pattern of inheritance explains all of the genetic data which are accepted as being valid for this condition. Most investigators in this field agree that even though genetic factors are important in the causation of schizophrenia, they are insufficient by themselves to account for the development of the illness. It is likely that what is inherited is a predisposition to schizophrenia, and whether or not an affected individual develops the full-blown illness depends to a large extent on his life experiences.

Affective Disorders

The primary affective disorders are characterized by a major disturbance in mood occurring in the absence of another preexisting psychiatric illness or an underlying physical ailment. They are generally divided into two types: unipolar depressive illness, which constitutes the vast majority of cases, and bipolar depressive illness. Recurrent episodes of depression occur in both of these; however, manic episodes are only seen in patients with the bipolar type (also called manic-depressive illness). Occasionally, bipolar patients have recurrent mania without clinically apparent depression.

Evidence derived from family risk, twin, and linkage studies indicates that genetic factors are important in the etiology of the primary affective disorders. The biologic relatives of affected persons have a higher expectancy rate for these conditions. Moreover, there are studies indicating that the same type of disorder (i.e., either unipolar or bipolar illness) tends to occur among family members.[53, 60] While there is general agreement that this is true for unipolar illness, some investigations have found this not to be the case for bipolar illness.[61]

Twin studies also indicate that a hereditary basis exists for the primary affective disorders. A summary of the major studies in the literature by Allen in 1976 revealed the following concordance rates: for all types of affective disorders, MZ 57%, DZ 14%; for the unipolar type, MZ 40%, DZ 11%, and for the bipolar type, MZ 72%, DZ 14%.[62] These figures contrast sharply with the expectancy rate of primary affective disorders in the general population, estimated to be 5–7%.[61] The data from twin studies also suggest that if one MZ twin has a unipolar or bipolar disorder, the co-twin, if ill, will most likely have the same disorder.

In contrast to schizophrenia, there are only a few reports of adoption studies in the affective disorders. What data are available show that there is a higher frequency of illness in adopted offspring of affected parents than in adoptees whose biologic parents were well.[63, 64]

On the basis of differences in family illness patterns, Winokur has suggested that unipolar depression can be subdivided into two types of depressive illness: depression spectrum disease and pure depressive disease.[61] The first condition is characterized by the onset of depressive episodes before age 40, a greater incidence among women, and a high rate of alcoholism and sociopathic behavior in male first-degree relatives of affected persons. The total rate of psychiatric disability due to depression, alcoholism, and antisocial personality is greater in the families with this condition than in those with pure depressive disease. Individuals with pure depressive disease generally have the onset of symptoms after age 40. There is equal sex distribution in this condition, and alcoholism and sociopathic disorder are not especially common among family members. Also, in families with pure depressive disease there is a marked similarity in the age of onset of the disorder. Whether these two conditions are genetically distinct disorders remains to be proved, but Winokur has some preliminary data indicating that depressive spectrum disease may be linked to such genetic markers as the third component of complement (C_3) or α-haptoglobin.[61]

The mode of inheritance of unipolar depression is unknown; however, evidence from linkage studies first reported in the early 1970s indicates that bipolar illness may be transmitted by a gene located on the X chromosome.[65] The mode of transmission is thought by some investigators to be a dominant type. The marker genes that bipolar depression has been linked to are those for red-green color blindness, the Xg blood group, and glucose-6-phosphate dehydrogenase deficiency, which are carried on the X chromosome.[66]

Information from some family pedigree studies has not supported the concept of X-linked transmission of bipolar illness. For example, there are instances reported of father to son transmission, something that is incompatible with this mode of inheritance. Also, the large chromosome distance between the gene locus for color blindness and that for the Xg blood group makes it unlikely that the gene for bipolar illness could be linked closely to both.

Because of these inconsistencies, linkage studies were recently conducted at the National Institute of Mental Health to test the hypothesis that bipolar illness is transmitted by a gene on the X chromosome.[67, 68] In these studies, no evidence for linkage between this disorder and the regions on the X chromosome for red-green color blindness and the Xg blood type was found.

This matter is at present a controversial one with conflicting data coming from different investigative groups. It is possible, as suggested by Mendlewicz and his co-workers, that bipolar illness is a genetically heterogeneous disorder, that in some families the condition is transmitted by a gene on the X chromosome while in others there is a different mode of transmission.[66]

GENETIC COUNSELING

As the knowledge of genetic disorders has increased, genetic counseling has become more and more important in the practice of medicine. It is essential that primary care physicians, especially those responsible for the care of young couples who are contemplating having children, be aware of the general developments in this area of medicine. Rainer points out that "genetic counseling today involves not only taking an accurate medical and family history, but also obtaining all necessary laboratory tests."[69] These services require specialized knowledge and facilities; therefore, persons in need of them are commonly referred to genetic centers.

The following are generally accepted indications for referral of a couple to a genetic counselor:

1. The presence of (in prospective parents or their immediate family):
   a. a congenital physical defect
   b. mental retardation
   c. unusually short or tall stature
   d. a chromosomal abnormality
   e. an inherited or metabolic disease, known or suspected
   f. abnormal development of the sexual organs
   g. failure to undergo pubertal development (with the development of secondary sexual characteristics)
2. Couples who have experienced repeated miscarriages
3. Couples in whom a routine infertility workup has failed to define a cause of conceptional difficulty.

Some of the functions performed by genetic counseling centers are to evaluate a family pedigree for genetic disease; to make definitive genetic diagnosis; to estimate the risk of specific genetic disorders occurring in the offspring of couples whose families have inherited defects; and to educate patients about genetic disorders and correct any misconceptions they may have. The ultimate responsibility for decision-making with respect to having children rests with the couple referred for counseling.

Prenatal diagnosis by amniocentesis is an important adjunct to effective genetic counseling (Fig 1–5). Amniotic fluid is obtained by suprapubic aspiration of the amniotic cavity

A FLOW CHART FOR THE STUDY OF FLUID OBTAINED BY AMNIOCENTESIS

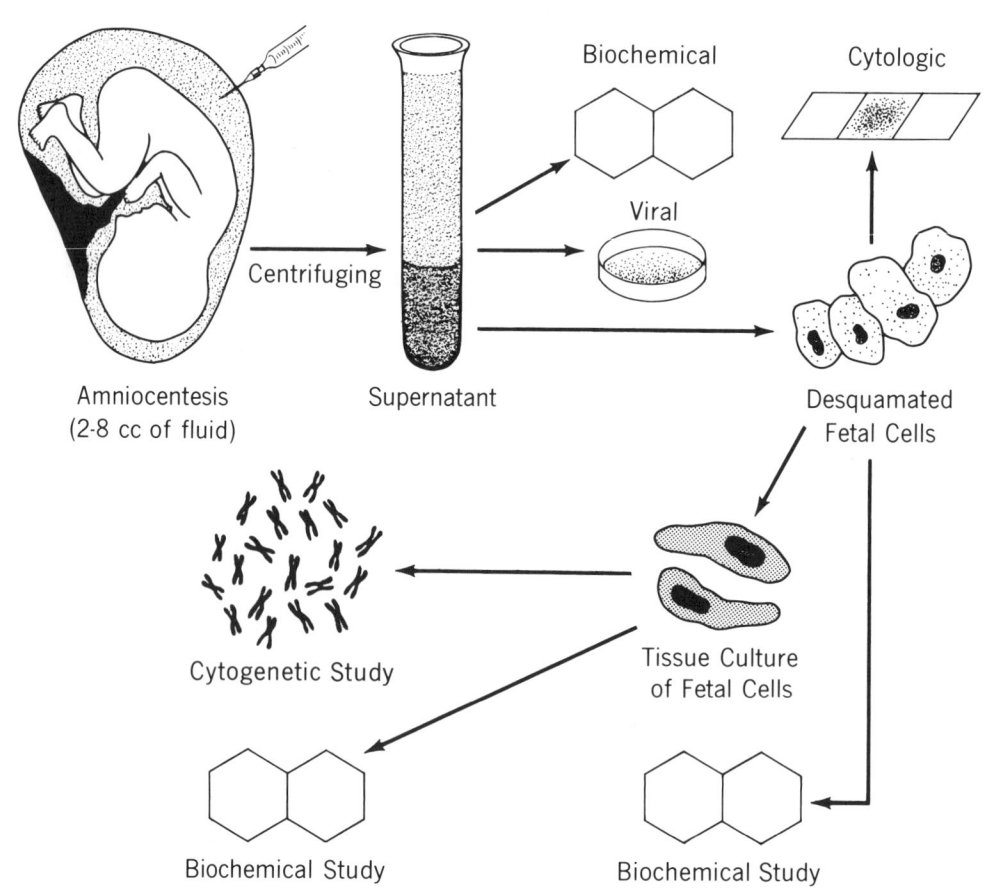

Fig 1–5.—Scheme for the analysis of amniotic fluid in prenatal diagnosis. (Adapted from figure by A. Spiegler from Dancis, J., "The prenatal detecton of hereditary defects," *Hospital Practice,* Vol. 4, No. 6, and from *Medical Genetics,* V.A. McKusick and R. Clairborne, eds., HP Publishing Co., Inc., New York, NY 1973. With permission.)

after careful localization of the fetal and placental positions by ultrasound. It is usually carried out after 14–16 weeks of gestation, a stage of pregnancy when the uterus is sufficiently large and yet there is still enough time to make a decision regarding the termination of the pregnancy before this constitutes a substantial risk to the mother. Table 1–6 gives the general indications for amniocentesis.

The aspirate from the amniotic cavity, a sample of the fluid surrounding the fetus, has cells from the fetus and the amniotic membrane derived from the zygote. After centrifugation, the supernatant is used for biochemical analysis. For example, a determination of the level of α-fetoprotein can be made which establishes, with more than 90% accuracy, the diagnosis of open neural tube defects. The centrifuged amniotic fluid cells grow well in tissue culture, and after 4 to 5 weeks the cultured cells can be studied by means of karyotype analysis and/or biochemical assay. It is now possible to diagnose more than 75 biochemical disorders by analysis of the cells.

TABLE 1–6.—GENERAL INDICATIONS
FOR PRENATAL DIAGNOSIS BY AMNIOCENTESIS

1. Any pregnancy in a woman who is 35 years of age or older.
2. A previous child has a proved or suspected chromosome abnormality.
3. Either parent is a known carrier for a chromosome abnormality.
4. Parents are thought to be carriers for an inherited disorder that is diagnosable in utero, e.g., spina bifida/anencephaly, galactosemia, Tay-Sachs disease:
   a. If there has been a previously affected child.
   b. If the parents have been demonstrated to be carriers by means of screening tests.
5. The mother is a carrier of a serious disorder that affects males only, e.g., Duchenne muscular dystrophy.

Source: Riccardi V.M.: *The Genetic Approach to Human Disease*. New York, Oxford University Press, 1977, p. 162. (Used by permission.)

Follow-up studies of women who have undergone diagnostic evaluation by amniocentesis and ultrasound scanning of the amniotic cavity have shown that these procedures are a valuable addition to prenatal care. Other forms of prenatal diagnosis such as fetoscopy (direct visualization of the fetus) and fetal blood sampling are currently under investigation.[70]

SUMMARY

Genetic factors are an important cause of some types of mental retardation and psychiatric illness, e.g., schizophrenia and the primary affective disorders. Evidence for this comes from chromosomal analyses and special genetic investigations including familial incidence and twin, adoptee, and linkage studies. Amniocentesis and analysis of the amniotic fluid allow for the identification of fetuses which are affected by severe genetic disorders that cause mental retardation and physical defects; this knowledge permits the parents to consider a planned abortion. For example, by means of karyotype analysis in translocation Down syndrome, it is possible to identify a parent who is a carrier of the translocation defect and predict the chances of a future child having the condition.

The chronic forms of schizophrenia and unipolar illness appear to be heritable, although the exact pattern of inheritance is unknown. Early linkage studies indicated that bipolar illness is transmitted by a dominant gene carried on the X chromosome; however, the data from more recent investigations have not supported this finding. It is possible that manic-depressive illness is a genetically heterogeneous disorder and that one form is transmitted in X-linked dominant fashion.

In many instances of mental retardation due to genetic defects, specific metabolic or structural abnormalities that impair neurologic function have been identified. The fact that genetic factors play a role in the etiology of schizophrenia and the affective disorders strongly suggests the presence of biochemical abnormalities in these disorders. A discussion of some theories of the biochemical pathogenesis of schizophrenia and the primary affective disorders appears in chapter 3.

REFERENCES

1. Dobzhansky T.: Of flies and men. *Am. Psychol.* 22:41, 1967.
2. Sparkes R.S. (moderator): Human gene mapping, genetic linkage, and clinical applications (UCLA Conference). *Ann. Intern. Med.* 93:469, 1980.
3. McBride G.: The newest thing in maps—one that localizes human genes. *J.A.M.A.* 237(1):8, 1977.
4. Jacob F.: Evolution and tinkering. *Science* 196:1161, 1977.
5. King M.C., Wilson A.C.: Evolution at two levels, molecular similarities and biological differences between humans and chimpanzees. *Science* 188:197, 1975.
6. Sager R., Kitchen, R.: Selective silencing of eucaryotic DNA. *Science* 189:426, 1975.
7. Barth L.G., Barth L.J.: Na[22] and Ca[45] uptake during embryonic induction in *rana-pipiens*. *Dev. Biol.* 28:18, 1972.
8. Kauffman S.A.: Control circuits for determination and transdetermination. *Science* 181:210, 1973.
9. McMahau D.: Chemical messengers in development: A hypothesis. *Science* 185:1012, 1974.
10. Krugman S. (ed.): Rubella symposium. *Am. J. Dis. Child.* 110:345, 1965.
11. McBride W.G.: Thalidomide and congenital abnormalities. *Lancet* 2:1358, 1961.
12. Towbin A.: Central nervous system damage in

the human fetus and newborn infant. *Am. J. Dis. Child.* 119:529–542, 1970.
13. Towbin A.: Nervous system damage related to hyaline membrane disease. *Lancet* 1:890, 1969.
14. Towbin, A.: Mental retardation due to germinal matrix infarction. *Science* 164:156–161, 1969.
15. Sameroff A.J., Chandler M.J.: Reproductive risk and the continuum of caretaking casualty, in Horowitz F.D. (ed.): *Child Development Research*. Chicago, The University of Chicago Press, 1975.
16. Werner E.E., et al.: *The Children of Kawai Honolulu*. Honolulu, University of Hawaii Press, 1971.
17. Present knowledge of the relationship of nutrition to brain development and behavior. *Nutr. Rev.* 31:242, 1973.
18. Read M.: Malnutrition hunger and behavior. *J. Am. Diabetic Assoc.* 63:379, 386, 1973.
19. Dobbing J.: Malnutrition and school progress. *Lancet* 1:284, Feb. 1, 1975; *J. Pediatr.* 88:702, 1976.
20. Werner E.E., et al.: Cumulative effect of perinatal complications and deprived environment on physical, intellectual, and social development of preschool children. *Pediatrics* 39:480–505, 1967.
21. Erbe R.W.: Current concepts in genetics. *N. Engl. J. Med.* 294(7):381, 1976.
22. McKusick V.A.: *Mendelian Inheritance in Man: Catalogs of Autosomal Dominant, Autosomal Recessive and X-Linked Phenotypes*. Baltimore, The Johns Hopkins University Press, 1978.
23. Riccardi V.M.: *The Genetic Approach to Human Disease*. New York, Oxford University Press, 1977.
24. Mussen P.H., Conger J.J., Kagen J.: *Child Development and Personality*. New York, Harper & Row, 1979.
25. Jensen A.R.: How much can we boost IQ and scholastic achievement? *Harvard Ed. Review* 39:449, 1969.
26. Bergsma D. (ed.): *Birth Defects: Atlas & Compendium*. Baltimore, Williams & Wilkins Co., 1973.
27. Sepe S.J., et al.: An evaluation of routine follow-up blood screening of infants for phenylketonuria. *N. Engl. J. Med.* 300:606, 1979.
28. Perry T.A., et al.: Unrecognized adult phenylketonuria. *N. Engl. J. Med.* 289(8):385, 1973.
29. Waisman H.A., Wang H.L., Palmer G., et al.: Phenylketonuria in infant monkeys. *Nature* 188:1124–1125, 1960.
30. Schlesinger K., et al.: Effects of experimentally induced phenylketonuria on seizure susceptibility in mice. *J. Comp. Physiol. Psychol.* 67:149, 1969.
31. Menkes J.H.: Cerebral proteolipids in phenylketonuria. *Neurology* 18:1003, 1968.
32. Shah S.N., Peterson N.A., McKean C.M.: Cerebral white matter and myelin in phenylketonuria. *J. Neurochem.* 19(10):2369, 1972.
33. Johnson R.C., Shah S.N.: Effect of hyperphenylalanemia on fatty acid composition of lipids of rat brain myelin. *J. Neurochem.* 21:1225, 1973.
34. Taub F., Johnson T.C.: The mechanism of polyribosome disaggregation in brain tissue by phenylalanine, *Biochem. J.* 151:173, 1975.
35. Siegel F.L., Aoiki K., Cobwell R.E.: Polyribosome disaggregation and cell-free protein synthesis in preparations from cerebral-cortex of hyperphenylalaninemic rats. *J. Neurochem.* 18:537, 1971.
36. Hughes J.V., Johnson T.C.: The effects of hyperphenylalaninemia on the concentrations of aminoacyltransfer ribonucleic acid in vivo. *Biochem. J.* 162:527, 1977.
37. Patel M.S., Grover W.D., Auerbach V.H.: Pyruvate metabolism by homogenates of human brain: Effects of phenylpyruvate and implications for etiology of mental retardation in phenylketonuria. *J. Neurochem.* 20:289, 1973.
38. Hsia D.Y.Y.: Phenylketonuria: Clinical genetic and biochemical aspects, In *Warsaw Congress Proceedings of the International Association for the Scientific Study of Mental Deficiency*, in press.
39. Berg J.M., Crome L.: Les phakomatoses dans la deficience mentale, in Michaux L., Feld M. (eds.): *Les Phakomatoses cerebrales* Paris, Spei-editeurs, 1963.
40. Gerald P.S.: X-linked mental retardation and an X-chromosome marker. *N. Engl. J. Med.* 303(12):696, 1980.
41. Lubs H.A.: A marker X-chromosome. *Am. J. Hum. Genet.* 21:231, 1969.
42. Turner G., et al.: Heterozygous expression of X-linked mental retardation and X-chromosome marker fra(X) (q27). *N. Engl. J. Med.* 303(12):662, 1980.
43. Jones K.L., Smith D.W., Streissguth A.P., et al.: Outcome in offspring of chronic alcoholic women. *Lancet* 1:1076, 1974.
44. German J., Kowal A., Ehlers K.H.: Trimethadione and human teratogenesis. *Teratology* 3:349–361, 1970.
45. Monson R.R., et al.: Diphenylhydantoin and selected congenital malformations. *N. Engl. J. Med.* 289:1049, 1973.
46. Nora J.J., et al.: Congenital abnormalities and first-trimester exposure to progestagen/estrogen. *Lancet* 1:313, 1976.
47. Shaul W.L., Emery H., Hall J.G.: Chondrodysplasia punctata and maternal Warfarin use

during pregnancy. *Am. J. Dis. Child.* 129:360, 1975.
48. Becker J.M., et al.: A biologic and genetic study of 40 cases of severe pure mental retardation. *Eur. J. Pediatr.* 124:231, 1977.
49. Smith S.D.: *Genetic Studies and Linkage Analysis of Specific Dyslexia*, thesis. Indiana University, Indianapolis, 1978.
50. Smith S.D., Pennington B.F., Kimberling W.J., et al.: Investigation of subgroups within specific reading disability utilizing neurological and linkage analysis. American Society of Human Genetics, 30th meeting, Minneapolis, Minnesota, 1979, p. 83A.
51. Kidd K.K., Heimbuch R.C.: Demonstration of transmission of stuttering. American Society of Human Genetics, 30th meeting, Minneapolis, Minnesota, 1979, p. 137A.
52. Kallmann F.J.: *The Genetics of Schizophrenia*. Locust Valley, N.Y., J.J. Augustin, Inc., 1938.
53. Slater E., Cowie V.A.: *The Genetics of Mental Disorders*. London, Oxford University Press, 1971.
54. Zerbin-Rüdin E.: Endogen psychosen, in Becker P.E. (ed.): *Humangenetik, ein kurzes handbuch*. Stuttgart, Thieme, 1967.
55. Kety S.S.: Genetic aspects of schizophrenia. *Psychiatr. Ann.* 6:11, 1976.
56. Tsuang M.T.: Genetic factors in schizophrenia, in Grenell R.G., Gabay S. (eds.): *Biological Foundations of Psychiatry*. New York, Raven Press, 1976, vol. 2.
57. Heston L.L.: Psychiatric disorders in foster home reared children of schizophrenic mothers. *Br. J. Psychiatry* 112:819–825, 1966.
58. Gottesman I.I., Shields J.: *Schizophrenia and Genetics: A Twin Study Vantage Point*. New York, Academic Press, 1972.
59. Kety S.S.: Mental illness in the biological and adoptive families of adopted individuals who have become schizophrenic: A preliminary report, in Fieve R., Rosenthal D., Brill H. (eds.): *Genetic Research in Psychiatry*. Baltimore, Johns Hopkins University Press, 1975.
60. Cadoret R.J.: Genetics of affective disorder, in Grenell R.G., Gabay S. (eds.): *Biological Foundations of Psychiatry*. New York, Raven Press, 1976, vol. 2.
61. Winokur G.: Unipolar depression. *Arch. Gen. Psychiatry* 36:47, 1979.
62. Allen M.G.: Twin studies of affective illness. *Arch. Gen. Psychiatry* 33:1476, 1976.
63. Cadoret R.J.: Evidence for genetic inheritance of primary affective disorder in adoptees. *Am. J. Psychiatry* 135:463, 1978.
64. Mendlewicz J., Rainer J.D.: Adoption study supporting genetic transmission of manic-depressive illness. *Nature* 268:327, 1977.
65. Mendlewicz J., Fleiss J.L., Fieve R.R.: Evidence for X-linkage in the transmission of manic-depressive illness. *J.A.M.A.* 222:1624, 1972.
66. Mendlewicz J., Linkowski P., Guroff J.J., et al.: Color blindness linkage to bipolar manic-depressive illness—New evidence. *Arch. Gen. Psychiatry* 36:1442, 1979.
67. Gershon E.S., et al.: Color blindness not closely linked to bipolar illness. *Arch Gen. Psychiatry* 36:1423, 1979.
68. Leckman J.F., et al.: New data do not suggest linkage between the Xg blood group and bipolar illness. *Arch Gen. Psychiatry* 36:1435, 1979.
69. Rainer J.D.: Genetics in behavior and psychiatry, in Grenell R.G., Gabay S. (eds.): *Biological Foundations of Psychiatry*. New York, Raven Press, 1976, vol. 1.
70. Antenatal diagnosis: What is standard? *J.A.M.A.* 241:1666, 1979.

2 / Neurologic Basis of Behavior

NEIL SCHNEIDERMAN, Ph.D.

THE BASIC DETERMINANT of human behavior is the nervous system; unless it functions properly, a person cannot interact successfully with the environment. Although psychological, social, and cultural factors greatly affect a person's thoughts and actions, in the final analysis adaptive behavior depends on a central nervous system that is more or less functionally and structurally intact. During the last century, it was discovered that certain areas of the brain subserve specific somatic functions, such as motor movements and sensory perception. Subsequently, it became apparent that many other psychological and behavioral functions (e.g., sleep, wakefulness, feeding, emotions, motivation, memory) also are integrated within the brain.

The initial studies relating the brain and behavior were based on lesion and stimulation experiments as well as on correlations between clinical findings in patients and brain pathology. Further advances in this area were facilitated by the introduction of sophisticated neurophysiological, neurohistologic, and biochemical analyses. These analyses indicated that changes in the central nervous system concentration of certain putative neurotransmitters are associated with changes in the emotional state and behavior of an individual. Moreover, progress has been made in relating these biochemical changes to specific neuroanatomical systems. It has also become clear that heredity has a significant influence on behavior, and that aberrations of psychological functioning can be genetically transmitted (see chap. 1). This has led to an intense search for enzymatic and biochemical factors that might explain these genetically induced illnesses (see chap. 3).

A thorough understanding of the relationship between the nervous system and behavior requires knowledge of (1) basic principles of neuronal transmission, (2) the effects of drugs on brain function and behavior, and (3) the relationship between central nervous system morphology and behavior. This chapter will examine briefly each of these aspects in an attempt to give the reader as broad a perspective as possible concerning the relationship between the nervous system and behavior.

NEURONAL TRANSMISSION

The human nervous system is a highly organized, interacting population of living cells that is specialized for the acquisition, transmission, and storage of information. These living cells, of which each of us has some 14 billion, are called neurons. They differ greatly from one another in structure, but all have a cell body or soma and at least one process. The individual neuron as well as the entire nervous system may be characterized by the activities of reception, analysis, transmission, and command.

The input elements of the neuron, called dendrites, receive information from other neurons, from specialized receptor cells, and from the environment itself. Dendrites often are found in great numbers and consist of arborized (treelike) processes. This makes it possible for a single neuron to receive information from many other neurons. Because information may be provided to the neuron via its many dendrites, neuronal information must be integrated before it is ready for transmission. The axon is the neuronal process that provides the means for the transmission of information over relatively long distances within the cell. Although each neuron has only one axon, this axon may branch into many collaterals, each of which carries the same information as the original axon. In this manner information from one neuron can be passed on to many others. The output element of the neuron is the axon terminal. Axon terminals in most neurons have synaptic vesicles that contain a chemical transmitter substance. When information is transmitted down the length of the axon in the form of a change in bioelectric activity, a transient release of chemical occurs from the synaptic vesicles located in the end terminals. This chemical transmitter in turn has the capacity to influence other neurons, muscles, or glands.

Bioelectric Properties of Nerve Cells[1,2]

If we take two electrodes and insert one of them into the neuron, we can record a potential difference such that the inside of the cell is about 60–70 mv negative with respect to the electrode on the outside of the cell. This potential difference across the cell membrane, called the resting potential, can be accounted for by the relative distribution of intracellular and extracellular ions. Extracellular fluid is relatively high in sodium ions (Na^+) and relatively low in potassium ions (K^+). In contrast, intracellular fluid is relatively high in potassium ions and very low in sodium ions. The low intracellular concentration of sodium ions is due to an energy-requiring process known as active sodium transport, or more colloquially as the sodium pump. This pump extrudes sodium ions from the cell against a concentration gradient. Because potassium ions can cross the membrane freely, they tend to flow along their concentration gradient, which is highest inside the cell. Potassium therefore tends to leave the cell. As a result of the loss of this positive ion, a relatively negative charge is left within the cell due to the negative charges of macromolecular proteins.

The chemical released from the end terminals of some neurons is capable of hyperpolarizing the cell membrane briefly to a slightly more negative level. In contrast, the chemical released from the end terminals of other neurons is capable of depolarizing the membrane briefly and slightly. When the cell begins to depolarize, current is carried across the membrane by potassium ions. As the membrane becomes more depolarized, the permeability of the membrane to sodium ions increases and sodium flows into the cell. At a critical threshold an action potential is initiated. The action potential is an all-or-nothing event that resembles that of an explosive charge. If the triggering energy is insufficient, nothing occurs; however, if the triggering energy is just sufficient, there is a full explosion.

During the initial phase of the action potential, the barrier to sodium ions that normally exists across the membrane suddenly breaks down and sodium rushes into the cell. The potential overshoots the zero line, thus reversing the polarity of the membrane to a positive 20–30 mv. The potential then returns more slowly to its resting potential level. The duration of the sequence is less than 1 msec and the amplitude of the action potential varies between 100 and 120 mv in different neurons under normal conditions.

Once an action potential is triggered, it is propagated down the axon at a constant amplitude with a fixed, nondecremental, relatively slow velocity of several meters per second. The conduction velocity is directly proportional to the diameter of the axon. In addition, a myelin sheath composed of lipid molecules that individually coats all but the thinnest axons further accelerates the conduction velocity. This is because the myelin sheath, which serves as an insulating layer, is regularly interrupted by constrictions known as nodes of Ranvier. It is only at these nodes that the axonal membrane is directly exposed to the extracellular fluid so that transmembrane ionic flow can occur. Therefore, instead of the action potential propagating from immediately contiguous sites along the membrane, the action potential in the myelinated axon leaps from node to node, constituting a process known as saltatory conduction. Whereas the conduction velocity is directly proportional to the diameter of the axon, the threshold level for the all-or-nothing action potential is inversely proportional; that is, the axons with the largest diameter are the most easily excitable and conduct at the most rapid velocities.

The Synapse

Neurons communicate with each other through junctions known as synapses. These synapses may be either electric or chemical in their mode of action, but chemical synapses are far more prevalent. In a chemical synapse, the transmitter substance crosses the synapse and influences the membrane of the receiving cell. In this manner most chemical synapses provide for one-way conduction of information. Reciprocal synapses, however, have been observed. In this case the receiving cell itself may become activated and release transmitter, which then crosses the synapse and influences the membrane of the original cell.

The neuron that releases the transmitter at the synapses is referred to as the presynaptic neuron, the neuron influenced by the transmitter is the postsynaptic neuron, and the 50–200 Å intercellular space between these neurons is the synaptic cleft. As mentioned, transmitter molecules are stored within the vesicles of the presynaptic nerve terminals. In response to action potentials reaching these terminals, calcium-dependent excitation-secretion coupling within the depolarized nerve terminal leads to the transient emptying of the contents of the vesicles into the synaptic cleft.

Release of transmitter into the synaptic cleft gives rise to transient excitatory or inhibitory potentials in the postsynaptic neuron.[3] Inhibition or excitation depends on the transmitter released by a given cell and the nature of the postsynaptic cell's receptor for the particular transmitter agent. Whereas excitatory postsynaptic potentials cause a transient, localized depolarization of the postsynaptic cell membrane, bringing the resting potential closer to the neuron's threshold for firing an action potential, inhibitory postsynaptic potentials cause a transient hyperpolarization of the postsynaptic cell membrane, moving the resting potential away from the threshold for triggering an action potential. These transient inhibitory and excitatory inputs to the postsynaptic neuron summate algebraically; moreover, they display temporal summation. If sufficient excitatory postsynaptic potentials summate temporally from the cell's various inputs, the postsynaptic cell will integrate these potentials and initiate its own all-or-nothing action potential down its axon. The presynaptic release of transmitter, the presence of a cleft, and the occurrence of localized, transient, bioelectric potentials in the postjunctional cell are also characteristic of the junctions between neurons and muscles.

Once a chemical transmitter influences the postsynaptic membrane, it must be removed from the receptor site in order to permit the postsynaptic membrane to return to its resting state. This may involve enzymatic destruction, presynaptic uptake, or simple diffusion from the synaptic area. In the case of some transmitters, such as the monoamines, all three methods of termination may be involved.

A schematic view of the events that occur at chemical synapses during neuronal transmission is outlined in Figure 2–1. When action potentials arrive at the presynaptic nerve terminal (event 1), there is a transient release (2) of transmitter, T, which diffuses across the cleft (3) and combines with a specialized receptor site in the postsynaptic membrane (4). This leads to a postsynaptic potential (5). Once the transmitter has exerted its effect, its action is terminated by its removal from the receptor sites by diffusion (6), enzymatic destruction (7), or uptake into the presynaptic terminals (8).

Identification of Synaptic Transmitters

In order to demonstrate conclusively that a particular chemical is the transmitter substance at a synapse, specific criteria must be satisfied. First, evidence must be presented that the presynaptic terminals contain the chemical or its immediate precursor. Second,

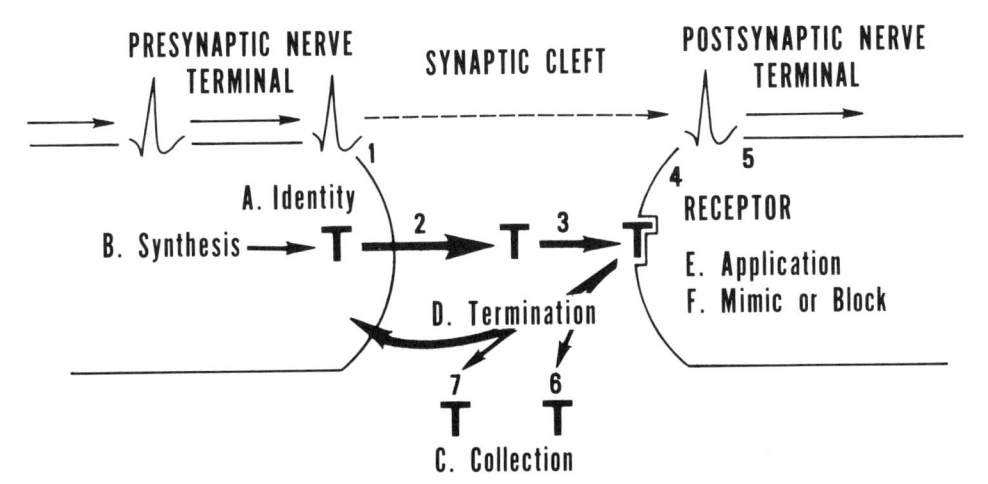

Fig 2-1.—Hypothetical transmission processes at a synapse; *T* represents a hypothetical chemical transmitter. The numbers refer to the events taking place, and the letters refer to the criteria for a transmitter. (From Rech R.H., Moore K.E. (eds.): *An Introduction to Psycho-pharmacology*, New York, Raven Press, 1971. Reproduced with permission.)

neural impulses in the presynaptic terminals must result in the liberation of the substance. Third, microiontophoretic injections of normal (i.e., physiologically compatible) amounts of the chemical must cause a change in the potential at the postsynaptic cellular membrane. (In a microiontophoretic injection the proposed transmitter is dissolved in water and ejected from the tip of a fine glass micropipette by means of a pulse of electric current.) Fourth, a suitable mechanism for the inactivation of the substance must be found in the vicinity of the synapse. Fifth, drugs that are known to facilitate or block the action of the putative transmitter must have the same effect at the synapse in question. Whereas these criteria have been met satisfactorily in the peripheral nervous system, it has been far more difficult to identify transmitters in the central nervous system.

In the peripheral nervous system acetylcholine is the transmitter at the neuromuscular junction of skeletal muscle. Acetylcholine is also the transmitter at autonomic ganglia and at the neuromuscular junctions of the parasympathetic nervous system. In contrast, norepinephrine is the transmitter at the neuromuscular junctions of the sympathetic nervous system. The fact that different chemicals block the transmission of acetylcholine at the neuromuscular junction involving skeletal muscle (e.g., curariform drugs), autonomic ganglia (e.g., hexamethonium), and the neuromuscular junction of the parasympathetic nervous system (e.g., atropine) is presumed to be due to differences in the configurations of receptor sites. Similarly, the fact that chemicals block norepinephrine transmission differentially at the arterioles subserving the skin and mucosa (α-adrenergic blockade) and at the heart (β-adrenergic blockade) has likewise been attributed to differences in receptor sites.

It is well accepted that acetylcholine is a neurotransmitter in the central nervous system (CNS), although the evidence is not so compelling as for the peripheral nervous system. One reason for this is that synapses in the CNS are less accessible than those in the periphery. Another is that central synapses are more heterogeneous, so that analyses must take into account the variety of chemical inputs that may concomitantly influence the postsynaptic membrane. To date the most convincing evidence for a CNS transmitter exists for acetylcholine, which is the transmitter at the motoneuron collateral to the Renshaw cell.[4] Convincing evidence also exists that acetylcholine is a neurotransmitter in the cortex and elsewhere in the brain.

Two other good candidates as CNS transmitters are the catecholamines, norepinephrine and its immediate precursor dopamine.[5] Catecholamines are organic compounds that contain a catechol nucleus (a benzine ring with two adjacent hydroxyl substituents) and an amine group. The strongest evidence for catecholaminergic synapses is in the cerebellum, olfactory bulb, and caudate nucleus. Almost invariably the response of single neurons to norepinephrine and dopamine is a depression of spontaneous activity. Convincing evidence has been provided that the responses to norepinephrine in the cerebellum are mediated by cyclic adenosine monophosphate. Thus, both electrophysiological and cytochemical studies have indicated that central β-adrenergic receptors of cerebellar Purkinje cells mediate their effects by the activation of adenylate cyclase.

Another important putative transmitter in the CNS is the indole amine, serotonin or 5-hydroxytryptamine. Almost all the serotonin-containing neurons in the CNS have their cell bodies in the raphe nuclei along the midline of the lower pons and midbrain. An understanding of serotinergic synapses appears to be a key to understanding important aspects of habituation to sensory stimuli, sleep, and the effects of lysergic acid diethylamide (LSD).

Two other strong candidates for classification as transmitters are γ-aminobutyric acid and glycine. The former appears to be an inhibitory transmitter in the cortex, while evidence has been presented that the latter may be an inhibitory transmitter in the spinal cord. Other substances such as glutamic acid, taurine, histamine, and various neuroactive peptides including substance P have also been proposed as transmitters, but supporting evidence has not been definitive.

In recent years, a large number of putative transmitters have been identified in the CNS. More than 20 substances have been suggested that may have neuroregulatory roles in normal and abnormal brain functioning. Numerous peptides, for instance, have a widespread distribution in the brain and when exogenously applied reveal potent effects on neuronal functioning and behavior. Nevertheless, little is known about their receptor mechanisms or about how they are synthesized or catabolized. Moreover, some neuroactive substances in the CNS remain active longer than the classical transmitter such as acetylcholine. This has given rise to a distinction between neurotransmitters and neuromodulators. The former are active only briefly, whereas the latter have relatively long-term effects. As present it is not known whether the two merely represent extremes along a continuum or actually have qualitatively different functions and modes of action.

Transmitter Dynamics and Synaptic Transmission: Acetylcholine As Example

The actions of most drugs that alter neuronal activity and behavior can be interpreted in terms of their effects on synaptic transmission. The synthesis of acetylcholine (ACh) in cholinergic neurons involves the transport of choline into the cell. This process is dependent on sodium and can be blocked by drugs called hemicholiniums. Once inside the neurons choline combines with acetyl-CoA to form ACh. The ACh appears to be stored in synaptic vesicles until released into the synaptic cleft. Botulinus toxin, the cause of certain cases of severe food poisoning, prevents the release of ACh from nerve terminals; death usually results from respiratory paralysis.

Once inside the synaptic cleft, ACh combines with specific cholinergic receptors on the postsynaptic membrane. Because low concentrations of nicotine mimic the actions of ACh at autonomic ganglia and at skeletal muscle, these receptors are referred to as "nicotinic." Because muscarine mimics the effects of ACh at postganglionic parasympathetic nerve endings, these receptors are referred to as "muscarinic." Just as some drugs mimic the effects of ACh at particular receptor sites, other drugs, called blocking agents, compete with the ACh molecules for receptor sites. Atropine, for instance, blocks the action of ACh at postganglionic parasympathetic nerve endings and is therefore known as a muscarinic blocking drug. Similarly, curare and hexamethonium block the actions of ACh at skeletal muscle junctions and at autonomic ganglia, respectively, and are called nicotinic blocking agents. The fact that both cholinergic agonists and antagonists are differentially effective at different synapses strongly suggests that there are at least slight differences among receptor sites.

Removal of ACh occurs when cholinesterase hydrolyzes the molecule into acetate and choline. Drugs that inhibit or inactivate cholinesterase are called anticholinesterases. These drugs cause ACh to accumulate at cholinergic sites, thereby producing continuous stimulation of cholinergic neurons. Because cholinergic neurons are widely distributed throughout the nervous system, anticholinesterase drugs have been used extensively as toxic agents in agricultural insecticides such as the organophosphates and tested as potential chemical warfare agents, so-called nerve gases. Therapeutically, anticholinesterase agents have been useful in counteracting atony of smooth muscle in the intestinal tract and urinary bladder and in treating myasthenia gravis, which is characterized by weakness and rapid fatigue in skeletal muscle.

The examples provided thus far have been based primarily on the interaction of drugs and transmitter dynamics in the peripheral nervous system. Many drugs that influence cholinergic synapses do not affect the CNS because they are unable to cross the blood-brain barrier at a significant rate. Atropine, scopolamine, and diisopropyl phosphorofluoridate, however, do penetrate the central nervous system. The amnesic effects of scopolamine and atropine have been attributed to the central effects of the drugs. Long-term administration of diisopropyl phosphorofluoridate to patients suffering from myasthenia gravis has been reported to produce nightmares, hallucinations, and confusion, while short-term use of anticholinesterases in normal human subjects has led to agitation, tenseness, and impaired performance on a variety of intellectual tasks.

Psychoactive Drugs and Transmitter Dynamics

There are many drugs that influence brain processes and behavior. Many of them have been linked to the dynamics of putative transmitters (see also chap. 3). The transmitters studied most thoroughly and linked most closely to the effects of psychoactive drugs are the catecholamines.

The catecholamines, with transmitter dynamics as shown in Figure 2–2 (see also Fig 3–1 for metabolic schema), are formed from their amino acid precursor, tyrosine. Tyrosine is taken up from the bloodstream and concentrated within catecholaminergic neurons by an active transport mechanism. In the presence of tyrosine hydroxylase, tyrosine is converted into dihydroxyphenylalanine (dopa). If aromatic amino acid decarboxylase is present, dopa may be synthesized into the putative transmitter dopamine, and if dopamine-β-oxidase is present in the cell, dopamine can be converted into norepinephrine. Both dopamine and norepinephrine are stored in synaptic vesicles and released in response to neuronal stimulation. Unbound catecholamines can be deaminated intraneuronally by monoamine oxidase (MAO). At postsynaptic receptors, however, the concentration of monoamines can be reduced by diffusion away from the receptor area, by active uptake into the presynaptic terminal, or by enzymatic destruction by means of catechol-O-methyl-transferase (COMT) and MAO. Although extraneuronal MAO may deaminate the catecholamines or their O-methyl derivatives, neither COMT nor extraneuronal MAO is believed to play an important role in terminating the actions of the catecholamines in the synaptic cleft.[6]

Both psychotherapeutic drugs and psychotomimetic agents have been linked to catecholaminergic transmitter dynamics. The antischizophrenic activity of phenothiazine drugs such as chlorpromazine, for example, has been closely correlated with the blockade of dopamine receptors.[7] Moreover, the extrapyramidal side effects often observed with these drugs have been related to a postsyn-

A SCHEMATIC REPRESENTATION OF THE FORMATION, ACTION, AND DEACTIVATION OF THE PUTATIVE NEUROTRANSMITTER NOREPINEPHRINE

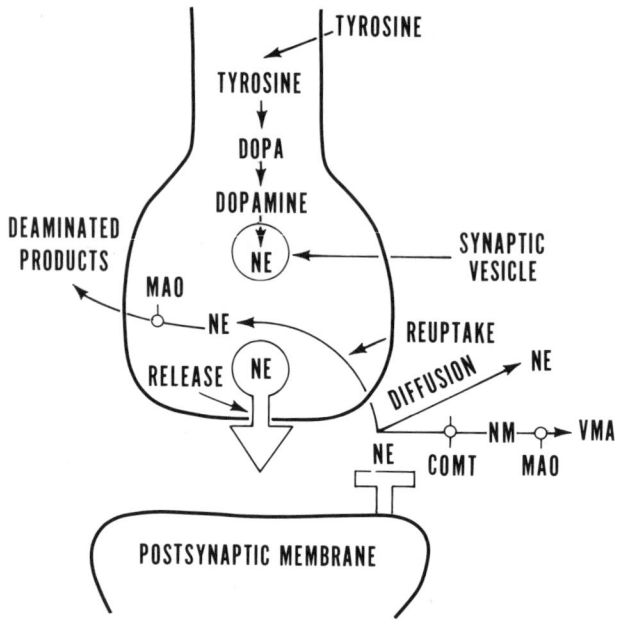

Fig 2-2.—Transmitter dynamics of the catecholamines. NE = norepinephrine; MAO = monoamine oxidase; COMT = catechol-O-methyltransferase; VMA = 3-methoxy-4-hydroxymandelic acid; NM = normetanephrine.

aptic reduction in the activity of dopamine. The catecholamines are believed to play a central role in the pathogenesis of the affective disorders and the two general classes of drugs most often used to treat major depression, the monoamine oxidase inhibitors and the tricyclic antidepressants, increase catecholaminergic activity at the synapses.

Psychoactive drugs have been linked to putative serotonergic as well as catecholaminergic synapses in the central nervous system. Serotonin (5-hydroxytryptamine), like other biogenic amines, does not enter the brain readily from the bloodstream because of its solubility characteristics. The primary substrate for the synthesis of serotonin in the brain is plasma tryptophan (see Fig 3-2 for metabolic schema). In the presence of tryptophan hydroxylase, the tryptophan molecule is hydroxylated at the 5 position to form 5-hydroxytryptophan. Following its synthesis, 5-hydroxytryptophan is almost immediately decarboxylated to yield serotonin.

The study of brain serotonin has aroused the interest of numerous investigators because of the possibility that a serotonergic system of neurons in the brain may be involved in mediating the effects of hallucinogenic drugs. Drugs such as d-lysergic acid diethylamine (LSD), psilocybin, psilocin, and bufotenine resemble serotonin structurally insofar as they, too, are indolealkyl amines.

Although the relationships between the effects of hallucinogenic drugs on behavior and their effects on serotonergic transmission are far from clear, several intriguing findings with respect to LSD have been reported that are relevant to this topic. These findings were facilitated by the discovery that the densest concentrations of serotonin-containing neurons in the entire brain lie in the raphe nuclei, which are located along the midline between the lower pons and the upper midbrain. One interesting finding is that following LSD administration raphe neurons have decreased firing rates. Another is that the decreased firing rates after LSD intake are accompanied by a decreased turnover of serotonin. Still a third provocative finding is that the activation of raphe neurons by iontophoretic injection of norepinephrine or serotonin can be blocked by LSD. This last finding suggests that LSD may inhibit serotonin-containing neurons by blocking the transmitters that normally activate these cells.

THE EFFECTS OF PSYCHOACTIVE DRUGS ON BRAIN FUNCTION AND BEHAVIOR

Most general classifications of psychoactive drugs have been based on differences in behavior induced by the drugs. Subcategorizations, however, have often been based on mixed criteria involving differences in molecular structure, intensity of the effect on behavior, or presumed action of drugs at the synaptic level. The need to resort to a mixed classification is not surprising when one considers that even a slight change in molecular structure or configuration can totally alter a drug's behavioral effect. Thus, for example, the stereoisomer of LSD, in which the positions of the side chains are reversed, has almost no effect on behavior. Another factor to consider is that even a thorough knowledge of a drug's action at the synaptic level cannot predict the effect of the drug unless the anatomical system it influences is also known. Chlorpromazine, for instance, presumably derives its antipsychotic effects from its actions on neocortical cognitive systems and the limbic system, and its Parkinson-like side effects from its action on the extrapyramidal system.

TABLE 2–1.—CLASSIFICATION OF PSYCHOACTIVE DRUGS (BRAND NAMES IN ITALICS)

A. Sedative-hypnotics (CNS depressants)
  1. Barbiturates
  2. Nonbarbiturates
    a. Glutethimide *(Doriden)*
    b. Methaqualone *(Quaalude, Sopor)*
  3. Ethyl alcohol
  4. Anesthetic gases
  5. Chloral hydrate
  6. Bromides
  7. Antianxiety agents
    a. Meprobamate *(Equanil, Miltown)*
    b. Chlordiazepoxide *(Librium)*
    c. Diazepam *(Valium)*
B. Stimulants and antidepressants
  1. Amphetamines
  2. Cocaine
  3. Convulsants
    a. Bicuculline
    b. Pentylenetetrazol *(Metrazol)*
    c. Picrotoxin
    d. Strychnine
  4. Methylphenidate *(Ritalin)*
  5. Nicotine
  6. Phenmetrazine *(Preludin)*
  7. Xanthines
    a. Coffee
  8. Clinical antidepressants
    a. Monoamine oxidase (MAO) inhibitors *(Parnate)*
    b. Tricyclic compounds or dibenzapines *(Elavil, Tofranil)*
C. Narcotic analgesics
  1. Opium
    a. Codeine
    b. Morphine
  2. Meperidine *(Demerol)*
  3. Methadone *(Dolophine)*
D. Antipsychotic agents
  1. Phenothiazines
    a. Chlorpromazine *(Thorazine)*
    b. Compazine
    c. Stelazine
  2. Reserpine *(Serpasil)*
  3. Butyrophenones
    a. Haloperidol *(Haldol)*
  4. Lithium
E. Psychedelic agents
  1. Acetylcholine psychedelics
    a. Atropine
    b. Scopolamine
    c. Muscarine
  2. Norepinephrine psychedelics
    a. Mescaline and mescaline derivatives: DOM(STP), MMDA, TMA
    b. Myristicin and elemicin (nutmeg and mace ingredients)
  3. Serotonin psychedelics
    a. Lysergic acid diethylamine (LSD)
    b. Dimethyltryptamine (DMT)
    c. Psilocybin, psilocin, bufotenine
    d. Ololiuqui (morning glory seeds)
  4. Harmine
  5. Anesthetic hallucinogens
    a. Ketamine *(Ketalar)*
    b. Phencyclidine *(Sernyl)*
  6. Cannabis
    a. Marijuana
    b. Hashish
    c. Tetrahydrocannabinol (THC)

Given the complexity of the issues involved, it is not surprising that classifications of psychopharmacologic agents have been based on mixed criteria. Table 2–1 presents one such classification.

Sedative-Hypnotic Drugs

The sedative-hypnotic drugs vary in chemical structure, but all are capable of depressing the CNS and behavior. Classification of these drugs as sedative-hypnotic tends to be somewhat misleading, because their effects depend on dose. At low doses they cause euphoria or relief from anxiety; at moderate doses they induce sedation; high doses of these drugs cause sleep; and very high doses produce anesthesia, coma, and even death. Death results from the depression of respiratory centers in the medulla.

Although the various CNS depressants differ in potency and in the manner in which they are metabolized, several general principles apply to the entire class. First, their effects summate with one another. Barbiturates, for example, exaggerate the depression induced by drinking alcohol. Second, low doses of these drugs may produce behavioral effects ranging from euphoria to excitement. In part, this is because of their ability to inhibit cortical functions that normally govern learned inhibition. Aside from this *disinhibition*, the inhibitory effects of these drugs on the neocortex and the limbic system reduce anxiety.

A third principle that seems to apply to this general class of CNS depressants is that when they are administered repeatedly over a prolonged period of time, physical dependence occurs. Withdrawal from the drug is followed by a period of hyperexcitability, which can be so severe that it leads to convulsions and death. A fourth principle is that the chronic use of these drugs can lead to tolerance related to the induction of drug-metabolizing enzymes in the liver and to the adaptation of synapses in the brain. Drugs that initially induce sleep may fail to do so after a period of time and may even cause insomnia. A fifth general principle is that sedative-hypnotic drugs tend to exhibit cross-tolerance with other drugs in this class. Thus, a person who is accustomed to drinking large quantities of alcohol will have concomitantly developed an increased tolerance for barbiturates. Both the tolerance and cross-tolerance are primarily restricted to the sedative effects of the drug, with the respiratory centers of the medulla showing considerably less tolerance.

The nonbarbiturate sedatives, glutethimide (Doriden) and methyprylon (Noludar), are virtually identical with the barbiturates except that each possesses one slight modification of the molecule. The differences are so insignificant that the receptors in the brain upon which barbiturates act probably cannot differentiate between them.

Some classifications of psychoactive drugs have distinguished between sedative-hypnotic drugs on the one hand and antianxiety agents or minor tranquilizers on the other. Because the so-called antianxiety agents have dose-response effects similar to those of the other sedative-hypnotics, and because they seem to be governed by the same principles previously described, many investigators feel that the distinction between antianxiety agents and sedative-hypnotics is unwarranted. Those who disagree feel that at least the benzodiazepams, diazepam (Valium) and chlordiazepoxide (Librium), have a specific tranquilizing action on the limbic system that decreases aggression. In addition, some benzodiazepines specifically block convulsions initiated within the hippocampus.

Stimulants

Stimulants are drugs that increase the behavioral activity of an individual. They differ widely in their molecular structures and mechanisms of action. Cocaine, amphetamines, methylphenidate, and phenmetrazine all are able to facilitate, mimic, or potentiate the action of norepinephrine. Cocaine and the amphetamines increase alertness, suppress fatigue, elevate mood, and to a limited extent reduce appetite. In larger doses they are capable of producing anxiety and even psychotic behavior. Methylphenidate (Ritalin), phenmetrazine (Preludin), and a similarly acting drug, benzphetamine (Didrex), are less potent than the amphetamines but are more potent than caffeine. Methylphenidate is used in the treatment of hyperactive children and in some cases of narcolepsy.

MAO inhibitors and tricyclic antidepressants elevate the mood of clinically depressed patients, especially those with major or primary depression. The MAO inhibitors inhibit the enzyme MAO and thereby increase the level of catecholamines and serotonin within the neuron that is available for release upon the arrival of action potentials. Tricyclic antidepressants block the active reuptake of catecholamines and serotonin into presynaptic terminals, thus presumably potentiating the action of these putative transmitters at the synapse. Current theory holds that both the MAO inhibitors and the tricyclic compounds owe their antidepressant action to facilitation of the synaptic action of these neurotransmitters (see also chap. 3).

Strychnine, picrotoxin, pentylenetetrazol (Metrazol), and bicuculline exert a generalized stimulant action on the CNS and are capable of inducing convulsions when given in sufficient quantities. They do not exert their effects on norepinephrine synapses and are not associated with mood elevation, increased alertness, or the suppression of fatigue. Strychnine, picrotoxin, and bicuculline exert their effects by selectively blocking inhibitory synapses in the CNS, whereas pentylenetetrazol appears to cause excitation by partially depolarizing the postsynaptic membrane.

The two most widely used psychoactive agents in our society are caffeine and nicotine. Both provide mild stimulation of the CNS. Caffeine is found in coffee, tea, cola drinks, and candy bars. The main pharmacologic effects of caffeine are exerted on the kidney and the heart as well as the CNS. Its effect on the heart and the CNS appears to be to increase the rate of cellular metabolism. By stimulating the cerebral cortex it increases wakefulness and improves psychomotor performance.

Nicotine appears to exert its effects by simulating acetylcholine in the peripheral nervous system and at all levels of the CNS, including the cerebral cortex. At low doses, such as those obtained by smoking cigarettes, nicotine can produce increased levels of behavioral activity; heavy smoking leads to increased irritability. At very high doses the drug can produce tremors and convulsions.

Narcotic Analgesics

The narcotic analgesics are drugs that reduce pain. Although sedative-hypnotics as well as narcotic analgesics induce sleep, sedative-hypnotic drugs lack the pain-killing properties of the narcotic analgesics. In addition, neither cross-tolerance nor cross-dependence occurs between the two classes of drugs.

The opiates are natural and synthetic drugs that produce effects on the body similar to those produced by morphine. Morphine and codeine are ingredients of the opium poppy. Codeine is structurally related to morphine and accounts for only a tiny fraction of the opium extract. Heroin is a semisynthetic derivative of morphine. Several totally synthetic opiates are also available; the two best known are meperidine (Demerol) and methadone (Dolophine).

The primary medical uses of the opiates have been for the relief from pain, treatment of diarrhea, and relief from cough. Opiates have also been used nonmedically to induce an extremely pleasant euphoric state associated with drowsiness, an absence of pain, and a clouding of mental faculties. Repeated use of the drug can lead to physical dependence and CNS tolerance.

There are three major criteria used to establish physical dependence on a drug. First, the individual who is physically dependent requires the drug in order to function normally. Second, withdrawal of the drug leads to a constellation of symptoms known as the abstinence syndrome. Third, the symptoms of withdrawal can be terminated by readministration of the drug. Physical dependence develops not only to the narcotic analgesics but also to the sedative-hypnotic compounds and the CNS stimulants (see chap. 12).

The narcotic analgesics exert their major effects primarily on the central nervous system, the eye, and the gastrointestinal tract. Although the major effects of the drug are sedation and analgesia, other prominent effects are decreased respiratory rate, chronic constipation, and constriction of the iris to form pinpoint pupils. With intermittent use of an opiate, little, if any, tolerance develops. However, with repeated use, CNS effects such as respiratory depression, analgesia, euphoria, and sedation show the development of tolerance, whereas peripheral nervous system effects such as pupillary constriction and constipation do not.

Recent research indicates that there are highly specific opiate receptors in neuronal membranes. These receptors are located in many regions of the brain including the frontal cortex, amygdala, caudate nucleus, medial thalamus, and periaqueductal region of the midbrain. Receptors appear to have two conformations with differential affinities for agonists and antagonists. The binding of agonists is decreased by sodium, whereas the binding of antagonists is increased. This enables investigators to predict whether drugs developed for clinical use have agonist, antagonist, or mixed properties.

Because it is unlikely that a highly stereospecific receptor that interacts only with alkaloids from the opium poppy would have developed in vertebrates, attention during the past decade has focused on the possibility that an endogenous ligand normally activates the opiate receptor. In 1974 two separate investigative teams found that this ligand is a neuropeptide.[9, 10] The term *endorphin* is now widely accepted as a descriptor of opioid peptides. Enkephalins are specific pentapeptides that belong to the endorphin class, which have been closely related to the endogenous ligand.

Among the interesting questions that have arisen concerning the endorphins and the stereospecific opiate receptors are those dealing with their possible physiological and pathophysiological roles. Because the characteristic effect of opiates in humans is less a specific blunting of pain (analgesia) than the production of a state of emotional detachment from the experience of suffering, it is conceivable that endorphins may play an important role in the regulation of affective states, even in individuals who are not dependent on opioids. One exciting prospect raised by this whole line of research is the possibility that either an endorphin deficiency or a change in the conformation of opiate receptors may play an important role in the development of dependence on opiates.

Antipsychotic Agents

Psychosis is a term that is applied to severe mental disorders (e.g., schizophrenia) characterized by personality disorganization and at least an intermittent inability to perceive reality and respond to it. The most widely used drugs for the treatment of schizophrenia are the phenothiazine derivatives. Chlorpromazine (Thorazine) is the best known and most widely studied phenothiazine derivative. The exact mechanism of action of chlorpromazine in the brain is not known, but evidence exists that among its effects is the blockade of postsynaptic dopamine receptors (see also chap. 3).

At appropriate dosages, chlorpromazine appears to improve the mood and behavior of schizophrenic patients by making them indifferent to external stimuli and reducing their anxiety. CNS-induced side effects sometimes include involuntary movements and tremors similar to those observed in persons who have Parkinson's disease.

Reserpine (Serpasil) is another drug that is effective in the treatment of psychoses. It is rarely used, however, because its pronounced side effects make phenothiazine administration preferable. The side effects of reserpine include severe mental depression, a marked decrease in blood pressure, insomnia, and diarrhea.

Reserpine's effects appear to be closely related to drug-induced depletion of the monoamines, dopamine, norepinephrine, and serotonin at central synapses. This occurs because the drug prevents the uptake of these presumed transmitters into storage granules within the presynaptic nerve terminal. The intraneuronal monoamines are thus more thoroughly exposed to MAO, which rapidly metabolizes them.

Haloperidol, a butyrophenone derivative, is another effective antipsychotic drug. It does not exhibit some of the serious toxicities such as jaundice that are occasionally seen with the phenothiazines, but its Parkinson-like symptoms are even more pronounced than those produced by chlorpromazine. Pharmacologically, haloperidol (Haldol) is similar to the phenothiazines, but it is metabolized and excreted at a much faster rate. Its mechanism of action appears to involve a blockage of dopamine and norepinephrine receptors. Haloperidol produces sedation, indifference to external stimuli, and reduction in anxiety and initiative.

The antipsychotic drugs mentioned have specific antischizophrenic effects in addition to sedative properties. Most are α-adrenergic-blocking drugs. In some patients they evoke motor dysfunction. The antipsychotic actions of the drug appear to involve blockade of dopaminergic pathways in the reticular activating system, hypothalamus amygdala and hippocampus, whereas the motor dysfunction seems to involve blockade of a dopaminergic pathway involving the globus pallidus and corpus striatum of the extrapyramidal system.

Institutionalized patients maintained on antipsychotic drugs such as chlorpromazine can often return to society and be seen as outpatients. In addition to a patient's other problems, however, the drug itself may cause complications because it produces sedation and a substantial reduction in initiative. As a consequence, the patient may cease to take medication. Initially, after discontinuing the drug the patient may feel better and function without psychotic symptoms. The healthful behavior in the absence of the drug may occur partly because of the cyclical nature of the illness or partly because metabolism of the phenothiazines is among the slowest of that for any group of drugs. Some metabolites of the phenothiazines may be present in the body months after the drug is discontinued. Unfortunately, the formerly psychotic patient who ceases taking the medication may lapse into psychotic behavior within a few weeks or months and again require hospitalization.

Long-term use of the phenothiazines, however, also poses risks. One of these is the possibility of inducing tardive dyskinesia. The essential feature of tardive dyskinesia is involuntary, spasmodic, repetitive, writhing movements (choreoathetosis) involving the lips, tongue, and extremities. A basic mechanism proposed for the syndrome is dopaminergic hypersensitivity in the striatonigral system, accompanied by a disruption in cholinergic functioning. Possibly long-term blockade of the dopaminergic synapse, and attempts of a known feedback system to compensate, may lead to alterations in the postsynaptic neuronal membrane, producing a denervation supersensitivity in which receptors become more sensitive to dopamine. In any event, after chronic administration of antipsychotic drugs, tardive dyskinesia may become severe and long-lasting.

RELATIONSHIPS BETWEEN THE ORGANIZATION OF THE NERVOUS SYSTEM AND BEHAVIOR

The General Divisions of the Nervous System

The human nervous system is made up of the CNS, which comprises the brain and spinal cord, and the peripheral nervous system, which comprises 12 pairs of cranial nerves and 31 pairs of spinal nerves. Although the distinction between the CNS and the peripheral nervous system is convenient, it should be noted that many neurons originating in the periphery terminate in the CNS, and that many neurons that have their cell bodies in the CNS project their axons via the peripheral nervous system.

The Peripheral Nervous System

The afferent axons of the peripheral nervous system transmit stimuli from sensory receptors toward the CNS. Efferent axons are of two types: (1) somatic motor fibers that terminate in skeletal muscle and (2) autonomic fibers that project toward smooth muscle, cardiac muscle, and glands.

The autonomic nervous system has two divisions. One of these, called the sympathetic (or thoracolumbar) division, originates from the thoracic and lumbar segments of the spinal cord. In contrast, the parasympathetic (or craniosacral) division originates from the brain and the sacral portion of the spinal cord.

In general, both divisions of the autonomic nervous system innervate target organs in a dual manner. In most instances the two divisions function in an antagonistic manner. The pair of vagus nerves to the heart, for instance, belongs to the parasympathetic division and is responsible for slowing the heart rate. In contrast, the cardioaccelerator nerves to the heart belong to the sympathetic division and are influential in increasing the heart rate and contractile force. It should be noted that while the vagus and cardioaccelerator nerves are capable of functioning antagonistically, they can also function synergistically. Thus, during vigorous exercise, for example, an increase in the firing rate of the cardioaccelerator fibers is accompanied by a decrease in vagal restraint (i.e., parasympathetic inhibition). Integrated behaviors may also require the synergistic functioning of the parasympathetic and sympathetic divisions. During sexual intercourse, for instance, erection in the male involves a parasympathetic response, whereas ejaculation reflects a sympathetic discharge.

The parasympathetic division is usually associated with vegetative, homeostatic functions such as digestion and excretion, whereas the sympathetic system more often discharges as a larger unit during emergency situations. In response to a stressful situation, for instance, the sympathetic division relaxes accommodation and dilates the pupil, thereby letting more light into the eye. An increase in blood pressure and a shunting of the blood supply lead to better perfusion of muscle. Concurrent constriction of peripheral blood vessels in the skin tends to limit bleeding if the organism is wounded. Large amounts of catecholamines liberated from the adrenal medulla, which incidentally has a cholinergic innervation, increase the amount of energy utilized by the organism.

The Central Nervous System

From the standpoint of morphology, the CNS may be conceptualized in terms of its embryologic development. During the course of prenatal development in mammals, the CNS begins to form as a tubular structure. The anterior portion of the neural tube develops into the brain, whereas the rest of the tube forms the spinal cord. Three conspicuous enlargements soon emerge within the anterior portion of the tube: forebrain, midbrain, and hindbrain. As embryologic growth and differentiation continue, the forebrain and hindbrain subdivide, but the midbrain does not. The most anterior portion of the forebrain becomes the telencephalon, consisting of the cerebral hemispheres, which form the outer mantle of the brain. The posterior portion of the forebrain becomes the diencephalon, which includes the thalamus and hypothalamus. Within the hindbrain, the anterior portion forms the pons and the cerebellum and the posterior portion forms the medulla.

The cerebral hemispheres in humans envelop the anterior brain stem and form the largest portion of the brain. A deep cleft along the midline (midsagittal) separates the two cerebral hemispheres. Communication between the two hemispheres is carried out over distinct bands of fibers. The most prominent band crossing the midline is known as the corpus callosum.

Behavioral integration occurs not only in the cerebral hemispheres but in the brain stem as well. The hypothalamus, for example, plays a key role in the regulation of virtually every homeostatic, motivational, and emotional state including thermoregulation, hunger, thirst, sexual drive, and defensive behavior. Through its direct connections with the pituitary, the hypothalamus plays an important role in water, fat, and carbohydrate metabolism. It coordinates nervous and endocrine activity and is the source of posterior pituitary hormones. A midventral core of neural tissue extending from the spinal cord through the diencephalon plays a critical role in the modulation of consciousness.

Correlation of Neurologic Structure and Function with Selected Aspects of Behavior

In this section, some specific relationships between the structural and functional organization of the central nervous system and certain aspects of behavior will be discussed. Several psychological states will be used as examples of conditions in which recent advances in knowledge show how the brain determines human behavior.

Modulation of Consciousness

Sleep and wakefulness in normal humans recur as a circadian or 24-hour rhythm. Variations occur within each of these behavioral states. Several distinct cycles occur during a night's sleep, and, in the course of a day, awake behavior may range from relaxed daydreaming to pronounced emotional excitement. At one time it was believed that sleep was merely the absence of wakefulness and that prolonged periods of inactivity led to sleep. Evidence has now accumulated that sleep and wakefulness involve somewhat separate mechanisms.

One of the most common ideas about sleep is that it provides rest for the body. In a general way this is true. If humans are deprived of sleep for a long enough time, their behavior may break down. They can become irritable, shows signs of emotional disturbance, and fall asleep on their feet. As yet, however, the precise biochemical and physiological needs that sleep fulfills are unknown. In addition, it now appears that many symptoms associated with sleep deprivation are associated with the stress of trying to keep the organism awake rather than with the deprivation of sleep itself.

ASCENDING RETICULAR ACTIVATING SYSTEM.—The reticular activating system (RAS) is part of the reticular formation, a midventral core of neural tissue extending from the spinal cord through the diencephalon. It is surrounded by long ascending fibers of the classic somatosensory pathways and by long descending motor pathways.

The RAS is uniquely capable of abstracting sensory information because it receives sensory input from most modalities. Its organization is complex, however, and the amount of synaptic convergence within it abolishes most modal specificity. Neurons within the RAS are typically activated with equal facility by several different sensory stimuli, although few, if any, of these neurons are influenced by all modalities of stimulation. In addition, many neurons in the reticular formation do not respond to stimulation from any sensory modality.

Electrical stimulation of the midbrain reticular formation in lightly anesthetized or conscious mammals produces an electroencephalographic (EEG) pattern of arousal in the cerebral cortex. Stimulation of the RAS also induces behavioral signs of arousal. Although studies with lesions have helped to elucidate the role of the RAS in wakefulness, these results have had to be interpreted cautiously. Initial studies in which massive one-stage bilateral lesions were made in the midbrain reticular formation reported that such lesions resulted in severe coma. This led some theorists to believe that the midbrain reticular formation was essential for all aspects of consciousness. Subsequent studies in which lesions were made in multiple stages, however, led to a modification of this position. Actually, when one considers that a large number of regulatory nuclei and projection fibers lie within the brain stem reticular formation, it is hardly surprising that animals lapse into coma and even die after massive one-stage lesions.

Carefully performed lesion studies have permitted a distinction to be made between the portions of the RAS involved in the EEG and those concerned with behavioral manifestations of arousal. Lesions in the posterior hypothalamic outflow of the RAS result in a behavioral somnolence that persists even when stimulation of the midbrain reticular formation produces an EEG pattern of wakefulness. In contrast, cats with lesions of the midbrain reticular formation are not completely somnolent but display an EEG pattern of sleep. Drugs such as atropine are also capable of producing an EEG pattern characteristic of sleep in the behaviorally awake person.

THE ELECTROENCEPHALOGRAM.—The simplest method of recording and studying the electrical manifestations of human brain activity is by means of the EEG. Wires are glued to the surface of a person's scalp to record the electrical activity generated by the underlying brain. Because the signals are in the microvolt range, they are first amplified and then displayed as a tracing on moving paper.

The EEG reveals a number of distinct patterns that are usually correlated with sleep and wakefulness (Fig 2–3). In the resting human with eyes closed, alpha waves are typically recorded. These are most pronounced in leads overlying the occipital cortex. The alpha rhythm consists of high-amplitude, well-synchronized sinusoidal waves with a frequency of 8–12 Hz. When the person opens his or her eyes, the synchronized alpha rhythm gives way to a desynchronized, lower-amplitude pattern in which some high-frequency responses—beta waves with a frequency of 18–30 Hz—can be detected by computer analysis. Desynchronization is characteristic not only of the transition between the closing and opening of the eyes but also of the most alert, attentive, or excited states. In excited states, low-amplitude gamma waves with a frequency of 30–50 Hz may be detected using computer analysis.

As a person becomes drowsy and drifts off to sleep, alpha waves tend to decrease in amplitude and rather low-voltage 4–6 Hz activity begins to show up in the record. Then spindle bursts begin to occur at a frequency of 12–15 Hz. In still deeper sleep, high-amplitude delta waves occur with a frequency of 2–4 Hz. Although fairly deep sleep is usually accompanied by delta wave activity, another deep stage of sleep is accompanied by EEG patterns that resemble those of wakefulness. At first glance the desynchronized EEG of this stage of sleep looks so much like the EEG of wakefulness, and so unlike the EEG of the slow-wave sleep characterized by delta waves, that the term "paradoxical sleep" has been applied to this stage of desynchronized sleep activity.

REGULATION OF SLEEP.—A comprehensive analysis of sleep states has been provided by Jouvet.[12] According to Jouvet the sleep of mammals is characterized by two states that can be readily distinguished on the basis of polygraph analyses (see also chap. 4). In one of these states, called slow-wave sleep, the EEG reveals a preponderance of delta waves. In the second state, which we have already identified as paradoxical sleep, the EEG activity resembles that of the waking state, but behaviorally the organism is in a state of deep sleep. Under normal circumstances approximately 80% of a night's sleep is spent in slow-wave sleep, whereas about 20% is spent in paradoxical sleep. This occurs during four or five cycles per night.

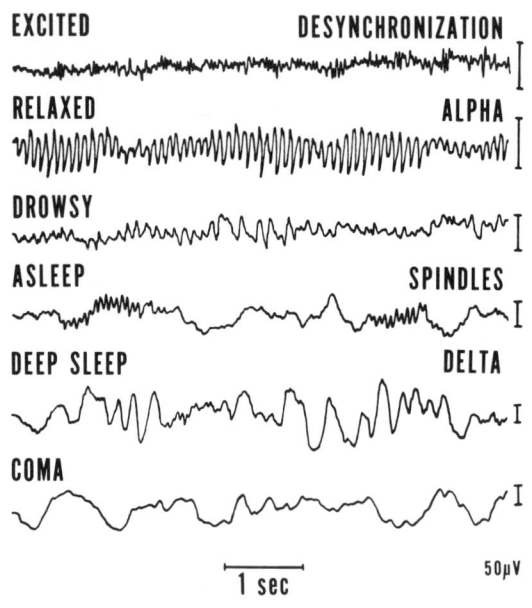

Fig 2–3.—Characteristic patterns of the electroencephalogram. (Adapted from Penfield W., Jasper H.: *Epilepsy and the Functional Anatomy of the Human Brain*, Boston, Little, Brown and Co., 1954.)

During paradoxical sleep, there is an almost total absence of electromyographic activity in the antigravitational jaw and neck muscles. This appears to represent a true paralysis that is induced by tonic inhibitory influences on motor output. Blood pressure drops but is accompanied by rapid oscillations. If one records ongoing brain activity from macroelectrodes placed within brain structures, large spiked brain waves can be detected periodically in the pons, lateral geniculate nucleus, and occipital cortex of the cat during paradoxical sleep. These PGO (abbreviated from pons, geniculate, occipital) spikes are closely related to bursts of rapid eye movements, which are characteristic of paradoxical sleep (also called rapid eye movement, or REM, sleep). The PGO spikes are not electrical artifacts of the eye movements, but rather large, synchronized neural discharges.

A sleeping person who is awakened during paradoxical (REM) sleep is much more likely to report dream activity than if awakened from slow-wave sleep. Although some authors have assumed that rapid eye movements and associated PGO spikes indicate that an animal or person is looking at objects in his or her dreams, findings that eye movements and PGO spikes occur in the normal pattern after removal of the cerebral cortex and other forebrain structures cast doubts on this assumption.

Several findings suggest that serotonin is involved in slow-wave sleep, whereas catecholamines such as norepinephrine and dopamine are involved in paradoxical sleep. A secondary injection of 5-hydroxytryptophan that increases the concentration of serotonin in the brain immediately restores slow-wave but not paradoxical sleep. Tertiary injection of dopa then restores normal sleep, including both slow-wave and paradoxical sleep.

Histofluorescence analyses have indicated that the cell bodies of serotonin-containing neurons are prevalent in the raphe or dorsal midline system of the lower midbrain and pons. In contrast, clusters of cell bodies that contain norepinephrine are located in the lateral part of the pontine tegmentum (locus ceruleus). The terminals of both the serotonergic and noradrenergic neurons are widely distributed throughout the brain stem, diencephalon, and cerebrum.

Bilateral lesions of the locus ceruleus in the pontine tegmentum suppress paradoxical sleep without altering slow-wave sleep. In contrast, lesions of the raphe system produce insomnia. Because paradoxical sleep usually appears only after slow-wave sleep has occurred, Jouvet has proposed that paradoxical sleep depends on (1) a serotonergic "priming" mechanism located medially in the raphe system, and (2) a noradrenergic "triggering" system located laterally in the pontine tegmentum.

A link between the slow-wave and paradoxical sleep systems was found in a study that examined the neuronal activity of giant reticular neurons in the cat.[13] During wakefulness or slow-wave sleep, these giant neurons, which course up and down the greater part of the brain, are very inactive. However, as the animal goes into paradoxical sleep, the activity of these neurons increases markedly. Moreover, the increased activity of these neurons begins to occur before the other signs of paradoxical sleep. In addition to showing tonic increases in firing rate during paradoxical sleep, the giant reticular neurons show bursts of activity that immediately precede rapid eye movements and the PGO spikes.

As soon as the firing rate of the giant reticular neurons begins to develop, a decrease occurs in the discharge rate of neurons in the locus ceruleus. The locus ceruleus neurons then cease to discharge during paradoxical sleep. This striking reciprocal relationship between the activity of the giant reticular neurons and the nerve cells in the locus ceruleus suggests that the two groups of neurons directly influence each other in a predominantly inhibitory fashion.

Although structures in the midbrain and pons appear to play a critical role in triggering both behavioral and EEG sleep patterns, rostral structures also seem to play an important role in regulating slow-wave sleep. Lesions of the anterior hypothalamus in the preoptic area of cats and rats cause the animals to remain awake for many days. Conversely, in normal animals, electrical stimulation in this area induces sleep. It should be noted in this context that the raphe neurons project through the medial forebrain bundle in their ascent to the limbic system, and that a descending control system passes through the preoptic region on its way back to the raphe system.

A region of the frontal-orbital cortex has also been localized that, when stimulated, produces slow-wave sleep. Removal of the neocortex eliminates slow-wave activity in the medial thalamus and the reticular formation for several months. Further evidence for a descending cortical synchronizing influence on the brain stem may be inferred from the finding that, following section of the brain stem at the junction of the midbrain and diencephalons, spindle activity persists above, but not below, the point of section.

Motivation and Emotion

During the course of evolution, important neuronal and hormonal control systems developed for such motivated behaviors as feeding, drinking, and sexual behavior. General approach and avoidance systems also developed. These approach and avoidance systems appear to play an important role in reinforcing particular behaviors. Positive reinforcers tend to strengthen the responses or behaviors that produce them, whereas negative reinforcers tend to strengthen the responses that terminate them. The hypothalamus and the limbic system play an important role in the regulation of these activities.

NEURAL SUBSTRATES OF REWARD AND PUNISHMENT.—Olds and Milner are credited with discovering the existence of a neuronal substrate that subserves reward.[14] Following this pioneering work, Olds and his collaborators initiated an important series of studies in which rats were trained to press a lever in order to receive a short train of electrical stimulation. The highest rates of lever pressing were observed for stimulation of the medial forebrain bundle of the lateral hypothalamus.

Previously, many investigators had trained rats to press a similar bar at high rates to receive food or water, but nobody had guessed that animals could be trained to press a bar to receive electrical stimulation of the brain.

Several investigators have shown that the rewards of brain stimulation may be influenced by altering the levels of catecholamines in the brain. In these experiments animals were initially trained to press a bar for electrical stimulation of the lateral hypothalamus. With each press, however, the intensity of the current was lowered. Finally the animal reached a point at which the intensity was so low that it ceased pressing. Administration of amphetamines or other drugs that increased the availability of catecholamines at central synapses led to a distinct lowering of the current intensity required to sustain bar pressing. Furthermore, it has been shown that catecholamines are released within the lateral hypothalamus following electrical stimulation of the medial forebrain bundle at the same parameter values that lead to high rates of bar pressing. When one considers that the clinically depressed person is an individual who no longer experiences environmental stimuli (e.g., praise, recognition) as being positively reinforcing, it is tempting to speculate that the reward pathway passing through the medial forebrain bundle is involved. It is interesting that antidepressants such as imipramine and the monoamine oxidase inhibitors make it easier to activate neurons in this pathway. Electrical stimulation of this region in humans is typically experienced as pleasant.

Electrical stimulation of the brain can motivate aversive as well as reward behavior. Stimulation of periventricular structures such as the midbrain central gray, the ventromedial hypothalamus, or the dorsomedial thalamus causes animals to behave as if they were receiving a noxious stimulus. These animals can be taught to avoid or escape the brain stimulation just as they are taught to avoid noxious stimuli.

Electrical stimulation of the hypothalamus has been used to elicit a number of behavioral patterns besides approach and avoidance.

These include eating, drinking, hoarding, stalk-attack, and sexual behavior. Each has been considered to reflect motivated behavior rather than a stereotyped motor act for several reasons. First, the stimulated animal does not engage in the behavior unless appropriate goal objects are present. Second, the animal from whom the behavior is elicited can be taught to perform some learned task, such as bar pressing, in order to obtain the goal object. Third, the animal usually tolerates a moderate amount of electric shock or other aversive stimulation in order to obtain the objects.

An interesting paradox is created by empirical observations that the lateral hypothalamus is the best site for stimulation that elicits feeding behavior as well as intracranial self-stimulation. Because the lateral hypothalamus contains a region in which neurons can be activated by low levels of glucose in the blood, activation of neurons in this region should make the organism feel hungry, not satisfied. An important paper by Olds and his collaborators appears to have resolved the paradox.[15] Whereas previous investigators who had elicited feeding and intracranial self-stimulation through the same electrodes had used relatively large macroelectrodes, Olds and his associates used a small microelectrode and weak currents so that a given stimulus activated a much smaller region of brain tissue. They found that only electrical self-stimulation was obtained from a fairly wide lateral region occupied by the medial forebrain bundle. Stimulation of the anterior hypothalamus yielded only drinking. Eating alone was obtained by stimulating a very dorsal portion of the middle lateral region immediately adjacent to the self-stimulation sites. Stimulation of the ventromedial nucleus tended to disrupt eating and did not elicit self-stimulation. It therefore appears that the hunger center and the self-stimulation zone in the lateral hypothalamus are distinct from one another but happen to be close anatomically.

NEURAL SUBSTRATES OF AGONISTIC BEHAVIOR.—Agonistic behavior refers to flight, defense, or attack. Integrated agonistic behavior requires an intact hypothalamus. Cats with all the brain tissue above the midbrain removed show only fragmented components of the rage reaction. For this reason the behavior is called sham rage. In contrast, cats with all brain tissue removed rostral to the hypothalamus display fully developed rage reactions.

Experiments using brain stimulation have, to a limited extent, distinguished among flight, rage, and stalking behavior patterns. Flight responses have been evoked by stimulation of the dorsomedial hypothalamus, rage responses characterized by hissing and snarling have been elicited from the ventromedial hypothalamus, and stalking behavior followed by killing has been obtained following electrical stimulation of the perifornical region of the posterior lateral hypothalamus. Injection of a cholinergic substance into this perifornical area can cause rats that have never killed spontaneously to stalk and kill mice. Conversely, injections of the anticholinergic drug, methylatropine, into the same region blocks the killing response in rats who kill naturally.

In the elaboration of aggressive behavior, the relationship of the hypothalamus to the amygdala seems to be particularly important. The amygdala lies deep within the temporal lobe. A corticomedial portion of the amygdala receives direct input from the olfactory bulb, whereas a basolateral portion does not. Other major inputs to the amygdala are from the reticular formation, the pyriform cortex, and the hippocampus. The amygdala also has connections with the orbitoinsulotemporal cortex. A major efferent outflow is to the septal region and the hypothalamus by way of the stria terminalis. Another connection between the amygdala and the hypothalamus is through the ventral amygdalofugal pathway provided by fibers lying just above the optic tract. Although section of the stria terminalis does not abolish the defensive reactions elicited by stimulation of the amygdala, the subsequent interruption of the ventral amygdalofugal pathway does.

Stimulation or lesion of different regions of the amygdala can facilitate or inhibit aggressive behavior depending on the site. The facilitating influence, which can be seen when the basolateral portion of the amygdala is stimulated, appears to be somewhat greater than the inhibiting influence, because the result of total bilateral amygdalectomy is usually increased docility. Stimulation of the amygdala in cats produces a pronounced defense reaction, including arching of the back, hissing, and bared teeth. Stimulation of the amygdala never arouses the quiet stalking response that can be caused by stimulation of the perifornical hypothalamus; in fact, it disrupts it.

The amygdala also appears to play a role in maintaining social dominance. Following bilateral amygdalectomy, monkeys show decreased social dominance in a group. In humans, bilateral stereotactic lesions in the amygdala have been reported to reduce emotional excitability and aggressiveness and to normalize social behavior in persons with severe antisocial behavior disorders.[16]

PSYCHOSURGERY.—Psychosurgery refers to the use of neurosurgical procedures to treat disorders that are primarily behavioral, at least insofar as symptoms are concerned. The term specifically excludes surgical procedures that are primarily aimed at relieving major seizure disorders, removing brain tumors, or treating head injuries, even though some of these events may have behavioral sequelae. Psychosurgical procedures have been used not only to control extreme violence but also to relieve intractable pain in terminally ill cancer patients, to eliminate severely debilitating compulsions, to relieve extreme fear and anxiety that have completely incapacitated the individual, and to treat severe psychoses. The problems surrounding the use of psychosurgery are very complex and not easily solved. Aside from the scientific and medical problems involved, there are also moral and ethical issues to be considered.

The first modern psychosurgical procedure was the prefrontal lobotomy, which consists of severing the connections between the frontal lobes and the rest of the brain. This operation was developed by a Portuguese neurosurgeon, Egas Moniz, to treat patients with severe emotional disturbances. For this "outstanding achievement," Moniz was awarded the Nobel Prize. The basic idea for the procedure stemmed from a 1935 paper by Fulton and Jacobsen, who in the course of their studies on monkeys and chimps observed that damage to the frontal cortex eliminated emotional responses in chimps.[17] Usually when animals make errors in a learning task, they become upset, but these damaged animals did not. Unfortunately, Moniz apparently missed the main point of the Fulton and Jacobsen research, which was that following surgery the animals had severe difficulty solving tasks that involved temporal memory.

In the years after the prefrontal lobotomy operation was introduced, it became apparent that the procedure is accompanied by severe side effects. Although patients did about as well as before on IQ tests, other performance deficits were noted. When given problems in which they had to change strategies in the course of the task, they tended to fall into set patterns and repeat responses, even when informed that these responses were incorrect. The patients seemed to lose social inhibitions that normally govern daily life. They became impulsive, did what they wanted when they wanted, and rarely concerned themselves with the consequences. Emotional reactivity was generally dampened.

The most systematic study of the effects of psychosurgery on humans was the Columbia Greystone Project, in which lesions were made in the prefrontal cortex in "volunteer" psychiatric patients. These lesions varied systematically in size. In general, the results were disappointing. The beneficial effects on psychotic behavior were at best variable. There were no substantial changes as recorded by IQ or other psychological tests. The most marked changes were in the patients' personalities. Relatives of the patients found them to be emotionally blunted and unresponsive. On the basis of such results, lobotomies were abandoned as a therapeutic approach.

In recent years, as the role of the limbic system in violent behavior has become more apparent, some neurosurgeons have performed psychosurgery by making lesions in the cingulate gyrus and amygdala. Mark and Ervin and their associates at Massachusetts General Hospital have made lesions in the amygdala to control episodic "attacks" of extreme, uncontrollable violence.[18] In some ways these attacks resembled the clinical epileptic condition of temporal lobe epilepsy.

In the first stage of Mark and Ervin's psychosurgical procedure, electrodes were implanted in deep structures such as the amygdala to detect abnormal epileptic brain-wave activity. Once such activity was clearly identified, stimulation of the relevant brain location was made in an attempt to produce symptoms characteristic of the beginning of a seizure. If this seizure activity could be reliably triggered and seemed to set off a fullblown seizure, the surgeons considered making a lesion at that site. Careful follow-up studies appear to indicate that minimum side effects occur in patients after small unilateral lesions are made in the amygdala.

The procedures used by Mark and Ervin may be criticized on ethical grounds but seem to have been well thought out scientifically. First, considerable animal experimentation has implicated the amygdala as participating in aggressive behavior. Second, before making their lesions, Mark and Ervin ascertained that abnormal electrical activity was occurring in the prospective lesion site. Third, the behavior of the patients resembled the clinical diagnosis of temporal lobe epilepsy. Fourth, the patients were extremely violent and clearly dangerous to themselves and others.

Many issues are raised by psychosurgery.[19] Cases in which there is an obvious relationship between a demonstrable brain disorder and behavioral pathology involving violent attacks are extremely rare. In contrast, the potential for abuse by subtle or not so subtle coercion is considerable. Most persons who show abnormal brain-wave activity, such as occurs in psychomotor epilepsy, exhibit no higher incidence of violent behavior than the rest of the population. Conversely, the vast majority of persons arrested for crimes of violence show little evidence of obvious brain-wave abnormality. Finally, even when correlations occur between brain-wave activity and behavioral pathology, they are not necessarily causally related. These and similar issues have made psychosurgery a controversial topic among scientists, physicians, and the general public.

Information Processing

The amount of information stored in the normal adult human brain is vastly greater than that stored in the brain of our nearest primate relative. This is due largely to language, although much more than a vocabulary is involved. Humans are able to evaluate what is important or relevant on the basis of a permanent memory store of information, a logic system, and the motivations and expectations they have at the time new information is assessed. In order to have some knowledge of the manner in which humans process information, we must have some notion of how and where information is coded, stored, and decoded.

LEARNING AND MEMORY.—Human memory can be characterized by several states or processes that have different durations or time courses. Iconic memory is very short-term memory, lasting less than a second. This is followed by primary or short-term memory, lasting a few seconds. An example of primary memory is a briefly remembered telephone number. If not disrupted, this short-term memory trace becomes consolidated into permanent memory. The consolidation hypothesis has been verified in numerous experiments in which very recent learning has been shown to be susceptible to interference and loss (e.g., by ether anesthesia or by electroconvulsive shock therapy), whereas older, well-learned habits have been almost impervious to loss. Several pathologic conditions have helped to clarify some aspects of short-term and long-term memory.

Wernicke-Korsakoff disease produces a pronounced defect in memory. The disease is characteristic of severe alcoholism and appears to be due almost entirely to extreme thiamine deficiency. A person who has Wernicke-Korsakoff disease suffers from anterograde amnesia or the inability to retain new memories for more than several minutes. To a lesser extent retrograde amnesia, or the loss of some memories formed before the beginning of the illness, is also observed. In contrast, intelligence test scores are reduced little, if at all, from the premorbid level, which is also true of motivation and perceptual abilities.

Structures most likely to be damaged during Wernicke-Korsakoff disease are those surrounding the third ventricle. Although the mammillary bodies of the hypothalamus are invariably affected, instances have been observed in which they were completely destroyed but memory was unimpaired.[20] In contrast, involvement of the dorsomedial thalamus, which is also adjacent to the third ventricle, always leads to anterograde amnesia, or the inability to store new memories permanently. The dorsomedial thalamus is a major relay in the limbic system and also has extensive projections to the frontal cortex in humans.

Several other clinical findings have been related to the inability to store new memories permanently. Occlusion of the posterior cerebral arteries, because of either atherosclerosis or embolism, causes both a bilateral infarction of the medial parts of the temporal lobes and anterograde amnesia. The fornix, hippocampus, and parahippocampal convolutions are particularly affected. Acute inclusion-body encephalitis also causes inflammatory necrosis of medial portions of the temporal lobes and amnesia. Surgical ablation of the medial and inferior parts of the temporal lobe bilaterally, or unilateral ablation of this area when the contralateral side is diseased, also leads to anterograde amnesia. The clinical data therefore indicate that the medial portions of the temporal lobe and their connections with the medial diencephalon are part of a circuit that is essential for the permanent storage of new memories.

There have been a few reports of a converse syndrome in which short-term memory itself is impaired, but the ability to store new memories permanently is not. Some persons with damage to the posterior association cortex of the left hemisphere, for instance, show an inability to comprehend verbal items that they hear, with no impairment of short-term memory for the same materials when presented visually. Such persons have difficulty with spoken language but not with reading. In contrast, other individuals have been described who have severe reading impairments but no difficulty with spoken language after the left hemisphere is damaged. On the basis of the present evidence, it appears that the posterior association cortex is involved in perceptual learning and short-term memory, and that the permanent storage of memories involves a circuit including the medial temporal lobes and the dorsomedial thalamus.

LANGUAGE.—Although many animals can both communicate and receive communications, *Homo sapiens* alone possesses a system of communication based on a sophisticated syntax, or set of formal rules for sequencing sounds or symbols. Man's closest relatives, the great apes, appear to have the rudimentary basis of language but have not evolved the specialized speech areas of humans.

The Gardners, in Nevada, have trained a chimp named Washoe in the American Sign Language.[21] Washoe has learned more than 100 signs and has strung them together in phrases as long as five signs. She uses sign language to initiate interactions, to get what she wants, and to comment on events, often with rather creative interpretations. Word order or syntax is much less important to Washoe than to human children, however. Based on this and similar studies, it appears certain that chimps have rather well-developed capacities for abstract and symbolic thought, which is consistent with their having a large association cortex. One may even conclude that the great apes can learn language, but not as people do, for they have not evolved the specialized speech areas of humans.

In 97% of all normal human adults, language is localized in the left cerebral hemisphere. Broca's area, which is adjacent to the region of the frontal motor cortex that controls the movements of the vocal cords, the tongue, the soft palate, the jaw, and the lips, appears to be important for the motor control of words and word sequences rather than for the conceptual aspects of language. Damage to Broca's area results in slow and labored speech, although comprehension of language remains intact. This is often referred to as motor or expressive aphasia.

The most permanent and devastating aphasias result from damage to a rather large area of the left posterior association cortex known as Wernicke's area. When Wernicke's area is damaged extensively, speech becomes relatively meaningless and comprehension is usually lost. This is sometimes referred to as receptive aphasia. Wernicke's and Broca's areas are joined by a tract called the arcuate fasciculus. According to Geschwind, each spoken phrase originates in Wernicke's area and is transmitted by the arcuate fasciculus to Broca's area.[22] In Broca's area the correct sequence of articulations is organized and transmitted to the motor cortex for speech. During conduction aphasia, in which the fasciculus is damaged but both Wernicke's area and Broca's area remain intact, the person has perfect comprehension of spoken and written language. Spoken language remains relatively fluent, but it is almost totally devoid of meaning.

ASYMMETRICAL ORGANIZATION OF THE CEREBRAL HEMISPHERES.—Extensive damage to the cerebral cortex of the left hemisphere essentially abolishes the ability to comprehend or speak intelligently. In contrast, similar damage restricted to the right hemisphere does not have that effect. A right-handed person with damage to the right hemisphere has great difficulty in performing spatial tasks, however, and experiences a substantial deficit in musical ability. Such a person may have great difficulty understanding complex diagrams or pictures and may get lost in relatively familiar surroundings. Experiments conducted on persons with epilepsy in whom the corpus callosum and anterior commissure were sectioned have helped to elucidate the disparate functions of the two hemispheres.

The most surprising thing about commissurotomy of the human brain is that it seems to have few obvious adverse effects on the patient. This is because most information normally continues to reach both hemispheres. In an interesting series of studies, however, Sperry and his collaborators took advantage of the fact that while each eye in humans projects information to both sides of the cortex, the left sides of the left and right eyes project only to the left cerebral cortex.[23] Conversely, the right side of each eye projects only to the right cerebral cortex. Therefore, by providing images only to the appropriate eye fields of each eye, information could be projected selectively to each hemisphere.

Sperry and his collaborators also took advantage of the fact that somatesthetic sensation in the left hand only projects to the right cerebral cortex, whereas somatesthetic sensation in the right hand only projects to the left hemisphere. The functioning of each hemisphere could therefore be evaluated by providing information selectively to each hemisphere.

The results of the experiments were unambiguous. If a word was flashed to the left hemisphere, the person could say it immediately. But this seldom occurred if a word was flashed to the right hemisphere. The right hemisphere, however, was quite capable of recognizing objects. When a picture of a spoon was flashed to the right hemisphere and the left hand was allowed to feel among several objects behind a screen, including the spoon, it would immediately select the spoon. However, because neither the visual image nor the somatesthetic sensation was projected to the left hemisphere, the subject still could not say what it was. But when the right hand was permitted to take the spoon from the left, the person immediately said "spoon."

In contrast to verbal performance, the right hemisphere was clearly superior to the left in solving spatial tasks such as arranging blocks, even though right-handed subjects had to use their left hands. Sperry and his associates also found that emotional perception and responsiveness were handled quite well, although nonverbally, by the right hemisphere. In one of these experiments a picture of a nude woman was flashed on the screen. This elicited an amused reaction from a female subject regardless of whether it was presented to the left or the right hemisphere. When flashed to the left hemisphere, the woman correctly identified the picture of a nude. But when the same picture was flashed to the right hemisphere, the woman chuckled but could not state what had elicited the reaction. The data from the split brain experiments seem to suggest that the nature and functions of consciousness may be quite different for the two hemispheres.

Pain

Pain is an unpleasant experience associated primarily with descriptions of actual or presumed tissue damage. It is usually discussed in terms of the stimuli that arouse it, the responses made to it, and the cognitive and affective variables that influence its perception.

PAIN PERCEPTION.—The perception of pain is poorly understood. To the classical if somewhat mythical sensory psychophysicist, somatosensation could be categorized in five basic qualities: touch, warmth, cold, kinesthesia (sensation arising from the positions and movements of joints and muscle), and pain. This basic formulation faced difficulties even at the perceptual level, in part because some of the supposed qualities are not always separable from one another. It is sometimes difficult, for instance, to distinguish between strong pressure and pain, or between burning or freezing and pain. In addition to these problems, some bodily sensations such as tickle and itch do not easily fit into a five-quality categorization of somatosensation.

The simplistic view of pain as merely a sensation runs into additional complications because the perception of pain can vary as a function of psychological, social, and cultural influences. As long ago as 1580 Montaigne wrote, "We feel one cut from the surgeon's scalpel more than ten blows of the sword in the heat of battle." More recently it was found that approximately 35% of more than 1,000 patients in some 15 studies reported marked relief from pathologic pain after receiving a placebo, which is an organically inactive substance.[24]

Some theorists have argued that the difficulties associated with the accurate measurement of pain can be reduced if a distinction is made between absolute pain threshold and pain tolerance. Absolute threshold is the point at which an individual first perceives a stimulation as painful 50% of the time. Tolerance, in the present instance, refers to the point at which an individual is unwilling to accept more pain. Two patients in a dentist's office may have very similar pain thresholds as measured by psychophysical methods, but one of the subjects may show less tolerance as evidenced by pronounced wincing or by a request for a local anesthetic. While the distinction between pain threshold and tolerance is useful, it is not a panacea. First, the absolute pain threshold is not a pure measure of sensation, because it can be influenced by cost-benefit adjustments. Second, separate measures of tolerance (e.g., wincing versus requesting a local anesthetic in the dental chair) may or may not be well correlated.

Another difficulty that has been encountered in pain measurement is equating laboratory pain with clinical pain produced by pathologic processes. In the clinic, for example, morphine can be effective in reducing pain reactions, whereas in the laboratory the effects of morphine cannot be distinguished from those of saline. What appears to be missing in the laboratory is the anxiety associated with the disease process, its threat of incapacitation or even death. Recent clinical investigations comparing alternative procedures for assessing pain thresholds and pain tolerance have helped to bridge the gap between controlled laboratory findings and clinical experience.

The sensation of pain can be aroused by mechanical, electrical, thermal, or chemical (e.g., prostaglandins, bradykinin) stimuli. Depriving tissue of its normal supply of blood can give rise to ischemic pain. An example of this is the substernal pain in persons with angina pectoris, which arises when the myocardium becomes ischemic during exertion.

Distention of a viscus produces pain, which may be felt in a somatic structure some distance away rather than at the site of the viscus. This phenomenon is called referred pain. The best-known example of it is the referral of cardiac pain to the inner aspect of the left arm. When visceral pain is both local and referred, it may seem to radiate from the local to the distant site.

The nerves from the visceral structures and the somatic structures to which pain is referred enter the central nervous system at the same level. One tentative hypothesis offered to explain the basis of referred pain is that visceral and somatic afferent neurons converge on the same neurons in the pain pathway. It also may be true that because somatic pain is much more commonly experienced than visceral pain, we "learn" that activity entering the CNS via a given pathway should be attributed to a pain stimulus in a particular somatic area. When either that pathway—or a closely related one—is stimulated by an activity transmitted via visceral afferent neurons, the pain stimulus is perceived as being somatic in origin.

The perception of deep pain, whether muscular-skeletal or visceral, is a complex sensation, because it is typically associated with general feelings of unpleasantness, anxiety, nausea, and autonomic changes such as hypotension and sweating. Pain elicited experimentally from the periosteum and ligaments by injection of hypertonic saline is associated with reflex contractions of nearby skeletal muscles. These muscle contractions are similar to the muscle spasms that occur as the result of injuries to bones, tendons, or joints. The protracted spasms cause the muscles to become ischemic, which in turn stimulates the pain receptors in the muscles. This creates a positive feedback loop, because the stimulation of pain receptors in the muscles leads to even more spasms.

Visceral inflammations of the abdomen also induce complex perceptual experiences. Classical signs of visceral inflammation include pain, tenderness to pressure, autonomic reactions, and spasm of the abdominal wall. The tenderness is related to increased sensitivity of pain receptors, the autonomic changes to the initiation of visceral reflexes, and the spasm to reflex contractions of skeletal muscle in the abdominal wall.

NEUROPHYSIOLOGICAL BASES OF PAIN PERCEPTION.—The perception of pain is only poorly understood, and its neurophysiological substrates remain even more obscure. In traditional theory, pain was postulated as being perceived through the activity of a specific sensory system. According to this theory, small peripheral fibers with free nerve endings are the receptors for pain. The afferent pain fibers enter the spinal cord and proceed through the lateral spinothalamic tract to the thalamus.

The specificity theory of pain perception has been criticized on several grounds. In its pure form, specificity theory requires the existence of identifiable receptors that only subserve pain. However, in studies using large samples of somatosensory fibers, only a very few fibers have been shown to respond exclusively to intense stimuli. Another troubling finding is that lesions of the lateral spinothalamic tract, including bilateral anterolateral cordotomy, are not invariably effective in terminating peripheral pain. Still another and even more puzzling finding is that under certain clinical conditions, pain in one region of the body may be triggered by mild stimulation of another unrelated area of the body surface.

Melzack and Wall have proposed an alternative to the specificity theory, which they call the gate control theory.[25] Basically, gate control theory is a form of pattern theory which proposes that pain is not the result of the activation of a limited set of pain receptors. Instead, it proposes that pain is a state that is triggered peripherally by a particular pattern of somatosensory input. According to Melzack and Wall a region in the dorsal horn of the spinal cord, known as the substantia gelatinosa, appears to act as a gate, thereby controlling access to the CNS of fibers that convey information about pain. Activation of small-diameter, slowly conducting, slowly adapting, unmyelinated fibers that are characterized by high thresholds to stimulation opens the gate. In contrast, activation of large-diameter, rapidly conducting, quickly habituating, myelinated fibers that have low stimulation thresholds is capable of closing the gate.

Figure 2–4 depicts the spinal mechanism proposed by Melzack and Wall in their gate control theory of pain. Accessibility of input from either the large- or small-diameter fibers onto T cells depends on the balance of activity between the two types of afferent fibers. According to the theory, the T cells project to activation and motivation systems in the brain that subserve pain. A prolonged intense stimulus, which is perceived as painful, tends to maintain excitation in the activation system long after the activity of the large-diameter, quickly adapting fibers is habituated. However, the theory also predicts that reactivation of the large fibers such as by softly rubbing a wound or gently stimulating the painful area electrically tends to attenuate the pain.

The original gate control theory proposed that the selection and modulation of the sensory input through the spinothalamic projection system provide the neurologic basis of the sensory discrimination of pain. In later formulations Melzack and Wall also emphasized that (1) activation of reticular and limbic system structures underlie the motivational drive and unpleasant affect that trigger the organism to action, (2) higher nervous system activity reflecting past experiences exerts control over both the discriminative and the motivational aspects of pain, and (3) higher centers in the brain appear to activate descending efferent fibers, which can influence afferent conduction at the initial synapses of the somatosensory system.[26]

Although the gate control theory has much to commend it, it appears to be too simplified in its present form to handle all the available evidence. First, the common finding in poly-

GATE CONTROL THEORY OF PAIN

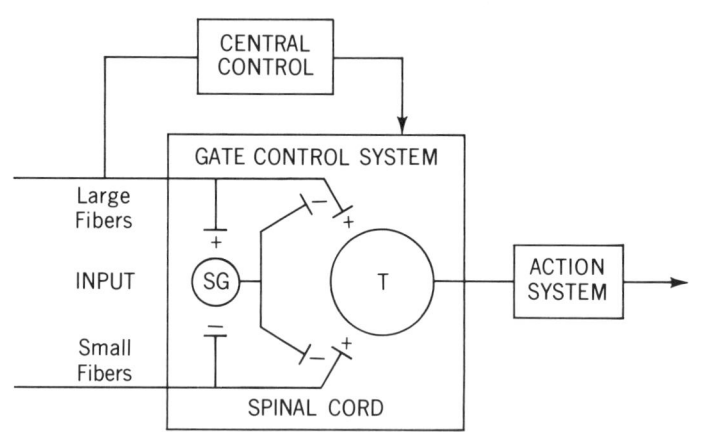

Fig 2–4.—Gate control theory of pain, a spinal mechanism proposed by Melzack and Wall. Large-fiber input excites the substantia gelatinosa, which acts to close the gate for both large and small fibers to the T cells. Small-fiber input has the opposite effect. Accessibility of input from either the large or the small fibers to the T cells depends on the balance of activity between these two classes of afferents. For this reason, the postulated gate acts as a spinal pattern detection device for the perception of pain. Central control of this mechanism probably also occurs as indicated above. T cells project to activation and motivational systems within the mammalian brain. (From Melzack R., Wall P.D.: *Science* 150:971–979, 1965. Copyright 1965 by the American Association for the Advancement of Science. Used by permission.)

neuropathy is a disproportionate destruction of large myelinated fibers with much less destruction of small-diameter fibers. This type of neuropathy is usually painless, and pain is not induced by mild stimulation. Second, neuropathies exist in which there is a relative decrease in the number of small-diameter to large-diameter fibers, but in which there is nevertheless a great deal of pain. In thallium neuropathy, for example, the large fibers are almost totally unaffected, whereas there is a large decrease in the number of small-diameter fibers. This is a very painful neuropathy in which most forms of stimulation cause pain. These as well as other findings reviewed by Nathan have led many investigators to conclude that the gate control theory of pain is incomplete in some respects and wrong in others.[27] Nevertheless, it is the most influential theory of pain presently espoused, and it has provided the theoretical underpinnings for treatments such as transcutaneous stimulation.

TREATMENT OF PAIN—The most widely used treatment for the relief of pain is the oral administration of salicylate compounds such as aspirin. Salicylates are particularly effective in relieving relatively low-intensity pain, whether circumscribed or widespread in origin. Headache, myalgia, and other pains arising from integumental rather than visceral structures respond particularly well to these compounds. Although the salicylates have a selective depressant effect on the central nervous system, the mechanism by which this is accomplished has not yet been elucidated. The primary action of aspirin (and other nonsteroidal anti-inflammatory and analgesic drugs) at the tissue level is the inhibition of prostaglandin biosynthesis.[28] Since the prostaglandins are chemical mediators of pain and inflammation, it is presumed that this effect is responsible for the analgesic properties of aspirin in many situations. What is clear is that salicylates primarily elevate the pain threshold rather than influence the willingness to withstand a painful stimulus. A 45% elevation of the pain threshold elicited by electrical stimulation of the dental pulp in humans has been reported after administration of 1.8 gm aspirin. In contrast to narcotic analgesics, salicylates have the advantage that chronic use does not lead to either tolerance or physical dependence.

Salicylates, however, are sometimes combined either with narcotic analgesics or with sedatives in mixtures designed to give more effective pain relief than is obtainable with any one class of these drugs alone. Although the effects of combining salicylate and narcotic analgesic are additive only in terms of raising the pain threshold, the opiate dissociates the perception of pain from the affective reaction to pain, reducing anxiety, providing a sedative effect, and in general making the subject more comfortable.

Although the salicylates are usually adequate for managing mild and moderate pain, the narcotic analgesics are the only drugs effective against chronic, severe pain. The major drawbacks to their long-term use in the treatment of pain are problems associated with tolerance and physical dependence. Before turning to an examination of some nondrug methods for dealing with chronic, severe pain, let us first examine the use of anesthetic agents in treating persons with acute pain.

Using general anesthetics for the abolition of pain in surgical operations was introduced in the middle of the 19th century. In 1844, Horace Wells, a dentist, had one of his teeth extracted while he was under nitrous oxide. Two years later William T. Morton used ether as a surgical anesthetic at Massachusetts General Hospital. Prior to that, major surgery without anesthetics was performed with great haste in order to shorten the agony involved. Amputations were usually accomplished in a few seconds, and surgeons prided themselves on the speed with which they performed major surgery.

General anesthetics decrease synaptic transmission, while axon conduction remains unimpaired. Although the general anesthetics produce a generalized, graded, dose-related depression of all CNS functions, it is commonly believed that synaptic depression within the midbrain reticular formation and its ascending diencephalic outflows are involved importantly in the loss of consciousness. As the level of anesthesia deepens, so does the level of unconsciousness, which is accompanied by a loss of reflexes and by analgesia. Pronounced analgesia occurs only at a very deep level of general anesthesia.

In contrast to general anesthetics, local anesthetics are drugs that, when applied locally as in a subcutaneous injection, block both the generation and the conduction of nerve impulses in the vicinity of the injection site, thereby causing analgesia in a relatively discrete area. Sigmund Freud and Karl Koller are generally credited with introducing cocaine as a local anesthetic in 1884, although VonAnrep had recommended its use several years previously. Procaine (Novocaine) was synthesized in 1905. Since then a great many other local anesthetics such as lidocaine (Xylocaine) have been introduced for both topical and injection-produced analgesia.

Other methods for the relief of pain include hypnosis, acupuncture, transcutaneous nerve stimulation, and surgery. All these procedures, as well as the administration of drugs, have led to both conspicuous successes and failures in the treatment of chronic pain.

Spectacular results have been claimed for hypnosis both in producing anesthesia during surgery and in treating mild to moderately intense chronic pain. In recent years, several carefully controlled studies have led to the conclusion that the positive results obtained under hypnosis are due to heightened motivation on the part of the patient, an increased readiness to accept suggestions from the physician, and a marked reduction in fear and anxiety. To some extent, these same factors govern the effectiveness of placebos. It therefore appears that the effectiveness of hypnosis or placebo in pain control depends mainly on a positive physician-patient relationship.

Acupuncture is an ancient Chinese approach to disease based on the restoration of an imbalance of opposing forces called yin and yang. Current interest in acupuncture centers on its use for the relief from pain. Acupuncture analgesia involves fairly intense, continuous stimulation of tissues by acupuncture needles. In some instances electric current is passed between two needles; in other instances the needles are rapidly twirled by hand. In either case, stimulation at a designated acupuncture site is reported to relieve pain at sites remote from the stimulation. Analgesia may outlast the duration of stimulation by several hours.

In our discussion about the perception of pain, it was indicated that deep pain is sometimes associated with a positive feedback loop involving the sequence of pain-spasm-pain. It is conceivable that any therapeutic intervention that interferes with the loop may lead to pain relief that may last for some time. To some extent the positive effects of acupuncture also seem explicable in terms of gate control theory. It is also possible that stimulation of some acupuncture points may influence either skeletomuscular or autonomic reflexes, thereby altering perceptual experience. Findings that somatic and visceral pain afferents enter the CNS at the same level and may utilize either the same or closely related CNS pathways could help to explain how the effects of stimulation at a somatic site relieve pain at a remote visceral site. Last but not least, factors associated with the positive effects of placebos such as heightened motivation and patient expectancy may be critical. Controlled experiments separating out all the relevant factors are currently needed.

In recent years cutaneously applied electrical stimulation, called transcutaneous nerve stimulation, has been used as a noninvasive means of treating persons incapacitated by chronic pain. Typically the application of this treatment is empirically based, with the site of electrode application and the parameters of stimulation heavily influenced by subjective reports of pain relief by the patient. Of more than 1,000 cases of chronic pain treated by transcutaneous nerve stimulation, about 30% of the persons so treated seem to have benefited over a long period of time. On the one hand, the finding that some 30% of persons incapacitated by chronic pain are helped by the procedure is encouraging because for most it was a treatment of last resort. On the other hand, there is a lack of carefully controlled studies examining this effectiveness.

The most drastic interventions for reducing pain involve surgery. Although many persons are helped by such surgery, the percentage of failures is significant no matter what procedure is used. Cordotomies, or sectioning the lateral spinal cord pathways to relieve pain, have been relatively successful for cancer victims suffering intractable pain. However, as survival time increases beyond 18 months there tends to be a return of chronic pain sensation. Another major problem associated with successful cordotomy is that the surgery requires the lesioning of a very large area in order to produce long-lasting pain relief. Unfortunately, the larger the area lesioned, the more other functions such as walking or bladder retention are impaired. Pain from the pelvic area, abdomen, and rectum in particular require bilateral lesioning in order to be effective.

Intracranial surgery has also been used to control pain. The relative long-term success of thalamic surgery is only about 30%. Frontal lobotomy and leukotomy have also been used in treating persons with intractable pain. Although the aversive feelings associated with pain seem to be reduced, this is frequently accompanied by a blunting of all emotional affect in these persons. Sympathectomy too has been used to control intractable pain, but the results after long periods of observation have usually been disappointing.

In contrast to the disappointing results obtained with some surgical procedures, others seem to be more effective. Surgery on the gasserian ganglion, the trigeminal root, or the trigeminal nucleus has proved useful in treating tic douloureux or idiopathic neuralgia of the trigeminal nerve. This pain is excruciating and paroxysmal and usually radiates from the angle of the jaw along the involved branch. Rhizotomy, or section of the dorsal roots of the spinal cord to relieve pain, has proved useful in dealing with the painful cramps suffered by spastics. In spite of their limitations, cordotomies and tractotomies of the spinothalamic tract are still useful procedures for dealing with intractable pain in terminally ill carcinoma patients.

SUMMARY

Demonstrations that specific physiochemical mechanisms in particular parts of the nervous system can be related to psychological and behavioral processes have opened up new approaches to our understanding of human behavior. These approaches are still relatively young, and it seems inevitable that many more psychological processes will eventually be explicable in terms of their underlying neurologic substrate. Even if we knew considerably more about the neuronal bases of behavior, however, detailed knowledge of the psychological, social, and cultural variables would still be necessary before human behavior could be fully comprehended. In this chapter, an attempt has been made to review some of the basic functional and structural aspects of the nervous system, and to show how a knowledge of these aspects provides a better understanding of the biologic mechanisms underlying behavior.

At the cellular level, synaptic transmission is a key factor in neurologic function. There is evidence that aberrations in neuronal transmission within the brain may be associated with mental illnesses (e.g., affective disorders, schizophrenia) and that the use of drugs that influence synaptic transmission is helpful in the treatment of persons who have these conditions (see chap. 3). An understanding of the biologic bases of many psychological processes (e.g., consciousness, motivation, emotion, linguistic behavior, memory) depends on a knowledge of neuronal transmission as it occurs in specific regions of the central nervous system. Comprehension of the neuronal bases of complex psychological processes such as pain, how persons respond to it, and how it is treated requires not only knowledge of neuronal transmission in sensory pathways, but also knowledge of how various neurally mediated systems operate and interact with one another. An understanding of psychosocial processes is also necessary.

REFERENCES

1. Hodgkin A.L., Huxley A.F.: Action potentials recorded from inside a nerve fibre. *Nature* 144:710, 1939.
2. Sheperd G.M.: *The Synaptic Organization of the Brain*, ed. 2. New York, Oxford University Press, 1979.
3. Eccles J.C.: *The Physiology of Synapses*. Berlin, Springer, 1964.
4. Eccles J.C., Fatt, P., Koketsu J.: Cholinergic and inhibitory synapses in a pathway from motor-axon collaterals to motoneurons. *J. Physiol. (Lond.)* 126:524, 1954.
5. Cooper J.R., Bloom F.E., Roth R.H.: *The Biochemical Basis of Neuropharmacology*, ed. 2. New York, Oxford University Press, 1978.
6. Molinoff P.B., Axelrod J.: Biochemistry of catecholamines. *Annu. Rev. Biochem.* 40:465, 1971.
7. Snyder S.H., et al.: The role of brain dopamine in behavioral regulation and the actions of psychotropic drugs. *Am. J. Psychiatry* 127:199, 1970.
8. Schildkraut J.J., Kety S.S.: Biogenic amines and emotion. *Science* 156:21, 1967.
9. Hughes J., Kosterlitz H.W., Leslie F.M.: Assessment of the agonist and antagonist activities of narcotic analgesic drugs by means of the mouse vas deferens. *Br. J. Pharmacol.* 51:139P, 1974.
10. Terenius L., Wahlstrom A.: Inhibitor(s) of narcotic receptors binding in brain extracts and cerebrospinal fluid. *Acta Pharmacol. Toxicol.* 35(suppl.):55, 1974.
11. Eccles J.C., Ito M., Szentagothai, J.: *The Cerebellum as a Neuronal Machine*. New York, Springer, 1967.
12. Jouvet M.: The states of sleep. *Sci. Am.* 216:62, 1967.
13. Hobson J.A., et al.: Selective firing by cat pontine brain stem neurons in desynchronized sleep. *J. Neurophysiol.* 37:497, 1974.
14. Olds J., Milner P.: Positive reinforcement produced by electrical stimulation of septal area and other regions of rat brain. *J. Comp. Physiol. Psychol.* 47:419, 1954.
15. Olds J., Allan W.S., Briese E.: Differentiation of hypothalamic drive and reward centers. *Am. J. Physiol.* 221:368, 1971.
16. Narabayashi H., et al.: Stereotaxis amygdalotomy for behavior disorders. *Arch. Neurol.* 9:1, 1963.
17. Fulton J.F., Jacobsen C.F.: The functions of the frontal lobes, a comparative study in monkeys, chimpanzees and man. *Adv. Mod. Biol.* 4:113, 1935.
18. Mark V.H., Ervin F.R.: *Violence and the Brain*. New York, Harper & Row, 1970.
19. Valenstein E.: *Brain Control. A Critical Examination of Brain Stimulation and Psychosurgery*. New York, John Wiley & Sons, 1973.
20. Adams R.D.: The anatomy of memory mechanisms in the human brain, in Talland G.A., Waugh N.C. (eds.): *The Pathology of Memory*. New York, Academic Press, 1969.
21. Gardner B.T., Gardner R.A.: Two-way communication with an infant chimpanzee, in Schrier A., Stollnitz F. (eds.): *Behavior of Nonhuman Primates*. New York, Academic Press, 1971.
22. Geschwind N.: Disconnexion syndromes in animals and man. *Brain* 88:237, 1966.
23. Sperry R.W.: Lateral specialization in the surgically separated hemispheres, in Schmitt F.O., Worden F.G. (eds.): *The Neurosciences: Third Study Program*. Cambridge, Mass., M.I.T. Press, 1974.
24. Beecher H.K.: *Measurement of Subjective Responses*. New York, Oxford University Press, 1959.
25. Melzack R., Wall P.D.: Pain mechanisms: A new theory. *Science* 150:971, 1965.
26. Melzack R., Wall P.D.: Psychophysiology of pain. *Int. Anesthesiol. Clin.* 8:3, 1970.
27. Nathan P.W.: The gate control theory of pain: A critical review. *Brain* 99:123, 1976.
28. Vane J.R.: Inhibition of prostaglandin synthesis as a mechanism of action for aspirin-like drugs. *Nature [New Biol.]* 231:232, 1971.

3 / The Biochemistry of the Functional Psychoses

JONATHAN J. BRAUNSTEIN, M.D., and SANFORD JACOBSON, M.D.

CONVINCING EVIDENCE EXISTS that the two major functional psychoses, the primary affective disorders and schizophrenia, have a genetic basis (see chap. 1). This strongly implies the presence of a heritable biochemical defect in persons with these conditions. Within the past 25 years, many studies have been carried out in an attempt to define such defects. While they have not yielded a definitive answer, they have given rise to a number of plausible hypotheses about the etiology of the primary affective disorders and schizophrenia. Most important, as a result of the application of modern scientific technology to these investigations, we have come a long way in our attempt to explain abnormal behavior in biologic terms.

BIOCHEMICAL ASPECTS OF THE AFFECTIVE DISORDERS

Most studies of the biochemistry of depression have involved persons with primary affective disorders, i.e., unipolar and bipolar depressive illnesses. They have focused on the functional state of the three biogenic amine neurotransmitter systems and the effects of psychoactive drugs on these systems. A hypothesis explaining the pathogenesis of the primary affective disorders, the so-called monoamine hypothesis, has been developed, which states: In depression there is a functional deficiency and in mania there is a functional excess of one or more of the biogenic amine neurotransmitters in the brain. This discussion will begin with a review of the synthesis and metabolism of these biogenic amines.

The Biogenic Amines

Dopamine and norepinephrine are both synthesized from the amino acid tyrosine (Fig 3–1), while serotonin is synthesized from the amino acid tryptophan (Fig 3–2). Regulation of the synthesis of a biogenic amine depends on many factors including the amount of substrate and enzymes. A metabolic feedback mechanism appears to operate so that the presence of large amounts of an amine inhibits the rate-limiting enzymatic reaction responsible for the synthesis of that amine.

After their formation within neuronal cell bodies, these neurotransmitters travel along the axon to the region of the presynaptic endplate, where additional synthesis of these compounds takes place. Here, these substances are stored in granules. The release of an amine into the synaptic cleft and its attachment to a receptor on the postsynaptic neuron account for the transmission of a nerve impulse across the synapse. After an amine is released into the cleft, its action is terminated by (1) an active process of reuptake into the axon terminal and (2) passive diffusion into the surrounding extracellular space. A secondary process of metabolic degradation takes place both in the synaptic cleft and within the cytoplasm of the neuron. The reuptake mechanism seems to be the most important in terms of inactivating the amine. The enzymes responsible for the degradation of norepinephrine and dopamine are catechol-*O*-methyltransferase (COMT) and monoamine oxidase (MAO); serotonin is broken down by MAO (see Figs 3-1 and 3-2).

Within a neuronal cell, there are three pools of an amine neurotransmitter. There is an *intragranular bound pool*, which is the principal form of storage for the amine. This bound pool is in equilibrium with an *intragranular mobile pool*, which is the source of the amine that is released into the synaptic cleft. Following the action of an amine on the postsynaptic receptor and its reuptake by the presynaptic neuron, amine that is not degraded to an inactive form enters a *cytoplasmic mobile pool*, which is in equilibrium with the intragranular mobile pool. Drugs and chemicals may alter the neuronal synthesis, release, storage, degradation, and reuptake of the biogenic amines, thereby modifying the function of the central nervous system.

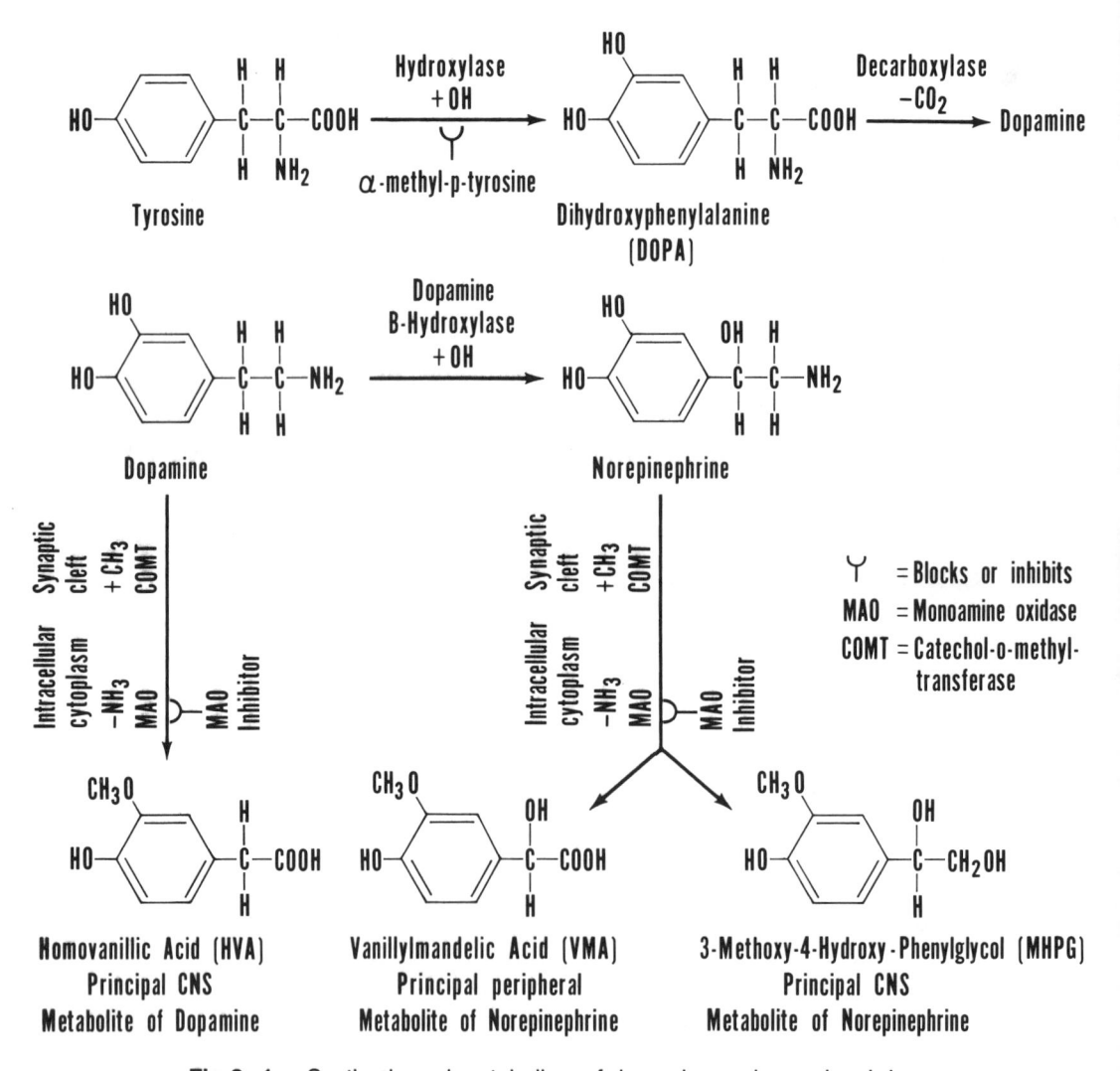

Fig 3-1.—Synthesis and metabolism of dopamine and norepinephrine.

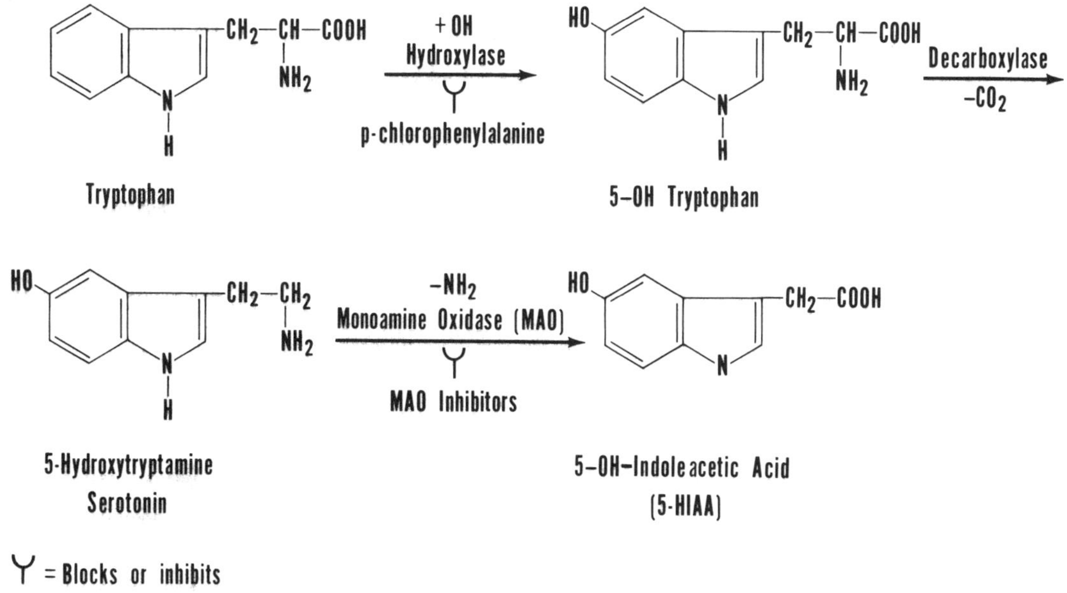

Fig 3-2.—Serotonin synthesis and metabolism.

The Monoamine Hypothesis of the Affective Disorders[1,2]

Pharmacologic Evidence.

Much of what is known about the role of the biogenic amines in the pathogenesis of psychiatric disorders has come from studies of the mechanism of action of the modern psychoactive drugs. One of the first of these agents to undergo careful scrutiny was reserpine, a derivative of the *Rauwolfia* plant. In the 1950s, this drug was widely used in treating persons with a psychosis, particularly schizophrenia. Studies of its mechanisms of action showed that it depleted the neuronal stores of biogenic amines, including serotonin, dopamine, and norepinephrine. It was discovered that this effect is due to a release of these transmitters from their intragranular pools, resulting in their degradation by monoamine oxidase.

Clinically, it was noted that persons who received reserpine developed drowsiness and sedation and that some (about 20%) became depressed. This observation stimulated considerable interest in the relationship between the concentration of monoamines in the brain and depression. It was postulated that a deficiency of these compounds led to depression, although it was not clear which of the transmitters was principally responsible for this effect.

Studies involving the administration of (1) amino acid precursors that increase the formation of monoamines, and (2) substances that block monoamine synthesis have been carried out in an attempt to resolve this matter. For example, it was demonstrated that dihydroxyphenylalanine (a catecholamine precursor) was more effective in reversing the depressive effects of reserpine than 5-hydroxytryptophan (a precursor of serotonin), suggesting that a depletion of catecholamines, particularly norepinephrine, was more important than a reduction of serotonin in the pathogenesis of depression. In other studies, α-methyl-*para*-tyrosine (which inhibits the enzyme tyrosine hydroxylase and decreases the synthesis of dopamine and norepinephrine) was found to produce mild depression in some subjects. However, the depression observed in persons treated with α-methyl-*para*-tyrosine is much less severe than that caused by reserpine, which indicates that serotonin depletion is also important in the pathogenesis of this state. Studies using *para*-chlorophenylalanine tended to confuse the issue further. Administration of this drug (which inhibits the enzyme tryptophan hydroxylase, and thereby blocks the synthesis of serotonin) produces anxiety, arousal, and psychotic manifestations, but no depression. Thus the question of which transmitter, the catecholamines or serotonin, is most important in the pathogenesis of depression was not resolved by these investigations.

Studies of other psychoactive medications that have a pronounced effect on mood were instrumental in elucidating the role of the biogenic amines in depression. Amphetamine, which produces a temporary elevation of mood, was found to release norepinephrine from its intragranular pools. In contrast to "depleters" like reserpine, however, the activity of norepinephrine is enhanced by this drug. This may be because amphetamine also inhibits monoamine oxidase and blocks the reuptake of norepinephrine into the cell—effects that increase the activity of this neurotransmitter. While initially this drug causes an elevation of mood, its long-term use may result in a "letdown" or depression after it is discontinued. The latter effect has been correlated with a depletion of norepinephrine from neurons.

The mechanism of action of the two groups of drugs most commonly used in the treatment of primary depression (monoamine oxidase inhibitors and tricyclic antidepressants) has given support to the monoamine hypothesis, since members of both groups increase the activity of the amine neurotransmitters at the postsynaptic receptor site. The monoamine oxidase inhibitors were among the first antidepressant drugs to be used. Originally, their use stemmed from the observation that iproniazid, a member of this class of drugs, elevated mood when it was given for the treatment of persons with tuberculosis. When the mechanism of action of iproniazid was discovered to be inhibition of the enzyme monoamine oxidase (MAO), it was reasoned that this might be responsible for the mood change. By blocking a major degradative pathway for the amine neurotransmitters, the MAO inhibitors permit greater amounts of these substances to accumulate presynaptically and more to be released into the synaptic cleft.

Tricyclic antidepressants block the "amine pump" responsible for the reuptake of biogenic amines into the presynaptic neuron. Since the reuptake process is the main mechanism for terminating the action of these transmitters, blockade of this process prolongs their activity and increases the stimulation of the postsynaptic receptors.

The different tricyclics have different effects on the neuronal reuptake of the biogenic amines (Table 3–1).[2,3] Those with a secondary amine structure (e.g., desipramine, nortriptyline) selectively prevent the reuptake of norepinephrine by adrenergic neurons, but have little or no effect on the "amine pump" in dopamine and serotonergic neurons. Of the tricyclics with a tertiary amine structure, imipramine inhibits the reuptake of both norepinephrine and serotonin, whereas the effect of amitriptyline is much more pronounced on serotonergic neurons. In the body, the tertiary amines are converted to their corresponding secondary amines (i.e., imipramine is partially metabolized to desipramine and amitriptyline is partially metabolized to nortriptyline), so the administration of a tertiary amine results in the presence of two active drugs in variable ratios.[3] This must be taken into account when considering the effects of a tertiary amine tricyclic on transmitter function.

As new drugs are introduced and found to be helpful in the treatment of persons with affective illnesses, attempts are made to correlate their clinical actions with their effects on the function of the amine neurotransmitters. Such is the case with lithium. In recent years, this drug, administered in the form of its salt, lithium carbonate, has gained wide

TABLE 3-1.—EFFECTS OF TRICYCLICS ON THE
AMINE PUMP

	BLOCKADE OF AMINE PUMP		
	For Serotonin	For Norepinephrine	For Dopamine
Secondary amines			
Desipramine	0	+++	0
Nortriptyline	+	++	0
Tertiary amines			
Imipramine	++	++	0
Amitriptyline	+++	0 or +	0

Source: Based on information in Maas J.W.: *Ann. Intern. Med.* 88:556, 1978; and Hollister L.E.: *N. Engl. J. Med.* 299:1106, 1978.

acceptance in the treatment of persons with mania. It is also used in some instances of primary depression, especially in bipolar illness. There is still some question as to its effectiveness in treating depression, particularly the unipolar type; however, it is clear that lithium is highly effective in alleviating and preventing the manic phase of manic-depressive illness. The mechanism by which lithium exerts its calming effect on manic individuals is not fully understood. However, there is evidence that this agent acts in two ways to alter neurotransmitter function in a manner consistent with the monoamine hypothesis.

First, studies suggest that lithium causes either an increase in transmitter reuptake or an inhibition of transmitter release by the presynaptic neuron.[1] It is hypothesized that, for norepinephrine, these changes are due to an alteration in the configuration of the substrate binding site on the carrier protein that transports this amine across neuronal membranes.[4] As a result, there is an intracellular accumulation of this neurotransmitter and a decreased activation of the postsynaptic receptors. There are data indicating that lithium increases transmitter turnover and the formation of deaminated transmitter metabolites, findings that would be expected to result from an increased intracellular accumulation of transmitter amines.[1]

Second, it is thought that lithium interferes with cyclic adenosine monophosphate (AMP)-mediated processes in the postsynaptic neuron that are activated by norepinephrine in its function as a neurotransmitter. This would decrease the response of the neuron to this neurotransmitter, or others that function in the same way.

Metabolites of the Biogenic Amines in Body Fluids

The introduction of techniques for measuring specific metabolites of the biogenic amines has allowed investigators to find out more about the central nervous system activity of these transmitters. Levels of these metabolites in the cerebrospinal fluid and urine have generally been used to assess biogenic amine function in the brain.

3-Methoxy-4-hydroxyphenylglycol (MHPG) is the major metabolite of norepinephrine in the brain (see Fig 3-1) and, therefore, levels of this substance have been thought to closely reflect the activity of this transmitter in the brain. This is true for measurements of MHPG in the cerebrospinal fluid (CSF). However, estimates of the fraction of MHPG in the urine that is derived from the brain have varied according to different investigators, with a recent study indicating it is only about 20%.[5] Studies of MHPG in the CSF show that *some* persons with primary depression have reduced concentrations and *some* with mania have elevated levels.[6,7] The excretion of this compound in the urine is also reduced in *some* individuals with primary depression.[8] In persons with bipolar illness, when the amount of urinary MHPG is decreased during the depressive phase it often increases with recovery; with the onset of mania, further elevations of the levels of this metabolite may occur. While some persons with depression have low levels of MHPG in their urine, others have normal or high values.

Reports that depressed persons have different levels of urinary MHPG (i.e., low, normal, high) suggest that there are subgroups that differ in terms of the pathogenesis of their illness.[2] It is thought that those with reduced amounts of MHPG have a decreased norepinephrine activity in the central nervous system, while those with normal or high levels have decreased function of the serotonergic system in the brain. A correlation has been noted between the excretion of MHPG in the urine of depressed persons and their response to the different tricyclic antidepressant drugs.[2,3,9] Individuals with low levels of MHPG appear to respond well to desipramine (which preferentially blocks the reuptake of norepinephrine) but not to amitriptyline—a finding that is consistent with the presence of a deficiency in noradrenergic neurotransmission in this group. On the other hand, depressives with normal or elevated levels of MHPG tend to have a good response to amitriptyline (which selectively blocks serotonin reuptake) but not to desipramine, suggesting deficient activity of the serotonergic neuronal system. These findings have not yet been completely validated and studies are still going on to determine whether or not the measurement of MHPG in the urine of a depressed person is a reliable guide for selecting the type of antidepressant medication that will work best for him.[10]

Studies of the level of homovanillic acid (HVA), an end product of dopamine catabolism, in persons with depression and mania have resulted in conflicting data. Most investigators report that the level of spinal fluid HVA is decreased in persons with depression.[1] In those with mania, some studies have found increased levels, while others report no change from the normal concentration. The level of 5-hydroxyindoleacetic acid (5-HIAA), the principal serotonin metabolite in cerebrospinal fluid, is either reduced or unchanged in depressed persons, depending on which studies one reads. A recent report indicates that the concentration of this compound is abnormally low only in certain persons with affective illness, and the rest have normal values.[11]

A special technique has been developed to assess changes in the level of amine metabolites in cerebrospinal fluid. The concentration of a substance in the spinal fluid is the result of its ingress into and its egress from this compartment. Since it is only the ingress of a metabolite that reflects its formation and metabolism in the central nervous system, it is important to separate these two processes (i.e., ingress and egress). Probenecid, a drug that blocks the egress of the major acid metabolites of dopamine and serotonin (i.e., HVA and 5-HIAA) from the cerebrospinal fluid, is used to make this differentiation.[12] After the administration of this drug, HVA and 5-HIAA accumulate within the spinal fluid compartment. By determining the rate of their accumulation, a much better idea of the central nervous system formation and metabolism of dopamine and serotonin can be obtained. It has been found using this procedure that HVA and 5-HIAA build up at a slower rate than normal in the spinal fluid of some depressed persons.

There is a good deal of variability in the data reported by studies measuring the levels of amine metabolites in persons with the affective disorders. Differences in the concentration of these metabolites among groups of depressed or manic persons may be due to several factors. First, there are a number of external variables, such as diet, motor activity, and age, that affect the concentration of these metabolites in the cerebrospinal fluid and urine. Second, the clinical diagnosis of depression encompasses a heterogeneous group of conditions. Even the primary affective disorders are undoubtedly made up of a number of conditions with different etiologies, so it is highly unlikely that all persons with depression, or even all those with primary affective disorders, have a uniform set of biochemical findings. In fact, the biochemical differences among these persons may be valuable clues to the presence of specific causes of their conditions.

Endocrine Abnormalities in Depression

Disturbances in endocrine function have been reported in the primary affective disorders (unipolar and bipolar depressive illness) that may be important in understanding their pathogenesis. Sachar points out that the suspicion that this might be so stemmed originally from two observations: first, the clinical symptomatology of these patients (e.g., disturbances in mood, appetite, sleep, sexual drive, and autonomic activity) suggests that there is hypothalamic dysfunction and, second, the same neurotransmitters that are postulated to play a role in the pathogenesis of depression modulate the secretion of hypothalamic-releasing hormones that, in turn, control the secretion of anterior pituitary hormones.[13, 14] Among the endocrine abnormalities reported in persons with primary depression are (1) hypersecretion of cortisol, (2) diminished human growth hormone (HGH) secretion in response to provocative stimuli, and (3) impaired release of thyroid-stimulating hormone (THS) following the administration of thyrotropin-releasing hormone (TRH). In clinical studies, a variable percentage of such persons are found to have these abnormalities, probably reflecting the biochemical heterogeneity of these disorders. In general, persons with secondary depression (associated with an underlying medical or psychiatric illness) do not demonstrate these disturbances of endocrine function, indicating that there may be fundamental biologic differences between primary and secondary depressive illness.

The most extensive investigations of endocrine function in depression have dealt with the hypothalamic-pituitary-adrenal (HPA) axis. These have documented three principal abnormalities in primary depressive illness:

1. *Elevated levels of urine and plasma cortisol.* When cortisol secretion is assessed by either measuring 24-hour urinary cortisol production rates (by isotope dilution methods) or 24-hour plasma cortisol concentrations (by sampling plasma at frequent intervals), about half of the patients with primary depression are found to be hypersecretors.[13, 14] In early studies by Sachar in which the level of plasma cortisol was measured every 20 or 30 minutes throughout the day and night using an indwelling venous cannula, the mean 24-hour value for 7 persons with primary depressive illness was 11.25 µg per dl as compared with a value of 7.28 µg per dl for 54 normal control subjects.[13] More recently, Sachar carried out 24-hour plasma cortisol measures on 17 additional patients with severe primary depression. Nine of the 17 were found to be hypersecretors with a mean 24-hour plasma cortisol of 10.0 µg per dl compared with mean values of 5.9 µg per dl for 8 nonhypersecreting cases and 6 normal controls.[14]

2. *Altered circadian rhythm of cortisol secretion.* Normally, cortisol is secreted in 9 to 11 discrete episodes during a 24-hour period (reflected by spikes in the plasma cortisol concentration). Approximately 40% of the total amount secreted daily occurs between the hours of 3:00 A.M. and 9:00 A.M. with relatively little secretion taking place in the late afternoon, evening, and early morning hours. In patients with primary depression who are hypersecretors of cortisol, there is a "flattening out" of the circadian curve of plasma cortisol (Fig 3-3). Those hypersecretors who were studied by Sachar had an increased number of secretory episodes which were associated with higher plasma levels of cortisol.[13, 14] Moreover, they did not have a reduction of cortisol secretion that normally takes place in the afternoon, evening, and early morning hours (see Fig 3-3).

The elevated levels of plasma cortisol and abnormal secretory pattern reverted to normal in these patients after recovery from their illness.

3. *Resistance of plasma cortisol to dexamethasone suppression.* Under normal circumstances, the administration of 1 or 2 mg of dexamethasone (a synthetic corticosteroid that inhibits the secretion of adrenocorticotropin) between 11:00 P.M. and midnight suppresses the concentration of plasma cortisol to

MEAN HOURLY CORTISOL CONCENTRATION
7 Depressed and 54 Normals

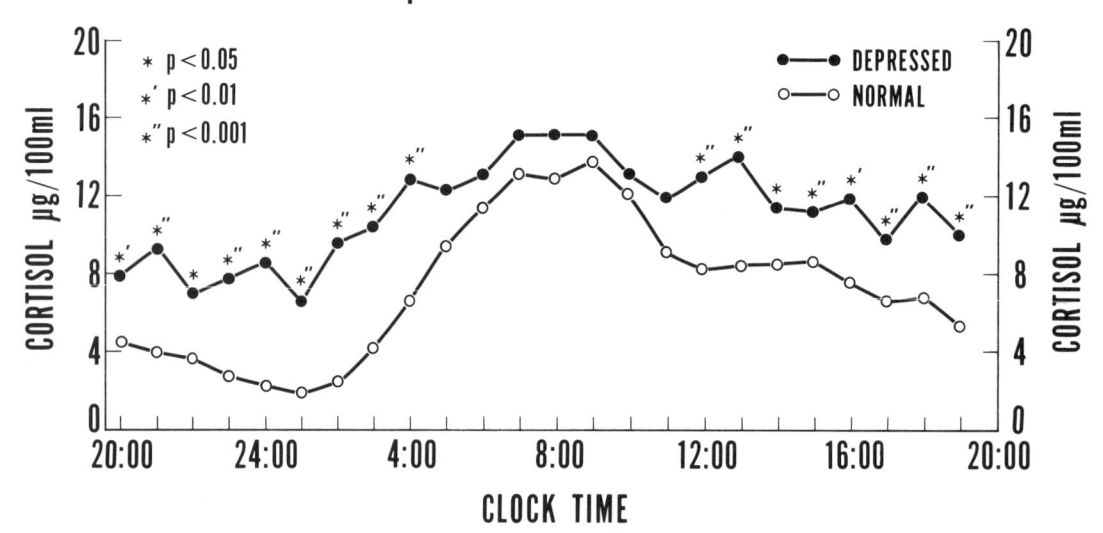

Fig 3-3.—Mean hourly concentration of cortisol in 7 severely depressed patients and 54 normals (the latter data provided by E.D. Weitzman). The largest and most significant differences between the depressed patients and the normals are in the afternoon, evening, and early morning hours. (From Sachar E.J.: *Annu. Rev. Med.* 27:392, 1976. Reproduced with permission.)

less than 6 μg per dl for at least the next 24 hours. About half of the persons who are ill with primary depression demonstrate a resistance to this suppression, although usually not of the magnitude seen in Cushing's syndrome.[14, 15, 16] In contrast to Cushing's syndrome, where there is a failure of normal suppression during the entire 24-hour period after dexamethasone, some individuals with primary depression may suppress normally in the early morning (following dexamethasone) only to escape from this suppression in the late afternoon or evening. After recovery from the depression, a normal response to dexamethasone occurs.

Nonsuppression to dexamethasone is rarely seen in patients with secondary depression and, therefore, it has been suggested that the dexamethasone suppression test may be useful in distinguishing between the primary and secondary depressive disorders.[16]

Thus, approximately 50% of patients with primary depression have dysfunction of the HPA axis that remits after their clinical recovery. One theory that attempts to explain this dysfunction relates it to the CNS activity of the biogenic amines that are postulated to play a role in the pathogenesis of depression. Under normal circumstances, these neurotransmitters influence endocrine function by their action on neurons (in the region of the median eminence of the hypothalamus) that discharge releasing factors (hormones) that regulate the secretion of anterior pituitary hormones. For example, it is believed that the noradrenergic system exerts a tonic inhibition on the discharge of corticotropin-releasing factor (CRF), while the serotonergic system has a stimulating effect on CRF discharge. A functional deficiency of norepinephrine in the brain (as is postulated to occur in depression) could account for an increased output of CRF that, in turn, would stimulate the anterior pituitary to secrete ACTH, causing the adrenal cortex to release excessive amounts of cortisol. In support of this theory, Sachar recently reported that the intravenous administration of dextroamphetamine (an adrenergic drug) to depressive hypersecretors of cortisol resulted in a rapid (and temporary) normalization of their cortisol levels.[14]

It has been reported that the secretion of human growth hormone (HGH) in response to insulin-induced hypoglycemia is diminished in some patients with primary depression.[14] The release of this hormone from the anterior pituitary is thought to be mediated by the action of both norepinephrine and serotonin, so a deficiency in the functional activity of either of these transmitters in the brain could explain the reduced secretion of HGH in depression.

Although thyroid function is normal in states of depression, abnormalities of the release of thyroid-stimulating hormone (TSH) following the infusion of thyrotropin-releasing hormone (TRH) have been reported in the primary affective disorders. A blunted TSH response to TRH occurs in a substantial number, varying from one third to three fourths depending on the test criteria used, of persons with unipolar depression.[14, 17, 18] Whereas the hypersecretion of cortisol in primary depression generally returns to normal after the individual recovers from his illness, the subnormal TSH response may persist despite clinical recovery.[14]

There is disagreement in the literature with respect to the results of the TRH test in bipolar depression. Some investigators have found no difference in the mean TSH responses of groups of unipolar and bipolar patients;[19] others report that a blunted TSH response occurs in bipolar depression but is less common than in unipolar depression.[14] The work of still others indicates that, in contrast to the blunted response in unipolar patients, there is an augmented TSH response in bipolar patients.[18, 20] On the basis of this finding, it has been suggested that the TRH test can be used as a clinical tool to distinguish the unipolar (low TSH responders) and bipolar (high TSH responders) subgroups of depression.[18, 20]

The reason for the impaired TSH response to TRH in primary depression is unknown. It is theorized by some workers in the field that the hypersecretion of cortisol that occurs in these disorders may be responsible, since both in Cushing's syndrome and with the chronic administration of adrenal corticosteroids there is a decreased TSH response to TRH. One group of investigators has found a

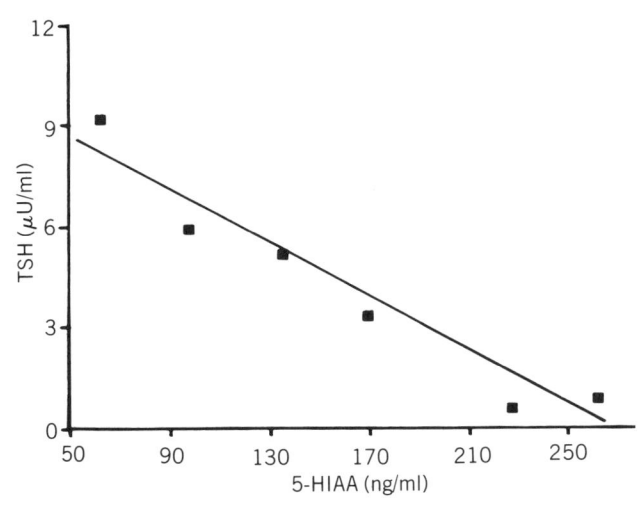

Fig 3–4.—Correlation between the age-corrected level of 5-HIAA in cerebrospinal fluid and the level of TSH in six persons with unipolar depression. (From Gold P.W., et al.: *Am. J. Psychiatry* 134(9):1029, 1977. Copyright 1977, the American Psychiatric Association. Reprinted by permission.)

significant inverse relationship between baseline serum cortisol levels and TRH-induced TSH release in depressive patients,[21] while another group reports no relationship between the elevated cortisol levels and impaired TSH response in primary depression.[14] A second theory explaining this decreased TSH response attributes it to a functional deficiency of one or another of the biogenic amines in the hypothalamus and pituitary regions. It is known that TSH release is inhibited by both dopaminergic and serotonergic neurons; thus, the decreased release of TSH observed in primary depression could be due to the enhanced activity of one of these neurotransmitter systems. Gold et al. reported that there was a significant negative correlation between the diminished TSH response to TRH and the probenecid-induced accumulation of 5-HIAA in the cerebrospinal fluid of the unipolar patients they studied (Fig 3–4), suggesting that increased activity of the serotonergic system may be at fault.[20] While this finding is in conflict with the theory of a deficiency of monoamine neurotransmitter activity in depression, it is in keeping with the concept of the primary affective disorders as a biochemically heterogeneous group of conditions.

BIOCHEMICAL ASPECTS OF SCHIZOPHRENIA[22]

The search for the etiology of schizophrenia has given rise to a number of theories, the majority of which have focused on the biochemistry of this disorder. Although the term *disorder* is used, it is more than likely that a number of *disorders* are included under the diagnostic heading of schizophrenia. It is probable that future medical research will define specific etiologic subgroups within the overall category of schizophrenia and that these will exhibit biochemical differences.

Two general models have evolved as a result of the biologic research on the pathogenesis of schizophrenia: a metabolic model and a pharmacologic model.[22] The metabolic model is based on the assumption that schizophrenia, as a genetically transmitted disorder, is associated with an inherited defect in body metabolism. The pharmacologic model was arrived at in a fashion similar to the pharmacologic model for the affective disorders. Certain drugs (e.g., the phenothiazines) were found to have a beneficial effect on the symptoms of persons who had schizophrenia, so it was reasoned that by studying the mechanism of action of these drugs one might discover the pathogenesis of this illness.

Metabolic Models

The Transmethylation Hypothesis[23]

Some of the early biochemical research designed to elucidate the etiology of schizophrenia was stimulated by the similarity that was noted between the symptoms produced by certain naturally occurring and synthetic hallucinogenic substances and the clinical picture of schizophrenia. It was found that several of these hallucinogens are methylated amines with chemical structures resembling those of the amine neurotransmitters. Specifically, mescaline is like dopamine and norepinephrine in structure, and N,N, dimethyltryptamine and bufotenine resemble serotonin (Fig 3–5). Because of these biochemical similarities, it was postulated that the abnormal transfer of methyl groups to a neurotransmitter, or to another endogenous substance, might result in the formation of a compound in the body that interferes with mental function.

It was proposed that the transmethylation of norepinephrine results in the production of 3,4-dimethoxyphenylethanolamine and/or the transmethylation of dopamine results in the synthesis of 3,4-dimethoxyphenylethylamine (DMPEA), substances that are psychotomimetic in nature. The main compound on which attention was focused was DMPEA. In the early 1960s, it was reported that this substance was recovered from the urine of 15 of 19 schizophrenics, but was not present in the urine of normal controls. Although this seemed to offer great support for the trans-

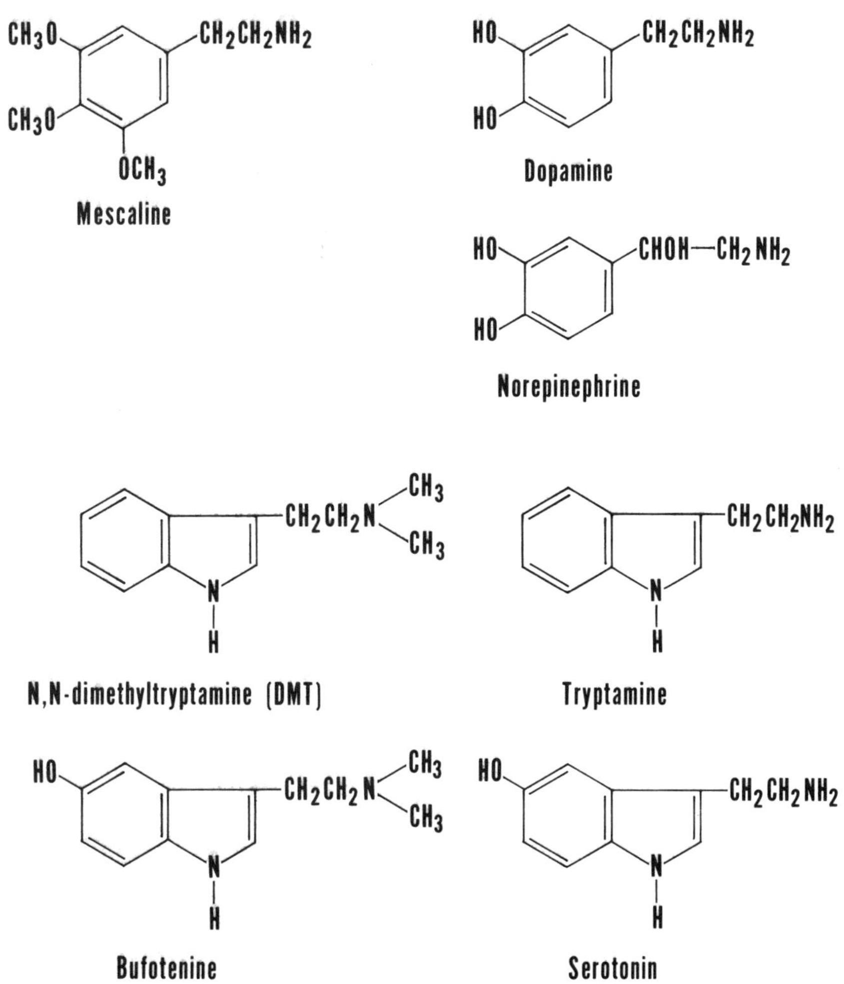

Fig 3-5.—Similarities in the chemical structure of psychotomimetics and amine transmitters.

methylation theory, subsequent investigations of DMPEA have resulted in controversial data. Apparently, this compound is recovered from the urine of nonschizophrenics as well as from that of schizophrenics. Also, foods such as tea have been reported to contain DMPEA. Perhaps the most damaging evidence against the role of DMPEA in schizophrenia is that its administration does not produce schizophrenic symptoms.

With respect to serotonin, it was postulated that tryptamine (which is derived from tryptophan) is methylated to form either 5-methoxy-N,N-dimethyltryptamine or N,N,dimethyltryptamine (DMT), both of which are hallucinogens. It is known that the enzyme that converts tryptamine to DMT, and serotonin to bufotenine, is present in human tissues including the brain. Tryptamine and serotonin are normal brain metabolites; thus, the ingredients for the synthesis of both DMT and bufotenine have been shown to exist in the central nervous system. Attempts to demonstrate significant differences in the levels of methylated serotonin derivatives in the blood and urine of schizophrenics and controls have resulted in conflicting data.

Thus far, the studies measuring methylated compounds in body fluids have not definitely confirmed the transmethylation hypothesis.

Perhaps future use of more sophisticated biochemical techniques in better controlled studies will make it possible to detect small amounts of these substances and differences between schizophrenics and controls.

While the inability to identify abnormal methylated compounds consistently in schizophrenics casts some doubt on the transmethylation hypothesis, the effect of methionine, a methyl group donor, on these persons provides support for the theory. In several studies, it has been noted that an exacerbation of psychotic symptoms occurs when large doses of this substance (10–20 gm), with or without a monoamine oxidase inhibitor, are given to chronic schizophrenics. In contrast to the conflicting reports on the recovery of DMPEA and other methylated compounds from persons with this disorder, the untoward effects of methionine in schizophrenia have been found consistently by investigators. The theoretical explanation for these effects is that methionine, in its biologically active form, S-adenosylmethionine, acts as a central nervous system methyl donor and promotes the formation of abnormal methylated derivatives from the amine neurotransmitters. In animal studies, Baldessarini et al. report that levels of S-adenosylmethionine increase in tissues, including the brain, after the administration of methionine; however, despite the greater availability of this methyl group donor, these investigators were unable to detect any increase in the production of methylated indoles or catechols by the animals.[24] The biochemical explanation for the ill-effects of methionine in schizophrenia is presently unknown.

In line with the transmethylation hypothesis, a number of investigators have attempted to treat schizophrenics with large doses of nicotinamide, a methyl acceptor, in the hope that this agent would divert methyl groups away from their use in the formation of toxic methylated substances in the brain. Initially, it was reported that schizophrenic patients seemed to improve with this therapy; however, subsequent evaluations have shown this not to be the case. One reason nicotinamide is not effective is that it is actually not a good methyl acceptor in the brain.

Baldessarini et al. point out that although interest in the transmethylation hypothesis has waned in recent years, the adverse effects of methionine on the symptoms of chronic schizophrenics is one of the few consistently reported clinical clues to a metabolic abnormality in this illness.[24] Moreover, the finding that persons with this illness have a lower activity of monoamine oxidase in their blood platelets also lends support to this theory (see section on Mechanisms of Dopaminergic Hyperfunction). At present, it is accurate to state that this hypothesis, while plausible, has yet to be validated, ideally by the isolation of the postulated toxic methylated compound or compounds from persons with schizophrenia.

Vitamin and Dietary Therapy for Schizophrenia

Pauling suggested the administration of large doses of vitamins in the treatment of schizophrenia.[25, 26] He pointed out that there may be significant differences in the daily requirements of individuals for vitamins and other nutrients and that it would be possible for a person to suffer from a deficiency of these substances even though he is ingesting what is considered to be the "recommended daily amounts." Pauling believes that the brain is particularly sensitive to its molecular environment and that "a localized cerebral avitaminosis or other localized cerebral deficiency disease" may exist, even though the rest of the body does not manifest a deficiency state.[25] He proposes that in certain individuals, a deficiency of essential nutrients (vitamins, minerals, and so on) could result in a mental illness like schizophrenia. Furthermore, he advises treating schizophrenics with large doses of vitamins and minerals in order to restore the optimal molecular environment for the brain.

This form of treatment is called orthomolecular psychiatry. It is defined as "the treatment of mental disease by the provision of the optimal molecular environment for the mind, especially the optimum concentrations of substances normally present in the human body."[25] Specifically, it consists of "the use of vitamins (in megadoses) and minerals; the control of diet, especially the intake of sucrose; and during the acute phase, the use of conventional methods of controlling the crisis, such as phenothiazines."[26] The vitamins usually given include ascorbic acid, nicotinamide, pyridoxine, and vitamins B_{12} and E.

Despite anecdotal reports of improvement of schizophrenia with this therapy, there is no definitive evidence that this illness is due to a localized cerebral deficiency of vitamins. Moreover, there are no well-controlled scientific studies that conclusively demonstrate that orthomolecular therapy is effective in the treatment of schizophrenia.[27] The fact that psychoactive drugs are often prescribed along with the vitamins and minerals in the orthomolecular approach makes it difficult to tell why improvement occurs in a patient's symptoms, if a response is noted. Since the administration of large doses of nicotinic acid or nicotinamide is associated with significant side effects (e.g., flushing, itching, liver damage, gastrointestinal problems, cardiac arrhythmias, increased levels of serum glucose and uric acid),[27] there is good reason *not* to use orthomolecular psychiatry in the treatment of schizophrenics.

Another interesting dietary theory of the cause of schizophrenia implicates a component of cereal grains, wheat gluten, as a pathogenetic factor. It is postulated that gluten may bring on or intensify the symptoms of schizophrenia in genetically predisposed individuals.[28,29,30] This substance is known to be a factor in the etiology of celiac disease in children and nontropical sprue (gluten-induced enteropathy) in adults. The hypothesis that gluten may be important in the pathogenesis of schizophrenia is based on the following findings:

1. A higher incidence of celiac disease in persons with schizophrenia and, conversely, a greater frequency of schizophrenia in adults with nontropical sprue. (In one study, the increased frequency of celiac disease among schizophrenics was not confirmed.)
2. A correlation between the rate of admission of women with schizophrenia to mental hospitals and the consumption of wheat in certain countries during World War II. The countries surveyed were the United States, Canada, Finland, Norway, and Sweden.
3. A therapeutic response by schizophrenics to the elimination of milk and cereal grain products from their diet. Moreover, the reintroduction of these substances to the diet of persons previously maintained on a diet without them interfered with this therapeutic response.

If the above findings can be reproduced by other investigators, a significant pathogenetic factor in schizophrenia will have been uncovered. The gluten hypothesis does not contradict the genetic basis for schizophrenia or the existence of an inherited biochemical defect that is fundamentally responsible for the disorder; it only points out the possible role of an environmental factor, diet, in determining the clinical manifestations of the illness.

Pharmacologic Models

Dopamine Hypothesis[31,32]

The dopamine hypothesis of the pathogenesis of schizophrenia is based primarily on the observation that the two main groups of neuroleptic drugs used in the treatment of this disorder cause a blockade of postsynaptic dopamine receptors in the brain. Because a drug-induced reduction in the activity of this neuron system is associated with an improvement in the symptoms of schizophrenics, it has been postulated that this illness is due to hyperfunction of the dopaminergic system. Some of the explanations of this hyperfunction are (1) the release of excessive amounts of dopamine into the synaptic cleft, (2) increased sensitivity of the dopamine receptors to normal amounts of dopamine, (3) a block in the conversion of dopamine to norepinephrine with a buildup in the levels of the former, or (4) the underactivity of another neuron system that is antagonistic to the dopamine system.[22]

EVIDENCE FOR DOPAMINERGIC HYPERFUNCTION.—Studies of the mechanism of action of the phenothiazines and butyrophenones, drugs with selective "antischizophrenic" action (i.e., they act on the basic symptoms), point to the presence of an overactive dopaminergic system in schizophrenia. The phenothiazines impair transmission across dopamine and norepinephrine synapses, while the butyrophenones primarily interfere with the function of dopamine synapses. There is indirect and direct evidence that both groups of drugs interfere with the activity of dopaminergic neurons by blocking postsynaptic receptors. The indirect evidence consists partly of experimental data demonstrating that phenothiazines inhibit the activation of dopamine-induced adenylate cyclase in the postsynaptic neuron and that they increase the turnover rate of dopamine in the brain. It has been reported that the degree of inhibition of dopamine-induced adenylate cyclase is proportional to the clinical potency of a phenothiazine in treating schizophrenia.

Indirect evidence has also come from studies of the release of the anterior pituitary hormone, prolactin. The secretion of prolactin is under the inhibitory control of the tuberoinfundibular dopamine pathway, so that blockade of the system results in an increased release of the hormone into the blood. Both normal persons and schizophrenics react to the administration of the antischizophrenic drugs (e.g., phenothiazines and butyrophenones) with a marked increase in the level of

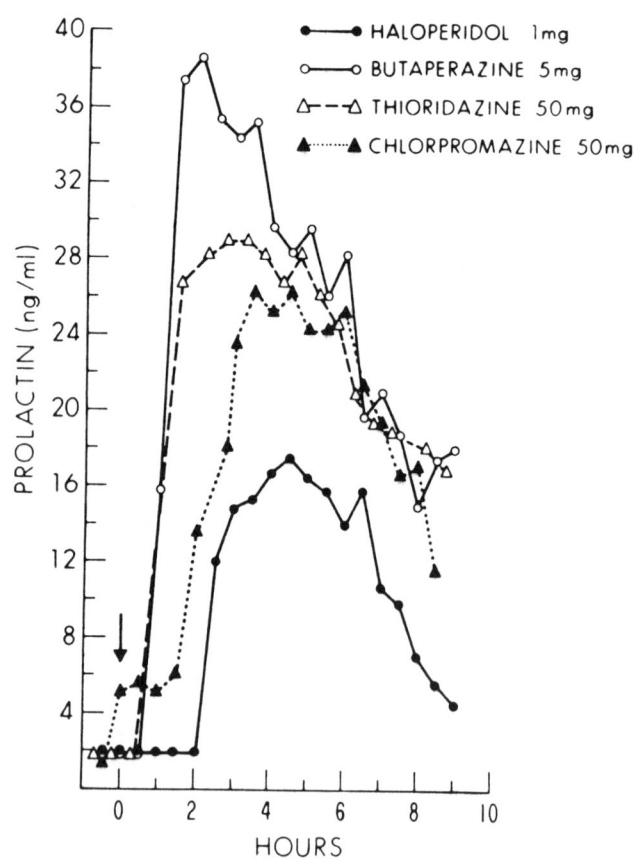

Fig 3–6.—Prolactin responses to four neuroleptics in a 22-year-old normal man. (From Gruen P.H., et al.: *Arch. Gen. Psychiatry* 35[1]:113, 1978. Copyright 1978, American Medical Association. Used by permission.)

prolactin in the blood, indicating that dopamine blockade has taken place (Fig 3–6).[33]

If psychoactive drugs are divided into two groups, those with antipsychotic activity (e.g., chlorpromazine, haloperidol) and those with little or no antipsychotic activity (e.g., promazine, promethazine, diazepam, imipramine), only the former appears to increase the secretion of prolactin. In addition, the clinical potency (on a milligram basis) of the antischizophrenic drugs can be correlated with the rise in the blood prolactin level after their administration.[33] In other words, the activity of these drugs in treating schizophrenia is directly proportional to their ability to block dopaminergic transmission.

Direct evidence for the mechanism of action of the phenothiazines has resulted from binding site studies on dopaminergic neurons. Snyder has identified the dopamine receptor in the brain biochemically by labeling the receptor through the binding of radioactive dopamine.[31, 32] He has shown that the phenothiazines compete with dopamine for receptor site binding; thus, they are true competitive inhibitors of dopamine. Moreover, he found that the relative potency of these drugs in competing for receptor binding closely parallels their clinical potency in treating schizophrenia (Table 3–2). This does not hold true for the butyrophenones. Haloperidol, which is much more effective clinically than chlorpromazine (on a milligram basis), is not particularly active in competing for dopamine receptor binding sites in in vitro tests. According to Snyder, this may be because haloperidol interacts with the dopamine receptor in a different way than does dopamine; the former binds to an "antagonist site" while the latter binds to an "agonist site."[31] He says that one can predict the clinical potency of the butyrophenones if this is correlated with their affinities for haloperidol antagonist sites.

Clinical evidence that the psychoactive drugs which are effective in treating schizophrenia act by blocking dopaminergic transmission in the brain is the extrapyramidal neurologic side effects that occur with their use. These symptoms closely resemble those of Parkinson disease, which is due to a deficiency of dopamine activity in the corpus striatum and other basal ganglia.

Pharmacologic studies dealing with the effects of amphetamines on animals and humans also suggest that excessive dopamine activity is important in the pathogenesis of the schizophrenic syndrome. Animals that are given amphetamines develop a rigid posture and a stereotyped pattern of compulsive behavior that varies with different species. This behavior often consists of a single activity, or a sequence of activities, that is repeated over and over despite outside distractions. In humans, a clinical syndrome very similar to acute par-

TABLE 3–2.—PHENOTHIAZINE AND THIOXANTHENE DRUG EFFECTS ON SPECIFIC DOPAMINE RECEPTOR BINDING

DRUG*	RELATIVE POTENCY IN COMPETING FOR DOPAMINE RECEPTOR BINDING† (CHLORPROMAZINE = 100)
Haloperidol (Haldol)	50
(+)-Butaclamol	1,200
α-Flupenthixol	625
Fluphenazine (Prolixin, Permitil)	465
Trifluoperazine (Stelazine)	181
Triflupromazine (Vesprin)	214
Perphenazine (Trilafon)	125
Chlorpromazine (Thorazine)	100
Promazine (Sparine)	27
(−)-Butaclamol	8

*Drugs are listed in approximate descending order of milligram potency in treating schizophrenia and eliciting extrapyramidal side effects.

†Potency in competing for binding to the dopamine receptor is defined as the reciprocal of the nanomolar concentration to occupy 50% of receptor binding sites × 1.5 × 10^5 in calf striatal membranes using the assay of Burt et al.[34] Larger values indicate greater potency. Thus (+)-butaclamol inhibits binding 50% at 1.25×10^{-7} M concentration.

Source: Snyder S.H.: *Psychiatr. Ann.* 6(1):60, 1976. (Used by permission.)

anoid schizophrenia occurs in otherwise normal individuals who take very large doses of this drug. Amphetamine psychosis mimics schizophrenia well enough to cause experienced psychiatrists to have difficulty separating the two conditions diagnostically. When taken by schizophrenic persons, even small doses of this drug may exacerbate their symptoms.

The amphetamines act by several means to increase the concentration of both norepinephrine and dopamine in the synaptic cleft. The question as to which of these two catecholamine neurotransmitters is responsible for the amphetamines causing an exacerbation of schizophrenia and amphetamine psychosis is unresolved; however, it is thought by some investigators that dopamine plays more of a role than does norepinephrine.[31]

The facts that the blockage of dopamine receptors by antipsychotic drugs, like the **phenothiazines**, alleviates the symptoms of **schizophrenia** and that the administration of **amphetamine**, which increases the synaptic levels of dopamine, exacerbates these symptoms constitute the major pharmacologic evidence for the existence of a hyperfunctional dopaminergic system in schizophrenia. The results of other drug studies, such as the administration of L-dopa and α-methyl-p-tyrosine (αMPT), are consistent with this hypothesis. L-Dopa, a precursor of dopamine, has been found to worsen symptoms when given to some schizophrenic persons; αMPT, which blocks the formation of dopamine, has been reported to decrease the amount of psychoactive drug necessary to control schizophrenic symptoms.

MECHANISM(S) FOR DOPAMINERGIC HYPERFUNCTION.—How might overactivity of the dopamine system arise? There is no information indicating that an excess of dopamine is released into the synaptic cleft. Measurements of HVA in the spinal fluid of untreated schizophrenics are within the normal range. If the formation of dopamine were increased in the brain of schizophrenics, one would expect the level of its degradation product (i.e., HVA) to be increased in the spinal fluid. Also, the level of prolactin in the blood is the same in schizophrenics as in normal persons. If an excess of dopamine were present in the brains of persons with this illness, prolactin levels should be decreased. Of course, it is possible that the increase in dopamine release in schizophrenics is limited to one or more local areas of the brain and does not involve the tuberoinfundibular dopaminergic system.

There is a report in which the enzyme dopamine-β-hydroxylase (DBH), which converts dopamine to norepinephrine, was found in significantly lower concentrations in postmortem assays of the brains of schizophrenics.[35] Such a deficiency would lead to a buildup of dopamine and a hyperdopaminergic state. However, this finding could not be confirmed by a later study. Measurements of CSF levels of DBH have failed to show any significant differences between schizophrenics and either controls or persons with other types of psychopathology. The fact that there is no evidence of excessive amounts of dopamine in the brains of schizophrenics, by HVA or prolactin studies, makes this enzymatic defect somewhat unlikely. Nevertheless, the finding of reduced levels of DBH in the brain deserves further investigation to see whether it can be substantiated.

Another enzyme that has been reported to be deficient in some schizophrenic persons is platelet monoamine oxidase (MAO). In the body, this intracellular enzyme plays a major role in the catabolism of the biogenic monoamines (see Figs 3–1 and 3–2). As a result of its action on dopamine, this neurotransmitter is inactivated. A number of studies have found that the mean level of activity of this enzyme is lower in platelets of chronic schizophrenics, particularly those with paranoid symptoms or hallucinations, than in those of control subjects (Fig 3–7).[36, 37] On the other hand, four studies have failed to confirm this finding. In those studies in which lower mean levels of platelet MAO activities are reported, a wide scattering of values has been observed so that there is significant overlap between the individual levels in the schizophrenic patients and controls (see Fig 3–7). Also, there are reports that platelet MAO activity is significantly less in persons with other forms of psychopathology (e.g., bipolar depression, alcoholism) than in normal controls, suggesting that low platelet MAO is not illness-specific but rather represents a nonspecific vulnerability factor increasing the risk of mental illness.

MAO exists in multiple forms within the body; various tissues have isoenzymes with different substrate and inhibitor specificities. A reduction of MAO activity in one tissue does not imply low activity in another. Thus, while studies have found platelet and skeletal muscle MAO to be lower in some schizophrenics, attempts by several investigators to demonstrate a similar reduction of MAO activity in the brain tissue of schizophrenics obtained at autopsy have failed. If a deficiency of MAO were discovered in the central nervous system of schizophrenics, this would support the dopamine hypothesis because low MAO activity would result in higher levels of dopamine. However, it could also be used to support the transmethylation theory, as a deficiency of MAO might cause a buildup of abnormal methylated neurotransmitters.

Due to a lack of evidence of excessive amounts of dopamine in the brains of schizophrenics, a number of alternative hypotheses have been developed to account for the postulated hyperactivity of the dopaminergic system. None of those mentioned at the beginning of this section have been confirmed experimentally, and so the basis for the hyperactivity—if, in fact, it exists—is unknown at the present time.

An offshoot of the dopamine hypothesis is the theory that a toxic metabolite of dopamine, 6-hydroxydopamine, is formed in the brains of schizophrenics, causing a disturbance of mental function. When given intraventricularly to animals, this compound damages catecholamine neurons in the forebrain and depletes forebrain stores of catecholamines. As a result of destruction of the norepinephrine reward system, it produces behavioral abnormalities in the animals. Both the damage to the catecholamine neurons and the behavioral disturbances are prevented by pretreatment with a phenothiazine (i.e., chlorpromazine). It has been postulated that because of a reduction in the activity of the enzyme dopamine-β-hydroxylase in the brain, a small amount of 6-hydroxydopamine is

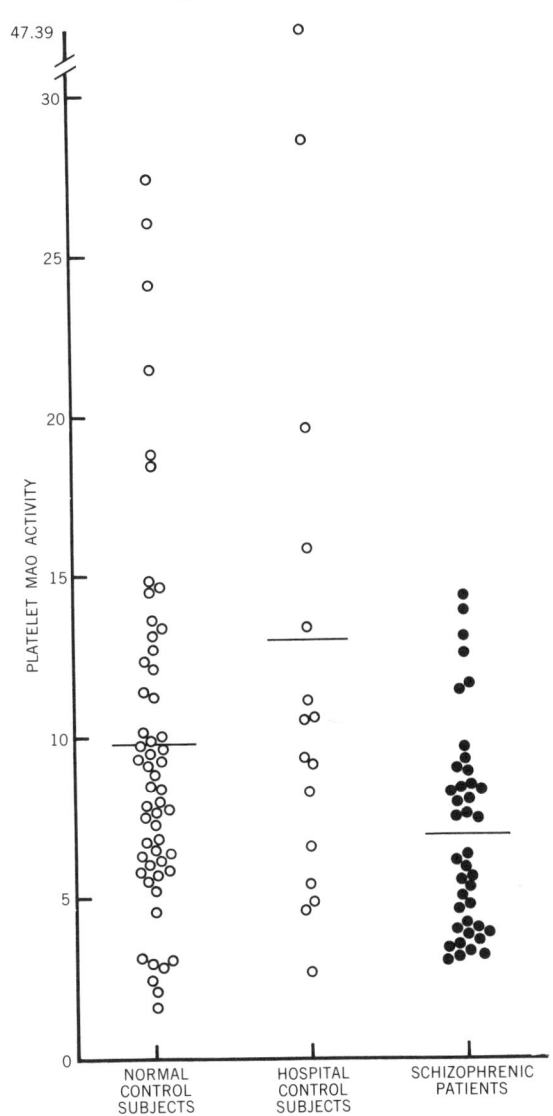

Fig 3–7.—Platelet MAO activity of 55 normal control subjects, 16 hospitalized control subjects, and 40 chronic schizophrenics. (Expressed in nanomoles of product per 10^8 platelets per hour.) (From Berger P.A., et al.: *Am. J. Psychiatry* 135[1]:97, 1978. Copyright 1978, the American Psychiatric Association. Reprinted by permission.)

formed, which destroys noradrenergic receptor sites and leads to the clinical syndrome of schizophrenia. According to this theory, the usefulness of chlorpromazine in treating schizophrenia is explained by its antagonism to the toxic effects of 6-hydroxydopamine.

The dopamine hypothesis is very much like the transmethylation theory in that it is a plausible explanation for schizophrenia but lacks sufficient documentation. Snyder has made the point that "nobody has found anything conclusively abnormal about dopamine in body fluids or brains of schizophrenics."[31] All of the evidence for this hypothesis is indirect, coming primarily from studies on the actions of various drugs. Great progress has been made in elucidating the mechanisms by which antischizophrenic drugs work, and this approach may be ultimately successful in defining the etiology of this disorder.

Norepinephrine Excess in the Brains of Schizophrenics

In addition to the studies on dopamine, recent investigations into the biochemistry of schizophrenia have focused on norepinephrine in the brain. Elevated concentrations of norepinephrine have been found in specific areas of the brains of schizophrenics, particularly the paranoid type, studied at autopsy. In 1980, investigators at the National Institute of Mental Health reported that the mean level of this putative neurotransmitter in the cerebrospinal fluid of 35 schizophrenic patients was significantly higher than it was for 29 healthy control subjects.[38] When the mean concentrations of norepinephrine for each of the three diagnostic categories of schizophrenia (paranoid, undifferentiated, and schizoaffective) were compared to that of the controls, only the paranoid subgroup (with the highest level) was significantly different. These investigators attributed the higher cerebrospinal fluid levels in the schizophrenics to an overflow of norepinephrine from the periventricular regions of the brain where its concentration is increased, due either to enhanced release or to diminished metabolism of the amine.

Some of the pharmacologic data discussed earlier with reference to the dopamine theory also support the concept that norepinephrine is a pathogenetic factor in schizophrenia. Neuroleptic agents that are effective in the treatment of schizophrenia block noradrenergic, as well as dopaminergic, neurotransmission and the amphetamines, which can produce a schizophrenia-like picture, increase the activity of both neurotransmitter systems in the brain.

Opioid Compounds and Schizophrenia[39, 40]

Chapter 2 introduced the topic of opiate receptors in the central nervous system. These receptors, which are widespread throughout the brain, bind both opiate agonist and antagonist drugs. They are stereospecific, having a greater affinity for the levo isomer. The presence of such highly specific receptors in the normal brain suggested to investigators that endogenous compounds might exist which interact with them. In 1975, after an intensive search, two peptides with opioid activity were isolated from pig brain. These were identified as pentapeptides that differ in only one amino acid, called methionine-enkephalin and leucine-enkephalin.

Since then, a number of opiate-like substances have been detected in the region of the hypothalamus and pituitary gland. A polypeptide hormone with 91 amino acids, β-lipotropin (β-LPH), appears to be the parent compound for these substances. Recent studies of pituitary tumor cells in culture have shown that β-LPH forms one end of a protein precursor that on enzymatic cleavage also yields adrenocorticotropic hormone (ACTH). β-LPH can be broken down to yield β-endorphin (β-END), and β-melanocyte-stimulating hormone (β-MSH) (Fig 3-8). β-END (amino acid sequence 61–91 of β-LPH) has potent opioid activity and constitutes most, if not all, of this activity in the pituitary. Three smaller fragments of this molecule that also possess opioid activity are α-endorphin (amino acid sequence 61–76), γ-endorphin (amino acid sequence 61–77), and methionine-enkephalin (amino acids 61–65). The

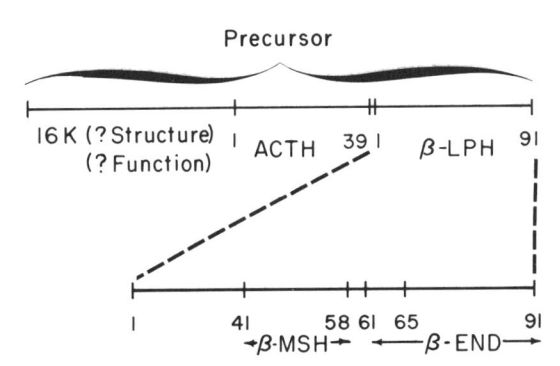

Fig 3–8.—Schematic representation of the chemical derivation of the pituitary opioids. (Adapted from Watson S.J., et al.: *Arch. Gen. Psychiatry* 36:35, 1979. Copyright 1979, American Medical Association. Used by permission.)

parent compound β-LPH itself is devoid of opioid activity.

Both the enkephalins and the β-LPH/β-END group of opioid compounds have pharmacologic properties similar to those of the naturally occurring plant opiates; however, their physiologic roles in the body are unknown. Speculations are that they may act as neurotransmitters or neurohormones. Opiate-enkephalin receptors are distributed throughout the brain (except for the cerebellum) and these compounds are rapidly broken down, consistent with a possible role as neurotransmitters. On the other hand, in animals the β-LPH/β-END system is located in a single set of hypothalamic neurons (with axons projecting throughout the brain stem), and the action of β-END lasts longer than that of the enkephalins, suggesting a neuromodulation function.[40] The pituitary gland has high concentrations of β-LPH and β-END and releases them, along with ACTH, into the blood in situations of acute stress and pain, consistent with their action as neurohormones.[39]

Of particular relevance to this discussion is the experimental evidence that the endogenous opiates are important in the regulation of normal and abnormal behavior and that they may play a role in the pathogenesis of schizophrenia. In animal experiments, the injection of β-END into the cisternal or ventricular spaces of rats has resulted in marked changes in behavior, including the production of a catatonic-like state.[41] The injection of this compound into the periaqueductal gray matter of rats causes marked sedation, catatonia, and blunted affect as if the animals were in a "dissociated" state.[42] These behavioral effects are reversed by the administration of an opiate antagonist, naloxone.

Although there are reports of elevations in the levels of certain endorphins in the cerebrospinal fluid of some schizophrenic patients,[43, 44] most of the research in humans pointing to a role for the endogenous opiate peptides in schizophrenia has dealt with the effects of these agents and their pharmacologic antagonists on the symptoms of persons with this disorder. Theoretically, if an excess of an endogenous opiate(s) is producing schizophrenic symptoms, then blocking its action by the use of an antagonist such as naloxone should have a beneficial effect. In 1977, Gunne et al. reported a reduction in auditory hallucinations in four of six chronic schizophrenics to whom naloxone (0.4 mg intravenously) was administered.[45] This study was not well designed or properly controlled and attempts by a number of investigators to replicate its findings were unsuccessful. However, using a larger dose of naloxone (10 mg intravenously), Watson et al., in a well-designed and carefully controlled study, found that six of nine schizophrenics reported decreased auditory hallucinations 60–90 minutes after receiving the drug.[46] The blockade of opiate receptors using a longer-acting oral antagonist, naltrexone, has also resulted in conflicting reports—two studies finding that there was no reduction in schizophrenic symptoms and one (pilot) study reporting some improvement in several schizophrenic subjects who took the drug.

Watson et al. summarize the investigations of the effects of opiate receptor blockade on schizophrenics as follows:

Although no clear conclusions can be drawn from these opiate antagonist studies, it seems that they are generally negative. It must be admitted that some subjects seem to be benefited by these agents. Our impression is that more thorough study designs must be used, that we must be alert to the possibility that some subjects may respond to opiate antagonists whereas others will not, and that dose level [may] be critical.[46]

Studies in which endorphins are administered to schizophrenics have been carried out in an attempt to determine whether these peptides affect the symptoms of persons with this illness. In one, the intravenous administration of β-END to three schizophrenics seemed to result in a worsening of their cognitive difficulties, while causing a reduction in their auditory hallucinations.[47] In another, the treatment of chronic schizophrenics with a derivative of γ-endorphin has been found to produce improvement.[48] The results of two other recently reported studies of the responses of schizophrenics to intravenous β-END were contradictory. One found that a slight but significant improvement in symptoms occurred,[49] while the other found the opposite effect, i.e., a worsening of schizophrenic symptoms.[50]

A most interesting study of the opioid compounds and their role in schizophrenia was conducted by Wagemaker and Cade.[51] These investigators treated schizophrenic patients using hemodialysis and found that an improvement in their symptoms occurred after 16 weeks of therapy. Unfortunately, the study was not double-blind and, therefore, dialysis cannot be accepted on the basis of this report to be an effective form of therapy for schizophrenia. Palmour et al. analyzed the dialysate fluid from some of these patients, finding a variant of the β-END molecule, leucine-5-β-endorphin.[52] It was postulated that this abnormal endorphin was a factor in causing the patients' symptoms and that its removal from the body by dialysis resulted in their improvement. While also of great interest, this finding is based on an investigation involving only small numbers of subjects and, so far, has not been confirmed by other workers in the field.

The investigations dealing with the endogenous opiates have raised the possibility of a new explanation for schizophrenia—one that may lead to specific therapeutic approaches in the future. The contradictory findings in some studies that, for example, both opiate agonists and antagonists seem to cause an improvement in some patients with schizophrenia indicate that, at this time, definitive answers to the many questions posed by the opiate theory of schizophrenia must await more careful studies.

SUMMARY

In this chapter, we presented some of the current biochemical theories of the etiology and pathogenesis of the functional psychoses. Much of the attention with respect to the biochemistry of these conditions has centered on the function of the biogenic amine neurotransmitter systems in the brain. For example, the effects of drugs on biogenic amine metabolism in the central nervous system have formed the basis for several theories. This kind of pharmacologic data constitutes only indirect evidence and, while it may be thought-provoking, it cannot be relied upon completely to validate a hypothesis. Such is the case with the monoamine theory of the affective disorders and the dopamine theory of schizophrenia. What is needed to validate these theories is the demonstration of a specific biochemical abnormality in one or more of these biogenic amine systems within the brain of affected individuals. So far, this has not been accomplished.

Even if it were possible to demonstrate such a biochemical defect, it would also be necessary to show that it occurred as a primary defect and not secondary (i.e., in response) to some other biologic abnormality. Thus, some reported disturbances of biogenic amine metabolism in persons with the functional psychoses may be due to extraneous factors such as anxiety or excessive psychomotor activity, instead of being causally related to the psychosis.

Of course, the hope is that by identifying the biochemical defects in persons with schizophrenia and the affective disorders, specific forms of therapy will result. However, the current emphasis on trying to discover etiologic biochemical defects does not diminish the importance of environmental factors in the development of clinical illness in these persons. There are many examples in medicine of diseases with a biochemical etiology in which the clinical course is profoundly affected by psychosocial variables such as stress, diet, physical activity, and drugs. These variables act as predisposing or precipitating factors, making it more likely that a person with the biochemical defect will become clinically ill. Thus, a comprehensive approach to patient care will probably still be necessary even when all the biochemical defects in schizophrenia and the affective disorders are eventually uncovered.

REFERENCES

1. Weil-Malherbe H.: The biochemistry of affective disorders, in Grenell P.G., Gabay S. (eds.): *Biological Foundations of Psychiatry*. New York, Raven Press, 1976, vol. 2.
2. Maas J.W.: Clinical and biochemical heterogeneity of depressive disorders. *Ann. Intern. Med.* 88:556, 1978.
3. Hollister L.E.: Tricyclic antidepressants. *N. Engl. J. Med.* 299:1106, 1978.
4. Bunney W.E., et al.: Mode of action of lithium. *Arch. Gen. Psychiatry* 36:898, 1979.
5. Blombery P.A., Kopin I.J., Gordon E.K., et al.: Conversion of MHPG to vanillylmandelic acid. *Arch. Gen. Psychiatry* 37:1095, 1980.
6. Gordon E.K., Oliver J.: 3-Methoxy-4-hydroxyphenylethyleneglycol in human cerebrospinal fluid. *Clin. Chim. Acta* 35:145, 1971.
7. Wilk S., et al.: Cerebrospinal fluid levels of MHPG in affective disorders. *Nature* 235:440, 1972.
8. Maas J.W., Fawcett J., Dekirmenjian H.: 3-Methoxy-4-hydroxy phenylglycol (MHPG) excretion in depressive states. *Arch. Gen. Psychiatry* 19:129, 1968.
9. Beckmann H., Goodwin F.K.: Antidepressant response to tricyclics and urinary MHPG in unipolar patients. *Arch. Gen. Psychiatry* 32:17, 1975.
10. Hollister L.E., Davis K.L., Berger P.A.: Subtypes of depression based on excretion of MHPG and response to nortriptyline. *Arch. Gen. Psychiatry*, 37:1107, 1980.
11. Åsberg M., et al.: "Serotonin depression"—A biochemical subgroup within the affective disorders? *Science* 191:478, 1976.
12. Goodwin F.K., et al.: Cerebrospinal fluid amine metabolites in affective illness: The probenecid technique. *Am. J. Psychiatry* 139:73, 1973.
13. Sachar E.J.: Neuroendocrine dysfunction in depressive illness. *Annu. Rev. Med.* 27:389, 1976.
14. Sachar E.J., et al.: Recent studies in the neuroendocrinology of major depressive disorders, in Sachar E.J. (ed.): *The Psychiatric Clinics of North America*. Philadelphia, W.B. Saunders Co., 1980, vol 3, p. 313.
15. Carroll B.J., et al.: A specific laboratory test for the diagnosis of melancholia. *Arch. Gen. Psychiatry* 38:15, 1981.
16. Brown W.A., Shuey I.: Response to dexamethasone and subtype of depression. *Arch. Gen. Psychiatry* 37:747, 1980.
17. Loosen P.T., Prange A.J.: Thyrotropin releasing hormone (TRH): A useful tool for psychoneuroendocrine investigation. *Psychoneuroendocrinology* 5:63, 1980.
18. Extein I., Pottash A.L.C., Gold M.S.: TRH test in depression. *N. Engl. J. Med.* 302:923, 1980.
19. Amsterdam J.D., Winokur A., Mendels J., et al.: Distinguishing depression subtypes by thyrotropin response to TRH testing. *Lancet* 2:904, 1979.
20. Gold P.W., Goodwin F.K., et al.: Pituitary thyrotropin response to thyrotropin-releasing hormone in affective illness: Relationship to spinal fluid amine metabolites. *Am. J. Psychiatry* 134(9):1028, 1977.
21. Loosen P.T., Prange A.J., Wilson I.C.: Influence of cortisol on TRH-induced TSH response in depression. *Am. J. Psychiatry* 135:244, 1978.
22. Matthysse S., Lipinski J.: Biochemical aspects of schizophrenia, in Creger W.P., et al. (eds.): *Annual Review of Medicine: Selected Topics in the Clinical Sciences*. Palo Alto, Cal., Annual Reviews Inc., 1976.
23. Wyatt R.J., Gillin J.C.: The transmethylation hypothesis: A quarter of a century later. *Psychiatr. Ann.* 6(1):33, 1976.
24. Baldessarini R.J., et al.: Methylation hypothesis. *Arch. Gen. Psychiatry* 36:303, 1979.
25. Pauling L.: Orthomolecular psychiatry. *Science* 160:265, 1968.
26. Pauling L.: On the orthomolecular environment of the mind: Orthomolecular theory. *Am. J. Psychiatry* 131(11):1251, 1974.
27. Herbert V.: Facts and fictions about megavitamin therapy. *J. Fla. Med. Assoc.* 66:475, 1979.
28. Dohan F.C.: Cereals and schizophrenia: Data and hypothesis. *Acta Psychiatr. Scand.* 42:125, 1966.
29. Dohan F.C., et al.: Relapsed schizophrenics:

More rapid improvement on a milk- and cereal-free diet. *Br. J. Psychiatry* 115:595, 1969.
30. Singh M.M., Kay S.R.: Wheat gluten as a pathogenic factor in schizophrenia. *Science* 191:401, 1976.
31. Snyder S.H.: Dopamine and schizophrenia. *Psychiatr. Ann.* 6(1):53, 1976.
32. Snyder S.H.: The dopamine hypothesis of schizophrenia: Focus on the dopamine receptor. *Am J. Psychiatry* 133:197, 1976.
33. Gruen P.H., Sachar E.J., Langer G., et al.: Prolactin responses to neuroleptics in normal and schizophrenic subjects. *Arch. Gen. Psychiatry* 35(1):108, 1978.
34. Burt D.R., et al.: Dopamine receptor binding in the corpus striatum of the mammalian brain. *Proc. Natl. Acad. Sci. USA* 72(11):4655, 1975.
35. Wise C.D., Stein L.: Dopamine-β-hydroxylase deficits in the brains of schizophrenic patients. *Science* 181:344, 1973.
36. Meltzer H.Y., et al.: Platelet monoamine oxidase activity and schizophrenia. *Arch. Gen. Psychiatry* 37:357, 1980.
37. Berger P.A., et al.: Platelet monoamine oxidase in chronic schizophrenic patients. *Am. J. Psychiatry* 135(1):95, 1978.
38. Lake C.R.: Schizophrenia: Elevated cerebrospinal fluid norepinephrine. *Science* 207:331, 1980.
39. Bunney W.E. (moderator): Basic and clinical studies of endorphins. *Ann. Intern. Med.* 91:239, 1979.
40. Watson S.J., et al.: Some observations on the opiate peptides and schizophrenia. *Arch. Gen. Psychiatry* 36:35, 1979.
41. Bloom F., et al.: Endorphins: Profound behavioral effects in rats suggest new etiological factors in mental illness. *Science* 194:630, 1976.
42. Jacquet Y.F., Marks N.: The C-fragment of β-lipotropin: An endogenous neuroleptic or antipsychotogen? *Science* 194:632, 1976.
43. Terenius L., et al.: Increased CSF levels of endorphins in chronic psychosis, letter. *Neuroscience* 3:157, 1976.
44. Domschke W., et al.: CSF β-endorphin in schizophrenia. *Lancet* 1:1024, 1979.
45. Gunne L.M., Lindstrom L., Terenius L.: Naloxone-induced reversal of schizophrenic hallucinations. *J. Neural Transm.* 40:13, 1977.
46. Watson S., et al.: Effects of naloxone on schizophrenia: Reduction in hallucinations in a subpopulation of subjects. *Science* 201:73, 1978.
47. Kline N.S., et al.: β-Endorphin-induced changes in schizophrenic and depressed patients. *Arch. Gen. Psychiatry* 34:1111, 1977.
48. Verhoeven W.M., et al.: Improvement of schizophrenic patients treated with (Des-Tyr¹)-γ-endorphin (DTγE). *Arch. Gen. Psychiatry* 36:294, 1979.
49. Berger P.A., Watson S.J., et al.: β-Endorphin and schizophrenia. *Arch. Gen. Psychiatry* 37:635, 1980.
50. Gerner R.H., Catlin D.H., et al.: β-Endorphin. *Arch. Gen. Psychiatry* 37:642, 1980.
51. Wagemaker H., Cade R.: The use of hemodialysis in chronic schizophrenia. *Am. J. Psychiatry* 134(6):684, 1977.
52. Palmour R., et al.: Characterization of a peptide from the serum of psychotic patients, in Usdin E., Bunney W.E., Kline N.S. (eds.): *Endorphins in Mental Health Research.* New York, Macmillan Publishing Co., Inc., 1979.

4 / Normal Sleep and Sleep Disorders

JONATHAN J. BRAUNSTEIN, M.D., and SANFORD JACOBSON, M.D.

IN CHAPTER 2, the physiology of sleep was discussed as it relates to the state of arousal of an organism. Here we will examine three aspects of the topic of sleep: first, the normal sleep patterns; second, the effects of drugs on sleep; and, finally, some of the pathologic conditions that affect sleep.

NORMAL SLEEP PATTERNS[1, 2]

Stages of Sleep

Five stages of sleep can be defined on the basis of the EEG recordings taken during a normal night's sleep (Fig 4–1). Stage 1 is a transitional phase that occurs as a person goes from wakefulness to full sleep. The EEG in this stage is characterized by waves that have low amplitude and mixed frequency. In stage 2, the EEG has sleep spindles (12–14 cps waves occurring periodically) and K-complexes (slow negative waves followed by a positive component). Stages 3 and 4 have similar EEG findings, that is, high-voltage, slow-frequency waves (delta waves). These stages are sometimes referred to as delta sleep. The stage of rapid eye movement (REM) sleep is associated with an EEG recording that is similar to, but not identical with, that of stage 1.

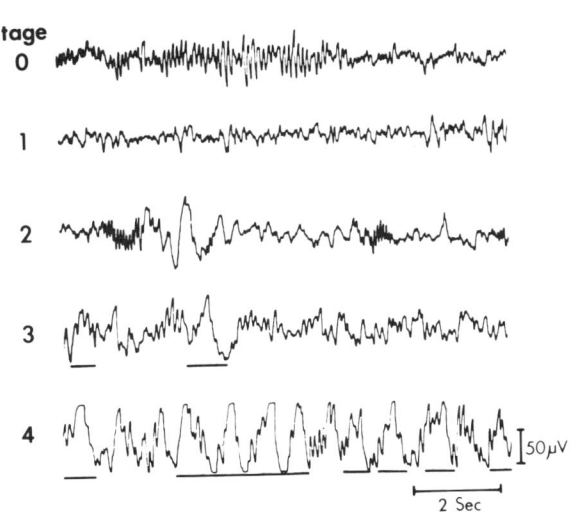

Fig 4–1.—The C_z–A_1 electroencephalogram during sleep. Stage 0 (wakefulness) shows alpha waves (8–12 Hz). Stage 1 shows low voltage, mixed frequency. Rapid eye movements (REM) and decreased muscle tone signify REM stage (1-REM). Stage 2 is defined by presence of sleep spindles (12–14 Hz) and K-complexes (negative sharp wave immediately followed by a positive component with total duration over 0.5 seconds). Stage 3 is defined when 20% to 50% of the tracing shows delta waves (0.5 to 3 Hz, 75 μV peak to peak), and stage 4, when over 50% does. (From Cohn M.A.: Sleep apnea. *Cardiopulmonary Technician's Journal*, 1980, in press.)

Stage 1, stage 2, and delta sleep are collectively referred to as non-REM (NREM) sleep.

A typical sleep pattern exhibited by a healthy young adult is depicted in Figure 4-2. The initial period of REM sleep usually occurs following stage 4 (deepest sleep), about 70–90 minutes after the person has gone to sleep. The time from the onset of sleep to the first REM period is called the first sleep cycle. Similar cycles recur four to six times during the night. REM sleep lasts about 15–20 minutes and takes up about 20–25% of the total sleep time of an adult. As the night goes on, the time spent in REM sleep tends to increase while that spent in stages 3 and 4 decreases. A person's sleep pattern is usually very much the same from night to night.

Williams has performed rather extensive studies on the sleep patterns of normal individuals between the ages of 3 and 79.[2] He found that "a U-shaped function best describes the relationship between total time in bed and age." In other words, time in bed was longest in childhood, decreased during the adult years, and increased again in old age. The total sleep time is also longer in childhood, decreasing gradually as one grows into adulthood. A further decline occurs with old age. The time spent awake during the night averages less than 2% until after middle age, when it gradually increases. Thus, older individuals have a lower sleep efficiency (sleep time/time in bed) than younger persons.

REM SLEEP.—The time spent in REM sleep varies according to age. The young child (3–5 years) spends about one third of the sleep period in this phase, the adult about one quarter, and the older person (over 65 years) approximately one fifth (Fig 4-3). When experimental subjects are deprived of REM sleep for several nights, there is a compensatory increase in the amount of time spent in this stage during ensuing nights.

The eye movements from which this stage of sleep gets its name are rapid bilateral horizontal movements resembling what one might see in an individual watching a tennis match. In addition to the rapid eye movements, there is considerable physiological activity during REM sleep. Wide fluctuations and increases in bodily functions occur, including a rise in blood pressure, heart rate, temperature, and respiration. In contrast, there are few changes in these physiological parameters during NREM sleep, and when they take place, they are generally reductions. Two other events that are regularly seen during REM sleep deserve mention: penile erections and episodic contractions of the skeletal muscles. This information is use-

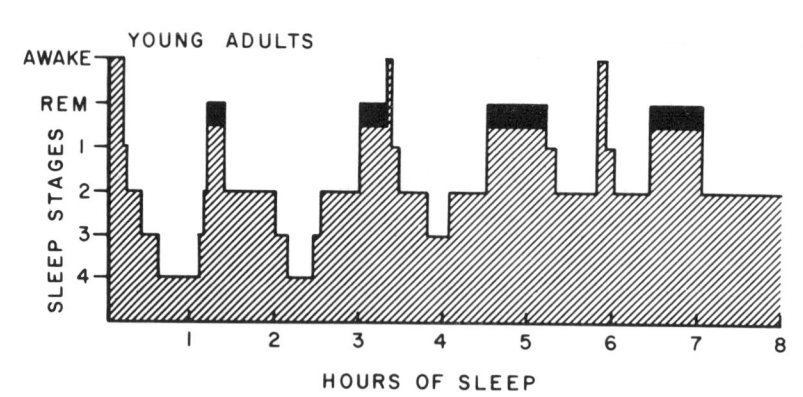

Fig 4-2.—Nocturnal sleep pattern in young adults. Note the absence of stage 4 and the decreased length of NREM periods during the latter part of the night, and the short first REM period. (From Berger R.J.: The sleep and dream cycle, in Kales A. (ed.): *Sleep: Physiology and Pathology—A Symposium*. Philadelphia, J.B. Lippincott Co., 1969, p. 20. Used by permission.)

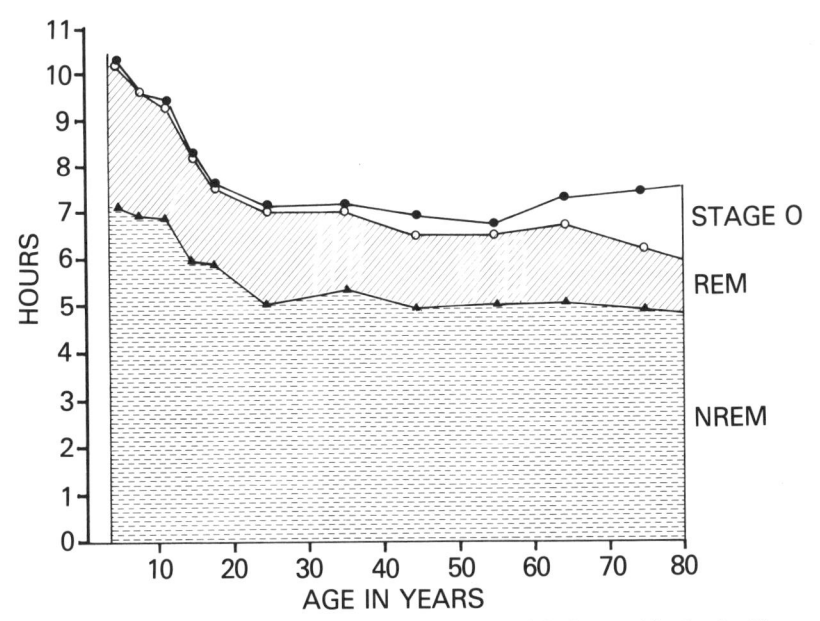

Fig 4–3.—Average total amount of nocturnal wakefulness (stage 0), REM, and NREM sleep for groups of healthy males between ages 3 and 79. (From Karacan I., Anch A.M., Williams R.L.: Recent advances in the psychophysiology of sleep and their psychiatric significance, in Grenell R.G., Gabay S. [eds.]: *Biological Foundations of Psychiatry,* vol. 1. New York, Raven Press, 1976, p. 458. Used by permission.)

ful in the evaluation of male impotence, since observation in a sleep laboratory can answer the question of whether or not a man is physically capable of having an erection. Although muscular contractions occur, muscle tone is markedly reduced during this stage. This is reflected in the electromyogram (EMG) by a "flat" baseline.

The recall of dreams is most common if one is awakened during REM sleep (Table 4–1). The literature is somewhat controversial with respect to the frequency of dream recall after NREM sleep (see Table 4–1). This is because of the varied definitions of dreams. Berger states that if one accepts the definition as being "a vivid multisensory imagery, frequently of a bizarre and unreal nature, in which the narrator himself often is actively involved," then the 7% incidence of dream recall after NREM sleep is a good estimate.[3] He says that if a broader definition of dreaming is used, one including a range of cognitive activities, then a greater frequency of dream recall will be reported after NREM sleep. "Thoughtlike" experiences are typical of the dreams recalled after NREM sleep.

NREM SLEEP.—The NREM stages differ in many ways from REM sleep. Most physiological functions (e.g., blood pressure, pulse, temperature) are decreased in the NREM stages when compared with their levels during the waking state or REM sleep. The body has active muscle tone during NREM sleep. The rate of occurrence of gross movements of the body is lowest in stages 3 and 4. In NREM sleep, the eyes move but in a slow, nonconjugate, drifting manner quite dissimilar to the eye movements during the REM stage.

DRUGS AND SLEEP

Sleeping pills are the most commonly prescribed medication in the world; more than 8 million people in the United States alone take them.[4] Almost without exception, the *chronic*

TABLE 4-1.—PERCENTAGE RECALL OF
DREAMS FOLLOWING REM AND NREM
AWAKENING IN 16 STUDIES

	REM	NREM
Aserinsky and Kleitman (1955)	74%	7%
Dement (1955)	88	0
Dement and Kleitman (1957)	79	7
Wolpert and Trosman (1958)	85	0
Goodenough et al. (1959)	69	34
Jouvet et al. (1960)	60	3
Snyder (1960)	62	13
Wolpert (1960)	85	24
Kremen (1961)	75	12
Foulkes (1962)	82	74
Orlinsky (1962)	86	42
Rechtschaffen et al. (1963)	86	23
Foulkes and Rechtschaffen (1964)	89	62
Goodenough et al. (1965)	76	21
Hobson et al. (1965)	76	14
Kales et al. (1967)	81	7

Source: Berger, R.J.: The sleep and dream cycle, in Kales A. (ed.): *Sleep: Physiology and Pathology—A Symposium.* Philadelphia, J.B. Lippincott Co., 1969, p. 24. (Used by permission.)

use of sleeping pills has the opposite effect of that for which they are intended; that is, they actually reduce the amount of time spent sleeping. Thus, these agents are often the cause of insomnia rather than its cure. At first, the administration of soporifics such as chloral hydrate, glutethimide, or the barbiturates increases sleep time; however, after a week or two tolerance develops and sleep time returns to or below the premedication level.[4] By increasing the dose of the medication, the same cycle of events is produced. Flurazepam, currently the most commonly prescribed sleep medication, is claimed to have more persistent effects on sleep and to influence sleep induction and maintenance over a longer period of time.

Many psychoactive drugs (e.g., sedatives, tranquilizers, and antidepressants) decrease the time spent in REM sleep. When they are discontinued there is a "rebound effect" so that the time spent in this stage is increased. Accompanying the increased REM sleep time may be increased dreaming and, at times, nightmares. With chronic use, these agents also cause a reduction in the time spent in sleep stages 3 and 4.

Alcohol, caffeine, and nicotine can interfere with normal sleep. Alcohol ingestion has effects on sleep similar to the other central nervous system (CNS) depressants mentioned. Consequently, chronic alcoholics frequently suffer from insomnia. Although they usually fall asleep easily, they awaken often during the night so that their total sleep time is reduced. In the sleep laboratory, it has been demonstrated that the recent onset of caffeine ingestion (i.e., coffee drinking) results in increased nocturnal wakefulness and reduced REM sleep time.[1] However, chronic ingestion is reported not to produce sleep difficulty, probably because of the development of tolerance to caffeine.[5] A recently published study by Soldatos et al. has shown that chronic cigarette smokers experience difficulty sleeping.[5] Compared to non-smokers, they are awake for a longer time during the night, primarily because they have greater difficulty falling asleep. The abrupt cessation of smoking results in improved sleep, in spite of daytime discomfort related to withdrawal.

The sudden and complete withdrawal of barbiturate hypnotics often results in withdrawal or rebound insomnia. Kales attributes this to psychological and physiological factors.[1,6] The person is usually quite apprehensive about his ability to go to sleep without the drug and experiences the CNS hyperactivity (nervousness, irritability) that accompanies the abrupt discontinuation of a CNS depressant. For these reasons, it is difficult for him to get to sleep. After falling asleep, he wakes up often and has difficulty staying asleep. Vivid and unpleasant dreaming associated with REM stage rebound may also disturb sleep.

Recently, Kales et al. described the withdrawal effects (on sleep) of five benzodiazepine drugs that were discontinued after short-term use. Flurazepam and diazepam were the only ones that did not cause rebound insomnia following their discontinuation, and this was attributed to their long half-lives.

It is best to gradually discontinue the use of ineffective hypnotics that are known to produce rebound insomnia. Kales recommends reducing the amount by one therapeutic dose every five or six days, being sure to inform the individual that some difficulty with sleep may occur, including excessive dreaming.[1] Another reason for being careful when reducing the dose of sleep medication is the side effect of REM rebound that can follow the abrupt withdrawal of REM suppressant drugs. This is potentially dangerous for the cardiac patient. The increased time spent in REM sleep with its associated increase in cardiovascular activity (blood pressure, heart rate, etc.) could precipitate an acute cardiovascular episode.

SLEEP DISORDERS[1, 7, 8, 9]

DIMS: Disorders of Initiating and Maintaining Sleep (Insomnias)

DIMS are a heterogeneous group of conditions in which patients complain of sleeplessness or insomnia. Since insomnia is a manifestation of disturbed function of the sleep mechanism, there should be a thorough search for its underlying cause(s). Too often, clinicians faced with a person complaining of insomnia merely respond by prescribing a sleeping pill. A much better approach is to consider carefully the different disorders that may cause this symptom, try to make an accurate diagnosis, and treat it appropriately.

What, in fact, is insomnia? This is not easy to answer if one relies entirely on the duration of sleep time. The mean total sleep time averages 7 hours for normal adults (ages 25–45); however, there is a wide variation in this value.[9] Some individuals report sleeping only 3 or 4 hours each night and yet function perfectly well during the day. Others routinely sleep 10 or 12 hours a night. In the elderly, the average time spent asleep diminishes to 6½ hours.[9] Hauri states that the "wide range in the sleep needs of apparently normal adults makes it necessary to define many sleep problems individually and subjectively."[9] His definition of insomnia is the inability to sleep that interferes chronically with efficient daytime function, regardless of the number of hours the person sleeps. Both the quality and the quantity of sleep should be considered when evaluating the symptom of insomnia by means of the medical history.

The term "pseudo-insomnia" has been used to describe the sleep problem of individuals who are concerned about a lack of sufficient sleep even though they are repeatedly observed by others to sleep soundly through the night. This may have several possible explanations. In some instances, this sleep complaint is used by a person to gain sympathy and attention; in other situations, it is the result of an inappropriate expectation about the length of time that one "should" sleep during the night. Finally, pseudo-insomnia may be due to subtle abnormalities of the sleep mechanism that interfere with the restorative properties of sleep. Older people often have a misconception about their sleep requirements, believing that they should sleep as long as they did when they were young. When they find themselves sleeping less, they become concerned and anxious. In response to their anxiety, they often take sleep medication in order to "get a full 8 hours of sleep." The fact that older persons spend less time in delta sleep (stages 3 and 4) may be responsible for the feeling they have in the morning of not having slept soundly.[10] This is another cause for the pseudo-insomnia that occurs in persons of this age group.

There are three types of sleep loss that are associated with insomnia: difficulty in falling asleep, disrupted sleep with multiple awakenings, and early morning awakening. Any of the three may occur alone, or they may all be present in a given insomniac. Generally, an insomniac's complaints accurately reflect the type (or types) of sleep problem(s) he is experiencing. This has been shown to be true of individuals with primary (or idiopathic) insomnia who were studied in the sleep laboratory.[11]

CAUSES OF DIMS.—DIMS are associated with a number of psychological and physical conditions (Table 4–2). Transient psychophysiological insomnia occurs with many different kinds of life stress that lead to emo-

TABLE 4–2.—CONDITIONS ASSOCIATED WITH DIMS: DISORDERS OF INITIATING AND MAINTAINING SLEEP (INSOMNIAS)

Psychophysiological reactions
  Transient and situational
  Persistent
Psychiatric disorders
  Symptom and personality disorders
  Affective disorders
  Other functional psychoses
Use of drugs and alcohol
  Tolerance to or withdrawal from CNS depressants
  Sustained use of CNS stimulants
  Sustained use of or withdrawal from other drugs
  Chronic alcoholism
Sleep-induced respiratory impairment
  Sleep apnea DIMS syndrome
  Alveolar hypoventilation DIMS syndrome
Sleep-related (nocturnal) myoclonus and "restless legs"
  Sleep-related (nocturnal) myoclonus DIMS syndrome
  "Restless legs" DIMS syndrome
Other medical, toxic, and environmental conditions

Adapted from Association of Sleep Disorders Centers. *Diagnostic classification of sleep and arousal disorders*, ed. 1, prepared by the Sleep Disorders Classification Committee, H.P. Roffwarg, Chairman. *Sleep* 2:1–137, 1979.

tional and physical upset.[7] Everyone has, at one time or another, suffered with this problem. To be classified as transient, the insomnia must not last longer than 3 weeks after the stressful situation or event passes. Temporary periods of insomnia are also seen with medical, toxic, and environmental conditions that interfere with sleep. Any illness that causes nocturnal pain or other physical discomfort can disrupt a person's sleep.

Persistent psychophysiological DIMS is a heterogeneous condition that is related to two factors that interfere with sleep: somatized tension-anxiety and conditioned association.[7] The former consists of restlessness, motor tension, autonomic hyperactivity, and hypervigilance. The latter refers to external cues (furniture, aroma, or sounds in the bedroom) or internal processes (e.g., apprehension about falling asleep) that, for some people, act as reinforcers of sleeplessness. The effects of these two factors in producing insomnia are additive, which accounts for the persistence of insomnia.

Dement and Guilleminault have drawn attention to four special conditions that cause insomnia: drug dependency, "restless legs" syndrome, sleep-related (nocturnal) myoclonus, and sleep apnea.[8] As noted, the chronic use of sleeping pills has the paradoxical effect of producing insomnia in some individuals. The "restless legs" syndrome is characterized by the presence of extremely disagreeable deep sensations (often described as something creeping or crawling) inside the calves, occurring intermittently during the day and night whenever the individual sits or lies down. These sensations cause an almost irresistible urge to move the legs, so that persons with this condition get out of bed and walk around when symptoms occur at night. Exercise of the legs is said to relieve the symptoms which, in severe cases, recur after the exercise is stopped. Sleep-related (nocturnal) myoclonus occurs in almost all persons with this syndrome.

Most persons with the "restless legs" syndrome have no underlying disease; however, there are some medical conditions that should be looked for whenever this diagnosis is considered. For example, chronic uremia and motor neuron disease occur in association with the syndrome.[7, 9] On the basis of his experience with 62 patients (over an 11-year period) with the "restless legs" syndrome, Lutz concluded that caffeine consumed in beverages or foods is a major factor in the causation of the syndrome.[12] A significant number of persons with the syndrome have a family history of it.[13] Treatment is directed to the underlying condition, if one exists. The elimination of caffeine and other xanthine derivatives from the diet is recommended by Lutz.[12] When the syndrome is familial or idiopathic, diazepam has been tried as well as an exercise program and relaxation techniques before bedtime.

Sleep-related (nocturnal) myoclonus occurs alone or in association with the much rarer "restless legs" syndrome. In this condition, periodic episodes of repetitive and stereotyped leg muscle "jerks" or twitches take place during sleep.[7] These episodes last for a few minutes to an hour or more. The jerks are usually bilateral but may involve only one leg. They always consist of an extension of the large toe along with a flexion of the foot and leg and are *followed* by a partial arousal or awakening. Patients may or may not be aware of the abnormal leg movements, but sleep is adversely affected and, therefore, they complain either of insomnia or of excessive daytime sleepiness. The incidence of this disorder among severe insomniacs is estimated to range from 1% to 15%.[7] The cause of many cases of sleep-related myoclonus is unknown; however, it is reported to occur in association with a number of conditions (e.g., chronic uremia, narcolepsy), and in some patients treated with tricyclic antidepressants. Withdrawal from a variety of drugs (e.g., anticonvulsants, benzodiazepines, and barbiturates) may also be associated with this disorder. No specific therapy is available for sleep-related myoclonus, although treatment with diazepam (Valium) seems to be helpful in reducing the severity of the problem.

IDIOPATHIC (PRIMARY) INSOMNIA.—About 10–15% of insomniacs who are carefully studied show no underlying psychological or physical condition that explains their sleep problem.[9] These individuals are sometimes referred to as having primary insomnia. It is thought that they have some dysfunction of the mechanisms regulating sleep; however, the basis for this dysfunction is unknown. Primary insomnia is chronic, often beginning in childhood or the teenage years.

Frankel et al. have reported on some of the differences in sleep patterns between 18 chronic primary insomniacs and their age- and sex-matched controls (Table 4–3).[11] The insomniacs had longer sleep latencies (time to sleep onset), less total sleep time, and a lower sleep efficiency (sleep time/time in bed). For 15 of 18 insomniacs sleep efficiency was less than 85%, whereas 14 of 18 controls had an efficiency greater than 85%. No statistical differences were reported in the amount of REM sleep experienced by the two groups; however, those in the group with insomnia had less slow-wave sleep (stages 3 and 4) than the controls. On repeated observations, the sleep of the insomniacs was found to have more night-to-night variability in terms of sleep latency and total sleep time.

It was found that the insomniacs tended to exaggerate their sleeping difficulty; that is, they overestimated their sleep latency and underestimated their total sleep time. Despite this, they accurately predicted the general pattern of their sleep dysfunction. Those who described difficulty with sleep onset did, in fact, have longer sleep latencies than those who did not complain of this problem. And those who said they had difficulty with sleep maintenance exhibited more night-time awakenings and more intermittent wake time than those who did not have this complaint.

Frankel et al. point out that the mean reduction of 43 minutes of total sleep time for the group of insomniacs (see Table 4–3) seems too small to account for their great concern about sleep loss. These investigators recommend using sleep efficiency as an aid in evaluating the complaints of these persons. A sleep efficiency of less than 85% is likely to be associated with the complaint of insomnia.

TABLE 4–3.—COMPARISON OF INSOMNIACS AND CONTROLS SLEEPING IN THE LABORATORY (BASED ON EEG DATA)

	INSOMNIACS Mean	SD	CONTROLS Mean	SD
Time in bed (min)	450.1	33.8	441.0	37.7
Sleep latency (min)	54.0	39.8	18.2	7.9
Total sleep (min)	339.5	29.4	382.8	33.0
Sleep efficiency (%)	76.5	6.9	87.8	5.9

Adapted from Frankel, B.L., et al.: *Arch. Gen. Psychiatry* 33:615, 1976.

In general, the findings reported by Frankel et al. are consistent with the results of studies by other investigators, except for disagreement with respect to whether or not delta or slow-wave sleep time (stages 3 and 4) is reduced in insomniacs compared with controls.

THE MANAGEMENT OF PERSONS WITH DIMS.—Persons with insomnia can suffer from a great deal of distress due to daytime sleepiness, fatigue, irritability, nervousness, and a nagging concern about not being able to "get a good night's sleep." Thus, this is an important medical problem.

In instances in which an acutely stressful event (e.g., loss of a loved one, business failure) results in insomnia, it seems quite reasonable to prescribe a hypnotic drug as a sleep aid. This type of insomnia is usually self-limited, making it unlikely that the person will take the medication for a long time or that drug dependence will occur. In addition to prescribing a hypnotic, the physician should take time to discuss the nature of the insomnia with the patient.

Successful treatment of the underlying psychological (e.g., depression) or physical (e.g., painful arthritis) condition is usually accompanied by an improvement in the person's insomnia. When dependence on sedatives and hypnotics is the cause of insomnia, gradual withdrawal of the drug(s) is indicated to avoid rebound insomnia. Also, the precipitous withdrawal of such drugs can result in serious medical consequences for someone who is physically dependent on them, another reason to proceed slowly in reducing the dose. Following drug withdrawal, a program of therapy for the insomnia should be instituted, including the management of any underlying psychiatric disorder.

The question as to whether to prescribe a hypnotic drug for chronic idiopathic insomniacs has recently received a great deal of attention.[4] When taken for more than two weeks, most hypnotics are ineffective in treating insomnia; in fact, they actually cause greater sleeplessness. Thus, in view of their hazards and ineffectiveness, the regular use of sleeping pills for longer than two to four weeks should be avoided.[4]

The choice of a hypnotic involves a number of considerations, and there are excellent reviews on this topic that should be read by a physician before prescribing this medication.[9, 14, 15] Barbiturates, which were formerly used extensively as sleep aids, are no longer widely prescribed by physicians because of their addictive potential and overdose risk. Currently, the most commonly prescribed drugs for sleep are the benzodiazepines, with flurazepam being the choice of most physicians. Like the other hypnotics, this drug has pronounced effects on the sleep EEG, suppressing the time spent in both REM and delta sleep.[16] Of importance to the physician prescribing flurazepam is the recent information that an active metabolite of this drug remains in the body for more than a day after its use; consequently, a person who takes the drug on consecutive nights will have increasing amounts of the metabolite build up in his system. By the end of a week, persons have four to six times the amount of the drug in their body than they had on the first night. This buildup can cause daytime sedation to develop, along with the risk of driving accidents.

Some conclusions reached by the Institute of Medicine of the National Academy of Sciences in a recent study on the use of sleeping pills in this country are:

1. Sleeping pills are prescribed far more often and with far less care than they should be.
2. Physicians should rarely, if ever, prescribe hypnotic drugs for periods beyond 2 to 4 weeks.
3. Studies show that half of all hospital patients are given sleeping pills. The casual (and in many cases unwarranted) prescribing of hypnotics in this environment may be expected to influence (physicians') future use of these drugs.
4. The elderly, who may experience (pseudo) insomnia as a natural consequence of aging, currently receive 39% of all sleeping pill prescriptions—a practice that is almost entirely unwarranted.[4]

DOES: Disorders of Excessive Somnolence

DOES is a term used to refer to a variety of conditions in which the chief complaint is excessive sleepiness during waking hours. Patients with DOES suffer from an actual increase in daytime sleep behavior (tendency to fall asleep quickly in the waking state, sleep "attacks"), not merely physical tiredness or loss of mental alertness.[7] The latter are awake state symptoms that frequently accompany DIMS. Table 4–4 lists the conditions associated with DOES, some of which can also cause DIMS.

NARCOLEPSY.[7, 8, 9]—This disorder has four cardinal manifestations:

1. *Excessive daytime somnolence and sleep attacks* that usually occur during times (after meals and in the late afternoon) when sleepiness is common. Affected individuals may have several sleep attacks, generally lasting 10 to 15 minutes, in the course of the day that can interrupt activities such as eating, talking, or physical exercise. Sleepiness and sleep attacks are generally the first of the tetrad of symptoms to develop, and nearly all persons with the syndrome experience them.

2. *Episodes of muscular weakness (called cataplexy)* lasting for only seconds during the day while the person is awake. These are almost always triggered by strong emotional reactions such as laughter or anger.[7] The degree of motor involvement varies from mild weakness to full paralysis. It can be generalized or localized to specific muscles, giving rise, for example, to postural collapse, facial sagging, loss of grip, or head-drop. About 70% of narcoleptics have this symptom, which may occur with a frequency of less than once a week to many times a day.[7]

3. *Sleep paralysis* that occurs just before falling asleep or just after awakening and consists of a feeling that one is unable to move any muscles except those that control eye motion. This lasts for only a few seconds or minutes.

4. *Vivid dreamlike experiences (called hypnagogic hallucinations)* occurring with the entry into or emergence from sleep. About half of all narcoleptics report having this symptom and/or sleep paralysis.[7]

The first two manifestations (daytime sleepiness with sleep attacks and cataplexy) are most important for the clinical diagnosis of narcolepsy; the last two (sleep paralysis and hypnagogic hallucinations) are not essential and are often referred to as auxiliary symptoms. Only 11–14% of narcoleptics have all four manifestations.[7] In addition to this tetrad of symptoms, patients with this disorder also complain of disturbed nocturnal sleep.

The etiology of narcolepsy is unknown; however, there is evidence that a genetic defect may be operative.[7, 17] The syndrome tends to run in families, and there is an animal model of the illness in dogs in which hereditary transmission has definitely been established. It is estimated that narcolepsy has an incidence of 4 cases per 10,000 with equal distribution among men and women.[7] In most

TABLE 4–4.—CONDITIONS ASSOCIATED WITH DOES: DISORDERS OF EXCESSIVE SOMNOLENCE

Psychophysiological
  Transient and situational
  Persistent
Psychiatric disorders
  Affective disorders
  Other functional disorders
Use of drugs and alcohol
  Tolerance to or withdrawal from CNS stimulants
  Sustained use of CNS depressants
Sleep-induced respiratory impairment
  Sleep apnea DOES syndrome
  Alveolar hypoventilation DOES syndrome
Sleep-related (nocturnal) myoclonus and "restless legs"
  Sleep-related (nocturnal) myoclonus DOES syndrome
  "Restless legs" DOES syndrome
Narcolepsy
Idiopathic CNS hypersomnolence
Other medical, toxic, and environmental conditions

Adapted from Association of Sleep Disorders Centers. *Diagnostic classification of sleep and arousal disorders*, ed. 1, prepared by the Sleep Disorders Classification Committee, H.P. Roffwarg, Chairman. *Sleep* 2:1–137, 1979.

cases, the syndrome has its onset in puberty and persists during the person's life. The degree of functional impairment due to daytime sleepiness, sleep attacks, and catalepsy varies from mild to severe. Accidents and habituation to stimulant drugs are complications and this syndrome not uncommonly leads to significant problems in interpersonal relationships (e.g., marital discord, employee-employer disagreements).

Narcolepsy is associated with a disturbance of REM sleep. In persons with this condition, REM sleep frequently occurs within 10 minutes after sleep onset,[18] whereas normally the REM stage does not occur until about 70–90 minutes after sleep begins. Laboratory diagnosis of narcolepsy is based on the finding of sleep-onset REM periods, although these periods are not pathognomonic of this syndrome since they can also be seen in other conditions (drug withdrawal, alcoholism, previous REM sleep deprivation, psychotic depression with DIMS).[7] Three of the symptoms of narcolepsy appear to be abnormal manifestations of REM sleep: cataplexy and sleep paralysis are related to the loss of muscle tone that occurs during the REM stage, while hypnagogic hallucinations represent dreams that are part of this sleep stage.

There is no cure for narcolepsy. Symptoms are treated if they interfere significantly with the person's life.[8,9] For those who complain primarily of excessive daytime sleepiness or sleep attacks, either methylphenidate (Ritalin) or one of the amphetamines can be prescribed. Because of the many side effects of the amphetamines and their strong tendency to produce dependence, these agents are less desirable than methylphenidate. For the person who experiences disabling episodes of cataplexy, imipramine may be effective. Recently, Kales et al. reported that propranolol in relatively large doses (240 mg to 480 mg a day, divided into 4 doses) was effective in treating persons with narcolepsy, especially in improving symptoms of daytime sleepiness and sleep attacks.[19] Since this study involved only 4 patients, these findings will have to be confirmed on a larger sample of naroleptics before this form of therapy is accepted.

SLEEP APNEA SYNDROMES.[8,9,20,21]—Sleep-induced apnea may be associated with either DIMS or DOES and is potentially a very serious, even life-threatening, medical problem. People with these syndromes suffer from recurrent episodes of apnea (defined as a cessation of air flow at the nose and mouth lasting 10 seconds or longer) during a night's sleep.[7] The episodes are due to either (1) *obstruction of air flow* in the upper respiratory tract; or (2) *absence of the central (neurologic) stimulation of respiration;* or (3) *a combination of these*. The first pattern is referred to as the obstructive type, the second as the central type, and the third as the mixed type of sleep apnea. In each patient with the sleep apnea syndrome, all three types of apneic patterns occur but one type usually predominates. Based on the predominant pattern, two basic sleep apnea syndromes are recognized, the predominantly obstructive sleep apnea syndrome and the predominantly central sleep apnea syndrome.[21] The former is much more common.

In the predominantly obstructive sleep apnea syndrome, the site of obstruction is the oropharynx.[21] The most common reason for blockage of the airway is an abnormal relaxation of the muscles of the pharynx plus a backward movement of the tongue. Many persons with this problem are obese and have a short thick neck and large jowls. Other less common reasons for the obstruction include enlarged tonsils and adenoids, acquired micrognathia, neurologic dysfunction involving the muscles of the pharynx, and posterior nasal packing used to stop nasal hemorrhage. Acromegaly and hypothyroidism are reported to be causes of mechanical upper airway obstruction resulting in sleep apnea.

Physiological studies of this type of sleep apnea show a cessation of air flow despite the presence of thoracoabdominal respiratory movements (Fig 4–4). Such persons make loud snoring noises during nighttime sleep

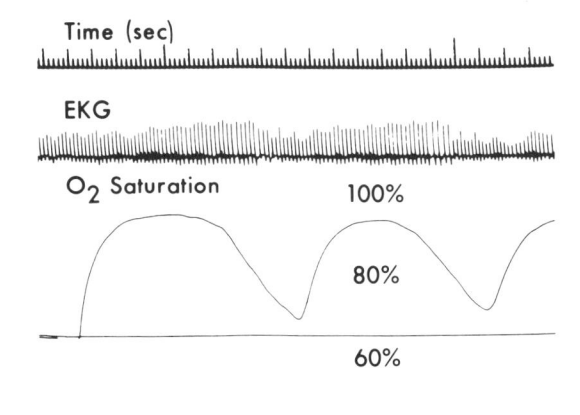

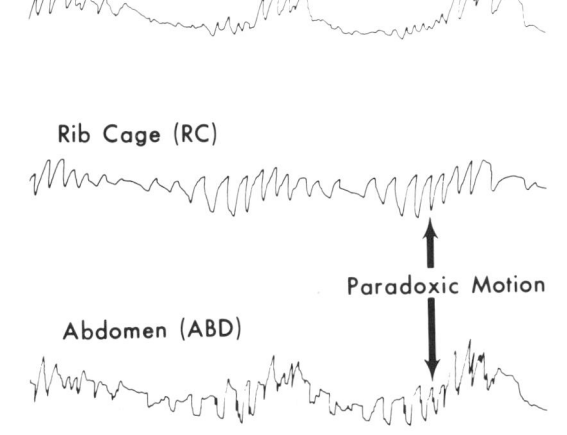

Fig 4-4.—Obstructive sleep apnea. Note paradoxic rib cage (RC) and abdominal motion (ABD) with nearly flat tidal volume (V$_T$(RC + ABD)) during obstructive apnea lasting for almost 30 seconds and associated with progressive oxygen (O$_2$) desaturation and bradycardia. (Compliments of M.A. Cohn, M.D., Sleep Disorders Center, Mount Sinai Medical Center, Miami Beach, Florida.)

due to the partial obstruction of air flow that takes place during nonapneic periods. Persons who have predominantly the obstructive syndrome complain of excessive daytime somnolence with or without sleep attacks (sleep apnea DOES syndrome).[7]

In the predominantly central sleep apnea syndrome, there is an absence of both air flow and respiratory movements (Fig 4-5). This indicates that the normal central (neurologic) stimulus for respiration has failed to occur, presumably due to some lesion of the central nervous system. Persons with this sleep apnea syndrome complain primarily of insomnia (sleep apnea DIMS syndrome).[7]

Although a few episodes of sleep apnea may occur in normal adults (especially the elderly), in the sleep apnea syndromes, periods of apnea (lasting anywhere from 10 to 90 seconds) occur many times during the night. With each episode of apnea the individual's sleep lightens and he experiences partial arousal, so the EEG recording for the night shows multiple awakenings and a decreased amount of delta (stage 3 and 4) sleep. These persons are generally unaware of their breathing difficulty or arousals; rather, they complain of daytime somnolence or insomnia and are often noted by those around them to have personality disturbances manifested by irritability, depression, and hostility.

Cardiovascular complications including hypertension and nocturnal cardiac arrhythmias occur commonly in patients with predominantly obstructive sleep apnea.[21] The alveolar hypoventilation that results from repeated episodes of apnea can lead to hypoxia and carbon dioxide retention. In severe cases, the hypoxia may produce pulmonary hypertension followed by right ventricular heart failure.[20]

Sleep apnea is not uncommon; it has been estimated that there are about 50,000 serious cases of this syndrome in this country. It occurs at all ages, although more than half of the cases are over 40 years old when diagnosed. Men outnumber women by more than 30 to 1. An average of 7% of insomniacs studied in sleep laboratories have the sleep apnea DIMS syndrome; 20% to 60% of persons with excessive daytime somnolence studied in these laboratories turn out to have the sleep apnea DOES syndrome.[7]

A diagnosis of sleep apnea should be suspected on the basis of the clinical picture, particularly a history of prominent snoring in a person who has daytime somnolence. Con-

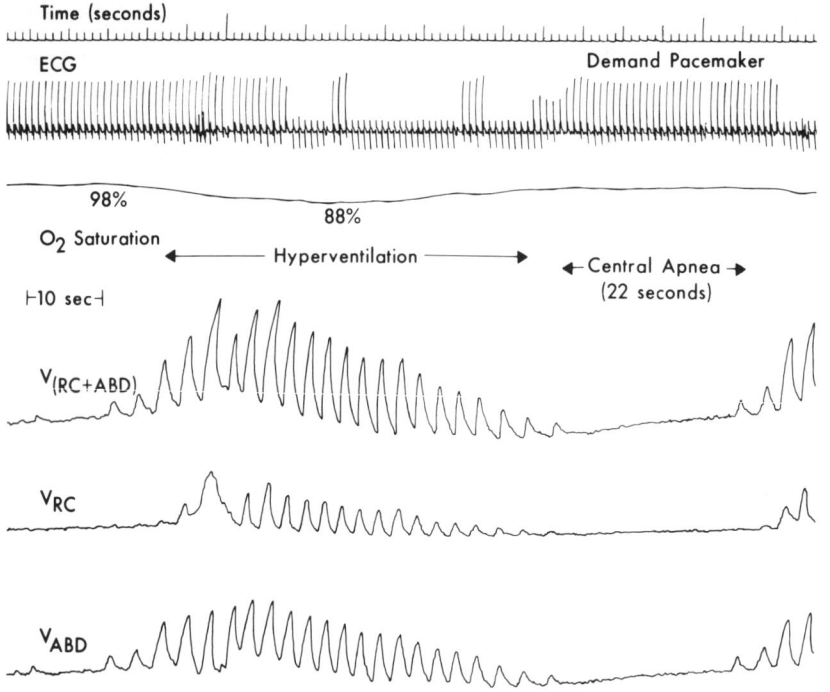

Fig 4–5.—Cheyne-Stokes respiration with central apnea alternating with hyperventilation. Note (a) absence of movement of rib cage (V_{RC}) and abdomen (V_{ABD}) as well as tidal volume ($V_{RC\ +\ ABD}$) during 22 seconds of central apnea; (b) triggering of demand pacemaker presumably secondary to bradycardia during apnea; and (c) oxygen desaturation as low as 88% occurring at time of hyperventilation. This pattern recurred during entire nocturnal study with arousals (not shown) during each hyperventilation phase. (From Cohn M.A.: Sleep apnea. *Cardiopulmonary Technician's Journal,* 1980, in press.)

firmation is made by monitoring the person's nighttime sleep using an EEG plus some measure of oronasal air flow and respiratory movements. The only specific therapy for sleep apnea is removal of the upper airway obstruction, which involves weight loss in instances where obesity is the major problem. Unfortunately, such persons are often unsuccessful in their attempts to reduce their weight. In the obstructive syndrome, it may be necessary in severe cases with cardiac involvement to establish a patent airway by means of a tracheostomy.[21] This is kept closed during the day and opened during the night. Of course, central type apneas will persist after tracheostomy. The response of the person with the obstructive syndrome to tracheostomy is usually dramatic. Sleep returns to a more normal pattern, there is no more daytime somnolence, and the cardiac complications and hypertension improve.

Successful treatment of some persons with the obstructive type of sleep apnea using progesterone has been reported, while progesterone and the tricyclic medications have produced improvement in some cases of the predominantly central sleep apnea syndrome.[21, 22] Most important, the physician should *not* prescribe any medication that might depress the respirations of persons with a sleep apnea syndrome. Thus, central nervous system depressant drugs are contraindicated.

Although most studies on sleep apnea in the literature deal with adults, Guilleminault has reported cases of children suffering from this syndrome. Evidence exists that some instances of the sudden infant death syndrome are due to sleep apnea.

Dysfunctions Associated with Sleep, Sleep Stages, or Partial Arousals (Parasomnias)[1, 7, 8, 9]

The *parasomnias* are a group of conditions in which undesirable activities occur while an individual is asleep. These activities include walking, urinating, and teeth grinding. In addition, frightening "dream experiences" are considered to be parasomnias. Some of these phenomena are related to specific sleep stages, while others appear to be disorders of partial arousal (transition from sleep to arousal) when a subject is in a state of confusion but is still able to carry out purposeful activities.[23]

SOMNAMBULISM.—Sleepwalking is said to occur in 1–6% of the population; thus, it is not a rare phenomenon.[1] It is seen mostly in children and, in some cases, there is a family history of the problem. Boys are affected more often than girls.

Somnambulism is initiated in the first third of the night during deep NREM (delta) sleep and is due, in the opinion of some, to an activation of the motor system in the state of partial arousal from delta sleep. It does not occur during REM sleep and, therefore, cannot be attributed to the acting out of a dream, as has been speculated in the past.

Sleepwalking consists of a sequence of complex behaviors (perseverative motor acts, semipurposeful automatisms) that, in addition to walking, may include dressing, opening doors, eating, and executing bathroom functions.[7] Episodes of sleepwalking usually last from a few minutes to more than a half hour. The somnambulist is generally unable to recall anything about the incident when questioned the next morning. In somnambulistic children, the EEG shows extremely high-amplitude slow waves in stage 4 sleep just before an attack.[24]

In children, somnambulism is fairly common (as many as 15% have one or more episodes) and does not imply the presence of a psychological disturbance. In the adult, this disorder may be associated with psychomotor epilepsy or a psychological disturbance.[25] As a general rule, children tend to outgrow somnambulism, usually before their twenties; consequently, no therapy is indicated except for taking the appropriate precautions so that the child is not injured during the sleepwalking episodes.

In the adult, treatment of the underlying illness may be effective in reducing the frequency of sleepwalking. When somnambulism is severe and persistent, the benzodiazepines (i.e., diazepam, flurazepam) have been prescribed in an attempt to suppress delta sleep, thereby decreasing the sleepwalking. The effectiveness of this medication is questionable.

SLEEP-RELATED ENURESIS.—(See chap. 15 for additional discussion.) Bed-wetting occurs in as many as 10–15% of otherwise normal children at age 5; however, only a small percentage (1.3%) of teenagers and young adults continue to suffer from it.[1] *Primary enuresis* is present when an individual has never stopped bed-wetting for any appreciable time since infancy; *secondary enuresis* exists when a person begins to wet the bed again after having undergone successful toilet training. By definition, both types are idiopathic.

Most bed-wetting episodes begin in deep NREM (delta) sleep or in the transition from delta sleep to lighter stages (in the course of arousal); thus they usually take place in the early part of the night when delta sleep is most prevalent. There is evidence that contractions of the urinary bladder start during delta sleep, followed by a lightening of the sleep to stage 1 or 2 as the individual is voiding.

The management of enuresis depends on whether the disorder is primary or secondary. Primary cases involving young children may represent only a delay in neurologic maturation (especially if there is a history of a similar disorder in the family), so that one need only be patient and the problem will spontaneously disappear. Although the possibility that organic cause exists should be investigated by means of a physical examination, this is not common in these persons. Other means of therapy are discussed in chapter 15.

Secondary enuresis usually can be explained by some psychological stress to which the child is exposed. Enuresis itself often produces emotional stress for the person involved and his family, especially if the problem is present in an older child or young adult, and this reaction may, in turn, aggravate the enuresis. So, managing the psychological reactions of the child and his family to enuresis is an integral part of the treatment.

SLEEP TERROR AND DREAM ANXIETY ATTACKS (NIGHTMARES).[1, 9, 26]—Generally, patients do not distinguish between these frightening experiences; however, from the standpoint of sleep physiology, they are quite different. A sleep terror has its origin in delta sleep, occurring most often in the early part of the night. The individual experiences a sudden arousal associated with a scream or cry, followed by intense anxiety and discharge of the sympathetic nervous system (markedly increased heart rate, increased rate and depth of respirations, sweating, mydriasis, etc.). The episode lasts about 5 to 10 minutes. During this time, the person is acutely aware of a feeling of impending doom; he is literally terrified. Children have sleep terrors (also called pavor nocturnus) more commonly than do adults. Stress may precipitate these attacks.

Nightmares are simply dreams that have a particularly frightening quality. They are far more common than sleep terrors and are experienced at all ages. As most dreams do, nightmares arise during REM sleep and, therefore, are more likely to occur in the mid to late portion of the night. They frequently accompany the increased REM sleep time (REM rebound) that occurs following the abrupt withdrawal of some hypnotic agents.

In addition to originating in different stages of sleep, nightmares differ in other ways from sleep terrors. The former are usually associated with a less intense emotional and physiological reaction than the latter. An individual experiencing a nightmare can generally give a detailed description of the dream, whereas someone experiencing a sleep terror can rarely recall much about the content of his dream experience.

The management of a person complaining of recurrent "bad dreams" requires that the physician distinguish between these two possibilities (sleep terrors and nightmares). Sleep terrors in children often go away with time. Generally, these episodes do not reflect any underlying psychological disturbance, so all that is necessary is to reassure the child and his family that this is not a serious problem. On the other hand, the adult who experiences sleep terrors may harbor a significant emotional problem, a situation in which psychological evaluation and treatment are indicated. Drugs that suppress delta sleep (e.g., diazepam) have been reported to be useful in treating persons with recurring sleep terrors.

Persistent and recurrent nightmares may be the consequence of an emotional disturbance, whether they occur in children or adults. When this is the case, psychological treatment can be effective.

A list of other dysfunctions associated with sleep, sleep stages, or partial arousals is shown in Table 4–5.

TABLE 4–5.—SOME DYSFUNCTIONS ASSOCIATED WITH SLEEP, SLEEP STAGES, OR PARTIAL AROUSALS (PARASOMNIAS)

Sleep-related epileptic seizures
Sleep-related bruxism
Sleep-related headbanging (jactatio capitis nocturnus)
Familial sleep paralysis
Impaired sleep-related penile tumescence
Sleep-related painful erections
Sleep-related cluster headaches and chronic paroxysmal hemicrania
Sleep-related abnormal swallowing syndrome
Sleep-related asthma
Sleep-related cardiovascular symptoms
Sleep-related gastroesophageal reflux
Sleep-related hemolysis (paroxysmal nocturnal hemoglobinuria)

Adapted from Association of Sleep Disorders Centers. *Diagnostic classification of sleep and arousal disorders*, ed. 1, prepared by the Sleep Disorders Classification Committee, H.P. Roffwarg, Chairman. Sleep 2:1–137, 1979.

Medical and Psychiatric Illnesses That Affect Sleep

Illness may disturb an individual's usual pattern of sleep. For example, someone who has cardiac or pulmonary disease may have difficulty sleeping because of symptoms of shortness of breath or cough. Conversely, sleep may be associated with the worsening of symptoms due to disease. For example, the dyspnea caused by heart failure may intensify during the night while the person is recumbent. Some medical conditions are adversely affected during specific stages of sleep. For instance, when the pain of angina pectoris occurs during the night, it is usually experienced during REM, rather than NREM, sleep. This is probably because of the marked fluctuations (and increases) in physiological activities such as heart rate and blood pressure that take place during REM sleep. Also it has been found that the secretion of acid in persons with peptic ulcer disease is greater during the REM stage of sleep.

Some of the observations linking physical illness to specific sleep stages have important clinical implications. For example, a physician caring for a patient with angina pectoris should exercise caution in prescribing barbiturate hypnotics. Although these drugs may initially suppress REM sleep, after a while a breakthough may occur with an increase in REM sleep time. When this happens, the angina may intensify.

A variety of other medical conditions occur during sleep or affect it in some way. "Sleep epilepsy" is a parasomnia in which seizures take place more or less exclusively while the individual is sleeping.[27] For some epileptics, sleep has been found to exacerbate their disorder, while in others sleep deprivation seems to worsen their condition. A sleep EEG may be of great diagnostic importance in instances where epilepsy is suspected as a cause of disturbed sleep. Insomnia may be experienced by persons who have hyperthyroidism. The sleep pattern of these individuals shows fragmented, brief periods of intense sleep (in which stages 3 and 4 are prominent). Hypothyroidism is associated with the reverse of this pattern—a greater amount of time spent sleeping and a paucity of stages 3 and 4 sleep.

The nutritional intake of an individual may affect his sleep. Almost everyone is familiar with the drowsiness that sometimes develops after a large meal. This may possibly be related to the caloric intake or to the ingestion of a specific nutritional substance, L-tryptophan. The latter is a precursor of serotonin and, by causing an increase in serotonin synthesis in the brain, could theoretically induce a state of somnolence. This may explain the successful use of a nighttime snack as a "hypnotic."

Persons with psychiatric illnesses, such as schizophrenia and depression, commonly complain of difficulty sleeping. Schizophrenics are most likely to be troubled with this problem when they are acutely ill. During this phase of the illness, the most common sleep complaints are sleep-onset insomnia and fragmentation of sleep by frequent arousals. The following abnormalities in EEG sleep recordings have been reported in schizophrenics: diminished total sleep time, less time spent in the REM stage, abnormal REM latency (the amount of time after falling asleep that the first REM period occurs), and a reduction in delta sleep time.[1, 2, 28] REM latency tends to be shortened in schizo-affective patients and prolonged in the other types of schizophrenic patients. It has been reported that, in contrast to normals, acutely ill schizophrenics fail to experience a compensatory increase in REM sleep time (i.e., REM rebound) on the nights following the experimental deprivation of REM sleep.[2] Remission from acute illness is associated with a gradual restoration of a normal sleep pattern.

The apparent similarity between dreams and hallucinations gave rise to the speculation that a disturbance in the dreaming process might play a role in the pathogenesis of schizophrenia.[2] In an attempt to resolve this question, comparisons have been made of the EEG, EOG, and EMG recordings of schizophrenics during hallucinations and those during the REM stage of sleep, when most dreaming takes place. As measured by these parameters, there are no similarities between hallucinations and dreams.

Depression is associated with alterations in sleep that range from insomnia to excessive sleep. Insomnia is most common, and people who are depressed often come to the physician with this as their principal complaint. Persons with primary depression have difficulty getting to sleep, but their major problem usually is staying asleep. They have repeated awakenings with a characteristic "early morning" arousal. EEG sleep studies of such persons show a reduction in total sleep time, a decrease in time spent in delta sleep, and a shortened REM sleep latency.[29] The last finding is a biologic marker of primary depression and usually is not found in secondary depression.[7, 29]

In an interesting and informative study, Gillin et al. compared the EEG sleep recording of 56 persons with primary depression with those from 18 primary insomniacs and 41 normal volunteers in order to gain information about the specificity of the sleep disturbance in primary depression.[30] The insomniacs had been previously described by Frankel.[11] The depressed persons showed less total sleep, longer sleep latency, more early morning awake time, more intermittent awake time, less delta sleep, lower sleep efficiency, and shorter REM latencies compared with the normal subjects. In comparison with the insomniacs, the depressed persons showed more early morning awake time, shorter REM latency, greater REM index (the sum of the eye movement scores during REM sleep for the entire night), and greater REM density (REM index/REM time). Using the statistical method of multivariate discriminant analysis, 73% of the depressed persons and 77% of the insomniacs could be accurately diagnosed on the basis of the variables studied in the sleep EEG. Particularly valuable in differentiating (primary) depression from (primary) insomnia is the short REM latency that occurs in the former.

SUMMARY

The prevalence of sleep disorders for which people either seek medical help or take medication has been estimated to be as high as 30% of the population in this country.[31] Thus, these disorders constitute a major medical problem. Prior to the last several decades, little objective information was available about the biologic aspects of sleep. Consequently, the diagnosis and treatment of sleep disorders had little scientific basis. This is no longer true. As a result of research conducted in sleep laboratories in this country and elsewhere in the world, the EEG pattern of normal sleep and the abnormalities present in a significant number of pathologic conditions have been reasonably well defined.

The recently published diagnostic classification of sleep and arousal disorders by the Association of Sleep Disorders Centers lists DIMS and DOES as two important categories of sleep disturbance.[7] In the past, it has been common practice among physicians to prescribe a hypnotic agent routinely for a person complaining of insomnia. To a significant extent, this is still occurring. More and more practitioners, however, are coming to realize that this approach is incorrect, that insomnia is a symptom of an underlying disorder and, as such, requires a careful diagnostic search. The same is true with respect to the symptoms of excessive daytime somnolence and sleep attacks. This search begins with a thorough medical and psychosocial appraisal of the person. In addition, the diagnosis of many sleep disorders is greatly facilitated by observing the person in a sleep laboratory overnight and closely monitoring his sleep by means of electronic recording devices (e.g., EEG, EOG, EMG).

As in other areas of medicine, the treatment of a sleep disorder should be based on an accurate diagnosis. In selected instances of insomnia, hypnotic drugs are effective and indicated for short-term (two weeks or less) use. However, they should not be given routinely "on demand" to patients, for extended periods without interruption, or in situations where dependence is likely to occur. In some conditions, such as sleep apnea, they are contraindicated. The overprescribing of hypnotics is prevalent among physicians in this country; the practice is to be deplored because of the limited effectiveness of these drugs and the serious hazards associated with their use.

REFERENCES

1. Kales A., Kales J.D., Humphrey F.J.: Sleep and dreams, in Freedman A.M., Kaplan H.I., Sadock B.J. (eds.): *Comprehensive Textbook of Psychiatry I*. Baltimore, Williams & Wilkins Co., 1975.
2. Karacan I., Anch A.M., Williams R.L.: Recent advances in the psychophysiology of sleep and their psychiatric significance, in Grenell R.G., Gabay S. (eds.): *Biological Foundations of Psychiatry*, vol. 1. New York, Raven Press, 1976.
3. Berger R.J.: The sleep and dream cycle, in Kales A. (ed.): *Sleep: Physiology and Pathology—A Symposium*. Philadelphia, J.B. Lippincott Co., 1969.
4. Smith R.J.: Study finds sleeping pills overprescribed. *Science* 204:287, 1979.
5. Soldatos C.R., et al.: Cigarette smoking associated with sleep difficulty. *Science* 207:551, 1980.
6. Kales A., et al.: Rebound insomnia. *J.A.M.A.* 241(16):1692, 1979.
7. Association of Sleep Disorders Centers. *Diagnostic Classification of Sleep and Arousal Disorders*, ed. 1, prepared by the Sleep Disorders Classification Committee, H.P. Roffwarg, Chairman. *Sleep* 2:1–137, 1979.
8. Dement W.C., Guilleminault C.: Sleep disorders: The state of the art. *Hosp. Practice* 8:57, 1973.
9. Hauri P.: The sleep disorders, in *Current Concepts*. Kalamazoo, Mich., The Upjohn Company, 1977.
10. Cohen S.: Sleep and insomnia. *J.A.M.A.* 236(7):875, 1976.
11. Frankel B.L., et al.: Recorded and reported sleep in chronic primary insomnia. *Arch. Gen. Psychiatry* 33:615, 1976.
12. Lutz E.G.: Restless legs: Anxiety and caffeinism. *J. Clin. Psychiatry* 39:693, 1978.
13. Boghen D., Peyronnard J.M.: Myoclonus in familial restless legs syndrome. *Arch. Neurol.* 33:368–370, 1976.
14. Johns M.W.: Sleep and hypnotic drugs. *Drugs* 9:448–478, 1975.
15. Greenblatt D.J., Miller R.R.: Rational use of psychotropic drugs. *J. Maine Med. Assoc.* 65:192–197, 1974.
16. Feinberg I., et al.: Flurazepam effects on sleep EEG. *Arch. Gen. Psychiatry* 36:95, 1979.
17. Leckman J.F., Gershon E.S.: A genetic model of narcolepsy. *Br. J. Psychiatry* 128:276–279, 1976.
18. Rechtschaffen A., Wolpert E., Dement W.C.: Nocturnal sleep of narcoleptics. *Electroencephalogr. Clin. Neurophysiol.* 15:599, 1963.
19. Kales A., Soldatos C.R., Cadieux R., et al.: Propranolol in the treatment of narcolepsy. *Ann. Intern. Med.* 91:741, 1979.
20. Sackner M.A., et al.: Periodic sleep apnea: Chronic sleep deprivation related to intermittent upper airway obstruction and central nervous system disturbance. *Chest* 67:164–171, 1975.
21. Guilleminault C., Cummiskey J., Dement W.C.: Sleep apnea syndrome: Recent advances. *Adv. Intern. Med.* 26:347, 1980.
22. Strohl K.P., Hensley M.J., Saunders N.A.: Progesterone administration and progressive sleep apneas. *J.A.M.A.* 27:1230, 1981.
23. Broughton R.J.: Sleep disorders: Disorders of arousal? *Science* 159:1070, 1968.
24. Jacobson A., Kales A., Lehmann D. et al.: Somnambulism: All-night electroencephalographic studies. *Science* 144:975–977, 1965.
25. Sours J.F., et al.: Somnambulism. *Arch. Gen. Psychiatry* 9:400, 1963.
26. Fisher C., et al.: A psychophysiological study of nightmares and night terrors: The suppression of stage 4 night terrors with diazepam. *Arch. Gen. Psychiatry* 28:252, 1973.
27. Gibberd F.B., Bateson M.C.: Sleep epilepsy: Its pattern and prognosis. *Br. Med. J.* 2:403–405, 1974.
28. Reich L., et al.: Sleep disturbance in schizophrenia—A revisit. *Arch. Gen. Psychiatry* 32:51, 1975.
29. Kupfer D.J.: REM latency: A psychobiologic marker for primary depressive disease. *Biol. Psychiatry* 11:159, 1976.
30. Gillin J.C., et al.: Successful separation of depressed, normal and insomniac subjects by EEG sleep data. *Arch. Gen. Psychiatry* 36:85, 1979.
31. Hartmann E.: Drugs for insomnia. *Ration. Drug Ther.* 11(12):1, 1977.

PART II
Psychological Factors in Behavior

5 / Theories of Psychological Function

Psychoanalytic Theory

SANFORD JACOBSON, M.D., and JONATHAN J. BRAUNSTEIN, M.D.

Learning Theory and Behavior Therapy

MALCOLM KUSHNER, Ph.D., and RICHARD P. TOISTER, Ph.D.

CONTEMPORARY PSYCHOLOGICAL THINKING embodies several different approaches to understanding and interpreting behavior. Two of the most influential are psychoanalytic and behavior or learning theories. From both the clinical and research standpoints these have dominated the fields of psychology and psychiatry for the past half-century. They have, in addition, greatly influenced art, literature, and even man's view of himself as a part of the natural universe.[1,2]

PSYCHOANALYTIC THEORY[3-10]

Freud, the founder of psychoanalytic theory, developed most of his concepts from observations he made while treating emotionally disturbed patients. Initially, these formulations stemmed from his studies of the treatment of hysteria and the effects of hypnosis on mental function. In his attempts to understand the basis for neurotic symptoms such as those experienced by hysterics, he focused his attention on past events in the lives of these patients that appeared to play a critical role in the pathogenesis of their illness. He also investigated the meaning of dreams reported by these patients, finding that they often contained, in disguised form, memories of traumatic events that had occurred previously in their lives. From these and later observations, Freud constructed topographic and structural models of the personality, which constitute the foundation of psychoanalytic theory. Also, as part of this theory he identified specific periods in the lives of children (called the psychosexual stages of development) in which critical experiences lead to the development of the adult personality. Although more recent psychiatrists and psychologists have modified Freud's concepts, contemporary psychoanalytic theory is still largely his creation.

Topographic and Structural Models

Freud's topographic model divides the mind into conscious and unconscious portions. The latter is the part of the psyche where ideas, wishes, and conflicts exist without the individual being aware of them. "Forbidden" material is held in the unconscious region of the mind by the active process of *repression*. Despite the individual being unaware of this unconscious material, it is able to exert an influence, sometimes pathologic, on his thoughts, actions, and behavior. Freud believed that it is from the unconscious that dreams originate, and that analysis of the content of dreams gives the examiner insight into the activities of this area of the mind.

A second concept of Freud's topographic model has to do with the presence of *instinctual drives,* or forces that act to motivate behavior. He theorized that these forces are of two principal types: a life (Eros) instinct and a death (Thanatos) or aggressive instinct. It should be noted that the psychoanalytic definition of instinct is not the same as that given by ethologists who define an instinct as an inherited fixed pattern of behavior arising from neurophysiological mechanisms. In psychoanalytic theory, instincts are forms of mental or psychic energy that express the biologic needs of an organism. Each of the two major drives has an aim: for the life instinct it is self-preservation, and for the death or aggressive instinct it is disorganization and destruction. Another term for the life instinct is the *libido,* or *sexual drive.* Used in this context the term *sexual* refers to pleasurable drives in general, not just to genital sex. While the concept of a life instinct has been generally accepted, that of the death instinct has met with a great deal of objection from psychologists and psychiatrists on the basis that it is not universally present in humans.

According to Freud, drives are part of the unconscious, where they are constantly striving to gain expression. The failure of a person to release drive energy results in a buildup of intrapsychic tension, along with the development of conflict between the drive forces and those psychic processes that act to prevent their expression. Besides these processes, there are external constraints that block the discharge of drive energy. For instance, as a person relates to the world, his instinctual urges often come in conflict with the demands of reality.

The topographic model can be viewed as a homeostatic system in which, under normal conditions, a balance exists between the drives that are seeking expression and the psychological processes that act to prevent the release of their energy. In this system, the emotional arousal produced by an instinctual urge causes a behavioral response that, if successful in venting drive energy, returns the psyche to the state of equilibrium that existed prior to the instinctual urge. If, on the other hand, the individual is unable to give expression to this drive, then intrapsychic tension mounts, giving rise to anxiety and emotional disequilibrium. Freud described certain unconscious psychic mechanisms that are designed to handle these emotional reactions and restore some degree of homeostatic balance—the so-called defense mechanisms, which will be discussed shortly.

Following his formulation of the topographic model, Freud realized that it was inadequate to explain all the complexities of mental function that he observed in his contact with patients. In 1923, he introduced a structural model that expanded his theory of mental function. In it, he described the personality as consisting of three interacting components: the *id,* the *ego,* and the *superego.*

ID.—The id is the repository of the inborn instinctual biologic energy or drives. It resides entirely in the unconscious. The behavior that results from id activity is dominated by the pleasure principle, i.e., the gratification of instinctual impulses without regard for the consequences. In this sense, the id is said to utilize *primary process thinking,* which is characterized by a lack of concern for reality and the absence of contradiction. In other words, in this form of thinking, there are no mutually exclusive ideas and the concept of "no" does not exist. Id activity is present at birth as a hereditary endowment, and gradually comes under control of the ego and superego with subsequent development and maturation.

EGO.—The ego functions in both the conscious and unconscious spheres. It can be conceived of as the "executive" portion of the mind. In contrast to the id, it is vitally concerned with the effects of its activity on the external world, and it is governed by the reality principle. In a sense, the ego acts as a liaison between the person and the environment in which he lives. Through its activity, an individual perceives, interprets, and reacts to the situations and events occurring about him.

The ego helps to regulate and control the drives of the id so that they gain expression in an acceptable fashion. To do this, it mediates among the id, reality, and the superego. The ego utilizes *secondary process thinking* (logic and reason) and, in contrast to the id, is able to delay the gratification of wishes and desires until circumstances in the outside world are appropriate.

The overriding task of the ego, according to Freud, is self-preservation. Other important functions include:
1. Reality testing
2. Regulation of the biologic systems that are under voluntary control (i.e., sensorimotor system)
3. Higher mental activities such as memory, judgment, and use of logic
4. Synthesis (or the bringing together in an organized fashion) of drives, feelings, and thoughts so that the individual can act in an integrated manner
5. Establishment of object relationships (the development of emotional attachment to others not based on id impulses)
6. The use of defense mechanisms to control psychic tension or anxiety

SUPEREGO.—The superego is derived from the ego and is the self-assessing part of the personality. It initially develops in a child at around 5 to 6 years of age when resolution of the Oedipus complex results in a child incorporating the beliefs and values of the parent of the same sex. Thus, to a large extent the superego represents internalized parental prescriptions and prohibitions. It also consists of internalized moral and ethical standards derived from the world in which the person lives.

The superego functions on both a conscious and an unconscious level. It is capable of generating both positive reactions of satisfaction and reward and negative reactions of guilt and self-criticism. By means of the latter, it acts to inhibit id impulses when these appear to violate the ideals and values that the person holds.

Specifically, superego activities include:
1. Regulation of ego function on the basis of "right" and "wrong"
2. Critical self-observation
3. Self-chastisement
4. Self-approval
5. Assistance to the ego in controlling id drives
6. Development of an ego ideal (a model of ideal behavior or standard of conduct)

Two other parts of the psychoanalytic theory deserve special mention: the psychosexual stages of development and the ego defense mechanisms.

The Psychosexual Stages of Development

Freud theorized that during infancy and childhood libidinous energies become focused on specific areas of the body and that these *erogenous zones* follow a predictable pattern that is related to the age of the individual. Indeed, these zones appeared to play such a critical role in personality development that Freud used them as labels to designate four of the five stages of his theory of psychosexual development. These periods are described in some detail in chapters 13, 14, and 15 and, therefore, will be discussed only briefly here.

ORAL STAGE.—In the infant (from birth to 12 months), the oral mucosa is the principal site of pleasurable sensations arising from activities such as feeding (sucking), biting, mouthing, and spitting.

ANAL STAGE.—At about 18 months to 3 years of age, libidinous energy becomes centered on the anus, particularly the anal sphincter. By this age, the child has acquired voluntary control of this sphincter, so toilet training is generally begun by the parents. Expelling and withholding feces become prime concerns and potential sources of conflict between the child and his parents.

PHALLIC STAGE AND THE OEDIPUS COMPLEX.—The phallic stage begins at about the third year of life and ends at approximately the sixth year. Children of this age become aware of differences between the sexes. In the boy, the penis becomes the focus of libidinal energy; among girls, there is concern about the absence of this organ. It is during this stage that a child develops a strong attachment to the parent of the opposite sex and resentment toward the parent of the same sex. In describing this conflict, Freud used the story of the Greek tragedy, Oedipus Rex, and labeled it the Oedipus complex.

LATENCY STAGE.—This stage covers the ages from about 6 to 12 or 13. During this phase, drive energy is directed toward the activities of learning and achievement. There is a reduction in internal conflict and, thus, id energy is freed for these outside activities.

GENITAL PHASE.—With the onset of puberty, at about 12 to 13 years of age, libidinal energy is again focused on the genital area, but there is a more mature form of drive expression than there was in the phallic stage. Drive energy is now directed toward members of the opposite sex.

Defense Mechanisms

Throughout childhood and adult life, there are frequent unconscious conflicts between the drives of the id, the demands of reality, and the censure of the superego. One consequence of these conflicts is anxiety, defined as an unpleasant state of tension, apprehension, or worry. When severe, it is associated with a feeling of impending doom. According to psychoanalytic theory, the ego utilizes mental stratagems or mechanisms of defense to protect the individual from conscious awareness of these conflicts as well as from the anxiety and emotional pain they cause. Functioning in this way, defense mechanisms have adaptive value; however, these mechanisms may be maladaptive if, for example, their use markedly distorts reality or causes emotional or physical symptoms.

Ego defense mechanisms operate on an unconscious level and are part of normal and abnormal mental function. They can be divided into several categories depending on the degree of reality distortion produced and, hence, their effect on adaptation.

DEFENSE MECHANISMS ASSOCIATED WITH MAJOR REALITY DISTORTION.—These include denial, projection, and dissociation.

DENIAL.—Denial refers to a refusal by an individual to admit the existence of some aspect of reality. Usually the material that is denied is psychologically threatening or conflictual so the ego represses or forces it into the unconscious.

A 48-year-old housewife brought her 19-year-old son to a psychiatrist on the advice of the family physician. She stated that her son was behaving in an unusual fashion and at times was observed to be staggering around the house. She was very concerned that he might have some neurologic disease, possibly a brain tumor. She was particularly upset about this because of her training as a nurse. From the history obtained from the young man and his mother, it was obvious that his unsteadiness of gait was due to drugs. The mother had been relatively "blind" to this reality. She had on one occasion found a pill in his shirt pocket and then accepted a rather ineffectual explanation the son offered about it. Even when told that his symptoms were related to drug abuse, she had great difficulty accepting this and insisted that he be hospitalized for a thorough battery of neurologic diagnostic tests.

This illustrates how the mechanism of denial works, in this instance to the detriment of the individual because it prevented the early recognition of a serious health problem—drug abuse.

People who are ill commonly use denial to deal with their symptoms and the anxiety they feel (see chap. 22).

PROJECTION.—Projection is the defense mechanism by which one attributes his own objectionable ideas, impulses, or traits to others. Thus, a person can escape responsibility for these qualities by "blaming" others for them. Projection may not always result in significant distortions of reality, but if utilized frequently, it is maladaptive.

A 17-year-old high school student was brought in for psychiatric consultation because of difficulty in sleeping, restlessness, and agitation. The family reported that he could not express himself as clearly as he once had. They noted that he rambled excessively and could not keep his mind on the subject matter. During the interview with him, he acknowledged auditory hallucinations and stated that he heard the voices of his schoolmates accusing him of being a homosexual. These voices were heard when he was in his room at home in the evening and when he was driving his automobile to school. He also thought he may have heard them over the radio on one occasion. Earlier in the year, he had been injured in football practice and was quite disappointed in his failure to make the first-string varsity squad. Coinciding with this was the rejection of him by his girlfriend after a relationship of 2 years.

The auditory hallucinations seemed to reflect his own anxiety about his adequacy as a man. The football injury and rejection by his girlfriend had impaired his self-esteem and threatened his somewhat fragile masculine identity. These fears were projected in the form of auditory hallucinations.

DISSOCIATION.—Dissociation is the splitting off of a group of ideas from the remainder of the psyche. When feelings are split off without associated ideas, the process is described as partial dissociation. Dissociation occurs along with the defense mechanism of repression.

A 19-year-old soldier in the midst of basic training rented a car while on a weekend pass and drove 800 miles to his hometown. When he arrived, his parents were quite surprised and asked him what he was doing at home, whereupon he became quite confused and upset. He claimed that he had been totally unaware of how he had driven 800 miles and could not recall any of the events that occurred during the trip. He appeared to be amnesic for about 18 hours, having been unaware of events from the time he left his military installation until he arrived at home. It became apparent upon interviewing him that he had many conflicts about military service. Under the influence of sodium amytal, he was able to recall what had happened during the trip and could even remember the restaurants at which he stopped and what he had eaten.

This type of dissociation is called a fugue state. Other types of dissociation, such as multiple personalities and prolonged periods of amnesia, are quite rare.

DEFENSE MECHANISMS ASSOCIATED WITH MODERATE DEGREES OF REALITY DISTORTION.—These mechanisms include repression, regression, conversion, reaction formation, displacement, and rationalization.

REPRESSION.—Repression is often described as the cardinal mechanism of defense. It is defined as the active process of forcing unacceptable or threatening thoughts, feelings, and impulses into the unconscious and keeping them out of conscious awareness. The anxiety-provoking material that is repressed may originate internally or externally. Examples of repression in everyday life are the unexplained forgettings of familiar names, places, appointments, or past events in one's life.

A 32-year-old woman entered psychotherapy because of fear of driving. The onset of her symptoms began about 12 years earlier. At that time she received psychotherapy and her symptoms resolved after 18 months of treatment. Over the following 9 years she was relatively free of this fear but at times experienced some anxiety related to driving. In the last year the fear returned and she became more limited in her ability to drive. She could venture only several blocks away from her home and could not cross large thoroughfares.

When questioned directly about the original cause of the fear, she could not give a specific answer. However, on recounting the circumstances that preceded the onset of her symptoms 12 years ago, she suddenly realized that the fear began while she was driving to her own wedding rehearsal, an event that produced a great deal of anxiety for her. Since her marriage was beset with significant problems, she had subsequently repressed the memory of this earlier event that was associated with psychological stress.

REGRESSION.—Regression is the return to an earlier, less mature stage of personality development, usually because of an inability to cope adequately with a situation of conflict or stress. By retreating to an earlier period of development, the person often feels less anxious in the face of the threatening situation.

A 6-year-old boy suddenly began wetting the bed at night after having been totally continent since age 3. The bed-wetting began during the toilet training of a younger brother who was receiving considerable attention from the family. The jealousy and rivalry experienced by the 6-year-old toward his younger brother resulted in a brief regression.

Individuals who become ill and are hospitalized often manifest childlike behavior, which is due to the mechanism of regression (see chap. 22).

CONVERSION.—In conversion, unconscious psychological conflict, due for example to repressed wishes or feelings, is expressed as a physical symptom(s). In the past, patients with this condition typically presented with a motor paralysis or a sensory deficit, such as a loss of sight; however, today the most common manifestation of conversion is psychogenic pain. In cases of conversion, there are no organic changes in the body to explain the patient's symptoms.

Symptoms of conversion symbolically represent repressed wishes or feelings, thus, giving partial vent to them and temporarily resolving the unconscious conflict. This partial expression is referred to as the *primary gain*. The term *secondary gain* refers to the advantage(s) the individual obtains as a result of being sick—for example, increased attention from others. Often, a patient with a conversion reaction is relatively indifferent to or unconcerned about his symptoms, something referred to as *la belle indifférence*.

While conversion is not universally considered to be a defense mechanism, it does protect the person from the anxiety caused by psychic conflict, so it is included here.

A 20-year-old married woman was referred for psychiatric evaluation because of persistent complaints of pelvic pain and weakness in her lower extremities, particularly after sexual intercourse. Diagnostic studies and thorough medical evaluation failed to disclose any abnormalities. She had been married for about 4 weeks and her symptoms began shortly after her honeymoon. She had a rather conservative family background with strong moral, ethical, and religious beliefs. On interview, it became apparent that her symptoms significantly interfered with her having sexual relations with her husband. The patient acknowledged that she had mixed feelings about their sexual relationship. There had been little physical contact prior to the marriage and her feelings about her own sexual functioning were confused. With treatment, her symptoms improved over a period of several months and she was able to develop more appropriate feelings about her sexual role.

REACTION FORMATION.—In reaction formation, attitudes or patterns of behavior are adopted that are the opposite of the ideas and feelings held unconsciously by the person. These ideas and feelings that are unacceptable to the person are repressed into the unconscious because they would create too much anxiety and conflict if the person became aware of them. By manifesting exactly the opposite attitude or behavior, the individual protects himself from this awareness.

A 39-year-old married woman, the mother of 4 children, became quite upset when she went with her husband and another couple to an R-rated movie. After the movie she was preoccupied with some of the material presented. She talked about it with her husband the next day and emphasized over and over again how disgusted she was by it. She complained of nausea and called her family physician to prescribe something for this symptom. The nausea persisted for several days.

When she was examined, the physician noted an extreme degree of anxiety. Closer inquiry revealed that she was not truly suffering from nausea, but was using the term to describe a feeling of emotional distress. He referred her for psychiatric consultation. Although it was difficult for the woman to acknowledge it initially, it became clear that the material she had seen in the movie was quite stimulating and yet, at the same time, threatening to her. She related various dreams in which she was involved with unknown men in sexual situations. The dream content was not overtly sexual but seemed to symbolize great sexual interest on her part.

In this example of reaction formation, the disgust that the patient experienced on seeing the movie was probably due to the fact that it brought into conscious awareness conflicting and forbidden feelings she had about sex. Rather than openly acknowledging her interest in this material, she adopted the opposite attitude, one of disgust. Other examples of this defense mechanism are a basically hostile person who puts on the appearance of being kind and concerned and an individual with strong dependency needs who acts very independent in his relationship with others.

DISPLACEMENT.—Displacement is a shifting of feelings (or emotions) from one person, object, or event to another. Generally, the shift is made because the individual finds it unacceptable to express his feelings toward the original person or object and, therefore, selects a "neutral" one on which he can safely vent them.

A 34-year-old married woman, mother of three children, suddenly developed a fear of driving her automobile. She was seen for psychiatric evaluation and related numerous difficulties with her husband that had developed over the past year. Some of the dreams that she was having were filled with material about traveling, particularly by airplane, and there appeared to be a strong desire to run away. This produced considerable guilt and ambivalence on her part.

This woman's fear of driving was due to a combination of the mechanisms of reaction formation and displacement. Her unconscious wish to leave was turned into a fear of running away (reaction formation) and then displaced onto the task of driving.

RATIONALIZATION.—Rationalization is the substitution of another explanation for the real reason for a thought or action. In such an instance, the individual usually finds that the real reason is unacceptable because it brings to mind emotionally charged material, and so he devises another reason that he can accept. A term often used by lay people to refer to this mechanism is "sour grapes."

A 25-year-old medical student entered his surgical rotation during his junior year with considerable enthusiasm. During the course of his surgical experience he found that he had some difficulty in functioning adequately in the operating room. After being criticized and teased in a rather friendly manner on several occasions because of his limited manual dexterity, he decided that surgeons were really nothing more than "technicians" and that his real interest was in internal medicine. He explained his difficulty in surgery as being due to a lack of interest and expressed the opinion that surgery is only a matter of practice.

MECHANISMS OF DEFENSE WITH MINIMAL REALITY DISTORTION.—Sublimation and altruism are not considered by some to be defense mechanisms; however, these processes are concerned with resolving psychic conflict and protecting the person from anxiety. Sublimation refers to the modification of a "forbidden" drive or impulse that allows the person to gratify it in a socially acceptable way. Thus, there is a change in the manner in which drive energy is expressed; unacceptable impulses are kept in check while the energy is dissipated through "safe" channels. Altruism, at least in some forms, permits a person to satisfy his drives vicariously by means of fulfilling the needs of others. Clinical examples of sublimation include a photographer who is gratifying voyeuristic impulses, actors and politicians who are gratifying some of their exhibitionist needs, and adolescents who gratify their sexual and aggressive drives by actively engaging in sports.

Clinical Application of Psychoanalytic Theory

Two aspects of psychoanalytic theory have been helpful in explaining the pathogenesis of some types of emotional illness, especially neurotic reactions:

1. The interaction between the three components of the personality—id, ego, and superego
2. The developmental process by which the personality matures—psychosexual stages of development

The first of these is the foundation of the *dynamic explanation* of psychopathology, while the second forms the basis for the *psychogenetic explanation*.[9] According to the dynamic explanation, symptoms of emotional illness occur when there is a disturbance in the homeostatic balance between the intrapsychic components. The psychogenetic explanation attributes psychopathology to arrests or distortions in personality maturation that result from emotional trauma or conflict during the psychosexual stages of development. Memories of these conflictual experiences in childhood may be repressed into the unconscious and reactivated later in life with untoward effects.

The dynamic mechanism focuses on the *present* function of the personality, while the psychogenetic mechanism stresses its *past* development. However, the two mechanisms are interrelated since a significant problem(s) in personality development early in life may result in a disturbance in homeostasis between the components of the psyche that persists into adulthood. Thus, the roots of *present* psychopathology can frequently be found in the *past*.

Both mechanisms usually produce symptoms through a common pathogenetic process: the repression of psychic conflict causing intrapsychic tension that exceeds an individual's capacity to deal with it. When this happens anxiety is experienced, a warning signal that forbidden impulses, emotions, or ideas are rising to a conscious level. In order to protect against anxiety and the conscious awareness of psychic conflict, defense mechanisms are utilized that, at times, are themselves the cause of emotional symptoms. The elements of this general pathogenetic process are specific for each person. Thus, the nature of the psychic conflict that develops, the ego defense mechanisms used to combat anxiety, and the reactions of the superego to the individual's behavior are matters that vary with one's psychological makeup, past experiences, and current relationships.

With these concepts of pathogenesis in mind, one can predict some of the goals of psychoanalytically oriented therapy. One of these is to alleviate unconscious conflict(s). In order to do this, therapy is aimed at enabling a patient to gain "insight" into his conflict(s) by bringing this material into conscious awareness and helping him to "work through" the problems surrounding it. Usually, this is a difficult and complex process requiring much time and effort on the part of the patient and therapist. Another goal, one that is often easier to reach, is to support and strengthen a patient's adaptive defense mechanisms, while at the same time discouraging his use of maladaptive mechanisms. Finally, one of the goals of therapy may be to reduce the influence of an overcritical superego.

Psychoanalytic theory is also useful to nonpsychiatric clinicians in attempting to understand the behavior of patients. People deal with the anxiety and emotional upset that accompany sickness using many of the same mental devices they employ when these reactions result from psychic conflict. For example, denial and rationalization are commonly employed to "defend against" the threatening realization that one is ill. There are studies indicating that denial plays a significant role in the outcome of disorders such as myocardial infarction and cancer by causing people to delay seeking medical care early in the course of the illness. Indeed, one of the ways of improving the mortality for these disorders is to develop methods of discouraging people from using these maladaptive defense mechanisms.

Many patients, especially men, have great difficulty in assuming a dependent role when they are ill. Actually, some have strong dependency needs but feel threatened by them, and so they repress these feelings and adopt the opposite behavior. Such individuals may become very anxious and emotionally upset when they are forced into a state of dependency by a serious medical illness. This anxiety can become so intense that seriously ill patients have been known to leave the hospital against medical advice because of the threat to their independence posed by hospitalization. Understanding the psychodynamics underlying these reactions enables medical personnel to help such patients deal with their feelings in a constructive manner.

Psychoanalytic theory is also useful in interpreting the interactions between patients and medical personnel. For example, many patients see in their physician or nurse a resemblance to authority figures to whom they have related in the past. When this happens, unconscious feelings or conflicts having to do with these authority figures may be reactivated, thereby influencing the patient's attitude and behavior toward the doctor or nurse. Freud referred to this as transference and felt that it played an important role in the therapist-patient relationship.

Many of the emotional reactions that patients have toward medical staff can be explained by the defense mechanism of displacement, whereby the anger and hostility caused by illness is directed inappropriately to the staff. Regression during a period of illness can result in a self-centered, hypochondriacal, and childlike attitude that interferes with the relationship between the patient and doctors or nurses.

LEARNING THEORY AND BEHAVIOR THERAPY

Whereas psychoanalytic theorists concern themselves primarily with the role of intrapsychic phenomena in determining behavior, learning theorists focus their attention on the influence of external situations and events. Thus, according to this approach, a maladaptive pattern of behavior is most effectively dealt with by helping the person to learn more adaptive coping skills. Clinically, this requires an understanding of the circumstances that influence the behavior(s) under consideration, i.e., the situations and events in the environment that determine the person's actions. Once these are understood, a desired change in behavior can be brought about by a systematic manipulation of the critical variables in these circumstances.

Historical Antecedents in the Development of Learning Theory

Psychology, as an experimental science, had its beginning in 1879 and was in its infancy at the end of the 19th and beginning of the 20th centuries. Consequently, little basic information was available from which to draw clinical insights. However, by the 1920s significant new experimentally derived information was appearing in the literature. Pavlov's[11] studies of classical conditioning in animals and Thorndike's[12] data on problem solving provided vital new evidence that certain behaviors are acquired. Watson and his students demonstrated that phobias could be learned as a result of traumatic experiences linked to environmental situations or events.[13] They further described, in what could be considered the first efforts at behavior therapy, that such phobias could be attenuated by controlling and manipulating critical variables in the environment.[14] Also, in the 1920s Krasnogorski directly exposed children to conflicting situations that resulted in neurotic responses—another demonstration of the learned nature of abnormal behavior.[15] (Because of the ethical issues involved, such clinical experimentation would not be conducted today.) In a very early application of aversion therapy, Kantorovich presented painful electric shocks to patients in conjunction with alcohol in order to "decondition" their attraction to this drug.[16]

In the 1930s, additional informaton was forthcoming from psychological laboratories dealing with emotion, perception, memory, motivation, and learning. Guthrie, seeing a clinical application for the conditioning principles that had been elucidated experimentally, suggested that individuals practice alternate and incompatible responses to cues that in the past had elicited undesirable reactions.[17] Skinner, another basic researcher and the originator of the expression *behavior therapy,* presented his initial findings on the nature of learning and introduced the concept of operant conditioning.[18] This form of learning emphasizes the importance of consequences influencing behavior.

As can be seen from the studies cited, which are only a small sample of the research going on during this time, a gradually increasing body of information was developing relative to behavior theory.

The latter part of the 1940s and the 1950s marked the onset of the surge of studies and papers that resulted in the development of contemporary behavior therapy as an effective psychotherapeutic modality. Wolpe, a psychiatrist, reported that cats with experimental neuroses could be deconditioned by first feeding them in an environment distantly removed from that in which they were traumatized, and then gradually bringing them closer and closer to the original experimental cage, which they could then tolerate.[19] This experiment was similar to earlier work reported by Jones on deconditioning a learned phobia.[14] From this research, Wolpe ultimately developed the technique known as *systematic desensitization,* which is effective in the treatment of human phobias and anxiety states.[20] Salter[21] described the use of assertive responses and various classical conditioning procedures in treatment; and Eysenck,[22] showing the limited effectiveness of conventional dynamic psychotherapy, advocated learning-based procedures. Skinner and Lindsley reported on their studies of behavior therapy with schizophrenics utilizing operant conditioning techniques.[23] Wolpe published *Psychotherapy by Reciprocal Inhibition,* in which he extensively discussed his theoretical position for the treatment of human neurosis based on learning principles.[20] This work was the most significant comprehensive clinical report up to that time and was a landmark in the practical application of behavior therapy to clinical problems.

The last two decades have seen a rapid proliferation of studies and reports dealing with behavior therapy and encompassing a wide variety of theoretical positions, including classical and operant conditioning, social learning processes,[24] and, most recently, cognitive processes.[25,26] Taken together, these underline the importance of behavior therapy as an important treatment modality.

Types of Learning

Fundamental to a behavioral approach are two general types of learning: classical (or respondent) and operant conditioning. The former originated from the work of Pavlov and the latter developed from the investigations of Thorndike and Skinner. The manner in which these types of learning operate can be understood from the following simple diagram:

$$A \leftrightarrow B \leftrightarrow C$$

where A stands for antecendent events, B stands for the behavior class under consideration, and C for consequent events. In classical conditioning, the events that come *before* a behavior are the key factors in learning; in operant conditioning, the events that come *afterward* are the principal determiners of behavior. Let's look at each of these types in a little more detail.

CLASSICAL CONDITIONING.—In Pavlov's well-known experiment with dogs, the ringing of a bell was paired with a stimulus (presentation of food) that elicited salivation. After repeated pairings he found that the ringing of the bell alone would elicit salivation. Thus, the dogs "learned" to respond to a previously neutral antecedent stimulus (bell) in a similar way that they responded to a natural one (food).

According to learning theory terminology, the food is the *unconditioned stimulus* and the salivation it elicits is the *unconditioned response.* After conditioning has occurred, when the ringing of the bell elicits salivation, the sound is called the *conditioned stimulus* and the salivation the *conditioned response.*

Watson attempted to demonstrate classical conditioning in infants by repeatedly exposing a child to a loud fear-provoking noise (unconditioned stimulus) in the presence of a white rat (conditioned stimulus).[13] After a time, the sight of the rat alone was enough to elicit the fear response (conditioned response). Moreover, this conditioned behavior became generalized so that it occurred when the child came in contact with objects bearing some similarity (e.g., a rabbit) to the conditional stimulus. While Watson's methodology has been criticized, his work was a pioneering effort to demonstrate classical conditioning in humans.

OPERANT OR INSTRUMENTAL CONDITIONING.—In this type of learning, the consequence(s) (C) of behavior (B) acts to determine the likelihood or probability of its being repeated. The term *operant* was coined by B. F. Skinner to denote the fact that behavior "operates" on the environment and is in turn modified by environmental consequences. In the remaining part of this section, we will discuss some of the processes by which this modification occurs.

REINFORCEMENT.—Reinforcement is the process by which behavior is increased or strengthened. A *positive reinforcer* is any consequent event the presentation of which strengthens the behavior on which it is contingent. An example of such an event is a parent's approving smile that follows some action by a child. Under ordinary circumstances the action that preceded the smile will increase in frequency; that is, it will be reinforced. It can be appreciated that the particular behavior reinforced by the smile need not be desirable—as in the familiar situation of parents smiling at "cute" but socially undesirable behavior which then, to their chagrin and discomfort, becomes a part of the child's repertoire. Thus, it is important to note that positive reinforcement refers only to the strengthening of behavior, not to its desirability.

A *negative reinforcer* is a consequent event the *removal* (partial or complete) of which strengthens behavior. An example is fine tuning a radio when static occurs; removal of the undesirable noise increases the likelihood that fine tuning will be used again whenever static recurs.

PUNISHMENT.—Negative reinforcement should not be confused with punishment, which is defined as a consequent event, usually noxious in quality, the presentation of which *decreases* the likelihood that behavior will recur. Reinforcement, therefore, involves *increasing* the probability of behaviors occurring, whereas punishment involves *decreasing* this probability. Examples of punishment abound in the natural environment and all too frequently are resorted to by parents, teachers, supervisors, and others in order to control social behavior. Punishment frequently results in resentment and anger (overt and covert), produces anxiety, and does little to actively mold new, more desirable behaviors. The use of positive reinforcement generally takes more time and thought to change behavior, and so punishment is often resorted to because of its immediate effects.

A mild form of punishment, referred to as *time-out from positive reinforcement*, or more simply as *time-out*, can be used to decelerate inappropriate behavior. This works as follows: the individual who is being punished because of some undesirable behavior is taken out of an environment which is ordinarily reinforcing. After a brief period (time-out) he is permitted to return to the reinforcing environment. The "go to your room" admonition of the parent is a frequently used example of this technique. However, in order for this to be truly a "time-out," the parent must be certain that the child's room does not contain reinforcers equal to or even more powerful than those from which the child is being removed (e.g., a color television set).

Another frequently used form of punishment is known as *response-cost*. In this situation, objects that have reinforcing value are removed contingent on undesirable behavior. A common example is a fine levied for some offense such as speeding, the rationale being that in order to avoid a similar cost, the speeder will be more likely to observe the traffic laws. Another example is removing a child's favorite toy in order to discourage behavior parents wish to eliminate.

The common goal in all punishment procedures is to decrease the probability of the occurrence of undesirable and unwanted behavior. As a generalization, it can be said that any consequent action or event that, when *added* to the environment, reduces the frequency of a behavior is a form of punishment.

However, punishment is not the only way to decrease the frequency of behavior. Another method is *extinction*. Here, consequences that were previously reinforcing are *withheld*, thereby resulting in a reduction in the behavior. For example, if a child's complaining and whining behavior was being reinforced by the attention paid to him by his mother, having her ignore the behavior will likely result in a decrease of whining. Of course, in such instances one must make certain that the child's demands for attention are not based on a bona fide need; otherwise, this response by the mother would be cruel. The famous "cry wolf" parable is an example of both reinforcement and extinction gone awry.

SHAPING.—By means of operant conditioning, complex behaviors can be established using the technique of *shaping*, whereby successive approximations to a final behavior are reinforced in a stepwise fashion. During childhood, this process is responsible for many developmental achievements as children learn a vast array of socially approved behaviors.

SCHEDULES OF REINFORCEMENT.—The contingent relationship between a behavior and a reinforcer or punisher is often termed a schedule of reinforcement. Reinforcement schedules have considerable effect on the acquisition, maintenance, and elimination of behavior. Generally, the relationship can be continuous (CRF) or intermittent. In continuous reinforcement every response or behavior produces a reinforcing consequence. For example, a parent going into a child's room each and every time the child called "Mom" would be continuously reinforcing this behavior. CRF usually produces a rapid acquisition of a behavior class but a rapid reduction in rate during extinction.

An intermittent reinforcement schedule can be either fixed or variable. In the former a fixed time interval (FI) or a fixed number of responses (FR) can be reinforced. In fixed interval (FI) reinforcement, for example, students can receive free play for 30 minutes of work or study. In fixed ratio reinforcement the students can receive free play for correctly finishing 20 math problems. In business a similar contingency would exist for workers paid by the hour (FI) or by piece work (FR).

Variable schedules are contingencies where reinforcers occur irregularly and often randomly. In variable interval (VI) schedules the reinforcers occur after variable time periods. In variable ratio (VR) schedules reinforcers are delivered after a variable number of behaviors, as in playing a slot machine. Often variable schedules produce high rates of behavior which are very resistant to extinction and hence give the "compulsive" nature to gambling, for instance. The gambler cannot often "predict" when he will win and therefore a high rate of behavior is emitted.

In real life, schedules can become very complex and difficult to describe but their effects can often be observed in the rate of behavior produced. Subsequently, treatment implications of reinforcement schedules are very important. For example, in helping to reduce tantrums in children the therapist must guide the parents so as not to accidentally place the child on a variable schedule of social reinforcement (attention) for occasional tantrums, thereby actually increasing the rate.

Table 5–1 compares classical and operant conditioning.

TABLE 5–1.—COMPARISON OF CLASSICAL AND OPERANT CONDITIONING

CLASSICAL CONDITIONING	OPERANT CONDITIONING
Behavior affected is usually experienced as involuntary—for example, reflexes (knee jerk, salivation, eye blink), feelings (fear, anxiety).	Behavior affected may be either voluntary—for example, actions (bar press), thoughts (plans for action)—or involuntary.
Key events (unconditioned and conditioned stimuli) are presented to the organism.	Key events (reinforcement and punishment) are produced by the organism's behavior.
Those events elicit the behavior; that is, they directly evoke it.	Those events control the behavior; that is, they determine how often the organism emits it.
In the absence of key stimuli, the behavior does not occur.	In the absence of specific stimuli, the behavior does occur; the effect of discriminative stimuli is to alter its frequency.

Source: Lazerson Arlyne (ed.): *Psychology Today: An Introduction*, ed. 3. New York, CRM Books, 1975.

Behavioral Assessment

As is true of medical treatment in general, effective behavioral intervention is dependent on a careful evaluation of the patient and his problems.

Traditional psychotherapeutic assessment typically focuses on what is considered to be the patient's basic personality traits; his actions are assumed to be a function of these traits. By contrast, behavioral assessment is concerned with the individual's behavior in response to environmental conditions that are relevant to the presenting problem(s). Emphasis, therefore, is placed on what a person *does* in specific circumstances rather than on what a person *has* (traits, etc.).[27]

It is assumed that behavior evaluated in a properly conducted behavioral assessment is representative of a range of meaningful, valid situations. In testing for assertiveness responses, for example, the therapist must obtain an adequate sample of situations that might potentially call for such a response, often referred to as a functional situational analysis.

Goldfried and Davison have differentiated between those variables that are associated with the occurrence of maladaptive behavior and those that are relevant to the selection of appropriate therapeutic techniques.[28] The first set of variables indicates what must be manipulated in order to modify the behavior in question, whereas the second set provides information about how to bring about this change most effectively. In determining the variables associated with the undesirable or maladaptive behavior, they suggest that the following be examined:

1. The *antecedent stimuli* (events) that are related to the maladaptive behavior.—These can be stimuli that arouse emotional responses or that act as cues for triggering the onset of undesirable responses.
2. The *maladaptive behavior*.—One should focus on the specifics of the behavior such as its duration, frequency, and intensity. It is also useful to differentiate between those aspects of the behavior that appear to be classically conditioned and those that seem to be due to operant conditioning, a distinction that is often difficult.
3. *Consequent events.*—A majority of our everyday behaviors are influenced and maintained by their consequences or effects on the environment. Such consequent variables include attention, nonattention, praise, approval, and monetary rewards—in other words, common everyday environmental events that influence behavior.
4. *Organismic factors.*—By this is meant the physiological and cognitive state of the individual that affects the way in which he perceives and interprets antecedent and consequent events. Factors such as health, fatigue, use of drugs, the manner in which the patient labels his own behavior, and his self-expectations must all be considered.

Two procedures are generally used to collect these four kinds of behavioral information: the clinical interview and direct patient observation.

CLINICAL INTERVIEW.—By far the most frequently used assessment procedure is the interview. Although on-the-spot observation is most desirable, conditions often do not permit this. Sensitive, astute, and experienced clinicians of varied theoretical persuasions are likely to proceed in a very similar manner in many aspects of the interview. The behavior therapist, however, tends to focus on "here and now" matters that are relevant to the presenting problem(s), as opposed to the psychoanalytically oriented therapist who might delve more into the patient's distant past. There are many situations in which past historical data are important to the behavior therapist.

In the interview, efforts are made to focus in detail on antecedent events, the specifics of the behavioral problem, the consequences of the behavior, and the physiological and cognitive state of the individual. There is also an attempt to determine the patient's expectations and behavioral strengths as well as to arrive at mutually acceptable treatment goals. Finally, time is spent describing the treatment program to the patient. All of this must be done in a manner that allows the patient to express himself freely. Also, undue pressure on the patient, which might arouse defensiveness or resistance, must be avoided.

DIRECT OBSERVATION—Wherever possible, direct observation of the patient in real-life situations is the most useful assessment technique. The observer can be the therapist, a trained observer, a family member, a teacher, or the patient himself. Family members or teachers who are unfamiliar with the specialized procedures of observation may collect less complex but nevertheless valuable data. They are generally asked to record the patient's responses to situations and events, being careful to note antecedent and consequent events. Patients are often asked to observe specific behaviors of their own, for example, thoughts, impulses, or responses. This kind of data has proved to be extremely important and effective in assessment. Questionnaires have been developed to assist patients in the self-report process. These include a Fear Survey Schedule,[29] an assertiveness questionnaire,[30] a Reinforcement Survey Schedule,[31] and a Test Anxiety Behavior Scale.[32]

With the advent of sophisticated electronic equipment, physiological measures have been utilized as indicators of conditions not otherwise readily observed. Various biofeedback instruments allow both patient and therapist to monitor bodily functions continually.

Behavior Therapy Procedures

Although the behavior therapist has a wide assortment of therapeutic techniques at his disposal, there is a significant problem in relating the findings obtained in the evaluation to particular treatment strategies. Many of the decisions regarding the type of therapy to use are made on the basis òf clinical judgment and experience. Of course, the nature of a problem may dictate the therapeutic approach. Compulsive behaviors, for instance, are most amenable to response-prevention procedures. Problems of a sexual nature that are most readily resolved with a partner require alternate techniques. A study by Kanter indicates that for situations in which social anxiety is the principal problem, rational restructuring is more effective than desensitization.[33]

It is clear that much more research must be done before particular patient characteristics and behaviors can be matched to specific treatment strategies and techniques. As Paul has stated, the basic question that must be answered is: "*What* treatment, by *whom*, is most effective for *this* individual with *that* specific problem, and under *which* set of circumstances?"[34]

With these reservations in mind, we will proceed to a discussion of some of the major procedures used in behavior therapy along with their general application to various clinical problems (see also chap. 8).

RELAXATION.—It has long been known that relaxation counteracts anxiety. Considerable empirical evidence exists demonstrating that the physiological accompaniments of deep-muscle relaxation (including a reduction in heart rate and blood pressure, slower and deeper respiration) are, in general, the opposite of those found in anxiety states.[35-37] Behavior therapy has incorporated the anxiety-inhibiting effects of relaxation into its armamentarium and this procedure has become an effective and easily taught form of therapy. (Also see chap. 7.)

Persons are told that, in general, anxiety is incompatible with muscle relaxation. They are also informed about the general fatiguing effects of muscle tension and the enhanced muscle efficiency resulting from relaxation. Learning how to relax is equated with the learning of other motor acts, such as driving and playing tennis, in which a skill is acquired through practice over a period of time. Persons are reminded that this takes effort and time and they are encouraged to persevere.

The actual procedure may be taught in several ways. Jacobson devised a method that involves alternately tensing and relaxing various muscle groups throughout the body.[38] This helps the person become aware of what is going on in his musculature, something to which he has been inattentive for the most part. An abbreviated approach is based on the person "letting go" of various muscle groups rather than tensing and relaxing. If the person has complaints relating to a particular area of the body, the Jacobson method can be used to relax the muscle of that area.

Another method for teaching relaxation is through the use of hypnosis. Persons can activate hypnotically learned cues in order to become relaxed under specific circumstances, or they may merely utilize the hypnotic state as a means of learning general relaxation. When a person becomes reasonably proficient, relaxation can be incorporated into other techniques in an overall treatment program. These techniques include systematic desensitization, assertiveness training, behavior rehearsal, and self-management.

SYSTEMATIC DESENSITIZATION.—This is a technique that uses deep-muscle relaxation as a means of reducing anxiety in conditions associated with high levels of anxiety, such as phobias. Wolpe is generally credited with developing an approach that combines deep-muscle relaxation with imagined scenes of the phobic situation, usually presented in a hierarchical order from least to most stressful.[20] He found that a person's ability to *imagine* such scenes without anxiety generalized to real-life phobic situations.

A careful behavioral assessment is necessary to determine the critical variables involved in constructing the hierarchy of imagined scenes. The therapist, with the patient's assistance, develops a list of incidents related to the phobia which will form the basis for the mental images the patient will be asked to consider. In order to facilitate arranging the images in an appropriately graded sequence, a scale based on a subjective rating of the degree of experienced discomfort for each image is developed. Relative values of 0–100 are used in the scale, where 0 indicates the total absence of anxiety or fear and 100 represents the worst anxiety ever experienced. Ordering the list of images (or scenes) should ideally provide an equally spaced sequence of experiences to which the patient would ordinarily respond with increasing anxiety. In practice, however, the items often need to be rearranged, new items included, and/or some deleted. The following is an example of a hierarchy for a patient with a phobia for driving. (The numbers in parentheses are subjective ratings of anxiety reported by the patient in the assessment phase.)

Imagine:
1. You are sitting alone in your car with the ignition turned off. (10)
2. You switch on the engine but leave the brake set and the transmission in neutral with the engine idling. (20)
3. The engine is idling quietly. You release the brake and put the car in reverse, slowly backing out to the end of your driveway, where you stop and set the brake again. (35)
4. You now release the brake and fully back out into the street. You put the car in forward and move at a slow speed to the end of the block, where you stop. (45)
5. You decide to continue around the block. You turn left. There is no traffic and you approach the next intersection, where you stop. Stay loose. Easy does it. You make a left turn again and are paralleling your street on the home leg. (60)
6. You are more than halfway home. You slow down at the next intersection. (60) There's no traffic so you turn into your street. You approach your house and now pull into your driveway, stop the car, set the brake, put the car in park, and release your seat belt. (20)

Similar hierarchies are utilized to extend the driving range. In carrying out this kind of desensitization, the patient is asked to be fully relaxed and is instructed to imagine the scene as clearly as he can. The scene is presented for about 10–15 seconds with approximately a 30–50-second interval between scenes. Some clinicians instruct the patient to signal as soon as he feels discomfort or anxiety so that consideration of the scene can be terminated, relaxation resumed, and then the scene again considered. Such repetitive exposure usually results in the patient being able to imagine the scene without experiencing fear or anxiety. Other clinicians feel that it is important for the patient to learn to actively cope with stress situations. Thus, when the patient signals that he experiences tension or anxiety, he is encouraged to try to relieve it while continuing to think about the scene rather than escape it by terminating the scene. He is instructed in various self-control measures to use at that time. This modification has proved to facilitate the learning of coping mechanisms that can be used in circumstances other than the specific phobia being treated.

After the patient works through the various scenes without anxiety or fear, he is encouraged to transfer this to the same situations in real life. Often patients need to be convinced that they can now do in fact what they have so long avoided, since they feel that desensitization may not be adequate to control anxiety in the real-life situation. However, desensitization results in a markedly improved ability to tolerate the previously phobic situation, and with encouragement most individuals attempt real-life exposure to the situation, eventually culminating in functioning without fear.

Flooding is a variant of systematic desensitization which can take place either in one's imagination (implosion) or in vivo, the latter being preferable. Here the patient is exposed (either by imagining scenes or by direct contact) to the fear-evoking situation and is urged to remain until the fear subsides. In most instances in which people continue to expose themselves to these situations in real life but still experience fear, it is because they escape from the situation before there is time for the fear to subside. Such escape behavior actually maintains the fear, since avoidance or escape from anxiety-evoking circumstances reinforces or strengthens anxiety on future occasions. On the other hand, the reduction in fear that comes with "riding it out" and not leaving the situation acts to reinforce approach responses. Rapid reduction in anxiety is often experienced following this procedure but the technique is utilized *only* with the full consent of the informed patient.

INTERPERSONAL RESPONSE TRAINING.—These procedures are designed to help people who have difficulty dealing with others, individually or collectively, because of deficiencies in social skills. The essential therapeutic task involves selecting critical situations and training the patient in socially approved and effective behavior. The emphasis is on the patient learning both *what* and *how* to respond appropriately. The procedures described below contain common elements and are frequently used within the same treatment program.

BEHAVIOR REHEARSAL.—This term is used interchangeably with role-playing and refers to the acting-out or simulation of real-life problems in the consulting room under the observation and direction of the therapist. It may easily be recognized that such an approach can deal with a wide range of situations including those involving health as well as business, industry, education, and other areas. This technique differs from another simulation procedure, psychodrama, where the primary goal is to reveal and clarify the emotional blocks that cause difficulties in interpersonal relationships.

In addition to providing an opportunity to practice appropriate behaviors, role-playing benefits the patient as a result of the desensitization and shaping properties of the procedure. Exposure to simulated situations that cause the patient difficulty in real life acts in much the same manner as does the systematic desensitization procedure described earlier. The step-by-step inclusion of more and more complex components of a new behavior in simulation is, in effect, a shaping process that gradually allows the patient to develop a new mode of responding to others.

The goals of this procedure are to provide

information and develop new behaviors, through the use of varying means. One approach involves having the patient interact with a therapeutic assistant. This allows for controlled situations or scenarios to be presented, and it also gives the patient the experience of interacting with someone with whom he has difficulty, for example, a person of the opposite sex. For instance, using a dating scenario, a female assistant could inform the male patient of her impressions of his efforts to start a conversation, such as the nature of the eye contact and the strength of voice.

Modeling techniques can be very useful in giving informational feedback about target skills. Using the dating scenario as an example, the therapist could "model" for the patient a more effective way of opening a conversation.

Another effective approach to behavior rehearsal is through the use of video and/or audio playback. Allowing the patient to see and hear himself is an ideal way to effect change, and this technique is a good time-saving device.

ASSERTIVENESS TRAINING.—Teaching an individual to attain his goals effectively in a socially approved manner is frequently done within a behavior rehearsal format. In assertiveness training, people are taught both how to stand up for their rights and how to express positive and negative feelings comfortably. A distinction is made between behaving assertively and behaving aggressively; the latter term implies some reduction in self-control with the expression of anger or hostility.

A lack of assertiveness may result from poor self-esteem, fear of disapproval or other negative outcomes, and lack of knowledge of when or how to assert oneself. Often the nature of a situation determines how a person responds; we all recognize that some situations foster a passive approach, while others result in assertive behavior. The crux of the issue, of course, is to what extent one is able to act in one's own best interests in a given set of circumstances.

Techniques such as desensitization to diminish anxiety, cognitive restructuring to correct false assumptions or self-esteem problems, and relaxation are used, either alone or in conjunction with behavior rehearsal, in assertiveness training. A group setting is useful in dealing with assertiveness problems because it readily allows for feedback as well as imitation of the assertive behavior of other group members.

SOCIAL SKILLS TRAINING.—This form of therapy is designed to help remedy behavioral problems involving difficulties in dealing with everyday types of interactions with such individuals as family members, coworkers, teachers, and members of the opposite sex. As with some of the previously mentioned problems, there are different ways of approaching such social skill deficits, although they are particularly well suited to behavior rehearsal procedures in a group setting. Here, too, the use of audio and/or video feedback and therapeutic assistants is often therapeutically helpful.

Specific training is given in what to do in certain situations as well as how to do it. Assuming that the principal problem is skill deficit, and that the apprehension or anxiety accompanying social interactions is secondary to this deficit, social skill training can be highly effective and relatively brief in duration. While simulation procedures are important in training, ultimately the patient must transfer or generalize learned skills to the real world. It is the responsibility of the therapist to suggest a graded sequence of real-life experiences for the patient to deal with to maximize his success and to provide him with encouragement, support, and follow-up assistance.

AVERSION THERAPY.—Aversion therapy attempts to suppress or eliminate undesirable behaviors or emotional responses by presenting a noxious stimulus contingent on the appearance of the behavior or response. Although Wolpe considers this to be a special case of reciprocal inhibition,[39] most workers in this field see it essentially as a punishment paradigm.[40,41] Prior to using such an uncomfortable procedure, the therapist must be assured that the behavior in question is not being maintained by or resulting from conditions amenable to other forms of treatment. Most frequently, this approach is used in the treatment of long-standing conditions over which the patient has little control, such as compulsions, fetishes, alcoholism, homosexuality, voyeurism, exhibitionism, smoking, and obesity. The treatment is usually relatively brief, uses varied stimulus modalities, and frequently requires ongoing booster sessions to maintain the benefits. Although patients often experience anxiety or apprehension during the active stimulation phase of treatment, they later generally report improvement in their problem; they are no longer concerned with or interested in their former attractions and anxiety is reduced in the presence of these attractions. With some problems, such as sexual disorders or obesity, it is not enough merely to suppress the old, inappropriate behaviors; the therapist must also be concerned with providing or teaching the patient new, more appropriate responses.

A commonly used and highly efficient stimulus modality is electric or faradic stimulation. This involves a shock source, usually battery powered and of low voltage and amperage, which delivers a brief, uncomfortable, nonconvulsive shock to the forearm or fingertips. Since such noxious stimulation may possibly result in anger, resistance, or avoidance of treatment, the therapist must be very sensitive to both the technical and the interpersonal aspects of this form of treatment. Of course, the patient is fully informed of the nature of the procedure and must give his approval and cooperation before aversion techniques are used.

Chemical agents, such as amphetamine and apomorphine, have been used to cause nausea—a noxious stimulus used in the treatment of alcoholism or certain types of food fads. Unpleasant odors (such as from hydrogen sulfide or valeric acid) and even curare-like drugs have been used in aversive therapy. While these have been successful in many instances, they are not so effective as electric shock from the standpoint of efficiency of conditioning. Control of the intensity of the stimulus, the time between its administration and effect, and its side effects are all very important in effective conditioning.

The noxious stimulus can also be administered while the patient imagines himself to be engaged in certain behavior or in the presence of actual objects such as photographs of fetishes. In general, the aversive stimulus is presented contingent with the undesired behavior. As noted earlier, the schedule of presentation must take into account the need to maintain long-standing avoidance of the formerly attractive but undesirable behavior in the absence of punishment; hence, a continuous or 100% schedule is used initially, followed by an intermittent schedule. Ambulatory treatment in real-life situations is sometimes important, particularly in dealing with the "urges" or cognitive elements of an attraction. Here, portable shock units or chemical vials are useful. Where appropriate, aversive therapy has proved to be very effective in the treatment of a wide variety of problems that in the past were considered to be intractable.

Another form of aversion therapy, developed by Cautela, is *covert sensitization*, which involves presenting a verbally induced noxious stimulus contingent on an imagined behavior.[42] This approach depends on the ability to elicit, through suggestion, ideation that is highly repulsive to the subject (the noxious stimulus), thus resulting in an adverse emotional reaction. Examples of this verbally induced noxious ideation are nausea and vomiting, excrement, or vermin. When this ideation is associated with a behavior that is undesirable, the behavior will tend to diminish. Of course, the aversive imagery selected is dependent on the idiosyncratic response of each individual. This approach has been useful in dealing with problems such as inappropriate sexual behaviors, alcoholism, and obesity.

Typically, during covert sensitization, an occurrence of the undesirable behavior results in the repulsive consequences, whereas cessation of the undesirable behavior and/or avoidance results in a return to the undisturbed state. This approach is often a preferable alternative to the more physically painful methods of aversive therapy.

COGNITIVE BEHAVIOR MODIFICATION.—In its early history, behavior therapy focused primarily on readily observable behavior. Thinking and mental processes in general were not considered to be amenable to this form of therapy. Although some behavior therapists still reject the notion that cognitive behavior modification is a legitimate extension of behavior therapy, this procedure is one of the newest areas of interest and activity. We will briefly discuss several methods by which cognitive processes can be modified to influence a person's attitudes, expectations, and beliefs; thereby helping him to develop more control over his behavior.

COGNITIVE RESTRUCTURING.—Ellis was one of the pioneers who focused attention on the importance of a patient's thoughts or self-statements in the understanding of his behavioral problems.[43] He developed rational-emotive therapy (RET), which views emotional problems as stemming from the irrational way in which people view their world and the assumptions derived from these perceptions. These assumptions result in self-defeating thoughts or statements that give rise to negative emotional reactions and ineffectual behaviors that, in turn, substantiate the original self-defeating thought. Thus, a cycle of events is established to maintain the undesirable behavior.

The therapist's tasks are (1) to help the patient to discover the situations and events that initiate this cycle, (2) to make him aware of the thoughts and assumptions that result in disturbed affect, and (3) to work with him in order to change his irrational beliefs and thought patterns. The rational-emotive therapist attempts to get the person to recognize that his problems derive from a faulty belief system by using various means such as challenging him and engaging him in Socratic dialogue, rational analysis, and behavioral assignments.

Different therapists emphasize different aspects of the patient's thought process. Beck focuses on their faulty thinking style by attempting to have them become aware of distortion in their thought patterns.[44] The attention of the patient is directed toward the occurrence of specific self-statements in particular situations, and then he is asked to test their validity. An analysis of his belief system is made; it is carefully examined and subsequently altered.

D'Zurilla and Goldfried focus on what they consider to be deficits in the patient's problem-solving ability.[45] They attempt to have the patient learn how to identify problems, develop various alternative solutions, select a tentative solution, and test the efficacy of that solution. The benefit of this approach is that it teaches the individual a variety of coping skills, which he can use to address a wide range of problems.

STRESS TRAINING.—The goal of this technique is to develop the individual's ability to deal with a wide variety of stress situations.[25] There are three phases to it: the first provides the patient with an understanding of the nature of his stressful responses; the second phase teaches the patient various behavioral and cognitive coping skills; and the final segment exposes him to a variety of stress situations wherein he can practice and refine his newly developed skills.

The initial or educational phase of stress inoculation training requires a behavior assessment of the patient's overt and covert responses to stress. Efforts are made to help the patient understand his thoughts and feelings while under stress. The stressful problem is conceptualized as being associated with affective or emotional as well as cognitive processes. The patient is informed of the priming or initiating quality of his self-statements and told that treatment will involve helping him control his emotional reactions as well as changing critical self-statements. He is also helped to see that his responses to stress progress through several phases rather than being an all-or-none reaction. These phases include preparing for a stress situation, dealing with it, and recovering from the stress.

The actual coping skills are taught in phase II, the rehearsal phase. Physical techniques such as muscle relaxation and deep, slow breathing are used as well as cognitive skills such as positive or appropriate self-statements. Examples of these kinds of self-statements are provided. Information is collected regarding the specific problem to be treated. Techniques such as thought-stopping are used to prevent or deflect negative or intrusive thoughts. The patient is urged to reflect on his performance, monitor his progress, and reinforce his efforts. Overall a positive, practical, problem-oriented approach is taught.

During the application phase, the patient practices his new skills and becomes more proficient and confident in their use. Such training has been found to be extremely beneficial in developing the attitude of "I can manage," which is of great benefit in all kinds of life situations and results in feelings of self-confidence.

The stress training technique outlined above has been used successfully with specific problems such as the control of anger, pain, and phobias.

In keeping with the concept that our thoughts initiate and influence attitudes, expectations, and overt behavior, *mental rehearsal techniques* have also been useful in helping people deal effectively with stress. Patients are encouraged to imagine various stressful or anxiety-laden tasks prior to engaging in them in real life. They are instructed to utilize relaxation and breathing techniques and positive self-statements as they talk themselves through their performance. While somewhat similar to systematic desensitization, the benefits of having patients actively engage in positive coping behaviors, either by giving themselves instructions or by imagining themselves involved in an action, provide a significant added dimension. This type of approach has recently become popular in training athletes and in learning athletic skills in general.

A technique similar to mental rehearsal called *self-instruction* has been found to be extremely useful, particularly in assisting children to deal with their impulses or to learn how to solve problems or perform new tasks. This essentially involves teaching the patient to alter his problem-solving styles by (1) trying to understand the task or experience in cognitive terms, (2) producing strategies and mediators for coping, and (3) using these mediators to guide, evaluate, and control his behavior. In effect, the patient is taught to ask himself what is required of him, to think how to go about it, and then to act while monitoring his performance.

Self-instruction techniques can be used fruitfully with socially deficient subjects, impulsive children, and schizophrenics.

THOUGHT-STOPPING.—The final technique of cognitive behavior therapy to be discussed is thought-stopping. Initially devised to deal with obsessive ruminations, it has been found to be equally effective with nonobsessive or neurotic thoughts. The procedure involves training the patient to interrupt the undesirable thought by subvocally shouting "stop" to himself whenever the thought appears. Persistent interruption of the intruding thought results in its gradual weakening until it is no longer disruptive. It is important that the patient initiate the thought-stopping as early as possible in the process of intrusion. On the surface this appears to be a simplistic technique and perhaps because of this patients frequently either do not attempt it or fail to follow through on it persistently. Commitment to the process and persistence in its application usually have beneficial results.

SUMMARY

The two most influential theories of behavior, psychoanalytic and learning theories, differ greatly in their explanation of normal and abnormal psychological function. The former is concerned primarily with intrapsychic phenomena, whereas the latter focuses mainly on events in the environment. According to Freud's topographic model, the psychic apparatus is divided into conscious and unconscious areas. Material in the unconscious, though not readily accessible to the person, can be the cause of psychic conflict. According to his structural model, mental function is due to the interaction of the three components of the mind—id, ego, and superego—which operate within these areas. There normally is a homeostatic balance among these components; if this is disrupted by internal conflict or external stress, mental dysfunction may occur. In addition, emotional trauma early in life, during the psychosexual stages of personality development, may leave psychological scars that can interfere with normal mental function later.

Learning theory attributes behavior, both normal and abnormal, to a process by which the environment "teaches" the individual to act in a certain way. Thus, by carefully examining the events coming *before* and those coming *after* a behavior, one should be able to identify the factors responsible for it. In classical (Pavlovian) conditioning, the learning process depends on the antecedent events; in operant conditioning, the process is influenced by the consequent events.

The approaches to the therapy for psychological dysfunction taken by psychoanalytic and learning theories are quite different, as one might expect considering their opposing views of pathogenesis. The former tries to help the patient understand and resolve his unconscious conflicts and develop more adaptive ways of handling the anxiety and emotional distress they cause. The latter attempts to have the patient decrease maladaptive patterns of behavior and develop more adaptive ones.

REFERENCES

1. Freud S.: *Civilization and Its Discontents*. New York, W.W. Norton & Company, Inc., 1962.
2. Skinner B.F.: *Beyond Freedom and Dignity*. New York, Alfred A. Knopf, Inc., 1971.
3. Brenner C.: *An Elementary Textbook of Psychoanalysis*, Rev. ed. New York, International Universities Press, 1963.
4. Freud S.: *The Ego and the Mechanisms of Defense*. New York, International Universities Press, 1946.
5. Freud S.: Introductory lectures on psychoanalysis (1956), in Rothgeb C.L. (ed.): *Abstracts of the Standard Edition of the Complete Psychological Works of Sigmund Freud*. New York, International Universities Press, 1973.
6. Freud S.: The ego and the id (1923), in Strachey J. (ed.): *The Standard Edition of the Complete Psychological Works of Sigmund Freud*. London, Hogarth Press, 1961, vol. XIX.
7. Freud S.: Inhibitions symptoms and anxiety (1926), in Strachey J. (ed.): *The Standard Edition of the Complete Psychological Works of Sigmund Freud*. London, Hogarth Press, 1959, vol. XX.
8. Freud S.: New introductory lectures on psychoanalysis (1933), in Rothgeb D.L. (ed.): *Abstracts of the Standard Edition of the Complete Psychological Works of Sigmund Freud*. New York, International Universities Press, 1973.
9. Meissner W.W.: Theories of personality; and Nemiah, J.C.: Dynamic basis of psychopathology, in Nicholi, A.M. (ed.): *The Harvard Guide to Modern Psychiatry*. Cambridge, Mass., Belknap Press of Harvard University Press, 1978.
10. Meissner W.W., et al.: Classical psychoanalysis, in Freedman A.M., et al. (eds.): *Comprehensive Textbook of Psychiatry*. Baltimore, Williams & Wilkins Co., 1975.
11. Pavlov I.P.: *Conditioned Reflexes*. London, Oxford University Press, 1927.
12. Thorndike E.L.: *The Psychology of Learning. (Educational Psychology, II)*. New York, Teachers College, 1913.
13. Watson J.B., Raynor P.: Conditioned emotional reactions. *J. Exp. Psychol.* 3:1, 1920.
14. Jones M.C.: A laboratory study of fear: The case of Peter. *J. Genet. Psychol.* 31:308, 1924.
15. Krasnogorski N.I.: The conditioned reflexes and children's neuroses. *Am. J. Dis. Child.* 30:754, 1925.
16. Kantorovich N.V.: An attempt at associative reflex therapy in alcoholism. *Psychol. Abstr.* No. 4282, 1930.
17. Guthrie E.R.: *The Psychology of Human Learning*. New York, Harper & Bros., 1935.
18. Skinner B.F.: *The Behavior of Organisms*. New York, Appleton-Century-Crofts, 1938.
19. Wolpe J.: *An Approach to the Problem of Neurosis Based on the Conditioned Response*, thesis. University of the Witwatersrand, 1948.
20. Wolpe J.: *Psychotherapy by Reciprocal Inhibition*. Stanford, Calif., Stanford University Press, 1958.
21. Salter A.: *Conditioned Reflex Therapy*. New York, Creative Age, 1949.
22. Eysenck H.J.: The effects of psychotherapy:

An evaluation. *J. Consult. Clin. Psychol.* 16:319, 1952.
23. Skinner B.F., Lindsley O.R.: *Studies in Behavior Therapy*. Status reports II and III. Office of Naval Research Contract N5 ori-7662.
24. Bandura A.: A social learning interpretation of psychological dysfunction, in London P., Rosenhan D. (eds.): *Foundations of Abnormal Psychology*. New York, Holt, Rinehart and Winston, Inc., 1963.
25. Meichenbaum D.H.: *Cognitive Behavior Modification*. Morristown, N.J., General Learning Press, 1974.
26. Mahoney M.J.: *Cognition and Behavior Modification*. Cambridge, Mass., Ballinger Publishing Company, 1974.
27. Mischel W.: *Personality and Assessment*. New York, John Wiley & Sons, Inc., 1968.
28. Goldfried M., Davison G.C.: *Clinical Behavior Therapy*. New York, Holt, Rinehart and Winston, Inc., 1976.
29. Geer J.H.: The development of a scale to measure fear. *Behav. Res. Ther.* 3:45, 1965.
30. McFall R.M., Lillesand D.V.: Behavior rehearsal with modeling and coaching in assertive training. *J. Abnorm. Psychol.* 77:313, 1971.
31. Cautela J.R., Kastenbaum R.A.: Reinforcement survey schedule for use in therapy, training and research. *Psychol. Rep.* 20:1115, 1967.
32. Suinn R.M.: The STABS, a measure of test anxiety for behavior therapy: Normative data. *Behav. Res. Ther.* 7:335, 1969.
33. Kanter N.J.: *Comparison of Self-control Desensitization and Systematic Rational Restructuring in the Reduction of Interpersonal Anxiety*, doctoral dissertation. State University of New York at Stony Brook, 1975.
34. Paul G.L.: Insight versus desensitization in psychotherapy two years after termination. *J. Consult. Clin. Psychol.* 31:333, 1967.
35. Jacobson E.: Variation of blood pressure with skeletal muscle tension and relaxation. *Ann. Intern. Med.* 12:1194, 1939.
36. Paul G.L.: Physiological effects of relaxation training and hypnotic suggestions. *J. Abnorm. Psychol.* 74:425, 1969.
37. Benson J.: *The Relaxation Response*. New York, William Morrow & Co., Inc., 1975.
38. Jacobson E.: *Progressive Relaxation*. Chicago, The University of Chicago Press, 1938.
39. Wolpe J.: *The Practice of Behavior Therapy*, ed. 2. Elmsford, N.Y., Pergamon Press, Inc., 1973.
40. Rachman S., Teasdale J.: *Aversion Therapy and Behavior Disorders*. London, Routledge & Kegan Paul, 1969.
41. Kushner M., Sandler J.: Aversion therapy and the concept of punishment. *Behav. Res. Ther.* 4:179, 1966.
42. Cautela J.: Treatment of compulsive behavior by covert sensitization. *Psychol. Record* 16:33, 1966.
43. Ellis A.: *Reason and Emotion in Psychotherapy*. New York, Lyle Stuart, Inc., 1962.
44. Beck A.: *Cognitive Therapy and Emotional Disorders*. New York, International Universities Press, 1976.
45. D'Zurilla T., Goldfried M.: Problem solving and behavior modification. *J. Abnorm. Psychol.* 78:107, 1971.

6 / The Classification and Evaluation of Psychological Dysfunction

SANFORD JACOBSON, M.D., RICHARD P. TOISTER, Ph.D., and JONATHAN J. BRAUNSTEIN, M.D.

UNDERSTANDING DISORDERS of human behavior requires the use of a system of classification.[1,2] Such a system is crucial to a scientific approach to the evaluation and diagnosis of these conditions. The initial step in the development of a classification scheme usually involves establishing guidelines that will help to distinguish between "normal" and "abnormal" behavior—a separation that is not always clear-cut.

WHAT CONSTITUTES PSYCHOLOGICAL DYSFUNCTION?

Several models have been used to help define normality and abnormality with respect to behavior that may appear to lie outside the accepted range. The most widely used of these, the medical model, takes the view that normal psychological function can be defined as an absence of symptoms and signs that cause discomfort to the person or to those about him. Based on the presence of specific clinical manifestations, a list of disorders can be made which can then be divided into categories, each representing a form of abnormal mental function. A standard classification system based on the medical model is found in the *Diagnostic and Statistical Manual of Mental Disorders (DSM)*.[1] The second edition of the *DSM* has been in use since 1968; a third edition has recently been published. Table 6-1 gives the major diagnostic categories listed in the current edition, *DSM-III*. Not all investigators agree with this scheme, and recently there has been discussion concerning the validity of such descriptive systems and the effects of labeling in general.[3,4]

Many of the current classifications of abnormal psychological function are based on a psychosocial model. Among these approaches are the Freudian or psychoanalytic and neo-Freudian theories,[5] social learning theory,[6] and humanistic theory as described by Rogers.[7] The psychosocial model attributes psychological dysfunction to disturbances in the interaction between an individual and his social environment. Thus, mental disorders can be classified in terms of pathogenetic factors such as abnormalities in interpersonal relationships, problems in patterns of learning, and coping with environmental stress.

Regardless of what model one subscribes to, it is clear that a differentiation between normal and abnormal mental function is in the last analysis made on a practical basis, that is, the effect of the behavior in question on the individual and those about him.[8,9] Four questions can be asked to determine whether or not a problem of abnormal behavior exists:

1. Is the behavior frequently associated with an anatomical, physiological, or biochemical abnormality in the brain?
2. Is the behavior associated with suffering, discomfort, or disability in the view of the great majority of the individuals exhibiting it?
3. Is the behavior viewed as an annoyance or a discomfort by the great majority of individuals who would come into contact with individuals who have the behavior?
4. Is the behavior, although acceptable or

TABLE 6–1.—DSM-III CLASSIFICATION: AXES I AND II CATEGORIES AND CODES

All official DSM-III codes and terms are included in ICD-9-CM. However, in order to differentiate those DSM-III categories that use the same ICD-9-CM codes, unofficial non-ICD-9-CM codes are provided in parentheses for use when greater specificity is necessary.

The long dashes indicate the need for a fifth-digit subtype or other qualifying term.

DISORDERS USUALLY FIRST EVIDENT IN INFANCY, CHILDHOOD OR ADOLESCENCE

Mental retardation
Code in fifth digit: 1 = with other behavioral symptoms (requiring attention or treatment and that are not part of another disorder), 0 = without other behavioral symptoms.
317.0(x)   Mild mental retardation, _____
318.0(x)   Moderate mental retardation, _____
318.1(x)   Severe mental retardation, _____
318.2(x)   Profound mental retardation, _____
319.0(x)   Unspecified mental retardation, _____

Attention deficit disorder
314.01   with hyperactivity
314.00   without hyperactivity
314.80   residual type

Conduct disorder
312.00   undersocialized, aggressive
312.10   undersocialized, nonaggressive
312.23   socialized, aggressive
312.21   socialized, nonaggressive
312.90   atypical

Anxiety disorders of childhood or adolescence
309.21   Separation anxiety disorder
313.21   Avoidant disorder of childhood or adolescence
313.00   Overanxious disorder

Other disorders of infancy, childhood or adolescence
313.89   Reactive attachment disorder of infancy
313.22   Schizoid disorder of childhood or adolescence
313.23   Elective mutism
313.81   Oppositional disorder
313.82   Identity disorder

Eating disorders
307.10   Anorexia nervosa
307.51   Bulimia
307.52   Pica
307.53   Rumination disorder of infancy
307.50   Atypical eating disorder

Stereotyped movement disorders
307.21   Transient tic disorder
307.22   Chronic motor tic disorder
307.23   Tourette's disorder
307.20   Atypical tic disorder
307.30   Atypical stereotyped movement disorder

Other disorders with physical manifestations
307.00   Stuttering
307.60   Functional enuresis
307.70   Functional encopresis
307.45   Sleepwalking disorder
307.46   Sleep terror disorder (307.49)

Pervasive developmental disorders
Code in fifth digit: 0 = full syndrome present, 1 = residual state.
299.0x   Infantile autism, _____
299.9x   Childhood onset pervasive developmental disorder, _____
299.8x   Atypical, _____

Specific developmental disorders
Note: These are coded on Axis II.
315.00   Developmental reading disorder
315.10   Developmental arithmetic disorder
315.31   Developmental language disorder
315.39   Developmental articulation disorder
315.50   Mixed specific developmental disorder
315.90   Atypical specific developmental disorder

ORGANIC MENTAL DISORDERS
Section 1. Organic mental disorders whose etiology or pathophysiological process is listed below (taken from the mental disorders section of ICD-9-CM).

Dementias arising in the senium and presenium
   Primary degenerative dementia, senile onset,
290.30   with delirium
290.20   with delusions
290.21   with depression
290.00   uncomplicated
Code in fifth digit:
1 = with delirium, 2 = with delusions, 3 = with depression, 0 = uncomplicated.
290.1x   Primary degenerative dementia, presenile onset, _____
290.4x   Multi-infarct dementia, _____

Substance-induced
   Alcohol
303.00   intoxication
291.40   idiosyncratic intoxication
291.80   withdrawal
291.00   withdrawal delirium
291.30   hallucinosis
291.10   amnestic disorder
Code severity of dementia in fifth digit: 1 = mild, 2 = moderate, 3 = severe, 0 = unspecified.
291.2x   Dementia associated with alcoholism, _____

   Barbiturate or similarly acting sedative or hypnotic
305.40   intoxication (327.00)
292.00   withdrawal (327.01)
292.00   withdrawal delirium (327.02)
292.83   amnestic disorder (327.04)

(continued)

Opioid
305.50 intoxication (327.10)
292.00 withdrawal (327.11)

Cocaine
305.60 intoxication (327.20)

Amphetamine or similarly acting sympathomimetic
305.70 intoxication (327.30)
292.81 delirium (327.32)
292.11 delusional disorder (327.35)
292.00 withdrawal (327.31)

Phencyclidine (PCP) or similarly acting arylcyclohexylamine
305.90 intoxication (327.40)
292.81 delirium (327.42)
292.90 mixed organic mental disorder (327.49)

Hallucinogen
305.30 hallucinosis (327.56)
292.11 delusional disorder (327.55)
292.84 affective disorder (327.57)

Cannabis
305.20 intoxication (327.60)
292.11 delusional disorder (327.65)

Tobacco
292.00 withdrawal (327.71)

Caffeine
305.90 intoxication (327.80)

Other or unspecified substance
305.90 intoxication (327.90)
292.00 withdrawal (327.91)
292.81 delirium (327.92)
292.82 dementia (327.93)
292.83 amnestic disorder (327.94)
292.11 delusional disorder (327.95)
292.12 hallucinosis (327.96)
292.84 affective disorder (327.97)
292.89 personality disorder (327.98)
292.90 atypical or mixed organic mental disorder (327.99)

Section 2. Organic brain syndromes whose etiology or pathophysiological process is either noted as an additional diagnosis from outside the mental disorders section of ICD-9-CM or is unknown.

293.00 Delirium
294.10 Dementia
294.00 Amnestic syndrome
293.81 Organic delusional syndrome
293.82 Organic hallucinosis
293.83 Organic affective syndrome
310.10 Organic personality syndrome
294.80 Atypical or mixed organic brain syndrome

SUBSTANCE USE DISORDERS

Code in fifth digit: 1 = continuous, 2 = episodic, 3 = in remission, 0 = unspecified.

305.0x Alcohol abuse, _____
303.9x Alcohol dependence (Alcoholism), _____
305.4x Barbiturate or similarly acting sedative or hypnotic abuse,
304,1x Barbiturate or similarly acting sedative or hypnotic dependence, _____
305.5x Opioid abuse, _____
304.0x Opioid dependence, _____
305.6x Cocaine abuse, _____
305.7x Amphetamine or similarly acting sympathomimetic abuse, _____
304.4x Amphetamine or similarly acting sympathomimetic dependence, _____
305.9x Phencyclidine (PCP) or similarly acting arylcyclohexylamine abuse, _____(328.4x)
305.3x Hallucinogen abuse, _____
305.2x Cannabis abuse, _____
304.3x Cannabis dependence, _____
305.1x Tobacco dependence, _____
305.9x Other, mixed or unspecified substance abuse, _____

304.6x Other specified substance dependence, _____
304.9x Unspecified substance dependence, _____
304.7x Dependence on combination of opioid and other nonalcoholic substance, _____
304.8x Dependence on combination of substances, excluding opioids and alcohol, _____

SCHIZOPHRENIC DISORDERS

Code in fifth digit: 1 = subchronic, 2 = chronic, 3 = subchronic with acute exacerbation, 4 = chronic with acute exacerbation, 5 = in remission, 0 = unspecified.

Schizophrenia,
295.1x disorganized, _____
295.2x catatonic, _____
295.3x paranoid, _____
295.9x undifferentiated, _____
295.6x residual, _____

PARANOID DISORDERS

297.10 Paranoia
297.30 Shared paranoid disorder
298.30 Acute paranoid disorder
297.90 Atypical paranoid disorder

PSYCHOTIC DISORDERS NOT ELSEWHERE CLASSIFIED

295.40 Schizophreniform disorder
298.80 Brief reactive psychosis
295.70 Schizoaffective disorder
298.90 Atypical psychosis

(continued)

TABLE 6–1.—DSM-III CLASSIFICATION: AXES I AND II CATEGORIES AND CODES (CONT.)

All official DSM-III codes and terms are included in ICD-9-CM. However, in order to differentiate those DSM-III categories that use the same ICD-9-CM codes, unofficial non-ICD-9-CM codes are provided in parentheses for use when greater specificity is necessary.

The long dashes indicate the need for a fifth-digit subtype or other qualifying term.

NEUROTIC DISORDERS: These are included in Affective, Anxiety, Somatoform, Dissociative and Psychosexual Disorders. In order to facilitate the identification of the categories that in DSM-II were grouped together in the class of Neuroses, the DSM-II terms are included separately in parentheses after the corresponding categories. These DSM-II terms are included in ICD-9-CM and therefore are acceptable as alternatives to the recommended DSM-III terms that precede them.

AFFECTIVE DISORDERS
Major affective disorders

Code major depressive episode in fifth digit: 6 = in remission, 4 = with psychotic features (the unofficial non-ICD-9-CM fifth digit 7 may be used instead to indicate that the psychotic features are mood-incongruent), 3 = with melancholia, 2 = without melancholia, 0 = unspecified.

Code manic episode in fifth digit: 6 = in remission, 4 = with psychotic features (the unofficial non-ICD-9-CM fifth digit 7 may be used instead to indicate that the psychotic features are mood-incongruent), 2 = without psychotic features, 0 = unspecified.

Bipolar disorder,
296.6x mixed, _____
296.4x manic, _____
296.5x depressed, _____

Major depression,
296.2x single episode, _____
296.3x recurrent, _____

Other specific affective disorders
301.13 Cyclothymic disorder
300.40 Dysthymic disorder (or Depressive neurosis)

Atypical affective disorders
296.70 Atypical bipolar disorder
296.82 Atypical depression

ANXIETY DISORDERS

Phobic disorders (or Phobic neuroses)
300.21 Agoraphobia with panic attacks
300.22 Agoraphobia without panic attacks
300.23 Social phobia
300.29 Simple phobia

Anxiety states (or Anxiety neuroses)
300.01 Panic disorder
300.02 Generalized anxiety disorder
300.30 Obsessive compulsive disorder (or Obsessive compulsive neurosis)

Post-traumatic stress disorder
308.30 acute
309.81 chronic or delayed
300.00 Atypical anxiety disorder

SOMATOFORM DISORDERS

300.81 Somatization disorder
300.11 Conversion disorder (or Hysterical neurosis, conversion type)
307.80 Psychogenic pain disorder
300.70 Hypochondriasis (or Hypochondriacal neurosis)
300.70 Atypical somatoform disorder (300.71)

DISSOCIATIVE DISORDERS (OR HYSTERICAL NEUROSES, DISSOCIATIVE TYPE)

300.12 Psychogenic amnesia
300.13 Psychogenic fugue
300.14 Multiple personality
300.60 Depersonalization disorder (or Depersonalization neurosis)
300.15 Atypical dissociative disorder

PSYCHOSEXUAL DISORDERS
Gender identity disorders
Indicate sexual history in the fifth digit of Transsexualism code: 1 = asexual, 2 = homosexual, 3 = heterosexual, 0 = unspecified.
302.5x Transsexualism, _____
302.60 Gender identity disorder of childhood
302.85 Atypical gender identity disorder

Paraphilias

302.81 Fetishism
302.30 Transvestism
302.10 Zoophilia
302.20 Pedophilia
302.40 Exhibitionism
302.82 Voyeurism
302.83 Sexual masochism
302.84 Sexual sadism
302.90 Atypical paraphilia

Psychosexual dysfunctions

302.71 Inhibited sexual desire
302.72 Inhibited sexual excitement
302.73 Inhibited female orgasm
302.74 Inhibited male orgasm
302.75 Premature ejaculation
302.76 Functional dyspareunia
306.51 Functional vaginismus
302.70 Atypical psychosexual dysfunction

Other psychosexual disorders

302.00 Ego-dystonic homosexuality
302.89 Psychosexual disorder not elsewhere classified

FACTITIOUS DISORDERS

300.16 Factitious disorder with psychological symptoms
301.51 Chronic factitious disorder with physical symptoms
300.19 Atypical factitious disorder with physical symptoms

DISORDERS OF IMPULSE CONTROL NOT ELSEWHERE CLASSIFIED

312.31 Pathological gambling
312.32 Kleptomania
312.33 Pyromania
312.34 Intermittent explosive disorder
312.35 Isolated explosive disorder
312.39 Atypical impulse control disorder

ADJUSTMENT DISORDER

309.00 with depressed mood
309.24 with anxious mood
309.28 with mixed emotional features
309.30 with disturbance of conduct
309.40 with mixed disturbance of emotions and conduct
309.23 with work (or academic) inhibition
309.83 with withdrawal
309.90 with atypical features

PSYCHOLOGICAL FACTORS AFFECTING PHYSICAL CONDITION

Specify physical condition on Axis III.
316.00 Psychological factors affecting physical condition

PERSONALITY DISORDERS

Note: These are coded on Axis II.
301.00 Paranoid
301.20 Schizoid
301.22 Schizotypal
301.50 Histrionic
301.81 Narcissistic
301.70 Antisocial
301.83 Borderline
301.82 Avoidant
301.60 Dependent
301.40 Compulsive
301.84 Passive-Aggressive
301.89 Atypical, mixed or other personality disorder

V CODES FOR CONDITIONS NOT ATTRIBUTABLE TO A MENTAL DISORDER THAT ARE A FOCUS OF ATTENTION OR TREATMENT

V65.20 Malingering
V62.89 Borderline intellectual functioning (V62.88)
V71.01 Adult antisocial behavior
V71.02 Childhood or adolescent antisocial behavior
V62.30 Academic problem
V62.20 Occupational problem
V62.82 Uncomplicated bereavement
V15.81 Noncompliance with medical treatment
V62.89 Phase of life problem or other life circumstance problem
V61.10 Marital problem
V61.20 Parent-child problem
V61.80 Other specified family circumstances
V62.81 Other interpersonal problem

ADDITIONAL CODES

300.90 Unspecified mental disorder (nonpsychotic)
V71.09 No diagnosis or condition on Axis I
799.90 Diagnosis or condition deferred on Axis I

V71.09 No diagnosis on Axis II
799.90 Diagnosis deferred on Axis II

Source: American Psychiatric Association: *Diagnostic and Statistical Manual of Mental Disorders (DSM-III)*, ed. 3. Washington, D.C., 1980. (Used by permission.)

---

desirable to a substantial number of individuals within a particular group, culture, or subculture, considered to be unacceptable or undesirable to the larger group or culture?

In Table 6–2 psychological disorders are listed along with the answers to the four questions for various groups of disorders. One can see that in each group there are several reasons for considering the behavior that occurs with these conditions as abnormal. The classic disorders that result in an affirmative reply to question 1 are the organic mental disorders and some cases of mental retardation. More and more evidence is accumulating to indicate that the major functional psychoses (schizophrenia, major affective disorders) are associated with a disturbance of neuronal function (see chap. 3), so these are included in this group of disorders.

Those conditions that result in an affirmative response to questions 2 and 3, but not to question 1, do not have an anatomical, physiological, or biochemical cause that is presently known, but they do result in disability and suffering. Thus, anxiety disorders are clearly a source of psychological distress to individuals with them. The same is true for some personality disorders.

Behaviors associated with an affirmative re-

TABLE 6–2.—A General System of Identifying Types of Psychological Disorders

QUESTION	DISORDER		
	Schizophrenia Major affective disorders Mental retardation Organic mental disorders	Anxiety disorders Some personality disorders (i.e., compulsive, schizoid)	Substance use disorders Psychosexual disorders
1. Is the behavior frequently associated with anatomical, physiological, or biochemical abnormality?	Yes	No	No
2. Is the behavior associated with suffering, discomfort, or disability in the view of individuals with the disturbance?	Yes	Yes	Yes (in some instances)
3. Is the behavior viewed as undesirable by individuals not having the disturbance?	Yes	Yes	Yes
4. Is the behavior viewed as desirable by individuals within a subgroup but unacceptable by the larger group?	No	No	Yes (in some instances)

sponse to question 4 are likely to be considered normal by members of the social subgroup to which the individual belongs, but people in the society at large consider them abnormal. Thus, among "gays" homosexual behavior is usually not felt to be deviant, while the heterosexual population generally regards it as abnormal. Culture-bound behavior (see chap. 10) may seem abnormal only when viewed from outside the individual's culture.

Questions 3 and 4 are based primarily on a statistical model of psychological function. Such an approach to normal and abnormal behavior relies on measures of deviation from a group norm (see also chap. 21). For example, if the average or mean height for a population is viewed as "normal," then a significant deviation above or below this value would be interpreted as atypical or "abnormal." While a statistical approach to defining behavior has the advantage of objectivity, there are several disadvantages. First, deviation from the norm may be "healthy" or adaptive for a given individual, and second, what is desirable or appropriate for the group is not necessarily reflected by group consensus. For instance, is it desirable to judge behavior according to a statistical norm if it means discriminating on the basis of sex or religion? Or, should political behavior be labeled abnormal and disturbed if it disagrees with the majority? Obviously not. Therefore, while the statistical model has several positive features, caution should be used in differentiating normal and abnormal behavior on the basis of statistical analysis alone.

CATEGORIES OF PSYCHOLOGICAL DISORDERS

The following disorders will be discussed in this section:
1. Mental retardation
2. Organic mental disorders
3. Schizophrenic disorders
4. Affective disorders
5. Anxiety disorders
6. Personality disorders
7. Psychosexual disorders

We plan to discuss them only briefly, so the reader will gain an appreciation of the range of psychopathology that is seen clinically without being overwhelmed by the details of diagnosis and management. For the latter, a standard textbook of psychiatry should be consulted.

Mental Retardation

The American Association of Mental Deficiency defines mental retardation as "significantly subaverage general intellectual functioning existing concurrently with deficits in adaptive behavior, and manifested during the developmental period."[10] Under this heading are included disorders both with (20–25%) and without (75–80%) an identifiable anatomical, biochemical, or physiological abnormality of the central nervous system (see also chap. 1). In the United States, there are approximately 6 million persons who, on the basis of intelligence testing alone, are diagnosed as being retarded. The majority of these individuals (about 75%) function at the borderline to mild level of retardation (Table 6–3).

Organic Mental Disorders (OMD)

The disorders in this category result from diffuse structural damage and/or functional impairment of the neurons of the cerebral cortex, which may be caused by a variety of factors including infectious, traumatic, vascular, degenerative, toxic (e.g., drugs and other substances), and metabolic ones. An OMD may be acute or chronic in nature. Generally, in persons with these conditions the results of neurologic examination and laboratory tests of neurologic structure and function are abnormal.

Schizophrenic Disorders

Clinically, schizophrenia is a diagnostic term applied to a heterogeneous group of psychotic disorders of unknown etiology and characterized by gross impairments of thinking, communication, perception, affect, and behavior (Table 6–4). While often referred to as a functional psychiatric illness, implying the absence of brain cell injury or dysfunction, there is compelling genetic, metabolic, and pharmacologic evidence that schizophrenia is an organic disease associated with a disturbance of neuronal function (see chaps. 1 and 3). In addition, psychological and social factors are of great etiologic importance.

Affective Disorders

These are conditions characterized by *major* disturbances in mood, that is, depression with or without mania. Symptoms of depression include sadness, loss of self-esteem, a feeling of hopelessness, difficulty in sleeping, reduced sexual drive, decreased appetite, and multiple somatic complaints. Mania is accompanied by an elevation of mood, a feeling of euphoria, flight of ideas, and hyperactivity. Paranoid and grandiose delusions may occur as a part of the clinical picture of mania, while hallucinations, delusions, and suicidal preoccupation are clinical features of psychotic depression.

Major affective disorders can be divided into unipolar and bipolar illness. Persons with bipolar illness (also called manic-depressive psychosis) suffer from depression and mania, while those with unipolar illness suffer only from depression. There is evidence that these clinical disorders have a genetic component and are associated with a disturbance in biogenic amine activity in the brain (see chaps. 1 and 3).

Anxiety Disorders

The current edition of DSM-III lists several types of anxiety disorders, conditions

TABLE 6–3.—LEVELS OF RETARDATION AND RELATED FUNCTIONING ABILITIES

LEVEL OF RETARDATION	FUNCTIONING SKILLS
Mild	Can learn basic academic skills and, as adults, can usually be employed in simple jobs; rarely institutionalized
Moderate	Can learn self-help skills and, as adults, can work under close supervision; social skills remain limited
Severe	Can learn some language and self-help skills with intensive training; generally in need of constant supervision
Profound	May be taught self-help skills using specialized techniques (behavior modification); otherwise require total care and may not learn to talk

Adapted from Calhoun J.F. (ed.): *Abnormal Psychology: Current Perspectives*. New York, CRM Books, 1977.

TABLE 6–4.—CLINICAL MANIFESTATIONS OF SCHIZOPHRENIA

AREA OF DISTURBANCE	EXPLANATION
Thinking	
Inappropriate associations (clang associations)	Word association by sound rather than meaning ("stump pump")
Overinclusion	Including irrelevant associations in speech or written expression
Conceptualization	Concrete thinking, as for example the inability to explain the meaning of a proverb such as "A rolling stone gathers no moss"
Delusions	Irrational beliefs that are seen as reality; common ones are delusions of grandeur, persecution, control, hypochondria, and guilt
Language	
Neologisms (new words)	Combining words or parts of words or using words in a unique way that is not comprehensible
Word salad	Using words in a disorganized manner without meaning or logic
Perception	
Hallucinations	A sensory perception without a corresponding external physical stimulus, for example, auditory (hearing voices) hallucinations
Affect	
Flat affect	Coarctated or restricted emotional reactions
Ambivalent affect	Expression of both positive and negative feelings simultaneously toward an individual
Inappropriate affect	Emotional reactions not correlated with the situation, as in becoming angry when promoted
Behavior	
Bizarre reactions	Tearing magazines, etc.
Lack of social interaction	Little or no interpersonal interactions; avoidance of social interaction
Catatonic state	Violent or reduced motor activity; sometimes severe withdrawal and mutism

Adapted from Calhoun J.F. (ed.): *Abnormal Psychology: Current Perspectives*. New York, CRM Books, 1977.

in which anxiety is the most prominent symptom:[1]
1. Generalized anxiety disorder
2. Phobic disorder
3. Obsessive-compulsive disorder
4. Panic disorder

GENERALIZED ANXIETY DISORDER.—This condition is probably the most common one in this group. It is characterized by recurrent symptoms of anxiety and autonomic nervous system discharge that appear to be *unrelated to specific events or experiences*. Persons with this disorder are often said to have "free-floating" anxiety because the reason for it is not apparent.

PHOBIC DISORDER.—A phobia is an intense and persistent fear of a specific object or situation, unrelated to reality, which causes the person to avoid it. Psychodynamically, it is explained as being due to a repression of unacceptable feelings or wishes and a displacement of the anxiety associated with these onto an external object or situation. Various types of phobias have been described:

Agoraphobia (fear of open spaces)
Claustrophobia (fear of closed places)
Acrophobia (fear of heights)
Hydrophobia (fear of water)
Hematophobia (fear of blood)
Pyrophobia (fear of fire)

Nyctophobia (fear of darkness)
Xenophobia (fear of strangers)

OBSESSIVE-COMPULSIVE DISORDER.—This condition is characterized by a preoccupation with a thought or idea (obsession) and/or the performance of a repetitive act or ritual (compulsion), both of which are very disturbing to the individual yet are seemingly beyond his control. Examples include obsessive rumination of being hurt or hurting someone else and compulsive hand-washing.

PANIC DISORDER.—The major feature of this disorder is recurrent panic (anxiety) attacks, usually of sudden onset, associated with widespread discharge of the autonomic nervous system (see also chap. 7). These attacks are characterized by extreme apprehension or fearfulness and symptoms of dyspnea, palpitations, chest pain or discomfort, dizziness, a choking or smothering sensation, feelings of unreality, etc. The condition differs from panic reactions due to specific stimuli (e.g., dog phobia) in that the person is never sure when a panic attack will occur. Panic disorder often has an onset in late adolescence or early adult life and is more common in women.

Personality Disorders

This category includes disorders in which longstanding and apparently ingrained patterns of behavior and character traits occur that interfere with successful social adaptation. Individuals diagnosed as having a personality disorder frequently are not overly concerned or apprehensive about their condition.

Table 6–5 lists several of the common personality disorders and their associated characteristics.

Psychosexual Disorders

Included in this category are (1) various dysfunctions of normal coitus and (2) disorders involving sexual behavior directed toward objects other than people of the opposite sex, sexual acts not usually associated with coitus, or coitus performed under unusual or bizarre circumstances. Deviant sexual activity is usually habitual and substitutes for "normal" heterosexual intercourse. Included in the list of sexual deviations (paraphilias) are fetishism (reliance on inappropriate body parts or objects for gratification), pedophilia (sexual relations with children), transvestism (dressing in the clothes of persons of the opposite sex as a means of achieving sexual excitement), exhibitionism (gratification by exposing one's genitals), voyeurism (sexual gratification by observing sexual activity or sexual anatomy of others), sadism (sexual pleasure by inflicting pain on others), and masochism (gratification by receiving pain).

TABLE 6–5.—PERSONALITY DISORDERS AND RELATED CHARACTERISTICS

PERSONALITY DISORDER	CHARACTERISTICS
Passive-aggressive	Stubbornness, sullenness, dissatisfaction, and a tendency to be obstructive; in other words, aggression expressed by passive means
Histrionic	Insecurity, and vain, self-dramatizing, attention-seeking behavior
Compulsive	Rigidity, strong inhibitions, perfectionistic tendencies, and meticulousness
Paranoid	Envy, hypersensitivity, suspiciousness, and a tendency to blame others or impugn their motives
Introverted	Difficulty in forming social relationships, bland or constricted affect, reserved, withdrawn, but with no eccentricities in thought, communication or behavior
Schizotypal	Odd thinking, perception, and communication, but not severe enough to warrant a diagnosis of schizophrenia
Narcissistic	Need for constant attention, grandiose feelings of importance, lack of empathy for others, and exploitativeness
Antisocial	Selfishness, callousness, impulsiveness, lack of remorse, and an inability to form close personal relationships

Source: Adapted from American Psychiatric Association: DSM-III, ed. 3. Washington, D.C. January 15, 1978.

EVALUATION OF PSYCHOLOGICAL FUNCTION BY MEANS OF THE MENTAL STATUS EXAMINATION

The interview is the fundamental clinical tool used to understand the patient and his presenting complaints.[11, 12] In the evaluation of individuals with behavior disorders, the psychiatric interview can be thought of as consisting of two major parts: a history of the person's illness and the mental status examination. The first is comparable to the traditional medical history in that the patient's principal problem(s) is elicited, all the circumstances associated with its onset and development are ascertained, and relevant information having to do with the individual's past medical history, family history, and social history is obtained. The second part constitutes an assessment of the following elements of psychological function:

1. General appearance and behavior
2. Thought processes, speech, and perception
3. Affect and mood
4. Orientation, memory, intellect, and judgment
5. Learned skills or activities

The skillfully conducted psychiatric interview should enable a physician to make an accurate diagnosis of the patient's behavioral problem, although at times objective psychological testing may be necessary. Since primary-care physicians are most likely to make initial contact with persons who are emotionally ill, it is essential that they be familiar with this kind of interview. As is the case with the usual medical history, the physician is primarily engaged in three activities: observing, questioning, and listening. In addition, there are special interviewing techniques, such as facilitation and confrontation, that are particularly helpful in enhancing communication with the person who has a psychological problem and is emotionally upset. The reader is referred to standard interviewing texts for a detailed description of these techniques.

The relationship that develops between the patient and the health-care professional is of the utmost importance in determining the kind and the degree of information obtained from the interview. This is particularly true with respect to mental illness, where there is often an understandable hesitancy on the part of the patient to reveal the details of his personal life and his innermost thoughts and feelings to a comparative stranger, even though it is his physician.

No single approach to the interview is successful with all patients; flexibility and improvisation are often essential. A physician who sees a person with a behavior disorder in an emergency room setting would obviously conduct the interview in a different manner than one who sees such a patient on an elective basis in his office. Likewise, a hospital consultation might be conducted quite differently than one held in a private office.

In this section, we are going to limit our discussion to the second part of the psychiatric interview—the mental status examination.

General Appearance and Behavior

Observation of the general appearance and behavior of the patient conveys a great deal of information about his emotional state. Some of the things about a person that should be noted are his dress and grooming, facial expression, posture, and movements. An unkempt and disheveled appearance is common among those who are psychotic or demented. Depressed persons often have a paucity of motor movements, walking slowly with head and shoulders bowed and eyes downcast. Conversely, manic persons exhibit increased activity, constantly moving about and shifting their attention from one subject to another. Schizophrenics may display unusual behavior that is not goal-directed and often seems purposeless. For example, such a person may engage in repetitive motor acts as if performing some ritual or imitate the behavior of others, including the physician. Schizophrenics who are catatonic are mute, immobile, and tend to assume unusual postures for long periods of time. Persons with anxiety reactions appear quite nervous, sitting on the edge of the chair, with signs of sympathetic nervous system discharge.

Thought Processes, Speech, and Perception

Schizophrenics do not display logical and goal-oriented thinking; rather, they have abnormal thought association, in which the thought processes are disorganized and do not lead to definite conclusions. They tend to think in very concrete terms and are often unable to deal with abstract notions. For example, proverbs such as "People who live in glass houses shouldn't throw stones" are interpreted literally. Patients with dementia may demonstrate a similar problem in thinking. Delusional thinking is also commonly found in schizophrenics as well as in persons with organic mental disorders.

When the type of thinking demonstrated by an individual is very personalized and seems to originate from internal experience and not from external reality, the term *autistic* is used. Autistic thinking is likely to be gratifying only to the individual. At times, very disturbed persons demonstrate thinking that is described as "magical." This refers to the belief that some thought or verbalization may have an effect in the physical world. While this is often seen in persons with mental disorders, it also occurs among normal individuals. Common superstitions are an example of magical thinking in everyday life. Some disturbances in thinking result in an unusual use of language and words, such as the coining of a new word, called a neologism. When the use of neologisms is frequent and words are scrambled together, the clinical picture seen in hebephrenic schizophrenia is produced. In another unusual speech problem seen in schizophrenics, words are chosen because of their sound, not their meaning—a form of speech called *clang association*. The term *blocking* refers to speech that is suddenly interrupted for no apparent reason. Blocking is often seen in schizophrenia and also in other disorders such as depression.

In disorders of mood and affect, the pattern of speech may be altered to a significant degree. There may be an excessive flow of words such as is seen in the manic stage of manic-depressive illness. Such individuals talk rapidly and move from one topic to another repeatedly. On the other hand, depressed persons often have reduced speech activity, talking in a low voice with a slow and halting rhythm. In anxiety disorders, verbal communication may also be affected: generalized anxiety reactions usually make the person overly talkative and obsessive-compulsives may go into excessive detail when describing a situation.

A person may lose the ability to communicate by means of language when there is damage to the dominant cerebral cortex. Thus, some persons with dementia suffer from dysphasia, a difficulty in understanding or utilizing language. In mild cases, individuals with dysphasia may have a problem thinking of the words they want to say or finding the exact name of an object they wish to discuss. In an effort to maintain their flow of speech, they often use substitutes for the real words they cannot think of, making mistakes in the process. Reading and writing, being forms of communication in which language is used, may also be impaired in persons with dysphasia. Mutism, or the absence of speech, is observed in those with various neurologic disorders as well as catatonic schizophrenia.

Individuals suffering from organic brain disease may have an excessive number of thought associations and be unable to suppress irrelevant information. In speaking, they may eventually get to the point they are attempting to make, but they often do so in a tangential manner.

Disturbances in perception are some of the most dramatic symptoms exhibited by psychiatric patients. Hallucinations are defined as false auditory, visual, tactile, or olfactory perceptions that cannot be changed by reason or logic. They may be experienced by persons with schizophrenia, manic-depressive illness, or organic mental disorder. Those that involve one sensory modality are more common in certain clinical illnesses. For example, visual hallucinations of animals or insects often occur in persons with delirium tremens, an acute organic mental disorder that is a manifestation of the alcohol withdrawal syndrome.

An illusion is a distortion of a real sensory perception, in contrast to a hallucination, which is an experience that originates within the person. The former are commonly associated with acute organic brain syndromes of a toxic or metabolic etiology.

Affect and Mood

A third element of psychological function that is assessed in the mental status examination is the feeling state (i.e., affect or mood) of the individual. A good appraisal of this can be made from observing a person's appearance, manner of speech, and behavior. Sometimes persons who seek medical help because of physical symptoms are really suffering from a disturbance of mood. For instance, someone with a depressive illness may come to the physician complaining of weight loss, insomnia, loss of sexual drive, or vague somatic symptoms—without realizing that he is actually depressed. Yet complaints such as these, particularly if no organic cause for them is readily apparent, should suggest the possibility of an underlying depression to the astute clinician.

Mood elevation, as seen in the manic phase of manic-depressive illness, is usually easily detected in the mental status examination. Such persons are "hyper" in their thoughts, speech, and actions. A similar clinical picture is seen in those with amphetamine intoxication.

Affect is said to be inappropriate when it is out of keeping with a person's thoughts or the situation being discussed. Inappropriateness of affect is typical of schizophrenics. Individuals with some forms of dementia may demonstrate a lability of affect in which there is marked variation in feeling state (i.e., mood swings) over a brief time. For instance, periods of crying and elation may alternate in rapid succession.

Orientation, Memory, Intellect, and Judgment

It is very important to determine whether or not a person with a behavioral disorder is oriented, as well as to assess his memory, intellect, and judgment. When severe, disorientation is easily recognized, but mild deficits are not uncommon, particularly with respect to time, and these may escape detection unless carefully sought. If a person is alert, has a good memory, and speaks intelligently about his problems, there is probably no need to inquire about orientation to time, place, or person. A loss of orientation is typically associated with organic mental disorders but may also occur in the psychoses. Patients in a hospital sometimes lose track of time, but if there is disorientation to place or person, then significant brain dysfunction is present.

A faulty memory is also usually evident during the interview when the person is asked to recall past events in his life. However, specific testing of this function should be carried out as part of the mental status examination, even in a person whose memory appears to be intact on superficial assessment. It is often helpful in clinical testing to divide memory function into three types: immediate, recent, and remote memory. In persons with dementia, it is common for recent memory to be lost, while the recall of events in the distant past is unaffected. Most of us are familiar with the stereotyped picture of a "senile" individual who dwells at great length on the occurrences in his life as a young man but cannot remember where he put his glasses or what he had to eat earlier in the day.

In Korsakoff's psychosis, an organic mental disorder seen in alcoholics, there is disorientation and memory loss, with the patient confabulating in an attempt to hide these defects. For example, if the interviewer asks him whether the two met the day before (knowing full well that they have never seen each other previously), the patient will make up a detailed story about such a meeting rather than admit that he cannot remember. The story is often so convincing that someone who didn't know better would tend to believe it.

Memory, concentration, and, to a certain degree, intellect can be assessed by asking the person to make a series of simple calculations such as successively subtracting 7 from 100, that is, continuing to subtract 7 from the previous answer obtained. Inability to do so is common in persons with moderate or severe dementia.

An individual's fund of information is obviously related to his education and life experiences; consequently, when assessing intelligence the physician must take into account the person's social and cultural background. Some people have a great deal of common sense and excellent judgment despite a lack of much formal schooling. Diagnostically, a general estimate of a person's intellectual function is important. A reduction in intellectual capacity and judgment is seen in persons who have psychotic disorders, mental retardation, and organic mental disorders. The interviewer should always keep in mind that the presence of extreme anxiety can adversely affect an individual's ability to perform higher intellectual functions such as abstract thinking.

Learned Skills or Activities

When there is brain damage involving the dominant cerebral cortex, execution of learned skills and activities may be impaired even though motor function and comprehension remain intact. The term that is applied to this disorder is *apraxia*. Examples of activities for which apraxias can develop are dressing, combing the hair, using a knife and fork to eat, and drinking from a cup. Difficulties with calculation may also result from lesions in the dominant cerebral cortex. These findings are seen only with organic disease of the brain and are not found in the functional psychiatric disorders.

PSYCHOLOGICAL TESTING

In this section, we will describe some commonly used psychological tests and discuss the clinical situations in which they are used. But before doing so, we will review some of the general principles that govern test design and interpretation. For the reader who is especially interested in psychological testing, several excellent texts are available that cover the topic more extensively.[13-16]

Test Design and Interpretation

An individual's performance on a psychological test constitutes a sample of his behavior. Based on the method used to interpret this information, two types of instruments are recognized: a *norm-referenced* test in which the performance of a subject is compared with that of other individuals in a normative reference group and a *criterion-referenced* test in which performance is judged on the basis of a set of predetermined criteria. Most psychological measures fall into the first category.

Before a norm-referenced test can be used to gather meaningful information on behavior, it must be standardized by administering it to a representative sample of the population (so-called normative group) for whom the instrument is intended. The performance of this group can be described in certain quantitative terms (called the norms of the test), which include the distribution curve, mean, and standard deviation of the scores. The distribution curve for tests that measure most complex behaviors approximates that of a theoretical "normal curve" (Fig 6–1). The variability of the scores of those in the normative group is indicated by the value of the standard deviation (SD). Given a normal distribution curve, approximately 68% of all scores fall within one SD above or below the mean and about 95% of the scores fall within two SD above or below the mean. The larger the SD, the wider is the variation in scores among the individuals tested.

Once a test has been standardized, the norms can be used to convert the raw scores obtained by test subjects to derived or standard scores. A derived score simply tells how much a raw score deviates from the mean. Figure 6–1 shows a number of different types of derived scores in relationship to a normal distribution curve. One that is very commonly used, the percentile score, indicates the percentage of persons in the normative group who scored below a particular raw score. The value of a derived score is that it permits comparisons to be made of the performances of different individuals taking a

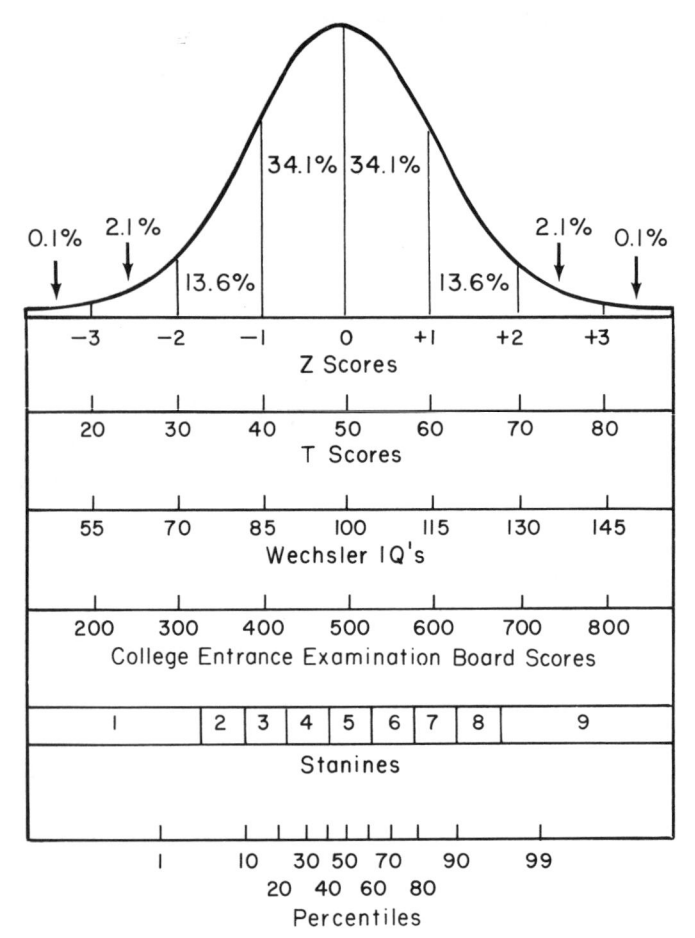

Fig 6–1.—The normal curve and derived scores. (Where: Z-scores represent one standard deviation from the mean; T-scores have a mean of 50 and a standard deviation of ±10; stanines divide the normal curve into half-standard deviations, the mid one straddles the mean.) (From Sundberg N.D.: *Assessment of Persons.* Englewood Cliffs, N.J., Prentice-Hall, Inc., 1977. Used by permission.)

test. Cross-comparisons of the derived scores from different tests can be made only if the distribution curves for the instruments approximate that of a normal curve and if the normative groups used to standardize them are similar.

For the proper standardization of a test, it is absolutely essential that the normative group is truly representative of the population to which the test is ultimately administered. For instance, if one were developing an instrument to assess the vocabulary of elementary school children, the normative group should consist of appropriate numbers of children of different age groups, socioeconomic levels, cultural backgrounds, and other variables. In this way, the test norms can be used to evaluate the performance of the wide variety of students in elementary schools.

Recently, criterion-referenced instruments have been gaining popularity in educational testing. In these measures, the level of a subject's performance is defined by predetermined standards (criteria), not by comparing his score with that obtained by some normative group.[17]

In both norm-referenced and criterion-referenced tests, two features are used to determine how well a test instrument is constructed: reliability and validity.

RELIABILITY.—Technically, reliability is a statistical estimate of the consistency of the test results, as, for example, on repeated administration of the instrument to the same person or group. Many variables influence this consistency, including the intrinsic properties of the test, the setting in which it is taken, and the condition of the individual taking it. The reliability of a test can be measured by testing the same persons on repeated occasions to see how much their scores vary over time.

Mathematically, reliability is expressed in terms of a standard error of measurement or a correlation coefficient. The former is equal to one SD (from the mean) in the distribution of scores that are recorded when an individual or group takes a test a number of times. In other words, if the mean score on repeated testing is 90 and the standard error is 4, this means that about two thirds of the times a person is retested, he will score between 86 and 94. The smaller the standard error, the more reliable is the test.

Information on reliability is also given in the form of a correlation coefficient that allows for estimates of the chance versus real fluctuations in test scores. If a positive linear relationship exists between two variables (e.g., scores on repeated testing), the correlation coefficient will range from +0.01 to +1.00, with the latter representing a perfect linear correlation. So, the higher the reliability coefficient, the greater is the degree of reliability of a test. For example, a coefficient of +0.60 for an instrument indicates that it is less reliable than one with a coefficient of +0.90.

VALIDITY.—This term refers to the accuracy with which a test measures what it has been designed to measure. Two specific types of validity are *content* and *criterion-related* validity. In assessing the former, an attempt is made to determine whether the items on a test (its content) accurately represent the material in the topic area that is being evaluated. This is usually accomplished by having "experts" in the field carefully analyze the test items. To determine criterion-related validity, the results of a test are compared with some external measure of the same behavior.[18] If there is agreement between the two, then the test is said to have criterion-related validity. For example, if performance on an intelligence test is really a valid predictor of future academic achievement, then those who score higher on the test should do better academically in school than those who obtain lower scores.

Different instruments measuring the same behavior often have different degrees of reliability and validity. Therefore, when the clinician interprets the results of a battery of psychological tests, the reliability and validity data of the instruments should always be consulted before any conclusions are reached.

Clinical Use of Psychological Tests

Psychological testing should be carried out in order to answer specific clinical questions or to arrive at certain decisions. If ordered for these purposes, the tests often provide objective information that is quite useful. Testing probably should not be done merely to satisfy one's curiosity, as, for example, in the case of parents who want to know their child's IQ. Careful attention should always be given to the confidentiality of psychological evaluations since diagnostic labeling based on test results can have far-reaching effects on an individual.

One should not rely on a single psychological test to make a definitive clinical diagnosis or decision. It is much more appropriate to administer several tests, each designed to assess a particular aspect of behavior. Such "test batteries" might include measures of cognitive ability (intellect or intelligence), specific skills or achievements (spelling, reading), and personality (social/emotional). The information gathered from these tests, plus that obtained from the clinical interview, physical examination, and other laboratory studies, allows for a comprehensive evaluation of a person who has a behavioral disorder.

TABLE 6-6.—INDIVIDUALLY ADMINISTERED PSYCHOLOGICAL TESTS

TYPE	TEST NAME	AGES USED (YEAR-MONTH)	DESCRIPTION
General intelligence			
Infant	Bayley Scales of Infant Development (Psychological Corp., 1969)	0-2 to 2-6	Assessment of early development, providing a separate mental and psychomotor score
	Cattell Infant Intelligence Scale (Psychological Corp., 1940)	0-3 to 2-6	Infant assessment used as a downward extension of the Stanford-Binet Intelligence Scale
Preschool and school age	Merrill Palmer Scale of Mental Tests (Harcourt Brace & World, 1931)	2-0 to 4-6	Test of general intelligence for young children
	Wechsler Preschool and Primary Scale of Intelligence (Psychological Corp., 1967)	4-0 to 6-6	Test of intelligence providing separate verbal and performance IQs
	Stanford-Binet Intelligence Scale, combined L and M form, third revision (Houghton Mifflin, 1960)	2-0 to 18-0	Intelligence test using an age scale with heavy verbal emphasis at school ages
	Wechsler Intelligence Scale for Children, revised (Psychological Corp., 1974)	6-0 to 16-0	Test of intelligence providing separate verbal and performance IQs
Adult	Wechsler Adult Intelligence Scale (Psychological Corp., 1955)	16-0 to adult	Test of intelligence providing separate verbal and performance IQs
Specialized intelligence tests			
	Arthur Adaptation of Leiter International Performance Scale (Stoelting Co., 1948)	2-0 to 12-0	Mental test requiring little or no verbal instruction
	Columbia Mental Maturity Scale (Harcourt Brace Jovanovich, 1954)	3-6 to 9-11	Mental test requiring no verbalization and limited motor response
	Hiskey-Nebraska Test of Learning Aptitude (Union College Press, 1966)	3-0 to 16-0	Learning aptitude test administered with either pantomime or verbal instructions for hearing-impaired child
Perceptual tests			
Visual-motor	Bender Visual Motor Gestalt Test for Children (Western Psychological Services, 1962)	5-0 to 10-0	Test of form copying used to detect organic involvement
	Berry-Buktenica Visual Motor Integration Test (Follett Publishing Co., 1967)	1-9 to 15-11	Visual-motor integration test of geometric form copying
	Frostig Development Tests of Visual Perception (Consulting Psychologist Press, 1961)	3-0 to 10-0	Test of visual perception including 9 subtests
Language	Illinois Test of Psycholinguistic Abilities (University of Illinois Press, 1969)	2-0 to 9-6	Test of language including 9 subtests measuring receptive, associative, and expressive processes
	Peabody Picture Vocabulary Test (American Guidance Service, 1959)	1-9 to 18-0	Test of receptive vocabulary through picture identification; no expressive verbal skills required

TYPE	TEST NAME	AGES USED (YEAR-MONTH)	DESCRIPTION
Achievement			
Cognitive skills	Wepman Auditory Discrimination Test (Language Research Associates, 1958)	5–0 to 8–0	Test of auditory discrimination for speech sounds; requires concept of same and different
	Wide Range Achievement Test (Psychological Corp., 1965)	Kindergarten to college	Short test of oral word reading, spelling, and arithmetic
	Peabody Individual Achievement Test (PIAT) (American Guidance Service, 1970)	Kindergarten to college	Test of achievement consisting of 5 scales measuring mathematics, reading recognition and comprehension, spelling, and general information
	Detroit Tests of Learning Aptitude (Bobbs-Merrill, 1967)	Preschool to high school	A comprehensive test consisting of 19 subscales measuring various mental abilities such as visual and auditory attention, verbal ability, practical judgment, motor ability, reasoning, and number ability
Social competency	Vineland Social Maturity Scale (American Guidance Service, 1965)	All ages	A measure of successive stages of social competency in acts of daily living
	Progress Assessment Chart, SEFA (N.A.M.H., 1963)	All ages	A behavioral checklist for 4 areas of social skills: self-help, communication, socialization, and occupation; developed initially for use with retarded children
Personality	Children's Appperception Test (C.P.S., 1949, 1965)	4–0 to 9–0	A projective test using 10 black-and-white pictures for story construction around childhood themes
	Thematic Apperception Test (Harvard University Press, 1935)	10–0 to adult	A projective test using 20 black-and-white pictures for story construction
	Rorschach Technique (Grune & Stratton, 1948)	All ages	A projective test utilizing 10 inkblot designs for personality diagnosis
	Minnesota Multiphasic Personality Inventory (MMPI) (Psychological Corp., 1966)	Older teenagers to adults	Objective or structured personality inventory

Adapted from Magrab P.: Psychology, in Johnston R.B., Magrab P. (eds.): *Developmental Disorders.* Baltimore, University Park Press, 1976.

In the following discussion, we will deal with some of the more widely used psychological tests. They can be conveniently divided into three categories: those that assess (1) intellectual abilities, (2) achievement, and (3) personality. A partial list of the individually administered tests in each category is shown in Table 6–6, along with the age groups in which they are generally used.

INTELLIGENCE TESTS.—Tests of intelligence evaluate the general cognitive abilities of an individual. They consist of a variety of mental tasks that assess the intellectual processes of comprehension, reasoning, judgment, and other factors, as well as a person's general fund of information. Measured intelligence is influenced by both hereditary and environmental factors. Examples of the latter include schooling, socioeconomic status, cultural background, acquired personality characteristics, language, and health.[19] These variables must be taken into account when standardizing any intelligence test that is to have wide applicability.

It must be emphasized that an IQ score reflects a person's intellectual level only at a particular time. Studies indicate that this score can change as a result of changes in the individual's life experiences. So no one should ever be stereotyped on the basis of an IQ test.

STANFORD-BINET SCALE.—Perhaps the best-known intelligence test is the Stanford-Binet (S-B) scale.[20] The instrument that is in current use (Form L-M) evolved from one originally constructed in France by Alfred Binet in the early 1900s in order to identify children who would not do well in school. It was revised in 1916 by Terman at Stanford University, hence the name Stanford-Binet. Subsequent test revisions were made in 1937 and 1960 and revised norms were published in 1972.

The S-B (Form L-M) is a developmental or age scale, meaning that there is a particular set of test items for each age or testing level, with the levels ranging from 2 years to superior adult. There are 6 items for each level (except for average adult, which has 8) and an individual is given credit (in months) for the age level of the item(s) that he answers correctly. As one ascends the test levels from preschool to adult, verbal items become progressively more common. Thus, at the upper age levels the test primarily stresses verbal abilities.

The S-B test yields a mental age score, which, when divided by the child's chronological age, gives a developmental index referred to as an IQ or intelligence quotient [IQ = (MA/CA) × 100]. For example, a child of chronological age 8 who is achieving a test or mental age score of 10 years would have an IQ of 125. Since 1960, these raw IQ scores have been converted to derived scores with a mean of 100 and a standard deviation of 16. These derived scores permit comparisons to be made between individuals at different age levels.

The reliability of the overall S-B (Form L-M) is very good; the standard error of measurement is 5 and the reliability coefficient is about 0.90. The test is primarily intended for children and usually is not used for adults of normal intelligence. Since the test tends to emphasize verbal ability in the older age levels, its use is of questionable value in persons who, for one reason or another, have language problems.

WECHSLER SCALES.—Currently there are three kinds of Wechsler intelligence scales: the Wechsler Pre-School Scale (WPPSI) for ages 4 through 6½, the revised Wechsler Intelligence Scale for Children (WISC-R) for ages 6 to 16 years, and the Wechsler Adult Intelligence Scale (WAIS) for ages 16 and above. Each of the Wechsler scales is divided into two parts: verbal and performance. In the WPPSI, the verbal and performance scales each have 5 subtests (plus one alternate subtest in the verbal); in the WISC-R, there are also 5 verbal and 5 performance subtests (plus one alternate test in *both* verbal and performance); while the WAIS is composed of 6 verbal subtests and 5 performance subtests (with *no* alternates). Table 6–7 shows the WISC-R subtests with the number of test items in each.[21] The Wechsler scales group test items covering a particular subject area into a single subtest (e.g., information, arithmetic, picture completion), in contrast to the Stanford-Binet in which items dealing with dissimilar subject areas are grouped together under the heading of an age or test level.

The Wechsler tests are "point scales," meaning that an individual's score is based on the total number of items answered correctly

TABLE 6-7.—DESCRIPTION OF ITEMS ON THE WECHSLER INTELLIGENCE SCALE FOR CHILDREN

	NUMBER OF ITEMS	DESCRIPTION*
Verbal tests		
Information	30	Questions and answers: How many weeks in a month?
Similarities	17	Questions, verbal abstracting and reasoning: How are a bird and an airplane alike?
Arithmetic	18	At very young ages counting objects on cards; for older children (8 years and above) questions requiring mental figuring: If one candy bar costs 5 cents what will be the price of two?
Vocabulary	32	Knowledge of word meaning; child verbally defines words.
Comprehension	17	Question and answer items involving social knowledge, rules, and information.
Digit span (alternate test)	Forward and reversed	Number recall, e.g., "say 567"; child repeats in order for forward, reversed for backward
Performance tests		
Picture completion	26	Pictures with one essential part missing; child names or points to missing part.
Picture arrangement	12 (timed)	Separate picture cards of a "story" requiring a correct sequencing to make a meaningful story.
Block design	11 (timed)	Blocks with red, white, and half-red, half-white sides; child must copy block design to sample and later to cards with pictured designs.
Object assembly	4 (timed)	Cardboard figure requiring child to put cutouts together correctly to make a complete figure; items: (1) girl, (2) horse, (3) car, (4) face.
Coding	50 (timed)	A paper and pencil copying task requiring child to insert a symbol under each figure; accuracy and rate measured.
Mazes (alternate test)	93 (timed)	Nine pencil mazes.

*Some items listed are not exact replicas of the test items.

on the subtests. The raw scores from the verbal subtests are converted to scaled scores and then summed to yield a verbal IQ score. Similarly, the performance subtests yield a performance IQ score. The total of the scaled verbal and performance scores equals the full-scale IQ score. All three of these (the verbal, performance, and full-scale IQ scores) are converted to derived scores with a mean of 100 and a SD of 15.

The Stanford-Binet and Wechsler tests are probably the most frequently used individually administered measures of intelligence. The reliability of the Wechsler scales is comparable to that of the S-B; however, it is lower for some of the subtests. The greatest degree of correlation in test performance is found between the S-B and the Wechsler verbal scales, as might be expected in view of the emphasis placed in this area by the S-B.

Some evaluators use subtest "profiles" (i.e., the results of the subtest scores) of the Wechsler scales for diagnostic purposes; however, there is insufficient experimental evidence to support this approach.[14] Nevertheless, factor analysis of the results of the WISC does suggest that clusters of common skills are being measured by the subtests.[22] Recent studies of the WPPSI suggest that two general types of intellectual abilities are being evaluated: a verbal comprehension factor and a perceptual organizational factor.[23] The WISC-R apparently tests for three factors: verbal comprehension, freedom from distractability, and perceptual organization.[24]

SPECIALIZED INTELLIGENCE TESTS.—Occasionally, because of sensory deficits (e.g., deafness, blindness) or language barriers, it is necessary to administer a specialized intelligence test. An example of such a test is the Arthur Adaptation of the Leiter International Performance Scale, an instrument designed for children aged 2 through 12 and requiring little or no vocal instruction. The test material consists of a slotted rack into which blocks can be fitted to correspond with drawings on a card placed along the top of the rack. The test is an age-graded scale with four tasks at each age level. These tasks become increasingly difficult with each higher age level; that is, they require a greater degree of conceptual as opposed to perceptual ability. The test yields a mental age and an IQ score.

The Columbia Mental Maturities Test, another specialized test of intelligence, requires that a child identify a drawing that does not belong with the other figures on a card. In order for the child to answer the items correctly, he must have developed the concepts of "similarities" and "differences." This test requires very little verbal instruction, and only simple motor responses (pointing) are required. For children with motor disabilities, such as cerebral palsy, this test enables the examiner to get a better picture of their overall capabilities than could be obtained by using a standardized intelligence test.

GROUP TESTING.—The aforementioned tests are usually administered on an individual basis; however, numerous group tests of "mental abilities" have been developed over the past 25 years, particularly for use in public school programs. These tests measure verbal, quantitative, and nonverbal skills such as perceptual-motor ability. More than two dozen such instruments are currently available, but the ones most commonly used are the ACT (Battery of the American College Testing Program), California Tests of Mental Maturity (1963 revision), College Board Scholastic Aptitude Tests (SAT), Graduate Record Examination (GRE), Miller Analogies Test, Otis-Lennon Mental Abilities Test, School and College Ability Test (SCAT), and SRA Primary Abilities Test (1962 edition).

ACHIEVEMENT TESTS.—In addition to intelligence tests that measure general intellectual abilities, achievement tests are often used in psychological evaluations to assess specific areas of competency such as reading, spelling, and mathematics. Two of the more popular achievement tests are the Wide Range Achievement Test (WRAT–revised) and the Peabody Individual Achievement Test (PIAT). The former can be administered in a relatively brief time and evaluates word recognition (or reading single words), arithmetic, and spelling. The Peabody Individual Achievement Test consists of five subscales—mathematics, reading recognition, reading comprehension, spelling, and general information. The testing levels cover preschool children through adults. The instrument was standardized on approximately 3,000 students in public schools from kindergarten through grade 12. It is an individually administered test that can yield a fairly accurate picture of a child's overall achievement level.

EVALUATING LEARNING DISABILITIES.—By definition, children with learning disabilities (LD) have at least average intelligence but experience difficulty in mastering academic or cognitive skills such as reading, writing, and mathematics. The relationship of this condition to attention deficit disorders, with or without hyperactivity, is discussed in chapter 15. The cause of LD can be traced to early studies on "dyslexia," "dysgraphia," "dyscalculia," and so on, which appeared in the literature prior to World War II.[25] Today it is generally felt that the disabilities are neurologically based; however, the evidence for this is far from conclusive.

A comprehensive psychoeducational evaluation should be performed on a child or adult prior to diagnosing a learning disability. A number of instruments are currently available that, when used in conjunction with intelligence and personality tests, are valuable in assessing these problems.

BENDER-GESTALT.—The Bender-Gestalt test was originally developed as a test of visual perception to assess the condition of persons with psychological disorders. However, of late it has been used to evaluate persons with learning disabilities and those with neurologic dysfunction. Several objective scoring systems are available for interpreting the performance of children[26] and adults.[27]

The test itself is very simple to administer; the person is simply asked to copy a series of nine designs, one at a time. Copying accuracy correlates with maturation in that children under the age of 5 or 6 tend to make numerous errors in copying, while those over the age of 7 or 8 progressively develop the ability to copy all the designs accurately. Errors in copying the designs form the basis for the interpretation of the test. Some clinicians believe that they are able to diagnose organic brain dysfunction from the test errors. Several studies have shown that these mistakes alone are insufficient evidence for this diagnosis, however, unless they are accompanied by clinical evidence of neurologic disease.

DETROIT TEST OF LEARNING APTITUDE.—This is a comprehensive measure that identifies specific cognitive deficits in children aged 3 through 18. The general areas evaluated include reasoning and comprehension, judgment, verbal ability, time and space relationships, arithmetic, auditory and visual attention, and motor abilities. The test itself consists of 19 subscales, which may be administered in various combinations to yield a profile of specific cognitive deficits. All the subscales rarely need to be given since as few as 6 may be sufficient to pinpoint a specific problem.

ILLINOIS TEST OF PSYCHOLINGUISTIC ABILITIES.—This test was originally developed from a theoretical psycholinguistic model[28] to assess the receptive, associative, and expressive aspects of language. The test has been given both positive and negative reviews in the research literature but remains one of the frequently used tests in a battery of measures designed to evaluate learning problems in children aged 2 through 9½.

PERSONALITY EVALUATION.—As a group, personality measures have considerably less reliability and validity than intelligence tests. One reason is that there is disagreement as to how to define precisely what is being measured, i.e., the personality of an individual. Another is that there are few acceptable external measures on which to base criterion-related validity. Suffice it to say that, in general, these tests assess the emotional-social aspects of thought and behavior, including motivation, attitude, feeling state, and other traits that characterize the psychological makeup of people. Their interpretation is often invalid without other data about an individual. Nevertheless, such tests, when coupled with other clinical information, can provide a basis for understanding an individual's psychological problems, as well as for planning a course of intervention.

There are two fundamental types of personality tests: objective or structured and projective or unstructured. In the former, the subject is given the opportunity to select from a limited number of responses on each test item (i.e., true-false, multiple choice); the latter gives the subject freedom to respond to the test items as he chooses.

OBJECTIVE TESTS.—One of the most widely used instruments to assess personality is the Minnesota Multiphasic Personality Inventory (MMPI).[29] This test was developed by obtaining the responses to a pool of more than 500 true-false items from groups of patients including depressed, obsessive-compulsive, and hypochondriacal individuals. The instrument consists of ten "clinical" scales and four "validity" scales. The results of the performance on each scale are expressed in terms of a derived T score, which is plotted on a graph. Test interpretations are based on the T scores obtained on the individual scales as well as on the "profile" or pattern of these scores for the entire test. Several recent adaptations of the MMPI involve automated scoring and analysis.

The literature is replete with studies of the MMPI in a multitude of populations and problem areas. The interested reader should consult any of several texts for more detailed descriptions of the use and interpretation of this test.[30,31]

Other objective personality tests and behavior checklists have been developed for both adults and children; two of these are the California Psychological Inventory and Behavior Problem Checklist for children. The Burros *Seventh Mental Measurements Yearbook*[14] and the text by Weiner[32] list and describe the instruments available in this testing area and provide validity and reliability information on them.

PROJECTIVE TESTS.—The so-called projective tests can be grouped into categories on the basis of the techniques used in eliciting subject responses. Lindzey identified the following five categories:[33]

1. *Association techniques.*—The person responds to some stimulus with the first word, image, or percept that comes to mind (e.g., Rorschach and word association tests).
2. *Construction techniques.*—The respondent produces something such as a story or a drawing (e.g., Thematic Apperception Test).
3. *Completion techniques.*—The subject must complete a partially finished task in any way he wishes (e.g., sentence completion procedure).
4. *Choice or ordering techniques.*—The subject selects one of several alternatives which may be ranked by preference or attractiveness (e.g., Szondi test).
5. *Expressive techniques.*—The subject performs some activity (e.g., free play, psychodrama, draw-a-person test).

Rorschach.—When a subject is asked to relate what he sees in an ambiguous drawing, he will "project" his personal views of the figure, thereby revealing important things about his personality and life experiences. This is the rationale underlying the Rorschach test, which was developed in 1921 by Herman Rorschach, a Swiss psychiatrist.

The test consists of ten inkblots, figures with ambiguous forms and lines that are subject to a variety of subjective interpretations.[34, 35] During the test administration, an individual is shown the ten inkblots, one at a time, and is asked to describe what he sees. The examiner carefully records his verbal descriptions and emotional responses. Then the examiner goes over each card with the subject again, asking *where* on the card the subject saw each percept and *what* about the blot made it look that way.

There are several elements of a person's responses that are important in scoring the test: his perception of form, color, movement, and shading; whether he responds to the whole blots or to their parts; the nature of the "things" he sees in the blots; and whether or not he describes the blots as others commonly do. Systematic scoring procedures have been developed to grade these responses. There are also several systems available for interpreting the test results, but for the most part they are based on the examiner's experience and theoretical orientation. Consequently, the reliability and validity of the test have come under considerable criticism.[14] Nonetheless, the Rorschach still is one of the most frequently used clinical tools for personality evaluation.

Thematic Apperception Test.—The Thematic Apperception Test (TAT) consists of a series of pictures on cards, which are shown to the subject one at a time. He is asked to make up a story about each picture, giving a detailed plot involving antecedent and consequent events.[36] The person is informed that there are no "right" or "wrong" stories but rather that this is a test of imagination.

The rationale for the test is that individuals will reveal how they perceive *themselves* from the person (i.e., the "hero") they identify with in their story, and they will reveal how they perceive significant *others* (e.g., parental figures) from their description of the interactions of the "hero" with others in the story. Test interpretation is based on the nature of the story that is made up plus other aspects of the patient's response, such as the latency of response (time between first looking at the card and beginning a story) and his emotional reactions. There are no generally accepted standardized scoring systems for the TAT, so that interpretation depends on the examiner's clinical experience and theoretical background. The lack of adequate reliability and validity data makes this test a clinical tool to be used *along with* other psychometric measures in psychological evaluation rather than by itself.

A children's version called the Children's Apperception Test (CAT) is available and consists of cartoon pictures. Also, there is an apperception test called Blacky Pictures, based on Freud's theory of psychosexual development, which uses cartoon drawings of a dog family to assess personality factors in young children.

Sentence completion.—This form of testing requires that a subject complete a series of sentences according to his or her own feelings. Table 6–8 lists 5 sample items from the High School Form of the Incomplete Sentence Blank, which has a total of 40 items. Clinical interpretation assumes frankness and veracity on the part of the subject as well as the ability to express ideas verbally. Scoring, as in most projective measures, is subjective, although Rotter suggests classifying responses into conflict, positive, or neutral categories.[37] Some studies indicate that the sentence completion method can be a very valuable technique in personality assessment.[38]

Drawings.—In this method, subjects are asked to simply "draw a person," and the resulting production is used as a basis for assessing personality factors. While human figure drawings can be scored and related to developmental age, personality interpretation using this technique has received negative reviews.[14]

TABLE 6–8.—SOME ITEMS FROM THE INCOMPLETE SENTENCE BLANK, HIGH SCHOOL FORM

ITEM	DESCRIPTION
2	The happiest time . . .
9	What annoys me . . .
13	My greatest fear . . .
17	When I was younger . . .
35	My father . . .
40	Most girls . . .

Source: Reproduced from the Rotter Incomplete Sentences Blank by permission. Copyright 1950 by The Psychological Corporation, New York, N.Y. All rights reserved.

SUMMARY

The classification of psychological dysfunction can be viewed from several perspectives and each of the nosologic systems that are in use today has its advantages and limitations. In fact, there is a considerable difference of opinion among psychologists and psychiatrists about the precise definition of abnormal behavior and how best to classify the behavioral disorders.

The current edition of the *Diagnostic and Statistical Manual (DSM III)* of the American Psychiatric Association gives the most widely accepted classification system. It lists a number of categories of psychological dysfunction, including mental retardation, organic mental disorders, schizophrenic disorders, affective disorders, anxiety disorders, personality disorders, and psychosexual disorders. The criteria for the diagnosis of these conditions are found in the manual; in this chapter, we have briefly described their basic elements to give the reader a general view of the range of clinical psychopathology.

The evaluation of a person with psychological dysfunction is primarily based on the psychiatric interview, which consists of two parts: the history of the person's illness and the mental status examination. The second part is discussed in some detail and examples are given of findings that occur in persons with the different mental disorders. At times, psychological testing is necessary to assess the intellectual abilities, achievement, and personality of an individual. When used in conjunction with the psychiatric interview and physical examination, these tests may be helpful in understanding a person's psychological problems.

REFERENCES

1. American Psychiatric Association: *Diagnostic and Statistical Manual of Mental Disorders*, ed. 3, (DSM-III). Washington, D.C., American Psychiatric Association, 1980.
2. Spitzer R.L., Wilson P.T.: Classification in psychiatry, in Freedman A.M., et al. (eds.): *Comprehensive Textbook of Psychiatry*. Baltimore, Williams & Wilkins Co., 1975.

3. Cromwell R.L., et al.: Criteria for classification systems, in Hobbs N. (ed.): *Issues in the Classification of Children*. San Francisco, Jossey-Bass, Inc., Publishers, 1975.
4. Phillips L., et al.: Classification of behavior disorders, in Hobbs N. (ed.): *Issues in the Classification of Children*. San Francisco, Jossey-Bass, Inc., Publishers, 1975.
5. Meissner W.W.: Theories of personality, in Nicholi A.M., Jr. (ed.): *The Harvard Guide to Modern Psychiatry*. Cambridge, Mass., Harvard University Press, 1978, chap. 8.
6. Bandura A.: *Social Learning Theory*. Englewood Cliffs, N.J., Prentice-Hall, Inc., 1977.
7. Rogers C.: A theory of personality, in Maddi S. (ed.): *Perspectives on Personality*. Boston, Little, Brown and Company, 1971.
8. Szasz T.: *The Myth of Mental Illness*. New York, Harper & Row, 1961.
9. Reiss S.: A critique of Thomas S. Szasz's myth of mental illness. *Am. J. Psychiatry* 128:71, 1972.
10. Grossman H.J. (ed.): A manual on terminology and classification in mental retardation, ed. 3. *Am. J. Ment. Defic.* (special publication series), no. 2, 1973.
11. Detre T.P., Kepfer D.J.: Psychiatric history and mental status examination, in Freedman A.M., et al. (eds.): *Comprehensive Textbook of Psychiatry*. Baltimore, Williams & Wilkins Co., 1975.
12. Evans H.S.: Mental status, in Prior J.A., Silberstein J.S. (eds.): *Physical Diagnosis*. St. Louis, C.V. Mosby Co., 1977.
13. Anastasi A.: *Psychological Testing*, ed. 4. New York, Macmillan Publishing Co., Inc., 1976.
14. Burros O.K. (ed.): *Seventh Mental Measurements Yearbook*. Highland Park, N.J., Gryphon Press, 1972.
15. Cronbach L.J.: *Essentials of Psychological Testing*, ed. 3. New York, Harper & Row, 1970.
16. Sundberg N.D.: *Assessment of Persons*. Englewood Cliffs, N.J., Prentice-Hall, Inc., 1977.
17. Ebel R.L.: Some limitations of criterion-referenced measurement, in Bracht G.A., Hopkins K.D., Stanley J.C. (eds.): *Perspectives in Educational and Psychological Measurement*. Englewood Cliffs, N.J., Prentice-Hall, Inc., 1972.
18. Lyman H.B.: *Test Scores and What They Mean*. Englewood Cliffs, N.J., Prentice-Hall, Inc., 1963.
19. Kessler J.W.: Environmental components of measured intelligence, in Millon T. (ed.): *Medical Behavioral Science*. Philadelphia, W.B. Saunders Co., 1975.
20. Terman L.M., Merrill M.A.: *Stanford-Binet Intelligence Scale*. Boston, Houghton Mifflin Company, 1972.
21. Wechsler D.: *Manual for Wechsler Intelligence Scale for Children—Revised*. New York, The Psychological Corporation, 1974.
22. Bush W.J., Waugh K.W.: *Diagnosing Learning Disabilities*, ed. 2. Columbus, Ohio, Charles E. Merrill Publishing Co., 1976.
23. Silverstein A.B.: Structure of the Wechsler Intelligence Scale for Children for three ethnic groups. *J. Educ. Psychol.* 65:408, 1973.
24. Kaufman A.S.: Factor analysis of the WISC(R) at eleven age levels between $6^{1}/_{2}$ and $16^{1}/_{2}$ years. *J. Consult. Clin. Psychol.* 43:135, 1975.
25. Orton S.T.: Word blindness in school children. *Arch. Neurol. Psychiatry* 14:581, 1925.
26. Kopitz E.M.: *The Bender-Gestalt Test for Young Children*. New York, Grune & Stratton, Inc., 1964.
27. Pascal G.R., Suttell B.J.: *The Bender-Gestalt Test: Quantification and Validity for Adults*. New York, Grune & Stratton, Inc., 1951.
28. Kirk S.A., McCarthy J.J., Kirk W.D.: *Examiner's Manual, Illinois Test of Psycholinguistic Abilities*. Urbana, Ill., University of Illinois Press, 1968.
29. Hathaway S.R., Meehl P.E.: *An Atlas for the Clinical Use of the MMPI*. Minneapolis, University of Minnesota Press, 1951.
30. Dahlstrom W.G., Welsh G.S., Dahlstrom L.E.: *An MMPI Handbook, Vol. 1, Clinical Interpretation*, Rev. ed. Minneapolis, University of Minnesota Press, 1972.
31. Dahlstrom W.G., Welsh G.S., Dahlstrom L.E.: *An MMPI Handbook, Vol. 2, Research Developments and Applications*. Minneapolis, University of Minnesota Press, 1975.
32. Weiner I.B. (ed.): *Clinical Methods in Psychology*. New York, John Wiley & Sons, Inc., 1976.
33. Lindzey G.: On the classification of projective techniques. *Psychol. Bull.* 56:158, 1959.
34. Beck S.J.: How the Rorschach came to America. *J. Pers. Assess.* 36:105, 1972.
35. Klopfer B., Kelley, D.: *The Rorschach Technique*. Tarrytown-on-Hudson, N.Y., World Book, 1942.
36. Murray H.A.: *Explorations in Personality*. New York, Oxford University Press, 1938.
37. Rotter J.B.: Word association and sentence completion methods, in Anderson H.H., Anderson L. (eds.): *An Introduction to Projective Techniques*. Englewood Cliffs, N.J., Prentice-Hall, Inc., 1951.
38. Goldberg P.: A review of sentence completion methods in personality assessment. *J. Project. Techn.* 29:12, 1965.

7 / Reactions to Stress

JONATHAN J. BRAUNSTEIN, M.D.

STRESS IS, and always has been, a normal part of life. It has both beneficial and harmful effects. On the one hand, it helps us to cope with challenging situations and events by evoking psychological and physiological responses that cause us to be more alert mentally and better able to meet the physical demands of these experiences. On the other hand, these same responses, if intense or prolonged, can have harmful effects on a person's physical and mental health. It is this feature of stress that makes it a particularly important area of medicine for physicians and others responsible for the care of the sick.

In this chapter, the following information about stress will be presented: its definition, the situations and events that produce it, its physical and psychological effects, and the results of studies indicating that it can adversely affect health. Chapter 8 deals with some of the diseases thought to be due to psychological and social stressors, the so-called psychosomatic disorders.

DEFINITION OF STRESS

Despite the fact that *stress* is a term frequently used by medical personnel, behavioral scientists, and lay persons, there is little agreement on its meaning.[1] It has been equated with an external force, a provocative situation or event, the response of the body to a demand, and other phenomena. For purposes of this discussion, stress is defined as any *change* requiring adaptation by an individual. Also included in this definition is the threat of change, i.e., a situation in which one anticipates that change may occur. That which produces change is called a stressor. This concept is graphically represented as follows:

Stressor ⟶ Change ⟶ Adaptation

There is a stimulus-response relationship between these variables, with the stressor being the stimulus for change and the adaptation being the response to it. Let's examine each element of this diagram.

Stressors

There are four general types of stressors: physical, psychological, social, and cultural. Extremes in temperature, inadequate nutrition, injury, and illness are examples of physical stressors. Psychologically, conflict in interpersonal relationships, frustration in satisfying basic needs and desires, and pressure and tension associated with work may act as stressors. The anticipation of adverse situations or events, even without their occurrence, can also be stressful, as for instance, the prospect of illness, economic reverses, or the loss of a loved one.

Many situations and events that people experience in their day-to-day lives are stressful. This fact was recognized more than 50 years ago by Adolf Meyer, a psychiatrist who originated the concept of the "life chart" as a means of studying their impact.[2] His method consisted of obtaining a detailed history of the important experiences occurring to his patients during their lifetime and correlating them with variations in their physical and emotional health. Meyer was able to show that events such as success or failure in school, occupational change, marriage, births, and deaths in a family often had an adverse effect on an individual's well-being.

A list of common life events that are associated with stress has been compiled by Holmes and Rahe in their Social Readjustment Rating Scale (Table 7–1).[3] The list was drawn from an analysis of over 5,000 case histories and the data obtained in laboratory experiments. The stressors in this scale can be divided into several categories depending on their social value: those that are desirable, undesirable, or neutral in value. Most of the events are undesirable and easily recognized as being adverse. Some of them, however, such as marriage, retirement, pregnancy, and outstanding personal achievement, are desirable social goals and, consequently, are less readily perceived to be stressors. The quality that all the events have in common is the ca-

TABLE 7–1.—SOCIAL READJUSTMENT RATING SCALE (SRRS)

RANK	LIFE EVENT	MEAN VALUE
1	Death of spouse	100
2	Divorce	73
3	Marital separation	65
4	Jail term	63
5	Death of close family member	63
6	Personal injury or illness	53
7	Marriage	50
8	Fired at work	47
9	Marital reconciliation	45
10	Retirement	45
11	Change in health of family member	44
12	Pregnancy	40
13	Sex difficulties	39
14	Gain of new family member	39
15	Business readjustment	39
16	Change in financial state	38
17	Death of close friend	37
18	Change to different line of work	36
19	Change in number of arguments with spouse	35
20	Mortgage over $10,000	31
21	Foreclosure of mortgage or loan	30
22	Change in responsibilities at work	29
23	Son or daughter leaving home	29
24	Trouble with in-laws	29
25	Outstanding personal achievement	28
26	Wife begin or stop work	26
27	Begin or end school	26
28	Change in living conditions	25
29	Revision of personal habits	24
30	Trouble with boss	23
31	Change in work hours or conditions	20
32	Change in residence	20
33	Change in schools	20
34	Change in recreation	19
35	Change in church activities	19
36	Change in social activities	18
37	Mortgage or loan less than $10,000	17
38	Change in sleeping habits	16
39	Change in number of family get-togethers	15
40	Change in eating habits	15
41	Vacation	13
42	Christmas	12
43	Minor violations of the law	11

Reprinted with permission from *Journal of Psychosomatic Research*, Volume II, Holmes T.H., Rahe R.H., p. 216, Copyright [1967], Pergamon Press, Ltd.[3]

pacity to produce change in one's pattern of life that requires adjustment—this is what accounts for their stressful effects.

The cultural aspects of life are also associated with the need to adapt, as for example, when a person moves from one cultural environment to another. This results in his being exposed to a new and different life-style, which is often quite stressful. Studies indicate that the demands and frustrations accompanying this experience may have adverse effects on physical and emotional health.

Change

The idea that man exists in a state of physiological and psychological balance is an old one dating back to the time of Hippocrates. In this century, the term *homeostasis* has been used by physiologists to refer to this concept. The change produced by a stressor causes a disruption of homeostasis, evoking adaptive responses designed to restore physical and psychological equilibrium.

Because of his unique mental makeup, man is predisposed to anticipate stressful situations and events prior to their occurrence. This is often enough to upset a person's physical or emotional balance. Indeed, this anticipation often creates as much or more change than the situation itself.

The impact of a stressor (i.e., the degree of change it produces) is determined by three factors: first, the nature of the stressor and the circumstances in which it occurs; second, the characteristics of the individual involved; and third, the meaning of the stressor to him. In general, novel situations or events have more of an impact than those with which a person has had previous experience. Also, the longer one is exposed to a stressor, the less of an impact it is likely to have on him. The SRRS (see Table 7–1) provides a quantitative estimate of the degree of change produced by different life events. Subjects were asked to rate 43 events in terms of the amount of effort and length of time required to accommodate to each of them. On this basis, relative values called life change units (LCUs) were assigned to the events, which were then arranged in rank order. The numerical values allow for a comparison of the magnitude of change caused by the events. Validation of this scale was accomplished in studies involving samples of our population and different cultural groups around the world.[4]

One cannot assess the impact of a stressor on an individual, however, without knowing a good deal about the person and his capacity to tolerate change. This capacity is related to physical, psychological, and social variables such as his state of health, personality, coping devices, and social support systems. Someone who is in a stable condition both physically and emotionally is more likely to maintain homeostasis when faced by a stressful experience. Conversely, physical illness, emotional upset, and inadequate social supports increase a person's vulnerability to change produced by a stressor.

The meaning that situations and events have for a person is very important in determining their impact. An event that is perceived as stressful by one person may not be viewed as such by another. It is an error for medical personnel to assume that the meaning they happen to attach to a situation or event is shared by the patient. Instead, they should always try to ascertain the significance of the experience for him.

A 35-year-old woman was seen by a physician because she had complaints of lower abdominal pain and diarrhea. These symptoms had been present intermittently for 5 years but had intensified during the past week. She had no other symptoms such as fever, weight loss, nausea, or vomiting. Physical examination revealed a young woman who appeared anxious. The only abnormalities were an increase in her pulse rate (110 beats per minute) and a moderate tenderness in the left lower quadrant of her abdomen overlying the sigmoid colon. Laboratory tests, including sigmoidoscopy and complete x-ray studies of her gastrointestinal tract, showed normal results.

On the basis of the clinical evaluation, the woman was felt to have the "irritable colon" syndrome, a functional bowel disorder known to be adversely affected by stress. Initially, no reason for the exacerbation of her illness could be found. However, during a subsequent office visit she admitted to being upset over the death of her brother, which occurred about a year earlier. Just prior to the intensification of her symptoms, she had visited the cemetery on the anniversary of his death. The woman also confided that she was very concerned because he had died from ulcerative colitis and she feared that she might have this disease. It soon became apparent to the physician that this concern plus the emotional reaction associated with the cemetery visit were acting as stressors, producing adverse effects on the woman's physical condition. Her management consisted of reassurance that her ailment was benign and had no relation to her brother's disease, dietary therapy, and the use of a mild tranquilizer, when necessary, to relieve her anxiety.

Up to this point in the discussion, the stress concept can be displayed as follows:

| Stressor | → | Change | → | Adaptation |

1. Physical
2. Psychological
3. Social
4. Cultural

Magnitude depends on:
1. Nature of stressor and prevailing circumstances
2. Characteristics of person involved
3. Meaning of stressor to him

Now, let's explore the nature of the adaptation that occurs in response to the change produced by a stressor.

Adaptation

There are two general types of responses to stress: physiological and psychological. Ordinarily, they are beneficial in that they help a person to cope with the stressor, to counteract the change it produces, and to restore homeostasis. Under certain circumstances, however, they can be harmful by reducing a person's adaptive capacity, causing physical and emotional symptoms, and predisposing him to disease. This is most likely to happen if the stress to which an individual is exposed is especially severe and prolonged, or if he reacts excessively or inappropriately to it.

Stress-induced physiological and psychological responses generally occur together as part of an integrated reaction pattern. However, in this chapter they will be dealt with separately for purposes of simplicity in presentation. In the following section, the interrelationship between them will be discussed in terms of the neuroanatomical basis for their occurrence.

PHYSIOLOGICAL RESPONSES
Basic Mechanisms

Many clinicians and scientists helped to elucidate the nature of these responses; however, the names of Walter Cannon, Hans Selye, Harold Wolff, and John Mason bear special mention. Cannon developed the concept of the "fight or flight response" based on his observations of the reactions of animals exposed to various stressors.[5] He noted that the animals exhibited an increase in blood pressure, heart rate, respiration, and blood flow to muscles—all of which seemed to prepare them either to engage a threatening foe in combat or to escape from danger. He also found that changes in the blood occurred during stress, including an increase in the level of glucose and a decrease in the clotting time. These appeared to serve an adaptive function by providing energy for meeting the stress and protecting the animal from excessive bleeding if injured. Cannon was able to identify the neuroendocrine basis for these responses, showing that they were mediated by the sympathetic division of the autonomic nervous system and the secretion of "adrenin" by the adrenal medulla.

Selye established the vital role of the adrenal cortex in adaptation. In 1936, he described a set of generalized body reactions in animals subjected to different types of stressors, which he called the general adaptation syndrome.[6] It occurred in three stages: an initial "alarm reaction" on sudden exposure of the organism to the stressful stimulus, a "stage of resistance" in which the organism acquired maximal adaptation, and a final "stage of exhaustion" associated with a loss of adaptation and death of the animal. The syndrome was accompanied by enlargement of the adrenal cortex along with histologic evidence of increased functional activity. In further studies, Selye demonstrated that the adrenal cortical response to stress results from initial activation of the hypothalamus, causing the release of adrenocorticotropin (ACTH) by the pituitary gland.

In a study of monkeys exposed to stress, Mason found a complex pattern of organization in their endocrine response (Fig 7–1).[7] During exposure to a stressor, there was an increase in the levels of adrenal corticoids (17-OHCS), adrenal medullary hormones (epinephrine and norepinephrine), thyroxine (BEI), and growth hormone, while the levels of insulin, estrogen, and testosterone declined. In the recovery phase, a reversal of this pattern took place. Mason interpreted these findings in terms of the action of the hormones on energy metabolism, dividing them into two types: those that were catabolic (adrenal corticoids, epinephrine, norepinephrine, growth hormone, and thyroxine) and those that were anabolic (insulin and testosterone). He reasoned that during the period of stress, the effects of the increased levels of catabolic hormones (i.e., the breakdown of glycogen, adipose tissue, and protein) produced a rise in the levels of blood glucose and free fatty acids, thereby providing the necessary sources of fuel for the organism. Later, in the recovery period, the action of the increased amounts of anabolic hormones (i.e. the synthesis of glycogen, adipose tissue, and protein) caused a restoration of the body tissues, which had been depleted during the stress.

Studies of the endocrine response to stress in man have included measurements of a variety of hormones in the blood and urine including cortisol, growth hormone, catecholamines, prolactin, and testosterone.[8] Acute exposure to stress, as for example in surgery, typically results in increased levels of all these hormones, except for testosterone, which decreases. The anticipation of the experience (i.e., surgery) often evokes the same general response as the experience itself.

In contrast to the early studies of stress in animals and man, which identified general and nonspecific patterns of endocrine response to a variety of stressors (e.g., fight or flight response, general adaptation syndrome), current research has focused on individual differences in the way organisms react. In man, these differences are attributable to variations in perception of the stressor, the presence and effectiveness of coping devices that "shield" the person from awareness of the stressor, and prior experience with the stressor.[8] It has been found that continued or repeated exposure to stressful stimuli

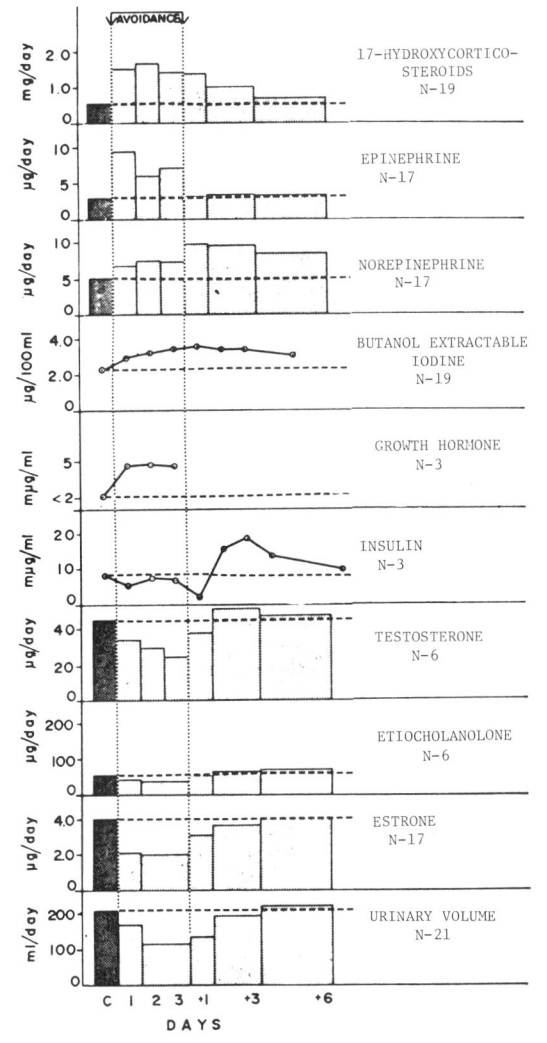

Fig 7–1.—Endocrine response to stress (72-hour avoidance sessions) in the monkey, with the levels of hormones in the blood and urine during the stress and recovery periods. (From Mason J.W.: *Psychosom. Med.* 30(suppl.):774, 1968. Used by permission.)

is associated with a diminished endocrine response, with the catecholamine response extinguishing more slowly than that for cortisol.

Adaptation to stress is associated with many alterations in the function of the body's organs. The extent of the alterations can be appreciated by considering the widespread physiological and metabolic effects of the neuroendocrine mechanisms discussed. These mechanisms are involved in the control of cardiac function, the activity of smooth muscle and glands, energy metabolism, fluid and electrolyte balance, tissue inflammatory response, and immunologic reactivity.

Wolff was one of the first investigators to conduct systematic studies of organ function during stress.[9] Figure 7–2, taken from his text, illustrates the changes in gastric acid secretion and blood flow occurring in a person exposed to chronic emotional conflict. When he surveyed the functions of other organs, such as the heart, lungs, skin, skeletal muscle, and colon, Wolff found stress reactions that were equally striking. He demonstrated that there is a significant variability in these reactions, depending on the nature of the stressor and the subject's emotional response. This variability can be appreciated by comparing Figures 7–2 and 7–3, which show opposite changes in gastric function occurring in the same person under stress—an increase in acid secretion and blood flow when he was angry and a decrease in these functions when he was frightened. Wolff found that the stress reactions of other organ systems were also subject to great variability.

In contrast to Wolff's observations, other investigators have described individuals with stereotyped physiological patterns of reaction to stress. These subjects had distinctive autonomic nervous system reactions that were reproducible when they were exposed to different stressors or to the same stressor at different times. Such persons are sometimes referred to as *cardiovascular reactors* or *gastrointestinal reactors*, depending on the organ system that is most reactive to stress. Whether these stereotyped responses to stress are innate or acquired is a question that is unresolved. There is evidence that infants

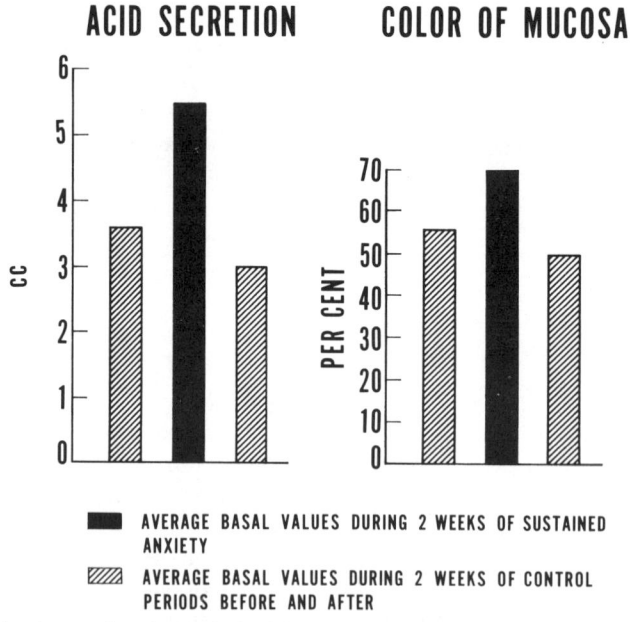

Fig 7–2.—Sustained acceleration of gastric function (acid secretion and blood flow into the mucous membrane) during chronic emotional conflict, with ensuing anger as a prevailing feeling state. (From Wolff H.G.: *Stress and Disease*, 1953. Courtesy of Charles C Thomas, Publisher, Springfield, Illinois.)

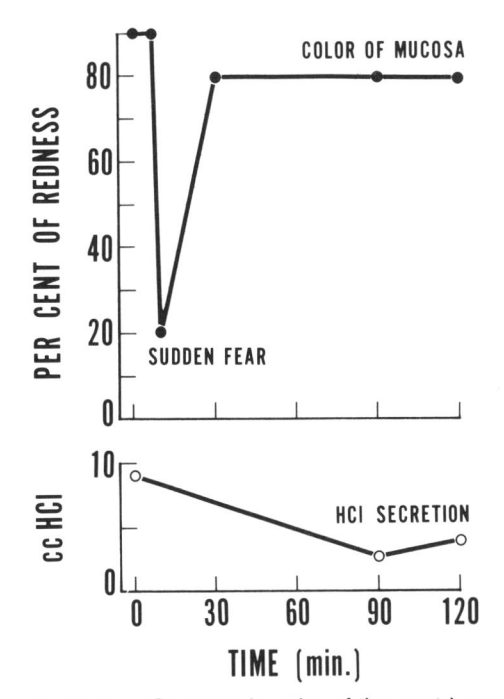

Fig 7–3.—Changes in color of the gastric mucosa (gastric fistula) associated with the subject's fear that he had lost a valuable protocol, had "lost face," and possibly had lost his job. (From Wolff H.G.: *Stress and Disease,* 1953. Courtesy of Charles C Thomas, Publisher, Springfield, Illinois.)

exposed to stress shortly after birth differ in the nature of their responses—some reacting primarily via the cardiovascular system and others by means of the respiratory system, the skin, or the gastrointestinal tract. While this seems to favor a role for genetic factors, it is quite possible that social learning is important in the development of stress-induced reaction patterns, since it has been shown that autonomic function can be modified by operant conditioning. For example, a child who develops a gastrointestinal reaction (e.g., nausea, vomiting, and abdominal discomfort) as a result of the stress of having to go to school may have this behavior reinforced by the attention he receives and by being allowed to stay home. If this reaction is rewarded again and again, over a period of time he may "learn" to respond to other kinds of stress in the same way, thus, becoming a "gastrointestinal reactor."

Clinical Syndromes Associated with the Physiological Responses

Physiological responses to stress may be accompanied by symptoms and signs which, in some individuals, produce significant distress and disability. With acute episodes, people develop symptoms of anxiety and enhanced activity of the autonomic nervous system and adrenal medulla. Several of the clinical syndromes that result from the effects of acute stress are listed in Table 7–2. For purposes of clinical diagnosis, the physician should be aware that the clinical syndromes resulting from acute stress can mimic a number of organic disorders such as hyperthyroidism, hypoglycemia, and an adrenal medullary tumor (pheochromocytoma).

Acute anxiety reactions are characterized by symptoms of extreme apprehension, restlessness, tremulousness, palpitations, and hyperventilation. These can be so severe that the person affected thinks he is suffering from an acute medical catastrophe, which causes a secondary emotional reaction that acts to intensify his original symptoms. Thus, a vicious cycle is set up, which can result in a state of panic. Anxiety reactions are usually precipitated by overt psychological stress; however, there are instances in which the stressor is not apparent and a careful medical history must be obtained in order to identify the cause of the reaction. Medical management consists of emotional support, reassurance, and, if necessary, the administration of a sedative or tranquilizer to calm the patient. In cases in which the episodes recur and are chronically disabling, psychiatric evaluation and therapy are often indicated.

A *vasovagal reaction* is the medical term for the common faint. This reaction generally follows acute stress of various types, for example, accidents and injuries, illness associated with severe pain, and situations in which there is extreme emotional upset. Persons typically develop symptoms of weakness, dizziness, and sweating followed by a loss of consciousness. Physiologically, the syndrome is explained by a decrease in cardiac output due to vasodilatation and a gravitational pooling of

TABLE 7-2.—CLINICAL MANIFESTATIONS OF ACUTE STRESS

	SYMPTOMS*	SIGNS
Acute anxiety reaction	Restlessness Irritability Tremulousness Breathlessness Palpitations Sweating, flushing Anorexia, nausea Epigastric distress	Cool moist skin Pallor Pupillary dilation Tachycardia Tachypnea Hyperpnea Increased blood pressure
Vasovagal reaction	Faintness, dizziness, and syncope Confusion Sweating Nausea Epigastric distress	Pallor Sweating Cool moist skin Bradycardia Decreased blood pressure
Hyperventilation syndrome	Faintness, dizziness Breathlessness Feeling of suffocation Tightness of chest Palpitations Paresthesias and numbness of fingers and circumoral region	Tachypnea Hyperpnea Signs of tetany—Chvostek and Trousseau signs, carpopedal spasm

*Anxiety and nervousness are present with all the reactions.

blood in the lower extremities. The diminished cardiac output is associated with a reduction in blood pressure and blood flow to the brain, causing syncope. Ordinarily, these hemodynamic changes would give rise to a compensatory increase in heart rate, but this fails to take place because the activation of parasympathetic (vagal) mechanisms produces a paradoxical bradycardia. The syncopal episode is short-lived because when the person faints, assumption of the supine position counteracts the gravitational pooling of blood, restoring cardiac output and cerebral circulation.

The hyperventilation occurring with acute stress is the cause of another syndrome characterized by faintness and dizziness.

An 18-year-old man was seen in a hospital emergency room; he complained of weakness and dizziness. These symptoms were associated with a sensation of "pins and needles" in his fingers and in the area about his mouth. He described himself as a "tense and nervous" individual, noting that these feelings had recently intensified because of his concern about an upcoming college examination. While studying for the examination, he first became aware of extreme nervousness, palpitations, and a feeling that he was suffocating. These symptoms were followed shortly by extreme weakness and dizziness. The episode lasted about 10 minutes, only to recur a half-hour later. He had four of these "attacks" before coming to the emergency room. Clinical examination revealed him to be apprehensive and hyperventilating. Signs of excessive sympathetic discharge were present, including tachycardia, cool moist skin, and dilated pupils. There was no evidence of tetany. A diagnosis of the hyperventilation syndrome was made by the emergency room physician, who, recognizing the emotional basis for the man's condition, attempted to calm him down by discussing his feelings and concerns about the upcoming examination. This approach was successful in ameliorating the symptoms.

The *hyperventilation syndrome* is associated with a reduction in the arterial content of carbon dioxide (Pa_{CO_2}) due to its loss through respiration, thus producing respiratory alkalosis. Acute reduction in Pa_{CO_2} causes a constriction of the cerebral arteries and a decrease in cerebral blood flow, while the alkalosis increases the binding of oxygen to hemoglobin, which tends to reduce the oxygenation of the tissues, including the brain. These two mechanisms are thought to be responsible for the lightheadedness and giddiness experienced by these persons. If the alkalosis is marked, symptoms and signs of tetany may also develop, which are presumably due to a reduction in the level of ionized calcium in the blood. During hyperventilation, electrocardiographic (ECG) changes can occur that simulate cardiac disease, and if chest pain is a part of the clinical picture, a mistaken diagnosis of organic heart disease may be made.

Persons exposed to chronic stress may develop many of the same clinical manifestations that occur in the acute reactions, except on a more protracted basis. In addition, acute episodes may punctuate the course of their illness. Symptoms, such as headache, weight loss, insomnia, and multiple ill-defined somatic complaints are prominent and may be a reason for repeated visits to the physician for medical evaluation.

One of the classic syndromes occurring in persons with chronic stress is *neurocirculatory asthenia*. Persons with this syndrome complain of dyspnea and fatigue with activity, palpitations, and chest pain. The dyspnea is usually a "sighing" type of breathlessness, while the chest pain is often located in the region of the apex of the heart—features that help differentiate these symptoms from those of organic heart disease. Anxiety and manifestations of increased sympathetic adrenal medullary activity are also present, as they are with other types of stress reactions. Evidence for the latter can be found in the physical examination, which often demonstrates a hyperkinetic pattern of cardiovascular function with a rapid heart rate, increased blood pressure, widened pulse pressure, and, frequently, systolic heart murmur. The most important aspect of the medical management of these patients is to reassure them that they are not suffering from an organic cardiac or pulmonary disease—a concern that is usually present and responsible for a great deal of anxiety.

PSYCHOLOGICAL RESPONSES

How a person responds psychologically to a stressor depends a good deal on his coping resources, which are determined by his personality, intellectual capacity, previous experiences with stress, and the support he receives from family and friends. The nature of these responses is critically important, since some are useful in coping with a stressor, while others interfere with the ability to do so. In deciding whether a particular response falls into the first or second category, it is helpful to consider the requirements for successful psychological adaptation. These include the following: first, one must be able to maintain adequate psychological balance during the period of stress; second, he must be able to assess the nature of the stressor accurately; third, he must be able to make appropriate judgments and decisions; and fourth, he must be able to interact effectively with the environment.

Specific Types of Psychological Responses

Exposure to stress commonly results in anxiety and mental arousal, which are potentially beneficial to the individual. The former serves to alert him to the presence of a stressor, while the latter makes him more aware of stimuli in the environment and enhances his intellectual function. The psychological responses that inhibit a person's adaptation include: excessive anxiety, emotional discharge and instability, disturbance of cognitive function, and loss of self-esteem. The adverse effects of these reactions are due to their interference with reality-testing and problem-solving, both of which are essential if one is to assess a stressful situation accurately, make the correct decisions, and take appropriate action. Responses of this type must be kept under control if the individual is to deal effectively with the stressor and the change it produces.

Anxiety, which is generally described as an uncomfortable feeling of tension, uneasiness, and apprehension, is the hallmark of the emotional response to stress. It varies in intensity depending on the degree of stress and the reactivity of the individual, and, as noted earlier, it is frequently accompanied by symptoms of sympathetic nervous system discharge (e.g., nervousness, restlessness, irritability, palpitations, sweating, and tremulousness). By acting as a warning signal for the presence of a stressor, anxiety and its accompanying manifestations can be valuable aids to adaptation. However, the usefulness of anxiety as a coping mechanism is lost when it becomes too intense or prolonged. In these instances, it reduces an individual's adaptive capacity and may also be the cause of significant distress and disability.

Because stress-induced anxiety produces discomfort, the individual tries in some way to alleviate it. One means is to eliminate the source of stress (stressor); however, this is frequently not possible and so he must rely on other methods such as ego defense mechanisms, role-playing devices, and physical activity. Any of the defense mechanisms described in chapter 5 may be used. Denial is commonly used, especially by persons trying to combat the anxiety associated with the stress of illness. Role-playing, or the assumption of a stylized pattern of behavior, sometimes helps to reduce the anxiety arising from certain stressful situations. For example, the haughty and official demeanor displayed by some physicians may be an attempt to discourage stressful challenges to their authority by patients. Engaging in physical activity can also be an effective method of reducing anxiety and tension. For instance, playing tennis or jogging can be a way of "letting off steam."

Many anxiety-reducing coping devices that are currently used by people originated earlier in their lives as a result of their experiences with conflict and stress. Those mechanisms that were successful in alleviating anxiety were positively reinforced and, with time, became part of the individual's repertoire of adaptive responses to be used in dealing with future adversity.

When confronted with a stressful challenge, an individual may become emotionally upset and develop feelings of helplessness, anger, or frustration. Whereas anxiety is a subjective experience, the *emotional discharge and instability* occurring with stress is usually apparent to others. In fact, it is one clue to the diagnosis of a stress reaction. Sometimes the individual under stress is unaware of the reason for an emotional outburst, and the physician has to discuss his behavior with him at some length before the cause of the reaction becomes clear. It is important for medical personnel to appreciate that those who are ill may be under considerable stress, which causes them to react emotionally. Indeed, one of the goals of medical care is to help a patient control this response so he can deal more effectively with the problems surrounding his sickness.

Another response to stress that may reduce one's coping ability is a *disturbance in cognitive function*. This is due primarily to a disruption of psychological homeostasis caused by the stressor, although anxiety and emotional instability are also contributing factors. Intellectual function is commonly impaired due to the stress of an illness. This accounts for the difficulty many people have in making sound judgments and decisions when they are sick. It also explains some instances of inappropriate behavior displayed by patients. Other aspects of cognitive function, such as concentration and memory, are also adversely affected by stress.

Anxiety, emotional instability, and impaired cognitive function all interfere with logical thought and action; consequently, a person exposed to a stressful situation or event often reacts impulsively. He frequently has to rely on others to help him interpret his experiences and make the right decisions. Their support and guidance are critical to his successful adaptation. Traditionally, family and close friends have assumed this supportive role; however, in recent years there has been a weakening of these traditional systems of support in our country. The nuclear family of modern America is less equipped to deal with stress than the extended family of the past, especially when the reason for the stress is an illness of one of the parents. Also, geographic mobility has reduced the availability of relatives, other than the immediate family, to act as sources of support during times of stress.

Many people experience a *loss of self-esteem* when exposed to stress. There are several reasons for this response. First, the disturbance in homeostasis caused by a stressor is damaging to one's sense of independence and self-sufficiency. For example, when a person becomes ill, he often loses confidence in his ability to control the events in his life and develops feelings of helplessness and dependency. Second, stressful experiences are often associated with the threat or actual loss of something important to an individual (e.g., love, approval, health), causing him to feel depressed and reducing his sense of self-worth. Finally, concern about not being able to deal successfully with a stressful challenge can be damaging to one's self-confidence.

Stages in Psychological Responses

The psychological reactions to acute stress occur in several discrete, but overlapping, stages. There is an initial *stage of impact* after exposure to a stressor. If the change it produces in homeostasis is very great, the person may experience feelings of shock, numbness, and bewilderment. In a study of the period immediately following community disasters, Tyhurst found that a majority of the people either became stunned and bewildered or reacted with confusion and hysteria.[10] Most were unable to recall the details of what had happened when questioned later. Only a few of those exposed remained "cool and collected" and were able to engage in purposeful activity. This shocklike state occurs only in response to severely stressful experiences; in situations of mild or moderate stress, the reaction is less intense, consisting mainly of anxiety.

Next, there is a *stage of stabilization* in which the individual tries to regain psychological balance after the impact of the stressor. To do so, anxiety, emotional upset, and impaired cognitive function must be controlled. This is accomplished mainly by the use of psychological defense mechanisms. The support that one receives from family and friends is also important. The degree to which a person is successful in stabilizing himself will determine his capacity to cope with the situation or event causing the stress.

Finally, there is the *stage of resolution* in which the individual turns his attention to the source of the stress and attempts to deal with it. Several approaches are open to him: he can try to cope with the stressor directly by either altering his behavior or modifying circumstances in the environment, he can avoid or "run away" from the stressor, or he can take no action. Each of these approaches can have adaptive value if used appropriately. The best method to use depends on the nature of the stressor and the resources of the individual. There are times when one should confront a stressful problem and try to cope with it by taking direct action. There are situations in which this is not possible, however (e.g., death of loved one), and the most that one can do is try to maintain psychological integrity until the impact of the stress passes.

Coping with a stressor directly requires good psychological function. One must be able to exercise emotional restraint so that impulsive action does not occur. The capacity for reality-testing and problem-solving must be maintained so that the individual can make use of logically planned action. Obviously, one can use many different styles and strategies when following this general approach to adaptation.

When confronted by a stressful experience, some persons try to cope by avoiding or "running away" from it. This can be accomplished by direct means (physically removing oneself from the situation) or indirect means (the use of alcohol or drugs). Using alcohol or drugs as an "escape mechanism" in dealing with stress has become commonplace in our society, often to the detriment of the individual. Not only do these agents interfere with one's coping ability but they also may be responsible for physical and mental illness. Work can also serve as a means of avoiding stress, particularly stress arising from unpleasant social situations. A person who is unhappy with his home life may become a "workaholic," spending long hours at his job so he does not have to be at home too much. Avoidance of a stressor may be successful in temporarily alleviating anxiety and discomfort; however, if the problem persists the individual may be forced to come to terms with it.

A person may elect to do nothing about a stressor even though it is a source of psychological discomfort. Conflict in interpersonal relationships is frequently handled in this manner. Generally, this mode of coping is unsatisfactory unless the stress is transitory and self-limited. If a person is exposed continually to a relationship that is stressful (e.g., an unhappy marriage), the resulting anxiety and emotional upset usually make the situation intolerable. Ultimately, he has to decide whether to face up to the conflict and try to resolve it, or avoid the situation completely (e.g., separation or divorce).

RELATIONSHIP BETWEEN PHYSIOLOGICAL AND PSYCHOLOGICAL RESPONSES

At this juncture in the discussion, the concept of stress can be pictured as follows:

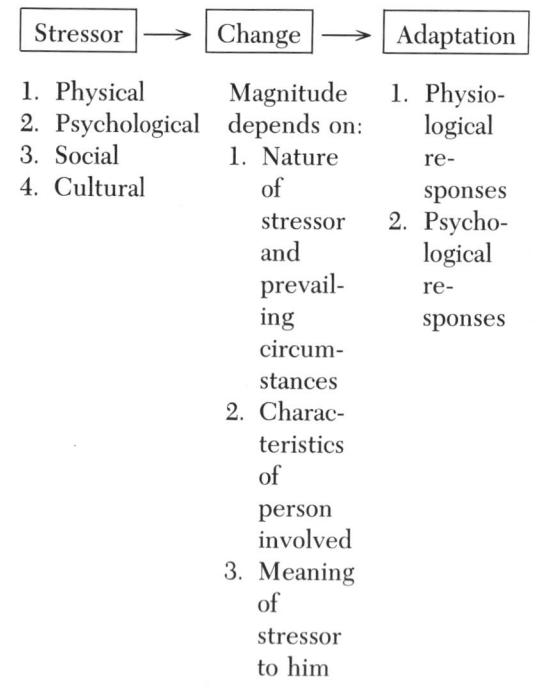

Stressor	→	Change	→	Adaptation
1. Physical 2. Psychological 3. Social 4. Cultural		Magnitude depends on: 1. Nature of stressor and prevailing circumstances 2. Characteristics of person involved 3. Meaning of stressor to him		1. Physiological responses 2. Psychological responses

The relationship between the physiological and psychological responses can be described in terms of the neuroanatomical basis for the body's reaction to stress, which will be summarized briefly. Stimuli from a threatening stressor in the environment impinge on sensory receptors in the eyes and ears, giving rise to impulses that travel via sensory pathways in the brain stem to the thalamus and reticular formation. These impulses are also conducted to areas of the brain concerned with the regulation of specific physiological (motor, autonomic, and endocrine) and psychological (cognitive and emotional) functions. These areas are the cerebral cortex for cognitive and motor function, the hypothalamus for autonomic and endocrine function, and the limbic system for emotional response. Neuronal pathways exist between these regions, which allow for the integration of their activities and thereby the coordination of the body's reactions to stress.

A typical pattern of reaction to the presence of an external stressor includes the following[11]: On suddenly being confronted with the stressor, the individual would become more alert (cortical activation), he would experience anxiety and fear (limbic system activation), his heart would beat faster and his blood pressure would rise (hypothalamic-autonomic nervous system activation), and there would be a discharge of cortisol from his adrenal gland (hypothalamic-endocrine activation). Thus, the activation of specific centers of the brain on exposure to a threatening situation leads to both physiological and psychological responses that prepare an individual to cope with the stressor. Similar responses take place with internal stressors, as for example, with the anticipation of adversity or with emotional conflict. Under these circumstances, information that originates in the cerebral cortex activates the other regulatory centers and gives rise to adaptive reactions.

While it is commonly thought that emotions are the cause of the physiological responses observed during stress, it is better to think of these reactions as occurring together, both being adaptations to the change produced by a stressor. The fact that persons under stress become anxious and emotionally upset at the same time that they experience physiological reactions should not be misinterpreted as indicating that the emotional response caused the physical responses.

LIFE STRESS AND ILLNESS

A middle-aged executive experiences a heart attack during a time of intense work, a young girl with asthma develops an acute episode after an argument with her parents, and a college student manifests signs of acute schizophrenia shortly after he is divorced from his wife. These are all examples of illness that seemingly has arisen as a result of stressful life events. The idea that stress can aggravate a preexisting physical and emotional illness is widely accepted by medical personnel; however, the question of whether or not it can cause disease to develop in a previously healthy individual has not been answered to the satisfaction of many physicians. Selye applied the term *diseases of adaptation* to illnesses such as hypertension, peptic ulcer, and ulcerative colitis, which he felt represented maladaptive responses to stress. In his studies, Wolff concluded that disease could arise whenever the physiological responses of the body to stress were excessive in degree or persisted over a long period of time. The concept of psychosomatic disorders (discussed in chap. 8) is based on the premise that the physiological responses induced by psychological stressors can cause pathologic changes in the body's organs.

An analysis of the relationship between stress and illness can be approached by posing three questions:
1. What clinical manifestations (symptoms and signs) occur in persons under stress?
2. What evidence is there that stress can exacerbate a preexisting illness?
3. Can stress, by itself or in combination with other causes, produce disease in a previously healthy individual?

The first question has been answered in the earlier sections of this chapter. To recapitulate, stress is responsible for causing a wide range of symptoms and signs for which persons may seek medical care. The rest of this chapter, and chapter 8 dealing with behavioral medicine, will focus on questions 2 and 3.

The Relationship Between Life Change and Onset of Illness

Empirical observations dating back to ancient times have indicated that people who suffer from excessive stress are more likely to become ill, but only in the past decade have medical personnel been able to establish a scientific basis for these observations. This basis was provided by the development of the Social Readjustment Rating Scale (SRRS) by Holmes and Rahe. Studies using the SRRS have shown that the onset of physical and emotional illness is sometimes preceded by a particularly stressful period in a person's life. Holmes and Rahe refer to this period in terms of a "life crisis," which they define as a clustering of stressful life events whose individual values, in life change units (LCUs), total at least 150 in one year. The greater the magnitude of the LCUs, the more severe is the crisis. In a retrospective analysis of the health of 88 resident physicians working in a Washington hospital, these investigators discovered that a correlation existed between the occurrence of a life crisis and a change in the health status of the physicians.[12] Furthermore, they found that there was a direct relationship between the severity of the crisis and the risk of developing an illness (Table 7–3). A health change followed a mild life crisis 37% of the time, a moderate life crisis 51% of the time, and a major life crisis in 79% of the instances. From this study, it appears that the occurrence of stress predisposes an individual to ill health, and that the more stress he experiences, the greater are his chances of becoming ill.

A number of investigators have studied the specific types of illnesses that are associated with stressful life events. Holmes and Holmes reported that minor ailments such as cuts, bruises, headaches, backaches, and colds

TABLE 7-3.—RELATIONSHIP OF LIFE CRISIS MAGNITUDE TO PERCENTAGE OF LIFE CRISES ASSOCIATED WITH HEALTH CHANGES

	NUMBER OF LIFE CRISES ASSOCIATED WITH HEALTH CHANGES	NUMBER OF LIFE CRISES NOT ASSOCIATED WITH HEALTH CHANGES	TOTAL NUMBER OF LIFE CRISES	LIFE CRISES ASSOCIATED WITH HEALTH CHANGES (%)
Mild life crisis (150–199 LCU)	13	22	35	37
Moderate life crisis (200–299 LCU)	29	28	57	51
Major life crisis (300 + LCU)	30	8	38	79
Total	72*	58	130	55

*Some life crises were associated with more than one health change.
Source: Holmes T.H., Masuda M.: Life change and illness susceptibility, in Dohrenwend B.S., Dohrenwend B.P. (eds.): *Stressful Life Events: Their Nature and Effects.* New York, John Wiley & Sons, Inc., 1974, p. 61. (Used by permission.)

were more likely to be experienced on days when an individual is exposed to an undue amount of stress.[13] The occurrence of more serious illness, of both a physical and an emotional nature, can also be related to the presence of life stress. In the medical history displayed in Figure 7–4, one can see that physical and emotional health problems occurred at times of maximal stress.

The following physical conditions have been reported to occur with greater frequency after a clustering of stressful life

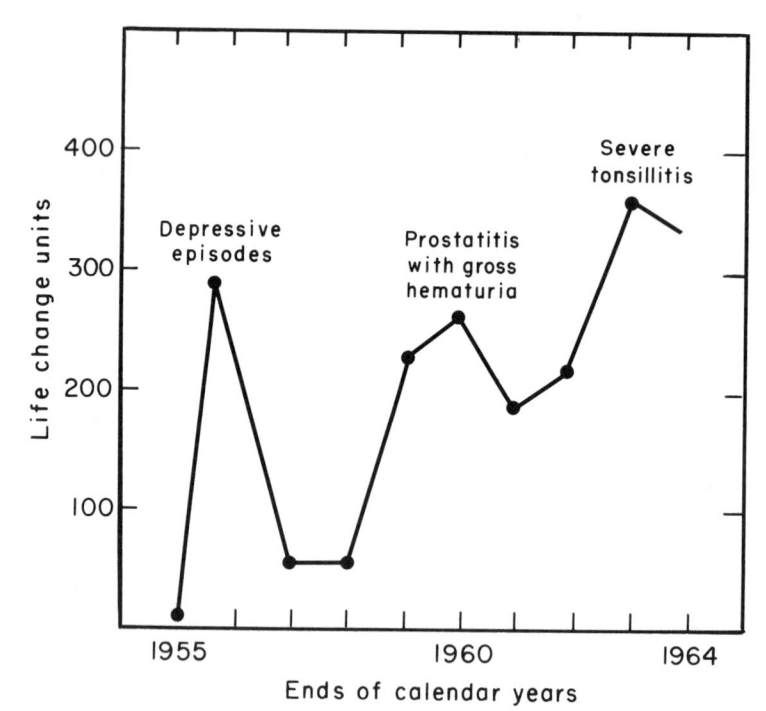

Fig 7–4.—Temporal relationship of life crisis and disease occurrence from a patient's medical history. (From Holmes T.H., Masuda M.: Life changes and illness susceptibility, in Dohrenwend B.S., Dohrenwend B.P. [eds.]: *Stressful Life Events: Their Nature and Effects.* New York, John Wiley & Sons, Inc., 1974. Used by permission.)

events (as indicated by a high value for life change units):

1. Myocardial infarction[14, 15]
2. Sudden cardiac death[16]
3. Diabetes mellitus[17]
4. Tuberculosis[18]
5. Fractures[12]
6. Athletic injuries[19]
7. Alcoholism[20]

Many other medical illnesses such as peptic ulcer disease, ulcerative colitis, asthma, hyperthyroidism, and migraine have been noted to have their onset, or become worse, after episodes of stress. Most of these reports represent anecdotal information or empirical observations, however, and do not have the kind of statistical support that is provided by the methodology used in the studies with the SRRS.

Of particular interest are the reports in the literature of sudden death occurring in association with stressful life experiences. Over a 6-year period, Engel was able to collect 170 cases from newspaper clippings in which the precipitating life event was clearly stated.[21] In most instances, death took place within an hour of the event. The peak age at which death occurred in the 99 male victims reported in this study was 45–55 years, for the 64 women, it was 70–75 years.* There were 3 children and 4 teenagers in the study group. The stressful circumstances under which death took place were divided into 8 categories, which are listed in Table 7–4 along with the numbers of deaths that occurred in each situation. Categories 1 through 5 represent situations in which a loss of some sort was the precipitating event; categories 6 and 7 represent circumstances in which personal danger or threat was present; while category 8 represents situations in which a happy ending occurred. The setting of loss accounted for 59% of the deaths, danger and threat for 34%, and happy ending for 6%. In this study, women were reported to be more likely to die in response to a loss than were men; the latter were more likely to die in reaction to danger and threat. All the life events that were thought to have precipitated death in this group of individuals shared the common quality of being an acute psychological

*The total of 163 men and women does not equal the 170 individuals in the study because in 7 instances the gender was not given.

TABLE 7–4.—STRESSFUL SITUATIONS AND NUMBERS OF ASSOCIATED DEATHS

CATEGORIES	MEN	WOMEN	GENDER NOT SPECIFIED	TOTAL
1. On the impact of the collapse or death of a close person	11 (11%)	25 (39%)		36 (21%)
2. During period of acute grief (within 16 days)	20 (20%)	15 (23%)		35 (20%)
3. Threat of loss of close person	10 (10%)	6 (9%)		16 (9%)
4. During mourning or anniversary	4 (4%)	1 (2%)		5 (3%)
5. Loss of status or self-esteem	9 (9%)	0	1	10* (6%)
6. Personal danger or threat of injury real or symbolic	27 (27%)	14 (22%)	5	46* (27%)
7. After danger is over	10 (10%)	1 (2%)	1	12* (7%)
8. Reunion, triumph, "happy ending"	8 (8%)	2 (3%)		10 (6%)
Total	99 (100%)	64 (100%)		170* (100%)

*Including cases where gender was not specified.
Source: Engel G.L.: *Ann. Intern. Med.* 74(5):773, 1971. (Used by permission.)

stressor that evoked intense psychological and physiological responses on the part of the victims. The most probable cause of death in these individuals was cardiac, i.e., the development of a disturbance of cardiac rhythm that was incompatible with life (e.g., ventricular asystole or tachyarrhythmia).

Paykel studied the relationship between life stress and the onset of psychiatric disorders.[22] According to his investigations, exposure to stressful events is most closely associated with the development of depression and attempts at suicide. Using a retrospective approach, he determined the number of stressful experiences occurring over a 6-month period to three groups of individuals: 53 depressives, 53 suicide attempters, and 53 subjects from the general population. For control purposes, these persons were matched according to age, sex, marital status, social class, and race. The suicide attempters experienced a mean of 3.3 stressful events in the 6 months prior to their attempt, while the depressives reported a mean of 2.0 events. In both instances, these values were significantly higher than the mean of 0.8 reported by the control subjects. Figure 7–5 shows the mean number of stressful events reported by the three groups in each month. Both the depressives and the suicide attempters had a peaking of stressful events in the month prior to the onset of their problem. This increase in stress was most prominent in the group attempting suicide, and careful analysis showed that this peaking occurred primarily during the week prior to their attempt.

According to Paykel, there is also a positive relationship between life stress and the onset of schizophrenia, although this association is not so strong as that found in depression and suicide attempts. Thus, suicide attempters report having the most stressful events, depressives experience the next highest number, and schizophrenics have the least number of stressful events of the three groups. With respect to the neurotic syndromes, Paykel found that there was a linear relationship between the degree of stress to which nonhospitalized persons were exposed and the severity of their symptoms. This relationship did not hold for depressed persons.

Rahe has recently reviewed the epidemiologic and clinical studies documenting the association between recent life change events and depression, schizophrenia, and neurosis.[23] The reader is referred to this article for a more complete discussion of this topic.

To recapitulate, the results of many studies

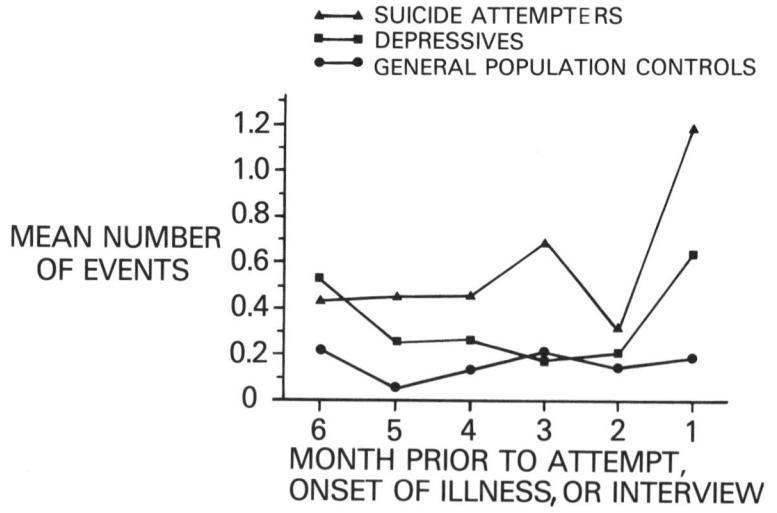

Fig 7–5.—Mean number of stressful events per month for suicide attempters, depressives, and general population controls. (From Paykel E.S.: Life stress and psychiatric disorder, in Dohrenwend B.S., Dohrenwend B.P. [eds.]: *Stressful Life Events: Their Nature and Effects*. New York, John Wiley & Sons, Inc., 1974, p. 145. Used by permission.)

show that there is a correlation between the occurrence of stressful life experiences (in the preceding 6 months to 1 year) and the clinical onset of a variety of physical and emotional illnesses. The highest correlation reported in these studies is relatively modest (0.36) so that, apparently, life change events do not have a strong primary effect on the onset of illness.[23] Some investigators have found that there is a linear relationship between the extent of a life change (i.e., degree of stress associated with the life event) and the risk of developing an illness; others report that the extent of the life change can be directly correlated with the severity of the illness that ensues.

Pathogenesis of Stress-Induced Illness

What do the results of the above studies linking stress to the onset of illness mean in terms of the role of this factor in causing disease? They do *not* mean that there is a direct cause and effect relationship between stressful life events and illness. These findings imply that stress exerts an adverse influence on the health of people such that it lowers their resistance to sickness. Rahe thinks of life change events as being "risk factors" for the onset of illness, an association that is analogous to that existing between an elevated level of serum cholesterol and the onset of coronary heart disease[23] (see chap. 11). As risk factors, stressful life events help to identify a segment of the population that has a greater likelihood of becoming ill than persons without these risk factors. The sensitivity and specificity of these predictors (of future ill health) are relatively low, however, since most people who are exposed to life stress do not become physically or emotionally ill and most illnesses are not preceded by stressful life events.

In speculating about the underlying mechanisms that would explain the relationship between stress and illness, it is helpful to utilize a multifactorial model of the cause of disease. According to this model, which is discussed in more detail in chapter 21, a number of factors (generally described as physical, psychological, or social in nature) interact in a complex manner in the cause of disease. One of these factors may be the stress produced by certain life events. By causing a disruption of homeostatic balance, which in turn evokes physiological and psychological responses, stress increases the vulnerability of some individuals to illness.

Whether or not someone who experiences a stressful life event becomes ill depends on a number of variables, including (1) the nature of the event; (2) the significance of the event to him based, for example, on his past life experiences; (3) his capacity to deal with the event and the change it produces (based, for example, on his psychological defenses and social supports); (4) his physical and psychological makeup, including the existence of underlying disease; and (5) the presence of a specific disease-causing agent. For instance, a person with preexisting coronary artery disease who experiences a series of stressful life events (a life crisis) that have great meaning to him *might* develop the symptom of angina or have a myocardial infarction. Similarly, a person who is exposed to tubercle bacilli, and who also experiences a life crisis with which he cannot adequately cope, *might* become ill with tuberculosis. Finally, an individual who has a genetic predisposition for diabetes mellitus *might* develop overt clinical illness following a number of stressful life events to which he responds by overeating and gaining an excessive amount of weight.

Clearly, stress is not a direct cause of disease in these instances but interacts with other variables to produce this effect. In other words, it acts as a *predisposing or precipitating factor* by either increasing one's susceptibility to a new illness or exacerbating a preexisting illness. Stress appears to have these effects in relation to many, if not all, physical illnesses. In addition, there is a special group of diseases, the so-called psychosomatic disorders, in which it is postulated that stress plays a major role in causation. Several of these conditions are discussed at length in chapter 8.

What has been said about physical illness

applies equally well to emotional illness such as schizophrenia. However, as Rahe points out, stress may act on a broader level in the pathogenesis of depressive and neurotic reactions, not only lowering a subject's resistence to these disorders but also influencing the formation of symptoms.[23]

Figure 7–6 illustrates the concepts that have been discussed.

Criticism of the Stress-Illness Relationship

There are critics of the previously mentioned studies of the relationship between stressful life events and the onset of illness. Rabkin and Struening point out that there are some deficiencies in the psychometric properties (reliability and validity) of the instruments used to measure the above relationship and in the methods of data analysis used to interpret the results.[24] In addition, these authors feel that the complex relationship between stress and illness has been oversimplified in the studies, and that the investigators have not paid sufficient attention to other important variables besides the stressful event, such as personal characteristics of the individual. Finally, they note, as Rahe has,[23] that there is actually a relatively low statistical correlation between the occurrence of life events and the onset of illness reported in most of these studies.

Mechanic has criticized the studies on stressful life events and illness for a different reason.[25] He feels that they have been too global in their approach and, consequently,

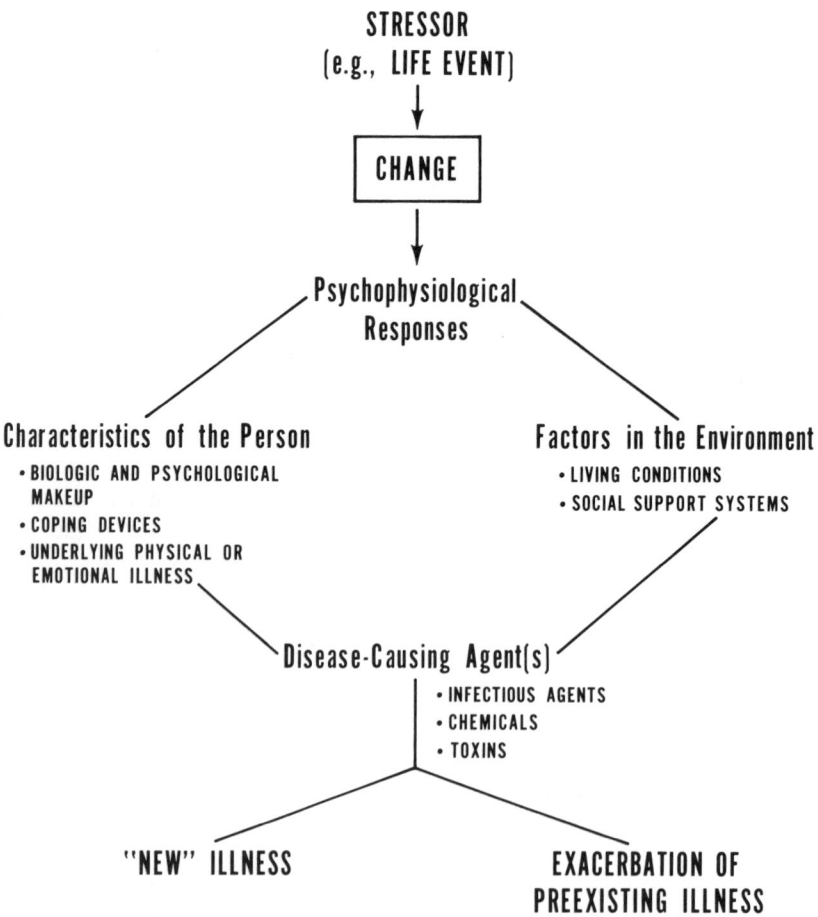

Fig 7–6.—Stress as a predisposing and precipitating factor in illness.

have left too many of the important variables uninvestigated in the relationship between stress and illness. He states:

> It is clear that stressful life events play some role in the occurrence of illness in populations. But any statement beyond the vague generalization is likely to stir controversy. The important issues in understanding how life events interact with social, psychological, biological, and intrapsychic variables require specification of *what* events influence *what* illnesses under *what* conditions through *what* processes. A prerequisite for fruitfully addressing these questions is greater specification of dependent variables and the intervening links that explain the association between global measures of life events and various more specific indices of illness.

Mechanic's comments are actually not so much a criticism as they are a statement of the present status of research in the area of stress-related illness. If, from a historical standpoint, this research is divided into phases, one can consider the present state to be part of the second phase. *Initially, the work of Cannon, Selye, Wolff, and others established the biologic basis for the effects of stress on the body.* In doing so, these investigators helped to define stress in concrete biologic terms. Prior to their studies, this phenomenon was more a theoretical concept than a documented reality in the world of medicine. This period might be referred to as the first phase of modern research into stress. Although there were strong hints that this factor might play an important role in the cause of human disease, the validity of this idea has yet to be proved.

The investigational work using the SRRS as a tool to measure the impact of stressful life events constitutes a second phase in this research. By placing the relationship between stressful life events and the onset of illness on a firm statistical basis, the information accumulated on the physiological and psychological effects of stress by earlier investigators was given greater relevance in terms of the cause of disease. In other words, the demonstration that an illness is, in fact, preceded by a stressor(s) lends credence to the theory that the physiological and psychological reactions, instead of adaptations that occur in response to stress may be important in the pathogenesis of the illness.

Of course, much work needs to be done to clarify the exact nature of the relationship between stress and health changes. In this regard, Mechanic's comments are quite valid. *Studies to elucidate the "dependent variables and intervening links" that explain this association can be viewed as the third phase in the evolution of research in this area.* A good deal of work has already been done linking stress to specific disease entities, and this material will be discussed in chapter 8. We are witnessing only the beginnings of a long process of investigation into one of the most complex factors in the cause of disease—stress and the adaptations to it.

SUMMARY

This chapter has attempted to define the concept of stress using a model that will be helpful to the clinician in understanding the relationship between this factor and illness. The impact of a stressor on a person (i.e., the degree of change it produces) and his responses to it depend not only on the nature of the stressor but also on his physical and psychological makeup, coping resources, social supports, and previous life experiences. While general patterns of stress response are observed in man and animals, there are individual differences in the way people react to stressful situations or events based on the variables listed above. This specificity of response means that the physician should individualize his approaches to the care of persons exposed to stress.

The organ dysfunction that is seen in persons exposed to stress is due to widespread physiological and metabolic changes including an activation of the autonomic nervous system (sympathetic and parasympathetic) and a stimulation of various endocrine systems in the body. Accompanying this dysfunction are psychological reactions associated with arousal of the cerebral cortical, hypothalamic, and limbic systems. Both the physiological and psychological responses to stress are of value in coping with a stressor and the change it produces. In this sense, stress is beneficial, even essential, to survival and adaptation. However, if these responses are excessive, are unduly prolonged, or occur to someone who is especially vulnerable to their effects, they can be maladaptive by causing distressing symptoms and, in some people, the onset of illness.

REFERENCES

1. Mason J.W.: A historical view of the stress field. *J. Human Stress* 1(1):6, 1975 (pt. I); 1(2):22, 1975 (pt. II).
2. Lief A.: *The Commonsense Psychiatry of Dr. Adolf Meyer*. New York, McGraw-Hill Book Co., 1948.
3. Holmes T.H., Rahe R.H.: The social readjustment rating scale. *J. Psychosom. Res.* 11:213, 1967.
4. Holmes T.H.: Development and application of a quantitative measure of magnitude of life change. *Psychiatric Clinics of North America* 2:289, 1979.
5. Cannon W.B.: *Bodily Changes in Pain, Hunger, Fear, and Rage*, ed. 2. New York, D. Appleton & Company, 1929.
6. Selye H.: A syndrome produced by diverse nocuous agents. *Nature* 138:32, 1936.
7. Mason J.W.: Organization of the multiple endocrine responses to avoidance in the monkey. *Psychosom. Med.* 30(suppl.):774, 1968.
8. Rose R.M.: Endocrine responses to stressful psychological events. *Psychiatric Clinics of North America* 3:251, 1980.
9. Wolff H.G.: *Stress and Disease*. Springfield, Ill., Charles C Thomas, Publisher, 1953.
10. Tyhurst J.S.: Individual reactions to community disasters. *Am. J. Psychiatry* 107:764, 1951.
11. Tilleard-Cole R.R., Marks J.: *The Fundamentals of Psychological Medicine*. New York, John Wiley & Sons, Inc., 1975.
12. Holmes T.H., Masuda M.: Life change and illness susceptibility, in Dohrenwend B.S., Dohrenwend B.P. (eds.): *Stressful Life Events: Their Nature and Effects*. New York, John Wiley & Sons, Inc., 1974.
13. Holmes T.S., Holmes T.H.: Short-term intrusions into the life style routine. *J. Psychosom. Res.* 14:121, 1970.
14. Theorell T., Rahe R.H.: Psychosocial factors and myocardial infarction, I. An inpatient study in Sweden. *J. Psychosom. Res.* 15:25, 1971.
15. Rahe R.H., et al.: Recent life changes, myocardial infarction and abrupt coronary death, studies in Helsinki. *Arch. Intern. Med.* 133:221, 1974.
16. Rahe R.H., Lind E.: Psychosocial factors and sudden cardiac death: A pilot study. *J. Psychosom. Res.* 15:19, 1971.
17. Kimball C.P.: Emotional and psychosocial aspects of diabetes mellitus. *Med. Clin. North Am.* 55:1007, 1971.
18. Hawkins N.G., et al.: Evidence of psychosocial factors in the development of pulmonary tuberculosis. *Am. Rev. Tuberculosis Pulmonary Dis.* 75:768, 1957.
19. Bramwell S.T., et al.: Psychosocial factors in athletic injuries: Development and application of the social and athletic social readjustment rating scale (SARRS). *J. Human Stress* 1:6, 1975.
20. Brill R.A., et al.: Alcoholism, life events, and psychiatric impairment: Work in progress on alcoholism. *Ann. N.Y. Acad. Sci.* 273:467, 1976.
21. Engel G.L.: Sudden and rapid death during psychological stress. *Ann. Intern. Med.* 74(5):771, 1971.
22. Paykel E.S.: Life stress and psychiatric disorder: Application of the clinical approach in Dohrenwend B.S., Dohrenwend B.P. (eds.): *Stressful Life Events: Their Nature and Effects*. New York, John Wiley & Sons, Inc., 1974.
23. Rahe R.H.: Life change events and mental illness: An overview. *J. Human Stress* 5:2, 1979.
24. Rabkin J.G., Struening E.L.: Life events, stress, and illness. *Science* 194:1013, 1976.
25. Mechanic D.: Discussion of research programs on relations between stressful life events and episodes of physical illness, in Dohrenwend B.S., Dohrenwend B.P. (eds.): *Stressful Life Events: Their Nature and Effects*. New York, John Wiley & Sons, Inc., 1974.

8 / Behavioral Medicine

(Psychosomatic or Psychophysiological Disorders)

NEIL SCHNEIDERMAN, Ph.D., WALLACE WILKINS, Ph.D., JONATHAN J. BRAUNSTEIN, M.D., and MARC SILBRET, M.D.

PSYCHOLOGICAL FACTORS were traditionally believed to play an important role in the etiology and pathogenesis of a relatively small number of organic illnesses. These included asthma, peptic ulcer, ulcerative colitis, migraine, neurodermatitis, and essential hypertension. Together, these disorders were subsumed under the heading of psychosomatic or psychophysiological diseases. In contrast to this limited view of the relationship between psychological factors and physical disorders, many physicians today believe that an intimate relationship exists between psychological and organic factors in many human illnesses. This is based on the following types of observations: (1) emotional upset can trigger the onset or exacerbate organic disease; (2) individuals suffering from emotional illness often complain of somatic symptoms; (3) people who are physically ill commonly have significant emotional reactions to their illness, which in turn seem to influence their prognosis; and (4) physical ailments can initiate or worsen mental illness.

In response to the growing awareness of the role played by psychological factors in human illness, the field of *behavioral medicine* has emerged. A meeting of senior biomedical and behavioral scientists at the National Academy of Sciences defined behavioral medicine as: "the interdisciplinary field concerned with the development and integration of behavioral and biomedical science knowledge and techniques relevant to health and illness and the application of this knowledge and these techniques to prevention, diagnosis and rehabilitation."[1] One important aspect of this definition is that it frees the field of behavioral medicine from the problem of mind/body dualism that plagued the early development of psychosomatic medicine.

This chapter will deal with a number of disorders in which the behavioral medicine concept has been shown to be useful. The intent is to provide the reader with a general overview of the behavioral medicine approach to illness.

GENERAL CONSIDERATIONS

One basic premise of this chapter is that psychological factors acting alone or together with other disease-causing agents are capable of producing structural damage to the body's tissues and organs. The mechanisms by which such damage might occur were discussed in some detail in chapter 7 and summarized in Figure 7–10. Three variables have traditionally been considered critical in the pathogenesis of psychosomatic diseases: (1) psychological factors, (2) physiological responses induced by these factors, and (3) constitutional and environmental factors that render the individual vulnerable to the ill effects of these responses. Let us briefly examine each of these variables from a historical perspective.

Psychological Factors

Several types of psychological factors have been implicated in the genesis of psychosomatic disease: emotionally upsetting situations and events, personality traits, and psychic conflict. A wide variety of life events are psychologically stressful, including those that are socially desirable and those that are undesirable (see Table 7–1 of chap. 7). A relationship has been shown to exist between the clustering of these events—at least the aversive ones—and the onset of physical illness. In addition, Engel[2] and Schmale[3] helped draw attention to a particular set of life circumstances that appears to predispose an individual to ill health. These investigators found that people faced with situations in which they experience intense feelings of helplessness and hopelessness are at a greater risk than others of becoming ill. They refer to this syndrome as the "giving up–given up" complex. The life circumstances that typically give rise to this complex involve a serious loss (e.g., death of a loved one) with which the person is unable to cope and to which he or she reacts with marked depression.

In the 1930s, Dunbar suggested that persons with certain personality types were more likely than others to develop psychosomatic disease.[4] Indeed, she felt that one could predict the nature of the disease by knowing the specific psychological profile of the person. For example, she postulated that hard-driving, tense, ambitious men were more likely to develop coronary heart disease. She described other personality traits that were supposedly associated with a tendency for persons to acquire specific psychosomatic disorders. While her theories have never been proved, in recent years a great deal of evidence has been advanced indicating that a particular behavior pattern (called type A) constitutes an important risk factor for coronary heart disease.

Freud was among the first to focus attention on the role of psychological conflict in the pathogenesis of disease. He considered this conflict to be a source of "dammed up" psychic energy which, when released through physiological channels, might have harmful effects on the body. Utilizing this concept, Alexander published a psychodynamic theory concerning the etiology of the psychosomatic disorders.[5] According to his theory, three factors are important in their cause: (1) the presence of an unresolved psychological conflict, (2) excessive arousal of the autonomic nervous system, and (3) the existence of a predisposing organ vulnerability. Alexander believed that, in most instances, the emotional conflict arose in early childhood, persisted, and was reactivated later in life by certain precipitating life events. When this occurred, the psychic energy that could not be expressed emotionally was discharged over the autonomic nervous system, causing dysfunction and injury to a vulnerable organ. Based on individual case study analysis, Alexander thought that he could predict the specific type of psychosomatic disorder from the nature of a person's emotional conflict.

The psychodynamic approach to understanding the psychosomatic disorders had many advocates during the quarter-century beginning around 1940. It stressed the role of the personality and psychic conflict in the etiology of these diseases. Some psychological factors that were thought to be important are shown in Table 8–1.

Almost all the studies on which the psychodynamic theories were based relied on data obtained from the psychological evaluation of patients *after* they became ill. Thus, the data were retrospective in nature, consisting of only the information that a person could recall about his or her past life. Great care must be used in interpreting this kind of data, however, since the psychological characteristics that people attribute to themselves retrospectively may not be accurate. Illness itself may produce marked personality disturbances and conflicts, so investigators must be certain that the psychological abnormalities that seem to be associated with a particular disorder *preceded* it, if they are to establish a role for these abnormalities in pathogenesis. As a matter of fact, there are few prospective studies of this type.

In one notable exception, Weiner et al. reported in 1957 on the results of a prospective study of duodenal ulcer disease involving a group of army recruits in basic training, some

TABLE 8–1.—SOME HYPOTHESIZED PSYCHOLOGICAL CORRELATES
OF PSYCHOPHYSIOLOGICAL DISORDERS

DISORDER	PSYCHOGENIC CAUSES, PERSONALITY CHARACTERISTICS, AND COPING AIMS
Peptic ulcer	Feels deprived of dependency needs; is resentful; represses anger; cannot vent hostility or actively seek dependency security; characterizes self-sufficient and responsible "go-getter" types who are compensating for dependency desires; has strong regressive wish to be nurtured and fed; revengeful feelings are repressed and kept unconscious.
Colitis	Was intimidated in childhood into dependency and conformity; feels conflict over resentment and desire to please; anger restrained for fear of retaliation; is fretful, brooding, and depressive or passive, sweet and bland; seeks to camouflage hostility by symbolic gesture of giving.
Essential hypertension	Was forced in childhood to restrain resentments; inhibited rage; is threatened by and guilt-ridden over hostile impulses which may erupt; is a controlled, conforming and "mature" personality; is hard-driving and conscientious; is guarded and tense; needs to control and direct anger into acceptable channels; desires to gain approval from authority.
Migraine	Is unable to fulfill excessive self-demands; feels intense resentment and envy toward intellectually or financially more successful competitors; has meticulous, scrupulous, perfectionistic and ambitious personality; failure to attain perfectionist ambitions results in self-punishment.
Bronchial asthma	Feels separation anxiety; was given inconsistent maternal affection; has fear and guilt that hostile impulses will be expressed toward loved persons; is demanding, sickly, and "cranky" or clinging and dependent; symptom expresses suppressed cry for help and protection.
Neurodermatitis	Has overprotective but ungiving parents; has craving for affection; has conflict regarding hostility and dependence; demonstrates guilt and self-punishment for inadequacies; is a superficially friendly and oversensitive personality with depressive features and low self-image; symptoms are atonement for inadequacy and guilt by self-excoriation; displays oblique expression of hostility and exhibitionism in need for attention and soothing.

Source: Millon T., Millon R.: Psychophysiologic disorders, in Millon T. (ed.): *Medical Behavioral Science*. Philadelphia, W. B. Saunders Co., 1975, p. 211. (Used by permission.)

of whom had high levels of pepsinogen in their blood.[6] The level of serum pepsinogen is an indirect measure of gastric secretory capacity; those persons with increased values are hypersecretors of gastric acid and have an increased risk of duodenal ulcer. On the basis of prospective interviews and psychological testing, Weiner et al. were able to: (1) separate the recruits with high levels of pepsinogen from those with low levels, and (2) predict those who would develop an ulcer under the stress of basic training. The men who developed an ulcer had both psychological problems similar to those that had been described by Alexander as typical for persons with ulcer and high levels of pepsinogen.

Weiner's study notwithstanding, the psychodynamic theories that attempted to relate specific types of unresolved psychological conflicts to specific illnesses have not been generally confirmed by appropriate prospective studies. Whereas many of the views expressed by psychodynamic theorists were based on insights derived from working with individual patients (i.e., the individual case study method), the scientific community today requires that convincing evidence not derived directly from controlled experimentation should at least be based on prospective studies using standardized instruments with independently assessed reliability and validity. Moreover, these studies should as far as possible be demonstrably free from investigator bias and should include appropriate control groups or control conditions.

An important question that has been posed concerning the relationship between psychological factors and illness is whether the differences in the forms of illness that occur among psychologically stressed individuals are based on: (1) the nature of the psychological factor, (2) differences in personality or psychological response styles, (3) physiochemical or morphological variations, or (4) aspects of the environment, including contaminants and microorganisms. Current research suggests that all of these may be important.

The nature of the psychological factor may be important since psychologically stressful situations that permit coping responses to be made apparently lead to one constellation of pathophysiological changes, whereas situations involving unavoidable stress lead to another.[7] Suggestions that personality or response styles may be important are supported by findings that individuals who display the Type A behavior pattern are at increased risk for coronary heart disease.[8] The hypothesis that physiochemical predispositions may be involved in specific disorders precipitated by stress is supported by the study of Weiner et al. previously cited.[6] Finally, the possibility that psychological stress may interact with specific infectious diseases is supported by a number of experiments indicating that various mammals display increased susceptibility to viral infections (e.g., herpes simplex, polyoma virus) as a function of environmental stress.[8]

Physiological Responses

As mentioned in chapter 7, Cannon, Selye, Mason, Wolff, and others have described bodily responses to stress. Because some of these responses may be triggered by psychological stimuli, the physiological responses have been thought to provide a pathogenic link between psychological factors acting as causes of illness and organ system pathology. Elucidation of this link, however, is not a simple matter. Before we can comprehend the relationship between psychological factors and a specific illness, we must be able to specify: (1) the psychological variables that initiate physiological responses, and (2) the manner in which these physiological responses induce or trigger specific pathologic changes. Moreover, the variables that govern each of these relationships are likely to be complex. In the case of psychological factors, we must know something about the individual's personality (i.e., predispositions to perceive and respond to the environment in certain ways) and the perceived psychosocial challenge that the individual is facing. The physiological responses are likely to be multiple and to influence a variety of substrates (target organs), which vary in susceptibility. Fortunately for scientific research: (1) distinctive behavior patterns, such as Type A, seem to occur repeatedly in certain individuals over a long period of time, (2) some of these behavior patterns have been reported to give rise to relatively fixed constellations of physiological responses, and (3) end-point pathology has been linked both to behavior patterns and to distinctive constellations of physiological responses. Because specific physiological responses appear to act as mediators between psychological factors and some illnesses, they are worth examining in further detail.

Based on clinical experience and an examination of the biologic literature, Engel suggested that individuals have two distinct modes of responding to psychological stressors.[2] One of these modes, acting through Cannon's sympathetic-adrenomedullary axis, was said to mediate "flight or fight" reactions, in which the organism struggles to cope actively with an external situation that is perceived as threatening. The other response mode, acting through the hypothalamic-pituitary-adrenocortical axis emphasized by Selye,[9] was said to mediate "conservation-withdrawal" reactions involving forms of passive coping, which come into play when active responses are perceived as being impossible.

The sympathetic-adrenomedullary axis is particularly efficient when vigorous skeletal motor activity is required. Thus, during situations that demand skeletal muscle activity, heart rate, myocardial contractility, cardiac output, and systolic arterial pressure are increased. The sympathetic nervous system also mobilizes lipids from adipose tissue, suppresses the secretion of insulin, and facilitates the effects of glucagon on carbohydrate metabolism.[10] When triglycerides in adipose tissue are mobilized, they are hydrolyzed to free fatty acids and glycerol. The free fatty acids can be utilized by skeletal muscles in the production of energy. However, free fatty acids that are not utilized in the production of energy are eventually taken up by adipose tissues and by the liver. The free fatty acids taken up by the liver form triglycerides and are secreted as very low density lipoproteins. During stressful situations the balance between the lipid mobilization and the utilization of free fatty acids for energy production determines the level of lipids in the blood and the rate at which the liver synthesizes and secretes very low density lipoproteins.

When individuals engage in strenuous exertion, they are likely to use large amounts of lipids. But what of situations in which we feel threatened and respond with anger? The sympathetic nervous system becomes engaged and lipids are mobilized, but unless we vent our frustrations physically, lipid mobilization may exceed lipid utilization.

The exact mechanisms that link sympathetic-adrenomedullary function to specific pathologies are presently a matter of speculation, but at least as far as fixed hypertension, atherosclerosis, stroke, and coronary heart disease are concerned, catecholamine influences on cardiovascular dynamics and/or lipid metabolism may be important mediators. Pathophysiological mechanisms that lead to atherosclerosis, for example, include damage to vascular endothelium and proliferation of smooth muscle cells. Ross and his collaborators have suggested that this damage to the vascular endothelium may be the result of hemodynamic factors associated with increased blood pressure and/or of chemical factors such as high levels of low density lipoproteins in the blood.[11] The Framingham study has established that the mortality risk for coronary heart disease is proportional to the level of lipid in the blood as well as the level of blood pressure,[12] and direct experimentation in animals has shown that the progress of lipid-induced atherosclerosis can be accelerated by raising the blood pressure. Detailed discussions of the relationships among psychological stress, the sympathetic-adrenomedullary axis, and cardiovascular pathology are beyond the scope of this chapter, but they have been presented elsewhere by Herd[10] and by Schneiderman.[7]

In contrast to the sympathetic-adrenomedullary axis, which appears to be related to fight or flight reactions and to active coping in the face of perceived threat, activation of the hypothalamic-pituitary-adrenocortical axis seems to be related to a conservation-withdrawal mode of responding to stress. This response constellation includes an increase in efferent vagal activity, increased adrenal corticosteroid secretion, decreased gonadal steroid secretion, and chronic elevation of blood pressure associated with an increase in total peripheral resistance. Behavioral correlates include an inhibition of skeletal motor activity and a suppression of environmentally directed activities. It has been suggested that prolonged activation of the hypothalamic-pituitary-adrenocortical axis may lead to increased susceptibility to infectious diseases, peptic ulcers, decreased reproductive capability, depression, and "sudden death."[13]

Organ Vulnerability

As mentioned in chapter 7, psychological stressors are thought to act as predisposing or precipitating factors for disease rather than as the sole cause. In other words, they are only one link in a chain of events that ultimately cause disease. Since only a relatively few people who are exposed to these psychological stressors develop illness, there must be additional factors involved. The concept of organ vulnerability helps to explain why some individuals exposed to pathogenic psychological factors develop illnesses whereas others do not.

Organ vulnerability may result from genetic or environmental factors. In the case of duodenal ulcer disease (an example of a stress-related disorder), the following evidence indicates that genetic influences are operative: (1) this condition is 2 to 2½ times more common in the siblings of persons who have a duodenal ulcer than among the general population, (2) it occurs with a much higher rate of concordance in monozygous as opposed to dizygous male twins, and (3) it is seen more frequently in individuals with blood group O.[14] Another indication that a hereditary basis exists for organ vulnerability in this disease is the high level of serum pepsinogen I (PG I) found in many persons who have a duodenal ulcer.[15] These persons are hypersecretors of gastric acid; one of the biologic markers of this excessive secretion is their high level of serum PG I. A recent study has shown that an elevated serum PG I level is inherited as an autosomal dominant trait in certain families with duodenal ulcer, a finding that supports the view that heredity is important in the pathogenesis of duodenal ulcer disease.[16]

Thus, duodenal ulcer disease may result from the impact of psychological stressors on an individual who has an increased organ vulnerability (i.e., one who is genetically programmed for the hypersecretion of gastric acid). Genetic factors are responsible for the increased capacity of the stomach to produce acid and pepsin, while the psychological stressors stimulate the stomach to hypersecrete these two substances. The increased amounts of acid-pepsin in the gastric secretions, in turn, cause autodigestion of the lining of the stomach (an ulcer). Environmental factors may also come into play in the causation of an ulcer as, for instance, when a person ingests drugs (i.e., coffee, cigarettes) that increase organ vulnerability and thereby enhance the risk of developing an ulcer.

In order to understand the etiology of psychosomatic disorders, it is necessary to consider the genetic and environmental factors that influence organ vulnerability, in addition to the psychological factors and physiological responses discussed. Incorporating these variables into a comprehensive scheme requires the use of a multifactorial model of the cause of disease (Fig 8–1). In this model, the three

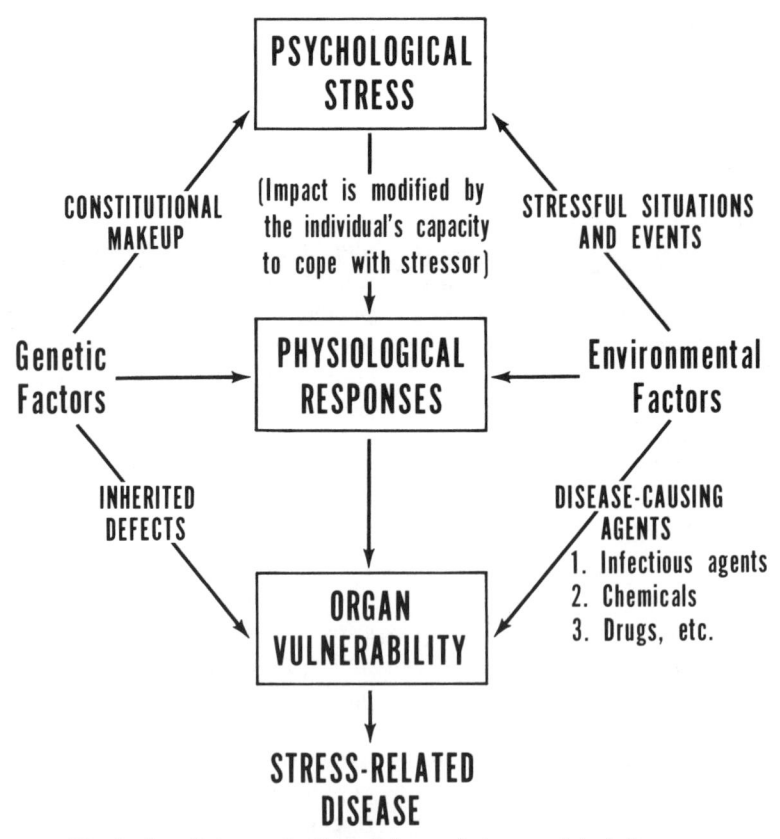

Fig 8–1.—Scheme for the etiology of stress-related diseases.

fundamental elements are the presence of pathogenic psychological factors (e.g., psychological stress), the physiological responses they elicit, and an underlying organ vulnerability. Both genetic and environmental factors influence these basic elements. In addition, the environment is a source of agents with disease-causing potential (e.g., organisms, drugs, antigens, chemicals) whose action may be important in the etiology of some disorders.

Now let us look at several examples of psychosomatic disease from the perspective of behavioral medicine and see how these variables interact.

CIRCULATORY DISORDERS

The relationship between behavioral (psychosocial) factors and cardiovascular pathology has long been suspected but difficult to demonstrate. As long ago as 1892, Sir William Osler contended that "heart attack" was related to "high pressure at which men live, and the habit of working the machine to its maximum capacity."[17] In the years since Osler's statement, psychological and social factors have been implicated in such circulatory problems as essential hypertension, coronary heart disease, and functional cardiac arrhythmias.

Essential Hypertension

Essential hypertension is one of the most common cardiovascular abnormalities and a cause of considerable morbidity and mortality. By definition the cause of this condition is unknown; however, a number of factors are thought to be important in its pathogenesis, including genetic, environmental, and psychological ones. There is evidence that the clinical entity called essential hypertension is really composed of a group of disorders, each having a different pathogenesis. Although multiple factors seem to be involved in the causation of essential hypertension, this section will emphasize the role of stress in the development of essential hypertension.

The importance of psychological stressors in the etiology of essential hypertension is suggested by both animal experimentation and controlled studies with humans. First, let's examine some of the animal studies.

In order to examine the development of hypertension as a function of emotional stress, Forsyth studied the blood pressure responses of rhesus monkeys to a long-term unsignaled shock-avoidance schedule.[20] On this schedule, the experimental animals worked for approximately 12 hours daily for several months on a task in which pressing a button delayed a mild electric shock for approximately 20 seconds. By pressing the button at exactly the right time, the animals could completely avoid receiving the shock. A control animal was yoked to the experimental animal in such a way that both animals received a shock if the experimental animal failed to press the button at the right time. Following the first few months of normal or low blood pressures, there was a steady increase in the blood pressure of the experimental animals to levels that averaged almost 30 mm Hg systolic and 20 mm Hg diastolic higher than those of the control animals or their prestress baseline. The elevated pressures were observed throughout the day, not just during experimental periods.

In another experiment, squirrel monkeys were trained to press a button at high rates for 2 to 4 hours per day to turn off a signal light associated with the delivery of a noxious shock.[21] Completion of the required number of button presses within a 5-minute period earned the animal a 60-second rest before the next trial and prevented any shocks from being delivered. Blood pressure was measured through catheters implanted in the aorta. As training progressed and each animal began to push the button rapidly, the number of noxious stimuli delivered decreased gradually, but the animal's blood pressure rose. After several months, in the majority of monkeys, blood pressure became elevated before, during, and after each session, even if the noxious stimuli were not delivered. In some monkeys, the pressure remained elevated 24 hours a day. The blood pressure changes that occurred during the 4–8-month experimental period were: normal blood pressure → transient hypertension in association with key-pushing → more sustained hypertension occurring before, during, and after sessions.

In the preceding experiments, pressing a button postponed an electric shock (i.e., button-pressing was the instrumental response). Other experiments have used an increase in blood pressure itself as the instrumental response. In one experiment conducted with baboons, both food delivery and shock avoidance were made contingent upon specified increases in arterial pressure.[22] Pressure elevations as large as 40 mm Hg developed and were maintained over periods lasting several months. The blood pressure elevations in these baboons during the initial training sessions were accompanied by increases in heart rate and cardiac output.

The experiments conducted on nonhuman primates suggest that psychological stress (i.e., sustained vigilance and/or the fear of aversive consequences) may be important in the development of hypertension. However, none of these experiments has demonstrated sustained hypertension lasting months or years after the stressful situation is removed. Moreover, these experiments have not demonstrated the development of arteriosclerosis as an accompaniment of the hypertension. Both sustained elevations in blood pressure during relatively quiescent periods and the progression of arteriosclerosis are characteristics of chronic essential hypertension in humans.

Perhaps the most convincing evidence that sustained hypertension and arteriosclerosis can be induced by stress has been reported by Henry and his collaborators.[13, 23] Henry and his co-workers originally found that CBA mice raised in isolation developed prolonged hypertension when as adults they were exposed to frequent confrontation with other mice in an "intercommunicating" box system. In contrast, control animals reared in groups remained normotensive under such circumstances. Other experiments provided evidence that the pressure elevations in the socially stressed isolates were related to a pronounced increase in activity of the sympathetic nervous system. Histologic examination of isolated mice subjected to Henry's experimental paradigm revealed the presence of interstitial nephritis, aortic arteriosclerosis, intramural coronary artery sclerosis, and myocardial fibrosis.[23]

With the exception of the studies on mice conducted by Henry and his colleagues, a large number of behavioral experiments with animals have failed to provide convincing evidence that psychological stress provides both necessary and sufficient conditions for producing sustained hypertension that adequately models chronic hypertension in humans. However, because psychological stress does lead to increased activity of the sympathetic nervous system and long-duration—if not permanent—hypertension, it is conceivable that such stress may precipitate chronic hypertension by interacting with various predisposing factors. Several of these potential predisposing factors have been identified through the development of different strains of rats.

Two of the most interesting strains of rats to be developed are: (1) the spontaneously hypertensive strain developed by Okamoto and his group[24] and (2) the Brookhaven hypertension-sensitive strain developed by Dahl and his colleagues.[26]

The spontaneously hypertensive rats developed by Okamoto and his co-workers have been studied extensively. Hypertension develops gradually in this strain but becomes elevated at a fairly early age. The primary mechanism involved appears to be a pronounced increase in sympathetic reactivity induced by the central nervous system. Of considerable interest for the present discussion is the finding by Okamoto's group that the hypertension in his experimental strain is potentiated by chronic psychological stress.[27]

Another rat strain of interest is the hypertension-sensitive rats developed by Dahl. These animals remain normotensive when maintained on low-salt diets, but they readily become hypertensive in response to sodium chloride loading. Although Dahl rats do not show such pronounced increases in blood pressure when subjected to psychological stress as do Okamoto rats, evidence exists that psychological stress does potentiate hypertension in the Dahl rats.[28]

Short-term effects of stress in producing transient hypertension in humans have been seen after battle[29] and after natural disasters.[30] More long-term effects have been seen in people who work as air traffic controllers, a job associated with a great deal of psychological stress. These air traffic controllers have been found to have higher rates of hypertension than a control population.[31] Prolonged exposure to noise has also been linked to hypertension in humans,[32] as has living in a stressful neighborhood.[33] These retrospective studies conducted on humans are generally consistent with the animal experiments, which have shown that organisms exposed to severe, prolonged stresses have a greater incidence of hypertension than do similar individuals not so stressed. For both the humans and animals studied, psychological stress appears to cause an increase in blood pressure by activating the sympathetic nervous system (Fig 8–2).

Studies with animals and humans have suggested that there are two stages in the development of stress-induced hypertension.[34–36] Initially, there is an increase in cardiac output with peripheral resistance being "normal"; later, peripheral resistance increases and cardiac output returns to normal. Actually, in the first stage, peripheral resistance is *relatively* high, since the normal physiological response to the increase in cardiac output would be a decrease in peripheral resistance. The sympathetic nervous system is thought to be hyperfunctioning in both stages of stress-induced hypertension.

Evidence for hyperfunction of the sympathetic nervous system in essential hypertension includes (1) the finding of elevated urine catecholamine levels in *some* hypertensives,[37, 38] and (2) the presence of increased tissue levels of enzymes involved in the biosynthesis of norepinephrine in hypertensives.[38] Drugs that are α- or β-sympathetic blockers are effective in lowering the blood pressure in hypertensive persons, which indicates that the sympathetic nervous system is important in this condition.[39] Moreover, the so-called relaxation response described by Benson, which uses a form of meditation to counteract the effects of the sympathetic nervous system discharge in the fight or flight response, has also been reported to be useful in lowering the blood pressure in persons with essential hypertension.[40]

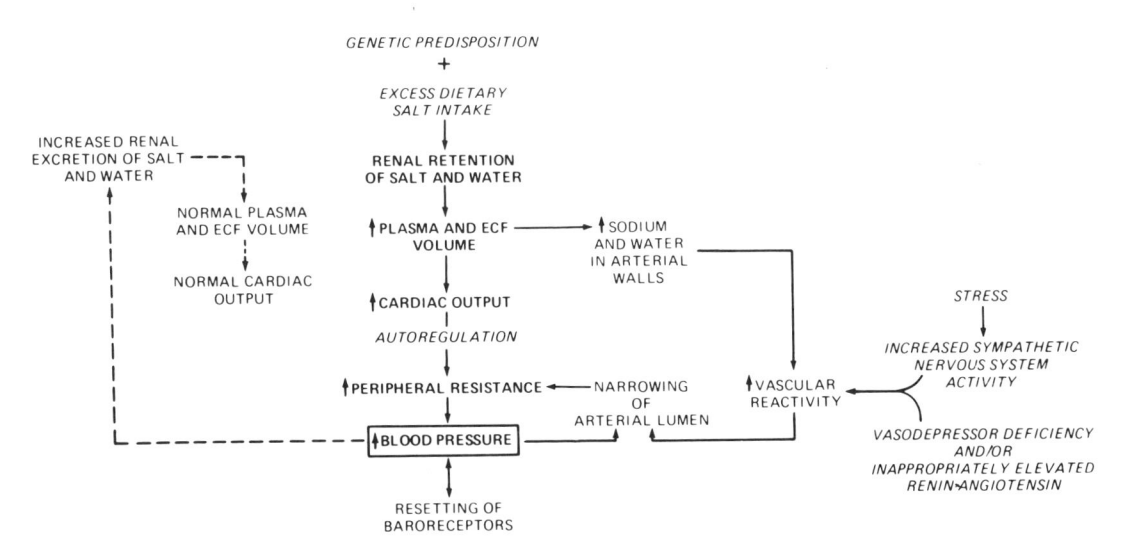

Fig 8–2.—An overall scheme for the possible pathogenesis of essential hypertension. ECF = extracellular fluid. (From Kaplan N.M.: *Clinical Hypertension,* ed. 2. Baltimore, Williams & Wilkins Co., 1978, p. 63. Used by permission.)

The sympathetically induced increase in peripheral resistance that is characteristic of severe hypertension of long duration may represent a secondary adjustment to the increase in cardiac output characteristic of the first stage of essential hypertension. For this reason some research attempting to link personality and behavioral profiles in humans with the development of hypertension have focused on borderline or early-stage hypertension.[41]

In an early study, Hamilton found that persons with borderline hypertension were less assertive, but more prone to anger than normotensive individuals.[42] Studies using various psychological measures (e.g., Catell's 16 PF test) have reported similar results.[43, 44] In one of these studies, the investigators devised a test of experimental yielding in which partners discussed topics on which they held opposite views.[42] The borderline hypertensive persons anticipated that they would not yield, but did so when confronted in the experimental situation. Although the self-description of "submissiveness" in borderline hypertensives obtained by the Catell 16 PF written test was thus confirmed in a test of actual behavior, the persons in the behavioral situation insisted that they yielded not to avoid further confrontation with their normotensive partner, but because they had genuinely changed their minds.

A relationship between repressed hostility and one form of borderline hypertension has been reported by Julius and his collaborators.[44] These investigators hypothesized that since the sympathetic nervous system plays an important role in regulating the release of renin by the kidney, and early essential hypertension has often been characterized by sympathetic nervous system activity, it is possible that an elevated level of plasma renin in mild hypertension reflects neural influences on the secretion of renin. The hypothesis was confirmed when it was found that persons with elevated levels of plasma renin also revealed increased concentrations of plasma norepinephrine and a greater decrease in cardiac output with β-adrenergic blockade when compared with hypertensive persons with low levels of renin.

Using the Catell 16 PF questionnaire, the Buss-Durkee personality inventory, and Harburg's anger in–anger out scale, Julius and his collaborators also found that the borderline hypertensives with high levels of renin as a group were controlled, guilt-prone, and submissive, with a high level of unexpressed anger. While this study by Julius and his coworkers did not show a direct *causal* relationship between personality factors and high-renin borderline hypertension, it is consistent with previous findings that anger elevates blood pressure, and that if anger is felt but cannot be expressed openly, the blood pressure response is greater than if an outlet for aggression is available.[45] Thus, there appears to be a link between hypertension related to sympathetic hyperactivity and unexpressed anger.

The research literature on both humans and nonhuman mammals strongly supports the hypothesis that psychological stress can produce hypertension in vulnerable individuals by activating the sympathetic nervous system. It is not entirely clear why some persons exposed to this stress develop hypertension while others do not. Some factors implicated thus far have included: (1) *hereditary predispositions* to hypertension, including a high level of sympathetic responsiveness and/or a low level of sodium excretion; (2) the presence of *environmental factors* such as severe psychological stressors and/or a large intake of sodium; and (3) the coping mechanisms used to deal with stress. Interactions among these variables appear to be of major importance in the development of essential hypertension, but these interactions are just beginning to be studied systematically.

Coronary Heart Disease

A behavior pattern, called Type A, has been identified by Rosenman and Friedman as a risk factor for coronary heart disease.[46] This pattern is characterized by hard-driving competitive behavior, impatience, aggressiveness, hostility, and insecurity, which are readily evoked in a variety of situations. In contrast, individuals classified as Type B show a relative absence of these characteristics. At present more than 40 prospective and retrospective studies have shown that the Type A behavior pattern is predictive of the major manifestations of coronary heart disease (e.g., myocardial infarction).[47] The most extensive prospective study of the relationship between the Type A behavior pattern and coronary heart disease was the Western Collaborative Group Study. An analysis of the data from this study, which followed a cohort of more than 3,000 working men for 8.5 years, found that Type A subjects had an estimated risk that was 2.37 times the risk for Type B subjects.[48] Thus, even though coronary heart disease was not one of the disorders usually considered to be psychosomatic by some psychodynamic theorists, the role of special personality factors in its cause is perhaps stronger in this disease than in any other.

An important question to be asked with regard to the Type A behavior pattern is whether it operates through one or more of the major traditional risk factors for coronary heart disease (e.g., hypertension, hypercholesterolemia, cigarette smoking). It is conceivable, for example, that an impatient, aggressive, hard-driving individual might smoke excessively and eat hurried, high-cholesterol meals at fast-food restaurants. In the Western Collaborative Group Study, however, the traditional risk factors for coronary heart disease correlated poorly with the presence of the behavior pattern. Adjustment for any of these factors, one at a time, reduced the relative risk from 2.37 to 2.25. Adjustment for all the factors simultaneously reduced the estimated relative risk to 1.97. These data, therefore, suggest that the Type A behavior pattern is a potent risk factor independent of the more traditional risk factors for coronary heart disease.

The Type A behavior pattern is a construct that encompasses several behavioral predispositions. As such, it represents an approximation of a coronary-prone behavior pattern the exact composition of which is as yet unknown. Classification of subjects as Type A or Type B was originally based on a standardized interview, which was the behavioral measure first used to predict the incidence of new cases of coronary heart disease in the Western Collaborative Group Study. The standardized interview depends not only on the content of the subjects' responses, but also on the manner or style in which the subject responds. During the course of the Western Collaborative Group Study, the Jenkins Activity Survey was introduced to supplement the standardized interview. The results of this self-administered questionnaire were in reasonably close agreement with the interview in identifying Type A individuals, and were themselves able to predict the future occurrence of coronary heart disease.[49]

The etiology of coronary heart disease is unknown, but a number of biologic and behavioral factors are thought to be important. The major risk factors include a hereditary predisposition, a dietary intake of excessive amounts of saturated fats and cholesterol, high levels of cholesterol in the blood, cigarette smoking, and hypertension. A large body of experimental data has linked these risk factors to the occurrence of coronary heart disease, although the exact mechanism(s) by which they exert their ill effects has not been worked out. The Type A behavior pattern is also considered to be a risk factor that leads to this disease; the question of how remains to be answered.

Glass has suggested that expression of the Type A behavior pattern represents an attempt by a person to cope with an environment that is perceived as hostile or threatening (i.e., stressful).[50] Such efforts are likely to lead to an increase in sympathetic nervous system activity, including increased secretion of catecholamines. A relationship between the Type A behavior pattern and augmented cardiovascular response to a psychomotor performance challenge has been reported.[51] The picture that is beginning to emerge, then, is that in the face of external stress, the individual manifesting the Type A behavioral pattern may respond with greater sympathetic activity than his or her Type B counterpart.

In chapter 7, evidence was presented to show that life stress, which may be responsible for eliciting the personality traits associated with the Type A behavior pattern, can be a factor in the cause of disease. It is conceivable that some of the stressful life events associated with a person's environment, including work, may be instrumental in bringing out the Type A pattern, and in causing physiological responses (e.g., changes in blood lipid levels, coronary artery spasm) that are injurious to the coronary vessels. In addition, external stress and the individual's perceptual and response styles to it (i.e., personality aspects of the Type A pattern) may lead to changes in life-style (i.e., overeating, excessive smoking, reduced recreational physical activity) that promote atherosclerosis. It is worth noting that occupational stress has been found to be associated with an increase in the level of serum cholesterol, a known factor in coronary heart disease.[52] As mentioned earlier, catecholamines have been found to play an important role in the mobilization of lipids. Thus, while the exact pathophysiological mechanisms relating the Type A behavior pattern and coronary heart disease are unknown, the foundations for future research have been laid.

BRONCHIAL ASTHMA

The fundamental abnormality in this condition is a hyperreactivity of the bronchi to a variety of stimuli (e.g., immunologic, physical, chemical, psychological).[53] On exposure to these stimuli, there is a widespread and intermittent narrowing of the air passages of the lungs, resulting in an obstruction to air flow, particularly during expiration. This narrowing is due to three processes occurring in the bronchial tree: (1) contraction of the smooth muscle, (2) edema and inflammation, and (3) accumulation of mucous secretions within the lumen of the airways. Persons who have bronchial asthma complain of dyspnea, wheezing, and cough, which typically occur in episodes lasting hours, days, or even weeks, and then remit spontaneously or in response to treatment. Between episodes, the asthmatic individual may have no complaints.

In many persons with asthma, the evidence for an immunologic cause is clear-cut. The most common example is so-called atopic asthma. On exposure to environmental antigens, individuals with this disorder produce a special type of antibody, called reagin, which belongs to the IgE class of immunoglobulins. These antibodies circulate in the blood and become attached to the surface of tissue cells (mast cells and basophiles). When the antibody on these cells combines with antigen, chemical mediators such as histamine and slow-reacting substance of anaphylaxis (SRS) are released. In the lung, these mediators react with the bronchial tissue, causing a narrowing of the airways and symptoms of asthma.[54] Because exposure to external antigens is critical in the pathogenesis of immunologic or allergic asthma, this form is referred to as *extrinsic asthma*.[53]

Some people with asthma have no evidence for an immunologic cause; that is, there is no sensitization to external antigens, and antigen-antibody reactions are not demonstrable. Since there is no evidence for external causes in this group, the term *intrinsic asthma* has been used to refer to their disorder.[53] Bronchial infection seems to precede the onset of asthma in some of these individuals.

As noted, persons with asthma (of either the extrinsic or the intrinsic type) have hyperreactive airways; that is, broncoconstriction occurs in response to a variety of chemical, physical, infectious, and psychological stimuli. These stimuli can precipitate an attack of asthma or exacerbate symptoms in a person already suffering from this disorder (Fig 8–3). In this section, we are particularly concerned with the role of psychological stimuli as precipitating or aggravating factors in asthma.

Role of Behavioral Factors in Asthma

Clinicians have recognized for many years, primarily on the basis of empirical observations, that psychological factors can aggravate bronchial asthma. Modern clinical investiga-

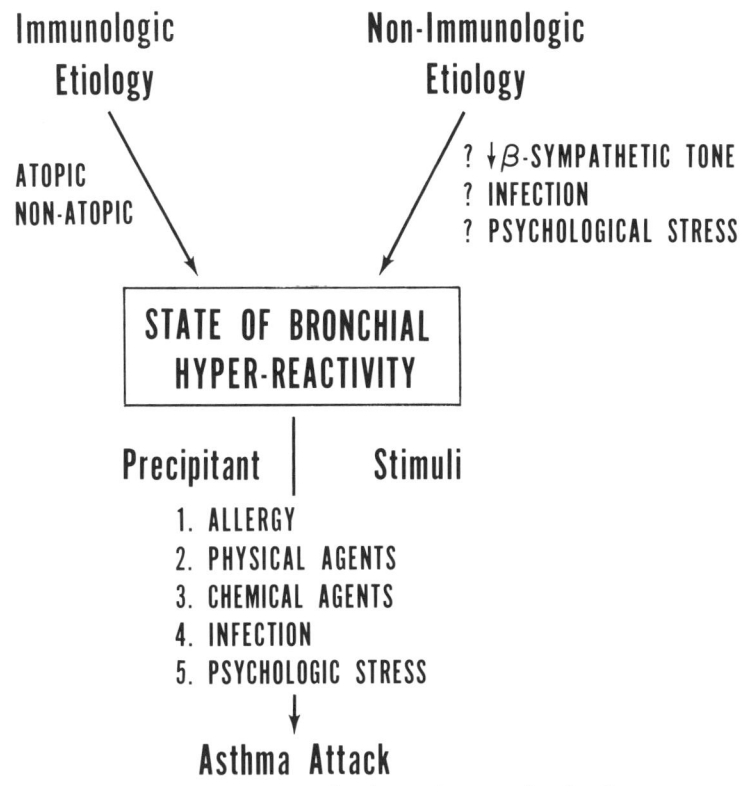

```
Immunologic                  Non-Immunologic
 Etiology                        Etiology

                              ? ↓β-SYMPATHETIC TONE
 ATOPIC                       ? INFECTION
 NON-ATOPIC                   ? PSYCHOLOGICAL STRESS
          ↘               ↙
        ┌─────────────────────┐
        │  STATE OF BRONCHIAL │
        │   HYPER-REACTIVITY  │
        └─────────────────────┘
                  │
        Precipitant │ Stimuli
        1. ALLERGY
        2. PHYSICAL AGENTS
        3. CHEMICAL AGENTS
        4. INFECTION
        5. PSYCHOLOGIC STRESS
                  ↓
            Asthma Attack
```

Fig 8-3.—A scheme for the pathogenesis of asthma.

tions have supported these observations by demonstrating that psychological stimuli do, in fact, play an important role in the pathogenesis of a large proportion of asthma cases. In attempting to establish a link between these stimuli and asthma, various studies have focused attention on (1) the personality structure of asthmatics, (2) the family relationships of persons who have asthma, (3) the emotional states during which asthmatic attacks tend to occur, and (4) the role of classical conditioning in asthma.

PERSONALITY STRUCTURE AND ASTHMA.—Personality differences have been described among persons who have asthma based on the severity of the disorder. For example, asthmatic children who require steroid medication for the control of symptoms can be discriminated by means of psychological evaluation from asthmatic children who do not require this medication.[55] While there has been documentation of differences in personality structure among certain groups of asthmatics, there is no evidence that a particular personality type predisposes one to asthma or that there are substantial differences between asthmatics and nonasthmatics in terms of the degree of psychopathology. Indeed, on a number of objective tests of psychopathology, persons with asthma have been found to have the same means and ranges as control subjects. Thus, it is important to bear in mind that the asthmatic who is referred for psychological assessment may resemble the nonasthmatic population more closely than he does other asthmatics.[56]

FAMILY RELATIONSHIPS.—The interaction that occurs between an asthmatic child and his parents may have adverse effects on the child's condition. In the 1930s, it was postulated by the psychodynamic theorists that conflict in the mother-child relationship was at the root of the cause of asthma, and that the asthmatic wheeze was, in effect, a cry for help on the part of the child. According to a more recent operant conditioning explanation, a parent who shows an asthmatic child attention primarily when that child reveals symptoms may selectively reinforce the occurrence of these symptoms and thereby increase the frequency of asthmatic behavior. These and other psychologically based theories are speculative. Recent studies, however, have confirmed that psychological problems arising from a disturbed relationship between the asthmatic child and his or her parents are inimical to the child's health.

Through the experimental manipulation of the family structure of children with atopic asthma, it has been found that the temporary removal of the parents from the environment has led on some occasions to a marked reduction in asthmatic episodes.[57] Parental separation had very little effect on the occurrence of episodes of asthma in persons in whom infection played a role in the cause, however. Some studies have shown that the parents of asthmatic children score higher on measures of neuroticism than those of nonasthmatic children. It is assumed that the factors responsible for the untoward effect of the parents on their asthmatic offspring are psychological ones. Separation of the parents from the child apparently eliminates psychological stress that acts as a stimulus for the attacks of asthma. It is important to point out, however, that these studies have been retrospective and it is possible that in some instances the psychological stress identified in the parent-child relationship is a *consequence* of the problems created by the child's asthma, rather than a *cause* of the illness.

EMOTIONAL STATES IN WHICH ASTHMA TENDS TO OCCUR.—Panic, fear, anger, and other states of emotional turmoil are known to be associated with the occurrence of asthma attacks. Much of the information linking these emotional states to the pathogenesis of asthma has come from retrospective self-reports by asthmatics. In addition, several investigators have demonstrated that when asthmatics are exposed to the psychological stimuli that they report as producing asthma, these stimuli do indeed produce the respiratory symptoms of asthma, even in the absence of allergic stimuli.[58]

Well-controlled experimental investigations have shown that asthma-like respiratory symptoms can be induced by stressful films and criticism.[59] It has also been reported that asthmatics seem to respond with significantly less anger than do nonasthmatic individuals to experimental situations of criticism.

CLASSICAL CONDITIONING.—Classical conditioning consists of pairing a stimulus known to elicit a particular response with a stimulus that is relatively neutral in such a way that the neutral stimulus acquires the capacity to elicit a response. One of the first descriptions of the psychogenic aspects of asthma was a report of a person who on a number of occasions developed asthmatic symptoms after being shown an artificial rose. This case of "rose asthma," as it has subsequently been referred to, may have been an example of classical conditioning. Many of the findings described in the previous sections are also consistent with what would be predicted if classical conditioning were occurring. However, it is important to keep in mind that just because a supposedly neutral stimulus is able to elicit an asthma-like response, this does not necessarily mean that the response has occurred because of classical conditioning. While it is conceivable that classical conditioning may play a role in some cases of asthma, there has been no scientific validation that this mechanism does, in fact, operate in its pathogenesis.

Although some symptoms of an asthma attack, such as dyspnea and wheezing, can be classically conditioned, it has usually not been possible to demonstrate that bronchoconstriction also has taken place and is responsible for the symptoms. In one investigation, an animal analogue experiment in which classical conditioning did result in bronchial obstruction to air flow, it was found that this response occurred in only a few of the animals and could not readily be generalized to other situations.[60]

Mechanisms by Which Psychological Stimuli Exert Their Effects in Asthma

There are several mechanisms by which psychological stimuli might precipitate asthma. One is by altering autonomic nervous activity via the central nervous system, that is, by either increasing parasympathetic activity or decreasing β^2-sympathetic activity to the lungs and bronchi. In a susceptible person, these neurologic changes could bring on an attack of asthma through direct and indirect effects on the bronchi: (1) a *direct effect* on the smooth muscle and glands of the bronchi (increasing bronchomotor tone and mucous secretion) to produce bronchoconstriction, and (2) an *indirect effect* involving the specialized cells in lungs and bronchi that secrete bronchoconstricting chemical mediators.[51] The elaboration of these chemical mediators in allergic asthma is modulated by the level of activity of the autonomic nervous system through its regulatory effects on the intracellular concentration of cyclic nucleotides, e.g., cyclic AMP, cyclic GMP (Fig 8–4). For example, the activation of the β^2-sympathetic division of the system increases the level of cyclic AMP in the mast cells and this, in turn, *inhibits* the release of chemical mediators in response to an antigen-antibody reaction. Conversely, a reduction in β^2-sympathetic activity decreases the level of intracellular cyclic AMP and *enhances* the release of these mediators. An increase in parasympathetic (vagal) tone raises the level of cyclic GMP and thereby *promotes* the secretion of these chemical substances. Thus, psychic stimuli could exacerbate allergic asthma by decreasing β^2-sympathetic and/or increasing para-

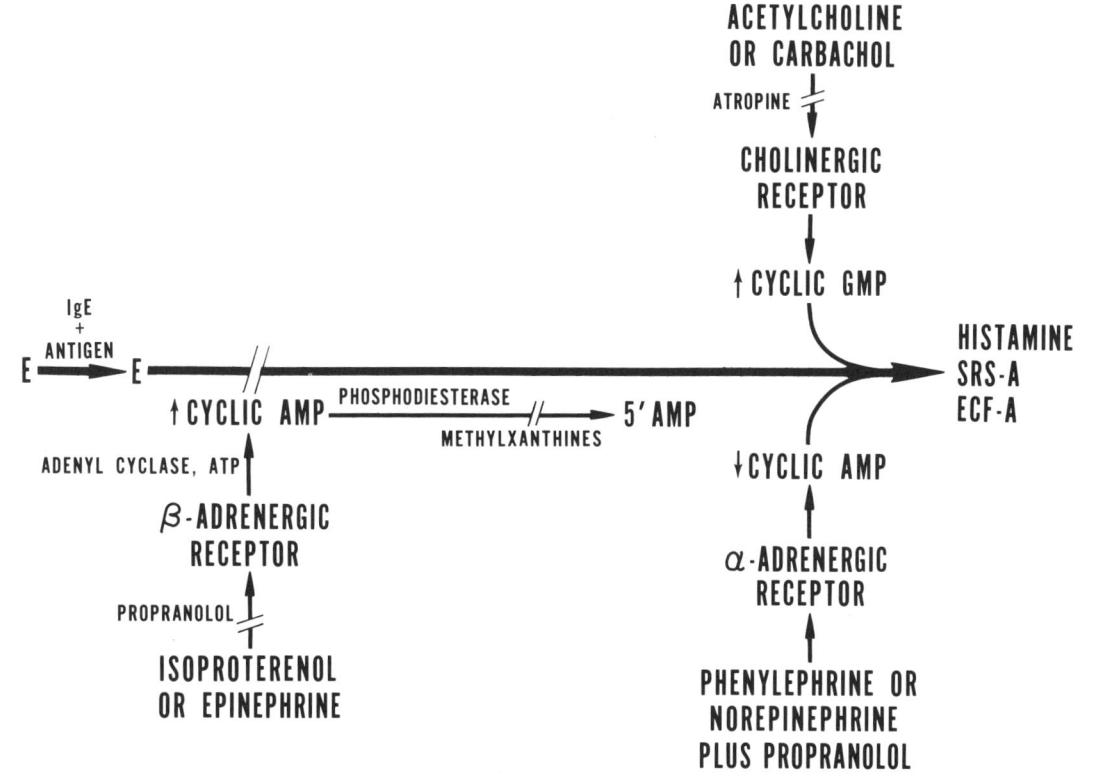

Fig 8–4.—Regulation of the release of the chemical mediators of immunologic (allergic) asthma. (From Austen K.F., Orange R.P.: *Am. Rev. Respir. Dis.* 112:423, 1975. Used by permission.)

sympathetic activity, either of which may cause a greater elaboration of the chemical mediators of asthma in response to an antigen-antibody reaction in the lung.

A second pathogenetic mechanism may also be important in psychologically induced asthma. It is known that stimulation of or injury to the hypothalamic area of the brain can not only produce changes in the function of the autonomic nervous system but also affect immunoreactivity.[61] Thus, it is possible that psychic stress acts at the level of the hypothalamus to enhance the immunologic reactivity of persons with allergic asthma. In keeping with this theory are animal studies showing that immune response and antibody titers can be affected by instrumental avoidance and conflict conditioning.[62]

PEPTIC ULCER DISEASE

Peptic ulcers are benign ulcerative lesions of the lining of the stomach or duodenum due to the effects of gastric acid and pepsin. Current theory states that in persons who have a gastric ulcer there is a disruption of the protective "mucosal barrier" of the stomach, which allows acid digestion to occur. Many studies have shown that the secretion of gastric acid is almost always normal or low when there is a gastric ulcer. In contrast, 50% of persons with a duodenal ulcer hypersecrete gastric acid, and it is felt that in this group the excessive amount of acid damages the duodenal mucosa, thus producing an ulcer. The rest of the persons with a duodenal ulcer (those with normal acid secretion) may have a defect in mucosal resistance that renders the tissue more vulnerable to acid-induced injury.

In a discussion of the pathogenesis of peptic ulcer disease, it is necessary to distinguish between acute and chronic ulcers. The former are typically found in the stomach and consist of superficial erosion(s) or ulceration(s) of the mucosa, without submucosal scarring. They generally occur a short time after an individual has been exposed to acute stress and, hence, they are often referred to as "stress ulcers." This is the type of peptic ulcer that is characteristically seen in animals subjected to experimental conditions that are ulcerogenic.

In chronic peptic ulcer disease, the mucosal ulceration involves the stomach or duodenum (typically the first part of the duodenum) and is associated with submucosal scarring. This is primarily a disease of humans, specifically civilized humans. The disease may extend over many years, during which the individual experiences periodic exacerbations followed by remission of symptoms. Men are affected more commonly than women, especially in the case of duodenal ulcer disease. Chronic duodenal ulcer disease differs from chronic gastric ulcer disease in a number of other respects, including age of onset, natural history, pathogenesis, and management.

The facts that acute and chronic peptic ulcer disease differ, and that a person with a gastric ulcer differs from one with a duodenal ulcer have made it somewhat difficult to interpret the data in the literature dealing with the pathogenesis of these conditions. In reports of laboratory and clinical investigations, there is a tendency to talk about these disorders as if they were one and the same when, in fact, they are quite distinct in many respects, particularly in their pathogenesis.

Biologic Factors in the Pathogenesis of Peptic Ulcer

In simplistic terms, the pathogenesis of all peptic ulcers can be explained by an imbalance between the aggressive forces of acid and pepsin and the defensive forces of mucosal resistance. As mentioned, about half of all persons with chronic duodenal ulcers have a higher than normal level of gastric acid, and it is felt that parasympathetic stimulation (excessive vagal drive) is responsible for a major part of this. Other physiological abnormalities that have been found to be important in the pathogenesis of chronic duodenal ulcer include (1) increased number of parietal and chief cells in the stomach, (2) increased sensitivity of the parietal cells to stimulation by the hormone gastrin, (3) increased secretion of gastrin following a meal, (4) impaired feedback inhibition of acid secretion in response to antral acidification, and (5) increased rate of gastric emptying.[63]

In the 50% of persons with duodenal ulcer, and those with gastric ulcer, who have normal or low levels of acid secretion, it is postulated that a breakdown in mucosal resistance occurs, and that this is the basis for the pathogenesis of the ulceration. A number of factors undoubtedly contribute to the resistance of the mucosa to ulceration. These include (1) a mucus layer overlying the mucosa, (2) the alkaline secretions in the lumen of the duodenum, (3) the adequacy of the blood supply, and (4) the intrinsic cellular defenses to damage.

Behavioral Factors in the Pathogenesis of Peptic Ulcer

THE EFFECTS OF PSYCHOLOGICAL STIMULI ON GASTRIC FUNCTION.—The fact that emotional reactions such as anger, hostility, and fear are associated with alterations in gastric function has been clearly established. Studies of persons with a gastric fistula (by Beaumont in 1833[64] and, more recently, by Wolff[65]) have shown that a number of changes in gastric physiology, including an increase in acid secretion and motility and a decrease in mucosal blood flow, may occur in response to psychological stressors. It is thought that these changes are brought about as a result of (1) the activation of the autonomic nervous system and (2) the secretion of hormones (such as the catecholamines and cortisol) or other humoral agents, both of which are induced by these stressors. For example, stimulation of the parasympathetic system (i.e., increased vagal discharge) would cause gastric hypersecretion and enhanced gastric motility and emptying, while increased discharge from the sympathetic nervous system would reduce mucosal blood flow. Thus, it is possible that psychological stimuli, by altering gastroduodenal secretions and blood flow, could either increase the magnitude of acid-pepsin forces or reduce the effectiveness of the forces of mucosal resistance.

Sun et al. described a person with a chronic duodenal ulcer who reacted to psychologically stressful interviews by a psychiatrist with an increase in the production of gastric acid.[66] This response was said to be conditioned. In other words, hypersecretion of acid was induced by the appearance of the psychiatrist, without the patient actually being interviewed. In addition to the studies showing that psychological stressors can cause gastric hypersecretion, it has been demonstrated that a reduction in this type of stress, as occurs for example in a state of hypnotically induced relaxation, diminishes gastric secretion.[67]

BEHAVIORAL ANTECEDENTS TO THE DEVELOPMENT OF PEPTIC ULCER DISEASE.—*Studies in humans* have provided some evidence for the role of stress in the etiology and pathogenesis of acute and chronic peptic ulcer disease. For instance, a number of investigations have found that, as a group, persons with *chronic* ulcer disease appear to have led a more stressful life when compared with groups of control subjects.[68-71] Moreover, there are reports indicating that the clinical diagnosis of chronic duodenal ulcer is often preceded by the occurrence of acute psychological stress.[68] In such cases, it is presumed that psychological factors precipitate this disease. In the study of air traffic controllers discussed earlier in this chapter, it was found that these individuals, who are exposed to a great deal of psychological stress, have a greater than normal incidence of chronic duodenal ulcer disease as well as hypertension.

Acute and severe stress is known to be associated with the development of *acute* peptic ulceration (stress ulcers) in humans. Persons exposed to acute illness, severe trauma, or burns may develop a stress ulcer(s), usually in the stomach.[72] This is probably the human counterpart of the ulcers described by Selye in his studies of the general adaptation syndrome in animals (described in chap. 7).

In the past, there has been a great deal of discussion about whether or not an ulcer-type personality exists; however, according to Fordtran, there is currently agreement among most investigators in this field that there is no specific personality that predisposes to this disorder.[73] Nor has there been adequate documentation of Alexander's theory that a particular psychological conflict involving unresolved dependency needs can be uniformly found in persons with chronic duodenal ulcer.

The results of *studies in animals* also attest to the ulcerogenic effects of stressful stimuli. However, it should be noted that the ulcers produced in these experiments are acute "stress ulcers," involving primarily the stomach, and they are not typical of chronic ulcer disease in humans. The following are two of the general experimental techniques used to produce peptic ulceration in animals.

FORCED ACTIVITY, FORCED RESTRAINT. — In animals, simple immobilization has been shown to cause peptic ulcers, particularly if the immobilization occurs during periods of the day in which the animal is usually active. Forced immobilization and forced activity have different effects on animals depending on their normal activity levels; the highest incidence of ulceration occurs in relatively active animals under conditions of forced immobilization and in relatively inactive animals under conditions of forced activity.[74]

In rat pups, forced immobilization, together with food deprivation, has been shown to interact with the effects of maternal separation in producing gastric erosions. The age of the pups at the time of maternal separation is a critical factor in determining the time of onset for the erosions. Pups that were separated from their mothers by 15 days after birth had a very high incidence of gastric erosions when evaluated on days 22 and 30, with the incidence generally decreasing on subsequent days. In contrast, animals separated from their mothers on day 21 or 25 showed a relatively low incidence of gastric erosions initially, with the incidence increasing thereafter.[75]

CONFLICT AND STRESS. — In Selye's classic studies of the responses of animals to stress, he noted that peptic ulceration (gastric) was a common finding in those that succumbed.

Other studies have shown that acute peptic ulcers result if animals are exposed to repeated unpredictable electric shocks. One method of doing this is the approach-avoidance conflict technique, in which animals are shocked when approaching food or water. Weiss conducted a series of investigations that showed that the likelihood of ulcer formation is greatest when the animal is unable to cope effectively with stress or when there is no positive feedback regarding the effectiveness of the coping responses.[76-78] Using the "yoked shock-avoidance" paradigm described in the section of this chapter on circulatory diseases, he found that while the delivery of shock per se could precipitate gastric ulcer formation, the ulcers occurred with greater frequency and severity in animals who received the shock and had no ability to terminate it, as compared with animals who were able to stop the shock. In particular, those animals who engaged in a high rate of responses in attempting to avoid the shock were more likely to develop ulcers than the more efficient animals who learned to avoid the shock with a lower overall frequency of avoidance responses. Weiss also noted that the more severe the ulcerations, the higher is the level of plasma corticosteroids.

Concepts About the Stress-Related Etiology of Peptic Ulcer Disease

In his extensive review of this subject, Fordtran listed three main suppositions in a psychosomatic theory of peptic ulcer formation in humans, along with his assessment of the validity of these suppositions.[73]

SUPPOSITION 1. — *Ulcer patients are exposed to long-standing psychic stress*. The evidence at hand strongly supports this supposition for duodenal ulcer, although it has not yet been proved. There are much less data dealing with this supposition in regard to gastric ulcer, but the data available support it.

SUPPOSITION 2. — *The chronic stress to which ulcer patients are exposed leads to some derangement in gastric function that predisposes to ulcer formation.* This supposition has been inadequately studied (lack of controlled, "blindly" recorded, and statistically analyzed studies) but is probably correct.

SUPPOSITION 3.—*A precipitating stressful event or situation precedes by a short time (4–7 days) the onset of an ulcer crater and ulcer symptoms.* To prove this supposition, it would be necessary to demonstrate (1) that the onset of peptic ulcer disease is more often preceded by a precipitating event than is the case with other nonpsychosomatic illnesses, and (2) that these events are more common prior to the time a person develops an ulcer than they are at other times in his life. These postulates are difficult to prove, according to Fordtran.

In those cases of peptic ulcer disease in which stress is felt to be a causative factor, it is believed that in most instances additional biologic factors are involved. Thus, a genetic predisposition is evident in some persons who have duodenal ulcer disease. This is manifested clinically by an increased level of serum pepsinogen I, presumably reflecting an excessive number of parietal and chief cells in the stomach and a greater than normal capacity for acid-pepsin secretion.

The mechanisms by which stress leads to the development of peptic ulcer probably involve a number of different neuroendocrine processes that regulate the secretory, motor, and vascular functions of the stomach and duodenum. For example, activation of efferent vagus impulses to these parts of the gastrointestinal tract by chronic stress could result in many of the pathophysiologic findings described in patients with duodenal ulcer disease (e.g., acid hypersecretion, increased parietal cell responsiveness to gastric secretagogues, and rapid gastric emptying). The pathogenesis of gastric ulcers resulting from acute stress may be related to the increased tissue levels of cortisol and catecholamines which impair gastric mucosal resistance, allowing the back diffusion of H^+ to damage the mucosa.

Finally, it is fairly certain that chronic peptic ulcer disease is not a single disease entity but rather a heterogeneous group of disorders with a similar pathologic picture. In some persons, the etiology of the ulcer may involve primarily biologic factors, while in others stressful stimuli may play an important role. It is possible that in the future persons with peptic ulcer will be subdivided on the basis of the relative degree of influence that stress has in the development or exacerbation of the illness. This, in turn, may lead to new approaches to prevention and treatment of this disorder.

THERAPEUTIC CONSIDERATIONS IN PSYCHOSOMATIC DISORDERS

In theory at least, it would seem that an effective form of treatment of psychosomatic disorders would be to reduce or eliminate the effects of the behavioral factors that precipitate and aggravate these disorders. Taking stress as an example of one of these factors, therapeutic interventions could logically be used at any of several points. First, an attempt could be made to remove the source of stress (i.e., the stressor) or to increase the person's capacity to cope with it successfully. Second, efforts could be directed toward modifying the physiological responses brought about by the stressors so that the impact of these responses on the body's organs is lessened. Third, therapy could be designed to reduce the degree of vulnerability of bodily organs to stress-induced physiological responses. In fact, all these approaches have been tried in order to combat stress-related illnesses, with a variable degree of success.

Prior to 1965, most reports of the use of these approaches in treating stress-related illness were uncontrolled and anecdotal. Fortunately, within the past decade and a half an increasing number of controlled studies have begun to appear in the literature. Few, if any, of the procedures have been subjected to large-scale clinical screening trials that could permit them to be selected as a treatment of choice, however. In this section we shall discuss such procedures as environmental modification, psychotherapy, pharmacologic agents, and behavioral methods.

Environmental modification is an obvious means of reducing the degree of life stress to which a person is exposed. The approach quite simply consists of changing the conditions under which the person works or lives. For a long time, it has been appreciated that hospitalization may lead to improvement in stress-related disorders, even though no specific pharmacotherapy is administered. This has been observed particularly for illnesses such as asthma, peptic ulcer, and ulcerative colitis. One reason for the improvement in these conditions might be that the person is no longer faced with the stressors in life that caused or aggravated the illness. There are other possible reasons for the improvement, or course, including physical rest, more orderly and conservative patterns of eating and sleeping, and the placebo effect brought about by the expectation of benefit from medical treatment. Ordinarily, hospitalization for stress-related illness is reserved for those patients who are quite ill and require intensive medical treatment, or as the first step in a comprehensive treatment plan for persons who have not responded well to treatment at home.

Stress-reducing changes in a person's environment can, of course, be made without resorting to hospitalization. Studies showing the beneficial effect of temporarily separating the child with asthma from his or her parents have been mentioned (this applies only to certain cases of atopic asthma). Changing a stressful job for one with less stress, avoiding acquaintances who by their behavior provoke stress, and changing one's personal life-style to reduce the amount of psychosocial stress are environmental modifications that have been reported to improve the health of persons with stress-implicated disorders. The availability of systems of social support (e.g., interaction with family, church groups, medical personnel) may protect against the adverse health consequences of stress.[79] Indeed, it has been reported that those persons who have these supports are less likely to become ill and die than those who are socially isolated.[80]

Psychotherapy has been used to effect changes in the personality, coping style, behavior, or interpersonal relations of persons with stress-related illnesses. If sufficiently interested and sensitive, most physicians and health-care practitioners should be able to carry out relatively uncomplicated, supportive psychotherapy. More sophisticated psychotherapy (e.g., analytically oriented therapy) requires a specially trained health professional such as a psychiatrist or psychologist. Individual or group psychotherapy has been reported to be successful in the treatment of various stress-related disorders, but the efficacy of such treatment needs to be established in controlled trials.[81]

When should a person with a stress-related disorder be referred for specific psychotherapy? In reviewing the current trends in psychosomatic medicine, Leigh and Reiser contend that the presence of a stress-related disorder is, by itself, not an indication for conventional psychotherapy.[82] They point out that as for any medical patient, psychotherapy for patients with stress-related illnesses is warranted only "if the psychological problems, in their own right, constitute a valid reason for it." Thus, only certain persons with stress-related illnesses are candidates for the psychotherapeutic approach.

It is important for the physician to keep in mind that even though it seems that psychological factors are significant contributors to the etiology of an illness, this does not mean that the illness will necessarily be helped by treating these factors.[81] Once an organic disease (e.g., peptic ulcer) is established, medical therapy for the disease (e.g., reduction or neutralization of gastric acid secretion) is of primary importance. Psychotherapy (if indicated) and the treatment of the physical disorder should go hand in hand in a comprehensive approach to patient care.

Pharmacologic treatment has been used to help persons control excessive psychophysiological responses to stress that may aggravate an organic illness. The judicious short-term use of the minor tranquilizers (e.g., Valium) to help a person cope with an acutely stressful life event (e.g., loss of a spouse) may be appropriate. The long-term administration of these drugs, however, is to be strictly avoided because of their adverse side effects and the risk of inducing drug dependency. Drugs that blunt the effects of discharge from the autonomic nervous system (sympathetic blocking agents) have also been used in the treatment of stress-related disorders, but their long-term side effects remain to be fully evaluated.

Behavioral methods such as self-control techniques and biofeedback have in recent years been used increasingly in the treatment of stress-induced illness.[83] Some of the self-control methods make use of clearly defined learning principles (e.g., contingent reinforcement, shaping of successive approximations toward a goal, discrimination training, extinction) to modify behaviors that may predispose, precipitate, or exacerbate organic disorders. Such self-control procedures include relaxation, cognitive behavior modification, and stress-management training (see chap. 5 for a detailed description of these behavioral methods). Other self-regulation techniques that do not stem from explicit learning theories include autogenic training[84] and meditation.[85]

In biofeedback therapy, information is provided on an immediate basis to the person about variations in physiological processes of which he or she is ordinarily not aware. This enables the person to make adjustments in those processes that would be difficult or impossible to achieve without the information feedback. During biofeedback training, the biologic information is provided to the person in the form of a light, a tone, or a counter that reflects some bodily function such as electromyographic (EMG) activity, electroencephalographic (EEG) activity, skin temperature, blood pressure, or heart rate. For example, in the course of biofeedback treatment the person might be instructed to try to get a light signal to go on and stay on as long as possible. When, by trial and error, the person makes the correct change in the physiological process being regulated, an output from a device used to record variations in this process triggers a signal light.[86] Once the person is able to keep the signal on continuously, the therapist can gradually increase the criterion level—the degree of change required to trigger the light signal. In this manner the person learns to alter the previously covert bodily function. If one considers the information that the subject receives concerning successful performance to be a positive reinforcer, then the biofeedback therapy can be considered a variant of operant conditioning.

The use of these behavioral methods (biofeedback, and self-control techniques such as the relaxation response and meditation) in the management of psychosomatic and other organic illnesses has recently gained greater recognition as a potentially important therapeutic modality. For this reason, several examples of the application of behavioral treatments to physical disorders will be described. A more detailed discussion of these treatments is presented elsewhere.[87]

Essential Hypertension

Presently the accepted treatment for essential hypertension consists of dietary restrictions (salt, calories if the patient is obese) and antihypertensive drugs. Although drug treatment is effective, it is sometimes difficult to convince patients, many of whom are asymptomatic, to undergo the inconvenience and expense associated with prolonged drug therapy. The problem is compounded when undesirable side effects occur. Biofeedback and self-control procedures have therefore been looked upon as potentially useful adjuncts or replacements for drugs in the management of mild or moderate essential hypertension.

An early clinical study using biofeedback of systolic blood pressure in hypertensive persons during multiple assessment and training sessions found that 5 of 7 subjects showed decreases in systolic pressure of 16 mm Hg or greater, although only 3 of the 7 were able to lower their blood pressure to normotensive levels.[88] In a subsequent single-group outcome study, Kristt and Engel also used biofeedback on systolic pressure in a within-subject design.[89] In this study 5 persons who were on medication and who had documented histories of essential hypertension of at least 10 years' duration were trained to control their systolic blood pressure. During the first phase of the study, lasting 7 weeks, the persons took their systolic and diastolic pressure readings at home and mailed these readings to the investigators daily. The second phase, which lasted for 3 weeks, took place in a hospital setting in which persons were trained to raise and lower their systolic pressure alternately. During the third phase of the study, lasting 3 months, the subjects again measured their blood pressure at home and mailed in their readings.

All the persons learned within the laboratory setting to increase or decrease their systolic blood pressure reliably during appropriate signals. Follow-up tests at 1 and 3 months provided evidence that this control was retained. Because heart rate, breathing rate, triceps brachia muscle tension, and EEG activity did not change systematically during the feedback for either systolic pressure increases or decreases, the investigators contended that it was unlikely for the blood pressure decreases to have been due to the subjects learning to relax.

The average baseline systolic pressure fell from 153 mm Hg during laboratory training to 135 mm Hg during a 3-month follow-up visit. Average systolic and diastolic pressures at home during the last phase of the study were 144 and 87 mm Hg, respectively. These compare with average readings of 163 and 95 mm Hg, respectively, during the initial phase. This study was particularly significant in a clinical sense because it demonstrated (1) relatively large blood pressure decreases in persons with long-standing hypertension, (2) transfer of the obtained decreases in blood pressure from the laboratory to the nonlaboratory setting, and (3) a long-term effect.

Although the preceding study provided evidence that the changes in blood pressure obtained were due to biofeedback training rather than to relaxation, relaxation techniques have also been shown to ameliorate hypertension. In one study, 19 persons who had modest elevation of blood pressure and who had never received antihypertensive therapy were studied for 6 months.[90] The 14 persons in the experimental group attended five 20-minute training sessions and were instructed in a meditation technique. This technique consisted of going to a quiet place, sitting upright in a comfortable chair, loosening tight clothing, attempting to relax one's muscles, and counting breaths subvocally in a continuous arithmetic progression. Members of the experimental group were instructed to repeat the technique twice daily for intervals of 10 to 15 minutes. Both the experimental group and the no-treatment control group were seen for blood pressure determinations once a month.

At the outset of the study mean arterial blood pressure averaged approximately 110 mm Hg in each group. During the 6 months of the study, this value declined by about 12 mm Hg in the experimental group, but showed almost no change in the control group. Reductions in mean arterial pressure were associated with decreases in the level of plasma dopamine-β-hydroxylase, which is the enzyme that converts dopamine to norepinephrine within the axon endings of sympathetic neurons. The reduction in pressure was also associated with a decrease in the activity of peripheral plasma renin without a significant change in plasma volume. These results suggest that the moderate drop in blood pressure observed in the experimental subjects with mild hypertension was due to reduced peripheral sympathetic activity. While the experiment did reveal that the experimental subjects experienced a decrease in mean arterial pressure, the absence of an attention-placebo control group precludes full attribution of the changes to the meditation technique.

In another study Patel and North used a combination of meditation-relaxation techniques and biofeedback-assisted relaxation training to treat hypertensives, some of whom were on medication.[91] The investigators enrolled 34 hypertensive persons in a randomized control study. Half the persons received relaxation and biofeedback-assisted relaxation training (first using galvanic skin response, then EMG) during 12 half-hour sessions over a 6-week period. The other half was given a similar number of sessions. In contrast to the experimental group, however, they rested on a couch but were not given specific instructions and were not connected to the biofeedback equipment.

Patel and North found that systolic and diastolic blood pressures decreased by 26 and 15 mm Hg, respectively, in the experimental group as opposed to 9 and 4 mm Hg, respectively, in the control group. After the end of a 3-month follow-up period, persons in the control group were given behavioral treatment and reportedly showed improvement comparable to that in the initial treatment group.

The results of the studies reviewed suggest that behavioral interventions can effectively reduce blood pressure in hypertensive persons. Use of a contact control group in the Patel and North study is particularly noteworthy, because the results of double-blind studies assessing the effects of antihypertensive drugs have clearly indicated that the expectations of subjects can lead to relatively large, sustained decreases in blood pressure that may take place over at least several weeks.[92] While the studies using behavioral methods to treat hypertension seem promising, they are by no means definitive. As yet, for example, it is not clear to what extent the decreases in blood pressure may have been due to changes in life-style (e.g., diet, exercise) and, where drugs were taken, to increased drug treatment compliance induced by engaging in the project. Even in the Patel and North study, which used a contact control group, the experimental group was asked to practice relaxation at home, whereas the control group was not. This, of course, might well have led to differences in motivation and adherence to good health practices in the two groups. In addition, because Patel and North did not use component analyses, it is not possible to determine whether the decreases in blood pressure were attributable to the biofeedback training, to the practice of meditation-relaxation techniques at home, or to a combination of the two. Another question with respect to relaxation training, i.e., whether the reduction in blood pressure generalizes to situations other than the training period, has been answered affirmatively. A recent study found that this carry-over (i.e., lowering of blood pressure) extends even to the nighttime while the person is sleeping.[93] All in all, the studies using behavioral techniques to treat hypertension suggest that this modality may prove to be effective as an adjunct or substitute for pharmacologic treatment in some cases of hypertension.

Cardiac Arrhythmias

During the past several years, evidence has accumulated that voluntary control of heart rate may be learned by means of biofeedback techniques. Such learning has been shown to influence the occurrence of selective arrhythmias, some of which may be related to stress. Engel and his collaborators have studied the effects of heart-rate biofeedback on persons with (1) premature ventricular beats, (2) tachyarrhythmias, and (3) conduction defects.[87, 94] All the investigations were single-group outcome studies.

The effects of biofeedback on the occurrence of premature ventricular contractions was studied because of the association of this arrhythmia with sudden death, and because in certain instances drug therapy is unsuccessful in suppressing these ectopic beats. The persons studied were trained to increase their heart rate in the presence of a green light and to decrease their heart rate in the presence of a red light. A yellow light informed them that they were performing successfully.[94]

Once the persons learned to increase and decrease their heart rate in response to the appropriate lights, they were trained to maintain their heart rate between preset upper and lower limits. Because a premature ventricular beat caused the heart rate to go above this range, and the compensatory pause following the premature beat caused the heart rate to go below this range, the light feedback the persons received informed them every time that they had a premature ventricular contraction. Eventually, the persons were gradually weaned from the light feedback and made to become aware of their premature ventricular contractions through their sensations.

Of 9 persons studied, 6 learned to control their premature ventricular contractions while in the laboratory, and 5 of the 6 showed evidence of being able to maintain this control outside the laboratory. Long-term follow-up on 2 persons—1 for 5 years and 1 for a year—showed that they continued to maintain good control as demonstrated by continuous 10-hour electrocardiogram recordings taken while they performed their normal daily activities.

Heart-rate biofeedback has also proved successful in the treatment of tachyarrhythmias including sinus tachycardia, paroxysmal atrial tachycardia, supraventricular tachycardia, and atrial fibrillation. In contrast, the procedure has been ineffective in treating bradyarrhythmias due to conduction defects such as third-degree heart block. These results indicate that heart-rate changes produced by biofeedback depend on appropriate efferent neuronal innervation of the heart. Because the extrinsic autonomic nerves to the ventricles do not mediate chronotropic (rate) function, the persons with third-degree block were unable to learn to modify their ventricular rates voluntarily.

Migraine

The syndrome of migraine is due primarily to vascular disturbance. In the pathogenesis of classic migraine there is an initial phase of vasoconstriction involving the intracranial and extracranial arteries that occurs prior to onset of the headache. Neurologic symptoms (the aura or prodroma) may be experienced at this time. Following the phase of vasoconstriction, there is a phase of vasodilatation during which the headache occurs.

As the migraine headache begins, large hydraulic pulsations of the arteries distend the pain-sensitive fibers surrounding the vessels. This results in painful throbbing. In addition, there is an accumulation of vasoactive substances about the dilated arteries that sensitizes them to pain. A sterile inflammation and edema of the arteries also occur in migraine.

A number of factors can precipitate a migraine attack in a person with this disorder. One of the most important is emotional upset associated with life stress. Ergotamine tartrate, a drug that produces vasoconstriction, has been found to be effective in relieving migraine headache if given shortly after the attack begins. This agent is not effective in all persons and it has significant adverse side effects. Thus, attempts have been made to treat migraine by nonpharmacologic means. An early behavioral study used autogenic training as a form of therapy. Briefly, the procedure consisted of training persons to increase their finger temperature, which is correlated with vasodilation. Although the investigators indicated that the training was effective, the study lacked quantified data. Nevertheless, it suggested that learned vasomotor control might be effective in the treatment of migraine.[95]

A more recent biofeedback experiment also focused on increases in the temperature of finger skin to treat migraine.[96] In this study, seven individuals suffering from migraine were given extensive biofeedback training in finger-warming until they could do so without having to resort to the feedback equipment. They were instructed to practice at home and to warm their finger temperature at the first sign of headache. Prior to receiving this training in finger-warming, three of the subjects received biofeedback training in finger-cooling. They served as a control group. None of the persons who received training in finger-cooling showed signs of clinical improvement in their migraine until after they received training in finger-warming. In contrast, the persons who were trained only to warm their finger temperature showed significant improvement in their headaches.

In another biofeedback experiment, persons with migraine who were trained to constrict their extracranial arteries experienced a reduction in the frequency of their migraine attacks.[97] A control group trained to vasoconstrict the arteries of the index finger on the side most often affected by migraine attacks showed no improvement. Although the experiment was convincing in demonstrating that biofeedback is successful in reducing the arterial pulse waves recorded from the surface of the skin using pressure plethysmographs, the reduction in the frequency of migraine attacks following vasoconstriction training was only moderate. Assessment of the utility of biofeedback as compared with that of other modalities in the treatment of migraine awaits further study.

Tension Headache

Approximately 70% of adults report having headaches and the vast majority have tension or muscle-contraction headaches. Tension headaches usually originate in the frontal or occipital region and are related to sustained contraction of scalp and/or neck muscles. Stress is thought to be a major factor in the pathogenesis of this type of headache.

In a pioneer biofeedback study, an experimental group that received electromyographic (EMG) biofeedback from the frontalis muscle and practiced relaxation at home was compared with a no-treatment control group and a control group that received noncontingent EMG feedback.[98] The investigators found that after training, the experimental group reported significantly fewer headaches, less need for medication, and a stable reduction of ancillary psychosomatic complaints. In addition, the investigators reported a high correlation between the decrease in frequency of headaches and the reduction in activity of the frontalis EMG in the experimental group. Although the study provided clear differences between the experimental and control conditions, it was not possible to tell whether the results were due to the EMG biofeedback, the home relaxation, or a combination of both.

In a subsequent experiment, 27 adults with chronic tension headaches were divided into (1) a group receiving EMG biofeedback from the frontalis, (2) a group receiving progressive relaxation instructions, and (3) a medication placebo group.[99] Each subject received 2 weeks of pretreatment and posttreatment assessment with 4 intervening weeks of treatment. Measures were taken of headache frequency, intensity, and duration as well as EMG activity, medication intake, and ancillary psychosomatic complaints. Assessment during the posttraining period, as well as at a 4-month follow-up visit, indicated that biofeedback and verbal relaxation instructions were equally superior to the placebo with respect to the clinical improvement of the persons on all measures. The finding that EMG biofeedback from the frontalis muscle and relaxation both gave equally superior results to a control group has also been reported in other studies.[100,101] It would therefore appear that behavioral interventions that are able to get persons to relax and reduce EMG activity from the frontalis muscle are likely to decrease the frequency, intensity, and duration of tension headaches.

SUMMARY

Three processes appear to be central to the etiology and pathogenesis of a psychosomatic disease: first, the impact of a behavioral factor (psychological or otherwise); second, the body's psychophysiological responses to the factor; and third, a biologically determined process that increases the vulnerability of the body to disease. Current evidence suggests that psychological stimuli may not directly cause disease but, rather, in most instances, they act as a precipitating or exacerbating factor, unmasking a previously latent disorder or aggravating a previously stable one. In other words, psychological factors appear to be necessary but insufficient pathogenetic factors in the occurrence of at least some physical disorders.

Many variables affect the three processes listed above. For example, in order to understand the impact of a psychological stressor on a given individual, one would have to know a good deal not only about the nature of the stressor, but also about its special meaning to the person, his or her personal coping devices, and the support the individual receives from others. These variables determine the magnitude of the impact of the stress on the person and this, in turn, influences the person's reactions to it. The body's physiological responses to stress are also affected by a number of variables including genetic factors, which are thought by some to program a person's physiological responses from birth, and environmental influences, which act to modify these responses through learned behavior. Organ vulnerability can also be attributed to genetic or environmental factors that produce either latent or overt dysfunction of a body organ, thereby rendering it more vulnerable to the ill effects of stress. For example, in asthmatics, this dysfunction is manifested as bronchial hyperreactivity; in persons with duodenal ulcer disease, it is characterized by the capacity for gastric hypersecretion.

Therapy for stress-related disorders can logically be thought of in terms of modifying the three processes described above—the impact of a behavioral factor, the psychophysiological responses to it, and the vulnerability of the involved organ.

A number of studies are described that indicate that some physical disorders lend themselves to specific types of behavioral therapy. Evidence has accumulated that the symptoms of essential hypertension, some kinds of cardiac arrhythmia, migraine headache, and tension headache can be ameliorated by behavioral self-control and biofeedback techniques. While the application of behavioral techniques to these conditions and others (including asthma and epilepsy) appears promising, there is a need for well-controlled group outcome studies to assess the efficacy of specific behavioral techniques. The findings that behavioral factors play a role in the etiology and pathogenesis of many disorders, and that behavioral techniques can modify some effects of stress on the individual suggest that biofeedback and behavioral self-control methods may prove useful in the prevention as well as the treatment of a variety of organic diseases.

REFERENCES

1. Schwartz G.E., Weiss S.M.: Behavioral medicine revisited: An amended definition. *J. Behav. Med.* 1:249, 1978.
2. Engel G.L.: A life setting conducive to illness: The giving-up–given-up complex. *Ann. Intern. Med.* 69:293, 1968.
3. Schmale A.H.: Giving up as a final common pathway to changes in health. *Adv. Psychosom. Med.* 3:20, 1972.
4. Dunbar F.: *Emotions and Bodily Changes.* New York, Columbia University Press, 1935.
5. Alexander F.: *Psychosomatic Medicine: Its Principles and Applications.* New York, W.W. Norton & Company, Inc., 1950.
6. Weiner H., Thaler M., Reiser M.F., et al.: Etiology of duodenal ulcer. *Psychosom. Med.* 19:1, 1957.
7. Schneiderman N.: Animal models relating behavioral stress and cardiovascular pathology, in Dembroski T.M., et al. (eds.): *Coronary-Prone Behavior.* New York, Springer-Verlag New York Inc., 1978.
8. Yamada A., Jensen M.M., Rasmussen A.F.: Stress and susceptibility to viral infections. III. Antibody response and viral retention during avoidance learning stress. *Proc. Soc. Exp. Biol. Med.* 116:677, 1964.
9. Selye H.: *The Stress of Life.* New York, McGraw-Hill Book Co., 1956.
10. Herd J.A.: Physiological correlates of coronary-prone behavior, in Dembroski T.M., et al. (eds.): *Coronary-Prone Behavior.* New York, Springer-Verlag New York Inc., 1978.
11. Ross R., Glomset J.A.: The pathogenesis of atherosclerosis. *N. Engl. J. Med.* 295:369, 1976.
12. Gordon T., Verter J.: Serum cholesterol, systolic blood pressure and Framingham relative weight as discriminators of cardiovascular disease, in Kannel W.W., Gordon T. (eds.): *The Framingham Study: An Epidemiological Investigation of Cardiovascular Disease.* U.S. Government Printing Office, 1969, section 23.
13. Henry J.P.: Mechanisms of psychosomatic disease in animals. *Adv. Vet. Sci. Comp. Med.* 20:115–145, 1976.
14. Chapman M.L.: Peptic ulcer. *Med. Clin. North Am.* 62:39, 1978.
15. Samloff I.M., Liebman W.M., Panities N.M.: Serum group I pepsinogens by radioimmunoassay in control subjects and patients with peptic ulcer. *Gastroenterology* 69:83, 1975.

16. Rotter J.I., Sones J.Q., Samloff M.I., et al.: Duodenal-ulcer disease associated with elevated serum pepsinogen. I. An inherited autosomal dominant disorder. *N. Engl. J. Med.* 300:63, 1980.
17. Osler W.: *The Principles and Practice of Medicine*. Edinburgh, Young, J. Reutland, 1892.
18. Forsythe R.P.: Regional blood flow changes during 72-hour avoidance schedules in the monkey. *Science* 173:546, 1971.
19. Hilton S.M.: Supramedullary organization of vasomotor control. *Prog. Brain Res.* 47:77, 1976.
20. Forsyth R.P.: Blood pressure responses to long-term avoidance schedules in the restrained rhesus monkey. *Psychosom. Med.* 31:300, 1969.
21. Herd J.A., Morse W.H., Kelleher R.T., et al.: Arterial hypertension in the squirrel monkey during behavioral experiments. *Am. J. Physiol.* 217:24–29, 1969.
22. Harris A.H., Gilliam W., Findley J.D., et al.: Instrumental conditioning of large-magnitude daily 12-hour blood pressure elevations in the baboon. *Science* 182:175, 1973.
23. Henry J.P., Ely D.L., Stephens P.M., et al.: The role of psychosocial factors in the development of arteriosclerosis in CBA mice: Observations of the heart, kidney and aorta. *Atherosclerosis* 14:203, 1971.
24. Okamoto K., Aoki K.: Development of a strain of spontaneously hypertensive rats. *Jpn. Circ. J.* 27:282, 1963.
25. Bianchi G., Fox U., DiFrancesco G.F., et al.: Hypertensive role of the kidney in spontaneously hypertensive rats. *Clin. Sci. Mol. Med.* 45:135s, 1973.
26. Dahl L.K., Heine M., Tassinari L.I.: Role of genetic factors in susceptibility to experimental hypertension due to chronic excess salt ingestion. *Nature* 194:480, 1961.
27. Yamori Y., Matsumoto M., Yamabe H., et al.: Augmentation of spontaneous hypertension by chronic stress in rats. *Jpn. Circ. J.* 33:399, 1969.
28. Friedman R., Iwai J.: Genetic predisposition and stress-induced hypertension. *Science* 193:161, 1976.
29. Graham J.D.P.: High blood pressure after battle. *Lancet* 1:239, 1945.
30. Ruskin A., Beard O.W., Schaffer R.L.: Blast hypertension: Elevated arterial pressure in the victims of the Texas City disaster. *Am. J. Med.* 4:228, 1948.
31. Cobb S., Rose R.M.: Hypertension, peptic ulcer, and diabetes in air traffic controllers. *J.A.M.A.* 224:489, 1973.
32. Jonsson A., Hansson L.: Prolonged exposure to a stressful stimulus (noise) as a cause of raised blood pressure in man. *Lancet* 1:86, 1977.
33. Harburg E., Erfurt J.C., Havenstein L.S., et al.: Socio-ecological stress, suppressed hostility, skin color, and black-white male blood pressure: Detroit. *Psychosom. Med.* 35:276–295, 1973.
34. Lund-Johansen P.: Hemodynamic alterations in essential hypertension, in Onesti G., Kim K.E., Moyer J.H. (eds.): *Hypertension: Mechanisms and Management*. New York, Grune & Stratton, Inc., 1973.
35. Julius S., Esler M.: Autonomic nervous cardiovascular regulation in borderline hypertension. *Am. J. Cardiol.* 36:685, 1975.
36. Frohlich E.D.: Hemodynamics of hypertension, in Genest J., Koiw E., Kuchel O. (eds.): *Hypertension: Physiopathology and Treatment*. New York, McGraw-Hill Book Co., 1977.
37. Chebanian A.V., et al.: Studies on the activity of the sympathetic nervous system in essential hypertension. *J. Hum. Stress* 4:22, 1978.
38. DeQuattro V.Y., et al.: Increased plasma catecholamine concentrations and vas deferens norepinephrine biosynthesis in men with elevated blood pressure. *Circ. Res.* 36:118, 1975.
39. Mehta J.: Adrenergic blockade in hypertension. *J.A.M.A.* 240:1759, 1978.
40. Benson H., et al.: The relaxation response. *Med. Clin. North Am.* 61:929, 1977.
41. Julius S.: Borderline hypertension: Epidemiologic and clinical implications, in Genest J., Koiw E., Kuchel O. (eds.): *Hypertension: Physiopathology and Treatment*. New York, McGraw-Hill Book Co., 1977.
42. Hamilton J.A.: Psychophysiology of blood pressure. I. Personality and behavior ratings. *Psychosom. Med.* 4:125–133, 1942.
43. Harburg E., Julius S., McGuinn N.F., et al.: Personality traits and behavioral patterns associated with systolic blood pressure levels in college males. *J. Chronic Dis.* 17:405–412, 1964.
44. Esler M., Julius S., Zweifler A., et al.: Mild high-renin hypertension. *N. Engl. J. Med.* 296:405–411, 1977.
45. Hokanson J.E., Burgess M.: The effects of status, type of frustration, and aggression on vascular processes. *J. Abnorm. Soc. Psychol.* 65:232–237, 1962.
46. Rosenman R.H., Friedman M.: Neurogenic factors in pathogenesis of coronary heart disease. *Med. Clin. North Am.* 58:269–279, 1974.
47. Jenkins C.D.: Recent evidence supporting

psychologic and social risk factors for coronary diseases. *N. Engl. J. Med.* 294:1033–1038, 1976.
48. Brand R.J., et al.: Multivariate prediction of coronary heart disease in the Western Collaborative Group Study compared to the findings of the Framingham Study. *Circulation* 53:348–355, 1976.
49. Jenkins C.D., Rosenman R.H., Zyanski S.J.: Prediction of clinical coronary heart disease by a test for the coronary prone behavior pattern. *N. Engl. J. Med.* 290:1271–1275, 1974.
50. Glass D.C.: *Behavior Patterns, Stress, and Coronary Disease.* Hillsdale, N.J., Lawrence Erlbaum Associates, 1977.
51. Dembroski T.M., et al.: Components of the Type A coronary-prone behavior pattern and cardiovascular responses to psychomotor performance challenge. *J. Behav. Med.* 1:159–176, 1978.
52. Friedman M., Rosenman R.H., Carroll V.: Changes in the serum cholesterol and blood-clotting time in men subjected to cyclic variation of occupational stress. *Circulation* 17:852–861, 1958.
53. Scadding J.G.: Definition and clinical categorization, in Weiss E.G., Segal M.S. (eds.): *Bronchial Asthma.* Boston, Little, Brown and Co., 1976.
54. Kaliner M., Austen F.K.: Biochemical characteristics of immediate hypersensitivity reactions, in Weiss E.G., Segal M.S. (eds.): *Bronchial Asthma.* Boston, Little, Brown and Co., 1976.
55. Block J., et al.: Interaction between allergic potential and psychopathology in childhood asthma. *Psychosom. Med.* 26:307–320, 1964.
56. Aitken R.C.B., Zealley A.K., Barrow C.G.: The treatment of psychopathology in bronchial asthmatics. Ciba Found. Symp., 1972.
57. Purcell K., Bernstein L., Bukantz S.: A preliminary comparison of rapidly remitting and persistently steroid dependent asthmatic children. *Psychosom. Med.* 23:305, 1961.
58. Dekker F., Groen J.: Reproducible psychogenic attacks of asthma. *J. Psychosom. Res.* 1:58–67, 1956.
59. Knapp P.H.: Psychosomatic aspects of bronchial asthma, in Reiser M.F., (ed.): *American Handbook of Psychiatry 4.* New York, Basic Books, 1975.
60. Ottenberg P., et al.: Learned asthma in the guinea pig. *Psychosom. Med.* 20:395–403, 1958.
61. Knapp P.H., Mathe A.A., Vachon L.: Psychosomatic aspects of bronchial asthma, in Weiss E.B., Segal M.S. (eds.): *Bronchial Asthma.* Boston, Little, Brown and Co., 1976.

62. Stein M., Schiavi R.: Psychophysiological respiratory disorders, in Freedman A.M., Kaplan H.I., Sadock B.J. (eds.): *Comprehensive Textbook of Psychiatry/II,* vol. 2. Baltimore, Williams & Wilkins Co., 1975.
63. Grossman M.I.: Abnormalities of acid secretion in patients with duodenal ulcer. *Gastroenterology* 75:524, 1978.
64. Beaumont W.: *Experiments and Observations on the Gastric Juice and the Physiology of Digestion.* Plattsburgh, N.Y., F.P. Allen, 1833.
65. Wolff S., Wolff H.G.: *Human Gastric Function.* New York, Oxford University Press, 1943.
66. Sun D.C.H., et al.: Conditioned secretory response following repeated emotional stress in a case of duodenal ulcer. *Gastroenterology* 35:155, 1958.
67. Stacher B., et al.: Effects of hypnotic suggestions of relaxation on basal and betazole-stimulated gastric acid secretion. *Gastroenterology* 68:656, 1975.
68. Davies D.T., Wilson A.T.M.: Observations of the life-history of chronic peptic ulcer. *Lancet* 2:1353, 1937.
69. Hamilton M.: The personality of dyspeptics with special reference to gastric and duodenal ulcer. *Br. J. Med. Psychol.* 23:182, 1950.
70. Hjer-Pederson W.: On the significance of psychic factors in the development of peptic ulcer. *Acta Psychiatr. Neurol. Scand.* 119 (suppl):v33, 1958.
71. Alp M.H., et al.: Personality pattern and emotional stress in the genesis of gastric ulcer. *Gut* 11:773, 1970.
72. Skillman J.J., Silen W.: Stress ulceration in the acutely ill. *Annu. Rev. Med.* 27:9, 1976.
73. Fordtran J.S.: The psychosomatic theory of peptic ulcer, in Schlesinger M.H., Fordtran J.S. (eds.): *Gastrointestinal Diseases.* Philadelphia, W.B. Saunders Co., 1973.
74. Ader R.: Gastric erosion in the rat: Effects of immobilization at different points in the activity cycle. *Science* 145:406–407, 1964.
75. Ackerman S.H., Hofer M.A., Weiner H.: Age at maternal separation and gastric erosion susceptibility in the rat. *Psychosom. Med.* 37:180–184, 1975.
76. Weiss J.M.: Effects of coping behavior in different warning signal conditions on stress pathology in rats. *J. Comp. Physiol. Psychol.* 77:1–13, 1971.
77. Weiss J.M.: Effects of punishing the coping response (conflict) on stress pathology in rats. *J. Comp. Physiol. Psychol.* 77:14–21, 1971.
78. Weiss J.M.: Effects of coping behavior with and without a feedback signal on stress pa-

thology in rats. *J. Comp. Physiol. Psychol.* 76:22–30, 1971.
79. Cobb S.: Social support as a moderator of life stress. *Psychosom. Med.* 38:300, 1976.
80. Berkman L.F., Syme S.L.: Social networks. Host resistance and mortality: A nine-year follow-up study of Alameda County residents. *Am. J. Epidemiol.* 109:186, 1979.
81. Hill O.: The psychological management of psychosomatic diseases. *Br. J. Psychiatry* 131:113, 1977.
82. Leigh H., Reiser M.F.: Modern trends in psychosomatic medicine. *Ann. Intern. Med.* 87:233, 1977.
83. Pomerleau O.F., Brady J.P. (eds.): *Behavioral Medicine: Theory and Practice*. Baltimore, Williams & Wilkins Co., 1979.
84. Schultz J.H., Luthe W.: *Autogenic Training: A Psychophysiological Approach in Psychotherapy*. New York, Grune & Stratton, 1959.
85. Wallace R.K., Benson H.: The physiology of meditation. *Sci. Am.* 226:84–90, 1972.
86. Schneiderman N., Dauth G.W., VanDercar D.H.: Electrocardiogram: Techniques and analysis, in Thompson R.F., Patterson M. (eds.): *Bioelectric Recording Techniques, Part C: Receptor and Effector Processes*. New York, Academic Press, 1974.
87. Schneiderman N., Weiss T., Engel B.T.: Modification of psychosomatic behaviors, in Davidson R.S. (ed.): *Modification of Pathological Behavior*. New York, Gardner Press, 1979.
88. Benson H., Shapiro D., Trusky B., et al.: Decreased systolic blood pressure through operant conditioning techniques in patients with essential hypertension. *Science* 173:740–741, 1971.
89. Kristt D.A., Engel B.T.: Learned control of blood pressure in patients with high blood pressure. *Circulation* 51:370–378, 1975.
90. Stone R., DeLeo J.: Psychotherapeutic control of hypertension. *N. Engl. J. Med.* 294:80–84, 1976.
91. Patel C.H., North W.R.S.: Randomised controlled trial of yoga and biofeedback in management of hypertension. *Lancet* 2:93–95, 1975.
92. Greenfill R.F., Briggs A.H., Holland W.C.: Antihypertensive drugs evaluated in a controlled double-blind study. *South. Med. J.* 56:1410–1414, 1963.
93. Agras W.S., Taylor C.B., Kraemer H.C., et al.: Relaxation training. *Arch. Gen. Psychiatry* 37:859, 1980.
94. Engel B.T., Bleecker E.R.: Application of operant conditioning techniques to the control of the cardiac arrhythmias, in Obrist P.A., Black A.H., Brener J., et al. (eds.): *Cardiovascular Psychophysiology*. Chicago, Aldine Publishing Company, 1974.
95. Sargent J.D., Green E.E., Walters E.D.: Preliminary report on the use of autogenic feedback training in the treatment of migraine and tension headaches. *Psychosom. Med.* 35:129–135, 1973.
96. Turin A., Johnson W.G.: Biofeedback therapy for migraine headaches. *Arch. Gen. Psychiatry* 33:517–519, 1976.
97. Friar L.R., Beatty J.: Migraine: Management by trained control of vasoconstriction. *J. Consult. Clin. Psychol.* 44:46–53, 1976.
98. Budzynski T.H., et al.: EMG biofeedback and tension headache: A controlled outcome study. *Psychosom. Med.* 35:484–495, 1973.
99. Cox D.J., Freundlish C., Meyer R.G.: Differential effectiveness of electromyographic feedback, verbal relaxation instructions and medication placebo. *J. Consult. Clin. Psychol.* 43:892–989, 1975.
100. Haynes S.N., Griffin P., Mooney D., et al.: Electromyographic biofeedback and relaxation instructions in the treatment of muscle contraction headaches. *Behav. Ther.* 6:672–678, 1975.
101. Nuechterlein K.H., Holroyd J.C.: Biofeedback in the treatment of tension headache: Current status. *Arch. Gen. Psychiatry* 37:866, 1980.

PART III

Behavior in Social and Cultural Perspective

9 / Social Aspects of Medicine

HARRIET P. LEFLEY, Ph.D.

THE PRACTICE OF MEDICINE is fundamentally a social phenomenon, since it affects the well-being and continuity of society.

In addition to the human suffering associated with disease, the disability it causes constitutes a serious "waste factor" in all societies, affecting productivity and the quality of life. In the United States, national health expenditures were $212 billion in 1979. Added to this are the human costs stemming from the disruption of personal and family life.

These short- and long-range costs to our society are determined to a large extent by social decisions such as the way in which we (as a society) allocate our health-care resources, including the degree of emphasis placed on basic and applied research, medical education, preventive health care, and health education for the public. The organization of our health care delivery system and the distribution of its resources critically affect the level of health of our population.

The kinds of specific issues that medical sociologists and other behavioral scientists are interested in confronting are briefly described in the following outline:

1. *Epidemiology of disease.*—This area deals with the effects of sociocultural variables on the incidence and prevalence of disease and disability. By identifying those factors that produce disease and then reducing their impact, it is hoped that mortality and morbidity will decrease.

2. *The ecology of health.*—This area is concerned with relationships between the level of health and social variables such as sanitation, housing, environmental toxins, life-style, diet, and various types of social stressors.

3. *The health-care system.*—A wide range of topics is subsumed under this heading, including the organization and structure of the health-care system, recruitment and training of medical personnel, institutional and practitioner interrelationships, the hospital as a social system, the distribution and utilization of medical services, social barriers to health-care delivery, and political factors influencing the health-care system.

4. *Sociocultural and social-psychological factors in health and illness.*—This is the most wide-ranging area of interest, focusing on psychological, social, and cultural variables that determine the onset of illness, the utilization of available health-care services, and the response to treatment. Some of the specific topics include:

a. Health attitudes and belief systems.—These are critical determinants of how people respond to symptoms of illness. They consist of normative beliefs regarding bodily function, traditional views about systems of healing, social attitudes toward the sick, and patient attitudes toward medical personnel.

b. Health maintenance mechanisms.—Included under this heading are the sociological factors relating to routine checkups, immunization procedures, proper exercise, and dietary habits. Also important in health maintenance are adequate food supplies, strategies for dealing with social stress, and group responses to family planning and genetic counseling.

c. Utilization patterns.—Patterns of selection and use of treatment modalities, including underutilization and overutilization of specific types of facilities, belong here. Also involved are selective variables such as delay in seeking treatment and compliance with medical advice. Alternative healing modalities (folk, psychological, medical, quasimedical, and the like) are subjects of study in this area.

d. Familial factors in medicine.—Patterns of health-oriented behavior and sick role definitions, transmitted to the individual by the family, are responsible for many reactions to illness. Family structure, dynamics, and transactional styles are critical in determining the effects of illness or disability on sick persons and their families.

5. *Patient-practitioner relationships.*—This issue focuses on the social factors that influence the interaction between patients and health professionals during the course of medical care. Some questions asked in studies dealing with this topic are: What are the areas of agreement and disagreement in patient-physician perceptions of an illness? How does the patient's socioeconomic or ethnic background affect diagnosis, prognosis, and treatment recommendation? What role does the physician's behavior play in determining the responses of the patient or her family? What social and cultural factors influence patient compliance?

In this chapter, it is obvious that only a few of the issues in this outline can be dealt with in any detail. In the discussion that follows, I have tried to (1) concentrate on issues that are germane to the everyday practice of medicine, and (2) describe actual clinical incidents. As a result of this approach, it is hoped that readers will gain an understanding of the close relationship between health and social phenomena on both the societal and individual levels; and become familiar with concepts that will be of practical value to them in their daily medical activities.

SOME SOCIOLOGICAL CORRELATES OF HEALTH AND ILLNESS

According to the federal government, the three major social concerns in the health area are long life, freedom from disability, and access to medical care.[1] A number of statistical indicators are used to assess these health matters: (1) average life expectancy at birth, (2) average number of days of disability per person per year, (3) number of visits to a physician's office per person per year, (4) personal confidence in the ability to obtain good medical care—a perception measure, and (5) percent of the population covered by health insurance. The last two are considered indirect measures of the availability of health-care services.

It is well known that there are significant differences in these indicators among various segments of our population. A discussion of these differences will illustrate the critical relationship between health status and social class variables such as income, occupation, education, and residence. Besides the variables on which social class is determined, other sociological factors are important in understanding the distribution and outcome of illness. These are age, sex, cultural background, religion, and race. The nature of the relationship between the health of an individual or group and social factors will be made clearer in the following discussion.

Longevity

Unfortunately, all babies are not born equal, at least in terms of their expected life span. Life expectancy varies according to year of birth, sex, and race. Table 9–1 shows the average longevity for persons born in the years 1900 to 1976. The dramatic increase in life span during this time is evident. The greatest change occurred in the period between 1900 and 1940 before the advent of modern advances in medical technology and therapeutics. Prior to 1900, epidemics of infectious diseases periodically ravaged urban populations. The increase in longevity in the 1920s and 1930s was due in large part to a reduction in mortality from these diseases, brought about primarily by general improvements in the living conditions of the public. Among these improvements were better housing, sanitation, and nutrition, all of which contributed to the decline in the death rates. While it is true that immunization procedures were beginning to be introduced in the

TABLE 9-1.—AVERAGE REMAINING YEARS OF LIFE AT BIRTH; SELECTED YEARS 1900–1977

YEAR	TOTAL POPULATION	WHITE (BOTH SEXES)	BLACK AND OTHER (BOTH SEXES)
1900	47.3	47.6	33.0
1910	50.0	50.3	35.6
1920	54.1	54.9	45.3
1930	59.7	61.4	48.1
1940	62.9	64.2	53.1
1950	68.2	69.1	60.8
1960	69.7	70.6	63.6
1970	70.9	71.7	65.3
1977	73.2	73.8	68.8

Data from U.S. Bureau of the Census, *Statistical Abstract of the United States: 1979*, ed. 100, 1979; and Grove R.D., Hetzel A.M.: *Vital Statistics Rates in the United States 1940–1960*. U.S. Department of Health, Education, and Welfare, National Center for Health Statistics, 1968.

1930s, they had not yet exerted a major influence on infection control. Nor could the use of antibiotics explain the improved mortality statistics from infections, as these were not available until the 1940s. Thus, it was probably the modification of social factors (i.e., the betterment of living conditions) that ultimately led to the striking improvement in longevity in the early part of this century.

The difference in longevity related to sex and race is depicted in Table 9-2. Despite all the medical advances of the 20th century, American women continue to outlive men by an ever-increasing margin. For white and nonwhite infants born in 1901, the life expectancy of a female was only 2.9 years longer than that of a male; in 1940, this difference

TABLE 9-2.—AVERAGE REMAINING YEARS OF LIFE AT BIRTH BY RACE AND SEX; SELECTED YEARS 1930–1977

	WHITE		BLACK AND OTHER	
YEAR	MALE	FEMALE	MALE	FEMALE
1930	59.7	63.5	47.3	49.2
1940	62.1	66.6	51.5	54.9
1950	66.5	72.2	59.1	62.9
1960	67.4	74.1	61.1	66.3
1970	68.0	75.6	61.3	69.4
1977	70.0	77.7	64.6	73.1

Data from U.S. Bureau of the Census, *Statistical Abstract of the United States: 1979*, ed. 100, 1979.

was 4.4 years; and in 1977, it had risen to 7.8 years. This discrepancy may be due in part to the effects of psychosocial factors, such as stress, work pressures, diet, and medical care.

In this country, life expectancy has always been substantially longer for whites than for blacks and other races (see Tables 9-1 and 9-2). Black people have been at a severe disadvantage compared with whites when it comes to living conditions, diet, and access to medical care. The adverse effect these disadvantages have on longevity is apparent in early life. The infant mortality (i.e., deaths in the first year of life) among blacks is significantly higher than that found in the white population (Fig 9-1).

In a comprehensive study, Katagawa and Hauser found that mortality in the United States varied significantly according to education, income, and occupation.[2] For example, when women with different educational backgrounds were compared, those with less education had an age-adjusted mortality that was 105% higher than those with more education. For white men, the less-educated had a 64% higher mortality. Among nonwhites, this educational differential was 70% for women and 31% for men. Similar differences in mortality were found when income level and occupation were taken as measures of social status; that is, those with higher socioeconomic status outlived those with lower socioeconomic status by substantial margins.

With respect to social class indicators such as income, education, and occupation, nonwhites typically rank lower than whites. Thus, the difference in longevity between the races reflects in part the correlation of mortality with social class standing.

In this country, people from the lowest socioeconomic group have substantially higher death rates from the four major causes of mortality (Table 9-3) than the more affluent. The gradient in mortality between higher and lower socioeconomic groups has been reported by numerous investigators, both contemporary and historical.[3, 4] In a detailed analysis of more than 30 comprehensive stud-

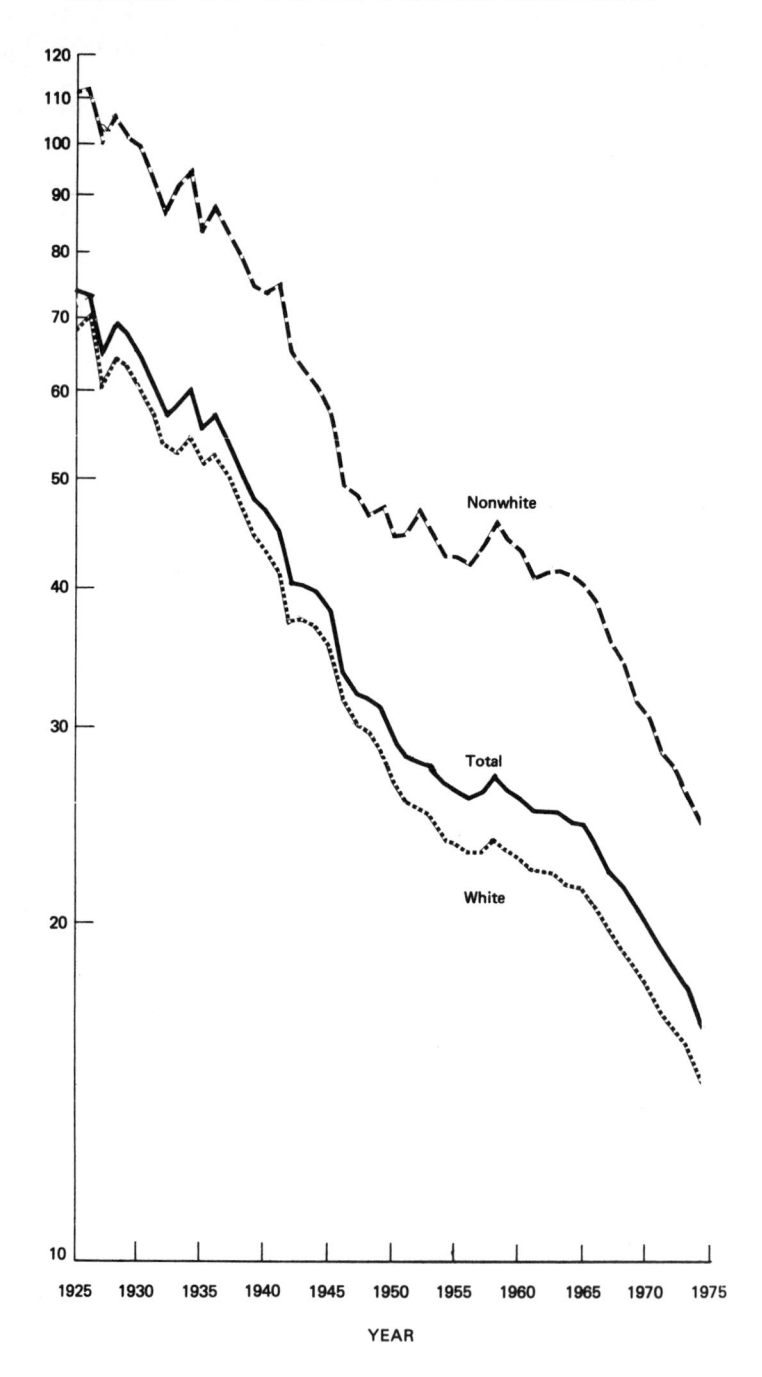

Fig 9–1.—U.S. infant mortality rates by color, 1925–1974. Rates are the number of deaths of children under 1 year of age per 1,000 live births. (From *Health United States 1975*. Rockville, Maryland, U.S. Department of Health, Education, and Welfare, Health Resources Administration, National Center for Health Statistics.

NOTES: 1925-1932 include Birth-Registration States only.
1932-1934, Mexicans are included with "nonwhite."
1962-1963, figures by color exclude data for residents of New Jersey.
1974, provisional.

TABLE 9-3.—DEATH RATES PER 100,000 POPULATION FOR THE LEADING CAUSES OF DEATH, 1977

CAUSE OF DEATH	RANK	DEATH RATE
All causes		878.1
Heart disease	1	332.3
Cancer	2	178.7
Stroke	3	84.1
Accidents	4	47.7
Influenza and pneumonia	5	23.7
Diabetes mellitus	6	15.2
Cirrhosis of liver	7	14.3
Arteriosclerosis	8	13.3
Suicide	8	13.3

Based on data from *Healthy People, The Surgeon General's Report on Health Promotion and Disease Prevention*, Department of Health, Education, and Welfare, Publication No. 79-55071, 1979.

ies, Antonovsky concluded that individuals from the lower socioeconomic classes have had a consistently lower life expectancy and higher mortality from most causes of death since the 12th century, when data relating to these questions were first compiled.[5]

In many ways, the living conditions and life-styles of those in the lower socioeconomic groups are more predisposing to illness. Poverty, poor nutrition, and lack of knowledge about health matters are often associated with inadequate health practices, particularly in infant and maternal care. Sometimes the poor do not make adequate use of preventive health services even when these are available (often because there is no culturally sensitive delivery system). Finally, those from the lower social strata have least access to good medical care, despite the fact that they suffer from a higher rate of illness. This description of the health characteristics of the poor has been true since earliest recorded medical history, and these problems still exist in the United States despite all our recent medical advances.

Disability

The term *disability* is used to describe any reduction of an individual's activities as a result of illness or injury. When calculating the days of disability per person per year, government health statisticians differentiate the following three types of disability: restricted activity (reduction in a person's normal activities), bed disability (person is confined to bed for most of the day), and work or school loss (person is absent from work or school). In addition, disability may be categorized as either short-term or long-term (institutional or noninstitutional).

Disability rates can be correlated with age, race, and social class. As one grows older, the likelihood of being disabled increases. Nonwhites suffer from chronic disability to a greater extent than does the white population (Table 9-4). Finally, by using income level as an indicator of social class standing, it can be demonstrated that for adults an inverse relationship exists between chronic disability and socioeconomic status (see Table 9-4).

The major causes of disability are chronic disorders such as heart disease, stroke, arthritis, lung disease, visual impairment, and mental illness. It is common knowledge that the aged have more of these kinds of physical ailments. What is not so well appreciated is that nonwhites suffer from more chronic debilitating physical illnesses than do whites (Table 9-5). The same holds true with respect to mental illness.

One explanation for the greater prevalence of chronic debilitating illness among black people lies in the disadvantaged social envi-

TABLE 9-4.—DAYS OF DISABILITY PER PERSON (AGES 17-44) PER YEAR BY COLOR AND INCOME

DEMOGRAPHIC CHARACTERISTIC	RESTRICTED ACTIVITY DAYS	BED DISABILITY DAYS	WORK LOSS DAYS
Total	13.6	5.4	5.1
Color			
White	13.0	5.1	4.8
All other	17.2	7.6	7.0
Family income			
Under $5,000	21.1	8.3	6.5
$5,000-$9,999	14.6	5.7	5.9
$10,000-$14,999	11.9	4.8	4.8
$15,000 and over	11.4	4.4	4.6

Adapted from *Health United States 1975*, No. (HRA) 76-1232. Rockville, Maryland, U.S. Department of Health, Education and Welfare, Health Resources Administration, National Center for Health Statistics, p. 491.

TABLE 9-5.—PREVALENCE OF SELECTED CHRONIC CONDITIONS REPORTED IN HEALTH INTERVIEWS BY SELECTED DEMOGRAPHIC CHARACTERISTICS, NUMBERS PER 1,000 PERSONS 45–64 YEARS OLD

DEMOGRAPHIC CHARACTERISTIC	ARTHRITIS (1969)	ASTHMA (1970)	CHRONIC BRONCHITIS (1970)	DIABETES (1973)	HEART CONDITIONS (1972)	HERNIA OF ABDOMINAL CAVITY (1968)	HYPERTENSION (WITHOUT HEART INVOLVEMENT) (1972)	ULCER OF STOMACH OR DUODENUM (1968)	IMPAIRMENT OF BACK OR SPINE (EXCEPT PARALYSIS) (1971)	HEARING IMPAIRMENTS (1971)	VISION IMPAIRMENTS (1971)
Total*	204.2	33.1	35.4	42.6	88.8	28.3	126.7	33.4	68.2	114.1	63.0
Color											
White	202.4	31.9	36.6	39.6	88.4	29.9	119.1	33.5	66.8	116.8	59.1
All other	221.8	44.5	23.5	70.0	91.6	13.3	196.8	32.6	80.7	88.7	99.6
Family income											
Under $5,000	297.8	53.5	44.2	74.1	139.3	40.5	172.7	45.2	102.8	158.9	114.1
$5,000–$9,999	200.3	33.5	38.7	43.8	92.5	26.7	125.4	31.8	67.2	118.1	57.4
$10,000–$14,999	163.7	23.7	29.0	37.8	74.3	23.1	121.3	28.3	62.3	107.3	45.9
$15,000 and over	159.8	22.7	30.3	30.5	66.6		105.3		52.2	85.9	48.9

*Includes unknown income.
Adapted from: Health United States 1975, No. (HRA) 76-1232. Rockville, Maryland, U.S. Department of Health, Education, and Welfare, Health Resources Administration, National Center for Health Statistics, p. 487.

ronment in which many live. Also to blame is their relative lack of access to good medical care, so that by the time blacks receive adequate treatment for an illness the condition is already in an advanced stage. The more advanced a disease is at the time of treatment, the more likely it is to result in disability and the less likely it is to respond favorably to therapy.

The pressures of social discrimination, adverse living conditions, and stressful lifestyles of many nonwhites are probably largely responsible for the higher morbidity they have for mental illness. As a group, the degree of stress to which they are exposed is many times greater than that experienced by the white population. There is another explanation for these higher rates, however; that is, the misdiagnosis of mental illness in blacks.[6,7] There is a tendency to diagnose mental illness as less severe in white patients and more severe in black patients. The literature consistently shows that black people are overdiagnosed for schizophrenia, a severe disorder that often leads to hospitalization, and underdiagnosed for depressive reactions, which are usually milder illnesses causing only short-term disability.[8] A comparison of morbidity for affective illness (primarily depression) indicates that for blacks the rate is only one-quarter to one-seventh that for whites.[9,10] In contrast, the morbidity for schizophrenia among blacks is 65–300% higher than among whites.[11,12]

Simon et al. investigated the possibility that the differences in the rates of mental illness between blacks and whites are due in part to diagnostic error.[7] In this study, the diagnosis of almost 200 black and white patients in nine state mental hospitals was reviewed. Using objective criteria to reclassify the patients, it was found that 40% of a group of blacks who were previously diagnosed as having schizophrenia actually had depressive illnesses.

Some reasons for the misdiagnosis of psychiatric illness in black patients include communication difficulties between these patients and white physicians, cultural differences in the responses of black and white patients to psychological screening tests, misinterpretation of the behavior of black patients by white physicians, and "social distance" between black patients and white providers of health care.[13] Racial bias affects not only the diagnosis but also the treatment of mental disorders in black patients. Research indicates that nonwhite patients are less often accepted for psychotherapy, more often assigned to inexperienced therapists, seen for shorter periods of time in therapy, and more likely to receive either custodial care or drugs alone.[14-19]

As mentioned, there is an inverse relationship between the socioeconomic standing of a group and the degree of disability from which it suffers (see Table 9-5). With respect to emotional illness, numerous comprehensive studies indicate that the lowest socioeconomic groups have the highest rates of severe psychiatric disorders.[20] Furthermore, the geographic areas with the greatest prevalence of these disorders are those with the greatest percentage of poor people, substandard housing, residential instability, and the highest crime and delinquency rates.[21] For the population as a whole, epidemiologic data compiled over the past 50 years indicate that hospitalization for mental illness increases during economic recession and decreases during periods of economic recovery.[22]

Disability due to physical illness is also more common among the lower socioeconomic groups. For example, in the age group 45–64 years, 43.7% of those with a family income of less than $3,000 are limited in their major activities because of a chronic condition, as opposed to only 7.1% of those with a family income of $15,000 and over.[1] This reflects the fact that the poor have a greater prevalence of many chronic diseases (see Table 9-6). Data from the National Center for Health Statistics indicate that families with incomes at or below the poverty level have four times as much heart disease, six times as much arthritis and rheumatic fever, and almost eight times as much eye disease as those in higher income brackets.[23, 24]

Access to Medical Care

According to federal reports, there are no direct measures of access to medical care for either individuals or families. Two indirect indicators are: (1) measures of the confidence people have in their ability to obtain good medical care, and (2) consumer expenditures for health care.[1]

PERCEIVED ADEQUACY OF THE HEALTH-CARE SYSTEM.—Statistics on people's confidence in their ability to obtain good medical care were collected in a national survey of 1,562 persons 18 years and over conducted in late 1971 by the Gallup organization.[25] In the survey, the following question was asked: "All things considered, how much confidence do you have in being able to get good medical care for you and your family when you need it—a great deal of confidence, a fair amount, not so much, or none at all?"

The responses of the study group indicated that 45% had a great deal of confidence, 39% had a fair amount, and 14% had little or no confidence in obtaining good medical care (with the remainder responding "don't know"). Within the group, there were significant differences in responses according to race, education, residence area, and income level. Forty-six percent of the whites reported a great deal of confidence, while only 41% of the blacks did so. People's confidence varied directly with their education—a great deal of confidence being expressed by 57% of the college graduates, 46% of the high school graduates, and only 37% of those who finished elementary school. In the group with the least education, more than a fifth of the respondents reported little or no confidence. A relationship was also found between the degree of confidence held by people and their income level—the higher the income, the greater was the confidence. In families with incomes of $15,000 and over, 58% reported high confidence, as compared with only 39% of those with incomes less than $5,000.

CONSUMER EXPENDITURES. — Expenditures for health services include monies spent for hospital care, physician's services, dental and other professional services, drugs and drug sundries, eyeglasses, prosthetics and other appliances, nursing and nursing home care, and other miscellaneous health services.

Statistics indicate that from 1960 to 1979 expenditures for health care rose from $27 billion to $212 billion—a staggering rise of almost 1,000%. Today, such spending accounts for about 9% of the gross national product as compared with less than 6% in 1960.

Current projections indicate that the United States may be spending more than 12% of its gross national product on health care by the end of the century—at an estimated cost of $3,200 per year for the average family of four.[26] The rapidly rising costs of health care have led to increasing public pressure for the government to play a greater role in providing medical services. Even though there has been a steady rise in the proportion of health-care costs covered by private insurance (from 12.2% in 1950 to 40.9% in 1973), this resource still covers less than half of these costs. In addition, there is a large discrepancy between insurance reimbursement for hospital care (75.3%) and for physicians' services (48.5%).

Those in our population who are in the moderate to low income brackets have the least amount of private health insurance coverage. Since access to private medical care is usually contingent on the ability to pay for these services, it is obvious why public health-care facilities have become increasingly overburdened with patients from the lower socioeconomic strata. To some extent this has changed as a result of Medicare and Medicaid, but even people with this coverage continue to use public facilities. While there are well-trained health professionals in both the private and the public sectors, the quality of medical care in the former setting is often much better than in the latter. Thus, the poor, who suffer from a greater amount of disabling physical and mental illness, find themselves having to rely on a lower level of health care because they cannot afford to pay for private medical services.

Utilization of Health-Care Services

We have seen that there are inequalities in the accessibility of medical care to consumers of different socioeconomic backgrounds. Any definition of *accessibility,* however, must include both the availability of the services and the disposition of people to use them. Once again, it appears that social class standing is a critical variable—this time, in determining whether or not people make use of available health-care resources. One's socioeconomic background is an important determinant of his level of information about disease, his ideas about the nature of health and illness, and his behavior while he is sick. In addition, one's social class standing is related to the actual and perceived barriers to obtaining adequate medical care. Research shows that lower socioeconomic groups demonstrate the following differences when compared with higher socioeconomic groups: less information about disease,[27-29] greater tendency to seek medical advice from lay persons,[27, 28, 30, 31] more skepticism and discontent about medical care,[27-31] greater preoccupation with illness,[32] higher degree of anxiety about health status,[33] and greater prevalence of acknowledged but untreated illness.[31]

Rosenblatt and Suchman, after studying blue-collar workers in urban slums, listed some of the barriers that discourage the utilization of orthodox health services by lower socioeconomic groups.[29, 30] These include communication problems with health-care professionals, impersonal attitudes of medical personnel in public clinics, and physical inconveniences encountered in these settings. In addition, these groups are predisposed to use alternative healing systems which derive from their cultural traditions.

DELAY IN SEEKING TREATMENT.—One of the most critical determining factors in medical treatment and prognosis is the tendency of many individuals to avoid seeking help until the disease process has reached an advanced stage (see also chap. 22). Numerous studies have found that this pattern of behavior is more characteristic of lower income groups. Why is this so? The most obvious reason people might avoid seeking immediate medical attention is an economic one—the inability to afford treatment. Even when there is no charge for medical care, the costs of time off from work, child-care arrangements, and transportation are often excessive for the very poor. These costs must be balanced against the urgency of the person's complaint. Of course, other barriers may be responsible for causing a person to procrastinate before going to the physician. Research shows that when various types of health-care services are offered free, social and demographic variables are often better predictors of the use of these services than the seriousness of the person's condition.[34]

In addition to social class standing, age and family relationships are important social variables that determine why people delay seeking medical care. A study by Gonda found that both older people and those from large families were more likely to complain persistently and to seek medical help for relief from pain.[35] Mechanic, in a study of 350 mother-child pairs, found that maternal attitudes toward illness were good predictors of whether or not medical aid would be sought.[36]

Delay is also related to a number of psychological characteristics, some of which are more likely to be found among the disadvantaged. For example, certain attitudes and beliefs about the body that presumably are held primarily by members of lower socioeconomic groups may delay treatment. Rainwater, describing the residents of a public housing project in St. Louis, suggested that poor people have a negative self-concept, which generalizes to their bodies.[37] Neugarten has found that lower-class people believe that they become "middle aged" at a much earlier time, chronologically, than do working-class or middle-class people.[38] In their study of utilization of medical services, Rosenblatt and Suchman stated that for blue-collar workers:

The body can be seen as simply another class of objects to be worked out but not repaired. Thus, teeth are left without dental care, and . . . false teeth may be little used. Corrective eye examinations . . . are often neglected, regardless of clinic facilities. It is as though the white-collar class thinks of the body as a machine to be preserved and kept in perfect functioning condition, whether through prosthetic devices, rehabilitation, cosmetic surgery, or perpetual treatment, whereas blue-collar groups think of the body as having a limited span of utility; to be enjoyed in youth and then to suffer with and to endure stoically with age and decrepitude.[29]

In describing the life of the poor, sociologists have used a constellation of terms that imply a fatalistic "what's the use?" attitude toward life. Feelings of alienation from the institutions of the dominant society, hopelessness (the expectation that no change will occur), and powerlessness (no control over one's own destiny) are all fairly obvious obstacles to seeking help actively.

In addition to various attitudes and beliefs, psychological ego defense mechanisms such as repression and denial may also be involved in the delaying process. These mechanisms minimize the importance of symptoms, prevent their entry into conscious awareness, or produce the type of magical thinking that tells the individual "it can't happen to me." While these psychological characteristics are found among people from all social strata, they tend to be more prominent in the subculture of poverty. The stress associated with a disadvantaged environment fosters the use of the defense mechanism of denial as a strategy for survival. Rainwater's work suggests that in ghetto life, the kind of self-esteem that encourages one to maintain a healthy body is perceived as "uppity" and may be subject to social sanctions.[37] The acknowledgment by low-income persons that something is wrong with their health may make them feel more vulnerable to environmental dangers. For example, an informal study of the prevalence of visual defects in persons in a low-income area elicited great anxiety from elderly respondents, who felt that identification of their problem would render them helpless to thieves and other malefactors.

Another reason for delay is a differing concept of how to manage sickness. Alternative belief systems regarding bodily functioning and appropriate remedies for illness are fairly widespread in the general population. They are especially common among the poor and ethnic minorities. For example, many individuals are drawn to cults that espouse specific dietary regimens, fasting, sulfur baths, discredited remedies such as laetrile and the like as preventive or therapeutic measures for a wide range of ailments.

The Implications of Social Stratification for Medical Practice

The material in this section is intended to demonstrate the importance of the concept of social stratification in three aspects of medical practice: encounter time, diagnostic accuracy, and treatment.

ENCOUNTER TIME.—This term refers to the quantity and quality of the time spent with a patient. In most service-oriented professions there is an unfortunate tendency to allocate time and attention to clients on the basis of not only their need but also their perceived status or social standing. Generally, the higher a person's status, the more consideration and respect he is accorded in social interactions. Consequently, it is not uncommon for medical personnel to spend more time with patients who are members of a higher social class. Usually the physician has a similar social background and finds it easier to communicate with these patients.

Yet patients from lower socioeconomic groups require *more* rather than less of the physician's time. Usually they have less knowledge about disease, are more reluctant to ask questions, and are less likely to understand the physician's explanation. The brief encounter time allotted to poor patients, often after they have spent hours waiting, is a common complaint. This is a function both of the health-care system and of the social distance between physician and patient. If the poor are to have equal access to health care, then medical practitioners must apportion time to patients on the basis of their medical needs, not their social class standing. They must try to communicate effectively with each patient, explaining the nature of the patient's illness in terms that are comprehensible to that individual. When advising a course of treatment, they must take into account the beliefs, practices, and resources of the patient, and how these might help or hinder the patient's compliance.

DIAGNOSTIC ACCURACY.—The literature indicates that persons from lower socioeconomic groups often bring minor symptoms to the physician's attention but ignore or minimize major symptoms. Further, because their understanding of body functions and the location of body organs is often faulty, symptoms are frequently misrepresented to the physician. Diagnostic accuracy can be improved by a careful medical history. Comprehending the lay terms that are used by ethnic groups to describe their complaints is sometimes of great importance in reaching the correct diagnosis.

The life-style of the poor often contributes to their ill health, so the recognition of disease-causing social factors is often important in diagnosis. The heavy ingestion of fats and carbohydrates, protein deficiency, exposure to toxic substances, and emotional stress are but a few factors that should be investigated in the medical history. In some cases, the patient's living arrangements (i.e., heating, sanitation, water sources) and occupational exposure provide a clue to a particular disease entity. While these are significant areas of investigation for most patients, they are especially critical in the medical evaluation of people from lower socioeconomic groups.

TREATMENT.—The treatment of an illness is often not so clear-cut as it might seem from the recommendations in medical texts. The therapeutic approach to disease depends on a number of variables. When there are various options available, the choice may be made on the basis of socioeconomic considerations such as the patient's economic situation, occupational activities, living arrangements, and social supports. With respect to infectious diseases, it is important to recognize that some people do not understand the concept of contagion, and that their living conditions may facilitate the transmission of infections. Many physicians have no comprehension of the living arrangements of the very poor, where several people may share one bed, there are no adequate bathroom facilities, and pests and vermin may be common.

An area of therapeutics that often involves problems in dealing with the poor is diet. Requesting that an indigent patient modify his diet may pose an insurmountable task for the individual. The poor simply cannot afford to purchase special foods and many times they do not have the knowledge to institute dietary changes using cheaper alternative foods. Thus, noncompliance with dietary prescriptions is common among persons from lower socioeconomic strata.

Compliance with other medical therapy is also a problem among the poor. Several reasons for this are that these patients have less encounter time with the physician and are less able to understand what is expected of them. Difficulty in communication is associated with a reluctance on the part of the patient to cooperate. This reluctance is rarely expressed overtly, however, as in an experience recounted by Crawford:[39]

A low-income elderly person living in a ghetto area, who had previously been seen at a clinic by an ophthalmologist, was told that she had "cataracts," and that this required an operation. The woman went home but would never have acted further on this matter had she not been selected as a subject in a research survey of health needs. The field interviewer was asked by the woman to explain, "What's cataracts?" and to deal with questions regarding the operation which had been unanswered by clinic personnel. . . . [T]he woman decided she would not have the surgery. When asked why, she stated: "Lord, child, you just don't know this neighborhood. If I were to leave this house (she lived alone in her own home) when I returned the windows would be broken and every stick of furniture would be stolen or broken."

Crawford notes that this incident points up several important social facts: "Treatment of this elderly woman necessitated not only that she understand the medical technology, but also the provision of a 'house sitter' to protect her property while she was in the hospital."

SOCIALIZATION AND HEALTH

Socialization is a process by which people are integrated into the society in which they live (see also chap. 10). It consists of a sequence of learning experiences that begin very early in a child's life. This process is initiated in child-rearing practices that reflect the parents' own socialization. Thus, it is the primary means by which the culture of a society is transmitted from generation to generation. Through socialization, a child acquires the values, attitudes, and mores that determine his concept of reality. This process of socialization extends to matters of health and illness.

Attitudes and Practices in Health Matters

During the socialization process, children develop attitudes toward themselves and their bodies. In the middle and upper social class milieu, emphasis is placed on health maintenance. Proper nutrition, exercise, dental care, periodic medical checkups, immunizations, and treatment for minor illnesses are considered important, so children incorporate these values as they grow up. In a lower-class milieu, health maintenance and medical care may also be perceived as desirable, but the problems of daily life often cause them to be relegated to a low priority. In households with many children, a working mother, and little money, procedures designed to maintain health are a luxury that few can afford.

Rainwater has suggested that lower-class people, perceiving their world as dangerous and chaotic, relate to their bodies in magical rather than instrumental ways.[37] Because of the conditions of their lives, the nonspecific complaint of "feeling sick" is ubiquitous. Remedies are resorted to frequently and typically involve the consumption of patent medicines and the use of herbal remedies, amulets, and other protective devices. However, the constant state of "feeling sick" and the sense of low self-esteem often delay the recognition of serious symptoms. In studying the residents of a housing project that he described as a "federal slum," Rainwater found that a high tolerance for physical disability or malfunctioning also extended to children. There was minimal concern or solicitude toward children's illnesses, particularly infections, colds, sores, and the like. The higher accident rate among children from lower socioeconomic groups may be attributed both to environmental dangers (more broken bottles, dangerous housing) and to lack of parental supervision. According to Rainwater:

> This . . . means that medical professionals cannot count on parents to exercise careful observation or supervision when their children are ill, and any program of treatment in which these attitudes are ignored is likely to fail. The acceptance of something short of good health has implications both in the care of people who are already ill and in preventive medicine, because it means that parents are not likely to carry out a consistent preventive regimen.[37]

Unfortunately, Rainwater and others do not stipulate what proportion of ghetto parents fall into this category. Without additional data, the implication that this is the modal or most widely prevalent pattern of behavior is open to dispute. Other studies indicate that preventive care is used when it is readily available, as for example in the case of prenatal and postnatal care. In an investigation of 806 mothers from three poor neighborhoods, Bullough found that 84% had taken their babies to a physician or clinic for a checkup within 2 months of the child's birth, and another 4% had been to a physician shortly thereafter.[40] However, 38% of the mothers could not remember the last time their older children had received a physical examination. The implication of this study is that preventive resources are used when and if they are available; failure to use them appears to be more a matter of limited accessibility than of indifference toward children's needs.

Rainwater suggests that the underutilization of health services for children by slum parents is due to low self-esteem. This idea is based on the sociological hypothesis that poor people do not attend to their health because, according to their perceptions, their bodies are not worthy of care. It is more likely, however, that children from the lowest socioeconomic groups are not brought in for care early in the course of an illness, when therapy is most effective, simply because minor symptoms receive less attention among the poor. The overworked ghetto mother can rarely afford the time and effort to minister to minor illnesses in crowded, multichild households. Further, mild illness is so common among poor adults that it is considered to be just another of life's many burdens. Children are conditioned to accept sickness as something to be endured stoically; therefore, they tend to ignore mild symptoms. There is little positive reinforcement for them to assume the sick role. The secondary gains, such as increased attention and sympathetic care, that are associated with this role in middle- and upper-class households are less likely to be present in poor families, unless the child is quite ill.

Another aspect of health in which the poor are at a disadvantage is nutrition. Among lower-class families, diet is determined by the cost of food rather than by its nutritive value. Consequently, there is a disproportionate consumption of cheaper carbohydrates, often leading to obesity. Today, obesity is significantly more prevalent among individuals in the lower socioeconomic groups, particularly women (see also chap. 12). In poor families with minimal knowledge of nutrition, there is little monitoring of proper food intake and sometimes a reliance on "junk food" as a means of quickly satisfying children's hunger.

Dietary preferences, which initially may be based on the availability and cost of foods, often become culturally ingrained over time. Eating habits develop with respect not only to types of food but also to the amount of food consumed. In some cultural groups, particularly those of Latin and Mediterranean descent, the fat child is considered a healthy child, and the good mother is one who constantly urges her child to eat. A mother's self-image is adversely affected if she is forced to "deprive" her child by restricting his food intake. Such attitudes and beliefs exist among many ethnic groups in this country.

Attitudes toward medication are also learned in the home or immediate social environs. In some families, use of aspirin, tranquilizers, antacids, and patent medicines is so prevalent that self-medication is perceived as normal behavior. The use of alcohol is also learned during socialization, sometimes in the family setting but more often in the larger social networks of adolescence. The relationships between drug and alcohol abuse later in life and the medication and alcohol consumption patterns learned by children during their socialization are still unclear, however (see also chap. 12).

Roles and Health Roles

During the process of socialization, an individual develops an identification with certain social and cultural reference groups. He learns to adopt specific behaviors when dealing with members of these groups and, in turn, comes to expect a particular type of behavior from them. The patterns of expected behavior among individuals engaged in social interaction are referred to as roles. A person learns a series of roles during his lifetime which enable him to function in a wide circle of social networks involving family, school, peer, vocational, and avocational relationships. One's social class, ethnicity, national origin, education, and religion are some of the determiners of the roles he develops. In adult life, career, marital, and parental roles predominate, and the behavior that derives from them affects both life-style and satisfaction.

In intact nuclear families, roles have typically been defined functionally, according to age and gender; fathers are breadwinners, mothers are housewives and nurturers, children are students. Although today there are many more women in the labor force, including mothers of preschool children, role changes have not kept pace. Despite more and more cases of father-nurturers and mother-careerists, social mores still dictate that the care of home and children is more appropriate for women than for men. Thus, many a working mother finds herself having to cope with excessive role demands. It is she who must shop, cook, clean, make child-care arrangements, care for the sick, and at the same time fulfill her responsibilities at work.

The illness of a family member almost always disrupts the social roles of the other members, something that must be taken into consideration in caring for the patient.

Since medicine is a social institution, the behavior of those who are ill and those who care for them is defined by specific roles (see also chaps. 22 and 24). Parsons has given the classic definition of the "sick role," including certain obligations that the sick person must fulfill in order to qualify for the role.[43] These are: he must be free of responsibility for causing his illness, he must seek competent medical help, and he must attempt to get well as soon as possible. In return, he is excused from performing his usual social roles—going to work, attending school, doing housework. Parsons also distinguishes between the "sick role," which involves withdrawal from customary responsibilities due to physical incapacity, and the "patient role," which governs the patient's behavior in his interaction with the providers of health care. Some researchers have indicated that individuals from the higher social classes accommodate themselves to these roles more easily than do those of lower socioeconomic status.

The socialization of an individual determines to a considerable extent how he or she will adapt to illness and to the roles that are associated with being sick and under medical care. A number of specific social factors influence how a person reacts to the expectations of the sick role and patient role. There is evidence that social class values are important in defining who is to be regarded as sick, and there are significant differences in the way higher and lower socioeconomic groups view this state.[41] In the immediate social context, family and job obligations determine a person's willingness to perceive himself as being sick. Situational demands are also involved in defining the sick role, as for example in wartime, when assumption of the sick role is based on far more stringent criteria than in peacetime.[42]

Adaptation to the sick role requires the mobilization of psychological resources to deal with anxiety, emotionality, dependency, and threat to self-esteem that comes with illness. This is discussed in detail in chapter 22 on illness behavior.

THE FAMILY IN MEDICINE

The important role played by the family in the health of its members cannot be overemphasized. It is the family that determines the patterning of health education and behavior and the priority placed on the use of health-care resources. The attitudes and beliefs toward illness that are shared by a family affect how the members will interpret symptoms, at what stage of an illness they will present themselves for treatment, and whether or not they will accept medical advice. Whenever a member becomes ill, there is an impact on family relationships, especially when long-term or serious illness occurs. This produces a challenge to the adaptive strengths of the family. The success with which this challenge is met may determine how well the affected member adjusts to being ill.

Family Structure and Dynamics

American history has seen marked changes in family structure. Within this century, the extended family of rural America has been replaced by the smaller nuclear family typically consisting of one or both parents and their children. Variant family forms, such as childless conjugal units or communal households with nonrelated persons in quasifamilial interaction, are increasingly seen. With the growing frequency and acceptance of divorce and the reduced stigmatization of mothers raising children born out of wedlock, the percentage of single-parent families is also on the rise. In the decade between 1960 and 1970 the number of households headed by women rose by more than 24%. In the same period, there was a 35% rise in the number of households composed of unrelated individuals. Since 1970, these trends have accelerated even more.

Other recent sociological changes have affected the family constellation. These involve the number of children per household, child-rearing practices, and the role performance of family members. Events are currently taking place that will have long-range and as yet unpredictable effects on family structure as it is now known. These include: (1) availability and increasing refinement of contraceptive techniques, (2) increasing legitimization of voluntary abortion, (3) a "zero population growth" ideology generating pressures to limit family size, (4) smaller housing units and migration patterns that tend to disperse kinship networks, and (5) rising consumer expectations and other economic pressures that encourage the maximal employment of adult family members, including mothers of young children. Related factors are the increasing emphasis on self-actualization for women outside the traditional mother-wife roles, variations in marital and mating patterns, and greater acceptance of childlessness in young couples as an alternative to parenting.

From the standpoint of the practice of medicine, the changes in family structure that have occurred and those that are evolving have important implications. It has been suggested by some noted sociologists that the contemporary American nuclear family is unable to provide adequate assistance and support for its sick members. Parsons and Fox maintain that the nuclear family has little margin for "shock absorption," because each relationship is critically important.[43] Ordinarily, there are only two adults to take the roles of major responsibility. The illness of the husband-father has an immediately disruptive effect on the family both economically and emotionally. In the case of the wife-mother's illness, the effects may be even more devastating.

The family unit is the place from which patients come and the place to which they return after medical treatment. The members of a family may constitute a support system or a source of conflict for the patient. They may play an antagonist or a protagonist role vis-à-vis the medical staff. They can be a source of inaccurate information, or they can aid in a correct diagnosis by bringing important symptoms or behaviors to the physician's attention.

Much of the family's role in the medical

setting depends on the kind of relationship the members have with the physician and other medical staff, that is, whether or not the medical personnel are able to empathize with the family's concerns, impart comprehensible information to them on the patient's condition, and involve them in the treatment process. For this reason, it is necessary for medical practitioners to have some degree of familiarity with the spectrum of family attitudes, behaviors, and interaction styles that may affect the care of the patient.

In almost all research on family process, the emphasis has been on the function of the family in maintaining a real or spurious homeostasis. In the presence of illness, even when it is minor, family homeostasis is usually disturbed. Under these circumstances, customary modes of interaction tend to become exaggerated. For example, the family that rallies to provide support and nurture for a member who is sick may have a tendency to overreact in the eyes of the medical personnel caring for the patient. Family members may pester the physician and other medical staff with questions concerning their relative's condition, visit at odd hours or overstay visiting times, bring unnecessary food supplements, and otherwise interfere with usual hospital routine. Although this behavior may be a nuisance to the staff, usually the support it provides for the patient more than counterbalances this effect. Conversely, a family that asks few questions and shows only slight concern for a sick member poses less of a problem for the medical staff, but also may provide less support for the patient.

Disturbed family dynamics sometimes precede a patient's illness and may even trigger its onset. In a comprehensive study of 161 patients hospitalized for medical reasons, Duff and Hollingshead posed the question whether family relationships had a bearing on the development of the patient's symptoms.[44] They found that 47% of the patients' illnesses were definitely linked to disturbed family relationships, while 53% were not. There was a significant correlation between family maladjustment and the mental status of the patient.

Sometimes the mental state that resulted adversely affected the patient's illness. When the data were examined in terms of the physician's knowledge, it was found that in approximately two cases out of three the physician had no idea of the impact the family had on the patient's illness.

The sensitive practitioner should be alert to detect patient problems that are related to disturbed family interaction. Excessive involvement in the patient's care, disproportionate concern over minor ailments, and expressions of hostility toward medical personnel are clues indicating that the relationship between the family and the patient should be examined closely. Not only should the physician be concerned with the behavior of "difficult" families, but those that seem to have little or no interest in their sick relative also deserve attention. Family behavior assumes critical importance when overinvolvement or underinvolvement is coupled with patient depression, resistance, or delayed recovery.

In such cases, some questions that might be asked are: What impact does the patient's illness have on the family's equilibrium? Does the patient's disability change dominance and power relationships within the family? Does any member benefit from the patient's incapacity? Is there competition or envy of the special attention focused on the patient? Finally, will there be a long-term role change, and, if so, how does one prepare the patient and family to adapt to this new situation?

While we have discussed this issue largely in terms of the family's effect on the patient, disturbed family dynamics often emanate from the patient himself. Patients may affect the family equilibrium by using their illness to gain personal ends. Duff and Hollingshead describe patients who utilize their visiting relatives as servants or as agents to demand special services from the hospital system.[44] Other patients view their sick state as a means of getting away from a spouse's nagging or sexual demands, or for regression to a childlike state. In their total study group, the authors found that 33% of the patients used illness as a manipulative device on the family, while 29% of the families manipulated the patients. The most common behavioral reactions to illness for both patients and family members, however, were those of empathic concern for each other, not manipulative actions.

Although some negative aspects of family dynamics have been indicated here, it should be emphasized that families usually do a great deal of good in providing the primary support system for the sick individual. The interaction that takes place between patients and medical personnel is necessarily limited, both temporally and therapeutically, and so it rarely provides the degree of support necessary for most patients. It is the patient's family that fulfills the major caring and support functions during illness. There is considerable documentation that social isolates who lack this family support have a shorter life span, a higher rate of disability, and a greater frequency of psychotic illness. Thus, the salutary effects of kinship bonds in the care of the sick should not be underestimated. In too many cases, health personnel view families as nuisances rather than as active collaborators in the therapeutic process. This has been particularly true in the mental health field. Currently, there is an increasing emphasis in the professional literature to "stop mistreating patients' families" and a move toward involving parents and other concerned relatives as cotherapists.[45, 46]

The Impact of Illness on the Family

Generally, the reaction of a family to the illness of one of its members is based on the nature of the disability (its acuteness and severity), the individual affected, the previous stability of the family system, and the economic impact. Depending on these factors, illness, like other crises, may be disruptive or unifying. Duff and Hollingshead observed two types of family coping strategies following the hospitalization of a principal member.[44] In one case, illness functions as a *centripetal force* that draws family members closer together for a mutual mobilization of resources. In the other reaction, the crisis is a *centrifugal force* that alters the social relations in a family group so that some members tend to withdraw from the demands of the situation.

Anderson and Meisel note that each family has its own social structure, involving expectations and individual roles, that maintains the system in homeostatic balance.[47] Family members have basically two types of roles. The most obvious are those assigned by society (parent, child, homemaker, breadwinner, etc.). There are, however, other roles deriving from the psychological needs and customary transactional styles of family members, such as "peacemaker," "blamer," "scapegoat," and the like.

We have noted that the psychodynamic function of the patient in the family system may well affect his or her response to illness. In turn, the absence of the patient from the family setting may also have an effect on their coping capabilities. For example, if an individual who has traditionally been the peacemaker is no longer able to perform that task, the family may erupt in conflict.[47] Conversely, the absence of a disruptive family member may facilitate the family's adaptation to stress.

In fragile family systems, even minor illness may exacerbate interpersonal tension. Conflict may develop regarding caretaking responsibilities, modes of dealing with the patient, and accommodation to even temporary financial burdens. Most research in this area has focused on the reaction to serious or long-term illness. Table 9–6 depicts some psychological effects on the modern urban (nuclear) family when a member is beset with serious illness.[48] These effects vary depending on which of the members is sick.

ILLNESS OF A SPOUSE.—In their hospitalization study, Duff and Hollingshead used four degrees of emotional impact to describe the reaction of a spouse to illness.[44] *Minimal* impact was likely when the illness was of minor or short duration, with no complications to handicap the patient at the end of convalescence. *Moderate* impact occurred when a

TABLE 9–6.—THE PSYCHOLOGICAL IMPACT OF SERIOUS ILLNESS ON THE PRECARIOUSLY BALANCED, EMOTIONALLY HIGHLY CHARGED SYSTEM OF THE MODERN URBAN FAMILY

FAMILY MEMBER	LIFE SITUATIONAL STRAINS	THE ILLNESS SOLUTION	THE ILLNESS IMPACT
Father-husband	As provider, primary status-bearer, classically the "scapegoat" or symbolic target for the hostility of the socializing child	The sick role offers semi-institutionalized respite from occupational demands and discipline	Worsens position of family, makes its adaptive problems more difficult, wife's focus on him withdraws attention from children, who must sacrifice part of maternal support
Mother-wife	As mediator between father and child, carrying the major socioemotional responsibility within the family, engendering solidarity and security, excluded generally from status and occupational satisfactions	The sick role offers escape from heavy "human relations management" responsibility or a compulsively feministic reaction to exclusion from the man's world	The most disturbing of all, subjecting husband and children to undersupport at a time when major demands are made on them—the greatest single source of danger to the family
Child-sibling	As socializer on the tension-ridden path toward maturity in competition with siblings	The sick role provides escape from growing-up obligations, gains care, concern, and close contact, furthers desired infantile regression, and gives advantage over siblings	Disturbs family equilibrium by making it difficult for mother to meet needs of father and siblings, making rivalry acute

Reproduced from Anthony E.J.: The impact of mental and physical illness on family life. *Am. J. Psychiatry* 127:138, 1970.

spouse had a physical disease with only a fair prognosis. Here there were usually some stressful sequelae for family relationships following hospitalization. Families in the category of *extensive* impact faced the necessity of adjusting to the long-term effects of a severe form of physical disability, such as a heart attack, malignancy, or stroke. In these situations, the affected spouse could no longer carry on his or her usual family role. Such patients were reduced to emotional and often economic dependency, with concurrent stress to the healthy spouse who now had to bear a substantial part of the family burden. Finally, *catastrophic* impact invariably occurred when the spouse's illness had a very poor prognosis and he or she faced early death. Such families adapted to untreatable physical or mental disease with significant alterations in role definitions and intense emotional strain.

The stress of an illness on a spouse is made even greater when it is accompanied by financial problems. In the study cited, the authors found that the impact of illness was signifi-cantly greater on the spouses of "ward" patients—those who could not afford private care—than on the spouses of private patients. There was also a strong relationship between the extent of the patient's physical disability and the spouse's emotional reaction to the illness, particularly when the sick person proved unable to perform his or her usual role in the family after the development of illness.

In most studies of long-term illness, the wife's sickness has a greater impact on the family than does a husband's illness, especially when there are young children in the family. In our society, women are expected to play a supportive and caretaking role with sick family members. Even though a wife may become overburdened by this role, particularly if she is also a breadwinner, the household usually continues to function. On the other hand, when the wife-mother is ill, structural adaptations are usually required to maintain family functioning. In studies of husbands' reactions to the long-term illness of their wives, it was found that there is a critical point at which expectations and tolerances change.[49] Husbands can usually make short-term adjustments to a wife's illness, even though this may involve taking time off from work, finding temporary placements for the children, and assuming unfamiliar housekeeping chores. When there are multiple hospitalizations or long-term disability, however, husbands tend to withdraw from their spouses, lower their role expectations, and make other arrangements for the continued functioning of the household. The provision of a permanent caretaker-substitute results in a strain on marital ties and tends to isolate the wife-mother as a marginal person in the family constellation. This leaves the woman without role or function and adversely affects her feelings of self-worth.

In families where either of the spouse-parents has a chronic deteriorating illness, there is often intolerable stress. The sick person must adapt to loss of role, reduced productivity within the family, loss of self-esteem, and feelings of "being a burden" to loved ones. Added to this are the pain, anxiety, and anticipatory grief about the terminal illness. Such individuals must have great ego strength to avoid displacing the frustration, irritability, and anger they feel onto other family members. Many families with long-term invalids, due to physical or mental illness, eventually exhaust their adaptive resources, so that the patients are no longer viewed as functional members of the family system. Psychological or even physical separation of the patient is sometimes a necessary coping mechanism to enable other family members to get on with their own lives. For many patients, this separation tends to confirm their feelings of worthlessness and may hasten the dying process, but paradoxically, for others the gradual weakening of psychological bonds is often a relief. It may enable them to cope with the guilt of being a burden to others and to dispense finally with the false cheerfulness and unrealistic hopes associated with the myth of recovery.

ILLNESS OF A CHILD.—Fatal or long-term illness in children is one of the most poignant problems encountered by medical personnel. The impact on the child's family is often drastic, and a good physician-family relationship is critical. Gordon and Kutner have delineated the following series of complex family reactions to the seriously ill child:[50]

1. An initial traumatic reaction when the diagnosis is revealed to the parents.

2. An alteration of the attitudes and relationships among the remaining family members, as well as with friends and neighbors.

3. A difficult period of adjustment to the medical needs of the sick child.

4. The establishment of a variety of relationships with physicians and other medical personnel in clinics and hospitals.

5. A long-term readjustment in the family's way of life, depending on the nature of the illness and the economic, biologic, and social consequences following in its wake.

6. The surfacing of latent emotional problems in response to the demands of the situation.

The initial reaction of the parents to a diagnosis of serious and potentially fatal illness in one of their children usually involves shock, anxiety, confusion, and disbelief. Typically, there is initial denial, followed by overwhelming grief and the unanswerable, painful query: Why *my* child? There may be feelings of rejection, particularly toward infants whose diagnosis and/or physical appearance indicates that they are unlikely ever to recover fully. With infants whose life span is limited, there may be avoidance of the child to prevent the development of a close relationship and the subsequent pain of separation. In this connection parents often have guilt feelings about their emotional reactions. In addition, they may feel that they are in some way responsible for the child's illness (e.g., through hereditary transmission of disease), and this leads to additional feelings of guilt.

Gordon and Kutner have pointed out that "the physician rendering the diagnosis may play a key role in managing the emotional reaction, reducing confusion and anxiety, and in helping parents approach the ensuing problems realistically."[50] Unfortunately, in this critical first stage medical personnel sometimes fail in their efforts to convey the "bad news" in as constructive a manner as possible.

In research on the impact of children's illness on their parents, a consistent parental reaction seems to be criticism of the diagnosing physician. While this criticism may well represent displacement of anger and frustration on the bearer of bad tidings, parents' complaints seem to be fairly specific regardless of the nature or severity of the child's condition. Physicians have been accused of crudeness, bluntness, lack of concern, evasion of issues, and the use of complicated terminology.[51] In a study of 100 families, almost 50% were critical of what and how they were told about the diagnosis and prognosis of their disabled child.[52]

The physician in this situation is in an extremely sensitive and difficult position. Bozeman et al., in discussing the impact of a diagnosis of leukemia, refer to the period following diagnosis as one of "intense parental anxiety manifested by hostility toward doctors."[53] Bruch has noted a conflict between the physician's need to instruct parents concerning the seriousness of the illness (in this case juvenile diabetes) and the concomitant wish to avoid kindling unnecessary anxiety and fright.[54]

Most physicians emphasize promptness and skill in transmitting an unfavorable diagnosis, with an emphasis on what Davis has termed "time perspective."[55] This means that the physician must communicate to the parents that any uncertainty in diagnosis or prognosis stems not from therapeutic incompetence or an attempt to mask the unpleasant truth, but rather from the nature of the disease itself or our current level of knowledge.[55]

Serious illness in children creates situational and emotional stress that may impose an intolerable burden on the family system. Gordon and Kutner[50] cite a study by Korkes[56] as one of the most significant investigations of parental reactions to serious illness in their children. The major aspect of the stress, according to Korkes, is the parents' lack of power to control the difficulty. This results in altered self-perception, changes in expectations and life goals, and social withdrawal. Four typical sociopsychological reactions occur: (1) a feeling of exclusion from the "normal community," (2) a loss of rewards of "free communication," (3) a loss of rewards of anticipated pleasures of child-rearing, and (4) a period of prolonged stress from which escape is impossible. Parents change their relationships to the larger social group through necessary or discretionary social isolation—the former because of homebound responsibilities to the sick child and the latter because of shame or guilt. Irrational guilt seems to accompany many types of disease, with parents imputing to themselves an instrumental role as carriers of a genetic error, or an actual causative role in generating the illness.

Gordon and Kutner note that children's illnesses may be divided according to degrees of parental "culpability," ranging from those with the least parental blame attached to them (infections, chance traumatic accidents) to those with the most blame associated with them (emotional or behavioral disorders, injuries from parental punishment).[50] The issue of perceived culpability seems to be a strong determinant of the way parents are treated by medical practitioners. This is almost always the case when a child's disability appears to be due to overt parental abuse or neglect. Medical attitudes may also be hostile when there is even a theoretical possibility that the parents played a role in causing or aggravating the child's illness (e.g., childhood autism or other types of mental illness). There is considerable evidence that changes in these inappropriate attitudes lag far behind new research findings that repudiate the theories themselves.[57]

In an article describing roadblocks to treatment of the chronic mentally ill, a psychiatrist pointed out that parents of schizophrenic children "felt that they were receiving far more than their fair share of the blame for what had happened to their children, and that no one in the professional ranks seemed to understand this, or for that matter, the problems inherent in being the parent of a schizophrenic. They wondered why the parents of a child with leukemia were treated with sympathy and understanding, while the parents of a child with schizophrenia received scorn and condemnation."[46]

The actual job of raising a chronically disabled child may take an extreme toll in terms of the psychological health of parents and siblings. S. Thomas Cummings of the Menninger Foundation in Topeka, Kansas, studied the impact of this life-style on both mothers and fathers. Mothers with a retarded child experienced a wide range of negative consequences, including depression, lowered self-esteem, and inhibited enjoyment of their normal children. Comparison with parents of normal children indicated that the mothers of chronically ill children seemed to repress their feelings to a great extent, or else worked them out in daily rituals on behalf of the afflicted child.

This study was replicated with fathers of children with medical illnesses (diabetes mellitus, rheumatic fever, cystic fibrosis, and others), mentally retarded children, and normal controls.[58] Parents in each category were matched for socioeconomic status and sex/age of the affected child. On a battery of tests, Cummings found significantly more depression, a lower sense of parental competence, and less enjoyment of *all* children in the family (the affected child and normal siblings) among fathers of medically ill or mentally retarded children. Fathers of mentally retarded children were significantly different from all other groups. They were more depressed, more preoccupied with their afflicted child, and more unhappy with the child than other fathers.

One of the most interesting findings in this study was that fathers of mentally retarded children scored considerably higher than control fathers in emphasizing neatness, orderliness, organization, and routine. Concomitantly, they were lower in dominance, assertiveness, and readiness to express an interest in the opposite sex. Cummings concluded that the situational stress of rearing a retarded child tended to produce "a constricted male accentuating his compulsive tendencies in order to suppress his aggressive and sexual drives." Cummings found little difference between the mothers and fathers of retarded children, but found much more stress among fathers of medically ill children than among their wives. He speculated that mothers were better able to relieve stress through direct caring for the afflicted child.

Types of Interaction Between Medical Personnel and Families

Generally, the interactions of physicians and other medical staff with the patient's family fall into four categories of behavior.

1. *Objectivity and distance.*—This is a common mode of interaction that maintains the "proper" scientific distance and prevents overinvolvement in the case. While this stance may save the physician psychic energy, it is often objected to by patients' families, who may perceive the physician as cold and noncommunicative. Physicians often adopt this interactional style when they have difficulty dealing with their own feelings and do not know how to impart an unfavorable diagnosis or prognosis.

2. *Irrelevant warmth.*—In this interaction, the physician establishes a brief pseudofriendship with family members, often recalling their names and occupations, exchanging in pleasantries and jokes, but excluding them from vital information on the progress of the disease. They will remember the physician as a "nice person" who gave them little substantive help.

3. *Masked hostility.*—In this type of communication, the family is viewed either as a precipitating agent in the patient's illness or as an obstacle to his effective treatment. Members of the family may be treated brusquely, indifferently, or

even with veiled contempt. This mode of interaction is most often used when the family actually interferes with hospital procedures or patient progress. However, it also occurs when the family is viewed as in some way culpable for the illness, particularly in the case of emotional disorders of children.[46]

4. *Communicative support.*—In the optimal kind of interaction, the attending staff is able to impart comprehensible information on the known etiology, course, and prognosis of the illness in an empathic and supportive manner. They suggest options for treatment or care that are acceptable within the family's cultural, religious, or socioeconomic framework. If they are not familiar with this framework, they are sufficiently sensitive to behavioral cues so that they can recognize signs of discomfort or reluctance on the part of the family. In response to this need, medical personnel call in resource persons who can provide appropriate input or act as "culture brokers" in the event this is needed.[59] Finally, family members are viewed as concerned individuals who should be involved in the therapeutic process for optimal patient care. They are treated with dignity and respect, including acknowledgment that they, as well as the patient, may be suffering through a period of emotional stress.

In the optimal interaction, the physician has three primary roles in dealing with patients and family members: *healer, educator,* and *facilitator*. Encounters with physicians must be helpful to the family on both an informational and an emotional level. Particularly in cases of long-term illness, the physician can make a critical contribution to a decision-making process that may have long-range effects on the lives of the patient and his family.

SUMMARY

In this chapter, the sociological factors in health and illness are discussed in terms of their relation to certain demographic variables—age, sex, race, and socioeconomic status—which can be correlated with specific measures of health. These measures include longevity, disability and morbidity rates, access to medical care (perceived adequacy of the health-care system and consumer expenditures), and utilization of medical services. In general, there is a discrepancy in the health status of rich and poor, white and nonwhite segments of our population, with the poor and nonwhite being at a serious disadvantage.

The development of health attitudes and practices is in large part a function of the process of socialization. Attitudes toward the body, nutrition and medication as well as health roles and adaptation to illness are acquired through this learning process as a child matures into an adult.

The importance to medicine of changing family structure is related to its effects on the caretaking capability of family members and the impact of illness on the family unit. Research findings on the impact of illness on the family indicate that there are four types of emotional impact—minimal, moderate, extensive, and catastrophic—which are related to the degree and type of illness of a spouse or spouse-parent. Parental reactions to the illness of a child, particularly the guilt feelings and/or social withdrawal that accompanies long-term or terminal illness, may have significant effects on the physician's ability to give proper care. To soften this impact and help families make appropriate life decisions, the roles of the physician or other medical staff member as healer, educator, and facilitator are of paramount importance.

REFERENCES

1. Executive Office of the President, Office of Management and Budget: *Social Indicators, 1973*. U.S. Government Printing Office, 1973.
2. Katagawa E.M., Hauser P.M.: *Differential Mortality in the United States*. Cambridge, Mass., Harvard University Press, 1973.
3. Syme S.L., Berkman L.F.: Social class, susceptibility and sickness, (unpublished manuscript).
4. Nagi M.D., Stockwell E.G.: Scoioeconomic

differentials in mortality by cause of death. *Health Serv. Rep.* 88:449, 1973.
5. Antonovsky A.: Social class, life expectancy and overall mortality. Quarterly Bulletin Milbank Memorial Fund, Part I 45:31, 1967.
6. De Hoyos A., De Hoyos G.: Symptomatology differentials between negro and white schizophrenics. *Int. J. Soc. Psychiatry* 11:245, 1965.
7. Simon R.J., et al.: Depression and schizophrenia in hospitalized black and white mental patients. *Arch. Gen. Psychiatry* 28:509, 1973.
8. Prange H., Vitols M.M.: Cultural aspects of the relatively low incidence of depression in southern negroes. *Int. J. Soc. Psychiatry* 8:104, 1961.
9. Malzberg B.: Mental disorders in the U.S., in Deutsch A., Fishman H. (eds.): *Encyclopedia of Mental Health.* New York, Franklin Watts, 1963, vol. 3.
10. Jaco E.G.: *The Social Epidemiology of Mental Disorders—A Psychiatric Survey of Texas.* New York, Russell Sage Foundation, 1960.
11. Taube C.: *Admission Rates to State and County Mental Hospitals by Age, Sex, and Color, United States, 1969.* U.S. Department of Health, Biometry Branch, Statistical Note 41, 1971.
12. Wilson D.C., Lantz E.M.: The effect of culture change on the negro race in Virginia as indicated by a study of state hospital admission. *Am. J. Psychiatry* 114:25, 1957.
13. Lefley H.P.: Ethnic patients and anglo healers: An overview of the problem in mental health care. Read before the ninth annual meeting of the Southern Anthropological Society, Blacksburg, Va., April 4–6, 1974.
14. Gross H., Heibert M.: The effect of race and sex on variation of diagnosis and disposition in a psychiatric emergency room. *J. Nerv. Ment. Dis.* 148(6):638, 1969.
15. Hunt R.: Occupational status in the disposition of cases in a child guidance clinic. *Int. J. Soc. Psychol.* 8:199, 1962.
16. Kohut H.: Introspection, empathy, and psychoanalysis. *J. Am. Psychoanal. Assoc.* 7:459, 1959.
17. Moss J.: Incidence and treatment variations between negroes and caucasians in mental illness. *Community Ment. Health J.* 3(1):61, 1967.
18. Singer B.D.: Some implications of differential psychiatric treatment of negro and white patients. *Soc. Sci. Med.* 1:77, 1967.
19. Yamamoto J., James Q., Palley N.: Cultural problems in psychiatric therapy. *Arch. Gen. Psychiatry* 19(1):45, 1968.
20. Fried M.: Social differences in mental health, in Kosa J., Antonovsky A., Zola I.K. (eds.): *Poverty and Health: A Sociological Analysis.* Cambridge, Mass., Harvard University Press, 1969.
21. Levy L., Rowitz L.: *The Ecology of Mental Disorder.* New York, Behavioral Publications, 1973.
22. Brenner M.H.: *Mental Illness and the Economy.* Cambridge, Mass., Harvard University Press, 1973.
23. *Preliminary Findings of the First Health and Nutrition Examination Survey, United States, 1971–72: Dietary Intake and Biochemical Findings.* U.S. National Center for Health Statistics, 1972.
24. Seham M.: *Blacks and American Medical Care.* Minneapolis, University of Minnesota Press, 1973.
25. Strickland S.P.: *U.S. Health Care: What's Wrong and What's Right?* Washington, D.C., Potomac Associates, 1972.
26. Morrow J.H., Edwards A.B.: U.S. health manpower policy: Will the benefits justify the costs? *J. Med. Educ.* 51(10):791, 1976.
27. Koos E.L.: *The Health of Regionville: What the People Thought and Did About It.* New York, Columbia University Press, 1954.
28. Feldman J.J.: *The Dissemination of Health Information: A Case Study in Adult Learning.* Chicago, Aldine Publishing Company, 1966.
29. Rosenblatt D., Suchman E.A.: Blue-collar attitudes and information toward health and illness, in Shostak A.B., Gomberg W. (eds.): *Blue-Collar World: Studies of the American Worker.* Englewood Cliffs, N.J., Prentice-Hall, Inc., 1964.
30. Rosenblatt D., Suchman E.A.: The underutilization of medical-care service by blue-collarites, in Shostak A.B., Gomberg W. (eds.): *Blue-Collar World: Studies of the American Worker.* Englewood Cliffs, N.J., Prentice-Hall, Inc., 1964.
31. Human M.D.: Some links between economic status and untreated illness. *Soc. Sci. Med.* 4:387, 1970.
32. Kadushin C.: Social class and the experience of ill health. *Sociol. Inquiry* 35:67, 1964.
33. Levine G.N.: Anxiety about illness: Psychological and social bases. *J. Health Hum. Behav.* 3:30, 1962.
34. Scheff T.: Users and non-users of a student psychiatric clinic. *J. Health Hum. Behav.* 7:114, 1966.
35. Gonda T.A.: The relation between complaints of persistent pain and family size. *J. Neurol. Neurosurg. Psychiatry* 25:277, 1962.
36. Mechanic D.: The influence of mothers on their children's health attitudes and behavior. *Pediatrics* 33:444, 1964.

37. Rainwater L.: *Behind Ghetto Walls: Black Families in a Federal Slum*. Chicago: Aldine Publishing Company, 1970.
38. Neugarten B.: *Personality in Middle and Late Life*. New York: Atherton Press, 1964.
39. Crawford C.: *Health and the Family: A Medical-Sociological Analysis*. New York, Macmillan Publishing Co., Inc., 1971.
40. Bullough B.: Poverty, ethnic identity, and preventive health care. *J. Health Soc. Behav.* 13:347–359, 1972.
41. Gordon G.: *Role Theory and Illness*. New Haven, Conn., College and University Press, 1966.
42. Mechanic D.: *Medical Sociology: A Selective View*. New York, The Free Press, 1968.
43. Parsons T., Fox R.C.: Illness, therapy, and the modern urban American family, *J. Soc. Issues* 8:31–44, 1952.
44. Duff R.S., Hollingshead A.B.: *Sickness and Society*. New York, Harper & Row, 1968.
45. Appleton W.S.: Mistreatment of patients' families by psychiatrists. *Am. J. Psychiatry* 131:655, 1974.
46. Lamb H.R., et al.: No place for schizophrenics: The unwelcome consumer speaks out. *Psychiatr. Ann.* 6(12):688, 1976.
47. Anderson C., Meisel S.: An assessment of family reaction to the stress of psychiatric illness. *Hosp. Community Psychiatry* 27(12):868, 1976.
48. Anthony E.J.: The impact of mental and physical illness on family life. *Am. J. Psychiatry* 127:2, 1970.
49. Kreisman D.E., Joy V.: Family response to the mental illness of a relative: A review of the literature. *Schizophrenia Bull.* 10:34, 1974.
50. Gordon B., Kutner B.: Long term and fatal illness and the family. *J. Heath Hum. Behav.* 6:190, 1965.
51. Waskowitz C.H.: The parents of retarded children speak for themselves. *J. Pediatr.* 54:319–329, 1959.
52. Koch R., Groliker B.V., Sands R., et al.: Attitude study of parents with mentally retarded children; evaluation of parental satisfaction with the medical care of a retarded child. *Pediatrics* 23:582–584, 1959.
53. Bozeman M.F., Orbach C.E., Sutherland A.M.: Psychological impact of cancer and its treatment. III. The adaptation of mothers to the threatened loss of their children through leukemia. *Cancer* 8:1, 1955.
54. Bruch H.: Physiologic and psychologic interrelationship in diabetes in children. *Psychosom. Med.* 11(4):200, 1949.
55. Davis F.: Definitions of time and recovery in paralytic polio convalescence. *Am. J. Sociol.* 61:582, 1956.
56. Korkes L.: *The Impact of Mentally Ill Children upon Their Families*. Trenton, N.J., State Department of Institutions and Agencies, 1955.
57. Arieti S.: *Interpretation of Schizophrenia*. New York, Basic Books, 1974.
58. Cummings S.T.: The impact of the child's deficiency on the father: A study of fathers of mentally retarded and of chronically ill children. *Am. J. Psychiatry* 46(2):246, 1976.
59. Weidman H.H.: Concepts as strategies for change, in Sussex J.N. (ed.): *Psychiatry and the Social Sciences*. Special edition of *Psych. Ann.* 5(8):17, 1975.

10 / Culture, Ethnicity, and Medicine

CLARISSA S. SCOTT, Ph.D.

PEOPLE THROUGHOUT THE WORLD have had to develop ways of meeting their needs for food, shelter, and clothing using what is available in their environment. Patterns of social relationships have had to be found in which children can be properly cared for and trained in the ways of that social group. Mechanisms have had to be devised to maintain cohesion within a society and stable values among its members.

Another human concern that is universal and with which every population has to deal is illness. Because social groups often have different gene pools, geographic environments, beliefs and customs, as well as resources and levels of technology, there is great variation in how they solve the problems related to the health and sickness of their members. In order to understand how they arrive at these solutions, one must understand the influence of *culture* on their lives.

A helpful way to look at culture is as an adaptive mechanism, that is, to see it as the solution to life's problems that a group provides for its members. Whether we build houses of stone or lumber may reflect the practical use of indigenous materials; whether we build them on the ground or on stilts may be the group's solution to the threat of flooding or the need for a cooling breeze to circulate underneath the house in a tropical climate. Even the language we use helps us to adapt to our particular environment and way of life. Every language has a vocabulary that is extremely full and precise in that area of life that is most vital to those speaking it. Eskimos, who depend to a large extent on seals for their survival, possess an extensive vocabulary to distinguish among the kinds and conditions of seals. The English language, in comparison, has an enormously expanded vocabulary relating to technology, a characteristic of our life.

In summary, culture consists of all the beliefs, behaviors, and values that are useful and functional for a particular group. These are integrated into a logical system and handed down from generation to generation. This system is functional because it provides the members of a cultural group with solutions to life's problems that earlier members have found, by trial and error, to work. Thus, culture is like a mental road map that is used to guide individuals in their surroundings and in their behavior with other people. Each member of a cultural group may have a slightly different version of the map; however, the general outline and many of the details are shared by the other members of the group.

When we speak of "American culture," we mean the shared system of beliefs, practices, and values that predominate within the United States, i.e., within the white middle class. The United States is a multiethnic country, however. Although the white middle class system is the predominant one, there are many other ethnic groups within the country, each with its own unique pattern of shared beliefs, practices, and values. Furthermore, members of each of these ethnic groups, as well as those within the white American group, are found in different socioeconomic class divisions. If we try to depict this for just one urban area, we might draw the triangle shown in Figure 10–1.

DIAGRAMMATIC REPRESENTATION OF THE ETHNIC GROUP AND SOCIAL CLASS POPULATION IN THE MIAMI (FLORIDA) COMMUNITY

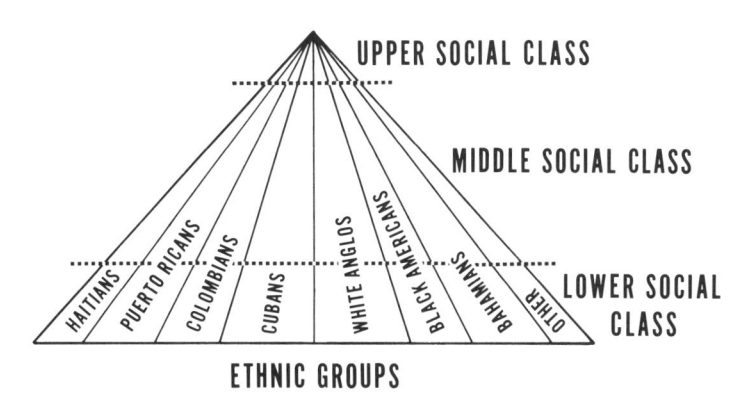

Fig 10–1.—This diagram was originally used in lectures by Hazel Weidman, Ph.D., to illustrate the influence of socioeconomic class and ethnicity on beliefs and behaviors. The populations within the triangle represent ethnic groups living with white Anglos in an urban area of the United States. Each ethnic group, as well as the white Anglo population, is composed of members found in each of the three socioeconomic classes.

We see that each ethnic group, as well as the white Anglos, has a proportion of members in each of the socioeconomic classes. Members from the upper class share certain class-oriented beliefs and behaviors in addition to various beliefs and behaviors derived from their own ethnic group. Taking the Cuban community as an example, we would expect a local Cuban physician to hold certain beliefs in common with others in the upper class, be they white Anglo, black American, or Haitian; however, we would also expect him to share some beliefs and behaviors with his fellow Cuban-Americans, regardless of their social class.

The terms *ethnic group* and *ethnicity* are used frequently in this chapter in the following way (again using Cubans as an example): Cuban culture, in toto is found on the island of Cuba. In the United States, the Cuban émigrés have brought part of this culture with them (religious beliefs, language used in the home, values about family life, and certain medicinal agents, for example). In Miami, however, where many have settled, they have had to incorporate certain parts of the American culture into their lives in place of aspects of the Cuban culture that are no longer available or are not adaptive here (e.g., the educational system, the language spoken in the larger community, the differing role of women). They no longer are able to embrace Cuban culture in its pure form. They are, in the United States, an *ethnic group*, that is, a group living in an alien environment yet remaining culturally distinct by virtue of sharing a common tie of nationality and cultural background.

HEALTH CULTURE

Among different cultures throughout the world we find variation in the incidence and type of illness, the way in which symptoms are expressed, etiologic explanations, and methods of treatment. Because life and death are of such importance to individuals in every culture, adults tend to retain tenaciously those health beliefs and practices with which they are familiar from childhood. These remain deep-rooted, having been learned consciously and unconsciously and incorporated into individual systems of beliefs and practices at very early ages. Despite the fact that we continue to utilize health beliefs and therapies that we learned were helpful in our childhood, we are also open to possible new effective methods of maintaining our health or curing illness. Rather than put all our eggs in one health basket, so to speak, we appear to be willing to *add to* our list of ways to heal, although we often hesitate to *relinquish* a particular health practice learned in childhood and *substitute* a different one.

All those beliefs and practices relating to health in any one culture are integrated into and reflect the total cultural pattern of that particular population. To illustrate with a very simple example, Western (American) medicine is characterized by the use of technology (from blood pressure gauges to x-ray machines), which "fits" our pattern of industrialization. A South American Indian population whose economic life is based on agriculture has, in comparison, a health culture characterized by extensive knowledge and use of medicinal plants.

The concept of health culture (see Weidman and Egeland[1] for a more comprehensive discussion of this concept) can be better understood with the help of brief descriptions of health cultures found among three ethnic populations within the United States: southern Appalachian whites, black Americans, and Mexican-Americans. Parts of the three systems are shared among themselves as well as with other diverse groups within the United States. For more complete descriptions, the reader is referred to references 2–6.

Southern Appalachian Whites

All the informants in a study by Stekert of southern Appalachian whites reported that they considered faith to be the most important factor in curing disease, and more than three fourths of them had a firm belief in faith healing.[7]

The healer to whom one turns for the treatment of common ailments is not the physician but the "skilled practitioner of home medicine . . . (usually an older woman, often the patient's mother or grandmother)," frequently described by respondents as "the greatest person in the world."[7] These women are the repositories for mountain medical lore and "always know" the most appropriate herbs and other ingredients necessary for the traditional cures (such as catnip tea and various poultices). One visits a physician "only when it is absolutely necessary." Mothers often assume the role of diagnostician, basing their decisions on traditional beliefs about disease: for example, all rashes on babies should be "encouraged" and the more the rash is "brought out," the better it is for the baby; if it does not break out, it will "go in." Syndromes and symptoms are grouped differently; for example, many different kinds of respiratory ailments are subsumed under the term *pneumonia*. The belief that "fate" rather than therapeutic behavior determines the outcome of illness is common.

Lay specialists treat a variety of ills; for example, a "thrash doctor," one who has special powers to heal the fungus irritation commonly called "thrush" by physicians, cures by blowing in the baby's mouth.

Beliefs involving diet include a prohibition against eating fresh fruits or vegetables when pregnant.

Pearsall has characterized this group as exhibiting "failure to identify certain abnormal states as true illness; willingness to accept and endure numerous symptoms fatalistically; and heavy reliance on prayer and home remedies."[4]

Black Americans

Among black Americans, the folk medical system classifies illness and misfortune into "natural" and "unnatural" categories. Illness that is "natural" is thought to be caused by forces of nature (going out in the cold with inadequate clothing) or by God as punishment for sin. Unnatural illness, in contrast, is the result of evil influences (meaning the devil) and witchcraft. Whether an individual defines his health problem as natural or unnatural, of course, affects his choice of a healer. Scientific medicine is not considered capable of curing a patient whom God is punishing; only He is the appropriate intercessor.[6]

The classification of practitioners depends on their healing methods and how they received the ability to heal. Those who have received the gift from God are thought to be the most powerful practitioners. Those who have learned to heal by education (physicians included) are able to cure only the most simple, natural illnesses.

Among the indigenous healers in this system are rootworkers (considered equally adept at casting spells that bring illness or misfortune to others and at removing spells and treating victims of witchcraft), faith healers (who practice healing as part of their ministry), spiritual healers (who are thought to possess the God-given gift to heal and utilize this gift outside the church), and owners of magic shops (which offer items such as candles, incense, and perfumes purporting to bring luck, insure money, and make one's spouse faithful).

Mexican-Americans

The specialist who is most commonly sought out for diagnosis and treatment of folk illnesses among Mexican-Americans is a *curandero(a)*. Some of these healers have a relatively simple knowledge of herbs, diet regulation, and folk remedies, while others have access to a vast repertoire of herbal mixtures and purgatives that are administered orally, and use massage, "cupping," diet prescriptions, and magical techniques.

Although Mexican-Americans do not consciously "classify" illnesses, Clark has grouped diseases that are "known" to this cultural group into six categories:[2]

1. Diseases in which there is an imbalance within the body of hot and cold.—These can often be treated by dietary changes.

2. Diseases resulting from the dislocation of internal organs.—"Fallen fontanelle," the symptoms of which are severe; diarrhea and vomiting; "fallen womb," which may be diagnosed as a cause of barrenness; and little lumps or balls that appear in arm or leg tissue are all examples.

3. Diseases of magical origin.—These are thought to be caused by evil spirits (the "evil eye" is one disorder of this type).

4. Diseases of emotional origin.—Interpersonal situations can give rise to excessive amounts of anger, hurt feelings, and sadness, and are thought to cause disease. Mexican-Americans cite one's emotions as playing a primary role in illness. Often these can be treated with herbal remedies alone, but some require the help of a curandera.

5. Other folk-defined diseases.—Preoccupation with gastrointestinal functioning is common among Mexican-Americans and is reflected in a disorder called *empacho* ("characterized by the presence of a large ball in the stomach which produces swelling of the abdomen"[2]).

6. Standard scientific diseases.—Measles, tuberculosis, whooping cough, and cancer are examples of many conditions recognized by Mexican-Americans. However, Mexican-Americans may often hold etiologic ideas about these that differ from those of physicians.

At this point, it is important to note that the situation represented in Figure 10–1 applies not only to culture in general but also to health culture specifically.

CULTURALLY DETERMINED CONCEPTS ABOUT THE BODY AND ITS FUNCTIONS

Concepts about the body and the way it functions are of extreme importance in determining whether an individual sees a bodily sensation or event as normal or abnormal, as well as what steps he takes in response to it. They also are important in making decisions in areas such as preventive health care and family planning. Differences in these concepts affect the practice of medicine among ethnocultural populations in the United States and elsewhere in the world.

Body Image (Body Concept)

The feelings that one has about one's own body and the bodies of those of the opposite sex can affect a person's response to questioning by a health professional, how he or she presents symptoms, and whether a recommended therapy is followed.

A critical problem today, when there are still so few women graduating from medical schools, is the genital examination of Puerto Rican and Mexican-American women by male physicians. Having been raised with feelings of "shame" about her genitalia and the idea that a "good woman" does not discuss sexual matters with or expose herself to a man, women from these cultures delay seeking treatment for a complaint in this area of the body. These feelings of shame inhibit Puerto Rican women not only from seeking care but also from even asking about birth control information and materials. The emotions surrounding this area of the body are so intense that it is a subject not commonly discussed between husband and wife. Clark has reported that a Mexican-American mother was horrified by even the suggestion that she manipulate her baby son's penis to ease some foreskin constriction, a request she perceived as analogous to asking her to perform an "indecent act."[2] (The father would have been the more appropriate adult to ask to do this.) The sexual area evoked deep feelings of modesty and shame when investigators attempted to elicit the terminology for body parts from five ethnic groups in Miami, Florida, by presenting drawings of the male and female bodies for them to label. In contrast to the Bahamian, Haitian, Cuban, and black American respondents, the characteristic Puerto Rican response was to refuse to label any part of the male or female body between the navel and the thigh.[8]

There are several clinical implications of these culturally derived attitudes and beliefs: (1) examinations of Puerto Rican and Mexican-American women should be done by female physicians, nurse-practitioners, or nurses when possible; (2) all reasonable means should be taken to preserve the patient's modesty; and (3) genitourinary problems of male children perhaps should be discussed with the father also.

Another example of how one's body image can influence the course of illness is drawn from the black American population. It is well documented that low-income black Americans do not use preventive health measures (such as the Pap smear) as frequently nor do they seek therapeutic care for overt symptoms of cancer as early as white Americans. Several investigators (Rainwater[9] among them) have suggested that this is due in part to their lower self-concept with accompanying inferior image of their body. The rationalization suggested by Rainwater follows these lines: "I am not as important a person as others in this society; my body is not as important either. If my body does not function as well as others' do, that is understandable and expected; neither do I as a person."

Neugarten[10] and Rosenblatt and Suchman[11] have found this same type of thinking in the lower/blue-collar class in general: that is, the body has only a limited number of years of utility; it is to be used and allowed to run down naturally but is not worth repairing.

Knowledge of Bodily Functioning

Many of us in the Western scientific world are guilty of thinking that if an individual does not have "scientific" knowledge about health, he does not have health knowledge—period. This is sometimes true. In the Miami study* in which subjects were asked to label drawings of parts of the body, many Puerto Ricans returned the drawing of the internal organs to the interviewer, saying, "I can't do that; I

---

*The Health Ecology Project, a 4-year investigation of health beliefs and practices of Bahamians, Cubans, Haitians, Puerto Ricans, and southern U.S. blacks in inner-city Miami, Florida, carried out by the Department of Psychiatry, University of Miami School of Medicine. Its principal investigators were James M. Sussex, M.D., and Hazel Weidman, Ph.D. The author was Field Coordinator of this project. The study was funded by The Commonwealth Fund and the report is available.[12]

don't know what's inside me." More often, a person does have knowledge about how his body works. However, it may be *cultural* knowledge rather than scientific, and it is absolutely essential for a physician to understand this. The same Miami investigation provides an illustration:

> On three separate occasions over a 2-month period, a Haitian mother brought her teenage daughter to the Emergency Room for treatment of a "heart attack." The first time, the physician explained that the rapid heartbeat, which the mother believed to be the onset of a heart attack, was simply palpitations attributable to "nerves," very understandable inasmuch as the daughter had recently arrived in the United States, could speak no English, had not yet made friends her age, missed her fiancé still in Haiti, etc. . . . The physician prescribed Valium and assured the mother it was nothing to worry about. On subsequent visits, during which the same complaint was presented, many attempts including an EEG were made in order to demonstrate to the mother that the daughter's heart was normal. Questions during this period revealed that the daughter had taken only one Valium pill, and that both the mother and daughter believed the pills would not help. As a result of field work, it was found that many Haitians believe that when there is insufficient blood in the body, the heart must beat harder and faster to circulate what little blood there is. Knowing this, it was now obvious why the daughter was not following the prescribed protocol. The Haitian expectation was that the doctor should prescribe a medicine to increase the amount of blood, *not* to "calm your nerves."

Often an uncomplicated drawing, simplified terms, and an unhurried manner are very helpful in dealing with patients. This is particularly true in regard to family planning and the effect of contraceptive methods on internal body parts. Many women have reported the fear that the condom may come off during intercourse and "get lost inside me." Some ethnic persons in Miami pictured the IUD as "closing" the "opening to the womb" in much the same fashion as a safety pin would. Asking the woman how she thinks a particular form of birth control works, and then describing the method using a simple drawing and an explanation that includes the message that her view is understandable and not to be ridiculed, may be the most helpful approach.

Far more challenging are those beliefs and behaviors (such as the Haitian example above) that are imbedded within a cultural system but are not in accord with scientific medicine. Unfortunately, there are very few studies concerned with this even though the implications are serious in terms of treatment, i.e., whether a sick individual decides to seek health care and whether he complies with a prescribed regimen. An individual's knowledge (whether from the scientific information of the orthodox system or from a different health cultural belief system) will affect his response to medical questioning, his presentation of symptoms, and his expectations of and response to therapies.

Although examples from many different parts of the body could be used to illustrate this point, we will look only at blood. Blood has been a major focus of folk beliefs for generations in all parts of the world and remains so for many ethnic groups in the United States today. Among Haitians, blood can be heavy, weak, quiet, turbulent, unclean, and sweet, as well as in too great and too small an amount.[13] Snow indicates that among ethnic groups in this country, blood is described as high, low, thick, thin, good, and bad.[6] It is believed by many that the body generates new blood each month and that blood picks up impurities, which are ingested and circulate within the body. A woman's menstrual period allows her to rid herself of (1) excess blood, which, if the amount grows too large, can rise to the head and cause a stroke; and (2) impure blood. Thus, the menses are seen as a way of maintaining good health.[8] It is also commonly believed that strong emotion can affect one's blood. These last two ideas (that blood is a carrier of impurities and that strong emotions can cause blood pathology) have been traced back hundreds of years* and noted in widely scattered parts of the world.[14] Snow has described blood beliefs among numerous American ethnic groups, categorizing them into four areas.[6]

---

*Trumbull notes a biblical reference concerning a leper having to purge his blood in order to achieve a cure.[15]

VOLUME.—The terms "high blood" and "low blood" are the most common conditions in this category and are prominent among black Americans, southern whites,[6] Haitians, and Bahamians.[13] Low blood literally means that the volume is dangerously reduced; high blood means that there is so much that it has no place to go but *up*, where it may collect in the chest and head with potentially dangerous results.

CIRCULATION.—Turbulence in nature[6] or in one's emotions[13] is thought to be reflected in a similar movement of the blood. The health of the individual is particularly unprotected during these periods. One can find almanacs in drug stores all over the United States that indicate (according to the signs of the zodiac) when a considerable amount of blood will be located at different sites within the body. It is considered dangerous to have dental or other surgery done at the time when bleeding might be excessive.

PURITY.—As discussed, impurities are thought to accumulate within the blood. By means of the body's circulatory system, they are thought to be carried throughout the body. One symptom of "impure" or "dirty" blood is a skin eruption. Snow states that any sort of skin eruption, from urticaria and diaper rash to measles or a syphilitic lesion, indicates that impurities are trying to come out.[6] Both black Americans and Appalachian whites turn to catnip tea as one means to help drive these out of the body.

VISCOSITY.—The thickness or thinness of one's blood can be affected by age, sex, diet, and environmental temperature.[6] Children, women, and the elderly are likely to have thin blood. It should thicken during the winter in order to protect the body against the cold damp air. Notions about the range of blood viscosity have been reported among the Haitians,[13] Mexican peasants, black Americans, and southern whites.[6] Women are especially at risk during menses, when cold might thicken the blood and stop its flow. One Appalachian white informant reported a particularly feared disease—"quick TB"—caused "when a menstruating woman took a shower or was caught in a rainstorm," during which the blood flow could stop and "back up," resulting in "sudden hemorrhaging from the lungs."[7] Reports have ascribed sterility, insanity, and tuberculosis to bathing and exposure to damp cold during the monthly period.[6]

Clinically, the differences in beliefs about bodily functioning exhibited by ethnic persons on one hand and health care providers on the other can be a cause of distrust between patient and physician, misunderstanding and miscommunication, inaccurate diagnosis and recommended therapy, and lack of compliance on the patient's part. Several examples of these situations are given below.

One of the most frequent areas of misunderstanding and miscommunication between rural black and white patients and white physicians is high blood pressure. A physician who tells a low-income black American or southern rural white patient that she has low blood pressure may be understood as meaning "low blood" (too little blood); conversely, a diagnosis of high blood pressure by the physician may be interpreted as "high blood" (too much blood). Inasmuch as proper foods are thought to be able to bring about changes in high or low blood, the patient often reasons that it will be easier and less expensive to change her eating habits than to take the medicine prescribed.[6]

Inaccurate diagnosis that leads to an incorrect medical regimen is not uncommon.

A Puerto Rican patient in Miami presented herself at the Department of Family Medicine in the University of Miami teaching hospital with complaints of stomach pains and swelling. X-rays were taken and palliative measures were suggested, although the cause of the problem was not clear to the physician. After several more visits, during which the physician felt dissatisfied with his understanding and diagnosis of the problem, he called in a medical anthropologist as consultant. The new line of questioning suggested by the consultant revealed that the patient was fearful that her symptoms were due to witchcraft. Her "recovery" occurred when she accepted the physician's suggestion that she take medication to alleviate the symptoms and go to a folk healer to have the witchcraft dispelled.

Obviously a physician (especially one in a multiethnic urban setting) cannot hope to be familiar with all the beliefs about the body and its functioning among the diverse ethnic populations he serves. However, he will have taken the first step in providing care that is valued and utilized by his ethnic patients if (1) he remembers that their frame of reference, though different from his own, may be just as valid in their eyes, and (2) he learns the most common folk medical concepts that might hinder understanding and compliance.

THE INFLUENCE OF ETHNICITY ON PATIENTS' SYMPTOMS

Just as ethnicity influences the beliefs we hold about our body and its functioning, it also affects the number and kinds of symptoms we experience, our perception of them, and the way in which we communicate them to others (see also chaps. 21 and 22).

Sometimes the recognition of a bodily sensation as abnormal is related to its prevalence in a population. Among many Mexican-American groups in the southwestern United States, diarrhea is such an everyday experience that it is seen as normal rather than symptomatic or unusual. Lower back pain is so common among lower-class white women that it is not considered to be indicative of a disease. In both these populations, children learn that these two symptoms are thought of as natural and inevitable and thus not to be acted on. In such situations the members usually lack a frame of reference and simply do not realize that other groups of people do not normally suffer from these same symptoms.

In a similar way, we learn which symptoms require concern and medical attention. Irving K. Zola, a medical sociologist, documented this in a study done in three outpatient clinics of Massachusetts General Hospital and the Massachusetts Eye and Ear Infirmary (the Eye Clinic; the Ear, Nose, and Throat Clinic; and the Medical Clinic).[16] Ethnic membership of the respondents enabled Zola to compare 63 Italian patients with 81 Irish. Most reported having between 10 and 12 years of schooling. Findings from an open-ended interview that included a number of objective measures revealed the following.

The Irish presented symptoms located in the eye, ear, nose, or throat. They did not complain of pain as frequently as the Italians, and some even denied its existence when asked directly. When Zola analyzed the number of presenting complaints, he found that the Irish voiced significantly fewer. The Italian patients, in comparison, did not describe symptoms as being located in the eye or ear *even when* they had a diagnosed disorder there. They complained about *more* symptoms and described them as being in significantly more areas of the body (often in the back, leg, and stomach regions).

Zola relates these differences in the perception of symptoms to the major values of these two groups. The Irish, he suggests, have learned to handle their greatly restricted daily life in which they endure long periods of "plodding routine" by using the psychological defense mechanism of denial. One person even said as much. Relating to the discomfort of her illness, she stated, "I ignore it like I do most things." The Italians, in comparison, may handle their problems by means of dramatization—a defense mechanism by which they overexpress anxiety and thus dissipate it.

To summarize, which symptom is presented and in what manner is learned within the family. If mothers in certain ethnic groups are accepting of or concerned about a child's complaint and give it extra attention, the child will probably grow up feeling free to express this complaint. Indeed, he or she may even use it later (unaware of the underlying motivational factor) to secure the concern and care of a spouse when a little extra reassurance is needed.

In the dependent period of life, a child quickly senses which symptom elicits his mother's concern and which is sloughed off as unimportant. In addition, he is positively or negatively reinforced in regard to the amount of complaining he does. Findings of a medical sociologist revealed that Jewish and Italian mothers were seen by their children as overprotective and overly concerned about their health.[17] This was supported by a study of 2,000 randomly chosen Army inductees, the results of which showed that the greatest number of symptoms were reported by the Italian and Jewish respondents.[18] These results have been used to suggest that "sensitivity to and concern with physical symptoms may be a general cultural trait of Jewish populations.[19]

It follows from this that children also learn the vocabulary to use in describing their discomfort; this affects the way in which they present their symptoms to the physician. In a classic study of patients in ear, nose, and throat clinics, Zola concluded that *the way in which patients presented their symptoms* to the examining physicians evidently *influenced how the physicians perceived, diagnosed, and treated them.*[20] The three ethnic groups in this study were the Italians, Irish, and those called Anglo-Saxons. In looking at the records of the cases in which there was *no medical basis* for symptoms, a surprising difference was found in the diagnoses: 11 of the 12 Italians in this category were reported by physicians as having a psychological problem; only 2 Anglo-Saxons out of 4 and 2 Irish out of 9 received this diagnosis. It is notable that the 2 Anglo-Saxons in which a psychogenic cause was diagnosed exhibited the most obvious psychopathology of the entire sample of 200 patients; one actually presented herself as being "mentally ill" and the other "reeled in," unsteady on her feet, with common signs of drunkenness. Zola's conclusion was:

Since psychosocial problems were equally present in all groups, there was no reason to expect one of the three ethnic groups to have more diagnoses in the "psychogenesis implied" category. Thus one can only conclude that the patient's ethnic background, which influenced the way she presented herself and her complaint, may have inordinately and inappropriately influenced the diagnosis by the examining physician.[20]

It is important that the examining physician be aware of what is considered normal by various ethnic groups when describing their state of health. What one population considers the proper way to present a health complaint may be thought by another to be overly dramatic, bordering on the hysterical, and indicative of emotional disturbance.

Another point to be mentioned here is that in certain ethnocultural groups, expression of emotional distress is discouraged. Members of these groups may have learned that difficulty in handling an emotional problem is a sign of weakness and that they will be ridiculed or deprecated if they express their fears and anxieties. Thus, they may learn to express their unhappiness or worries in somatic terms. Their physical complaints, usually of a diffuse nature, are ones which the physician has a difficult time explaining. They are frequently asking for help with stress of a social nature but are unable to express it in those terms.

Previous investigators, in coming to the conclusion that "the threshold of pain is more or less the same for all human beings, regardless of sex, age or nationality," provided the basis for the investigation of pain in terms of differential ethnic responses.[17] Zborowski undertook this study among patients in a large metropolitan Veterans Administration hospital.[17] The ethnic groups represented were Irish, Italian, Jewish, and "Old American" (defined as "white, native-born individuals, usually Protestant, whose grandparents, at least, were born in the United States and who do not identify themselves with any foreign group"). The conclusion of the study was that those of similar cultural backgrounds respond to pain in a similar way and that these responses are learned by children on the basis of approval or disapproval by family members.

In the VA hospital where Zborowski observed patients, the Italians and Jews moaned, cried, complained, and called for help. They expected sympathy and assistance. The Irish and "Old Americans," by contrast, were more reserved in their reactions. Unfortunately, most of the health professionals in the hospital were of "Old American" stock and interpreted the Italian and Jewish behavior as exaggerated and overly emotional. Rather than giving the hoped-for sympathy, the nurses and physicians reacted negatively. Zborowski recorded many cases in which Jewish and Italian patients who expressed pain in "overexaggerated" and "overemotional" ways were identified as "mental" and sent to the psychiatric ward.

Whether symptoms are considered "serious" or "inconsequential" also depends on ethnic membership and socialization within a particular group. In field work among five ethnic groups in inner-city Miami (described earlier), mothers were asked whether they or any members of their families had (in the preceding 12 months) experienced any of the symptoms on a 22-item list. The results were interesting: The three most frequent symptoms were the same for the Bahamians, Cubans, American blacks, and Puerto Ricans, i.e., cough, fever, and aches and pains. The surprise was the Haitians, whose most frequently cited symptoms were cough, tiredness, and loss of appetite. The reason these symptoms were recalled and listed by members of this particular ethnic group may be due to the fact that tuberculosis is still one of the leading causes of death in Haitians over 1 year old. Cough, tiredness, and loss of appetite are realistic causes for concern in every Haitian family and may be remembered long after someone complains of a pain or feeling hot.

Results from the same Miami study revealed another finding of interest here. A difference was noted in the numbers of symptoms exhibited by respondents in different ethnic samples. For example, the Puerto Rican mothers volunteered significantly more symptoms for their families than did the black American mothers. It was not believed that this necessarily indicated that the Puerto Ricans actually suffered from more symptoms. Instead, the investigators suggested that it was a reflection of the way children are "taught" to react to illness and the ways in which mothers respond to their children's physical complaints. A Puerto Rican mother is typically very protective of her children and voices great concern if they appear ill. Children learn that it is perfectly acceptable to share feelings of illness within their families. On the other hand, though caring just as deeply for her children, the black American mother discourages complaints (in much the same way as white Anglo mothers do): "Don't be a baby! Don't run to me with every little thing!"

A physician, knowing that a black American mother may feel that a child is a "complainer" if he talks about all his symptoms, might want to encourage the child to talk more during the history about how he feels in order to get the complete picture. Similarly, medical personnel might not want to accept the Haitian patient's history at "face value" and without question, knowing that certain symptoms are realistically dangerous in Haiti and may take on greater importance in the patient's eyes than others of equal medical concern.

CULTURALLY RELATED DIFFERENCES IN THE INCIDENCE OF DISEASE

Most of us today are aware of the role played in many diseases by racial factors (characterized by genetic differences) and ethnic factors (characterized by cultural differences). Tay-Sachs disease, which is associated with the U.S. Jewish population, and sickle cell disease, which is linked to persons of African or Southeast Asian descent, may be the first to come to mind. McKusick has prepared two tables that present the differential ethnic prevalence of inherited disorders (Table 10-1) and multifactorial disorders (Table 10-2).[21] The latter conditions are ones in which either complex genetics may be found or genetic factors are not yet proved. Disorders linked to specific racial/cultural groups may be due to both genetic and cultural factors, each working separately or in association with each other. These tables have been modified to show only those disorders that are commonly recognized by medical personnel.

TABLE 10–1.—THE ETHNICITY OF DISEASE: SIMPLY
INHERITED DISORDERS

ETHNIC GROUP	RELATIVELY HIGH FREQUENCY	RELATIVELY LOW FREQUENCY
Ashkenazi Jews	Bloom's syndrome Niemann-Pick disease Spongy degeneration of brain Stub thumbs Tay-Sachs disease	Phenylketonuria
Mediterranean peoples (Italians, Greeks, Sephardic Jews)	Thalassemia (mainly β) G6PD* deficiency, Mediterranean type Familial Mediterranean fever	Cystic fibrosis
Africans	Hemoglobinopathies, especially HbS, HbC, α- and β-thalassemia, persistent HbF G6PD deficiency, African type Adult lactase deficiency	Cystic fibrosis Hemophilia Phenylketonuria
Chinese	G6PD deficiency, Chinese type Adult lactase deficiency	
Armenians	Familial Mediterranean fever	G6PD deficiency
Finns	Congenital nephrosis	Phenylketonuria

From McKusick V.: *Isr. J. Med. Sci.* 9(9–10):1376, 1973.
*G6PD = glucose-6-phosphate dehydrogenase.

A few remarks concerning several disorders in each group may stimulate the reader to dig deeper into this fascinating and as yet largely unexplored territory. Just as certain language similarities that appear in groups now widely separated indicate a common cultural link in the past, so can rare recessive genes indicate a genetic affinity between groups. We see this in the widely separated Athabaskan Indians of Alaska and the Navajo Indians (residents of the southwestern United States) who share not only the Athabaskan language grouping but also a disorder resulting from deficiency of the enzyme methemoglobin reductase.

In Table 10–2, the fact that skin cancer, osteoporosis, and fractures of the hip and spine are seen so infrequently among Afro-Americans has been related to the protective pigmentation of their skin and their heavier bone structure.[21] Comparison of responses to alcohol between Caucasians and numerous other ethnic groups have been reported by (1) Fenna et al., who describe less rapid metabolization of ethanol by Canadian Eskimos and Indians,[22] and (2) Wolff, who noted marked facial flushing and symptoms of intoxication earlier among Japanese, Taiwanese, and Koreans than among Caucasians.[23]

Graham and Reeder suggest that ethnicity is implicated in the epidemiology of numerous diseases because of the homogeneity within ethnic groups of such things as diet, education, hygiene, and religious practices.[24] The finding that Polish-Americans are at high risk for cancer of the esophagus and lungs, whereas Italian-Americans are more frequently victims of cancer of the bladder, large intestine, and pharynx, has motivated research into the dietary and drinking habits of these groups. An unusually low rate of cervical cancer has been found among Jewish and Moslem women. The Jewish religious prac-

TABLE 10-2.—THE ETHNICITY OF DISEASE: DISORDERS WITH COMPLEX GENETICS OR IN WHICH GENETIC FACTORS ARE NOT PROVED

ETHNIC GROUP	HIGH FREQUENCY	LOW FREQUENCY
Ashkenazi Jews	Diabetes mellitus Hyperuricemia Ulcerative colitis and regional enteritis Kaposi's sarcoma Buerger's disease Leukemia	Cervical cancer Tuberculosis Alcoholism
Irish	Major central nervous system malformations (anencephaly, encephalocele)	
Northern Europeans	Pernicious anemia	
Chinese	Nasopharyngeal cancer	
Japanese	Cleft lip–palate Cerebrovascular accidents Gastric carcinoma Gallbladder carcinoma (in females) Pulseless disease (in females)	Otosclerosis Acne vulgaris Breast cancer Chronic lymphatic leukemia
Filipinos	Hyperuricemia (in United States)	
Polynesians (Hawaiians)	Clubfoot Coronary heart disease Diabetes mellitus	
Africans	Polydactyly Sarcoidosis Tuberculosis Hypertension Esophageal cancer Uterine fibroids Corneal arcus Cervical cancer Keloids Lupus erythematosus, systemic	Major central nervous system malformations (anencephaly, encephalocele) Multiple sclerosis Skin cancer Osteoporosis and fracture of hip and spine Gallstones Psoriasis Emphysema Chronic myeloid leukemia Legg-Perthes disease Duodenal ulcer
American Indians and Mexicans	Gallbladder disease Diabetes mellitus Tuberculosis Cleft lip–palate	
American Indians, Lapps, North Italians	Congenital dislocation of hip	
Icelanders	Glaucoma	
Eskimos	Salivary gland tumors, otitis, deafness	

From McKusick V.: *Isr. J. Med. Sci.*: 9(9–10):1377, 1973.

tice of circumcision, and hygienic practices among Jewish and Moslem men have been suggested as reasons for this finding. The results of the studies in the literature have been somewhat contradictory, however. Neither male circumcision nor Jewish and Moslem hygienic practices have clearly been shown to be critical factors. Yet to be disproved is the possibility that Jews may possess genes that provide protection against cervical cancer. The fact that this type of cancer is found so rarely in these two ethnic groups has been the basis for the investigations of other variables including age at intercourse and marriage and number of sex partners.[24]

There are undoubtedly many more disorders linked in some way to either racial or cultural factors, but we will not discover these unless ethnic membership is carefully recorded with diagnoses on medical records and such relationships are analyzed. An illustration of this is a study in New York that unexpectedly provided evidence that Puerto Ricans are at high risk for myopia. It began with the invention of a device to test vision called an Ophthalmetron, which was used to evaluate students in fourth-grade classes in several New York City schools. Fortunately, ethnicity and diagnosis were both recorded during the study. The unexpected finding by the investigators was that a significantly higher incidence of myopia occurred among the Puerto Ricans (31% for boys and 44% for girls) than among the black Americans and white Anglos.[25] The New York school system is now alerted to the need to test this high-risk group (the Puerto Rican children) before or on entering first grade.

Some of the most interesting current research compares the incidence of a particular disease in the "home" country with the incidence among migrants from that country now living in the United States. Does it remain the same for the migrant group, lending support to a genetic predisposition, or does it change, sustaining the implication of cultural factors (e.g., diet, occupation, physical activity)? Gordon reported a surprising differential in mortality from cardiovascular disease between Japanese in Japan and persons of Japanese descent living in the United States.[26] He found that the death rates of male residents of Japan (aged 55-64) due to heart disease were approximately half the rates for persons of Japanese descent living in the United States. This finding has been followed up by a study of the health of Japanese-Americans who live in northern California.[27] From this study, it appears that "the increase in CHD (coronary heart disease) rates amongst Japanese-Americans cannot be accounted for solely by differences in dietary intake, nor by differences in any of the other known biological risk factors for CHD."[27] The findings *do* show that those Japanese in the United States who have the highest degree of maintenance of the traditional Japanese way of life (the least assimilated into the American culture) have a CHD rate very similar to that of the Japanese in Japan. In contrast, those Japanese with the greater degree of acculturation into the American life-style have the greater prevalence of CHD. The *least* acculturated group has a rate *five times less* than that of the *most* acculturated Japanese.[27]

CULTURE-BOUND SYNDROMES

There are some illnesses that have no genetic basis but are restricted to certain ethnocultural groups. These are called culture-bound (or ethnic-specific) syndromes because they are recognized and defined only in a particular culture or cultural area of the world. They have been defined as "folk illnesses"—"syndromes from which members of a particular cultural group claim to suffer and for which the culture provides the etiological explanation, diagnostic criteria, preventive measures and regimens of healing."[28] Frequently cured by folk practitioners who attribute their skill in healing to a God-given gift or to knowledge gained during apprenticeship to those who are more powerful and experienced, these syndromes are not thought to be amenable to scientific, orthodox medication—"Doctors do not understand them."

This section contains a discussion of some examples of culture-bound syndromes described among ethnic groups in this country. These syndromes are important because their manifestations can be confused with illnesses recognized within the orthodox system. This may result in misdiagnosis and mistreatment that, at the least, can cause lack of trust and confidence and, at worst, can have tragic results. It is important for medical personnel to recognize that these syndromes are not simply an odd collection of superstitions but are useful within a culture to (1) provide a means of social control and (2) alleviate anxieties that build up within a social group and, if allowed to continue unchecked, might have more serious repercussions.

Within the health belief system that provides the context for culture-bound syndromes among the Mexican-Americans, folk illnesses have been classified into three types.[29] (These are also known within the Cuban and Puerto Rican populations, but in somewhat varied form.)

1. *Certain folk diseases are thought to have a "natural" origin.*—**Empacho** has been described as the "failure of the digestive system to pass a chunk of food through the intestinal tract."[5] (It is also related to "slow digestion" and "poor digestion" within the Miami Cuban community.) The cause is often related to conflict or stress, as in a situation where a guest is invited by the host to eat but does not want to and cannot refuse without appearing to be impolite.

2. *Some folk illnesses are thought to have an emotional origin.*—To Mexicans, the mind-body dichotomy of Western medicine does not exist. Instead, there is a continual interaction between psyche and soma, and emotion is commonly thought to influence one's physical well-being. **Susto** is an example of this. (Cubans and Puerto Ricans also experience *susto*, but in these populations it is not thought to have the serious consequences attributed to it by Mexican-Americans.) Almost any emotionally disturbing experience can bring on *susto*: an unexpected noise, an accident, or the experience of anger or fear (sometimes even acute embarrassment). These incidents can cause one's soul (or spirit) to leave the body and bring about physical disability; listlessness, loss of appetite, stomachache, diarrhea, high temperature, and vomiting are all possible symptoms. Recognized early, these can be treated fairly simply by a folk healer's use of psychotherapy and a ritual designed to bring the wandering soul back to the body. Before this ritual, the healer and the patient talk over the situation in which *susto* has occurred and the feelings that might have been involved. During the ritual, the healer prays calmly and quietly, and the climax takes place when the healer suddenly emits a shower of water or other liquid from his mouth, "bathing" the patient's face. The patient "feels" that his wandering spirit has returned to his body; he "begins to feel whole once again."[5] When the condition of *susto* is not recognized early in its appearance, it can become alarmingly serious and require intense treatment. If completely untreated, death can occur by slow "wasting away" of the victim. This later stage has very practical implications for the delivery of health care to Mexican-Americans because it can be confused with tuberculosis by those health professionals who are unfamiliar with it as a culture-bound syndrome.[5]

3. *Several folk diseases are thought to have a magical origin.*—**Mal de ojo** (the evil eye) is a culturally defined illness that is widespread throughout Spanish America. It is thought to have a magical cause in that certain individuals can bring harm to others (especially children) by looking at them (a compliment such as "What a beautiful child" is particularly hazardous), although not necessarily with malice. However, several writers have linked the action to feelings of covetousness and envy on the part of the person producing the illness.[5] This is another condition in which stressful social relations can endanger the equilibrium of the individual.

The symptoms of the evil eye vary somewhat according to national origin but can include fever, vomiting, diarrhea, abnormal crying, loss of weight or appetite, and restlessness[29-31] The treatment of *mal de ojo* (as well as *susto*) is seen as restoring the harmony within the individual and within his social relationships. First, the patient is quieted and enveloped in a therapeutic atmosphere in which are collected those who are most deeply concerned about him. The "monotone of prayer," "the relaxed ministrations of the healer," and the recreating of and conversation about the episode in which the "shock" or "loss" was incurred all conspire to restore balance within the individual and between him and his social group.[5]

Magical amulets are helpful in protecting against *mal de ojo*, and in every clinic with Spanish-speaking patients, one sees a black stone *(azabache)* pinned to a baby's garment or on a necklace to ward off the effects of this magic. It is thought that if someone does cast an evil eye at the wearer, the stone will absorb the evil and crack, deflecting the power. That *mal de ojo* is not restricted to Spanish-speaking people or to the rural lower class is attested to in an article by Smith describing folk medicine among Sicilian-Americans in Buffalo, New York.[32] Individuals who reported personal experiences with the evil eye *(malocchio)* were often college graduates, who were sometimes fourth-generation Americans.

Another example of a culture-bound syndrome occurring in a Latin American ethnic group is the "Puerto Rican syndrome." Five patterns of this syndrome have been described. Three were during the field investigation of the Health Ecology Project in Miami:

1. *Mal de pelea* (literally, "the fighting sickness"), characterized by *violent* behavior of an assaultive, destructive nature (a family member may bite or beat another one severely) without any *apparent* reason.

2. *Ataque de nervios* (nervous attack), which resembles an epileptic attack and is characterized by falling to the ground, convulsive movements, hyperventilation, and salivation.

3. "*Suicidal fit*," a suicide attempt described as having a fitlike character, unplanned, and usually involving the ingestion of a poisonous household substance.

Miami field work has added two more (not yet described in the medical literature):

4. *Ataque de risa*, in which the victim literally laughs hysterically for as long as 30 minutes.

5. *La pulga del parto* (literally, "the childbirth flea"), in which the female "acts like she's crazy, *loca*."

The various patterns of the Puerto Rican syndrome share five features: (1) a suddenness of onset and termination, (2) a transient state of partial loss of consciousness, (3) a self-limiting quality (episodes last from a few hours to 3 weeks), (4) an association with occurrences in the individual's social environment, and (5) hyperkinetic behavior. Rubio et al. note that because these patterns of the Puerto Rican syndrome bear clinical resemblance to conditions such as schizophrenia and epilepsy, they "present a problem in medical management and admission disposition."[33] A study by these writers conducted in a military hospital in Puerto Rico illustrates this problem. Sixty-one Puerto Rican patients in the armed services who exhibited the symptoms described for the Puerto Rican syndrome were evacuated from overseas back to the Puerto Rican military hospital with the following diagnoses: 52 as psychotics, 4 as epileptics, and 5 as having character disorders. After observation and tests in Puerto Rico, only 14 of the 52 were confirmed as psychotic, and 3 of the 4 diagnosed epileptics had normal electroencephalograms and were presumed to suffer from hysterical seizures (a term used to describe this is *ataque de nervios*). The 5 cases of character disorders were confirmed.

We believe this type of behavior is an example of the cultural elaboration of a defense mechanism. Another explanation that has appeared in the literature is that it is a hysterical reaction to great anxiety and to a range of minor to severe stresses.[33-38] On a second level, it has been said that the underlying cause of the anxiety that triggers this behavior relates to the inability of the Puerto Ricans generally to handle anger.[36, 39, 40] A third explanation concerns the influence of socialization and child-rearing practices on the development of this syndrome. Rothenberg remarks on two Puerto Rican ideals that are incorporated into socialization practices and that may lead to the angry feelings "so frequently seen in all types of psychiatric illnesses in Puerto Rico": "repression of assertiveness and aggressiveness, and the need to preserve an appearance of outward dignity at the expense of inner psychological needs."[40]

CULTURAL DIFFERENCES IN ETIOLOGIC EXPLANATIONS

In all cultures, therapeutic methods are related to what the cause of illness is thought to be. This is an important fact to keep in mind for those who provide health care to persons from various ethnic populations. If a patient ascribes a cause to an illness that is different from the one assigned to it by the examining physician, the patient's trust in the physician may falter and noncompliance with the prescribed therapeutic regimen may result.

Zola has pointed out that modern scientific etiologic explanations are not so markedly different from those of primitive magic.[41] He notes that both utilize invisible agents to explain ill health: loss of soul, possession by spirits, and witchcraft, on the one hand; filterable viruses, chromosomes, and the unconscious, on the other. While *they* blame mental illness on "the internal struggle of soul and spirit," *we* argue for the struggle between ego, id, and superego. We disparage the claim that sorcery based on hatred and envy can cause sickness, but say "he gives me a pain in the neck" or "she makes me sick to my stomach." Finally, Zola wonders whether there is such a great gulf between "primitive" people searching for "etiological clues in broken taboos, frightening sights, sins of, or offenses to, ancestors," and our equally intensive search into childhood traumas and "the deprivations, feelings and emotions toward and by our parents." Numerous authors have pointed out that many African medical practices are every bit as pragmatic and founded on practical experience as ours are.[42, 43]

The demonic theory of disease (espoused and recorded as early as 1500 B.C. in India, as well as in China, Egypt, and Greece) is one with which we are still acquainted; it has been firmly implanted in Christian thinking in the New Testament of the Bible (from the fourth chapter of St. Matthew on). European history also gives testimony to this etiologic concept; St. Augustine stated that "all diseases are to be ascribed to demons."[43] Witch-hunting continued in both the Old and the New World to the 17th century. Humans everywhere, even today, project human desire and the capacity to harm others onto supernatural powers. These supernatural powers may be seen as gods, spirits, ancestors, or ghosts. Often, among many ethnic groups as well as among the white Anglo population, persons think of illness as God's punishment for sin. Mexican-Americans voice the belief that certain kinds of illness are willed by God as a *castigo* (punishment), while Appalachian whites acknowledge that "the wrath of God may cause ill health which gives the sinner time to contemplate his misdeeds." One black American has said: "So many times we have to be taught a lesson, a sickness sometime bring us down to make us serve the Lord's will. . . . Sickness is like a whuppin'. A reminder."[6]

If a person is sick as a result of God's punishment for his sin, the physician will be unable to cure him. As one Baptist minister was heard to say to his congregation: "Medicine cannot reach the mind, nor a heart diseased by sin."[6] A clinical implication here is that those who believe that their sickness has been visited on them because of their misdeeds may not seek out a physician. They may first go to a faith healer or to a minister who will put them "right" with God.

As mentioned, many ethnic populations in America classify illness as either "natural" or "unnatural." Illness sent by God can be "natural"; that is, it has to do with the world as God made it and He intended it to be.[6] Other illnesses that would be classified as natural are those that have their source in nature (being caught in damp, cold air without suitable protection). Air is seen as a frequent cause of illness among Mexican-Americans and individuals of Caribbean origin. It is thought possible for air, or bad air (*aire* or *mal aire*), to enter body cavities and cause illness. Care is taken, for example, to keep the vagina covered for a prescribed number of days after childbirth to protect against air entering into the body through this opening.

"Unnatural" sicknesses represent the forces of evil and the work of the devil; as such, they are beyond the capability of man to cure. Evil influences (referred to by Spanish-speakers as *malas influencias* and which often connote witchcraft) are thought to cause a wide variety of problems among numerous ethnic groups (among them, Haitian, Bahamians, Puerto Ricans, black Americans, Mexican-Americans, and Cuban-Americans). It has been estimated that one third of the black patients at a southern psychiatric center and one fourth of the patients of a Spanish-speaking physician in California hold the belief that they are victims of witchcraft.[6] That belief in witchcraft (called *vodun* by Haitians, *rootwork* by black Americans, and *brujeria* by Cubans, Puerto Ricans, and Mexican-Americans) is viable among low-income urban ethnic groups received support from a 9-month investigation into folk healers and their patients at the University of Miami School of Medicine. Evil influences are most commonly associated with interpersonal rivalry, jealousy, and envy; these occur most often in connection with a love problem. Wintrob has explained the continued popularity of witchcraft among blacks as reflecting their

socioeconomic and political exclusion . . . from the dominantly white community, along with their corollary sense of powerlessness, futility, and suppressed rage. The greater the uncertainty of people about the chances of achieving socially valued goals, the greater the tendency to seek and accept alternative paths to these goals, magic among them. Within the same theoretical framework it is possible to explain occult practices as a socially approved and valued outlet for the displacement of suppressed rage, characteristic of powerless, excluded social groups living within what the late Oscar Lewis defined as the "culture of poverty."[44]

Wintrob does not see migration to urban areas as decreasing the use of a supernatural explanation of illness.[45] On the contrary, he suggests that the attempts by urban immigrants to cope with the increased stress of urban life with fewer supports from the extended family and a dropping away of traditional methods of enculturation will be followed by a greater reliance on the supernatural.

For those who believe, rootwork can cause not only illness but also death. One account of a psychogenic (voodoo or magical) death at Johns Hopkins was reported in 1971.[46] Numerous explanations of how a belief that one has been rooted (hexed) can actually lead to one's death have been proposed. Walter B. Cannon, a physiologist, explained it in terms of the sympathetic nervous system; the hypothesis of Curt Richter, a psychophysiologist, pointed to the parasympathetic nervous system; and Barbara Lex suggests that death may occur as a result of both systems being activated simultaneously. These physiological explanations, as well as several psychological, social, and cultural ones, are reviewed in "Magical Death Reconsidered: Some Possible Social and Cultural Correlates," a paper presented by David Landy at the American Anthropological Association in 1975.

Clinically, medical personnel can sometimes help patients who fear they may be hexed, but they must first be aware of the symptoms that suggest this possibility ("acting crazy," "feeling bad," loss of weight, depression, sleeplessness, swelling, lack of appetite, and gastrointestinal complaints). The patient will rarely volunteer his fears because he expects ridicule, but he is often relieved to share them when a concerned, sensitive nurse or physician asks, "Do you think something has been done to you?" or "Do you think you've been rooted?"

The Miami investigation findings indicate clearly that the orthodox system is most commonly the first source of help sought for physical symptoms by ethnic group members. In those cases where the patient thinks witchcraft is involved, he hopes that the physician will prove him wrong and provide a medical answer to the problem. In those cases where the patient does *not* think the symptom is caused by evil forces, the physician may inadvertently cause the patient to come to this conclusion. Uncertainty on the part of the physician and suggestions that tests should be made to rule out this or that disease plant a seed of concern in the patient's mind that the symptom may indeed be caused by someone working against him. It is extremely important that the physician assure the patient that his symptoms are curable, if this is true. If the physician determines that the symptoms are psychogenic, he should instigate palliative, supportive measures and accept, without ridicule, tandem treatment by rootworkers or spiritual healers whose job it is to neutralize or remove the spell.

Another explanation that many groups use to help them understand why a particular illness occurs is psychological or physiological imbalance. Many white Anglos account for their sickness by implicating too much or too little food, insufficient rest, or not enough exercise. Our attempts to provide the "right" amount of food, rest, and exercise are reflected in our books, courses, and even television programs on proper diet and exercise. In other countries, achieving the proper physiological balance in the body is also important but is viewed from a different perspective. The idea is commonly held that illness results from an imbalance of elements, humors, or vital forces in the body. Probably originating as a folk explanation in the Mediterranean area, this was common during ancient Egyptian, Greek, and Roman times, eventually becoming known as the "humoral theory," of disease (see chap. 21). This theory, widespread in time and space, is still found in the United States, especially among Spanish-speaking populations. In these ethnic groups, foods, medicinal agents, and illnesses are classified as being "hot" or "cold" (this does not necessarily have any relationship to temperature). If one has an illness that is "hot," the natural balance in the body is restored by counteracting it with a "cold" food or medicine.

The following example from Harwood's paper on what has come to be known as the hot-cold theory illustrates how differing etiologic beliefs held by the physician and patient may influence the patient's compliance.[47] A Puerto Rican woman who is pregnant (considered to be a "hot" condition) and is advised by her physician to take iron supplements and vitamins will probably not comply with this directive. Iron and vitamins are believed to be "hot" also and, in conjunction with the woman's already "hot" condition, will upset the body's natural balance and render her vulnerable to illness. The physician who is aware of her belief in the hot-cold theory will suggest that she take her iron supplements and vitamins *with* fruit juice. Because fruit juice is classified as "cool," it will offset the "hot" iron and vitamins and help to maintain the proper balance of hot and cold in her body. The patient, in all likelihood, will in this case comply with the physician's advice and, furthermore, her trust in his judgment will probably increase.

DIFFERENCES IN CHOICE OF THERAPIES AND THERAPISTS

Most of the social factors that affect whether or not persons will seek treatment and what system of health care they utilize are discussed in chapters 9 and 22. In this chapter, some factors associated with the cultural background of people will be examined. One of these is the degree of health cultural "fit" between the patient and the medical personnel. By health cultural "fit" is meant the extent to which the health beliefs and practices of the patient, on the one hand, and the health care professional, on the other, "match." We have seen that attitudes and beliefs about health matters such as bodily functioning, symptoms, and causes for illness differ among persons from different ethnic groups. Most important, many ethnically based health beliefs are at variance with those held by our scientific system of medicine. When a health-care consumer and provider with similar health cultural backgrounds interact (i.e., a white middle-class Anglo-Saxon patient and a physician from the same cultural group), the problems that arise are not likely to be serious. When the patient comes from a health cultural tradition that is quite dissimilar to that of his physician (as in the case of an American Indian, Haitian, or Vietnamese), however, the misunderstandings that develop can be so many and so basic that both parties often feel dissatisfied with their encounter.

Studies of the differential use of orthodox health-care facilities by various ethnic groups in both New York[48] and Miami[49] have revealed that Puerto Ricans in the two areas have consistently been the group least likely to avail themselves of these services. It is safe to assume that this is due partly to the ethnic mismatch (lack of cultural fit). The Puerto Ricans are not the only ones who may turn to their traditional healers and therapies because of a mismatch of health expectations, beliefs, and behaviors, however. The Appalachian white patient, whose traditional expectation is that a healer is concerned with alleviating emotional as well as physical stress, may well be dissatisfied with an urban physician who treats only the physical symptom and ignores his mental suffering. He may "continue to shop around for new doctors in the city, return to his home in the Southern mountains for treatment, or retreat into the old attitude that doctors are not much help."[7]

Two studies of an Italian community in Boston describe much the same problem there. Spiegal described the dominant American attitude toward health and health care as follows: Each citizen is expected to stay abreast of the latest scientific findings and take responsibility for keeping himself healthy; as for the physician, he is to be impersonal, utilize the newest technical aids when appropriate, and produce a cure rather than comfort. In contrast, for Italian-Americans, who have different cultural values,

illness is something that just happens to people . . . as a part of man's fate. . . . It may happen more often and in a more severe form to some people, either because they are unlucky or a punishment for their evil ways. . . . The doctor's job is to give comfort, relieve pain and suffering, and if everyone is lucky, help nature or supernature effect a cure.[50]

Gans is in agreement that it is this value mismatch that underlies the fact that some Italian-Americans assign the physician a marginal role in their health care. He states that

The [Italians in this community] view illness as resulting either from a breakdown in self-control, or from conditions beyond the individual's control.

The first type is thought to require self- or group-inflicted punishment as part of the treatment. In the second type of illness, the doctor's services may be used, but the possibility of a cure rests to a considerable extent on the workings of fate.[51]

However, the picture is not all negative by any means. In vitually all ethnic populations, it is accepted as common knowledge that there are certain illnesses that physicians can cure more quickly and efficiently than folk healers. In this category are fever, unusual pain, and serious injuries. These problems are usually brought promptly to the physician for treatment. Furthermore, there is evidence from studies of inner-city ethnic groups in Miami that when it is not clear whether an illness is due to unnatural causes (and therefore properly treated by a healer with supernatural help) or to a causal agent readily susceptible to orthodox treatment, the patient commonly presents himself first to the physician for help. This can be interpreted in part as utilization of the orthodox system as a diagnostic aid (i.e., to rule out unnatural causes). If the physician cannot produce results in a relatively short time, this is often seen as evidence that "something else" is at work; if he can cure the symptom or condition quickly, so much the better.

In the Miami study of 57 patients (30 Bahamians, 11 black Americans, 10 Cubans, and 6 Puerto Ricans) who described their step-by-step action in response to their current symptom or condition (and who had utilized a folk healer at some point in their illness episode), 27 went first to a private physician and 11 sought help first from a hospital (clinic or emergency room). Fourteen of these went to *both* a private physician and a hospital *before* seeing a folk healer. In other words, 38 (67%) gave the orthodox system first crack at treatment, and 14 of these (25% of the total number of patients) gave it *two* chances.

Those who use folk therapies (e.g., dietary changes, prayer) or folk healers in tandem with treatment by a physician are reacting in an adaptive manner to a stressful situation (illness) that produces anxiety. The herbal teas and rituals give them the same sense of comfort and mastery over this threat in their lives that prayer gives a white Anglo Catholic and that a "chicken soup" remedy gives a Jew. As long as the folk remedy is harmless and does not interfere with the treatment of the patient's disease, the physician is wise to encourage its use.

Other investigations indicate that there may be consultations with healers within the patient's ethnic health-care system before he goes to a physician. Madsen reports that among lower- or middle-class Mexican-American families, if one has a minor illness that does not respond to home remedies, the help of an "experienced" and "knowledgeable" neighbor or *compadre* (a child's godparent) is solicited.[52] If this step does not produce a cure, the family then seeks out a diviner (who can diagnose the ailment) and/or a *curandero* (folk healer). Professional physicians are viewed with suspicion and hostility by conservative members of the lower class, who point out that a curandero "knows" how to treat a patient, but a physician has to consult books and colleagues or rely on x-rays to discover the cause of an ailment; a curandero petitions God and the saints for aid in the cure, but a physician generally ignores the possibility of divine assistance.

The typical physician and nurse fail to achieve the close affective relationship with Mexican-American patients that is so characteristic of curandero-client relationships. The most obvious reason for this failure is the language barrier between Anglo physician or nurse and the Mexican-American patient who speaks little English. A second reason is the authoritarian attitude that the physician and nurse assume with Mexican-American patients. The patient feels that the physician and nurse are not concerned with his welfare, his feelings, and the obligation of his family to be part of the therapeutic activity. As a final insult, the physician may ridicule the patient's self-diagnosis on the basis of folk disease theory. On the other hand, the curandero maintains close relationships with both the client and his family. He patiently explains the cause and nature of the affliction and the reasons behind each step of the treatment. These explanations are meaningful in the context of the Mexican-American value system, and therefore great reliance is placed on them. The curandero often uses great skill in manipulating interpersonal relations within the family so as to relieve pressures that produce stress and anxiety in the patient.

The conservative Mexican-American consults a physician only as a last resort, when all other curing techniques have failed. His attitude is comparable to that of an educated Anglo who places his life in the hands of a faith healer when his physician has told him his disease is fatal and incurable.

In regard to this topic, the findings from the Value Orientation Scale[53] administered to Amish, Italians, and white Anglos in Pennsylvania,[54] and from a modified version of the scale administered in Miami, are of interest. The theory underlying this instrument is that there are five common problems in life to which *every* culture must devise a solution, and, further, that there are only three possible solutions to each. Among the three ethnic groups in Pennsylvania and five groups in Miami, the results from the scale indicated that there is a cultural pattern in the responses to every problem area *except* that of health. In this area, respondents showed not only a reluctance to put all their eggs in one health basket, as it were, but also a willingness to try several approaches to health care. The fact that these individuals with varied ethnic backgrounds clearly chose to be pragmatic in their health behavior suggests that health professionals should not feel that they must *change* the health beliefs and practices of their patients. The values that guide health behavior can evidently support a wide range of health practices, both orthodox and otherwise.*

SUMMARY

Culture can be defined as an adaptive mechanism consisting of all the beliefs, be-

---

*This point is made in the Miami Health Ecology Project Report, vol. II, by Janice Egeland.

haviors, and values that are useful to a particular group. Throughout history, cultural groups have responded to the needs of their members for such things as shelter, food, communication, and health care by developing specific ways of dealing with these issues. The cultural solutions to life's problems have often been arrived at empirically, by trial and error.

As children, all of us acquire health-related beliefs and practices from our contact with members of our particular social class and ethnic or cultural group. Because ways of coping with illness are learned at an early age, they tend to remain with us in adult life as deeply ingrained concepts. We accept them as being true or correct. Included as part of our health culture are notions about our body and how it functions, and ideas that can affect our perception and interpretation of bodily sensations. Whether we regard a sensation as being indicative of ill health and the type of action we take in response to it are determined to a large extent by culturally derived health beliefs.

Culture influences the manner in which a patient presents himself to the physician. As a result of their experiences as children, individuals from some ethnic groups express their emotional reactions to illness openly and freely, while others are reserved and stoic. It is important that the physician be aware of the basis for these differences so that he does not misinterpret the behavior of his patients. For example, someone who has been taught to express himself freely may be incorrectly regarded as a "complainer" unless his cultural background is taken into consideration.

Culture is a determinant of the incidence of disease. This influence is exerted through the effects of culture on diet, occupation, lifestyle, health-care practices, mating patterns, and other psychosocial factors. The occurrence of a special category of illness, culture-bound syndromes, is closely linked to the cultural environment.

Of great importance are patients' ideas concerning the cause of illness because these concepts often determine what kind of treatment is sought and whether there will be compliance with a suggested therapeutic regimen. When the concepts held by patients are at variance with the scientific ideas of medical personnel, serious disagreements can arise that adversely affect the patient's care. Thus, it is essential that a physician caring for patients of ethnic groups other than his own be as knowledgeable as possible about their views of the cause of disease.

REFERENCES

1. Weidman H., Egeland J.A.: A behavioral science perspective in the comparative approach to the delivery of health care. *Soc. Sci. Med.* 7:845, 1973.
2. Clark M.: *Health in the Mexican-American Culture*. Berkeley, University of California Press, 1970.
3. Fabrega H., Manning P.K.: An integrated theory of disease: Ladino-Mestizo views of disease in the Chiapas Highlands. *Psychosom. Med.* 35(3):223, 1973.
4. Pearsall M.: *Little Smoky Ridge: The Natural History of a Southern Appalachian Neighborhood*. Birmington, Al., University of Alabama Press, 1959.
5. Rubel A.J.: Concepts of disease in Mexican-American culture. *Am. Anthropologist* 62(5): 795, 1960.
6. Snow L.: Folk medical beliefs and their implications for care of patients. *Ann. Intern. Med.* 81(4):82, 1974.
7. Stekert E.J.: Focus for conflict: Southern Mountain medical beliefs in Detroit, in Paredes A., Stekert E.J. (eds.): *The Urban Experience and Folk Tradition*. Austin, University of Texas Press, 1971.
8. Scott C.S.: The relationship between beliefs about the menstrual cycle and choice of fertility regulating methods within five ethnic groups. *Int. J. Gynaecol. Obstet.* 13:105–109, 1975.
9. Rainwater L.: *Behind Ghetto Walls*. Chicago, Aldine Publishing Company, 1970.
10. Neugarten B.: *Personality in Middle and Late Life*. New York, Atherton Press, 1964.
11. Rosenblatt D., Suchman E.: The under-utilization of medical-care services by blue-collarites, in Shostak A.B., Gomberg W. (eds.): *Blue Collar World: Studies of the American Worker*. Englewood Cliffs, N.J., Prentice-Hall, Inc., 1964.
12. Weidman H.H., et al.: *Miami Health Ecology Report*. Dept. of Psychiatry, University of Miami School of Medicine, vol. 1, 1978.

13. Scott C.S.: The theoretical significance of a sense of well-being, in Bauwens E. (ed.): *The Anthropology of Health*. St. Louis, C. V. Mosby Co., 1978, pp. 79–87.
14. Scott C.S.: Competing health care systems in an inner city area (brief communications). *Hum. Organ.* 34(1), Spring, 1975, pp. 108–110.
15. Trumbull H.C.: *The Blood Covenant*. Philadelphia, J.T. Wattles Co., 1893.
16. Zola I.K.: Culture and symptoms—An analysis of patients' presenting complaints. *Am. Sociol. Rev.* 31(5):615, 1966.
17. Zborowski M.: Cultural components in response to pain, in Apple D. (ed.): *Sociological Studies of Health and Sickness*. New York, McGraw-Hill Book Co., 1960.
18. Croog S.H.: Ethnic origins, educational level, and responses to a health questionnaire. *Hum. Organ.* 20:65, 1961.
19. Mechanic D.: Religion, religiosity and illness behavior: The special case of the Jews. *Hum. Organ.* 22:202, 1963.
20. Zola I.K.: Problems of communication, diagnosis and patient care: The interplay of patient, physician and clinic organization. *J. Med. Educ.* 38:829, 1963.
21. McKusick V.: Ethnic distribution of disease in non-Jews. *Isr. J. Med. Sci.* 9(9–10):1375–77, 1973.
22. Fenna D., Mix L., Schaefer O., et al.: Ethanol metabolism in various racial groups. *Can. Med. Assoc. J.* 105:472, 1971.
23. Wolff P.H.: Ethnic differences in alcohol sensitivity. *Science* 175:449, 1972.
24. Graham S., Reeder L.G.: Social factors in chronic disease, in Freeman H., Levine S., Reeder L.G. (eds.): *Handbook of Medical Sociology*. Englewood Cliffs, N.J., Prentice-Hall, Inc., 1972.
25. Safir A., Kulikowski C., Deuschle K.: Automatic refraction: How it is done: Some clinical results. *Sight-Sav. Rev.* 43:137, 1973.
26. Gordon T.: Mortality experience among the Japanese in the United States, Hawaii, and Japan. *Public Health Rep.* 72:543, 1957.
27. Marmot M., Syme S.L.: Culture, Disease and Acculturation in Japanese Men. Read before the 74th annual meeting of the American Anthropological Association, San Francisco, December 1975.
28. Rubel A.J.: The epidemiology of a folk illness: *Susto* in Hispanic America. *Ethnology* 3:268, 1964.
29. Tharp R., Meadow A.: Differential change in folk disease concepts. *Interam. J. Psychol.* 7(1–2):55, 1973.
30. Baca J.: Some health beliefs of the Spanish-speaking. *Am. J. Nurs.* 69(10):2172, 1969.
31. Foster G.M.: Relationships between Spanish and Spanish-American folk medicine. *J. Am. Folklore* 66:201, 1953.
32. Smith E.: Folk medicine among the Sicilian-Americans of Buffalo, New York. *Urban Anthropol.* 1(1):87, 1972.
33. Rubio M., Urdaneta M., Doyle J.L.: Psychopathic reaction patterns in the Antilles command. *U.S. Armed Forces Medical Journal* 6(part 2):1767, 1955.
34. Fernandez-Marina R.: The Puerto Rican syndrome: Its dynamics and cultural determinants. *Psychiatry* (brief communication) 24:79, 1961.
35. Maldonado-Sierra E., Trent R.: The sibling relationship in group psychotherapy with Puerto Rican schizophrenics. *Am. J. Psychiatry* 117:239, 1960.
36. Leavitt R.R.: *The Puerto Ricans*. Viking Fund Publication in Anthropology, No. 51. Tucson, University of Arizona Press, 1974.
37. Berle E.: *Eighty Puerto Rican Families in New York City*. New York: Columbia University Press, 1958.
38. Padilla E.: *Up from Puerto Rico*. New York, Columbia University Press, 1958.
39. Mehlman R.D.: The Puerto Rican syndrome. *Am. J. Psychiatry* 118:328, 1961.
40. Rothenberg A.: Puerto Rico and aggression. *Am. J. Psychiatry* 120:962, 1964.
41. Zola I.K.: The concept of trouble and sources of medical assistance—to whom can one turn, with what and why. *Soc. Sci. Med.* 6:673–679, 1972.
42. Harley G.W.: *Native African Medicine*. Cambridge, Mass., Harvard University Press, 1941.
43. Amorin J.K.E.: The notion of the prevention of disease in the African traditional thinking. Bulletin of the International Union against Tuberculosis, 1968 Meetings, vol. 62, August 1969.
44. Wintrob R.: Hexes, roots, snake eggs? M.D. vs. occult. *Med. Opinion* 1(7):54, 1972.
45. Wintrob R.: The influence of others: Witchcraft and rootwork as explanations of behavior disturbances. *J. Nerv. Ment. Dis.* 156(5):318, 1973.
46. Webb J.Y.: Louisiana voodoo and superstitions related to health. *HSMHA Health Reports* 86(4):291, 1971.
47. Harwood A.: The hot-cold theory of disease. *J.A.M.A.* 216(7):1153, 1971.
48. Suchman E.A.: Sociomedical variations among ethnic groups. *Am. J. Sociol.* 70:319, 1964.
49. Scott C.S.: Health and healing practices among five ethnic groups in Miami, Florida. *Public Health Rep.* 89(6):524, 1974.
50. Spiegal J.P.: Cultural variations in attitudes to-

ward death and disease, in Grosser E., et al. (eds.): *The Threat of Impending Disaster*. Cambridge, Mass., M.I.T. Press, 1971.
51. Gans H.: *The Urban Villager*. New York, The Free Press of Glencoe, 1962.
52. Madsen W.: *Mexican-Americans of South Texas*. New York, Holt, Rinehart and Winston, Inc., 1964.
53. Kluckhohn F., Strodtbeck F.: *Variations in Value Orientation*. New York, Row, Peterson & Co., 1961.
54. Egeland J.A.: Belief and behavior as related to illness, unpublished doctoral dissertation, Yale University, 2 vols., 1967.

11 / Life-Styles and Health

MARC SILBRET, M.D., NEIL SCHNEIDERMAN, Ph.D., AND
JONATHAN J. BRAUNSTEIN, M.D.

STUDYING THE EFFECTS of life-style on health helps to bring into sharper focus the clinical relevance of the material in chapters 9 and 10, and to demonstrate why health professionals should be conversant with these sociological and anthropological concepts. In this chapter, we will examine a group of diseases whose incidence is specifically related to environment and life-style and discuss how they can be prevented through the reduction or elimination of adverse factors.

LIFE-STYLE IN OUR MODERN URBAN SOCIETY

What do we mean by the term *life-style?* In its broadest sense, this refers to the many experiences and events that make up the daily pattern of living of an individual, including:

1. Where he lives and the conditions of his home environment
2. What type of work he does and the conditions surrounding this activity
3. The food he eats and drinks
4. His personal habits (e.g., smoking, drinking, use of drugs)
5. The degree of physical activity in which he engages
6. The kinds of recreational activities in which he participates
7. His associates, that is, his family and friends

All are vital components of an individual's life-style and also play an important role in determining his state of health.[1]

The technological advancement of our country in this century has greatly altered human life. Clearly, the life-style of the majority of our present population differs markedly from what it was 100 or 200 years ago when our society was agrarian. This difference can still be seen when comparing the patterns of living of those in the urban and rural areas of our country. Similarly, the life-style that characterizes urban America differs considerably from that found in Asian and African countries that have yet to participate in the modern technological revolution. To a large extent, the changes that have come with industrialization have benefited our population, for nowhere in the world do people live in such affluence. On the other hand, these changes have brought with them new threats to our health. In the ensuing discussion, we will be examining some ways in which industrialization and technology have adversely affected the well-being of our population.

Air Pollution[2]

Atmospheric pollution is a prominent side effect of technological advancement and industrialization. The chemical toxins in the air we breathe cause acute irritation of the lungs and exposed mucous membranes. Low-level chronic exposure to atmospheric pollution has been implicated as a factor in the cause of certain types of cancer and chronic respiratory diseases such as emphysema and asthma. Higher mortality in urban versus rural areas due to several kinds of respiratory and gastrointestinal cancer has been demonstrated in both the United States and England. This suggests that contaminants, perhaps in the air, are important factors in the cause of these disorders.

An increased incidence of bronchial asthma has been found in the highly industrialized areas of Japan, the United States, and Great Britain. Chronic bronchitis, which is unusually prevalent in England, has been associated with air pollution in the following ways. First, during acute episodes of air pollution, there is a flare-up of symptoms in persons who have chronic bronchitis.[2] Second, on days of atmospheric inversion and large amounts of pollution, an abnormally high mortality occurs in these individuals.

Two types of air pollution can be distinguished. The first includes photochemical smog, ozone, and other oxidants, which are formed from hydrocarbons and oxides of nitrogen in the presence of sunlight. Although a serious nuisance, the chronic effects of this type of air pollution on health have yet to be clearly demonstrated. The second category of air pollutants is the sulfur oxides. When industrial and domestic combustion of coal is extensive, high levels of sulfur dioxide, sulfates, and even droplets of sulfuric acid are found in the air. These agents are suspected of contributing to the relatively high morbidity and mortality due to respiratory illnesses found in the densely populated and industrialized areas of Great Britain. While high concentrations in the air of these agents alone may not be sufficient to irritate the respiratory tree directly, the adverse effects of sulfur oxides in the presence of small-particle aerosols have been demonstrated in laboratory animals.

Occupational exposure to particulate matter in the air may cause serious illness. The "classic" disease of this type is silicosis, which typically develops in miners, iron and steel workers, and sandblasters who are exposed to silica dust. When inhaled into the lungs, this substance acts as an irritant, producing a fibrotic tissue reaction that, in some cases, results in severe lung disease. In recent years, attention has been focused on the injurious effects of asbestos, a fibrous mineral used in many diverse industries in this country and abroad. Statistics indicate that people engaged in occupations in which asbestos is used have a higher incidence of lung cancer and mesothelioma (a malignant tumor of the lining cells of the pleural or peritoneal space).[3] This group of workers is also at risk of developing chronic lung disease.

Radiation

Radiation exposure is another problem that has accompanied the development of modern technology. The effect of radiation on tissue is largely related to whether the radiation possesses sufficient energy to produce ionization. Hence, a distinction is made between nonionizing and ionizing radiation.

NONIONIZING RADIATION. — The wavelengths of nonionizing radiation range from long radio waves of about 500 m, through the spectrum of visible light, and down to near ultraviolet, which is about 1,700 Å. A primary effect of these types of radiation is to produce heat when absorbed. Penetration is directly related to wavelength, with ultraviolet rays being completely absorbed in the superficial layers of the skin. Changes in human skin leading to certain forms of skin cancer appear to be a function of the amount of ultraviolet radiation received from the sun. The degree of exposure to this type of radiation depends on the state of the earth's atmosphere. Recently it has been discovered that the discharge of fluorinated hydrocarbons, which are commonly used as propellants for aerosol sprays (i.e., hair sprays, perfumes), into the air destroys the ozone layer of the atmosphere. Since this layer acts as a protective "screen" to filter out the damaging ultraviolet rays from the sun, its destruction has a potential for resulting in serious skin disease. Because of this, the government has taken action to ban the use of fluorocarbon propellants.

Infrared or microwave radiation penetrates increasingly deeper in proportion to its wavelength. Radar and radiotransmission equipment are the major generators of heat-producing microwaves. These microwaves may adversely affect (1) the lens of the eye, which because of its lack of vascularity is unable to dissipate heat adequately, and (2) gonadal tissue, which has high sensitivity to heat. Prevention is effective if exposure is minimized and protective clothing and goggles are worn.

IONIZING RADIATION.—In contrast to non-ionizing radiation, ionizing radiation possesses sufficient energy to split atoms into positive and negative ions as it passes through air and tissue. The greatest medical interest is in (1) very high frequency electromagnetic waves such as x-rays and gamma rays, and (2) high-velocity neutrons, alpha and beta particles. Gamma rays and x-rays are highly penetrating, whereas alpha particles, which are positively charged helium nuclei, produce minimal penetration but dense ionization and tissue injury. Beta particles are electrons that can pass through several millimeters of tissue but create low ion density. Finally, neutrons can pass through more than a centimeter of tissue and unite with protons upon collision to produce ions and isotopes.

Absorption of radioactivity is expressed in ergs per gram (energy per amount of tissue). The roentgen (R), which is a measure of the absorption of gamma and x-irradiation in air, is 83 ergs/gm. A roentgen equivalent in man (Rem) is the quantity of radiation of any kind (alpha particles, beta particles, neutrons) that produces the same biologic effects in man as those resulting from the absorption of 1 R of gamma or x-irradiation. Another unit, the radiation absorbed dose (rad), which is equivalent to 100 ergs/gm, is slightly greater than the roentgen in air but is approximately equal to the roentgen in body tissue. Because high-energy particles cause more damage to biologic tissue than gamma or x-rays for a given amount of radiation energy, a relative biologic effectiveness (RBE) rating can be combined with the pure energy rating (roentgen or rad) to provide an index of biologic injury.

Cataracts, for example, can be caused by either gamma or neutron irradiation. For equivalent quantities of radiation energy absorption (in rad), however, the biologic injury caused by neutrons is ten times more severe. An RBE of 10 is assigned to neutrons in cataract formation, whereas an RBE of 1 is assigned to gamma rays.

Radiation causes biologic damage by disrupting cellular macromolecules. This can lead to cellular death, to the alteration of chromosomal material, or to a delay in mitosis. The basis of cancer radiotherapy is that rapidly dividing cells are most sensitive to radiation injury. Thus, in cancer radiotherapy the rapidly dividing cancer cells are highly vulnerable, whereas normal tissue is somewhat less vulnerable.

Given sufficient dose, rate of exposure, and lowered oxygen tension, normal as well as cancer tissue can, of course, also be destroyed. The most susceptible normal tissues are the gastrointestinal epithelium, skin, gonadal cells, and blood-forming cells. Acute radiation sickness, which reflects injury to these susceptible tissues, causes symptoms of epilation (loss of hair), diarrhea, petechia (small purplish, hemorrhagic spots on the skin), and sore throat.

Humans are exposed to natural sources of radioactivity such as cosmic rays and radionuclides including uranium and potassium-40. There is some fear that the use of aerosol propellants, by damaging the ozone layer of the earth's atmosphere, will result in humans being subjected to damaging levels of radioactivity from the sun. In addition to exposure to natural sources of radioactivity, people are susceptible to additional exposure from medical and other man-made sources. Suggested exposure limits for individuals up to age 30 from other than natural sources is 10 R, 5 R of which are expected to be from cumulative exposure to medical x-ray and the remainder from possible exposure to occupational and man-made radiation.

Medical and dental x-rays done in technologically advanced countries have exposed populations to approximately the same dose as already exists from natural sources, with the two sources being additive. Weapons testing is a more serious potential source of increased global radioactivity. This is especially true for such long-lived substances as strontium-90, cesium-137, and carbon-14. Background radiation has already increased almost 10% from these sources. Industrial

TABLE 11–1.—Dose-Effect Relationships of Ionizing Radiation in Humans

BIOLOGIC EFFECTS	ACUTE EXPOSURE	CHRONIC EXPOSURE
Death	400–1,000 Rem whole body penetrating dose for 30 days is lethal for 50–100% of those exposed	1 R/day is lethal in 3–6 years; 10 R/day is lethal in 3–6 months
Leukemia	30–50 rad exposure to bone marrow can increase incidence of leukemia up to twice unexposed rate	1 R/day for prolonged periods
Cancer		
Bone	1,500–2,000 rad (delayed effects after 5–20 years)	1 R/day for prolonged periods
Thyroid	200 rad to thyroid of children (adult thyroids appear resistant to exposures as high as 2,000 rad)	1 R/day for prolonged periods
Genetic	30–50 Rem may increase risk of mutations to twice normal	
Cataracts	600 R produce complete opacity in 50% of exposed lenses within 1 year	
Radiation sickness	100-R exposure appears to be minimum dose required to induce symptoms	

Adapted from Whittenberger J.L.: The physical and chemical environment, in Clark D.W., MacMahon B. (eds.): *Preventive Medicine*. Boston, Little, Brown and Co., 1967, from data tabulated by J.J. Fitzgerald and B.G. Ferris, Jr. Used by permission.

plants that process uranium are also potential sources of environmental contamination because of the discharge of radioactive products into the environment during the separation process. Stream pollution from radioactive liquid residues was a problem for some time in the tributaries of the Colorado River. An even more significant potential danger arises from the possibility of environmental leakage of high-level, slow-decaying radioactive wastes.

The atomic bombs that destroyed Hiroshima and Nagasaki produced a whole range of long-term illnesses including leukemia.[4] During peacetime, radon and its radioactive derivatives absorbed by dust in the air of mines have been implicated in the high incidence of lung cancer among German and Czechoslovakian miners during the early part of this century, and among uranium miners of the Colorado plateau during the 1950s. The relationship between doses of ionizing radiation and biologic effects in humans is summarized in Table 11–1.

Agricultural Chemicals

Pesticides, herbicides, fungicides, and nematocides have been effective in increasing agricultural production, and this has stimulated the expansion of their use. Because the action of these agents depends on their ability to affect biologic systems adversely, they represent a potential health hazard to humans who receive either occupational or general exposure. Occupational risk is greatest for the highly toxic organophosphorus anticholinesterase agents; significant numbers of deaths and serious injuries have occurred among handlers and disseminators of these compounds.

Broad-spectrum chlorinated hydrocarbon pesticides, such as DDT and dieldrin, may persist for many years in soils and increasingly penetrate other phases of the environment. Some soils in concentrated agricultural areas are so heavily polluted with these chemicals that food grown on them contains higher than acceptable levels of pesticide residues. These substances have a high resistance to biologic and physiochemical degradation and may gradually enter ground and surface waters. Eventually they may reach man, with the possibility of toxic or carcinogenic effects.

Water Pollution

Discharge of domestic wastes and cropland runoff of fertilizers and other chemicals into lakes and streams promote the propagation of algae. The taste of water and operation of filtration plants may be affected. Waste products from chemical industries are also being found downstream from these sites. Stable organic chemicals from these wastes can pass through water treatment facilities. Some are known to be carcinogenic to animals, but their effect on humans in concentrations found is as yet unknown.

Certain enteric viruses, such as the agent of infectious hepatitis, are more resistant to treatment by chlorination than are bacterial pathogens. In India a waterborne epidemic affected more than 28,000 persons. Usually such waterborne epidemics can be traced to the use of water that has been inadequately treated. Ingestion of contaminated water has also been associated with bacillary dysentery, typhoid, and cholera. Waterborne diseases can also be transmitted by contaminated shellfish, oysters, or clams, which appear to act as mechanical vectors, or certain species of water snails, which are the intermediate hosts of the nematode disease, schistosomiasis. Even in urban areas of the United States where the collection of sewage and other refuse is fairly well organized, its disposal and the consequent contamination of harbors, rivers, lakes, and beaches are still serious problems.

The increasing contamination of fresh water supplies by salt is a potential problem in places where the water supply is small and there is growing utilization. Large losses of water from evapotranspiration in dry areas and absorption of salts from irrigation tend to promote increased salt content.

Environmentally Induced Accidents[1]

Accidental injury is the leading cause of death in the United States for individuals aged 1 to 44 years. Nearly half of the more than 100,000 accidental deaths that occurred in 1977 in the United States were due to motor vehicle accidents. Automobile accidents also account for about 1.8 million disabling injuries. Occupational accidents account for approximately 13,000 deaths per year in the United States and for more than 9 million nonfatal injuries.

Although poorly constructed vehicles, faulty highway design, and inadequate safety standards for occupational equipment contribute to high accident mortality and morbidity, these variables interact with social factors (i.e., work schedules) and individual factors (i.e., poor eyesight). Many behavioral characteristics can be related to the occurrence of accidents. Among these are fatigue, boredom, anxiety, and the ingestion of drugs and alcohol, which alter consciousness, concentration, and motor coordination. The greatest risk factor for fatal automobile accidents is the use of alcohol by the driver. In about 50% of these accidents, drivers have had blood alcohol concentrations higher than 100 mg/dl, which is considered in most states to be presumptive evidence of intoxication. Physical and emotional illnesses are also contributing factors. For instance, it has been found that individuals with diabetes, epilepsy, cardiovascular disease, and mental illness average more than twice as many accidents per 1,000 miles of driving as people who are free of these diseases.[5]

Impairments associated with aging also lead to accidents. About 28,000 persons 65 and older die annually from this cause, and more than 3 million are injured. Two thirds of these accidents occur at home. Although people over 65 constitute only a tenth of the population, they account for more than a quarter of all fatal accidents, three quarters of all fatal falls, and a third of all pedestrian deaths. Much of this is ascribed to defects in their control of posture and gait, but faulty judgment due to impairment of cerebral function appears also to play some role.

Some controversy has arisen as to whether an accident-prone personality exists. Several *retrospective* studies have examined the personality characteristics of individuals who have had frequent or severe accidents. These studies have suggested that individuals who repeatedly suffer accidents have poor control over hostility, are depressed, and/or may have an unconscious wish to escape or avoid painful or humiliating experiences. Those who have poor control over hostility have been reported to be verbally or physically aggressive. They have also been said to have a tendency to be impulsive and to "act out" rather than to be introspective when faced with a conflict. So-called accident-prone persons suffering from depression have been characterized as being unable to express aggression and having strong guilt feelings and a need for expiation.

The concept of an accident-prone personality has been criticized on several grounds. First, it has not yet been supported by *prospective* studies. Second, some *retrospective* studies have not properly matched subjects on the basis of relevant variables. For instance, some studies have failed to take into account the variation in degree of exposure. A person who drives 100,000 miles per year is obviously exposed to a greater risk of an automobile accident than one who drives 1,000 miles per year. Third, studies that have attempted to identify an accident-prone personality have often failed to take into account the large number of individuals with the same personality characteristics who have few accidents. Fourth, studies have seldom distinguished those who have accidents while under the effects of alcohol from those who do not. Since alcohol plays a major role in a large proportion of accidents, it would be important to determine whether the characteristics of the so-called accident-prone personality differ from those associated with heavy alcohol consumption.

In order to provide a broader perspective of the impact of our modern urban life-style on our health, two of the most important medical disorders will be discussed—cancer and atherosclerotic cardiovascular disease.

CANCER

The largest group of diseases that has been causally related to life-style and environmental factors is cancer. At one time viruses and radiation were thought to be the two greatest causes of cancer; today chemical agents are believed to play a preeminent role in the etiology of this disease. Statistics indicate that since 1900 the incidence of cancer has increased dramatically in this country. This appears to be one of the adverse consequences of the life-style and environment created by our technological progress. As a result of this progress, the public has been exposed to carcinogenic chemicals in the air, water, and food.

The link between environmental chemicals and cancer can be appreciated by studying the geographic distribution of U.S. cancer mortality. Information from the National Cancer Institute indicates, for example, that the incidence of lung cancer is highest along the coast of the Gulf of Mexico, particularly in Louisiana, where there is a great amount of air pollution from industry and cigarette smoking. The highest incidence of bladder cancer is in Salem County, New Jersey, where 25% of the workers are employed in chemical and allied industries. Some chemicals with which these workers come in contact have been shown experimentally to cause bladder cancer in animals.

Besides environmental chemicals, other specific cancer-causing agents are known to exist that are related to life-style. These agents are associated with our diet, personal habits such as cigarette smoking and alcohol consumption, work conditions, and even the medical care we receive. One of the most interesting hypotheses currently being investigated is that there is a relationship between nutrition and cancer. Research on two of the most common cancers, colon and breast, have shown that there is a correlation between their prevalence and the dietary intake of specific foods. In the case of colon cancer, a diet high in animal protein and fats and low in plant fiber has been implicated in causation, although this is a matter of some controversy.[1, 6, 7] Breast cancer has been linked to a diet rich in polyunsaturated fats.

Lung Cancer and Smoking

The data indicating that cigarette smoking causes lung cancer are almost incontrovertible. It is unlikely that we shall ever have totally conclusive *experimental* proof of this in humans because it would be ethically wrong to compel one group of people to smoke and another group not to smoke. However, the cumulative weight of the direct experimental evidence in animals combined with the indirect evidence derived from a large number of human studies make it quite clear that smoking cigarettes is causally related to lung cancer.[8]

With respect to animal experiments, evidence has been presented that dogs trained to smoke through tracheostomy tubes develop pulmonary neoplasms,[9] as do hamsters and rats subjected to intratracheal administration of components of cigarette smoke condensate. In humans, prospective studies have shown that death rates from lung cancer are as much as 40 times higher for heavy smokers than for nonsmokers. Moreover, there is a strong dose-response effect, with the greatest amount of smoking leading to the highest mortality. The considerable strength of the association between smoking and lung cancer can also be seen in the retrospective finding that 85% of all deaths from lung cancer occur among cigarette smokers.

A consistent association between cigarette smoking and lung cancer has been found in both retrospective and prospective studies of diverse groups in countries throughout the world. In addition, the time relationship between the onset of cigarette smoking and the development of lung cancer that has been found in these studies corresponds to the long latent period characteristic of carcinogenesis. Finally, when individuals gave up cigarette smoking, the decrease in mortality from lung cancer that was observed has been directly related to the duration of time since they had stopped.

In addition to these correlations between cigarette smoking and lung cancer, the relationship of these two variables is supported by the following information. First, cigarette smoke contains a number of carcinogens, and inhalation of cigarette smoke brings these carcinogens into intimate contact with tissues. Second, autopsy studies in humans have identified what are believed to be precancerous changes, such as the presence of atypical cells, in the bronchial trees of smokers.

One criticism that has been directed at the thesis that cigarette smoking causes lung cancer is based on the observation that not every person who smokes develops lung cancer. This does not rule out a causal relationship, however, but only suggests that one or more other factors interact with cigarette smoking to cause the disease. Another criticism is that not everyone who develops this disease has smoked. This is not a particularly damaging criticism, because the inhalation of carcinogens other than by smoking cigarettes is also known to increase the risk of lung cancer. For instance, increased risk may occur secondary to occupational exposure to asbestos, chromates, nickel, and chloromethyl methyl ether.[10] Also, a relationship between air pollution and lung cancer seems possible.

Cigarette smoking appears to be a causal risk factor for tumors other than lung cancer. Table 11-2 depicts the mortality ratio (i.e., ratio of observed to expected deaths) of cigarette smokers versus nonsmokers for a variety of diseases, including several cancers.[11] Although the mortality ratio for cancer of the

TABLE 11-2.—Ratio of Observed (O) to Expected (E)* Deaths for Smokers of Cigarettes

UNDERLYING CAUSE OF DEATH	MORTALITY RATIO (O/E)
Cancer of lung	10.8
Bronchitis and emphysema	6.1
Cancer of larynx	5.4
Cancer of esophagus	4.1
Stomach and duodenal ulcer	2.8
Cancer of bladder	1.9
Coronary heart disease	1.7
General arteriosclerosis	1.5
Cancer of the rectum	1.0
All causes of death	1.7

Source: U.S. Public Health Service. *Smoking and Health Report of the Advisory Committee to the Surgeon General*, pub. 1103. Washington, D.C., U.S. Government Printing Office, 1964.
*Based on mortality rates in nonsmokers.

lung is by far the highest, ratios also are quite high for cancer of the larynx and esophagus.

Asbestos-Associated Tumors

Asbestos workers have higher death rates from several forms of cancer, especially from mesothelioma (Table 11–3).[2] The occurrence of this tumor is so unusual that its presence is a strong indication that the affected individual has been exposed to asbestos. The risk of developing a mesothelioma extends to workers who have jobs that bring them in close proximity to where asbestos is being handled, even though they themselves are not directly involved in handling the material. Also, the immediate family of asbestos workers and people who live within a quarter-mile of an asbestos plant have higher than normal incidences of asbestos-associated diseases. It may be difficult to obtain a positive history of exposure to asbestos from persons with these diseases for two reasons: (1) only a brief period of contact (as little as one month) with asbestos is necessary for these conditions to occur, and (2) there is a long latent period of up to 30 or 35 years before the diseases are clinically evident. The combination of asbestos exposure and cigarette smoking increases the lung cancer risk 90 times, so it is especially important for people who work or have worked with asbestos to avoid cigarette smoking.[1]

Thyroid Tumors Following Head and Neck Irradiation

Prior to the 1950s, radiation therapy was commonly used in treating certain benign conditions (enlargement of the thymus, tonsils, and adenoids; mastoiditis; sinusitis; and skin lesions such as acne or hemangiomas) involving the head, neck, and chest. Infants and children often received this therapy, which is no longer acceptable because of its effects on the thyroid gland.[12, 13] Both benign and malignant thyroid tumors are reported to occur some years after the irradiation, with the former being at least three times as common as the latter. On clinical examination, about 20–30% of the individuals who had head or neck radiation therapy in the past will have a palpable thyroid abnormality, and about 30–40% of those operated on will be found to have thyroid cancer (2–6% of the total number of subjects examined). The latency for the development of these cancers is 5–35 years from the time of irradiation. They are generally small when detected (less than 1.5 cm) and have a good prognosis. On the other hand, some of these tumors are multicentric so that extensive thyroid surgery may be necessary.

From studies it appears that low doses of radiation (in the range of 50–700 rad) are more carcinogenic than large doses (more than 2,000 rad), apparently because of the inhibition of cell replication that is produced by the high doses. This may explain why the high dose of radiation accompanying ^{131}I radiotherapy for hyperthyroidism has not resulted in an increased incidence of thyroid cancer.

Other Forms of Cancer

A number of environmental chemicals have been causally related to cancer of the urinary bladder. In this regard, exposure to beta-

TABLE 11–3.—DEATHS AMONG 17,800 ASBESTOS INSULATION WORKERS IN THE UNITED STATES AND CANADA, JANUARY 1, 1967–JANUARY 1, 1977

	EXPECTED*	OBSERVED
Total deaths, all causes	1,660.96	2,270
Total cancer, all sites	319.90	994
Lung cancer	105.97	485
Pleural mesothelioma	†	66
Peritoneal mesothelioma	†	109
Cancer of esophagus	7.01	18
Cancer of stomach	14.23	22
Cancer of colon-rectum	37.86	59
All other cancer	154.83	235
Asbestosis	†	162
All other causes	1,351.06	1,114

*Expected deaths are based upon white male age-specific mortality data of the U.S. National Center for Health Statistics for 1967–1975 and extrapolation to 1976.
†These are rare causes of death in the general population.
Note: The membership of the International Association of Heat and Frost Insulators and Asbestos Workers, AFL-CIO, CLC, was enrolled on January 1, 1967, and has been observed since.
Source: Selikoff I.J., Hammond E.C.: C.A. 28(2):88, 1978. (Used by permission.)

naphthylamine and other aromatic amines used in the aniline dye industry has been known to be an occupational hazard throughout this century. A cause-effect relationship between these chemical agents and bladder cancer seems certain. As indicated in Table 11–2, cigarette smoking also seems to be related to bladder cancer, although the strength of the association is considerably less than that between cigarette smoking and lung cancer. The risk of bladder cancer for cigarette smokers, however, is also dependent on dose, and in smokers of more than two packs per day the risk is about five times higher than for nonsmokers.[14] Although a number of the end products of inhaled smoke are excreted in the urine, the particular carcinogen responsible has not yet been identified.

Tobacco in forms other than cigarettes has been linked to cancer of the oral cavity. In India, where dried betel nut, tobacco, and spices wrapped in a betel leaf are chewed for prolonged periods of time, cancers of the cheek, tongue, and other buccal sites are common. In countries in which betel chewing does not include the use of tobacco, buccal cancer is not particularly prevalent. In the United States the chewing of tobacco has been shown to be a factor in the cause of oral cancers, and it has been suggested that the marked decrease in the prevalence of these tumors during the past half-century can be attributed to the decline of this habit.

The combination of drinking hard liquor and smoking tobacco has a strong association with esophageal cancer.[15, 16] Because of the high correlation between smoking and drinking habits, however, it has been difficult to determine the extent to which each of these two factors alone contributes to the causation of this tumor.

Sexual practices are an integral part of life-style and numerous studies have attempted to establish a relationship between these activities and cancer. At present, the data on this subject are controversial and open to the criticism that they come from poorly designed studies. The following observations, however, can be found in the literature and deserve comment: (1) higher incidences of cancer of the uterine cervix have been associated with sexual promiscuity and the onset of sexual activity early in life;[17] (2) cancer of the penis occurs more often in uncircumcised males, particularly where there is phimosis (i.e., the foreskin cannot be pushed back over the glans penis) and poor penile hygiene; and (3) a higher frequency of breast cancer is found in unmarried women, women who have never had children, and those who have had their first pregnancies after age 30. Since the specific etiology of these cancers is unknown, the precise role that sexual practices play in contributing to their cause is not clear at this time. There are several hypotheses, however. With respect to penile cancer, it is known that smegma (a cheezy secretion from the glands of Tyson, which is found under the prepuce) causes cancer in experimental animals. Furthermore, studies have shown that this form of cancer can be prevented by circumcision, an operation that reduces the skin contact with smegma. One theory that attempts to explain the higher rates of breast cancer among women who do not have children or have them later in life is that the increased cyclic ovarian activity they experience stimulates tissue changes in the breasts that lead to cancer.

Cancer of the colon has an annual incidence in the United States of about 30 per 100,000, whereas in Japan, where fish and rice are an important part of the diet, the incidence is only 4 per 100,000. When Japanese move to the United States and adopt a westernized diet, their incidence of cancer of the colon increases and approximates that found in the United States. Mention has been made of the correlation between the westernized diet, which is high in animal protein and fats and low in fiber, with the occurrence of this type of cancer. Perhaps this explains why the Japanese experience a rise in the incidence of colonic tumors after coming to this country.

The medicines we have developed as a result of our technological progress may at times be responsible for causing cancer. A case in point is the administration of estrogens to control the symptoms and signs accompanying the menopause in some women. While these agents are effective in relieving certain menopausal complaints (i.e., vasomotor instability, vaginal atrophic changes), there has been a tendency to overuse them and prescribe them for symptoms that are primarily emotional in nature. For a long time this was justified on the premise that no serious harm came from their use. In the past several years, however a number of case-controlled studies have established that prolonged and continuous administration of estrogens to postmenopausal women is associated with an increased risk (estimated to be 3 to 8 times as great as that of women of the same age not taking estrogens) of endometrial cancer (cancer of the lining of the uterus).[18, 19] The Food and Drug Administration (FDA) has strongly cautioned physicians against using these drugs for treating the menopausal syndrome unless there are compelling reasons, and then the drugs should be given cyclically, for the shortest possible time, and at the lowest effective dose.[18]

A serious health problem has been reported to occur as a result of the administration of diethylstilbestrol (DES), a synthetic estrogen, to pregnant women in order to prevent miscarriage. It was discovered that some female offspring of these mothers developed vaginal cancer as a consequence of their in utero exposure to this hormonal medication. DES-related vaginal cancer occurs at an early age, usually becoming clinically evident in the first or second decade of life, i.e., at a time when gynecologic malignancies are extremely rare. A question has been raised as to whether the mothers who received DES have an increased risk of developing breast cancer.[20]

ATHEROSCLEROTIC CARDIOVASCULAR DISEASE

More than one third of all deaths among adults in the United States are due to cardiovascular diseases, principally coronary artery (heart) disease and stroke.[1] These disorders are also the leading cause of mortality in other Western industrialized nations. It is noteworthy, however, that a substantial decline in mortality from cardiovascular diseases has occurred in this country since the mid-1960s. For the period 1968 to 1976, this reduction amounted to about 20% for coronary artery disease and 32% for stroke.[1]

Extensive clinical research has shown that life-style factors play a critical role in the pathogenesis of atherosclerosis, the pathologic lesion underlying most cases of coronary artery disease and stroke. These life-style factors constitute *risk factors* for the development of atherosclerotic cardiovascular disease (ASCVD). Since the precise cause of this condition is unknown, risk factors are very important in predicting who will experience the effects of ASCVD. Most important, modification of these factors is the principal means of preventing this serious disease, and there are data indicating that the recent decline in mortality from it is related to a reduction in these risk factors. In view of the great significance of risk factors, a brief description of what they are and how they operate seems in order at this point.

Risk Factors Defined

When we speak of a phenomenon having only a single cause, we mean that the presence of a specific factor is necessary for the occurrence of the phenomenon. Conversely, the absence of this factor precludes the occurrence of the phenomenon. When a phenomenon is determined by multiple factors, the presence of only one of the factors may not lead to the occurrence of the phenomenon. Moreover, when more than one factor determines the occurrence of a phenomenon, their effects may not be simply additive. The nature of the interaction between these factors must be understood before a cause-effect relationship can be fully specified.

The finding that two or more variables are *correlated* does not necessarily imply that one variable causes the other. Instead, some as yet unidentified variable may explain their association. Suppose, for example, that the softness of the asphalt in the street is found to be positively correlated with sweating in nonexercising individuals. This, of course, implies neither that the softness of the asphalt causes sweating nor that sweating causes the asphalt to soften. Instead, a third factor, the heat of the sun, causes both sweating and soft asphalt. Now consider the relationship between coronary heart disease and cigarette smoking. These two variables are positively related. Although it is possible that the cigarette smoking causes coronary heart disease through some as yet unknown mechanism, it is also conceivable that a third factor such as nervousness or anxiety leads to both.

When a disease has only a single cause, the major criterion for identifying this cause is its specificity of association with the disease (as in Koch's postulates). However, some of the major disorders that afflict us, such as coronary heart disease, cancer, and stroke, appear to be multiply determined. In such instances it is difficult to isolate the specific causative agents; consequently, several criteria have been established to help distinguish whether a specific factor is causally related to a disease. When these criteria are reasonably satisfied for a particular factor, it is called a *risk factor* for the disease. The criteria used for identifying a risk factor as being associated with a disorder include (1) strength of association, (2) consistency of association, (3) temporal correctness of association, and (4) coherence with existing knowledge.

Strength of association refers to the incidence of a disorder in those who possess the risk factor in question as opposed to those who do not. For example, if hypercholesterolemia is to qualify as a risk factor for coronary heart disease, the occurrence of this disease in a population should be positively correlated with increased levels of blood cholesterol. *Consistency of association* depends on the extent to which a relationship between a disorder and a potential risk factor is found in various studies using very different experimental designs. *Temporal correctness of association* refers to whether or not the latent period (i.e., the period of time during which the potential risk factor is present prior to the onset of the disorder) is consistent with the known latent period for the disorder. Finally, *coherence with existing knowledge* refers to the extent to which the information linking the potential risk factor and the disorder is consistent with other available information. The relationship between cigarette smoking and lung cancer, for example, is coherent with available information insofar as cigarettes contain carcinogens and inhalation can be shown to bring these carcinogens into contact with lung tissue.

Prospective epidemiologic studies have established that the following life-style factors affect the risk of developing atherosclerotic coronary artery disease:

1. Hypertension
2. Diet high in saturated fats and cholesterol
3. High level of cholesterol in the blood
4. Cigarette smoking
5. Physical inactivity
6. Type A coronary-prone behavior

Moreover, this risk is much greater if an individual is in the upper part of the distribution for several of these risk factors than if for only one or two. When one considers certain risk factors such as a diastolic blood pressure above 90 mm Hg, serum cholesterol level above 250 mg, and smoking more than 20 cigarettes per day, the simple addition of these factors seems to lead to a geometric increase

TABLE 11–4.—RATES OF FIRST CORONARY EVENT ACCORDING TO NUMBER OF RISK FACTORS

	RATE PER 1,000
No risk factor	20
One risk factor	48
Two risk factors	90
Three risk factors	171

Source: U.S. Public Health Service: *Multiple Risk Factors in Arteriosclerosis*. Report by National Heart and Lung Institute Task Force on Arteriosclerosis, vol. 2. Washington, D.C., U.S. Government Printing Office, 1971.

in risk. Table 11–4 shows the rates of first coronary events according to the number of risk factors present as determined in the National Cooperative Pooling Project for men aged 30 to 59 years.[21] Let us examine these risk factors more closely.

Hypertension

Hypertension is one of the most important risk factors for coronary artery disease and stroke.[22] It is estimated that in the United States there are at least 24 million hypertensives (i.e., those with a diastolic blood pressure above 90 mm Hg). In the early 1970s it was estimated that half of all hypertensives went undetected, and about half of those who were diagnosed either went untreated or received inadequate therapy. The explanation for this lies partly in the fact that hypertension is asymptomatic for most individuals. In 1972, the government initiated a nationwide program to detect and treat this disorder. Significant progress has been made in these efforts, which may partly explain the reduction in mortality from both coronary artery disease and stroke during this period.

From the standpoint of etiology, hypertension can be divided into two main categories: primary or essential hypertension and secondary hypertension. Approximately 85–95% of all cases are essential hypertension—a disorder or group of disorders in which an organic cause has not been identified. The remaining cases of secondary hypertension are attributable to diverse causes such as renal parenchymal disease, renovascular constriction, coarctation of the aorta, and adrenal diseases such as Cushing syndrome or pheochromocytoma. In addition to the organic factors operative in the etiology of hypertension, several life-style factors have been found to play an important role in the development of this condition: diet and stress.

Two dietary components have been shown to contribute to the development of high blood pressure—the number of calories and the amount of salt. A general correlation between hypertension and obesity has long been known. Recent studies have found that this association is manifest in three ways: (1) obesity is more common among hypertensives than among normotensives, (2) normotensive overweight persons are more likely to develop hypertension, and (3) hypertensive individuals have a greater risk of becoming obese than do normotensive individuals.[22] The prevalence of hypertension in obese subjects increases in proportion to the degree of obesity. Most important from a therapeutic standpoint is that a loss of weight is associated with a reduction in blood pressure in obese hypertensives.[23] While it is clear that obesity increases the risk of hypertension and weight loss lowers blood pressure, the overweight state is not a sufficient cause by itself for hypertension, as there are many overweight persons who are normotensive.

Salt intake is a relevant factor in the genesis of hypertension in both humans and experimental animals.[24, 25] Epidemiologic studies have consistently shown a positive (and linear) correlation between the average daily intake of sodium chloride and the prevalence of hypertension among populations in different areas of the world (Fig 11–1).[24] When a primitive people who have previously been exposed to a low intake of salt change their res-

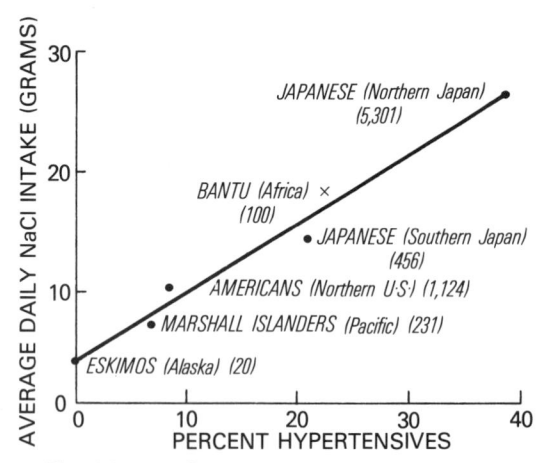

Fig 11–1.—Correlation of average daily salt intake with the incidence of hypertension in different geographic areas and among different races. The number of persons studied is given in parentheses. (From Weinsier R.L.: *Prev. Med.* 5(1):7, 1976. Used by permission.)

idence and adopt a modern life-style in which they ingest a large amount of salt, their incidence of hypertension rises significantly. In the United States, the mean daily intake of salt has increased over the past several decades due in part to a life-style that encourages people to use more and more processed foods to which excess salt has been added. The current intake of salt by Americans is far greater than bodily needs dictate, and this may play a role in the pathogenesis of hypertensive disease. It should be noted, however, that there are variations in the blood pressure response to a large salt intake. Some people are able to eat a lot of salt without penalty, while others who ingest the same amount develop high blood pressure. Heredity is probably important in determining such differences in the blood pressure effects of salt intake in humans.

Another aspect of our modern life-style that may be important in the pathogenesis of hypertension is the stress created by the conflicts, pressures, and frustrations that we all experience. Stressful stimuli of an acute nature can provoke a transient rise in blood pressure. The "flight or fight" response to stress, as described by Cannon (see Chap. 7), is characterized by a pronounced discharge of the sympathetic nervous system and a temporary increase in blood pressure. It is possible that this response, if prolonged or repetitive, may play a role in the development of sustained hypertension.

Dietary Fats and Serum Cholesterol

Nutrition plays a critical role in the pathogenesis of ASCVD. Epidemiologic studies of populations throughout the world have established that a diet high in saturated fats and cholesterol is associated with the development of this disorder. Figure 11–2, taken from a report of the International Cooperative Study on the Epidemiology of Cardiovascular Disease, illustrates the positive correlation between the intake of saturated fats and the mortality and morbidity due to coronary heart disease.[26] In this prospective study, men (aged 40–59) from seven countries (Finland, Greece, Italy, Japan, the Netherlands, United States, and Yugoslavia) were observed over an extended period of time to determine the incidence of this disease. The composition of their diets varied according to the geographic area from which they came. Men from the United States were among those with the highest intakes of saturated fats; their incidence of coronary heart disease was also among the highest. On the other hand, subjects from countries where the dietary in-

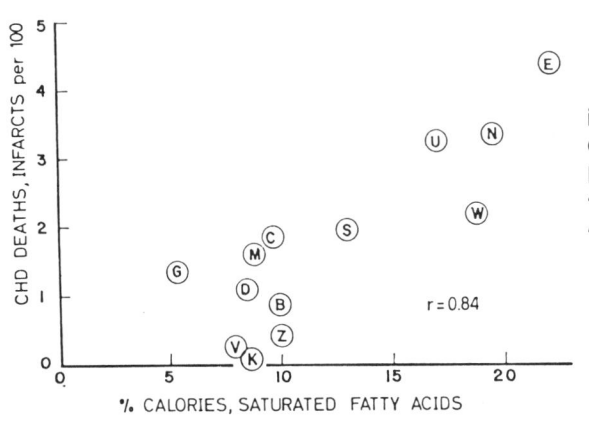

Fig 11–2.—Correlation between the intake of saturated fats and the incidence of coronary heart disease in several populations. (From Keys A.: *Circulation* 41(4):1, 1970. Used by permission of the American Heart Association, Inc.)

Ⓑ-BELGRADE FACULTY, Ⓒ-CREVALCORE, Ⓓ-DALMATIA
Ⓔ-EAST FINLAND, Ⓖ-CORFU, Ⓚ-CRETE, Ⓝ-ZUTPHEN
Ⓜ-MONTEGIORGIO, Ⓢ-SLAVONIA, Ⓤ-U.S. RAILROAD
Ⓥ-VELIKA KRSNA, Ⓦ-WEST FINLAND, Ⓩ-ZRENJANIN

take of saturated fats was low exhibited a low incidence of this disease.

Two other key findings emerged from this study: (1) the level of serum cholesterol is directly related to the amount of saturated fats in the diet, and (2) the incidence of coronary heart disease shows a positive correlation with the level of serum cholesterol. The last finding is of particular significance and has been confirmed by many other investigations.

One of the best known of these is the Framingham study in which the residents of the city of Framingham, Massachusetts, participated in a long-term epidemiologic survey to determine the effects of variables, such as serum cholesterol, on the incidence of cardiovascular disease.[27] The relationship between the risk of developing coronary heart disease and the level of serum cholesterol can be seen in Figure 11–3. This relationship is a continuous one; that is, as the concentration of cholesterol in the boood rises, the degree of risk increases. This is true even at the lower concentrations. According to the Framingham study, men in the age range 30–49 who have a serum cholesterol concentration of 250 mg/dl have approximately three times the risk of developing coronary heart disease as those with a concentration of 200 mg/dl. The risk of stroke is also increased by elevated serum cholesterol, although the association is not as strong as for coronary artery disease.[1]

The relationship between the level of serum cholesterol and the risk of coronary heart disease is more complex than indicated in Figure 11–3. Cholesterol, along with other blood lipids, circulates in combination with serum proteins, forming molecules called lipoproteins. On the basis of their physical and chemical properties, the lipoproteins can be divided into various types, each having a different percentage of cholesterol. The low-density (LDL) and high-density (HDL) lipoproteins are most important in terms of the risk of developing coronary heart disease. There is a *direct* relationship between the level of LDL cholesterol and this risk, but an *inverse* relationship between the HDL cholesterol level and this risk. Current research suggests that, in some persons, measuring the

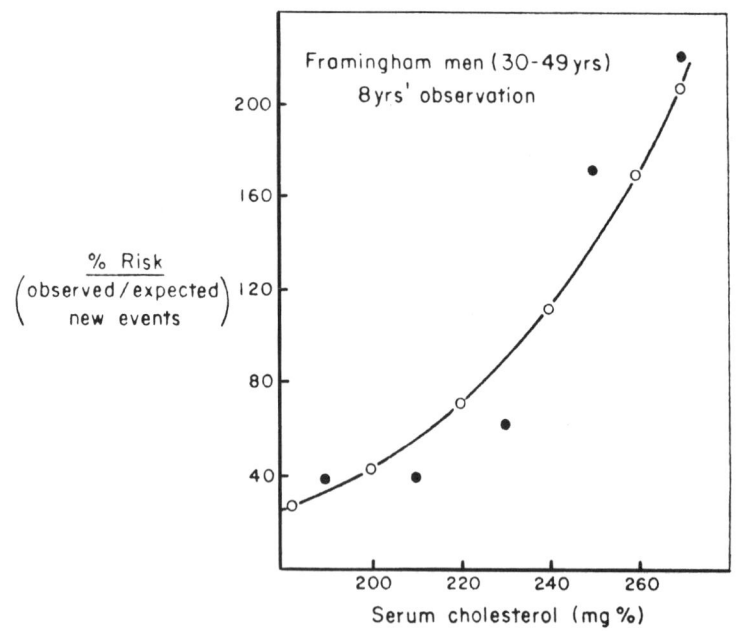

Fig 11–3.—The relation between levels of serum cholesterol in men (30–49 years old) and their relative risk of coronary heart disease (0). This curve is the best fit to the data (0) from the Framingham study. (From Ahrens E.H.: *Ann. Intern. Med.* 85:87-93, 1976. Used by permission.)

blood level of HDL and LDL may be a more accurate way of predicting the risk of coronary artery disease than measuring serum cholesterol alone.[1, 27]

Experimentally, it is possible to produce atherosclerotic vascular lesions by feeding animals a diet high in saturated fats and cholesterol. Not only does this diet result in the animals developing atherosclerosis, but it also leads to an elevation in the level of serum cholesterol. The "lipid" hypothesis of atherogenesis is based on epidemiologic, pathologic, and experimental data indicating that there is a direct relationship between diet (the ingestion of saturated fats and cholesterol), the total level of serum cholesterol, and the development of the lipid-laden atherosclerotic vascular lesion that underlies most instances of heart attack and stroke.

A number of factors interact to determine the serum concentration of lipoproteins and cholesterol besides diet. Those that are related to life-style include physical activity, cigarette smoking, alcohol consumption, and stress.[28, 29] Heredity and hormonal factors are also important in this regard.[30, 31]

One reason diet and other life-style determiners of serum lipid levels have received so much attention with respect to the pathogenesis of atherosclerosis is that these factors are potentially under the control of the individual. Information suggests that diet was in large part responsible for the epidemic of atherosclerotic vascular disease that began in the 1940s, and perhaps earlier, in the Western industrialized countries. Moreover, dietary trends may also explain a portion of the decline in mortality from coronary artery disease that occurred in this country after the mid 1960s. When one surveys the nutritional intake of our population during the period in which the epidemic of atherosclerotic cardiovascular disease was evolving, one feature stands out—the increasing content of fat in our diet. From the early 1900s until the 1950s, the American diet underwent a marked change, with increased consumption of meat, poultry, and dairy products and decreased intake of cereals, potatoes, and starchy foods. As a result, there was an increase in the proportion of calories derived from fat, particularly saturated fat and cholesterol. This nutritional change can be correlated with a rising incidence of and mortality from coronary heart disease. Since the early 1950s, however, the consumption of saturated fats and cholesterol has decreased while the intake of linoleic acid, the principal polyunsaturated fat in the diet, has increased. This dietary trend has been accompanied by a decline in the average serum cholesterol level and mortality from coronary artery disease in the United States.

The evidence cited above suggests that it may be possible to prevent coronary heart disease by modifying the typical American diet so that less saturated fat and cholesterol are ingested. It makes a difference whether one eats saturated or unsaturated fats in terms of one's level of serum cholesterol. Diets rich in saturated fats (animal fats) increase the level of serum cholesterol, while diets rich in polyunsaturated fats (vegetable fats) lower it. In the average American diet, the ratio of polyunsaturated to saturated fatty acids is about 0.3, indicating a superabundance of the saturated types of fat. The average cholesterol intake is more than 600 mg a day. It has been recommended that Americans (1) decrease their total fat intake to approximately 35% of their total calories (from the present level of about 40%); (2) change the fats in their diet from predominantly saturated to approximately isocaloric amounts of saturated, monounsaturated, and polyunsaturated; and (3) decrease the amount of cholesterol in their diet to about 300 mg a day in order to reduce the incidence of coronary heart disease.[30] Adjusting the total calorie intake to avoid obesity is also a part of this dietary recommendation. The hoped-for results of these recommendations are a lowering of the level of blood cholesterol and prevention of coronary heart disease.

These recommendations are based on the "lipid" hypothesis of atherogenesis and the premise that "reducing the level of plasma cholesterol in an individual or in a population group will lead to a reduction in the risk of suffering a new event of coronary heart disease."[32] A number of studies have been conducted in which diet, drugs, or both have been utilized to lower the level of blood lipids; however, this premise is as yet unproved. Changing an aspect of the life-style of a population, in this case their dietary habits, requires a great deal of time, effort, and money. So it stands to reason that there should be substantial evidence that such a change is beneficial before attempting to institute it on a large scale. Nevertheless, for the individual, these recommendations seem quite appropriate when there is a family history of atherosclerotic cardiovascular disease or if a person has had an episode of coronary or cerebrovascular disease. With respect to the therapy for hyperlipidemia, it is essential to determine the exact profile of the lipid abnormality before prescribing a specific diet. For some lipoprotein disturbances, a low-fat diet is important; for others, a restriction in the dietary intake of carbohydrate is crucial.

Other Important Risk Factors

CIGARETTE SMOKING.—Data accumulated from studies in this country and elsewhere show that there is a strong correlation between the average per capita consumption of cigarettes and the mortality from coronary heart disease. In the National Cooperative Pooling Project (consisting of the pooled data from several long-term prospective studies of the incidence of coronary heart disease in men in this country), it was found that for men aged 30–59 who smoked more than 20 cigarettes a day, the risk of having a first major coronary event was three times greater than that for nonsmokers (Fig 11–4).[28, 33] As can be seen from this figure, there is a linear increase in the incidence of these events as the number of cigarettes smoked increases. Pipe and cigar smokers had only a slightly higher incidence of coronary artery disease, as did cigarette smokers who had discontinued the habit. The death rate from coronary heart disease among men in this age group who smoked more than 20 cigarettes a day

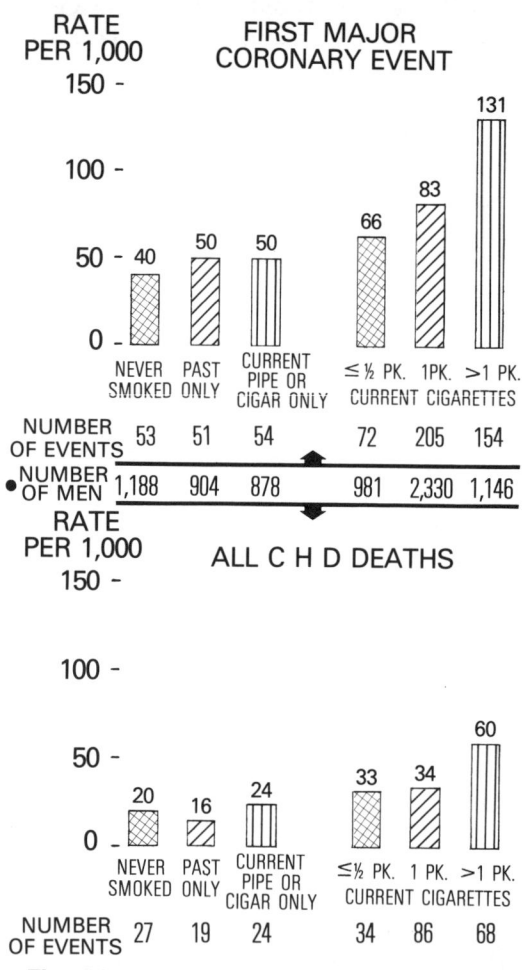

Fig 11–4.—Relationship between tobacco smoking and morbidity-mortality from coronary heart disease (CHD) in men aged 30–59. Data from the National Cooperative Pooling Project. (From Inter-Society Commission for Heart Disease Resources: *Circulation* 42:A 55, 1970. Used by permission of the American Heart Association, Inc.)

was also three times greater than that for nonsmokers (see Fig 11–4). The mortality from cerebrovascular disease (stroke) shows a similar correlation with cigarette smoking, although this is not quite as great as that for coronary heart disease for a comparable amount of smoking.

Recently it has been found that women, especially those over 40 years of age, also share in the risk of coronary artery disease if they smoke cigarettes. This enhanced risk is particularly evident if they are taking oral contraceptives. The results of these investigations have prompted the FDA to issue a strong warning to women on the pill to avoid cigarette smoking.

PHYSICAL INACTIVITY.—A lack of physical exercise, so common in our sedentary life-style, has been linked to the premature development of coronary heart disease. Numerous investigations from many countries have found that there is an inverse relationship between the degree of physical activity in which people engage and the incidence of and mortality from coronary heart disease.[34] The initial studies purporting to show this came from England, where observations were made indicating that workers in occupations requiring little physical activity had a higher risk of coronary heart disease than those who had jobs that kept them physically active. A number of occupations were evaluated; however, the best known of these studies compared the incidence of myocardial infarction in drivers and conductors working on double-decker London buses. It was found that the former had a higher rate of infarction than the latter. This was attributed to the difference in the physical exercise in which the two groups engaged; the drivers had a sedentary job, whereas the conductors were much more active as a result of frequent climbing up and down the stairs during their tour of duty.

In the recently reported Framingham study, men who engaged in less physical activity had a higher morbidity and mortality rate from coronary heart disease than their more active counterparts.[35] The effect on mortality of being sedentary was modest compared to the effects of other coronary risk factors, but it persisted even when these factors were taken into account. For women, this study showed the adverse effects of physical inactivity to be negligible.

Another often-quoted study of the relationship between physical activity and coronary artery disease was conducted by Paffenbarger, et al.[36] These investigators surveyed the health of 16,936 Harvard male alumni, aged 35–74 years, over spans of 16–50 years since matriculation, and found that the risk of having a first heart attack was inversely related to energy expenditure and physical activity.

The protective influence of physical exercise against coronary artery disease as reported in the literature may be due in part to a favorable effect on other coronary risk factors. It has been shown that men who exercise regularly and vigorously have higher plasma levels of high-density-lipoprotein cholesterol, which are associated with a lower risk of coronary heart disease.[29] Also, those who are physically active during their leisure activities may have better health habits that lead to lower body weight, less cigarette smoking, and lower blood pressure.[35] Another reason for the protective effects of physical activity in coronary heart disease is an augmentation of fibrinolytic activity in the blood in response to thrombotic stimuli.[37]

Although the epidemiologic data are strongly suggestive, proof is lacking that physical exercise, related to either occupation or leisure activities, will prevent or delay the development of coronary heart disease. There is, in fact, an ongoing debate about the issue of selection versus protection. Are those who exercise regularly a self-selected group with a lower risk of coronary artery disease or does regular exercise protect them against this disease? Further studies are needed to answer this question conclusively.

CORONARY-PRONE BEHAVIOR PATTERN.— A specific type of behavior has been identified as a risk factor for coronary heart disease (see also Chap. 8).[38] This coronary-prone behavior pattern, called Type A, is characterized by:

1. Excessive competitive drive
2. Striving for achievement
3. Aggressiveness and hostility
4. A strong sense of time urgency and impatience
5. Restlessness and tenseness

All these features need not be present simultaneously. The behavior is not considered to be a personality trait or a stress reaction, but rather the observable behavior that emerges when a person predisposed by his character is confronted by a triggering situation. Such a situation is provided by many occupations in which people are engaged in our achievement-oriented "high-pressure" society. While the Type A behavior pattern or syndrome is recognized by the presence of the above traits, Type B is marked by their absence.

Persons with the Type A pattern tend to be overly dedicated to their work, so much so that in many instances they neglect other important aspects of their life. In fact, this excessive involvement in a vocation or profession is one of the most typical features of the life-style of the Type A individual.

A number of retrospective studies have demonstrated that there is an association between the Type A behavior pattern and the development of clinical coronary heart disease. The most impressive data have come from a prospective investigation known as the Western Collaborative Group Study.[39] In this study, a cohort of more than 3,000 working men aged 30–59 were followed for more than 8 years. Those with Type A behavior had more than twice the incidence of clinical coronary heart disease as those with Type B. This was true even after allowance was made for the effects of other risk factors such as hypertension, high levels of serum cholesterol, and cigarette smoking. So, there is evidence to support the idea that the coronary-prone behavior pattern carries with it a significant risk for heart attack—one that acts independently of the other known risk factors for this disease.

Frank et al. conducted a study designed to see whether a correlation exists between the severity of atherosclerotic coronary artery disease and the prevalence of the Type A behavior pattern.[40] One hundred forty-seven consecutive patients with clinical manifestations of this disease who underwent coronary angiography were evaluated by means of psychiatric and psychological studies. On the basis of the standardized Rosenman-Friedman interview, the patients were assigned to one of four points on the dimension of the coronary proneness of their personality: A1, A2, B3, B4. It was found that those patients with the greatest degree of proneness (A1 and A2) had more severe involvement of their coronary arteries (measured by the number of arteries stenosed by 50% or more) when compared with those individuals with a lesser degree of proneness. Thus, based on a rather precise measure of the extent of the coronary atherosclerotic process, an association was demonstrated between the severity of this process and the risk factor of a Type A personality pattern. Furthermore, this association persisted even after adjustments had been made for the effects of five other major coronary risk factors.

Problems in the Prevention of Atherosclerotic Cardiovascular Disease

The practical importance of identifying the life-style risk factors associated with ASCVD lies in the application of this knowledge in disease prevention. That such an effort can be effective is indicated by a recent analysis of the reasons for the 20% decline in mortality from coronary artery disease in this country from 1968 to 1976, which showed that improvements in these risk factors were partly responsible.[41] Table 11–5 gives the percent decrease in these factors between the early 1960s and mid-1970s.

A nationwide program to modify coronary risk factors and further reduce mortality from ASCVD would have to be directed toward changing the behavior patterns that underlie and support them. This involves public education.

A recent survey of the public's knowledge of the preventive aspects of coronary heart disease showed a widespread lack of information.[42] Interviews with a sample of 617 adults (aged 20–59) in the Chicago area were conducted to ascertain whether they were able to identify the major risk factors commonly associated with coronary heart disease. When asked the question: What do you feel are the major likely causes of heart attacks in persons under 60 years of age? cigarette smoking was

TABLE 11-5.—PERCENT DECREASES IN RISK FACTORS FOR CORONARY HEART DISEASE*

RISK FACTOR	APPROXIMATE PERCENT DECREASE	TIME PERIOD
Cigarette smoking (% who smoke):		
Men	26	1964–1975
Women	8	
Per capita consumption of:		
Tobacco	22	1963–1975
Fluid milk and cream	20	
Butter	32	
Eggs	13	
Percent with high cholesterol (260 mg/100 ml plus):		
Men aged 45–54	6	c1962–c1975
Men aged 55–64	14	
Women aged 45–54	13	
Women aged 55–64	29	
Percent hypertensives untreated:		
In U.S.	10	c1962–c1974
In 14 U.S. cities†	25	

*Note: Coronary heart disease deaths (to which these risk factors are related) declined by 20 percent in the period 1968–1976.
†Part of a special National Heart, Lung, and Blood Institute study program.
Source: *Healthy People, The Surgeon General's Report on Health Promotion and Disease Prevention*, Department of Health, Education, and Welfare, Publication No. 79-55071, Washington, D.C., 1979.

listed by only 28% of the respondents, high blood pressure by only 21%, and cholesterol or fat in the diet or blood by only 13% (Table 11-6). Half the people interviewed did not name any of these major risk factors, while only 1% correctly identified all three. Despite their lack of information about the nature of the specific risk factors, 76% of the respondents believed that heart attacks could be prevented.

The results of this study are similar to those reported from a nationwide survey published in 1973 by Louis Harris and associates. Both reports show evidence of an extensive lack of information on the part of the general public with respect to the etiology of ASCVD. This

TABLE 11-6.—WHAT DO YOU FEEL ARE THE MAJOR LIKELY CAUSES OF HEART ATTACKS IN PERSONS UNDER 60 YEARS OF AGE?*

	EDUCATION			
RESPONSE	NOT HIGH SCHOOL GRADUATE	HIGH SCHOOL GRADUATE	FOUR-YEAR COLLEGE GRADUATE	TOTAL†
Stress, worry, nervous tension, pressure	20%	36%	47%	36%
Overweight	27	29	34	30
Cigarette smoking	24	28	32	28
High blood pressure	20	18	30	21
Not enough exercise	9	16	25	17
Don't know	28	17	9	16
Cholesterol, fat in diet or blood	12	12	15	13
Heredity, family history	3	11	16	11
Not enough rest, working too hard	10	12	8	11

*Survey of Chicago-area adults, 1976 to 1977.
†Percentages do not add to 100% because each respondent could give several responses. Responses given by less than 10% of respondents have been omitted.
Source: Shekelle R. B., Liu S. C.: *J.A.M.A.* 240(8):757, 1978. (Used by permission.)

includes even the more educated in our society, since in the Chicago study 41% of college graduates could not name any of the three major risk factors for coronary heart disease.

It seems only reasonable to conclude that, since a modification of these risk factors is the only means of prevention presently available to reduce the morbidity and mortality due to ASCVD, better education of the public in this area is a critical first step in any program of prevention. However, this does not mean that the increased knowledge that people acquire will necessarily cause them to change their life-style in such a way as to reduce the impact of these factors. In fact, studies dealing with patient compliance indicate that treatment programs that require people to abandon established patterns of behavior, such as dietary habits, smoking, and drinking, are less likely to be followed than those that do not involve a disruption of their usual daily routine (see also chap. 23).[43] Since a modification of the risk factors for ASCVD requires that people change deeply ingrained habit patterns, this will undoubtedly prove to be a difficult task.

There is evidence, however, that specific programs designed to increase the public's knowledge about the preventive aspects of ASCVD and to change their life-style to reduce the impact of ASCVD risk factors can be successful. The National High Blood Pressure Education Program, which was initiated in 1972 by the government, is designed to alert people to the high frequency and dangers of hypertension. This program is partly responsible for the increase in the proportion of people with this disorder who know they have it, from 50% in 1972 to the current figure of 70%.[1] Moreover, a much higher percentage of hypertensives is now under effective treatment as a result of public health measures such as this.

The report of a preventive health program for ASCVD initiated by Stanford University indicates that community health education using mass media campaigns and face-to-face counseling can reduce the risk of ASCVD.[44] In this study, people from two small California communities who received health education were compared with the people in a third control community (who did not receive this education) in terms of (1) their knowledge and behavior related to ASCVD and (2) the physiological indicators of ASCVD risk. In the control community the risk of ASCVD increased over the two-year period of observation, while in the two treatment communities there was a substantial and sustained decrease in risk (Fig 11–5).

Another successful community program de-

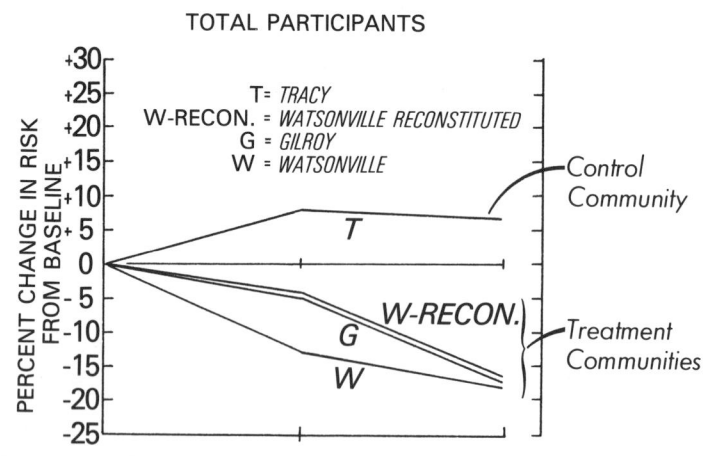

Fig 11–5.—Percentage change from baseline (0) in the risk of coronary heart disease after one and two years of health education among participants from three communities. (From Farquhar J.W., et al.: *Lancet* 1(2):1192, 1977. Used by permission.)

signed to reduce the levels of three of the main risk factors for coronary heart disease (i.e., cigarette smoking, serum cholesterol concentration, and high blood pressure) was carried out in East Finland, where the prevalence of this disease is greater than in any other country (see Fig 11–2).[45] Not only did the levels of these risk factors fall, but there was a reduction in the incidence of acute myocardial infarction and stroke, as well as a decrease in mortality from cardiovascular disease, during the period of the study (1972–1977).[46]

SUMMARY

Through the use of the concept of life-style we have tried to demonstrate the manner in which social and cultural factors affect the health of our population. The ill effects of dietary excesses, cigarette smoking, lack of exercise, and exposure to environmental contaminants on our well-being can be profound. Only recently have we become aware that, as a result of the technological advancements of the past 100 years, we are being confronted by a myriad of new health hazards.

The practical value of recognizing these life-style and environmental disease-causing factors lies in the application of this knowledge in the prevention of disease. Once disorders such as cancer, heart attack, and stroke occur, the outlook for recovery is dismal in most instances. On the other hand, modification of the risk factors that predispose people to these conditions may help to prevent or delay their onset. Of course, public health measures of a broad scope are necessary in order to deal effectively with the problems of environmental contamination; however, there is much that an individual can do to alter his own life-style and thereby reduce the impact of personal risk factors on his health.

Medical personnel attempting to implement a therapeutic program requiring a change in life-style should realize that patterns of living are deeply rooted in socially and culturally derived attitudes and beliefs. To change these patterns is very difficult. For people to reduce the salt and fat content of their diet (assuming that this is advisable) is not so simple a matter as it may seem. It is common knowledge that cigarette smoking is a habit that is extremely hard to break. Of the people who attempt to lose weight by dieting, many more fail than succeed.

Two categories of disease, cancer and atherosclerotic cardiovascular disease (ASCVD), were selected for discussion in this chapter because (1) they are the chief causes of mortality in our society, and (2) they are prime examples of conditions in which environmental and life-style factors play a key role in causation. The changes in environment and life-style that accompanied the industrial transformation of our society in the first half of this century appear to be the reasons for the steady increase in the incidence of cancer and ASCVD during this period. The same may be true for other degenerative diseases that currently plague us. The knowledge gained from the study of these changes will provide both a clue to the etiology of these disorders and methods of reducing their prevalence. A prudent diet, the control of hypertension, the cessation of cigarette smoking, the judicious use of physical exercise, and the adoption of better ways of coping with stress may have a greater impact on ASCVD than all the medications and surgical procedures currently used. There is, in fact, evidence that the recent decline in mortality from coronary artery disease is due in part to a reduction in these risk factors. The future success of public health programs designed to modify these factors depends on medical personnel having a better understanding of the social and cultural aspects of medicine and how they affect our life-style.

REFERENCES

1. *Healthy people: The Surgeon General's Report on Health Promotion and Disease Prevention, 1979*, No. 79–55071. U.S. Department of Health, Education and Welfare, Public Health Service.
2. Drinker P.: Health aspects of air pollution. *Arch. Environ. Health* 4:221, 1962.
3. Selikoff I.J., Hammond E.C.: Asbestos-associ-

ated disease in United States shipyards. *CA.* 28(2):87–99, 1978.
4. Brill A.B., et al.: Leukemia in man following exposure to ionizing radiation: A summary of the findings in Hiroshima and Nagasaki, and a comparison with other human experiences. *Ann. Intern. Med.* 56:590, 1962.
5. Waller J.A.: Chronic medical conditions and traffic safety: A review of California experience. *N. Engl. J. Med.* 273:1413, 1965.
6. Modan B., et al.: Low-fiber intake as an etiologic factor in cancer of the colon. *J. Natl. Cancer Inst.* 55(1):15, 1975.
7. Hill M.J.: Colon cancer: A disease of fiber depletion or of dietary excess? *Digestion* 11:289, 1974.
8. U.S. Public Health Service: *Health Consequences of Smoking*, pub. 73–8704. Washington, D.C., U.S. Government Printing Office, 1973.
9. Auerbach O., et al.: Effects of cigarette smoking in dogs. II. Pulmonary neoplasms. *Arch. Environ. Health* 21:754, 1970.
10. Figueroa W.G.: Lung cancer in chloromethyl methyl ether workers. *N. Engl. J. Med.* 288:1096, 1973.
11. U.S. Public Health Service: *Smoking and Health Report of the Advisory Committee to the Surgeon General*, Pub. 1103. Washington, D.C., U.S. Government Printing Office, 1964.
12. DeGroot L.J.: Radiation-associated thyroid carcinoma. *Thyroid Today* 1:1, 1977.
13. Walfish P.G., et al.: Irradiation-related thyroid cancer. *Ann. Intern. Med.* 88(2):261–262, 1978.
14. Wynder E.L., et al.: An epidemiologic investigation of cancer of the genito-urinary tract. *Cancer* 16:1388, 1963.
15. Bradshaw F., et al.: Smoking, drinking and oesophageal cancer in African males in Johannesburg, South Africa. *Br. J. Cancer* 30:157, 1974.
16. Feldman J.G., et al.: A case-control investigation of alcohol, tobacco and diet in head and neck cancer. *Prev. Med.* 4:444, 1975.
17. Singer A.: Promiscuous sexual behavior and its effect on cervical morphology. *Br. J. Obstet. Gynaecol.* 82:588, 1975.
18. *Estrogens and Endometrial Cancer*, FDA Drug Bulletin, vol. 6, no. 1. U.S. Department of Health, Education, and Welfare, February–March 1976.
19. Weinstein M.C.: Estrogen use in postmenopausal women—costs, risks, and benefits. *N. Engl. J. Med.* 303:308, 1980.
20. *DES and breast cancer*, FDA Drug Bulletin, vol. 8, no. 10. U.S. Department of Health, Education, and Welfare, 1978.
21. U.S. Public Health Service: *Multiple Risk Factors in Arteriosclerosis,* report by National Heart and Lung Institute Task Force on Arteriosclerosis, vol. 2. Washington, D.C., U.S. Government Printing Office, 1971.
22. Smith W.M.: Epidemiology of hypertension. *Med. Clin. North Am.* 61(3):467, 1977.
23. Reisin E., Abel R., Modan M., et al.: Effect of weight loss without salt restriction on the reduction of blood pressure in overweight hypertensive patients. *N. Engl. J. Med.* 298:1, 1978.
24. Weinsier R.L.: Overview: Salt and the development of essential hypertension. *Prev. Med.* 5(1):7–14, 1976.
25. Dahl L.K.: Salt and hypertension. *Am. J. Clin. Nutr.* 25:231, 1972.
26. Keys A.: Coronary heart disease in seven countries. *Circulation* 41(4):1–211, 1970.
27. Kannel W.B., et al.: Cholesterol in the prediction of atherosclerotic disease: New perspectives based on the Framingham study. *Ann. Intern. Med.* 90:85, 1979.
28. Stamler J.: Epidemiology of coronary heart disease. *Med. Clin. North Am.* 57:5, 1973.
29. Hartung G.H., Foreyt J.P., Mitchell R.E., et al.: Relation of diet to high-density-lipoprotein cholesterol in middle-aged marathon runners, joggers, and inactive men. *N. Engl. J. Med.* 302:357, 1980.
30. Christakis G., Rathmann D.: Position statement on diet and coronary heart disease. *Prev. Med.* 1(1–2):255, 1972.
31. Gordon T., et al.: Menopause and coronary heart disease: The Framingham study. *Ann. Intern. Med.* 89(2):157–161, 1978.
32. Ahrens E.H.: The management of hyperlipidemia: Whether, rather than how. *Ann. Intern. Med.* 88:87–93, 1976.
33. Stamler J., Epstein F.: Coronary heart disease: Risk factors as guides to preventive action. *Prev. Med.* 1:27, 1972.
34. Clarke H.H. (ed.): Physical Fitness Research Digest, Series 2, No. 2. President's Council on Physical Fitness, 1972.
35. Kannel W.B., Sorlie P.: Some health benefits of physical activity. *Arch. Intern. Med.* 139:857, 1979.
36. Paffenbarger R.S., Wing A.L., Hyde R.T.: Physical activity as an index of heart attack risk in college alumna. *Am. J. Epidemiol.* 108:161, 1978.
37. Williams R.S., Logue E.E., Lewis J.L.: Physical conditioning augments the fibrinolytic response to venous occlusion in healthy subjects. *N. Engl. J. Med.* 302:987, 1980.
38. Friedman M., Rosenman R.H.: *Type A Behavior and Your Heart*. New York, Alfred A. Knopf, Inc., 1974.
39. Rosenman R.H., Friedman M.: Neurogenic

factors in the pathogenesis of coronary heart disease. *Med. Clin. North Am.* 58:269, 1974.
40. Frank K.A., et al.: Type A behavior pattern and coronary angiographic findings. *J.A.M.A.* 240(8):761, 1978.
41. Stern M.P.: The recent decline in ischemic heart disease mortality. *Ann. Intern. Med.* 91:630, 1979.
42. Shekelle R.B., Liu S.C.: Public beliefs about causes and prevention of heart attacks. *J.A.M.A.* 240:756, 1978.
43. Mathews D., Hingson R.: Improving patient compliance, a guide for physicians. *Med. Clin. North Am.* 61:879, 1977.
44. Farquhar J.W., et al.: Community education for cardiovascular health. *Lancet* 1(2):1192, 1977.
45. Puska P., Juomilehto J., Salonen J., et al.: Changes in coronary risk factors during comprehensive five-year community program to control cardiovascular diseases (North Karelia Project). *Br. Med. J.* 2:1173, 1979.
46. Salonen J.T., Puska P., Mustaniemi H.: Changes in morbidity and mortality during comprehensive community program to control cardiovascular diseases during 1972–1977 in North Karelia. *Br. Med. J.* 2:1178, 1979.

12 / Substance Abuse

JONATHAN J. BRAUNSTEIN, M.D., NEIL SCHNEIDERMAN, Ph.D., AND MARC SILBRET, M.D.

IN THIS CHAPTER, we will examine the psychological, social, and cultural aspects of substance abuse. No attempt is made to cover this complex subject in its entirety. The pharmacologic properties of the drugs will be dealt with only in terms of their general effects on the central nervous system. Treatment, although a very important topic, will be discussed only briefly because for most forms of substance abuse there is no specific curative therapy, and many of the treatments presently used are still under investigation to determine their ultimate value.

GENERAL CONCEPTS

Understanding the problem of substance abuse is facilitated by thinking of it in terms of the interplay of three factors: the substance, the individual who abuses it, and the social and cultural milieu in which he lives.

The Substance or Drug

A wide spectrum of substances are subject to abuse, and different criteria have been used to classify them. The following is a simple classification that has great practical value for medical personnel:
1. Food
2. Social drugs
    a. Alcohol
    b. Nicotine
    c. Caffeine
3. Licit agents (over-the-counter and prescription drugs)
    a. Analgesics
    b. Sedatives–tranquilizers
    c. Stimulants
4. Illicit agents
    a. Opium derivatives (e.g., heroin)
    b. Stimulants
    c. Hallucinogens (e.g., marihuana)

Food, although not usually considered a chemical agent, is a substance that is commonly abused—a fact that is corroborated by the high prevalence of obesity in this country. The remainder of the substances on the list are psychoactive or mind-altering, i.e., their use causes changes in thinking, perception, mood, or consciousness.

For purposes of this discussion, a drug is defined as any substance that, when taken into the body, produces alterations in physiological and biochemical processes. According to this broad definition, socially used substances such as alcohol, nicotine, and caffeine belong in this category just as much as those chemical agents that have a medical use. The latter constitute the group of licit drugs, over-the-counter and prescription medications. By contrast, the so-called illicit drugs (e.g., marihuana, heroin, LSD) are not generally used for medical purposes, although, as we shall point out later, there are exceptions to this generalization—as, for example, marihuana.

The distinction between the use and the abuse of a drug may not be clear-cut. One definition of drug abuse is the taking of a psychoactive medication for nonmedical purposes. This definition applies best to the licit drugs designed to alleviate the manifestations of physical and emotional illness. When they are taken for this purpose, they are being used appropriately; when they are taken for pleasure or recreation, they are being abused.

Even when licit drugs are utilized to combat the symptoms of ill health, however, they can be abused if they are self-administered without medical supervision.

The social drugs (alcohol, caffeine, and nicotine) and illicit agents (marihuana, heroin, LSD) present a somewhat different problem in terms of the definition of abuse. Because these drugs were not intended for any specific purpose other than pleasure and recreation, abuse often becomes a matter of whether or not their use has harmful effects on the individual and those about him. For some illicit agents (heroin, LSD), use and abuse are really synonymous since any exposure to them is potentially harmful. For the social drugs, use and abuse can usually be distinguished on the basis of the amount of the agent that is taken in and the frequency with which it is used, since these are the primary factors determining their harmful effects.

Certain pharmacologic properties of the psychoactive drugs play a critical role in their abuse. First and foremost among these is the ability to induce *psychological dependence,* meaning that exposure to one of these agents may cause a person to develop a psychological need or desire for it, which impels him to seek out the agent again and again. In varying degrees, this is a property of all drugs of abuse. With the use of some drugs (e.g., heroin), this dependence is so strong that it can only be described as a "craving" that must be satisfied whatever the cost.

A second pharmacologic property of some psychoactive drugs that leads to their abuse is the capacity to induce *physical dependence* after repeated administration. This is typical of the central nervous system (CNS) depressants, for example, alcohol, barbiturates, and opiates. In this form of dependence, exposure to the drug is associated with biochemical and physiological changes in the body's tissues and organs (e.g., central nervous system), which make them unable to function appropriately unless a certain amount of the drug is present. When the concentration of the drug in the body falls below a critical level, a withdrawal or abstinence syndrome occurs, which is characteristic for each of the categories of CNS depressants. This syndrome not only is a painful experience, but in some instances it can also be medically very serious and even lethal.

A third property that is shared by the psychoactive drugs of abuse is the capacity to produce a state of *tolerance* in the individual. Repeated administration of a given dose of a drug has progressively less effect, so that increasing amounts are required in order to achieve the same effect as the original dose. Thus, a person who abuses the drug finds that he must take more and more to experience the desired psychological reactions. Tolerance may develop to some actions of a drug, but not to others. *Cross-tolerance* exists when the development of tolerance to one drug is associated with the occurrence of tolerance to another pharmacologically related drug(s).

Tolerance occurs because of two types of drug-induced changes: (1) metabolic changes (e.g., hepatic enzyme induction) that affect the biotransformation of the drug in the body, and (2) molecular changes in the body's tissues that cause them to adapt to the presence of the drug. For a detailed discussion of the biologic basis for drug tolerance and physical dependence, the reader is referred to several excellent reviews of this subject that have recently appeared.[1,2]

The Person Who Abuses Drugs

If people who misuse drugs are asked, why did you initially become involved in this problem? a variety of answers will be given. Among their responses are likely to be the following: to relieve anxiety, tension, boredom, or depression; to improve social interaction; to compensate for feelings of alienation and isolation; to satisfy curiosity; to achieve a sense of self-identity; and to just feel good.[3,4] The point to be made is that there is no single reason why people start to abuse drugs but rather a number of different explanations.

Since there is no unanimity of opinion with regard to why people initially become involved in drug abuse, perhaps there is an accepted explanation for their persistence in this behavior even though it is harmful. Again, there is no single reason but rather a number of factors (physical, psychological, and social) that perpetuate drug-taking behavior. In animals, biologic factors have been shown to play a role in some instances. Experimental studies with some species indicate that susceptibility to narcotic addiction is under genetic control, at least in part. In the past decade, evidence has been obtained indicating that genetic factors play a role in the development of alcoholism. One of the early investigations that separated the genetic from the environmental determinants of this disease was carried out in Denmark by Goodwin and his co-workers.[5] They interviewed two groups of men: one consisting of the offspring of alcoholics who were separated from their biologic parents soon after birth and raised by nonrelatives, the other of adoptees of nonalcoholic biologic parents. The rate of alcoholism in the first group was almost four times that of the second group. Moreover, alcoholism in the parents who adopted the two groups of children did not explain this difference. The smaller number of alcoholic women in Denmark made it difficult for Goodwin et al. to ascertain the exact significance of genetic factors in this sex.

PSYCHOLOGICAL FACTORS IN DRUG ABUSE. —The psychological status of drug abusers often varies according to the type of agent that is used and the extent of its misuse. For instance, while the use of social drugs is common among people who are well adjusted, the abuse of an illicit drug like heroin is an indication of serious maladjustment. Those who experiment briefly with a drug and than give it up are less likely to have significant psychopathology than those who chronically abuse drugs.

Cohen has described the population of *chronic drug abusers* as being made up of the following different personality types:[6]

1. Immature
2. Depressed
3. Antisocial
4. Schizoid or schizophrenic
5. Environmentally handicapped
6. Mature

The *immature person* is unable to deal with the day-to-day problems of life without developing an inordinate degree of tension, anxiety, and frustration. He is unable to function adequately in society, and for him drug abuse offers a means of coping. The chronically *depressed individual* experiences real emotional pain and discomfort for which psychoactive drugs appear to be a remedy. Both CNS stimulants and depressants may be abused by such people in an attempt to get more enjoyment out of life. Those with *sociopathic* or *antisocial personalities* are unable to accept society's rules and regulations. Their behavior is self-centered and narcissistic and often does not reflect a sense of responsibility and conscience. For these individuals, personal needs and gratification come first in life. This description fits a large number of the abusers of "hard" drugs like narcotics.

Some of those who engage in drug abuse have serious emotional illnesses (e.g., psychoses such as *schizophrenia*); however, in the majority of instances this is not so. On the other hand, *schizoid personality* disturbances are probably not uncommon. People with this personality type have great difficulty in establishing meaningful interpersonal relationships; they are "loners" with limited intellectual abilities. For them, drugs offer a means of breaking down the barriers to communication, allowing them to "fit in" with the society. *Environmentally deprived* individuals, as for example, those living in the urban ghetto areas of our country, are more susceptible to drug abuse. Their dismal living conditions cause them to turn to drugs to escape from the harsh realities of life.

The spectrum of individuals who are susceptible to and engage in drug abuse is a broad one. At one end are those who apparently have no psychopathology, while at the other end are those who are severely maladjusted and emotionally ill. Between these two extremes are a variety of types of psychological problems, as for instance: the adolescent trying to "find himself," the college student seeking to ingratiate himself with his peer group, the depressed middle-aged homemaker attempting to cope with her loneliness and depression, and the driving achievement-oriented business executive searching for a means of relaxation from the "pressures" of work.

THE ROLE OF OPERANT CONDITIONING.—The drug-taking behavior of people, regardless of their psychological makeup, can be explained in terms of the *social learning theory* or *operant conditioning* (Fig 12–1). In other words, substance abuse can be viewed as a form of conditioned behavior.[7]

When the self-administration of a psychoactive drug produces a pleasurable reaction (or reduces psychological pain due to anxiety, tension, or depression), there is a tendency for the person to want to take it again to reexperience this feeling. The "reward" (the pleasurable reaction) that accompanies the use of the substance acts as a positive reinforcer for this behavior. Over a period of time, a pattern of drug-seeking behavior may be established in which the individual repeatedly takes the substance for its pleasurable effects. This form of drug dependence is called *primary psychological dependence* and is the initial step in the development of drug abuse.

The problem of substance abuse is more complex than this, however, because some agents also produce a state of *physical dependence* in the individual. This is true for the CNS depressants but not for the stimulants and the hallucinogens. Once this occurs, the person is at risk of developing a withdrawal or abstinence syndrome if he reduces the intake of the drug. Withdrawal is a physically and psychologically painful experience that acts as a negative reinforcer to perpetuate the individual's drug-taking behavior; he seeks out the drug to avoid experiencing the painful symptoms of withdrawal. This form of drug dependence is called *secondary psychological dependence*.

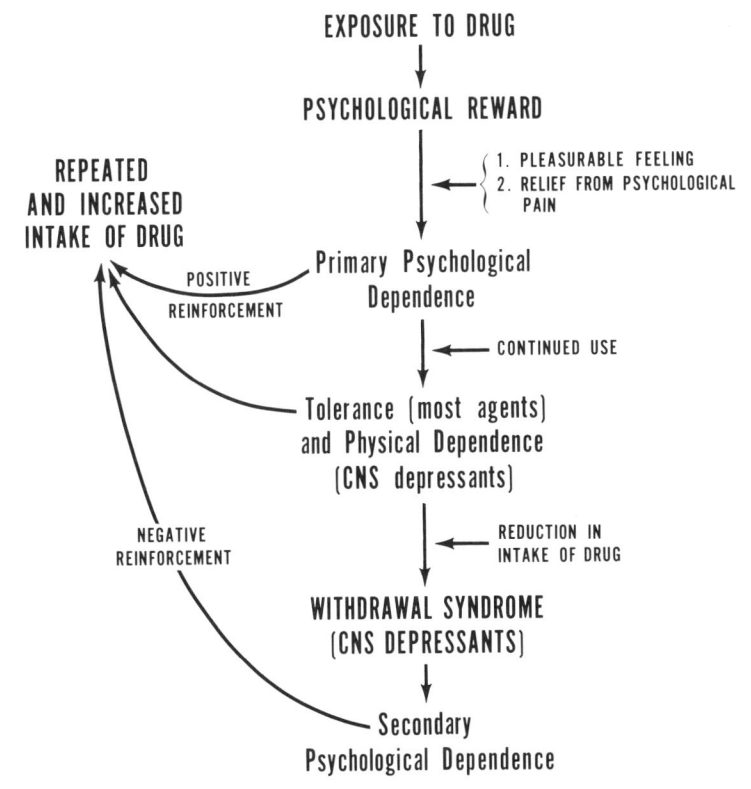

Fig 12–1.—The operant conditioning of drug-taking behavior in susceptible persons.

Drug *tolerance* further compounds the problems faced by the individual who is physically dependent. In this situation, the effects of the drug on the person—its pleasure-producing qualities and its capacity to forestall the development of abstinence symptoms—can be maintained only by taking larger and larger doses. In the case of a drug like heroin, the addict may become so tolerant to its pleasurable effects that he no longer gets "high" from the drug, and the principal reason he continues to seek out the agent is to prevent the manifestations of withdrawal.

Social and Cultural Milieu in Which Drug Abuse Occurs

The social and cultural environment in which an individual lives has a great bearing on whether or not he will engage in drug abuse and, if so, what agent he will select. The urban American life-style, with its many stressful experiences, is a predisposing factor for the development of drug-taking behavior. For example, those who live in the poverty areas of inner cities face a life that is in most respects so bleak that drugs often seem a welcome alternative to reality. Even those in the middle and upper social strata encounter the stresses of our modern life-style, since they too have to meet the demands and pressures of our "dog eat dog" competitive society. Environmental influences in the form of peer pressure and media advertisements are additional incentives for this drug-taking behavior.

In addition to acting as a predisposing factor, the social and cultural milieu determines both the *accessibility* and the *acceptability* of psychoactive substances. Throughout history, man has abused those chemical agents that his particular life-style has made readily available. For example, in Europe, alcoholic beverages have been the mainstay; in Moslem countries, where alcohol is prohibited by religious dictates, hashish (a close relative of marihuana) has been a favorite recreational drug. For many centuries, cocaine chewed from the leaves of the coca plant was widely utilized as a psychotropic agent in South American civilizations. In Mexico, peyote and certain mushrooms have been used to achieve a psychic "high."

The same general principle applies to the abuse of drugs in our country. Since the average person has easy access to tobacco, alcohol, and licit drugs (such as over-the-counter and prescription medications), these agents are most frequently misused. Illicit agents (i.e., heroin, cocaine, and LSD), which are not so readily available, are less commonly abused, even though more publicity surrounds this abuse problem.

A marked increase in the prevalence of substance abuse has occurred in this country over the past half-century.[8] There is good reason to believe that social change and pharmacologic discoveries have been mainly responsible, since this increase cannot be accounted for by a rise in the number of susceptible individuals. These may have resulted in more drug abuse by: (1) increasing the availability of psychoactive agents, (2) making the use of these agents more acceptable to the public, and (3) giving rise to the belief that the use of drugs is an appropriate means of solving life's problems. There is no question that mind-altering drugs are more plentiful in today's society than ever before. This is especially true with respect to psychoactive medications since the introduction of tranquilizers in the early 1950s. By their prescribing habits, physicians have unwittingly increased not only the availability but also the acceptability of these agents. There was a time when taking a psychoactive drug was considered undesirable, and even dangerous, by most of the public. The liberal attitude of many physicians in prescribing tranquilizers and sedatives has convinced people that their use is both a safe and an appropriate means of dealing with the psychological problems due to life stress.

Within each social group, certain drugs are more acceptable than others and are more likely to be misused. For example, adolescents and college students are likely to use alcohol and marijuana as the drugs of choice, a middle-aged businessman may be drawn most to alcohol, while the middle-aged or elderly housewife is likely to turn to sedatives or tranquilizers. Urban ghetto residents and counterculture youths are more likely to use hard drugs like heroin and LSD. Cocaine is coming more and more into vogue with those in the middle and upper classes. Not only is the misuse of single drugs a problem, but also multiple drug abuse is popular among certain counterculture youth and other individuals in our society.

OBESITY

Obesity, which is defined as an excess of body fat, affects a large proportion of the adult population of this country.[9] As seen in Figure 12–2, the frequency of this condition varies with age, sex, race, and socioeconomic status. Being obese and being overweight are usually, but not necessarily, synonymous. This is because not all overweight persons have excessive body fat. For example, a 230-pound fullback on a football team may be overweight because of his large muscle mass. Similarly, a person with abnormal fluid retention may be overweight because of an excess of body water.

The diagnosis of obesity is usually made by general inspection. Since the vast majority of overweight individuals are obese, a comparison of a person's height and weight with the ideal or desirable values on a standard height-weight table (prepared by insurance actuaries) is usually enough to substantiate the diagnosis. The measurement of skinfold thickness in certain body areas is another simple, objective way to determine whether someone is obese.

Those who exceed their ideal or desirable weight by more than 20–30% have a significant medical problem. Such individuals have a greater prevalence of a number of serious physical disorders including hypertension, diabetes mellitus, gout, atherosclerosis, endometrial cancer, osteoarthritis, and gallbladder disease. In addition, they suffer from psychological, social, and economic problems as a result of their obesity. Most important, their

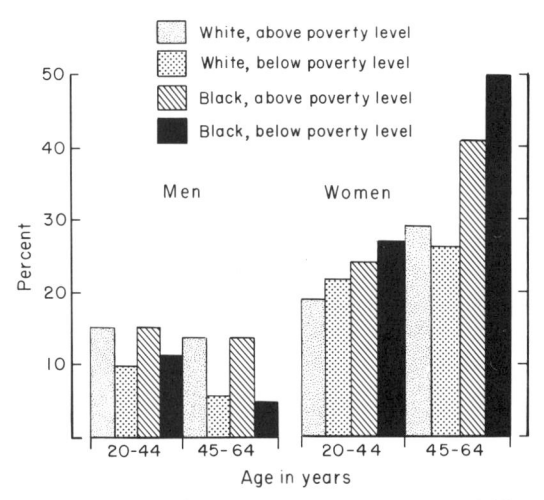

Fig 12–2.—Obesity among persons aged 20–74 according to sex, age, race, and poverty level: United States, 1971–1974.
Note: Obesity measure is based on triceps skinfold measurements and is defined as greater than the sex-specific 85th percentile measurements for persons aged 20–29.
Source: *Health, United States, 1978.* Third Annual Report on the Health Status of the Nation. Hyattsville, Md., U.S. Department of Health, Education, and Welfare, Public Health Service, Publication No. 78–1232. December 1978, p. 215.

longevity is reduced in proportion to the degree of their overweight condition. It was previously thought that even minor degrees of obesity reduce survival but recent investigations, such as the Framingham study, have found that minimal mortality actually occurs at weights that are somewhat above the so-called ideal or desirable levels.[9]

Causative Factors in Obesity

Fundamentally, obesity is due to an energy imbalance. When energy intake exceeds output, the excess is stored in the body as adipose tissue. Both excessive food intake (hyperphagia) and insufficient physical activity play a causative role in human obesity; however, food abuse is generally considered to be the main culprit.

A metabolic basis for obesity has been looked for, but until recently no evidence of a specific defect has been found. In 1980, however, De Luise, Blackburn, and Flier described a reduction in activity of the energy-consuming red cell sodium-potassium pump (sodium and potassium-dependent adenosine triphosphatase) in a group of obese persons, a finding that also has been reported to occur in an animal model of obesity (ob/ob mouse).[10] If this enzyme abnormality is confirmed and found to be present in other tissues of individuals with obesity, it would provide a molecular basis for a considerable decrease in energy use by the body. This would lead to an energy imbalance (as long as food intake did not decrease) and the deposition of excess body fat.

In animal models, genetic, neurologic, and endocrine factors are important determinants of obesity. Human obesity also appears to be heterogeneous in terms of etiology. In the vast majority of instances of this condition, no underlying disease can be found. Such patients are referred to as having *primary obesity*, which, in turn, can be subdivided into childhood-onset and adult-onset obesity. Psychological, social, and cultural influences are thought to be of great importance in the development of primary obesity. Besides the primary type, there are also *secondary forms of obesity*, i.e., those due to an underlying medical disorder.

In a recent review of the *genetic factors* in human obesity, Foch and McClearn analyzed the results of familial resemblance, twin, and adoption studies in the literature.[11] They concluded that (1) obesity clearly is familial (over two thirds of obese persons have at least one obese parent) and (2) genes play a significant role in the etiology of this condition. In cases of primary obesity in which heredity is a causal factor, a polygenic mode of inheritance appears to be operative. In addition, there are secondary forms of obesity due to single gene defects. These constitute a rare group of disorders, transmitted as mendelian recessives, including the Laurence-Moon-Biedl syndrome, the Alström syndrome, and the Prader-Willi syndrome.

Neurologic diseases (e.g., tumors, inflammatory diseases) or injuries involving the hypothalamus account for some cases of secondary obesity. The incidence of these disorders is very low, and patients who have them invariably have neurologic findings that indicate damage to this area of the brain. A number of *endocrine conditions* also can result in obesity. These include hyperinsulinism, due either to exogenous administration or to endogenous overproduction (e.g., by an insulin-secreting tumor of the pancreas); an excess of adrenal cortical steroids, from exogenous or endogenous sources; and hypothyroidism.

The Role of Psychosocial Factors in Primary Obesity

Hyperphagia can be viewed as a type of food abuse. The latter term applies specifically to individuals who overeat *not* in response to physiological hunger but because psychological, social, and cultural influences impel them to do so. For instance, hyperphagia is often a reaction to the stress of everyday life. Also, people often find themselves eating in order to be sociable. They eat at parties, at ball games, while watching television, and at other social events when they are not especially hungry. Food has become a sort of "social drug" similar to caffeine, nicotine, and alcohol in that it is used to facilitate social interaction, to relax, and as a way to cope with the trials and tribulations of life.

The role of the psyche in the pathogenesis of primary obesity deserves special comment. Early in life, the psychological effects of the mother-child relationship may predispose a child to develop obesity. Some mothers are apparently "obesogenic" for their children in that they encourage them in one way or another to overeat. At times this is related to misinformation these mothers have about nutrition, as for example, the idea that chubbiness is a sign of good health in a baby. In addition, mothers convey social attitudes and beliefs about diet to their children, including what type and how much food to eat. They may inadvertently "teach" a child to overeat or consume fattening foods. Finally, there are instances in which a mother may have psychopathology that is instrumental in causing obesity in her child.

When obesity develops in childhood, the person is more likely to suffer from psychological dysfunction than when the condition is acquired in adult life. One important psychological difference between childhood and adult-onset obesity is that a distortion of body image is commonly experienced by persons in the former category. Attempts to define a particular personality type that is associated with primary obesity have been unsuccessful.

There appears to be a reciprocal relationship between emotional distress and obesity: on the one hand, emotional conflict may lead to obesity; on the other, obesity may be responsible for the genesis of emotional problems. The social rejection experienced by overweight adolescents and adults can adversely affect their self-esteem, resulting in anxiety, anger, and depression. These reactions, in turn, often stimulate the person to overeat, thus compounding the obesity problem.

Guggenheim describes two specific types of psychological obesity: reactive hyperphagia and symbolic obesity.[12] The first is typically seen in situations in which a person has experienced an acutely stressful life event (e.g., death of a loved one, divorce). In response to this stress, he overeats to the extent that he becomes significantly overweight. Reactive hyperphagia may be transitory, abating when the acute event has passed, or chronic and recurrent in instances where people react to even mild stress by overeating. In symbolic obesity, the increased body size of the overweight person has symbolic meaning to him. In other words, a secondary gain results from the obesity, at least in the mind of the individual. Two examples of symbolic obesity are: an obese executive who equates his size with the power he exerts over others and an obese woman who attempts to discourage potential male suitors (whom she cannot accept psychologically) by becoming very obese and, hence, unattractive. For those with symbolic obesity, the gain associated with their overweight condition represents a serious obstacle to therapy, for to lose weight is to give up this gain.

While the psyche is often given the most attention in discussions of the development of obesity, the importance of social and cultural factors cannot be overstated. Evidence supporting this can be found in the different rates of obesity in countries throughout the world and among the various social classes in this country. In a study of coronary artery disease in men from seven countries around the world, Keys found that those from the United States had by far the greatest prevalence of obesity (Fig 12–3).[13]

In the United States, recent data indicate that there is a relationship between the prevalence of obesity and social class standing. In the age range 45–64, 35% of women below the poverty level are obese in contrast to only 29% of those with incomes above this level.[14] Comparable figures for men are 5% and 13%. There is also a racial difference in the prevalence of obesity, with a higher rate among white men as compared with black men (see Fig 12–1). This finding is reversed for women, with black women having a greater prevalence of obesity than white women.

The life-style of many people in this country predisposes them to obesity. People have become accustomed to high-calorie diets (rich in animal fats and simple sugars) and a sedentary mode of living. In most instances, primary obesity is due to this combination. Once a person becomes obese, his condition tends to limit the degree of spontaneous physical activity in which he engages, further reducing his energy output and creating a vicious cycle in which a positive energy balance is maintained.

Counteracting this obesogenic life-style is a recent social trend in the United States emphasizing the importance of physical fitness and of being thin. This trend is evident in the advertising in news media and accounts for a large number of the commercial diet and exercise programs that have been introduced in the last few years.

Treatment of Obesity

The fundamental principle in the treatment of obesity is to establish a negative energy

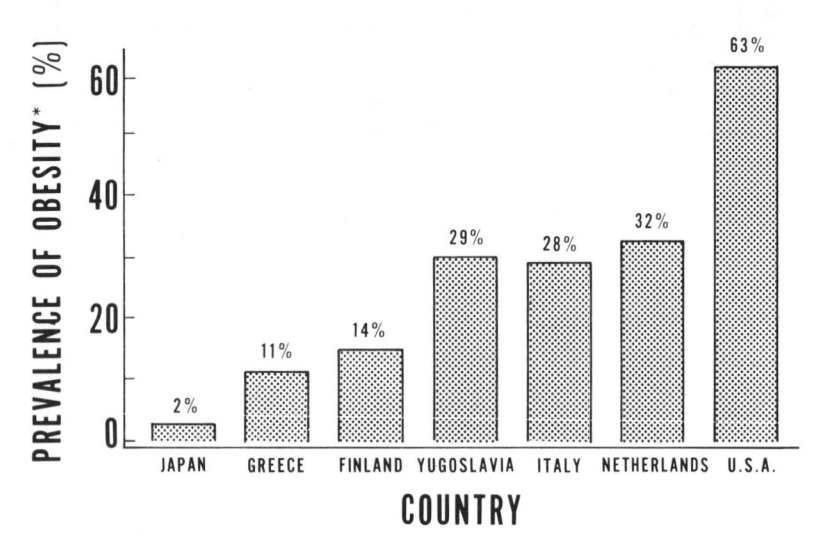

Fig 12-3.—Prevalence of obesity in groups of men from seven countries. (Data from Keys A.: Coronary heart disease in seven countries. *Circulation* [suppl. 1] 41[4]:1, 1970. By permission of the American Heart Association, Inc.)

balance by reducing energy intake (i.e., by dieting), increasing energy expenditure (i.e., by exercise), or both. Dieting is the key to any successful program of weight reduction, being a much more effective way of losing weight than exercise alone. This is true because it takes a great deal of exercise to use up the energy contained in a small quantity of food. For example, eating a piece of cake is calorically equivalent to briskly walking for approximately two hours. Clearly, it is easier to eliminate the cake from one's diet. In practice, *both* dieting and exercise are used to treat the overweight person since they complement each other in producing a negative energy balance. In addition, exercise increases cardiopulmonary fitness. Of course, the physician should be knowledgeable about the person's physical, emotional, and social status before prescribing a program of diet and exercise.

It is a fact that most therapeutic attempts at weight reduction meet with failure. Of those overweight persons who seek medical help, and they constitute the minority, only a small percentage follow medical advice and are able to lose a significant amount of weight. Moreover, the vast majority of persons who are successful in initially reducing their weight eventually regain it after a variable period of time.

Why is it so difficult for obese persons to lose weight? The basic reason is that in order to do so they must change their life-style, something that is very difficult for most individuals. Patient compliance with therapeutic regimens that involve an alteration of long-standing patterns of behavior (e.g., eating, physical activity) is generally poor. Successful therapy for obesity depends essentially on a highly motivated person because life-style habits are supported by strong psychological and sociocultural forces, which are usually extremely resistant to change.

The simplest and most practical therapeutic plan for obesity is a balanced diet that is low in calories and a supervised program of exercise. The average person must ingest each day a number of calories equivalent to about 15 times his body weight in order to maintain this weight. In obesity, a reduction in caloric intake to below this maintenance level will cause an increased catabolism of body fat and, consequently, a loss of weight. For example, a 500-calorie net deficit per day will result in a loss of one pound of fat tissue a week.

Anorexigenic drugs have little, if any, place in the routine treatment of obesity. Their usefulness is short-lived due to the tolerance to them that develops, and they have significant side effects. Unfortunately, for the obese person there is no simple alternative to changing his patterns of eating and activity.

Some self-help groups have proved to be as effective as medical programs in the treatment of obesity, or more so. Groups such as TOPS and Overeaters Anonymous have a relatively good record for weight reduction. The support and understanding that the obese share with one another are critical factors in the success of these self-help groups.

A number of other medical approaches have been introduced to help the overweight person reduce. For example, brief periods of total fasting in the hospital with close medical supervision have been used in an effort to produce large weight losses rapidly.[15] This technique is effective and well tolerated by most obese persons. However, a large part of the weight loss is due to a diuresis of body water and a breakdown in lean body tissue (protein), the latter being very undesirable. Also, long-term follow-up of persons who lose weight by fasting shows that there is a high incidence of recidivism.

When a fast is supplemented with moderate amounts of protein (1.5 gm/kg ideal body weight) with high biologic value, along with other essential nutrients, the breakdown of body protein is reduced. This has formed the basis for the use of the Protein-Sparing Modified Fast (PSMF) as a means of treating obesity.[16] This form of therapy, which does not require hospitalization, is effective in causing significant weight loss but carries with it the potential for side effects, some of which are serious. In fact, a number of unexplained deaths have occurred in otherwise healthy women who fasted and took a liquid protein supplement (containing hydrolyzed collagen fortified with the amino acid tryptophan), a protein source of poor biologic value.[17,18] It is clear that therapeutic programs using extreme dietary restriction (i.e., fasting, semifasting) are potentially dangerous to health and should be undertaken only when: (1) the person is very obese (i.e., at least 30% over desirable body weight) and a large weight loss is necessary, (2) the program is carefully supervised by a physician who understands the physiological effects of severe dieting, (3) there are no medical contraindications to the program, and (4) the person has been thoroughly informed about the potential risks.

One of the newer approaches to the therapy for obesity that has shown great promise is behavior modification.[19,20] Not only do persons in behavioral programs lose weight, but many are able to maintain this weight reduction for a relatively long time (i.e., up to a year). Since this technique appears to offer a good deal of hope for the therapy for obesity in the future, it will be described in some detail.

A typical program using behavior modification contains the following four elements: (1) record keeping, (2) control of stimuli that precede eating, (3) use of techniques to control the act of eating, and (4) modification of the consequences of eating. The crux of these programs is that they pay specific attention to the circumstances surrounding eating and the mood of the person—modifying both in order to encourage dieting. One form of record keeping is a graph showing the loss of weight that has occurred over a period of weeks. Such a graph provides both feedback about the effectiveness of diet and positive reinforcement. Each time the person loses a pound, marking the graph serves as a self-reinforcer for dieting behavior. Looking at the entire pattern of weight loss each morning also seems to have reinforcement value. A second form of record keeping consists of a diary indicating what, where, how much, and with whom one ate, and how one felt while eating. Such diaries increase one's awareness of internal and external stimuli that are associated with eating behaviors. A third form of record keeping consists of tabulating the number of calories eaten at each meal.

The control of stimuli that precede eating

is important because obese persons seem to be markedly influenced by external cues. An effort is made to limit the amount and accessibility of high-calorie food in the house. Dieters are asked to confine all eating to a specific place and to eat only at prescribed times. Specific techniques are also used to control the act of eating, such as decreasing the speed of eating (e.g., having persons put down their eating utensils after every third mouthful). Persons are also encouraged to stop combining their eating with such activities as reading the newspaper or watching television.

The last specific element in the program is to modify the consequences of eating. Instead of setting up rewards for accomplishing long-term goals, an attempt is made to reward successful dieting on a short-term basis. Loss of 2 or 3 pounds at the end of a week is typically rewarded by strong praise from the therapist and encouragement for the persons to reward themselves for their accomplishment. Friends and immediate relatives are also encouraged to be positively reinforcing.

Stunkard and Penick have recently reviewed the long-term results of behavior modification therapy for obesity.[20] They found that while this technique is initially successful in a large percentage of cases, the weight losses are not well maintained over an extended period of time. Specifically, these authors studied a group of 32 obese persons who received 12 weeks of behavioral modification therapy. Fifty-three percent of the patients lost a substantial amount of weight by the end of the treatment—a figure that increased to 60% at the end of one year. However, during the next 4 years the patients began to regain the weight they had lost, so that at the end of the 5-year follow-up period, only 27% had maintained their initial weight loss.

Finally, in the past decade a form of surgical therapy has been introduced for the control of *massive* obesity. Selected individuals who are markedly overweight and resistant to medical therapy have had an operation bypassing a major portion of their small intestine in order to reduce the absorption of nutrients. Jejunoileal bypass, the most widely used operation, is effective in causing a large weight loss in such persons; however, the mortality and serious complications associated with the procedure limit its use.[21]

THE USE AND ABUSE OF ALCOHOL

Approximately two thirds of all adult Americans drink alcoholic beverages at least occasionally. In this sense, the use of alcohol can be considered an integral part of the American life-style. For most people, alcohol poses little or no problem; however, for an estimated 10 million adults and 3 million teenagers in the United States who abuse this drug, it is the cause of serious psychological, medical, and social problems.[22]

Alcohol Abuse Defined

Imagine a horizontal line representing the population of alcohol consumers, with the extreme left composed of people who take an occasional drink with meals or at a party, the extreme right consisting of those who are the grossest abusers of alcohol, and in between the two extremes individuals with varying degrees of alcohol use and abuse. The main point of this schema is to emphasize that the use and abuse of alcohol are best conceived of as a continuum. The exact point at which use crosses over and becomes abuse is not clear-cut and has been the subject of considerable discussion and debate. In general, alcohol abuse can be said to exist whenever the chronic ingestion of alcohol produces dysfunction of a physical, psychological, or social nature for the person and his family.

Two general kinds of alcohol abusers can be recognized: (1) *problem drinkers*, those who experience physical, psychological, and social problems associated with excess alcohol consumption but are not physically dependent on alcohol, and (2) *alcoholics*, those who experience these problems and, in addition, are physically dependent on this chemical agent. Table 12–1 gives the currently accepted definitions of alcoholism, problem drinking, and alcohol-related disability. The following are some signs that can be used as evidence of alcohol abuse (i.e., problem drinking or alcoholism):

1. Repeated intoxication
2. Drinking in order to function socially or at work
3. Drinking in order to overcome unpleasant emotional states
4. Drinking that results in problems at work, at home, or among friends
5. Alcohol-seeking behavior that interferes with life activities and social roles
6. Illness or injury due to alcohol

TABLE 12–1.—DEFINITIONS OF ALCOHOL-RELATED DISABILITY, ALCOHOLISM, AND PROBLEM DRINKING

- **Alcohol-related disability** is a broad term that includes alcoholism but doesn't require that alcoholism be present.

An alcohol-related disability exists when there is an impairment in the physical, mental, or social functioning of an individual, so that it may be reasonably inferred that alcohol is part of the cause of that disability. Impairment includes actual health problems related to a specific drinking bout; offensive behavior caused by heavy drinking; injuries, death, and property loss caused by accidents related to drinking; failure of the chronic excessive drinker to fulfill his or her role in the family or on the job; and mental problems, such as depression and anxiety, related to drinking.

People manifesting alcohol-related disabilities, although not necessarily alcoholics, have an increased risk of becoming alcoholics.

- **Alcoholism** is addiction to alcohol. It is also defined as alcohol dependence syndrome by WHO and in the ninth revision of the International Classification of Diseases. Alcoholism is characterized by a compulsion to take alcohol on a continuous or periodic basis to experience its psychological and physical effects, and sometimes to avoid the discomfort of its absence. Tolerance may or may not be present.

The fact that a person is addicted to alcohol (an alcoholic) implies a probable impaired behavioral responsiveness to social control.

- **A problem drinker** is a person who drinks alcohol to an extent or in a manner that an alcohol-related disability is manifested. Therefore, the term problem drinker generally is applied to those who demonstrate problems in relation to drinking alcohol.

Source, Noble E.P. (ed.): *Alcohol and Health*. National Institute on Alcohol Abuse and Alcoholism, preprint copy, June 1978, p. 9.

7. Withdrawal manifestations of alcohol

Among alcoholics, the amount of alcohol consumed and the frequency of ingestion vary considerably. Some are steady drinkers, while others are binge or spree drinkers.

Epidemiology of Alcohol Abuse

The Surgeon General's 1979 Report on Health Promotion and Disease Prevention states that "the proportion of heavy drinkers in the population grew substantially in the 1960s to reach the highest recorded level since 1850, though it has leveled off in recent years."[14] It is estimated that the population of alcohol abusers (problem drinkers and alcoholics) in this country consists of 10 million adults (18 years and older) and 3.3 million teenagers (14–17 age range).[22] Of the adult group, it is thought that two thirds to three fourths are men and one fourth to one third are women. One in ten adults who drink will go on to abuse alcohol. While the popular stereotype of the alcoholic is the "skid-row bum," in actuality, this form of alcoholism is seen in only about 5% of the people with this disorder. The vast majority of the 5 million alcoholics in this country merge imperceptibly with the rest of the public; they are professionals, business people, blue-collar workers, homemakers, and adolescents.

Over the past 25 years, alcohol abuse has become increasingly prevalent among teenagers and women. A recent national survey examined teenage drinking among students in grades 7 through 12 (Fig 12–4). Seventy-four percent were found to be drinkers—79% of the boys and 70% of the girls. Most significantly, 19% of the students were problem drinkers—23% of the boys and 15% of the girls. As can be seen in Figure 12–4, the percentage of students who used and abused alcohol rose steadily with each succeeding grade.

A significant number of adult women in this country abuse alcohol (current estimates range from 1.5 to 2.25 million), even though taken as a group there is a lower percentage of problem drinkers and alcoholics among women than among men (about 3% of adult

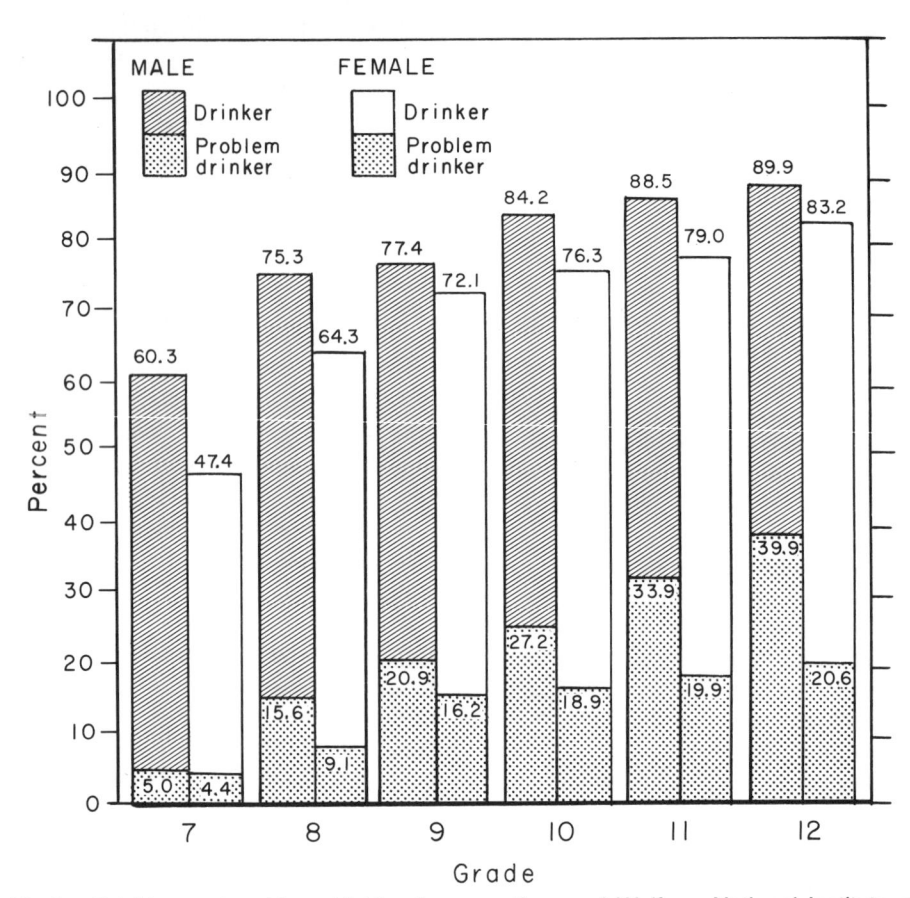

Fig 12–4.—Drinking and problem drinking by sex and grade in school. (From Noble E.P. [ed.]: *Alcohol and Health.* Third Special Report to the U.S. Congress from the Secretary of Health, Education, and Welfare. National Institute on Alcohol Abuse and Alcoholism, preprint copy, June 1978, p. 24. Data from Donovan J.E., Jessor R.: *J. Stud. Alcohol* 39(9):1506–1524, 1978.)

women are alcohol abusers as compared with about 10% of adult men). It has been said that the data for women may be falsely low because of the hesitancy of women to admit to this problem due to the greater social stigma associated with alcohol abuse in women. Also, women who abuse alcohol tend to do their drinking at home and, therefore, are less visible than men.

Race, ethnic background, and generational status are important determinants of drinking patterns. For example, compared with whites, problem drinking is more prevalent among American Indians and less common among Orientals. As a general rule, alcoholism tends to be uncommon among groups whose drinking habits are well integrated into the rest of their culture. First-generation Jewish-Americans and Italian-Americans have typically come from cultures in which drinking takes place in the family setting (with meals) or in a religious context. While the use of alcoholic beverages is a part of their lifestyle, strong sanctions are applied against drunkenness by both groups. Thus, although alcohol is frequently used, first-generation members of these groups have very low rates of alcoholism.[23] On the other hand, later generations of these same cultural groups have a greater number of alcohol problems presumably because they have become integrated into the general American life-style.

In contrast to Jewish-Americans and Italian-Americans, Irish-Americans come from a tradition in which drinking is done in pubs. Little drinking is associated with important rituals and intoxication is often deliberately sought. Although first-generation Italian-Americans drink more frequently than Irish-Americans, the latter have a higher rate of alcoholism. However, by the third generation both groups have approximately the same rate of alcohol abuse.

Causes of Alcohol Abuse

The exact cause of this disorder is unknown. Most current concepts incorporate the idea that a multiplicity of factors (genetic, psychological, sociocultural) are involved. The fundamental mechanism by which alcoholism develops may be operant conditioning. Initial exposure to alcohol in *susceptible* individuals is followed by repeated use of the drug because of the development of psychological dependence. Over a period of time, with repeated intake, some people also develop physical dependence and continue to drink in order to avoid the pain of withdrawal. The chronic alcohol abuser experiences both euphoria and dysphoria as a result of alcohol ingestion; the former acts as a positive reinforcer (i.e., person drinks to restore the euphoria), while the latter acts as a negative reinforcer (i.e., person drinks to relieve the dysphoria).

The key word in this description is *susceptibility*. Since only about one of ten alcohol users becomes an abuser, there must be factors that predispose the abuser to this disorder. One of these is heredity. Nearly all studies dealing with the familial incidence of alcoholism have found that there is a greater risk of developing this condition if one has a close family member who is an alcoholic. Current estimates are that 25% of the male and 5–10% of the female relatives of alcoholics have this condition. This amounts to about four times the expected incidence. While these findings could be due to environmental determinants, studies have definitely shown that genetic factors are important in the etiology of at least some cases of alcoholism.[5, 24]

Psychological factors are believed to be involved in much of the alcohol abuse in this country. As a generalization, it can be said that people who have some degree of psychopathology (mild, moderate, or severe) are at a greater risk of misusing alcohol than those who are stable and well adjusted. This applies to teenagers as well as adults. While psychopathology predisposes to problem drinking and alcoholism, no specific personality type has been clearly identified as typical of the alcohol abuser. Persons who have difficulty handling life stress, tension, and frustration appear to be at a greater risk of developing alcohol-related problems. Indeed, studies have shown that drinking alcohol increases during times of stress, particularly when an individual faces a loss of self-esteem or feels he has lost control.[22]

People who are subjected to significant psychological trauma are more likely to abuse alcohol.[22] For example, some alcohol abusers have had childhoods in which a relationship with a parent was disrupted due to death, divorce, or desertion. Among teenage problem drinkers, a history of a broken home and a poor parent-child relationship is not uncommon. Among younger women, the crisis of a divorce or separation is responsible for increased numbers of problems related to alcohol.

Sociocultural factors are also critical in the development of alcohol abuse. Societies in which heavy drinking is condoned have a greater prevalence of alcohol-related disability. Conversely, when heavy drinking meets with social disapproval, there is a lower rate of alcohol abuse. The last statement may account for the fact that there is a lower prevalence of this disorder among women in the United States, since our society generally attaches a greater stigma to excessive drinking by women. Parental attitudes have a strong influence on the use of alcohol among adolescents; heavy drinking by parents is associated with a tendency for this behavior in their offspring. Problem drinking is less frequent among members of some groups (Jews) than others (Irish, Spanish-speaking population, and American Indians), differences that may be based on the attitudes and beliefs about drinking held by these groups.[22]

Effects of Alcohol on the Individual and the Society

GENERAL EFFECTS OF ALCOHOL ON THE BODY.—Ethyl alcohol is a central nervous system depressant, being closely related to some of the sedative-hypnotic agents, especially the barbiturates. It also shares many pharmacologic effects with the minor tranquilizers (e.g., benzodiazepines). Low doses of alcohol are thought to produce disinhibition of cortical functions. The behavioral reaction to this disinhibition varies from person to person, being determined to a large extent by the individual's personality, his or her mental set at the time of drinking, the social circumstances, and his past experiences with alcohol. Also, the same person may be affected differently at different times. In one situation, he may become relaxed and carefree, whereas under another set of circumstances, he may become withdrawn and bellicose. As the dose of alcohol is increased, sensorimotor coordination is impaired, reaction time slows down, judgment is adversely affected, and the person becomes sedated. At high doses the intoxicated person may pass out, and upon awakening be amnesic for events that occurred while drinking. These episodes are referred to as "alcoholic blackouts" and are quite characteristic of chronic abusers of this agent. Levels of alcohol greater than 500 mg/100 ml in the blood are associated with coma and are potentially lethal.[25] Occasionally, a person will develop marked dysfunction after drinking only a small amount—a condition that is referred to as "pathologic intoxication."

Alcohol is rapidly and completely absorbed from the entire gastrointestinal tract. The absorption rate varies depending on (1) whether the stomach is empty or contains food and (2) the volume of fluid in which the alcohol is taken. The absorption rate is greater and the level of alcohol in the blood increases far more rapidly in someone who is drinking on an empty stomach than in someone who has recently completed a large meal. Also, because absorption depends on how concentrated alcohol is in the stomach, diluted alcohol solutions—such as beer, which contains about 3% alcohol—are absorbed much more slowly than are cocktails, which may contain close to 50% (100 proof) alcohol.

About 95% of the alcohol that is consumed is metabolized before it is excreted. Metabolism of alcohol occurs in the liver by the action of three enzyme systems: alcohol dehydrogenase, which accomplishes the greatest part of this activity; catalase; and the microsomal ethanol oxidizing system, which functions most after heavy chronic alcohol consumption.[22] It has been theorized that differences in the susceptibility to alcohol abuse among various racial and ethnic groups might be related to differences in rates of alcohol metabolism. However, studies of certain Indian groups with a high prevalence of alcoholism have not revealed any consistent differences in their rates of (alcohol) metabolism compared with those of whites.[25] So at present the available evidence does not support this theory.

The consumption of alcohol can produce tolerance as early as 3–6 hours after drinking.[25] Studies have shown that tolerance is accompanied by an increased catabolism of alcohol, up to twice the basal rate.[25] Cross-tolerance for other sedative-hypnotic drugs (e.g., barbiturates) also occurs as a result of chronic alcohol ingestion.

In the alcoholic who is physically dependent, symptoms and signs of withdrawal may result when there is a reduction in the intake of alcohol. The *alcohol withdrawal syndrome* consists of a number of neurologic manifestations including tremulousness, hallucinations, seizures, and delirium tremens (Table 12–2). Administering alcohol ameliorates the manifestations of withdrawal, indicating that they are due to a decreasing level of alcohol in the blood and the central nervous system.

When alcohol is taken together with another sedative-hypnotic (e.g., a barbiturate or a minor tranquilizer), their effects on neuro-

TABLE 12–2.—WITHDRAWAL SYMPTOMS

ALCOHOL		BARBITURATES (SEDATIVES)	MORPHINE	
Tremors	Impaired level of consciousness	Anxiety	Yawning	
Anxiety	Impaired quality of contact	Sleep disturbances	Lacrimation	Restlessness
Sweats	Impaired sensorium	Nausea and vomiting	Rhinorrhea	Insomnia
Depression	Gait disturbance	Irritability	Perspiration	Vomiting
Nausea	Nystagmus	Restlessness	Muscle tremor	Diarrhea
Tinnitus	Convulsions	Tremulousness	Gooseflesh	Weight loss
Hallucinations	Fever	Postural hypotension	Loss of appetite	
Pruritus	Tachycardia	Seizures (severe intractable)	Dilated pupils	
Agitation		Withdrawal psychosis	Fever	
Insomnia		Hyperpyrexia	Increase in respiratory rate	
Muscle pain				

Source: Kissin B.: Alcoholism and drug dependence, in Simons R. C., Pardes H. (eds.): *Understanding Human Behavior in Health and Illness*. Baltimore, Williams & Wilkins Co., 1977, p. 642. (Used by permission.)

logic function are synergistic. No doubt this accounts for some of the accidental deaths that have occurred when a person ingested barbiturate sleeping pills while under the influence of large doses of alcohol. The cross-tolerance that develops between alcohol and the other sedative-hypnotics can be therapeutically useful, since the latter can be administered in order to ameliorate the effects of withdrawal from alcohol. Hence, drugs such as diazepam (Valium) are used to control the manifestations of delirium tremens.

Tolerance to alcohol may be lost, sometimes rapidly, by chronic alcohol abusers. Under these circumstances, an alcoholic may find himself becoming intoxicated by doses of the drug that he formerly could drink without difficulty.

ADVERSE EFFECTS OF ALCOHOL ON THE INDIVIDUAL AND THE SOCIETY.—It is estimated that more than 10% of the deaths in the United States each year are related in some way to alcohol misuse—an astounding figure.[14] Table 12–3 lists the causes of the deaths attributable to alcohol in 1975. A large proportion of the nearly 46,000 highway fatalities that took place that year were associated with alcohol intoxication. In fact, in about 50% of all fatal automobile accidents drivers have been found to have alcohol levels of more than 100 mg/dl in their blood at the time of death. A large percentage of the accidents at home and at work are also attributable to drinking.

Crimes of physical violence are commonly associated with the misuse of alcohol. Homicide is typically related to alcohol. In one study of 588 homicides in Philadelphia, for example, alcohol was absent from the blood of both killer and victim in only 36% of the cases. Moreover, alcohol was shown to be associated with specific methods of homicide. In approximately 70% of the homicides caused by stabbings or beatings, alcohol was involved, as compared with only 55% of shootings. Alcohol is a significant factor in child-beating cases in which the child requires hospitalization (i.e., battered child syndrome). At least 25% of suicide attempts are associated with alcohol misuse (see Table 12–3).

It is estimated that in 1975 the cost to our society for alcohol-related problems was close to $43 billion. A breakdown of this figure indicates that it is based on (1) the loss of productivity due to the dysfunctional effects of alcohol on the individual, (2) an increased need for certain goods and services (i.e., health care, police and fire protection) required to deal with the problems caused by alcohol abusers, and (3) damage to property

TABLE 12–3.—ESTIMATED DEATHS RELATED TO ALCOHOL IN THE UNITED STATES, 1975

CAUSE OF DEATH	NUMBER OF DEATHS	PERCENT RELATED TO ALCOHOL	ESTIMATED NUMBER RELATED TO ALCOHOL
Alcohol as a direct cause			
Alcoholism	4,897	100	4,897
Alcoholic psychosis	356	100	356
Cirrhosis	31,623	41–95	12,965–30,042
Total	36,876		18,218–35,295
Alcohol as an indirect cause			
Accidents			
Motor vehicle	45,853	30–50	13,756–22,926
Falls	14,896	44.4	6,614
Fires	6,071	25.9	1,572
Other*	33,026	11.1	3,666
Homicides	21,310	49–70	10,442–14,917
Suicides	27,063	25–37	6,766–10,013
Total	148,219	29–40	42,816–59,708
Overall total	185,095		61,034–95,003

*Includes all accidents not listed above, but excludes accidents incurred in medical and surgical procedures.
Source: Noble E.P. (ed.): *Alcohol and Health*. National Institute on Alcohol Abuse and Alcoholism, preprint copy, June 1978, p. 13. Data from Day, Nancy: *Alcohol and Mortality*, paper prepared for National Institute on Alcohol Abuse and Alcoholism under Contract No. NIA-76-10(P), January, 1977; and National Center for Health Statistics, *Vital Statistics of the United States, 1972, Vol. II*. Washington, D.C., U.S. Government Printing Office, 1975.

that occurs as a result of the accidents and crimes in which alcohol plays a role. It is important to note that of the $43 billion, only about $2 billion was spent for the management of alcohol-related problems.

Even before an individual is born, he may experience the adverse effects of alcohol, since it has been established that this agent causes birth defects and behavioral impairment (including mental retardation) in children born to mothers who drink while they are pregnant.[22, 26, 27] Table 12–4 shows the various manifestations of the so-called fetal alcohol syndrome (FAS), all or part of which may be present in a given case. The estimated incidence of the FAS in the United States is one case for every 5,000 births,[14] making it the third leading cause of birth defects with associated mental retardation (Down's syndrome and spina bifida are one and two), and the only one of the three that is preventable.

The risk of developing the FAS and the extent of the abnormalities appear to increase with the amount of alcohol consumed; that is, they are dose-related. Safe levels of drinking are unknown, but it is believed that the ingestion of 3 or more ounces of absolute alcohol a day (approximately six drinks) by a pregnant woman establishes a risk. The effects of drinking between 1 and 3 ounces a day are still uncertain, but it is advised that the expectant mother drink no more than 1 ounce of absolute alcohol per day.

Pregnant women who are heavy drinkers have a higher incidence of spontaneous abortions, stillbirths, and premature infants. It has also been speculated that behavioral problems developing later in childhood, such as difficulty learning in school and the symptom complex of the attention deficit disorder, may in some instances be due to fetal exposure to alcohol.[27]

A host of serious physical disorders are attributable to alcohol, either due to its direct effects or as a consequence of alcohol-associ-

TABLE 12-4.—MOST CONSISTENT FEATURES OF THE FETAL ALCOHOL SYNDROME

Growth and performance
  Prenatal onset growth deficiency, more pronounced in length than in weight
  Concomitant microcephaly (small head circumference) even when corrected for small body weight and length
  Postnatal growth deficiency in weight and length, usually below 3d percentile
  Delay of intellectual development and/or mental deficiency (mean IQ from Seattle study = 64, range 16-92)
  Fine motor dysfunction (poor coordination)
Head and face
  Microcephaly
  Short palpebral fissures (narrow eye slits)
  Midfacial (maxillary) hypoplasia (underdevelopment of midfacial region)
  Flattened, elongated philtrum (middle of upper lip) associated with thin, narrow vermilion lip borders (highly specific to FAS)
  Minor ear anomalies including low set ears
Limbs
  Abnormal creases in the palm of the hand
  Minor joint anomalies
    Syndactyly (fingers or toes joined together)
    Clinodactyly (abnormal bending of fingers or toes)
    Camptodactyly (one or more fingers constantly flexed at one or more phalangeal joints)
Heart
  Ventricular and atrial septal defect (valve defects)
Brain
  Absence of corpus callosum
  Hydrocephalus (excess fluid in cranium)
  Brain cell migratory abnormalities
Other
  Minor genital anomalies
  Hemangiomas (benign tumors made up of blood vessels) in infancy

Source: Noble E.P. (ed.): *Alcohol and Health*. National Institute on Alcohol Abuse and Alcoholism, preprint copy, June 1978, p. 56. Data from Jones Kenneth L., and Smith David W.: *Teratology* 12(1):1-10, 1975.

ated malnutrition and vitamin deficiency. Virtually every organ in the body may be injured by alcohol. The gastrointestinal system is especially vulnerable, with gastritis, pancreatitis, and liver disease frequently encountered in chronic alcohol abusers. Cirrhosis of the liver ranked as the sixth most common cause of death in the United States in 1975, and up to 95% of cirrhosis is estimated to be related to alcohol.[22] This agent is also involved in the causation of cancer. In comparison with the general population, heavy consumers of alcohol show higher mortality from cancers of mouth, esophagus, and liver.[22] Other conditions associated with alcohol abuse are hematologic abnormalities, skeletal muscle damage, cardiomyopathy, and neurologic disorders involving both the central and the peripheral nervous systems. Alcoholics are also more vulnerable to bacterial infections, pneumonia and tuberculosis being two examples. Finally, withdrawal manifestations are a source of significant morbidity among chronic alcoholics. The most serious of these, delirium tremens, is reported to have a mortality as high as 10%.

Treatment of Alcohol Abuse

Over the years, a variety of methods have been used to treat alcohol abuse, including drug therapy, psychotherapy, behavior modification therapy, and other interventions such as halfway houses and Alcoholics Anonymous. Often two or more treatment modalities have been combined. The sooner therapy is begun, the more effective it is likely to be—hence the importance of early diagnosis while the illness is still mild. By the time alcoholism reaches its late stages, the patient is generally suffering from severe physical, psychological, and social dysfunction—problems that are very difficult to reverse.

Traditionally, the basic principle common to all treatment modalities has been abstinence; the alcoholic must give up all drinking. Recently this principle has been challenged—with some people arguing in favor of controlled drinking for selected types of abusers—but the general consensus is still that abstinence is the most important aspect of treatment for the alcoholic.[22] Of course, abstinence is not the only treatment goal; improvement in physical, psychological, and social functioning are also of prime importance.

A period of detoxification in which alcohol is withdrawn usually is the first step in the treatment process. In a series of 564 consecutive outpatient admissions for detoxification, only 8% of the persons had to be ultimately brought into the hospital for the management of withdrawal symptoms.[28] Thus, in most cases it is not necessary to utilize expensive inpatient hospital facilities to discontinue the use of alcohol. Sedatives or tranquilizers are commonly used to manage the person during the period of withdrawal (detoxification). In a recent review of the prevention and treatment of alcohol withdrawal, Khantzian and McKenna state that either diazepam (Valium) or chlordiazepoxide (Librium) is the drug of choice, and that the oral and intravenous routes (in acute situations) are preferred because of poor or erratic absorption via the intramuscular route.[29] After the period of detoxification is over, sedatives or tranquilizers should be discontinued, since they are habituating and there may be a tendency for the alcoholic to substitute dependence on these agents for dependence on alcohol. In the management of acute and severe withdrawal symptoms (e.g., delirium tremens), hospitalization is necessary so that intensive medical care can be given in order to combat dehydration, electrolyte imbalance, and the other medical complications.

After withdrawal and detoxification, drugs play a very minor role in the treatment of alcoholism. One, however deserves special mention: disulfiram (Antabuse). This agent inhibits the action of the enzyme acetaldehyde dehydrogenase, which metabolizes acetaldehyde to acetate during the catabolism of alcohol. As a result, when a person drinks after taking disulfiram, acetaldehyde accumulates in the body, giving rise to unpleasant symptoms such as headache, nausea, vomiting, and "cold sweats." Thus, an alcoholic who takes disulfiram finds that alcohol makes him feel so sick that he avoids drinking. This drug seems to be most useful for the highly motivated recovering alcoholic, who uses it to prevent a brief relapse. However, when used as a sole treatment, persons tend to avoid taking the drug, in which case drinking can be resumed after a few days. In one study, for example, less than 1% of all persons receiving maintenance doses of disulfiram following detoxification in the hospital continued to take the drug after their release.[30] So, if it is used, disulfiram should be part of a comprehensive program of management. Furthermore, the drug should be used with great caution in persons with arteriosclerotic heart disease, diabetes mellitus, hypertension, cirrhosis, renal disease, or any other medical condition that would reduce the person's tolerance to the acetaldehyde-induced reactions.

Although it is not the purpose of this chapter to review the various modes of therapy for alcoholism, one in particular deserves comment, Alcoholics Anonymous (A.A.), which was begun in 1935. From an initial two-person group, the organization has grown to more than 18,000 autonomous groups in North America, which meet weekly. Upon referral to A.A. by oneself, a friend, a relative, a clergyman, or a physician, the alcoholic is provided with a sponsor. This sponsor is a recovered alcoholic who assumes responsibility for helping the new member deal with the personal crises that accompany the decision to stop drinking. The sponsor accompanies the "prospect" to A.A. meetings, where the new member learns A.A. philosophy, rules for living, and expectations. Among the basic tenets of A.A. philosophy are the following: a member of A.A. must have full recognition that he or she is and always will be an alcoholic; an A.A. member must also recognize that because he or she is an alcoholic, total abstinence is required; instead of concentrating on the long-term problem of alcoholism, the A.A. member must concern himself or herself with abstaining "one day at a time." By following these tenets, having the support of a group of like-minded individuals, and having a committed volunteer sponsor who is on call day and night, A.A. seems to have the highest long-term "cure" rate for alcoholism. Even so, this rate is less than 35%.

Success in the long-term management of alcohol abuse is measured in terms of alcohol consumption, behavioral (psychological and physical) impairment, and social adjustment[22]—an improvement in the first category being generally, but not always, reflected by improvement in the others. Moore states that an old rule of thumb is that success in therapy occurs in one third of alcoholics, partial success in another third, and failure in the final third.[31] Recent reports from the National Institute of Alcohol Abuse and Alcoholism (NIAAA) have been more encouraging. Even without specific therapy, some alcohol abusers and alcoholics recover from their illness by experiencing a spontaneous remission.

As is the case with many chronic illnesses, persons with alcoholism commonly suffer relapses during the course of treatment. All too often, physicians become irritated and angry with the alcoholic when he or she returns to drinking after apparently responding to therapy, "blaming" the patient for loss of control. The same physicians would probably think it ridiculous to have such an attitude toward a cardiac or arthritic patient who had a relapse, yet they feel justified in reacting to the alcoholic in a judgmental way. Clearly, it is necessary for the physician to have realistic expectations about the management of alcoholism and not to "personalize" the success or failure of therapy. A moralistic attitude on the part of a health professional toward the alcoholic is rarely helpful and often leads to a rejection of the patient by the physician.

LICIT AND ILLICIT DRUGS (OTHER THAN ALCOHOL)

Among the licit agents, the rising incidence of the use and abuse of the minor tranquilizers, the so-called antianxiety agents, is a most important development in recent years. Also, the widespread abuse of propoxyphene (Darvon), an oral narcotic analgesic, has gained attention. Its abuse is estimated to result in 1,000 to 2,000 deaths a year across the nation, ranking second only to the barbiturates as the leading prescription drug associated with drug fatalities. Concern about the illicit drugs centers on the opiates (e.g., heroin), marijuana, cocaine, and hallucinogens such as LSD. The misuse of multiple drugs has become a serious problem in this country, with abusers taking various agents in combination.

Space does not permit a thorough review of all these agents, so we will only attempt to give the reader an overview and perspective of the main issues concerning their abuse.

Narcotic-Analgesic Drugs

Opium is an air-dried product of the sap of the poppy seed capsule *(Papaver somniferum)* and contains a number of alkaloids including morphine and codeine. A minor chemical change in morphine transforms it into heroin, which is much stronger but otherwise has identical effects. In addition to the opium alkaloids and their semisynthetic derivatives, there are four other chemical classes of narcotic analgesics, which are listed (along with representative compounds from each class) in Table 12–5.

OPIATE ABUSE.—Heroin abuse constitutes about 90% of this problem. Initially this drug may be taken by "sniffing," but those who continue to use it usually go on to subcutaneous injections ("skin popping") and eventually to intravenous ("mainline") administration. An immediate effect of mainlining heroin is the "rush," which has been described as a whole body orgasm lasting up to 15 minutes. Another effect of taking heroin is drowsiness (the "nod"), which may be accompanied by a simple state of satisfaction and the temporary absence of such negative feelings as anxiety, failure, and guilt.

For the individual who is physically dependent on heroin, abstinence for more than 5 or 6 hours can lead to withdrawal symptoms (see Table 12–2). In addition to these physical manifestations (so-called nonpurposive behav-

TABLE 12–5.—NARCOTIC ANALGESICS

Opium alkaloids and their semisynthetic derivatives	Morphine
	Codeine
	Heroin
	Dihydromorphinone (Dilaudid)
	Oxycodone (Percodan)
Diphenylpropylamine derivatives	Methadone
	Propoxyphene (Darvon)
Phenylpiperidine derivative	Meperidine (Demerol)
Morphinan derivative	Levorphanol
Benzomorphan derivative	Pentozocine (Talwin)

Adapted from Jaffe J.J., Martin W.R.: Narcotic analgesics and antagonists, in Goodman L.S., Gilman A. (eds.): *The Pharmacological Basis of Therapeutics.* New York, Macmillan Publishing Co., Inc., 1975.

ior), drug-demanding and attempts to acquire the drug for relief (so-called purposive behavior) are common. Without treatment, most symptoms disappear in 7–10 days. Although extremely uncomfortable, acute abstinence from heroin is less dangerous to life than is withdrawal from alcohol or barbiturates.

The long-term effects of heroin addiction are extremely serious. Because the addict devotes his very existence to acquiring and using the drug, his other interests (i.e., family, employment) are abandoned. Usually he must steal to maintain the costly habit. The diet of the heroin addict is frequently inadequate so that malnutrition and lowered resistance to disease are common. Other medical complications also occur.[29, 32] Addicts often grow careless about the sterility of injection needles, with the result that tetanus, bacterial infection (e.g., skin abscesses, endocarditis), and hepatitis are often found in this group of individuals. The intravenous injection of opiate drugs and adulterant mixtures may lead to embolization of particulate matter (starch, talc, cotton) in the lungs, causing a foreign-body reaction (granulomatosis) and infection. The injection of an overdose of an opiate can lead to serious toxicity due to cardiovascular and respiratory depression. The triad of impaired consciousness, small pupils, and depressed respirations are classically found in opiate intoxication—a diagnosis that calls for the prompt administration of naloxone (an opiate antagonist). Acute pulmonary edema is a life-threatening side effect of intravenous heroin overdose.[33] At the mercy of drug dealers, the heroin addict may inject a contaminated dose, one mixed with another drug, or a dose much larger than that to which he is accustomed. Any of these eventualities can result in death.

The epidemiology of opiate abuse is an interesting story.[34] From the 1930s to the early 1960s, two patterns of opiate dependence were observed: (1) morphine addiction among southern, rural, middle-class whites who had often been introduced to this drug by a physician treating them for a medical problem, and (2) heroin addiction among urban minority group members in their late twenties or thirties. In the mid-1960s, a new pattern of heroin addiction emerged involving teenagers and those in their early twenties. The typical heroin user at this time was a member of a minority group, an inner-city, unemployed, unmarried man. Indeed, between 1965 and 1970 a veritable *epidemic* of heroin abuse occurred among these individuals.[35] Although there was an abrupt drop in incidence (number of new cases) in the early 1970s, most of those individuals who were already addicted to heroin continued to be active drug users. In other words, the prevalence (number of total cases in the community) was still much higher than it had been in past decades, even though the incidence had declined significantly. Also, during this period heroin addiction had spread from the urban ghettos to the suburbs and smaller cities.

In the latter part of the 1970s, the prevalence of heroin abuse appears to have declined. Although the exact number is unknown, it is estimated that there are between 400,000 and 800,000 heroin addicts in the United States, with the Surgeon General's report giving a figure of 450,000 for 1978.[14, 36] In comparison to the number of individuals who abuse alcohol, thought to be around 10 million, heroin addiction is a far less common drug abuse problem.

There is a clear correlation between the use of heroin and crime. In contrast to alcoholism, a situation in which illegal acts are usually perpetrated *because* the individual is under the influence of the drug, heroin addicts engage in crime primarily to obtain money to buy narcotics. For the most part, this is not violent crime but rather shoplifting, burglary, and prostitution. Muggings and armed robbery, however, also occur. The major reason for the correlation between heroin use and crime is that the addict has to come up with a substantial amount of money every day in order to support the habit, something that is usually not possible by legal means. An estimate has been made that in New York City alone, the crimes committed by heroin addicts to finance their habits cost more than $10 million per day.

Since the etiology of opiate abuse is related to personal, social, and pharmacologic variables, the management of persons who are dependent on these drugs requires a comprehensive medical approach. The first step is detoxification, whereby the addicting drug is withdrawn from the individual. In the usual treatment of opiate withdrawal, methadone (a synthetic narcotic) is given to reduce the severity of the abstinence syndrome. However, recent studies indicate that clonidine, a drug commonly used in the treatment of hypertension, also is effective in controlling the symptoms and signs of withdrawal.[37] Second, a program of rehabilitation is instituted with the ultimate goals of enabling the individual to maintain a drug-free state and to reintegrate himself into society. Most narcotic addicts have significant physical disability, psychological dysfunction, and social problems that need to be addressed before they can assume a productive and satisfying life.

Methadone may be used as maintenance therapy to help the addict stay off the addicting drug. The administration of methadone in order to rehabilitate the heroin addict was initially described in 1964 and since then has been found to be an effective mode of therapy. Ketchum and Jarvik explain the effects of methadone on the addict as follows: "By virtue of its more gradual buildup and decline in concentration at central sites of action, methadone provides sustained relief from the craving that follows each short-lived heroin 'high' and at the same time reduces the pleasurable 'rush' which tends to reinforce an obsession with the next 'fix.' "[36] For heroin abusers who qualify and are willing to participate in a methadone maintenance program, it provides them with a means of returning to a productive social life without the necessity of having to seek out heroin.

Levo-alpha-acetylmethadol (LAAM), a narcotic with even more long-lasting effects than methadone, is currently being investigated as an alternative to methadone in rehabilitation programs. LAAM need be given only three times a week in contrast to methadone, which must be taken daily by the addict. Since maintenance programs using methadone or LAAM have really only replaced one addiction with another, the addict should be withdrawn from these drugs if it is possible. Deviations from such programs are common, with addicts still abusing heroin while on methadone and some even trading take-home methadone for street heroin. In addition to the use of narcotic agents as substitutes for heroin, some treatment programs have used narcotic *antagonists*, such as cyclazocine and naltrexone, in order to "block" the euphoriant effects of heroin and thus eliminate one reason for the addict's drug-seeking behavior.

Nonpharmacologic strategies are also used for the treatment of opiate dependence, relying on psychosocial rehabilitation usually in a residential setting for periods of one year or more.[36] The results of both the pharmacologic and nonpharmacologic methods indicate that many addicts are amenable to therapy and that the prognosis for heroin abusers is not so bleak as was once thought. Many heroin addicts relinquish their drug habit for periods of time during their drug-taking career without being forced to do so.[36] In a follow-up of 500 Vietnam veterans who were heroin abusers, it was found that 90% were no longer using opiates one year after being discharged from military service.[36] Vaillant reported that of a group of opiate addicts treated in the early 1950s, roughly half of those surviving 20 years later had achieved stable abstinence.[38]

PROPOXYPHENE (DARVON) ABUSE.—Darvon was developed for use as an alternative to the stronger narcotic agents for persons who have mild to moderate pain. When it was first brought out, it was said to be equal to codeine in pain-relieving properties but without codeine's potential for abuse. The last supposition proved to be incorrect, for time has shown that Darvon is indeed capable of inducing psychological and physical dependence. An early study of Darvon abuse was reported by Chambers, who identified the following five patterns:[39]

1. *Overuse as a medication.*—This was by far the most common pattern, occurring primarily among middle-class families who had originally been given a prescription for Darvon by a physician. Once it had been used as an analgesic and remained in the household, more than 80% of the families interviewed in the study said they medicated themselves with it for other pains without being told to do so by a physician.

2. *Chance experimentation.*—In this pattern, Darvon was taken at irregular intervals as an experiment by adolescents naive about drugs.

3. *True drug dependence.*—Persons were identified who regularly abused Darvon as the drug of preference.

4. *As a substitute for opiates.*—This occurred when persons addicted to opiates were unable to obtain these agents, because either "street opiates" were in short supply or the addict was hospitalized or incarcerated.

5. *Part of a situation of multiple drug abuse.*—This pattern occurred mostly among young white abusers who were taking either sedatives or tranquilizers in addition to Darvon.

This study demonstrates the variety of ways in which a licit drug can be misused. Depending on their personal characteristics, people seem to develop a particular pattern of abuse that is consistent with their life-style. Similar patterns are observed with the abuse of other prescription drugs such as sedatives and tranquilizers.

As previously noted, Darvon abuse is responsible for a large number of deaths in this country. Most of these are overdoses resulting in suicides; however, some appear to be "accidental", having occurred to individuals taking Darvon in conjunction with other CNS depressants, e.g., alcohol, sedatives, or tranquilizers.[40] Some of those in the latter group were not habitual drug abusers and apparently suffered the fatal consequences of Darvon misuse after taking doses only slightly greater than the upper limits of the recommended doses. Persons who take an overdose of Darvon have severe respiratory and circulatory depression as is true of the other narcotic agents but, in addition, may experience seizures. Darvon intoxication may not respond completely to naloxone and may necessitate more prolonged respiratory support.

Darvon (in doses of 32–65 mg) is said to be approximately two thirds as potent as codeine and no more effective than the usual doses of aspirin or acetaminophen. It is often prescribed in combination with aspirin or acetaminophen in order to enhance their effectiveness, and it is felt by some that the contribution of Darvon to the pain-relieving properties of these medications is minimal. Thus, Darvon is not a very effective medication, yet despite this, Darvon products are frequently prescribed brand-name analgesics, with more than 30 million prescriptions written in 1978.[40] In view of its abuse potential and the seriousness of the effects of intoxication, the Food and Drug Administration has called on physicians to monitor the prescribing of Darvon more carefully and to warn persons of the risks of taking Darvon along with other CNS depressants.

Sedatives and Tranquilizers

This category of drugs includes (1) barbiturates, (2) nonbarbiturate sedatives such as glutethimide (Doriden) and methaqualone (Quaalude), (3) "minor" tranquilizers like meprobamate and the benzodiazepines, (4) antidepressants, and (5) "major" tranquilizers of which chlorpromazine (Thorazine) is the prototype. In addition, there is a variety of over-the-counter sedatives of which the public makes extensive use. The first three groups of drugs apparently produce much the same effects; by inhibiting the higher cortical regulatory centers they relieve anxiety, decrease inhibitions, and in many cause a sense of euphoria.

Since their rise in popularity in the late 1930s, the barbiturates have been among the most frequently abused prescription drugs, particularly in suicide attempts. Barbiturate intoxication (with or without alcohol) is responsible for more overdose fatalities each year than any other prescription drug. It has been estimated that there are about 300,000 barbiturate abusers in this country. If taken on a continuous basis and at high doses, these agents are capable of producing tolerance, physical dependence, and, upon withdrawal, a medically serious abstinence syndrome (see Table 12-2). This syndrome is of variable severity but is potentially life-threatening and is associated with a worse prognosis than withdrawal from narcotics.[41] For this reason, the abrupt discontinuation of these drugs by someone who is physically dependent is extremely dangerous, and the detoxification of a barbiturate addict should be carried out gradually while the person is in the hospital under close medical supervision. Symptoms of CNS hyperactivity are characteristic of the abstinence syndrome, including tremulousness, irritability, seizures, and delirium. Death may occur. The severity of the abstinence syndrome is related to the duration and the amount of the drug used.

Of all the drugs listed in this category, the "minor" tranquilizers have shown the greatest increase in use and abuse in this country over the past decade. The benzodiazepines, e.g., chlordiazepoxide (Librium), diazepam (Valium), and flurazepam (Dalmane), are the most popular of this group of psychotropic agents. In fact, the most widely prescribed drug in the United States today is Valium. It is fair to say that the extent of its use exceeds all reasonable estimates of the medical necessity for this agent, so misuse must be quite common. As with the barbiturates, physical dependence and symptoms of withdrawal occur in chronic abusers of the minor tranquilizers.

It is estimated that as many as 60% of the adults in this country have had experience with one or another of the sedative-tranquilizers, either proprietary or prescription.[8] Many people take these agents for medical reasons, but approximately 10% of the adult population use these psychoactive agents for nonmedical purposes. Any of the five patterns of abuse described by Chambers for Darvon may occur with these drugs.

The spectrum of sedative-tranquilizer abusers is wide. At one extreme are young persons who use illicitly obtained drugs; at the other are individuals, usually women, who utilize over-the-counter or prescription medications.[42] The former are usually looking for the excitement or "high" that comes with the drug experience, while the latter are often trying merely to cope with the tensions and problems of everyday life. Studies indicate that women are the most frequent abusers of sedative-tranquilizer prescription drugs.[8] Much of this medication is prescribed for anxiety reactions associated with life stress or functional symptoms (i.e., complaints for which no organic basis is found). When caring for such persons, some physicians routinely prescribe a sedative or tranquilizer to help the individual "relax," a practice that is often not warranted. Other types of sedative-tranquilizer abusers include the teenager who is curious about the effects of these agents and the harried businessman trying to survive in a pressurized world of deadlines.

Stimulants and Hallucinogens

The agents in this category differ in a number of important ways from the CNS depressants. Foremost among these differences is, of course, that the stimulants and hallucinogens primarily enhance and excite psychic function and motor activity. The hallucinogens produce distorted sensory phenomena (hallucinations, illusions) at a lower point on the dose-response curve than the stimulants; otherwise these two groups have the same general psychotoxicity. While both the CNS depressants and the stimulant-hallucinogens cause psychological dependence, the latter do not produce physical dependence and, therefore, have no discrete abstinence syndrome associated with them as is the case with the former. A possible exception to this rule is the amphetamines, which, at least in animals, have been shown to be associated with the development of physical dependence.[1] The cessation of amphetamine or cocaine use by a chronic high-dose abuser is usually associated with a "letdown" or "crash" in which the individual experiences lassitude, lethargy, and depression.[29] Tolerance to some of the stimulants and hallucinogens (particularly the amphetamines) does occur, but, in general, it plays a lesser role in the chronic abuse of these drugs than it does with the CNS depressants.

THE STIMULANTS.—The most commonly abused stimulants (excluding caffeine and nicotine) are the amphetamines and cocaine. At one time, the amphetamines were considered to be an important part of the treatment of obesity, and many of the people who ultimately ended up abusing them were originally introduced to these drugs by their physician. Once their great potential for misuse was appreciated, the utilization of these drugs by physicians as a means of helping persons reduce their weight was curtailed. Because of the abuse problem, in 1979 the Food and Drug Administration initiated action to remove the prescribing indication, for the management of obesity, from the labeling of amphetamine-containing drugs. Today most of the amphetamines that are abused are gotten from the black market, supplied by clandestine laboratories and sources outside the United States.[43] These drugs are either taken orally or injected parenterally. Those who misuse these drugs commonly do so in an attempt to enhance their physical and psychological performance in situations in which fatigue occurs. Other individuals take these drugs primarily for the euphoria they produce. Many of them have significant psychological and social problems and are misusing several drugs (e.g., amphetamines with sedatives or alcohol).

In addition to having a pronounced stimulatory effect on the CNS, amphetamines are similar to other sympathomimetic agents in terms of their action on the autonomic nervous system, cardiovascular system, and smooth muscle.[43] Thus, the manifestations of toxicity include both physiological and psychological signs. Small doses are often associated with mood elevation and feelings of well-being. Larger amounts consumed by nontolerant individuals cause restlessness, hyperactivity, volubility, tremulousness, insomnia, paranoia, aggressiveness, and at times violent and assaultive behavior. The latter may be responsible for antisocial behavior, including destructive and illegal acts. An overdose of these drugs can produce a psychotic reaction that is clinically indistinguishable from paranoid schizophrenia. Physical signs accompanying these behavioral aberrations include elevated blood pressure, tachycardia, dilated pupils, dry mouth, and hyperreflexia. Rarely, hyperthermia and convulsions occur.

Overshadowed in the 1960s by the publicity given to other illicit agents, such as heroin and marijuana, cocaine emerged in the 1970s as one of the most popular illegal drugs in the United States. It is estimated that about 4.4 million Americans now use this drug.[44] Cocaine use is reported to be more common among men, urban dwellers, college students, and those with higher levels of income and education. Its high cost ($100–$120 a gram) tends to restrict the use of cocaine to those who are relatively affluent.

This drug is a vasoconstrictor, local anesthetic, sympathomimetic, and CNS stimulant. The last effect is similar to that produced by the amphetamines, that is, increased alertness, euphoria, reversal of fatigue, and excitement, although the duration of action of cocaine is much shorter. Some investigators question whether tolerance occurs with the chronic use of cocaine, but there is clinical evidence of this phenomenon, with some abusers taking as much as 10 grams daily.[44] Cocaine can be injected, swallowed, mixed with liquor, and applied directly to the mucous membranes, but by far the most popular method of abuse is nasal insufflation (snorting). Snorting cocaine causes mucosal inflammation, congestion, and even perforation of the septum due to its vasoconstrictive properties.

There is widespread belief that cocaine is a relatively harmless drug. This is clearly not the case, since this drug can be highly dangerous when abused. A recent report by Wetli and Wright of 68 deaths associated with the recreational use of this drug certainly makes this point.[45] The authors found that with intravenous use, respiratory collapse and death occurred shortly after injection; oral or nasal ingestion was followed by a latency of up to an hour before the onset of generalized seizures and death. Besides these acute lethal effects, there are milder side effects associated with chronic cocaine abuse. These are similar to the side effects seen with amphetamine abuse and include weight loss, insomnia, anxiety, anorexia, and increased psychomotor activity.[44] Confusion, paranoia, and hallucinations may also occur with chronic high-dose use of cocaine.

THE HALLUCINOGENS.—Marijuana is by far the most frequently abused hallucinogen, more than 40 million Americans having used this agent on at least one occasion. Experience with this drug has increased sharply over the past several decades (Fig 12–5). The use of marijuana is more prevalent among certain segments of the population than others; for instance, approximately 28% of youth (aged 12–17) and 60% of young adults (aged 18–25) *have tried* this drug as compared with only 15% of older adults (aged 26 or older).[46] The Surgeon General's 1979 Report on Health Promotion and Disease Prevention states that about 17% of men aged 20 to 24 who have tried this drug are *daily users* and that among a group of high school students surveyed 10% said they used it *daily*.

Marijuana and hashish are products of the weedlike hemp plant *Cannabis sativa*, whose

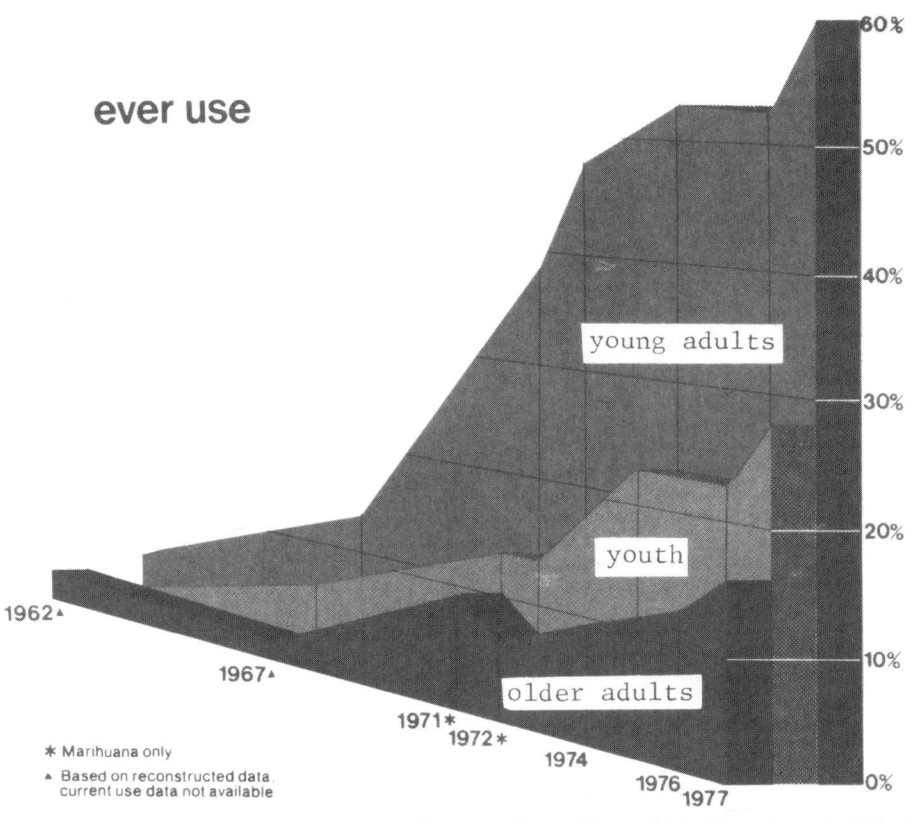

Fig 12–5.—Trends in lifetime experience with marijuana/hashish. (From Cisin I., Miller J.D., Harrell A.V.: *Highlights from the National Survey on Drug Abuse.* U.S. Department of Health, Education, and Welfare, National Institute on Drug Abuse, 1977.)

derivates have been used since 400 to 500 B.C. throughout the Eastern and Western worlds as "recreational drugs." Natural marijuana is made from the plant's flower clusters and leaves, while hashish, a more potent derivative, comes from the resin secreted from the flowering tops of the female plant.

The principal chemical responsible for the effects of marijuana, Δ-9-tetrahydrocannabinol (THC), has a number of psychological and physiological actions in humans. The psychological effects of marijuana vary depending on the potency (the amount of THC) and the dose of the material used, the route of administration (inhalation or ingestion), the setting in which the agent is used, the previous experience the individual has with the drug, and his emotional state at the time.[47] Descriptions of typical psychic reactions include an alteration in mood (euphoria, dreaminess); a distortion of sensory perception (visual illusions, altered perception of the body and space); and a general feeling of drowsiness, detachment, and unreality. Although there is usually an overall calming effect, some persons react with anxiety, hyperactivity, and agitation. There are even reports of a type of toxic psychosis following marijuana use. Among the physical actions of natural marijuana or synthetic Δ9 THC are an engorgement of the conjunctival vessels, a speeding up of the heart rate, a dilatation of the small airways of the lungs, a lowering of intraocular pressure, and an antinausea antiemetic effect.[48] The last two properties are of *potential* benefit in medical practice: the reduction of intraocular pressure in the treatment of glaucoma, and the antinausea antiemetic effect in the control of gastrointestinal upset that occurs with cancer chemotherapy. Controlled studies comparing THC with placebos and traditional antiemetics (e.g., phenothiazines) have shown that THC is effective in preventing nausea and vomiting in many patients receiving cancer chemotherapy, even when other antiemetics are ineffective.[49, 50]

Lysergic acid diethylamide, or LSD, is the best known and most widely used potent hallucinogen. Synthesized in 1938 by Stoll and Hoffman, it became one of the chemicals used to create a "model psychosis" (i.e., a psychotomimetic compound). Some other agents with strong hallucinogenic properties are peyote, mescaline, and dimethyltryptamine (DMT). These hallucinogens are generally taken orally and their repeated ingestion is associated with tolerance and psychological dependence (physical dependence does not occur). The age groups usually abusing these illicit drugs are adolescents and young adults who typically are emotionally and socially maladjusted.

Although the misuse of LSD is less common than it was in the 1960s, it still occurs with sufficient frequency to be a significant medical concern. The psychological effects of LSD are dramatic, with delusions, depersonalization, lability of mood, and pronounced distortions of sensory perception including visual hallucinations and illusions. The individual may panic while under the influence of the drug and this effect combined with the psychotic-like reactions described above may lead to personal injury and even suicide. The onset of drug action after an oral dose is short, usually within minutes, and its effects generally begin to dissipate after 12 hours. The effects of the drug may recur without the individual retaking it—the so-called flashback phenomenon.

A person taking LSD may experience a "bad trip," and it is usually this toxic reaction that makes the LSD abuser seek medical care. First-time users have a higher rate of these reactions, which are due to a combination of drug effects and the panic that occurs in response to them. However, a bad trip may occur even to habitual users. The care of the person with this type of drug reaction involves minimizing the input of sensory stimuli (by having the person stay in a quiet room away from the general activity of the emergency room), having someone stay in the room with him at all times, and attempting to "talk him down" by reassurance and reorientation. Occasionally, sedative medication is necessary, pentobarbital or one of the benzodiazepines (e.g., Librium or Valium) being the drugs of choice.[29] The bad trip should last no longer than 24 hours and, if it does, another diagnosis should be suspected.

Phencyclidine hydrochloride (PCP) is another commonly used hallucinogen with a reputation for producing "bad trips." In 1977, the abuse of this drug resulted in over 4,000 emergency room visits and at least 100 deaths.[14]

SUMMARY

We have approached the issues associated with substance abuse by describing the nature of the substances abused, the types of individuals who abuse them, and the reasons they engage in this form of self-destructive behavior. Judging from the prevalence of obesity in this country, the abuse of food is perhaps the most common abuse problem in our society. Alcoholism and problem drinking also stand out as critical abuse problems. Whereas the health hazards associated with cigarette smoking have been widely publicized, the risks attendant on the misuse of alcohol have not received the widespread attention they deserve. Yet the toll exacted by alcoholism is very great as measured by its adverse effects on the physical, psychological, and social aspects of life.

Another serious abuse problem is the misuse of licit drugs, i.e., the sedatives, tranquilizers, and analgesics. Overprescribing of these agents by medical personnel plays a major role in the cause of this problem. For example, 30 million prescriptions were written for products that contain propoxyphene (Darvon) in 1978,[40] and currently more than 25 million prescriptions are written annually for "sleeping pills."[51] The extent of their distribution indicates that a considerable degree of misuse of these drugs must exist.

The abuse of illicit drugs such as marijuana, cocaine, heroin, and LSD tends to occur among special segments of the population, for example, teenagers, young adults, counter-culture groups, and urban ghetto residents. The publicity surrounding this problem has diminished somewhat as of late, but it still constitutes a significant medical and social concern. In fact, statistics indicate that there has been a progressive rise in the incidence of marijuana use over the past 10 years. While there may be a philosophical basis for the argument to legalize some of the illicit drugs, specifically marijuana, from the medical standpoint they are all potentially harmful to a person's health and, thus, their misuse is to be strongly discouraged.

REFERENCES

1. Ehrenpreis S., Teller D.N., Lajtha A.: Drug tolerance and dependency, in Grenell R.G., Gabay S. (eds.): *Biological Foundations of Psychiatry*. New York, Raven Press, 1976.
2. Mendelson J.H., Mello N.K.: Behavioral and biochemical interrelations in alcoholism. *Annu. Rev. Med.* 27:321, 1976.
3. Ray O.S.: *Drugs, Society and Human Behavior*. St. Louis, C. V. Mosby Co., 1972.
4. Girdano D.D., Girdano D.A.: *Drugs*. Reading, Mass., Addison-Wesley Publishing Co., Inc., 1973.
5. Goodwin D.W., et al.: Alcohol problems in adoptees raised apart from biological parents. *Arch. Gen. Psychiatry* 28:238, 1973.
6. Cohen S.: Profiles of drug abusers, in Pradhan S.N., Dutta S.N. (eds.): *Drug Abuse*. St. Louis, C. V. Mosby Co., 1977.
7. Seevers M.H.: Etiological considerations in drug abuse and dependence. *J.A.M.A.* 206:1263, 1968.
8. Greene M., et al.: Evolving patterns of drug abuse. *Ann. Intern. Med.* 83:402, 1975.
9. Bray G.A. (ed.): *Obesity in America*. U.S. Department of Health, Education, and Welfare, National Institutes of Health, Publication No. 79-359, November, 1979.
10. De Luise M., Blackburn G.L., Flier J.S.: Reduced activity of the red-cell sodium-potassium pump in human obesity. *N. Engl. J. Med.* 303:1017, 1980.
11. Foch T.T., McClearn G.E.: Genetics, body weight, and obesity, in Stunkard A.J. (ed.): *Obesity*. Philadelphia, W.B. Saunders Co., 1980.
12. Guggenheim F.G.: Basic considerations in the treatment of obesity. *Med. Clin. North Am.* 61:781, 1977.
13. Keys A.: Coronary heart disease in seven countries. *Circulation* (Suppl. 1)41(4):1–211, April 1970.
14. *Healthy people: The Surgeon General's Report on Health Promotion and Disease Prevention 1979*. Department of Health, Education, and

Welfare, Public Health Service, Publication No. 79-55071.
15. Duncan G.G., et al.: Intermittent fasts in correction and control of intractable obesity. *Am. J. Med. Sci.* 245:515, 1963.
16. Bistrian B.R.: Clinical use of a protein-sparing modified fast. *J.A.M.A.* 240:2299, 1978.
17. Michiel R.R., et al.: Sudden death in a patient on a liquid protein diet. *N. Engl. J. Med.* 298:1005, 1978.
18. Van Italie T.B.: Liquid protein mayhem (editorial). *J.A.M.A.* 240:144, 1978.
19. Currey H., et al.: Behavioral treatment of obesity: Limitations and results with the chronically obese. *J.A.M.A.* 237:2829-2831, 1971.
20. Stunkard A.J., Penick S.B.: Behavior modification in the treatment of obesity. The problem of maintaining weight loss. *Arch. Gen. Psychiatry* 36:801, 1979.
21. Scott H.W., et al.: Metabolic complications of jejunoileal bypass operations for morbid obesity. *Annu. Rev. Med.* 27:397, 1976.
22. Noble E.P. (ed.): *Alcohol and Health*. Third Special Report to the U.S. Congress from the Secretary of Health, Education, and Welfare, U.S. Department of Health, Education, and Welfare, National Institute on Alcohol Abuse and Alcoholism, June 1978.
23. Cahalan D., Cisin I.H., Croseley H.M.: *American Drinking Practices: A National Survey of Drinking Behavior and Attitudes*. New Brunswick, N.J., Rutgers Center of Alcohol Studies, 1969.
24. Goodwin D.W.: Alcoholism and heredity. *Arch. Gen. Psychiatry* 36:57, 1979.
25. Mendelson J.H., Mello N.K.: Biologic concomitants of alcoholism. *N. Engl. J. Med.* 301:913, 1979.
26. Hanson J. W., et al.: Fetal alcohol syndrome—experience with 41 patients. *J.A.M.A.* 235:1458, 1976.
27. Shaywitz B.A.: Fetal alcohol syndrome: An ancient problem rediscovered. *Drug Ther.* January, 1978, p. 95.
28. Pattison E.M.: Management of alcoholism in medical practice. *Med. Clin. North Am.* 61:797, 1977.
29. Khantzian E.J., McKenna G.J.: Acute toxic and withdrawal reactions associated with drug use and abuse. *Ann. Intern. Med.* 90:361, 1979.
30. Lubetkin B.S., Rivers P.C., Rosenberg C.M.: Difficulties of disulfiram therapy with alcoholics. *Q. J. Stud. Alcohol*. 32:168, 1971.
31. Moore R.A.: Dependence on alcohol, in Pradhan S.N., Dutta S.N. (eds.): *Drug Abuse*. St. Louis, C.V. Mosby Co., 1977.
32. Becker C.E.: Medical complications of drug abuse. *Adv. Intern. Med.* 24:183, 1979.
33. Frand U.I., Chang S.S., Williams M.H.: Heroin-induced pulmonary edema. Sequential studies of lung function. *Ann. Intern. Med.* 77:29, 1972.
34. Greene M.H., Dupont R.L.: Heroin addiction trends. *Am. J. Psychiatry* 131:545, 1974.
35. Dupont R.L.: Profile of a heroin-addiction epidemic. *N. Engl. J. Med.* 285:320, 1971.
36. Ketchum J.S., Jarvik M.E.: Pharmacotherapy for the opioid addict: Agonists or antagonists. *Ration. Drug Ther.* 13(1):1, 1979.
37. Gold M.S., Pottash A.C., Sweeney D.R., et al.: Opiate withdrawal using clonidine. *J.A.M.A.* 243:343, 1980.
38. Vaillant G.E.: A twenty-year follow-up of New York narcotic addicts. *Arch. Gen. Psychiatry* 29:327, 1973.
39. Chambers C.D., Moffett A. D.: Five patterns of Darvon abuse. *Int. J. Addict.* 6:173, 1971.
40. FDA Drug Bulletin, vol. 9, no. 1, February–March 1979.
41. Chambers C. D., Brill L.: Some considerations for the treatment of non-narcotic drug abusers. *Indust. Med. Surg.* 40:29, 1970.
42. Sutherland E.W.: Dependence on barbiturates and other CNS depressants, in Pradhan S.N., Dutta S.N. (eds.): *Drug Abuse*. St. Louis, C.V. Mosby Co., 1977.
43. Council on Scientific Affairs: Clinical aspects of amphetamine abuse. *J.A.M.A.* 240:2317, 1978.
44. Byck R., Weiss B.L., Wesson D.R. (symposium participants): Cocaine: Chic, costly, and what else? *Patient Care* 14:136, 1980.
45. Wetli C.V., Wright R.K.: Death caused by recreational cocaine use. *J.A.M.A.* 241:2519, 1979.
46. Cisin I., Miller J.D., Harrell A.V.: *Highlights from the National Survey on Drug Abuse*. National Institute on Drug Abuse, Department of Health, Education, and Welfare, 1977.
47. Grinspoon L.: *Marijuana Reconsidered*. Cambridge, Mass., Harvard University Press, 1971.
48. Tashkin D.P. (moderator): Cannabis 1977. *Ann. Intern. Med.* 89:439, 1978.
49. Sallan S.E., Zinberg N.E., Frei E. III: Antiemetic effect of delta-9-tetrahydrocannabinol in patients receiving cancer chemotherapy. *N. Engl. J. Med.* 293:795, 1975.
50. Sallan S.E., et al.: Antiemetics in patients receiving chemotherapy for cancer. *N. Engl. J. Med.* 302:135, 1980.
51. Smith R.J.: Study finds sleeping pills overprescribed. *Science* 204:287, 1979.

PART IV

The Life Cycle

13 / Introduction to Human Development

MICHAEL C. HUGHES, M.D., AND JONATHAN J. BRAUNSTEIN, M.D.

CURRENT CONCEPTS of human development stress the importance of the interaction of heredity and environment. Human beings possess a genetic endowment, the product of millions of years of evolution, which gives them the inborn potential for a wide variety of biologic, psychological, social, and intellectual functions. However, realizing this potential depends on having certain requirements met by the environment in special ways and at special times. The genetic and environmental factors influencing a person's development are highly specific for him and, as a result, he acquires special characteristics and traits that make him a unique individual. Yet there are also certain aspects of development that he shares in common with all other people. For example, the two fundamental biologic processes, *growth* and *aging*, are universal and cause all people to travel similar developmental pathways. The former is an incremental process, starting at the time of conception, which is responsible for an embryo developing into a mature adult; the latter is a decremental process, beginning in the early thirties, which results in a regression in body structure and function. In addition, there are life experiences that are shared by all humans; for instance, the prolonged period of helplessness and dependency during infancy and the decline of physical vigor and stamina in old age.

The universal elements of human development have formed the basis for a concept of the life cycle as a series of stages. According to this concept, successful passage through an earlier stage is a prerequisite for success in the next. Thus, many theorists have viewed normal development as both a continuous and a cumulative process, with each new advancement taking place upon a previously established foundation.

While there is a basic continuity to the developmental process, this does not mean that it is smooth and linear. Rather, it proceeds in a saltatory fashion, i.e., at different rates during different times of life. There are phases in which it progresses at a rapid pace and times when it slows almost to a halt so that the individual seems to have reached a plateau. Lidz gives the following graphic description of personality development:

The process is not like climbing up a hill and down the other side, but more akin to a Himalayan expedition during which camps must be made at varying altitudes, guides found, the terrain explored, skills acquired, rests taken before moving up to the next level, and the descent is also made in stages.[1]

In addition to natural variations in the rate of development, life problems (e.g., physical illness, malnutrition, emotional trauma) may cause a transient arrest, regression, or distortion of maturation. If these obstacles are successfully overcome, normal development again ensues; if not, development may be hindered with subsequent physical, emotional, social, or intellectual handicaps.

Continuity in development is a concept supported by the work of A. Freud,[2] Fries,[3] and Thomas.[4] Freud introduced the theory of "developmental lines" to emphasize the continuity of certain basic human functions throughout the life cycle. She identified six of these lines, the prototype being the one associated with the development of object relations, that is, relationships with other people. This function progresses from the helpless dependency of infancy and early childhood, through the struggle of adolescence to disengage from parents and establish more independent relationships outside the family, and, finally, to the achievement of adult relationships with others. Another developmental line deals with the individual's control over bodily needs, impulses, and the like. This line progresses from the domination of these internal demands in infancy, through the development of bowel and bladder control, motor skills, and rational attitudes toward bodily care, and, finally, to the relative independence from these demands that is typical of normal adult behavior.

Longitudinal studies of human development have demonstrated that there are prominent differences among individuals almost from the time of birth, and that these may persist in later life. Fries has described variations in activity levels in infants that were still evident years later. Thomas and his co-workers have identified certain temperament characteristics in children as young as 3 months that were predictive of their emotional reactions later.[4] In a carefully designed longitudinal study of 130 middle-class children, he found the following traits apparent in early infancy: activity level, rhythmicity, approach or withdrawal, adaptability, threshold of responsiveness, intensity of reaction, quality of mood, distractibility, and attention span and persistence. Later in life, 27 of the children developed psychiatric problems, many of which were related to these early temperament characteristics.

ESSENTIAL HUMAN NEEDS

Man is a physical, psychological, social, and intellectual being; development involves changes in each of these areas of function. For these changes to occur in a normal fashion, the environment must provide certain essentials. The environmental contribution to the physical needs of an individual is fairly clear-cut: unless appropriate nutrients, water, clothing, and shelter are made available, survival, let alone normal development, is impossible. There are also critical psychological and social needs that must be met if a person is to survive and prosper. The importance of the proper psychosocial "nutrients" to human development can be highlighted by noting the effects of a deficiency of these elements, as illustrated by the following examples.

During infancy, when growth is occurring at a rapid rate, a child is extraordinarily sensitive to environmental conditions of a psychosocial as well as a physical nature.[5] An appropriate degree of sensorimotor stimulation is necessary for the maturation of the nervous system, and certain kinds of social experiences (nurturing experiences) are required for emotional and intellectual development to proceed normally. Studies in both humans and animals have clearly demonstrated that a lack of these experiences is detrimental to the infant. Not only do such environmentally deprived infants fail to acquire some of the psychological and social traits that are characteristic of the normal child, but their physical development may also be greatly impaired. They may not eat properly even though food is offered, growth becomes retarded, and neurologic and motor development is adversely affected.

When one looks at the opposite end of the life span, the geriatric period, the same kind of vulnerability to psychosocial deprivation is found. The elderly who are impoverished, who reduce their social activities, and who no longer have a confidant (i.e., spouse or close personal friend) to relate to experience a decrease in life satisfaction. This often leads to depression, which in turn may have adverse effects on physical health and mental function. For example, it is not uncommon for an older person who is placed in a nursing home, after having lived with his family for many years, to deteriorate physically and mentally as a result of a paucity of stimulating experiences in his new environment. Thus, there is a parallel between the pathologic consequences of environmental deprivation in the very young and in the very old.

In each phase of life man must have the appropriate environmental conditions, from a physical, psychological, and social standpoint, in order to realize his genetic potential and to meet successfully the challenges and tasks of normal development. To put this idea in the form of a metaphor: If the roots of the developmental process are represented by the genetic makeup of an individual and the soil that nurtures the process is composed of the life experiences and environmental conditions to which he is exposed, then it should be obvious that both the roots and the soil will have a significant influence on the type of tree that emerges.

Now, let us review some general concepts of physical, psychosocial, and cognitive development—ideas that will be discussed in more detail in subsequent chapters dealing with the specific periods of the life cycle.

GENERAL CONCEPTS OF DEVELOPMENT

One important concept having to do with human development is the epigenetic principle, which states, in effect, that each phase of life is associated with specific tasks or challenges that must be surmounted at the proper time if this process is to proceed normally. One way of thinking about these tasks is as stepping-stones along a developmental pathway, each one being a prelude to the next. An inability to negotiate a preceding step successfully makes it more difficult for a person to negotiate the following one, and the one after that, and so on.

Achieving the physical, psychosocial, and cognitive tasks at each stage prepares the individual to deal with those at the next level. This is why the failure to accomplish a task (or set of tasks) is so detrimental to development. However, during the life cycle circumstances may allow a person a number of chances to complete a task and to correct previous deficiencies. So, even though he was unsuccessful at accomplishing a task at the proper time, this does not mean that he will never master it. Indeed, each new developmental step provides an opportunity for an individual to review past experiences, integrate them into his personality, and use them to meet new challenges.

The different types of developmental tasks (physical, psychosocial, and cognitive) are interrelated such that achievement in one area is often a requirement for achievement in another. Conversely, the failure to meet a challenge in one area may lead to failures in others. For example, a brain-damaged toddler who does not achieve the milestones of neuromuscular function and is unable to walk will have difficulty developing the sense of autonomy that comes to the normal 3-year-old as a result of his active explorations of the environment. Or, the young adult who has problems establishing an intimate relationship with a member of the opposite sex will have great difficulty in assuming the social responsibilities entailed in marrying and rearing a family.

Physical Development

The physical changes occurring during childhood and adolescence are due primarily to the process of growth. As is true of development in general, the rate at which this process evolves varies at different times of life and from child to child.

Figure 13–1 illustrates the patterns of growth for the body and several of its organs from birth to age 20. There are two periods of rapid general body growth: the first of these is during fetal life and infancy; the second is the well-known adolescent growth spurt during the early and middle portions of the second decade of life. The interval between them—from about age 2 to age 10—is a time of relatively slow uniform growth.

It is obvious from Figure 13–1 that there are significant differences in the rate of growth of the body's organs. For example, the size of the brain increases rapidly during infancy. Roughly 50% of total brain growth oc-

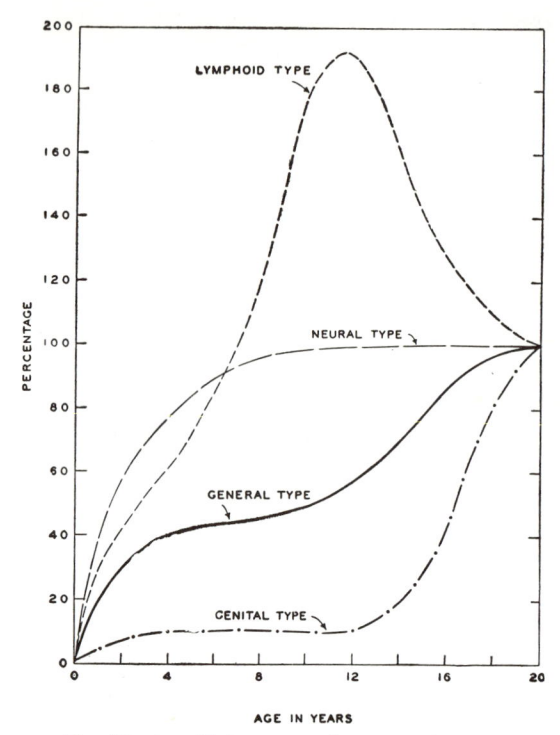

Fig 13-1.—Main types of postnatal growth of various parts and organs of the body. (From Vaughan V.C.: Growth and development, in Vaughan V.C., McKay R.J., Behrman R.E. [eds.]: *Nelson Textbook of Pediatrics.* Philadelphia, W.B. Saunders Co., 1979, p. 29. Used by permission. Cited after Scammon: The measurement of the body in childhood, in Harris et al.: *The Measurement of Man.* Minneapolis, University of Minnesota Press, 1930.)

curs during the first year of life, and it is 95% completed by the second year. Appropriate environmental stimulation during this time is most important for the full development of neurologic potential. Measurement of head circumference is a valuable index of brain growth and is used by pediatricians to follow this aspect of development. In contrast to the brain, the genital organs grow at a slow pace during the first 10 years of life and then enter a period of rapid growth during the second decade. The growth pattern of the lymphoid tissue of the body is different from that of most other tissues in that it actually diminishes in volume after the first decade. At age 10, the normal child has nearly double the amount of this tissue that is present at maturity. This must be kept in mind when assessing the size of the tonsils and lymph nodes in children.

Gesell and his co-workers did the early pioneering work that established normal parameters of physical growth. In these and other studies, it has been demonstrated that there is considerable individual variation among children in these parameters. Because of this, developmental norms are properly thought of as consisting of a range of values, not a single fixed standard. For example, when the appearance of a physical feature is charted for a large number of children, a typical bell-shaped distribution curve results. Normal val-

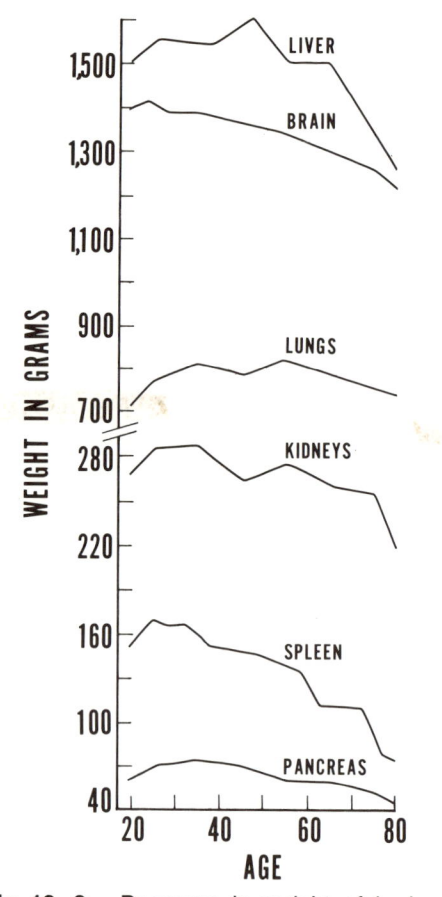

Fig 13-2.—Decrease in weight of body organs with aging. (From Rossman I.: The anatomy of aging, in Rossman I. (ed.): *Clinical Geriatrics.* Philadelphia, J.B. Lippincott Co., 1979, p. 19. Used by permission.)

ues for this aspect of development may deviate from the average in either direction. Of course, the larger the deviation, the greater are the chances that the parameter being measured is abnormal.

Just as there are variations in the rate of growth among normal individuals, the process of aging occurs at different rates in different people. Some persons at age 75 are younger physiologically than others at age 65. Thus, chronological age is not necessarily a good indicator of physiological age. Another similarity between the growth and aging processes is that the various organs of the body do not participate equally in the changes that take place. Figure 13–2 shows the decline in weight of several body organs with progressive age.

Normal biologic variability has many determinants, including genetic, environmental, racial, and ethnic factors. Illness, injury, and malnutrition may interfere with physical development, as may emotional and social problems. Thus, a comprehensive medical evaluation is in order for any child with a disturbance of normal growth, as well as for any adult who appears to be aging prematurely.

Psychosocial Development

Two men, Freud and Erikson, have had a particularly great influence on contemporary thinking with regard to psychosocial development. Working with adults in psychoanalysis, Freud reconstructed experiences that had occurred during childhood and established their significance in the pathogenesis of adult psychopathology. From such studies, he ultimately evolved a psychosexual theory of childhood development.[6] In it, he described five stages in the formation of the adult personality: the *oral stage* of infancy; the *anal stage*, occurring at about ages 2 through 3; the *phallic stage,* seen in the preschool child; the *latency stage,* in the school-age child; and the *genital stage,* beginning with adolescence and continuing through adult life.

Freud believed that human behavior is greatly influenced by biologically derived instinctual or drive energy of two primary types: sexual or libidinal and aggressive or destructive. In individuals of all ages, psychic conflict occurs between the source of this drive energy, which seeks to gain discharge, and the forces that act to socialize and sublimate its expression. Freud postulated that during the early stages of development libidinal energy is invested in the activities associated with certain erogenous zones of the body, such as the mouth, anus, and phallus, and that events and experiences that result in either overinvestment or interference in the expression of this energy could interfere with subsequent personality development. He observed that adults with psychosomatic problems and other forms of psychopathology had experienced such difficulties as children.

Prior to Freud, the impact of early childhood experiences on psychosocial development was given little consideration and was not well understood. "Infantile amnesia" generally shields people from the recollection of their early childhood experiences and most remember only isolated events from the time prior to their sixth or seventh year of life. Freud's contribution in uncovering the relevance of these experiences revolutionized the study of human psychology.

The developmental psychologist Erik Erikson elaborated the psychosexual theories of Freud and others by focusing attention on the significance of social experiences and interactions, not only those occurring during childhood but also the ones taking place later in life. Erikson's approach involved the synthesis of the psychological and social aspects of development. In his psychosocial theory, he emphasized particular developmental tasks to be accomplished by the individual during the course of his life. For example, in infancy the goal is to achieve basic trust as a result of intimate interactions with mother. The failure to have his needs met in an appropriate fashion causes the infant to develop a feeling of mistrust, which carries over to his relationships with others in the future. In adolescence, the task is to develop a sense of self-identity apart from one's family. If this is not accomplished, the individual ends up in a

ERIKSON'S EIGHT AGES OF MAN

	1	2	3	4	5	6	7	8
I INFANCY	TRUST vs. MISTRUST				Unipolarity vs. Premature Self-Differentiation			
II EARLY CHILDHOOD		AUTONOMY vs. SHAME, DOUBT			Bipolarity vs. Autism			
III PLAY AGE			INITIATIVE vs. GUILT		Play Identification vs. (oedipal) Fantasy Identities			
IV SCHOOL AGE				INDUSTRY vs. INFERIORITY	Work Identification vs. Identity Foreclosure			
V ADOLESCENCE	Time Perspective vs. Time Diffusion	Self-Certainty vs. Identity Consciousness	Role Experimentation vs. Negative Identity	Anticipation of Achievement vs. Work Paralysis	IDENTITY vs. IDENTITY DIFFUSION	Sexual Identity vs. Bisexual Diffusion	Leadership Polarization vs. Authority Diffusion	Ideological Polarization vs. Diffusion of Ideals
VI YOUNG ADULT					Solidarity vs. Social Isolation	INTIMACY vs. ISOLATION		
VII ADULTHOOD							GENERATIVITY vs. SELF-ABSORPTION	
VIII MATURE AGE								INTEGRITY vs. DISGUST, DESPAIR

Fig 13-3.—Erikson's eight ages of man. (From Erikson E.H.: *The Life Cycle*, with the permission of W.W. Norton & Company, Inc., Copyright © 1980 by W.W. Norton & Company, Inc. Copyright © 1959 by International Universities Press, Inc.)

state called an "identity crisis" with confusion about himself and his future roles in life.

Erikson's classic work, *Childhood and Society*, further elaborated his theory of human development.[7] In it he discusses the eight ages of man, which are illustrated graphically in Figure 13-3. This figure depicts the changing developmental tasks along the diagonal dimension; the theme of continuity in development is represented, although still in preliminary fashion at this period in Erikson's work, along the vertical and horizontal dimensions. The more recent work of Anna Freud and her associates on the concept of developmental lines has done much to clarify these last two dimensions, which were only briefly introduced by Erikson.

Until recently most of the attention with respect to psychosocial development has been focused on childhood, adolescence, and old age. The long period following maturity (adulthood) was largely ignored in studies of the life cycle, even though observations strongly suggested that this is a time of continued change and development.

The young adult years are the special time for achieving a meaningful relationship with someone of the opposite sex and for developing work skills. The adult years are times for strengthening the intimacy and meaning of a marital relationship, perhaps rearing children, and for becoming productive, skillful, and satisfied with one's work and livelihood. Finally, in old age, it is hoped, life can be reviewed with some sense of satisfaction and accomplishment, with an acceptance of life's successes, limitations, and disappointments.

The investigations of Gould, Levinson, and others have shown that the adult stage of life is indeed a very dynamic one in terms of psychosocial change.[8,9] *Stable periods* have been identified which alternate with *transitional* or *unstable periods*. According to Levinson, the primary developmental task of a stable period is to make certain crucial choices, build a life structure, and seek to attain particular goals and values within this structure. Although many changes occur during these periods, the basic life structure remains relatively intact. The primary developmental task of a transitional period is to terminate the existing structure and to work toward the initiation of a new structure, which generally involves significant changes in life-style.

Cognitive Development and Learning

The higher intellectual functions set man apart from the rest of the animal kingdom; consequently, a great deal of attention has been given to the study of how man acquires his cognitive abilities. In this regard, the work of the Swiss psychologist Jean Piaget provides the broad theory of the development of cognition.[11] His objective has been to trace the evolution and development of rational, logical, scientific thinking from its early beginnings in the newborn to the adolescent or young adult where these processes reach their fruition. Piaget considers intelligence to be but one aspect of the general biologic principle of adaptation. Just as an organism ingesting a new kind of food must make certain adjustments or accommodations in terms of chewing and digesting in order to assimilate it, Piaget notes that a parallel process of accommodation must occur for intellectual adaptation or problem-solving if the individual is to assimilate a new piece of information. These fundamental processes underlie all cognitive development throughout the life of the individual, whether the problem confronting him is learning how to grasp a new object at 6 months of age, how to tell time at 5 years, how to solve an abstract calculus problem at 18, or how to make an accurate medical diagnosis at 35.

Like the investigators dealing with other developmental processes, Piaget described cognitive development in terms of sequential stages that occur during the life cycle. The *sensorimotor stage,* the first one described by Piaget, is ushered in as the infant comes in contact with an increasing number of environmental stimuli. Primary and secondary "circular reactions" are described as taking place during this time, meaning that the child responds to and then acts upon his environment in a circular repetitive fashion. Tertiary circular reactions occur as the infant begins the process of actively exploring the environment. New objects are integrated into the infant's internal schema (i.e., his mental image) as a consequence of their similarity with previous objects. This process is called assimilation by Piaget. Ultimately, the infant's internal schema and behavior become modified as a result of his exposure to new and different experiences—a process called accommodation.

The *preoperational stage* of cognitive development, Piaget's second stage, usually occurs between the ages of 2 and 7. Even though the child can still focus his attention on only one perceptual feature at a time, he begins the process of symbolic thinking as he starts to reason logically and deductively on the basis of past experiences.

Concrete operations, the third stage, evolves between ages 7 and 11. Now the child has progressed to a point where he can consider two or more variables at once, and his thinking is no longer bound to immediate circumstances and perceptions. The environment can be described and explored based on relationships that exist between objects and classes of objects. The principle of conservation is also established at this time: the same amount of water, although placed in beakers or containers of varying sizes and shapes, is understood to remain the same.

Formal operations, the final stage of cognitive development, begins at about age 12, reaches its peak at ages 14 and 15, and continues throughout life. Now ideas as well as objects can be manipulated by establishing hypotheses and using these to plan ahead. The ability to generalize from the specific releases one from the concrete world of present experience. These forms of more abstract thinking are by no means achieved by everyone and, even at best, are achieved incompletely.

Learning, another aspect of the developmental process, results from interactions between the individual's cognitive growth and his environment. According to traditional paradigms within experimental psychology, learning takes place through classical conditioning and operant conditioning. Both types of learning are described at length in chapter 5.

Behaviors are learned not only by conditioning but also by imitation or observational learning.[10] Among children, this kind of learning is especially common. They observe the actions of those about them (parents, teachers, friends) and then at some later time attempt to copy all or part of what they have witnessed. In this way, complex behaviors (e.g., helping, aggressive behavior) may become part of a child's response pattern. Studies indicate that certain models are more likely than others to be imitated by children, for example, people they admire, other children, and persons whose actions are rewarded. Also, Bandura has shown that if a child is given an incentive (a reward) to imitate a behavior, he is more likely to do so. Thus, operant conditioning and observational learning often occur together, one facilitating the other.

A vast array of new behaviors that children and adults acquire during their life span are learned by means of these three paradigms. Of course, learning is not the only explanation for changes in behavior, since intrapsychic processes are also responsible for motivating people to think or act in new ways.

CULTURE AND DEVELOPMENT

Up to this point, we have described development from a physical, psychosocial, and cognitive standpoint. In order to complete this discussion, however, another aspect of this process must be considered, man's cultural endowment.[1] This is a force that exerts a tremendous influence in all facets of life, molding human behavior from the time of birth.

Chapter 10 described how each social group defines for its members those beliefs, attitudes, and values that are desirable. In effect, these tell people how to think and act in relation to important matters in life. From the time of infancy, a child is taught to accept the system of beliefs and values in his society—a process called enculturation or socialization. The family is the primary agent transmitting this information, although peers, teachers, and other influential persons also play a role in helping a person learn the ways of his culture. Most of the time this learning process occurs so naturally that it is hardly noticeable unless one consciously thinks about it.

Physical, psychological, and cognitive development are guided by cultural determinants. Language, the basic tool of cognitive function, is a product of culture. The richness and precision of a particular language may assist in maximizing cognitive potential while a more primitive language may inhibit the full unfolding of intelligence for a given cultural group. Most social events, situations, and relationships also are influenced by culture and social tradition.

Physical development, of course, determines the timetable for the appearance of such functions as the capacity to digest solid foods, the control of bowel and bladder, and sexual reproduction. The decline in physical functions that comes with old age also follows a biologic clock. However, the meaning, expression, and even to some extent the timing of key activities related to these functional changes (e.g., weaning, toilet training, courtship and marriage, and retirement) are largely determined by societal custom. Without understanding the impact of culture on our daily lives and the manner in which it guides development, the life cycle cannot be seen in its full perspective.

Let us briefly examine some specific effects of culture on development, using, as we did previously, examples from both ends of the life span. Studies indicate that cultures vary greatly in the practices of infant care. With respect to the feeding of infants, some provide food (by breast or bottle) on demand and others at scheduled time periods; some wean the child at an early age, others prefer late weaning. Bathing an infant is also handled differently by different cultures. In some societies, frequent cleansing is the rule; in others it is infrequent. Even the positioning of an infant at rest varies from culture to culture. In some, an infant's activities are restricted by using swaddling or cradle boards; in others, the child is carried close to the mother in a sling where he is allowed to nurse whenever he is hungry.

Culture also exerts a marked influence on the lives of the elderly. Palmore and Maddox have compared the status of the aged in agricultural and industrial societies, noting that in the former they are generally accorded great prestige and privilege and are revered for their greater knowledge and experience.[12] This is typical of many of the Far Eastern cultures. In some industrial societies, such as ours, there is a tendency to show less regard for the elderly. It is fair to say that in the United States, the aged are *not* venerated; in fact, there is a widespread bias against them, which has been referred to as "agism." These cultural views can greatly affect the attitude and behavior of the elderly. For instance, in an agrarian society, where the aged are encouraged to play an active role in the affairs of the family and community, their sense of self-worth is maintained, whereas in our society, where the older population is frequently pressured to give up work and community responsibilities, their self-esteem is likely to decline.

METHODS OF STUDY

Of all the parts of the life cycle, child development has received the most intense scrutiny. The information on this subject that is currently available has come from a variety of sources, both clinical and experimental. Studies of children, as well as laboratory investigation of animal behavior, have contributed much to our understanding of specific parameters of growth and psychosocial development. At this point in the discussion, it is worthwhile to examine some approaches that have been used in these studies to unravel the mysteries of growth and development.

Clinical Studies of Children

Studies of the neurophysiology of the newborn have shed considerable light on subsequent physical, emotional, and cognitive development. Variations in neurologic responses among infants have been described that point out that the period of rapid brain growth in early infancy is a time of critical importance.[13] Clinical neurologic observations have shown that major differences exist between adults and children, and that one must take into consideration the age of a child and the sensory input he has been exposed to when evaluating his neurologic status.[13] Some basic biologic rhythms have been studied by Wolff, who found that many of these are part of an innate pattern of behavior. Included in this category are the rate and rhythm of sucking, the cycle of sleep and wakefulness, and the endocrine and psychophysiological correlates of the menstrual cycle.[14] Investigations of the neurophysiology of infant sleep,[15] psychological and physiological correlates of the sleep cycle in the young and old,[16] and sleep deprivation[17] have shed light on the interface between neurophysiological and psychological development.

Clinical medicine has served as a resource for understanding child development and its variations. While one would not intentionally subject children to experimental situations (such as nutritional deficiency, mother-child separation, sensory deprivation) that might be harmful, the vicissitudes of life do, in fact, bring them into contact with these kinds of circumstances. These "experiments in nature" lead to developmental abnormalities of a physical, emotional, and social nature and, as a result, have shed considerable light on normal and abnormal developmental processes. The adverse effects of nutritional deficiency, particularly in early infancy during the period of rapid brain growth, have been documented. Studies have been conducted on the interplay of emotional stimulation and nutrition in Mexican infants.[18] Two groups of infants with a marginal nutritional intake were evaluated for parameters of growth: one group having adequate maternal care and stimulation, the other group with inadequate care. Neurologic and cognitive development was found to be impaired to a greater degree in the latter group.

Much has been learned about the process of early mother-infant attachment through studies of disruptions in this relationship. Spitz discovered that prolonged hospitalization, with maternal separation and a lack of good institutional care, resulted in impaired physical development, a significant infant mortality, and psychological impoverishment.[19] Bowlby's classic monograph reviewed factors involved in maternal deprivation.[20] Other investigators, who attempted to reduce the emotional deprivation due to maternal separation by providing optimal care for the children while their mothers were hospitalized, have clarified the specific consequences of separation and loss in the early years of life. Studies of institutional care have led to the demise of orphanages and emphasized the importance of early placement in an adoptive home or, at least, in foster-care family situations.[21, 22]

Studies of blind infants have demonstrated the impact of specific sensory impairments on general development.[23] The importance of the smiling response has been graphically illustrated in blind infants in whom smiling does occur but is not related to the infant's visual perception of the mother's facial expressions. In this situation, the maternal contribution to the mother-infant relationship may be diminished due to the mother's feeling that her child does not respond to her because he does not react with a smile to her facial expressions. This clearly illustrates the *reciprocal* nature of the interaction that takes place between mother and child—something that will be discussed at greater length in chapter 14.

Autistic children, in their most disturbed form, do not find solace, comfort, or gratification in human relationships. Recent studies of children with this disorder suggest that there is a strong biologic component to their illness.[24]

Animal Studies

Ethology, the observation and study of animal behavior, has made significant contributions to the understanding of human development, although observations of animals are to be applied to humans with considerable care. A special advantage of animal work, however, is that it allows much wider experimental latitude. In birds, a newly hatched offspring becomes "imprinted" upon an object (usually the mother) that moves and produces sound; this special form of social attachment occurs very early in development and in a predictable sequence. Under experimental conditions in which the mother is absent, however, birds may become attached or imprinted to inanimate objects or fail to develop any social attachments at all, resulting in isolation from the flock and an inability to mate. True imprinting has not been demonstrated in humans or in other primates, yet an analogy does exist in the attachment of infants to their mother's face. Infants prefer complex movement and sound for early visual stimulation. Their mother's face is by far the most interesting object to them, so they are attracted to her facial expressions and verbal communication.[25] Despite early psychoanalytic theorizing about the infant's attraction to the breast, current child observation studies demonstrate that it is the mother's face that is the most important "attention getter" for the infant and the most critical in the process of mother-infant attachment.

The significance of physical contact, one of the critical features of maternal care in primates, has been evaluated by Harlow in his work with monkeys. When these animals are deprived of a maternal figure, they turn to surrogate mothers or to mechanical objects made of either wire or soft material.[26] Harlow has also studied the importance of social bonding, including the particular problems that develop when mothering is absent. For example, monkeys raised without mothers have great difficulty in establishing social contact, are unable to learn mating behavior, and, if artificially impregnated, are unable to rear their young subsequently. Recently, a most interesting experiment demonstrated that monkeys raised without mothers will develop more normal social relationships if provided daily interaction and contact with peers.[27]

Lorenz, in his classic ethological work *On Aggression*, described ways in which aggression is controlled, ritualized, and integrated within the animal kingdom.[28] Territoriality, behavioral analogies to moral concepts, instinctual behavior, and productive social applications of aggression are discussed from the perspective of the social behaviors of animals and birds.

From physical anthropolgy we learn that the most rapid growth of the human brain occurs *after* birth, in contrast to animals in which much of brain growth occurs *prior* to birth. Postnatal maturation in humans is greatly prolonged, particularly neurologic development, leading to significant dependency and immaturity for longer periods than occur in animals. This prolonged maturation has the advantage of allowing a longer time for the socialization of the individual.

SUMMARY

Past explanations of development have varied: to some theorists, the development of a person was analogous to a lump of clay that is molded and shaped by the environment; to others, development was seen as a genetically programmed sequence that is relatively unaffected by life experiences. This age-old debate about the relative importance of "nature" and "nurture" is outdated, since present developmental theory emphasizes the importance of *both* genetic and environmental factors in this process. Physical development is interwoven with psychological, social, and cognitive development. All are affected by life experiences that may be harmful, such as physical illness, emotional insults, and social deprivation, or experiences that may be helpful, such as an intact and supportive family, a good education, and good medical care. The uniqueness of the genetic and environmental influences to which each person is exposed is what makes him like no other individual in the world.

Growth is an incremental process with a built-in time table for the unfolding of certain potentials. In the clinical practice of medicine, we are concerned with this unfolding as well as with those factors that either support or impede it. On the other hand, aging is a decremental process with a built-in timetable for the regression of body function. The physical changes that occur during growth and aging are associated with a succession of needs and opportunities in relationship to the person's interaction with his environment. A long period of relative dependence in the early part of maturation, less noteworthy within the animal kingdom, is a special aspect of the human life cycle that plays a vital role in the social development of the individual. The increasing life span that has resulted from medical advances has presented people with a new and different problem, that is, how to cope with the challenges of old age.

Both change and continuity are integral parts of human development. The individual travels an evolutionary road from the dependence of infancy and childhood to the achievement of partial autonomy and independence in adolescence, to the attainment of the adult responsibilities of marriage and parenthood, and, finally, to the retirement of old age where, for some, dependency occurs once again. It is true that our past experiences form the foundation for our later development; thus, each phase of life is closely linked to the next in a continuous developmental process.

REFERENCES

1. Lidz T.: *The Person*. New York, Basic Books, Inc., Publishers, 1976.
2. Freud A.: *Normality and Pathology in Childhood*. New York, International University Press, 1965.
3. Fries M., Woolf P.: Some hypotheses on the

role of congenital activity type in personality development. *Psychoanal. Study Child* 8:48–62, 1953.
4. Thomas A., Chess S.: *Temperament and Development*. New York, Brunner-Mazel, Inc., 1977.
5. Hunt J.M.: Psychological development: Early experience. *Annu. Rev. Psychol.* 30:103, 1979.
6. Freud S.: *Three Essays on the Theory of Sexuality*, standard ed. London, Hogarth Press, 1953.
7. Erikson E.: *Childhood and Society*, ed. 2. New York, W.W. Norton & Company, Inc., 1950.
8. Gould R.L.: The phases of adult life: A study in developmental psychology. *Am. J. Psychiatry* 129:5, 1972.
9. Levinson D.J.: *The Seasons of a Man's Life*. New York, Alfred A. Knopf, Inc., 1978.
10. Bandura A., Walters R.H.: *Social Learning and Personality Development*. New York, Holt, Rinehart and Winston, Inc., 1963.
11. Flavel J.H.: *The Developmental Psychology of Jean Piaget*. New York, D. Van Nostrand Company, 1963.
12. Palmore E., Maddox G.L.: Sociologic aspects of aging, in Busse E.W., Pfeiffer E. (eds.): *Behavior and Adaptation in Late Life*. Boston, Little, Brown and Co., 1977.
13. Richmond J., Lipton E.: Some aspects of the neurophysiology of the newborn and their implications for child development, in Jessner L., Pavensted E. (eds.): *Dynamic Psychopathology of Childhood*. New York, Grune & Stratton, Inc., 1959.
14. Wolff P.H.: The role of biological rhythms in early psychological development, in Chess S., Thomas A. (eds.): *Annual Progress in Child Psychiatry and Child Development*. New York, Brunner-Mazel, Inc., 1968.
15. Anders T., Hoffman E.: The sleep polygram. *Am. J. Ment. Defic.* 77:506–514, 1973.
16. Mack J.: *Nightmares and Human Conflict*. Boston, Little, Brown and Co., 1970.
17. Dement W., Fisher C.: Experimental interference with sleep cycle. *Can. Psychiatr. Assoc. J.* 3:400–405, 1963.
18. Cravioto J.: Nutrition and its contributions to mental functions, Kitty Scientific Foundation, 1973. *Hospital Tribune*, May 21, 1973.
19. Spitz R.A.: Hospitalism. *Psychoanal. Study Child* 1:53–74, 1945.
20. Bowlby J.: *Maternal Care and Mental Health*, ed. 2. World Health Organization Monograph 2, Geneva, 1952.
21. Freud A., Burlingham D.: *Infants Without Families*. New York, International Universities Press, 1970.
22. Provence S., Lipton R.: *Infants in Institutions* New York, International Universities Press, 1962.
23. Fraiberg S.: Smiling and stranger reaction in blind infants, in Helmuth J. (ed.): *Exceptional Infant*. New York, Brunner-Mazel, Inc., 1971, vol. 2, pp. 110–127.
24. Fish B.: Biological Antecedents of Psychosis in Children, in Freedman, D.X. (ed.): *Biology of the Major Psychoses*, Association for Research for Nervous System and Mental Disease, Publication No. 54. New York, Raven Press, 1977.
25. Lewis M.: *Clinical Aspects of Child Development*. Philadelphia, Lea & Febiger, 1971.
26. Harlow H.F.: The nature of love. *Am. Psychol.* 13:673, 1958.
27. Suomi S., Harlow H., McKinney W.: Monkey psychiatrists. *Am. J. Psychiatry* 27:200–203, 1972.
28. Lorenz K.: *On Aggression*. New York, Harcourt, Brace & World, 1966.

14 / The Early Years

JEFFREY M. SEIBERT, Ph.D., and RICHARD P. TOISTER, Ph.D.

This chapter will deal with the major developmental changes occurring from birth to 4 years of age. It will focus on the physical, cognitive, and psychosocial aspects of behavior in the infant and toddler. In addition, the acquisition of language, one of the most important developmental tasks of this period, will be described.

THE INFANT

The stage of infancy covers the time from birth to about 18 months of age. During that relatively brief period of development, change is rapid and complex as the immature human organism begins to acquire some mastery of motor, language, and social skills. The first 30 days of life are often referred to as the neonatal period. At birth the neonate appears to be a relatively helpless creature, totally dependent on the ministrations of others. Despite the appearance of helplessness, however, he enters the world equipped with sophisticated reflexive behavior patterns that enable him to make the adaptations to the environment necessary for survival (Table 14–1). Every healthy newborn quickly demonstrates the capacity to suck, grasp, vocalize, and respond to light and sound. These primitive behavior patterns not only are the infant's basic tools of survival (e.g., sucking enables him to take in the necessary nutrients; crying signals hunger, pain, or discomfort) but they also provide the basic building blocks for all future development.

Physical Development

The most striking feature of the physical development of the infant is the rapid rate at which he grows. At no other time in an individual's life, except perhaps adolescence, does he experience so great a change in his physical being in such a short time. A normal infant's birth weight doubles in 6 months and triples by the age of 12 months. The organ system that undergoes the greatest degree of growth and maturation during this time is the neurologic system (see Fig 13–1 in chap. 13). Myelination of the nerve fibers of the brain and spinal cord occurs to a large extent in the first year of life and is responsible for the progressive increase in the coordination of neuromuscular function that takes place during this period.

The rapid rate of growth and development characteristic of infancy is associated with increased nutritional requirements, making the infant particularly vulnerable to nutritional deficiency. During this period, drugs, chemical toxins, and infectious diseases may have serious effects on the infant by interfering with the physiological and metabolic processes that are so active at this time.

Motor development in infancy proceeds sequentially in a *cephalocaudal* (from head to extremities) and *proximodistal* (central to peripheral) direction. By about 15 months of age, most infants are ambulatory and capable of fine motor adaptive responses such as the pincer grasp. Of course, motor development is essential for the infant to acquire socially important behaviors such as speech. Since articulation involves the control and coordination of the muscles of the tongue and pharynx, it is common for children under 3 years who have not experienced this degree of motor development to make a high rate of errors in articulation.

As motor development proceeds in infancy,

TABLE 14–1.—NEONATAL REFLEXES AND ELICITING STIMULI

NAME	STIMULUS	REFLEX PATTERN
Rooting	Touch or stroke corner of mouth with baby in supine position (lying on back)	Head turns toward stimulus and mouth opens
Moro	Body supported and head let drop a few inches with sudden but not forceful movement	Arms outstretch then cross chest as if to grasp
Tonic neck reflex (TNR)	Baby supine; head turned slowly to right side	Jaw and arm on right side extended out, left arm flexes
Babinski	Baby supine; sole of foot scratched on lateral side from toes to heel	Dorsal flexion of big toe and fanning of smaller toes
Plantar grasp	Baby supine; thumbs pressed against balls of infant's feet near toes	Flexion of all toes simultaneously
Palmar grasp	Baby supine; touching only palmar surface, press fingers from ulnar side into hands and press palmar surface	Flexion of all fingers around examiner's fingers
Sucking response	Baby supine; index finger placed about 3 cm into mouth	Rhythmic sucking movement

Modified from Prechtl H., Beintema D.L.: *The Neurological Examination of the Full Term Newborn Infant.* London, Spastics International Medical Publications in association with William Heinemann Ltd., 1965, pp. 1–75.

the child becomes more capable of interacting directly with his physical world. This increased capability permits him to manipulate the environment, which stimulates the learning process.

Learning and Cognition

LEARNING PROCESSES.—The two basic learning paradigms, classical and operant conditioning, were discussed in detail in chapter 5. Given these two paradigms, the question that has intrigued developmental psychologists is how they can be demonstrated to be operative early in infancy.[1-5] The evidence suggests that infants cannot be classically conditioned until about 3 or 4 months of age, but that operant conditioning of at least some responses, such as components of the sucking response, can be demonstrated even in the first days after birth.[3, 4, 6]

Sameroff has argued that the cognitive demands are much greater in learning to associate an arbitrary neutral stimulus with an unconditioned stimulus in classical conditioning than in increasing the rate of a response as a function of its consequences.[4, 6] Even for operant conditioning, however, response and reinforcer selection must be done carefully. Early operant conditioning is possible only with adaptive responses basic to survival, such as sucking, and when meaningful consequences are associated with the response, such as delivery of milk to the mouth.[3, 6] The operant conditioning of vocalizations, reinforced by the gentle stroking of the abdomen, has been reported only for infants about 3 months of age.[7]

During the past decade, interest has been developing in a different kind of learning, called *habituation*, which has the potential for providing clues to the kinds of information young infants process and how their memory functions. The procedure to demonstrate habituation involves the presentation of an attention-eliciting stimulus such as a visual pattern or a tone of a certain frequency. After repeated presentations of the stimulus, its attention-eliciting properties diminish until the infant no longer attends to it. Infants typically fail to habituate to repeated visual stimulus presentations until 2 to 3 months of age, which suggests that the young infant is not encoding the information in his memory.[8] Successful habituation implies memory for the habituated stimulus, provided that fatigue and sensory adaptation can be ruled out as causes for the observed response decrement. This learning paradigm can be used to provide information on the infant's processing capacities simply by changing the presented stimulus after the infant has habituated to it. Recovery of attention indicates that the infant has discriminated the difference. By changing various components of the original habituated stimulus (e.g., changing the frequency of a tone or presenting a red square or a blue circle after producing habituation to a blue square) and observing whether the infant begins to attend again, one can determine what in the original stimulus the infant must have been attending to.

The habituation paradigm has been used as a way to explore the infant's discriminative powers and his memory for various stimuli such as geometric shapes and patterns, human faces, simple concepts, and sensitivity to auditory, including linguistic, input. Evidence suggests that 4-month-old boys are more likely to habituate to geometric patterns than are girls;[9] that by the second half of the first year, most infants can discriminate male faces from female faces;[10, 11] and that by about 7 months, infants can recognize pictures of the same persons in various orientations.[12] In addition, there is evidence that infants in the first months of life can discriminate among small but important changes in speech sounds (such as [ga] versus [ba] or [pa] versus [ba]), suggesting that infants may be innately predisposed auditorially to attend to some important but subtle linguistic cues.[13, 14]

PIAGET'S SENSORIMOTOR STAGE.—The cognitive theories of Piaget were summarized in chapter 13.[15-19] It is during the first 18 to 24 months of life, according to Piaget, that the processes of accommodation and assimilation are most readily observable, because the infant's intelligence is limited to the plane of action; that is, he can solve problems only by acting.[17] The infant during this time is incapable of symbolic, representational thinking. For this reason, Piaget has labeled this first period of cognitive development the period of sensorimotor intelligence.

The infant passes through a series of stages in the transition from basic reflexive behavior to representational thinking during these first 2 years. The neonate's world is one of fleeting, nonsubstantial, nonpermanent images, uncoordinated with sound and touch, lacking depth and three-dimensionality. The infant has no awareness of a distinction between self and environment and has no understanding of temporal or cause-effect relationships. By modifying his behavior, first by repeated practice of his reflexive behavior patterns in response to various environmental inputs, the child learns both about his own actions and about the objects and persons in the world around him. Gradually, he organizes the information from his various senses into a coordinated whole. He then develops an understanding about the continued existence of objects, about persons in three-dimensional space subject to physical laws, and about himself as an object in this spatiotemporal system. By the end of the sensorimotor period of intelligence, the infant has begun to develop mental representations of his world and can act mentally without having to act physically. He is no longer totally dependent on immediate perceptual input but can represent things to himself mentally that are no longer perceptually present. The child has left the plane of action and will develop now on the plane of thought.

Language Development

Perhaps the most important and difficult learning task facing a child is the acquisition of language. Mature language involves complex, rule-governed use of socially determined symbols in order to communicate thoughts and feelings. Its origins have been examined by studying the development of the various components that constitute the linguistic system, including: (1) sound production and the reception system for the units of sound; (2) the units of linguistic meaning, morphemes and words (semantics); (3) the rules of grammar used for combining the units of meaning (syntax); and (4) the different ways in which language can serve as a communication system (pragmatics). During the first 18 months of life the infant is developing his sound production and reception system, acquiring a basic vocabulary of single words, and developing an understanding of some ways to use language to communicate with others. Syntactic development, i.e., the acquisition of rules to combine words, emerges only after 18 months.

As noted earlier, it has been demonstrated that infants have the innate ability to discriminate at least some important speech sounds. This finding is supported by the observation that infants in the first weeks of life will synchronize their body movements to the rhythm and pattern of adult speech.[20] Other studies, however, suggest that there are limits to this innate capacity to discriminate speech sounds and point out the important role played by experience in the child's acquisition of many speech perceptual skills.[21, 22]

In terms of vocalization skills, it appears that most infants pass through a series of stages in developing their capacity to vocalize. Their earliest vocalizations are primarily vowel sounds, but by 3 to 5 months infants begin to produce squeals, growls, and raspy sounds. During the next several months, infants start to babble, combining consonants with their vowel sounds and expanding their productions to include strings of these combinations (such as bababa). Finally, before mature speech emerges, the infant between 11 and 14 months begins to produce complex combinations of meaningless sounds called gibberish. With this final stage, the infant's vocal system is sophisticated enough to produce most sounds necessary for adult speech.[23]

The infant's first meaningful words are usually produced somewhere near the end of his first year,[24, 25] although evidence is accumulating that the infant may already understand several words before he produces any.[26] By 18 months, the average child's productive vocabulary has expanded to about 50 words[27] and he is on the verge of producing his first word combinations. It has been observed by several language researchers that the infant's earliest vocabulary is focused primarily on actions and objects that move or change.[26, 28]

Despite his limited vocabulary, the infant even as young as 11 or 12 months is using his vocalizations intentionally to communicate his wants and needs to others,[29] and over the next 6 months he will use his single-word utterances to convey many different meanings about what is happening around him.[24]

Psychosocial Aspects of Development

THEORIES OF FREUD AND ERIKSON.—Freud called the period of infancy the oral stage of life because he perceived that most of the child's psychic energy was centered about activities in which the mouth was used. Besides feeding, the infant seems to use his mouth as sort of a "sensing organ" to communicate with the outside world. Now objects that are new are investigated by placing them in the mouth, presumably to detect size, shape, and taste.

In his writings, Erikson stated that the fundamental psychosocial task of infancy is the establishment of a trusting relationship between the infant and his caregiver, mother. To him, she represents "the world" insofar as she is by far the most important individual in his life. The trust that develops on the part of the infant is based on how well she meets his needs and the type of social attachment that occurs between them. If the mother is able to meet the child's physical and emotional requirements satisfactorily, then he is likely to view the world in an optimistic fashion and will be better prepared to deal with the problems and frustrations that he encounters in the future. On the other hand, if a feeling of mistrust is established at this early stage of development, it is possible that the child will carry this feeling with him as he tries to cope with life in the future.

It is difficult for some to understand how such a fundamental aspect of psychological makeup—trust—can be determined so early in human development, yet this seems to be the case. It is clear that the infant, although appearing to be simply a reflexive organism, is undergoing profound psychological changes that will influence his behavior for the remainder of his life. Of course, it is only the foundation for trust that is laid during infancy, and this part of the individual's personality is subject to continued modification as he grows older.

MOTHER-INFANT RELATIONSHIP.—This aspect of infant development has been subjected to a great deal of scientific study in the last 20 years. Previous conceptualizations of infant behavior were based on natural observations and clinical case reports. These tended to describe the infant as more passive than active, as a tabula rasa (blank tablet) upon which experience writes, or in general the "receiver" in the early interaction that takes place between mother and child.

Recent investigations using controlled observations, however, have strongly supported the thesis that the infant, even in the neonatal period, is an active participant in these early social exchanges. In fact, the social behavior and/or temperament of the infant can directly affect the responsiveness of the mother or other caregiver.[30] The concept of *reciprocity* in the mother-infant relationship, or the thesis that the behavior of each party influences the actions of the other, is basic to an understanding of this social dyad. In addition to its great importance in normal development, this concept is extremely useful in the analysis of situations of abnormal development, such as the syndrome of autism, which will be discussed later in this chapter.

The concept of *social attachment* is critical to an understanding of the nature of the mother-infant relationship. The dictionary defines "attachment" as a "feeling that binds one to a person, thing, cause, idea, etc." The important words are "feeling" and "binds," implying a close emotional tie or relationship to another person. With respect to the first 2 years of life, one source notes that the "term attachment refers to the infant's tendency during the first and second years to approach particular people, to be maximally receptive to being cared for by these people, and to be least afraid when with these people."[31] Thus, in infancy social attachment is best demonstrated in the reciprocal relationship that develops between the infant and his caregiver (parent).

Since establishing a feeling of trust is the major psychosocial goal in infancy, it follows that the mother-infant relationship is the most important psychosocial feature of this stage of life. The personal attributes of both parties affect the kind of social attachment that develops between them. Some mothers possess the qualities that allow them to meet their child's needs effectively, while others have a difficult time adjusting to their infant's demands. Some infants are by temperament easy to care for, while others are more difficult. In addition to the personal makeup of the mother and child, there are environmental factors that affect their interaction, including the number of children in the household, the presence of one or two parents in the family, whether or not the mother works, and the socioeconomic status of the family.

Often it is very difficult to observe social attachment directly and, therefore, investigators have relied on other indicators of this phenomenon, such as smiling, "stranger anxiety," and "separation anxiety," to evaluate the early bond between the infant and his mother. These parameters of social attachment are not the only ones that can be observed (one investigator lists more than ten[32]); however, they are usually considered to be most important.

Studies on *social smiling* in infancy indicate that spontaneous responsive smiling usually appears between 2 and 5 months of age, with the average age of appearance about 2½ months.[33] The reciprocal reactions of the mother to this behavior, such as holding and touching the infant after a smile, can alter the frequency of the smiling.[34]

The smile of her infant may be interpreted by the mother as having special significance. First, it is a source of great pleasure to her, often serving as a "reward" for the great deal of attention and care she has given her infant. Second, it helps to reassure her that she is a "good" mother who is able to care for her child successfully, and it encourages her to continue to put forth her best efforts. Expressed in terms of operant conditioning theory, the infant's smile acts as a powerful reinforcer for the mother's caretaking activities. Conversely, if the infant for one reason or another does not smile in response to the mother, she may feel that she is unable to meet his needs successfully. This may cause her to become concerned, anxious, and emotionally upset, resulting in an impairment in social attachment. The delay or absence of appropriate social smiling may indicate developmental problems[35] as well as difficulties in the social attachment between the infant and the caregiver.

Social attachment between mother and infant is also illustrated by the occurrence of stranger anxiety. Infants typically learn by 7 or 8 months of age to discriminate (respond differentially) among various visual and auditory stimuli in their environment. For instance, infants can separate face from nonface stimuli as well as respond differentially to male versus female characteristics of faces at this time. At about 8–10 months of age (range from 3 to 19 months) most infants react emotionally (e.g., crying, avoidance) to the presence of strangers. This fearful behavior is usually referred to as stranger anxiety and is interpreted by many developmental scientists as evidence for the development of social attachment. The rationale is that as the infant matures cognitively and becomes able to recognize different people, those who are new to him cause him to react with fear. Thus, when confronted by a stranger, he clings to the parent or caregiver for emotional comfort and support. Various factors such as the infant's previous experience with strangers and the stranger's behavior can influence this reaction. Stranger anxiety is seen in all cultures,[32] and animal studies have found similar behavior in kittens faced with novel situations.[36]

At approximately 10–14 months of age, infants usually become anxious and fearful when separated from their mother or caregiver. For instance, an infant may be sitting in a highchair and observe the mother leave the room, whereupon the child begins to cry. When she returns, the infant reaches out to be held and then quiets when picked up by the mother. Emotional behavior on the part of the infant in response to a temporary separation from the mother is usually called separation anxiety. By about 22 months of age, it begins to disappear.

Many factors in the infant's environment, as well as individual temperament, influence the age of onset, intensity, and persistence of separation anxiety. For example, if an infant is hospitalized during the age period in which separation anxiety is prominent, the emotional reaction can be quite intense, resembling adult depression with initial agitation followed by sadness and a decrease in food intake. Severe reactions of this nature are called marasmus and can have profound developmental effects of a social and physical nature on the infant. To avoid these problems, most health care facilities have parent-child accommodations. The problem of separation anxiety must be considered in the decision on the timing of adoption and placement.

PERSONALITY DIFFERENCES AMONG INFANTS.—Variations in response to environmental stimuli, which are thought to be due to basic differences in temperament, have been described among young infants.[37, 38] The eventual outcome of these early temperamental differences is not totally understood, but follow-up studies have indicated that certain of these behavior patterns may persist into school age and adolescence, affecting family and school adjustment. Whether the variations in responsiveness in infancy are due primarily to genetic factors, environmental influences, or both is problematical.

In an interesting book on personality and temperament, Buss and Plomin list four qualities of temperament along with a "reaction range" for each:[38]
1. Activity (active–lethargic)
2. Emotionality (emotional–impassive)
3. Sociability (gregarious–detached)
4. Impulsivity (impulsive–deliberate)

According to their theory, this reaction range is genetically acquired and underlies temperamental differences between individuals. As a person develops, his inherited potential or range is modified through his interaction with the environment.

Investigators who have observed groups of infants over time and studied their temperamental differences have concluded that these early variations predict later adjustment problems.[39] As a result of such observations, three types of infants have been identified on the basis of nine dimensions of temperament (Table 14–2): the easy to manage, the difficult to manage, and the slow to warm up (i.e., shy in novel situations). Follow-up studies showed that a significant percentage of children with the difficult temperament pattern often required professional intervention later for problems of social and emotional adjustment. These kinds of studies demonstrate that early individual differences in temperament may persist throughout childhood with effects on subsequent development.

Biologic differences between boys and girls in rate of growth (height, weight, etc.) have been well documented, but recently there has been additional evidence on sex-related personality differences. Findings from psychological studies conducted in the past few years show that by age 3 or 4 boys tend to be more active and physically aggressive, less dependent, and more competitive than girls of a similar age and background.[40] Both biologic and environmental factors probably play a role in the evolution of these differences. Given an inherited reaction range or temperament, the early acquisition of specific personality traits may depend on the differential manner in which caretakers respond to boy and girl infants. As the child grows older, this differential treatment is continued and he or she is "taught" how to behave in various life situations. For example, a young girl may learn that it is accepted for her to cry if she is hurt, whereas a boy learns that he must be "brave" and not indulge in this kind of emotional response. In the later stages of toddlerhood, differences associated with sexual roles become more apparent as the child learns gender labels ("I am a boy" or "I am a girl"), associated behavior (boy toys versus girl toys), and emotional expression. The circumstances surrounding this learning process are often subtle, consisting mainly of observation and imitation on the part of the child. Of course, differential social responsiveness based on gender does not end with infancy or toddlerhood but continues throughout the life cycle, molding the individual's behavior.

In recent years, cultural attitudes toward the behavior patterns of men and women have undergone change in our country, so that both sexes are permitted a wider latitude of expression of personality traits. These views are, in turn, communicated to children by their parents during the early developmental periods of life.

The Impact of Socioeconomic Factors on Infant Development

In the United States, a variety of socioeconomic factors affect prenatal and postnatal development. Their impact is particularly evident when one compares the health status of infants and children born to parents at opposite ends of the social class spectrum, i.e., the poor and the affluent. In general, the offspring of the poor are at a serious disadvantage in terms of health. For example, the following adverse health statistics characterize the poor in this country:
1. Higher infant mortality
2. Higher rates of prematurity
3. Higher incidence of neurologic disorders at birth

TABLE 14–2.—SAMPLE CLINICAL QUESTIONS RELATED TO A CHILD'S TEMPERAMENTAL TRAITS

DIMENSIONS OF TEMPERAMENT	TYPICAL QUESTIONS	TYPICAL PARENTAL DESCRIPTION
1. Activity level	As an infant, did the child kick off his blanket at night? Did he move around in his crib a lot? Has he always been active? Did you feel a lot of activity before he was born?	He moved all around, even when he was asleep. He was always on the go. He never was still even as a baby; he wiggled all the time. (High activity level)
2. Rhythmicity	Did the child eat, sleep, and have bowel movements pretty much on a predictable schedule? Was it easy to develop a good feeding schedule?	I could never tell when he'd want to be fed; sometimes every two hours, then every six, then two again. He has always gone to bed at different times. (Low degree of rhythmicity)
3. Approach/withdrawal	Does the child tend to respond to a new situation by moving into it? Does he tend to hang back in response to a new situation? As a baby, did he like new foods?	He always goes right after new things. (Approach) He tends to hang back in a strange situation. (Withdrawal)
4. Adaptability	Does the child tolerate change easily? Does he tend to respond easily to suggestions? Does he tend to respond to discipline by changing his behavior in the direction you want? Do strange situations seem to disturb him (this reaction should be differentiated from withdrawal; the child is not upset but simply responds to novelty by "hanging back").	He has always been comfortable in new situations. Changes in the environment, or what we expect, etc., don't seem to upset him.
5. Intensity of reactions	Does the child tend to react full-scale whether laughing or crying? When he was a baby, did he scream about a wet diaper or just complain? Does it seem that everything, good and bad, is a big deal?	He just doesn't have a mid-range. If something strikes him funny, he screams with laughter. If he's even a little hurt, he howls at the top of his lungs. (Intense reactions)
6. Quality of mood	Is he generally cheerful? Does he tend to be irritable and fussy?	He's always been a happy, cheerful baby. (Positive mood) He was colicky as a baby and he's usually whiney and ornery. (Negative mood)
7. Persistence, attention span	Does the child stick to a task? Does he work for long periods of time on one thing?	Once he started something, he would stick to it no matter what. He didn't get tired of playing with the same toy for a long time. (High persistence attention span)
8. Distractibility	Is the child easily pulled away from something he is doing?	Any noise or somebody entering the room was enough to get his attention away from a toy or even food. (High degree of distractibility)
9. Threshold to stimuli	Would you describe your child as a hair-trigger kid? Does it take much to set him off, one way or another?	Anything at all was enough to get a reaction: a whisper was as good as a shout. (Low threshold)

Source: French A.P.: *Disturbed Children and Their Families*. New York, Human Sciences Press, 1977. (Used by permission.)

4. Higher incidence of fetal loss (miscarriages, stillbirths)
5. Lower birth weights for full-term infants
6. Increased numbers of home deliveries
7. Inferior and less frequent prenatal care
8. Higher maternal death rates
9. Higher rates of intellectual retardation (infants and young children)

The fact that in 1974 there were more than 4½ million families in the United States below the poverty level[41] indicates that a health problem of great magnitude needs to be overcome if children in this social class are to reach their developmental potential. In one review, it was concluded that socioeconomic status has a more important influence on child development than biologic perinatal factors.[42]

Since the black population in this country has a much higher percentage of poor individuals than the whites, the infants born to black parents suffer from more health problems than those born to white parents. Infant mortality is significantly higher among blacks—a statistic that is considered to reflect the basic health status of a population (see Fig 9-1). Besides the disadvantage with respect to health, blacks are also confronted by social circumstances that impede child development. Inadequate housing, sanitation, and nutrition contribute to the social problems facing children in the black population. Another problem that adversely affects child development is the higher incidence of single-parent families among blacks. In 1975, only 49% of black children lived with both parents, compared with 85% of white children.[41] Thus, socioeconomic factors are responsible for serious difficulties for black children at the very beginning of life.

Studies indicate that the various social class and ethnic groups in our country differ significantly with respect to styles of parenting and child-rearing practices. However, the information derived from these reports must be used with caution for several reasons. First, there is wide variation in these styles and practices within any given group; and second, in the clinical setting one is usually concerned with an individual child and family and, thus, group generalizations may be of little value.

In general, infants and children raised by parents in the lower social class are exposed to a less enriching environment from a psychological standpoint. For example, studies show that these children tend to have fewer opportunities to expand their linguistic abilities.[42] Another observation is that lower-class parents tend to emphasize physical punishment, while middle- and upper-class parents rely more on psychological punishment (loss of love) to discipline their children.

Developmental Problems in Infancy

SOCIAL DEPRIVATION.—Ever since Freud wrote about the importance of infancy as a basis for the individual's later development, it has been generally accepted that experiences during this period of life are of great significance. Consistent with this view are the results of studies showing that infants raised in environments that are inadequate, from a psychological and social standpoint, fail to develop normally. The pioneering work of Spitz[43, 44] and the extensive observations of Provence and Lipton[45] have documented the deleterious effects of institutionalization on the physical and psychosocial development of the infant and young child. It has been suggested that the nature of the institutional environment produces a kind of learned helplessness on the part of children; it gives them a general feeling that their actions have no consistent effects on others or any predictable consequences.

On the other hand, there are reports that mild degrees of environmental deprivation in early life may not be harmful. In a study of children from remote villages in the mountains of Guatemala, it was found that a lack of varied experiences in the first 12 to 18 months of life does not necessarily have detrimental effects later on.[46] Infants in this culture are provided little stimulation beyond that necessary for caretaking functions until the child himself is capable of locomotion and can move himself out of the dark hut that has been his home for his first year and a half. Despite this deprivation, by middle childhood the performance of these children on various culture-fair tests of cognitive functioning revealed no differences from the American middle-class norms.

Animal studies have shown that the first year of life is a "critical period" in development, meaning that certain stimuli and/or events must be present if this process is to proceed normally. In the human infant, development of the visual system is critically dependent on the proper visual experiences; however, except for receptor systems such as this, there is no evidence that critical periods exist (i.e., with respect to psychosocial development) for humans.[47]

The ethological concept of critical periods is well demonstrated in studies of the process by which young ducklings acquire the early following response, a process referred to as imprinting. It has been shown that there is a crucial time period shortly after birth for imprinting to occur. If for any reason imprinting fails to take place at that time, it becomes difficult or impossible to establish the following response as the animal grows older. These kinds of experiments have implications for early social attachment and social development in human infants, even though imprinting, as such, does not occur in humans.

Harlow and his associates conducted the now classic animal studies on the effects of maternal separation and social deprivation on the infant.[48] These studies showed that socially deprived baby monkeys (reared without contact with members of their species and having only a surrogate mother made of either wire or cloth) manifested distinctly abnormal behavior as adults. For example, they were withdrawn, had difficulty mating, and after giving birth failed to mother their young. Contact with peers or adults during the early months of their development seemed to lessen these effects, even though the animals had no contact with their biologic mothers. It is interesting that the baby monkeys preferred cloth-surrogate to wire-surrogate mothers, suggesting that touching and clinging ("contact comfort") are important in the development of social bonding in monkeys.

In human infants, the clinical signs of maternal and social deprivation include:
1. Apprehension, sadness, weepiness
2. Lack of eye contact, environmental rejection, withdrawal
3. Developmental delays (vocalization), slow movements
4. Dejection
5. Loss of appetite, refusal to eat, weight loss
6. Sleep problems

Many of these signs are similar to those seen in depressed older children and adults, and in Spitz's original study the term "anaclitic depression" ("anaclitic" meaning dependent) was used to describe the behavior of these infants.

In his classic review of the effects of social deprivation, Bowlby concluded that these were irreversible and permanent.[49] Studies by Skeels, however, clearly demonstrated that this damage could be reversed providing adequate care was given to the deprived infant later in life.[50] In a subsequent study, Bowlby himself came to the same conclusion as Skeels.[51] Thus, while the impact of maternal and social deprivation on the infant can be far-reaching, the plasticity of the child early in life allows him to correct past deficiencies if given the opportunity. Many variables influence the outcome of these adverse experiences in infancy, including the infant's sex, age at separation, duration of separation, previous attachment experiences, individual temperament, and quality of the new environment.

Appropriate environmental stimulation is essential not only in infancy but also throughout childhood for normal physical and psychosocial development. In fact, some recent data suggest that active maternal behavior is necessary to maintain normal polyamine metabolism in the brain of the neonatal rat.[52] These data provide a physiological basis for the effects of maternal care and stimulation and suggest areas for future research directed at pinpointing neurologic and biologic abnormalities associated with deprivation.

AUTISM.—Perhaps no other behavioral disorder in infancy is as dramatic as infantile autism. *Autism* is a descriptive term and not a definitive diagnosis. In fact, recent studies attempting to define the condition have often had to deal with conflicting criteria.[53] The term *infantile autism* was coined by the psychiatrist Leo Kanner in the 1940s to describe a condition in which the subjects demonstrated:[54]

1. A disturbance in interpersonal relation-

ships characterized by a failure to relate to others as "persons" (aloofness)
2. Abnormal behavior associated with self-stimulation and the performance of repetitive acts
3. Language disorders (echolalia, little or no appropriate speech)

The incidence of this condition is 2–4 per 10,000 with some studies indicating a boy-girl ratio of about 2.6/1. The major and associated symptoms of autism are listed in Table 14–3.

Early conjectures were that autistic behavior in infants and toddlers was the direct result of a "cold" or emotionally rejecting mother figure, but recent studies have not supported this view. In fact, it has been suggested that the socially unresponsive autistic infant or child elicits the atypical mother-child interaction often observed, since the infant's lack of responsiveness provides the mother with little or no positive feedback for care-giving. Present thinking is that biologic factors are important in the pathogenesis of this syndrome. One study found that:[35]

1. Twenty percent of autistic patients have a low birth weight
2. Fifty percent or more of the mothers of these patients had toxemia and/or bleeding during pregnancy
3. Neurologic findings are similar in autistic and organically brain-damaged comparison groups
4. Approximately 75% of autistic children have some form of seizure disorder

In another investigation the pneumoencephalograms of autistic children indicated an enlargement of the left lateral ventricle in 15 of 18 patients. The authors suggested that atrophy of the medial temporal lobe may be a contributing factor in the condition.[55]

In general, the developmental quotient (DQ) or intelligence quotient (IQ) is a good indicator of prognosis; that is, higher functioning children at the time of diagnosis tend to remain brighter, while dull children become duller (even more so if they are institutionalized).

The picture in Figure 14–1 shows a 3-year-old child diagnosed as autistic. It illustrates hand posturing and complete inattentiveness to the social environment. This youngster often spent extended periods just looking at his hands and shadows on the ground and would not respond to adults calling his name.

The differential diagnosis between autism and childhood schizophrenia is often difficult and may rest on the historical information provided by parents, such as age of onset (au-

TABLE 14–3.—DEFINING AND ASSOCIATED SYMPTOMS OF AUTISM

DEFINING SYMPTOMS OF AUTISM	ASSOCIATED SYMPTOMS
Lack of social interest or responsiveness	Periodic hypoactivity and hyperactivity
Delayed or deviant development of language	Stereotyped movements, usually of the hands and fingers
Resistance to change or stereotyped behaviors	Self-abuse
	Short attention span
	Abnormally intense responses to sounds or lack of response
	Apparent insensitivity to pain
	Unusual fears
	Feeding difficulties
	Temper tantrums
	Aggression
	Enuresis
	Encopresis

Adapted from Stewart M.A., Gath A.: *Psychological Disorders of Children: A Handbook for Primary Care Physicians*. Baltimore, Williams & Wilkins Co., 1978.

Fig 14–1.—Hand positioning or self-stimulatory behavior in a three-year-old autistic boy.

tism generally occurs at an earlier age, i.e., before 36 months). Autistic children are abnormal almost from birth while schizophrenics often have a period of normal development followed by regression when they become ill.

In autism, traditional treatment such as psychotherapy is largely unsuccessful, but behavior modification, early family intervention with parent training, and educational training for the child, including speech therapy, can be very helpful in fostering language and social development. Prognosis, however, regardless of treatment, is poor, with studies indicating that only about 10% of autistic children make a normal social adjustment as adults. Table 14–4 compares the social adjustment of two groups of adolescents, one composed of individuals who were diagnosed as autistic in childhood and the other (a control group) composed of persons who were seen as children in the same psychiatric clinic for other problems. The data indicate that most autistic children (over 60%) make a poor adjustment as teenagers. Parents of autistic children require continued support in their efforts to provide a positive environment for their child. Such support often requires the expertise of speech therapists, educators, and psychological-psychiatric management programs.

THE TODDLER

This period covers the ages from 1½ to about 3 years. Several changes occur during this time that are particularly important from a developmental standpoint. First, formal language is mastered; second, critical social skills are learned (toileting, the manipulation of tools and toys, and the ability to exercise some self-control); third, formal social relationships with peers are established (usually in the context of environments such as day-care centers); and, finally, the young child begins to separate from parental dependency and to exhibit self-directed behavior.

Physical Development

By 2 years of age, the average weight of boys and girls is about 28 pounds and their average height or length is approximately 34 inches.

The growth in height and weight from 18 months to 3 years shows a general deceleration so that, after tripling in weight and increasing in length by about one third from birth to 1 year, the child gains only about 6

TABLE 14–4.—Social Adjustment of Autistic Children in Adolescence

ADJUSTMENT	AUTISTIC NUMBER	(%)	CLINIC CONTROLS NUMBER	(%)
Normal	1 } 9	(14)	7 } 20	(33)
Good	8		13	
Fair	16	(25)	19	(31)
Poor	8	(13)	7	(11)
Very Poor	30	(48)	15	(25)
Total	63	100	61	100

Adapted from Stewart M.A., Gath A.: *Psychological Disorders of Children: A Handbook for Primary Care Physicians*. Baltimore, Williams & Wilkins Co., 1978.

pounds in weight and 5 inches in height during the second year of life.

As the name for this period implies, motor development is a cardinal feature of the toddler period. The most important physical achievement for the child in this age group is walking, which takes place at about 12–14 months. After the onset of walking, there is a rapid acceleration in the development of both motor and language skills. The acquisition of motor and language skills markedly increases the toddler's capacity to cope with the demands of his physical and social environment.

The clinical evaluation of neuromuscular functions is an important aspect of the examination of the infant and toddler. Normal appearance of these developmental parameters implies that the maturation of the central nervous system is proceeding in an appropriate fashion. Delay in their appearance is often the first obvious indication of the presence of underlying illness of psychological dysfunction.

However, this may also be due to variability in the rate of maturation.

The question of whether environmental factors influence physical development is an important one. Several studies have shown that even with restricted opportunities for motor practice, infants and toddlers eventually achieve all the major motor skills by the age of 3, although they may exhibit delays in reaching some milestones such as standing or walking.[56] The adverse effects of atypical social environments are felt primarily in the areas of emotional and social development, not in the acquisition of motor skills. Some psychosocial factors, however, can result in delayed physical growth and a condition referred to as the "failure to thrive" syndrome (i.e., a state in which an infant or toddler loses or fails to gain weight without apparent cause).[57] Since this syndrome may be caused by organic disease, the health-care professional should always make a thorough evalua-

TABLE 14-5.—SOME OBSCURE CAUSES OF FAILURE TO THRIVE AND RELATED SCREENING PROCEDURES

CAUSE	SCREENING TESTS
ENVIRONMENTAL	
Inadequate food intake	History, hospital observation
Emotional deprivation	History, hospital observation
Environmental disruptions	History, hospital observation
Rumination	Observation in hospital
ORGANIC	
Central nervous system abnormalities	Neurologic exam, developmental assessment, brain scan, transillumination of skull
Intestinal malabsorption	Observation in hospital, stool fat
Cystic fibrosis of pancreas	Sweat test
Intestinal parasites (rarely in temperate climates)	Stool for ova and parasites
Partial cleft palate	Physical exam, observation of feeding
Chronic heart failure	Physical exam, roentgenogram of chest
Endocrine disorders	Construction of growth chart, thyroid-blood test, bone age films
Idiopathic hypercalcemia	Serum calcium
Turner's syndrome (girls)	Buccal smear
Other chromosomal disorders	Chromosomal analysis in children with peculiar facies or multisystem defects
Renal insufficiency	Urinalysis, blood urea nitrogen
Renal tubular disorders	Urinalysis, urinary amino acid screen
Chronic infection (usually tuberculosis or mycotic)	Tuberculin test, chest roentgenogram, temperature pattern in hospital
Chronic inflammation (e.g., rheumatoid arthritis)	Physical exam
Malignancies (especially of the kidney, adrenal, brain)	Roentgenogram of abdomen and chest, intravenous urography, brain scan

Source: Barbero G.J., McKay R.J.: Failure to thrive, in Vaughan V.C., McKay R.J., Behrman R.E. (eds.): *Nelson Textbook of Pediatrics*, ed. 11. Philadelphia, W.B. Saunders Co., 1979, p. 311.

tion of the child's health status. Table 14–5 lists some of the psychosocial and organic causes of the failure to thrive syndrome and the screening procedures used to detect them. These illnesses can markedly retard learning and cognitive development; therefore, prompt therapy is essential for the child's physical and psychological well-being.

Learning and Cognition

DEVELOPMENT OF THE REPRESENTATIONAL SYSTEM.—The major cognitive advances made by the toddler involve the development of his representational or symbolic ability, of which language is perhaps the most significant aspect. Operating with a symbolic-representational system means that the child is no longer restricted to physical action on his environment to solve problems but can perform mental actions; that is, he can think. The development of this capacity during these 18 months involves the child's increasing ability to represent his experiences mentally and to use these representations to guide his actions. So, for example, rather than trying to fit a round object into a square hole on a form board, the child can now look at the object and the hole, anticipate mentally the outcome of his actions, and look for the appropriate hole in which to place the object.

The child passes through a series of stages in developing this capacity to deal symbolically with his world. One of the earliest indications that the child is actually representing aspects of his experience mentally is when he imitates a novel action, something he has never done before, hours or more after observing someone else perform the action. For example, when a child throws his first tantrum the day after observing another child throwing a tantrum, it can be concluded that he is using some representation of what he observed the previous day to guide his reproduction of the actions.

Further representational development can be observed in the emergence of symbolic play, in which the child pretends with his actions or uses objects to stand for other objects. Initially the child's symbolic play may involve pretending to sleep or eat or cry. Later he uses objects in his play, pretending perhaps to feed his doll or that an old shoe is a doll bed. More sophisticated symbolic play emerges still later when the child pretends to perform a series of actions that he has only observed others perform, such as when the little boy pretends to shave like his father or the little girl pretends to apply makeup like her mother.[19] Obviously, besides indexing the child's level of symbolic development, these examples suggest that the child at this point in development is capable of learning many behavior patterns simply by observing others. Further developments of the symbolic representational capacity generally involve language as well as action.

THE DEVELOPMENT OF CATEGORIES.—The habituation paradigm has been used with children in this age range to determine whether they can categorize objects as a means of organizing their experiences. Faulkender, Wright, and Waldron report habituation to conceptual categories (such as animals, fruits, and patterns) upon repeated presentation of examples within the categories,[58] suggesting that children in the third year do organize objects categorically. This finding is especially interesting in light of other observations of children in this age range, which indicate that they do not consistently categorize when asked to group together similar objects from an array of various categories of objects. Inhelder and Piaget observed that the child will group objects together in order to make a picture or tell a story, but not on the basis of perceptual or conceptual similarity.[16] Vygotsky has made similar observations of children asked to group objects together; that is, they group objects based on similarities derived from the child's own imaginings and not from any properties intrinsic to the objects or their categories.[59]

CONSTRAINTS ON THE CHILD'S THOUGHT.—There are other limitations on the child's thinking during this period that prevent him from using his mental abilities logically and consistently. The child's mental actions seem to exist and occur in relative isolation from each other, rather than being organized into a coherent system in which it is possible to move back and forth facilely between them. The relative independence of these mental actions from each other produces the inconsistencies and illogic that characterize the young child's thinking at this stage, according to Piaget.[16] For this reason, the child is described as lacking operations in his mental actions (operation, in the mathematical sense, implies organization into an interrelated system) and is placed in what is called the *preoperational stage* of intellectual development.

Another characteristic of the child's thinking in the early part of this period is its lack of true concepts; the child's definition and understanding of concepts are more fluid and less systematized than the adult's. A few examples demonstrate the fluid, prelogical nature of the child's thought at this period: Piaget observed his 2½-year-old daughter, Jacqueline, seeing her sister Lucienne in a new bathing suit with a cap, asking:

"What's the baby's name?" Her mother explained that it was a bathing costume, but Jacqueline pointed to Lucienne herself and said: "But what's the name of that?" (indicating Lucienne's face) and repeated the question several times. But as soon as Lucienne had her dress on again, Jacqueline exclaimed very seriously: "It's Lucienne again," as if her sister had changed her identity in changing her clothes.[18]

And another time, Piaget observed that Jacqueline

used the term "the slug" for the slugs we went to see every morning along a certain road. At two years, seven months, she cried: "There it is!" on seeing one, and when we saw another ten yards further on she said: "There's the slug again." I answered: "But isn't it another one?" Jacqueline went back to see the first one.[18]

Piaget observes that she did not seem to comprehend the question as to whether the slug was the same one or a different one. The question seemed to have no meaning for her.

Language Development

Language, of course, is one manifestation of the symbolic process for representing the world (the alternatives being images and personal symbols). There are various hypotheses about the relationship between language and the more general representational cognitive system. Investigators have argued that certain general developments in the symbolic system are necessary for the symbolic use of language, including reference to nonpresent objects and the combination of words syntactically.[60, 61]

SEMANTIC DEVELOPMENT.—Vocabulary growth becomes more rapid by the end of the second year, with the average child knowing 272 words by age 2 and 896 words by age 3.[62] It is reported that children in this age period characteristically extend the use of words beyond the set of objects to which they apply. So, for example, the child calls all men "daddy" or all small, furry animals "doggie." Originally, these overextensions were assumed to indicate the fuzzy, ill-defined nature of the child's concepts,[63] but more recent evidence suggests that these concepts are apparently clear in the child's mind.[26] His problem may simply be that he does not have the necessary vocabulary to refer to an object and so uses a word that he does know, despite its lack of appropriateness. Furthermore, it has recently been suggested that some instances of overextension may not be errors but rather attempts by the child to categorize objects according to concepts he already understands.[64] For example, when a child calls a grapefruit "moon," he may be commenting on the object's similarity to the moon rather than claiming that the grapefruit actually is the moon.

SYNTACTIC DEVELOPMENT.—Somewhere between 18 and 24 months, most children put together their first two-word utterances. A goal of many investigators has been to devise a set of linguistic rules that can predict and explain all the young child's early word combinations. Most of the attempts in the 1960s were unsuccessful because they focused primarily on frequency counts of words and combinations, independent of the context in which they were occurring, or what the child seemed to be trying to accomplish with his speech.[65-67]

Bloom was one of the first investigators to argue that knowing the context in which an utterance occurs is necessary for any analysis of the possible rules governing children's early language productions.[68] Clearly, typical two-word combinations, such as "Mommy sock," "baby table," or "give doggie" are ambiguous without more information about how they are being used. More recently, child language theorists[24] have turned to the literature on adult semantic-based grammar[69] for help in analyzing children's speech. There is optimism that the semantically based approach to syntax will provide important insights into the process of acquiring language in these early stages.

Some specific syntactic developments that emerge between 2 and 3 years include the appearance of the plural morpheme (-s), the development of the forms to express the present progressive tense (-ing) and past tense (-ed), the use of prepositions of location (in and on), the use of markers for possession (-'s), and the use of the articles "a" and "the."[70]

Psychosocial Aspects of Development

THEORIES OF FREUD AND ERIKSON.— Freud described this period of life as the anal stage of development to emphasize that the focus of the child's psychic energy is on the anal area. He conjectured that pleasurable experiences become centered around the defecatory act, i.e., the movement or retention of feces, cleaning of the anal area by the mother after defecation, etc. Psychoanalytic theorists have speculated that if toilet training is undertaken too early or if it is associated with a great deal of conflict between parent and child, personality development may be adversely affected, giving rise to personality traits that persist into adulthood. Those traits that are said to reflect a disturbance of personality development in the anal stage include stubbornness, excessive concern for orderliness, compulsiveness, and stinginess. However, empirical data derived from the study of patients do not support a literal interpretation of this theory. In other words, one cannot assume that problems in the anal stage will necessarily lead to a specific personality disorder, nor can one diagnose with certainty a disturbance in personality development in this stage from a given set of personality traits.

Erikson takes a broader view of toddlerhood, emphasizing that the most important aspect of psychosocial development is the acquisition of a sense of autonomy by the child, acquiring toilet skills being just one component of this task. In fact, the potential crisis facing the child, as expressed by Erikson, is one of "autonomy versus self-doubt." If the child is unsuccessful in his early attempts at independent action, then he may fail to develop confidence in his own abilities and will be saddled with feelings of self-doubt later on. This may occur if the limits set by his parents are excessive. Thus, there is an obvious conflict during this period: the parents' need to protect the child and insure his safety by limiting his activities versus the child's need to express himself and develop a feeling of self-confidence. The child's strivings for autonomy are reflected in his frequent negative reactions to parental restrictions and his strong desire to do things for himself. This is a critical phase for parent-child interaction since parents are constantly having to decide between rule-setting and allowing the child to move toward independence. Mastery of this basic issue (autonomy versus self-doubt) by the toddler permits the child to enter the preschool age with positive feelings of independence tempered by a respect for adult guidance and authority.

SOCIAL RULES AND SELF-CONTROL.—The physical and motor development that occurs during this period (e.g., walking) opens up a whole new world to the child, exposing him to interesting and sometimes dangerous situations. Increasingly, he is using independent thought and action. In the context of such rapidly developing motor, cognitive, and verbal skills, parents are often frustrated by the negative behavior of children in this age group, hence the term the "terrible two's." This reflects the many problems that occur when the attempts at independent actions by the child of this age come into conflict with the social discipline and training that are necessary to insure his safety. The instances in which mother has to restrain the toddler's activities with a "no" are many, and these cause the child to feel frustrated. Reactions to frustration at this age are often characterized by increased motor activity (kicking, throwing objects, lying on the floor) and vocalizations (crying, yelling). The above is a polite way of describing what all parents know as a temper tantrum. Tantrums in toddlerhood have been studied by several investigators and general findings indicate that there are sex-related differences; boys are more physically aggressive and girls are more vocal in expressing or reacting to frustration. In addition, variations in temperament may explain differences in this behavior (see Table 14–2), such as the more frequent and intense tantrums of the so-called difficult child. Language deficits that make it difficult for a child to communicate his wants and needs can result in frequent tantrums.

Parental management of such tantrums is important for the child eventually to learn more socially acceptable ways of expressing anger and frustration. Parents may unwittingly make the situation worse by giving in or yielding to tantrums, thereby increasing their frequency. Common parental practices of dealing with tantrums include distracting the child to other activities, ignoring or attempting to reason with him, and punishing him. Parents often find themselves in a vicious cycle in which punitive action produces more aggression and anger on the part of the child.

In most attempts at teaching self-control, parents are really trying to help the child internalize the accepted social rules of the family. The most important guideline for the parents to follow in disciplining their children is to be fair and consistent. Some parents are by nature more consistent and adept at positive rule-setting and management than others. Factors that may interfere with parental consistency include the parent's mood, marital conflicts, interference of relatives such as grandparents, and the presence of other siblings in the household. Studies indicate that some parents of preschool children with behavior management problems find child-rearing to be very stressful, resulting in frustration on their part and expressions of hostility and anger toward the child.

Knowing when to refer parents for counseling is important, since some problems can only be dealt with using proper management techniques. In this context, parental education programs and written manuals often help interested parents acquire the knowledge and skills for appropriate management.[71]

Clinical Issues—Toilet Training

Perhaps no other developmental task has received as much attention during the toddler stage as the teaching of appropriate toileting skills. In fact, surveys of pediatricians on parental concerns during this age period show that toilet training and problems of bowel and bladder control stand out as the major concern, especially for parents who are attempting this task for the first time.[72] Historically, if one reviews the child-rearing advice given to parents it will be found that, in general, the professional opinions of any period can be correlated with the prevailing theories of psychological development. For instance, in the 1920s and 1930s, when Watsonian behaviorism was in vogue, strict discipline and scheduling for toilet training were generally recommended in popular publications. Subsequently, the increase in popularity of psychoanalytic theory, with its emphasis on avoiding psychological trauma and fixation in the anal stage of development, resulted in a climate that was more permissive.

Empirical research tends to indicate that appropriate toilet training involves a positive and consistent approach with emphasis on appropriate feedback to the child. In this regard, Azrin and his co-workers have shown that even profoundly retarded adults can be toilet trained with patience and specific management techniques. With normal toddlers, the data indicate that when parents approach the task armed with specific management principles, as well as a positive attitude, most normal 22–26-month-old children can become toilet trained within an average of 4–5 hours of actual training time.[73]

Parents often are concerned about when to initiate training. There is a wide age range in which this training can be started—6 months to 3 years. The studies of Azrin et al. show that 20–24 months is a good time to begin, provided the child has mastered certain cognitive and communicative skills such as knowing the difference between "wet" and "dry."

Contrary to early conjectures that poor toilet training experiences invariably lead to personality problems later in life (e.g., obsessive-compulsiveness), surveys show that this is not necessarily so.[74] It does appear that inappropriate or punitive toilet training results in a higher incidence of toileting problems later on, such as enuresis and encopresis.

SUMMARY

In the first 4 years of life, the child develops from an essentially helpless infant totally dependent on his mother to an ambulatory, inquisitive, and somewhat independent toddler. Physically, there is considerable growth and, most important, a progressive maturation of the central nervous system. Parameters of neuromuscular function (so-called motor milestones of development) are monitored closely by physicians who care for children in this age group to make certain that physical development is occurring normally.

By far the most significant psychosocial aspect of infancy is the mother-infant relationship, i.e., the social attachment and interaction between the two parties. Much of the cognitive, emotional, and social development occurring during this stage of life is dependent on the adequacy of this relationship. Achieving the basic psychosocial task of acquiring a sense of trust is closely related to how effectively the infant's needs are met by his mother. A disturbance in mother-infant bonding or the absence of a mother figure may have dire consequences for the infant.

In contrast to older views of the infant as a passive recipient of environmental stimuli, current information indicates that he is an active learner, interacting with and influencing the people about him. In particular, there is a reciprocal relationship in the behavior of the mother and infant as they interact with one another.

By the end of the second year, the toddler is a mobile and talkative youngster, actively investigating his environment. He is becoming increasingly independent in thought and action, and his needs often conflict with the wishes of his parents. He is often called upon to discipline himself in a number of ways, including toilet training, which frequently leads to frustration on his part. According to Erikson, the acquisition of a sense of autonomy is the principal psychosocial task of this stage of life. If the toddler is excessively restrained by his parents in his early attempts at independent action, he may fail to develop confidence in his ability to act on his own. Thus, instead of a sense of autonomy, he will experience self-doubt.

Cognition proceeds from the sensorimotor stage of infancy to the preoperational stage of the toddler. In the first, the child's thinking is limited to the plane of action; that is, he is incapable of symbolic representational thinking. He learns mainly by acting on his environment. In the second, he begins to function mentally (without physical action) in such a way as to represent things that are not actually present. He demonstrates imitative behavior and acquires much of the mature language system, indicating that he is dealing symbolically with his world.

REFERENCES

1. Lipsitt L.P., Kaye H.: Conditioned sucking in the human newborn, in Bijou S.W., Baer D.M. (eds.): *Child Development: Readings in Experimental Analysis.* New York, Meredith Publishing Co., 1967.
2. Marquis D.P.: Can conditioned reflexes be established in the newborn infant? *J. Genet. Psychol.* 39:479–492, 1931.

3. Sameroff A.: The components of sucking in the human newborn. *J. Exp. Child Psychol.* 6:607-623, 1968.
4. Sameroff A.: Can conditioned responses be established in the newborn infant? *Dev. Psychol.* 5:1–12, 1971.
5. Siqueland E.R., Lipsitt L.P.: Conditioned head-turning in human newborns, in Bijou S.W., Baer D.M. (eds.): *Child Development: Readings in Experimental Analysis.* New York, Meredith Publishing Co., 1967.
6. Sameroff A.: Learning and adaptation in infancy: A comparison of models. *Adv. Child Dev. Behav.* 7:169, 1972.
7. Rheingold H.L., Gewirtz J.L., Ross H.W.: Social conditioning of vocalizations in the infant, in Bijou S.W., Baer, D.M. (eds.): *Child Development: Readings in Experimental Analysis.* New York, Meredith Publishing Co., 1967.
8. Jeffrey W.E., Cohen L.B.: Habituation in the human infant, in Reese H.W. (ed): *Advances in Child Development and Behavior.* New York, Academic Press, vol. 6, 1971.
9. Pancratz N., Cohen L.B.: Recovery of habituation in infants. *J. Exp. Child Psychol.* 9:208–216, 1970.
10. Cornell E.H.: Infants' discrimination of faces following redundant presentation. *J. Exp. Child Psychol.* 18:98–106, 1974.
11. Fagan J.F.: Infants' recognition of invariant features of faces. *Child Dev.* 47:627-638, 1974.
12. Cohen L.B.: Concept acquisition in the human infant. Read before the Society for Research in Child Development meeting, New Orleans, March 1977.
13. Eimas P., Siqueland E.R., Jusezyk P., et al.: Speech perception in infants. *Science* 171:303–306, 1971.
14. Moffitt A.R.: Consonant cue perception by twenty to twenty-four week old infants. *Child Dev.* 42:717–732, 1971.
15. Inhelder B., Piaget J.: *The Growth of Logical Thinking from Childhood to Adolescence.* New York, Basic Books, Inc., Publishers, 1958.
16. Inhelder B., Piaget J.: *The Early Growth of Logic in the Child.* New York, W.W. Norton & Company, Inc., 1964.
17. Piaget J.: *The Origins of Intelligence in Children.* New York, International University Press, 1952.
18. Piaget J.: *The Construction of Reality in the Child.* New York, Basic Books, Inc., Publishers, 1954.
19. Piaget J.: *Play, Dreams and Imitation in Childhood.* New York, W.W. Norton & Company, Inc., 1962.
20. Condon W.S., Sander L.W.: Neonate movement is synchronized with adult speech: Interactional participation and language acquisition. *Science,* 183:99–101, 1974.
21. Eilers R.E., Wilson W.R., Moore J.M.: Developmental changes in speech discrimination by infants. *J. Speech Hear. Res.* 20:766, 1977.
22. Trehub S.E.: Infants' sensitivity to vowel and tonal contrasts. *Dev. Psychol.* 9:9–16, 1973.
23. Oller D.K.: Language research with young retarded children. Application to National Institutes of Health, 1977.
24. Greenfield P., Smith J.: *The Structure of Communication in Early Language Development.* New York, Academic Press, 1976.
25. Nelson K.: Structure and strategy in learning to talk. *Monogr. Soc. Res. Child Dev.* 38(149):1, 1973.
26. Huttenlocher J.: The origins of language comprehension, in Solso R.L. (ed.): *Theories in Cognitive Psychology.* Potomac, Md., Lawrence Earlbaum Associates, 1974.
27. Nelson K., Benedict H., Gruendel J., et al.: Lessons from early lexicons. Read before the biennial meeting of Society for Research in Child Development, New Orleans, March 1977.
28. Nelson K.: Concept, word, and sentence: Interrelations in acquisition and development. *Psychol. Rev.* 81:267–285, 1974.
29. Bates E., Camaioni L., Volterra V.: The acquisition of performatives prior to speech. *Merrill-Palmer Q.* 21:205–226, 1975.
30. Lewis M., Rosenblum L.A. (eds.): *The Effect of the Infant on Its Caregiver.* New York, John Wiley & Sons, Inc., 1974.
31. Mussen P.H., Conger J.J., Kagan J.: *Child Development and Personality,* ed. 4. New York, Harper & Row, 1974.
32. Ainsworth M.D.S.: *Infancy in Uganda.* Baltimore, Johns Hopkins University Press, 1967.
33. Foss M.: *Determinants of Infant Behavior.* London, Methuen, 1965, vol. 3.
34. Brackbill Y.: Extinction of the smiling responses in infants as a function of reinforcement schedule. *Child Dev.* 29:115, 1958.
35. Knobloch H., Pasamanick B. (eds.): *Gesell and Amatruda's Developmental Diagnosis,* ed. 3. Hagerstown, Md., Harper & Row, 1974.
36. Collard R.R.: Fear of strangers and play behavior in kittens with varied social experience. *Child Dev.* 38:817, 1967.
37. Thomas A., Chess S., Birch H.: The origin of personality. *Sci. Am.* 223:102, 1970.
38. Buss A.N., Plomin R.: *A Temperament Theory of Personality Development.* New York, John Wiley & Sons, Inc., 1975.
39. Thomas A., Chess S., Birch H.J.: *Temperament and Behavior Disorders in Children.* New York, New York University Press, 1968.

40. Feshbach S.: Aggression, in Mussen P.H. (ed.): *Carmichael's Manual of Child Psychology*. New York, John Wiley & Sons, Inc., 1970, vol. 2.
41. *Statistical Abstract of the United States*, ed. 9. U.S. Government Printing Office, 1976.
42. Berstein B.: A sociolinguistic approach to socialization: with some reference to educability, in Williams F. (ed.): *Language and Poverty*. Chicago, Markham Publishing Co., 1970.
43. Spitz R.A.: Hospitalism: An inquiry into the genesis of psychiatric conditions in early childhood. *Psychoanal. Study Child*. 1:53–74, 1945.
44. Spitz R.A., Wolf K.M.: Anaclitic depression: An inquiry into the genesis of psychiatric conditions in early childhood, II. *Psychoanal. Study Child*. 1:53, 1945.
45. Provence S.A., Lipton R.C.: *Infants in Institutions*. New York, International University Press, 1962.
46. Kagan J., Klein R.E.: Cross-cultural perspectives on early development. *Am. Psychol*. 29:947–961, 1973.
47. Hunt J.M.: Psychological development: Early experience. *Annu. Rev. Psychol*. 30:103, 1979.
48. Harlow H.F., Harlow M.H.: Learning to love. *Am. Sci*. 54:244, 1966.
49. Bowlby J.: Maternal care and mental health, WHO Monogr. Ser. 2, 3:355, 1951.
50. Skeels H.M., Dye H.B.: A study of the effects of differential stimulation on mentally retarded children. *Proc. Am. Assoc. Ment. Def*. 44:114, 1939; Skeels H.M.: Adult status of children with contrasting early life experiences. *Monogr. Soc. Res. Child Dev*. 31(ser. 105, no. 3), 1966.
51. Bowlby J., et al.: The effects of mother-child separation: A follow-up study. *Br. J. Med. Psychol*. 29:211–247, 1956.
52. Butler S.R., Suskind M.R., Schanberg S.M.: Maternal behavior as a regulator of polyamine biosynthesis in brain and heart of the developing rat pup. *Science* 199:445, 1978.
53. Meeting of the Florida Study Group on Developmental Disabilities, Autism Study Section, Miami, Florida, December 1977.
54. Kanner L.: Autistic disturbances of affective contact. *Nerv. Child* 2:217, 1943.
55. Hauser S.L., DeLong G.K., Roseman N.P.: Pneumographic findings in the infantile autism syndrome. *Brain* 98:607, 1975.
56. Dennis W.: Infant reactions to restraint. *Trans. N.Y. Acad. Sci*. 2:202, 1940.
57. Barbero G.J., McKay R.J.: Failure to thrive, in Vaughan V.C., McKay R.J. (eds.): *Nelson Textbook of Pediatrics*, ed. 11. Philadelphia, W.B. Saunders Co., 1979.
58. Faulkender P.V., Wright J.C., Waldron A.: Generalized habituation of concept stimuli in toddlers. *Child Dev*. 45:1002–1010, 1974.
59. Vygotsky L.S.: *Thought and Language*. Cambridge, Mass., M.I.T. Press, 1962.
60. Edmonds M.: New directions in theories of language acquisition. *Harvard Educ. Rev*. 46:175–198, 1976.
61. Bloom L.: *One Word at a Time: The Use of Single Word Utterances Before Syntax*. The Hague, Mouton, 1973.
62. Dale P.S.: *Language Development: Structure and Function*. Hinsdale, Ill., The Dryden Press, Inc., 1972.
63. Clark E.V.: What's in a word? On the child's acquisition of semantics in his first language, in Moore T.E. (ed.): *Cognitive Development and the Acquisition of Language*. New York, Academic Press, 1973.
64. Nelson K., Benedict H., Gruendel J., et al.: Lessons from early lexicon. Read before the biennial meeting of SRCD, New Orleans, March 1977.
65. Brown R., Fraser C.: The acquisition of syntax, in Cofer C.N., Musgrave B. (eds.): *Verbal Behavior and Learning: Problems and Processes*. New York, McGraw-Hill Book Co., 1963.
66. Braine M.D.S.: The ontogeny of English phrase structure: The first phase. *Language* 39:1–14, 1963.
67. McNeill D.: Developmental psycholinguistics, in Smith F., Miller G. (eds.): *The Genesis of Language: A Psycholinguistic Approach*. Cambridge, Mass., M.I.T. Press, 1966.
68. Bloom L.: *Language Development: Form and Function in Emerging Grammars*. Cambridge, Mass., M.I.T. Press, 1970.
69. Filmore C.: The case for case, in Bach E., Harms R.T. (eds.): *Universals in Linguistic Theory*. New York, Holt, Rinehart and Winston, Inc., 1968.
70. Brown R.: *A First Language: The Early Stages*. Cambridge, Mass., Harvard University Press, 1973.
71. Patterson G.R.: *Families: Applications of Social Learning to Family Life*. Champaign, Ill., Research Press, 1971.
72. Toister R.P., Worley L.M.: Behavioral aspects of pediatric practice: A survey of practitioners. *J. Med. Educ*. 51:1019, 1976.
73. Azrin N.H., Foxx R.M.: *Toilet Training in Less than a Day*. New York, Simon & Schuster, Inc., 1974.
74. Caldwell B.M.: The effects of infant care, in Hoffman M.L., Hoffman L.W. (eds.): *Review of Child Development Research*. New York, Russell Sage Foundation, 1964, vol. 1, pp. 9–87.

15 / Preschool and School Age

RICHARD P. TOISTER, Ph.D., and JEFFREY M. SEIBERT, Ph.D.

PRESCHOOL AGE (3–6 YEARS)

DURING THIS STAGE of development, the child becomes much more sophisticated psychologically and begins to acquire some of the personal qualities that will enable him to interact socially. For instance, he greatly expands his capacity to communicate with others and acquires a rudimentary concept of a standard of appropriate conduct. In addition, the child begins to develop a sense of self, including his gender identity. Children of this age generally have a very lively imagination and this, coupled with their increasing cognitive and motor abilities, explains why they are so searching and inquisitive.

This stage is a time when most children experience their first peer relationships, often as a consequence of attending formal nursery school programs. This socialization depends on the child's mastery of some elementary social tasks such as toilet training and language. Also, when he plays with his new-found friends, he is called upon to control some of his naturally impulsive behavior, which can be difficult for most young children. Parental discipline has a pronounced effect on the behavior and personality of the child of this age.

Physical Development

The Denver Developmental Screening Inventory (Fig 15–3) lists the common achievements in motor, language, and social development during the preschool years. The acquisition of such skills enables him to engage in a broader range of activities, including more social interaction with others. The basic abilities of numeration and copying and the enhanced capacity for communication make it possible for the preschooler to participate in more formal learning situations. This further increases the already rapid rate of his psychosocial development.

Physical development between 3 and 5 years of age is relatively constant, with a 4–5-pound gain in weight and a 2–3-inch increase in height per year.[1] By 4 years of age, "handedness" is usually well established, although ambidexterity may be observed in some children. Characteristically, children in this age group are physically very active, using their newly acquired motor skills to explore the world about them. Whatever they do, they do with a great deal of energy and adults often find it difficult to keep up with them.

Cognitive Development

By 3 years of age, the child has a well-developed representational system and a linguistic system adequate for considerable communication. But his mental actions, still not organized into a consistent system, continue to place him at the preoperational period of intellectual development. In fact, his increased linguistic competencies provide better insights into the deficiencies in his system of thought.

Piaget has devised several classic tasks to demonstrate the shortcomings of the child's cognition. Among them is the seriation task in which a child is shown an ordered array of sticks of increasing size and is asked to reproduce the ordered pattern from a disordered pile of the sticks. The problem is beyond the capacities of the preoperational child. Another task, rooted in classification skills, involves comparing an entire set of objects with one of its subsets. So, for example, the child is shown an array of six dogs and three cats

1. **Conservation of substance (6–7 years)**

A

The experimenter presents two identical plasticene balls. The subject admits that they have equal amounts of plasticene.

B

One of the balls is deformed. The subject is asked whether they still contain equal amounts.

2. **Conservation of length (6–7 years)**

A

Two sticks are aligned in front of the subject. The subject admits their equality.

B

One of the sticks is moved to the right. The subject is asked whether they are still the same length.

3. **Conservation of number (6–7 years)**

A

Two rows of counters are placed in one-to-one correspondence. Subject admits their equality.

B

One of the rows is elongated (or contracted). Subject is asked whether each row still has the same number.

4. **Conservation of liquids (6–7 years)**

A

Two beakers are filled to the same level with water. The subject sees that they are equal.

B

The liquid of one container is poured into a tall tube (or a flat dish). The subject is asked whether each contains the same amount.

5. **Conservation of area (9–10 years)**

A

The subject and the experimenter each have identical sheets of cardboard. Wooden blocks are placed on these in identical positions. The subject is asked whether each cardboard has the same amount of space remaining.

B

The experimenter scatters the blocks on one of the cardboards. The subject is asked the same question.

Some simple tests for conservation with approximate ages of attainment.

Fig 15–1.—Some simple tests for conservation. (From Lefrancois G.R.: *Of Children, An Introduction to Child Development.* Belmont, Calif., Wadsworth Publishing Co., Inc., 1973, p. 305. Reprinted by permission of the publisher.)

and is asked whether there are more dogs or more animals. The preoperational child seems incapable of making this part-whole comparison and invariably asserts that there are more dogs than animals.

Probably the most well-known set of tasks involves questions about conservation of some quantity (such as length or weight) of an object or set of objects following perceptual transformation of the object or set of objects. The following is an example of this kind of task. A child is shown two equal-sized balls of clay, one of which is then rolled into a sausage or flattened into a pancake. He is asked whether there is still the same amount of clay in both pieces. The preoperational child asserts that they are no longer equal as a result of the observed transformation. There is a series of tests for conservation, graded in difficulty, ranging from conservation of number problems to conservation of volume (Fig 15–1). The preoperational child fails to solve these problems. Examination of the child's responses reveals certain consistent characteristics of his thinking that account for his errors. First, the child's thinking is "irreversible"; that is, after he has performed a certain mental action based on an observed transformation, he seems to be incapable of reversing the action and mentally reconstructing the situation that existed prior to transformation. For example, he does not seem to realize that the clay pancake can be rolled back into a ball so that it is once again the same as the other ball. Second, the child's thinking is "centered"; that is, he attends to or centers on only one dimension at a time. He notes that the clay pancake now covers more area but fails to coordinate this information with the fact that there has been a corresponding decrease in thickness. Third, the child's thinking is "static"; that is, he focuses on states rather than dynamic transformations. An adult presented with the pancake and ball made of clay could only guess about their equality, because he sees them only in their final state. The preoperational child acts as if he too has information only about their final states and knows nothing about the previous transformation of the ball to a pancake.

The major challenge to Piaget's theory of the role of operations in solving these problems and thinking logically comes from training studies that have attempted to teach children the correct responses to some of these tasks and then demonstrate the generalization of this knowledge to the solution of different but related tasks. The training itself usually involves no attempt to teach the supposed underlying operations. Gelman has demonstrated success in teaching conservation of number and found generalization even to tasks involving conservation of mass.[2] Other researchers also report successful early training in several tasks that, according to Piaget, should require operational intelligence.[3,4] These findings, while not invalidating Piaget's theory, do suggest caution in interpreting his claims about what is necessary for various levels of logical thinking.

The child's increasing verbal skills also allow for a more sophisticated assessment of his memory capacity and skills. The general conclusion seems to be that on memory tasks that do not require the use of strategies to aid in remembering (such as most recognition tasks where the subject is shown a series of pictures and then shown a second set and asked to select those he has seen before), there are no differences between the young child and the adult. In tasks where the use of strategies aids performance, however, striking differences are observed.[5] The kinds of memory tasks that depend on the use of strategies include those that require recall or reconstruction of information rather than merely recognition. Some of the strategies used are rehearsal (repeating the information to oneself), thinking or organizing the information into meaningful categories, labeling, and pairing images with the information to be remembered.

Given that the younger child fails to use strategies where they would be helpful for remembering, the question naturally arises whether the child is even capable of using such strategies. The evidence suggests that the child, if instructed in relevant strategies, will make use of them provided he is constantly prompted. But despite his greater success, the child will not generalize the strategies to new but similar tasks. The problem for the child at this point in development appears to be a metamemorial deficiency. Metamemorial refers to the ability to assess one's memory capacity and limits, to recognize the various strains that different tasks might place on one's memory and to recognize the need to make use of mnemonic strategies to aid memory when necessary. It is these metamemorial skills that the young child seems to lack. Several studies have documented the young child's wild overestimates of his memory capacity and his inability to use feedback on his memory performance to modify those estimates.[6,7]

Language Development

From 3 to 6 years of age, the average child's vocabulary expands from less than 1,000 words to more than 2,500.[8] Insight into the structure of the child's semantic categories is provided by studies that look at the word associations children produce in response to word presentations. Children younger than 6 or 7 tend to give responses across grammatical categories from the stimulus word (called syntagmatic responses). So, for example, the child at this period of development is likely to say "mountain" in response to "high." After about 7 or 8 years of age, the child is more likely to give responses that are in the same grammatical category as the stimulus word (called paradigmatic responses), such as "low" in response to "high."[9]

It is an impressive feat of the young child that by the end of his fifth or sixth year, he has mastered most of the complexities of the mature grammar of his native language. The primary developments from 3 to 6 years involve the addition of various types of transformations to the child's array of syntactic rules. The kinds of transformations mastered include negative sentence constructions,[10] questions,[11] and passive transformations of active sentences.

Psychosocial Development

THEORIES OF FREUD AND ERIKSON.—Traditional Freudian theory refers to this period as the phallic stage—a time when libidinal energy is focused on the genital area. The Oedipus complex, which is based on the young child developing a possessive attachment to the parent of the opposite sex, occurs during this stage. The boy, motivated by fear of retaliation by his father, resolves this conflict by repressing his "desires" for his mother and identifying with his father. In the case of the girl, fear of the loss of her mother's love causes her to repress her "desires" for her father and identify with her mother. Freud felt that the "heir" to the Oedipus complex was the superego or conscience. Thus, as the child identifies with the parent of the same sex, he incorporates many of his or her rules and regulations regarding social conduct. Future emotional problems were seen by Freud to be related to difficulties during this psychosexual stage of development.

In Erikson's theory of psychosocial development, the major task facing the preschool child is "initiative versus guilt." By this, Erikson means that the preschooler must cope with the conflict created when he is called upon to restrain his exploratory and aggressive behavior. If this issue is successfully resolved, the child retains a sufficient degree of initiative, while at the same time acquiring a socially acceptable degree of control over his behavior. Alternatively, if the child's behavior is excessively suppressed, he may develop a feeling of guilt when he attempts to think or act independently; thus, he may fail to develop an adequate degree of individuality and spontaneity.

MORAL BEHAVIOR.—Perhaps the most comprehensive cognitive approach to moral development has been the work of Kohlberg.[12] He describes moral judgment as evolving through related stages dependent on:

1. External reward and punishment
2. Naive hedonism (doing what feels good)
3. Approval of others (good boy, etc.)
4. Authority figures (standards based on significant adults)
5. Contractual obligation or democratic laws

6. Individual principles of conscience

Even though much of his data are retrospective, Kohlberg has attempted to correlate age levels with the above sequence of stages. Young children (as well as some adults) are seen to function in stages 1–4 and mature adults in stages 5 and 6. Kohlberg's work has been criticized on several grounds including methodology (retrospective reports); however, his concept provides a useful approach to understanding a very complex area.

As mentioned previously, the psychoanalytic explanation of moral development is based on the resolution of the Oedipal conflict, which results in the formation of the superego or conscience. Learning theorists point to the importance of reward and punishment, as well as the role of imitative learning, in the evolution of moral behavior.

Data from studies on aggressive behavior in childhood indicate that, in general, aggressive acts are related to previous learning and current circumstances. In addition, studies show that in children between 2 and 5 years of age, three types of problems account for more than 70% of anger outbursts: problems of social interaction, conflicts over routine (going to bed), and conflicts with authority. Analyses of the arguments that occur between preschool children during play in a nursery school setting indicate that:[13]

1. The arguments average three to four per hour.
2. The average argument lasts less than 30 seconds.
3. Arguments tend to decrease with age.
4. Boys argue more frequently and aggressively than girls.
5. Children argue more with those of the same sex.
6. Most arguments concern possessions.
7. Pushing, hitting, and pulling are the most common motor correlates.
8. Crying, commanding, and forbidding are the most common vocal components.
9. The arguments are mostly settled by the children.
10. Most children recover quickly and show no resentment.

The following learning principles are useful in managing the behavior problems of preschool children that involve anger and aggression: reduce stimuli for aggression, provide cues for nonaggressive behavior, reduce exposure to aggressive models, provide models of nonaggressive behavior, reduce aversive stimuli, train in skills (other ways of coping), and provide differential reinforcement (rewarding acceptable behavior and providing unfavorable consequences for aggression).

The development of a sense of morality involves the learning of honesty and truthfulness. Telling the truth often becomes a key issue during early moral development, with most parents reducing the punishment given for wrongdoing if the child tells the truth about what happened.

Observations of parental discipline have indicated that the techniques can generally be categorized into (1) power-assertive techniques, including physical punishment, shouting, and threats, and (2) psychological techniques, which are divided into (a) love withdrawal and guilt, whereby love is made contingent on good behavior, and (b) induc-

TABLE 15–1.—PARENTAL DISCIPLINE TECHNIQUES AND RELATED OUTCOMES IN THE CHILD'S BEHAVIOR AND PERSONALITY

TECHNIQUE*	PERSONALITY CORRELATES	MORAL BEHAVIOR(S)
Power assertion	Aggressive behavior and fantasy	Minimal internalization of moral prohibitions
Love withdrawal	Anxiety and dependence	No clear-cut relationship
Inductions	Autonomy and concern for others	Advanced moral development

*See text for definition.
Source: Newman B., Newman P.R.: *Development Throughout Life: A Psychosocial Approach.* Homewood, Ill., Dorsey Press, 1975, pp. 91, 162. © 1975 by Barbara and Philip Newman. (Used by permission.)

tions, whereby reasons and explanations about the social consequences of an act are emphasized. Newman and Newman have summarized the general effects of such techniques on the behavior and personality of the child[14] (Table 15–1).

Other studies have shown that hostile parental attitudes coupled with a lack of, or inconsistent, discipline usually result in aggressive and impulsive behavior in children. In general, it can be said that firm consistent discipline, along with reasons for appropriate conduct, usually produces the best results in terms of the development of moral behavior in children.

SEX ROLES.—Sex roles evolve over the first few years of life and by the preschool period they are fairly firmly established. Most young children learn their sex role in the following sequence: first, they learn gender labels (I am a boy; I am a girl); second, they learn sex role standards (males are _____; females are _____); third, they learn sex preferences (I'd rather be a *boy, girl*); and finally, they identify strongly with the parent of the same sex (I want to be like Mom, like Dad).[14] Concepts of what is "masculine" (e.g., football, toy guns) and "feminine" (e.g., dolls, tea parties) are acquired by age 3 or 4. The assigned sex role is a very powerful psychological force in determining a person's sex orientation. Studies of genetic males and females who acquire opposite sex roles during their childhood show that everyone ultimately had a sexual identity in keeping with the assigned role.[15] This finding underlines the important contribution of psychological and environmental factors in the development of one's sexual identity.

Parental comments such as "be a nice boy" or "be a good girl" play a role in gender labeling at a very early age. In the preschool-age period, children experience reactions from teachers and peers in nursery school that are based on sex roles. Statements such as "boys line up here," "girls over there" continually reinforce labeling distinctions during this period. As role behavior and preferences develop, so do attitudes regarding one's gender. Cultural and familial influences also affect gender labeling.

Although some attitudes about "maleness" and "femaleness" are based on biologic differences, many are merely cultural stereotypes. There have been recent challenges to these stereotypes, primarily as a result of the "women's liberation" movement, and over the past decade there has been a noticeable change in the traditional roles of men and women in our society.

Developmentally, sexual standards and preferences change according to age level, expectations, and abilities. For instance, if crying or passivity is seen as feminine in a family, a boy is given to understand that he should avoid this emotional reaction. This message is related to age, however; so the parents might condone crying in a 2-year-old boy but not when he reaches the age of 4 or 5. Children as they develop experience different social consequences depending on their sex role. When their behavior, temperament, or disposition is out of keeping with social sex role expectations, emotional and behavioral problems can result. For example, a boy may be labeled as a "sissy" or a girl seen as a "tomboy."

Parents in particular may become concerned if the activities or interests of an older child are incongruous with his assigned sex role (cross-gender behavior), such as, effeminate mannerisms in boys or masculine interests in girls. Often this concern is based on fears that such behavior may indicate future sexual deviations, such as homosexuality. There have been few systematic and comprehensive analyses of whether or not cross-gender behavior and interests in boys and girls of early school age predict later heterosexual or homosexual preferences.

Identification—the desire to "be like" or to emulate an "ideal" person—has particular relevance in the formation of the concept that one has of his or her sexual identity. In the psychoanalytic model of development, the successful resolution of the Oedipus conflict results in the boy identifying with his father and the girl identifying with her mother. Learning theory views sexual identification as related primarily to imitation of parental behavior by the child, with differential reinforcement of those behavior traits that approximate those exhibited by the parent of the same sex.

Whatever one's theoretical approach, most students of child development agree that by age 3 or 4 most children have a relatively fixed concept of their gender identity. In fact, attempts to alter this concept after this age are generally unsuccessful.

SOCIAL RELATIONSHIPS.—The world of the youngster of this age greatly expands when he attends nursery school, interacts socially with peers in the neighborhood, and travels with the family on outings. In recent years, as more working mothers place young children in day care centers, interaction with others apart from the immediate family is becoming more common. The possible ill effects of this kind of social environment on a child have been a concern for some people. Early conjectures about "group rearing" suggested that future emotional or social problems might develop; however, investigations have failed to support these speculations. For example, studies of infants and toddlers raised in the Israeli kibbutzim indicate that there are no specific psychological or social differences between these children and those raised in the usual home environment, when both groups are evaluated in later years. One reason is that in the kibbutzim young children spend a good deal of time with their parents and therefore progress through the typical stages of attachment early in life. Whatever the rearing environment, as the young child enters and proceeds through the preschool stage, there are strong pressures on him to socialize and develop relationships with others.

Social interaction with peers may occur in formal settings (such as nursery schools) or in informal interactions (such as free play in the park or neighborhood). At this age, an older person is usually in close proximity to monitor and regulate this interaction. In the nursery school or day-care setting, daily routines may be established so that the preschool child learns to regulate his behavior by "time" or "activity." For example, during story time there is an emphasis on quiet listening and not disturbing others. This requires that the child restrain his natural impulse to talk or shout, which is difficult for many preschoolers. Gradually, there is a shaping of acceptable social behavior and the child learns what he can and cannot do in certain circumstances. Regulating their behavior is hard for some children because of their history and temperament. Children who are impulsive, shout out, interrupt others, and cry easily when frustrated may be labeled as "immature" during this period of development. Such children are generally not liked by their peers and may even be avoided since they do not have the capacity for appropriate social interactive play.

Most children of this age, however, develop the ability to regulate their behavior in social settings. They proceed from parallel play (playing along side one another with little or no cooperative interaction) to interactive play (play in which there is cooperation between the children). By age 4, most children can participate in simple games and such activities are commonplace. Of course, competition for desired toys or leadership often results in altercations, but these are usually brief. However, at times physical aggressiveness (pushing, hitting) is observed in such situations and, if such behavior occurs frequently with a given child, intervention may be needed to prevent his attempts to resolve all play problems by physical force. Adults who supervise children in the nursery school environment are particularly sensitive to positive social behaviors such as sharing, cooperating, and showing consideration for others. Erikson has postulated that discipline that excessively suppresses self-expression may thwart or inhibit social development, resulting in an overly inhibited child with little initiative. Therefore, while cooperation during this age is important for social maturation, so is competition; while physical expression of anger and frustration should be discouraged, verbal assertiveness and expression of feelings should be encouraged; while conformity to group rules to achieve common goals is necessary, so is the individuality of the child. The balance achieved between these often conflicting goals in the preschool child is very important for future emotional and social development.

In addition to developing the capacity to control his behavior, the child needs to learn how to express his emotions (e.g., anger, frustration) appropriately during this stage of development. For example, the older preschool child should be helped to understand that there is nothing wrong with the angry "feeling" that he experiences when another child grabs his toy; it is what he does about it (hitting versus telling) that is the issue.

Two other related factors should be emphasized at this point; these are the importance of peer imitation and group acceptance, especially for the older preschool child. Imitating the behavior of a more dominant child and copying the act receiving the most peer attention are common among children this age. Being accepted by others is an important goal for most preschoolers and represents one of the prime factors influencing the behavior they adopt. Behavior that develops as a result of conforming to the social expectations of others first begins to be expressed overtly in this age period. Occasionally, a child's behavior creates problems because he becomes either an "overconformist" or an "underconformist." The former shows a lack of individuality (to the point of imitating peers or others even when the behavior produces negative reactions from adults), while the latter has little or no regard for social rules and, in serious cases, may be negativistic and oppositional. When an "oppositional" child fosters great concern in his parents, comprehensive evaluations should be initiated, since identifying serious problems early and providing management are important in preventing future social difficulties and attenuating power struggles between the child and adults.

Illustrative Clinical Problems

ENURESIS (see also chap. 4).—Enuresis is defined as the involuntary discharge of urine after the age when bladder control should have been established. Daytime enuresis is diagnosed if a child continues to wet after the age of 3 (despite appropriate training); the diagnosis of nocturnal or sleep-related enuresis is made if there is frequent bed-wetting after age 4. Sleep-related enuresis is more common, and it is estimated that at age 5 as many as 10% to 15% of otherwise normal children suffer from this problem. It is slightly more common among boys. As children get older, the incidence of this disorder decreases, with about 2% of those aged 12 diagnosed as having nocturnal enuresis (Table 15-2). Diagnostically, a distinction is made between primary enuresis (children who never had bladder control) and regressive or secondary enuresis (children who achieved control and later regress).

Treatment of nocturnal enuresis generally has been approached using three management techniques: (1) direct training (bell and

TABLE 15-2.—PREVALENCE OF NOCTURNAL ENURESIS BY AGE AND SEX

AGE (Years)	N	BOYS (% Wet)	GIRLS (% Wet)	SEX RATIO
5	395	13.4	13.9	1.00
7	359	21.9	15.5	1.41
9–10	1,814	9.0	5.6	1.61
14	1,913	3.0	1.7	1.77
Average (all ages)		14.0	9.1	1.4

Adapted from Stewart M.A., Gath A., *Psychological Disorders of Children: A Handbook for Primary Care Physicians*. Baltimore, Williams and Wilkins Co., 1978.

pad), (2) medication (imipramine), and (3) counseling and/or psychotherapy. The most effective treatment as shown in several well-controlled studies is the so-called bell and pad method developed by Mowrer in 1938.[16] In this method, the sleeping child is awakened soon after he urinates by a bell alarm connected to a moisture-sensing pad under the sheet. Several companies market such devices and surveys indicate that hundreds of thousands are sold. The overall training program should include counseling sessions with both the child and the parents to explain the goals of this treatment approach. If the program is carefully followed, success rates generally average between 80% and 85% within 6 months of initiating treatment.

Although not so successful in terms of the cure rate and the rapidity at which bladder control is achieved, the tricyclic antidepressant imipramine has been used in the treatment of nocturnal enuresis. This approach sometimes has negative implications for the child and family regarding the nature of the problem in enuresis; the use of a pill to control the disorder seems to indicate to some that bed-wetting is a "disease" rather than a habit that the child himself can solve with help.

Psychotherapy has not been very successful in altering bed-wetting. When the social restrictions of bed-wetting (especially with older children), such as not being able to sleep at friends' homes, result in significant emotional problems, however, psychological counseling (along with direct training for the bed-wetting) may be indicated. Studies show that there are improvements in many areas of psychosocial function (school, peer relationships, and family interaction) when the enuresis is treated successfully with direct training, even though no psychotherapy is used.[17] The following case study illustrates a direct training approach.

The patient was a 6-year-old boy referred by his pediatrician because of primary nocturnal enuresis. All physical evaluations proved normal and the parents described his physical and social development as normal. The child was the oldest of two siblings; a younger brother was aged 3.

Both parents reported that the child had developed normally throughout his life and was attending first grade and doing well. They stated that his social relationships were good and that he was outgoing and friendly. They stated that other than the

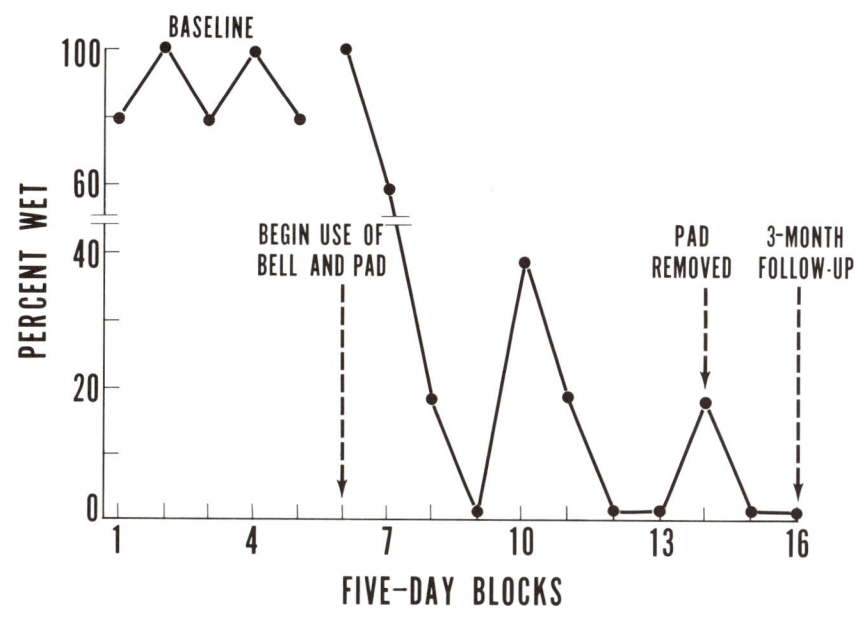

Fig 15–2.—Percent wet days during baseline (no treatment), use of the bell and pad for treating enuresis and follow-up.

normal problems of child-rearing there were no difficulties except for the enuresis.

A psychological screening indicated normal achievement levels in basic academic skills as well as high average intellectual potential.

The child and his parents were given an explanation of the "bell and pad" approach or direct training method. Both parents agreed that they would purchase the device and consult the psychologist before it was used. Subsequently, in about 3 weeks, the family called and was seen regarding the use of the alarm bell and pad for training.

A 30-minute session was held with the child and his parents during which use of the device was explained, as well as the incentive or reinforcement program enabling the child to receive prizes of increasing value for being dry on *consecutive* nights.

Before using the device, the parents kept a baseline record of wet and dry nights (Fig 15–2). During this time, the child was wetting the bed 22 out of 25 nights, or 88% of the time. Once the training program was initiated, there was a decrease in wetting until finally the bell and pad were removed. A 3-month follow-up indicated that there was no recurrence of the bed-wetting. The parents described the child as doing well in all areas and they had almost "forgotten" about the earlier bed-wetting problem.

Such data are fairly characteristic of the direct training approach to bed-wetting with cooperative normal children and families. As in all learning, there are regressions on the part of the individual, as can be seen in the data, but it should be noted that regression peaks were lower than the previous baseline and the performance right after intervention. If regression peaks in the learning curve (frequency of wetting) do go above past performance levels after 2 weeks of treatment, the parents and/or child should be seen to determine whether the procedures are being followed closely (getting up at night with the child, resetting the alarm, helping the child to remake the bed, making no critical comments, providing rewards, etc.).

DEVELOPMENTAL DELAYS—SCREENING AND MANAGEMENT.—Another important problem in this stage is behavioral or cognitive delays in development. It is becoming routine for pediatricians to gather developmental information using formal screening instruments such as the Denver Developmental Screening Test (Fig 15–3) throughout the preschool period.[18] In fact, some pediatricians are currently using trained consultants or developmental specialists routinely to screen children in their practice. It is at this stage of development that children who may be mildly or moderately retarded intellectually begin to show clear-cut developmental deficits or disabilities compared with normal children.[19]

Parents often have a great deal of concern about intellectual development and, consequently, have great difficulty in accepting such findings. Hence, appropriate counseling and direction regarding management and training are always indicated. This may involve consultation with professionals in several disciplines such as psychology, education, speech therapy, and social casework. In situations in which a developmental delay is due to hereditary disorders, appropriate genetic counseling for the parents becomes necessary. All parents feel more or less responsible for such genetically induced delays and, therefore, feel varying degrees of guilt about the child's difficulties. Proper management should attempt to reduce this feeling of guilt and at the same time help the parents to shoulder the responsibilities of child-rearing.

SCHOOL-AGE PERIOD (6–12 YEARS)

During the school years, many important cognitive and social skills develop as the child enters the world of formal education. In this environment, he not only learns the "three Rs" but also formulates his early attitudes toward work and achievement. He also undergoes a process of self-assessment, for as he interacts with others in the school setting he measures his qualities and capabilities against theirs. Success and failure in school have far-reaching effects on his feelings of self-worth. The child emerges from this period with a more crystallized self-concept that carries with it important implications for his development in the next stage of adolescence.

Physical Development

Most children grow 1–2 feet and add 25–30 pounds between the ages of 6 and 12, so that the average child of 12 is approximately 5 feet tall and weighs 65 pounds. As in other periods, there is considerable individual variability in the rate of growth.

Children may become stereotyped because of their body dimensions or build; in fact, people may react to them differently on this basis. Sheldon advanced the theory that there is a relationship between body build and personality.[20, 21] He categorized people in terms of three basic body types—mesomorph, endomorph, and ectomorph—and described personality traits that were supposedly characteristic of each (Fig 15–4). His research has been criticized on several points, but especially because the same individuals rated both body type and personality factors. While the specific aspects of his theory have never been validated, it did give rise to a great deal of discussion and debate among psychologists. What can be said is that physical appearance and capability do influence a child's self-image and that this, in turn, determines to a large extent how he relates to others in his environment.

Cognitive Development

Somewhere around age 6 or 7, the child enters the period of concrete operations in his intellectual development. During this period, he shows evidence of systematic thinking, but his logic is limited to concrete aspects of his world. He remains incapable of operating on an abstract hypothetical level. Over the course of this stage of development (which extends to early adolescence), the child masters the various conservation problems discussed earlier, with the exception of conservation of volume, since volume is a more abstract concept and beyond the scope of concrete operations. He exhibits some adult-like concepts and demonstrates mastery over various seriation and classification problems, provided the objects of his operations are real. In order to understand the child's continuing deficiencies during this period of development, it may help to consider an example of a seriation problem modified to make it abstract. The concrete operational child can, of course, order an array of sticks from shortest to longest and will use a systematic strategy for positioning each stick in the series. If the same type of problem is presented to him in the abstract, however, he fails to solve it. For instance, given the following question—Alice is taller than Barbara, and Cynthia is shorter than Barbara, who is the tallest?—he will be unable to answer it correctly. Since the problem must be solved by operating on symbols rather than on concrete objects, the child at this period of development cannot handle it successfully.

Success in solving such problems awaits achievement of the final period of cognitive development—the period of formal operations—sometime in early adolescence. The adolescent can deal not only with the concrete and the real but also with the abstract, the possible, the hypothetical. His thinking is truly mature and rational by adult standards (or perhaps more accurately, his thinking may not always be on the highest level, but he is at least capable of such a level of thought if he sets his mind to it). The age of development of formal operations explains why algebra is usually not taught until junior high school, and why it is not until adolescence that a preoccupation with the future, the hypothetical, the possible, begins to dominate the individual's thinking.

While we have not stressed this point, it is Piaget's assertion that the sequence of intellectual development is both constant and universal. There are others, however, who challenge this claim and the assumption that thinking in the final period of development is based on logic rather than on simple empiricism (i.e., based on some sense of logical inevitability rather than on common experience). For example, college students have been persuaded to give up a belief in the conservation of volume or weight following perceptual transformations. This shift in judgment should not occur if the individual's original conclusion were based on logic. There is,

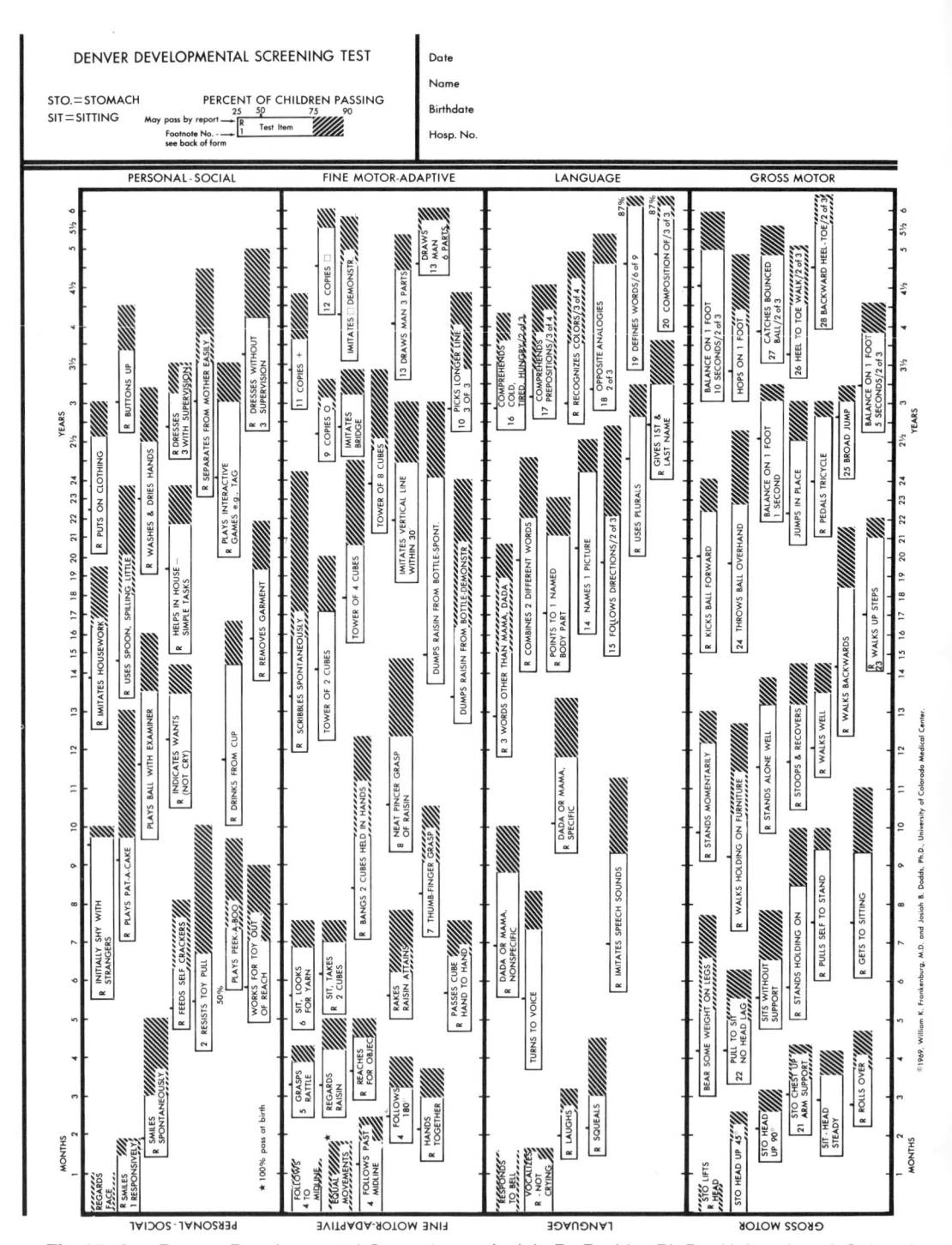

Fig 15-3.—Denver Developmental Screening Test. © 1969, William K. Frankenburg, M.D., and Josiah B. Dodds, Ph.D., University of Colorado Medical Center. Used by permission.

PRESCHOOL AND SCHOOL AGE

```
                    DATE
                    NAME
    DIRECTIONS      BIRTHDATE
                    HOSP. NO.
```

1. Try to get child to smile by smiling, talking or waving to him. Do not touch him.
2. When child is playing with toy, pull it away from him. Pass if he resists.
3. Child does not have to be able to tie shoes or button in the back.
4. Move yarn slowly in an arc from one side to the other, about 6" above child's face. Pass if eyes follow 90° to midline. (Past midline; 180°)
5. Pass if child grasps rattle when it is touched to the backs or tips of fingers.
6. Pass if child continues to look where yarn disappeared or tries to see where it went. Yarn should be dropped quickly from sight from tester's hand without arm movement.
7. Pass if child picks up raisin with any part of thumb and a finger.
8. Pass if child picks up raisin with the ends of thumb and index finger using an over hand approach.

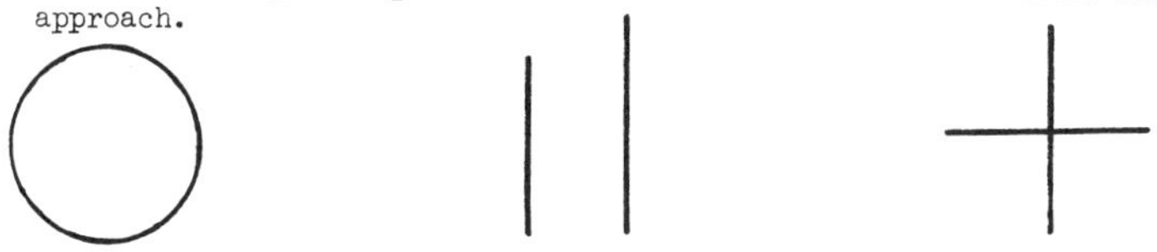

9. Pass any enclosed form. Fail continuous round motions.
10. Which line is longer? (Not bigger.) Turn paper upside down and repeat. (3/3 or 5/6)
11. Pass any crossing lines.
12. Have child copy first. If failed, demonstrate.

When giving items 9, 11 and 12, do not name the forms. Do not demonstrate 9 and 11.

13. When scoring, each pair (2 arms, 2 legs, etc.) counts as one part.
14. Point to picture and have child name it. (No credit is given for sounds only.)

15. Tell child to: Give block to Mommie; put block on table; put block on floor. Pass 2 of 3. (Do not help child by pointing, moving head or eyes.)
16. Ask child: What do you do when you are cold? ..hungry? ..tired? Pass 2 of 3.
17. Tell child to: Put block on table; under table; in front of chair, behind chair. Pass 3 of 4. (Do not help child by pointing, moving head or eyes.)
18. Ask child: If fire is hot, ice is ?; Mother is a woman, Dad is a ?; a horse is big, a mouse is ?. Pass 2 of 3.
19. Ask child: What is a ball? ..lake? ..desk? ..house? ..banana? ..curtain? ..ceiling? ..hedge? ..pavement? Pass if defined in terms of use, shape, what it is made of or general category (such as banana is fruit, not just yellow). Pass 6 of 9.
20. Ask child: What is a spoon made of? ..a shoe made of? ..a door made of? (No other objects may be substituted.) Pass 3 of 3.
21. When placed on stomach, child lifts chest off table with support of forearms and/or hands.
22. When child is on back, grasp his hands and pull him to sitting. Pass if head does not hang back.
23. Child may use wall or rail only, not person. May not crawl.
24. Child must throw ball overhand 3 feet to within arm's reach of tester.
25. Child must perform standing broad jump over width of test sheet. (8-1/2 inches)
26. Tell child to walk forward, 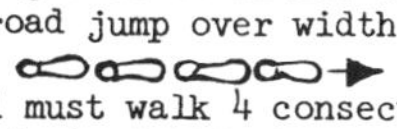 heel within 1 inch of toe. Tester may demonstrate. Child must walk 4 consecutive steps, 2 out of 3 trials.
27. Bounce ball to child who should stand 3 feet away from tester. Child must catch ball with hands, not arms, 2 out of 3 trials.
28. Tell child to walk backward,  toe within 1 inch of heel. Tester may demonstrate. Child must walk 4 consecutive steps, 2 out of 3 trials.

DATE AND BEHAVIORAL OBSERVATIONS (how child feels at time of test, relation to tester, attention span, verbal behavior, self-confidence, etc.):

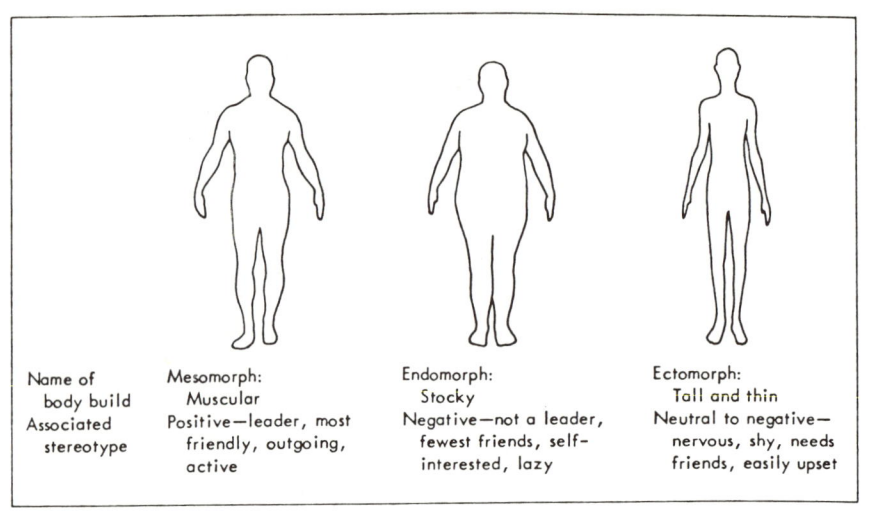

Fig 15–4.—Schematizations of three basic body builds and brief descriptions of social stereotypes of each found in the United States. (From Strommen E.A., McKinney J.P., Fitzgerald H.E.: *Developmental Psychology: The School-Aged Child.* Homewood, Ill., The Dorsey Press, 1977, p. 11. Used by permission.)

| Name of body build / Associated stereotype | Mesomorph: Muscular / Positive—leader, most friendly, outgoing, active | Endomorph: Stocky / Negative—not a leader, fewest friends, self-interested, lazy | Ectomorph: Tall and thin / Neutral to negative—nervous, shy, needs friends, easily upset |

in addition, a large body of evidence to indicate that, even for college students who might be expected to be the most likely members of society to achieve the final stage of formal operations, logical hypothetico-deductive reasoning is relatively rare, and context can override the elements of logic in a problem.[22]

The other attack on Piaget's theory comes from those who contend there is an additional stage of intellectual development, which involves the ability not only to solve problems but also to generate significant and meaningful questions to which the problem-solving tools can then be applied. In other words, the path to further development lies not in the search for equilibrium, but in the search for conflict and disequilibrium achieved by placing oneself in situations that require additional adaptations.[23] It is at this level of intellectual performance that the highest achievements of civilization are generated.

The major changes in memory that occur during the school-age period involve an increasing appreciation of one's limitations as well as one's strengths, that is, an increase in metamemorial skills with a subsequent greater reliance on mnemonic strategies. Efficient use of strategies, such as organization of material into meaningful categories, improves with age as the child's semantic domain develops. By the age of 12 or 13, the child has nearly the full battery of memory strategies available to the adult.

Language Development

The child's vocabulary continues to expand at a phenomenal rate during this period of life. Around age 7 or 8, his semantic organization apparently undergoes a qualitative change as indicated by word association tests. On these tests, his responses are more likely to be paradigmatic (responding to the word "soft" by saying "hard") than syntagmatic (responding to "soft" by saying, for example, "pillow").[9]

While it is commonly assumed that syntactic development is complete by about age 5 or 6, Chomsky has reported some interesting failures in comprehension among 6- to 10-year-olds.[24] These may occur with syntactically complex constructions, as in the following example. The situation involves presenting a blindfolded doll to the child and asking the question, "Is the doll easy to see or hard to see?" Many children younger than 7 or 8 interpret the question to mean, "Is it easy or is it hard for the doll to see?" and answer incorrectly that the doll is hard to see because it is blindfolded. Errors of comprehension may also occur when a child is directed to ask someone about information that is already available to them both. For example, the child may be instructed to say to another child, "Ask Billy what is the color of the car," when it is clearly visible to them both. Children under about 8 years of age will respond with the answer rather than asking the other child for the information. In other words, children of this age have a tendency to interpret instructions of this kind as directions to tell rather than to ask.

Most first language acquisition is complete by the end of the first 12 years of life. Also, it has been found that acquisition of a second or a third language is more difficult after adolescence. Mastery of the phonological and syntactic rules of a language is more complete the earlier the child is exposed to the language. This fact, plus the observation that recovery of language function following damage to the language areas of the brain is most complete in children younger than 5 or 6 and least complete in individuals after adolescence, has led to the postulation that a critical period exists for the acquisition of language.[25] The ease with which a preschooler can master additional languages is impressive, particularly when one considers the difficulty experienced by many college students attempting to learn a second language. While there is controversy over the extent to which a child is innately "preprogrammed" to learn a language, there is general agreement that there is a species-universal predisposition for the acquisition of language during the first decade of life.

Psychosocial Development

THEORIES OF DEVELOPMENT.—Freud considered the school years a time when id forces were relatively stable or quiescent and, thus, he referred to these years as the latency stage. During this period, the child's energy is thought to be focused on learning and cognitive development.

In 1975, there were almost 60 million children enrolled in public and private schools in the United States. Of these, approximately 34 million or about 57% were of elementary school age.[26] It is during the school-age period that most individuals develop the fundamental attitudes and behavior patterns that are crucial for their future adjustment in society. In this context Erikson theorized that the primary psychosocial issue of school age is "industry versus inferiority"; that is to say, the child striving for achievement and mastery in school will acquire a sense of accomplishment and self-pride if he is successful, whereas if he fails he will develop a poor self-concept.

Specific tasks facing the child during this period include:[27]

1. Learning to work well with peers
2. Becoming more independent from the family
3. Developing skills and ideas necessary for everyday life
4. Learning the basic academic skills of reading, writing, and arithmetic
5. Developing a more mature scale of values and morality
6. Developing ideas and attitudes toward social groups and institutions

These areas are interrelated, and often development in one area has significant effects on progress in others. While all are important for future social adaptation, several have special significance because of their great influence on adjustment during this age. These include peer relationships, self-concept, and performance in school.

PEER RELATIONSHIPS.—School-age children socialize in formal settings (i.e., school) and in informal play groups organized by themselves. Examples of the latter are the familiar neighborhood "gangs" and groups designed for sports activities and other games. Gang membership involves close personal relationships between the children often with a special meeting place (e.g., a tree house) for the group. Generally, the informal gangs (or play groups) have the following characteristics:[27]

1. The "gang" is more of a club or play group.
2. Members are of the same sex.
3. Usually three or four members are involved.
4. Activities are stressed (e.g., games, sports).
5. There is usually a special meeting place away from adults.
6. There may be a characteristic name or symbol for the group.

As the school-age child relates to his peers outside the home and away from family influences, he is given the opportunity to express certain personality traits such as leadership and independence. How well he fares in his interaction with peers can have significant effects on the development of his self-concept. In addition, he may acquire behavioral qualities as a consequence of identifying with other children with whom he has contact. For example, they may encourage him to be friendly, cheerful, and enthusiastic, and discourage behavior such as talkativeness and restlessness.[28]

As the child matures, informal group activities take on more formal, competitive qualities with games becoming more complex and focused on teams. Team-oriented activities have a significant influence on the social attitudes of the school-age child, particularly as these relate to cooperativeness among group members and competition with opposing groups. Newman and Newman refer to these as "in-group" and "out-group" attitudes.[14]

The impact of peer relationships on the psychosocial development of children of this age cannot be overemphasized. This is supported by animal studies that show that appropriate peer interaction can attenuate the ill effects of early social deprivation.[29]

SELF-CONCEPT.—In the course of informal and formal group interactions, school-age children acquire attitudes toward others and themselves. As a result of the approval and criticism they receive from peers, older children, and adults, they begin to develop a mental picture of themselves in relation to the rest of their world. Although many factors can affect the child's self-concept at this age, Hurlock believes that there are eight important ones:[27]

1. *Physical condition.*—A child with poor health or physical defects may be limited in peer interactions and, consequently, may develop feelings of inferiority.
2. *Intelligence.*—Individuals who are below average in intellectual abilities may feel inferior and are often made fun of or rejected by their peers. Very bright children may also be seen as "different" (the so-called brain of the class) and rejected by their classmates; alternatively, they may develop a feeling of superiority and in this way become alienated from their friends.
3. *Physical build.*—Obesity or very short stature may result in rejection and feelings of inferiority.
4. *Social acceptance.*—Social acceptance by peers is an important factor in the development of self-concept. Being very popular and being isolated are the two extremes along this dimension.
5. *Names or nicknames.*—Family names or nicknames that suggest minority group status or are humorous can result in rejection and damage to the child's self-concept.
6. *Socioeconomic status.*—Having more toys, a better home, etc., may result in feelings of superiority, while coming from a "poor" home may cause a child to feel envious and inferior.
7. *Success and failure.*—Success in tasks or activities, especially in competition with peers, tends to produce a feeling of self-confidence and self-worth. Failure, especially if repeated, has the opposite effect.
8. *School environment.*—Teachers who are understanding and encouraging can enhance a child's self-esteem, while harsh or overly critical teachers can diminish it.

PERFORMANCE IN SCHOOL.—The school environment, with its teacher-pupil interaction and the demands on the child made by formal instruction, represents one of the most important socializing influences in Western society. In the early school years, the cognitive and social skills of the preschool period are strengthened and expanded. Children who have not developed these prerequisite skills (e.g., attending to teacher, cooperating with classmates, sitting quietly during class) are sometimes considered to be immature. In fact, there is great variation among children of the 5–7 age group in terms of their preparedness for school. Educators are generally well aware of this problem, and recent instructional programs have emphasized individualized teaching, i.e., instruction that is tailored to each pupil's needs using "behavioral objectives." Regardless of the instructional program or materials available, one of the most important determiners of success in school is the relationship between the child and the teacher.

While "good teaching" is often said to be more of an art than a skill, various studies have attempted to identify those qualities or skills that are associated with successful teaching and learning. The following list of qualities was identified by students as being found in "good" teachers:[30]

1. Human qualities—sympathetic, cheerful, good disposition
2. Physical appearance—neat, attractive, good manner of talking
3. Discipline—fair, consistent, does not scold or shout
4. Participation—joins in games, permits play activities
5. Performance—explains well, permits expression of opinion

Of course, these characteristics also describe "good" parenting and "good" child-rearing in general. Qualities associated with academic achievement by children at this age include: intellectual level (IQ), emotional and social maturity, and parental factors including a good parent-child relationship, positive parental attitudes toward school, and parental interest in the child's performance. Some studies show that mothers who encourage independence and are warm and affectionate have children who are higher achievers.

The atmosphere of the classroom is also important in determining a child's school performance and in influencing his ideas about social interaction during this period. The classroom environment can be autocratic, democratic, or laissez-faire. Studies generally indicate that children in an autocratic environment, where the teacher represents total authority, have a low acceptance of group goals, a low morale, a high degree of dependence on the leader, and a difficulty in establishing friendly peer relationships. If the autocratic teacher is aggressively dominant, the children, by identifying with her behavior, may manifest aggression toward each other. In democratic classrooms, the group generally shows a high acceptance of group goals, good morale, and ability to work together constructively. Laissez-faire or permissive classrooms have been associated with quarrelsomeness, low morale, disorganized group interaction, and boredom.[31]

Illustrative Clinical Problems

Many developmental problems occur in the school-age period. Some of the most common are psychological reactions to school and behavioral abnormalities that interfere with school performance.[32]

SCHOOL PHOBIA.—While this term has been used to describe persistent absence from school with parental knowledge (as distinguished from truancy, in which school absence usually occurs without parental knowledge), a more exact definition is an intense fear of some aspect of the school environment and/or anxiety about separating from parents (especially the mother) which causes the child to avoid going to school.

School phobia is a serious problem for the child because it adversely affects school performance, peer relationships, and family interaction. The attitude of parents is usually anxious concern and, at times, even anger at continued school absence. Often the problem is associated with physical complaints such as headaches, nausea, fainting, and "feeling ill" on the part of the child. These symptoms usually become worse on Sunday evenings before the start of the school week or on Monday mornings, and they lessen if the child is allowed to remain at home instead of attending school. If he does go to school, the symptoms tend to abate as the school day progresses.

Thus, in school phobia a vicious cycle is created, which illustrates the negative reinforcing effects of fear avoidance; that is, avoiding a fearful situation (in this case, school or separation from a parent) reduces anxiety and this, in turn, increases the avoidance behavior (staying away from school). For this reason, treatment often means getting the child into the school environment as quickly as possible. The following case illustrates a direct treatment approach involving the cooperation of several professionals.

This case involves a rather severe school phobia in a 10-year-old, otherwise normal, girl who was attending fourth grade. The parents described the child's previous social and emotional history as being normal; however, they did state that she was somewhat shy and quiet, especially in new situations.

The school problem began a year earlier when the girl developed "fainting" and "dizziness" for the first time. The parents stated that she also became "moody." Because of these symptoms she was seen for a complete physical examination, which provided normal results. She had been an average to above-average student, and until the onset of the "dizziness" appeared to be enjoying school. Subsequently, she became extremely anxious and upset when getting ready to go to school in the morning, complaining of stomachaches and headaches. On several occasions when attending school she became pale and dizzy, was taken to the nurse's office, and eventually sent home. The child became concerned about fainting in public and had one such episode during a vacation with the family while she was eating lunch at a restaurant. All medical evaluations for these symptoms proved normal.

The child and family were seen in consultation for a total of eight sessions. A history was taken and an academic achievement screening performed. The school history was normal prior to the first episode of dizziness, after which the child became increasingly anxious when attending school. At the time of the initial referral, she had been out of school for 9 consecutive weeks. She had a homebound teacher and apparently was keeping up with her work.

In discussions with the girl, she was able to describe her physical symptoms fairly accurately and stated that she was extremely anxious about her "problem." After rapport was established, the basics of relaxation and desensitization were explained as well as the overall goals of the management program. She was rehearsed in muscle relaxation and asked to visualize mentally several school-related scenes that in real life would elicit anxiety and stress. In addition, it was emphasized to the child and family that school attendance was necessary and required by law and that, while it would be uncomfortable in the beginning for the child to attend, with patience and practice her symptoms would diminish. (In all school phobias, getting the child back to school as soon as possible is important for successful treatment.)

A motivational program was established in which the child kept a record of her symptoms when attending school (Fig 15–5). In this recording system, the child was required to place a check when she felt "okay" during each period of the school day and to place a minus sign for each time she experienced anxiety, or the "ill feelings" in her stomach, as she described it. In addition, if she went to the nurse's office she was to record an "O." As can be seen on the data card, initially there were some minuses with checks in the early morning (which is common in school phobias). These reported ill feelings abated as she remained in school. Besides self-recording, the child and parents agreed that when she earned 70 checks she would be able to purchase the puppy she wanted.

The child was seen weekly for supportive counseling, and both parents were to be counseled on management if any "attacks" recurred. Written instructions were given to school personnel to avoid paying undue attention to her because of her symptoms, so as to minimize any "secondary gain" she might obtain from being ill. If she became ill, the school officials were instructed to place the child quietly in the nurse's office and monitor her periodically. Her parents were not to be called until 30 minutes after she rested and/or if there were any significant problems (fever or vomiting). This approach was approved by the girl's physician.

Within a short time the child was attending school on a full-time basis, and follow-up showed that progress was maintained. She remained in school for the rest of the term with a B average. A progress check the following year showed she had excellent attendance with no recurrence of the symptoms. The parents reported that the girl had become more socially outgoing and assertive, had joined an after-school girls' softball team, was in-

PERIOD	M	T	W	T	F	M	T	W	T	F	M	T	W	T	F
Up A.M.(home)		−✓	−✓	−✓	−✓	−✓	✓	✓	✓	✓	✓	✓	✓	✓	✓
Homeroom		✓	✓	✓	✓	✓	✓	✓	✓	✓	✓	✓	✓	✓	✓
Lang. Arts	NO SCHOOL	✓	✓	✓	✓	✓	✓	✓	✓	✓	✓	0	✓	✓	✓
Lunch		✓	✓	✓	✓	✓	✓	✓	✓	✓	✓	✓	✓	✓	✓
Math.		✓	✓	✓	✓	✓	✓	✓	✓	✓	✓	✓	✓	✓	✓
Science		✓	✓	✓	✓	✓	✓	✓	✓	✓	✓	✓	✓	✓	✓
3:00 P.M.		✓	✓	✓	✓	✓	✓	✓	✓	✓	✓	✓	✓	✓	✓
BONUS POINTS		✓				✓					✓				
Daily Total		8	7	7	7	8	7	7	7	7	8	6	7	7	7
Cumulative		8	15	22	29	37	44	51	58	65	72	78	85	92	99

✓ Feeling "O.K."
− Feeling "ill"
0 Went to nurse's Office

Fig 15−5.—Record sheet as self-recorded. First three weeks of program to combat school phobia.

teracting better with her peers, and in general seemed happy and well-adjusted.

This case illustrates a direct approach to treating school phobia, coordinating the expertise of psychological, medical, and educational professionals to achieve the desired goal for the child. School phobias that involve more complex emotional problems might require more intensive psychotherapy and family guidance.

ATTENTION DEFICIT DISORDERS.—In previous classification systems terms such as "minimal cerebral dysfunction," "hyperkinetic syndrome," and "minimal brain damage" were often used interchangeably to describe disorders associated with impulsivity and inappropriate attention. These terms were sometimes employed as diagnostic labels by health professionals, even though they really were only descriptive terms that did not indicate a specific disease entity.[33] The history of this field and the evolution of these terms have been summarized by Ross, who has pointed out that medical personnel should be cautious in applying them.[34, 35]

The new DSM-III (see chap. 6) describes attention deficit disorders involving two conditions, those with hyperactivity and those without associated hyperactivity. Hyperactivity itself is somewhat difficult to define. One of the reasons is that a large percentage of normal children are described by their mothers as "restless" or overactive.[36] Werry defined hyperactivity or hyperkinesis as "a level of daily motor activity which is clearly greater (ideally by more than two standard deviations above the mean) than that occurring in children of similar sex, mental age, socioeconomic and cultural background."[37] After reviewing many clinical case reports, he concluded that there *is* a hyperactivity syndrome associated with specific perinatal, cerebral, and cognitive abnormalities.[38] These abnormalities interfere with normal development, especially academically and socially. Prevalence data show that about 6% of 10-year-old children were judged as hyperactive, with a boy/girl ratio of about six to one.[39]

A behavioral checklist (Table 15–3) has been developed for rating children thought to be hyperactive. Other checklists have been developed, such as the Connors rating scale. In addition to excessive motor activity, children who are hyperactive characteristically have difficulty maintaining their attention span. Because they experience problems in school performance and social interaction, management is also an important consideration. Contrary to what one might think, the treatment of this disorder with sedatives has led to a worsening of symptoms, while stimulants to the central nervous system (e.g., methylphenidate) have been found to be of

TABLE 15–3.—THE WERRY-WEISS-PETERS ACTIVITY SCALE

	NONE	SOME	MUCH
During meals			
Up and down at table	—	—	—
Interrupts without regard	—	—	—
Wriggling	—	—	—
Fiddles with things	—	—	—
Talks excessively	—	—	—
Television			
Gets up and down during program	—	—	—
Wriggles	—	—	—
Manipulates objects or body	—	—	—
Talks incessantly	—	—	—
Interrupts	—	—	—
Doing homework			
Gets up and down	—	—	—
Wriggles	—	—	—
Manipulates objects or body	—	—	—
Talks incessantly	—	—	—
Requires adult supervision or attendance	—	—	—
Play			
Inability for quiet play	—	—	—
Constantly changing activity	—	—	—
Seeks parental attention	—	—	—
Talks excessively	—	—	—
Disrupts other's play	—	—	—
Sleep			
Difficulty settling down for sleep	—	—	—
Inadequate amount of sleep	—	—	—
Restless during sleep	—	—	—
Behavior away from home (except at school)			
Restlessness during travel	—	—	—
Restlessness during shopping (includes touching everything)	—	—	—
Restlessness during church/movies	—	—	—
Restlessness while visiting friends, relatives, etc.	—	—	—
School behavior			
Up and down	—	—	—
Fidgets, wriggles, touches	—	—	—
Interrupts teacher or other children excessively	—	—	—
Constantly seeks teacher's attention	—	—	—
Subtotal score	× 0	× 1	× 2
Total score		—	

Source: Werry J.S.: *Pediatr. Clin. North Am.* 15:581, 1968. (Used by permission.)

benefit. Double-blind studies have shown that this medication decreases hyperactive behavior, increases attention span, and improves social relationships. However, several studies have shown that the most effective use of medication is in a combined program with behavior management involving teacher and parent cooperation and training.[40, 41]

It has been pointed out that approximately 2% of all elementary school children in the United States were receiving stimulant medication in 1976.[40] This is a striking statistic and indicates that many children may be receiving these drugs for behavior problems without adequate evaluation. In every case of suspected hyperactivity, the health professional should obtain a careful history, including a good description of the child-family interaction and the child's school performance, and perform a thorough physical examination before medication is prescribed. If it is given, the treatment goal should include a plan to discontinue the medication at some point, thus ultimately shifting the locus of behavioral control from the drug to the child. Several strategies to accomplish this through behavior and educational management are available.[42]

The above descriptive or labeling difficulties notwithstanding, attention deficit disorders with hyperactivity are described in the new DSM-III as the manifestation of developmentally inappropriate attention, impulsivity, and hyperactivity. Specific diagnostic criteria include:

A. *Inattention*. At least three of the following:
   1. Often fails to finish things he or she starts
   2. Often doesn't seem to listen
   3. Easily distracted
   4. Has difficulty concentrating on school work or other tasks requiring sustained attention
   5. Has difficulty sticking to a play activity
B. *Impulsivity*. At least three of the following:
   1. Often acts before thinking
   2. Shifts excessively from one activity to another
   3. Has difficulty organizing work (not due to cognitive impairment)
   4. Needs a lot of supervision
   5. Frequently calls out in class
   6. Has difficulty awaiting turn in games or group situations
C. *Hyperactivity*. At least two of the following:
   1. Runs about or climbs on things excessively
   2. Has difficulty sitting still or fidgets excessively
   3. Has difficulty staying seated
   4. Moves about excessively during sleep
   5. Is always "on the go" or acts as if "driven by a motor"
D. *Onset before the age of seven*
E. *Duration of at least six months*
F. *Not due to schizophrenia, affective disorder, or severe or profound mental retardation*

Attention deficit disorder without hyperactivity has the same features as the above with the exception of criterion C (hyperactivity). Usually, this condition is milder than attention deficit disorder with hyperactivity.

SPECIFIC DEVELOPMENTAL DISORDERS.—Previously, specific developmental disorders were usually described under the category of learning disability (LD). As with hyperactivity, the term "LD" has often been used to designate a heterogeneous group of children who show significant variability in their behavior. Ross has reviewed the disorder and suggests the following "exclusive" definition:

A learning disability is present when a child does not manifest general mental subnormality, does not show an impairment of visual or auditory functions, is not prevented from pursuing educational tasks by unrelated psychological disorders, and is provided with adequate cultural and educational advantages but nonetheless manifests an impairment in academic achievement.[34]

In other words, children who have normal intelligence, intact sensory function, and adequate educational opportunities but still show deficits in academic achievement (reading, writing, or arithmetic) qualify for this diagnosis. The prevalence of this disorder has been estimated to be as high as 4–10% of all school-age children; however, the estimate may be inflated because of problems of diagnosis that lead to an inclusion of children with other conditions in this category. The DSM-III lists several specific developmental disorders, including developmental reading disorder, developmental arithmetic disorder, developmental language disorder (receptive or expressive), developmental articulation disorder, and mixed specific developmental disorder.

Special educational programs, involving smaller numbers of children in the classroom and individualized techniques of instruction, have been introduced to help these children. In an interdisciplinary approach, the efforts of the pediatrician, teachers, and psychologist may be coordinated to help the child.

Parental guidance is an important part of any treatment program since negative attitudes on the part of the parents can exacerbate the child's problem. For example, some parents feel that their child is "lazy" or "retarded," and proper information is required to educate them about the problem of LD. The role of the family physician or pediatrician is important not only in coordinating intervention but also in supporting parental efforts in dealing with the problem of LD by providing guidance, accurate information, and encouragement.

SUMMARY

Children in the preschool and school-age periods have greater access to the world outside their home. The resulting interaction with adults and peers greatly influences their psychological and social development. The preschooler begins to develop a sense of right and wrong partly as a result of the incorporation of his parent's system of values and partly due to effects of the rewards (approval) and punishment he receives from his parents and others. He (or she) also acquires a gender identity and a sex role, which serve to mold behavior. Most significant, he begins to manifest some degree of self-control—something that is necessary if he is to interact successfully with others.

According to psychoanalytic theory, this period is the time when the Oedipus complex is manifest. The successful resolution of this complex is believed to be responsible for the formation of the superego and the child's assumption of the appropriate sex role, both being due to the child's identification with the parent of the same sex. Examples of clinical problems at this time include enuresis and developmental delays.

During the school years, major strides in cognitive and psychosocial development are made by the child. Piaget's stage of concrete operations begins usually about the time at which he enters school. That is to say, during this period the child's mental actions become organized into a coherent system and he evidences logical thinking, but only in terms of the concrete aspects of his world. He still cannot function mentally on an abstract hypothetical level. Language acquisition is largely completed by the end of the school-age period.

The child's self-concept becomes increasingly crystallized as he interacts with school chums, teachers, and other adults, mainly as a result of the feedback they give him about his appearance and behavior. His performance in school, if successful, can give him a sense of "industry," whereas if he meets with failure, he may acquire a feeling of "inferiority." Thus, a person's self-esteem and attitude toward work and achievement are based to a certain extent on early school experiences.

Two problems of the school-age period are school phobia and the group of disorders referred to as the hyperactivity syndrome, learning disability, and minimal cerebral dysfunction.

REFERENCES

1. Vaughan V.C., McKay R.J., Behrman R.E. (eds.): *Nelson Textbook of Pediatrics*, ed. 11. Philadelphia, W.B. Saunders Co., 1979.
2. Gelman R.: Conservation acquisition: A prob-

lem of learning to attend to relevant attributes. *J. Exp. Child Psychol.* 7:167–187, 1969.
3. Bryant P.E., Trabasso T.: Transitive inferences and memory in young children. *Nature* 232:456–458, 1971.
4. Kohnstamm G.A.: *Piaget's Analysis of Class Inclusion: Right or Wrong?* The Hague, Mouton, 1967.
5. Brown A.L.: The development of memory: Knowing, knowing about knowing, and knowing how to know. *Adv. Child Dev. Behav.* 10:104–152, 1975.
6. Flavell J.H., Freidrichs A.G., Hoyt J.D.: Developmental changes in memorization processes. *Cognitive Psychol.* 1:324–340, 1970.
7. Markman E.M.: Factors affecting the young child's ability to monitor his memory. Unpublished Ph.D. dissertation, University of Pennsylvania, 1973.
8. Dale P.S.: *Language Development: Structure and Function.* Hinsdale, Ill., The Dryden Press, Inc., 1972.
9. Brown R., Berko J.: Word association and the acquisition of syntax. *Child Dev.* 31:1–14, 1960.
10. Bloom L.: *Language Development: Form and Function in Emerging Grammars.* Cambridge, Mass., M.I.T. Press, 1970.
11. Brown R. Gazden C., Bellugi U.: The child's grammar from I to III, in Hill J.P. (ed.): *Minnesota Symposium on Child Psychology.* Minneapolis, University of Minnesota Press, 1969, vol. 2.
12. Kohlberg L.: Development of moral character and moral ideology, in Hoffman M.L., Hoffman L.W. (eds.): *Review of Child Development Research.* New York, Russell Sage Foundation, 1964, pp. 383–431.
13. Herbert M.: *Emotional Problems of Development in Children.* New York, Academic Press, 1974.
14. Newman B., Newman P.R.: *Development Throughout Life: A Psychosocial Approach.* Homewood, Ill., Dorsey Press, 1975.
15. Hampson J.D., Hampson J.G.: The ontogenesis of sexual behavior in man, in Young W.C., Corner G.W. (eds.): *Sex and Internal Secretions*, ed. 3. Baltimore, Williams & Wilkins Co., 1961, vol. 3.
16. Mowrer O.H., Mowrer W.: Enuresis: A method for its study and treatment. *Am. J. Orthopsychiatry* 8:436, 1938.
17. Baker B.L.: Symptom treatment and symptom substitution in enuresis. *J. Abnorm. Soc. Psychol.* 74:42, 1969.
18. Frakenberg W.K., Dodds J.B.: Denver Developmental Screening Test. *J. Pediatr.* 1969, 71:181.
19. Knobloch H., Pasamanick B. (eds.): *Gessel and Amatruda's Developmental Diagnosis*, ed. 3. Hagerstown, Md., Harper & Row, 1974.
20. Sheldon W.H.: *The Varieties of Human Physique.* New York, Harper & Row, 1940.
21. Sheldon W.H.: *The Varieties of Temperament.* New York, Harper & Row, 1942.
22. Ennis R.H.: An alternative to Piaget's conceptualization of logical competence. *Child Dev.* 47:903–919, 1976.
23. Arlin P.K.: Cognitive development in adulthood: A fifth stage? *Dev. Psychol.* 11:602–606, 1975.
24. Chomsky C.: *The Acquisition of Syntax in Children from 5 to 10.* Cambridge, Mass., M.I.T. Press, 1969.
25. Lenneberg E.: *Biological Foundations of Language.* New York, John Wiley & Sons, Inc., 1967.
26. *Statistical Abstract of the United States*, ed. 9. U.S. Government Printing Office, 1976.
27. Hurlock E.B.: *Child Growth and Development*, ed. 5. New York, McGraw-Hill Book Co., 1978.
28. Laughlin F.: *The Peer Status of Sixth and Seventh Grade Children.* New York, Bureau of Publications, Teachers College, Columbia University, 1954.
29. Harlow H.F., Harlow M.H.: Learning to love. *Am. Sci.* 54:244, 1966.
30. Jersild A.T.: Characteristics of teachers who are "liked best" and "disliked most." *J. Exp. Educ.* 9:139, 1940.
31. Johnson R.C., Medinnus G.R.: *Child Psychology: Behavior and Development.* New York, John Wiley & Sons, Inc., 1967.
32. Toister R.P., Worley L.M.: Behavioral aspects of pediatric practice: A survey of practitioners. *J. Med. Educ.* 51:1017, 1976.
33. Skinner B.F.: *Science and Human Behavior.* New York, Macmillan Publishing Co., Inc., 1953.
34. Ross A.O.: *Psychological Aspects of Learning Disabilities and Reading Disorders.* New York, McGraw-Hill Book Co., 1976.
35. Ross A.O.: *Learning Disability: The Unrealized Potential.* New York, McGraw-Hill Book Co., 1977.
36. Tuddenham R.D., Brooks J., Milkovich L.: Mothers' reports of behavior of ten-year-olds. Relationships with sex, ethnicity, and mother's education. *Dev. Psychol.* 10:959, 1974.
37. Werry J.S.: Developmental hyperactivity. *Pediatr. Clin. North Am.* 15:581, 1968.
38. Werry J.S.: Organic factors in childhood psychopathology, in Quay H.C., Werry J.S. (eds.): *Psychopathological Disorders of Childhood.* New York, John Wiley & Sons, Inc., 1972, pp. 83–121.
39. Stewart Mark A., Gath A.: *Psychological Dis-*

orders of Children. Baltimore, Williams & Wilkins Co., 1978.
40. O'Leary S.G., Pelham W.E.: Behavior therapy and withdrawal of stimulant medication in hyperactive children. *Pediatrics* 61:211, 1978.
41. Ayllon T., Layman D., Kandal W.: A behavioral-educational alternative to drug control of hyperactive children. *J. Appl. Behav. Anal.* 8:137, 1975.
42. Rosenthal R.H., Allen T.W.: An examination of attention, arousal and learning dysfunctions of hyperkinetic children. *Psychol. Bull.* 85:689, 1978.

16 / Child Abuse—A Problem of Family Dysfunction

IRENE MOLNER SCHATZ, A.C.S.W., and LUCY ESTRIN, A.C.S.W.

THE FAMILY is fundamental to the social matrix of our society. Not only does it play a crucial role in the development of the individual, but it is also an important factor in the maintenance of the health and well-being of people. It has been shown that on the average married persons outlive those who are unmarried and that they are sick less often.[1] On the other hand, when there is family dysfunction, it can result in illness on the part of its members. A graphic example of such a situation is child abuse—a major medical and social problem in this country that is caused in most instances by a breakdown in family relationships. In this chapter, we will briefly review some functional characteristics of the healthy family and then discuss the problem of child abuse as an example of what can happen when these functions go awry.

GENERAL CONCEPTS OF FAMILY FUNCTION

The Nuclear Family

The family is the optimal vehicle for transmitting cultural values, social mores, and tradition. In our society, it is in fact the principal institution guiding the development of the individual. Families that function well and provide an environment in which their individual members flourish appear to have several distinguishing characteristics:

1. *Good communication among members.*—Communication is open and congruent, with pain and disapproval as well as affection being expressed openly. A child in such a family is listened to and given consideration. He is willing to take risks because he feels like a valued member of a group—loved and respected. As a consequence, he learns to listen to and love others.

2. *Flexibility.*—A nurturing family is flexible in that it shows a respectful appreciation for the individual differences of its members. Disappointment and frustration do not evoke panic but rather adjustment and an ability to move on. Mistakes are tolerated without continued harassment or ridicule.

3. *Sense of interdependency among members.*—The family members view their being together as a mutual survival system. They are aware that what affects one affects all. Meaning and purpose to life come from their mutual relationship.

Just as a normal person exhibits a variety of changes in his day-to-day behavior, families are fluid, dynamic, and continually changing. At one time, a family may find that things are going well and relationships are harmonious; at another, it may be caught up in adversity and disharmony. The capacity to deal effectively with disruptive situations and maintain its integrity is the mark of healthy family function. Just as a person's behavior is a result of forces both within and outside him, a family is a social system that is affected from within as well as from without. It is a carefully balanced system of relationships that must have a dynamic stability in order to absorb successfully the shocks of stress that originate internally and externally.

Currently the nuclear family is going

through a time of transition and strain. It has come under attack in recent years and its viability has been seriously questioned. More and more young adults are selecting a "single" life, and those who do elect to marry are doing so later in life than did their parents and grandparents.

The disappearance of the extended family in this country is being followed by a decline in the number of nuclear families. In 1975, 84% of the families in this country were of the husband-wife variety—a figure that has been steadily declining since the 1960s.[1] Among black families, this figure was only 61% in 1975, compared with 75% in 1960.[1] The marriage rate is falling and the divorce rate rising—statistics that indicate that the survival of the nuclear family is clearly being threatened. These data also suggest that the nuclear family is failing to meet the needs of many contemporary Americans and, further, that this failure may be a manifestation of a pervasive form of family dysfunction.

Parenthood

Even families that begin with love marriages often have difficulty surviving. As Lefer points out, "the capacity to be intimate, to share, and to develop mutuality is not innate."[2] These qualities are, in fact, developmental tasks that are acquired by the young adult. Many young adults are able to accomplish these tasks; unfortunately, some do not. It is when the latter group marry that family dysfunction is most likely to occur.

In other words, romantic love is not enough to insure a successful marriage. After a period of marriage, routine and familiarity replace the excitement and mystery of romance. Conflict is bound to arise. Various issues must be worked through by the marriage partners, including issues of dependence, privacy, authority, management of labor, responsibility, competition, and jealousy. So even without the added burden of parenthood, there are many sources of stress on the family. Ultimately, successful husband-wife families reach an equilibrium in which they experience some degree of mutual satisfaction in the relationship.

When a child is born to a family, extra demands are placed on the husband and wife, along with the joys and pleasures of parenthood. Parents are, after all, people who happen to have children. They are not imbued with any special powers or any superior intellect. Some are well prepared to assume this new function of nurturing a dependent human being; others are quite unable and even unwilling to take on this responsibility. One thing is very clear: the addition of a child to a dysfunctional family rarely improves the state of affairs, since it is another source of stress with which the family must cope. Likewise, becoming a parent will not by itself cause an immature and neurotic individual to change for the better. Rather, it may only bring into sharper focus his or her difficulty in adapting to new situations.

The Family as a Social System

Since the beginning of time, we have accepted the cliché "as the twig is bent so shall it grow." Only through the results of recent research in the field of mental health (particularly in family therapy) have we come to understand the impact of the family on the child and, conversely, the child's impact on his family. The concept of reciprocity that was discussed in chapter 14 is very important to an understanding of the functioning of the nuclear family. A child with developmental problems (physical, psychological, or social) may be regarded as part of a functional family system that operates reciprocally (i.e., the family members influence the child's health and behavior and he or she influences theirs). In other words, behavioral disturbances such as depression, school failure, withdrawal, or delinquency often indicate family dysfunction rather than exclusively a problem of the individual.

If it is accepted that in some instances the abnormal behavior of a family member is really a manifestation of dysfunction of the total family unit, then it follows that the person who is experiencing problems may not recover unless his family life is realigned into a proper state of balance. Of course, we do not mean to imply that all, or even most, of the difficulties that befall family members are attributable to family dysfunction. Many are, however, and unless the reciprocal relationship between the behavior of family members is understood, these families will not receive the proper help. Moreover, even when the aberrant behavior (or illness) experienced by a family member is not due to family dysfunction, it still has an impact on the other members and may cause them considerable distress and disability.

Thus, it is appropriate to view the nuclear family as a social system with each member linked to the others by physical, emotional, and social ties. It is a reverberating system such that when one of its "parts" is malfunctioning, the other "parts" feel the impact. From time to time, both internal and external pressures are exerted on the system. Its stability and resiliency depend on a dynamic equilibrium between the members. When this equilibrium is disrupted, the consequences can be serious, for example, illness on the part of a member or even the dissolution of the family.

CHILD ABUSE

Throughout history, children have been the targets of a multiplicity of types of abuse.[3] Many children were mutilated and even destroyed for political, economic, or religious reasons that reflected the times. Epileptic children were often brutalized in an attempt to expel the devil, and others were beaten just because they were girls. A review of history reveals that many children were flogged by schoolmasters as well as by parents, and that severe treatment and punishment of children were generally condoned by society. During the Industrial Revolution, children were forced to work for long hours in unbearable conditions and were beaten when they could not withstand the pressures or meet the demands.

In describing one of the first reported cases of child abuse in this country, Fontana cites the story of Mary Ellen, a young girl living in the latter part of the 19th century who was maltreated by her adoptive parents.[4] Several local church workers noted the obvious malnourishment and the recurrent brutalization of the child but were unable to convince authorities to take action against the parents. At this time, parents were still granted the right to discipline their children in any way they saw fit, and there were no laws to protect children. The church workers took their case to the Society for Prevention of Cruelty to Animals (S.P.C.A.), which was able to have Mary Ellen taken away from her parents. They accomplished this on the grounds that she was a member of the animal kingdom and could therefore be protected under the existing laws prohibiting cruelty to animals. As a result of this case, the Society for Prevention of Cruelty to Children was formed in New York in 1871.

Until recently, a child was regarded as the property of his parents, without rights of his own. Indeed, some parents still believe this is so. They feel they have the right to discipline their children at their own discretion and, moreover, they resent and resist social interference. It is only recently that society has come to view children as individuals with legal and moral rights, one of which is the protection from parental injury. Children are now entitled to advocates acting on their behalf to insure them of their rights.

In the United States, medicine did not become involved in the child abuse problem until the 1950s. In 1962 Kempe et al. published their classic article describing the "battered child syndrome," a particularly severe form of physical abuse.[5] Since this report focused the attention of the public and the medical profession on this problem, much has been done in an attempt to cope with the different kinds of child abuse. Child abuse reporting laws have been established in all 50 states. Most important, a greater awareness of this problem among pediatricians and other primary-care physicians has developed, which is essential if child abuse is to be diagnosed at an early stage so that the proper therapy can be instituted before irreparable injury, even death, occurs to the child.

Child abuse is a significant problem in many countries, and in 1979, the International Year of the Child, "the rights of children to be free from maltreatment have again been recognized worldwide."[6]

Classification of Child Abuse

There are several forms of child abuse—physical abuse and neglect, emotional abuse and neglect, and sexual abuse.[6] These may occur alone or, as is often the case, two and even three are seen together. It is not unusual for a child to be hospitalized for one type of abuse, and then it is discovered, after a more careful evaluation, that there is evidence of other types.

PHYSICAL ABUSE AND NEGLECT.—Physical abuse is best defined as the nonaccidental physical injury of a child by his or her parents or guardians. Physical damage may occur as part of "normal" punishment, but when the injuries sustained by a child are sufficient to require medical attention, child abuse should be strongly suspected. Physical neglect is defined as the failure to provide adequate food, clothing, medical care, and supervision for a child. When this occurs willfully, it constitutes a form of child abuse. On the other hand, if this neglect is unintentional, as in the case of the family that is financially incapable of providing these necessities, it is not considered to be child abuse.

EMOTIONAL ABUSE AND NEGLECT.—Emotional abuse and neglect occur when a parent denies a child a loving environment in which to thrive, learn, and develop. Because it can be subtle and complex in nature, this type of abuse is often difficult to identify and manage. Emotional abuse and neglect may be the result of an active process (e.g., the parent who is excessively demanding, demeaning, and hostile) or a passive process (e.g., the parent who withdraws both physically and emotionally from the child and therefore fails to provide necessary support and comfort). Despite its subtle nature, this form of abuse may have extremely adverse effects on a child's psychological and social development. Many emotionally abused or neglected children have serious learning difficulties that may lead secondarily to behavior problems.

SEXUAL ABUSE.—In the past 5 years sexual abuse, which can be broadly defined as any sexual activity between a child and an adult, has received greater attention.[6,7] Nonviolent sexual abuse is frequently not identified because of the absence of physical injury. Moreover, its effects are often subtle and late in developing. Violent attacks of sexual abuse, however, leave both physical and psychological scars, which have a deleterious effect on the child's subsequent psychosexual development.

Incidence

The actual incidence of child abuse is unknown as many cases never reach the physician's office or emergency room and, of those that do, many go unreported. Furthermore, the system of reporting and documenting confirmed versus suspected cases varies from state to state. Despite these reservations, it is clear that the number of reported cases of child abuse has increased dramatically over the past decade. Currently, the number of children being abused in this country is thought to range from 70,000 to 4 million per year. If we assume that a reasonable estimate is 1.5 million cases per year, then it is possible that as many as 2,000 children a year die as a result of abuse.[8] Although only estimates, these figures are staggering.

Child abuse occurs among people in all religions, races, and nationalities. Although in surveys of this problem families in the lower socioeconomic groups are more often identified as being involved, this appears in part to be statistical bias. These families tend to go to emergency rooms and public clinics where the likelihood of a case of child abuse being diagnosed and reported is greater than it is in the office of a private physician. Moreover, lower social class groups frequently depend on community agencies to obtain welfare, food stamps, housing support, and family services. Thus, they come under professional scrutiny much more often than do the upper classes. In addition to these sources of statistical bias, there are elements in the life-style of the economically disadvantaged that might predispose to child abuse. For example, poor families are often subjected to life stresses, such as unemployment and lack of adequate housing, that not only make their day-to-day existence difficult but can also be a precipitating factor in child abuse.

Pathogenesis

In order for an act of child abuse to occur, three factors must be present: an abuser, an abusee, and a crisis. An abuser is a parent or guardian who possesses the potential for child abuse, a potential that generally has its genesis in the parent's own childhood. The abusee is a child who, for a multiplicity of reasons, is singled out by the parent or guardian as being "special." The crisis may be any occurrence or circumstance that serves as a stimulus or catalyst for the abusive event. When all three of these factors are present, the possibility that child abuse will occur is great.

ABUSER.—An abusive parent frequently is someone who was the subject of parental abuse in his or her own childhood. The behavior of a parent toward a child provides a role model that the individual tends to emulate when he or she grows up and becomes a parent. Thus, parental role models are passed on from generation to generation. In view of this, it is not at all surprising that parenting behavior that is associated with child abuse tends to be repetitive in nature and, therefore, predictable.

Often one parent will actively abuse a child while the other passively allows the abuse to occur repeatedly. Mothers are most frequently found to be the active abuser principally because, as the primary caretakers, they spend the most time with the children. In approximately 95% of cases, the parent is found to be the abuser, with babysitters, relatives, and other adults constituting the remaining 5%. A small proportion of abusive parents are psychotic, and in some instances alcohol and drug abuse play a role; however, many of these parents do not have a defined psychiatric illness.[6] Nor are they criminals, although the legal interpretation of this behavior may vary from state to state depending on the specific laws governing this issue. The children of the 10–20% of child abusers who do exhibit severe psychopathology are at greatest risk for severe injury.

To understand the child abuse cycle, we must examine the manner in which the tendency for child abuse develops. As noted, the potential for child abuse begins in the parents' own infancy or childhood, a time during which they were often victims of unrealistic expectations and were forced to comply with excessive demands. These range widely from parental expectations regarding crying, sleeping through the night, toilet training, walking, and achieving other developmental and behavioral milestones, even extending to comforting the parent when he or she is distraught. Moreover, many of these children were conceived for a variety of inappropriate reasons such as saving a marriage, relieving loneliness, or providing the parent with constant love. The failure of a child to meet these unrealistic expectations often results in criticism and punishment. In such an environment, children often come to regard their own needs as secondary in importance and, consequently, grow up with many basic childhood needs unmet. When such children grow up and become parents, they may rely on their children to satisfy these unmet needs and, as a result, make unrealistic demands of them, just as they experienced as children. Thus, the cycle is perpetuated.

In view of such a childhood, it is easy to understand why abusive parents often have a difficult time trusting others. This lack of trust has detrimental effects on their capacity to form interpersonal relationships throughout their lifetime.

Erikson lists the acquisition of "basic trust" as the primary developmental task of the infant. By *trust* is meant a sense of confidence that develops in an infant exposed to consistent and empathetic caretaking.[9] It is this early trust in mothering figures that enables the individual later in life to develop close and meaningful adult relationships. The lack of trust on the part of abusing parents is evident in their attempts to try to manage life problems without asking for external help, in contrast to normally reared parents who, when faced with similar kinds of stress, are able to reach out for help from a spouse, relative, neighbor, or other external source. Abusive parents view these outside sources of help as potentially threatening, much like their own punitive parental figures. In a hospital setting with its many "authority" figures, this threat becomes magnified, often to an unbearable degree.

In addition to a lack of trust, abusive parents are characterized by a significant degree of social isolation, for their inability to form positive relationships as children persists into adulthood. They tend to marry early in an attempt to find someone to love and care for them, and to escape from their unhappy home. Often, however, they form relationships with people from similar backgrounds, and their marriages may not be satisfying, frequently paralleling those of their parents. As a result of their respective childhoods, both parents have many unmet needs but lack the capacity to express them. Such a marriage, although sometimes stable, usually does not meet the needs of the two parties, so their feelings of isolation are thereby reinforced. Abusive parents, moreover, tend to show little interest in social or community activities. This, of course, only further contributes to their isolation.

As a result of both the lack of trust and the social isolation, abusive parents possess very little self-esteem. Secondary to their deprecation as children, they have difficulty forming the types of satisfying relationships that contribute to a positive self-image. They are especially vulnerable to stress and lack the internal resources to handle things maturely. Consequently, they are extremely sensitive to criticism and disapproval. This type of parent is likely to interpret a child's "bad" behavior as a reflection of his or her own inadequacy. Therefore, discipline tends to be severe.

Because of their inadequate childhood experiences, abusive parents tend to have little knowledge of normal child development.[6] Having been deprived of much of the freedom and spontaneity of being a child, such as having an occasional temper tantrum, exploring the environment, or simply expressing feelings, they have, as parents, distorted perceptions of what really constitutes normal child behavior. They place great emphasis on punishment as the sole form of discipline, based on the only role model they know—their own parents. This punishment is often repetitive and used by the parent to correct "bad" behavior. It is the parent's distorted perception of what constitutes "bad" behavior, coupled with the extreme degree of punishment, that differentiates the abusive from the nonabusive parent.

ABUSEE.—The abusee is a child who, for various reasons, is perceived by the abusive parent as being "special."[6] Such a child may be regarded in this way because of his physical condition, psychological state, or behavior; for example, he may have a congenital anomaly, suffer from mental retardation, or exhibit hyperactive behavior. Or, his being "special" may be based only on the parent's subjective impressions that he is less attractive, less bright, or less well behaved than other siblings in the family. The child may even remind the parent of one of his own siblings with whom he did not get along. The important point is that, in many instances, the "special" child is perceived as such because of the parent's unique psychological makeup and background. It is interesting to note that often it is only one of several children in a family who is singled out for abuse, while the others escape maltreatment.

As noted in chapter 14, a major factor affecting the parent-child relationship is the psychological attachment that develops between them very early in life—during childbirth, during the postpartum period, and in infancy. This is known as parent-infant bonding. Positive affective ties are crucial to the quality of the parent-child relationship. Bonding is normally a very natural and easily observed process but can, on occasion, be disrupted by a separation of the parents and child following birth. This separation may be due to either physical factors, such as prematurity or maternal or neonatal illness, or psychological factors, as for example, in maternal postpartum depression. In this country, children who are separated from their parents, especially their mothers, during infancy have an increased risk of abuse. It is important to note, however, that there are many families in which there is a temporary separation of the mother and infant and yet strong affectional bonds still develop between the two. Also, there are cultures (e.g., in China) in which separation of mother and child during infancy is commonplace and yet the problem of child abuse apparently does not exist.[6]

There are many characteristic behavior patterns seen in abused children that can alert one to the presence of this problem. Any extreme behavior, be it aggressive or passive, can be a signal that a child is being abused. Many physically and emotionally abused children are withdrawn and passive, frightened of their parents, and wary of contact with other adults. When admitted to hospital pediatric units they often demonstrate behaviors that, although atypical for a normal child, are quite characteristic and at times even diagnostic of the abused child. Frequent among these is overcompliance. When a medical procedure is being performed, for example on a 2-year-old, it is normal for the child to cry. An abused child will often refrain from crying for fear of punishment.

Some abused children are nondiscriminating in their relationships to strangers, clinging to each new individual (physician, nurse, social worker, etc.) without specific preference. This shows a lack of attachment to a specific parenting figure. Other abused children are particularly anxious and frightened, not knowing what to expect or what will happen to them next. These children may become acutely apprehensive upon merely hearing another child cry. Still other behaviors common to the abused child are reactions of aggression, hostility, and rage toward both adults and other children.

Children who are chronically abused frequently have difficulties in school both academically and in their peer relationships. They may have little interest in extracurricular activities and demonstrate a general lack of motivation.

THE CRISIS.—In a situation involving a potential abuser and an abusee, the third factor necessary for an abusive event to occur is the precipitating crisis. The crisis is not necessarily a major event; rather, it is a turning point—an event that acts as a catalyst in an already potentially abusive situation. The nature of these crises varies widely from major occurrences such as the death of a relative, illness, divorce, or the loss of a job to seemingly insignificant happenings such as a flat tire, a pot of soup boiling over, the television not working, or a child's crying. Obviously, the definition of a crisis differs widely from family to family and from time to time in the same family. Thus, what constitutes a crisis to one family may not be viewed as such by another family, or even by the same family at a different time.

Because of the social isolation characteristic of abusive families, these parents often have inadequate support systems. They not only lack the trust to turn to others in time of crisis but also lack the internal resources and skills to cope with these stressful situations themselves. They therefore tend to handle this stress in an inadequate way, which only magnifies the impact of the situation. Crises often leave the abusive parent feeling helpless and overwhelmed, and this, in turn, may be enough to trigger child abuse.

Clinical Presentation[10]

The diagnosis of child abuse is often dependent on the physician's awareness of the multiplicity of ways in which this disorder is manifested clinically. Unless a high index of suspicion is maintained, many cases of abuse will go undiagnosed.

PHYSICAL ABUSE.—The diagnosis of physical abuse should be considered in every child who has an injury. After taking a detailed history and doing a thorough physical, the physician should make sure that the injury is adequately explained by and consistent with the history. While recognition of this problem in a severely battered child is not difficult, diagnosis of the more subtle forms of physical abuse is often overlooked.

There are a number of clues in the history that should alert the astute diagnostician to the possibility of child abuse. The first of these is a discrepancy in the history as given by the parents. For instance, each of them may have a different explanation of how the "accident" occurred, or one or both parents may change their original story. A second clue is an unexplained delay between the time of the injury and the date medical attention is sought. A third is an explanation of an injury that is inconsistent with the developmental age of the child. For example, a statement by a parent that a 2-month-old baby was burned after reaching up and turning on the hot water faucet in the bathtub is clearly in error. Fourth, a recurrence of accidents in young children should stimulate the physician to elicit a more detailed explanation of the nature of each accident. While true accidents can be plausibly explained by most parents, abusing parents tend to be vague and evasive as well as inconsistent. A fifth clue is inappropriate parental behavior as seen in the parent who shows little concern over a serious injury, refuses medical attention, or leaves the child in the emergency room and goes home. Finally, one should look for disturbed parent-child interaction. This may be evident when the parent fails to attempt to comfort the child, ignores him, or is openly hostile toward him, or when the child does not go to the parent for comfort.

Physically abused children have physical findings of bruises, burns, fractures, abdominal injuries, lacerations, and human bite marks. The bruises and welts are often seen in various stages of healing, which indicates repeated punishment. Moreover, careful examination may reveal the type of instrument used to inflict the injuries, e.g., a cord or belt mark. The most common burns are cigarette burns most frequently found on the palms, soles, or buttocks. As with bruises, burns are often seen in various stages of healing and may be in the shape of the object used, e.g., an iron or hot plate. Rope burns are usually found on the wrists or ankles, and immersion burns are often symmetrical. This symmetry is often a helpful diagnostic clue. As one might imagine, a child's normal response to contact with hot liquid would be to withdraw one leg quickly, not to leave both legs in together; thus, symmetric immersion burns are usually forced. Abdominal injuries are the most common cause of death in physically abused children, usually secondary to intra-abdominal hemorrhage. Fractures are common in these children, and although they can occur almost anywhere in the body, there are certain diagnostic clues to look for. As with bruises and burns, fractures in various stages of healing indicate repeated trauma. Other findings that should alert the physician are multiple fractures, spiral fractures of the long bones (indicating a twisting injury), and fractures of any kind occurring in a child less than 2 years of age.

Green reported on a study of 60 physically abused children and their parents who were seen at the Downstate Medical Center from 1970 to 1972.[11] The children ranged in age from 5 through 12. Thirty "neglected" children and 30 normal children (and their parents) served as controls. The physically abused children exhibited marked impairment on psychiatric, psychological, and neurologic evaluations as compared with the normal controls. Almost all had significant academic and behavioral problems in school. Even though the physical effects of abuse had passed, the children were left with serious emotional scars due to their experiences.

PHYSICAL NEGLECT.—Physically neglected children can often be recognized by their characteristic appearance, for they are frequently underweight, improperly dressed, and dirty. They are, moreover, often listless, withdrawn, and uncommunicative. Routine medical care has often been neglected, and unattended medical problems such as "cradle cap," severe diaper rash, and multiple infected skin lesions are not uncommon. Whenever a child's height, weight, head circumference, or motor development is found to be significantly less than average, the possibility of physical neglect should be considered.

"Failure to thrive" is a serious medical condition in which a child, without an overt cause, fails to gain and often loses weight (see also chap. 14). It is most frequently seen in infants, but may occur in older children. After careful medical evaluation, some of these cases are found to have an organic cause such as cardiac, metabolic, or gastrointestinal disease (see Table 14–5). Others can be accounted for by understandable and unintentional errors in feeding techniques on the part of the mother. The remainder have no evidence of organic disease and, in most instances, the condition is secondary to psychosocial factors, including disturbed parent-child interaction. Such children usually fall below the third percentile in the standard height and weight curves, but, unlike the organically caused cases, many improve dramatically when separated from their parents and given proper care in the controlled environment of a hospital. Children suffering from nonorganic failure to thrive are often developmentally retarded with respect to motor, social, and intellectual function. These disturbances may respond to appropriate care, nourishment, and stimulation; however, early intervention is imperative if the child is to recover.

EMOTIONAL ABUSE/NEGLECT.—Although varying degrees of this type of maltreatment may be common, evidence to substantiate the diagnosis is difficult to obtain because of its intangible nature. The diagnosis is made principally through observations of the behavior patterns of both the child and the parents. Such children frequently exhibit extremes in behavior: appearing on the one hand overly compliant, passive, and undemanding or, on the other hand, very aggressive, demanding, and angry. They may exhibit other types of atypical behavior, as for example, a young child who acts like an adult by parenting his siblings or an older one who behaves inappropriately infantile by sucking his thumb or wetting the bed. Emotionally abused children often have poor peer relationships and, in general, lag in their physical, emotional, and intellectual development. As a result, learning and discipline problems in school are common.

The parents of the abused child often lack consistency in parenting behavior and may belittle or even terrorize a child for no apparent reason. They may also be cold and rejecting or may seem totally unconcerned about their child's problems. Because of the often subtle nature of these diagnostic clues, it is usually only the most flagrant cases that are diagnosed. Some remain unidentified because of the lack of a sufficiently high index of suspicion on the part of the physician.

SEXUAL ABUSE.[7]—When the sexual abuse of a child is assaultive or violent in nature, his or her physical appearance may be all that is necessary to make the proper diagnosis. One should look for torn, stained, or bloody underclothing as well as bruises, lacerations, and bleeding in the genital and anal areas. In some cases, semen may be found around the mouth or genitals or on the clothing of even small infants. In an older girl, a pregnancy should be viewed with suspicion of possible abuse by the parent or caretaker.

In the absence of obvious physical evidence, one must rely on diagnostic clues obtained from observation of the behavior patterns of both the children and the parents. Such children often appear withdrawn or engage in fantasy or inappropriately infantile behavior. They may have trouble forming adequate peer relationships and are frequently unwilling to participate in physical activities. They may engage in delinquent acts and may run away from home. The parents, often victims of sexual abuse in their own childhood, may encourage the children to perform sexual acts in front of them or may encourage prostitution or pornography. They may appear overly protective of the children and, at times, even jealous of a child's friends. Not unexpectedly, in such families marital problems are common, as are alcohol and drug abuse. Sexual abuse is the least frequently reported type of child abuse. Not only is physical injury frequently not in evidence, but also, since the abuser is usually the parent, other family members are frightened and hesitant to reveal what has happened.

Management

The physician's role in the management of child abuse may be divided into four major areas of responsibility—diagnosis, treatment, reporting, and prevention.

The diagnosis of abuse begins with the physician having a sufficiently high index of suspicion and evaluating beyond the simple treatment of an injury. The history and physical examination, as well as the characteristic behavior patterns of the children and parents, should alert the physician to this diagnosis. Once identification of the problem has been made, certain laboratory studies should be ordered. Although it is beyond the scope of this chapter to discuss these studies in detail, radiologic studies such as a bone survey and photographic documentation of the injuries are usually part of the diagnostic evaluation. It is obvious that the treatment of the child's injuries is an essential aspect of management, but it must not be forgotten that treatment of the parents is also critical, for without this intervention the abuse is likely to recur. Many child abuse centers have instituted treatment programs for parents with the idea that this better serves the long-term interests of the children than incarceration of the parent under existing criminal statutes.

Reporting a suspected child abuse case to the appropriate child welfare service is essential. Since the children are too young or too frightened to act as their own advocates, someone else must do so by contacting the proper authorities. The advocate may be a concerned friend, neighbor, or relative, as well as a professional. When the report is received by the agency, a caseworker is usually assigned to investigate whether or not child abuse or neglect has indeed occurred. Once a decision has been made that child abuse exists, disposition must be determined. Frequently this is done via court action. The basic decision that must be made is whether or not the home is safe for the child. If not, temporary shelter or foster home placement may be necessary.

As Green points out, therapy for a case of child abuse is directed to the three underlying pathogenetic factors: the abusing parent, the child, and the environmental situations that act as crises.[12] In other words, an attempt is made to "strengthen the family and its childrearing capacity."[12] A multidisciplinary approach is most effective, in which the family physician, psychiatrist, or psychologist, social worker, and nurse collaborate to help the family make the necessary changes that will enable it to have a constructive, instead of a destructive, effect on the child's health and development.[6] Psychotherapy (individual or group), counseling, and child-rearing education are indicated for the parents, along with various types of home assistance (e.g., homemaking services, day care for children). These parents require a great deal of support and encouragement for they are usually hesitant to accept help because of their nontrusting attitude and long history of social isolation.

The abused child also needs rehabilitative psychotherapy to enable him to cope with the effects of the abuse. Long after the physical evidence of mistreatment has cleared, many of these children continue to suffer from "a wide range of cognitive, developmental, neurological and emotional deficits."[12] Unless the emotional effects are reversed, there is a chance that the abused individual will become an abusing parent—a link in the recurring cycle of abuse that was described earlier. Finally, there must be some means developed to help the family deal more effectively with the life stresses that befall the members. The availability of immediate assistance in case of an emergency (an emergency hot-line) and regular home visits by social workers or nurses will provide a supporting crutch. With successful psychotherapy, the parents may be able to modify their reactions to stress, so that instead of acting impulsively and hostilely, they will become more mature in their responses.

Prognostically, it has been estimated that a majority of the families in which child abuse occurs can be rehabilitated so that the family provides a safe and constructive environment for the child. Thus, while the initial impression of many health professionals upon seeing an abused child is that the situation is hopeless, such is not the case in most instances. In addition to avoiding a pessimistic attitude, medical personnel must also refrain from being judgmental or having hostile feelings toward the abusing parent if they are to provide meaningful help and support.[13] After all, child abuse is really a symptom of an illness that affects the family; the parents require treatment and understanding if the illness is to be successfully resolved. Of course, the optimal form of treatment is prevention. Some medical centers now have programs designed to identify the potentially abusing parent in the prenatal and postpartum periods and to institute preventive measures at that point.

SUMMARY

Lying at the root of the vast majority of cases of child abuse is a disturbance in family function, specifically in the parent-child relationship. Defective parenting is usually the result of learned behavior, the abusing parent having been exposed to poor parental role models as a child. Abusing parents are characterized as being nontrusting, having little self-esteem, tending toward social isolation, and lacking the capacity to deal effectively with stressful situations and events. They have unrealistic expectations of their children and, consequently, make demands that the children cannot meet. Frequently there is marital discord between husband and wife, neither of whom is sufficiently mature to serve as a good marriage partner or function in the role of a parent.

Given a child who is in some way seen by them as being "special" (in a negative sense) and a precipitating stressful event, such parents are liable to become abusive to the child. This abuse may be physical, psychological, or sexual. While there are mild forms, the effects of child abuse can be very serious, even lethal. Children who recover from the immediate effects of physical abuse may be emotionally scarred for life. For these children, academic, social, and behavioral problems are frequently the long-term residuals of abuse.

Most significant, the individual who was abused as a child has a greater risk of later becoming an abusive parent. Thus, a repetitive cycle is established whereby the abusive parent is both the cause and the result of child abuse. Interrupting this cycle requires that therapy be directed to both the parent and the child. Obviously, the prevention of child abuse is the best way of dealing with this problem; if the tendency for abuse can be recognized in a new parent, prophylactic measures can be instituted.

REFERENCES

1. Somers A.R.: Marital status, health, and use of health services. *J.A.M.A.* 241(17):1818–1822, 1979.
2. Lefer G.L.: Marriage and the stages of parenthood, in Simons R.C., Pardes H. (eds.): *Understanding Human Behavior in Health and Illness*. Baltimore, Williams & Wilkins Co., 1977.
3. Radbill S.X.: *A History of Child Abuse and Infanticide*. Chicago, The University of Chicago Press, 1965.
4. Fontana V.J.: *The Maltreated Child: The Maltreated Syndrome in Children*. Springfield, Ill., Charles C Thomas, Publisher, 1964.
5. Kempe C.H., et al.: The battered child syndrome. *J.A.M.A.* 181:17, 1962.
6. Taylor L., Newberger E.H.: Child abuse in the international year of the child. *N. Engl. J. Med.* 301:1205, 1979.
7. Tilelli J.A., Turek D., Jaffe A.C.: Sexual abuse of children. *N. Engl. J. Med.* 302:319, 1980.
8. McNeese M., Hebeler J.: The abused child, *CIBA Found. Symp.* 29(5), 1977.
9. Erikson E.: *Childhood and Society*, ed 2. New York, W.W. Norton & Company, Inc., 1950.
10. U.S. Department of Health, Education, and Welfare Interdisciplinary Glossary on Child Abuse and Neglect: *Legal, Medical, Social Work Terms*, 1978.
11. Green A.: Parental dysfunction and child abuse, in Simons R.C., Pardes H. (eds.): *Understanding Human Behavior in Health and*

Illness. Baltimore, Williams & Wilkins Co., 1977.
12. Green A.H.: Current perspectives on child maltreatment. *Resident & Staff Physician* 25(5):150, May 1979.
13. Stechler G.: Facing the problem of the sexually abused child (editorial). *N. Engl. J. Med.* 302:348, 1980.

RECOMMENDED READING

Giovannoni J.M., Becerra R.M.: *Defining Child Abuse.* New York, Free Press, 1979.

Helfer R.E., Kempe C.H. (eds.): *The Battered Child.* Chicago, The University of Chicago Press, 1974.

Helfer R.E., Kempe C.H. (eds.): *Child Abuse and Neglect: The Family and the Community.* Cambridge, Mass., Ballinger Publishing Company, 1976.

Helfer R.E.: *The Diagnostic Process and Treatment Programs.* National Center on Child Abuse and Neglect. U.S. Department of Health, Education, and Welfare, Publication No. (OHD) 75-69, 1975.

Kempe C.H.: Approaches to preventing child abuse. *Am. J. Dis. Child.* 130:941, 1976.

Kempe C.H., Helfer R.E. (eds.): *Helping the Battered Child and Family.* Philadelphia, J.B. Lippincott Co., 1972.

Martin H.P. (ed.): *The Abused Child: A Multidisciplinary Approach to Developmental Issues and Treatment.* Cambridge, Mass., Ballinger Publishing Company, 1976.

Steele B.F.: *Working with the Abusive Parent from a Psychiatric Point of View.* National Center on Child Abuse and Neglect. U.S. Department of Health, Education, and Welfare, Publication No. (OHD) 75-70, 1975.

17 / An Introduction to Adolescent Development

ANTHONY NOWELS, M.D., RICHARD P. TOISTER, Ph.D., and JONATHAN J. BRAUNSTEIN, M.D.

THERE ARE ABOUT 40 million teenagers in the United States, nearly 20% of our population. A brief overview of the effects of illness in this age group on the individual and society will emphasize the medical importance of this stage in the life cycle. In 1971 mental health care for teenagers cost nearly $500 million.[1] This figure reflects only the tip of the iceberg when the cost to society due to disability and unfulfilled potential is also included in the analysis. It is astounding that nearly one out of every ten teenagers will consult a mental health professional.[1] Another indicator of the magnitude of the psychological difficulties occurring in adolescence is the National Institute of Mental Health estimate that nearly 250 million school days are lost each year because of emotional and family problems.

There is general agreement that emotional problems contribute significantly to the more than 1 million juvenile offenders who go before our courts each year and the more than 1 million "runaways" reported annually.[2,3] Certain severe debilitating mental disorders originate during the teenage years: acute psychotic decompensations, which probably reflect early manifestations of schizophrenia; severe depressions, which recent studies suggest are far more common than previously suspected; and manic-depressive illness, which has only recently been recognized to have its onset during adolescence.[4,5] Finally, over the past several decades the suicide rate among 15–19-year-olds has nearly tripled, making this a relatively common cause of death in this age group.[6]

Teenagers also suffer from a variety of serious physical ailments. Some idea of their prevalence can be gained from Figure 17–1, which lists the causes of death in teenagers and young adults. Other medical problems common in adolescence are venereal disease, parasitic infections, and dermatologic disorders. Of great medical concern is the incidence of teenage pregnancies. Recent data indicate that alcohol and drug abuse are prevalent problems among adolescents (see chap. 12).

This overview should not be interpreted to mean that mental and physical illnesses are an integral part of adolescence; far from it, most teenagers manage to go through this stage of life without such problems. Still, the information strongly supports the need for careful analysis and management of the special problems that teenagers bring to the health care community.

GENERAL CONCEPTS

Different specialists choose to see adolescence from different vantage points. The psychoanalyst may view adolescence as a period of awakening genital sexuality with accompanying adjustment of the psychic apparatus to the tensions so created. The endocrinologist may focus on the development of secondary sexual characteristics, hormonal blood levels, or the role of hypothalamic-releasing factors in the elaboration of the pituitary hormones that regulate gonadal function.[7,8]

Social scientists might emphasize as the im-

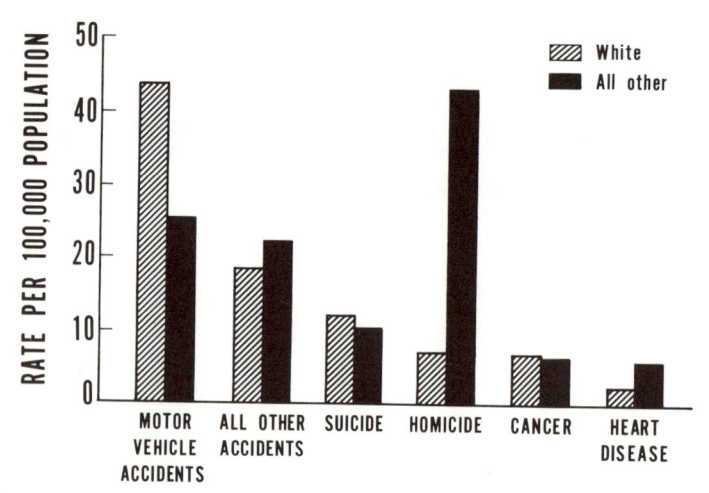

Fig 17–1.—Major causes of death in the United States, 1976, for persons aged 15–24. (From *Healthy People,* The Surgeon General's Report on Health Promotion and Disease Prevention, Department of Health, Education, and Welfare, Publication No. 79-55071, 1979.)

portant events of adolescence the social changes that occur, including the teenager's separation from his or her family, the assumption of adult responsibilities, and the selection of a career.[9] Cognitive theorists might stress the significant changes in intellectual ability that take place during this period, pointing out that these developing skills have enormous impact on later functioning and adjustment in society.[10,11] Whatever one's point of view, however, the adolescent period is usually considered to encompass the years 11–20, during which all the above facets of development take place. For many in our society, however, especially those who acquire a higher education, adolescence extends well into the twenties.

Both historians and anthropologists have pointed out that the social definition of adolescence has varied depending on the time in history and the culture in which it has been studied. One does not have to go far back into the Industrial Revolution to find a time when childhood seemed to merge quickly with adulthood. In the early part of this century, teenagers in our society were expected to assume adult roles at an earlier age. Anthropological studies have found that in some cultures the adolescent period is extremely brief and regimented, offering little opportunity for the complex behavior seen in Western society.[12,13]

With the onset of adolescence, the relative psychological and social stability that characterizes the grade-school years is upset, primarily as a result of biologic and physical changes that begin to take place. Rapid acceleration of growth and sexual development occurs during the adolescent period, and by the time it is over a sexually mature adult has emerged in place of the child. Sexual maturation is due to the effects of increased levels of sex hormones, primarily androgens in boys and estrogens in girls.[8,14] The activity of these hormones produces the clinical manifestations of puberty: the *secondary sexual characteristics* (consisting in women of breast enlargement, the growth of pubic hair, and the development of a female body contour, and in men of enlargement of the penis and testes, the growth of pubic, axillary, and facial hair, and the development of a muscular body build), the *onset of menarche* (in girls), and *sperm production* (in boys).

The specific neuroendocrine mechanisms responsible for the onset and progression of these pubertal changes have been the subject of intensive investigation. It is known that the hypothalamus elaborates a chemical agent known as gonadotropin-releasing hormone

(GRH), which stimulates the pituitary to secrete FSH and LH, the gonadotropic hormones that control the function of the gonads. In response to FSH and LH, estrogens and testosterone are elaborated by the ovaries and testes, respectively. The secretion of GRH is regulated by the effects of other areas of the brain on the hypothalamus and by the level of sex hormones in the blood. In the man, testosterone acts by a negative feedback mechanism to inhibit the secretion of FSH and LH; in the woman, estrogens have this inhibitory effect and, in addition, stimulate the release of LH in the mid-menstrual cycle (a positive feedback effect).

In the early stages of puberty, there is a gradual increase in the prepubertal levels of FSH and LH in the blood, which continues throughout adolescence.[8,14] One of the first indications of a change in the output of pituitary gonadotropin from the constant low-grade secretion of the child to the episodic secretion of the adult is the pulsatile release of LH that occurs during sleep in the pubertal period, a phenomenon that is unique to this time of life.[15] As puberty proceeds in the girl, the secretion of the gonadotropins comes to resemble the monthly cyclical pattern characteristic of the mature woman.

The enhanced release of the gonadotropins that occurs at the time of puberty is thought to be due to a decrease in the sensitivity of the hypothalamus to the inhibitory effects of the low levels of circulating sex hormones present in the prepubertal child. Also, the pituitary responsiveness to GRH increases with the onset of puberty. The heightened output of sex hormones by the gonads can be explained by both the effect of the higher levels of gonadotropins in the blood and the greater sensitivity of the gonads (in males) to these hormones. In addition to the gonadal secretion of sex hormones, the adrenal glands (stimulated by the adrenocorticotropic hormone) increase their output of androgens at this time. The complex hormonal events that are postulated to take place during sexual maturation are listed in Table 17–1. It seems that the sexual development of the adolescent is the consequence of physiological events that occur at several different functional levels, including the hypothalamus, pituitary, gonad, and adrenal gland.[8]

The biologic and physical changes experienced by the adolescent are accompanied by psychological and behavioral reactions. Some of these reactions are related to an increase in the teenager's sexual drive; others can be at-

TABLE 17–1.—HORMONAL EVENTS ASSOCIATED WITH SEXUAL MATURATION

Hypothalamic-pituitary axis	Decreasing sensitivity of hypothalamus (and pituitary?) to negative feedback by gonadal steroids	
	Increasing capacity to secrete gonadotropins (non-feedback related)	Increasing levels of serum LH and FSH
	Pubertal sleep-induced episodic release of LH	
	Development of adult pattern of episodic release of gonadotropins	
	Increasing pituitary response to GRH	
	Development of positive feedback response to gonadal steroids in females	Cyclic preovulatory gonadotropin surge resulting in ovulation
Gonads	Increasing gonadal sensitivity to gonadotropins (in males)	
	Increasing gonadal steroid secretion associated with increasing gonadotropin levels	Increasing serum levels of gonadal steroids and adrenal androgens
Adrenal	Increasing adrenal secretion of androgens	

Source: Swerdloff R.S.: *Med. Clin. North Am.* 62(2):351, 1978. (Used by permission.)

tributed to the effects of the physical and sexual changes taking place on the adolescent's body image.[6,16] The increased sexual drive is manifested as an ill-defined sense of bodily tension and restlessness and a heightened interest in sexual activities. For many adolescents, the emerging feelings of sexuality are a source of concern and anxiety, and coping with this aroused sexual drive poses a significant psychological problem. A stable body image is dependent on a constancy in one's physical appearance. An adolescent who is experiencing rapid changes in body size, proportions, and sexual characteristics may find it difficult to adjust psychologically to these alterations. Indeed, one of the fundamental tasks of this stage of life is to integrate these changes into the individual's emerging sense of "who he or she is."

The physical and sexual development of adolescence is also associated with social demands for changes in roles and behavior. In other words, as the child gradually becomes more like an adult physically, he is expected to begin to act in a more adult fashion. Increasing independence from parents, the assumption of self-responsibility, the development of the capacity for heterosexual relationships, and the choosing of a career are all psychosocial tasks that confront the adolescent as he emerges into the adult world. Most important, the teenager must acquire a new sense of his own identity, especially with respect to his relationships with those about him, in the face of the rapid social changes that are occurring in his life. These challenges generate significant psychological conflicts as the adolescent tries to meet them, at times making this period of life one of great emotional turmoil for the child and, as a result, one of great concern for his or her parents. Ultimately, the successful resolution of these conflicts and the achievement of these psychosocial tasks result in an individual ready to assume the roles, privileges, and responsibilities of the young adult.

In describing the period of adolescence, we have chosen to divide it into three phases: early adolescence, mid-adolescence, and late adolescence. These three phases will be discussed in terms of the individual's (1) physical and biologic development, (2) psychosexual development, (3) psychosocial development, and (4) cognitive development.

EARLY ADOLESCENCE (AGES 11–13 IN GIRLS AND 13–15 IN BOYS)

This phase is characterized by rapid physical growth and biologic change, increasing conflict with parental authority regarding independence, and a growing sense of peer pressure and group conformity.

Physical and Biologic Changes[17]

As adolescence begins, there is a marked increase in the rate of growth, sometimes referred to as a "growth spurt." The increase in height and weight that occurs usually takes place earlier in girls (Fig 17–2), so that they are generally taller and heavier than boys between the ages of 12 and 13. Studies have shown that there are differences among normal adolescents with respect to the age of onset of the growth spurt. For instance, boys may experience the spurt as early as $10^1/_2$ or as late as 16; among girls, it may begin anywhere from $9^1/_2$ to $14^1/_2$ years of age.

The age at which the other physical changes of puberty, such as secondary sexual characteristics, make their appearance also varies. Thus, at 13 some adolescents are well on their way to sexual maturity, while others this same age have hardly begun to develop sexually. Once it begins, sexual development proceeds in an orderly fashion. The secondary sexual characteristics commonly appear in a predictable sequence, the usual order of events being shown in Table 17–2. Of particular diagnostic significance for the physician is the presence of straight pubic hair in an adolescent, which indicates that puberty has begun. This finding can be used to reassure worried parents who are concerned that their teenager may not be developing adequately.

Boys generally feel positive about their increased size and weight as it heralds the onset of "manhood." Such rapid growth, especially

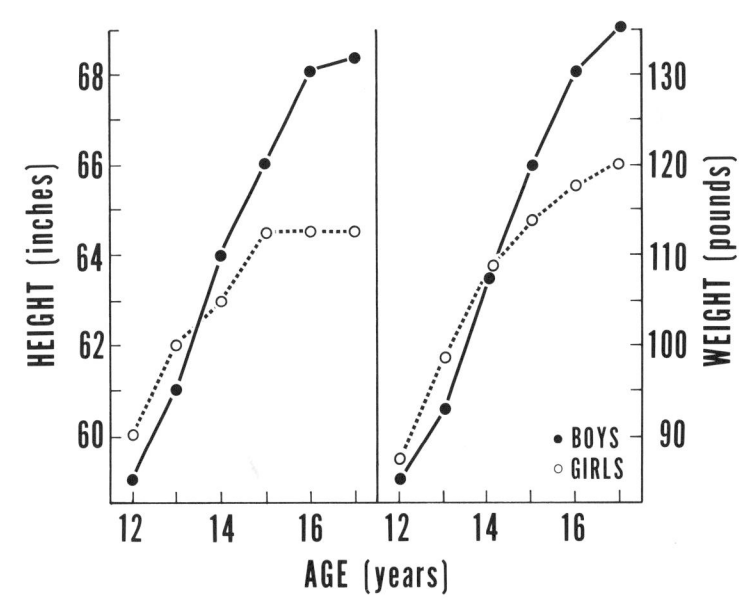

Fig 17-2.—Average height and weight for boys (●) and girls (○) during adolescence. (Adapted from Vaughan V.C. III, McKay R.J. Jr., Behrman R.E. [eds.]: *Nelson Textbook of Pediatrics,* ed. 11. Philadelphia, W.B. Saunders Co., 1979.)

in the younger adolescent boy, however, is often accompanied by a stage of awkwardness that can adversely affect his developing self-concept and impair his self-esteem and self-confidence. Girls are particularly sensitive to changes in body height and weight and that early in adolescence they are usually larger than boys of the same age. Pre-adolescent and early adolescent girls are often worried about becoming obese. Fad diets and concern over "fattening foods" become popular topics of conversation at this age. The health professional should be aware of the pathologic implications of overconcern with weight in this age group. A severe psychiatric disorder, usually seen in girls, called anorexia nervosa may arise at this time and is characterized by a reduction in appetite or a refusal to eat, leading to severe loss of weight.

Pubertal changes in sexual characteristics also result in concern on the part of teenagers. Teens with erroneous or inappropriate information, as for instance the girl who is not emotionally or informationally prepared for menstruation, may become embarrassed and self-conscious. If, on the other hand, an adolescent has received proper guidance within an accepting home atmosphere, these physical changes are seen as part of growing up and are generally accepted.

TABLE 17-2.—Order of Appearance of Secondary Sexual Characteristics

MALE	FEMALE
1. Growth of testes	1. Breasts enlarge—"budding"
2. Straight pubic hair	2. Straight pubic hair
3. Increased penile size	3. Growth spurt
4. Voice change	4. Kinky pubic hair
5. First ejaculation	5. Menarche
6. Kinky pubic hair	6. Axillary hair
7. Growth spurt	7. Rounding out of breasts
8. Axillary hair	
9. Beard	

Psychosexual Development

Traditional psychoanalytic theory describes early adolescence as a time when endocrine changes signal an increase in instinctual drives. This "awakening" sexuality may produce anxiety, which reduces ego control, often resulting in emotional lability and a confusion of purpose. At one moment the young adolescent is cooperative and content; the next, he is argumentative and irritable. Parents often find these sudden behavioral changes both frustrating and perplexing.

Freud viewed adolescence as the genital stage of development, in which libidinal energy begins to be directed toward heterosexual love objects. Early in this stage, intense romantic "crushes" may develop, so that rock or movie stars may be "worshiped" by the teenager. In this way, sexual drives are worked out in a safe fashion; that is, sexual feelings are released in a situation in which there is little chance for the actual expression of physical urges or for rejection by the admired figure. During the course of adolescence, however, more direct expressions of sexuality become increasingly common.

Studies have shown that adolescent sexual attitudes and behavior are influenced greatly by social and cultural variables such as socioeconomic background, race, religious views, and the prevailing social attitudes. Youth from the upper social classes, those without strong religious affiliations, and blacks tend to be more liberal in their sexual attitudes and behavior than their counterparts.[6, 18] Changes have taken place in teenage sexual activity in this country over the past 25 years (Table 17–3). In particular, there has been a striking increase in premarital sex among girls, while the frequency of premarital sex for boys has remained about the same. Even more recent data indicate that over 50% of girls aged 15–19 in the United States are sexually active.[19] Whether this finding is due to sampling differences or to the changing social atmosphere (media and public attitudes regarding sex) is difficult to say. There is no doubt that teenagers today have more opportunity to view sexual themes in movies and television and read about sex in popular publications. Also, the advent of oral contraceptives has played a significant role in bringing about the changes in female adolescent sexual behavior.

Psychosocial Development

While Erikson sees the psychosocial crisis of adolescence as one of "identity versus role diffusion," other investigators have chosen to separate psychosocial development in this period into two related issues.[18] The first of these, which is associated with early adolescence, has been characterized as the issue of "group identity versus alienation"; the second, which is associated with later adolescence, has been described as a problem of "individual identity versus role diffusion." The latter corresponds to Erikson's conceptualization. Thus, in early adolescence the main social theme is the development of peer relationships and a concept of oneself as related to the group. During this time, it is very important for the individual to be like his peers, and adolescents share common heroes (rock groups), wear the same "uniform" (jeans), and so forth.

Interaction among teenagers occurs in several settings: in large groups or crowds, in smaller more intimate groups or cliques, and among individual friends. Dunphy points out that there is a gradual change in teenage relationships as one moves from early to late adolescence.[20] Specifically, he lists the following five stages of adolescent group interaction:

TABLE 17–3.—
ADOLESCENT SEXUAL ACTIVITY

	PERCENT HAVING SEXUAL INTERCOURSE	
	BEFORE AGE 16	BY AGE 19
Males		
1948	39	72
1973	44	72
Females		
1953	3	20
1973	30	57

Source: Newman B., Newman P.R.: *Development Through Life: A Psychosocial Approach.* Homewood, Ill., Dorsey Press, 1975, p. 195. (Used by permission.)

Early adolescence

Stage 1   Precrowd stage. Isolated unisexual cliques.
Stage 2   Beginning of the crowd. Unisexual cliques in group-to-group interaction.

Stage 3	Transition. Unisexual cliques with upper-status members forming a heterosexual clique.
Stage 4	Fully developed crowd. Heterosexual cliques in close association.

Late adolescence

Stage 5	Beginning of crowd disintegration. Loosely associated groups of couples.

In this model, the young adolescent usually functions in stages 1 and 2; that is, peer groups are "mono" or "uni" sexual, meaning that social relationships occur in cliques of same-sexed individuals. Because of wide individual differences at this age, however, it is not uncommon to see social gatherings of boys and girls where some members relate heterosexually on an individual basis, while others relate to members of the opposite sex only via the clique or group. For example, if 13–14-year-olds attend a party, some boys might interact with girls on a one-to-one basis (dancing), while others interact only in small groups of two or three boys to two or three girls. This is an example of stages 2 and 3 in the above model. As the adolescent matures physically and socially, individual heterosexual relationships become more frequent. Popularity in the peer group depends on many factors such as physical attractiveness, athletic skills, intelligence, common religious membership, and special attributes or talent.

Young adolescents who have difficulty adjusting emotionally to the social changes taking place or have inadequate social skills may find this stage of development very disturbing. On the one hand, there is growing social pressure to become independent from the family and to rely more on peer relationships, while, on the other, their own insecurity and lack of ability may make it difficult to socialize or identify with a group.

Cognitive Development

According to Piaget, the adolescent goes through the final phase of mental development or the period of formal operations. In this period, the individual begins to develop a true symbolic sense of the world. He begins to think in hypothetical terms and is capable of conceptualizing what are and what are not logical possibilities. Intellectually, the young adolescent begins to "manipulate" the world symbolically. While it is not possible to identify a specific age during which each adolescent enters the period of formal operations, most children become more capable of complex symbolic reasoning by age 13 or 14.[21]

The development of these cognitive abilities affects social and emotional development. The teenager begins to think about himself and his relationship to others. At times, this takes on the qualities of egocentrism or excessive self-interest. As a type of reasoning, formal operational logic becomes of interest in and of itself; the process becomes enjoyable. Thus, adolescents may enjoy "thinking about thinking" and nuances of thought may become self-rewarding and exciting. Adults often are puzzled by the many variations on a theme that young adolescents present in discussions, not realizing that the symbolic manipulation itself is what is being attempted. If adults misinterpret this as "argumentativeness" or "negativity," a great deal of misunderstanding and problems in communication may arise. Therefore, while increased cognitive abilities in adolescence can be exciting for both the child and the parent, they can also lead to frustration and confusion.

MID-ADOLESCENCE (AGES 14–16 IN GIRLS AND 15–17 IN BOYS)

Physical and Biologic Changes

By age 16, most girls have achieved approximately 100% of their mature height and about 90% of mature weight. Boys, on the other hand, continue to show significant increases in both height and weight beyond this age. During mid-adolescence the average boy will grow 2–3 inches in height and add about 15 pounds in body weight. As a result, boys become taller, heavier, and physically stronger than girls as mid-adolescence is completed. Associated with these physical

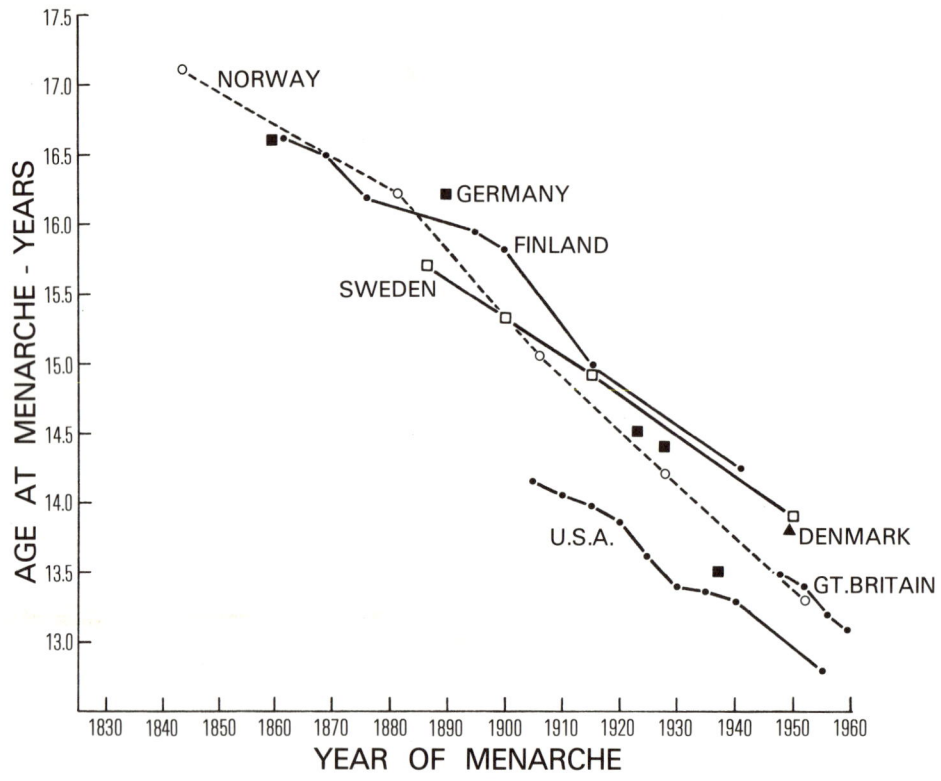

Fig 17-3.—Cross-cultural trend in average age at menarche, 1840–1960. (From Tanner J.M.: *Growth at Adolescence.* Oxford, Blackwell Scientific Publications, 1962. Used by permission.)

changes are corresponding changes in sexual maturation.

Menarche or the onset of menses takes place in mid-adolescence, about 2 years after the beginning of puberty. An interesting observation is that the average age of menarche has shown a steady decline since the 19th century (Fig 17–3). Today in the United States it occurs on the average at about 12½ years of age, with a range of 10–16½. Several explanations have been given for this trend, the most popular of which is that better nutrition associated with modern diets has led to earlier sexual maturation. Since ovulation usually occurs about 1 to 2 years following menarche, the age at which adolescents can conceive has also been steadily declining. This, along with the greater degree of sexual activity among adolescent girls, may be a factor in the rising number of teenage pregnancies over the past quarter-century.

Another interesting trend is the increase in physical size of children and adolescents over the past half-century. Figure 17–4 shows the height differences of white male children and teenagers in North America in the years 1880 and 1960. Fifteen-year-old boys in 1960 were on the average 5 inches taller than boys in 1880. Again, nutrition appears to be a contributing factor in the greater physical development of modern-day children and adolescents.

Psychosexual Development

During mid-adolescence, the teenager is "moving away" from the family and acquiring closer peer relationships. An important part of this growing independence is the development of heterosexual relationships and the beginning of regular dating. According to the psychoanalytic view, at this time there is a gradual return to ego control, allowing the

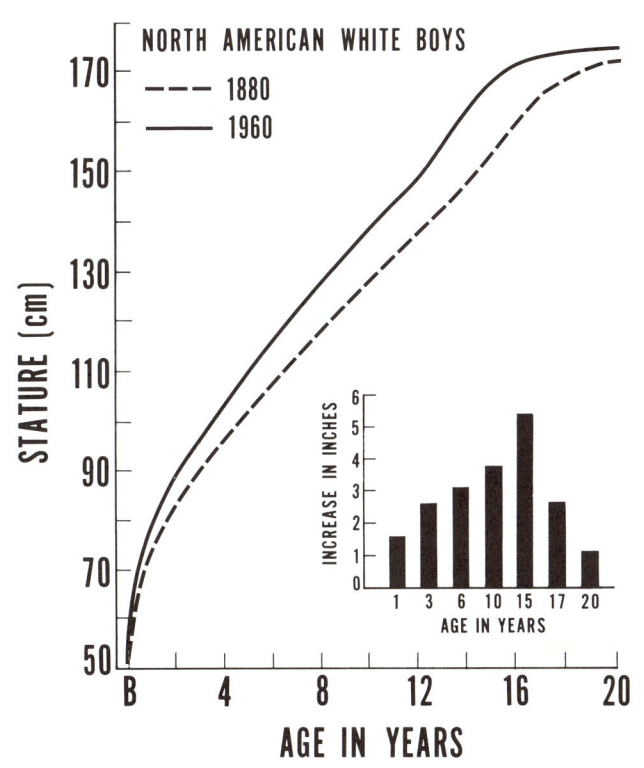

Fig 17–4.—Schematic curves of mean height in 1880 and 1960. Inset shows differences between the curves at selected ages. (From Meredith H.V.: *Adv. Child Dev. Behav.* 1:90 1963. Used by permission.)

expression of sexual drives through the development of more stable relationships with members of the opposite sex. These relationships do not necessarily have the tenderness and intimacy that are associated with them in later adolescence and adulthood, since most adolescents at this stage have not acquired the capacity to integrate the feelings of sexuality with those of love and tenderness. Nor is overt sexuality expressed; rather there is a gradual exploration of sexual feelings and behavior, which may progress from hand-holding, to kissing, and to petting. For some adolescents, however, overt sexual relationships do occur.

There is often a reawakening of feelings of the Oedipus complex, with their associated fears and inhibitions, in teenagers during this period. Therefore, some may find it very threatening to acknowledge strong sexual or physical feelings.

As indicated, the percent of male teenagers experiencing sexual intercourse has probably not changed much in the last 25 years. However, a much larger percentage of girls have reported sexual experience by ages 16 and 19 (see Table 17–3). Engaging in sexual intercourse at this age can be related to many psychological, cultural, and sociological factors. Reiss suggests that in this country we have four basic attitudes or beliefs regarding premarital sex;[22] these influence an adolescent's decision about whether or not to engage in it.

1. *Abstinence.*—Premarital sex is wrong for both men and women.
2. *Permissiveness with affection.*—Premarital sex is right for men and women under certain conditions (e.g., if there is a stable relationship with love).
3. *Permissiveness without affection.*—Premarital sex is right without any reference to affection or stability.

4. *Double standard.*—Premarital sex is accepted for men but wrong for women.

Psychosocial Development

Middle adolescence is a time when teenagers begin to gain greater autonomy from family ties and concomitantly to form close-knit social groups and individual friendships. In Dunphy's model of group interaction discussed previously, the mid-adolescent period is when heterosexual groups or cliques become more common; that is, the teenager develops close friendships and heterosexual relationships within the context of particular group affiliations. Since the family still serves as a reference point for the adolescent at this stage, he must reconcile the expanding influence that his peer group has on him with parental values and restrictions.

FAMILY RELATIONSHIPS.—One major area of conflict for the adolescent is giving up childhood dependence in order to become an independent, self-sufficient adult member of society. The rejection of adult values as a step toward this autonomy is characteristic of this stage of adolescence, giving rise to the term "adolescent rebelliousness." The way in which parents handle the teenager's attempts to achieve independence becomes a critical factor in family relationships. Parents who are overly strict (either because of their own fears of losing control of the child or because of insecurity that prevents their accepting outside influences on him) and parents who are overly permissive (because of an inability to tolerate conflict) are examples of undesirable extremes of parental behavior. If parents provide firm guidelines, coupled with encouragement for the teenager to discuss parental restrictions openly, the transition will be less stressful for both parties. To follow this approach, however, parents must themselves have resolved their emotional conflicts in the areas of dependence and control. Since most adolescents are ambivalent about gaining autonomy, it is important for parents to provide an atmosphere of understanding along with guidelines for achieving this independence.

Garrison and Garrison have summarized the effects of different home atmospheres on adolescent behavior (Table 17–4).[23] A firm but warm and democratic home environment, where respect is shown for the teenager's opinions, seems to provide the best atmosphere for the development of positive social characteristics and attitudes in the teenager. Where parents are inconsistent in their guidance and discipline, rebellion on the part of the adolescent is not uncommon, as if he is searching for some sense of direction to assist him in achieving independence and self-responsibility. On the other hand, an overly strict, dominating home atmosphere can result in unquestioned obedience or determined resistance. The latter may occur overtly (i.e., a direct challenge to authority) or covertly (i.e., forgetting to do chores, underachieving in school), both of which are extremely frustrating to parents and teachers alike. An overly protective parental attitude may prevent the adolescent from breaking away from his dependence on the family, stifle his attempts at self-direction, and, in general, delay his psychosocial maturation. Thus, conflicts arising from unhealthy home environments can adversely affect a teenager's personality and his relationships with "authority" figures.

PEER RELATIONSHIPS.—In this phase of adolescence, teenagers develop close personal relationships and begin to interact with members of the opposite sex on an individual basis. While many factors influence an adolescent's choice of friends, similarity (someone like oneself), age, and proximity (living nearby) appear most important. Surveys indicate that the closeness and stability of friendships increase with age during this time. The formation of close friendships has a critical effect on the identity (the formation of self-concept) of an adolescent. Teenagers who are popular are likely to feel more self-confident and have higher self-esteem than those who are isolated and have few friends. One method of assessing popularity or social status among adolescents is the technique of sociometry.[24] In this procedure, individuals are asked to rank others on the basis of who they

TABLE 17–4.—RELATIONSHIP OF THE HOME ATMOSPHERE TO BEHAVIOR PATTERNS OF ADOLESCENTS

HOME ATMOSPHERE	RESULTING BEHAVIOR PATTERNS
Firm, warm, democratic	Self-direction
	Lack of tension
	Realistic compliance
	Initiative, independence
	Friendship with peers
	Exchange of ideas
	Social interaction
Indulgent, protective	Delayed maturity
	Lack of self-direction
	Lack of responsibility
	Low self-reliance
	Social interaction
Pressure for compliance	Slavish conformity or rebellious independence
	Withdrawal, moodiness
Inconsistent discipline	Lack of self-direction
	Lack of growth in independence
	Open rebellion
	Lack of responsibility
Stern, autocratic	Blind obedience or aggressive independence
	Conflict over dependence
	Covert or overt rebellion
	Lack of responsibility
	Withdrawal, moodiness

Adapted from Garrison K.C., Garrison K.C., Jr.: *Psychology of Adolescence*, ed. 7. Englewood Cliffs, N.J., Prentice-Hall, Inc., 1975.

would most prefer as chums or friends. The results can be depicted in a diagram called a sociogram that visually shows the relative degree of popularity of individuals in a group.

With respect to adolescent heterosexual relationships, most societies provide standard guidelines for courtship or dating between the sexes. Dating may occur irregularly with different partners or take the form of "going steady" or being "pinned." Most mid-adolescents date many individuals before seeing only one person on a steady basis. Going steady implies a more permanent commitment both socially and sexually. While mid-adolescents date individually, group parties and double dating are still common. Couples often serve as role models for each other as boys and girls imitate a friend's approach to a date. While "making out" or petting is common, sexual intercourse is not frequently done at this stage.[25]

Dating patterns can be related to social class variables. Studies suggest that dating in middle-class children today begins at earlier ages than in previous decades. Perhaps the trend toward earlier physical maturation discussed previously explains this. Also, contemporary middle-class parents seem to encourage the earlier development of social relationships, especially for their daughters.

THE DEVELOPMENT OF IDENTITY.—The term "identity" is difficult to define exactly but a good working concept of it is the individual's "awareness of who he is as well as his perception of the assessment of others regarding who he is."[18] Thus, identity is defined partly by the person and partly by those around him. There are many dimensions to one's total sense of self-identity, including intellectual, emotional, vocational, ethical, socioeconomic, sexual, and familial components.[18] While a person's self-concept is in the process of being formed from the earliest period of life throughout childhood, the development of identity that takes place during adolescence is especially critical because of the marked physical and psychosocial changes that the individual undergoes. The adolescent's view of himself as an autonomous person really begins to take shape as he separates from his family and assumes a greater degree of independence in his interaction with others.

Feedback from others regarding appearance and capabilities, as well as exploring different roles, are examples of ways the adolescent develops a sense of identity. The variety of behaviors and changes in personality that he exhibits may be confusing to adults who do not recognize the underlying reason for his actions. Unfortunately, these behaviors are often interpreted by adults as being exceedingly narcissistic or self-indulgent, causing them to become upset with the adolescent.

Second, the teenager begins to contemplate himself actively in relationship to the world about him. He develops a "future sense" of himself apart from his immediate surroundings—something that requires the capacity for abstract thought and the ability to utilize fantasy in exploring the future. For instance, career choices can be considered and a self-assessment of the individual's personal qualities made in relation to various occupational demands.

Third, by means of identification with peers and adults (parents, teachers, etc.), the adolescent incorporates the attitudes, values, and beliefs of others around him. Without realizing it, he becomes more and more like his parents and the members of the social and cultural reference groups with whom he regularly associates, while still maintaining his own special attributes. Thus, he acquires a moral and ethical identity, a religious identity, a political identity, and others.

The self-image that the adolescent finally acquires serves as a basis for the individual's self-esteem and becomes a foundation that helps to determine both his thoughts and his conduct. Such a foundation, if positive and stable, is not easily changed by external events or internal stress. As a result of knowing "who he is" and what others "think of him," he will be able to interact more effectively with people. Moreover, if these two views are congruent, life will be more predictable for him and he will acquire a self-confidence based on a realistic appraisal of his position in the world.

On the other hand, if the adolescent fails to develop a positive and stable identity or if the one he develops is not based on a realistic assessment of his personal qualities, then he will enter adulthood without a strong sense of direction and self-confidence. Erikson was one of the first social scientists to point out the critical importance of achieving a sense of identity in adolescence, calling this the central task of this period of life. The development of identity does not stop in middle or late adolescence, however, but is an ongoing process. It is during adolescence that the *direction* of the emerging identity becomes crystallized in preparation for young adulthood.

LATE ADOLESCENCE

When the individual enters the period of late adolescence, much has happened over the past 5 or 6 years. Most of the physical and sexual development that will take place is complete, there is a greater degree of emotional stability, and some of the desired independence has already been attained. From this point on, a consolidation of identity occurs with the development of meaningful heterosexual relationships, some decisions are made about occupation and career goals, and the assumption of adult roles and responsibilities begins to take place.

Physical Changes

The older adolescent has reached a peak of physical maturation and prowess, so that it is not uncommon to find older teenagers successfully competing with adults in athletic events. Record accomplishments in track and field, swimming, and other activities may be set by individuals in this age group.

While variations exist in rates of physical growth, the majority of 18–19-year-olds have approximately reached their full adult size. The average height and weight for 18-year-old boys are 68.7 inches and 139 pounds. For girls of this age, the figures are 64.0 inches and 119.9 pounds.[17]

Physical differences in size and strength between the sexes are clear-cut at this age, with men predominating in both categories. Although traditionally men have utilized these physical advantages by engaging in sports activities, recent changes in sexual-coded roles[26] (culturally determined roles based on gender) have resulted in greater participation by women in these kinds of typical "male activities."

Psychosexual Development

Normally, the ego attains control over the person's impulses and drives and is able to integrate them successfully with the other aspects of physical and psychological function. Therefore, the older adolescent's energy is more effectively directed toward intellectual, athletic, and social endeavors. According to Lidz, by this age the individual should have achieved an ego identity and should be capable of developing close intimate relationships with others.[27] If there are still unresolved problems about gender identity and sexuality, however, the person may fail to acquire this capacity. The older adolescent's psychosexual attitudes, feelings, and behavior are molded by social mores or codes of conduct about such matters as sexual activities, pregnancy, and abortion. Parental views are also very important in determining adolescent behavior with respect to these matters.

Psychosocial Development

In late adolescence, three related tasks form the major themes of development: achieving a greater degree of independence (from parents) approaching that of an adult; developing a code of morality or ethics; and making a career or vocational choice.

PARENTAL RELATIONSHIPS.—During this period, social and maturational forces combine to act as the final catalysts stimulating the person to achieve an independent identity and to function on his own. In this context, family relationships take on new meaning. The family becomes a source of emotional and social support, a sort of "home base" for the older adolescent as he moves toward complete adult autonomy.

A brief disclaimer of sorts seems appropriate here vis-à-vis the much-discussed conflict between teenagers and parents during adolescence. The traditional view of this period as a time of emotional turmoil and rebelliousness may be something of a myth.[25] King, after reviewing the studies dealing with the turmoil and rebellion supposedly associated with adolescence, concluded that this is not the norm but that most healthy teenagers are able to cope with the stress of this period while still maintaining their emotional equilibrium a good deal of the time.[28] Moreover, they demonstrate a remarkable resourcefulness in adapting to the problems they face. There are several possible reasons why there has been an overemphasis on adolescent rebellion in the past: first, the preoccupation of professionals with the extremes of adolescent behavior; second, a dramatization of adolescence by the media; and third, inaccurate generalizations formed from biased studies of this period.[29]

Meissner's observations tend to support the view that teenagers generally have positive feelings toward their parents.[30] He studied more than 10,000 high school boys, interviewing them to obtain their opinion of their parents. More than 70% were proud of their parents, and more than 80% indicated that they spent half their free time at home with their parents.

PEER RELATIONSHIPS.—As the older adolescent expands his degree of independence, peers become a primary source of social and emotional support. According to Dunphy's model, late adolescence is a time when teenagers relate to each other in loosely associated groups of couples. At this age, the capacity for more intimate and less egocentric relationships develops as the adolescent solidifies his or her identity.

A major task of late adolescence is to achieve the capacity to form close intimate relationships with other people, including the ability to love. Such intimacy requires the development of a stable and positive identity and at least some degree of independence from the family. Given these prerequisites, the individual can commit himself to another person, gradually becoming comfortable with the emotional sharing that intimacy involves. This increasing comfort with closeness is often dependent on the teenager having previously experienced successful interfamily relationships.

In the development of heterosexual relationships, there is a sampling process by which the individual interacts with various partners, guided in his selections by the limits of society's standards. The older teenager appears to search for qualities in partners that are complementary, rather than identical, to those he possesses. Very intense feelings of affection and love can develop toward the partners so that separation from a loved one can be very painful. These feelings lack the impulsivity associated with earlier adolescent development. "Going steady" and even overt sexuality, including intercourse, are accompanied by genuine feelings of love rather than being "conquests" or a collection of sexual successes.

For the older adolescent, the need to conform and be accepted by his peer group becomes less important and is gradually replaced by a recognition of the importance of individuality. Studies of conformity have shown that it is less prominent among 15–21-year-olds than among those in the 11–13 age group.[31] This suggests that older adolescents have a more stable identity and, therefore, feel less need to conform. In other words, older adolescents tend to be more responsive in their behavior to internal values and attitudes than to external factors.

As the person matures, the stability of friendships increases so that he often has a number of ongoing stable relationships. A boy or girl is valued as a friend for what he or she is and because of the feelings that the teenager has for him or her, not on the basis of the person's status with the rest of the peer group.

MORALITY AND ETHICS.—In late adolescence, acquiring an internalized set of standards and values that guide behavior is an important task. In chapter 15 Kohlberg's cognitive approach to the development of morality was discussed.[32] According to this conceptual model, the older adolescent holds views on morality that are based on social contracts, mutual or utilitarian values, and ethical principles. While individuals of this age differ in the "stage" of morality in which they function, most older adolescents have the cognitive capability to conceptualize moral behavior in formal principles. Whereas the young adolescent thinks of morality in terms of authoritative judgments and absolute extremes of "right" or "wrong," the older adolescent is able to apply universal principles of moral judgment and behavior on a relative basis to specific issues of living. In gathering data on this issue, Kohlberg posed hypothetical problems to adolescents in the form of brief anecdotes in which they were asked to judge the behavior of the main characters in the story. Older teenagers relied more on conscience and "higher" universal laws of morality to make these judgments, whereas younger adolescents based their opinions on absolute social rules and/or authority.

Adolescents who do not develop a set of internalized values and rules seem to have difficulty understanding another person's point of view and tend to rely on set rules or authority. Under these circumstances, right and wrong become absolute, and in judgmental situations these adolescents are rigid and uncompromising. On the other hand, teenagers who do develop a set of internalized standards and moral principles are able to appreciate another individual's viewpoint and consider this in arriving at a solution to a moral issue. Thus, they can begin to relate to others with mutual respect and trust.

The absence of moral feeling or conscience is characteristic of persons with a "psychopathic" or "sociopathic" personality disorder. However, health professionals should be cautious in using these terms, even descriptively, for adolescents, since the development of moral values is variable at this age. For example, some adolescents who are socially anxious or insecure may appear to be morally "callous" because of their attempts to cover up these problems by acting with a bravado that masks their real concern for the opinions of others.

Weiner suggests that true principled thinking is not reached until adulthood, and that most adolescents and adults function at a level of morality that is based on presenting a good picture to others and adhering to duty and obligations.[33] He feels that the adolescent delinquent is more egocentric and relates behavior only to the expected consequences.

VOCATIONAL CHOICE.—To be an adult in our society implies that one is independent, not only psychologically and socially, but also economically. This is certainly so for men and, in recent years, has also become true for many women. Thus, an important consideration for the adolescent, particularly the older adolescent, is his or her future vocation. While the final decision on a lifelong occupation is often delayed until the mid-twenties, for teenagers who do not intend to go to college, it is an immediate concern.

Actually, children begin to fantasize about what they will do as adults early in life, but these notions generally have little to do with reality. Early in adolescence, tentative decisions are often made about one's future work, and as adolescence progresses, more and more serious and realistic thinking with respect to this matter begins. Some factors that influence this thinking include:[27]

1. The anticipated enjoyment or satisfaction associated with the work
2. The security, prestige, and financial gains that appear to accompany the occupation
3. The "fit" between the individual's perceived personality and capabilities and the apparent requirements of the vocation
4. Parental desires and advice
5. Identification with parents and other esteemed adults
6. The attitudes of peers
7. Actual contact with aspects of certain jobs
8. Advice and suggestions of teachers and school counselors

It is important to recognize that although vocational choices are usually made in late adolescence and in young adulthood, these choices are not necessarily final; as we will see in chapter 18, career changes occur throughout adult life, even into old age.

One dilemma that faces the adolescent in contemporary America who is pondering about a future vocation is the wide variety of choices theoretically open to him. In fact there are certain limitations: some are obvious as, for example, a person's abilities or the finances necessary for extensive schooling; others are more subtle, such as social class influences (i.e., some occupations are more acceptable to the members of a particular social class than others). Until recently, gender was a prominent restricting factor, since certain occupations were felt to be more appropriate for men while others were intended primarily for women. Now increasing numbers of women are going into vocational fields that were not readily open to them in the past (e.g., medicine, law, government) and, conversely, men are taking jobs that had been traditionally "closed" to them (e.g., flight attendants, nurses, secretaries). For many career women, their vocational choice involves a postponement of marriage and having children—a decision that weighs heavily on the minds of some adolescent girls.

Almost inevitably, the extensive period of education that is required for jobs at the higher socioeconomic level leads to a prolongation of adolescence. Whereas the individual who goes straight to work after high school, marries, and begins to raise a family has clearly entered the adult world, the person who puts off getting married and goes on to college may still remain dependent on his parents for financial aid and guidance. Thus, although the latter is chronologically an adult, in terms of accomplishing the tasks of this period he has not yet qualified for this status. Such a prolongation of adolescence is unique to societies where there are opportunities for higher education in preparation for future life work. This situation is sometimes accompanied by psychological conflict, both on an *internal* level, as the older "adolescent" tries to reconcile himself to this prolonged dependency, and on an *external* level, as disagreements arise between the adolescent and his parents, who attempt to couple their financial aid with "advice and guidance" as to how to run his life.

A facet of economic life in this country that is of particular importance to the older teenager is the high unemployment rate among individuals in this age group.[6] Over the past several years, the rate for white teenagers has been around three to four times the overall unemployment rate; for black teenagers, it is approximately eight to ten times the overall rate. Many adolescents who enter the labor market are unskilled with little education, and the types of jobs available to them are limited. This is particularly true for blacks in the urban ghettos. The inability to find gainful employment may be one factor responsible for the relatively high prevalence of juvenile delinquency in this country, particularly among adolescents from lower socioeconomic classes who live in ghetto areas of our metropolitan cities.

Cognitive Development

There is a progression of intellectual development between childhood and adolescence. While Piaget stresses the qualitative nature of the difference between adolescent thinking and that of younger children, several reviews indicate that this difference is more quantitative than qualitative.[33]

As stated earlier, formal operational thinking begins between 12 and 15 years of age. The older adolescent finds satisfaction in considering different premises and outcomes in the exploration of a problem. The ability to use formal operational logic permits him to do so. This reflective thought may give rise to conflict between an "idealistic" (in a logical sense) adolescent and a more experienced "pragmatic" adult. The battleground of ideas between these two generations can be political, moral, social, or scientific. It is important for professionals who work with adolescents to recall that not all teenagers engage in formal operational thinking and, when they do, it may not be consistently demonstrated.

PROBLEMS OF ADJUSTMENT IN ADOLESCENCE

At the beginning of this chapter, we gave an overview of some of the physical and emotional problems that beset adolescents in our society. In this section, two of these problems will be briefly discussed: juvenile delinquency and teenage pregnancy.

Juvenile Delinquency

The term "juvenile delinquency" is a legal one referring to people younger than 17 or 18 who commit a crime. In recent years, this problem has become a major social concern because of the increase in the number of crimes by minors. Table 17–5 shows that a large percentage of serious crimes are committed by juvenile offenders. By far the most frequent criminal acts performed by members of this age group are breaking and entering and theft. While recent data suggest that there has been a downward turn in the number of juvenile offenses, the overall trend since 1960 is quite alarming. A 70% increase in juvenile court cases occurred from 1960 to 1973. While this increase may partially reflect different reporting and recording practices

TABLE 17-5.—Arrests by Age and Offense, 1975*

OFFENSE CHARGED	TOTAL (000)	UNDER 15 YEARS OLD (%)	UNDER 18 YEARS OLD (%)	18–24 YEARS OLD (%)
Total	8,013	8.9	25.9	31.0
Serious crimes	1,901	17.0	43.1	32.1
Murder and nonnegligent manslaughter	16	1.1	9.5	35.3
Manslaughter by negligence	3	2.6	12.1	38.5
Forcible rape	22	3.9	17.6	40.4
Robbery	130	9.6	34.3	42.7
Aggravated assault	202	5.2	17.6	32.0
Burglary (breaking or entering)	449	20.1	52.6	32.6
Larceny—theft	959	20.1	45.1	30.4
Motor vehicle theft	120	14.4	54.5	30.1
All other charges Total	6,112	9.5	27.3	33.8

*Includes persons arrested but not charged reported by 8,051 agencies with a total population of 179,191,000 as estimated by the FBI.
Source: *Uniform Crime Reports for the United States*. U.S. Federal Bureau of Investigation, 1975.

over the years, it does underscore a rather striking upsurge in juvenile crime.

Overall incidence figures suggest that from 3% to 10% of all children between the ages of 10 and 17 are involved in criminal acts in the United States. These figures may even be low since many offenders either do not get caught or are not charged. Suggested causes underlying juvenile crime are many and varied, including:

1. Parental and family factors
   a. Parental absence
   b. Parental rejection
   c. Inconsistent discipline
   d. Parental conflict
   e. Parental criminality
   f. Large families
2. Sociological factors
   a. Low socioeconomic status
   b. Peer or gang influence
   c. Unemployment

It is possible that future delinquent behavior may be predictable in children as young as 10 years of age. The data in one study indicated that a pattern of behavior in 10-year-olds consisting of disobedience, truancy, quarrelsomeness, inattention, and unkempt appearance was predictive of later juvenile arrest.[34]

Personality theorists have suggested that delinquents are characteristically aggressive, egocentric, impulsive, and antisocial—a profile that is also felt by many to be descriptive of psychopathic or sociopathic personality disorders. Research indicates that delinquents from middle- and upper-class environments are more likely to be emotionally maladjusted than are children from lower socioeconomic classes. Parental factors, such as a father's occupational status and the type of discipline (erratic or consistent) to which the child has been exposed, seem to be related to juvenile delinquency.[35] Social deprivation, as found among those living in inner-city slums, can also be correlated with juvenile crime. Similarly, coming from a broken home is a risk factor for this problem. Thus, in order to understand the pathogenesis of juvenile delinquency it is probably best to think of it in terms of the interaction of psychological, social, and economic factors.

Most efforts at intervention have produced discouraging results. Individual psychotherapy, casework, group or peer programs, and traditional incarceration or punishment have generally not been successful. Current efforts aimed at producing alternative behaviors, which result in economic services or marketable skills, within a comprehensive program of counseling and social and educational training may produce higher success rates. One area of prevention, namely, improving deficient parenting, is largely unexplored. It seems paradoxical that even though there is documentation that poor parenting is a factor in causing juvenile delinquency, few major efforts at direct family intervention have been undertaken. One exception is a current project called "Achievement Place," in which foster parents provide consistent role models for delinquent youth.[36] As longitudinal data from this and other related intervention efforts accumulate, better strategies for treatment and prevention may emerge.

Teenage Pregnancy

Teenage pregnancy is a serious problem in the United States, where the birth rates for women of this age are among the highest for advanced countries. The increased incidence of this problem since the 1940s is related to the increase in premarital sex among adolescent girls and to a widespread lack of proper contraceptive measures by persons in this age group. Despite this trend, teenage pregnancy has not reached the epidemic proportions often alluded to in the press. In fact, there has been a reduction in its incidence since 1973 in terms of both the proportion of teenagers having babies and the absolute number of these pregnancies.[37] The exception to this statement is for girls under 14 years of age, where births have occurred at about the same rate over this period of time.

Approximately one in ten adolescent girls become pregnant each year, resulting in more than 1 million pregnancies and 600,000 births. However, approximately 360,000 of these births are to married 18- and 19-year-olds.[37] Pregnancy during adolescence occurs more frequently in girls from lower socioeconomic groups and is much more prevalent in the nonwhite community—statistics that have important prognostic implications.

There is an increased medical risk for both mother and child associated with teenage pregnancy. The maternal death rate is higher, as are complications of pregnancy such as toxemia and anemia. The age of the mother at the time of pregnancy is a determiner of medical risk for the infant, as it has been shown that prematurity occurs more frequently with teenage mothers under 15 years of age (those who are within 2 years of menarche).

Many reported complications of teenage pregnancy are due to the fact that a large proportion of these mothers come from lower socioeconomic groups in which obstetric risks are greater, rather than being attributable solely to the youth of the mother. Another reason for the poorer medical outcome of pregnancy in this age group is that adolescents are less likely to seek obstetric care and, when they do, they frequently do not comply with medical advice. As a matter of fact, teenage pregnancy can be managed quite successfully if the mother receives good prenatal care.

In addition to the medical risks associated with this problem, there are social and psychological repercussions. Adolescent girls who become pregnant tend to drop out of school and never catch up educationally with peers. They are much more likely to end up on welfare, to have unsuccessful marriages, and to have repeated unwanted pregnancies. Thus, teenage mothers often come from and tend to remain in the lower socioeconomic strata of society.

Many adolescent mothers are deficient in parenting skills. They have unrealistic expectations of the ages at which their infants will achieve developmental milestones, are likely to use techniques of control that rely excessively on punishment, and provide little stimulation for the infant by means of verbal interaction and play. Also, the offspring of teenage mothers are more likely than their age mates to have had a variety of primary caregivers, including grandmothers, aunts, and foster parents. As a consequence of these and other differences in rearing, these children have an increased risk of experiencing developmental problems. In the first few months of life, developmental delays may not be apparent, but by school age an increasing number of scholastic problems appear, especially in reading and numeration. Conduct and acting-out problems are also more common among these children as compared with children born to older mothers with a similar social background.[37]

SUMMARY

Adolescence is defined as the period between childhood and adulthood and is generally considered to cover ages 11–20. However, for some segments of our population (those who go to college to prepare for a career), adolescence can be prolonged into the twenties. It is a time of great physical, psychological, and social change during which the individual gradually develops an increasing degree of independence and self-sufficiency. Most important, he is involved in the process of forming a self-identity that will influence his behavior and interpersonal relationships from this time on. Although the teenage period has been viewed by many professionals in the past as one of turmoil and rebellion, this aspect of adolescence has probably been overstated since for most persons the transition to adulthood is a satisfying and rewarding experience.

We divided adolescence into early, middle, and late phases; however, the reader should keep in mind that these phases are really a continuum, with teenagers progressing from one to another at varying rates. In a successful transition, a child evolves into a young adult from a physical, sexual, psychological, and social standpoint. One particularly important aspect of this maturation is acquiring the capability of relating heterosexually in a warm, intimate manner, thus, preparing the person for marriage and parenting. By understanding the many facets of adolescent development, the health professional who works with adolescents will be better able to aid them at a crucial stage of their lives.

A number of health-related problems occur in adolescence, most of which are psychosocial in nature. These include psychiatric disorders, drug and alcohol abuse, and suicide. Delinquency and teenage pregnancy are two health concerns discussed in this chapter.

REFERENCES

1. National Institute of Mental Health, Statistics from the Biometry Branch, Publication on Mental Health. U.S. Government Printing Office, 1972.
2. *Statistics on Juvenile Delinquency*. National Institute of Juvenile Justice, Law Enforcement Assistance Administration. U.S. Government Printing Office, 1972.
3. Haley J.: Family therapy, in Theager C.J., Kaplan H.F. (eds.): *Progress in Group and Family Therapy*. New York: Brunner-Masel, 1972.
4. Helgason T.: Epidemiology of mental disorders in Iceland. *Acta Psychiatr. Scand.* 40:Suppl. 173:1+, 1964.
5. Hudgens R.W.: *Psychiatric Disorders in Adolescence*. Baltimore, Williams & Wilkins Co., 1974.
6. Mussen P.H., Conger J.J., Kagen J.: *Child Development and Personality*. New York, Harper & Row, 1979.
7. Williams R.H. (ed.): *Textbook of Endocrinology*. Philadelphia, W.B. Saunders Co., 1968.
8. Swerdloff R.S.: Physiological control of puberty. *Med. Clin. North Am.* 62(2):351, 1978.
9. Erikson E.: *Identity, Youth and Crisis*. New York, W.W. Norton & Company, Inc., 1968.
10. Piaget J.: *The Origins of Intelligence in Children*. New York, International Universities Press, 1952.
11. Piaget J., Inhelder B.: *The Growth of Logical Thinking from Childhood to Adolescence*. New York, Basic Books, Inc., Publishers, 1958.
12. Plos P.: *On Adolescence*. New York, The Free Press, 1961.
13. Erikson E.: *Childhood and Society*. New York, W.W. Norton & Company, Inc., 1950.
14. Reiter E.O., Root A.W.: Hormonal changes of adolescence. *Med. Clin. North Am.* 59:1289, 1975.
15. Boyar R.M.: Regulation of gonadotropin secretion in man. *Med. Clin. North Am.* 62:367, 1978.
16. Sider R.C., Kreider S.D.: Coping with adolescent patients. *Med. Clin. North Am.* 61:839, 1977.
17. Vaughan V.C., McKay R.J., Behrman R.E. (eds.): *Nelson Textbook of Pediatrics*, ed. 11. Philadelphia, W.B. Saunders Co., 1979.
18. Newman B., Newman P.R.: *Development Throughout Life: A Psychosocial Approach*. Homewood, Ill., Dorsey Press, 1975.
19. Zelnik M., Kim Y.J., Kanter J.F.: Probabilities of intercourse and conception among U.S.

teenage women, 1971 and 1976. *Fam. Plann. Perspect.* 11:177, 1979.
20. Dunphy D.C.: The social structure of urban adolescent peer groups. *Sociometry* 26:230, 1963.
21. Piaget J.: *The Construction of Reality in Children.* New York, Basic Books, Inc., Publishers, 1954.
22. Reiss I.L.: The sexual renaissance in America. *J. Soc. Issues* 22:123, 1966.
23. Garrison K.C., Garrison K.C., Jr.: *Psychology of Adolescence.* Englewood Cliffs, N.J., Prentice-Hall, Inc., 1975.
24. Lindzey G., Borgatta E.F.: Sociometric measurement, in Lindzey G. (ed.): *Handbook of Social Psychology.* Reading, Mass., Addison-Wesley Publishing Co., Inc., 1954.
25. McKinney J.P., Fitzgerald H.E., Strommer E.A.: *Developmental Psychology: The Adolescent and Young Adult.* Homewood, Ill., Dorsey Press, 1977.
26. Money J.: Sex roles and sex coded roles. *J. Pediatr. Psychol.* 2:108–109, 1977.
27. Lidz, T.: *The Person.* New York, Basic Books, Inc., Publishers, 1968.
28. King S.: Coping and growth in adolescence. *Semin. Psychiatry* 4:355–366, 1972.
29. Bandura, A.: The stormy decade: Fact or fiction? *Psychol. Schools* 1:224–231, 1964.
30. Meissner W.W.: Parental interaction of the adolescent boy. *J. Genet. Psychol.* 107:225–233, 1965.
31. Costanzo P.R., Shaw M.E.: Conformity as a function of age level. *Child Dev.* 37:967–975, 1966.
32. Kohlberg L.: Development of moral character and moral ideology, in Hoffman M.L., Hoffman L.W. (eds.): *Review of Child Development.* New York, Russell Sage Foundation, 1964, vol. 1.
33. Weiner A.S.: Cognitive and social-emotional development in adolescence. *J. Pediatr. Psychol.* 2:87–92, 1977.
34. West D.J., Farrington D.P.: *Who Becomes Delinquent?* London, Heinemann, 1973.
35. Stanfield R.E.: The interaction of family variables and gang variables in the etiology of delinquency. *Soc. Probl.* 13:411–417, 1966.
36. Phillips E.L., Phillips E.A., Fixen D.L., et al.: Achievement place: Modification of the behaviors of predelinquent boys within a token economy. *J. Appl. Behav. Anal.* 4:45–49, 1971.
37. Scott K., Field T., Robertson E.: *Teenage Parents and Their Offspring.* New York, Grune & Stratton, in press.

18 / Young and Middle Adulthood

CLARISSA S. SCOTT, Ph.D.

UNTIL RECENTLY, little systematic research had been done on the adult period of the life cycle. Most studies of human development dealt with childhood, adolescence, or old age. One reason for this may have been that the physiological and psychosocial changes taking place during these stages are often more dramatic than those experienced by the adult. From the physical standpoint, men and women remain very much the same in general appearance until the effects of aging become apparent. Perhaps the plateau of physical development that characterizes adulthood lulled investigators into believing that psychosocial development is also quiescent. Even today, there is a widely held, but mistaken, notion that adults are rational beings who enter into a relatively stable, integrated life pattern with no major crises or developmental changes.[1] As we shall soon see, this is apparently not the case, for current studies indicate that this phase of life is one of dynamic change in which psychosocial development continues to occur. A variety of psychosocial challenges confront the adult; indeed, adaptation is as much a part of this period as it is of childhood, adolescence, and old age.

THEORETICAL BASIS FOR THE STAGES OF ADULTHOOD

Erikson identified the psychosocial tasks of the young and middle-aged adult in his sixth and seventh stages of human development.[2] In the period of young adulthood, the issue that must be faced is one of "intimacy versus isolation." By the term "intimacy," Erikson means the capacity to combine feelings of tender love with those of a sexual nature in a relationship with a partner of the opposite sex, i.e., to be able to merge one's life with that of a love partner. To achieve intimacy, an individual should have successfully resolved the identity crisis of adolescence and acquired a firm sense of his ego identity. This permits him to become closely involved with another person without being fearful of losing his own identity in the process. The consequence of failing to develop the capacity for intimacy is isolation, living one's life without a deep and meaningful relationship with a love partner.

In middle age, Erikson sees the psychosocial issue confronting a person as being "generativity versus stagnation." The first term refers to a person's commitment to the future as demonstrated by his "interest in establishing and guiding the next generation." The result of a failure to achieve generativity is increasing self-absorption or personal stagnation; as Erikson puts it, "individuals who do not develop generativity often begin to indulge themselves as if they were their one and only child."[2]

In contrast to his detailed description of the earlier stages of development, Erikson provided only a rough outline for those occurring during adulthood and old age and, in his writings, he urged other investigators to delve more deeply into these periods.

In Austria, the findings of research carried out under the leadership of Charlotte Buhler were first reported in the 1930s.[3] Using a unique approach to elicit the general principles that are valid for the human life span, Buhler and her colleague, Else Frankel, critically studied approximately 400 biographies of individuals from various nations, social classes, and occupations. In addition, letters and diaries were used as well as direct questioning of elderly, poor, and working-class individuals for whom no biographic data were available. From this material, an inventory was obtained of the external events that took place in their lives, their internal reactions to those events, and their accomplishments during the different periods of their lives.

Buhler and Frankel attempted to find out whether there is a psychosocial pattern of development that parallels the five biologic periods, which they describe as: (1) birth to the time at which one can reproduce, (2) from this time to the mid-twenties, (3) from the mid-twenties to the loss of reproductive ability, (4) from approximately 45–50 years old to retirement from one's occupation, and (5) from approximately 65 years of age until death. The first two stages are identified as growth periods, the third as one of stability, and the last two as periods of decline. The psychosocial data provided a relatively good match in terms of these periods. The first psychosocial stage, in which the child lives at home with a relatively narrow field of interests, corresponds to the first biologic period. The second begins as the adolescent enters a self-chosen activity and leaves the dependent relationship with his or her family. The third behavioral stage, which closely parallels the middle biologic period, is a time in which a definite choice of vocation is made, the greatest number of social activities occur, and a new home is created. This is called the *culmination period* and is characterized by expansiveness of interests and activities. In contrast to the first three psychosocial stages (which are associated with the building up of life), the fourth signals a decrease in the number of activities and the appearance of negative aspects (such as sickness and loss of strength, friends, family members, and financial ability). The final stage is marked by complete retirement from one's usual occupation and involves a continued restriction in the number of activities. This restriction is usually tied to the decline in vital processes. This need not be completely negative; indeed, these investigators found that as physical vitality declines, most of their sample adapted to this by refocusing on the mental aspect of life.

In summary, Buhler and Frankel see the biologic and psychosocial characteristics of the first half of life as being determined by the normal physical and psychological *needs* of the individual; in contrast, the second half is dominated by behavior as a reaction to *duties* that are imposed either externally (by society) or internally (by one's ideals or conscience).

Keniston introduced the concept of *youth*—which he described as "a new stage in the life cycle" between adolescence and the assumption of adult status.[4] He sees this period, through which only a relatively few young people pass, as being associated with the complexities of industrialism. It is only when a young person leaving adolescence senses "conflict and disparity between his emerging self-hood and his social order" that the term applies.[5] The central task for an individual in this stage is to acknowledge the realities of a society from which he feels estranged and to cope with them. One coping method is to conform to the social norms (e.g., "selling out" by joining the Army or one's father's business). This, of course, can mean a denial of self and one's sense of values and integrity. Another method is to preserve one's sense of self and work to bring about social reform by means of joining a group that is fighting for the desired changes (e.g., the civil rights movement, ERA). A harmful variant of this is "dropping out" of society altogether by the abuse of psychedelic drugs. Most young people are able to find a relatively comfortable "fit" between their self-image and the demands of the society in which they live and, thus, move directly from adolescence to young adulthood without passing through the period Keniston calls "youth."

Studies of Gould and Levinson[6-8]

GOULD.—In the 1960s, exciting new research in the field of the developmental psychology of adulthood began on several fronts within the United States. Roger Gould and his colleagues at UCLA focused their investigation on the age-related psychological changes that occur over the adult life span, specifically, on the individual's "sense of the world" (i.e., the "interior, gut-level organizing percepts of self and non-self, safety, time, size, etc., that make up the background tone of daily living and shape the attitude and value base from which decisions and action emanate"[6]). Their first study took place in 1968 at the UCLA Psychiatric Out-Patient Clinic with all the patients who were participating in group therapy. They separated these patients into seven age groups (16–18, 18–22, 22–28, 29–34, 35–43, 43–50, 50 and over) and observed them over a 12-month period. On the basis of this study, Gould and his co-workers were able to delineate important differences between these seven phases of life.

To see whether these differences also occurred in a nonpatient population, they next studied 524 white middle-class individuals. Their final sample included 20 subjects for each age between 16 and 33, and 20 subjects for each 3-year age span between 33 and 60. The male-female ratio was approximately 1 to 1 (although there was an uneven distribution in the over-45 groups, with more women than men). As in the initial study, seven distinct periods (approximately 16–17, 18–21, 22–28, 29–36, 37–43, 44–50, and 51–60) again emerged from the data, with only minor differences in the results of this investigation compared with the first one.

The findings from these two studies highlight certain "themes" for each of the seven periods:

16–17: The subjects repeatedly voiced the idea: "We have to get away from our parents." At the time, they were living in the family house and considered themselves family members.

18–22: The same theme is repeated, but now most subjects are either living away from home or living at home and paying rent. "They feel themselves to be halfway out of the family and are worried that they will . . . not make it out completely."

22–28: This is a period in which most individuals felt quite autonomous and "engaged in the work of being adults." Their energy is expended in mastering their roles rather than questioning whether their choices of commitments (to job, spouse, etc.) are correct or not.

29–34: Serious questions are asked during this period. "What is this life all about now that I am doing what I am supposed to?" "Is what I am the only way for me to be?" Individuals are aware of an inner aspect of self that has not been satisfied.

35–43: The existential questioning of self, values, and life continues, "but with a change of tone toward quiet desperation and an increasing awareness of a time squeeze." The questions are "Have I done the right thing?" and "Is there time to change?"

44–50: During this period, many come to terms with the reality of finite time and the prospect that they may never achieve their dreams. A characteristic of this period seems to be an acknowledgment that the "die is cast."

51–60: Although a mellowing appears along with a more positive view of parents, children, and spouse, "there is a renewed questioning about the meaningfulness of life as well as a review of one's own work contributions to the world."

During each period, Gould believes that we must come to grips with these specific issues and questions and find a satisfactory way of resolving them. He has been quoted in a newspaper article as saying:

If you meet your growth tasks, if you challenge certain restrictive ideas, you'll feel alive and vital. . . . If you don't, you'll feel stagnant, stuck, and generally miserable. It's like driving a car with the brakes on. You move along, but it's a pretty bumpy ride.[9]

LEVINSON.—At virtually the same time Gould began his investigations at UCLA,

Daniel Levinson (a psychologist in the Department of Psychiatry at Yale) was beginning studies that independently led to a concept of adult developmental periods similar to Gould's.[7] To understand Levinson's work, one must know something about his concept of a life structure, which he sees as having three aspects:

1. The nature of the man's sociocultural world, including class, religion, ethnicity, race, family, political systems, occupational structure, and particular conditions and events such as economic depression or prosperity, war and liberation movements of all kinds.
2. His participation in this world—his evolving relationships and roles as citizen, worker, boss, lover, friend, husband, father, member of diverse groups and organizations.
3. The aspects of his self that are expressed and lived out in the various components of his life; and the aspects of the self that must be inhibited or neglected within the life structure.[10]

Levinson does not see each of these aspects as being equal. Rather, he believes that components such as family and occupation are primary in that they call for the most time and energy and play the most significant role in influencing the concept of self. While ethnic membership, religion, and one's peer groups are important components, they require less investment of the self and, therefore, are less critical than the primary factors.

Adult development is viewed by Levinson as "the evolution of life structure" in a sequence of stable periods alternating with transitional ones. The findings from the Yale investigations have shown that stable periods usually last approximately 6–8 years, while the transitional ones usually extend for 4–5 years.

Levinson describes these two types of periods in these terms:

> The primary developmental task of a *stable period* is to make certain crucial choices, build a life structure around them, and seek to attain particular goals and values within this structure. Each stable period also has its own distinctive tasks which reflect the requirements of that time in the life cycle. Many changes may occur during a stable period, but the basic life structure remains relatively intact.

> The primary developmental task of a *transitional period* is to terminate the existing structure and to work toward the initiation of a new structure. This requires a person to reappraise the existing life structure, to explore various possibilities for change in the world and in the self, and to move toward the crucial choices that will form the basis for a new life structure in the ensuing stable period. Each transitional period also has its own distinctive tasks reflecting its place in the life cycle.[10]

Levinson's mode of research lies roughly midway between the highly detailed analysis of a single man (such as Erikson's examination of the lives of Luther and Gandhi) and the extensive study of a large sample (such as Gould used). Levinson and his co-workers selected 40 men on a random basis through their work settings; 10 men in each of four occupational categories (hourly workers in industry, business executives, academic biologists, and novelists). Each man was interviewed to reconstruct the story of his life, focusing on the late adolescent and adult years. The components of living that were important for the interviewee (e.g., education, work, peer relationships, family of origin, lineage and family of procreation, leisure, religion, and politics) were followed over the course of his life. It was felt that the study group of 40 men was small enough to permit a detailed biographic analysis, yet sufficiently large to allow valid data to be obtained for the whole sample as well as its subgroups. In addition to these subjects, the lives of men described in biographies, autobiographies, poetry, plays, and novels were examined by Levinson.

The research undertaken by Levinson and his colleagues was of a multidisciplinary nature. Psychologists, psychiatrists, and sociologists worked together to plan the study and carry it out. The publication of findings from the study on men first appeared in 1974; the results of the study on women, which began somewhat later, have not yet appeared in journals.

Levinson and his colleagues identified four *eras* within the life cycle, each lasting approximately 25 years and with several years overlapping between them (Fig 18–1):

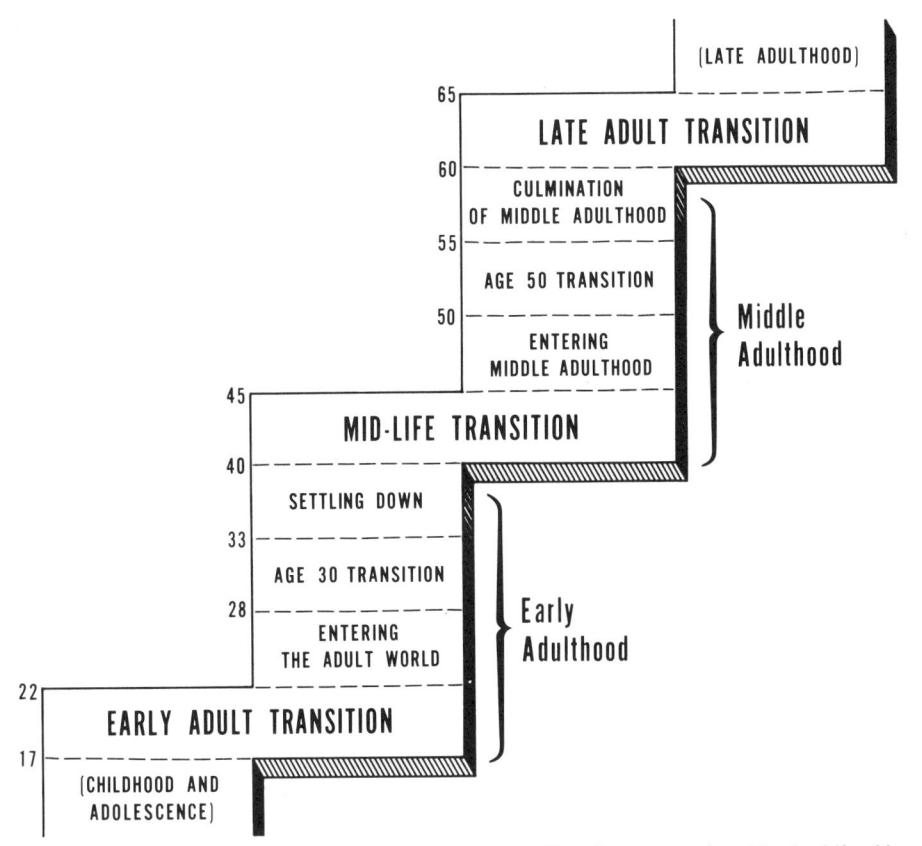

Fig 18–1.—Levinson's developmental periods in early and middle adulthood. (From Levinson D.L.: *The Seasons of a Man's Life.* New York, Alfred A. Knopf, Inc., 1978. Used by permission.)

1. Childhood and adolescence (0–22)
2. Early adulthood (17–45)
3. Middle adulthood (40–65)
4. Late adulthood (60–?)

The sequence of these eras provides the macrostructure of the life cycle, the framework within which the developmental periods occur. Levinson repeatedly makes the point that the year at which an era is said to begin or end is not "standardized" but merely represents the "average or most frequent age" of onset or completion. However, the variability occurs within surprisingly narrow limits (usually no more than 5–6 years).

The data indicate that early adulthood begins at about 17 years of age. Levinson calls the transitional period that forms the bridge between adolescence and early adulthood (17–22) the Early Adult Transition. This is the time during which the young man terminates his preadult self and makes the choices that will lead him to his initial place in the adult world. Two tasks have been identified for this period:[7]

1. To start moving out of the preadult world; to question the nature of that world and one's place in it; to modify or terminate existing relationships with important persons, groups, and institutions; to reappraise and modify the self that had formed in it.
2. To make a preliminary step into the adult world; to explore its possibilities, to imagine oneself as a participant in it, to consolidate an initial adult identity, to make and test some preliminary choices for adult living.[10]

The Early Adult Era for men (spanning approximately 25 years) represents the peak years of biologic functioning in terms of strength, sexual capability, and general biologic capacity. During this stage, a man usually forms a preliminary adult identity and makes major decisions in regard to marriage, job, residence, and life-style.

Levinson refers to the first stable period of this era as Entering the Adult World. The research data indicate that young men are working on two major tasks from about ages 22 to 28. An important point concerning these dual tasks is that they are not compatible with each other. The first one requires the man "to explore the possibilities for adult living: to keep his options open, to avoid strong commitments, and to maximize the alternatives." The young adult must come to the realization that to survive, he must now look to himself rather than to his family. Today this period of "trying out" often includes not only jobs but also partners of the opposite sex. With increased social approval of the practice of sharing an apartment or home with a member of the opposite gender (either as a trial marriage or just for convenience and/or enjoyment), young people no longer feel so much pressure to marry as in the past. The second task is "to create a stable life structure: to settle down (and) become responsible." Each individual works out a different balance between these two tasks. Some place greater emphasis on "hanging loose" and trying a variety of jobs and relationships; others make strong commitments to a marital partner and occupation early in the period, expecting that both will remain fulfilling choices throughout their lives.

Another writer, Lidz, has summarized this young adult period as follows:

> The lengthy developmental process as a dependent apprentice in living draws to a close as individuals attain an identity and the ability to live intimately with a member of the opposite sex, and contemplate forming families of their own. They have attained adult status with the completion of physical maturation, and, it is hoped, they have become sufficiently well integrated and emotionally mature to utilize the opportunities and accept the responsibilities that accompany it. They have reached a decisive point on their journeys. They have dropped the pilot and now start sailing on their own—but they have been taught to navigate and they have been provided with charts, albeit charts that can be but approximately correct for the currents and reefs change constantly. They have practiced under more or less competent supervision, taken trips in sheltered waters, and now they assume responsibility for themselves and must accept the consequences of their decisions. Usually couples decide to share the journey, and soon others join them, bidden and unbidden, whose welfare depends upon their skills and stability.
>
> However, some will still tarry undecided about where they will journey, or the course they will take to an unfamiliar place, or whether to try out partners imaginatively or in actuality before setting forth. Some are still uncertain about where they will find their place in the scheme of things, whether they wish to find a place in the scheme, or whether there is a scheme of things at all.[11]

During the late twenties, this stable period draws to a close and young men move into another transition—this one called the *Age Thirty Transition*. Lasting from approximately 28 to 33, it is a time to question preliminary choices and make changes in parts of one's life-style before they become concretized. Some make this transition smoothly, with little internal or external disruption and with only minor modifications being made. For others, the Age Thirty *Transition* may become the Age Thirty *Crisis*. The majority of the subjects in Levinson's study were in the latter category, having great difficulty working through the developmental tasks of this period. The data revealed a high frequency of marital problems, job changes, and psychotherapy as the young men wrestled with feelings of great dissatisfaction with their present life structure while not knowing how to make necessary changes for the better.

Levinson sees the end of this transitional period as a critical point in adult development. If the decisions the young man makes here "are congruent with his dreams, values, talents, and possibilities, they provide the basis for a relatively satisfactory life structure. If the choices are poorly made . . . , he will pay a heavy price in the next period."[10]

At about age 32 or 33, the second stable period appeared in the lives of the young men in Levinson's study. During the next 7 years,

each man was found to be working at two major tasks:
1. Establishing a niche in his world by developing competence in his chosen field and by becoming a valued member of society.
2. "Making it" up the "ladder" according to the American imagery of rungs of a ladder representing levels of advancement in terms of social class, income, quality of family life, social contributions, and so on. "Making it" means different things to different individuals but each tries to meet an inner timetable and progress toward his dream of achieving "the good life" (however he defines it).

Somewhere around age 39 or 40, the *Midlife Transition* begins, which provides a link between early and middle adulthood. Spanning approximately 5 years, it emerged from the research data as a "highly defined transition at mid-life." It was a time to ask oneself difficult questions about the meaning, value, and direction of one's life. Although some of the men studied were apparently undisturbed by these concerns, about 80% suffered "tumultuous struggles within the self and with the external world." For these, it was a time of crisis, not merely transition. In the type of profound reappraisal that takes place during this period, the individual is hindered by old anxieties and guilt, dependencies and animosities carried over from earlier years. Furthermore, a man of 40 who attempts any radical changes at this age will often find powerful forces (family, employer, parents, and social pressures from various other parts of the system) aligned against him.

In the United States, where there are so many options available in terms of marital partner, occupation, vocation, and so on, there is no way that an individual can indulge all his interests. He must make difficult choices, opting for those with highest priority and rejecting others. During the thirties, as the young adult attempts to "make it," he often has to neglect certain personal needs and desires; during the Mid-life Transition these come to mind. In Levinson's words:

He hears the voice of an identity prematurely rejected; of a love lost or not pursued; of a valued interest or relationship given up in acquiescence to parental or other authority; of an internal figure who wants to be an athlete or nomad or artist, to marry for love or to remain a bachelor, to get rich or enter the clergy or live an essentially care-free life—possibilities set aside earlier to become what he now is.[10]

This is a period where some make one more effort to grab the "golden ring" (whether that means to love and be loved, to indulge a creative need, to win fame and fortune, or simply to be free of an intolerable relationship). As Lidz puts it, "life is a one-time matter and it is difficult to cope with the feeling that the chance has been wasted."[11] For some for whom life has gone well and who have reached their goals, the middle years can be a period of great satisfactions. For others, there is a sense of increasing regret, dissatisfaction, and "a bitter resentment that life has slipped through their fingers."[11] Depressive reactions are not uncommon when one's expectations of life are still unmet.

The Mid-life Transition, and also the era of middle adulthood, can be a time of "de-illusionment." During early adulthood, a young man's dreams that he will be a success, have a happy marriage, and fulfill valued goals are helpful and necessary. Later, in middle age, he comes to grips with the fact that some of these may not happen and that he must reduce his expectations of life. A limited reduction of expectations at middle age is both appropriate and constructive—especially if the individual can accept part of the responsibility for a less than satisfactory marriage, choice of occupation, or whatever.

The life structure that emerges early in the era of middle adulthood varies greatly in its satisfactoriness, that is, in its suitability for the self and its viability in the world. Some men have suffered such irreparable defeats in childhood or early adulthood, and have been able to work so little on the tasks of their Mid-life Transition, that they lack the inner and outer resources for creating a minimally adequate structure. They face a middle adulthood of constriction and decline. Other men form a life structure that is reasonably viable in their world. They keep busy, perform their social roles, and do their bit for themselves and others. However, this structure is poorly connected to the self, and their lives are lacking an inner excitement. . . . [For others, who are able to rework their lives appropriately, achieving an optimal balance between society's and their unique individual needs], middle adulthood is often the fullest and most creative season in the life cycle.[7]

It was at this point in the lives of their subjects (i.e., their late forties) that Levinson's study ended. However, he and his team of psychologists, psychiatrists, and sociologists see evidence that alternating stable and transitional periods continue to the end of one's life cycle. They propose an Age Fifty Transition during which those who did not make sufficient changes in earlier transitional periods can still modify an unsatisfactory life structure. A stable period between 55 and 60 (roughly) is described as being the counterpart to the Settling Down stage of early adulthood. Finally, it is suggested that from about 60 to 65, men move through a Late Adult Transition, focusing on the task of concluding their middle years and preparing themselves for the final era to come.

A Word of Caution in Interpreting Gould's and Levinson's Studies

These studies have come under criticism for several different reasons. Some investigators in the field do not accept the concept of stages in the adult period of life. Butler, for example, wrote in 1975 (when only preliminary data from Levinson's study were available):

Stage theory is most useful in childhood and perhaps has its greatest validity there. . . . In early development there are more clearly defined links between physiology and mental development. But as man moves along in the course of the life cycle, his situation becomes more elaborately intricate, the environment has increasing impact, and there is greater variance or wider deviations from the mean in psychological, physiological, and other measures. Stage theory, therefore, appears to have limited usefulness for the understanding of the course of life, including middle life.[12]

Levinson answers,

Of course, men traverse [developmental periods] in myriad ways, as a result of differences in class, ethnicity, personality and other factors. . . . At a more conceptual level, however, we are interested in generating and working with hypotheses concerning relatively universal, genotypic, age-linked, adult developmental periods within which variations occur.[1]

According to Levinson these periods are conceived of as having origins in "both the nature of man as a biosocial and biopsychological organism, and in the nature of society as an enduring . . . form of collective life."[1] An important distinction is made between Freudian and Piagetian stages of childhood development, on one hand, and the adult developmental stages described in this chapter, on the other. The Freudian and Piagetian stages represent "an unfolding of maturational potentials from within," while the adult stages reflect the operation of "a variety of biological, psychodynamic, cultural, social-structural, and other time tables which operate in only partial synchronization."[1]

Neugarten has criticized the work of Levinson's group because of the small numbers of subjects involved, and on this basis she questions the validity of their findings.[13] Conclusions drawn from studies in which only small numbers of subjects participate must indeed be viewed with great circumspection since a relatively small sample may not be representative of the group as a whole. It is possible, however, to derive valid information from such studies. Kluckhohn is an example of a behavioral scientist who developed a research instrument which could successfully be used to elicit values which guide behavior from a carefully selected small group and which allows the results to be generalized to an entire cultural population.[14] Neugarten also does not take into consideration Levinson's extensive use of data from biographies, autobiographies, poetry, plays, and novels—a technique pioneered successfully during World War II.

Neugarten has also questioned the value of trying to delineate an invariant sequence of stages during adulthood in view of the recent biologic and social changes taking place within our society—changes that alter the timing and rhythm of events in the life cycle.[13] It is a biologic fact that puberty is occurring earlier and people are living longer than in the past. From the social standpoint, men are entering the labor force at a later time in their lives and retirement is coming earlier. More women are postponing marriage until their late twenties or early thirties, and of those who do marry, more are deciding not to bear children. And these are only a few of the social changes enumerated by Neugarten.

According to Hirschhorn, our life cycle has become a "fluid" one, meaning that in addition to changes in the timing of events during the life cycle, there is an increasing tendency for people to change their roles during adulthood.[15] Also, exceptions to traditional age-related roles are becoming more and more commonplace. As Neugarten puts it:

> While there are few studies in which this social change has actually been measured, our society is becoming accustomed to the 28-year-old mayor, the 30-year-old college president, the 35-year-old grandmother, the 50-year-old retiree, the 65-year-old father of a preschooler, and the 70-year-old student, and even the 85-year-old mother caring for a 65-year-old son.[13]

Finally, the notion that each period in adult life has specific tasks or goals that do not occupy the attention of the individual at other times is misleading. As Neugarten points out: "the psychological preoccupations of adults are recurrent. They appear and reappear in new forms over long periods of time."[13]

Certainly at this juncture in the study of adult development we must not accept uncritically and in all respects the concept of adulthood as an invariant succession of discrete stages, each with its special tasks or goals. This would lead to dangerous oversimplification. The work of Gould and Levinson at least indicates the need for further empirical investigations to confirm or deny their findings. Such studies should involve subjects from a variety of populations in our country and elsewhere. Within our country alone, there is great diversity in life patterns not only among people of different cultural backgrounds but even among individuals who belong to the same ethnic group but perhaps a different social class.

WOMEN DURING ADULTHOOD—MYTHS AND REALITIES

In discussions in the literature about the differences in developmental stages between women and men, it has been suggested that the task of developing an identity and sense of autonomy may be only partially dealt with by young women during the Early Adult Transition period. Women who marry during their dependent period (i.e., while still living in their parents' house and/or depending on them for shelter, food, college expenses, etc.) move immediately into *another* dependent role, this time vis-à-vis their husbands. This is especially true if they begin to raise a family. It is not until after they experience motherhood and after their children are older that they return to the task of resolving identity and autonomy problems (often not until the middle years). Some, as we are aware, never accomplish this goal.

Young women today have several special problems. They often feel torn between the opposing demands of our society. On one hand, they are aware that new careers and positions of authority are being opened to them, while on the other, they sense society's expectations (with accompanying social pressures) that they should devote their early adult years to marriage and raising a family. These young women are still of a generation in whom this latter idea was deeply ingrained in their formative years. They are also of a generation in which there are few models available to show them how to handle the combination of a career and motherhood successfully. Reared with the traditional goal of becoming a wife and mother, they are also concerned with a woman's role in the society at large, with equal pay, equal opportunities, and the widespread biases against women. Many believe "that women can be achievement-oriented and still retain expressive characteristics and that men should incorporate expressive as well as achievement-oriented instrumental characteristics."[11] The bind for many young women who are career-oriented is reflected by investigative findings that "bright, highly competent college women have feared success, considering that achievement requires competition, that competition is aggressive, and that aggression is unfeminine." A further finding was that "2/3 of college men did better in competitive than noncompetitive situations, as compared with fewer than 1/3 of the women subjects."[11] Our society is making changes in its fundamental beliefs about women and their roles, and it is likely that women will continue to feel "caught in a bind" for some time to come.

Role changes are becoming more common among women in our society. It is most frequently between the ages of 35 and 40 that women change the course of their lives, either resuming their education or entering the work force as their children enter school.

Age Markers

Neugarten, who is in the forefront of the few who have studied middle age, found that women (and men) in this period of life use chronological age less as an important marker than do younger or older people.[16] Women base their sense of middle age on different criteria than do men, however. While women define their age status in terms of timing of events within the family circle, men tend to use career or work position to mark their life stage. Neugarten reports (as we would expect) that married women define the period at which their children take their place in the adult world as middle age; however, a surprising finding is that even unmarried career women often describe middle age in terms of the family they might have had.[16]

Writers have often noted that women's lives are more closely tied to biologic variables than are the lives of men. And, in a sense, this is true—certainly in terms of reproductive events. However, it now appears that this biologic influence may have been unduly stereotyped as being inevitably *central* and *critical* in woman's life (especially as we are changing sex and age roles in our society).

The Impact of Age 30

Notman has stated that women also sense the age 30 crisis (which Levinson noted for men). "For many, 30 is the important birthday which makes the transition out of 'youth' . . . the loss of youth is more critical socially for women than for men."[17] Sontag (a journalist to whom Notman refers the reader in lieu of being able to find articles in medical journals on this subject) says:

For the normal changes that age inscribes on every human face, women are much more heavily penalized than men. . . . In a man's face lines are taken to be signs of "character." They indicate emotional strength, maturity—qualities far more esteemed in men than in women. (They show he has "lived.") Even scars are often not felt to be unattractive; they too can add "character" to a man's face. But lines of aging, any scar, even a small birthmark on a woman's face, are always regarded as unfortunate blemishes. In effect, people take character in men to be different from what constitutes character in women.

There is no way to keep certain lines from appearing, in one's mid-twenties, around the eyes and mouth. From about thirty on, the skin gradually loses its tonus. In women this perfectly natural process is regarded as a humiliating defeat, while nobody finds anything remarkably unattractive in the equivalent physical changes in men. Men are "allowed" to look older without sexual penalty.[18]

In addition, when a man reaches age 30 it does not have the same impact on reproductive decisions as it does for a woman. Under pressure from prevailing medical and social opinion about the best time for pregnancy, many women feel that they must make a decision to have or not to have children by the age of 30. Notman states that even those women who are not interested in having children are aware of the choice they have made as they approach 30—and they may even need to rework their earlier decision. Among young professional women, the same reexamination of life plans is said to take place as was noted for young men by Levinson.

The "Empty Nest" Period

Two periods of a middle-aged woman's life are especially noteworthy: the time when all her children have left home and the years of the climacterium. In the past, it was thought that the former was one in which most women experience a significant "letdown" or depression. The term "empty nest syndrome" has been used to characterize this "crisis." In a recent study of middle and lower middle class men and women whose youngest child was about to leave home, however, the concept of the empty nest syndrome has been challenged.[19] The subjects in the study were not questioned directly about their evaluation of this period of their lives but were asked to rate all the periods of their lives from adolescence through age 65 on a scale from 1 to 5 (with the higher numbers indicating greater satisfaction). These evaluations showed that the two periods of life that received the lowest number of points (i.e., indicating dissatisfaction) were adolescence and early middle age (a phase that roughly corresponds to Levinson's Mid-life Transition). In contrast, the so-called empty nest period was perceived by both men and women as a "promising" one. A typical comment from the female respondents (most of whom did not hold jobs outside the home) was: "I feel my job with them is done. I don't have to discipline them anymore, it's their problem. . . . I hope I can always be a mother, but we will treat each other as adults. I have a much more relaxed feeling now."

The respondents appeared to be looking forward to enjoying a less complex, less encumbered life-style. Rather than a crisis or a challenge, the period of the youngest child's departure was perceived as a relief to the majority in this study. Of course, the findings in this investigation must be replicated before they can be accepted without reservation.

The Menopausal Period

The climacterium is another phase of middle-aged life that may have been mistakenly stereotyped. In women, it designates the period of gradual diminution of ovarian function, beginning anywhere from the early forties to early fifties and lasting generally from 5 to 10 years. The laity, and even many physicians, commonly refer to this time in a woman's life as the menopause. Since menopause (technically defined as the *cessation* of the menses) is only one of the events taking place in the climacterium, however, it is incorrect to use this term to describe the entire period. Nevertheless, because of its widespread usage, we will also use the term "menopausal period" interchangeably with the "climacterium."

In a 1974 review of the literature dealing with the climacterium, McKinlay and McKinlay noted that research in this field has been both sparse and of poor quality.[20] Many of the existing studies consist only of case histories and reports of the clinical experiences of gynecologists and psychiatrists, who see women with problems. They are not based on systematically gathered data from a random sample of women, including both those who are and those who are *not* under psychiatric or medical treatment during this period of their lives. Thus, some of the traditional beliefs held about this period of life (e.g., that it is a highly stressful time for most women and that disabling physical and emotional symptoms are common) may reflect investigational bias. There is no basis for assuming that the information about the climacterium obtained from patients can be generalized to nonpatients—a common mistake made in interpreting the data in the literature.

An article by Lennane and Lennane points out that certain beliefs among physicians regarding female (or female-related) disorders often persist in the face of overwhelming contradictory evidence.[21] For three of these disorders (dysmenorrhea, nausea of pregnancy, and labor pain), scientifically gathered data have contradicted prevailing beliefs. For the climacterium, a similar body of reliable and valid data is now beginning to appear. It, too, may take a while to become generally accepted, especially if it contradicts current thinking.

Let us turn now to several of these recent articles. Winokur, a psychiatrist at the University of Iowa College of Medicine, wondered whether depressive episodes that had their onset around the time of the climacterium, and as a result were attributed to it, might be only a chance occurrence.[22] Inasmuch as approximately 40% of the first attacks of manic-depressive disease occur during the two decades between the ages of 40 and 60 and this is *also* the period during which the climacterium takes place, he reasoned that perhaps physicians were incorrectly assuming the two were related. He studied 71 women, all consecutive admissions to a psychiatric ward with diagnoses of an affective disorder. Applying the appropriate formulas to determine whether the women were at greater risk during the menopausal period than at other times during the life span revealed "a 7.1% risk of developing an affective disorder during the menopausal years and a 6% risk during other times" (not a significant difference).[22]

In reviewing the endocrinologic data regarding the nature and extent of symptoms related to the climacterium, Perlmutter states, "There are multiple disorders that have been ascribed to the changing hormonal balance and are equated with the menopause. In reality, not all the changes that are noted are due to hormonal imbalance; some are the consequences of aging and others have a basis in psychological factors and life patterns."[23] In fact, as of 1973, there was still some question as to the exact composition of the "menopausal syndrome."[20]

The following is from a study of women who were *not* selected from a patient population:

Results of a postal questionnaire survey of 638 women aged 45 to 54, living in the London area in 1964–65, indicate (consistent with other recent surveys) that hot flushes and night sweats are clearly associated with the onset of a natural menopause and that they occur in the majority of women. Hot flushes were reported to occur more frequently (usually daily) and over more of the body by women whose menstrual flow showed evidence of change or cessation, and for 25% of those women whose menses had ceased for at least one year, hot flushes persisted for five years or more. The other six symptoms specified, namely, headaches, dizzy spells, palpitations, sleeplessness, depression, and weight increase, showed no direct relationship to the menopause but tended to occur together, each being reported by approximately 30 to 50% of the respondents with little variation according to menopausal status. None of the six sociodemographic variables investigated, i.e., employment status, school leaving age, social class, domestic workload, marital status, and parity, had any marked association with the reported frequency of symptoms. The majority of respondents did not anticipate or experience any difficulties and only about 10% expressed regret at the cessation of menses. Despite embarrassment and/or discomfort from hot flushes reported by nearly three-quarters of those experiencing this symptom, only one-fifth had apparently sought medical treatment.[24]

As one part of Neugarten's classic study of personality in middle age, she and her colleagues administered an "Attitudes-Towards-Menopause Checklist" to a sample of 100 women between the ages of 45 and 55 drawn from lists of mothers of graduates of two Chicago high schools. Even though many of the respondents professed not to believe in what they called "old wives' tales," most were aware of such common beliefs as "women are especially prey to mental breakdown at this period" and "the menopause ends female attractiveness and sexual desires." In spite of this, a substantial number did not appear to be unduly concerned about the period. Three questions from the checklist and the percentage of women in agreement with them follow:[25]

II. 17. After the change of life, a women feels freer to do things for herself. (74% agreed)
III. 12. Going through the menopause really does not change a woman in any important way. (74% agreed)
IV. 7. Women who have trouble in the menopause are those who are expecting it. (76% agreed)

Although 58% agreed with the statement that "menopause is an unpleasant experience for a woman," a typical added comment was: "Yes, the change of life is an unpleasant time, no one enjoys the hot flushes, the headaches, or the nervous tension. . . . But I've gone through changes before, and I can weather another one. Besides, it's only a temporary condition."

The preceding discussion alerts the reader to the fact that recent investigations are casting doubt on some traditionally held concepts about the climacterium. Cross-cultural data are providing increasing evidence that hot flushes and "night sweats" are the only true hormonal-related symptoms of the menopausal period.[26] The other symptoms which in the past have been associated with the climacterium (e.g., depression, headaches, insomnia) are apparently of psychological, social, or cultural origin.[26, 27] The major influence of the sociocultural environment in modifying female response to this period was revealed in a study of 483 Indian women of the Rajput caste. Premenopausal women are kept veiled and secluded within their quarters (according to the Indian custom of purdah). Postmenopausal women, however, are no longer considered to be contaminated by menstrual blood, nor are they required to wear a veil, but are granted a higher status and can leave their quarters at will to visit with men as equals. The perception of menopause is thus quite different among women in this caste who see it as liberating and as a reward, contrary to the perception held by females in many other cultures. It is not surprising that investigators found that few of the Rajput women experienced nonhormone-related symptoms, in contrast to the United States where the menopause is thought by some women to signal "the end of the road."[26, 27] Clearly, more attention needs to be devoted to the role of sociocultural factors in structuring symptom formation during the climacterium.

ACTIVITIES AND ISSUES IN THE ADULT YEARS

The Young Adult

Central to one's life structure is making the right choices and dealing with their consequences, and the most critical choices one must make relate to work, family, religion, friendships, and love relationships. Of these, two appeared frequently in Levinson's data as primary: work and marriage-family. Inasmuch as these are universal characteristics of human life, let us look at these specifically—reminding ourselves that they are experienced at different times and in different ways by adults and that, indeed, some do not experience either.

WORK.—Within our society, occupation touches the individual in many ways. It determines his physical and social environment 8 hours a day; it influences the individual's lifestyle and status within the community; it is also the medium most frequently used to pursue one's dreams. As Levinson analyzed it:

At best, his occupation permits the fulfillment of basic values and life goals. At worst, a man's work life over the years is oppressive and corrupting, and contributes to a growing alienation from self, work and society. In studying a man's life, we need to understand the meaning of work and the multiple ways in which it may serve to fulfill, to barely sustain or to destroy the self.[7]

Work even has been associated with one's personality traits. A common example of this last relationship from the medical profession is the difference in personality attributes needed for work in the emergency room and in family medicine. In the emergency room, patient-physician contact is on a short-term basis, focused on the presenting problem only, with critical decisions having to be made under stress of time and often without knowing anything about the patient except a number of demographic characteristics. In contrast, a family medicine practitioner works in a slower-paced treatment setting in which he or she can establish a long-term relationship with patients and provide holistic care based on knowledge of the individual's social context and physical, spiritual, and mental needs.

The earliest considerations about one's future often are *unrealistic* ones, fueled by children's stories and games (counting buttons to find out whether one will be "doctor, lawyer, Indian chief, richman, poorman, beggarman, or thief"). Television has made children aware of an enormous variety of jobs to be considered, and children "try these out" in play activities. Gradually, the child begins to take into consideration his or her special interests, abilities, and limitations, and to focus on certain jobs that are realistically within reach.

Unfortunately, the choice of occupation for many is largely determined for them by such factors as the geographic region in which they are born (e.g., the coal-mining area of West

Virginia or the midwestern farm belt), their parents' social class (how much opportunity is there to obtain the education necessary to achieve their occupational goal?), and their gender (a middle-aged woman today had little opportunity or encouragement to train as a telephone lineman or trial lawyer no matter how well suited she might have been). Women can now be increasingly expected to enter virtually every occupation. In the United States, the custom has been for women not to enter occupations that require considerable strength (such as stevedores and truck drivers). However, there is apparently no physiological basis for this, since in other cultures, women perform jobs that would be thought, in the United States, to be outside their capability. (Lidz gives examples of this: the Soviet Union, where women clean and repair roads, and New Guinea, where "everyone knows that women are built" so that they can carry heavier loads than men). We can expect that as more women are raised to believe that to be aggressive and competitive is acceptable, more will also be seen in high administrative positions.

The well-known term TGIF (Thank God It's Friday) attests to the fact that many workers do not find satisfaction and stimulation in their jobs. Studs Terkel, in his well-researched bestseller of several years ago, supported this; his findings indicated widespread dissatisfaction of workers with their jobs. Only recently in this country have any substantial numbers of people had a reasonable choice of occupation. The knowledge that many individuals are unable to choose an occupation that reflects their interests, values, and abilities should alert us to the possible role this might play in psychosomatic illness. Although many physicians are now aware of the need to question a patient about his or her marital or family relationships when it is difficult to identify a physiological basis for the presenting complaint, they are not so likely to relate psychologically based somatic difficulties to job dissatisfaction.

MARRIAGE.—Although there are socially acceptable alternatives to marriage and the formation of a nuclear family (e.g., sharing an apartment or home with someone of the opposite sex, remaining unmarried, joining a commune), marriage is still the preferred way of life for the majority. Sexuality per se certainly does not explain why two people marry. Indeed, in our society most adults do not believe that marriage is a necessary condition for sexual activity. Rather, it appears that a marital relationship (over generations and across cultures) provides the most consistently stable context for the rearing of young. Further, it enables a man and a woman (each possessing different abilities and filling different roles) to complement each other in providing a child with a secure foundation.

Marriage entails entering into a legal commitment (and, in most cases, a religious one as well) with another person. This relationship acknowledges a reciprocal responsibility to each other to share economically and sexually in the establishment of a new family unit. A lengthy list of reasons why people devote themselves to marriage has been formulated by Bowden and Burstein:[28]

1. Love.—Here, they note that there can be romantic love ("a state of intense but often transient passion" and a poor basis for marriage) as well as marital love. This term, "marital love," is used to imply feelings of mutual responsibility as well as a reciprocity of "intense psychological investment" in each other.
2. Completion of one's identity.—Marriage is seen as providing a feeling of self-adequacy and a sense of completion to one's idealized self-concept.
3. Procreation.—The wish to become parents in terms of contributing productive members to the next generation.
4. Sexuality.—The opportunity to meet sexual needs while at the same time filling affectional and security needs.
5. Security and escape.—There are some who desire to have economic security, to achieve a higher social status, or to be cared for by another. These can be legitimate concerns; danger arises when one of them is the primary motivating factor.
6. Unconscious needs.—Most readers will

be able to think of at least one emotional relationship that can be described as sadomasochistic (i.e., one spouse enjoys mentally and/or literally beating up the other—who has an equal need to be beaten up). Neither is aware of his or her behavior. It is worth noting here that the wish to have a spouse fill the role of a parent is not necessarily neurotic or harmful in a marriage. Indeed, in times of stress, disappointment, or illness, a maternal or paternal nurturant attitude on the part of the spouse can be particularly comforting and helpful.

7. Pregnancy.—A significant number of brides are pregnant at the time of marriage (and the proportion is even higher among youger persons and those in the lower socioeconomic groups).

The developmental history of marital choice is similar to that of occupation. It begins with fantasies: the incestuous wish to marry one's parent ("I Want a Girl Just Like the Girl That Married Dear Old Dad") or a parent substitute such as a teacher. During adolescence, the individual commonly has a "crush" on an older adolescent (a high school football hero or cheerleader) who is imagined to embody perfection and ideal love. During this period, the young person is gaining familiarity with members of the opposite sex and important information regarding what type of person he or she feels most comfortable with. The adolescent is also finding out what kind of person *he* or *she* attracts. Finally, the young adult actually "tries out" potential partners in dating and courtship.

When final decisions are made and the wedding is over, adjustment on the part of both partners becomes central. They must work together to find "reciprocally interrelating roles that permit the meshing of activities with minimal friction; it includes the reorganization of the family patterns which each spouse learned at home, and which may involve differing ethnic and social class patterns."[11] This is of special concern in the United States where many persons marry others of a different religious persuasion, ethnic background, and social class. In such situations, each will be bringing different beliefs, values, and behaviors into the union.

Ideally, both partners characterize their marriage as good. Although a satisfactory marriage can be many things to many people, depending on the needs of the particular partners, the "good marriage" has been described as having "a minimum of tension, certainty of the esteem of one's partner, a steady warmth of affection, the sense of mutual support in the face of inescapable life crises and, perhaps centrally, the sense of reciprocal gratification."[28] Unfortunately, the "good marriage" seems to be increasingly difficult to achieve, with approximately 50% of all marriages currently ending in divorce.[28] This is all the more poignant in view of the impact of divorce on children.

Often marital problems can be explained in terms of one spouse not meeting the needs of the other. These needs frequently are not recognized by one or both. An example of this pattern might be a man who marries a young woman whom he sees as a very nurturant kind of person because she has been successfully and warmly raising several younger brothers and sisters after the death of their mother. He is drawn to her to fill an unconscious need for "mothering." She, on the other hand, is not aware of this and is delighted to be relieved of her unexpected mother-substitute role by virtue of her marriage.

A second pattern may be illustrated by a marriage in which goals are mutually inconsistent. A young man marries with the expectation that he has found a partner with the traditional values and needs to establish a family. This wife soon becomes involved in the women's movement and joins the local zero population group; she becomes sincerely convinced that it is in the best interests of mankind that they give up any plans to have children. This situation reminds us of the problems that many young (and not so young!) couples have today in attempting to build equity in marriage. The data from a study by the Rapoports indicate that there is a point (which the investigators have called the "identity tension-line") at which one spouse may feel such great discomfort in experimenting with a new unfamiliar sex role that it is wisest not to push beyond that limit at that time.[29] To do so would jeopardize that spouse's emotional health or the integrity of the marriage.

FAMILY.—As mentioned, marriage is the mechanism by which a new family unit is formed. As the basic unit in social systems all over the world, the family has two critical functions—nurturance and enculturation/socialization. Nurturance applies whether there are children or not; enculturation/socialization pertains only to the raising of children.
1. Nurturance.—The family is the means by which the physical, emotional, affectionate, and security needs of all its members are met.
2. Enculturation and socialization.*—Enculturation is the process by which children are taught the values, customs, and language of their cultural group. Socialization is another type of learning that is critical in human development. Closely associated with enculturation, this is the process by which the child learns how to get along within the social groups of his culture (or, said another way, how he is trained for social participation in groups).

If the marital partners decide to become parents (or inadvertently find themselves having to prepare for that role), new tasks await them. Having worked before marriage to establish their own individual identities and having developed within marriage a relationship of intimacy and interdependence, they now must make emotional room for a third person for whom they will be primarily responsible for almost two decades.

The Middle Years

CRITICAL ISSUES.—Peck has identified several positive qualities that, if developed by middle-aged individuals, can enable them to make successful adjustments to this period.[30] He has described them along with their negative counterparts.

VALUING WISDOM VERSUS VALUING PHYSICAL POWERS.—One issue of the middle years is depicted by Peck as "valuing wisdom versus valuing physical powers." He suggests that those individuals who are able to change their earlier hierarchy and now place using their "heads" ahead of using their "hands" will weather the middle years most successfully. A waning in physical strength, stamina, and attractiveness (attractiveness being associated in the United States with youthfulness) is inevitable during middle adulthood. A middle-aged individual, however, can utilize life experience and wisdom (defined as "judgmental powers") to solve problems for which younger people use physical powers. Wisdom should be thought of not only as one's chief resource in problem-solving but also as a standard for self-evaluation.

SOCIALIZING VERSUS SEXUALIZING IN HUMAN RELATIONSHIPS.—Here, Peck suggests that a positive outcome of middle age (and the climacterium) is the ability to see others to a much greater extent than previously as "individual personalities, rather than primarily as sex-objects." Deeply satisfying interpersonal relationships may accompany this ability to redefine others as primarily individuals and companions and less in terms of sexual gender.

CATHECTIC FLEXIBILITY VERSUS CATHECTIC IMPOVERISHMENT.—This issue deals with a quality (or ability) that is helpful in any developmental period but takes on a more important value during the middle years: "the capacity to shift emotional investments from one person to another and from one activity to another." Children are leaving home, parents are dying, and the middle-aged adult is beginning to see contemporary friends and relatives die. (Fortunately, this is also frequently the period of widest contacts and most numerous friendships.) An individual's emotional life may suffer in the next stage if he or she cannot "reinvest" emotionally in dif-

---

*Many sociologists and psychologists use the two terms interchangeably, although most anthropologists make a distinction between the two.

ferent people and different activities. Peck sees an important task of this period as not only learning to transfer cathexis from individual A to individual B and from activity A to activity B but also learning the *generalized* skill of making new cathexes.

An additional issue has been described by other writers. It deals with how the middle-aged individual copes with the change in body and self-image. The adult in his or her middle years "becomes conscious of a . . . changing body image—greyness, baldness, loss of teeth, longsightedness, and the onset of [various chronic] diseases."[31] This leads to a realization of death, which in turn directs the individual to a changing time perspective; the period ahead is now seen as limited and one measures life in terms of not how long one has lived but how long one has left. The changes in body image can lead the individual to take one of two different paths. Some, reflecting social expectations and stereotypes, react to their changing body image by viewing themselves as vulnerable and no longer strong and healthy. This may lead to underfunctioning physically and/or to the development of neurotic worries concerning health (overconcern with daily aches and pains, fatigue). Others, perceiving their body image in more youthful terms than is realistic, may react by "unrealistic self-driving" (overtaxing the body, ignoring significant symptoms). In either of these two paths, there is a discrepancy between the individual's body image and the objective facts.

Self-imagery is an area in which the transcultural approach is of great interest. For example, in China, the traditional cultural beliefs are that the most enjoyable time of life is the period after retirement from work. The culture's most highly valued pursuits (contemplation, poetry, arts, philosophy) are all well suited to retirement. The period between ages 40 and 50 is thus too young in China to be valued as the prime of life. In contrast, in most English-speaking countries, where physical activity is more highly prized, the forties and fifties are considered *past* one's prime!

SUMMARY

Until recently little systematic research had been done on the adult period of the life cycle. Current studies indicate that this phase of life may be a continuation of psychosocial development begun in childhood and adolescence. The data from these investigations indicate a sequence of psychosocial stages in the young and middle years. Each stage is characterized in terms of issues to be dealt with and tasks to be worked through. Decisions in regard to these issues and tasks are crucial in providing the base for a satisfying or unsatisfactory life structure. Caveats from other researchers in the field, however, caution against accepting uncritically an invariant sequence of stages during adulthood with accompanying tasks or goals.

Although there is a great need for more systematically collected data on women in the young and middle adult years, it now appears that the biologic influence in a woman's life may have been unduly stereotyped as being inevitably central and critical. The empty nest syndrome and the concept of the menopausal period as a time of great stress and disabling physical and emotional symptoms are being challenged by new evidence.

REFERENCES

1. Levinson D.J., et al.: The psychosocial development of men in early adulthood and the mid-life transition, in Ricks D.F., et al. (eds.): *Life History Research in Psychopathology*. Minneapolis, University of Minnesota Press, 1974.
2. Erikson E.G.: *Childhood and Society*. New York, W.W. Norton & Company, Inc., 1950.
3. Buhler C.: *Der menschliche Lebenslauf als psychologisches Problem*. Leipzig, Verlag von S. Hirzel, 1933.
4. Keniston K.: Youth: A "new" stage of life. *Am. Scholar* 39:631, 1970.
5. Keniston K.: Youth and its ideology, in Arieti S. (ed.): *American Handbook of Psychiatry*. New York, Basic Books, Inc., Publishers, 1974, vol. 1.
6. Gould R.L.: The phases of adult life: A study in developmental psychology. *Am. J. Psychiatry* 129(5):521, 1972.
7. Levinson D.J.: *The Seasons of a Man's Life*. New York, Alfred A. Knopf, Inc., 1978.

8. Levinson D.J.: Eras: The anatomy of the life cycle. *Psychiatric Opinion* 15(9):10, September 1978.
9. Gould R.: "Is *Passages* Leading Us Astray?" *Miami Herald*, January 15, 1979.
10. Levinson D.J.: The mid-life transition: A period in adult psychosocial development. *Psychiatry* 40:99, 1977.
11. Lidz T.: *The Person*. New York: Basic Books, Inc., Publishers, 1976.
12. Butler R.M.: Psychiatry and psychology of the middle aged, in Freedman A.M., et al. (eds.): *Comprehensive Textbook of Psychiatry*. Baltimore, Williams & Wilkins Co., 1975, vol. 2.
13. Neugarten B.L.: Time, age and the life cycle. *Am. J. Psychiatry* 136(7):887, 1979.
14. Kluckhohn F.R., Strodtbeck F.L.: *Variations in Value Orientations*. Evanston, Ill., Row, Peterson & Co., 1961.
15. Hirschhorn L.: Social policy and the life cycle: A developmental perspective. *Soc. Serv. Rev.* 51:434, 1977.
16. Neugarten B.: The awareness of aging, in Neugarten B. (ed.): *Middle Age and Aging*. Chicago, University of Chicago Press, 1968.
17. Notman M.T.: Women and mid-life: A different perspective. *Psychiatric Opinion* 15(9):15, September 1978.
18. Sontag S.: The double standard of aging. *Saturday Review of Literature*, 55(39):29, September 23, 1972.
19. Lowenthal M.F., Chiriboga D.: Transition to the empty nest. *Arch. Gen. Psychiatry* 26:8, 1972.
20. McKinlay S.M., McKinlay J.B.: Selected studies of the menopause. *J. Biosoc. Sci.* 5:533, 1973.
21. Lennane K.J., Lennane R.J.: Alleged psychogenic disorders in women—A possible manifestation of sexual prejudice. *N. Engl. J. Med.* 288:288 1973.
22. Winokur G.: Depression in the menopause. *Am. J. Psychiatry* 130(1):92 1973.
23. Perlmutter J.: The menopause: A gynecologist's views, in Notman M., Nadelson C. (eds.): *The Woman Patient*. New York, Plenum Publishing Corp., 1978.
24. McKinlay S.M., Jeffreys, M.: The menopausal syndrome. *Br. J. Prev. Soc. Med.* 28(2):108, 1974.
25. Neugarten B.L., et al.: Women's attitudes toward the menopause, in Neugarten B.L. (ed.): *Middle Age and Aging*. Chicago: The University of Chicago Press, 1968.
26. Utian W.H.: *Menopause in Modern Perspective*. New York, Appleton-Century-Crofts, 1980.
27. Fink P.J.: Psychiatric myths of the menopause, in Eskin B.A. (ed.): *The Menopause*. New York, Masson Publishing USA, Inc., 1980.
28. Bowden C.L., Burstein A.G.: *Psychosocial Basis of Medical Practice*, ed. 2. Baltimore, Williams & Wilkins Co., 1974.
29. Rapoport R., Rapoport R.: Men, women, and equity. *Family Coordinator* 24:421, 1975.
30. Peck, R.C.: Psychological developments in the second half of life, in Neugarten B.L. (ed.): *Middle Age and Aging*. Chicago, The University of Chicago Press, 1968.
31. Soddy K.: *Men in Middle Life*. London, J.B. Lippincott Co., 1967.

19 / The Geriatric Period

JONATHAN J. BRAUNSTEIN, M.D.

THE GERIATRIC PERIOD is generally considered to begin at age 65, although the aging process actually begins in the thirties. As in earlier stages of the life cycle, this period is associated with important biologic, psychological, and social changes. This chapter will describe some of these changes and how they affect the medical care of the elderly.

DEMOGRAPHIC ASPECTS OF AGING IN THE UNITED STATES*

Number of Older Persons

During the past 75 years there has been a progressive increase in the size of our aged population. In 1900, the number of people 65 and over in the United States was 3.1 million, by 1940 this figure had increased to 9.0 million, and by 1976 it had risen to 23 million. Furthermore, projections indicate that by the year 2000 there will be approximately 32 million elderly.

Since 1900 the size of the geriatric age group has grown more rapidly than the rest of the population. At that time, members of this age group constituted about 4% of our total population, whereas today they make up about 11%. During the period 1960–70, the size of the geriatric population increased 21%, as compared with an increase of only 13% for the population as a whole. In addition, it should be noted that the group 75 years and over (the "old-old") is growing even more rapidly than those aged 65–74 (the "young-old"). By the year 2000, there will be about 17 million "old-old" in the United States.

Sex and Race Composition

Women in the 65-and-older age group are the fastest-growing segment of the U.S. population.[2] There has been a gradual decline in the sex ratio (men per 100 women) of those over age 65 during the past 40 years. In 1970, it was estimated that there were only 72 men per 100 women over age 65. This trend is expected to continue so that by the year 2000 there will be only 68 men for every 100 women in the geriatric age group. Measured in terms of longevity, women are clearly the "stronger" sex.

The greater number of women in the geriatric age group is the result of higher mortality among men in all segments of the population. Despite the general improvement in health in the past 50 years, the mortality of men has declined much less than that of women. When compared with the white population in this country, the black population has a much smaller proportion of its members who are 65 and over, which can be attributed to higher mortality among blacks in younger age groups.

Geographic Variations

The geographic distribution of elderly persons follows that of the general population. The most populous states, i.e., New York, California, Pennsylvania, and Illinois, have nearly one third of the population 65 years and over. Of all the states, Arizona, Nevada,

---

*The data for this part of the discussion are taken from an article by Jacob Siegel on the demographic aspects of aging[1] and the special report on aging (1979) prepared by the National Institute on Aging.[2]

and Florida have had the largest percentage increase in the number of people in the geriatric age group, growing by more than 70% between 1960 and 1970. Considering that the overall geriatric population grew by only 21% during this time, it is obvious that there was a large influx of the elderly into these states. In 1970, Florida ranked first in the nation in the percentage of elderly, with 14.6% of its population aged 65 and over and 5% aged 75 or over.

Mortality and Survival

Life expectancy from birth has shown a great increase since 1900 (see Table 9–1). Since this statistic is a function of lower death rates at all ages, it does not reveal the extent to which those over 65 years old have benefited. In fact, most of the progress in extending life expectancy from birth is due to a reduction in mortality in the younger population, especially in the neonatal period. In 1900–1902, 39% of the newborns could expect to reach age 65, while in 1969 this figure was 72%. The percentage of persons aged 65 who could expect to survive to age 80 was 33% in 1900–1902, increasing to 49% in 1969. Thus, there was a greater improvement in survival statistics for those under 65 compared with those over 65.

Life expectancy for men is less than that for women for all races in this country. Also, the black population is at a disadvantage when compared with the white in terms of survival.

Causes of Death

Diseases of the heart far outrank the other causes of death among persons 65 and over. Table 19–1 gives the mortality (number of deaths per 100,000 population) for the leading causes of death in this age group in 1977. The first three (diseases of the heart, malignant neoplasms, and cerebrovascular disease) account for 75% of the deaths.

The death rates for men aged 65 and over due to diseases of the heart, malignant neoplasms, influenza and pneumonia, accidents, bronchitis, emphysema, and asthma are greater than those for women. Also, there is a marked difference in the death rates between the white and black population over age 65, with the rates for the black population being much higher for every major disease except bronchitis, emphysema, and asthma.

TABLE 19–1.—MORTALITY FOR PERSONS 65 AND OVER IN 1977

RANK	CAUSE	RATE*
1	Diseases of heart	2,334.1
2	Malignant neoplasms	988.5
3	Cerebrovascular disease	658.2
4	Influenza and pneumonia	169.7
5	Arteriosclerosis	116.5
6	Accidents	102.6
7	Diabetes mellitus	100.5
8	Bronchitis, emphysema, and asthma	69.3
9	Cirrhosis of liver	36.7

*Number of deaths per 100,000 population.
Based on data from *Healthy People: The Surgeon General's Report on Health Promotion and Disease Prevention 1979.* DHEW (PHS), Pub. No. 79–55071.

Social and Economic Characteristics

Some important social aspects of the elderly include education, marital and family characteristics, work status, and income. In 1969–70, only 28% of those in the geriatric age group were high school graduates. Half of them had completed less than nine years of school. This educational experience is much less than that of the current population aged 25–65. This situation is changing rapidly, however, as younger persons with more education move into the geriatric age group.

The marital situation and living arrangements of the elderly differ according to sex (Tables 19–2 and 19–3). Most men 65 and over are married and live with their wives; most women in this age group are widowed and a significant number live alone. Contrary to the popular belief, only about 5% of the elderly live in institutions.

The work status of the elderly has changed in recent years. In 1950, 46% of men 65 years and over were members of the labor force; by 1971, this figure was 26%, and it was projected to drop to 22% by 1980. This decline is the result of the increased number of voluntary retirement programs, more stringent retirement policies by employers, and the decline in self-employment. The recent passage

TABLE 19–2.—
DISTRIBUTION OF
POPULATION 65 YEARS AND
OVER IN 1971, BY MARITAL
STATUS AND SEX

	MEN	WOMEN
Single	7.1%	7.3%
Married	73.1	36.2
Widowed	17.1	54.2
Divorced	2.7	2.3

Based on data from Siegel J.: Some Demographic Aspects of Aging in the United States, in Ostfeld A.M., Gibson D.C. (eds.): *Epidemiology of Aging*, DHEW Publication, NIH, No. 75–711, 1972.

TABLE 19–3.—LIVING ARRANGEMENTS OF PEOPLE 65 YEARS AND OVER IN 1971

	MEN	WOMEN
Total	8,473	11,620
Living alone	13.9%	34.8%
Spouse present	70.1%	34.5%
Living with someone else	15.9%	30.7%

Based on data from Siegel J.: Some Demographic Aspects of Aging in the United States, in Ostfeld A.M., Gibson D.C. (eds.): *Epidemiology of Aging*, DHEW Publication, NIH, No. 75–711, 1972.

of a law by Congress extending the age of retirement to 70 may reverse this trend somewhat.

The income of a substantial number of people who are 65 and over is below the poverty level. The U.S. Census Bureau reports that in 1979 there were 3.6 million poor elderly, up from a figure of 3.2 million in 1978.

BIOLOGIC CHANGES WITH AGING

Age-related biologic and physical changes begin to appear in the thirties and reach their full expression in the geriatric period. At times, it may be difficult for the clinician to distinguish the effects of disease on the body from the changes due to aging. In contrast to disease, however, aging is universal; the fact that it occurs to everyone makes it a normal phenomenon. The cause of the aging process is unknown but it is probably related to both genetic and environmental factors. Externally, the effects of aging are readily apparent as they alter the physical appearance of the individual. Internally, the effects may not be so obvious, but nonetheless they are very significant.

As a consequence of aging, there is a reduction in the size and functional capacity of most of the body's organs due primarily to a loss of cell mass. In the elderly, an organ system may function perfectly well at rest but fail to respond appropriately when challenged by a stressful situation. This is often the case with respect to the heart, lungs, and kidneys. Adjustments to changes in the internal environment of the body are impaired. Many of the effects of aging render the elderly more vulnerable to disease.

Although the aging process is inevitable, the rate at which it occurs and the extent of the biologic and physical changes it produces vary from person to person. Two people of the same chronological age (say, 65 years) may differ considerably from a biologic standpoint. One may have the physiological makeup of a person in his fifties, while the other may appear to be in his seventies in terms of this physical condition. The clinician responsible for the care of geriatric persons should be aware of the distinction between chronological and biologic age, and that the former may not be an accurate reflection of the latter.

In the following sections, some biologic changes that accompany the aging process will be described. Most of the studies quoted are *cross-sectional*. In this type of study, single measurements of biologic phenomena are made in healthy individuals in various age brackets, i.e., 30–40, 40–50, 50–60, 60–70, etc. The mean values are obtained for each age group, and on the basis of these values comparisons are made between the groups to determine (1) the extent of the biologic changes that take place with aging and (2) the rate at which they occur. The major drawback of cross-sectional studies is that they do not detect individual variations in either of these two parameters. To obtain this information, *longitudinal* studies are necessary, in which the same individual is observed over a prolonged period of time, with repeated measurements taken to determine the effects of aging. These studies are much more difficult to carry out and they take a long time to complete; consequently, only a few have been reported in the literature. Duke University's longitudinal studies and the National Institute of Aging's Baltimore longitudinal study are the prototypes of these kinds of studies of aging.

Body Composition

The following characteristic changes in body composition occur in the elderly:

1. Decrease in lean body mass
2. Increase in amount of adipose tissue
3. Decrease in total body water
4. Decrease in intracellular water
5. Decrease in total body potassium

The total number of cells in the body decreases about 30% from age 35 to 75. This is reflected by a decrease in lean body mass and total body water. The reduction in metabolically active cells is associated with a decline in basal oxygen utilization as measured by the basal metabolic rate (BMR). Thyroid function is normal in the elderly in the absence of disease; therefore, one can assume that the metabolic activity of the existing cells is also normal.

Bone mass decreases after age 40 in both men and women, although the loss of bone mass is more severe in women. Their rate of loss per decade (after age 40) has been estimated to be 8%, as contrasted to only 3% in men.[3] The loss of bone structure results in characteristic changes in body stature in the elderly (e.g., loss of height, kyphosis of spine) and predisposes them to fractures.

Cardiovascular System

Structurally, the most striking age-related change in the heart is the presence of a lipofuscin pigment.[4] There is a progressive accumulation of this pigment within the myocardial fibers after the age of 20. In the very old it may constitute as much as 30% of the total solids of a fiber, although it does not seem to interfere significantly with myocardial function.

The heart valves, particularly the mitral and aortic, become thickened with age due to degenerative changes in the collagen fibers, deposition of fibrous tissues, and accumulation of lipid and calcium.[5] The endocardium of the left ventricle may also undergo local thickening and fibrosis. It is generally felt that these changes are due to hemodynamic factors associated with blood flow and repeated valve closure and, in the absence of specific heart disease, do not interfere significantly with cardiac function.

An increased amount of collagen is found in the subendothelial region and media of the medium and large arteries.[6] Other changes take place, including a straightening, fragmenting, and splitting of the elastic fibers and a deposition of calcium in the media of these vessels. The effects of these changes are to decrease the resiliency and to increase the rigidity of the major arterial vessels. Physiologically, this is reflected by a higher intra-aortic systolic pressure and an increase in the velocity of the aortic pulse wave.

The resting arterial blood pressure and pulse vary with age. Systolic and diastolic blood pressures both increase in persons in the geriatric age group.[7] The systolic pressure may rise to 140–150 mm Hg and the diastolic to 85 mm Hg. The diastolic pressure does not exceed 90 mm Hg as a result of aging, so any value greater than this should be considered an indication of hypertension, just as in the young. The resting heart rate tends to slow with age, and older individuals do not achieve so great an increase in their heart rate when undergoing maximal exercise.

Cardiac output at rest decreases progressively with age after the third decade[8] (Fig 19–1). This change is estimated to be about 1% per year. The decrease in cardiac output is not necessarily due to impaired myocardial capacity; rather, it seems to be related to the diminished metabolic needs of the body which result from an age-related loss of metabolically active cells. Studies of left ventricular function indicate that it diminishes with

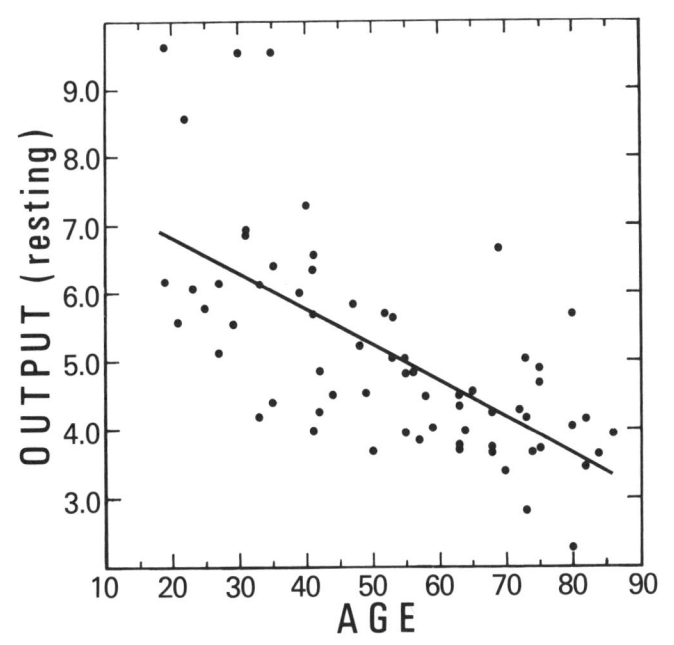

Fig 19–1.—The relation between resting cardiac output and age in 67 men without circulatory disorders. The line represents the linear regression on age. (From Brandfonbrener M., Landowne M., Shock N.W.: *Circulation* 12:557-566, 1955. By permission of the American Heart Association, Inc.)

age, particularly when there is a need for increased cardiac output. It is likely that aging diminishes the "myocardial reserve" and makes the elderly person more susceptible to heart failure when excessive demands are made upon his heart by disease.

Respiratory System

In the elderly, the chest wall becomes less mobile due to degenerative changes in the spine and costal cartilages of the rib cage. Kyphosis of the dorsal spine is often seen. As a result of these changes, there is a reduction in the compliance of the chest wall, which increases the work of breathing.

Respiratory function declines with age.[9] Vital capacity (VC) and maximal voluntary ventilation (MVV) fall progressively between the third and ninth decades. The forced expiratory volume at one second (FEV_1) shows a similar decrease. Values for the partial pressure of oxygen in arterial blood (PaO_2) are lower in the geriatric age group. Measurement of the lung volumes demonstrates a progressive increase in residual volume (RV) after the age of 40. The ratio of residual volume to total lung capacity (RV/TLC) increases linearly with age.

The effect of some of the age-related changes in the structure and function of the respiratory system is to reduce the reserve capacity of the lungs. Many persons in the geriatric age group have a reduced cough efficiency and this may result in increased susceptibility to pulmonary complications (i.e., pneumonia) after surgery or when they are subjected to prolonged bed rest.

Renal Function

Changes in renal structure and function begin after the fourth decade and slowly progress throughout the lifetime of the individual. Structurally, the kidneys decrease in size, with a reduction of about 30% in mass by age 85. Renal blood flow and glomerular filtration rate diminish with age, both decreasing about 50% between the ages of 40 and 85.[10]

Renal tubular function shows a degree of reduction similar to that of glomerular function in the geriatric age group when measured by the tubular secretion of Diodrast or para-aminohippurate or the maximum tubular reabsorption of glucose. With progressive age, there is a reduction in the ability of the kidneys to concentrate and dilute the urine. The maximum specific gravity of 1.032 observed in the young decreases to 1.024 by age 80.[9] The maximum urine osmolality decreases from 1,040 at age 20 to 750 at age 80.[9] As a consequence, the elderly are much more vulnerable to dehydration when faced with diminished fluid intake or increased fluid loss.

The basis for all these functional changes is probably a decrease in the number of functional nephrons. From this standpoint, the aged kidney is similar to the diseased kidney in that the major change is a reduced number of intact nephrons. In general, decreased renal function due to the aging process does not result in symptoms; however, it does render the older person less able to respond to changes in the internal environment of the body that result from disease.

Endocrine Function

Adlin and Korenman have recently reviewed a symposium on this topic in which much of the following information was presented.[11]

The basal levels of most of the commonly measured hormones are within the normal range in healthy older persons. Exceptions to this generalization are the sex hormones (estrogens and testosterone) and the pituitary gonadotropins. Postmenopausal estrogen levels usually are low and accompanied by increased serum concentrations of follicle-stimulating hormone and luteinizing hormone. There is some disagreement in the literature with respect to the changes in testosterone levels with age. Previous studies indicated that these levels begin to decline in the sixth decade along with a rise in gonadotropin levels. However, a recent study of 76 healthy, nonobese men ages 25 to 79 failed to demonstrate a decrease in testosterone levels with age. In these men, testicular volume decreased and there was an increase in gonadotropins in the blood, suggesting that testicular function was reduced and that the testosterone levels were maintained in the normal range because of the compensatory increase in gonadotropins.

One of the most important endocrine-related functions to be affected in the elderly is glucose tolerance, which decreases progressively with advancing age. The following is a good "rule of thumb" to use in estimating the degree of change in blood sugar that normally occurs with age:

	Amount of Increase per Decade
Fasting blood glucose	1–2 mg/dl
Blood glucose 1 hour after a glucose load	10 mg/dl
Blood glucose 2 hours after a glucose load	5 mg/dl

Of course, before making the diagnosis of diabetes mellitus in an elderly person one must take into consideration the age-related changes in blood sugar.

The most important reason for the decline in glucose tolerance with age appears to be decreased tissue sensitivity to insulin. This, in turn, may be related to a decrease in cellular hormone receptors that has been found in the majority of the elderly.

Immune System

Age-related changes occur in the immune system that some physicians consider to be important in the genesis of the aging process and certain diseases of the elderly. There is a reduction in the amount of thymic tissue and in the number of circulating lymphocytes derived from the thymus (so-called T cells). Decreased immunologic responsiveness (both cellular and humoral) to external antigens is commonly found among the aged. As a consequence, their antibody responses to various vaccines may be impaired, as well as their reactions to diagnostic skin tests such as the tuberculin test. Decreased immunologic responsiveness may in part explain the increased susceptibility to infections seen in the geriatric age group.

In contrast to the decreased responsiveness

to external antigens, the elderly exhibit increased immunologic reactivity to internal or autoantigens. An example of the increased tendency to form autoantibodies is a higher incidence of a positive test for rheumatoid factor (in the absence of diseases causing the abnormality). An increase in the formation of autoantibodies has been attributed to a decrease in the number of suppressor T cells, those that inhibit the antibody response of plasma cells that come from bone marrow–derived lymphocytes (so-called B cells). In the opinion of some investigators, the failure of the immune system to recognize as "self" various components of the body may lead to an autoimmune process that can cause disease locally or, if generalized throughout the body, act as a mechanism for the aging process.

Nervous System and Special Senses

Anatomically, there is a progressive decrease in the weight of the brain, associated with a loss of neurons, after the sixth decade. It has been estimated that brain weight declines 10–15% from the time of young adulthood to age 70.[12] The loss of neurons is not uniform throughout the brain; certain parts suffer more than others. The cells of the cerebral cortex are particularly vulnerable. Focal abnormalities of the electroencephalogram have been reported in approximately 30% of healthy individuals over the age of 60.[12] With age, there also appears to be a progressive reduction in cerebral blood flow and cerebral oxygen consumption, associated with a rise in cerebrovascular resistance.[9] These changes may be related to arteriosclerotic cerebral vascular disease.

One of the most common misconceptions of the elderly is that they experience a progressive decline in intellectual function. This is supported by the stereotyped picture of the older person as forgetful and mentally slow. While these characteristics are found in some individuals who have organic disease of the brain, they are certainly not typical of the healthy geriatric population. In fact, less than 5% of these persons have manifestations indicating significant deterioration of mental function, i.e., so-called senile dementia. The remainder continue to function adequately from an intellectual or cognitive standpoint.

Early cross-sectional studies of intelligence in the general population were reported to show a "bow-shaped" curve, with scores on intelligence tests rising during the late teens and early thirties and declining progressively thereafter. Longitudinal studies conducted at Duke University, however, failed to show a decline in this function in the older age groups; for example, in a 10-year follow-up study of a group of healthy persons aged 60–69, no significant decrease in intellect was detected.[13] Of course, intelligence is affected by physical, psychological, and social factors in addition to intrinsic brain function. For example, it is reported that the elderly do better on tests in which there is no time limitation in making a response. If they are hurried, they frequently become anxious and withhold answers rather than risk making a mistake. Those aged persons who maintain normal intellectual function until very late in life are usually in good physical and emotional health and often come from the middle and upper socioeconomic classes.

Whether or not there is a "normal" decline in cognitive function in the elderly is as yet unresolved, but if there is one it is very mild. If a significant impairment in intellectual function occurs in an elderly person, it should not be attributed to "old age"; rather, this change indicates the need for a thorough medical evaluation to detect the presence of an organic or psychiatric illness.

Many different conditions may affect the brain in old age and give rise to diffuse impairment in cerebral function. The term "senility" is commonly used to refer to this mental deterioration, which is characterized by the loss of memory, judgment, intellect, and orientation. While a few of the diseases causing "senility" are irreversible (e.g., cerebral arteriosclerosis, senile dementia, Alzheimer's disease), some 100 reversible conditions can also produce this clinical picture.[2] Less than 5% of those over 65 develop senile dementia, but it is these patients who make up a large portion of the elderly population living in institutions.

Vision and hearing are affected by the aging process. Visual accommodation is impaired due to a loss of the pliability of the lens; consequently, almost everyone older than 45 requires reading glasses. The aged experience a reduction in the size of their visual fields, a decrease in the speed of dark adaptation, and an elevation in the threshold of minimal light perception. They have a limited ability to see in dim or dark environments, and therefore bright lighting should be used to illuminate darkened areas where they live. The pupil gets smaller with old age, making the examination of the ocular fundus difficult.

Hearing is diminished as a result of aging, particularly hearing the higher frequencies. The ability to hear and understand speech, even though speech frequencies are relatively low, may also be affected. The term "presbycusis" is given to the changes in hearing that occur in the elderly.

Taste and smell change with age. Studies comparing young and elderly subjects have shown that the latter are less able to identify, by taste and smell, a variety of foods and flavors.[2] Reduced sensitivity to odors, rather than lack of taste, appeared to be the main reason for the difficulty in identifying foods by the older subjects.

PSYCHOSOCIAL ASPECTS OF AGING

From the psychosocial as well as the physiological standpoint, the elderly population is heterogeneous. While certain generalizations can be made about psychosocial adaptation, there is a great deal of variability in the responses of the aged to psychosocial change. Adaptation to old age, as in other stages of life, is an individual matter that can best be understood by knowing the makeup of the person under consideration and his special life circumstances.

In his theory of psychosocial development, Erikson regards the principal issue facing the aged as "ego integrity versus despair."[14] The geriatric period can be one in which developmental progress continues to be made by the individual, but it can also be a time of despair and depression. It is a period when most people reflect about their earlier life with its successes and failures. To a significant extent, ego integrity is based on a feeling by the older person that his past activities have been worthwhile, constructive, and self-satisfying. Those who enter the geriatric period with positive feelings about what has come before in their life are much more likely to adapt successfully to the stresses they encounter. The elderly who have successfully completed the developmental tasks associated with the previous stages in the life cycle are better equipped to deal with the problems of old age.

Some of the experiences in the geriatric period that may impair ego integrity include (1) losses sustained by the individual, (2) physical and social inactivity, (3) retirement, and (4) dependency on others. In addition, negative social attitudes toward the elderly may have this effect. These constitute barriers to successful aging for many of the elderly.

The Losses of Old Age

In order to understand the psychological impact of aging, one must know something of the nature of the losses that occur to many in this stage of life.[15] These include:

1. *Loss of status.*—Although frequently referred to by the respectful title of "senior citizens," the elderly in our society are often treated as though they were a burden to their family and community.

2. *Loss of income.*—The median income of the elderly is much less than that of the rest of the adult population and the quality of life, insofar as it is related to money, is thereby diminished for them. This reduced financial status contributes to many of their other social problems.

3. *Loss of health.*—The geriatric segment of our population has many more health problems than the younger segments and utilizes the health care system to a far greater extent. In 1977, this group, amounting to about 11% of our population, accounted for 29% of the total health care dollars spent in this country.[16] The number of chronic illnesses in-

creases greatly with advancing age and impaired physical capacity is a major impediment to an adequate psychosocial adjustment. Public Health Service reports indicate that almost half the population aged 65 and older has some limitation of physical activity due to chronic disease. Figure 19–2, depicting the number of restricted-activity and bed-disability days per person per year by age and sex in 1971, shows how much greater the degree of disability is among the elderly when compared with other age groups.

4. *Loss of company.*—Retirement and the death of family and friends are responsible for a certain degree of social isolation. A lack of transportation and physical disability limits the older person's contacts with his dwindling circle of acquaintances. Many older individuals, particularly women, live alone. The consequences of this social isolation can be profound, resulting in a general dissatisfaction with life. The presence of a confidant (spouse, relative, or close friend) is extremely important in helping the older individual to cope with the stresses of old age.

5. *Loss of independence.*—The infirmities of old age make the elderly increasingly dependent on others. Some people handle this well, but others have great difficulty accepting it without a loss of self-esteem. Such persons may deny their need for help or react with anxiety and depression.

6. *Loss of living arrangements.*—Many old people live in unsuitable housing, principally because of their inadequate income. They commonly reside in neighborhoods with high crime rates, so that they live in fear of their physical security. Some elderly who are chronically ill or debilitated must stay in nursing or convalescent homes, although the number of these is quite small (about 5%) relative to the total population of the elderly.

7. *Loss of life.*—The elderly are aware of the nearness of death as they see their family, friends, and associates die.

Depression is a common psychological reaction to the losses of old age. It may take several forms including overt sadness and despondency, irritability and anger, or "masked" depression in which the person has

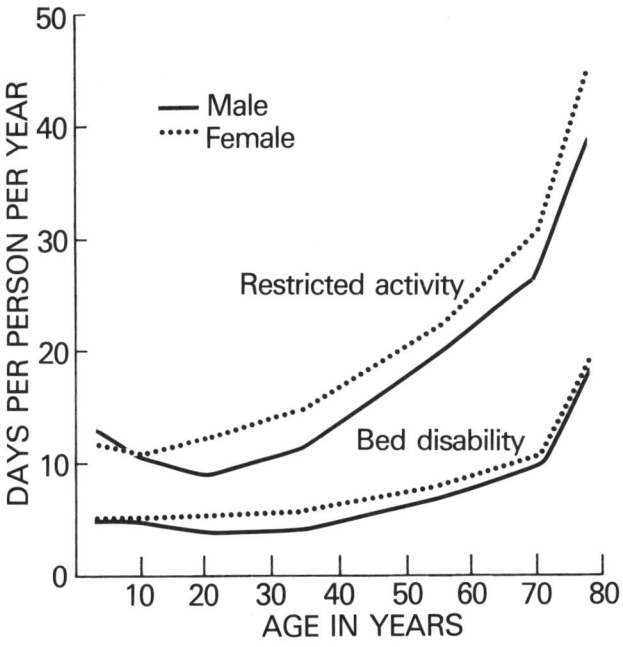

Fig 19–2.—Number of restricted-activity and bed-disability days per person per year by sex and age in 1971. (From Disability Days, United States, 1971, in *Vital and Health Statistics,* Department of Health, Education, and Welfare, Series 10, no. 90.)

physical complaints such as headaches, insomnia, and weight loss. Depression may also be responsible for causing impaired intellectual function, at times even mimicking the syndrome of senile dementia. This condition has been referred to as "pseudodementia." Since a mistaken diagnosis of senile dementia can lead to institutionalization, recognition of this disorder is important.

Insomnia and weight loss are symptoms of depression that have special significance in the elderly. Improper therapy for the insomnia with sedatives and hypnotics can lead to serious side effects in this population group. At times, the weight loss simulates the picture of malignant disease. It is easy to see how an unwary clinician can be led to suspect the presence of a tumor in an elderly person who has multiple aches and pains and a progressive loss of weight.

Suicide is common among the elderly, particularly men, so depression in this age group is not to be taken lightly (Table 19-4).[17] In fact, white men over the age of 65 have the highest suicide rate of any segment of our population. Not uncommonly, the suicidal individual seeks medical help for his problems before taking his life, so the physician may be able to institute preventive measures.[18, 19] Since a significant number of suicides are carried out with the use of sedatives and other psychoactive drugs, the physician who cares for the elderly person with depression should avoid prescribing these drugs, except when clearly indicated, and then give only small amounts at a time.[18, 19]

Social Activity in Old Age

Two conflicting theories that deal with social activity in the geriatric period are relevant to this discussion. The *theory of disengagement*, which was proposed a decade and a half ago, states that social withdrawal of the aged is a necessary, even inevitable, process for successful aging. In contrast, the *activity theory*, which is more widely accepted today, holds that disengagement is *not* necessary or inevitable; rather, maintenance of a substantial level of social activity is a requirement for successful adaptation. Longitudinal studies carried out at Duke University, which provide support for this theory, have shown that healthy elderly subjects experience only a small decline in social activities with progressive age.[20]

The Duke studies notwithstanding, there is a tendency for some elderly people to reduce their level of social activities. There are a number of reasons for this, including physical disabilities, lack of adequate transportation, and financial restrictions. Also, the death of relatives, close friends, and neighbors often results in less social interaction on the part of the survivors. In addition to these factors that influence activity patterns, the life-style of an individual during earlier periods of his life, as well as his psychological makeup, are important. Thus, an elderly person with an outgoing personality who has always been socially active is likely to continue this pattern later in life if his health permits.

There is a growing belief among gerontologists that social activity (staying in the mainstream of life) has adaptive value for those in the geriatric population. Conversely, it is thought that inactivity lies at the root of some of the physical disability and much of the life dissatisfaction experienced by some of the aged. Inactivity may lead to a vicious cycle in which the resulting disability and dissatisfaction causes the older person to become depressed and lose his self-esteem, making

TABLE 19-4.—1976 DEATH RATES* FROM SUICIDE IN VARIOUS AGE GROUPS

AGE RANGE	MALES WHITE	MALES BLACK	FEMALES WHITE	FEMALES BLACK
5-14	0.7	0.3	0.2	0.4
15-24	19.2	14.7	4.9	4.0
25-34	23.7	22.8	8.6	6.5
35-44	23.6	16.8	11.0	4.7
45-54	27.7	13.5	13.8	4.3
55-64	31.6	12.3	12.1	2.8
65 & over	39.7	14.5	8.3	3.2
All ages	19.8	11.0	7.2	3.2

*Deaths per 100,000 population
Data from U.S. Bureau of the Census, *Statistical Abstract of the United States: 1978*, ed. 99. Washington, D.C., 1978.

1. PHYSICAL DISABILITY
2. PSYCHOLOGICAL MAKEUP
3. LOSS OF SPOUSE, FRIENDS
4. GEOGRAPHIC SEPARATION FROM CHILDREN
5. LACK OF TRANSPORTATION
6. LACK OF FINANCES

↓

DIMINISHED PHYSICAL AND SOCIAL ACTIVITY

PSYCHOLOGICAL REACTIONS, e.g., DEPRESSION, LOSS OF SELF-ESTEEM

REDUCED FUNCTIONAL CAPACITY OF MUSCLES, CARDIOPULMONARY SYSTEM, etc.

DISSATISFACTION WITH LIFE

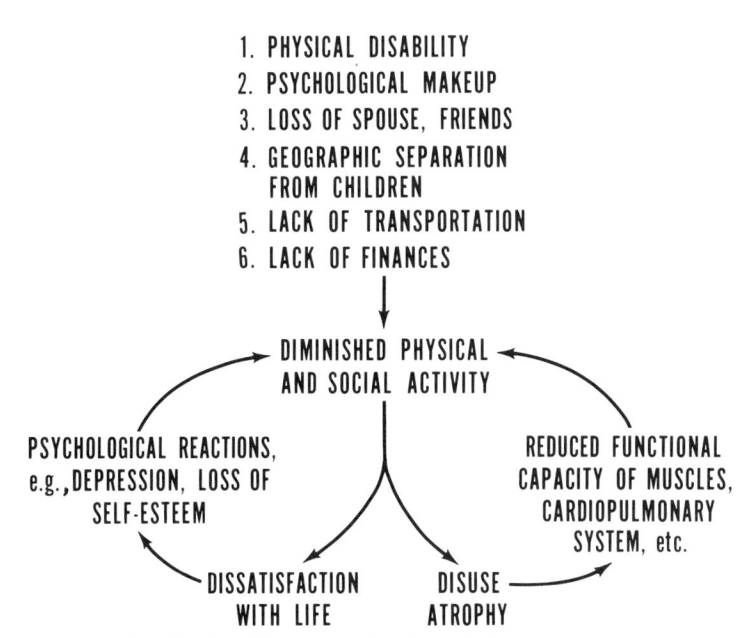

DISUSE ATROPHY

Fig 19–3.—Vicious cycle of inactivity in the aged.

him want to withdraw even further socially (Fig 19–3).

RETIREMENT.—Retirement greatly affects the level of social activity of many of those in the geriatric population, especially men. In the past, the legal age of retirement in this country was 65 years; however, recently this has been extended to 70 by an act of Congress.

In addition to being a cause of social inactivity, retirement carries with it a change in social status that may be difficult for an older person to accept. In our society, a person's social status is very much related to the work he does; consequently, to give up an occupational role without assuming another role with an equal or better status may adversely affect one's self-image. Forced retirement may be interpreted by the individual as being "put out to pasture." Because of this change in status, many people dread their retirement.

Other consequences of retirement include an increase in the amount of free or leisure time and a reduction in income. An increase in leisure time can be a blessing or a problem depending on the individual. When work has been an integral part of one's life and he has derived great satisfaction from it, he may be quite reluctant to retire. Conversely, when a job has been only a means of obtaining an income, an individual may look forward to retirement, providing that his income does not decrease too much afterwards. The increased amount of free time changes the relationships between family members. After retirement, a husband who has usually been at work during the day is now at home, which often requires considerable adjustment on the part of his wife. The inability of some men to develop a new pattern of life in which the excess leisure time is utilized in a meaningful way can lead to problems at home.

Many of those who face retirement in our society do so with mixed feelings. On the one hand, they look forward to a well-earned respite from the rigors of work, to more free time in which to enjoy leisure activities, and to an opportunity to fulfill wishes that were made during their working years. On the other hand, they are concerned about some of the changes that follow retirement—changes in status, income, and patterns of living. For some of the elderly the positive aspects of retirement far outweigh the negative features, while for others the reverse is true.

SEXUAL ACTIVITY.—One of the misconceptions about old age is that interest in sex and sexual activity cease. In fact, studies have shown that people in the geriatric age group continue to be sexually active, even into their eighties.

In the Duke longitudinal study, healthy people 60–94 years of age were observed over a 10-year period. At the outset, 80% of the men reported that they had an interest in sex; follow-up 10 years later showed that this percentage had not decreased significantly.[21] Seventy percent of the men indicated that they were still active sexually at the beginning of the study; after 10 years this number had declined to 25%. Women differed from men in that only about a third said that they still had an interest in sex, and only 20% were sexually active at the beginning of the study—figures that did not change significantly over a 10-year period. Not only do sexual interest and activity continue with advancing old age, but a significant proportion of the elderly men studied at Duke actually had an increase in sexual interest and activity as they grew older.

The Duke studies indicate that people who have an interest in sex and are active sexually in their later years are generally those who had these habits earlier in their lives. In these studies, married and unmarried men differed little with respect to their degree of sexual activity, whereas married women were more active than unmarried women. It appears that the levels of sexual interest and activity among women in the geriatric age group depend to a great extent on the availability of a socially acceptable and sexually capable partner.[22]

Information derived from studies, such as this one, into the sexual life of the aged has important implications for the care of geriatric persons. Physicians and others who provide health care should be prepared to discuss sexual problems with their elderly patients if such matters are brought up. Moreover, these professionals should have an "open mind" with respect to the sexual behavior of the elderly, recognizing that there is great variability in this aspect of human behavior in both the young and the old.

Dependency in Old Age

The geriatric age group contains a broad spectrum of individuals in terms of their degree of independence. At one end are those who are physically healthy and active, mentally alert and financially secure, while at the other end are those who are ill, senile, and poverty stricken. In between these extremes are the majority of the aged who, despite some health and financial problems, carry on a fairly independent life. Naturally, as they reach the age of the "old-old," even they tend to rely more on others for help and assistance.

For many elderly, especially the poor and infirm, living a relatively independent existence in the community depends on having certain basic needs met. Medical care, transportation, companionship, assistance with physical tasks around the home, and even help in getting adequate meals are some of these necessities. Assistance may come from family, friends, or, at times, community agencies set up for this purpose. The availability of support services such as home health care, homemaker services, "meals-on-wheels," and senior citizen centers is often a deciding factor in determining: (1) whether an elderly person lives independently in the community or has to go into an institution that provides continual care, (2) whether he will be hospitalized for a mild illness, and (3) how soon he can be discharged from a hospital after an admission.

A particular instance in which dependency becomes a critical issue is when an elderly parent can no longer care for himself and comes to live with his children. When grown children assume the responsibility for part or all of the care of a mother or father, there is a reversal of the roles that previously existed. Parents who are used to interacting with their children on the basis of the earlier parent-child relationship may have great difficulty in accepting a situation in which they are dependent and have to take direction from their offspring. In such circumstances, painful disagreements may lead to alienation between the aged parents and their children, with resulting depression on the part of the former and guilt on the part of the latter.

Providing help for the elderly requires that the health professional understand the psychological reactions experienced by the patient and his family as he becomes more and more dependent with progressive age. It is also essential that physicians be aware of the support services that exist in the community so that these will be fully utilized when necessary.

Social Attitudes toward the Aged

To a certain extent, growing old is a state of mind. If someone thinks of himself as "old," he will act this way; if he thinks of himself as "young," he will act in accordance with this view. Thus, the self-image that a person in the geriatric age group has is very important in determining his attitudes and behavior.

One of the most important factors influencing this self-image is the prevailing social attitudes toward the aged. In our society, there is a general fear or hatred of the elderly, which has been referred to as "gerontophobia."[23] Each year, millions of dollars are spent by the middle-aged and elderly to disguise the physical effects of aging, for example, gray hair and sagging wrinkled skin. For these individuals, it is apparent that growing old is not very pleasant, something to be avoided at all costs.

Underlying the negative attitudes toward the aged in our society are a number of misconceptions that exist about people in this age group. The following are some of these misconceptions along with the actual facts:

1. There is a widespread belief that most older people are infirm and debilitated, that they spend much of their time in bed due to illness, and that many have to live in institutions. In fact, only about 15% of the elderly rate their health as "poor," as a group they are bedridden due to illness only 5% of the total days in the year, and only 5% reside in institutions that provide continual care.[20]
2. The aged are not interested in and do not participate in sex. This is, of course, erroneous, as has been discussed.
3. Older persons are generally less capable mentally; they are slow, forgetful, and unable to learn new things. In fact, longitudinal studies have shown that little, if any, significant reduction in intellectual function occurs with age in healthy middle- and upper-class individuals.
4. Members of the geriatric population are generally dissatisfied with life and are irritable, "grouchy," and "cranky." The Duke University longitudinal studies indicate that little or no significant decline in happiness or life satisfaction occurred in a group of healthy elderly persons observed over a 10-year period.[20]
5. Productivity. The older worker is unproductive, inefficient, or unreliable. In fact, there is evidence that a positive correlation exists between productivity and age, and that absenteeism and accidents occur less frequently among older workers. Certainly creativity continues, for many of the outstanding world scholars, scientists, and people in the arts are in the geriatric age group.
6. Isolation. That the elderly are for the most part isolated and lonely is incorrect. In fact, the majority live either with their family or in close proximity to a relative, usually a child. Because of widowhood, older women are more likely to be living alone than men, but even so 60–70% of them still reside with a family member(s).

Discrimination against the aged in our society (so-called ageism) based on these misconceptions takes several forms. It is particularly evident in employment practices where there is a great reluctance on the part of many employers to hire the elderly, but it also is found in many other areas of life.

If one accepts as true the negative stereotypes about the aged when he is young, it is likely that he believes that he will acquire these characteristics as he grows older. Thus, these stereotypes can become a self-fulfilling prophecy.

The negative attitudes we hold about the aged in our youth-oriented society are not universal. There are many cultures in which the elderly are held in great esteem, even reverence. It is well known that the Oriental people have this view of the aged. In the past, when our country was agrarian, the old were treated with greater respect than they are now. In those times of the extended family made up of children, parents, and grandparents, the eldest of the group often occupied a position of great esteem. In today's industrialized society, geographic mobility has made the extended family a phenomenon of the past. Elderly parents do not usually live in the same household as their grown children and they are rarely consulted for advice or guidance. Achievement and productivity are valued highly in our country, so those who are retired and not a part of the work force are considered to have little value in the eyes of many of the public.

MEDICAL CARE OF THE ELDERLY

A comprehensive plan, involving the analysis and treatment of physical, psychological, and social problems, should be used in the medical care of the elderly. Often, this is best accomplished with the "team approach" in which different health professionals (physician, nurse, social worker, physical therapist, dietician, etc.) cooperate in the patient's management.[24] While this concept of patient care is also valid for the younger population, it is especially critical for the elderly. The geriatric patient, especially if he is over 75 years old, is generally in a delicate balance physically, psychologically, and socially. A disturbance in function in any one area may disrupt the function in the others.

Unfortunately, many medical personnel have had little formal training in the care of geriatric patients, and they believe the negative stereotypes of the elderly that are so common in our society. There is a special professional bias against geriatric patients. The "ideal" patient medical personnel like to care for is someone who is young and has an acute illness involving a single organ system. Such a person is easy to work with and his disease usually can be cured. This model of acute reversible illness is the one with which health professionals are most familiar as a result of their medical education.

Things are quite different with the elderly who have different kinds of medical problems. First, they tend to have multiple diseases. Butler states that "on the average, each person 65 years and over suffers from five different disease entities."[24] Most of these are chronic and irreversible. Second, several organ systems are usually affected by disease. The symptoms, signs, and laboratory abnormalities that geriatric persons develop during an illness reflect this multiorgan involvement.

Dysfunctions of multiple organ systems in the geriatric patient sometimes make it difficult to identify the disease that was responsible for the initial insult. For instance, an elderly patient with pneumonia may present with signs of cerebral dysfunction (e.g., coma), suggesting the diagnosis of a primary disorder, or he may be in congestive heart failure, leading the physician to think that he primarily has a cardiac problem.

Older patients respond to disease differently than those in the younger age groups, at times causing errors in diagnosis by the physician. The frequent occurrence of mental confusion during an acute illness makes the geriatric patient a poor historian. Those suffering from chronic illness may not be able to give an adequate medical history because of deafness, inability to concentrate, or faulty memory. The symptom of pain is frequently less prominent in the elderly; a heart attack or an acute abdominal catastrophe may occur without much discomfort being felt. Many of the physical signs of disease are either absent or atypical in the aged. For example, there may not be the expected rise in temperature with an infection or the usual abdominal findings in acute appendicitis.

Treatment of disease in the aged poses certain problems that are specific for this age group. Drugs affect these patients differently. The incidence of adverse drug reactions is higher in the geriatric population. There are several reasons for this, including: (1) the dose given to the elderly, which is often the same as that used for the young, may be excessive because of the reduced amount of metabolically active tissue in these patients; (2) diminished renal function (due to the aging process) renders the body less capable of excreting drugs and their metabolities; (3) many organs have increased susceptibility to the effects of drugs; and (4) many elderly persons are taking several medications, which makes drug interactions common. The elderly are less able to tolerate rapid changes in homeostasis due to drugs. Diuretics, antihypertensive agents, sedatives, and tranquilizers, even in "normal" doses, may so alter the physiological equilibrium that serious side effects result.

In general, medical personnel should be careful when administering drugs to persons in this age group. There must be a clear-cut indication for a drug before it is prescribed, the use of multiple drugs should be avoided, and the treatment schedule for a drug should be simple and easy to follow in order to minimize errors in taking the medication. Most important, when a drug is no longer needed by the patient, it should be stopped.

The goals of the management of geriatric patients are often different from those of younger patients. When treating children and younger adults with acute disease, dramatic cures are frequently possible. The elderly, however, are far more likely to have several chronic ailments that are not amenable to cure and so the physician often must be content with controlling or slowing down the progress of disease.[25]

When caring for a geriatric patient, the primary goals are to maintain as much of the functional capacity of the body's organ systems as possible, to restore his general psychological and social well-being, and to enable the individual to realize his maximal potential for independent living.

The effect of illness on psychological and social function is generally much greater for the elderly than for the young. Patients in the geriatric age group, who are already depressed about the various losses associated with aging, frequently react to illness with an intensification of their depression. The lack of a spouse (more often the case for women) or other close family members makes it very difficult for many of the aged to cope with the social problems caused by sickness.

Geriatric patients are particularly susceptible to the complications associated with bed confinement and hospitalization. When acutely ill they may be obtunded, incontinent, and relatively immobile, thereby increasing the risk of pressure sores of the skin. Pneumonia occurs more commonly in elderly patients subjected to prolonged bed rest, either after surgery or because of a medical illness. These kinds of problems make the nursing care that the geriatric patient receives one of the most important aspects of his management in the hospital.

Rehabilitation—physical, psychological, and social—plays a critical role in the comprehensive care of the geriatric patient. Many of the changes due to disease and disuse are modifiable so that the individual's performance may be greatly improved by these measures.[25] When the patient is in a hospital, most of the necessary supportive and rehabilitative services are readily available; however, it is often difficult for the elderly person to obtain these services when he is at home. Those who care for the aged should be fully aware of the community agencies and services available and how to make the necessary arrangements for them.

SUMMARY

The geriatric segment of our population is increasing in numbers more rapidly than any other segment. Because the elderly are sick more often than the young, they have a greater impact on the health care system than their absolute numbers would suggest. One need only visit the office of a primary-care physician to see that a large proportion of his patients are in this age group.

The elderly differ in many respects from the young. Some of the physical changes associated with aging are attributable to the aging process, others are due to various diseases, while still others are secondary to disuse. In comparison to their younger counterparts, geriatric patients have a greater prevalence of multiple, chronic, and irreversible disorders. In the aged, many organ systems are usually affected by disease. The overall effect of the changes due to the aging process and those resulting from disease is to reduce the functional capacity of the body's organs. Consequently, when an older person develops an acute illness it is frequently more devastating than it would be to a younger individual.

The aged respond differently to illness than do the young. For example, many of the characteristic symptoms and signs of disease are either absent or atypical. Also, physical illness is more likely to disturb psychosocial function in this age group. The medical care of the geriatric patient has as its main goal the restoration and maintenance of the maximal degree of physical, psychological, and social function. A comprehensive approach is essential to achieving this goal.

REFERENCES

1. Siegel J.: Some demographic aspects of aging in the United States, in Ostfeld A.M., Gibson D.C. (eds.): *Epidemiology of Aging*. U.S. Department of Health, Education, and Welfare, NIH, No. 75-711, 1972.
2. Special Report on Aging: 1979. U.S. Department of Health, Education, and Welfare, NIH, No. 80-1907, February, 1980.
3. Avioli L.V.: Senile and postmenopausal osteoporosis. *Adv. Intern. Med.* 21:391-415, 1976.
4. Strehler B.L., et al.: Rate and magnitude of age pigment accumulation in the human myocardium. *J. Gerontol.* 14:430, 1959.
5. Pomerance A.: Aging changes in human heart valves. *Br. Heart J.* 29:222, 1967.
6. Goldman R.: Speculations on vascular changes with age. *J. Am. Geriatr. Soc.* 18(10):765-779, 1970.
7. Master A.M., Lasser R.P.: Blood pressure elevation in the elderly, in Brest A.M., Moyer J.H. (eds.): *Hypertension: Recent Advances*. Philadelphia, Lea & Febiger, 1961.
8. Brandfonbrener M., Landowne M., Shock N.W.: Changes in cardiac output with age. *Circulation* 12:557-566, 1955.
9. Goldman R.: Decline in organ function with aging, in Rossman I. (ed.): *Clinical Geriatrics*. Philadelphia, J.B. Lippincott Co., 1971.
10. Davies D.F., Shock N.W.: Age changes in glomerular filtration rate, effective renal plasma flow, and tubular excretory capacity in adult males. *J. Clin. Invest.* 29:496-507, 1950.
11. Adlin E.V., Korenman S.G.: Endocrine aspects of aging. *Ann. Intern. Med.* 92:429, 1980.
12. Busse E.W.: Biologic and sociologic changes affecting adaptation in mid and late life. *Ann. Intern. Med.* 75:115-120, 1971.
13. Eisdorfer C.: Intelligence and cognition in the aged, in Busse E.W., Pfeiffer E. (eds.): *Behavior and Adaptation in Late Life*, ed. 2. Boston, Little, Brown and Co., 1977.
14. Erikson E.: *Childhood and Society*. New York, W.W. Norton & Company, Inc., 1950.
15. Pitt B.: *Psychogeriatrics: An Introduction to the Psychiatry of Old Age*. London: Churchill Livingstone, 1974.
16. Kane R., et al.: The future need for geriatric manpower in the United States. *N. Engl. J. Med.* 302(24):1327, 1980.
17. Busse E.W., Pfeiffer E. (eds.): Functional psychiatric disorders in old age, in *Behavior and Adaptation in Late Life*, ed. 2. Boston, Little, Brown and Co., 1977.
18. Murphy G.E.: The physician's responsibility for suicide, I. An error of commission. *Ann. Intern. Med.* 82:301-304, 1975.
19. Murphy G.: The physician's responsibility for suicide, II. Errors of Omission. *Ann. Intern. Med.* 82:305-309, 1975.
20. Palmore E., Maddox G.L.: Sociological aspects of aging, in Busse E.W., Pfeiffer E. (eds.): *Behavior and Adaptation in Late Life*, ed. 2. Boston, Little, Brown and Co., 1977.
21. Pfeiffer E.: Sexual behavior in old age, in Busse E.W., Pfeiffer E. (eds.): *Behavior and Adaptation in Late Life*, ed. 2. Boston, Little, Brown and Co., 1977.
22. Pfeiffer E., Davis, G.C.: Determinants of sexual behavior in middle and old age, in Palmore E. (ed.): *Normal Aging II*. Durham, N.C., Duke University Press, 1974.
23. Bunzel J.H.: Recognition, relevance and deactivation of gerontophobia: Theoretical essay. *J. Am. Geriatr. Soc.* 21(2):77-80, 1973.
24. Butler R.N.: Geriatrics and internal medicine. *Ann. Intern. Med.* 91:903, 1979.
25. Fries J.F.: Aging, natural death and the compression of morbidity. *N. Engl. J. Med.* 303:130, 1980.

20 / Death and Dying

JONATHAN J. BRAUNSTEIN, M.D.

SINCE EARLIEST recorded history, man has tried to understand and cope with the inevitability and finality of death. A great deal of philosophy and religion is really an attempt to reconcile us to this fate. Indeed, a concern about dying has had more to do with the way people think and live than any other aspect of human existence. Despite the obvious relevance of this topic to the practice of medicine, until relatively recently insufficient attention has been given to it by medical personnel. In part, the reluctance of those in medicine to confront death reflects the general attitude of the public. Our society has been called "death denying" because of the many conscious and unconscious attempts we make to avoid examining it. Within the past several decades, however, death has become a more acceptable topic for discussion both by those in the medical profession and by the lay public. Thanatology, the discipline dealing with the physical, psychological, and social aspects of death, has developed into an important area of study.

Throughout history, man has had two general interpretations of death: the first is that death constitutes annihilation or the end of one's existence, and the second is that death is a transition to another phase of existence, a prelude to an afterlife. The second interpretation assumes that even though man's physical being ceases to exist, his spiritual being continues to survive. This view has been adopted by many cultures and religions, although they often vary in their ideas of the nature of spiritual existence after death.

While these philosophic views occupy everyone's thoughts from time to time, most people deal with the issue of death through the use of the defense mechanism of denial. In her writing, Kübler-Ross points out that all of us engage in potentially lethal activities from time to time (e.g., driving a car at fast speeds, riding in an airplane) without major concern.[1] We are saying, in effect, that death can happen to others but not to us.

Denial is used to avoid thinking about death because this idea creates a great deal of anxiety and fear for most people. There are several reasons why death is feared. It represents the separation of the person from everyone and everything he knows and loves on earth. It is a completely unknown experience and, therefore, very threatening. Death is often equated with pain and suffering because it frequently results from an external destructive force, such as injury or illness. Perhaps the greatest fear for most people is that death is followed by "nothingness," a total loss of existence.

MODERN CHANGES IN DEATH

Although it might seem that death, as an event, would be the same regardless of the times, changes have taken place in this century with respect to its definition, where it occurs, and the types of diseases that cause it. These changes have had a significant impact on people's attitudes toward dying and on the management of the terminally ill.

The Definition of Death

Twenty years ago it would have seemed ludicrous for someone to ask, "How do I know when a person is dead?" Since that time, this has become a very practical question, particularly for medical personnel. In the past, the criteria for death were the cessation of heartbeat and breathing. With the advent of modern life-support systems that can artificially maintain cardiac and respiratory function for indefinite periods of time, however, these criteria have become inadequate for certain situations.

A 55-year-old man was involved in a serious automobile accident. He was brought to the emergency room in a coma with severe cranial injuries. Part of the management of the patient consisted of artificially supporting his breathing with a respirator and treating him with drugs to maintain cardiovascular function. Subsequent evaluation in the hospital showed that the patient had irreversible brain damage. Despite being comatose, however, he continued to breathe and his heart continued to beat with the assistance of the machine and drugs. On temporarily stopping these measures, the patient was unable to initiate respiration and his blood pressure dropped significantly. The patient was still in this condition after three days. At that time, an electroencephalogram showed no brain wave activity.

Advances in medicine (e.g., drugs and life-support systems) have allowed medical personnel to prolong artificially the process of dying. These advances make it possible to maintain brain function in the absence of spontaneous cardiorespiratory activity. So, even though a person has no spontaneous heartbeat or respirations, he can be "kept alive." Also, it is now possible to maintain a person's cardiorespiratory function even after his brain has been destroyed. This was the situation with the patient previously described. Sometimes, in situations similar to this, efforts to support the patient go on for days or even weeks. As a result, family and friends are put through unnecessarily long periods of suffering and anguish, even though the outcome is certain.

The development of organ transplantation as an important form of medical therapy provided another reason to question the adequacy of the old criteria for death. In order to obtain a transplantable organ, it has to be removed from the body promptly after death; otherwise, the tissue will lose its viability. After circulation and respiration cease, there are only a few minutes before most of the body's organs are irreparably damaged. To rely on the cessation of heartbeat and breathing to diagnose death means that medical personnel have very little time to remove and preserve an organ for transplantation.

Many potential organ donors are young, previously healthy individuals who have sustained lethal brain injuries. As in the case of the patient described earlier, it is often possible, with life-support systems, to maintain cardiorespiratory function and the integrity of most of the body's organs for relatively long periods. If a diagnosis of death could be made on the basis of irreversible brain damage, then medical personnel could prepare for the removal and preservation of a transplantable organ before the life-support systems for these patients are discontinued.

Both humanitarian concerns and the problems associated with organ transplantation were instrumental in causing a reevaluation of the criteria for death. In 1968, a group of physicians from Harvard Medical School published a definition of brain death to replace the older criteria for death based on cardiac and respiratory function.[2] The Harvard criteria defined brain death as irreversible coma and gave the clinical and laboratory findings on which a diagnosis of this condition could be made. In a subsequent report in 1977, the Harvard criteria were reassessed in the light of clinical and research experience accumulated since 1968.[3] Table 20–1, based on infor-

TABLE 20–1.—THE HARVARD CRITERIA OF BRAIN DEATH

Complete cessation of brain function for a 24-hour period as manifested by:
1. Unresponsiveness to all stimuli
2. Absence of spontaneous movements
3. Absence of spontaneous respiration
4. Absence of reflexes
5. Isoelectric EEG

Exceptions in which the above criteria do not apply:
1. Hypothermia
2. Intoxication with central nervous system depressants

mation obtained from this report, lists some of the current recommendations for the diagnosis of brain death.

Among those in medicine, the Harvard criteria were generally accepted as a basis for determining when death had occurred. Significant questions were raised by the public, however, with respect to whether or not brain death should be used as a definition of death.[4] Perhaps the most serious objection was the fact that in most states death was legally defined by the older criteria, i.e., the cessation of heartbeat and breathing. In these states, a physician who disconnected the life-support apparatus that maintained a patient's circulation and respiration, even though brain death had occurred, ran the risk of criminal prosecution.

During the past decade, there has been increasing recognition by the public of the merit of using the criteria of brain death to determine when a person has died. This is reflected in many court decisions and changes in the laws of a number of states to make these criteria legal.[4] Several advantages for both the lay public and the medical profession result from the legalization and use of the criteria of brain death. First, the family and friends of a patient with irreversible coma will not be subjected to prolonged suffering while their loved one is being maintained on a life-support apparatus after all hope of recovery is gone. Second, the physician is spared the threat of being prosecuted for discontinuing lifesaving measures for a patient who is, for all intents and purposes, already dead. Third, by being able to anticipate the time of death, medical personnel are better able to secure viable organs for transplantation, thereby extending the duration and improving the quality of life for many individuals who receive them.

Where and Why People Die

There has been a change in both the place where people die and what they die of in the past 75 years. In the early 1900s, death usually occurred at home with the individual surrounded by family and friends. Most people were familiar with what dying was like as a result of having witnessed the death of a loved one. Today things are quite different. It is far more common for a person to die in an institution, such as a hospital, than in his own home. There are two basic reasons for this. First, advances in the diagnosis and treatment of disease have made the hospital the place to go when one is very sick; and second, in contrast to the extended family of 19th-century America, the contemporary nuclear family lacks the capacity to cope effectively with the problems brought about by serious illness. With death occurring away from the home more often, many people grow up without having personally witnessed death and, consequently, are totally unprepared to deal with it when they have to confront it later in life.

The major causes of death in this country have changed since the early part of this century. At that time, acute infectious diseases were the principal menaces to life. However, in the past 75 years there has been a dramatic decline in the mortality from these conditions, largely as a result of improvements in the general standard of living, sanitation, nutrition, and medical care. A new group of diseases has taken their place as the number one "killers" in our society: the degenerative and neoplastic diseases, of which heart disease, cancer, and stroke are the prime examples (see Table 9–3).

The longer a person lives, the more likely he is to develop one of the degenerative or neoplastic diseases, so there is a particularly high incidence of these conditions in people over 65 years old. For older individuals with these diseases, death is usually preceded by a period of chronic illness and debility. When their condition worsens and they cannot be cared for at home, they are taken to a hospital or chronic-care institution. When death finally comes, they are often alone in the world, their spouse and close friends having died earlier, and their children living in another part of the state or country. For such individuals, dying is a lonely experience.

When one develops a disease for which there is no definitive treatment and death is imminent, he faces a unique set of experiences and problems. More and more, medical personnel have to care for patients with terminal illnesses because of the greater prevalence of degenerative and malignant diseases for which there is no cure. The psychosocial needs of these patients are quite different from those of patients with a treatable condition.

THE TERMINALLY ILL PATIENT

The manner in which a patient reacts to the knowledge that he is dying depends on a number of personal factors including his psychological makeup, religion, education, and previous experiences with terminal illness and death among family members and friends. However, several general statements can be made about the process of dying *today* that help to explain some of the behavior exhibited by the terminally ill.

First, as already noted, many individuals die away from the familiar surroundings of their home, separated from family and friends. Despite the presence of medical personnel, a feeling of aloneness commonly develops.

Second, a terminally ill patient in the hospital may receive little emotional support from medical personnel, who with all of their scientific knowledge are poorly equipped to help him deal with his psychosocial needs. Such a patient, whose disease is not amenable to treatment, often feels himself to be a "burden" to the medical staff. Unfortunately, this attitude is often communicated to the patient by the staff, who think that their time and effort are better spent treating patients who will recover. Studies have shown that once it is determined that a patient will not recover, medical personnel tend to spend less and less time with him.

Third, the process of dying in the hospital is often a dehumanizing experience; it produces a kind of social death for the patient while he is still alive.[5] He is often cared for medically as though he did not exist as a person. The status of his disease may be discussed by medical personnel at his bedside without paying much attention to him. Decisions about his care may be made without consulting his views. At a time when his most important need is to communicate with an understanding and compassionate person, the "system" of care he is exposed to seems to be organized in a manner that prevents him from satisfying this need.

What Terminally Ill Patients Fear

Patients who know they are going to die fear most of all pain and suffering, because of both the psychological meaning of death and the fact that many diseases that cause death produce discomfort. They also fear being alone, particularly when they die. Separated from family and friends as a result of being hospitalized, the dying patient is often subjected to further isolation as a consequence of the attitudes of the medical staff toward the dying. To suffer is bad enough, but to suffer alone is an unbearable thought for many of the terminally ill.

A loss of hope is another fear that the terminally ill experience. Strangely enough, even though an individual is aware that he has a serious illness and is dying, he often finds things to hope for. Hope may be found in some new treatment that his physician has told him may help, or it may be a result of his denial of the true nature of his illness. Most dying patients vacillate between states of hopefulness and despair—a situation referred to as "middle knowledge." Hackett attributes this state to two opposing forces—the reality of the situation as told to the patient and perceived by him, and his intense desire to negate the dreaded information.[6]

Finally, patients who are dying fear the unknown with respect to both what their future life holds for them and what the effects of death will be. Most people are more fearful of the process of dying than of death itself.[6] Not knowing exactly what to expect, the patient often assumes that the worst will happen—that there will be great pain and suffering, that he will have to face these problems alone, and that he will lose control of himself emotionally and panic.

To recognize the fears of the terminally ill

and to help them deal with them successfully is one of the major goals of those caring for the dying. To do so, medical personnel should be familiar with the ways in which patients react to these fears emotionally.

Psychological Responses to Terminal Illness

Kübler-Ross describes these responses as occurring in five stages: denial, anger, bargaining, depression, and acceptance.[1] According to her, not every terminally ill person goes through all the stages, nor is the order in which they take place always the same. If looked for carefully, however, this sequence of responses will be found in many dying patients when the process of dying occurs over an extended period of time.

DENIAL.—In the first stage, the patient uses the defense mechanism of denial to deal with the anxiety and emotional upset that come with the knowledge that he is terminally ill. Often critically ill patients are not told explicitly by medical personnel that they are dying. Most of the time these patients have some degree of awareness that they have a serious illness based on indirect evidence acquired from their observations and through discussions with physicians and nurses. Under these circumstances it is somewhat easier for a person to deny the facts than when he is directly informed of his prognosis. However, even those who are told they are terminally ill usually use denial to cope with the emotional impact of this news.

A 57-year-old businessman was admitted to the hospital because of a mass in his neck. In the previous 3 months, he had lost 20 pounds and complained of mild indigestion. Examination of a biopsy specimen of the mass showed it was due to a metastatic tumor. X-rays of the upper gastrointestinal tract demonstrated that the tumor had originated in his stomach. There was evidence of spread of the tumor to his liver and lungs on other studies. Despite these findings, he felt generally well and had no debilitating symptoms. When he was told of his diagnosis and the fact that without treatment he might live only several months, the patient at first became emotionally upset. Later, after he had calmed down, he asked about the type of treatment that would be necessary and how long he would have to stay in the hospital. He seemed to be rationally planning to undergo the therapy. However, the next day he abruptly made preparations to leave the hospital, saying he had to get back to the office because the work was piling up and the business would fail if he wasn't there. Even though his family tried to persuade him to remain in the hospital for treatment, he refused to do so.

Another example of the use of denial as a coping mechanism is the situation in which a person goes from physician to physician after being told he has a terminal illness, trying to find one who will give him a more hopeful prognosis.

A dying patient may only partially deny the truth about his condition. Although he knows he is terminally ill and would say so if asked, he is able to maintain hope by putting this thought out of his mind much of the time. This denial may wax and wane from day to day. During those times when he is more aware of the seriousness of his illness, he appears anxious and depressed; when he is able to suppress this information from consciousness, he becomes more hopeful.

Denial can be very beneficial to a patient with terminal illness by helping him to face a seemingly intolerable situation. It is particularly useful early in the course of his illness because it provides him with time to adjust gradually to the realization that he is dying. As the illness progresses and his condition deteriorates, denial is more difficult to maintain because the reality of the situation becomes more and more apparent. But by this time, other stabilizing forces, both psychological and social, can be mobilized to help the person cope.

Some degree of denial is a healthy adaptation to the knowledge that one has a terminal illness, and it is to be encouraged by medical personnel. Of course, when it is so marked that it interferes with the proper treatment of a patient or is injurious to him or his family in other ways, it should be discouraged. Usually this can be accomplished by discussing the patient's concerns with him and giving him time to reconcile himself to his illness.

ANGER.—The second stage of the patient's response to terminal illness is characterized by anger. With the realization that the worst of all calamities has befallen him, he reacts by asking, "Why me?"[1] The anger he feels is often directed to the environment and those about him, not uncommonly toward the hospital and medical personnel. The nursing care, food, hospital schedules, and laboratory and x-ray services may become the object of the patient's wrath. Arguments between a patient and the physician, nurse, or other hospital staff may ensue. The hospital personnel, who have been conscientiously trying to help him, may feel he is ungrateful because of his irritability and anger. In return, they may avoid him, spending less and less time with him, which only intensifies his anger. Not only are medical personnel the targets for his anger, but even members of the patient's family may be treated in this way.

The dying patient sometimes seems to be angry at everyone and yet, despite his feelings, there is really nobody he can justifiably blame for his misfortune except "cruel fate." The reason for his anger is not hard to understand when one considers what is happening and what will happen to him. He is experiencing a progressive illness associated with physical discomfort. He is going to lose his life, thereby separating himself from everyone and everything that he loves. When a terminally ill patient sees others alive and well and enjoying life, it is quite understandable that he should feel angry that he has been singled out for this most severe punishment.

Many times family, friends, and even medical personnel fail to recognize this reaction of anger for what it is, and instead respond to the patient with anger themselves. This is unfortunate because what the patient needs most at this time is to be understood and allowed to express his feelings without the fear of losing the love and respect of those around him. If he is permitted to express his feelings, he will be better able to tolerate the psychological stress he is going through. It is particularly important that medical personnel do not react defensively to the patient with anger and avoidance. Not only is their support desperately needed, but they also often have to interpret the patient's actions for family and friends.

BARGAINING.—The third stage that the dying patient goes through is described by Kübler-Ross as bargaining. In this phase, the patient attempts to enter into some agreement that may temporarily delay the inevitable. Like so much of adult behavior, this response has its origins in childhood. Bargaining is commonly used by children to get their way. For example, when a child is told he cannot have something he wants very much, he initially becomes upset and angry; however, after a while he frequently will attempt to bargain for the object by offering to do something in return. The terminally ill often use the same approach except that their bargaining is an attempt to postpone pain, suffering, and death. In essence, they seek the granting of a special wish in return for good behavior. The pact is made with either medical personnel or "the Supreme Being." The special wish consists of time, a period in which they are free from pain and discomfort, or an extension of life; in return, the person may agree to cooperate with his treatment or to undergo a procedure, i.e., to be a "good patient."

A 47-year-old woman was hospitalized with a diagnosis of metastatic cancer of the breast. In the past month, she had been suffering a great deal with pain in her back due to deposits of tumor in the spine. She was being treated with chemotherapy and local radiation, both of which were responsible for her experiencing marked nausea and vomiting. As a result of the pain and vomiting she became very irritable and uncooperative. In fact, one day she became so upset about these symptoms that she told her physician she wished to be discharged so that she might go home to die. However, a day later when the physician came to see her, the patient told him that she had reconsidered and would agree to undergo any treatment he suggested if he would only assure her that she would be home with her family for the Christmas holidays in 2 months. The physician explained that while he could not guarantee this, he felt it was quite possible that she would be able to do so if the treatment were successful.

DEPRESSION.—The fourth stage of terminal illness is characterized by depression. Kübler-Ross refers to this type of depression as *preparatory* to distinguish it from the *reactive* depression the patient experiences earlier in the course of his illness. The former prepares the person to separate himself from the world, while the latter occurs in response to the many losses he has experienced during the illness (loss of health, loss of contact with family and friends, financial loss, etc.).

Reactive depression is felt by all persons who are dying at some time during their illness. The management of the patient with this kind of depression differs from that of the patient with preparatory depression since the reactive type may respond to encouragement and reassurance. On the other hand, preparatory depression is a prelude to death. Little can or should be said or done to raise false hope and, thereby, interfere with the grieving process. While our initial reaction is usually to try to "cheer up" the depressed, this is inappropriate for the patient at this stage of dying.

While little needs to be said at this stage, the presence of a loved one is important to many patients. Gradually, as the patient prepares himself for death, worldly things and people become less and less meaningful, except for those who have been very close to him during life. As previously noted, one of the great fears of those who are dying is to die alone; therefore, special family members should be encouraged to stay with the patient as the end approaches.

ACCEPTANCE.—The final stage is one in which acceptance occurs; that is, the person has successfully passed through each of the preceding stages and is able to meet death with calm and serenity. During this period, the need of the patient for emotional support lessens, while that of the family increases. Frequently the person just wishes to be alone, except for a special loved one nearby. Visitors are not desired and the patient says very little, spending most of the time resting or sleeping. Communication with his family takes place mostly on a nonverbal level.

Some patients seem to be able to cope with the psychological effects of dying better than others. Carey studied some factors that determine an individual's capacity to deal with terminal illness, his ability to "make the most" of the remaining days and to live them out in relative comfort.[7] Using an Emotional Adjustment (EA) Scale designed to measure the extent to which patients were able to cope emotionally with their illness and limited life expectancy, he evaluated 84 patients who were aware that they had an incurable illness that would result in their death within one year. The evaluation was based on information obtained from the patients, their families, and the hospital staff. Carey found that a patient's emotional adjustment was closely related to the following factors: (1) the degree of physical discomfort he experienced as a result of the illness, (2) his previous contact with dying persons, (3) his religious orientation, (4) the degree of concern for him demonstrated by his family and friends, and (5) his educational background. The more discomfort a patient experienced from his illness, the less able he was to maintain a high level of emotional adjustment. If the individual had known someone who accepted death with equanimity, he was better able to adjust to dying, whereas if his previous contact with the terminally ill was limited to those who died with great emotional upset, he was less able to adjust. Individuals who had made religion an intimate part of their life-style adjusted best. Also, the more extensive one's education, the better was his emotional adjustment. Other factors that were found to be important in determining a patient's capacity to cope with terminal illness were his ability to deal successfully with other stressful situations in the past; a feeling of having had a meaningful and fulfilling life; a warm and supporting relationship with his spouse; and an explanation of his illness by his physician that was tactful, candid, and contained the assurance of support.

THE RESPONSES OF MEDICAL PERSONNEL TO THE DYING

Caring for the terminally ill and witnessing death are stressful experiences with which many health care professionals have to deal. Not only are those in medicine more commonly exposed to the dying, but they often see people dying before their time (i.e., the young and middle-aged), which is especially upsetting. Coping successfully with death is particularly important for them because they are the ones to whom the patient and family turn for guidance and support during terminal illness. Unless a physician is comfortable discussing this topic, he will be unable to tell a patient the truth about his impending death or allow a patient to communicate his feelings about death; in other words, the physician will be ineffective in caring for the dying patient and his family.

Physicians and other members of the medical staff each have their own ideas about death based on personal factors such as their psychological makeup, social background, religion, and life experiences. Since these ideas greatly influence how they relate to dying patients, it is very important for medical personnel to examine them before attempting to help others deal with the issue of death. In addition to their personal views, those in medicine acquire attitudes and beliefs about terminal illness and death as a result of their special training. The health professions place great emphasis on the preservation of human life, and the education of medical personnel equips them to achieve this goal. Unfortunately, they may have had little, if any, preparation to deal with the problems of the dying patient and his family.

The Hospital Setting

The setting in which medical personnel are trained and in which most people die—the hospital—has certain built-in barriers to the appropriate care of the dying. The basic orientation of patient care is on the management of the physical aspects of illness; emotional and social problems have a lower priority. Since the mission of the hospital is considered by the staff to be primarily that of saving lives, they may find themselves somewhat at a loss as to what to do when faced with the care of a terminally ill patient. All the knowledge about the treatment of disease, all the sophisticated diagnostic equipment, and all the lifesaving devices are useless in caring for a patient whose death is inevitable. Confronted with this situation, is it any wonder that medical personnel feel ill at ease?

Physicians, nurses, and other hospital personnel often feel a sense of personal defeat and failure when caring for a dying patient. Even though they are not responsible for the patient's condition, they may still blame themselves for not having done more to help the person get well. Often this guilt is handled by avoiding the issue. There may be a hesitancy in discussing his illness with a patient or his family and they may spend less time with the patient.

A situation commonly develops in the hospital in which a terminally ill patient is unaware of his impending death, even though the physician and hospital staff know this to be the case. Strauss has called this "closed awareness."[8] He has listed five reasons for it. First, patients are not experienced at recognizing the signs of impending death. Second, physicians frequently do not tell patients that they are going to die. Many excuses are given for not telling the patient, but most are merely rationalizations to avoid becoming involved in an emotionally upsetting experience. Third, families tend to guard the secret of impending death. Family members rarely take the initiative to tell a terminally ill patient about his impending death if the physician does not inform him. Fourth, hospitals are arranged in such a way as to hide medical information from patients. Records are kept out of reach, discussions about the patient's illness are held outside the patient's room, and those that do occur within earshot of the patient are in medical terms that he cannot understand. Fifth, the terminally ill patient has no allies who will help him discover that he is dying. The physician, nurses, family, and even other patients withhold this information from him as a result of their well-meaning intent to save him from emotional trauma.

Sometimes medical personnel even hide

the truth about a patient's imminent death from themselves. In their anxiety to treat and to cure, they may fail to appreciate that their patient's disease has progressed to a point where no medical treatment will control it. They may persist in doing diagnostic studies, administering potent drugs, and performing "lifesaving" procedures even after the patient's condition has become terminal. Not only are these efforts inappropriate and ineffective, but they interfere with one of the most important goals of the management of the dying patient—that is, to make him as comfortable as possible. Being able to recognize when a patient's disease becomes untreatable is an important part of a clinician's diagnostic acumen for it tells him when to shift his efforts from treating a disease to caring for a dying patient.

Psychological Reactions of the Physician

A physician's reactions to a dying patient can be understood in terms of the effects of this experience on three subconsciously held self-concepts: his image of himself as a "powerful healer," his idea of an "indestructible self," and his view of himself as a "destructive force."[9] Caring for a terminally ill patient reminds the physician of his inability to heal and, consequently, is a blow to his self-esteem. Emotional reactions of frustration and anger may cause him to spend less time with the patient. His behavior in avoiding the patient may be rationalized with the statement "There is nothing further I can do for this patient," meaning, of course, that he can no longer treat the patient's disease. Alternatively, he may attempt to use excessive measures to treat a patient whose death is inevitable in order to assuage his feelings of helplessness and guilt.

A physician may identify with a dying patient, particularly if the person is in the same age group and of the same sex, and become fearful that he might develop a similar illness. Since he cannot save the patient's life, he may not be able to save his own, which seriously challenges the subconscious view he has of himself as "indestructible." He also may compare a dying patient to a family member or a friend who had a terminal illness, and in doing so transfer the feelings he had about that individual to the patient. In this instance, the physician may be unable to care for his patient effectively because of his emotional reactions.

A 75-year-old man was admitted to the hospital because of abdominal pain and weight loss, which had been progressive over the past 3 months. Examination revealed the patient to be cachectic with a markedly enlarged and "hard" liver indicative of a malignant process. A diagnosis of stomach cancer with metastasis to the liver was made on the basis of x-rays and a liver biopsy. Although the physician suggested that the patient have chemotherapy in an attempt to control the disease, the patient refused. The physician's attitude toward the patient, which initially had been very empathetic and supportive, changed after the patient made this decision. He became short and abrupt in his daily discussions with the patient. He realized that being near the patient made him anxious and angry but could not explain why he felt this way. Because he was concerned about these feelings and his relationship with the patient, he asked another physician to take over the management of the case.

With more time to reflect on his attitude, the physician became aware that he had identified many of this patient's personal characteristics and disease problems with those of his father who had died of cancer 6 months earlier. He had been very close to his father and felt particularly bad because he could do nothing to help him medically. The emotional impact of his father's death was still fresh in his mind when he was confronted by an individual of similar age and personal characteristics who was also dying of cancer.

A physician may react to a dying patient with a feeling of guilt because he believes that he may have been responsible in some way for the person's condition. This concern may take several forms: the physician may wonder whether he might have diagnosed the patient's condition earlier, whether he might have used another drug that would have been more effective, or whether the treatment he gave might have had ill effects. The psychodynamic basis for the guilt is the subconscious belief that if he is a "powerful healer" then he also has the potential to injure his patients through a misuse of his powers.

It is not unusual for a physician to become upset and even depressed when caring for a terminally ill patient with whom he has developed a close physician-patient relationship. Indeed, this reaction is quite natural and poses no problems unless it prevents the physician from making the necessary decisions about the patient's illness. When he can no longer be objective in dealing with the patient and his family, then the physician should question whether or not he has become too emotionally involved with the case to function effectively. On the other hand, some physicians try to suppress completely their feelings about a dying patient, perhaps in order to protect themselves from emotional upset. As a result, they are unable to relate to the patient with the concern and empathy that are required to communicate effectively with the dying. Both extremes are to be avoided in caring for the terminally ill.

CARING FOR THE DYING PATIENT

The management of the dying patient is first and foremost a humanistic task. When a physician determines that there is nothing more that can be done to control a patient's disease and that his death is inevitable, the care of the patient changes. If one divides medical care into four major components— diagnosis, treatment, relief, and safe conduct—the care of the dying is based on the latter two elements.[10]

Complete relief from symptoms, particularly pain, is not always possible, but every effort should be made to achieve this goal. Weisman points out that almost everything else in the management of the dying patient's illness is secondary to pain relief.[10] To accomplish this, analgesic drugs must be used appropriately. Studies have shown that physicians often use less than effective doses of narcotics and do not give them frequently enough when treating patients in pain.[11] These errors may be due to a lack of information about the pharmacology of these drugs or a concern about overmedicating and harming the patient. Also, physicians are accustomed to placing a limit on the duration of time for which narcotics are prescribed based on a concern for their addiction potential. However, this concern is generally not relevant to patients with terminal illness, whose suffering is great and life expectancy is limited. The physician should prescribe analgesic medication so that the patient will not have to wait until he has pain to receive a pain-relieving drug. Rather than ordering this medication on an as-needed basis for frequent and intense pain, the physician should make it available on a regular schedule prior to the time the pain recurs.

Providing safe conduct is essentially a matter of communication and trust. Another great fear of the terminally ill, in addition to having pain and other discomfort, is being left alone, being deserted. That is why the relationship between the dying patient and medical personnel assumes such great significance. The communication, both verbal and nonverbal, between a physician or nurse and a terminally ill patient should provide the patient with the feeling that those caring for him will be "beside him" to the end giving whatever support and care are necessary.

What should the physician tell the dying patient and what should he allow the patient to reveal to him? These questions are at the "heart" of the communication between physician and patient. The first question asks whether it is all right to tell the patient the truth about his illness and, if so, how to go about it. In the past, it was generally considered wrong to discuss death frankly with a terminally ill patient because this topic was too emotionally upsetting for him. This view is no longer held by most physicians. In a poll of physicians reported by the American Medical Association in 1977, 78% stated that they do discuss imminent death with terminally ill patients who are able to respond.[12] When asked how often they do so, 14% said they "always" discussed this matter with the patient, 49% said they do "most of the time," and 28% said they do so only "in a few cases." In keeping with this recent change in attitude, the poll indicated that younger physicians were more likely to enter into this discussion than older physicians (Table 20–2).

If the physician decides to tell a patient about the nature of his terminal illness, then there is still the important matter of how and how much to tell him. Certainly no physician would want to present this information in a way that would cause unnecessary psychological pain and suffering for the patient. To avoid this, the physician should know how much of the truth the patient is able to accept emotionally, how much he already knows, and how much he wishes to know about his illness at a particular time. Conveying this information requires, most of all, an individualized approach by the physician. In this regard, Meyer stated:

What is imparted to a patient about his illness should be planned with the same care and executed with the same skill that are demanded by a potentially therapeutic measure. Like a blood transfusion, the dispensing of certain information must be distinctly indicated; the amount given must be consonant with the needs of the recipient; and the type must be chosen with the view of avoiding untoward reactions.[13]

Medical personnel tend to underestimate the amount of information a patient has about his illness. Most dying patients know the truth about their illness, even though they are not told directly and do not talk about it. This knowledge is usually acquired by indirect means, including observations made by the patient about his condition, contact with someone who had the same or a similar medical problem, and clues left by medical personnel as a result of their attitudes and behavior toward the patient. For example, one can assume that a patient who smokes cigarettes and develops an illness characterized by the coughing of bloody sputum, progressive weight loss, and an abnormal chest x-ray will wonder whether he has lung cancer. If the patient is advised to have a diagnostic procedure, such as a bronchoscopy, in which a biopsy specimen of tissue is taken, his suspicions about this diagnosis are even further aroused. If the course of the patient's illness is one of progressive deterioration, the truth about his illness is probably quite clear to him, whether or not he is told directly. Transfer to a special part of the hospital in which cancer patients are treated and the administration of chemotherapy or radiation therapy only confirm the patient's impression about his diagnosis.

Providing the physician communicates with the patient in a tactful and considerate manner, he can discuss the facts about his illness and still allow the person to maintain some hope. As Cousins puts it, "The physician's obligation to tell the truth can be upheld even as the patient's interests are served."[14] When explaining the nature of his illness to the patient, the physician should attempt to present the information in such a way as to keep alive his morale and prevent a sense of panic from developing. Knowing that everything that can be done to help him will be done serves to reassure the patient, helping to counterbalance the depressing news about his illness.

The importance of encouraging the dying patient to share his feelings and concerns cannot be overemphasized. This takes both time and a receptive listener. Medical personnel should realize that the dying patient usually needs more, not less, of their time than patients with treatable conditions. One cannot hurry discussions with the dying. The physician should cultivate the ability to communicate effectively with the dying, allowing the patient to express his emotions and ask questions about his illness and what the future

TABLE 20–2.—RELATIONSHIP BETWEEN AGE OF PHYSICIAN AND DISCUSSION OF DEATH WITH TERMINALLY ILL PATIENTS

AGE	WILLING TO TALK ABOUT THE PROSPECTS OF DEATH WITH TERMINALLY ILL PATIENTS
Under 35	88%
36–49	83%
50–64	70%
Over 65	56%

Source: American Medical Association: What do you tell the dying patient? *American Medical News* 20(4):3, 1977. (Used by permission.)

holds. This is by no means an easy or pleasant task for the physician, but it is an essential part of the care of the dying.

THE FAMILY

Caring for a terminally ill patient involves helping his family to deal with the crisis with which they are confronted. Family members often turn to medical personnel for assistance during the patient's illness and after he has died. This may be in the form of emotional support or advice about practical matters such as whether to have additional private nursing help, whether to care for the patient at home or send him to a medical care facility, and when to make the necessary arrangements of his personal and business affairs in preparation for his death.

Adequate communication with the family members is very important. At all times, the family must feel that they, along with the physician and other medical staff, share in the responsibility for the patient's safe conduct. The nature of the patient's illness and his prognosis should be tactfully and carefully discussed with them and they should be given an opportunity to ask questions. Their role in helping the patient to avoid the isolation and loneliness that come with dying should be emphasized to them, and they should be encouraged to visit with the patient as much as they wish.

Psychological Reactions of the Family

Faced with the loss of someone dear to them, people react emotionally with shock, anxiety, and depression. In addition, there are often feelings of anger and guilt. The sudden realization that a loved one is going to die has a far greater impact than if awareness of this develops gradually, as might be the case when the dying individual has had a prolonged illness. In the first instance, the family has had no chance to prepare psychologically for the situation, whereas in the second, they have been able to mobilize some of their psychological defenses. Other factors that affect the way in which a family reacts to the impending death of one of its members are the nature of their relationship with the dying person, their personalities and coping styles, their previous experiences with illness and death in the family, and their religious orientation.

Most human relationships have a mixture of positive and negative features. Even those who love each other very much have arguments and, at times, become angry with one another. When a loved one is terminally ill, family members may feel guilty as they recall some of the disagreements that took place between themselves and the dying person. Guilt may also arise because they feel they were responsible for not getting the individual to the physician earlier in the course of his illness.

Anger is another common reaction to the burdens placed on the family by a terminally ill patient. The shift in roles that occurs as a result of the patient's illness places stress on the other family members. Because of a spouse's illness, a woman may have to go to work to meet the daily living expenses or a man may have to assume the household chores and care of the children. Even though the healthy wife or husband intellectually realizes that the dying spouse is not to blame for this, feelings of annoyance and anger may well up uncontrollably at times.

Guilt, anger, and depression may cause family members to become irritable and emotionally unstable. At times, this may result in anger being directed toward the physician, nurse, or other medical staff for "not being able to do more to help their loved one get well." Medical personnel should never personalize these kinds of emotional reactions and become defensive. Instead, they should try to understand what is going on, to empathize with the psychological and social trauma the family is experiencing, and attempt to help them cope with their feelings. Open discussion between the physician and the family members in which they are encouraged to express their concerns and feelings is very helpful in enabling them to adjust to the situation.

Telling the family that a loved one has died

is an especially difficult task with which most clinicians are faced some time. There is no easy way to convey this information. It is best to take the relatives into a quiet room where they can be alone before telling them about the death of a loved one. They should be seated, if this is possible. It is usually better to tell the family members while they are together so that they can support one another. Often one will be emotionally stronger than the rest and able to help the others deal with the shocking news. The expression on the physician's face and his general demeanor will usually make the family aware that something serious has happened. So, even before he speaks to them, they are alerted to the possibility that the patient has died. For this reason, a simple and direct statement by the physician to the effect that the patient has died is all that is necessary. He may simply say, "I am sorry to have to tell you that your father has just passed away." After this statement, the relatives should be encouraged to express their natural feelings.

Grieving—The Response to the Loss of a Loved One

Engel has likened grief to the healing of a physical wound, stating that "if we define grief as the typical reaction to the loss of a source of psychological gratification, we can compare the experience of the loss to the wound, while the subsequent psychological responses to the loss may be compared to the tissue reaction and the processes of healing."[15] He has divided the psychological responses to the loss of a loved one into four stages: shock and disbelief, development of awareness, restitution, and resolution of the loss.

The first reaction of a survivor to the death of a relative, particularly if it was unexpected, is shock. He may be immobilized, unable to move physically or react emotionally. He may not accept what has happened, saying "No, this can't be true." This period of shock may last for only several minutes or for as long as several days. While in this state, the person experiences feelings of anguish and despair. He may just sit and stare, dazed by what has happened.

Not all survivors react in this way. Some are able to accept the death of a loved one with relative equanimity because during the course of the person's terminal illness they have prepared themselves psychologically. In a sense, their grieving began while the person was still alive. There are circumstances in which the death of a family member who has suffered a long and painful illness may be welcomed by his relatives because it brings relief from his suffering. Occasionally a surviving family member shows no significant emotion on learning of a loved one's death. This reaction may indicate that the relative has not accepted the reality of the situation, that he has denied what has happened. Later on, when the "truth" of what has taken place becomes evident to him, he may have a particularly severe emotional reaction.

In the second stage of the grieving process, the survivor begins to comprehend more fully the meaning of the loss he has sustained and, consequently, experiences feelings of emptiness, sadness, and helplessness.

How one expresses these feelings depends on his personality, religion, and cultural background. Some cultures, such as those in the Latin American countries and about the Mediterranean Sea, encourage the grieving individual to do so openly and loudly; other cultures encourage their members to exercise restraint.

In general, the closer the relationship the more severe is the emotional reaction. Crying is a natural physical response to sadness and the physician should not attempt to discourage the grieving individual from expressing himself in this way. Failure to give vent to grief indicates an inability to go through the grieving process in a normal way. "Bottling up" one's emotions can prolong the period of grief and prevent the individual from successfully resolving the loss.

In stage three, restitution, the main work of mourning takes place. All cultures "institutionalize" this process with rituals, such as the funeral. The purpose of these rituals is to enable those remaining to accept the death of their loved one and to give some meaning to the tragedy. They also provide an opportunity for the survivors to express their grief and to lend support to one another.

The final stage of mourning involves the acceptance of the loved one's death and a return to a normal pattern of living by the survivors. This can be a long process during which the individual learns to fill the void left by the dead person. This may require that he develop a new set of social relationships and activities that will help to gratify his emotional needs.

The mourning process may go on for as long as a year before successful resolution occurs. Time is the eventual healer. When grieving goes on for a longer period or is associated with an extreme degree of emotional upset and depression, it can be considered pathologic. Under normal circumstances, the grief process comes to an end and emotional healing takes place just as the physical healing of a body wound occurs with time. Gradually, the family is able to accept the loss of their loved one, to remember him and the time they spent together without undue sadness, to relinquish their emotional attachment to him, and to reinvest it in other persons.

In his original work with the grief-stricken victims of the Coconut Grove Fire of 1942, Lindemann described the emotional response to loss and observed that unless people pass through the various stages of grief successfully they do not fully recover from their loss.[16] In other words, grief must run its natural course before the mourner can feel better. Lindemann also found that a person's recovery was enhanced if he was given the opportunity to express his emotions.

Whether or not a grief reaction is handled successfully by an individual may determine its impact on his health. Many studies have shown that grieving can adversely affect the physical and emotional well-being of the bereaved.[17-21] The loss of a loved one is a crisis that produces a dramatic change in the life of a survivor, thereby acting as a potent stressor. By evoking physiological and psychological responses, this stressor may precipitate physical or emotional illness.

People who are recently bereaved often complain of symptoms such as anxiety, fatigue, nervousness, loss of appetite, and insomnia, which are directly attributable to the "normal" grief reaction. It is also known that recent widows and widowers have an increased number of psychosomatic symptoms including headaches, dizziness, indigestion, palpitations, and general aching of the body.[17, 18] The incidence of hospitalization increases for persons who have recently lost a loved one.[19] Finally, there is evidence that grief is a cause of death. Those who are grieving have a higher mortality than expected during the first year following the death of a loved one.[17, 20, 21] Parkes found that in three quarters of the mourners who died in the first 6 months of bereavement, the cause of death was heart disease, specifically arteriosclerotic heart disease and myocardial infarction.[17] Thus, people do die of a "broken heart" as has been suggested by writers and poets since the beginning of time.

SUMMARY

In order to be most effective in caring for the dying patient, the physician should first try to understand his own views about death. His education, which is oriented principally to the diagnosis and treatment of disease, i.e., the maintenance of life, may not have adequately prepared him to deal with the psychological and social problems surrounding death. Feelings of inadequacy and helplessness may result from his inability to cure the patient's disease and prevent him from dying. This, in turn, may cause the physician to avoid the patient or impair communication between the two at the very time when the physician's presence and help are most needed.

There are several important goals in caring for the terminally ill, including keeping the patient as free from pain and discomfort as possible, allowing him to discuss his thoughts and feelings about his illness, and helping him to avoid the loneliness and isolation that come with dying. Today most physicians tell such patients something about their illness and imminent death. The questions "How?" and "How much?" to tell should be answered on an individual basis, depending on the particular patient's needs and capacity to accept the truth. However much the physician decides to tell the patient, he must never do so in a way that destroys his morale, causes him to panic, or removes hope entirely.

There are several stages in the psychological responses of the dying patient and his grieving family. Medical personnel should be aware of these and know how to help the patient and family cope with these reactions. It may be particularly difficult for the hospital staff to deal with some of the negative feelings of anger and resentment that a patient and family may develop toward them. The staff should recognize that under the circumstances these are understandable reactions when one considers the degree of stress the patient and family are going through.

The ability of a dying patient to endure a terminal illness without undue psychological pain is to a large extent dependent on the understanding and support he receives from those caring for him. The knowledge that his physician is "standing by his side" and will continue to care for him in a concerned and dignified manner throughout his illness is extremely important to the dying patient. The fear of abandonment, isolation, and loneliness can best be allayed by attention from empathetic medical personnel and support of close family members.

REFERENCES

1. Kübler-Ross E.: *On Death and Dying*. New York, Macmillan Publishing Co., Inc., 1969.
2. A definition of irreversible coma, Report of the Ad Hoc Committee of the Harvard Medical School to Examine the Definition of Brain Death. *J.A.M.A.* 205:337, 1968.
3. Walker E.A., et al.: An appraisal of the criteria of cerebral death. *J.A.M.A.* 237:10, 1977.
4. Veith F., et al.: Brain death, Part I. A status report of medical and ethical considerations. *J.A.M.A.* 238:1651-1655, 1977; Part II. A status report of legal considerations. *J.A.M.A.* 238:1744-1748, 1977.
5. Kastenbaum R.: Psychological death, in Pearson L. (ed.): *Death and Dying: Current Issues in the Treatment of the Dying Person*. Cleveland, The Press of Case Western Reserve University, 1969.
6. Hackett T.P.: Psychological assistance for the dying patient and his family. *Annu. Rev. Med.* 27:371, 1976.
7. Carey R.G.: Living until death: A program of service and research for the terminally ill, in Kübler-Ross E. (ed.): *Death: The Final Stage of Growth*. Englewood Cliffs, N.J., Prentice-Hall, Inc., 1975.
8. Strauss A.L.: Awareness of dying, in Pearson L. (ed.): *Death and Dying: Current Issues in the Treatment of the Dying Person*. Cleveland, The Press of Case Western Reserve University, 1969.
9. Spikes J., Holland J.: The physician's response to the dying patient, in Strain J.J., Grossman S. (eds.): *Psychological Care of the Medically Ill: A Primer in Liaison Psychiatry*. New York, Appleton-Century-Crofts, 1975.
10. Weisman A.D.: Care and comfort for the dying, in Troup S.B., Greene W.A. (eds.): *The Patient, Death, and the Family*. New York, Charles Scribner's Sons, 1974.
11. Reuler J.B., Girard D.E., Nardone D.A.: The chronic pain syndrome: Misconceptions and management. *Ann. Intern. Med.* 93:588, 1980.
12. American Medical Association: What do you tell the dying patient? *American Medical News* 20(4):3, 1977.
13. Meyer B.C.: Truth and the physician. *Bull. N.Y. Acad. Med.* 45(1):59, 1969.
14. Cousins N.: A layman looks at truth telling in medicine. *J.A.M.A.* 244:1929, 1980.
15. Engel G.L.: Grief and grieving. *Am. J. Nurs.* 64:93, 1964.
16. Lindemann E.: Symptomatology and management of acute grief. *Am. J. Psychiatry* 101:141, 1944.
17. Parkes C.M.: The broken heart, in Schneidman E.S. (ed.): *Death: Current Perspectives*. Palo Alto, Calif., Mayfield Publishing Co., 1976.
18. Maddison D., Viola A.: The health of widows in the first year following bereavement. *J. Psychosom. Res.* 13:297, 1968.
19. Glick I.O., Weiss R.S., Parkes C.M.: *The First Year of Bereavement*. New York, John Wiley & Sons, Inc., 1974.
20. Young M., Benjamin B., Wallis C.: Mortality of widowers. *Lancet* 2:454, 1963.
21. Rees W.D., Lutkins S.C.: Mortality of bereavement. *Br. Med. J.* 4:13, 1967.

PART V

The Patient and the Doctor

21 / Concepts of Health, Illness, and Disease

JONATHAN J. BRAUNSTEIN, M.D.

AT FIRST, it might seem that the terms *health*, *illness*, and *disease* would be easy to define; however, they actually represent complex concepts that vary according to one's point of view and system of values.[1] Historically, the definitions of these conditions have undergone many changes. Even today in our medically sophisticated society there are a variety of different viewpoints with respect to what constitutes these states. This is particularly evident when the concepts of lay persons and medical personnel are compared, but even those in the health professions have differing views of health and ill health.

A physician's approach to diagnosis and treatment is based on his view of the nature of disease and illness. At times, the concepts held by a physician and his patient differ, and when this occurs, the care of the patient may suffer.

A 36-year-old woman was seen by her physician. She complained of nervousness, headaches, and difficulty sleeping for the past 2 months. These symptoms developed shortly after she separated from her husband to whom she had been married for 15 years. The separation occurred after a long period of severe marital discord because of his excessive drinking. She was obviously quite distressed over her symptoms, which she felt were preventing her from effectively doing her work as a school principal. The physician examined her thoroughly and performed a series of x-ray and laboratory tests to evaluate her complaints. The results from both the clinical exam and the tests were normal. On a return visit, he informed her that he could find nothing wrong with her. He further advised her to go home and try to "get hold of herself." He did not give her a return appointment.

This case points out the type of problem that may arise when there is disagreement between a patient and a physician about the definition of illness. The patient felt sick; she had symptoms that caused her great discomfort and interfered with her work. She went to her physician expecting to receive medical attention for her illness. According to his concept of illness, however, she was not *really* sick because there was no physical basis for her symptoms. He did not consider symptoms of an emotional upset to be a significant medical problem and, therefore, felt no obligation to help her. Thus, this patient went without treatment simply because of the way in which her physician defined illness.

The concepts of health, illness, and disease held by medical personnel affect not only the type of care given individual patients but also the delivery of medical services to the general public. For those in medicine who define health in negative terms, as merely the absence of disease, the primary goal of medical care is the treatment of the sick. On the other hand, those who define health in positive terms, as the optimal physical, psychological, and social functioning of the individual, see the need for a more comprehensive program of medical care in which greater emphasis is given to the promotion and maintenance of health. These different approaches to the delivery of medical services have been referred to as "sick care" and "health care."[2]

Before going on with this discussion of concepts in medicine, it is essential that the reader understand something about the nature of concepts in general and how they influence behavior.

WHAT ARE CONCEPTS?

Concepts are ideas that are used to convey the meanings that situations, events, objects, and relationships have for people. They enable a person to express his thoughts about these matters in a few words, instead of having to resort to a long and detailed description. For example, the terms *majority rule* and *human rights* represent concepts that are used and generally understood by those in our society. To explain their meaning to someone from another society who was unfamiliar with them would take a great deal of time and effort.

Concepts are used by people because they facilitate communication and social interaction, but this is true only when individuals understand each other's ideas. For example, many organizations in our society use the concept of majority rule in making group decisions, such as selecting officers. No one has to explain this to the members; they understand that when a vote is taken the majority opinion will prevail. However, if someone from another society in which this idea was foreign were to join the organization, he might have difficulty communicating with the other members in respect to matters involving majority rule.

For concepts to be effective in promoting social interaction, there must be some degree of uniformity in the way people view life experiences. This uniformity is brought about as a result of the system of values we acquire from our social and cultural reference groups (i.e., family, peer group, social class, and ethnic group). In general, people with the same social and cultural background share similar concepts about important matters in life; consequently, communication between them is made easy. Conversely, individuals with different backgrounds often have a great deal of difficulty communicating with each other.

In addition to aiding communication and social interaction, concepts provide guidelines for behavior. One of the basic tenets of psychology is that people act in accordance with the way in which they see the world. The views a person has about child-rearing, education, nutrition, and health are important in determining his behavior in these matters. If one understands these views, he can anticipate how the individual will behave when faced with these issues. Because people acquire many of their concepts by incorporating the attitudes and beliefs of their social and cultural reference groups, one can also anticipate an individual's behavior by knowing something about his social and cultural background.

The meanings that situations and events have for a person are determined by other factors besides his social and cultural background (Fig 21–1). Age, sex, psychological makeup, education, religion, and previous life experiences all influence the way in which one sees the world. These are some of the variables that explain why people exposed to similar situations and events develop different

Age and sex
Psychological makeup
Social and cultural background
Education
Religion
Life experience

↓ Formulation of

Beliefs, attitudes, and perceptions of life

↓

Concepts

↓ Influence on

Communication and Behavior

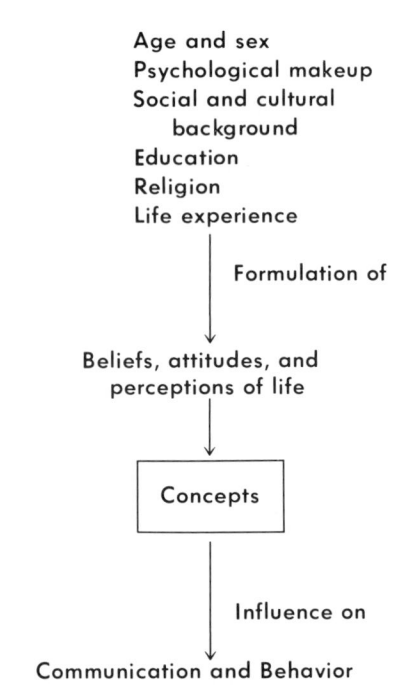

Fig 21–1.—Factors influencing the development of concepts.

concepts about them. For example, a lower-class black living in Mississippi has a different understanding of majority rule and human rights than a middle-class white Bostonian.

Many important concepts are acquired early in life as a result of the socialization of a child (see chap. 13). Children are taught by their parents to view situations, events, and relationships in certain ways. This learning process usually takes place without either the parent or the child being consciously aware of it. A child assumes that the concepts he acquires from his parents represent the "correct" way of preceiving the world. Later on, he incorporates into these concepts the attitudes and beliefs of his peers and other social reference groups. Education and religious training also play an important role in molding a person's views.

For most people, reality is defined by the concepts they hold. In other words, people believe that their perceptions of the world accurately reflect the true state of affairs. This is so even when their views are illogical and inconsistent with reality. For example, people in many cultures throughout the world still believe in the supernatural. To them, spirits and apparitions really exist. No matter how strange and unusual these beliefs may appear to someone living in a modern Western society, they are very real to those who subscribe to them.

One of the most important things to remember about the way concepts exercise their influence on communication and behavior is that, for the most part, people are unaware of their effects. In other words, concepts function on an unconscious level; they are considered by a person to be the "normal" way of thinking about things. Most of us spend very little time reflecting about our views of situations and events in life, yet we usually have very definite ideas about these matters. Moreover, each of us tends to regard our concepts as being "right", the proper way of viewing these matters. When we are confronted by someone who holds concepts that differ from our own, we often think that the person's ideas are somewhat strange and unusual. As we learn more about him, however, we begin to see that his concepts are just another way of viewing life by someone with a different background and life experiences.

CONCEPTS OF ILL HEALTH—ILLNESS VERSUS DISEASE

Ill health can be perceived in several ways; it can be viewed as an abnormal feeling state or as a loss of some function, physical, psychological, or social. A lay person's concept is usually based on these considerations. He judges himself to be ill when he feels bad and is unable to participate in his usual daily activities. On the other hand, ill health can be viewed as a biologic entity. This is the way medical personnel tend to see it, in terms of the morphological, physiological, and biochemical changes that occur.

A fundamental distinction can be made between illness and disease.[3] The former is a psychological and social experience. It is what the patient is talking about when he complains about being sick. He means he has some sort of discomfort or is disabled in some way. Because illness is a subjective experience, it is open to interpretation by both the individual and the society in which he lives. Two people with the same symptom may disagree as to its significance. One of them may consider himself to be ill and seek medical help, while the other may pass the symptom off as being unimportant. The concept of illness is shaped by social and cultural forces that affect people's perceptions, explanations, and methods of dealing with this experience (also see chaps. 9 and 10).

In contrast to illness, disease is a biologic process that affects the organs and tissues of an individual. It is characterized by structural, functional, and biochemical changes. Wherever and whenever a specific disease occurs, these basic features are the same. For example, tuberculosis has been known since the earliest periods of history and in every part of the world. No matter when or where is occurs, it is the same disease; that is, it is caused by the same organism and has the same general pathologic features. Thus, disease is an objective and scientifically measurable entity. It is what medical personnel usually mean when they talk about ill health.

Illness may occur in the absence of disease. In other words, a person may complain about feeling sick when there is no disease affecting the tissues and organs of his body. The previous case of the woman who came to her physician with symptoms of nervousness, headaches, and difficulty sleeping, but who had no clinical or laboratory evidence of disease, is an example. The term *functional illness* is sometimes applied to a situation in which a person has symptoms with no apparent biologic basis (no disease).[4] A significant percentage of all visits to physicians are because of this type of illness, so it is by no means uncommon.

Conversely, disease may be present when the person does not feel ill. Physicians often refer to this state as the *preclinical phase of disease*. It may precede the clinical phase (i.e., the one in which the patient has symptoms) by a period of time as short as a few hours or as long as 40 or 50 years. Sometimes an existing disease never becomes clinically apparent. For example, many persons with coronary artery disease, gallstones, and diverticulosis of the colon are totally unaware of their conditions during life; only at autopsy are these diseases discovered. In the preclinical phase, the diagnosis of a disease often has to be made by a laboratory test, an x-ray, or a biopsy of tissue. The person is entirely asymptomatic and his physical examination may give no indication of a disease being present.

The relationship between illness and disease is illustrated in Figure 21–2. The circle with the solid line represents disease, with the open area in it being the preclinical phase (disease with no clinical manifestations). The circle with the dashed line represents illness, with the open area corresponding to the state of functional illness (symptoms but no demonstrable disease). The area where the circles overlap represents the clinical phase of disease, in which both disease and illness are present.

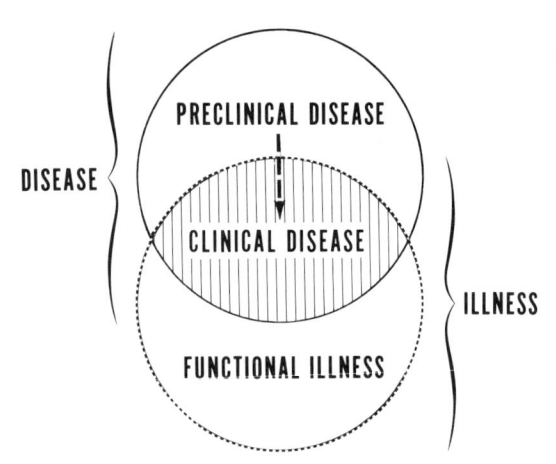

Fig 21–2.—Relationship between illness and disease.

This information has practical value for medical personnel who must evaluate patients. In general, patients present to them in one of three ways. Many are ill because of a disease. This is the type of patient the physician expects to see and with which he is best prepared to deal. However, some patients are suffering from a functional illness or are in the preclinical phase of disease. It is important that the physician be able to diagnose these conditions correctly and provide appropriate treatment. Many times, the physician has a great deal to offer the person with functional illness in terms of alleviating his symptoms. The challenge to the physician in caring for the person with preclinical disease is to prevent the development of clinical disease by instituting the proper treatment.

The Changing Concept of Disease

Man's concept of disease has undergone many changes since the earliest periods in history. The historical evolution of this concept is not only an interesting story but also an important one for medical personnel to understand. If nothing more, it reminds us that our current concepts of disease are also subject to change with time. No matter how correct they may seem to us now, they may be found to be in error by those who come after us.

Prior to the period of modern medicine, most theories of disease had a magical or religious orientation. Today these concepts seem outmoded and even ridiculous to health professionals. However, some of them continue to be important in the life of people from certain social and cultural groups. One example is "folk medicine," a system of medical beliefs and practices based on magic, religion, and empiricism. A large number of lay persons rely on this method of dealing with illness. It includes treatments such as home remedies, body manipulation, and the wearing of charms or amulets. These beliefs and practices have been passed on by word of mouth from generation to generation since the earliest times. The fact that this system of medicine has persisted in modern technological societies like ours is evidence that magicoreligious beliefs are still a vital part of the concepts of disease held by many individuals.

Primitive man believed that disease was due to the malevolent influence of a god or supernatural being. He attributed it to either the introduction of some noxious material into the body or a separation of the soul from the body. Treatment was carried out by a "medicine man", who by rituals and incantations attempted to counteract this influence, eliminate the evil substance, and restore the integrity of the body and soul. Even in primitive times, however, it was appreciated that there were mild diseases that could be managed at home without calling for the help of a medicine man. Various remedies such as plants and herbs were used to treat symptoms. Through a process of trial and error some of these were found to be helpful and became part of the system of folk medicine. Many valuable drugs (e.g., digitalis, colchicine, opiates, and belladonna) were originally folk remedies and were discovered to be of value for treating certain diseases as a result of empirical use.

Primitive man's magicoreligious view of disease was challenged by Hippocrates, who was the first to describe disease as a natural phenomenon. In his book *The Sacred Disease* (believed to be epilepsy), Hippocrates emphasized the importance of observation and logical reasoning in the analysis of disease, especially with regard to its diagnosis and prognosis. He was conservative in the treatment of disease, advising the avoidance of "meddlesome interference" by physicians so that natural healing could occur. Hippocrates's contributions to medical thinking about disease were revolutionary and set the stage for future developments in this area. Despite this advancement, Greek and Roman medicine was characterized by a return to imaginative and fanciful theories of disease. One of these was the theory of the "four humors", which Galen (a Roman physician) subsequently elaborated into a medical doctrine that held sway during the Middle Ages. According to this theory, the body was composed of four humors: blood, phlegm, yellow bile, and black bile. Health was attributed to a proper balance of these substances, while disease was felt to be due to an imbalance. A variation of this theory held that there were four qualities—heat, cold, moisture, and dryness—and four elements—air, fire, earth, and water. It was thought that disease was the consequence of the dominance of one of these qualities and elements and, therefore, treatment was designed to restore their balance.

This concept of disease still persists as a cultural belief in many Latin American countries, where it is referred to as the "hot-cold theory of disease."[5] People from these countries have immigrated to the United States, so medical personnel here may encounter patients who subscribe to this system of medicine. According to this theory, diseases, foods, and medications are classified as either hot or cold, wet or dry. The designation of a particular quality is made without regard to the physical characteristics of the food or medicine. For example, hot tea is considered a cool substance, while cold beer is considered hot. A "cold" disease is typically treated with a "hot" food or medicine, and vice versa.

If a physician prescribes a medication that conflicts in some way with this system, a patient who subscribes to the hot-cold theory will not take it. Therefore, it is important for medical personnel who care for such persons to be aware of their beliefs about disease.

With the advent of the Renaissance, the magicoreligious concepts of disease began to change. Vesalius, an early anatomist, accurately described for the first time many structural features of the human body. His dissections showed that many anatomical facts taught by the medieval physicians were in error. In addition to discrediting the old concepts, his studies marked the beginning of the use of the scientific method in the study of disease. Humoral theories still persisted in medical teaching and writing, however. One of these was the "chemical concept", proposed by Paracelsus in the 16th century, in which the body was thought to be composed of three elements: sulfur, mercury, and salt.

Harvey revolutionized medicine and man's view of disease with his description, in 1628, of the physiology of circulation. His account of cardiovascular function, in which he demonstrated that the heart is the force that propels the blood throughout the circulatory system, was responsible for establishing a scientific basis for body function, just as Vesalius had done for body structure. The scientific approach used by Harvey in his studies provided a model for medical researchers in the future. As anatomy and physiology began to emerge as distinct disciplines, the older ideas of supernatural causes of disease began to fade.

In the early part of the 17th century, two general theories of disease arose as the consequence of scientific advances in physics and chemistry. One theory, the iatromechanical or iatrophysical, held that the body was a machine and that disease could be best explained in mechanical or physical terms. The iatrophysical school of medicine was composed of scientists who concentrated their efforts on the development of apparatus to measure the physical events taking place in the body. These instruments included the thermometer and the balance or weighing machine. The other theory, called iatrochemical, pictured the body as a "test tube" with disease being the consequence of abnormal chemical reactions. The iatrochemists studied the chemical changes that take place in the body fluids, such as saliva, pancreatic juice, and bile, in the hope of discovering the factors that cause disease.

The 17th and 18th centuries were a time in which many important biologic phenomena were described for the first time. These discoveries were made possible by the development of new scientific instruments. One of these, the microscope, enabled man to see the cellular structure of the body's organs and to discover the world of microorganisms existing within and about him. The first of these advances gave rise to the discipline of pathology. Virchow, the most eminent early pathologist, originated a new theory of disease, the *cellular theory*. The second of these advances led to the emergence of the science of bacteriology, established through the work of men such as Pasteur and Koch in the 19th century. During the same time that bacteriology and pathology were evolving, physiologists were beginning to construct the modern concept of body function.

Even though scientific advances that would give rise to the modern concepts of disease were taking place, many imaginative and fanciful ideas were still in vogue. For example, in the 17th and 18th centuries, the theories of animism and vitalism were widely accepted explanations for health and illness. According to animism, a soul or *anima* was present in everyone as the source of all vital function and as a protection against disease. The theory of vitalism was similar; it held that a "vital principle" existed in a person as the primary factor responsible for health and illness. This substance was felt to keep the body in a state of tonic equilibrium, with disease resulting from an excess or a deficiency of tonus. Treatment was based on counteracting excessive tonus with a sedative and deficient tonus with a tonic. Even today people often speak of "taking a tonic" to increase their well-being and vigor.

The latter half of the 19th century ushered in the modern scientific era and with it came new concepts of disease. One of these was the *germ theory*, which was based on the work of the early bacteriologists, Pasteur and Koch. It stressed the role of infectious agents (i.e., bacteria) in the etiology of disease and suggested that treatment depended on the control of these agents. In 1885 Lister, applying this theory, used an antiseptic substance (carbolic acid) to prevent postoperative infection, an achievement that ranks among the most important in modern medicine. The germ theory was expanded as a result of studies on the epidemiology of the tropical diseases and the emergence of the new specialty of preventive medicine at the turn of this century. In the *epidemiologic model of disease*, disease is attributed to the interaction of three factors: a causative (e.g., infectious) agent, the environment, and the host. The agent acts as the primary etiologic factor; the environmental and host factors are important in determining (1) whether or not a person is exposed to it and (2) his susceptibility to its ill effects.

The importance of the germ theory and the epidemiologic model in the practice of medicine in the early part of this century cannot be overemphasized. This is because the infectious diseases were the major contributors to the high morbidity and mortality that existed at that time. Diphtheria, measles, scarlet fever, pneumonia, and tuberculosis were responsible for large numbers of deaths, particularly among the young. Epidemics of cholera, yellow fever, typhoid fever, and typhus periodically ravaged the population of the cities in this country. The marked reduction in mortality from these disorders that occurred in the 1920s and 1930s was due to the application of the newer concepts of disease (germ theory and epidemiologic model) that evolved over this period.

The *cellular concept of disease*, originally proposed by 19th-century pathologists, gained wide acceptance in the early part of this century. This concept focused attention on the structural abnormalities in the tissues and organs of the body as a result of disease. These changes formed the basis for a pathologic classification of disease, which allowed physicians to diagnose a disease from a tissue specimen obtained by biopsy during life or at postmortem. The development of the electron microscope in the 1940s allowed the detailed examination of a previously unknown region of the body—the ultrastructure of the cell. This advance gave physicians vital new information about the cellular alterations in disease. Today medical personnel continue to think of disease primarily as a pathologic entity, showing that the cellular concept has had a great impact on the practice of medicine.

The discovery that biochemical abnormalities are associated with clinical disease led to the development of the *molecular model of disease*. This model looks at disease in terms of the changes in body chemistry that take place. Initial research in this area focused on conditions caused by a deficiency of body nutrients, such as vitamins and minerals. Later progress in biochemistry gave rise to analytic methods that allowed researchers to determine the structure of complex molecules. It was discovered that certain genetic disorders were accompanied by biochemical defects (e.g., disturbed enzymatic activity) that resulted in clinical disease. Thus, a new basis for disease was found and a new group of diseases, called the "inborn errors of metabolism," was identified. In 1948, Pauling discovered that sickle cell anemia is caused by a genetically acquired defect involving a single amino acid in the hemoglobin molecule. This is the classic example of a molecular disease.

Other concepts or models of disease were developed in this century. Two that deserve comment are the *physiological or mechanical model* and the *immunologic model*. Each was based on the perspective of a particular medical discipline or specialty. The first was concerned with the pathophysiological abnormalities that occur during the course of a disease, especially with the way in which these abnormalities produce clinical symptoms and signs. The second model was an offshoot of the new science of immunology. It dealt with the role of the body's immune system in the cause of disease. A new group of diseases, called "autoimmune diseases," were described in which a disturbance was thought to occur in the body's immune mechanisms, resulting in self-destruction of body tissues and organs. Systemic lupus erythematosus is the prototype of these conditions.

Thus, there have been many different concepts of disease since man first attempted to define this process. There have also been a number of ideas about the nature of illness, which will be discussed in a subsequent section of this chapter. The fact that medical personnel have concerned themselves primarily with the concept of disease, rather than with illness, accounts for the greater volume of knowledge dealing with this aspect of ill health.

The ideas of normality and abnormality are an essential part of all concepts of disease and illness, since both states are generally regarded as deviations from "normal" health. A physician diagnoses a disease on the basis of specific structural, functional, or biochemical abnormalities, whereas patients define illness in terms of abnormalities in the way they feel or function. However, *normal* and *abnormal* are relative terms; that is, their definition depends on the perspective of the individual. Frequently the distinction between the two is vague and uncertain.

Normality and Abnormality

Several guidelines are used by people to determine normality and abnormality. One way of defining these terms is on the basis of the *prevalence* of a condition. Something that occurs commonly in a population is often considered to be normal, while something that occurs infrequently is called abnormal. This generalization applies to both physical and mental disorders. Reliance on the prevalence of a condition as a criterion for normality, however, can lead to errors in the recognition of a disease or illness. For example, Bloom states that the Kuba of Sumatra, a primitive tribe living in the jungle, have skin diseases and injuries so commonly that they do not regard them as abnormal.[6] In our own society, obesity is an example. For many years the accepted values for normal body weight in this country were based on average weights. Eventually, it was shown that these "normal" values were too high to be considered ideal for health. The reason for this is that many people in this country are overweight. By taking the average or most prevalent weight as a standard of normality, values were accepted as normal that actually represented a mild degree of obesity.

Another instance in which using the prevalence of a condition to determine normality is misleading, in terms of the recognition of a harmful disorder, is the interpretation of the proper level of serum cholesterol.[7] If one accepts the average value of serum cholesterol in population groups in this country as being normal, he will be certifying as normal a level that is, in fact, higher than what is ideal for an individual's health. Cross-cultural comparisons of people in our country with those in non-Western countries show that we have higher average levels of cholesterol and that these levels are associated with a greater incidence of coronary heart disease. Thus, our average (or most prevalent) values of cholesterol are abnormally high when compared with those found in other population groups, and they indicate a significant medical problem.

Another way of looking at normality and abnormality in health is in terms of the *desirability* of a condition. Body weight can also be used as an example to illustrate this point. In some cultures, a slight or moderate degree of obesity is thought to be physically attractive and, therefore, is considered desirable or normal. In other cultures, the ill effects of obesity on the health of the individual make it undesirable and abnormal. Current medical thinking in our country is that the latter view of obesity is correct. So obesity can be looked upon as normal or abnormal depending on whether one views this condition from the standpoint of its cosmetic appearance or its effects on one's health.

Behavior can also be judged as normal or abnormal depending on its desirable or undesirable effects. A person's behavior is usually considered to be within the range of normality as long as it does not interfere with his interactions and relationships with others. When his behavior disrupts the usual pattern of life for those around him or has ill effects on them, it is generally regarded as abnormal. For example, someone who drinks a small amount of alcohol at a party in order to be sociable is called a "social drinker," behavior that is regarded as desirable and normal. If he drinks too much and becomes loud and offensive in his language, however, he is referred to as being "drunk," behavior that is considered abnormal because of its disruptive effects on others. To carry this point one step further, if he becomes intoxicated on repeated occasions, he may be labeled an "alcoholic," behavior that is defined medically as a serious disorder.

Finally, it is important to recognize that abnormalities in health can be viewed on a right-wrong or *moralistic basis*. According to this perspective, some diseases and illnesses are considered to be moral, rather than medical, issues. Emotional illness was interpreted in this way for many years. Prior to 1795, when Pinel removed the chains from the insane in a Paris prison, the mentally ill were treated as if they were criminals. Even today, there is a tendency on the part of medical personnel and lay persons to judge deviations of behavior on a moral basis. For example, the alcoholic is frequently judged to be depraved. In the past, if someone was found intoxicated in a public place, he was usually taken to jail even though he had committed no specific offense. This attitude prevailed until 1968, when the first state laws were introduced to remove drunkenness from the criminal code. Today there is widespread acceptance that alcoholism is an illness that requires medical treatment and not a moral or legal issue.

Other medical problems that are commonly evaluated on a moralistic basis are drug addiction, homosexuality, and neurotic behavior. Functional illness is often judged in this way by medical personnel. A person who complains of being ill but has no disease is looked upon with suspicion and distrust by many physicians. Disparaging terms such as *crock* or *turkey* are often used to describe him.

Clearly, defining a health problem in moral terms is incorrect. Most important, this definition frequently affects the type of medical care the patient receives. If medical personnel believe that the alcoholic or the person with a functional illness is wrong instead of sick, they are not likely to give him the best medical care.

The distinction between normality and abnormality is more obvious when it comes to defining disease as opposed to illness because of the objective nature of disease. The structural, functional, and biochemical deviations that take place can be measured scientifically and, therefore, are clearly demonstrable. On the other hand, the deviations from normality that constitute illness are subjective and, consequently, are often determined on the basis of the prevalence, desirability, and "correctness" of a condition.

CONCEPTS OF HEALTH

It is easier for one to understand the concepts of health after he has been introduced to the definitions of disease and illness. This is the reason these concepts are being discussed at this point in the chapter. Health is generally considered to be a "normal" condition. Many physicians define a healthy person as one in whom no disease can be found. A person undergoing an evaluation by his physician will be told he is in good health so long as there are no symptoms, signs, or laboratory abnormalities. The main focus of attention in the evaluation is the physical condition. Emotional and social problems are not accorded the same degree of importance as physical problems, unless they are severe and incapacitating.

The negative concept of health, as a state characterized by the absence of disease, initially gained wide acceptance in the early and middle portions of this century. The advent of modern methods of diagnosis and treatment resulted in the cure of many diseases that previously had been incurable. As a consequence, a change occurred in the approach to the delivery of medical care, away from a consideration of the "entire" patient to the treatment and cure of his disease. While the latter is a highly desirable goal, it is often unattainable simply because there is no curative therapy presently available for many diseases. The list of these conditions is long and contains some of the most serious disorders in terms of morbidity and mortality. Among them are atherosclerotic coronary artery disease, cancer, stroke, and chronic inflammatory disorders such as rheumatoid arthritis.

During the same period, there was a growing awareness of the importance of psychosocial factors in the etiology of many of these so-called refractory disorders. It became more and more apparent that health is related to psychological and social as well as physical well-being. Many people, health professionals and lay persons alike, began to question the validity of the negative concept of health. If it is true that health is based solely on the presence or absence of disease, what about the individual who is ill but has no disease? Or the person who cannot function socially without experiencing symptoms of stress? Or those people who live in such poor and squalid surroundings that they are unable to provide themselves with adequate food and medical care?

Are these health matters the legitimate concern of medical personnel? Many thought they were. So did the World Health Organization (WHO), when in 1948 this group officially defined health as "a state of complete physical, mental and social well-being and not merely the absence of disease or infirmity." Not everyone agreed with this new definition, however. Some physicians felt it was too idealistic and impractical, that to use it as a basis for the delivery of health care would involve medicine in areas that were not within its proper sphere of interest. Other critics said that the implied goal of the WHO definition of health—to have a major segment of the population function optimally from a physical, psychological, and social standpoint—is unrealistic and unattainable. These objections notwithstanding, a majority of the informed public seemed to agree that this definition was a step in the right direction.

In contrast to the negative concept, the positive concept of health stresses the vital role played by psychosocial factors in the health of an individual. This idea has been succinctly expressed by Feinstein in a recent editorial:

> Good health is not an attribute of a person or group of people which happen(s) by chance, or which exists unrelated to other aspects of living. It is an integral part of life affected by education, social class, diet, income, and many other factors.[8]

Some of the other factors (to which Feinstein is referring) are:

1. Environment (living and work)
2. Life-style
3. Interpersonal relations
4. Personal habits
5. Access to health care
6. Occupation

The importance of psychosocial factors such as these in the health of our population is clearly indicated in the 1979 Surgeon General's Report on Health Promotion and Disease Prevention, which estimates that they are related directly or indirectly to disorders that account for as much as 70% of the mortality experienced by Americans.[9] One thing is clear: any definition of health that is to be useful in combating the major health problems of today (i.e., chronic degenerative and neoplastic diseases) must give adequate consideration to the psychosocial as well as the physical aspects of human function.

THE PRACTICAL APPLICATION OF THE CONCEPTS OF HEALTH AND ILL HEALTH

This subject will be discussed from two perspectives: those of medical personnel and those of the lay public. In the following section, the traditional medical model of disease will be compared with a theoretical medical-behavioral model of health and ill health. When used as a basis for health-care delivery, the former has many deficiencies related to its restricted view of health matters. The latter attempts to correct these deficiencies through a more comprehensive approach to patient evaluation and care.

The Medical Perspective

THE TRADITIONAL MEDICAL MODEL OF DISEASE.—According to the contemporary medical model of disease (Fig 21–3), etiology is attributed to a biologic agent that may originate either internally (e.g., genetic defect) or externally (e.g., infectious agent). The means by which the agent produces disease is referred to as pathogenesis, a process that is described in biochemical and physiological terms. The cardinal manifestations of any disease are the changes that occur in the body's tissues and organs; pathologic diagnosis is based on these structural abnormalities. Clinical diagnosis depends on an analysis of a patient's symptoms and signs plus the use of ancillary diagnostic methods such as laboratory tests and x-rays. Treatment of disease is designed to control or eliminate the causative agent and reverse the biochemical, physiological, and structural changes that have taken place.

This model, which clearly emphasizes the physical and biologic aspects of disease, gradually evolved over the past 75 years. During this period there were dramatic improvements in medical care, resulting in a significant reduction in morbidity and mortality from many diseases. However, despite the many important benefits that accrued from this disease-oriented approach, it became obvious in the 1960s that there were serious deficiencies in our system of health care. A crisis of sorts had developed because of the inability of the system to meet the needs of many segments of the public. There were several reasons for this crisis: first, the cost of medical

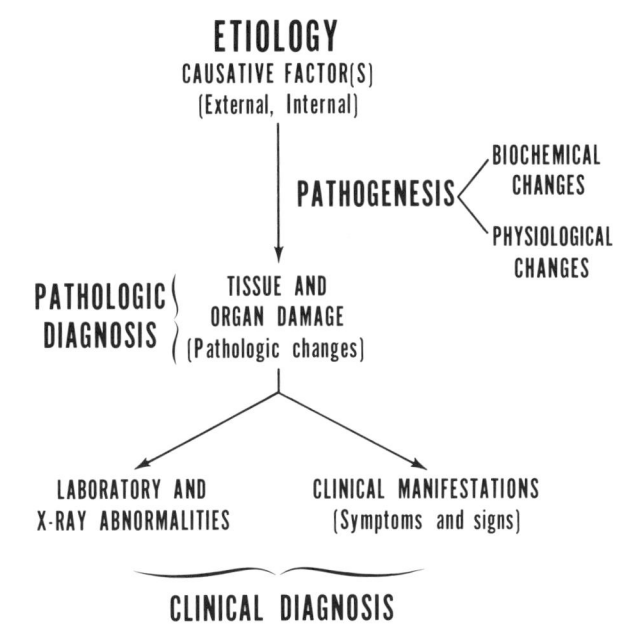

Fig 21–3.—The traditional medical model of disease.

care became excessive; second, medical services were not easily available to certain segments of our population (e.g., the poor and those in rural areas); third, the medical services being rendered to many people were unsatisfactory in that they were episodic and not comprehensive; and fourth, there were insufficient numbers of physicians, particularly in the area of primary care. The advocates of our system pointed with great pride to its accomplishments, specifically to the fact that the United States was the acknowledged world leader in medical science and technology. On the other hand, critics of the system noted that people in this country were in poorer health than those in many other Western nations when criteria such as infant mortality and life expectancy were used to evaluate health status. According to data available in 1973, the United States ranked only 15th in infant mortality and only 19th in life expectancy for men.[8]

Clearly, a problem existed in translating the advances in biomedical science into better medical care for the public. To a large extent, this problem was due to the narrow perspective of the medical model—its failure to give adequate attention to several important aspects of health-care delivery. While concentrating most of their efforts on the evaluation and treatment of disease, medical personnel had neglected those measures designed to promote and maintain health (in a positive sense), especially preventive care. By focusing primarily on the biologic and technologic aspects of medicine, medical personnel had lost sight of the importance of behavioral (psychological, social, and cultural) factors in the determination of both health and ill health.

A second development in the past half-century raised further doubts about the efficacy of the medical model in health-care delivery. This was the dramatic change in the pattern of disease in the Western countries of the world.[10] At the turn of this century, the leading causes of mortality were the acute infec-

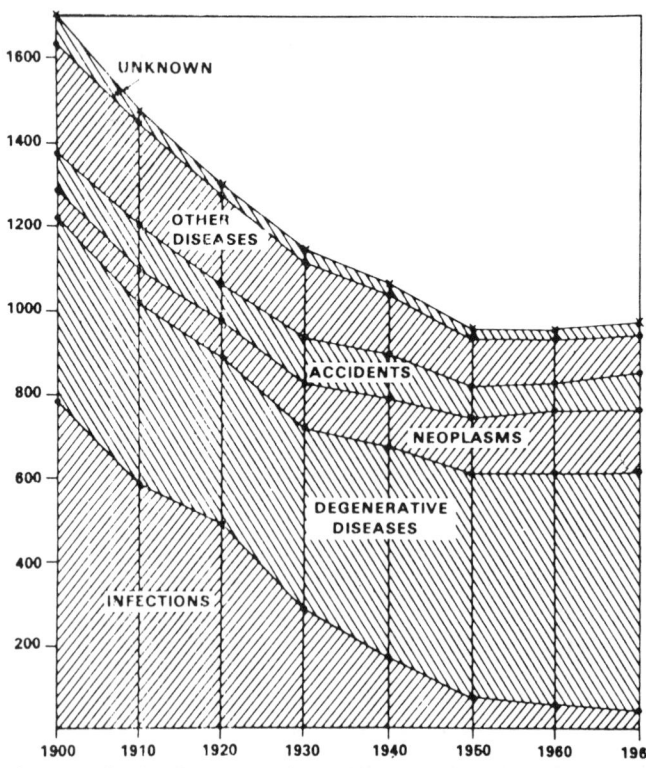

Fig 21–4.—Death rates from all causes, by major categories. Figures are for the United States, 1900–1969. (From Peery T.M.: *Am. J. Clin. Pathol.* 63:453, 1975. Used by permission.)

tious diseases (Fig 21–4). In the ensuing 50 years, these conditions ceased to be a major cause of death as a result of the introduction of higher standards of living (housing and sanitation) and modern methods of diagnosis, treatment (i.e., antibiotics), and prevention (i.e., immunization) of disease. Life expectancy increased dramatically, and because of this people found themselves threatened by a new group of chronic degenerative disorders (e.g., heart disease, stroke, cancer, and arthritis). The medical model, which had played such an important role in the conquest of the infectious diseases, proved to be less effective in dealing with many of these disorders for which there is no known cause or specific therapy.

A new model of health and ill health was needed, one that would be able to deal more effectively with the contemporary problems of health-care delivery.

A MEDICAL-BEHAVIORAL MODEL OF HEALTH AND ILL HEALTH.—This model is based on a comprehensive picture of a person as a biologic, psychological, and social being. Health is defined in positive terms as an optimal degree of function in all these areas, while ill health is defined as dysfunction in one or more of these spheres. According to the medical-behavioral model, disease is a biologic process in which psychological and social factors are important in terms of both etiology and treatment. Thus, this model retains the fundamental biologic viewpoint of the traditional medical model of disease, but broadens it to include a role for those psychological and social factors that are relevant to health.

The relationship of biologic, psychological, and social dysfunction to disease and illness is depicted in Figure 21–5, adapted from the work of Reading.[11] Three points deserve emphasis with respect to this diagram: first, psychosocial dysfunction can result in ill health directly or indirectly as a consequence of its effects on the biologic systems of the body; second, disease, although by definition a biologic process, is often due to the interaction of biologic and psychosocial factors; and third,

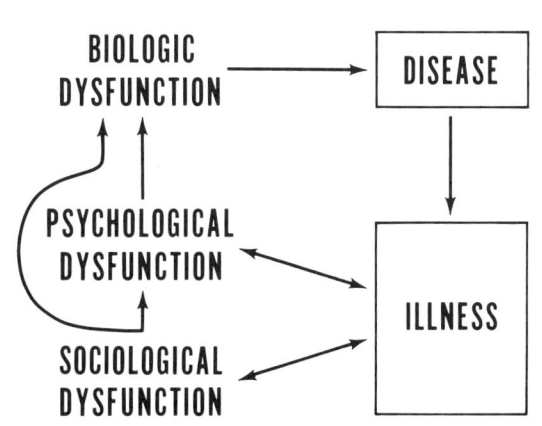

Fig 21–5.—Behavioral and biologic factors in disease and illness.

clinically evident disease commonly results in an illness in which the patient experiences psychological and social dysfunction. The first and third points are discussed at length in chapters 7, 8, and 22. Let us examine point two in more detail here, since it has particular relevance to the current problems of health-care delivery facing this country.

In the medical-behavioral model, disease causation is attributed to the interaction of multiple factors, both biologic and behavioral. The immediate etiologic agent is generally biologic; this factor is necessary for disease to occur. Psychosocial factors usually act indirectly by predisposing an individual to the effects of biologic agents. For example, take tuberculosis. The immediate cause or necessary factor is the tubercle bacillus. Without infection by this agent, the disease cannot occur. Psychosocial factors, such as age, race, poor nutrition, and crowded living conditions, act as predisposing factors by increasing a person's chances of exposure to the bacillus and lowering his resistance to the organism. Surveys using skin tests and chest x-rays to determine the incidence of tuberculosis have shown that while many people are infected by the bacillus, few develop evidence of clinical disease. Those that become ill generally do so because a predisposing factor(s) has made them more susceptible.

The occurrence of many of the degenerative and neoplastic diseases that constitute the major health problems of today is also determined by multiple biologic and psychosocial factors. Some of the risk factors associated with atherosclerotic coronary heart disease are described in chapter 11 and include hypertension, a diet high in saturated fats and cholesterol, cigarette smoking, physical inactivity, and the type A pattern of behavior. The interaction of these factors, along with heredity, is important since the presence of more than one greatly increases the chances of an individual developing the disease (see Table 11–4). With respect to cancer, it is generally acknowledged that this group of disorders is causally related to life-style factors (e.g., cigarette smoking, alcohol consumption, diet) and occupational exposure to carcinogenic substances. Heredity is also an etiologic factor of significance.

The fact that the etiology of disease is multifactorial has implications for the delivery of health care to the public, especially in the area of prevention. Since the immediate biologic cause of many of the major disorders (e.g., cancer, atherosclerotic coronary heart disease, stroke) affecting our population is either unknown or untreatable, medical personnel often have to rely on the modification of predisposing psychosocial factors in order to control them. The 1979 Surgeon General's Report on Health Promotion and Disease Prevention states:

Of the 10 leading causes of death in the United States, at least seven could be substantially reduced if persons at risk improved just five habits: diet, smoking, lack of exercise, alcohol abuse, and use of antihypertensive medication.[9]

There is, in fact, evidence that public health measures designed to modify coronary risk factors have been responsible in part for the declining mortality rate from this disease since 1968.[12]

When it comes to the management of the individual patient, the multifactorial concept of disease dictates that therapy be directed to the psychosocial, as well as the biologic, factors that play a role in disease causation. A comprehensive approach is especially important in treating patients who have disorders that are chronic and incurable, since the effects of these disorders on a person are also multifactorial. In other words, for patients with these conditions, psychosocial problems constitute an integral part of their illness, and medical care that does not attempt to deal with them is doomed to failure.

In summary, the medical-behavioral model views a person's health as being influenced by genetic and environmental factors. His genetically determined physical and psychological makeup constitute the basic substrate upon which his health is based. As he passes through life, he is confronted by a host of biologic, psychological, and social determiners of health. These interact with one another to constitute the "health milieu" of the individual. When attempting to evaluate the health status of an individual, one must take into consideration all of the variables (biologic and behavioral) that affect his physical, psychological, and social well-being.

The goals of the medical-behavioral model are twofold: first, the promotion of health and the prevention of ill health, and second, the proper diagnosis and management of disease and illness. By health is meant the "desirable" aspect of normality, that is, optimal physical, psychological, and social well-being. Thus, a healthy person is not only free of disease but is also able to realize the maximal degree of physical, psychological, and social function of which he is capable.

The Patient's Perspective

The concepts that patients have of ill health often differ from those held by medical personnel. Since it is the patient's concepts that determine his expectations and behavior in the medical setting, it is important that health professionals know as much as possible about how people think about disease and illness. Lay concepts of ill health are based to a large extent on socially and culturally determined attitudes and beliefs. These affect people's perceptions of symptoms, the diagnostic labels they attach to them, the manner in which they respond to sickness, and their communication with physicians. In addition to social and cultural factors, there are a variety of personal factors that affect a person's views of ill health, including his education, his previous experiences with illness, and the extent of his contact with medical personnel.

In order to understand the influence that social and cultural values have on a person's concept of health matters, one must recognize that health and ill health are social as well as personal matters. Ill health occurs in a social setting and the decision as to whether or not a person is sick is a social as well as a medical one. Every culture defines for its members the conditions that are to be labeled as illness. The criteria that are used vary among different cultures and among different social groups within a particular culture. Various social and cultural groups also differ with respect to their beliefs about the causes and treatment of disease (see chaps. 9 and 10). These differences are reflected in the behavior of the members of these groups. For example, a person of Latin American background who believes in the hot and cold theory of disease will react differently to symptoms than a middle-class American who subscribes to the more modern concepts. In the first instance, the individual will initially medicate himself with remedies designed to counteract the imbalance of hot or cold forces. If this is not successful in alleviating his symptoms, he may then elect to go to a nonmedical cultural "healer" who shares his beliefs. Only when his illness becomes severe and incapacitating is he likely to consider going to a physician for help. In the second instance, the person may also try some home remedy before seeking professional help; however, if this is unsuccessful he will probably go directly to a physician for treatment.

In our society, the lay concepts of ill health are of three general types: *scientific, magicoreligious,* and *folk*.[13] The scientific viewpoint encompasses many of the ideas that are held by medical personnel. The magicoreligious and folk orientations were described in the discussion of the historical evolution of the concept of disease (see also chaps. 9 and 10). The ideas that most lay people have of disease and illness are composed of elements of all three concepts. One or another of these views may dominate depending on a person's age, sociocultural background, and education. Thus, a college professor is more likely to view health matters in scientific terms, whereas an impoverished member of a minority group is more likely to have concepts that are made up of magicoreligious and folk beliefs. The nature of an illness may also influence a person's perspective. When seriously ill, most people go immediately to a physician, believing that scientific medical care is necessary in this circumstance. On the other hand, when people are confronted by a mild illness, they may choose to medicate themselves by using folk remedies or look for a "magical" cure for their symptoms by going to a "faith healer."

People initially obtain their ideas about health and ill health from their family. In the process of socialization, a young child acquires his parents' views about health matters. Later these ideas are modified as he expands his social horizons and is exposed to different concepts. As an older child and adolescent, his contact with medical personnel influences his views about disease and illness. Of course, his education in school is also a major contributor to these views.

The concepts that children of various ages have of illness were the subject of a study by Cambell.[14] He found that a young child defines illness primarily on the basis of the way he feels; in other words, if he has symptoms (i.e., pain or discomfort) then he considers himself to be sick. As the child grows older, he begins to incorporate into this concept some of the psychosocial effects of being sick, such as the inability to participate in one's usual daily activities (play or go to school) and the need to withdraw from the environment (go to bed). As he matures further, he begins to develop more sophisticated ideas about illness as a result of being able to recognize specific types of illnesses (e.g., a "cold" or the "flu"). Over a period of time, the knowledge he acquires about health matters and his personal experiences with sickness and medical personnel lead to the development of concepts of illness that are more like those of an adult.

Members of the same social and cultural groups tend to share similar concepts about illness just as they do about other important matters in life. This fact was clearly pointed out in the classic study by Koos in which he demonstrated that a person's perception of the significance of symptoms could be correlated with his social class ranking.[15] Koos surveyed people with different social backgrounds in the rural community of Regionville, New York, to find out how they interpreted various somatic complaints. He divided the community into three social classes: Class I, the "successful people" (bankers, doctors, businessmen); Class II, the major portion of the town's "breadwinners" (wage earners); and Class III, those at the lowest economic level. Representatives of each class were asked to evaluate a number of symptoms in order to determine which ones they thought required medical attention. On the basis of their responses, Koos was able to show that there was a clear-cut relationship between an individual's social position and the meaning he attached to these symptoms (Table 21–1). The people in Class I had a greater awareness of the medical importance of symptoms than the individuals in Class II; those in Class III were least able to recognize the significance of symptoms. For example, shortness of breath was felt to be a complaint requiring medical attention by 77% of the respondents in Class I, whereas only 55% of those in Class II and 21% of those in Class III recognized the importance of this symptom.

Another study demonstrating that concepts of illness are related to social class was conducted by the National Opinion Research Center (quoted by King[13]). This study showed that people with different occupations, income, and education responded differently to questions about their expectations and knowledge of illness. For example, those persons with the least education and income agreed most often with statements such as: "A person has to expect a good deal of illness and one might as well get used to some aches and pains" and "Nobody should go to a hospital

TABLE 21–1.—PERCENTAGE OF RESPONDENTS IN EACH SOCIAL CLASS RECOGNIZING SPECIFIED SYMPTOMS AS NEEDING MEDICAL ATTENTION

SYMPTOM	CLASS I ($N = 51$)	CLASS II ($N = 335$)	CLASS III ($N = 128$)
Loss of appetite	57%	50%	20%
Persistent backache	53	44	19
Continued coughing	77	78	23
Persistent joint and muscle pains	80	47	19
Blood in stool	98	89	60
Blood in urine	100	93	69
Excessive vaginal bleeding	92	83	54
Swelling of ankles	77	76	23
Loss of weight	80	51	21
Bleeding gums	79	51	20
Chronic fatigue	80	53	19
Shortness of breath	77	55	21
Persistent headaches	80	56	22
Fainting spells	80	51	33
Pain in chest	80	51	31
Lump in breast	94	71	44
Lump in abdomen	92.	65	34

Note: Percentages rounded to nearest whole number.
Source: Koos, Earl Loman, *The Health of Regionville*. New York, Columbia University Press, 1954, p. 33. (Reprinted with permission of the publisher.)

unless there is just no other way." Knowledge about ill health was directly related to an individual's level of income and education. When the respondents were asked to name any of the symptoms of cancer, diabetes, and poliomyelitis, the number of people who could *not* name any symptoms was greatest among those with the least education and income. When asked whether they thought cancer was contagious, more than twice as many respondents in the lowest education and income group thought this was so, when compared with the highest group.

The results of studies such as these, indicating that individuals with different social backgrounds have different concepts of disease and illness, are important in understanding how people react to being sick. They suggest, for instance, that those at the lower socioeconomic levels will react differently to ill health than those at the higher levels; that the former tend to ignore mild illness and delay seeking medical care, while the latter are more responsive to mild and moderately severe symptoms in terms of obtaining this care.

Some studies have shown that there is a direct relationship between income level and the use of medical services. This relationship is illustrated in a study by Ludwig and Gibson,[16] where people who considered themselves to be in poor health were interviewed and divided into two groups: those who had and those who had not sought medical help. The proportion of individuals who had *not* seen a physician or visited a health-care facility was much greater for persons at the lower income levels.

Concepts of ill health are very important in communication within the medical setting. The poor and members of ethnic minority groups are more likely to subscribe to magicoreligious and folk beliefs about illness, which are at variance with the scientific views of medical personnel. Consequently, people from these groups often have a great deal of difficulty communicating with health professionals. This communication gap is the basis for a feeling of alienation on the part of the poor and of ethnic minorities with respect to our health-care system and is another reason they frequently delay seeking medical help when they are sick.

According to a study by Suchman, social isolation and ethnocentrism are the principal reasons why members of the lower classes and minority groups tend to have more parochial views about health and illness.[17] He found that these individuals had limited contact with people outside their social and cultural groups. As a result, they were rarely exposed to up-to-date ideas about ill health. Suchman found that there was a positive correlation between ethnocentrism and a lack of knowledge about the scientific aspects of disease. He also noted that people who were socially isolated tended to have a less favorable attitude toward medical practitioners.

The concept of health, like that of illness, varies among different segments of our population. Baumann conducted an interesting study in which she surveyed people of different backgrounds to determine their definitions of health.[18] She used three criteria of health in the study: (1) the presence of a general feeling of well-being (feeling-state orientation), (2) the absence of symptoms of illness (symptom orientation), and (3) the ability to perform the activities that one wishes (performance orientation). In response to the question, "What do you think people mean when they say they are in good physical condition?" most lay persons considered the first (feeling-state) and the third (performance) criteria to be most important in defining health. When asked the same question, medical students selected the second (symptom) and third (performance) criteria. A concept of health that stresses the symptom orientation was more common among educated people and those in the upper socioeconomic classes, while a concept emphasizing the feeling-state orientation was found more often among people without much education and those in the lower socioeconomic classes. Baumann noted that there was a tendency for people to become symptom-oriented once they accepted the role of a patient, because after one receives a diagnosis by medical personnel, he begins to focus on symptoms to which he previously may have been indifferent.

In the aged population, the criterion of performance is more important than the criteria of feeling-state and symptoms. The elderly often come to accept some aches and pains as a normal part of growing old, so long as they do not interfere too much with the performance of their daily activities.

Thus, health is defined somewhat differently by people depending on their age, social background, and education. Most lay persons agree that a positive feeling-state, the absence of symptoms, and the ability to perform one's daily activities are important; the differences that occur among people in their concepts of health are based on which of these criteria they feel are most important.

In the medical setting, it is crucial that the physician attempt to understand his patient's concepts of health and ill health. In general, patients are hesitant to share their views with the physician, simply because they are not sure he will understand and accept their ideas and explanations of disease and illness. Unless these views are recognized and taken into account during the course of medical evaluations and treatment, however, it is unlikely that a satisfactory physician-patient relationship will develop. In such a situation, with the patient having one set of ideas about health matters and the physician another, communication between them is difficult and patient compliance is bound to suffer.

SUMMARY

Differences in the way medical personnel and lay persons look at health matters are often based on the different concepts they have of health and ill health. The former define ill health in terms of a disease concept; the latter view ill health in terms of an illness concept. Disease is an objective biologic process that affects a person's tissues and organs, causing structural, biochemical, and functional changes. Traditionally, the physician's primary goals have been to diagnose, treat, and if possible cure a patient's disease. There are times, however, when medical care is needed even though there is no disease present. This is true with respect to preventive care administered before a person becomes sick. There are also a number of conditions in which a person is ill but has no disease (e.g., functional illness, drug abuse, emotional illness).

Illness is a subjective state in which a person has symptoms or is unable to perform certain activities. It can be caused by disease but, as noted above, a person may feel ill for other reasons. Psychological and social problems often result in illness; consequently, these problems may be the basis for a patient's visit to his physician. For a lay person, the seriousness of an illness is gauged in terms of the amount of distress he experiences and the extent to which his activities are curtailed.

Lay persons have different concepts of disease and illness depending on variables such as age, education, and social and cultural background. These concepts play a vital role in determining the behavior of the sick. For this reason, it is crucial that health professionals develop an understanding of the lay as well as medical concepts of ill health and incorporate both views in their approach to the evaluation and care of patients.

Concepts of health and ill health have important implications for the delivery of medical care to the public. A concept of health that takes into consideration the psychological and social as well as the physical function of the individual will lead to a more comprehensive approach to the delivery of medical services than one based on the absence of disease. The traditional medical perspective has tended to focus too much on the diagnosis and cure of the disease and not enough on the prevention of disease and the maintenance of health. A medical-behavioral model, which takes into consideration both the biologic and the psychosocial aspects of health and ill health, has significant advantages as a guide in the delivery of medical services to the public.

REFERENCES

1. Hudson R.P.: The concept of disease. *Ann. Intern. Med.* 65(3):595, 1966.
2. Lanning J.A.: Are medical education dollars buying what they should? *J.A.M.A.* 238:1153–1157, 1977.
3. Cassell E.: *The Healer's Art*. Philadelphia, J.B. Lippincott Co., 1976.
4. Tumulty P.A.: The approach to patients with functional disorders. *N. Engl. J. Med.* 263:123–128, 1960.
5. Harwood A.: The hot-cold theory of disease. *J.A.M.A.* 219(7):1153, 1971.
6. Bloom S.W.: *The Doctor and His Patient*. New York, Russell Sage Foundation, 1963.
7. Wright I.S.: Correct levels of serum cholesterol, average vs normal vs optimal. *J.A.M.A.* 236:261–262, 1976.
8. Feinstein R.J.: The forgotten Americans. *Miami Medicine*, vol. L, no. 10, November 1980.
9. *Healthy People: The Surgeon General's Report on Health Promotion and Disease Prevention 1979.* Department of Health, Education, and Welfare, Public Health Service, publication no. 79-55071.
10. Perry T.M.: The new and old diseases. *Am. J. Clin. Pathol.* 63:453, 1975.
11. Reading A.: Illness and disease. *Med. Clin. North Am.* 61:703–710, 1977.
12. Stern M.P.: The recent decline in ischemic heart disease mortality. *Ann. Intern. Med.* 91:630, 1979.
13. King S.H.: *Perceptions of Illness and Medical Practice*. New York, Russell Sage Foundation, 1962.
14. Cambell J.D.: Illness is a point of view: The development of children's concepts of illness. *Child Dev.* 46:92, 1975.
15. Koos E.L.: *The Health of Regionville*. New York, Columbia University Press, 1954.
16. Ludwig E.G., Gibson G.: Self perception of sickness and the seeking of medical care. *J. Health Soc. Behav.* 10(2):125, 1969.
17. Suchman E.A.: Social factors in medical deprivation. *Am. J. Public Health* 55:1725, 1965.
18. Baumann B.: Diversities in conceptions of health and physical fitness. *J. Health Hum. Behav.* 2:39, 1961.

22 / Illness Behavior

JONATHAN J. BRAUNSTEIN, M.D.

IN THIS CHAPTER, the expression *illness behavior* refers to the health-oriented actions of a person from the time he first experiences symptoms until his illness runs its course. These actions take place in two time periods: while he is sick but has not yet made contact with the health-care system and while he is a patient being cared for by medical personnel. During the first period, he decides when and where to go for help. This decision is important, since the longer a person delays before going to a physician for care, the greater is the likelihood that his disease will be in an advanced stage and, consequently, less responsive to therapy.

A 65-year-old woman came to her physician because of a lump in her right breast. Although she had noticed a progressive enlargement of the lump during the previous 8 months, this was the first time she had sought medical help. She had discussed the presence of the lump with her husband and several of her friends, and although they strongly advised that she go to a physician, she refused to do so until the skin of the breast overlying the lump developed a weeping ulcer. Examination by the physician revealed a hard mass 6 by 7 cm in diameter in the upper outer quadrant of the right breast. The skin over the mass was ulcerated and draining a serosanguineous material. There were two hard axillary lymph nodes palpable on the right side. A biopsy of the mass at the time of surgery showed that it was cancer of the breast, which had spread to the axillary lymph nodes. Despite a radical mastectomy and postoperative chemotherapy, the woman died 8 months later of metastatic cancer.

The prognosis of breast cancer is related to the size of the primary tumor mass and whether or not lymph node metastases have occurred. In general, the longer a tumor is present, the larger it is likely to be and the greater are the chances that it has spread to the lymph glands. In this woman, the extensive size of the tumor mass and the presence of axillary node metastases were very ominous prognostic signs. The unnecessary wait after she first became aware of the lump in her breast was a critical factor in determining the fatal outcome of her disease.

After a sick person enters the traditional health care system, his behavior continues to be an important determinant of how well he does medically. Even though a physician makes an accurate diagnosis and prescribes the proper therapy, the success of treatment usually depends on a patient following medical advice. A lack of compliance with medical instructions can adversely affect the course of such a patient's illness.

A 35-year-old man had been diagnosed as having pulmonary tuberculosis 3 months earlier. At that time, he was hospitalized with symptoms of cough, hemoptysis, fever, and weight loss. Physical examination and x-rays of the chest revealed an infiltrate involving the upper lobes of his lungs. The results of smears and cultures of his sputum confirmed a diagnosis of tuberculosis. He was treated for this disease with three drugs (isoniazid, ethambutol, and pyridoxine) and was discharged on these medications after being in the hospital one month. Three months after his discharge, he returned to see his physician with a recurrence of the same symptoms that had led to his hospitalization. Although he had been given an appointment to see the physician 2 weeks after his discharge, he had failed to keep it. On talking with the patient, the physician found out that he had stopped taking all his medicines. He gave no specific reason for doing this except that he had run out of the pills and it was "too much trouble to come back to get some more." Examination of the patient and x-rays of his lungs showed that the tuberculosis had progressed and he had to be hospitalized for further treatment.

In describing and interpreting the actions of the sick, various authors have defined *health-oriented behavior* in different ways. For instance, to Mechanic this term means "the ways in which given symptoms may be differentially perceived, evaluated and acted upon (or not acted upon) by different kinds of persons."[1] This definition encompasses only the first period of an illness, prior to the time the person comes under medical care. Kasl and Cobb have identified three types of health-related behavior, which they called health behavior, illness behavior, and sick role behavior.[2] The first of these refers to the actions of people that are designed to maintain their health, the second to the actions taken by people who feel ill in an attempt to define their condition, and the third to the behavior of people who consider themselves to be sick and are attempting to get well. The actions of people in the patient role have been described by Suchman and constitute an additional kind of health-oriented behavior.[3]

A broader definition of illness behavior is used in this discussion to bring together under one heading the behavior exhibited by people during all the different phases of an illness. The outline that will be followed to describe this behavior is shown in Table 22–1, which lists the various periods and stages of an illness.

THE PERIOD PRIOR TO CONTACT WITH THE HEALTH-CARE SYSTEM

The Symptom Experience Stage

A symptom is an abnormal feeling state associated with discomfort or pain, a disturbance of physical or mental function, or an alteration in the appearance of the body. It is a subjective experience—something a person complains about to family, friends, or medical personnel. Barsky points out that a symptom can be thought of as consisting of two elements: a peripheral sensation (perceptual component) and a cortical elaboration of that

TABLE 22–1.—PERIODS AND STAGES OF ILLNESS BEHAVIOR

I. The period prior to contact with the health-care system
   A. The symptom experience stage
   B. The assumption of the sick role stage
II. The period of medical care
   A. The medical care contact stage
   B. The stage of patienthood
   C. The recovery or rehabilitation stage

Adapted from Suchman E.A.: *J. Health Hum. Behav.* 6:114, 1965.

sensation (reactive component).[4] Both must be taken into consideration if one is to understand this stage of illness.

INTERPRETATION OF SYMPTOMS.—Everyone experiences symptoms of one sort or another in their day-to-day lives. A pain in the abdomen, an ache in the back, a cough, nervousness, and a skin rash are all common complaints. Most symptoms are so mild and transient that people generally pay little attention to them.

What makes a person decide that a symptom is important and should not be ignored? His decision is related to the nature of the two components previously mentioned. With respect to the *perceptual component*, people generally use three criteria to distinguish symptoms that are significant and need further attention from those that are inconsequential. The first has to do with the intensity and duration of the physical sensation. A pain that is severe or prolonged will be taken more seriously than one that is mild and short-lived. The second criterion is the degree to which a sensation interferes with a person's physical or mental function. Shortness of breath that prevents a person from walking about the house is more likely to produce alarm than if it occurs only after strenuous physical activity. Symptoms that interfere with eating, urination, defecation, or body movement are usually considered important medical problems. A third criterion is whether or not a symptom interrupts a person's usual social activities, such as going to school or working. If it does, it becomes a concern not only to the person but also to those who expect him to perform the activity (i.e., teacher, employer, fellow workers).

The *reactive component* may cause a person either to minimize or to amplify a peripheral sensation. It partly explains why different degrees of symptomatic impairment occur to people who have similar amounts of tissue pathology.[4] This component is determined by one's psychological makeup, social and cultural background, education, past history of illness, and recent life situation. For instance, personality traits influence a person's interpretation of a sensory experience. Some people are stoic and tend to ignore discomfort, while others are attentive to even the mildest distress. People with a low level of self-esteem may react with greater anxiety to symptoms than those who are more self-confident. Also, those who place a high value on being independent are usually more concerned by signs of ill health than those who are comfortable in a situation of dependency.

Psychological problems often increase one's awareness of symptoms. People who are depressed, from whatever cause, generally pay more attention to evidence of physical dysfunction. In fact, somatic symptoms can be a prominent part of the clinical picture of depression, even though no organic disease is present. Those who have recently experienced an undue amount of stress are more likely to amplify symptoms than those who have not (see chap. 7).[5, 6] Neurotic persons often react excessively to relatively minor ailments, which may cause their family and even medical personnel to overestimate the seriousness of their illness.

Social background may account for differences in the reaction to symptoms. Persons in the lower part of the socioeconomic scale have a tendency to ignore symptoms and to delay seeking medical care.[7, 8] Unless they are severely ill, health matters have a relatively low priority for them. They live a "crisis-oriented" existence, confronted daily by a myriad of critical problems such as paying the rent, getting enough food on the table, and finding a job. Health matters must compete with all these other problems for the time and energies of the poor. On the other hand, those in the upper social strata do not have these life stresses and, therefore, are able to pay more attention to symptoms.

Minimizing or amplifying a symptom can also be related to one's cultural background.[9, 10] Among some ethnic groups, it is common for people to display a heightened sensitivity to physical sensations, while others seem to encourage their members to make light of physical discomfort unless it is severe (see chap. 10). These types of behavior are often learned early in life. Thus, a child from one of the former groups is taught to go to his parents for help as soon as he notices a symptom, even if it is very mild, whereas a child from the latter group is told not to "run to mother with every little complaint."

Education and experience with illness should also be taken into consideration when attempting to understand the interpretation of symptoms. Those who have little knowledge of medical problems are more likely to ignore mild symptoms because they do not understand their significance. On the other hand, previous experience with an illness generally makes a person more aware of the meaning of particular symptoms and when to seek medical help.

RESPONSE TO SYMPTOMS.—When someone develops what he considers to be a significant symptom, he usually reacts with anxiety and concern. The extent of this reaction is primarily related to how much of a threat the symptom seems to pose to his health. In general, the greater the severity of a symptom, the greater is the anxiety it produces. Symptom-induced anxiety may be accompanied by other manifestations of a stress reaction such as nervousness, irritability, sweating, palpitations, and sleeplessness. These secondary symptoms can alter the individual's perception of his original complaint and cause him to modify his description of it.

This anxiety reaction often causes a person to take some action to remedy his condition. This may entail going to a physician to find out what is wrong with him and what, if any, treatment is needed. There are other ways of dealing with the anxiety, however, for instance by the use of defense mechanisms such as denial, counterphobia, or rationalization. By means of denial, an individual ignores a symptom and acts as though it does not exist. An extension of this mechanism is counterphobia, whereby someone who is sick not only ignores a symptom but also engages in activities designed to prove to himself and others that he is, in fact, in good health. For example, someone who exhibits a counterphobic reaction to back pain might attempt to play 18 holes of golf just to show that his back is "all right." Rationalization is a common psychological device by which the sick attempt to cope with symptom-induced anxiety. An individual who uses this device may attribute a potentially serious symptom to a minor ailment that is less of a threat to his health. Thus, someone who has an episode of severe chest pain that would make the average person think first about the possibility of a heart attack rationalizes the episode by calling it "indigestion." Instead of going immediately to a physician, he takes an antacid for relief. All these psychological mechanisms help to relieve a person's concern about his symptom and allay his anxiety. The price he pays for this relief can be great, however: a delay in obtaining the appropriate medical care.

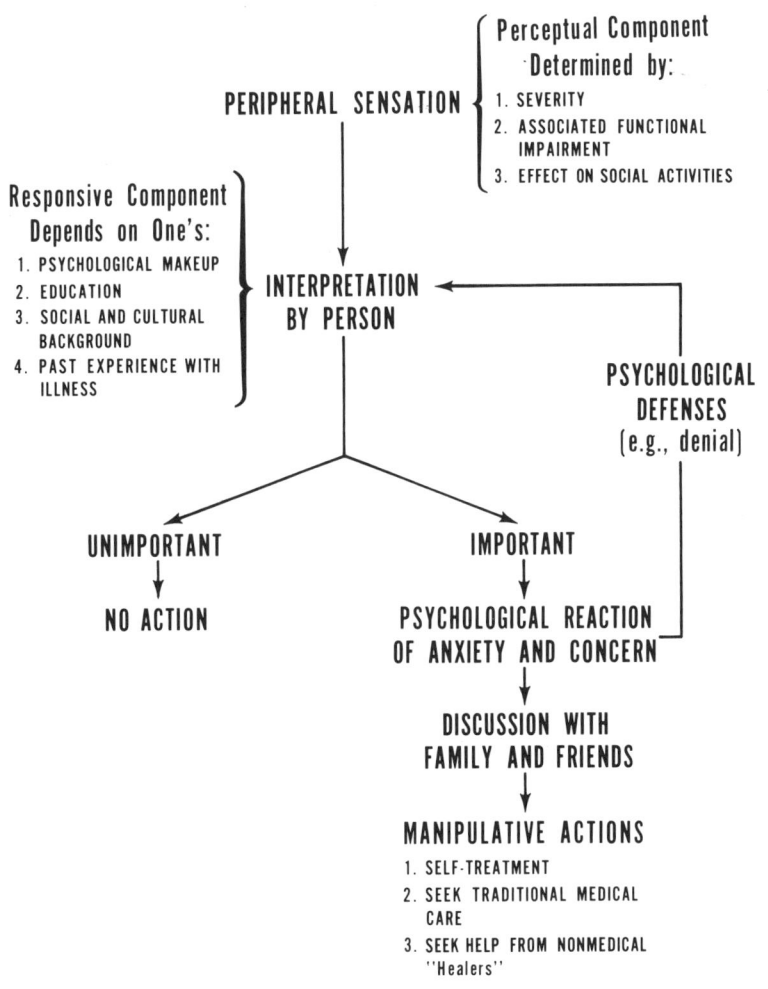

Fig 22-1.—The symptom experience stage.

When a symptom is severe and incapacitating, the individual is usually compelled to seek immediate medical care. If it is only mild or moderate in degree, however, there are other sources of help that he can turn to before going to a physician. In fact, one of the first things people do when they think they may be sick is to seek the advice of family or friends, which is referred to as a lay consultation. Usually they are looking for help in answering two questions: What is the meaning of their symptom? and What should they do about it? By sharing their problem with others, they are also taking the initial step in assuming the sick role.

Even if a person decides, after lay consultation, that he is ill he may not go directly to a physician. Instead, many people treat themselves with either home remedies or over-the-counter medications. Some home remedies are part of the system of folk medicine, which originated in earliest recorded history and has been passed on from generation to generation to the present time. In this system, a mixture of hot tea, butter, and rum may be used to treat a "cold", and a charm, such as a copper bracelet, may be used to ward off arthritis. A wide variety of over-the-counter medications is available to the public at the local pharmacy. Most families have a supply of these in the medicine cabinet, so that a person does not have to go to the physician for every symptom. Often the mother in the family is the "lay physician" for her children and husband, diagnosing their symptoms and prescribing either a folk remedy or a patent medicine. In our society, it is a rare patient who has not tried one of these types of medications prior to seeing his physician.

There are other sources of help besides the traditional health care system that are used to obtain relief from a symptom and to allay symptom-induced anxiety. Various ethnic groups in our society have their own "healers" who diagnose and treat illness (see also chap. 10). For example, southern blacks have "root doctors," Haitians have voodoo priests and priestesses, and Cubans have "espiritistas" and "santeros." When sick, members of these cultural groups commonly turn to these "healers" first, particularly if they have a culture-based illness that physicians do not recognize. There is also a variety of nonspecific "faith healers" who are used by lay people.

Figure 22–1 summarizes the important points made in this discussion of the symptom experience stage.

The Assumption of the Sick Role Stage

In chapter 21 it was pointed out that illness is a matter of social as well as medical concern. Every culture defines the conditions that are to be labeled as sickness and provides its members with guidelines for their behavior while they are ill. One of the ways the actions of the sick are regulated is through the mechanism of role-oriented behavior.

A social role is a pattern of expected behavior with characteristic obligations and privileges. It reflects the attitudes and beliefs of a society toward the matter with which the role is concerned. In medicine, social roles are important in guiding the behavior and interaction of patients and physicians.[11] Both have expectations about how the other will act based on a tacit assumption that behavior will conform to a social role. In the case of the patient, this is the sick role; there is also the physician's role. The manner in which the sick role affects the behavior of the ill and their interaction with medical personnel is discussed below. The physician's role will be described in chapter 24.

When a person develops a symptom and is identified by others as being ill, he is treated differently and is expected to behave in a different manner. He is accorded certain privileges and, in turn, has certain obligations to fulfill; in other words, he is expected to assume a sick role. This role varies in different cultures depending on the particular value system of the people. The classic description of the sick role in our society was given by Parsons[12] (Table 22–2). According to Parsons, a person who is ill is accorded the privilege of being exempt from his usual social responsibilities providing three obligations are met: first, he must not be responsible for his con-

TABLE 22-2.—THE SICK ROLE

I. Privilege—Exemption from normal responsibilities
II. Obligations
   A. Initial—to qualify for the sick role
     1. Person must not be responsible for his condition
     2. He must be motivated to get well as soon as possible
     3. He must seek technically competent help
   B. Secondary—to continue in the sick role
     1. He must cooperate with medical personnel
     2. He must be willing to resume his former social resonsibilities if and when he recovers

Adapted from Parsons T.: *The Social System*. New York, The Free Press, 1951; and Balint M.: *The Doctor, His Patient, and the Illness*. New York, International Universities Press, 1957.

dition; second, he must be motivated to get well as soon as possible; and third, he must seek technically competent help in an effort to recover. This definition implies that illness is an undesirable event beyond the control of the individual and that the sick need assistance from others (medical personnel) in order to get well.

The theory of the sick role as a primary factor governing the actions of the sick is a generalization about illness behavior and, like all generalizations, has certain limitations when applied to real life. In contrast to other social roles, which go on for long periods of time in a person's life, Parsons's description of the sick role seems to imply that it is relatively short-lived. From this standpoint, the role seems to apply best to persons who have an acute self-limited illness, those who are sick for a brief period and then recover. While ill, they relinquish their usual social roles; after recovery, they resume these activities. This concept of the sick role does not apply so well to a person who has a chronic illness. He may be sick for years and may never recover his health to the extent that he is able to return to his previous social roles.

Despite some limitations to its practical application, Parsons's theory of the sick role is very useful in understanding many interactions that take place between medical personnel and patients. When a person violates, or is thought to have violated, the obligations associated with this role, significant problems can arise that may interfere with his care.

A 22-year-old man was admitted to the hospital because of severe infection in his right forearm. He had a history of drug addiction for the past 3 years. The infection occurred as a direct result of injecting heroin into the veins of his arm. Physical examination of the patient showed that he had a fever of 104 F; a markedly swollen, reddened, and tender right forearm; and enlarged right axillary lymph glands. Appropriate laboratory tests were carried out and he was started on a program of management including antibiotics and local heat treatments to the right arm.

On the second day in the hospital, it became apparent to his private physician that the hospital staff (the interns, nurses, and aides) had a different attitude toward this patient than toward the others on the ward. Although the patient was cooperative, they did not care for him in a concerned and empathetic manner. For example, instead of personally giving the local heat treatments to the patient as they did in other cases, the nurses would leave the hot packs by the bedside for him to apply to his arm. One nurse described her feelings about the patient as follows, "He caused his own illness, let him treat himself." A similar view was held by an intern, who stated, "Anyone who has abused himself like this patient has doesn't deserve our sympathy."

The reason for the hospital staff's animosity can best be understood in terms of the patient's *apparent* violation of one obligation of the sick role, that is, to be free from responsibility for one's own illness. Of course, their assumption that the patient had "made himself sick" is probably incorrect, for drug addiction is generally acknowledged to be a disorder that is often beyond the control of the individual. The attitude expressed by the members of this hospital staff is not uncommon and shows the effect that a violation of the "rules and regulations" of the sick role can have on the medical care of a patient.

People with other medical conditions, such as alcoholism, cigarette smoking, and obesity, may also appear to have violated the obligation of the sick not to be responsible for their own illness. When one eats too much, drinks too much, or smokes too many cigarettes, it is often assumed that he could control this behavior if he really wanted to and, thus, any diseases that result from these excesses are self-inflicted.

The benefits of the sick role consist of more than an exemption from one's normal social obligations and include certain secondary gains that accrue as a result of being sick. While someone is ill, he receives special consideration and care from his family and friends; he becomes the center of attention. In addition, there may be financial benefits, such as disability insurance payments, which come to him as a consequence of his illness. So long as the individual's behavior conforms to the sick role, he is considered to be entitled to these secondary gains; however, if he fails to comply with the obligations of the role, he may not be accorded these benefits.

One of the most serious violations of the sick role is to pretend to be sick, when in fact one is not, in order to obtain certain secondary gains. This is defined as malingering. If discovered, the malingerer generally receives the disapproval of both family and friends for having tried to "put one over on them." If there is disagreement as to whether a person with a symptom is really ill and entitled to the privileges of the sick role, he is sent to a physician. In addition to diagnosing and treating disease, the physician acts as a "legitimizing agent" for the sick role.

To view all the actions of the sick as being due to role-oriented behavior is much too narrow a perspective. There are many other factors that influence how a person acts during this stage of an illness, including psychological makeup, previous experiences with illness, and social and cultural background. The behavior of the sick is also determined by the responses of others to them; in other words, their actions can be modified by operant conditioning. In a given person, one or more of these variables may play a critical role in behavior. For instance, a person with a preexisting medical condition who develops a recurrence of symptoms often reacts quite differently than someone with the same symptoms who has never had this condition. Moreover, if an individual has never had much experience with illness, he may have great difficulty adjusting to the psychological effects of being sick. He may be unable to give up his usual social roles and accept the sick role. This is especially true of people who depend on being active and independent for a great deal of their ego strength.

A 55-year-old man was admitted to the hospital because of an acute myocardial infarction. He was an executive with a manufacturing firm. During most of his life, he had been in good health and had no previous history of cardiac disease. While at the office one day, he developed chest pain and was taken to the emergency room at a nearby hospital. The diagnosis of a myocardial infarction was confirmed by the appropriate tests and he was sent to the coronary care unit. Because his condition was stable after 3 days, he was transferred to a regular ward of the hospital. His pain gone, the patient felt relatively good, whereupon he announced to the hospital staff that he intended to resume his business activities from his hospital bed. He stated that he wanted his secretary brought to the room so they could work on some upcoming contracts. Despite explanations by his physician about the seriousness of his condition, the patient persisted in his demands that he be allowed to work in the hospital, saying "If you won't let me work here, I'll go home and work." Finally, after much discussion, a compromise was reached whereby the patient agreed to do a limited amount of paperwork for an hour or so a day.

THE PERIOD OF MEDICAL CARE

The Medical Care Contact Stage

Only a small percentage of those who experience symptoms come under the care of a physician. Why does a person who seeks medical care decide on this course of action? There are several reasons, the most obvious being to find out why he is sick and to get relief from his symptoms. In addition, there are other factors that motivate him to go to a physician: one has to do with the anxiety and concern he has about his symptoms; another is based on the obligation of the sick role, which requires that he obtain technically competent help. Thus, there is a physical (symptoms), psychological (anxiety), and social (sick role obligation) basis for the decision of the sick to seek medical care.

Prior to seeing a physician, a person usually discusses the matter with family or friends, and often it is at their insistence that he finally decides to take this step. In addition, certain situations and events can trigger this decision, including a family crisis created by the illness or a loss of income resulting from an inability to work.[13, 14]

Certain features of the health-care system also determine whether or not someone who is sick will seek medical care. One of these is the *availability* of services. In some parts of this country, good medical care is difficult to obtain. This is particularly true in the inner cities and rural areas where there is a large number of poor and ethnic minority groups. On the other hand, the middle- and upper-class suburban areas have an abundance of good medical facilities and personnel. If one lives in an area where medical services are not easily available, he is likely to put off going to a physician when he first becomes ill. Instead, he may wait until the illness is so severe that he is forced to seek help. The knowledge that medical services are not available without making an extraordinary effort to obtain them is often responsible for the fact that the poor and minority group members delay seeking medical care until late in the course of an illness.

Medical care must also be *accessible* to a person before he can utilize it. This refers to the ease with which a person can make use of available medical services. A private physician's office may be within several miles of an individual's home, but if he is unable to get to the office because of a lack of transportation or a physical disability, it is as if these services did not exist for him.

The *cost of health care*, which has risen at a rapid rate over the past 25 years, is a major barrier to some persons in their attempt to get adequate medical services. Despite the advent of Medicaid and Medicare, there are still large segments of the population that cannot afford to be hospitalized with a major illness. The high cost of health care deters people from using preventive medical services; instead, they wait until they become ill and "have to go to the doctor."

The *acceptability* of medical services is important in determining a person's use of them. Acceptability depends on whether or not the services that are offered to a patient meet his particular needs. Certain needs are common to all patients, such as being treated with concern and dignity. Compare the difference in care in an office of a private physician with that in a public clinic where there are crowded conditions and long waits and patients are frequently treated in an impersonal and undignified manner. The physicians and nurses who work in the clinics are usually from the middle or upper classes, and many have little understanding of the social problems that confront the poor who come there. Communication barriers exist between the patients and the medical personnel in these clinics because of their dissimilar backgrounds.

The Stage of Patienthood

THE DEPENDENT PATIENT ROLE.—Being a patient means that one has to rely to a certain extent on his physician and, in doing so, he assumes a dependent role. The degree of dependency associated with this role varies with the nature of the patient's illness. Szasz and Hollender describe three patterns of interaction between physicians and patients; these differ in the degree of control that the physician exercises over the patient.[15] When someone is critically ill, as for example in a coma, the physician has to assume almost total responsibility for what is done to him medically. In this situation, called the "active-passive" type of relationship by Szasz and Hollender, the patient is completely dependent on his physician. In circumstances in which a patient is acutely ill but is able to cooperate in his management, a different kind of physician-patient interaction takes place. This type is referred to as "guidance and cooperation" by Szasz and Hollender. Here, the patient is very much dependent on his physician to guide his actions; however, he has some independence because his cooperation is necessary for the treatment to be successful. Finally, there is the situation of chronic illness in which the patient is still dependent on his physician but able to interact with him on a more equal footing. This relationship is called "mutual participation" by Szasz and Hollender because the patient is encouraged to participate actively with his physician in making decisions concerning his care.

The personalities of a physician and patient also determine the extent to which a patient is dependent. Some physicians are more comfortable in a relationship in which they make the medical decisions for the patient, while others prefer to share some of the responsibility for decision-making with the patient. Similarly, there are patients who would rather rely completely on a physician and have him tell them what to do, and there are those who like to participate as much as possible in their own care.

There are both positive and negative aspects to the dependency associated with the patient role. On the positive side, it gives the physician added influence with the patient, besides that stemming from his medical knowledge and prestige, and enables him to control what takes place in the medical setting. On the negative side, it sometimes leads to conflict in their relationship because the needs and expectations of the patient are unmet.[16]

What are some of these needs and expectations? Most patients want their physician to give them an amount of time and attention that is consistent with the severity of their illness. They want to have sufficient information about their condition so they can understand what is happening to them and what is likely to happen in the future. And they want to be treated in a considerate and dignified manner. Because of their dependency, patients rely on the physician to meet these and other basic needs. If he fails to do so, then they are likely to feel disappointed and disillusioned. Sometimes the reason for this disappointment is that patient expectations are excessive and unrealistic; other times it is because the physician has failed to live up to expectations that are quite appropriate. In either case, the natural consequence of this disappointment and disillusionment is conflict between patient and physician.

In an interesting study dealing with the patient role, Tagliacozzo and Mauksch interviewed 86 hospitalized patients to ascertain their views of this role.[17] The patients were very much aware of the degree to which they were dependent on those who cared for them (i.e., physicians and nurses). Because of this dependence, most felt that it was extremely important for them to gain the favor of and be accepted by the medical staff. The following excerpt from the study makes this point.

Being on good terms (i.e., with the hospital staff) was seen by these patients not only as a convenience but as an essential factor for their welfare. They (i.e., the patients) directly expressed their awareness of their inability to control those who are in charge of their care. Patients felt that they were subject to rewards and punishment and that essential services could be withheld unless they made themselves acceptable. Some of these patients were dependent on intimate forms of physical assistance and their points of view reflected their awareness of this dependence on others.

When the patients in the study were asked what they thought was expected of them by the medical staff, several aspects of patient behavior were consistently mentioned. They believed that they were expected to be cooperative, that is, to adhere to the hospital routine and follow medical orders. They also felt that their physician expected them to have trust and confidence in him, while the nurses expected them to be considerate and to refrain from making too many demands. Many patients thought that a failure on their part to conform to these expectations would endanger their relationship with the staff and might cause the staff to withhold services that the patients needed.

Although the study by Tagliacozza and Mauksch was restricted to the hospital setting, the description of the expectations that medical personnel have of the patient role applies equally well to the office or clinic setting. Fulfilling these expectations is necessary in order to be considered a "good patient."

The price often paid by patients who fail to comply with them is conflict with the physician and other medical personnel. The dependent status of the patient makes this conflict very undesirable and, consequently, he usually attempts to conform. Unfortunately, this places undesirable restrictions on his behavior, often preventing him from (1) questioning or objecting to medical advice, (2) assertively expressing his needs, or (3) criticizing the actions of those caring for him.

THE STRESS OF ILLNESS AND HOSPITALIZATION.—Patients are often exposed to stress that affects not only their behavior but, at times, the outcome of their illness.[18, 19, 20] In general, the magnitude of this stress is directly related to the severity and prognosis of their illness. For example, the diagnosis of cancer carries with it a much greater impact on a person's psyche than does the diagnosis of a benign condition. Other medical disorders that cause a great deal of stress include heart attack and stroke, the former because of the threat of sudden death and the latter because of the resulting disability. Severe illness that requires hospitalization is a particularly potent stressor. The patient is usually in pain and discomfort, concerned about bodily injury, separated from family and friends, and almost totally dependent on the hospital staff. What's more, if he is acutely ill or undergoing surgery, he is even faced with the possibility of losing his life.

Many people find the dependent patient role to be stressful. This is especially true for individuals who take pride in being self-sufficient. In our society, this is typically a man, because masculinity is equated with being physically and emotionally "strong." As noted, those who have rarely been sick also have difficulty adjusting to the patient role.

The nature of the medical setting also contributes to the stress of being a patient. For most persons, a visit to a physician's office produces anxiety. The long wait that so often occurs before being seen, the impersonal attitude frequently displayed by physicians and nurses, and the uncomfortable examinations and treatments are partly responsible for this emotional reaction. When hospitalized, a person is exposed to an environment that is both stressful and frightening. The variety of medical personnel and the vast array of complex technical equipment in a hospital can be bewildering to a person who is already anxious and concerned because of his illness. He usually has to undergo diagnostic and therapeutic procedures of which he has little, if any, understanding. Often the language used by those caring for him is so filled with medical jargon that he finds it almost incomprehensible.

Intensive care units are unique in terms of the stressors that patients are exposed to. In these areas, there is a monotonous repetition of sights, sounds, and sensations, causing many to become emotionally upset, disoriented, and even delirious.[21] The following are descriptions of the intensive care environment given by patients:

"It was like something I could never have imagined existing"; "it was like being on a different planet where everything was unfamiliar"; "I didn't know where I was, nothing looked like anything I had ever seen before"; ". . . even the smells and sounds were unfamiliar"; "everyone was in some kind of uniform or mask"; "there was no way of telling day from night, the lights were always on and there were no windows"; "things were constantly happening, people coming and going, patients dying . . . sometimes you didn't know if it was you or someone else."[21]

Patients in a hospital are especially concerned about the risks involved with the tests, procedures, and treatments to which they are exposed. For example, both the anticipation and the actual experience of surgery are very stressful. Psychological complications of surgery are relatively common and appear to be related to how well the patient has been prepared emotionally and the kind of physician-patient relationship that exists.[22] In a study of persons undergoing surgery, Janis noted a relationship between their emotional state before and their psychological adjustment afterward.[23] He divided them into three groups: those with a low, moderate, or high degree of preoperative anxiety. He found that patients who had a moderate degree of anticipatory fear adjusted better emotionally after surgery than those who had either a low or a high degree of anxiety. They appeared to have a more realistic view of the aftereffects of the procedure and, therefore, were better able to deal with the postoperative pain and discomfort. Patients who were inappropriately calm and unworried prior to surgery seemed to make excessive use of denial to allay their anxiety. Consequently, when they experienced pain and suffering after surgery they reacted with dismay and anger—emotions that interfered with their care. Patients who exhibited extreme apprehension and anxiety before surgery were usually psychoneurotic and appeared to lack the necessary coping resources to deal with the situation. After the operation, they continued to display the same type of emotional reaction.

Adequate communication between the surgeon and patient prior to an operation is essential if the patient is to cope successfully with the psychological aspects of the procedure.[24, 25] The goals are to (1) give the patient a realistic view of the procedure and risks involved, (2) help him to mobilize appropriate psychological defenses, and (3) enable him to reduce the use of inappropriate defenses such as excessive denial. The hyperanxious patient has an increased risk of postoperative complications, both physical and psychological, and so the management of excessive anxiety is mandatory.[22]

ADAPTATION TO THE PATIENT ROLE AND ILLNESS-INDUCED STRESS.—This involves the use of certain coping mechanisms, one of which is regression or the return to an earlier, more childlike form of behavior. It is an adaptive response to illness and hospitalization because it allows the individual to accept the dependent-patient role. When a patient regresses, he becomes more self-centered, concerned primarily with his own needs and discomforts. In addition, he may become impatient, demanding, and hypochondriacal. The last three reactions can cause problems in his relationship with the medical staff.

Patients are usually ambivalent with regard to regression and the dependency associated with it. On the one hand, they welcome the care they receive while they are sick and disabled, but on the other, they resent being placed in a situation in which they are forced to rely on others for help. Some people have a particularly difficult time accepting this situation without sacrificing their self-esteem. Such persons are generally unable to tolerate regression without developing a great deal of anxiety and emotional tension.

A 65-year-old former professional baseball player was admitted to the hospital because of acute cellulitis in his right leg. During the medical history, the patient attempted to minimize the severity of his symptoms despite the fact that his leg was markedly swollen and inflamed. His attitude toward the hospital staff was one of annoyance whenever they tried to assist him in any way. At one point, he became emotionally upset when one of the nurses tried to help him walk to the bathroom. On being informed that he would have to use a bedside commode instead of the bathroom, he threatened to leave the hospital. In order to help the patient adjust to hospitalization, efforts were made by the staff to enable him to be as self-sufficient as possible while continuing his medical care.

Another way in which patients attempt to deal with the stress of illness is by using ego defense mechanisms such as denial, displacement, and rationalization. Displacement sometimes leads to problems in the relationship between a patient and medical personnel. Through its use, a person shifts his feelings concerning a stressful situation or event to someone or something else in the environment. For example, the emotional upset and anger that a patient feels as a result of his predicament (sickness and hospitalization) can be directed toward the medical staff or hospital. Consequently, he may become suspicious, distrustful, and uncooperative; trivial occurrences may cause him to react with anger and hostility. The staff, puzzled by his seemingly unwarranted behavior, may respond in a similar fashion, thus leading to disagreement and conflict. One clue to the recognition of this mechanism is a disparity between the nature and magnitude of a patient's emotional reaction and the degree of stress associated with the inciting situation or event.

A 35-year-old woman was admitted to the hospital for evaluation and treatment of ulcerative colitis. When the intern attempted to examine her, she became emotionally upset and angry, stating "You young doctors have no business taking care of sick people." On greeting her attending physician, she suspiciously asked, "What are you going to do to me?" Nothing the nursing staff did seemed to please her and she was continually getting into arguments with the nurses and aides. She even asked to see the director of the hospital and presented him with a list of complaints ranging from a lack of attention by the nurses to the quality of the food. While some of her complaints were justified, most were without foundation.

Her behavior alienated her from most of the hospital personnel. Finally, the attending physician attempted to discuss these problems with the patient, whereupon she broke down and cried bitterly. She said that she was terrified about her illness, that she had heard cancer was a complication of ulcerative colitis and she feared she had developed this. She was also worried that she might require an ileostomy to treat her colitis. It became apparent that her anxiety and fear had been displaced onto those in the environment, resulting in an intolerable situation for her and the medical staff.

The nature of a patient's illness and the setting in which he is cared for influence his psychological reactions and methods of adaptation. On the basis of a study of 145 patients referred for psychiatric consultation after admission to a coronary care unit (CCU) because of a myocardial infarction, Cassem and Hackett identified a characteristic pattern of psychological response (Fig 22–2).[26] Anxiety is greatest on day one shortly after the infarction, when the patient first comes to the unit. At this time, he is concerned about a recurrence of cardiac symptoms and the possibility of death. After the acute episode of illness subsides and he is relatively free of symptoms (days two and three), denial is used as a coping mechanism. Later on, as he begins to fully appreciate what has happened, depression sets in. This reaction tends to evoke coping behavior that is based on the particular personality of the individual. Thus, the obsessive-compulsive person manifests these kinds of traits while the impulsive person demonstrates this kind of reaction.

Adaptation of a patient to prolonged illness can be particularly difficult. The extended period of dependency, the persistence of functional impairment, and the need for repeated medical visits, tests, and treatments all have an extremely detrimental effect on a person's self-esteem and self-concept. Depression is an especially prominent part of a patient's emotional response to prolonged illness because of the many losses he sustains. Over a period of time, the failure to improve or the deterioration of his condition may overwhelm his psychological defenses. Anger over his predicament is directed internally and this, along

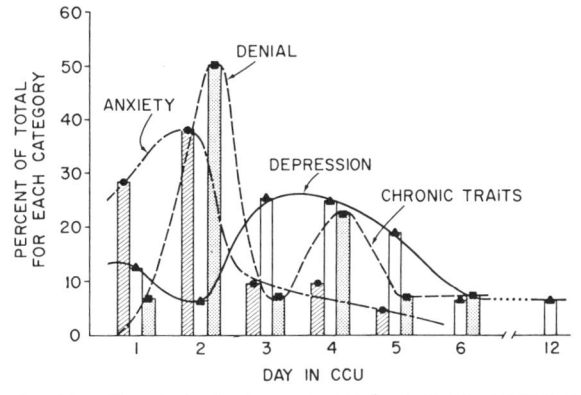

Fig 22–2.—Psychological responses in a coronary care unit. (From Cassem N.H., Hackett T.P.: *Ann. Intern. Med.* 75:9–14, 1971. Used by permission.)

with the helplessness, dependency, and loss of self-esteem, results in despondency. When depression becomes too severe or prolonged, it can be a major impediment to the patient's successful management.

Medical personnel have an important role to play in helping a patient cope with the stress of illness and hospitalization. This aspect of patient management should accompany the treatment of a patient's disease if medical care is to be maximally effective. When providing this help, medical personnel ought to have definite goals in mind. During an illness, they should try to facilitate the patient's acceptance of the patient role, including the dependency and regression associated with it. At the same time, they should set some limits on the regression and try to prevent the person from experiencing too great a loss of self-esteem. Depression needs to be treated at an early stage before it interferes with the management of the rest of the patient's illness. The appropriate use of defense mechanisms by the patient to control his emotional reactions should be supported, and their inappropriate use should be discouraged. To prevent the development of uncertainty and unwarranted anxiety, a physician should describe in detail any examination, test, or procedure that a patient is to undergo and give a realistic view of the risks involved.

The Recovery or Rehabilitation Stage

For most patients, a period of convalescence and recovery follows the acute phase of an illness. The principal tasks for the person in this period are to reintegrate the functioning of his mind and body, to adjust to any losses that may have occurred, and to begin to resume those activities that he is capable of performing. Sometimes there are problems in accomplishing these tasks. For example, some patients are reluctant to give up the sick role despite an improvement in health. Their behavior is exactly the opposite from what one might expect, since it would seem logical that someone who was fortunate enough to have gotten well would be eager to resume his previous activities. There are a number of reasons why this logic may not prevail. For instance, it is common for a patient who has recovered from a serious illness to be hesitant about engaging in physical activities that, in his view, might cause him to suffer a relapse. This is especially true for cardiac patients.

A 52-year-old man was hospitalized for 3 weeks with an acute myocardial infarction. Following the hospitalization, he was sent home to recuperate. His convalescence was uneventful and at the end of 3 months his physician stated that it was all right for him to resume his occupation as a truck driver. Although he appeared to have fully recovered, he refused to go back to work, saying he was "just not up to it."

The patient complained of becoming weak and tired whenever he exerted himself. He had no other symptoms. A complete medical checkup failed to show any abnormalities that might be responsible for causing his complaints. In the view of his physician, there was no organic basis for his physical debility. On the other hand, his wife noted that he appeared to be depressed and worried. She had tried to discuss this with him on several occasions but he had refused.

Finally, on a return visit to his physician, he acknowledged that he was very much afraid that if he resumed his former work activities he would have another heart attack. This fear caused him to be anxious and depressed because he felt that he would never be able to go back to work again.

Convalescing patients not only worry about resuming physical activity but also may be apprehensive about returning to a home situation or a job that has a great deal of psychological stress. Another aspect of daily living that is sometimes of concern for the recuperating patient is sexual activity. A patient with a heart condition may be quite fearful of engaging in sex because he thinks it may exacerbate his condition. Needless to say, this can pose a major problem for the spouse as well. The thought that he is unable to function at work or sexually is a blow to the patient's self-esteem, which may cause him to become anxious, depressed, and angry. These emotional reactions can make full recovery from an illness more difficult and prolonged.

There are other reasons people hesitate to give up the sick role. The desire to be well may be counterbalanced by the secondary gains (e.g., attention from family and friends, exemption from social responsibilities, and financial benefits such as disability income) a person receives while he is ill. These may act as positive reinforcers, causing him to want to remain in the sick role so that he can continue to benefit from the advantages that accompany it.

There are, of course, other outcomes for someone who is sick besides recovery. Some patients enter a period of chronic illness and disability, either deteriorating gradually or remaining at about the same level of functional impairment for years. For the chronically ill, rehabilitation instead of recovery is the principal goal of medical care. Studies of persons who have chronic disorders, such as obstructive pulmonary disease, renal failure, and rheumatoid arthritis, have shown that psychological and social factors are important determinants of the success or failure of rehabilitation. Chronic obstructive pulmonary disease (COPD) is one of the leading causes of long-term disability in this country. Patients with this condition suffer from a progressive impairment of lung function, which, if severe, causes marked shortness of breath with minimal physical activity. Treatment is palliative, designed to improve symptoms and to prevent a deterioration of lung function. The emotional reactions of patients with COPD are similar to those experienced by individuals with other chronic disorders; they include anxiety (and its accompanying manifestations), depression, and excessive preoccupation with bodily functions.[27] These patients are particularly anxious about their shortness of breath and develop a "phobia" about engaging in any physical activity that brings on this symptom.

Emotional reactions such as those mentioned may have adverse physiological effects on patients with severe COPD.[28] For example, when such a patient becomes very angry he may experience marked dyspnea along with laboratory evidence of a worsening of pulmonary function (i.e., a decrease in arterial oxygen tension and an increase in arterial carbon dioxide tension).

Rehabilitation of such patients involves the development of a close physician-patient relationship and management of the individual's psychological problems, in addition to the institution of the appropriate medical therapy and physical reconditioning.[27] Helping the individual to overcome his fear of becoming short of breath with activity and alleviating his symptoms of depression are especially important. Moreover, medical personnel must understand the patient's need to avoid emotionally upsetting situations and to use defense mechanisms to control excessive emotional reactions.

In an investigation of 21 men with COPD who had completed a year's rehabilitation program, Agle and Baum et al. found that improvement in the patients' performance of physical activities was positively correlated with the successful management of their psychological problems.[29] Thus, the "responders" to rehabilitation were those patients who had a significant reduction in their symptoms of anxiety, depression, and preoccupation with their body, whereas the "nonresponders" had little or no decrease in these symptoms. Improvement in the amount of activity in which the responders could engage was *not* associated with a like improvement in their physiological measures of lung function (except in one patient), which suggests that the psychological symptoms exhibited by these patients prior to rehabilitation played a major role in their disability.

Patients with chronic renal failure who are being treated with long-term hemodialysis are a unique group with respect to the problems of rehabilitation. Since they are dependent on a form of therapy that itself produces disability, they are rarely able to return to the full level of physical activity in which they participated prior to the onset of their illness. Moreover, their dependence on a "machine" and medical personnel to sustain life places a special psychological burden on them.[30,31] Levy divided the psychological adaptation of patients on chronic hemodialysis into three periods: the "honeymoon" period, the period of disenchantment and discouragement, and the period of long-term adaptation.[31]

The honeymoon period usually occurs in

the first 6 months after the individual begins hemodialysis. It is characterized by feelings of confidence and hope—a "rebirth"—following the realization that the procedure can save their life. Prior to hemodialysis, most patients with terminal renal failure are severely depressed about their poor physical condition and prognosis. With the use of hemodialysis, however, a marked improvement in their physical well-being takes place, along with a brightening of their emotional outlook. During the honeymoon period, dependence on the "machine" and the medical staff is generally well accepted, although anxiety is a prominent symptom.

Levy describes the period of disenchantment and discouragement as occurring quite abruptly after the honeymoon period, when the patient recognizes that he will need to resume some of his former independent social activities. A conflict occurs: the individual is torn between his desire to continue in a dependent role and the expectations of others that he begin to return to some productive social role (e.g., school, work). During this period, patients are likely to feel anxious and depressed as they try to resolve this conflict.

The period of long-term adaptation is characterized by some degree of acceptance by the patient of his dependence on the "machine" and his limitations in function. In his studies, Levy found that there were wide variations in the quality of life experienced by patients on hemodialysis, and that a good life adjustment was related to a patient's ability to cope successfully with the stress of the procedure. This seemed to depend on his personality structure and the nature of his system of social support.

A recent study by Yelin et al. of some of the variables contributing to work disability in persons with rheumatoid arthritis (a chronic debilitating illness with less of an immediate threat to life than COPD or renal failure) found that social and work-related factors had a far greater effect on disability than all disease factors including therapy.[32] According to these investigators, the role of the physician in the work rehabilitation of patients with this disorder is largely an educational one, making the patient aware of the interaction between his disease and the social and physical characteristics of his job.

SUMMARY

During each phase of an illness, a person's behavior may either increase or decrease the chances of a favorable outcome. For example, early in the course of most illnesses there is a crucial period during which the individual decides whether or not a symptom is significant. A wrong decision can have dire consequences. If he chooses to ignore a symptom that is caused by a serious underlying disease, the delay in obtaining medical care could jeopardize his chances of recovery. Even if he decides that help is necessary, his behavior is still very important in determining if and when he goes to a physician. There are, in fact, a number of other options available, including self-treatment (with either proprietary medicines or folk remedies) and the assistance of various types of nonmedical healers. Regardless of the action taken by a sick person, his decision is usually preceded by one or more lay consultations, in which he solicits the advice of family members and friends and in effect requests permission to assume the sick role.

Once he is under the care of a physician, a patient may encounter a good deal of stress, especially if he is acutely ill and hospitalized. His ability to control his reactions to this stress, using certain psychological coping devices, will largely determine whether or not he adapts successfully to the dependent-patient role. One of the important goals of medical personnel is to facilitate this adaptation. Recovery from acute illness means that the individual must relinquish both the patient and the sick roles, which is difficult for some people to do because of a concern about (1) relapsing or (2) a loss of secondary gains.

Chronic disease is generally accompanied by profound emotional reactions and social changes, which can interfere with medical treatment and rehabilitation. The management of such patients requires an understanding of the psychological and social, as well as the physical, aspects of their illness, since the success of rehabilitation may depend on the appropriate modification of all of these components.

REFERENCES

1. Mechanic D.: The concept of illness behavior. *J. Chronic Dis.* 15:189, 1962.
2. Kasl S.V., Cobb S.: Health behavior, illness behavior, and sick-role behavior. *Arch. Environ. Health* 12:246, 531, 1966.
3. Suchman E.A.: Stages of illness and medical care. *J. Health Hum. Behav.* 6:114, 1965.
4. Barsky A.J.: Patients who amplify bodily sensations. *Ann. Intern. Med.* 91:63, 1979.
5. Rahe, R.H., Ransom A.J.: Life change and illness studies: Past history and future directions. *J. Human Stress* 4:3, 1978.
6. Mechanic D.: Effects of psychological distress on perceptions of physical health and use of medical and psychiatric facilities. *J. Human Stress* 4:26, 1978.
7. Pratt L.: The relationship of socioeconomic status to health. *Am. J. Public Health* 61:281, 1971.
8. Rainwater L.: The lower class: Health, illness, and medical institutions, in Deutscher I., Thompson E.J. (eds.): *Among the People: Encounters with the Poor.* New York, Basic Books, Inc., Publishers, 1968.
9. Zola I.K.: Culture and symptoms—An analysis of patients' presenting complaints. *Am. Sociol. Rev.* 31:615, 1966.
10. Zborowski M.: Cultural components in response to pain. *J. Soc. Issues* 8:16, 1952.
11. Bloom S.W.: *The Doctor and His Patient.* New York, The Free Press, 1965.
12. Parsons T.: *The Social System.* New York, The Free Press, 1951.
13. Balint M.: *The Doctor, His Patient, and the Illness.* New York, International Universities Press, 1957.
14. Zola I.: Illness behavior of the working class, in Shostak A., Gomberg W. (eds.): *Blue-Collar World: Studies of the American Worker.* Englewood Cliffs, N.J., Prentice-Hall, Inc., 1964.
15. Szasz T.S., Hollender M.H.: A contribution to the philosophy of medicine: The basic models of the doctor-patient relationship. *Arch. Intern. Med.* 97:585, 1956.
16. Friedson E.: *Profession of Medicine.* New York, Dodd, Mead & Company, 1971.
17. Tagliacozzo D.L., Mauksch H.O.: The patient's view of the patient's role, in Jaco E.G. (ed.): *Patients, Physicians, and Illness,* ed. 2. New York, The Free Press, 1972.
18. Psychological reactions to medical illness and hospitalization, in Strain J.J., Grossman S. (eds.): *Psychological Care of the Medically Ill: A Primer in Liaison Psychiatry.* New York, Appleton-Century-Crofts, 1975.
19. Mechanic D.: *Medical Sociology,* ed. 2. New York, The Free Press, 1978, chap. 9.
20. Volicer B.J.: Hospital stress and patient reports of pain and physical status. *J. Hum. Stress* 4:28, 1978.
21. Kimball C.P.: Reactions to illness: The acute phase, in *Symposium on Liaison Psychiatry.* Psych. Clin. North Am., vol. 2, p. 307. Philadelphia, W.B. Saunders Co., 1979.
22. Rockwell D.A., Pepitone-Rockwell F.: The emotional impact of surgery and the value of informed consent. *Med. Clin. North Am.* 63:1341, 1979.
23. Janis I.L.: Psychological stress among surgical patients, in Millon T. (ed.): *Medical Behavioral Science.* Philadelphia, W.B. Saunders Co., 1975.
24. Sime A.M.: Relationship of preoperative fear, type of coping, and information received about surgery to recovery from surgery. *J. Pers. Soc. Psychol.* 34:716, 1976.
25. Williams J.G., et. al.: The psychological control of preoperative anxiety. *Psychophysiology* 12:50, 1975.
26. Cassem N.H., Hackett T.P.: Psychiatric consultation in a coronary care unit. *Ann. Intern. Med.* 75:9, 1971.
27. Agle D.P., Baum G.L.: Psychological aspects of chronic obstructive pulmonary disease. *Med. Clin. North Am.* 61:749, 1977.
28. Dudley D.L., Wermuth C., Hague W.: Psychosocial aspects of care in the chronic obstructive pulmonary disease patient. *Heart Lung* 2:389, 1973.
29. Agle D.P., Baum G.L., Chester E.H., et al.: Multidiscipline treatment of chronic pulmonary insufficiency, 1. Psychologic aspects of rehabilitation. *Psychosom. Med.* 35(1):41, 1973.
30. De-Nour A.K., Shaltiel J., and Czaczkes J.W.: Emotional reactions of patients on chronic hemodialysis. *Psychosom. Med.* 30:521, 1968.
31. Levy N.B.: Psychological studies at the downstate medical center of patients on hemodialysis. *Med. Clin. North Am.* 61:759, 1977.
32. Yelin E., Meenan R., Nevitt M.: Work disability in rheumatoid arthritis: Effects of disease, social, and work factors. *Ann. Intern. Med.* 93:551, 1980.

23 / Patient Compliance

CLARISSA S. SCOTT, Ph.D.

THE IDEAL WORLD

Mr. Owen has been bothered by headaches and dizziness and goes to his physician. Doctor Evans diagnoses the problem as high blood pressure and prescribes medication to be taken two times a day. She also tells Mr. Owen that he should relax more and stop smoking. Mr. Owen stops by the pharmacy on the way home and fills the prescription. He takes the medicine in the prescribed dose at the designated time of day, stops smoking, and relaxes more. He feels better and continues this regimen until his next scheduled visit the following month.

THE REAL WORLD

Mr. Owen has been bothered by headaches and dizziness and goes to his physician. Doctor Evans diagnoses the problem as high blood pressure and prescribes medication to be taken two times a day. She also tells Mr. Owen that he should relax more and stop smoking. Mr. Owen is not sure he fully understands everything the physician has said, but he is hesitant to ask "stupid" questions. He stops by the pharmacy on his way home and fills the prescription. When he gets home, he talks over the diagnosis and prescribed treatment with his wife and sister-in-law. Later that evening he and his neighbor meet while taking out the garbage and Owen shares the news of his high blood pressure. All these individuals know others who have used either different medication or a special diet to lower the "pressure." Doubt assails Mr. Owen. The medication is expensive and if it would be possible to get the same results with fewer pills or a different diet, why not try it? He decides to take one pill a day instead of two and decrease the amount of salt in his diet. He feels better and continues this regimen until the next scheduled appointment with the physician.

Many medical professionals harbor the comfortable assumption that the patient believes the physician is the only person who can "legitimately make rational pronouncements on the use of medications."[1] It does not occur to them that perfectly sane, intelligent patients will pay for an office visit, laboratory tests, and x-rays (i.e., the best diagnostic skills the physician can apply); purchase the prescribed medication; and, following this, decide unilaterally (or with the advice of friends, family, and neighbors) to take more or fewer pills at different times than instructed!

It has only been in recent years that physicians have become fully aware of the magnitude of the problem of noncompliance. They have come to realize that although they can instruct a patient to eat or not eat certain foods, to take medicine at specific times of the day, and to appear for checkups, it is the patient who has the last word; *he* ultimately evaluates these instructions and decides whether or not to follow them. Very often patients choose not to do so. In terms of medications, physicians can control *what* medicine and *how much* the patient is able to obtain, but the patient controls how much he takes and when he takes it.

DEFINITION AND SCOPE OF THE PROBLEM

The term *compliance* refers to "the extent to which a patient's behavior . . . coincides with the clinical prescription."[2] It is one of the most important aspects of patient behavior, because whether or not a person follows the instructions given by his physician often determines the effectiveness of his treatment and, hence, the outcome of his illness.

Kasl has listed various types of patient behavior that are encompassed by the term *compliance*, including entering into and continuing with a treatment program; keeping appointments; taking prescribed medications; and following recommended changes in one's activities, such as smoking, diet, and exercise.[3] The issue of compliance becomes quite complicated when one considers that a treatment program often calls for several different behaviors, such as taking one or more medications, exercising, and avoiding certain foods. A patient may comply with all, some, or none of these. For example, he may take one of the two medications prescribed and avoid some of the proscribed foods but not others. Finally, he might comply with medical advice at one time but not at another.

What is the magnitude of the problem of noncompliance? It depends to a certain extent (as we shall see) on the clinical situation and is affected by variables such as the nature of the illness and the treatment program. Findings from the following selected studies indicate that a significant problem exists.

1. In one study involving outpatient and general practice situations, the percent of noncompliers ranged from 19 to 72.[1]
2. In another study, only 11% of asthmatic children on oral medication were found to be taking the prescribed dosage, 23% had *no* measurable amount of the medication in their systems, and the rest (66%) were taking less than what was considered a therapeutic dose.[4]
3. Stewart and Cluff's 1972 review article noted that between 20 and 82% of all patients do *not* take medication as prescribed.[5]
4. Bergman and Warner found that compliance was sometimes as low as 8%.[6]
5. In Sackett's discussion of the magnitude of compliance and noncompliance, he cites 54% as the weighted average rate of compliance with different long-term medication regimens for different illnesses in different settings.[2]
6. In Podell and Gary's review, they state that "a good rule is that one-third of patients take their medicines; one-third sometimes take them; and one-third almost never do."[7]

Clearly, medical personnel cannot assume their patients will follow the instructions that are given them. To the contrary, physicians and nurses must be aware of the high probability of patient noncompliance and be on the alert for this problem.

METHODOLOGICAL PROBLEMS OF THE STUDY OF COMPLIANCE

Until the 1960s, the investigations of compliance had been both sparse and relatively unsophisticated in methodology. Since that time there has been a steadily increasing number of investigations as well as an increased level of sophistication with which they are designed and carried out. Most early investigations followed a medical model of compliance, that is, one that looks for easily identified and quantifiable factors that have to do with the patient (e.g., age and education), the regimen (e.g., type and complexity), and the illness (e.g., acute, chronic). There are several shortcomings to this approach:

1. These factors are relatively constant, and even if it were possible to prove that there is a strong relationship between, for example, age or type of disease and noncompliance, there is little that can be done to alter these factors.
2. These factors rarely relate to underlying motivations of patients; they do not help to explain why certain patients who have features characteristic of noncompliers *do* follow directions, or why certain patients who do *not* possess features characteristic of compliance *do* comply.
3. Perhaps the most important criticism of the medical model for studying compliance is that it "relies on a 'shotgun' method of selecting items for study, rather than upon the prior development of a unified conceptual approach to, or hypothesis about, compliance as a starting point."[8] As Kasl and Cobb noted, the early studies were mainly concerned with "superficial demographic and back-

ground variables rather than with fundamental, theoretically derived attitudes and subjective perceptions. This has an advantage in the area of measurement, but the disadvantage that one does not always understand well the meaning of such associations."[9]

A characteristic of the reports of research findings from compliance studies using the medical model is that they are often in conflict with one another. Suspecting that this might be due in part to the methodology used by individual investigations, a group of medical researchers at McMaster University Medical Centre in Toronto decided to analyze and score the quality of the methodological techniques of the 185 published studies dealing with compliance.[10] For the following list of factors, standards were developed and each of the 185 investigations was assigned a numerical value indicating the rigor of the methodology used in assessing these factors (the higher the numerical value, the more valid the findings could be considered).

1. *Study design.*—A randomized trial received 4 points, a quasiexperimental design was assigned 3 points, and so on.
2. *Selection and specification of the study sample.*—In many early studies, researchers did not even adequately describe the study sample, much less use appropriate safeguards in the selection of patients so that the study population was not biased in ways that might distort conclusions drawn from the results. For example, is there a randomized selection of the patient sample from several clinics (3 points) or has the investigator simply "grabbed" patients from one clinic and interviewed those willing to participate (0 points)?
3. *Specification of the illness or condition.*—Are diagnostic criteria included (with inclusion/exclusion criteria) so that the study can be replicated in another setting?
4. *Description of the therapeutic regimen.*—A complete description (2 points) would include such features as name of the drug, dose schedule, cost of the prescription, and side effects.
5. *Definition of compliance.*—The researcher should share with the reader exactly how she or he has divided the study population into compliers and noncompliers. The definition should be precise, unambiguous, and appropriate. What percentage of the medicine was it necessary to consume in order to be defined as compliant? 75%? 90%? Unfortunately, "a substantial number of compliance investigators have failed to provide a proper definition [of compliance]."[2]
6. *Measure of compliance.*—There are direct and indirect methods of measuring compliance.

Direct measures include:

a. Determining the level of the prescribed drug in the blood.
b. Measuring the urinary excretion of either the medication itself or a metabolic by-product.
c. Determining the amount of a tracer substance that has been added to the prescribed medication.

Indirect measures include:

a. Checking the outcome (assuming, for example, that someone who is taking medication for high blood pressure in the prescribed way will have a lower blood pressure reading).
b. Getting the impression of the physician as to the compliance of the patient.—All research data indicate that this is the poorest indicator of all.
c. Asking the patient directly.—Research findings suggest that patients who say they are *noncompliant are* in fact *noncompliant*. The problem lies with those who say they are compliant; an unfortunate number of patients who say they are taking medication as prescribed are not actually doing so. There is a growing feeling, however, that questioning of the patient in his home (apart from the clinic setting) by an interviewer who is *not* associated in any way with the medical

care team may be an effective way to elicit an accurate report by the patient.

d. Taking a "pill-count."—This method compares the number of pills (ounces of liquid) that *actually* remain in the patient's bottle with the number that *should* be there if she or he is complying with directions. When the medication is one that can be used by other family members (such as an antibiotic or antacid), the validity of pill-counts is questionable, since family members may take the medication for minor infections or gastrointestinal upsets. The Toronto investigators gave 4 points to any study that used urinalyses for tracer substances on at least three separate occasions for at least 80% of the subjects. Two points were allotted for the use of pill-counts, because this obviously is a less valid measure.

e. Checking whether prescriptions are filled.—This measure is even less valid than pill-counts. The mere filling of a prescription tells us nothing about whether the patient has taken the drug at all, much less whether it was consumed according to directions.

CURRENT STATE OF KNOWLEDGE

The following discussion of compliance findings is based in large part on the analysis by the Toronto group of the 185 published re-

TABLE 23–1.—DEMOGRAPHIC FEATURES OF PATIENTS ASSOCIATED WITH COMPLIANCE

	ASSOCIATION WITH COMPLIANCE		
	POSITIVE ASSOCIATION*	NEGATIVE ASSOCIATION†	NO ASSOCIATION‡
Age			
young vs. old	5 studies	—	27 studies
Sex			
female vs. male	1	3	22
Education	3	—	21
Socioeconomic status			
high vs. low	1	1	8
Occupational status	4	—	8
Income	2	—	6
Marital status	Correlations found:§	5	10
Race			
white vs. black	3	—	6
Ethnic background	—	—	4
Religion	—	—	3

*Positive association indicates that the two variables under study vary in the same direction (e.g., as patient satisfaction with visit/clinic increases, so does compliance).

†Negative association indicates that the two variables under study vary in opposite directions (e.g., as the complexity of the regimen increases, compliance decreases).

‡No association indicates that the variable under study apparently does not have a significant influence on patient compliance (e.g., socioeconomic level does not significantly affect compliant/noncompliant behavior).

§"Correlations found" relate to factors which have more than two nominal categories. Most of the features listed in Tables 23–1 and 23–2 have only two (e.g., young vs. old, higher vs. lower income, presence of symptoms contrasted with their absence). There are several features, however, that include more than two categories; i.e., in Table 23–1, marital status subsumes the married, the separated, the divorced, and so on.

From Haynes R.B.: A critical review of the "determinants" of patient compliance with therapeutic regimens, in Sackett D.L., Haynes R.B. (eds.): *Compliance with Therapeutic Regimens*. Baltimore, Johns Hopkins University Press, 1976, Table 3.1.

ports of investigations.[10] These medical researchers evaluated the data in these studies according to the rigor of their methodology; that is, greater weight was given to the findings of studies in which greater stringency was observed in terms of study design, selection of study sample, and so on.

In looking at these reports, they found that the determinants of compliance that had been studied could be classified under the following headings:

1. Demographic features of patients
2. Features of the disease
3. Features of the therapeutic regimen
4. Features of the therapeutic source
5. Features of the patient-therapist interaction
6. Sociobehavioral features of the patients

Each of these factors will be discussed in turn.

DEMOGRAPHIC FEATURES OF THE PATIENT.—A glance at Table 23–1 shows that few of the studies that assessed this factor found any association between the demographic features of patients and compliance.

FEATURES OF THE DISEASE.—In Table 23–2, we see that there are few associations between *disease features* and compliance; diagnosis is the exception. On reading these three studies in which a correlation was found, however, we find that all compared mental patients with those suffering from a physical illness (mental patients were shown to be less compliant in taking medication).

FEATURES OF THE THERAPEUTIC REGIMEN.—Here we have some very interesting findings. Note in Table 23–3 that correlations were discovered between compliance and the type of medication. An illustration of this is a study in which psychotic patients who were taking the medication thioridazine were more compliant than those who were taking chlorpromazine; we can hypothesize that differential side effects were a factor here. Studies concerned with the degree of behavioral change involved in a therapeutic regimen all showed the same finding—that the greater the change in behavior called for, the less compliance one can expect. In addition, data are clear that compliance by patients who must *acquire new* habits (such as taking a particular medication) is greater than among patients who are asked to *change old* behaviors (such as dietary habits), which exceeds, in turn, the degree of compliance among those who must *break personal* habits (such as smoking or drinking).

Table 23–3 shows a preponderance of findings that indicate a negative association with compliance when the regimen is complex (i.e., the more complex the regimen, the less likely a patient is to be compliant). Of the three reports with positive findings, one was based on patient interviews only and the "no association" study provided *no* supporting evidence!

There have been surprisingly few studies (only two) that look at the cost factor. The study that reported no association was done

TABLE 23–2.—SELECTED FEATURES OF THE DISEASE ASSOCIATED WITH COMPLIANCE

	ASSOCIATION WITH COMPLIANCE		
	POSITIVE ASSOCIATION*	NEGATIVE ASSOCIATION	NO ASSOCIATION
Diagnosis	Correlations found: 3		8
Severity	—	1	7
Duration	—	—	4
Symptoms	—	2	3

*See footnotes to Table 23–1.
From Haynes R.B.: A critical review of the "determinants" of patient compliance with therapeutic regimens, in Sackett D.L., Haynes R.B. (eds.): *Compliance with Therapeutic Regimens.* Baltimore, Johns Hopkins University Press, 1976, Table 3.2.

TABLE 23-3.—FEATURES OF THE THERAPEUTIC REGIMEN ASSOCIATED WITH COMPLIANCE

	ASSOCIATION WITH COMPLIANCE		
	POSITIVE ASSOCIATION*	NEGATIVE ASSOCIATION	NO ASSOCIATION
Type of medication	Correlations found: 6		9
Degree of behavioral change	4	—	—
Complexity	3	12	1
Cost	1	—	1

*See footnotes to Table 23-1.
From Haynes R.B.: A critical review of the "determinants" of patient compliance with therapeutic regimens, in Sackett D.L., Haynes R.B. (eds.): *Compliance with Therapeutic Regimens*. Baltimore, Johns Hopkins University Press, 1976, Table 3.3.

in a clinic where the cost of treatment was determined by the ability to pay! Obviously, more research is needed in this area, especially involving patients with chronic diseases.

FEATURES OF THE THERAPEUTIC SOURCE (Table 23-4).—The finding that health professionals are unable to distinguish between compliers and noncompliers among their own patients is fairly clear and has obvious implications for those who study health behavior. The tendency is for physicians to overestimate the degree of patient compliance. The data relating to the effect of having a particular therapist are rather surprising. Most of us probably expect that having a regular, or private, physician (in contrast to a physician in a public clinic) would make a difference in compliance. The findings do not support this, however.

FEATURES OF THE PATIENT-THERAPIST INTERACTION (Table 23-5).—A serious problem with the research on patient-physician interaction is that much of the data are "circumstantial, highly subjective, and of uncertain validity. Furthermore, so few investigations have ventured into the study of this complex subject from the viewpoint of compliance that not even the replicability of results can be assessed."[10] Because of these factors, the Toronto group decided to analyze only those features of patient-physician interaction "for which the data are both sufficient and of a consistent nature."[10] Utilizing these guidelines, two clear findings stand out.

1. All the studies indicate the importance of the degree of supervision in determining patient compliance; hospital patients are more compliant than day patients, who in turn are more compliant

TABLE 23-4.—FEATURES OF THE THERAPEUTIC SOURCE

	ASSOCIATION WITH COMPLIANCE		
	POSITIVE ASSOCIATION*	NEGATIVE ASSOCIATION	NO ASSOCIATION
Therapist's prediction of compliance	—	—	5
Particular physician	1	—	3
Private vs. public physician	—	1	3

*See footnotes to Table 23-1.
From Haynes R.B.: A critical review of the "determinants" of patient compliance with therapeutic regimens, in Sackett D.L., Haynes R.B. (eds.): *Compliance with Therapeutic Regimens*. Baltimore, Johns Hopkins University Press, 1976, Table 3.4.

TABLE 23-5.—Features of the Patient-Therapist Interaction

	ASSOCIATION WITH COMPLIANCE		
	POSITIVE ASSOCIATION*	NEGATIVE ASSOCIATION	NO ASSOCIATION
Amount of supervision	3	—	—
Patient's satisfaction with specific visit, doctor, clinic	4	—	—
Patient's expectations met	2	—	—
Patient's attitudes toward health professionals and care in general	—	—	5

*See footnotes to Table 23-1.
From Haynes R.B.: A critical review of the "determinants" of patient compliance with therapeutic regimens, in Sackett D.L., Haynes R.B. (eds.): *Compliance with Therapeutic Regimens*. Baltimore, Johns Hopkins University Press, 1976, Table 3.5.

than outpatients. In addition, "before-after" studies have given support to this (e.g., compliance improves when the frequency of outpatient visits is increased or when home visits are added).

2. The patient's subjective feelings of satisfaction with his medical care are also associated with compliance. Related to this is the positive correlation between compliance and patients' beliefs that the physicians have met their expectations for care. Note, however, that patients' attitudes toward physicians or the health-care system in *general* do not appear to influence compliance.

Several researchers have attempted to correlate the interaction and communication between physician and patient with patient compliance.[11, 12] However, the research methodology is not sufficiently rigorous in these studies to permit reliance on their findings.

SOCIOBEHAVIORAL FEATURES OF THE PATIENT.—Six sociobehavioral factors are of interest, as outlined in Table 23-6. Patients' *perceptions of the efficacy* of the treatment they are receiving are subjective beliefs that are independent of both factual knowledge and the truth of the situation (i.e., they are unrelated to any scientific evidence of benefit). An example might be a person with cancer who believes that laetrile is helpful and chemotherapy is not.

TABLE 23-6.—Sociobehavioral Features of Patients

	ASSOCIATION WITH COMPLIANCE		
	POSITIVE ASSOCIATION*	NEGATIVE ASSOCIATION	NO ASSOCIATION
Patient perception of efficacy of therapy	4	—	4
Knowledge of therapy/disease	4	—	8
Intelligence	—	—	5
Influence of patient's family	5	—	1
Family stability	4	—	2

*See footnotes to Table 23-1.
From Haynes R.B.: A critical review of the "determinants" of patient compliance with therapeutic regimens, in Sackett D.L., Haynes R.B. (eds.): *Compliance with Therapeutic Regimens*. Baltimore, Johns Hopkins University Press, 1976, Table 3.6.

A comment is needed in regard to the lack of clear correlation between compliance and patient knowledge of the therapy/disease. Common sense would seem to dictate that the more one understands about his disease and his therapeutic regimen, the greater care he would take in following the prescribed protocol. Although some studies have indeed shown this, an analysis of the methodologies used, when compared with those in the studies that showed no association, leads to the conclusion that the latter were carried out with more rigor and sounder methodology. Accordingly, more reliance should be placed on those studies that showed no association. This is supported by the lack of association between patient education and compliance (see Table 23–1) and between intelligence and compliance (see Table 23–6). This finding has special importance for those involved in patient care.

In summary, there is no description that fits all, or even most, of the compliant patients. With respect to the influence of patient attributes and the medical setting on compliance, the conclusion reached by Podell and Gary seems justified:

> Indeed, the most important lesson derived from the research—i.e., compliance—must be that noncompliance is found among all socioeconomic groups, among all types of persons, and in all medical settings. While certain patients who frequently will not comply can be identified (such as the alcoholic and the angry, dissatisfied patient), these highly visible groups are but a tiny minority of the noncompliers. The majority of noncompliers are quite similar in most respects to patients who do comply. Noncompliance is a complex and multifaceted phenomenon, one which most patients display from time to time. It usually cannot be written off as simply inherent to particular individuals or certain socioeconomic or personality groups.[7]

Persons who have more knowledge about their condition and treatment program do not seem to have a higher rate of compliance when compared with those who are less well informed. On the other hand, the attitudes and beliefs that patients have about their illness and therapy are important in determining compliance. This is so whether or not their beliefs are, in fact, correct. When people believe that they have a severe illness, that it poses a serious threat to their health and life, and that the treatment prescribed is very effective, they are much more likely to adhere to the treatment program.[13]

From the above data, it appears that one important factor in determining compliance is the physician-patient relationship, specifically, the degree of supervision of the patient and his satisfaction with his care. When there are problems in communication between a physician and his patient, compliance is likely to be adversely affected.[14] A physician-patient relationship in which there is effective communication and close patient supervision, plus satisfaction on the part of the patient with respect to his care, may act as an incentive for the patient to comply with medical advice.

HEALTH BELIEF MODEL

Large numbers of studies using the medical model of compliance have failed to identify clearly the critical variables that determine this aspect of patient behavior. Recall that this model confined the search for significant variables to such factors as demographic and social characteristics of the *patient,* the type and complexity of the *regimen,* and the nature of the *illness.* Researchers have thus increasingly turned to social-psychological theory in formulating hypotheses that might explain compliance behavior.

In the mid-1960s, Rosenstock drew on social-psychological theory to construct a *health belief model,* which could predict who would engage in *preventive* health behavior (such as an immunization program). This health belief model hypothesizes that one can predict compliance/noncompliance from knowing (1) the *value of an outcome* to an individual and (2) that individual's *expectation that a given action will result in that outcome.* The model also includes the idea that a "cue to action" must be present to "trigger" the suggested behavior (e.g., the perception of a symptom or a television announcement).

Although this model seems to provide a good basic approach, it had to be modified to predict and explain compliance with prescribed medical regimens by the (already) ill patient. This was accomplished largely through the work of Marshall Becker, a psychologist.[8] The factors in his model (Fig 23-1) are of considerably greater value to the clinician than those in the medical model because they have been demonstrated to be alterable; they allow the physician or other health worker to tailor a regimen "to suit the particular needs of each patient."[8] Note the importance assigned to *"subjective estimates"* in the second and third boxes on the left of the figure (under Readiness to Undertake Recommended Compliance Behavior). It cannot be overemphasized that the critical factor is "the person's subjective perceptions rather than . . . some medical or objective estimate of the illness or therapy."

To summarize:

[T]his model suggests that patients (a) who feel *susceptible* to problems or complications because of their illness, or to further attacks of the illness itself; (b) who believe that their illness could pose *severe* consequences for their health and daily functioning; (c) who feel that the proposed treatment plan will be highly *effective* in treating their illness; and (d) who do not foresee such major *obstacles* to compliance as adverse drug effects, cost of the regimen, or perceived lack of safety of a medication, will be more likely to follow regimens offered to them than patients *not* holding these beliefs.[13]

It is impossible to discuss each of the elements in Becker's model (see Fig 23-1), but let us look at two: (1) subjective estimate of the proposed regimen's efficacy (under left-hand column, Readiness to Undertake Recommended Compliance Behavior) and (2) interaction between physician and patient (under Modifying and Enabling Factors).

Subjective Estimate of the Proposed Regimen's Efficacy

Roth et al.'s classic study of "Patient's Beliefs about Peptic Ulcer and Its Treatment" is a good example here.[15] After a study con-

Fig 23-1.—Hypothetical model for predicting and explaining compliance behavior. (From Becker M.H.: Sociobehavioral determinants of compliance, in Sackett D.L., Haynes R.B. [eds.]: *Compliance with Therapeutic Regimens.* Baltimore, The Johns Hopkins University Press, 1976, p. 48. Used by permission.)

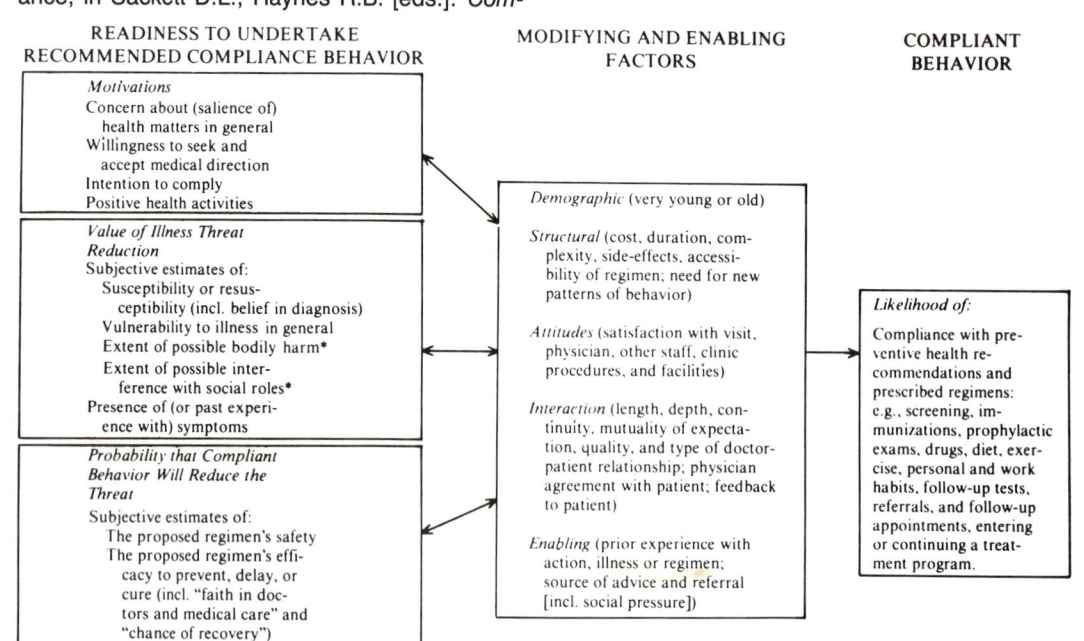

READINESS TO UNDERTAKE RECOMMENDED COMPLIANCE BEHAVIOR	MODIFYING AND ENABLING FACTORS	COMPLIANT BEHAVIOR

Motivations
Concern about (salience of) health matters in general
Willingness to seek and accept medical direction
Intention to comply
Positive health activities
 	
Value of Illness Threat Reduction
Subjective estimates of:
  Susceptibility or resusceptibility (incl. belief in diagnosis)
  Vulnerability to illness in general
  Extent of possible bodily harm*
  Extent of possible interference with social roles*
  Presence of (or past experience with) symptoms
 	
Probability that Compliant Behavior Will Reduce the Threat
Subjective estimates of:
  The proposed regimen's safety
  The proposed regimen's efficacy to prevent, delay, or cure (incl. "faith in doctors and medical care" and "chance of recovery")
	Demographic (very young or old)
	
	Structural (cost, duration, complexity, side-effects, accessibility of regimen; need for new patterns of behavior)
	
	Attitudes (satisfaction with visit, physician, other staff, clinic procedures, and facilities)
	
	Interaction (length, depth, continuity, mutuality of expectation, quality, and type of doctor-patient relationship; physician agreement with patient; feedback to patient)
	
	Enabling (prior experience with action, illness or regimen; source of advice and referral [incl. social pressure])
		Likelihood of:
		Compliance with preventive health recommendations and prescribed regimens: e.g., screening, immunizations, prophylactic exams, drugs, diet, exercise, personal and work habits, follow-up tests, referrals, and follow-up appointments, entering or continuing a treatment program.

*At motivating, but not inhibiting, levels.

ducted at a Veterans Administration Hospital revealed that patients with peptic ulcers took only 40% of the prescribed medication that was placed at their bedside, Roth and his colleagues undertook to find the explanation for this behavior. In a rigorously designed and executed study, they placed bottles of antacid on patients' bedside tables. Each patient was instructed to take a certain number of ounces before breakfast, lunch, and dinner and at bedtime. The nursing staff inconspicuously noted how many ounces of the medicine had been consumed at these times. Compliance was high in terms of drinking the antacid at mealtimes but fell off significantly at bedtime. When these investigators examined the patients' subjective beliefs about the healing process of ulcers and the purpose of antacids, they found that most patients thought of acid as coming from food (and did not know that acid was produced internally). Furthermore, the patients used the analogy of healing of sores on the surface of the body to understand the healing of ulcers (conceived of as internal sores) inside the body. Thus, many did not see any need to follow physicians' directions to take antacid at bedtime because:

1. They saw acid as being a problem only at those times when food was ingested (i.e., mealtimes).
2. They viewed the healing ulcer as being protected by a "scab" or "thin skin" that could be "knocked off" by ingested food, and that this "skin" or "scab" could be protected by coating the stomach at mealtimes by the antacid.

Absolutely critical here is the point that simply informing the patient about the scientific facts is probably going to be of little help. When information is given to a patient that does not "fit" that patient's existing belief system, it will often be rejected. The physician must ask the patient what he or she believes and start from there to modify these views.

Interaction between Physician and Patient

As mentioned, the interaction between patients and physicians seems to influence the degree of compliance. Several factors that have appeared to be significant in the existing studies of patient-physician interaction and noncompliance are as follows:

1. Davis found that noncompliance was associated with a clinician who "exhibited disagreement, formality or rejection of the patient, and asked for information without giving any feedback."[16]
2. Korsch et al. noted that "failure to receive an explanation of diagnosis and cause of the child's illness were key factors in noncompliance."[11]
3. Patient beliefs that their expectations are not being met or that their physicians are not behaving in a friendly manner are associated with noncompliance.[11,12]

Unfortunately, most studies of physician-patient interaction have not been undertaken with a sufficient degree of rigor that we may rely confidently on the findings. It is to be hoped that future investigations will be carried out using objective measurements of compliance and testing the health belief model of compliance in different settings, among different populations, and with various kinds of therapeutic regimens.

STRATEGIES FOR IMPROVING COMPLIANCE

In a discussion of improving patient compliance, a distinction should be made between those problems of noncompliance that are due to *errors on the part of the patient* and those that are attributable to *deliberate changes made by the patient*.

Errors

Errors are most frequently due to inadequate communication between physician and patient. The physician should be sure that the patient understands every item of the treatment program before he or she leaves the office. The most common errors in taking medication occur in the *frequency* of consumption per 24 hours and the *number of units* taken (i.e., the patient takes more or fewer spoonfuls, pills, etc., than prescribed).

A situation that frequently leads to confusion is one in which the physician gives verbal directions to the patient in the consultation room and expects these to be recalled accurately an hour or so later when the patient opens the package from the pharmacy and sees the label on the bottle "Take as directed." All too often, the patient (whose anxiety level in a physician's office may be higher than usual) has forgotten at least part of the directions. In the hospital setting, instructions regarding diet, medications, and limitation of activity are often given to the patient in the last few hours prior to discharge. Unfortunately, the patient's thoughts are centered on other concerns such as whether a neighbor can get off work to pick him up and how he is going to pay the hospital bill!

Findings from several studies illustrate the frequency of noncompliance that occurs because of misunderstanding on the part of the patient.

1. One investigation found that between 9% and 64% of the patients misinterpreted the written instructions on the bottle label (e.g., one capsule three times daily; one tablet daily).[16]
2. Another study discovered that of 90 prescribed medications, 27 were being taken inaccurately. Seven were omitted completely because the patients seemed unaware that they had been part of the regimen, while 20 were being taken in incorrect dosages due to errors in understanding.[17]
3. In studies of middle-class patients who had a continuing relationship with a private physician, the average rate of taking less or more medication than was prescribed because of error was nearly 20% and the scheduling misconceptions averaged 17%.[18-20]
4. Galloway and Eby surveyed residents of poverty areas and discovered that 80% could not correctly interpret what the physicians and druggists assumed to be easily understood prescription labels.[21]

As the reader can imagine, a population at greatest risk for misunderstanding and making errors is the elderly. Because of failing eyesight, for example, they may misread the small type on labels; because of impaired hearing, they may misunderstand the physician's verbal directions. One study of 178 outpatients, 60 years and older, found that 59% were making an error in taking or omitting a medicine;[22] another investigation of elderly patients revealed that nearly three of five made medication errors.[20]

To prevent noncompliance due to errors, the following steps should be taken by a physician:

1. Print the directions on paper.
2. Ask the patient (especially if elderly) to read them back.
3. Explain that many people are confused by medical "jargon," and ask the patient if he has any questons, e.g., does "3 times a day" mean *at* meals, *before*, or *after*, etc.
4. When the patient comes back for follow-up, ask him to tell you when and in what amount he has been taking medication.

Therapeutic Changes by Patient

The Toronto medical researchers who evaluated the 185 published reports of compliance investigations in terms of research design also rated those that dealt with strategies for improving compliance. They assigned a "+" to those in which improvement in compliance was statistically significant ($P = <.05$) and a "+" to those in which the effect on the associated therapeutic outcome was statistically significant. In studying these reports, Sackett, Haynes, and their colleagues classified the strategies tested into three broad categories: educational, behavioral, and combined (a mixture of educational and behavioral). Educational strategies were defined as "those which attempt to improve compliance through the transmission of information about a disease and its treatment to patients." Types of educational strategies included "fixed-content" health messages (these tended to be brief and exposed subjects to information that was intended to promote the use of seat belts, glaucoma screening, and so on); individual patient counseling (in regard to the need for following the diabetic regimen, for example); and programmed instruction (on the diabetic regimen). Behavioral strategies, on the other hand, include attempts (1) to reduce barriers to compliance (such as expense or inconvenience), (2) to cue or stimulate compliance, and (3) to reward or reinforce compliance. In these latter approaches, a patient's knowledge of his disease and its treatment was not of direct concern. Types of behavioral strategies embraced behavior modification (one of these studies sought to motivate proper dental hygiene by giving token rewards); home visits to retrieve patients who did not attend clinic (hypertension and tuberculosis clinics, for example); and free medication given at the clinic (free iron tablets to antenatal patients).

Although descriptions of patient education projects appear frequently in the medical literature, few have built evaluation into their programs. Table 23–7 is therefore of great interest. It is clear from this comparison that behavioral and combined strategies are more effective than educational strategies in terms of both increases in compliance and improvement in therapeutic outcomes.

Two types of strategies have either firm theoretical bases or well-demonstrated effectiveness in improving patient compliance with therapeutic regimens. One of these involves behavioral modification. A physician skilled in this can (1) identify the behavior to be controlled, (2) determine those events or circumstances in the patient's environment that lead to the occurrence and nonoccurrence of the behavior, and (3) help the patient to design a self-care regimen by which the patient receives encouragement for compliance behavior and either no encouragement or actual discouragement for noncompliance. Although many physicians and members of patients' families have always used this technique *informally*, research has demonstrated the greatest effectiveness when reinforcement is applied systematically.

Another strategy is to utilize a "patient contract." This is a method whereby the physician and patient *together* specify what the patient can expect of the physician, and vice versa. It can include any aspect of the therapeutic regimen (medications, dosages, acceptable and unacceptable side effects, amount and type of exercise, etc.). These contracts are individualized to "fit" each patient. If either physician or patient does not achieve the agreed upon goals, the contract should be renegotiated. Furthermore, these contracts can be modified in the event that the diagnosis and prognosis of the disease change. This strategy implies a collaborative working-together of the patient and physician—a therapeutic alliance that involves shared goals and mutual participation in the therapeutic process. With this relationship, the patient feels free to suggest ways to simplify the regimen, to help schedule medication times to involve the least disruption of his routine, and to share his concern about the cost of the pro-

TABLE 23–7.—METHODOLOGICAL AND SUCCESS RATINGS OF STRATEGIES FOR INCREASING COMPLIANCE

APPROACH	AVERAGE METHODOLOGICAL RATING	SUCCESS IN INCREASING COMPLIANCE	THERAPEUTIC SUCCESS
Educational	10.3	18 studies out of 28 (64%)	5 studies out of 10 (50%)
Behavioral	10.9	34 studies out of 40 (85%)	18 studies out of 22 (82%)
Combined	9.9	14 studies out of 16 (88%)	9 studies out of 12 (75%)

Source: Haynes R.B.: Strategies for improving compliance: A Methodologic Analysis and Review, in Sackett D.L., Haynes R.B. (eds.): *Compliance with Therapeutic Regimens*. Baltimore, Johns Hopkins University Press, 1976, p. 75. (Used by permission.)

posed treatment. Both patient and physician are free to negotiate the elements in the regimen. It appears that the physician who is aware of his or her patient's beliefs, feelings, and habits and enlists the patient in becoming a participant in designing the medical regimen will achieve the greatest degree of compliance.

Ethics Regarding the Use of Strategies Designed to Change Patient Behavior

One theme that surfaced repeatedly during the 1974 workshop/symposium at McMaster University Medical Centre was ethics. Some argued that for a physician to utilize a strategy specifically designed to change the patient's behavior amounts to "mind-bending." Because of this, and because it makes therapeutic sense, Sackett suggests that four conditions must be met prior to attempting to modify patient behavior to gain compliance:

1. The diagnosis must be correct.
2. The therapy must do more good than harm.
3. Neither the illness nor the proposed therapy can be trivial.
4. It must be established that the patient is an informed, willing partner in the execution of any maneuver designed to alter compliance behavior.[2]

SUMMARY

Physicians have traditionally looked at compliance through *their* eyes rather than those of the patient. In the past, the view was maintained that the patient "ought" to be obedient in following the physician's directions; reflecting this view was the terminology used in describing a noncompliant patient—"unreliable," "deviant," "uncooperative." An increasing number of studies indicate that, upon leaving the physician's office, patients evaluate what they have been told and make their own decisions regarding whether to follow the prescribed treatment exactly, partially, or not at all. The weighted average of compliance with different long-term medication regimens for different illnesses in different settings has been cited as 54%.

Early investigations followed the medical model, that is, the model that looked at: easily identifiable and quantifiable patient characteristics (e.g., age and education), the regimen (e.g., its type and complexity), and the illness (e.g., its type, severity, and duration). This model has been unsatisfactory and researchers have turned increasingly to social-psychological theory in formulating hypotheses that might explain health behavior. In the health belief model, prediction of compliance is based on the *value* of a particular health outcome to an individual and on the individual's *expectation* that a given health action on his part will result in that outcome. The many methodological problems associated with compliance research help to explain why reports of study findings are often in conflict with one another.

Demographic features generally have not been helpful in identifying compliant patients (age, sex, education, and ethnic background are examples). Likewise, many features of the illness (such as severity and duration) and sociobehavioral characteristics of patients (including patient knowledge of the therapy/disease and level of intelligence) are not helpful.

The following variables have been shown to be associated with compliant/noncompliant behavior:

1. Patients with psychiatric diagnoses are less likely to be compliant than those suffering from physical illness.
2. The more behavioral change a patient must make, the less compliant he tends to be.
3. The more complex the regimen, the less compliant is the patient.
4. The greater the degree of supervision of the patient, the more compliance is achieved.
5. The greater the patient's satisfaction with the specific visit, physician, or clinic, the more compliant is the behavior shown.

Strategies for improving compliance include those that are educational (e.g., television ads to encourage being tested for glaucoma), behavioral (e.g., behavior modification programs), and a combination of these two. In a comparison of the three different methods, it was found that educational strategies are least effective in terms of increased compliance and therapeutic outcome.

REFERENCES

1. Stimson G.V.: Obeying doctor's orders: A view from the other side. *Soc. Sci. Med.* 8:97, 1974.
2. Sackett D.L.: Priorities and methods for future research, in Sackett D.L., Haynes R.B. (eds.): *Compliance with Therapeutic Regimens*. Baltimore, Johns Hopkins University Press, 1976.
3. Kasl S.V.: Issues in patient adherence to health care regimens. *J. Hum. Stress* 1(3):5, 1975.
4. Eney R.D., Goldstein E.O.: Compliance of chronic asthmatics with oral administration of theophylline as measured by serum and salivary levels. *Pediatrics* 57(4):513, 1976.
5. Stewart R.B., Cluff L.E.: A review of medication errors and compliance in ambulant patients. *Clin. Pharmacol. Ther.* 13:463, 1972.
6. Bergman A.B., Werner R.J.: Failure of children to receive penicillin by mouth. *N. Engl. J. Med.* 268:1334, 1963.
7. Podell R.N., Gary L.R.: Compliance: A problem in medical management. *Am. Fam. Physician* 13:74, 1976.
8. Becker M.H.: Sociobehavioral determinants of compliance, in Sackett D.L., Haynes R.B. (eds.): *Compliance with Therapeutic Regimens*. Baltimore, Johns Hopkins University Press, 1976.
9. Kasl S., Cobb S.: Health behavior, illness behavior, and sick role behavior. *Arch. Environ. Health* 12:246, 1966.
10. Haynes R.B.: A critical review of the "determinants" of patient compliance with therapeutic regimens, in Sackett D.L., Haynes R.B. (eds.): *Compliance with Therapeutic Regimens*. Baltimore, Johns Hopkins University Press, 1976.
11. Korsch B.M., et al.: Gaps in doctor-patient communication. 1. Doctor-patient interaction and patient satisfaction. *Pediatrics* 42(5):855, 1968.
12. Francis V., et al.: Gaps in doctor-patient communication: Patients' response to medical advice. *N. Engl. J. Med.* 280(10):535, 1969.
13. Matthews D., Hingson R.: Improving patient compliance, *Med. Clin. North Am.* 61:879, 1977.
14. Mumford E.: The responses of patients to medical advice, in Simons R.C., Pardes H. (eds.): *Understanding Human Behavior in Health and Illness*. Baltimore, Williams & Wilkins Co., 1977.
15. Roth H.P., et al.: Patients' beliefs about peptic ulcer and its treatment. *Ann. Intern. Med.* 56:72, 1962.
16. Davis M.S.: Variation in patients' compliance with doctors' orders: Medical practice and doctor-patient interaction. *Psychiatry in Medicine* 2:31, 1971.
17. Curtis E.B.: Medication errors made by patients. *Nurs. Outlook* 9:290, 1961.
18. Hulka B.S., et al.: Communication, compliance, and concordance between physicians and patients with prescribed medications. *Am. J. Public Health* 66(9):847, 1976.
19. Charney E.: Patient-doctor communication. *Pediatr. Clin. North Am.* 19:263, 1972.
20. Neely E., Patrick M.L.: Problems of aged persons taking medications at home. *Nurs. Res.* 17:52, 1968.
21. Galloway S.P., Eby C.E.: Poverty area residents look at pharmacy services. *Am. J. Public Health* 61:2211, 1971.
22. Schwartz D., et al.: Medication errors made by elderly, chronically ill patients. *Am. J. Public Health* 52:2018, 1962.

24 / The Physician-Patient Relationship

Communication Between the Physician and the Patient

JONATHAN J. BRAUNSTEIN, M.D.

The Traditional and Humanistic Models

GAIL SILVERMAN, Ph.D.

BEFORE THE ADVENT of modern scientific medicine, the relationship that developed between a patient and a physician was a major element in the therapeutic armamentarium of the physician. Little could be done to alter the natural history of disease in favor of the patient and cure was impossible with the methods of treatment then available. The "art of medicine," i.e., the establishment of a therapeutically beneficial relationship between the physician and the patient, was relied on quite heavily by both parties in coping with illness. With the technological revolution in medicine that has occurred over the past several decades, however, there has been a weakening of the ties between the physician and the patient. This is reflected in part by a widespread public disenchantment with the medical profession. Some of the public have come to view the physician as a highly skilled technician who seems more interested in a disease than in the person who harbors it.

Of course, this generalization does not accurately reflect the attitude of many patients toward their own personal physician. As a matter of fact, there is still a great deal of respect for the medical profession, as indicated in Table 24–1, which shows the results of a study conducted by the Gallup organization in 1976. When a nationally representative sample of the public was asked to rank the honesty and ethical standards of 11 occupations, physicians received the highest rating. Even so, the fact that 44% of this group did *not* feel that physicians are highly ethical and honest should be of concern to all those in the medical profession. It suggests that all is not well with the physician-patient relationship.

COMMUNICATION BETWEEN THE PHYSICIAN AND THE PATIENT

In this discussion the word *physician* (as used in *physician-patient relationship*) refers to a special kind of physician, that is, a clinician. Tumulty defines a clinician as "one whose prime function is to manage a sick person with the purpose of alleviating most effectively the total impact of the illness upon that person."[1] He points out that managing a person's illness is entirely different from simply diagnosing and treating his disease. In the first instance, the total function of the individual (physical, psychological, and social) must be taken into consideration along with the effects of the illness on those about him.

To fulfill the requirements of his role, a cli-

TABLE 24-1.—How the Public Rates Physicians and Others on Honesty and Ethics, June 6, 1976*

	VERY HIGH	HIGH	AVERAGE	LOW	VERY LOW
Physicians	17%	39%	35%	6%	3%
Engineers	10	39	43	3	1
College teachers	9	35	44	7	2
Journalists	7	26	49	13	3
Lawyers	6	19	48	18	8
Building contractors	5	18	54	18	3
Business executives	3	17	58	16	4
Senators	3	16	51	22	7
Congressmen	3	11	47	27	11
Labor union leaders	2	10	38	31	17
Advertising personnel	2	9	43	29	15

*Percentages are rounded.
Note: Physicians head the list when a nationally representative sample of the public is asked to rank the honesty and ethical standards of 11 occupations. Fifty-six percent say physicians have very high or high standards of ethics and honesty. Following the physicians are two other professional groups—engineers and educators. Rated lowest in ethics and honesty are politicians, labor leaders, and advertising personnel.
Source: *American Medical News*, March 28, 1977, p. 7. (Used by permission.)

nician has to be skillful in communication. He must be able to convey his ideas and feelings to his patients in a meaningful way. Moreover, he should be equally adept at encouraging them to do the same. Above all, he needs to be a good listener.

As in most relationships, the interaction that takes place between a physician and a patient occurs on two different levels: a technical and a nontechnical one. On the technical level, the physician is involved in diagnosing and treating the patient's disease. A medical history is taken, a physical examination is performed, laboratory tests are ordered, and treatment is prescribed. To accomplish these objectives, the physician makes use of his technical medical knowledge. Although his directions and explanations are conveyed to the patient in lay terminology, the basis for their communication on this level is the physician's application of medical science. On the nontechnical level, interaction between the physician and the patient consists of a more personal type of communication; that is, the two parties relate to one another as any two human beings would who are involved in a social relationship.

These two levels of communication become intermixed as the physician and the patient relate to each other. Most important, they are interdependent so that, for example, success in communication on the nontechnical level helps to insure success on the technical level. Conversely, the failure to interact effectively on one level impairs interaction on the other.

Individuals "talk" to each other in several different ways. Mayerson has divided human language into three types: the lexical, which refers to human speech activities; the kinesic, which includes body movements; and the somatic, which consists of the observable manifestations of autonomic nervous system activity.[2] Another categorization of these methods of communication makes use of the terms *verbal* and *nonverbal*. When interacting with a patient, a physician should be aware that the spoken word is only one facet of their communication. He should be on the alert to detect the nonverbal (i.e., kinesic and somatic) messages that the patient sends him. They can be of diagnostic value. For example, kinesic signals such as facial expression, body posture, and gestures may clearly point to the presence of depression, even though the patient may not be consciously aware of this feeling state. The nonverbal cues that the physician sends a patient may either enhance or interfere with their interaction. For instance, a facial expression that indicates concern on the part of the physician and a demeanor that shows he is interested in listening to the patient are very helpful in establishing an atmosphere in which the patient will readily communicate his thoughts and feelings.

Three groups of factors influence communication between a physician and a patient, those relating to:

1. The psychological aspects of their interaction
2. The sociocultural aspects of their relationship
3. The nature of the patient's illness

Psychological Aspects of the Physician-Patient Interaction

PERSONALITIES OF PHYSICIAN AND PATIENT.—In all human relationships, the psychological makeup and function of the parties involved determine to a large extent the manner in which they interact. Both the physician and the patient bring to their encounter a personality that has been molded over years of living, and it is obvious that similarities and differences in their attitudes and beliefs about medical and nonmedical issues will affect their relationship. This is a generalization that does not require further elaboration. There are several psychological aspects of the physician-patient relationship that do bear special comment, however. One has to do with personality traits that are commonly found among physicians.

Many physicians can be characterized as being mildly to moderately obsessive, perfectionistic, and inhibited in terms of emotional expression. They have learned through experience to suppress many of the feelings they have toward situations and people. While these qualities may be of some value to them in adapting to their professional role, they often interfere with establishing warm personal relationships.

Physicians also tend to be somewhat authoritarian in their interactions with others. During their training, they become used to "taking charge" of a situation—giving advice and directing the actions of patients. Some patients who are passive by nature feel quite comfortable in letting the physician assume this role; others who are more independent may resent this aspect of the physician's personality. The inability of some physicians to establish warm personal relationships and to allow certain patients to participate as partners in the decision-making process lies at the root of many communication problems that beset the physician-patient relationship.

A second psychological aspect of the physician-patient relationship that deserves comment is the process of transference and countertransference.[3] There is a tendency for people to attribute to the authority figures with whom they have contact the qualities they have found in these kinds of individuals earlier in their lives. Thus, the relationships that a person had with his parents, teachers, and physicians in the past will influence his attitude and behavior toward his current physician. If his experiences in these previous relationships were positive and associated with the development of confidence and trust, then he is likely to relate to his physician in a similar manner. On the other hand, if some of these experiences were negative, he may have difficulty establishing a trusting relationship with a physician.

The process by which someone attributes to his physician the qualities that existed in key individuals in his life (and then interacts on this basis) is called transference. In situations of illness, the psychological regression experienced by a patient serves to facilitate this process. It is usually associated with the development of feelings and expectations on the part of a patient that are unrealistic and resistant to change. Transference explains many of the inappropriate reactions, both positive and negative, that patients have toward their physicians. Excessive affection, seductiveness, resentment, suspicion, or hostility expressed by a patient may be due to transference.

On their parts, physicians often attribute

unrealistic qualities to their patients based on past relationships they have had with significant people in their lives—a process referred to as countertransference. Sometimes a patient has physical or psychological characteristics that remind the physician of someone he was previously close to, and this facilitates countertransference. Since this process may be the basis for attitudes and feelings that adversely affect communication with patients, physicians should be alert to recognize it. Countertransference should be suspected whenever a physician finds himself reacting either very positively or very negatively toward a patient without apparent reason, i.e., in a manner that seems inappropriate to the situation at hand.

THE STRESS EXPERIENCED BY THE PATIENT AND THE PHYSICIAN.—One of the most influential factors affecting communication between a physician and a patient is the stress to which they are exposed in the medical setting. It was pointed out in chapter 22 that, for the patient, there are several causes for this stress, including his concern about his illness, his need to go to a relative stranger (the physician) for help, the situation of dependence in which he finds himself, and his apprehension about the tests and treatments that he may have to undergo. The psychological reactions to these stressors are predictable. Thus, when someone who is sick comes to a physician for help, he is usually anxious, even fearful, especially if he is acutely ill. He frequently experiences a sense of helplessness and dependency, a feeling that he is no longer in control of his life. In addition, if an illness is severe or protracted, depression is common.

These emotional reactions can impair a patient's ability to communicate. For example, he may be unable to recall important information about his medical history accurately and he may not remember the physician's instructions to him, no matter how carefully the physician has given them. Besides being unable to communicate effectively, patients under stress often react emotionally and impulsively, thereby placing a strain on the physician-patient relationship.

The physician may also be under stress when he enters into the relationship, although it is usually not so intense as that experienced by the patient. It stems from several sources, including the need to diagnose and treat the patient's illness correctly; a concern that he might order the wrong test or prescribe the wrong treatment and, as a result, injure the patient; and his desire to be accepted by the patient. Today, physicians are expected to do more than diagnose and treat disease; they are expected to help the patient solve his psychological and social problems. Some physicians are unprepared to deal with these kinds of problems and feel a great deal of discomfort when called upon to do so. The long hours of work and heavy caseload that many physicians carry tire them physically and limit their ability to deal effectively with the stressors that confront them.

Like the patient, a physician who is stressed may react psychologically in ways that compromise the physician-patient relationship. In addition to interfering significantly with his practice, these reactions can even cause serious disability.[4] There is statistical evidence that the incidence of drug abuse and alcoholism is higher among physicians than in the rest of the population.[5] Also, the suicide rate for physicians is considerably greater than it is for the general adult population.[6]

CONFLICT BETWEEN THE PATIENT AND THE PHYSICIAN.—Since the interaction between the physician and the patient supposedly has a common goal—the patient's medical welfare—one would think that there is little basis for disharmony in their relationship. Unfortunately, this is not the case. Most studies of the physician-patient relationship have shown that conflict is actually quite common and that it impairs communication between the parties. One reason for the conflict is the inequality that exists in the relationship, with most of the "power" on the side of the physician. This inequality stems from the physician's expertise in medical matters, the high regard in which the medical profession is held by the public, and the dependency of the patient on the physician. In social relationships in which the distribution of power is unequal, there is a tendency for the weaker party (the patient) to feel that he is being exploited by the stronger (the physician), thus giving rise to conflict.

A second reason disagreements sometimes occur between a physician and a patient is that their expectations of each other are not met. Because of the inequality of their positions, patients often find it difficult, if not impossible, to communicate their needs to the physician in an open and forceful manner. Under these circumstances, they have to rely on the hope that the physician will anticipate and respond to these needs on the basis of his knowledge and training. By contrast, the physician, as the more powerful of the two parties, is generally able to express his expectations directly to the patient.

Often a sort of competition develops between the physician and the patient to control the relationship, each trying to establish his prerogatives. On the one hand, the physician strives to get the patient to comply with his instructions, and on the other, the patient endeavors to assert his special needs. The physician may openly react with displeasure, irritation, and even anger if a patient fails to "act as he should." The patient, who cannot overtly express his feelings of disapproval toward the physician because of a fear of alienating the person on whom he depends for care, usually has to rely on indirect means of showing his displeasure. Passive-aggressive behavior is one way of doing this; failure to comply with medical advice is another.

In other areas of life, when a person becomes displeased with someone who is providing services to him, he will usually just change to another provider. This is certainly the case in the business world. It is not so simple in medical practice, however, where the patient depends on a particular physician for his health and even his life. There is a great hesitancy on the part of many patients to change physicians, particularly when they have gone to one for a long time and the physician has knowledge of their special medical problems. So, instead of abrogating the relationship when their expectations are not met, they continue to see the physician. In this case, patients often have hidden animosity toward the physician that hinders communication between them.

Sociocultural Aspects of the Physician-Patient Relationship

In describing the sociocultural factors that affect the physician-patient interaction, medical sociologists have looked at this relationship from both *functional* and *structural* standpoints.

FUNCTIONAL CONCEPTS.—Bloom has been the principal proponent of the first approach, which explains this interaction in terms of the effects of *social forces* and *roles*. Relying on earlier works by Henderson and Parsons,[7,8] he developed a model of the physician-patient relationship as a dynamic social system (Fig 24–1).[9,10] In this system, communication between the doctor (A) and the patient (B) occurs within a field of social forces that determine their attitudes, beliefs, and behavior. The patient is influenced most by his primary reference group, his family (B'), whereas the doctor is influenced mainly by his primary reference group, the medical profession (A'). Both parties relate to specific subcultural groups (D and E), e.g., social class, ethnic, and religious groups, which also mold their thoughts and actions. Finally, there is an overall sociocultural matrix (C), which determines the general values and beliefs held by the doctor and the patient.

Contrary to the common belief that the behavior of the patient and the doctor is governed primarily by rational problem-solving motives, Bloom asserts that it is actually determined to a large extent by the social forces that have been enumerated. It must be emphasized that the influence of these forces occurs mostly on an unconscious level, neither the doctor nor the patient being aware of their effects. For instance, it is generally ac-

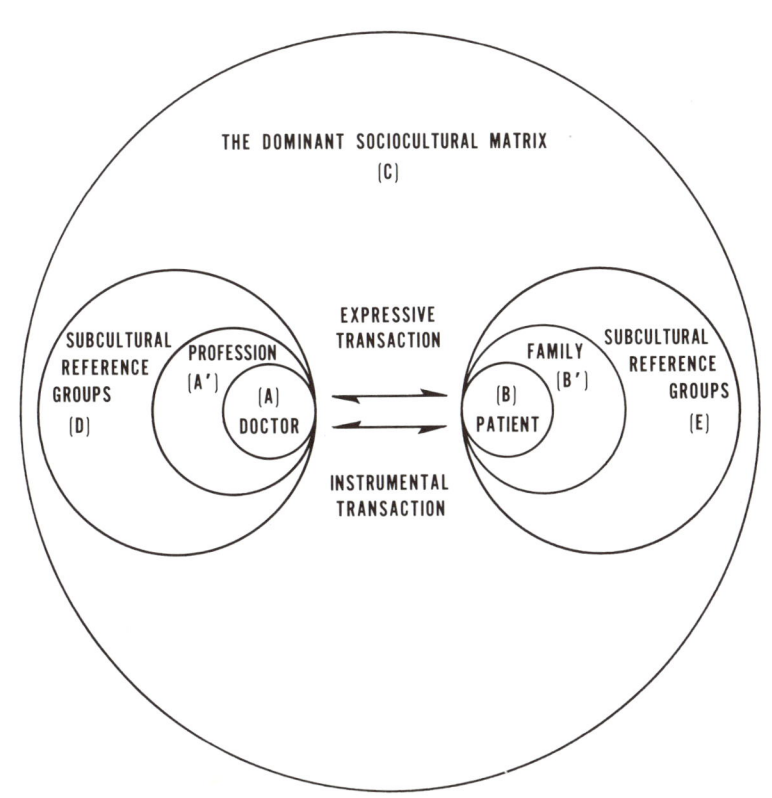

Fig 24-1.—The total transactional system. (From Bloom S.W.: *The Doctor and His Patient.* New York, Russell Sage Foundation, 1963, p. 256. © 1963 Russell Sage Foundation. Reprinted with permission. Further reproduction prohibited without permission of copyright holder.)

cepted that people with different ethnic and social class backgrounds differ in the way in which they view many aspects of life, including matters of health and sickness. Without realizing exactly how they have come by these views, individuals assume them to be correct and communicate with others on this basis. Thus, it is easy to see that a person from the lower social groups might experience difficulty communicating with a doctor who comes from the middle or upper social strata. Similarly, if a patient and a physician are from different ethnic groups, they may have problems relating to each other.

Bloom also makes the point that the behavior of the sick and those who care for them is determined by the adoption of social roles (patterns of expected behavior) by the two parties. While these role designations are only generalizations describing ideal forms of behavior, they do have a great deal of validity and are of considerable help to those attempting to understand the physician-patient relationship. In chapter 22, Parsons's concept of the sick role was described. Parsons has also given the classic description of the social role of the physician in our society (Table 24–2).[8] It is expected that a physician will (1) possess and apply a high degree of knowledge and skill in medical matters and (2) act primarily for the benefit of the patient as opposed to his own self-interest. The second expectation is rooted in the concept of a profession as a service-oriented occupation. Thus, in contrast to business occupations in our society, in which self-interest and profit are the principal motivating forces, those in medicine are supposed to be guided primarily by altruistic motives. A suspicion on the part of the public that physicians or other medical personnel are mainly guided in their actions by their own interests, as opposed to those of their patients, usually

TABLE 24-2.—THE ROLE OF THE PHYSICIAN

Expected to:
1. Act for the welfare of the patient (orientation to collective vs. self)
2. Be guided by the rules of professional behavior (universalism vs. particularism)
3. Apply a high degree of achieved skill and knowledge to problems of illness
4. Be objective and emotionally detached (affective neutrality)

Privileges:
1. Professional self-regulation
2. Access to physical and personal intimacy

Parsons, Talcott: *The Social System*. Glencoe, Ill.: The Free Press, 1951. Reprinted with permission of Macmillan Publishing Co., Inc., Copyright 1951 by Talcott Parsons.

leads to disappointment and some loss of confidence in these personnel. In fact, one of the major complaints expressed by patients with respect to the modern-day physician is that, despite being extremely well trained in medical science, he appears to be less committed to the personal welfare of his patients.

In his concept of the physician's role, Parsons defines the proper attitude of the physician toward his patients as one of *affective neutrality*. By this he means that the physician is expected to be objective and emotionally detached from the patient, while at the same time showing a sincere concern for the patient's welfare. Bloom points out that it is extremely difficult for physicians to maintain this emotional distance and that most are, in fact, affected by the behavior of their patients. The word *empathy* is often used to describe the appropriate attitude of the physician toward the patient. This means that the physician should be able to "place himself in the patient's shoes" to understand the kinds of difficulties and problems that the patient is experiencing.

Most important, the physician's role requires that medical personnel remain neutral in their judgment of the patient's actions and beliefs. In other words, they should try to *understand* what motivates a patient's behavior *instead of judging* it in moralistic terms. Unfortunately, many physicians do not follow this approach. Thus, it is not uncommon to hear a physician refer to patients as "good" or "bad" depending on their attitude, dress, or behavior.[11] Some physicians are even judgmental when it comes to a patient's disease, preferring to treat certain types of illnesses as opposed to others.[11] Clearly, this kind of judgmental or moralistic attitude may prevent a physician from acting in the best interests of patients who behave in some way that he does not approve of, or who happen to have a disease he does not like to treat.

In exchange for fulfilling the expectations of the physician's role, medical personnel are granted certain privileges including access to personal information about the patient's life and authority to examine the patient. In addition, the medical profession is allowed a great degree of autonomy in regulating its own affairs and the professional conduct of its members. Thus, the profession is expected to monitor the proficiency of its members and to discipline those who fail to meet the standards it sets.

STRUCTURAL CONCEPTS.—Several structural elements of our present health-care system greatly affect the physician-patient interaction. Over the past 50 years, profound changes have occurred in the way in which medicine is practiced in this country, and these have altered both the technical and the nontechnical aspects of the physician-patient relationship. The changes to which we refer are:

1. A greater reliance on technology in diagnosis and treatment
2. An increasing number of medical specialists
3. The emergence of group practice
4. The bureaucratization of the health care system

TECHNOLOGY.—The introduction of sophisticated medical technology, along with the dramatic increase in knowledge in the biomedical sciences, has greatly enhanced the diagnostic and therapeutic skills of physicians. These advances have focused the attention of the medical profession on the technical aspects of health-care delivery, often at the expense of the nontechnical or humanistic ones. Medical students are introduced to this kind of thinking early in their training.

Patients expect their physician to be technically competent; indeed this is taken for granted by most people. In addition, they expect him to relate to them on a warm personal basis and to demonstrate a sincere concern for their welfare. When this attitude and behavior are not demonstrated, patients become disappointed and disenchanted with their medical care. Thus, a modern dilemma faces the physician-patient relationship, stemming from excessive reliance by physicians on science and technology in patient care. It partly explains why the public has lost some of its admiration and respect for the medical profession, and it may also account for the rising number of malpractice suits against physicians at a time when the technical level of medical care is the highest in history.

SPECIALIZATION.—Another development in medical practice in this country that has had adverse effects on the physician-patient relationship is the trend toward specialization and subspecialization by physicians. The specialist is, by definition, a physician who is highly trained in a specific area of medicine, such as anesthesiology, surgery, or psychiatry. A subspecialist is even more limited in his area of expertise. For example, a surgeon may restrict his practice to diseases involving the chest or heart, or an internist may decide to treat only the heart, kidneys, or blood. This is in contrast to the approach taken by primary-care physicians (i.e., those who are in family practice, general internal medicine, and pediatrics), which is to care for the entire patient.

In the early 1930s, more than 90% of the practicing physicians in the United States were involved full time in primary care. By 1970, this figure had fallen to about 50%, and by 1975 it had dropped to 38%.[12, 13] During this time, there has been a corresponding increase in the proportion of specialists and subspecialists in practice (Fig 24–2).

Specialization has brought with it many

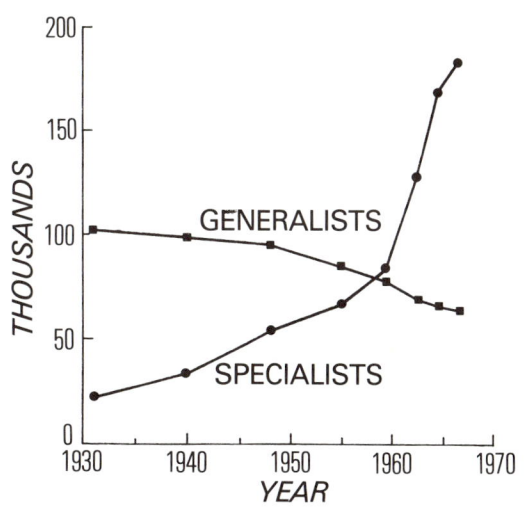

Fig 24–2.—Numbers of generalists and specialists in private practice in the United States. (From Code C.F.: *N. Engl. J. Med.* 283:679, 1970. Reprinted by permission.)

benefits; the most important is a higher quality of medical care for the public. Most specialists are better prepared by far to diagnose and treat the diseases in their area of expertise than the generalist. One drawback of specialized training in medicine is that a compartmentalization occurs with respect to the physician's view of the patient. Instead of considering "the whole patient" when evaluating and treating someone who is sick, there is a tendency to think only in terms of his diseased organ. To patients, it sometimes seems as though the specialist sees them as a "heart," a "brain," or a "kidney," depending on which organ is involved with the disease. When this happens, the technical medical needs of the patient are usually well taken care of (i.e., diagnosis and treatment of his disease), but his nontechnical needs are often neglected (i.e., the psychological and social aspects of his illness).

GROUP PRACTICE.—Another recent change in medical practice in this country has been the emergence of group practice as a means of health-care delivery. By *group practice*, we are referring to significant numbers of physicians (more than five) with varying specialty or subspecialty interests who practice together to benefit their patients and themselves. Group practice is a way of bringing several medical disciplines together "under one roof," thereby making readily available to the patient the expertise of a number of specialists. There are other advantages: for the patient, the cost of medical care is sometimes less, particularly if the group operates as a prepaid health maintenance organization (i.e., the patient pays a set fee in advance for all his medical care during the year); for the physician, it provides a means of sharing the work load, responsibility, and financial overhead of medical practice.

There are also disadvantages for the patient who is taken care of by physicians in group practice. One of these is the difficulty he may experience in finding a physician who will act as "his" physician. In other words, when he is ill he may see different specialists in the group, depending on his complaints, and may never establish a meaningful ongoing relationship with any one of them. Since it takes repeated contacts and shared experiences for a good physician-patient relationship to develop, the group practice arrangement tends to work against this goal.

BUREAUCRATIZATION.—Recent advances in medical knowledge and technology have been accompanied by public demand for more and better health-care services. This demand places a burden on the health-care system as increased numbers of people attempt to make use of it. Specialization, group practice, and the participation of various government and private agencies have made the system very complex indeed. Today, a patient seeking medical care is faced with several potential problems, including:
1. Finding a place where appropriate care is offered
2. Paying for the care
3. Finding his way among the various types of available care
4. Deciding what to do and who to go to if things don't go right[14]

The complexity of the health system and the difficulties experienced by people who try to make use of it have resulted in the growth of a bureaucratic organization of medical practice. McKinlay notes that "the single feature which most distinguishes present day medical practice from earlier forms—indeed has altered it almost beyond recognition—is its high degree of bureaucratization."[15] The familiar family physician who was in solo practice and made house calls has been replaced by a complex health-care delivery system. This system is centered about the modern community hospital with its multiple health-care personnel and sophisticated medical instrumentation. In addition to the community hospital, there are university medical centers, community health centers, health maintenance organizations, and so forth. A recent development in American medicine is the rise of a new medical-industrial complex, one in which private corporations are engaged in the business of providing health-care services for a profit.[16] It is estimated that in 1979 this industry had a gross income of 35-40 billion dollars, about a quarter of the amount spent for personal health care that year.[16] The direct line that the patient had to the physician in days past is being replaced with a bureaucratic organization in which the patient now interacts with institutions and representatives of institutions.

Bureaucratization of medical practice carries with it serious disadvantages, including a threat to the physician-patient relationship as we have known it in the past. Perhaps the greatest drawback is the tendency for a bureaucracy to deal with people in an impersonal manner. There is a certain built-in rigidity in the operation of bureaucratic organizations, which does not allow adequate consideration for the personal needs of the people using them. Thus, instead of being seen as an individual with special problems and concerns, the patient is likely to be considered as just another part of the "system."

Nature of the Patient's Illness

SCOPE OF ILLNESS.—To a large extent, the scope of an illness determines the nature of the physician-patient relationship that should develop. According to Fabrega and Van Egeren, sickness affects three distinct areas of human behavior.[17] First, it interferes with a person's capacity to carry out his physical activities and tasks. Second, there is a "social cost" created by illness since people who are ill may be unable to carry out their usual social roles, whether these be occupational, familial, recreational, or religious. Third, ill health has a psychological impact, causing emotional distress and disability.

The hope, indeed the expectation, of most patients is that the physician will try to understand and help them deal with their emotional and social problems as well as the physical aspects of their illness. In the opinion of some, this is best accomplished by a holistic or comprehensive approach to the delivery of health care, one that has been defined as the integration of knowledge of the body, mind, and environment in an effort to prevent disease, maintain health, and manage a patient's illness.[18] Although this approach is sometimes regarded as novel, Relman points out in a recent editorial that the precepts of holistic medicine are actually part of the tradition of medicine (as he puts it, "old friends" to the experienced clinician).[19] He admits, however, that they may "need a fresh introduction to some of our more technologic and narrowly focused colleagues."

SEVERITY OF AN ILLNESS.—Three models of the physician-patient interaction have been described by Szasz and Hollender (see also chapter 22) based on the severity of the patient's illness (Table 24–3).[20] In the *active-passive model*, the patient is acutely ill or in a coma. The physician does something *to* the patient, who is merely the passive recipient of his actions. There is no real human interaction between the two because the patient is almost inanimate.

When illness is less severe, the model of *guidance-cooperation* may form the basis for the physician-patient relationship. Here, the physician *directs* the patient's actions and the patient is expected to *cooperate* with the instructions he is given. This model is appropriate for certain types of serious illness, where the patient's welfare depends on following the physician's orders to the letter.

The model of *mutual participation*, in which the physician and patient work together as partners, is best suited for situations in which the patient is able and willing to play an active role in his medical care. Ostensibly, this would apply in the vast majority of nonacute medical illnesses. According to Szasz and Hollender, three elements should be present in a physician-patient relationship in order to utilize this model: first, the two parties should have approximately equal power; second, they should be dependent on each other; and third, they should be engaging in an activity that is mutually satisfying.

Szasz and Hollender note that the "control" exercised by the physician diminishes as one moves from the active-passive to the guid-

TABLE 24–3.—THE THREE BASIC MODELS OF THE DOCTOR-PATIENT RELATIONSHIP

MODEL	PHYSICIAN'S ROLE	PATIENT'S ROLE	CLINICAL APPLICATION OF MODEL	PROTOTYPE OF MODEL
Activity-passivity	Does something to patient	Recipient (unable to respond or inert)	Anesthesia, acute trauma, coma, delirium, etc.	Parent-infant
Guidance-cooperation	Tells patient what to do	Cooperator (obeys)	Acute infectious processes, etc.	Parent-child (adolescent)
Mutual participation	Helps patient to help himself	Participant in "partnership" (uses expert help)	Most chronic illnesses, psychoanalysis, etc.	Adult-adult

Source: Szasz T.S., Hollender M.H.: *Arch. Intern. Med.* 97:586. © 1956 by the American Medical Association. Reprinted with permission. Further reproduction prohibited without permission of copyright holder.

ance-cooperation to the mutual participation model. Conversely, the patient's identity as a "person" increases as one moves in the same direction. Thus, in these models of the physician-patient relationship there appears to be an inverse relationship between the physician's "control" of the interaction and the patient's identity as a "person."

In actual medical practice, it is not uncommon for a physician and a patient to shift from one model to another as the physical condition of the patient changes. For instance, a patient who is admitted to a hospital in a coma will be cared for according to the active-passive model; as he improves and becomes awake and alert, the relationship changes to one of guidance-cooperation; and finally, after the patient is discharged and begins a process of rehabilitation, the model of mutual participation applies.

Up to this point, the discussion has dealt with some of the psychological, sociocultural, and illness-related factors that affect communication between a physician and a patient. The material that was presented is mostly theoretical, because until recently there were few systematic studies dealing with the physician-patient relationship. One reason for this is that, for the most part, this relationship is a secluded and private element in the health-care system—one that is not easily amenable to objective assessment.[21]

With this discussion as a background, let us now turn our attention to a comparison of two models of the physician-patient relationship: the traditional and the humanistic.

THE TRADITIONAL AND HUMANISTIC MODELS OF THE PHYSICIAN-PATIENT RELATIONSHIP

In Figure 24-3, the interaction between a physician and his patient is depicted as a continuing range of behaviors on the part of the physician, with those representing the traditional model of the physician-patient relationship on the left and those that are part of the humanistic model on the right. Traditionally, the physician has assumed the role of an expert authority figure; in the humanistic model, his role is one of an educator-advisor. In any particular physician-patient relationship, the appropriate choice of the behaviors listed will depend on the goals and values of the physician and the condition of the patient.

The Traditional Model

DEFINITIONS.—Excerpts from the medical literature related to the role of the physician include the following:

When one looks at the literature of the field of Evaluation of Medical Care . . . it becomes apparent that the focus is on the management of pathological processes with little or no attempt to measure the degree to which the patient's problem, as he perceives it, has been solved. It deals more with the expectations of the physician and the Medical Model than the acceptance and satisfaction of the consumer. . . . The standards [of medical care] . . . are almost entirely concerned with the management of disease, the amount of scientific knowledge, and the facile use of standard technical practices.[22]

[The] image projected by textbooks for the beginning clinician may often be one of the doctor as investigator—a mind primarily involved in the collection of information. . . . the doctor does not express his own emotions. . . . He is seen most often as radically separate from the patient—an observer, a cataloguer and an analyzer.[23]

Thus, the professional model often presented to the student of medicine is one in which a rational scientific approach to diagnosis and therapy is emphasized, along with a relative lack of personal involvement. According to this model, the physician is to act primarily as a scientist in his interactions with patients. It is also recognized, however, that

Fig 24-3.—Developing the physician-patient relationship. Along the continuum the physician has a range of behaviors from which to choose and will move back and forth somewhat for each situation.

the physician cannot be totally oblivious to his own feelings or those of the patients. So he is advised to adopt a position of affective neutrality toward patients, meaning that he is to demonstrate empathy, consideration, insight, and intuition, but at the same time maintain a certain emotional distance.[24]

But affective neutrality is a contradiction in terms—affective relating to emotion and neutral to noninvolvement. The basic notion is that since the physician is often called on to deal with difficult situations of a life-and-death nature, he will become exhausted physically as well as emotionally if he gets too involved with his patient's problems. This seems logical, but there is a difference between being emotionally involved, as you would be with your own family or with intimates, and being a receptive, caring person. Few patients expect the first type of involvement, but most would consider the second to be quite desirable. The need for some degree of personal involvement on the part of the physician has been eloquently stated by Peabody:

> The essence of the practice of medicine is that it is an intensely personal matter. . . . At first sight this may not appear to be a very vital point, but it is, as a matter of fact, the crux of the whole situation. The treatment of a disease may be entirely impersonal; the care of a patient must be completely personal. The significance of the intimate personal relationship between physician and patient cannot be too strongly emphasized, for in an extraordinarily large number of cases both diagnosis and treatment are directly dependent on it, and the failure of the young physician to establish this relationship accounts for much of his ineffectiveness in the care of patients.[25]

THE INTERACTION BETWEEN THE PHYSICIAN AND THE PATIENT.—According to the traditional model, the physician, by virtue of his medical knowledge, is supposed to be the responsible, able participant. He is to "take charge," to direct the evaluation and care of the patient. He is active; the patient is passive and follows orders. In this model, a "good patient" is one who is

totally cooperative, trusts the doctor implicitly and does not question the reason or purpose of testing or therapy, is not curious, has no relatives who may become emotional or demand explanations, has emotions well under control and is stoical about pain, is a thorough and accurate observer of symptoms and an accurate historian of the past, and has a bodily disease which can be diagnosed and cured.[23]

The traditional model leaves little room for emotional interchange between the physician and the patient. The physician is supposed to keep his emotional involvement with the patient's problems to a minimum. Underlying this approach are several assumptions. One is that the physician "can think or can care, but . . . can't do both at the same time."[23] Another is that "you can feel or you can act, but you can't do both at the same time."[23] Clearly, these assumptions are largely misconceptions. They imply that a physician's thoughts and feelings must be separated, and that emotional involvement is incompatible with thinking and doing—ideas that are disproved by our everyday experiences. All of us know people who are very committed to the work they do, who render valuable service to people, and who, quite obviously, think and care simultaneously.

There is another false notion having to do with human interaction that, in effect, states that each person has a limited capacity for giving, caring, and loving, and that emotional conservation is necessary to preserve this capacity. So, if a physician expresses these feelings in his day-to-day work with patients, he will have little or no capacity left to interact on this level with those who are close to him, such as his family. Of course, this is not the case. In actuality, as you express feelings of caring and acceptance to others, you generate a greater capacity to do so.

In the traditional model, the behavior of the patient occurs in response to the role of the physician as described above. When the physician "takes charge," the patient relies on his judgment and decisions. Statements such as "Doctor, whatever you say I'll do" or "Please do something; I don't feel well" reflect this reliance on the physician. The physician, on the other hand, replies "Leave everything to me" or "Don't worry, I'll take care of you," indicating a paternalistic attitude toward the patient. This is a dependent-counterdependent type of interaction, which typically occurs when one person in a relationship is superior and the other is subordinate.

The Humanistic Model

Humanistic medical care can be traced back to Hippocrates, who is reported to have said, "Medicine is an art; one cannot know the nature of the body without knowing the nature of the universe."[26] In other words, the patient should not be looked upon as just someone with a disease; he also has a cultural heritage, social expectations, a life environment, and feelings about his illness.

ASSUMPTIONS OF THE HUMANISTIC MODEL.—Humanistic medical care can be described in terms of a series of assumptions that underlie this approach to the patient. One of these is: "The patient is more than his disease." A corollary to this is: "The health professional is more than a scientifically trained mind using technical skills."[27] That is to say, healing reaches its maximum potential when there is interaction between two "whole persons." This type of healing is more potent than treatment of just the disease itself.

A second assumption is: "A person is more than his body."[27] The patient has a body, mind, emotions, and a spirit, all of which have to be considered when interacting with that patient.

Third: "Each person has the capacity to define himself and be increasingly responsible for himself."[27] If the physician has this attitude, then he can guide the patient to an awareness of the patient's potential to help himself get better.

Fourth: "The health of each person involves an intricate relationship between past, present and future happenings."[27] The medical history should include material, social, ethical, and spiritual goals.

The fifth assumption is: "Physical disease and other apparent calamities of life, such as pain, suffering, aging and even death, can at times be seen as valuable and meaningful events in the life of an individual."[27] Thus, relieving symptoms or problems is not a sufficient strategy for dealing with the totality of human suffering.

Finally, the sixth assumption is: "A more fully humanistic medical approach will depend not only on the application of conventional skills, but also on other equally vital qualities such as intuition, inventiveness, and empathy, among many others."[27] These assumptions are not new ideals, but they have been somewhat forgotten in our modern technological approach to medical care. Presently, there is a rediscovery of the importance of these ideals, and humanistic medical care is the outgrowth of this movement.

NATURE OF THE INTERACTION BETWEEN THE PHYSICIAN AND THE PATIENT.—The basic approach to medical care in the humanistic model involves a contract or convenant* made between the physician and the patient, which establishes the roles, responsibilities, and expectations of each party.[28] In this contract, the physician and patient become collaborators, sharing responsibility for the patient's health care.

What is the role of the physician? He acts as a collaborator, an educator, a source of emotional and social support, and a technical consultant for the patient, as well as fulfilling his usual roles of diagnostician and therapist. He assumes that his patients will share the responsibility for the maintenance of their health and for their care if they become ill. The humanistic physician helps his patients to understand the nature of an illness and its effects on their lives.

What role does the patient play in the humanistic model? He is a participant in his care, sharing authority and responsibility with his physician. Above all, there is a sharing of decision-making, so that the patient maintains "freedom and control over his own life and destiny when significant choices are to be made."[28] The patient is the "expert" when it comes to himself and the impact of illness on

---

*The terms *contract* and *covenant* are used in a symbolic, not a legalistic, sense.

his life; the physician is the medical expert. The patient is an active, responsible adult; although a part of his body may be dysfunctional due to disease, the remainder, including his mind, is functional. He has feelings about his illness, and when treated he expects his entire being to be taken into consideration. He can take an active part in healing himself.

The humanistic model of the physician-patient relationship requires a major alteration in traditional medical thinking. In this model, the physician is no longer in control since the responsibility of patient care is shared with the patient. In fact, one of the physician's principal concerns is how he can help the patient regain control of his life after this control has been disrupted by illness. Obviously, the humanistic model involves a different kind of communication with the patient than the traditional model, on both the technical and the nontechnical levels. The patient who is oriented to the humanistic model might ask, "What can I do to help myself get better?" or "What is my responsibility in treatment?" If the physician is not accustomed to a humanistic model, he will be unable to respond to these questions.

Sometimes a physician who is oriented to a humanistic approach encounters a patient who expects a traditional type of physician-patient relationship. The physician should educate the patient by explicit statements, such as: "Here's what I can do to help you; here's what you will have to do. Is that clear? Any questions?" or "Let's review; you will do X, and I will do Y." Or, "Do you feel clear about why you are getting these treatments and what the medicine will do?"

It is not only what the physician says, but how he says it. Nonverbal communication is important! The tone of voice that is gentle yet strong, direct yet available to questions, is essential. A demeanor that communicates "I am interested in you and concerned about you" says more than words. Conversely, tapping fingers, glancing at a watch or chart, or talking without looking at the patient sends the opposite message—that the physician is not *really* interested. The patient knows from a physician's nonverbal behavior when he is impatient, bored, or feeling pressure.

ADVANTAGES OF THE HUMANISTIC MODEL.—The most significant reason to use a humanistic model rather than a traditional one in the care of patients is that it is a more effective means of delivering health care. This is true with respect to both the maintenance of health and the treatment of disease. Where and how an individual lives and works have more to do with his health than perhaps any other factors. From this standpoint, the responsibility for the state of a person's health lies to a large extent with the individual. The nature of his diet, life-style, personal habits, home and work environment, activity pattern, and life stress can be modified only through the efforts of the person involved. Thus, a model of the physician-patient relationship that gives full recognition to the patient's responsibility in these areas, i.e., the humanistic model, is far more realistic than one that places most of the responsibility in the hands of the physician. One goal of the humanistic model is to have the patient work along with his physician as a partner to maintain the patient's health at an optimal level. In the area of health maintenance, the physician serves mainly as an educator and a consultant.

What about the treatment of disease? This aspect of medical care often involves changing a patient's personal life. Without the patient's cooperation (which means accepting the responsibility to make the change), this form of therapy cannot be successful. Moreover, patient compliance is obviously a critical factor in the success of drug therapy. Under the traditional model of the physician-patient relationship, patient compliance with programs of medical care has been rather poor, with as many as 50% of all patients failing to adhere to their physician's advice. Undoubtedly, some of this noncompliance can be explained by a lack of proper communication between physician and patient, and the failure of the physician to share the responsibility for medical care with the patient. For example, a physician who is alert to verbal and nonverbal clues indicating that the patient is not grasping treatment instructions will be more likely to take the time, when necessary, to explain properly to a patient what he is to do and why. Also, a physician who is sensitive to his patient's feelings will have a greater chance of picking up clues of resistance, confusion, and lack of motivation—all of which indicate the need to help the patient understand more about his illness and treatment.

In general, patients who participate with their physician in making decisions about their medical care are more committed to carry out this care successfully. A patient who is actively involved in planning his own care will have a greater motivation to comply with medical instructions than one who is a passive recipient of orders.

A second major advantage of the humanistic approach is that it aids in the early diagnosis of disease. A patient will more likely go to his physician with mild symptoms and subtle changes in his health if the physician is his collaborator, someone who is very receptive and interested in his concerns. Being readily available to his patients is a cardinal element of the physician's role in the humanistic model. Being receptive and interested in even the smallest of his patient's problems is another of these elements.

Most patients are hesitant to "bother their doctor" with complaints unless they are quite ill, because they consider him to be a very busy person (a feeling, by the way, that many physicians and office staffs intentionally convey to their patients). The humanistic physician actively encourages his patients to call him and makes them feel at ease when they do so. Such a physician is much more likely to have patients consult him in an early stage of their illness, while their symptoms are still mild. Since early diagnosis and treatment often lead to a more favorable outcome of an illness, this approach is clearly in the patient's best interests.

A third advantage of the humanistic approach, and by no means the least important, is that it makes the delivery of medical care a more rewarding experience for both the physician and the patient. A physician who thinks in terms of people rather than just the diseases they have will find the practice of medicine more fulfilling emotionally. A practice will become a source of an infinite variety of people, with their strengths and weaknesses, hopes and disappointments, successes and failures, rather than an endless array of symptoms and signs. Because the humanistic physician explores with the patient the unique meaning of his illness within his life, the patient greatly benefits. "Going to the doctor" will produce less anxiety and fear if the physician is an open, warm, caring individual. By participating with his physician in decision-making, the patient will feel that he is at least partly in control of what happens to him—a very reassuring feeling when one is sick and under medical care.

In describing his personal experiences "fighting cancer," Fiore has graphically described the importance that patients attach to the humanistic approach and how much they benefit from its use.[29] Referring to cancer treatment programs that incorporate the humanistic model, he states:

These programs offer patients an opportunity to participate actively in their own recovery, to take responsibility for their own health care, and to regain a sense of control over their bodies. Such programs clearly communicate to patients that they need not act like helpless victims.[29]

Fiore goes on to define the role of the patient that he feels should be part of all cancer therapy programs:

[This] approach to the patient with cancer uses a team of experts, including the patients, as experts on their own feelings and the reactions of their bodies, and the ones ultimately responsible for their lives.[29]

WHAT IS NEEDED TO BE A HUMANISTIC PHYSICIAN.—It goes almost without saying that a strong commitment on the part of the physician is necessary if he is to utilize the humanistic model effectively in his interaction with patients. There must be a willingness to "give of himself" and to take the time to educate his patients to their role and responsibilities in the relationship. To some physicians, this approach comes easier than it does to others by virtue of their personalities and social background. Some are never able to adopt the humanistic model for the same reasons.

Initially it may take extra time for a physician to interact on a humanistic basis, to act as an educator and consultant to his patients, and to involve them in the decision-making process. However, such time is well spent. This is clearly pointed out by Blumgart:

> One frequently hears the comment, "Well there is the problem of time. We are too busy ascertaining the fundamental organic status of the patient to probe into his personality and ascertain the kind of person who has the disease." My reply is clear. In the first place, unless one knows the person, the diagnosis will frequently be incomplete or inaccurate. In the second place, if the physician tries to learn about the person with the disease from the very first moment they meet, it will take very little more time, and in some cases no more time, than the usual trite, narrow approach to the patient. In the third place, the treatment may not be effective. And, lastly, the physician will be missing one of the most fascinating and rewarding aspects of our profession.[30]

In the long run, the time spent with the patient may actually be shorter using the humanistic approach as opposed to the traditional one, because the patient will become more self-sufficient. Once he has a better understanding of his illness and the rationale of treatment, a patient is less likely to need repeated visits or to make unnecessary phone calls to clarify confusing matters about his medical care.

Having a commitment and taking the time to implement the humanistic model are not enough; the physician must also possess special skills. Truax and Carkhuff identified three qualities that are necessary for a helping relationship—empathy, genuineness, and warmth.[31] Being able to communicate these to a patient requires the development of the capacity for listening, giving "caring" attention, reflecting, expressing emotions, exhibiting judgmental understanding, and providing psychological support. It is most important that the physician demonstrate a willingness to listen to *all* aspects of the patient's illness, not just a recitation of his symptoms. Only by doing so will a physician discover what an illness means to a patient within the context of his life and how he feels about being ill.

The physician should not only listen, but listen with "caring attention" to the patient. In other words, by means of verbal and nonverbal communication he should try to convey to the patient that he is listening with *concern and empathy*, that he is sincerely involved in an effort to help the patient solve his problems.

Reflecting requires that the physician restrains himself from voicing his own viewpoint on a subject and, instead, becomes a mirror for his patient. This skill would be demonstrated by a statement such as "It sounds as though you're worried about something" rather than "Have you thought of doing such and such?" The first response conveys great caring and empathy to the patient. It also models the notion that solutions to human problems are in the patient and that the physician serves as a catalyst by enabling the patient to find his own solution. The physician can provide information, educate him about his options, and urge him to seek another opinion, but in the end it must be the patient's decision, assuming he is physically and mentally able to make decisions.

Being able to recognize how one feels about someone or something and having the capacity to express one's emotions appropriately are critical skills for the physician who wishes to adopt the humanistic model. Many people have lost these skills, which they had as children, as a result of the socialization process. For a long time, medical education has inculcated in the physician the need to control his feelings and emotions, so it is common to find physicians who are out of touch with their feelings and who deny their emotions. Obviously, this restricts the kinds of relationships they can develop with other people, especially their patients. For such physicians, a reeducation of emotions may be necessary. Of course, the goal is not to produce emotionality per se, but rather to encourage the utilization and acceptance of a wide range of behaviors on the part of the physician. The fully functioning human being is, according to Carl Rogers, "congruent": He is aware of what he is feeling or thinking and can make choices about how to communicate.

Every physician treats patients who say or do things that he thinks are "wrong." Being human, physicians may find that they like some patients more than others because of their personal characteristics, background, life-style, or even the illness they have. The humanistic physician, while recognizing the human tendency to "judge others" on the basis of one's own values, tries to care for his patients as much as possible with nonjudgmental understanding.

In addition to the humanistic skills listed above, the physician who uses this approach in his practice should have adequate knowledge of the behavioral sciences as these apply to medical practice. Educational programs covering these subjects have been introduced into most medical schools, primarily at the preclinical level. Unfortunately, there is still a hesitancy on the part of many clinical faculty members to incorporate this kind of learning experience into the clinical training of physicians. Medical psychology, sociology, and anthropology are essential ingredients of a well-rounded medical education today, and they have critical importance to the humanistic physician in his day-to-day practice.

SUMMARY

Recent advances in medical technology and biomedical science, although threatening to change the nature of the physician-patient relationship, have not diminished its importance. This relationship has always been and will continue to be the central element of medical practice. Nevertheless, it appears to many of the public as though physicians are paying less attention to the nontechnical or humanistic aspects of patient care than they did in the past. Concern about this trend is reflected by a decreasing level of respect and admiration for the medical profession, at a time when the diagnostic and therapeutic skills of physicians are the most highly developed in history.

Communication between the physician and patient is influenced by many psychological and sociocultural factors, some of which are discussed in this chapter. It should be clear that the interaction that occurs on both the technical and nontechnical levels is a complex process that defies simple analysis.

Two models of the physician-patient relationship, the traditional and the humanistic, are compared in order to give the reader some idea of the change in thinking about this relationship that is taking place in our society. In the traditional model the physician assumes a paternalistic role, that of an authority figure who makes the medical decisions and ministers to the patient's needs. The humanistic model encourages the patient to participate actively in his medical care, sharing the decision-making process with his physician, who acts primarily as an educator-advisor.

REFERENCES

1. Tumulty P.A.: What is a clinician and what does he do? *N. Engl. J. Med.* 283:20, 1970.
2. Mayerson E.W.: *Putting the Ill at Ease*. Hagerstown, Md., Harper & Row, 1976.
3. Freud S.: The dynamics of transference, in *The Standard Edition of the Complete Psychological Works of Sigmund Freud*. London, Hogarth Press, 1958, vol. 12.
4. Vaillant G.E., Sobowale N.C., McArthur C.: Some psychologic vulnerabilities of physicians. *N. Engl. J. Med.* 287:372, 1972.
5. Vaillant G.E., Brighton J.R., McArthur C.: Physicians use of mood-altering drugs. *N. Engl. J. Med.* 282:365, 1970.
6. AMA Council on Mental Health: The sick physician: Impairment by psychiatric disorders, including alcoholism and drug dependence. *J.A.M.A.* 223(6):684, 1973.
7. Henderson L.J.: The patient and physician as a social system. *N. Engl. J. Med.* 212:819, 1935.
8. Parsons T.: *The Social System*. Glencoe, Ill., The Free Press, 1951.
9. Bloom S.W.: *The Doctor and His Patient*. New York, The Free Press, 1965.
10. Bloom S.W., Summey P.: Models of the doc-

tor-patient relationship: A history of the social system concept, in *The Doctor-Patient Relationship in the Changing Health Scene*, U.S. Department of Health, Education, and Welfare Publication No. (NIH) 78–183, 1976.
11. Papper S.: The undesirable patient. *J. Chronic Dis.* 22:777, 1970.
12. Code C.F.: Determinants of medical care—A plan for the future. *N. Engl. J. Med.* 283:679, 1970.
13. Califano J.: The government-medical education partnership. *J. Med. Educ.* 54:19, 1979.
14. Ehrenreich B., Ehrenreich J.: The system behind the chaos, in Millon T. (ed.): *Medical Behavioral Science*. Philadelphia, W.B. Saunders Co., 1975.
15. McKinlay J.B.: The changing political and economic context of the patient-physician encounter, in *The Doctor-Patient Relationship in the Changing Health Scene*. U.S. Department of Health, Education, and Welfare Publication No. (NIH) 78–183, 1976.
16. Relman A.S.: The new medical-industrial complex. *N. Engl. J. Med.* 303:963, 1980.
17. Fabrega H., Van Egeren L.: A behavioral framework for the study of human disease. *Ann. Intern. Med.* 84:200, 1976.
18. Menninger R.W.: Psychiatry 1976, time for a holistic medicine, editorial. *Ann. Intern. Med.* 84:603, 1976.
19. Relman A.S.: Holistic medicine, editorial. *N. Engl. J. Med.* 300:312, 1979.
20. Szasz, T.S., Hollender, M.H.: A contribution to the philosophy of medicine: Three basic models of the doctor-patient relationship. *Arch. Intern. Med.* 97:585, 1956.
21. Gallagher E.B.: Conference background and objectives, in *The Doctor-Patient Relationship in the Changing Health Scene*, U.S. Department of Health, Education, and Welfare Publication No. (NIH) 78–183, 1976.
22. Schatz B.: Evaluation of the humanistic component of the quality of medical care, in Miller S., Miller S. (eds.): *First Report of the Program in Humanistic Medicine*. San Francisco, The Program in Humanistic Medicine, 1974, p. 67.
23. Remen N., Blau A.A., Hively R.: *The Masculine Principle, The Feminine Principle and Humanistic Medicine*. San Francisco, Institute for the Study of Humanistic Medicine, 1975.
24. Braunstein J. (ed.): Introduction to Medicine and Behavioral Science: A Syllabus. Part II—Social and Cultural Aspects of Medicine, personal document, p. 32.
25. Peabody F.W.: The care of the patient. *J.A.M.A.* 88:877–882, 1927.
26. Heidel W.A.: *Hippocratic Medicine: Its Spirit and Method*. New York, Columbia University Press, 1941.
27. Belknap M.M., Blau R.A., Grossman R.N.: *Case Studies and Methods in Humanistic Medical Care*. San Francisco, Institute for the Study of Humanistic Medicine, 1975.
28. Veatch R.M.: Models for ethical medicine in a revolutionary age. What physician-patient roles foster the most ethical relationship? *Hastings Cent. Rep.* 2(3):5–7, June 1972.
29. Fiore N.: Fighting cancer—One's patient's perspective. *N. Engl. J. Med.* 300:284, 1979.
30. Blumgart H.L.: Caring for the patient. *N. Engl. J. Med.* 270:449, 1964.
31. Truax E., Carkhuff R.: *Toward Effective Counseling and Psychotherapy: Training and Practice*. Chicago, Aldine Publishing Company, 1967.

Name Index

Numbers in italics refer to material in this book.

A

Abel, B., 262
Ackerman, S.H., 190
Adams, R.D., 54
Ader, R., 190
Adlin, E.V., 406, 416
Agle, D.P., 467, 469
Agras, W.S., 191
Ahrens, E.H., 254, 262
Ainsworth, M.D.S., 325
Aitken, R.C.B., 190
Alexander, F., 164, 165, 180, 188
Allan, W.S., 54
Allen, M.G., 20, 25
Allen, T.W., 350
Alp, M.H., 190
Amorin, J.K.E., 239
Amsterdam, J.D., 75
Anastasi, A., 142
Anch, A.M., 79, 93
Anders, T., 306
Anderson, C., 210, 217
Anderson, H.H., 142
Anderson, L., 142
Anthony, E.J., 211, 217
Antonovsky, A., 199, 216
Aoki, K., 24, 189
Apple, D., 239
Appleton, W.S., 217
Arieti, S., 217, 399
Arlin, P.K., 349
Åsberg, M., 75
Aserinsky, 80
Auerbach, O., 262
Auerbach, V.H., 24
Austen, K.F., 177, 190
Avioli, L.V., 416
Axelrod, J., 54
Ayllon, T., 350
Azrin, N.H., 323, 324, 326

B

Baca, J., 239
Bach, E., 326
Baer, D.M., 324, 325
Baker, B.L., 349
Baldessarini, R.J., 66, 75
Balint, M., 469
Bandura, A., 118, 142, 306, 382
Barbero, G.J., 319, 326
Barlingham, D., 306
Barrow, C.G., 190
Barsky, A.J., 469
Barth, L.G., 23
Barth, L.J., 23
Bates, E., 325
Bateson, M.C., 93
Baum, G.L., 467, 469
Baumann, B., 451, 453
Bauwens, E., 239
Beard, O.W., 189
Beatty, J., 191
Beaumont, W., 190
Becerra, R.M., 362
Beck, A., 118
Beck, S.J., 142
Becker, C.E., 292
Becker, J.M., 25
Becker, M.H., 478, 483
Becker, P.E., 25
Beckmann, H., 75
Beecher, H.K., 54
Behrman, R.E., 13, 298, 319, 348, 367, 381
Beintema, D.L., 308
Belknap, M.M., 501
Bellugi, U., 349
Benedict, H., 325, 326
Benjamin, B., 431
Benke, P.J., *1–25*
Benson, H., 171, 189, 191
Benson, J., 118
Berg, J.M., 24
Berger, P.A., 71, 75, 76, 78, 79, 80, 93
Bergman, A.B., 471, 483
Bergsma, D., 24
Berkman, L.F., 191, 215
Berko, J., 349
Berle, E., 239
Bernstein, L., 190
Berstein, B., 326
Bianchi, G., 189
Bijou, S.W., 324, 325
Birch, H.J., 325

Bistrian, B.R., 292
Black, A.H., 191
Blackburn, G.L., 269, 291
Blau, A.A., 501
Bleecker, E.R., 191
Block, J., 190
Blombery, P.A., 75
Bloom, F., 54, 76
Bloom, L., 322, 326, 349
Bloom, S.W., 453, 469, 488, 489, 490, 500
Blumgart, H.L., 501
Boghen, D., 93
Borgatta, E.F., 382
Bowden, C.L., 396, 400
Bowlby, J., 306, 316, 326
Boyar, R.M., 381
Bozeman, M.F., 213, 217
Bracht, G.A., 142
Brackbill, Y., 325
Bradshaw, F., 262
Brady, J.P., 191
Braine, M.D.S., 326
Bramwell, S.T., 162
Brand, R.J., 190
Brandfonbrener, M., 405, 416
Braunstein, J.J., *1–25, 55–93, 97–105, 119–191, 241–306, 363–382, 401–431, 435–453, 454–469, 484–494,* 501
Bray, G.A., 291
Brener, J., 191
Brenner, C., 117
Brenner, M.H., 216
Brest, A.M., 416
Briese, E., 54
Briggs, A.H., 191
Brighton, J.R., 500
Brill, A.B., 262
Brill, H., 25
Brill, L., 292
Brill, R.A., 162
Brooks, J., 349
Broughton, R.J., 93
Brown, A.L., 349
Brown, R., 326, 349
Brown, W.A., 75
Bruch, H., 213, 217

503

Bryant, P.E., 349
Budzynski, T.H., 191
Buhler, C., 383, 384, 399
Bukantz, S., 190
Bullough, B., 217
Bunney, W.E., 75, 76
Bunzel, J.H., 416
Burgess, M., 189
Burros, O.K., 142
Burstein, A.G., 396, 400
Burt, D.R., 76
Bush, W.J., 142
Buss, A.N., 325
Busse, E.W., 306, 416
Butler, R.M., 390, 400, 414, 416
Butler, S.R., 326
Byck, R., 292

C

Cade, R., 74, 76
Cadieux, R., 93
Cadoret, R.J., 25
Cahalan, D., 292
Caldwell, B.M., 326
Calhoun, J.F., 125, 126
Califano, J., 501
Camaioni, L., 325
Campbell, J.D., 449, 453
Cannon, W.B., 146, 161, 162, 166, 234
Carey, R.G., 423, 431
Carkhuff, R., 499, 501
Carroll, B.J., 75
Carroll, V., 190
Cassell, E., 453
Cassem, N.H., 465, 469
Catlin, D.H., 76
Cautela, J., 114, 118
Chambers, C.D., 286, 292
Chandler, M.J., 24
Chang, S.S., 292
Chapman, M.L., 188
Charney, E., 483
Chebanian, A.V., 189
Chess, S., 306, 325
Chester, E.H., 469
Chiriboga, D., 400
Chomsky, C., 340, 349
Christakis, G., 262
Cisin, I., 289, 292
Clairborne, R., 22
Clark, D.W., 244
Clark, E.V., 326
Clark, M., 221, 222, 238
Clarke, H.H., 262

Cluff, L.E., 471, 483
Cobb, S., 189, 191, 455, 469, 471, 483
Cobwell, R.E., 24
Code, C.F., 491, 501
Cofer, C.N., 326
Cohen, L.B., 325
Cohen, S., 93, 266, 291
Cohn, M.A., 77, 87, 88
Collard, R.R., 325
Condon, W.S., 325
Conger, J.J., 10, 24, 325, 381
Cooper, J.R., 54
Cornell, E.H., 325
Corner, G.W., 349
Costanzo, P.R., 382
Cousins, N., 427, 431
Cowie, V.A., 18, 25
Cox, D.J., 191
Crampton, D.R., 1–25
Crandall, B.F., 16
Cravioto, J., 306
Crawford, C., 205, 217
Creger, W.P., 75
Crome, L., 24
Cromwell, R.L., 142
Cronbach, L.J., 142
Croog, S.H., 239
Croseley, H.M., 292
Cummings, S.T., 214, 217
Cummiskey, J., 93
Currey, H., 292
Curtis, E.B., 483
Czaczkes, J.W., 469

D

Dahl, L.K., 170, 171, 189, 262
Dahlstrom, L.E., 142
Dahlstrom, W.G., 142
Dale, P.S., 326, 349
Dancis, J., 22
Dauth, G.W., 191
Davidson, R.S., 191
Davies, D.F., 416
Davies, D.T., 190
Davis, F., 213, 217
Davis, G.C., 416
Davis, K.L., 75
Davis, M.S., 479, 483
Davison G.C., 109, 118
DeGroot, L.J., 262
De Hoyos, A., 216
De Hoyos, G., 216
Dekirmenjian, H., 75
Dekker, F., 190
DeLeo, J., 191

DeLong, G.K., 326
De Luise, M., 269, 291
Dembroski, T.M., 188, 190
Dement, W., 80, 82, 93, 306
Dennis, W., 326
De-Nour, A.K., 469
DeQuattro, V.Y., 189
Detre, T.P., 142
Deuschle, K., 239
Deutsch, A., 216
Deutscher, I., 469
DiFrancesco, G.F., 189
Dobbing, J., 24
Dobbs, J.B., 338
Dobzhansky, T., 3, 23
Dodds, J.B., 349
Dohan, F.C., 75
Dohrenwend, B.P., 156, 158, 162
Dohrenwend, B.S., 156, 158, 162
Domschke, W., 76
Donovan, J.E., 276
Doyle, J.L., 239
Drinker, P., 261
Dudley, D.L., 469
Duff, R.S., 209, 210, 217
Dunbar, F., 164, 188
Duncan, G.G., 292
Dunphy, D.C., 368, 372, 376, 382
Dupont, R.L., 292
Dutta, S.N., 291, 292
Dye, H.B., 326
D'Zurilla, T., 115, 118

E

Ebel, R.L., 142
Eby, C.E., 480, 483
Eccles, J.C., 54
Edmonds, M., 326
Edwards, A.B., 216
Egeland, J.A., 220, 237, 238, 240
Ehlers, K.H., 24
Ehrenpreis, S., 291
Ehrenreich, B., 501
Ehrenreich, J., 501
Eilers, R.E., 325
Eimas, P., 325
Eisdorfer, C., 416
Ellis, A., 115, 118
Ely, D.L., 189
Emery, H., 24
Eney, R.D., 483
Engel, B.T., 183, 191

Name Index

Engel, G.L., 157, 162, 164, 166, 188, 429, 431
Ennis, R.H., 349
Epstein, F., 262
Erbe, R.W., 24
Erfurt, J.C., 189
Erikson, E., 299, 300, 306, 310, 322, 333, 341, 355, 361, 368, 381, 383, 399, 416
Erikson, E.H., 300
Ervin, F.R., 45, 54
Eskin, B.A., 400
Esler, M., 189
Estrin, L., *351–362*
Evans, H.S., 142
Extein, L., 75
Eysenck, H.J., 106, 117

F

Fabrega, H., 238, 493, 501
Fagan, J.F., 325
Farquhar, J.W., 260, 263
Farrington, D.P., 382
Fatt, P., 54
Faulkender, P.V., 320, 326
Fawcett, J., 75
Feinberg, I., 93
Feinstein, R.J., 444, 453
Feld, M., 24
Feldman, J.G., 262
Feldman, J.J., 216
Fenna, D., 228, 239
Fernandez-Marina, B., 239
Ferris, B.G., 244
Field, T., 382
Fieve, R., 25
Figureroa, W.G., 262
Filmore, C., 326
Findley, J.D., 189
Fink, P.J., 400
Fiore, N., 501
Fischer, 19
Fish, B., 306
Fisher, C., 93, 306
Fishman, H., 216
Fitzgerald, H.E., 340, 382
Fitzgerald, J.J., 244
Fixen, D.L., 382
Flavell, J.H., 306, 349
Fleiss, J.L., 25
Flier, J.S., 269, 291
Foch, T.T., 270, 291
Fontana, V.J., 361
Fordtran, J.S., 179, 180, 190

Foreyt, J.P., 262
Forsyth, R.P., 169, 189
Foss, M., 325
Foster, G.M., 239
Foulkes, 80
Fox, R.C., 208, 217
Fox, U., 189
Foxx, R.M., 326
Frailberg, S., 306
Francis, V., 483
Frand, U.I., 292
Frank, K.A., 258, 263
Frankel, B.L., 83, 84, 93
Frankel, E., 383, 384
Frankenburg, W.K., 338, 349
Fraser, C., 326
Freedman, A.M., 93, 117, 141, 142, 190, 400
Freedman, D.X., 306
Freeman, H., 239
Frei, E., III, 292
Freidrichs, A.G., 349
French, A.P., 314
Freshbach, S., 326
Freud, A., 295, 305, 306
Freud, S., 52, 97, 98, 99, 100, 117, 164, 299, 310, 315, 322, 341, 306, 500
Freundlish, C., 191
Friar, L.R., 191
Fried, M., 216
Friedman, M., 172, 189, 190, 262
Friedman, R., 189
Friedson, E., 469
Fries, J.F., 416
Fries, M., 295, 296, 305
Frohlich, E.D., 189
Fulton, J.F., 44, 54

G

Gabay, S., 18, 19, 25, 75, 79, 93, 291
Galen, 439
Gallagher, E.B., 501
Galloway, S.P., 480, 483
Gans, H., 236, 240
Gardner, B.T., 54
Gardner, R.A., 54
Garrison, K.C., 372, 373, 382
Garrison, K.C., Jr., 372, 373, 382
Gary, L.R., 471, 481
Gath, A., 317, 318, 334, 349
Gazden, C., 349

Geer, J.H., 118
Gelman, R., 329, 348
Genest, J., 189
Gerald, P.S., 24
German, J., 24
Gerner, R.H., 76
Gershon, E.S., 25, 93
Geschwind, N., 47, 54
Gesell, A., 298
Gewirtz, J.L., 325
Gibberd, F.B., 93
Gibson, G., 451, 453
Gilliam, W., 189
Gillin, J.C., 75, 92, 93
Gilman, A., 283
Giovannoni, J.M., 362
Girard, D.E., 431
Girdand, D.D., 291
Girdano, D.A., 291
Glass, D.C., 173, 190
Glick, I.O., 431
Glomset, J.A., 188
Gold, M.S., 75, 292
Gold, P.W., 63, 64, 75
Goldberg, P., 142
Goldfried, M., 109, 115, 118
Goldman, R., 416
Goldstein, E.O., 483
Gomberg, W., 216, 238, 469
Gonda, T.A., 203, 216
Goodenough, 80
Goodman, L.S., 283
Goodwin, D.W., 266, 291, 292
Goodwin, F.K., 75
Gordon, B., 212, 213, 217
Gordon, E.K., 75
Gordon, G., 217
Gordon, T., 188, 230, 239, 262
Gottesman, I.I., 19, 25
Gould, R.L., 300, 306, 384, 385, 386, 391, 399, 400
Graham, J.D.P., 189
Graham, S., 228, 239
Green, A., 361, 362
Green, E.E., 191
Greenblatt, D.J., 93
Greene, M., 291, 292
Greene, W.A., 431
Greenfield, P., 325
Greenfill, R.F., 191
Grenell, R.G., 18, 19, 25, 75, 79, 93, 291
Griffin, P., 191
Grinspoon, L., 292
Groen, J., 190

Groliker, B.V., 217
Gross, H., 216
Grosser, E., 240
Grossman, H.J., 142
Grossman, M.I., 190
Grossman, R.N., 501
Grossman, S., 469
Grover, W.D., 24
Gruen, P.H., 68, 76
Gruendel, J., 325, 326
Guggenheim, F.G., 291
Guilleminault, C., 82, 83, 93
Gunne, L.M., 73, 76
Guroff, J.J., 25
Guthrie, E.R., 105, 117

H

Hackett, T.P., 420, 431, 465, 469
Hague, W., 469
Haley, J., 381
Hall, J.G., 24
Hamilton, J.A., 172, 189
Hamilton, M., 190
Hammond, E.C., 248, 261
Hampson, J.D., 349
Hampson, J.G., 349
Hanson, J.W., 292
Hansson, L., 189
Harburg, E., 189
Harley, G.W., 239
Harlow, H.F., 304, 306, 316, 326, 349
Harlow, M.H., 326, 349
Harms, R.T., 326
Harrell, A.V., 292
Harris, A.H., 189
Harris, L., 259
Hartmann, E., 93
Hartung, G.H., 262
Harwood, A., 235, 239, 453
Hathaway, S.R., 142
Hauri, P., 81, 93
Hauser, P.M., 197, 215
Hauser, S.L., 326
Havenstein, L.S., 189
Hawkins, N.G., 162
Haynes, R.B., 473, 474, 475, 476, 478, 480, 481, 483
Haynes, S.N., 191
Hebeler, J., 361
Heibert, M., 216
Heidel, W.A., 501
Heimbuch, R.C., 25
Heine, M., 189
Helfer, R.E., 362
Helgason, T., 381

Helmuth, J., 306
Henderson, L.J., 488, 500
Henry, J.P., 170, 188, 189
Hensley, M.J., 93
Herbert, M., 349
Herbert, V., 75
Herd, J.A., 167, 188, 189
Heston, L.L., 19, 25
Hill, J.P., 349
Hill, M.J., 262
Hill, O., 191
Hingson, R., 263, 483
Hilton, S.M., 189
Hirschhorn, L., 391, 400
Hively, R., 501
Hjer-Pederson, W., 190
Hobbs, N., 142
Hobson, J.A., 54, 80
Hodgkin, A.L., 54
Hofer, M.A., 190
Hoffman, 290
Hoffman, E., 306
Hoffman, L.W., 326, 349, 382
Hoffman, M.L., 326, 349, 382
Hokanson, J.E., 189
Holland, J., 431
Holland, W.C., 191
Hollender, M.H., 461, 462, 469, 493, 501
Hollingshead, A.B., 209, 210, 217
Hollister, L.E., 59, 75
Holmes, T.H., 144, 155, 156, 162
Holmes, T.S., 155, 162
Holroyd, J.C., 191
Hopkins, K.D., 142
Horowitz, F.D., 24
Hoyt, J.D., 349
Hsia, D.Y.Y., 24
Hudgens, R.W., 381
Hudson, R.P., 453
Hughes, J., 54
Hughes, J.V., 24
Hughes, M.C., 295–306
Hulka, B.S., 483
Humphrey, F.J., 93
Hunt, J.M., 306, 326
Hunt, R., 216
Hurlock, E.B., 342, 349
Huttenlocher, J., 325
Huxley, A.F., 54
Hyde, R.T., 262

I

Ing, P., 4
Inhelder, B., 325, 381

Ito, M., 54
Iwai, J., 189

J

Jaco, E.G., 216
Jacob, F., 23
Jacobsen, C.F., 44, 54
Jacobson, A., 93
Jacobson, E., 111, 118
Jacobson, S., 55–93, 97–105, 119–142
Jacquet, Y.F., 76
Jaffe, A.C., 361
Jaffe, J.J., 283
James, Q., 216
Janis, I.L., 469
Jarvik, M.E., 292
Jasper, H., 40
Jeffrey, W.E., 325
Jeffreys, M., 400
Jenkins, C.D., 189, 190
Jensen, A.R., 10, 24
Jensen, M.M., 188
Jersild, A.T., 349
Jessner, L., 306
Jessor, R., 276
Johns, M.W., 93
Johnson, R.C., 24, 349
Johnson, T.C., 24
Johnson, W.G., 191
Johnston, R.B., 135
Jones, K.L., 24
Jones, M.C., 105, 117
Jonsson, A., 189
Jouvet, M., 40, 54, 80
Joy, V., 217
Julius, S., 172, 189
Juomilehto, J., 263
Jusezyk, P., 325

K

Kadushin, C., 216
Kagan, J., 325, 326
Kagen, J., 10, 24, 381
Kales, A., 78, 80, 86, 93
Kales, J.D., 93
Kaliner, M., 190
Kallmann, F.J., 18, 19, 25
Kandal, W., 350
Kane, R., 416
Kannel, W., 188, 262
Kanner, L., 316, 326
Kanter, J.F., 381
Kanter, N.J., 110, 118
Kantorovich, N.V., 105, 117

NAME INDEX

Kaplan, H.F., 381
Kaplan, H.I., 93, 190
Kaplan, N.M., 171
Karacan, I., 93
Kasl, S., 455, 469, 470, 471, 483
Kastenbaum, R., 118, 431
Katagawa, E.M., 197, 215
Kauffman, S.A., 23
Kaufman, A.S., 142
Kay, S.R., 76
Kaye, H., 324
Kelleher, R.T., 189
Kelley, D., 142
Kempe, C.H., 353, 361, 362
Keniston, K., 384, 399
Kepfer, D.J., 142
Kessler, J.W., 142
Ketchum, J.S., 292
Kety, S.S., 25, 54
Keys, A., 253, 262, 271, 272, 291
Khantzian, E.J., 282, 292
Kidd, K.K., 25
Kim, K.E., 189
Kim, Y.J., 381
Kimball, C.P., 162, 469
Kimberling, W.J., 25
King, M.C., 23
King, S., 375, 382
King, S.H., 453
Kirk, S.A., 142
Kirk, W.D., 142
Kissin, B., 279
Kitchen, R., 23
Klein, R.E., 326
Kleitman, 80
Kline, N.S., 76
Klopfer, B., 142
Kluckhohn, F.R., 240, 390, 400
Knapp, P.H., 190
Knobloch, H., 325, 349
Koch, 440, 441
Koch, R., 217
Kohlberg, L., 330, 331, 349, 376, 382
Kohnstamm, G.A., 349
Kohut, H., 216
Kojw, E., 189
Koketsu, J., 54
Koller, K., 52
Koos, E.L., 216, 450, 453
Kopin, I.J., 75
Kopitz, E.M., 142
Korenman S.G., 406, 416
Korkes, L., 213, 217
Korsch, B.M., 479, 483

Kosa, J., 216
Kosterlitz, H.W., 54
Kowal, A., 24
Kraemer, H.C., 191
Krasnogorski, N.I., 105, 117
Kreider, S.D., 381
Kreisman, D.E., 217
Kremen, 80
Kringlen, 19
Kristt, D.A., 183, 191
Krugman, S., 23
Kübler-Ross, E., 417, 421, 422–423, 431
Kuchel, O., 189
Kulikowski, C., 239
Kupfer, D.J., 93
Kushner, M., *105–116*, 118
Kutner, B., 212, 213, 217

L

Lajtha, A., 291
Lake, C.R., 76
Lamb, H.R., 217
Landowne, M., 405, 416
Landy, D., 234
Langer, G., 76
Lanning, J.A., 453
Lantz, E.M., 216
Lasser, R.P., 416
Laughlin, F., 349
Layman, D., 350
Lazerson, A., 108
Leavitt, R.R., 239
Leckman, J.F., 25, 93
Lefer, G.L., 352, 361
Lefley, H.P., *195–217*
Lefrancois, G.R., 328
Lehmann, D., 93
Leigh, H., 182, 191
Lennane, K.J., 393, 400
Lennane, R.J., 393, 400
Lenneberg, E., 349
Leslie, F.M., 54
Levine, G.N., 216
Levine, S., 239
Levinson, D.J., 300, 301, 306, 384, 385, 386, 387, 388, 389, 390, 391, 392, 395, 399, 400
Levy, L., 216
Levy, N.B., 467, 468, 469
Lewis, J.L., 262
Lewis, M., 306, 325
Lex, B., 234
Lidz, T., 295, 305, 375, 382, 388, 389, 396, 400
Liebman, W.M., 188
Lief, A., 162

Lillesand, D.V., 118
Lind, E., 162
Lindemann, E., 430, 431
Lindsley, O.R., 106, 118
Lindstrom, L., 76
Lindzey, G., 142, 382
Linkowski, P., 25
Lipinski, J., 75
Lipsitt, L.P., 324, 325
Lipton, E., 306
Lipton, R., 306
Lipton, R.C., 315, 326
Lister, 441
Liu, S.C., 259, 263
Logue, E.E., 262
Loman, E., 450
London, P., 118
Loosen, P.T., 75
Lorenz, K., 305, 306
Lowenthal, M.F., 400
Lubetkin, B.S., 292
Lubs, H.A., 24
Ludwig, E.G., 451, 453
Lund-Johansen, P., 189
Luthe, W., 191
Lutkins, S.C., 431
Lutz, E.G., 93
Lyman, H.B., 142

M

Maas, J.W., 59, 75
McArthur, C., 500
McBride, G., 23
McBride, W.G., 23
McCarthy, J.J., 142
McClearn, G.E., 270, 291
McFall, R.M., 118
McGuinn, N.F., 189
Mack, J., 306
McKay, R.J., 13, 298, 319, 326, 348, 367, 381
McKean, C.M., 24
McKenna, G.J., 282, 292
McKinlay, J.B., 393, 400, 492, 501
McKinlay, S.M., 393, 400
McKinney, J.P., 340, 382
McKinney, W., 306
McKusick, V.A., 6, 9, 22, 24
McMahau, D., 23
MacMahon, B., 244
McNeese, M., 361
McNeill, D., 326
Maddi, S., 142
Maddison, D., 431
Maddox, G.L., 303, 306, 416
Madsen, W., 240
Magrab, P., 135

Mahoney, M.J., 118
Maldonado-Sierra, E., 239
Malzberg, B., 216
Manning, P.K., 238
Mark, V.H., 45, 54
Markman, E.M., 349
Marks, J., 162
Marks, N., 76
Marmot, M., 239
Marquis, D.P., 324
Martin, H.P., 362
Martin, W.R., 283
Mason, J.W., 146, 147, 166, 162
Master, A.M., 416
Masuda, M., 156, 162
Mathe, A.A., 190
Matsumoto, M., 189
Matthews, D., 263, 483
Matthysse, S., 75
Mauksch, H.O., 462, 469
Mayerson, E.W., 485, 500
Meadow, A., 239
Mechanic, D., 162, 216, 217, 239, 469
Medinnus, G.R., 349
Meehl, P.E., 142
Meenan, R., 469
Mehlman, R.D., 239
Mehta, J., 189
Meichenbaum, D.H., 118
Meisel, S., 210, 217
Meissner, W.W., 117, 142, 375, 382
Mello, N.K., 291, 292
Meltzer, H.Y., 76
Melzack, R., 49, 50, 54
Mendels, J., 75
Mendelson, J.H., 291, 292
Mendlewicz, J., 21, 25
Menkes, J.H., 24
Menninger, R.W., 501
Meredith, H.V., 371
Merrill, M.A., 142
Meyer, A., 143
Meyer, B.C., 431
Meyer, R.G., 191
Michaux, L., 24
Michiel, R.R., 292
Milkovich, L., 349
Miller, G., 326
Miller, J.D., 289, 292
Miller, R.R., 93
Miller, S., 501
Millon, R., 165
Millon, T., 142, 165, 469, 501
Milner, P., 42, 54

Mischel, W., 118
Mitchell, R.E., 262
Mix, L., 239
Modan, B., 262
Modan, M., 262
Moffett, A.D., 292
Moffitt, A.R., 325
Molinoff, P.B., 54
Money, J., 382
Moniz, E., 44
Monson, R.R., 24
Mooney, D., 191
Moore, J.M., 325
Moore, K.E., 29
Moore, R.A., 282, 292
Moore, T.E., 326
Morrow, J.H., 216
Morse, W.H., 189
Morton, W.T., 51
Moss, J., 216
Mowrer, O.H., 335, 349
Mowrer, W., 349
Moyer, J.H., 189, 416
Mumford, E., 483
Murphy, G., 416
Murphy, G.E., 416
Murray, H.A., 142
Musgrave, B., 326
Mussen, P.H., 10, 24, 325, 326, 381
Mustaniemi, H., 263

N

Nadelson, C., 400
Nagi, M.D., 215
Narabayashi, H., 54
Nardone, D.A., 431
Nathan, P.W., 51, 54
Neely, E., 483
Nelson, K., 325, 326
Nemiah, J.C., 117
Neugarten, B., 203, 217, 222, 238, 390, 391, 392, 400
Nevitt, M., 469
Newberger, E.H., 361
Newman, B., 331, 332, 342, 349, 368, 381
Newman, P.R., 331, 332, 342, 349, 368, 381
Nicholi, A.M., 117
Nicholi, A.M., Jr., 142
Noble, E.P., 275, 280, 281, 292
Nora, J.J., 24
North, W.R.S., 184, 185, 191
Notman, M.T., 392, 400

Nowels, A., *363–382*
Nuechterlein, K.H., 191

O

Obrist, P.A., 191
Okamoto, K., 170, 171, 189
Olds, J., 42, 43, 54
O'Leary, S.G., 350
Oliver, J., 75
Oller, D.K., 325
Onesti, G., 189
Orange, R.P., 177
Orbach, C.E., 217
Orlinsky, 80
Orton, S.T., 142
Osler, W., 169, 189
Ostfeld, A.M., 416
Ottenberg, P., 190

P

Padilla, E., 239
Paffenbarger, R.S., 257, 262
Palley, N., 216
Palmer, G., 24
Palmore, E., 303, 306, 416
Palmour, R., 74, 76
Pancratz, N., 325
Panities, N.M., 188
Papper, S., 501
Paracelsus, 440
Pardes, H., 279, 361, 483
Pare, 7
Paredes, A., 238
Parkes, C.M., 430, 431
Parsons, T., 207, 208, 217, 459, 469, 488, 489, 490, 500
Pasamanick, B., 325, 349
Pascal, G.R., 142
Pasteur, 440, 441
Patel, C.H., 184, 185, 191
Patel, M.S., 24
Patrick, M.L., 483
Patterson, G.R., 326
Patterson, M., 191
Pattison, E.M., 292
Paul, G.L., 110, 118
Pauling, L., 66, 75, 441
Pavensted, E., 306
Pavlov, I.P., 105, 106, 117
Paykel, E.S., 158, 162
Payronnard, J.M., 93
Peabody, F.W., 501
Pearsall, M., 220, 238
Pearson, L., 431
Peck, R.C., 398, 399, 400

NAME INDEX

Peery, T.M., 446
Pelham, W.E., 350
Penfield, W., 40
Penick, S.B., 274, 292
Pennington, B.F., 25
Perlmutter, J., 394, 400
Perry, T.A., 24
Perry, T.M., 453
Peterson, N.A., 24
Pfeiffer, E., 306, 416
Phillips, E.A., 382
Phillips, E.L., 382
Phillips, L., 142
Piaget, J., 301, 309, 320, 321, 325, 337, 369, 378, 381, 382
Pitt, B., 416
Plomin, R., 325
Plos, P., 381
Podell, R.N., 471, 483
Pollin, 19
Pomerance, A., 416
Pomerleau, O.F., 191
Pottash, A.L.C., 75, 292
Pradhan, S.N., 291, 292
Prange, A.J., 75
Prange, H., 216
Pratt, L., 469
Prechtl, H., 308
Prior, J.A., 142
Provence, S.A., 306, 315, 326
Purcell, K., 190
Puska, P., 263

Q

Quay, H.C., 349

R

Rabkin, J.G., 160, 162
Rachman, S., 118
Radbill, S.X., 361
Rahe, R.H., 144, 155, 158, 159, 160, 162, 469
Rainer, J.D., 21, 25
Rainwater, L., 203, 205, 206, 217, 222, 238, 469
Ransom, A.J., 469
Rapoport, R., 397, 400
Rasmussen, A.F., 188
Rathmann, D., 262
Ray, O.S., 291
Raynor, P., 117
Read, M., 24
Reading, A., 453
Rech, R.H., 29
Rechtschaffen, A., 80, 93

Reeder, L.G., 228, 239
Rees, W.D., 431
Reese, H.W., 325
Reich, L., 93
Reiser, M.F., 182, 188, 190, 191
Reisin, E., 262
Reiss, I.L., 382
Reiss, S., 142
Reiter, E.O., 381
Relman, A.S., 493, 501
Remen, N., 501
Reuler, J.B., 431
Rheingold, H.L., 325
Riccardi, V.M., 23, 24
Richmond, J., 306
Richter, C., 234
Ricks, D.F., 399
Rivers, P.C., 292
Robertson, E., 382
Rockwell, D.A., 469
Roffwarg, H.P., 82, 85, 90, 93
Rogers, C., 119, 142
Root, A.W., 381
Rose, R.M., 162, 189
Roseman, N.P., 326
Rosenberg, C.M., 292
Rosenblatt, D., 202, 203, 216, 222, 238
Rosenblum, L.A., 325
Rosenhan, D., 118
Rosenman, R.H., 172, 189, 190, 262
Rosenstock, 477
Rosenthal, D., 25
Rosenthal, R.H., 350
Ross, A.O., 347, 349
Ross, H.W., 325
Ross, R., 167, 188
Rossman, I., 298, 416
Roth, H.P., 483
Roth, R.H., 54
Rothenberg, A., 239
Rothgeb, C.L., 117
Rothgeb, D.L., 117
Rotter, J.B., 142
Rotter, J.I., 189
Rowitz, L., 216
Rubel, A.J., 238, 239
Rubio, M., 232, 239
Ruskin, A., 189

S

Sachar, E.J., 61, 62, 75, 76
Sackett, D.L., 471, 473, 474, 475, 476, 478, 480, 481, 483

Sackner, M.A., 93
Sadock, B.J., 93, 190
Safir, A., 239
Sager, R., 23
Sallan, S.E., 292
Salonen, J., 263
Salter, A., 106, 117
Sameroff, A., 308, 325
Sameroff, A.J., 24
Samloff, M.I., 188, 189
Sander, L.W., 325
Sandler, J., 118
Sands, R., 217
Sargent, J.D., 191
Saunders, N.A., 93
Scadding, J.G., 190
Schaefer, O., 239
Schaffer, R.L., 189
Schanberg, S.M., 326
Schatz, B., 501
Schatz, I.M., *351–362*
Scheff, T., 216
Schiavi, R., 190
Schildkraut, J.J., 54
Schlesinger, K., 24
Schlesinger, M.H., 190
Schmale, A.H., 164, 188
Schmitt, F.O., 54
Schneiderman, N., *26–54, 163–191, 241–292*
Schneidman, E.S., 431
Schrier, A., 54
Schultz, J.H., 191
Schwartz, D., 483
Schwartz, G.E., 188
Scott, C.S., *218–240, 383–400, 470–483*
Scott, H.W., 292
Scott, K., 382
Seevers, M.H., 291
Segal, M.S., 190
Seham, M., 216
Seibert, J.M., *307–350*
Selikoff, I.J., 248, 261
Selye, H., 146, 161, 162, 166, 180, 188
Sepe, S.J., 24
Shah, S.N., 24
Shaltiel, J., 469
Shapiro, D., 191
Shaul, W.L., 24
Shaw, M.E., 382
Shaywitz, B.A., 292
Shekelle, R.B., 259, 263
Sheldon, W.H., 337, 349
Sheperd, G.M., 54
Shields, J., 19, 25
Shock, N.W., 405, 416

Shostak, A.B., 216, 238, 469
Shuey, I., 75
Sider, R.C., 381
Siegel, F.L., 24
Siegel, J., 401, 403, 416
Silberstein, J.S., 142
Silbret, M., *163–191, 241–292*
Silen, W., 190
Silverman, G., *494–501*
Silverstein, A.B., 142
Sime, A.M., 469
Simon, R.J., 200, 216
Simons, R.C., 279, 361, 483
Singer, A., 262
Singer, B.D., 216
Singh, M.M., 76
Siqueland, E.R., 325
Skeels, H.M., 316, 326
Skillman, J.J., 190
Skinner, B.F., 105, 106, 117, 118, 349
Slater, E., 18, 25
Smith, D.W., 24
Smith, E., 232, 239
Smith, F., 326
Smith, J., 325
Smith, R.J., 292
Smith, S.D., 25
Smith, W.M., 262
Snow, L., 238
Snyder, 80
Snyder, S.H., 54, 69, 72, 76
Sobowale, N.C., 500
Soddy, K., 400
Soldatos, C.R., 80, 93
Solso, R.L., 325
Somers, A.R., 361
Sones, J.Q., 189
Sontag, S., 392, 400
Sorlie, P., 262
Sours, J.F., 93
Sparkes, R.S., 23
Sperry, R.W., 47, 54
Spiegal, J.P., 236, 239
Spiegler, A., 22
Spikes, J., 431
Spitz, R.A., 306, 315, 316, 326
Spitzer, R.L., 141
Stacher, B., 190
Stamler, J., 262
Stanfield, R.E., 382
Stechler, G., 362
Steele, B.F., 362
Stein, L., 76
Stein, M., 190
Stekert, E.J., 220, 238
Stephens, P.M., 189

Stern, M.P., 263, 453
Stewart, M.A., 317, 318, 334, 349
Stewart, R.B., 471, 483
Stimson, G.V., 483
Stockwell, E.G., 215
Stoll, 290
Stollnitz, F., 54
Stone, R., 191
Strachey, J., 117
Strain, J.J., 431, 469
Strauss, A.L., 424, 431
Strehler, B.L., 416
Streissguth, A.P., 24
Strickland, S.P., 216
Strodtbeck, F., 240, 400
Strohl, K.P., 93
Strommen, E.A., 340, 382
Struening, E.L., 160, 162
Stunkard, A.J., 274, 291, 292
Suchman, E.A., 202, 203, 216, 222, 238, 239, 451, 453, 455, 469
Suinn, R.M., 118
Summey, P., 500
Sun, D.C.H., 179, 190
Sundberg, N.D., 132, 142
Suomi, S., 306
Suskind, M.R., 326
Sussex, J.M., 217, 222
Sutherland, A.M., 217
Sutherland, E.W., 292
Suttell, B.J., 142
Sweeney, D.R., 292
Swerdloff, R.S., 365, 381
Syme, S.L., 191, 215, 239
Szasz, T.S., 142, 461, 462, 469, 501
Szentagothai, J., 54

T

Tagliacozzo, D.L., 462, 469
Talland, G.A., 54
Tanner, J.M., 370
Tashkin, D.P., 292
Tassinari, L.I., 189
Taub, F., 24
Taube, C., 216
Taylor, C.B., 191
Taylor, L., 361
Teasdale, J., 118
Teller, D.N., 291
Terenius, L., 54, 76
Terkel, S., 396
Terman, L.M., 142
Thaler, M., 188

Tharp, R., 239
Theager, C.J., 381
Theorell, T., 162
Thomas, A., 295, 296, 306, 325
Thompson, E.J., 469
Thompson, R.F., 191
Thorndike, E.L., 105, 106, 117
Tienari, 19
Tilelli, J.A., 361
Tilleard-Cole, R.R., 162
Toister, R.P., *105–116, 119–142, 307–350, 363–382*
Towbin, A., 7, 23, 24
Trabasso, T., 349
Trehub, S.E., 325
Trent, R., 239
Trosman, 80
Troup, S.B., 431
Truax, E., 499, 501
Trumbull, H.C., 223, 239
Trusky, B., 191
Tsuang, M.T., 18, 19, 25
Tuddenham, R.D., 349
Tumulty, P.A., 453, 484, 500
Turek, D., 361
Turin, A., 191
Turner, G., 24
Tyhurst, J.S., 162

U

Urdaneta, M., 239
Usdin, E., 76
Utian, W.H., 400

V

Vachon, L., 190
Vaillant, G.E., 292, 500
Valenstein, E., 54
VanDercar, D.H., 191
Vane, J.R., 54
Van Egeren, L., 493, 501
Van Italie, T.B., 292
Vaughan, V.C., 13, 298, 319, 326, 348, 367, 381
Veatch, R.M., 501
Veith, F., 431
Verhoeven, W.M., 76
Verter, J., 188
Viola, A., 431
Vitols, M.M., 216
Volicer, B.J., 469
Volterra, V., 325
VonAnrep, 52
Vygotsky, L.S., 320, 326

W

Wagemaker, H., 74, 76
Wahlstrom, A., 54
Waisman, H.A., 24
Waldron, A., 320, 326
Walfish, P.G., 262
Walker, E.A., 431
Wall, P.D., 49, 50, 54
Wallace, R.K., 191
Waller, J.A., 262
Wallis, C., 431
Walters, E.D., 191
Walters, R.H., 306
Wang, H.L., 24
Warner, R.J., 471
Waskowitz, C.H., 217
Watson, J.B., 105, 106, 117
Watson, S., 73, 76
Waugh, K.W., 142
Waugh, N.C., 54
Webb, J.Y., 239
Wechsler, D., 142
Weidman, H., 217, 219, 220, 222, 238
Weil-Malherbe, H., 75
Weiner, A.S., 377, 382
Weiner, H., 164, 165, 166, 188, 190
Weiner, I.B., 140, 142
Weinsier, R.L., 252, 262
Weinstein, M.C., 262
Weisman, A.D., 426, 431
Weiss, B.L., 292
Weiss, E.B., 190
Weiss, E.G., 190
Weiss, J.M., 180, 190
Weiss, R.S., 431
Weiss, S.M., 188
Weiss, T., 191
Welsh, G.S., 142
Wermuth, C., 469
Werner, E.E., 24
Werner, R.J., 483
Werry, J.S., 346, 349
Wesson, D.R., 292
West, D.J., 382
Wetli, C.V., 289, 292
Whittenberger, J.L., 244
Wilk, S., 75
Wilkins, W., *163–191*
Williams, F., 326
Williams, J.G., 469
Williams, M.H., 292
Williams, R.H., 381
Williams, R.L., 79, 93
Williams, R.S., 262
Wilson, A.C., 23
Wilson, A.T.M., 190
Wilson, D.C., 216
Wilson, I.C., 75
Wilson, P.T., 141
Wilson, W.R., 325
Wing, A.L., 262
Winokur, A., 75
Winokur, G., 20, 25, 393, 400
Wintrob, R., 234, 239
Wise, C.D., 76
Wolf, K.M., 326
Wolff, H.G., 146, 148, 149, 155, 161, 162, 166, 190
Wolff, P.H., 228, 239, 306
Wolff, S., 190
Wolpe, J., 105, 111, 113, 117, 118
Wolpert, E., 80, 93
Woolf, P., 305
Worden, F.G., 54
Worley, L.M., 326, 349
Wright, I.S., 453
Wright, J.C., 320, 326
Wright, R.K., 289, 292
Wyatt, R.J., 75
Wynder, E.L., 262

Y

Yamabe, H., 189
Yamada, A., 188
Yamamoto, J., 216
Yamori, Y., 189
Yelin, E., 468, 469
Young, M., 431
Young, W.C., 349

Z

Zborowski, M., 226, 227, 239, 469
Zealley, A.K., 190
Zelnik, M., 381
Zerbin-Rüdin, E., 25
Zinberg, N.E., 292
Zola, I.K., 216, 225, 226, 233, 239, 469
Zweifler, A., 189
Zyanski, S.J., 190

Subject Index

A

Abnormality: discussion of, 442–443
Abstinence: sexual, in mid-adolescence, 371
Abuse
  alcohol, 274–283
    causes, 277–278
    definition, 274–275
    epidemiology of, 275–277
    susceptible individuals for, 277
    treatment, 281–283
  of analgesics, 283–286
  child (see below)
  Darvon, 285–286
    dependence on, true drug, 286
    experimentation with, chance, 286
    in multiple drug abuse, 286
    overuse as medication, 286
    as substitute for opiates, 286
  drug, 264–292
    antisocial personality and, 266
    chronic, 266
    classification of, 264
    concepts in, general, 264–269
    cultural milieu of, 268–269
    depressed individual and, 266
    environmentally deprived individuals and, 266
    immature person and, 266
    learning theory and, social, 267
    operant conditioning and, 267–268
    person who abuses drugs, 265–268
    psychological factors in, 266–267
    schizoid personality and, 266
    schizophrenia and, 266
    social milieu of, 268–269
    sociopathic personality and, 266
  hallucinogens, 287–291
  of illicit drugs, 283–291
  of licit drugs, 283–291
  of narcotics, 283–286
  opiate, 283–285
  sedatives, 286–287
  stimulants, 287–291
  tranquilizers, 286–287
Abuse, child, 353–362
  abusee, 356–357
  abuser, 355–356
  classification, 354
  crisis and, 357
  emotional abuse, 354
    presentation, clinical, 359
  incidence, 354–355
  management, 360–361
  neglect, 354
    presentation, clinical, 358–359
  pathogenesis, 355–357
  physical abuse, 354
    presentation, clinical, 357–358
  sexual abuse, 354
    presentation, clinical, 359–360
Acceptance: of death, 423
Accessibility: of health-care services, 202
Accidents: environmentally induced, 245–246
Achievement tests, 138
Active-passive model, 493
Activity theory, 410
Adaptation
  diseases of, 155
  stress and, 146
Adjustment
  disorders, 123
  problems in adolescence, 378–381
Adolescence
  anxiety disorders of, 120
  development in, 363–382
    concepts in, general, 363–366
  disorders evident in, 120
  early, 366–369
    biologic changes in, 366–367
    development in, cognitive, 369
    development in, psychosexual, 367–368
    development in, psychosocial, 368–369
    physical changes in, 366–367
  height in, 367
  late, 374–378
    development in, cognitive, 378
    development in, psychosexual, 375
    development in, psychosocial, 375–378
    ethics and, 376–377
    morality and, 376–377
    parental relationships in, 375
    peer relationships in, 375–376
    physical changes in, 374–375
    vocational choice in, 377–378
  mid-adolescence, 369–374
    biologic changes in, 369–370
    development in, psychosexual, 370–372
    development in, psychosocial, 372–374
    double standard in, sexual, 372
    family relationships in, 372
    peer relationships in, 372–373
    physical changes in, 369–370
    sexual abstinence in, 371
    sexual permissiveness in, 371
  problems of adjustment in, 378–381
  relationship of home atmosphere to behavior patterns in, 373
  sexual activity in, 368

513

Subject Index

Adolescence (cont.)
  weight in, 367
Adoption studies, 18
Adulthood
  Gould studies, 384–391
    interpretation of, caution concerning, 390–391
  Levinson studies, 384–391
    developmental periods, 387
    interpretation of, caution concerning, 390–391
  middle, 383–400
    cathectic flexibility vs. cathectic impoverishment, 398–399
    issues in, critical, 398
    socializing vs. sexualizing during, 398
    valuing wisdom vs. valuing physical powers, 398
  stages of, theoretical basis for, 383–391
  women during (see Women during adulthood)
  young, 383–400
    activities of, 395–398
    family and, 398
    issues in, 395–398
Affect, 130
Affective disorders, 20–21, 122, 125
  biochemical aspects of, 55–64
  monoamine hypothesis of, 57–61
    pharmacologic evidence, 57–59
Affective neutrality, 490
Age
  arrests by, 379
  cardiac output and, 405
  enuresis by, 334
  markers of women, 392
  at menarche, 370
  obesity and, 269
  old (see Aged)
  preschool (see Preschool age)
  school (see School age)
  Thirty
    Crisis, 388
    impact of, for women, 392
    Transition, 388
Aged
  dependency of, 412–413
  inactivity of, 411
  losses of, 408–410
  medical care of, 414–415
  sexual activity of, 412
  social activity of, 410–412
  social attitudes toward, 413–414

Ages: Erikson's eight ages of man, 300
Aging
  biological changes with, 403–408
  body composition and, 404
  cardiovascular system and, 404–405
  demographic aspects of, 401–403
  economic characteristics in, 402–403
  endocrine function and, 406
  geographic variations and, 401–402
  immune system and, 406–407
  nervous system and, 407–408
  number of older persons, 401
  psychosocial aspects of, 408–414
  race composition in, 401
  renal function and, 405–406
  respiratory system and, 405
  senses and, 407–408
  sex composition in, 401
  social characteristics in, 402–403
  weight decrease with, 298
Agonistic behavior: neural substrates of, 43–44
Agricultural chemicals, 244
Airflow: obstruction, 86
Air pollution, 241–242
Alcohol
  abuse (see Abuse, alcohol)
  effects on body, general, 278–279
  fetal alcohol syndrome, features of, 281
  individual and, 278–281
    adverse effects of alcohol, 279–281
  related
    disability, definition, 275
    mortality, 280
  society and, 278–281
    adverse effects of alcohol, 279–281
  use of, 274–283
  withdrawal syndrome, 278–279
Alcoholism: definition, 274, 275
Amine(s)
  biogenic, 55–56
  metabolites of, in body fluids, 59–61
  pump, and tricyclic

antidepressants, 59
  transmitters, and psychotomimetics, 65
Amniocentesis: for prenatal diagnosis, indications, 23
Amniotic fluid: analysis in prenatal diagnosis, 22
Analgesics
  abuse of, 283–286
  narcotic, 35–36
Anencephaly, 17
Aneuploidy, 12
Anger: about death, 422
Anima, 440
Animal studies: and development, 304–305
Anomalies
  chromosome, and mental retardation, 12–17
  multiple congenital, and mental retardation syndrome, 15–17
Antecedent stimulus, 109
Antidepressants: tricyclic, and amine pump, 59
Antipsychotic drugs, 36–37
Antisocial personality: and drug abuse, 266
Anxiety, 151–152
  attacks, dream, 90
  disorders, 122, 125–127
    of adolescence, 120
    of children, 120
    generalized, 126
  reactions, acute, 149
  separation, 312
  stranger, 312
Apnea
  central, 88
  sleep (see Sleep, apnea)
Appalachian Whites: Southern, 220
Arrests: by age and offense, 379
Arrhythmia: cardiac, treatment, 185–186
Asbestos
  -associated tumors, 248
  insulation workers, mortality of, 248
Assertiveness training, 113
Association
  clang, 129
  consistency of, 251
  correctness of, temporal, 251
  strength of, 251
Asthenia: neurocirculatory, 151
Asthma
  behavioral factors in, 174–177

bronchial, 174–178
  conditioning and, classical, 176–177
  emotional states and, 176
  extrinsic, 174
  family relationships and, 175–176
  immunologic, chemical mediators of, 177
  intrinsic, 174
  pathogenesis of, 175
  personality structure and, 175
  psychological stimuli in, mechanisms, 177–178
Ataque
  de nervios, 232
  de risa, 232
Atherosclerotic (*see* Cardiovascular disease, atherosclerotic)
Attention deficit disorder, 120, 345–347
Attitudes: health, 195, 205–207
Autism, 129, 316–318
  hand-positioning in, 318
  infantile, 316
  self-stimulatory behavior in, 318
  social adjustment after, 318
  symptoms of, 317
Aversion therapy, 113–115
Azabache, 232

B

Bargaining: and death, 422
Behavior
  agonistic, neural substrates of, 43–44
  assessment, 109–110
    consequent events in, 109
    interview, clinical, 109–110
    observation in, direct, 110
    organismic factors in, 109
  biology of, 1–93
  class and, socioeconomic, 219
  cognitive, modification, 115
  compliance, model in, 478
  coronary-prone pattern, 257–258
  in cultural perspective, 193–292
  development and, 3–25
  ethnicity and, 219
  general appearance and, 128
  genetics and, 3–25
  health-oriented, 455
  illness (*see* Illness behavior)

maladaptive, 109
moral, 330–332
neurologic basis of, 26–54
neurologic structure and function and, 39–53
patient, strategies in changing, and ethics, 482
patterns, and home atmosphere, in adolescents, 373
psychoactive drugs and, 33–37
psychological factors in, 95–191
rehearsal, 112–113
relationship to nervous system organization, 37–53
self-stimulatory, in autism, 318
in social perspective, 193–292
therapy, 105–116
  procedures, 110–116
Behavioral
  antecedents, of peptic ulcer, 179–180
  factor(s)
    in asthma, 174–177
    in disease and illness, 447
    in peptic ulcer pathogenesis, 179–180
  -medical model of health and ill health, 447–448
  medicine, 163–191
  methods, in psychosomatic disorders, 183
  organ vulnerability in, 167–169
  physiological response in, 166–167
  sociobehavioral features of patient, 476–477
Belief
  class and, socioeconomic, 219
  ethnicity and, 219
  systems, 195
Bender-Gestalt, 138–139
Biochemistry: of functional psychosis, 55–76
Bioelectric properties: of nerve cells, 27–30
Biogenic amines, 55–56
  metabolites of, in body fluids, 59–61
Biologic
  changes with aging, 403–408
  factors in peptic ulcer pathogenesis, 178–179
Biology: of behavior, 1–93
Birth: average remaining years of life at, 197
Black Americans, 220–221
Blocking, 129
Blood volume, 224
Body
  build (*see* Build)
  composition, and aging, 404
  concept, 222
  culturally determined concepts about, 221–225
  effects of alcohol on, general, 278–279
  functions, knowledge of, 222–225
  image, 222
Brain
  death, Harvard criteria of, 418
  function and psychoactive drugs, 33–37
  syndromes, organic, 121
Bronchial asthma, 174–178
Brujeria, 234
Build, physical
  self-concept and, 342
  social stereotypes and, 340
Bureaucratization: and doctor-patient relationship, 492

C

Cancer, 246–250
  lung, and smoking, 246–248
Cardiovascular disease, atherosclerotic, 250–261
  prevention problems in, 258–261
  risk factors in, 250–252, 256–258
  definition of, 250–252
Cardiovascular reactors, 148
Cardiovascular system: and aging, 404–405
Care
  coronary care unit, psychological responses in, 465
  of dying patient, 426–428
  health (*see* Health, -care)
  medical (*see* Medical, care)
Cataplexy, 85
Catecholamines: transmitter dynamics of, 32
Categories: development of, 320

SUBJECT INDEX

Cathectic flexibility vs. cathectic impoverishment: in middle adulthood, 398–399
Cell(s)
 hybrid, 5
 nerve, bioelectric properties of, 27–30
 sperm, 3
Cellular
 concept of disease, 441
 theory, 440
Central nervous system, 38–39
 malformations, 17
Centrifugal force: crisis as, 210
Centripetal force: illness as, 210
Cephalocaudal direction: of motor development, 307
Cerebral hemispheres: organization of, 47–48
Change: and stress, 145–146
Chemical(s)
 agricultural, 244
 mediators of immunologic asthma, 177
Cheyne-Stokes respiration, 88
Child abuse (*see* Abuse, child)
"Childbirth flea," 232
Childhood: disorders evident in, 120
Children
 anxiety disorders of, 120
 clinical studies of, and development, 303–304
 illness of, 212–214
 temperamental traits, questions related to, 314
 thought of, constraints on, 320–321
Cholesterol
 levels, and coronary heart disease, 254
 serum, and dietary fats, 253–256
Chromosome, 4–5
 anomalies, and mental retardation, 12–17
 syndromes, imbalance, 13
Chronic conditions: and demographic characteristics, 200
Cigarette smoking (*see* Smoking, cigarette)
Circadian rhythm: of cortisol secretion, 61
Circulation, 224
 disorders, 169–174
Clang association, 129

Class: socioeconomic, influence on beliefs and behaviors, 219
Classical (*see* Conditioning, classical)
Cognition: of toddler, 320–321
Cognitive
 behavior modification, 115
 development (*see* Development, cognitive)
 function, disturbance in, 152
 restructuring, 115
Coherence: with existing knowledge and potential risk factor, 251
Color (*see* Race)
Communication: in family, 351
Communicative support: in interaction of medical personnel and family, 215
Company: loss of, by aged, 409
Compliance, 470–483
 behavior, model in, 478
 definition of, 472
 demographic features and, 473, 474
 disease features and, 474–475
 errors and, 479–480
 knowledge about, current state of, 473–475
 measure of, 472–473
 patient-therapist interaction, features of, 475–476
 problem of, definition and scope of, 470–471
 with regimen
  complexity of, 477
  efficacy of, subjective estimate of, 478–479
  therapeutic, 472
  therapeutic, features of, 475
  type of, 477
 sociobehavioral features of patient, 476–477
 strategies for improving, 479–482
 study
  design, 472
  problems in, methodological, 471–473
  sample for, 472
 therapeutic changes by patient, 480–482
 therapeutic source, features of, 475

Compulsive-obsessive disorder, 127
Concepts, 435–453
 definition of, 436–437
 development of, factors influencing, 436
 of disease, 435–453
  cellular, 441
  changing, 438–442
  of health (*see* Health, concepts of)
  of ill health (*see* Ill health, concepts of)
 of illness, 435–453
Concrete operations: in cognitive development, 301
Conditioned
 response, 106
 stimulus, 106
Conditioning
 classical, 106
  asthma and, 176–177
  comparison with operant conditioning, 108
 instrumental, 106
 operant, 106
  comparison with classical conditioning, 108
  drug abuse and, 267–268
Conduct disorder, 120
Conflict(s)
 between patient and doctor, 487–488
 peptic ulcer and, 180
Consciousness: modulation of, 39–42
Consequent events: in behavior assessment, 109
Conservation: simple tests for, 328
Consistency: of association, 251
Consumer expenditures, 201–202
Contract, 496
Conversion, 102
Coronary
 care unit, psychological responses in, 465
 event, risk factors in, 251
 heart disease (*see* Heart, disease, coronary)
 -prone behavior pattern, 257–258
Correlation: of variables, 250
Cortisol
 concentration in depression, 62
 elevated levels, 61

resistance to dexamethasone
   suppression, 61–62
   secretion, altered circadian
      rhythm of, 61
Counseling: genetic, 21–23
Covenant, 496
Crisis
   Age Thirty, 388
   as centrifugal force, 210
   child abuse and, 357
   life (see Life, crisis)
Cross-tolerance: to drugs, 265
Cultural
   differences in etiologic
      explanations, 233–235
   milieu of drug abuse,
      268–269
   perspective, behavior in,
      193–292
Culturally
   determined concepts about
      body, 221–225
   related differences in disease
      incidence, 227–230
Culture, 218–240
   -bound syndromes, 230–232
   development and, 302–303
   health, 219–221
   medicine and, 218–240
Curandero, 221
Curve: normal, 132
Cytoplasmic mobile pool, 56

D

Darvon (see Abuse, Darvon)
Death, 417–431
   (See also Mortality)
   acceptance of, 423
   anger about, 422
   associated with stress, 157
   bargaining and, 422
   brain, Harvard criteria of,
      418
   causes of, 419–420
      in ages 15–24, 364
   changes in, modern, 417–420
   definition of, 417–419
   denial of, 421–422
   depression and, 422–423
   family and, 428–430
   in hospital setting, 424–425
   place of, 419–420
Defense mechanisms, 100–103
   with reality distortion
      major, 100–101
      minimal, 103
      moderate, 101–103

Delay: in seeking treatment,
   202–204
Delinquency: juvenile, 378–380
Dementia, 120
   substance-induced, 120–121
Demographic
   aspects of aging, 401–403
   characteristics, and chronic
      conditions, 200
Denial, 100
   of death, 421–422
Denver Developmental
   Screening Test, 338–339
Dependency: of aged, 412–413
Dependent
   role of patient, 461–463
   variables and stress, 161
Depressed individual: and drug
   abuse, 266
Depression
   cortisol concentration in, 62
   death and, 422
   endocrine abnormalities in,
      61–64
   preparatory, 423
   reactive, 423
   stress and, 158
Deprivation: social, 315–316
Desensitization: systematic,
   106, 111–112
Desirability: of condition,
   442–443
Detroit test of learning
   aptitude, 139
Development, 295–306
   in adolescence (see under
      Adolescence)
   animal studies, 304–305
   behavior and, 3–25
   of categories, 320
   children, clinical studies of,
      303–304
   clinical problems in, 7–8
   cognitive, 301–302
      in adolescence, early, 369
      in adolescence, late, 378
      concrete operations, 301
      formal operations in,
         301–302
      preoperational stage, 301
      in preschool age, 327–330
      in school age, 337–340
   concepts of, general,
      297–302
   culture and, 302–303
   discussion of, 295–306
   disorders
      pervasive, 120
      in school age, 347–348

in early years, 307–326
genetic function during, 6–7
of identity, 373–374
of infant (see Infant,
   development of)
intellectual, preoperational
   stage of, 321
language
   of infant, 309–310
   in preschool age, 330
   in school age, 340–341
   in toddler, 321–322
methods of study, 303–305
motor (see Motor
   development)
physical, 297–299
   of infant, 307–308
   in preschool age, 327
   in school age, 337
   of toddler, 318–320
in preschool age (see
   Preschool age,
   development in)
psychosexual (see psychosexual, development)
psychosexual stages of (see
   Psychosexual, stages of
   development)
psychosocial, 299–301
   in adolescence, early,
      368–369
   in adolescence, late,
      375–378
   in mid-adolescence,
      372–374
   in preschool age, 330–334
   in school age, 341–343
of representational system,
   320
semantic, 321
in school age (see School age,
   development in)
syntactic, 321–322
theories of, in school age, 341
of toddler (see Toddler,
   development of)
Developmental periods: of
   Levinson, 387
Dexamethasone suppression:
   cortisol resistance to,
      61–62
Diagnostic
   accuracy, and social
      stratification, 204
   and Statistical Manual of
      Mental Disorders, 119,
      120–123
Dietary therapy: of
   schizophrenia, 66–67

Disability, 199–201
  by income, 199
  by race, 199
Discipline techniques:
    outcomes of, 331
Disease
  behavioral factors in, 447
  biologic factors in, 447
  concepts of, 435–453
    cellular, 441
    changing, 438–442
  ethnicity of, 228–229
  folk, origin of, 231
  incidence, culturally related
      differences in, 227–230
  relationship to illness, 438
  vs. illness, 437–443
Disengagement: theory of, 410
Disinhibition, 34
Disorder: discussion of term, 64
Displacement, 103
Dissociation, 101
Dissociative disorders, 122
Distance: in interaction of
    medical personnel and
    family, 214–215
Doctor
  communication with patient,
      484–494
  conflict with patient,
      487–488
  as educator, 215
  ethics of, 485
  as facilitator, 215
  as healer, 215
  honesty of, 485
  humanistic, 498–500
  and patient, 433–501
  -patient relationship, 196,
      479, 484–501
    bureaucratization and, 492
    concepts in, functional,
        488–490
    concepts in, structural,
        490–491
    developing the
        relationship, 494
    features of, 475–476
    group practice and,
        491–492
    model (see Model, in
        doctor-patient
        relationship)
    nature of illness, 492–494
    psychological aspects of,
        486–488
    scope of illness, 492–493
    severity of illness, 493–494
    sociocultural aspects of,
        488–492

  specialization and, 491
  technology and, 490–491
  transactional system, total,
      489
  personality of, 486–487
  psychological reactions to
      dying, 425–426
  role of, 490
  stress of, 487
Dominant inheritance, 8, 9
Dopamine
  hypothesis of schizophrenia,
      67–72
  metabolism of, 56
  receptor binding,
      phenothiazine and
      thioxanthene, 69
  synthesis of, 56
Dopaminergic hyperfunction
  evidence for, 68
  mechanisms for, 70–72
Double standard: of sexual
    behavior in mid-
    adolescence, 372
Down syndrome, 12
Drawings, 141
Dream
  anxiety attacks, 90
  recall after REM and NREM
      sleep, 80
Dreamlike experiences: vivid,
    85
Drives
  instinctual, 98
  sexual, 98
Drug(s)
  abuse (see Abuse, drug)
  antipsychotic, 36–37
  cross-tolerance to, 265
  exposure, in multiple
      congenital anomalies and
      mental retardation
      syndrome, 16
  illicit, abuse of, 283–291
  licit, abuse of, 283–291
  physical dependence on, 265,
      267
  psychoactive (see
      Psychoactive drugs)
  psychological dependence on
      (see Psychological,
      dependence on drugs)
  sedative-hypnotic, 34
  sleep and, 79–81
  tolerance to, 265, 268
Dying, 417–431
  caring for, 426–428
  medical personnel responses
      to, 423–426
  psychological reactions of

    family to, 428–429
Dyslexia, 17

E

Early years: development in,
    307–326
Eating disorders, 120
Ecology: of health, 195
Economic characteristics: and
    aging, 402–403
Education: health, and coronary
    heart disease, 260
Educator: physician as, 215
Ego, 98–99
Elderly (see Aged)
Electroencephalography, 40
  characteristic patterns of, 40
  during sleep, 77
Emotion, 42–45
Emotional
  conflict, and gastric function,
      148
  discharge, 152
  instability, 152
  origin of folk illnesses, 231
  states, and asthma, 176
Empacho, 231
Empathy, 490
"Empty nest" period: for
    women, 392–393
Encephalocele, 17
Encounter time: and social
    stratification, 204
Endocrine
  abnormalities, in depression,
      61–64
  conditions, and obesity, 270
  function, and aging, 406
  response to stress (in
      monkey), 147
Endorphin, 36
Enuresis, 334–336
  by age, 334
  bell and pad for, 335
  primary, 89
  secondary, 89
  by sex, 334
  sleep-related, 89
Environment: school, and self-
    concept, 342
Environmental
  factors, in hypertension, 172
  modification in psychosomatic
      disorders, 182
Environmentally
  deprived individuals, and
      drug abuse, 266
  induced accidents, 245–246
Epidemiology: sociocultural

variables in, 195
Erikson's eight ages of man, 300
Erikson's theories
  infant and, 310–311
  preschool age and, 330
  toddler and, 322
Erogenous zones, 99
Errors: and compliance, 479–480
Escape, 396
Essential human needs, 296–297
Ethics
  adolescence and, late, 376–377
  of doctor, 485
  strategies in changing patient behavior and, 482
Ethnic group, 219
Ethnicity, 218–240
  of disease, 228–229
  influence on beliefs and behaviors, 219
  influence on symptoms, 225–227
  medicine and, 218–240
Etiology: explanations of, cultural differences in, 233–235
Expenditures: consumer, 201–202
Experimentation: chance, with Darvon, 286
Extinction, 107

F

Facilitator: physician as, 215
Factitious disorders, 122
Failure
  self-concept and, 342
  to thrive, causes of, 319
Family
  communication in, 351
  death and, 428–430
  dynamics, 208–210
  factors in medicine, 196
  flexibility in, 351
  function, general concepts of, 351–353
  impact of illness on, 210
  interaction with medical personnel, 214–215
  interdependency of members in, 351
  in medicine, 208–215
  nuclear, 351–352
  relationships
    asthma and, 175–176

in mid-adolescence, 372
risk studies, 18
as social system, 352–353
structure, 208–210
young adulthood and, 398
Fat
  dietary, and serum cholesterol, 253–256
  saturated, and coronary heart disease, 253
Fear
  gastric mucosa and, 149
  in terminal illness, 420–421
Fetal alcohol syndrome: features of, 281
"Fighting sickness," 232
Flea: "childbirth," 232
Flexibility: in family, 351
Flooding, 112
Fluids: body, metabolites of biogenic amines in, 59–61
Folk
  concepts of ill health, 449
  diseases, origin of, 231
Formal operations: in cognitive development, 301–302
Freud's theories
  infant and, 310–311
  preschool age and, 330
  toddler and, 322

G

Gain
  primary, 102
  secondary, 102
Gastric (see Stomach)
Gastrointestinal reactors, 148
Gate control theory: of pain, 50
Gender identity disorders, 122
Gene, 5
General appearance: and behavior, 128
Genetic
  concepts in medicine, 3–9
  counseling, 21–23
  factors in obesity, 270
  function during early growth and development, 6–7
  map, 6
Genetics, 3–25
  behavior and, 3–25
  of mental retardation, 9–12
  of psychiatric disorders, 18–21
Genotype, 8
Geographic variations: and aging, 401–402
Geriatric period, 401–418

Germ theory, 441
Gould studies, 384–391
  interpretation, caution concerning, 390–391
Grieving, 429–430
Group
  ethnic, 219
  practice, and doctor-patient relationship, 491–492
  testing, psychological, 138
Growth
  early
    clinical problems in, 7–8
    genetic function during, 6–7
  postnatal, main types of, 298
Guidance-cooperation: model of, 493

H

Habituation, 308
Hallucinations: hypnagogic, 85
Hallucinogens: abuse, 287–291
Hand positioning: in autism, 318
Harvard criteria: of brain death, 418
Hashish: lifetime experience with, 289
Head radiotherapy: thyroid tumors after, 248
Headache: tension, treatment, 187
Healer: physician as, 215
Health
  attitudes, 195
  belief model, 477–479
  -care
    cost of, 461
    services, utilization of, 202–204
    system, 195
    system, perceived adequacy of, 201
  changes, and life crisis, 156
  concepts of
    medical perspective on, 445–448
    patient's perspective on, 448–452
    practical application, 445–452
  culture, 219–221
  ecology of, 195
  education and coronary heart disease, 260
  ill health (see Ill health)
  life-style and, 241–263
  loss of, by aged, 408–409

SUBJECT INDEX

Health (cont.)
  maintenance mechanisms, 195
  matters, attitudes and practices in, 205–207
  model of, 447–448
  -oriented behavior, 455
  roles, 207–208
  socialization and, 205–208
  sociological correlates of, 196–205
Heart
  (See also Cardiovascular)
  aging and, 404–405
  arrhythmia, treatment, 185–186
  attack in persons under 60, causes of, 259
  disease, coronary, 172–174
    cholesterol levels and, 254
    fats and, saturated, 253
    health education and, 260
    morbidity-mortality of, and smoking, 256
    risk factors for, decreases in, 259
  output, and age, 405
Height
  in adolescence, 367
  curves, comparison of 1880 and 1960, 371
Hemispheres: cerebral, organization of, 47–48
Hereditary predispositions: to hypertension, 172
Heterozygous, 8
5-HIAA: and TSH, 63
Home atmosphere: and behavior patterns in adolescents, 373
Homozygous, 8
Honesty: of doctor, 485
Hormonal events: in sexual maturation, 365
Hospital setting: death in, 424–425
Hospitalization: stress of, 463–464
Hostility: masked, in interaction of medical personnel and family, 214–215
Humanistic doctor, 498–500
Hybrid cells, 5
Hydrocephalus, 17
Hyperactivity, 347
Hypertension, 252–253
  environmental factors in, 172
  essential, 169–172
    pathogenesis of, 171
    treatment, 183–185

hereditary predispositions to, 172
  incidence, and salt intake, 252
Hyperventilation, 88
  syndrome, 150–151
Hypnagogic hallucinations, 85
Hypnotic-sedative drugs, 34
Hypothalamic injury: and obesity, 270

I

Id, 98
Identity
  completion of, 396
  development of, 373–374
Ill health
  concepts of, 437–443
    folk, 449
    magico-religious, 449
    medical perspective on, 445–448
    patient's perspective on, 448–452
    practical application of, 445–452
    scientific, 449
  model of, 447–448
Illicit drugs: abuse of, 283–291
Illinois test of psycholinguistic abilities, 139
Illness
  behavior (see below)
  behavioral factors in, 447
  biologic factors in, 447
  of child, 212–214
  concepts of, 435–453
  folk, origin of, 231
  impact on family, 210–214
  -induced stress, 464–466
  life stress and, 155–161
  onset, relationship to life change, 155–159
  relationship to disease, 438
  sleep, illnesses associated with, 91–92
  sociological correlates of, 196–205
  of spouse (see Spouse, illness of)
  stress of, 463–464
  stress-induced, pathogenesis of, 159–160
  -stress relationship criticism of, 160–161
  terminal (see Terminal illness)
  vs. disease, 437–443

Illness behavior, 454–469
  medical care contact stage, 460–461
  patienthood stage of, 461–466
  period
    of medical care, 460–468
    prior to contact with health-care system, 455–460
  recovery stage of, 466–468
  rehabilitation stage of, 466–468
  sick role stage, assumption of, 458–460
  summary of, 455
  symptom experience stage, 455–458
Image: body, 222
Immature person: and drug abuse, 266
Immune system: and aging, 406–407
Immunologic asthma: chemical mediators of, 177
Impact
  of illness on family, 210–214
  stage in psychological response to stress, 153
  of stress, 161
Impulse control disorders, 123
Impulsivity, 347
Inactivity
  of aged, 411
  physical, 257
Inattention, 347
Incidence of disease: culturally related differences in, 227–230
Income
  disability by, 199
  loss, by aged, 408
Incomplete sentence blank, 141
Independence: loss by aged, 409
Infancy: disorders evident in, 120
Infant, 307–318
  autism of, 316
  cognition of, 308–309
  development of, 307–318
    language, 309–310
    physical, 307–308
    problems in, 315–318
    psychosocial aspects of, 310–313
    socioeconomic factors and, 313–315
  Erikson's theories and, 310–311

Subject Index

Freud's theories and, 310–311
learning of, 308–309
mortality rates, 198
-mother relationship, 311–312
personality differences among infants, 312–313
smiling of, social, 311–312
Information processing, 45–48
Inheritance, 7
dominant, 8, 9
mendelian, 8–9
patterns of, 8–9
polygenic, 9
recessive, 8, 9
Insomnia, 81–84
idiopathic, 83–84
primary, 83–84
Instinctual drives, 98
Instrumental conditioning, 106
Intellect, 130–131
Intellectual development: preoperational stage of, 321
Intelligence
self-concept and, 342
tests, 135–136
specialized, 137–138
Interaction: between medical personnel and families, 214–215
Interdependency of members: in family, 351
Interpersonal response training, 112
Intervening links: and stress, 161
Interview: clinical, in behavior assessment, 109–110
Intestine: reactors, 148
Intragranular pool
bound, 56
mobile, 56
Irradiation (see Radiation)

J

Judgment, 130–131
Juvenile delinquency, 378–380

K

Karyotype
of female, normal, 4
XXX, 14
XYY, 14

Kidney function: and aging, 405–406
Klinefelter syndrome, 12

L

La belle indifférence, 102
Language, 46–47
development (see Development, language)
La pulga del parto, 232
Learned skills or activities, 131
Learning, 45–46, 301–302
aptitude, Detroit test of, 139
disabilities, evaluation of, 138
processes, 308–309
theory, 105–116
historical antecedents in development of, 105–106
social, and drug abuse, 267
of toddler, 320–321
types of, 106–108
Levinson studies, 384–391
developmental periods, 387
interpretation, caution concerning, 390–391
Libido, 98
Licit drugs: abuse of, 283–291
Life
change, relationship to illness onset, 155–159
crisis
disease occurrence and, 156
health changes and, 156
cycle, 293–431
stress, and illness, 155–161
-style, 241–263
definition, 241
health and, 241–263
in urban society, 241–246
Linkage studies, 5
Living arrangements
loss by aged, 409
for 65 and over, 403
Longevity, 196–199
by race, 197
by sex, 197
Love, 396
Lung cancer: and smoking, 246–248

M

Magico-religious concepts: of ill health, 449
Maladaptive behavior, 109
Mal aire, 233

Malas influencias, 234
Mal de ojo, 231–232
Mal de pelea, 232
Malocchio, 232
MAO activity: in schizophrenia, 71
Marijuana: lifetime experience with, 289
Marital status: for 65 and over, 403
Marriage, 396–398
Maternal toxins, 7
Medical
attention, symptoms needing, and social class, 450
-behavioral model of health and ill health, 447–448
care
access to, 201–202
of aged, 414–415
contact stage of illness behavior, 460–461
model (see Model, medical)
personnel
interaction with families, 214–215
responses to dying, 423–426
perspective on disease, 445–448
practice, implications of social stratification for, 204–205
services (see Services, medical)
Medicine
behavioral (see Behavioral, medicine)
biologic, organ vulnerability in, 167–169
culture and, 218–240
ethnicity and, 218–240
family in, 208–215
family factors in, 196
social aspects of, 195–217
Memory, 45–46, 130–131
Menarche
age at, 370
onset of, 364
Mendelian inheritance, 8–9
Menopausal period, 393–395
Menses: cessation of, 393
Mental disorders: organic, 120–121, 125
Mental rehearsal techniques, 116
Mental retardation, 120, 125
cause of, factors in, 11
chromosome anomalies and, 12–17

Mental retardation (cont.)
  genetics of, 9–12
  levels, and related
    functioning abilities, 125
  "pure," 17
  syndrome, and multiple
    congenital anomalies,
    15–17
  X-linked, 16–17
Mental status examination, 128
Metabolic disorders, 14–15
Mexican-Americans, 221
Middle adulthood (see
    Adulthood, middle)
Middle years (see Adulthood,
    middle)
Mid-life Transition, 389
Migraine: treatment, 186–187
Model(s)
  active-passive, 493
  in compliance behavior, 478
  in doctor-patient relationship,
    493–500
    humanistic, 496–500
    humanistic, advantages of,
      497–498
    humanistic, assumptions of,
      496
    humanistic, interaction in,
      496–498
    interaction in, 495–496
    traditional, 494–496
    traditional, definitions,
      494–495
  of guidance-cooperation, 493
  health belief, 477–479
  medical
    -behavioral, of health and
      ill health, 447–448
    of disease, traditional,
      445–447
  of mutual participation, 493
  in psychoanalytic theory,
    topographic and
    structural, 97–99
  of schizophrenia (see
    Schizophrenia, models)
Monoamine hypothesis of
  affective disorders,
  57–61
  pharmacologic evidence,
    57–59
Mood, 130
Moral behavior, 330–332
Morality: and late adolescence,
  376–377
Morbidity
  of coronary heart disease and
    smoking, 256

risk in schizophrenia, 18
Mortality
  (See also Death)
  alcohol related, 280
  of asbestos insulation
    workers, 248
  of coronary heart disease and
    smoking, 256
  in geriatric period, causes of,
    402
  infant, 198
  rates
    by causes, leading, 199,
      446
    from suicide, 410
    for 65 and over, 402
    in smoking, cigarette, 247
Mother
  -infant relationship, 311–312
  injury to, 7
Motivation, 42–45
Motor development
  cephalocaudal direction, 307
  proximodistal direction, 307
Movement disorders:
  sterotyped, 120
Muscle: weakness, episodes of,
  85
Mutual participation: model of,
  493
Myelomeningocele, 17

N

Names: and self-concept, 342
Narcotic(s)
  abuse of, 283–286
  analgesics, 35–36
Neck radiotherapy: thyroid
  tumors after, 248
Needs
  essential human, 296–297
  unconscious, 396–397
Nerve cells: bioelectric
  properties of, 27–30
Nervous attack, 232
Nervous system
  aging and, 407–408
  central, 38–39
  malformations, 17
  divisions of, 37–39
  organization, relationship to
    behavior, 37–53
  peripheral, 37–38
Neural substrates
  of behavior, agonistic,
    43–44
  of punishment, 42–43
  of reward, 42–43

Neurocirculatory asthenia, 151
Neuroleptics: prolactin
  responses to, 68
Neurologic
  basis of behavior, 26–54
  diseases, and obesity, 270
  structure and function, and
    behavior, 39–53
Neuronal transmission, 26–33
Neurophysiological bases: of
  pain perception, 49–51
Neurosis, 122
  hysterical, dissociative type,
    122
Neutrality: affective, 490
Newborn: reflexes of, 308
Nicknames: and self-concept,
  342
Nightmares, 90
Nondisjunction, 4
Norepinephrine
  excess in schizophrenia, 72
  synthesis and metabolism, 56
Normal curve, 132
Normality: discussion of,
  442–443
NREM sleep, 79
  dream recall after, 80
Nuclear family, 351–352

O

Obesity, 269–274
  age and, 269
  causative factors in, 269–270
  endocrine conditions and,
    270
  genetic factors in, 270
  hypothalamic injury and, 270
  neurologic diseases and, 270
  poverty level and, 269
  prevalence of, 272
  primary, 270
  psychosocial factors in,
    270–271
  race and, 269
  secondary, 270
  sex and, 269
  treatment, 271–274
Objectivity: in interaction of
  medical personnel and
  family, 214–215
Obsessive-compulsive disorder,
  127
Old age (see Aged)
Operant (see Conditioning,
  operant)
Opiate
  abuse, 283–285

substitute, Darvon for, 286
Opioids
 chemical derivation of, 73
 schizophrenia and, 72–74
Organismic factors: in behavior assessment, 109
Orientation, 130–131

P

Pain, 48–53
 gate control theory of, 50
 perception, 48–49
  neurophysiological bases of, 49–51
 treatment, 51–53
Panic disorder, 127
Paralysis: sleep, 85
Paranoia, 121
Paraphilia, 122
Parasomnia, 89–90
Parental relationships: in late adolescence, 375
Parenthood, 352
Patient
 behavior, strategies in changing, and ethics, 482
 communication with doctor, 484–494
 compliance (*see* Compliance)
 conflict with doctor, 487–488
 and doctor, 433–501
 doctor-patient relationship (*see* Doctor, -patient relationship)
 personality of, 486–487
 perspective on disease, 448–452
 role
  adaptation to, 464–466
  dependent, 461–463
  stress of, 487
  terminally ill, fear of, 420–421
 therapeutic changes by, 480–482
 -therapist interaction, features of, 475–476
Patienthood stage: of illness behavior, 461–466
Peer relationships
 in adolescence, late, 375–376
 in mid-adolescence, 372–373
 in school age, 341–342
Peptic (*see* Ulcer, peptic)
Perception, 129–130
Permissiveness: sexual, in mid-adolescence, 371

Personality
 antisocial, and drug abuse, 266
 differences among infants, 312–313
 disorders, 123, 127
  related characteristics, 127
 of doctor, 486–487
 evaluation, 139
 of patient, 486–487
 schizoid, and drug abuse, 266
 sociopathic, and drug abuse, 266
 structure, and asthma, 175
Personnel (*see* Medical, personnel)
Phakomatosis, 15
Pharmacologic treatment: in psychosomatic disorders, 182–183
Phenothiazine: and dopamine receptor binding, 69
Phenotype, 8
Phobia, 126–127
 school, 343–345
  program to combat, 345
Physical
 build (*see* Build, physical)
 condition
  psychological factors affecting, 123
  self-concept and, 342
 dependence on drugs, 265, 267
 development (*see* Development, physical)
 inactivity, 257
Physician (*see* Doctor)
Physiological response
 in behavioral medicine, 166–167
 to stress (*see* Stress, physiological response)
Piaget's sensorimotor, 309
Pneumonia: and Southern Appalachian Whites, 220
Pollution
 air, 241–242
 water, 244–245
Polygenic inheritance, 9
Postnatal growth: main types of, 298
Poverty level: and obesity, 269
Practice: medical, implications of social stratification for, 204–205
Practices: in health matters, 205–207

Practitioner-patient relationships (*see* Doctor, -patient relationship)
Pregnancy, 397
 teenage, 380–381
Prenatal diagnosis
 by amniocentesis, indications for, 23
 amniotic fluid analysis in, 22
Preschool age, 327–336
 development in
  cognitive, 327–330
  delays, screening and management of, 336
  language, 330
  physical, 327
  psychosocial, 330–334
   Erikson's theories and, 330
   Freud's theories and, 330
 problems of, clinical, 334–336
 sex roles in, 332–333
 social relationships in, 333–334
Prevalence: of condition, 442
Problem drinking
 definition, 274, 275
 grade in school and, 276
 sex and, 276
Procreation, 396
Projection, 100–101
Projective (*see* Test, projective)
Prolactin: responses to neuroleptics, 68
Propoxyphene (*see* Abuse, Darvon)
Proximodistal direction: of motor development, 307
Psychiatric disorders
 associated with sleep, 91–92
 genetics of, 18–21
Psychoactive drugs
 behavior and, 33–37
 brain function and, 33–37
 classification, 33
 transmitter dynamics and, 31–33
Psychoanalytic theory, 97–105
 application of, clinical, 103–105
 models in
  structural, 97–99
  topographic, 97–99
Psycholinguistic abilities: Illinois test of, 139
Psychological
 aspects of doctor-patient relationship, 486–488

Psychological (cont.)
  correlates of
    psychophysiological
      disorders, 165
  dependence on drugs, 265
    primary, 267
    secondary, 267
  disorders
    categories of, 124–127
    classification, 119–142
    definition, 119–124
    evaluation, 119–142
    identifying types, general
      system of, 124
  factors
    affecting physical
      condition, 123
    in behavior, 95–191
    in drug abuse, 266–267
    in psychosomatic disorders,
      163–166
  function
    evaluation, 128–131
    theory of, 97–118
  reactions
    of family to death, 428–429
    of physician to dying,
      425–426
  responses
    in coronary care unit, 465
    to stress (*see* Stress,
      psychological response)
    to terminal illness,
      421–423
  -social factors in health and
    illness, 195
  stimuli
    in asthma, mechanisms,
      177–178
    gastric function and, 179
  test (*see* Test, psychological)
Psychopathology
  dynamic explanation of, 103
  present, with roots found in
    past, 104
  psychogenetic explanation of,
    103
Psychophysiological disorders,
  163–191
  psychological correlates of,
    165
Psychosexual
  development
    in adolescence, early,
      367–368
    in adolescence, late, 375
    in mid-adolescence,
      370–372
    stages of (*see below*)

disorders, 122, 127
dysfunction, 122
stages of development,
  99–100
  anal stage, 99
  genital phase, 100
  latency stage, 100
  Oedipus complex, 99–100
  oral stage, 99
  phallic stage, 99–100
Psychosis, 121
  functional, biochemistry of,
    55–76
Psychosocial
  aspects
    of aging, 408–414
    of development in infant,
      310–313
    of development of toddler,
      322–323
  development (*see*
    Development,
    psychosocial)
  factors in obesity, 270–271
Psychosomatic disorders,
  163–191
  behavioral methods in, 183
  environmental modification
    in, 182
  pharmacologic treatment in,
    182–183
  psychological factors in,
    163–166
  therapeutic considerations in,
    181–187
Psychosurgery, 44–45
Psychotomimetics: structure of,
  65
Pump: amine, and tricyclic
  antidepressants, 59
Punishment, 107
  neural substrates of, 42–43
Purity, 224

R

Race
  composition in aging, 401
  disability by, 199
  longevity by, 197
  obesity and, 269
Radiation, 242–244
  ionizing, 243–244
    dose-effect relationships of,
      244
  nonionizing, 242–243
Radiotherapy: of head and
  neck, thyroid tumors
  after, 248

Rationalization, 103
Reaction
  anxiety, acute, 149
  formation, 102
  vasovagal, 149–150
Reactive component: to
  peripheral sensation, 456
Reactors
  cardiovascular, 148
  gastrointestinal, 148
Recessive inheritance, 8, 9
Reciprocity, 311
Recovery stage: of illness
  behavior, 466–468
Reflexes: of newborn, 308
Regression, 101–102
Rehabilitation stage: of illness
  behavior, 466–468
Rehearsal
  behavior, 112–113
  techniques, mental, 116
Reinforcement, 106–107
  positive, time-out from, 107
  schedules of, 108
Reinforcer
  negative, 107
  positive, 106
Relaxation, 110–111
Reliability: of psychological
  tests, 133
REM sleep, 78–79
  dream recall after, 80
Renal function: and aging,
  405–406
Representational system:
  development of, 320
Repression, 97, 101
Resolution stage: in
  psychological response to
  stress, 153
Respiration
  central stimulation, absence
    of, 86
  Cheyne-Stokes, 88
Respiratory system: and aging,
  405
Response
  conditioned, 106
  endocrine, to stress (in
    monkey), 147
  interpersonal, training, 112
  physiological
    in behavioral medicine,
      166–167
    to stress (*see* Stress,
      physiological response)
  psychological (*see*
    Psychological, responses)
  unconditioned, 106

Subject Index

Retardation (see Mental retardation)
Reticular activating system: ascending, 39
Retrospective studies, 245, 246
Reward: neural substrates of, 42–43
Roles, 488
  of doctor, 490
  health, 207–208
  patient
    adaptation to, 464–466
    dependent, 461–463
  sex, 332–333
Rootwork, 234
Rorschach test, 140
Rules: social, 322–323

S

Salt intake: and hypertension incidence, 252
Schizoid personality: and drug abuse, 266
Schizophrenia, 18–20, 121, 125
  biochemical aspects of, 64–74
  dietary therapy of, 66–67
  dopamine hypothesis of, 67–72
  drug abuse and, 266
  manifestations of, clinical, 126
  MAO activity in, 71
  models
    metabolic, 64–67
    pharmacologic, 67–74
  morbidity risk in, 18
  norepinephrine excess in, 72
  opioids and, 72–74
  in twins, concordance rates, 19
  vitamin therapy of, 66–67
School
  age (see below)
  environment, and self-concept, 342
  grade in, and problem drinking, 276
  performance in, 343
  phobia, 343–345
    program to combat, 345
School age, 336–348
  development in
    cognitive, 337–340
    disorders of, 347–348
    language, 340–341
    physical, 337

    psychosocial, 341–343
    theories of, 341
  peer relationships in, 341–342
  problems of, clinical, 343–348
  self-concept in, 342
Scientific concepts: of ill health, 449
Scores: derived, 132
Security, 396
Sedative
  abuse, 286–287
  -hypnotic drugs, 34
Self-concept, 342
Self-control, 322–323
Self-esteem: loss of, 152–153
Self-instruction, 116
Self-stimulatory behavior: in autism, 318
Semantic development, 321
Sensation: peripheral, reactive component to, 456
Senses: and aging, 407–408
Sensorimotor stage: of Piaget, 309
Sentence completion, 141
Separation anxiety, 312
Serotonin: synthesis and metabolism, 57
Services, medical
  acceptability of, 461
  accessibility of, 461
  availability of, 461
  utilization of, 202–204
Sex
  composition in aging, 401
  enuresis by, 334
  longevity by, 197
  obesity and, 269
  problem drinking and, 276
  roles, 332–333
  for 65 and over, 403
Sexual
  abstinence in mid-adolescence, 371
  abuse of child, 354
    presentation, clinical, 359–360
  activity
    in adolescence, 368
    of aged, 412
  characteristics, secondary, 364
    appearance of, order of, 367
  drive, 98
  maturation, hormonal events in, 365

  permissiveness in mid-adolescence, 371
Sexuality, 396
Sexualizing vs. socializing: in middle adulthood, 398
Shaping, 107–108
Sick role stage: of illness behavior, 458–460
Sleep
  apnea
    obstructive, 87
    syndromes, 86–88
  attacks, 85
  disorders, 81–92
  drugs and, 79–81
  dysfunctions associated with, 89–90
  electroencephalography during, 77
  illnesses associated with, medical and psychiatric, 91–92
  initiating and maintaining, disorders of, 81–84
    causes of, 81–83
    conditions associated with, 82
    management, 84
  normal, patterns, 77–79
  NREM, 79
    dream recall after, 80
  paralysis, 85
  regulation of, 40–42
  -related enuresis, 89–90
  REM, 78–79
    dream recall after, 80
  somnolence (see Somnolence)
  stages of, 77–79
    dysfunctions associated with, 89–90
  terror, 90
Smiling: social, of infant, 311–312
Smoking, cigarette, 256–257
  coronary heart disease morbidity-mortality and, 256
  lung cancer and, 246–248
  mortality in, 247, 256
Social
  (See also Psychosocial)
  acceptance, and self-concept, 342
  activity of aged, 410–412
  adjustment after autism, 318
  aspects of medicine, 195–217
  attachment, 311
  attitudes toward aged, 413–414

Social (cont.)
  characteristics, and aging, 402–403
  class, recognizing symptoms needing medical attention, 450
  deprivation, 315–316
  forces, 488
  learning theory and drug abuse, 267
  milieu of drug abuse, 268–269
  perspective, behavior in, 193–292
  -psychological factors in health and illness, 195
  readjustment rating scale (SRRS), 144, 161
  relationships in preschool age, 333–334
  rules, 322–323
  skills training, 113
  smiling, of infant, 311–312
  stereotypes, and physical build, 340
  stratification, implications for medical practice, 204–205
  system, family as, 352–353
Socialization: and health, 205–208
Socializing vs. sexualizing: in middle adulthood, 398
Society
  alcohol and, 278–281
    adverse effects of, 279–281
  urban, life-style in, 241–246
Sociobehavioral features: of patient, 476–477
Sociocultural
  aspects of doctor-patient relationship, 488–492
  factors in health and illness, 195
Socioeconomic
  class, influence on beliefs and behaviors, 219
  factors in development of infant, 313–315
  status, and self-concept, 342
Sociological correlates: of health and illness, 196–205
Sociopathic personality: and drug abuse, 266
Somatoform disorders, 122
Somnambulism, 89
Somnolence, excessive daytime, 85
  disorders of, 85–88

conditions associated with, 85
Southern Appalachian Whites, 220
Specialization: and doctor-patient relationship, 491
Speech, 129–130
Sperm
  cell, 3
  production, 364
Spouse, illness of, impact of, 210–212
  catastrophic, 211
  extensive, 211
  minimal, 210
  moderate, 210–211
SRRS (Social readjustment rating scale), 144, 161
Stabilization stage: in psychological response to stress, 153
Stanford-Binet scale, 136
Status: loss by aged, 408
Stereotypes: social, and physical build, 340
Stimulants, 34–35
  abuse, 287–291
Stimulus
  antecedent, 109
  conditioned, 106
  psychological (see Psychological, stimuli)
  unconditioned, 106
Stomach
  function
    emotional conflict and, 148
    psychological stimuli and, 179
  mucosa, and fear, 149
  reactors, 148
Stranger anxiety, 312
Strength of association, 251
Stress, 143–162
  adaptation and, 146
  biologic basis for, effects of, 161
  change and, 145–146
  death associated with, 157
  definition of, 143–146
  dependent variables and, 161
  depression and, 158
  of doctor, 487
  endocrine response to (in monkey), 147
  of hospitalization, 463–464
  of illness, 463–464
  illness-induced, 464–466
  -illness relationship, criticism of, 160–161

impact of, 161
-induced illness, pathogenesis of, 159–160
intervening links and, 161
life, and illness, 155–161
manifestations of, clinical, 150
of patient, 487
physiological response, 146–151
  cause of, 154
  clinical syndromes associated with, 149–151
  mechanisms, basic, 146–149
  relationship to psychological response, 154–155
as precipitating factor, 159, 160
as predisposing factor, 159, 160
psychological response, 151–161
  relationship to physiological response, 154–155
  specific types of, 151–153
  stage of impact, 153
  stage of resolution, 153
  stage of stabilization, 153
reactions to, 143–162
related
  diseases, etiology of, 168
  etiology of peptic ulcer, 180–181
suicide attempts and, 158
training, 115–116
ulcer, 179
ulcer and, peptic, 180
Stressors, 143–145
Stuttering, 17
Style (see Life, -style)
Substance
  abuse (see Abuse, drug)
  use disorders, 121
Success: and self-concept, 342
"Suicidal fit," 232
Suicide
  attempts, and stress, 158
  mortality rates from, 410
Superego, 99
Support: communicative, in interaction of medical personnel and family, 215
Survival: for 65 and over, 402
Susceptible individuals: for alcohol abuse, 277

Susto, 231
Symptom(s)
  influence of ethnicity on, 225–227
  experience stage of illness behavior, 455–458
  interpretation of, by patient, 455–456
  response to, 456–458
Synapse, 28
  transmission processes at, 29
  transmitter dynamics and, 30–31
  transmitters, identification of, 28–30
Syntactic development, 321–322

T

Technology: and doctor-patient relationship, 490–491
Teenage pregnancy, 380–381
Temperamental traits: of children, questions related to, 314
Temporal correctness of association, 251
Tension headache: treatment, 187
Terminal illness, 420–423
  fears of patient, 420–421
  psychological responses to, 421–423
Terror: sleep, 90
Test
  achievement, 138
  Detroit, of learning aptitude, 139
  group, 138
  Illinois, of psycholinguistic abilities, 139
  intelligence, 135–136
    specialized, 137–138
  projective, 140–141
    association techniques in, 140
    choice techniques in, 140,
    completion techniques in, 140
    construction techniques in, 140
    expressive techniques in, 140
    ordering techniques in, 140
  psychological, 131–141
    criterion-referenced, 131
    design, 131–133

individually administered, 134–135
  interpretation, 131–133
  norm-referenced, 131
  objective, 139–140
  reliability of, 133
  use of, clinical, 133–141
  validity of, 133
  validity of, content, 133
  validity of, criterion-related, 133
Rorschach, 140
thematic apperception, 140–141
Thematic apperception test, 140–141
Theory(ies)
  activity, 410
  cellular, 440
  of development in school age, 341
  of disengagement, 410
  of Erikson (see Erikson's theories)
  of Freud (see Freud's theories)
  germ, 441
  learning, 105–116
    historical antecedents in development of, 105–106
  psychoanalytic (see Psychoanalytic theory)
  of psychological function, 97–118
Therapist(s)
  differences in choice of, 235–237
  -patient interaction, features of, 475–476
Therapy
  (See also Treatment)
  aversion, 113–115
  behavior, 105–116
  procedures, 110–116
Thinking, process
  primary, 98
  secondary, 99
Thioxanthene: and dopamine receptor binding, 69
Thirty (see Age, Thirty)
Thought
  of child, constraints on, 320–321
  processes, 129–130
  -stopping, 116
Thyroid tumors: after head and neck irradiation, 248
Toddler, 318–324

cognition of, 320–321
development of
  language, 321–322
  physical, 318–320
Erikson's theories and, 322
Freud's theories and, 322
issues concerning, clinical, 323–324
learning of, 320–321
toilet training of, 323–324
Toilet training: of toddler, 323–324
Tolerance: to drugs, 265, 268
Toxins: maternal, 7
Training
  assertiveness, 113
  interpersonal response, 112
  social skills, 113
  stress, 115–116
Tranquilizers: abuse, 286–287
Transactional system: and doctor-patient relationship, 489
Transition
  Age Thirty, 388
  Mid-life, 389
Translocation, 4
  analysis of, 5
Transmission
  neuronal, 26–33
  processes at synapse, 29
  synaptic, and transmitter dynamics, 30–31
Transmitter(s)
  amine, and psychotomimetics, 65
  dynamics
    of catecholamines, 32
    psychoactive drugs and, 31–33
    synaptic transmission and, 30–31
  synaptic, identification of, 28–30
Treatment
  (See also Therapy)
  delay in seeking, 202–204
  differences in choice of, 235–237
  social stratification and, 204–205
Tricyclic antidepressants: and amine pump, 59
TSH: and 5-HIAA, 63
Tumors
  asbestos-associated, 248
  thyroid, after head and neck irradiation, 248
Turner syndrome, 14

Twin(s)
  schizophrenia in, concordance rates, 19
  studies, 18

U

Ulcer
  chronic, 179
  peptic, 178–181
    acute, 179
    (in animals), 180
    behavioral antecedents of, 179–180
    conflict and, 180
    etiology of, stress-related, 180–181
    forced activity in, 180
    forced restraint in, 180
    pathogenesis, behavioral factors in, 179–180
    pathogenesis, biologic factors in, 178–179
    stress and, 180
  stress, 179
Unconditioned
  response, 106
  stimulus, 106
Unconscious needs, 396–397
Unrealistic considerations: about one's future, 396
Urban society: life-style in, 241–246

Utilization: of health-care services, 202–204

V

Validity (see Test, psychological, validity of)
Variables: correlation of, 250
Vasovagal reaction, 149–150
Vessels
  (*See also* Cardiovascular)
  aging and, 404–405
Viscosity, 224
Vitamin therapy: of schizophrenia, 66–67
Vocational choice: in late adolescence, 377–378
Vodun, 234

W

Warmth: irrelevant, in interaction of medical personnel and family, 214–215
Water pollution, 244–245
Wechsler scales, 136–137
  items on, description of, 137
Weight
  in adolescence, 367
  decrease with aging, 298
Werry-Weiss-Peters Activity Scale, 346

Whites: Southern Appalachian, 220
Wisdom: valuing in adulthood, 398
Withdrawal
  symptoms, 279
  syndrome, alcohol, 278–279
Women during adulthood, 391–395
  age markers, 392
  age thirty, impact of, 392
  "empty nest" period, 392–393
  menopausal period, 393–395
  myths concerning, 391–395
  realities concerning, 391–395

X

X-linked
  inheritance
    dominant, 9
    recessive, 9
  mental retardation, 16–17
XXX karyotype, 14
XYY karyotype, 14

Y

Young adulthood (*see* Adulthood, young)